Contents

International Sevens Tournaments

Women's Rugby

International Records and Statistics

The Countries

Elite Competitions

Referees

The Back Row

Rugby's biggest year

WORLD RUGBY™

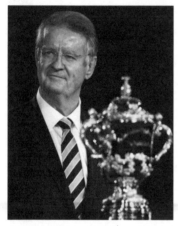

A message from Bernard Lapasset, World Rugby Chairman

Welcome to the 10th edition of the World Rugby Yearbook. It has been a stellar year for rugby with the biggest and best Rugby World Cup to date, the road to Rio 2016 gathering pace and rugby participation topping 7.2 million as our sport reaches and inspires new audiences in record numbers.

Rugby World Cup 2015 was a truly special and global celebration of rugby that elevated our sport to new levels on and off the field. It was certainly the biggest and most successful Rugby World Cup to date with a total attendance of 2.4 million, a global television audience of 780 million homes and a phenomenal social media reach of one billion as the world's top players competed to win our sport's greatest prize, the Webb Ellis Cup.

Yet, for me, RWC 2015 was about much more than statistics, it was undoubtedly the best Rugby World Cup to date. Full and vibrant stadia the length and breadth of England and into Cardiff and a further million watching in fanzones set the stage for the world's top players to showcase their talents in what was the most compelling and competitive Rugby World Cup.

Unforgettable moments were created. We witnessed extraordinary feats of courage. We shared the elation of dreams fulfilled as Japan recorded rugby's biggest ever upset and we were moved by tears of elation and tears of disappointment as an incredible story was played out on rugby's greatest stage.

The players certainly made us proud. They are role models who lived and breathed rugby's character-building values and reminded us that even in the most competitive of environments at the very top of sport, it is possible to compete with a spirit of friendship, respect and fair play.

Nowhere was the tournament and its unforgettable moments and friendships better reflected than on social media. This was the 'social' Rugby World Cup and the most talked about sporting event of the year, projecting rugby beyond its traditional nations and audiences and connecting a potential global audience of nearly one billion.

Great people make great events and tribute should be paid to the venues and cities for being exceptional, welcoming hosts, the Rugby Football Union for being a wonderful host union and the England Rugby 2015 and World Rugby teams for ensuring that Rugby World Cup 2015 stayed true to its objective of having teams and fans at heart.

But most of all, praise should go to the hundreds of players, thousands of wonderful volunteers and millions of fans who played their full part in making RWC 2015 such a special tournament on and off the field and who elevated our showcase tournament to new heights.

The legacy for the host nation and global rugby will be strong and long-lasting and as the hosting ball is passed from England to Japan, we can look forward with great excitement to a game-changing Rugby World Cup 2019 in Asia. The tournament venues and dates have already been set and the qualification process and a vibrant new logo announced, and while the dust has barely settled on Rugby World Cup 2015, fans and teams alike can now start planning for 2019.

As we look ahead to RWC 2019, World Rugby is determined to capitalise on the commercial and sporting success of Rugby World Cup 2015 and its predecessors, which is enabling record investment in rugby from the playground to the podium across our 120 national member unions.

Between 2009 and 2016 £350 million will have been injected into rugby at all levels ensuring a competitive and sustainable future for all. We are already seeing tangible benefits of that investment on and off the field and at the community level more than one million children have tried, played and stayed in our sport through our dedicated Get Into Rugby programme run in more than 120 nations worldwide.

As an inclusive sport for all, it is important that we continue to nurture rugby outside of our traditional markets and I am delighted to say that Asia and Africa in particular are a major success story, while a quarter of all participants are female. By the time we make our Olympic Games debut at Rio 2016, we hope to have a global playing population of more than eight million.

Off the field, we are investing record sums in player welfare, which is World Rugby's number one priority and we continue to work with leading independent medical experts to ensure that our game is as safe and enjoyable to play for all as possible.

Rugby World Cup 2015 set new standards of care in rugby, particularly in the area of concussion and together we must ensure that the #RecogniseAndRemove concussion education message gets through to all. RWC 2015 demonstrated that culture is changing, but we will not be complacent and will continue to ensure that we build upon the 500,000 players, coaches, match officials, medics, parents and teachers who have received concussion education worldwide.

On the field our quadrennial law review process, for which trials are already underway in selected domestic competitions, will have player welfare at its heart to drive enhancements wherever possible at all levels of the game and while injury rates are not increasing, we must continue to ensure that players are appropriately and adequately supported.

On the field at international level, we must continue to drive opportunities to bridge the competition gap between tier one and tier two teams. The superb performances at Rugby World Cup 2015 highlighted the progress made, but we are committed to delivering appropriate structures and fixture schedules that will ensure that these teams arrive at RWC 2019 in Japan in the best-possible shape.

Underpinning our mission to grow the global rugby family must be good governance. The game is thriving and we are reaching, engaging and inspiring more audiences than ever before. We are redistributing record sums in the development and sustainability of the game. Together we are successful and growing as a sport. That is the best reason for change, and in November we announced an historic programme of reform to World Rugby's decision-making structures which will drive greater union and regional representation on Council and independence on a more dynamic Executive Committee.

This exciting new model, which will operate from May 2016, will ensure that World Rugby, and by extension, the sport, has the governance structures to support and drive the future growth of rugby around the world.

If 2015 was a stellar year for rugby, then 2016 will be ground-breaking as we look forward to our Olympic Games return after an absence of 92 years. Rugby sevens is a global success story and its exciting blend of iconic international locations, high-octane action and festival atmosphere is proving to be a hit with fans, broadcasters and commercial partners alike.

Rugby sevens' debut at Rio 2016 will be a game-changer. We are already seeing the tangible benefits of inclusion through National Olympic Committee and Olympic Solidarity support around school curriculum inclusion, but we are also seeing broadcast and social media engagement reach record levels. The Rio 2016 Olympic Games will project our sport to new nations, communities and audiences and inspire participation and involvement. It will deliver a new and youthful audience to the Olympic Games. The world's top players are excited about the opportunity to be Olympians and showcase our sport on the greatest stage and I have no doubt that sevens will be great for the Olympics, great for Brazil and great for rugby worldwide.

The Front Row

RUGBY WORLD CUP 2015

End of an iconic All Black era

By Iain Spragg

Richie McCaw holds aloft the Webb Ellis Cup for the second time after the All Blacks created Rugby World Cup history.

When Richie McCaw announced his retirement, 19 frenetic days after captaining the All Blacks to their successful and scintillating defence of the Webb Ellis Cup at Twickenham, the decision was tinged with sadness. By his own admission, reports of the tragic death of his former team-mate Jonah Lomu just 24 hours earlier cast a sombre shadow on proceedings but there was amongst the sense of loss also celebration as the game paid tribute to McCaw and his glittering career.

The news that McCaw had pulled on the world famous black jersey for the last time in New Zealand's victory over the Wallabies in the Rugby World Cup 2015 final was not unexpected. After a record-breaking 148 tests over 14 bruising years and two World Cup triumphs with the All Blacks, not even the seemingly indestructible 34-year-old could continue forever but the realisation that he would never again grace the international stage was nonetheless a bitter sweet moment.

The All Blacks captain applauds the Twickenham crowd after the RWC 2015 final.

McCaw's own mantra that no individual player was more important than the team was unquestionably heartfelt, but after more than a decade as the heartbeat of the world champions his retirement created a void that even the mighty All Blacks conceded would be hard to fill.

"The last two weeks have given me the chance to reflect a bit and, I guess, I sit here today with no regrets about what I've done as a rugby player," McCaw said as he faced the media. "That last game [at Twickenham], to have that as the lasting memory of your last time on the pitch is pretty satisfying.

"Professional rugby has been great to me. It's allowed me to pursue my passion, to be involved with great people, hopefully make those close to me proud and travel the world. I've had some wonderful experiences for which I'm very grateful and I'd like to thank New Zealand Rugby for the opportunities they have given me.

"The support and encouragement from my family and friends has been huge throughout my career and I want to thank them. Mum and Dad haven't missed many of my games and I thank them, [my girlfriend] Gemma and the rest of my family for everything they have done.

"I've also been really fortunate to have had some great coaches and played with some outstanding players over the years, from my teenage years through to Canterbury, the Crusaders and the All Blacks. I'd like to thank them too for all they have done for me throughout my career.

"I'd also like to thank the fans who have supported me, both here and overseas. Your unwavering and passionate support for myself and the other players has always given us a huge lift, wherever we have played. We play the game to make you proud and I hope I have managed to do that over the years.

"I'm hanging up my boots having accomplished everything I could have ever dreamed about in the game. Knowing that I was able to end my career by helping the All Blacks win the Rugby World Cup final is a hugely satisfying feeling.

"It has been a hell of a journey over the last 15 years. I've been privileged to do what I love for so long. Here's to new adventures."

The list of McCaw's personal milestones and achievements is as long as his incredible career. First capped at the age of 20 against Ireland in Dublin in November 2001, just eight months after making his Super Rugby debut for the Crusaders, he was named man of the match after the All Blacks' 40–29 victory at Lansdowne Road and despite his inexperience and tender years, he immediately established himself as a regular starter for New Zealand.

An ever-present during his World Cup debut in Australia in 2003, he first captained the All Blacks against Wales in Cardiff in November 2004 and following the retirement of Tana Umaga the following year he was handed the armband by Graham Henry on a permanent basis. In 2006 he was named the World Rugby Player of the Year and along with team-mate Dan Carter is the only man to have collected the coveted accolade three times.

His 50th test as captain came in August 2010 when he led the team to a 20–10 triumph in the Tri-Nations against Australia in Christchurch and the following month he eclipsed Sean Fitzpatrick's national record of 51 tests as captain when he played in the 23–22 victory over the Wallabies in Sydney, scoring a try to mark the occasion. His third World Cup in 2011 saw him become New Zealand's first test centurion in the pool stages against France.

No-one in the history of the game has played more tests than McCaw. His 131 victories in those 148 internationals is also a record while his 110 tests as captain is a milestone that is difficult to envisage anyone ever surpassing.

Under his captaincy the All Blacks claimed 10 Bledisloe Cup triumphs, four Tri-Nations and three Rugby Championship titles but as glittering as those achievements are, even they are eclipsed by his feat of leading New Zealand to back-to-back Rugby World Cup successes, the first team to achieve the feat.

The first came on home soil in 2011 when the All Blacks edged out France 8-7 in an epic encounter in the final in Auckland. Victory ended the nation's agonising wait to be crowned champions for the first time since they won the inaugural tournament in 1987 and the end of the 24-year-long wait was a cathartic experience for the players and the public alike.

The triumph cemented McCaw's status as a national icon but admiration turned to adulation in 2015 when the flanker successfully steered the side back to the climax of the World Cup in England, New Zealand lifting the Webb Ellis Cup for a third time after overcoming Australia 34–17 at Twickenham in what is generally regarded as the greatest final in the history of the tournament.

The All Blacks stormed into a 21–3 lead early in the second half with tries from winger Nehe Milner-Skudder and centre Ma'a Nonu and 11 points from the boot of Carter but were pegged back to 21–17 by two Wallaby scores before they reasserted their supremacy with a Beauden Barrett try and eight points from the redoubtable Carter. It was a thrilling, free-flowing performance and one which McCaw insisted had been four years in the making.

"We played damn good rugby," he said. "We had the better of the first half but didn't quite get the reward we wanted out of it but we said at half-time there would be a period when they came back into it and we were down to 14 and the big thing wasn't to panic. We knew we would

McCaw is the most-capped player (148 tests) and captain (110 tests) in the history of the game.

get it back at some point but we didn't want the damage to be too much.

"We lost the momentum in the second half but we kept our composure and came home strong, which has been a hallmark of this team the last four years. I wouldn't say I felt anxious [when the score was 21–17], we knew the momentum was against us and we've been in those situations before. It's a matter of doing the simple things to get the ball back and get back the control and every man did that.

"The game got tight but there was a sense that we came here to do a job and we did it. We knew if we did our best we would give ourselves a pretty good chance. The pieces of the puzzle came together. We've done it a lot of times over the years but to do it when it really counts in a World Cup final, it shows the calibre of the men we've got.

"We said four years ago after the last one that we'd get on the road again with the end goal being playing here at Twickenham in a World Cup final and try and do something that no one else has done. I'm proud of the way the guys have done it.

"The big thing was after that game in 2011 we wanted to perform like world champions in between and give ourselves another chance and we don't have an off day, and that is what I am always hugely proud of about the All Blacks is they go about their work no matter what the day is, they are expected to go and perform and we've done that.

"The win in 2011 was significant because there had been a bit of heartbreak in New Zealand from our point of view for 24 years, so to tick that off was a magnificent achievement, a massive relief too, not only for us as rugby players but for New Zealand as a nation.

"Winning at Twickenham, doing something that no-one had done before, had a different specialness to it. To go and do something no other team had done, to achieve that. It was all about getting the monkey off the back in 2011 but four years later it was about forging a new way."

Players with the mental strength and physical resilience to play test rugby for more than a decade are a rare breed indeed. McCaw's legendary dedication in training in part explained his remarkable longevity at the very highest level but the man himself insisted in the wake of the World Cup final that it was the pride in the iconic shirt and the honour of leading out the test team that kept him going for 14 punishing years in the unforgiving environment of international rugby.

McCaw's elation at lifting the Webb Ellis Cup for the first time at RWC 2011 is clear to see.

"Every time I run out onto that field with the All Black jersey on, first of all I acknowledge how lucky I am to do that and make sure I do my bit to ensure the team do well," he said. "When you become an All Black, you realise that there are a lot of good men that have gone before. You feel that responsibility straight away, that there's no one person bigger than the team.

"It's been a privilege to lead this group of players. To captain a bunch of men like we've got is an honour and I pinch myself every time I get that opportunity. We had a great mix of youth, young guys who've come in with sheer enthusiasm and talent, everything you'd expect from those young fellas, and a good bunch of men who've been around for a long time and understood what test rugby is all about, understood what it took and had the skill and the desire and, I guess, the thing that ticks under the chest to direct the team the way we wanted."

The superlatives that followed after McCaw announced his retirement were as richly deserved as they were numerous and New Zealand head coach Steve Hansen was among the first to pay tribute to the loyalist of all All Black servants.

"He's been an inspiration to us all," Hansen said. "Not only has he enhanced the jersey during his time, but he has left a lasting legacy that will be talked about by many people long after we're all gone. It's been an absolute pleasure to have shared the road with him.

McCaw performs the haka before New Zealand's semi-final with South Africa at Twickenham.

"In my opinion, he will go down not only as the greatest All Black of all time, but the greatest captain we have ever had and possibly the greatest player to have ever played the game in the modern era. On behalf of the All Blacks, we want to congratulate Richie on everything he has achieved in his career. All this success couldn't have happened to a better bloke and we wish him all the very best for the future.

"To play 148 tests is something to be marvelled at on its own, particularly with the physical demands of the position he plays. But the more impressive thing about those 148 games is the quality of the performances he produced. Having been involved in the majority of those test matches, I can't recall him ever playing a bad game."

It may take rugby, and All Black supporters in particular, a little while to adjust to the prospect of a New Zealand side without McCaw at the coal face, knocking down opposition players and competing for the ball in the dark recesses of the breakdown. His retirement represented the quintessential end of an era but the great man himself was already busy making plans for the future.

"I've got an opportunity to be part of a helicopter business in Christchurch, so that's going to be my thing going forward," he said. "I'm excited about the opportunities there and I'm going to carry on flying and work towards getting my commercial pilot licence. It's something that I'm hugely passionate about and I know it will never replace the thrill of running out in front of 80,000.

"The iSport Foundation charity, which I set up with Dan Carter and Ali Williams, also gives us the opportunity to help talented teenagers reach their potential in their chosen sport, which is a cool way for us to give back. I'm now really excited about starting the next chapter of my life. I'm looking forward to the future and what it may hold."

IRB RUGBY WORLD CUP 2015

The stuff of dreams

By Stephen Jones, *The Sunday Times*

If Rugby World Cup 2015 had simply consisted only of the game between South Africa and Japan at the Brighton Community Stadium, then we would still be looking back on a gorgeous autumn. You can hardly count the ways in which that game elevated the sport, the spirit, and the aura of the whole activity.

Looking back, you sometimes feel the need to check the DVD replays, in case it never really happened – and after you check, you're still relieved that you did not imagine the colossus of an ending.

Yet the priceless aspect of that special day is that looking back, it does not tower over the rest of the proceedings. Yes, for South Africa to go down to Japan was the shock of all times in rugby, and conceivably one of the top five in all sports, ever. It turned on a vast audience new to rugby. How many times in the succeeding hours, days and weeks did people who had previously exhibited no interest in the grand sport, come up and express their wonder at what the Japanese had done.

But there were many wonders. The debate on the endless battle for recognition against the odds of the tier two nations is a feature of every World Cup, and God bless rugby followers, it is also clearly one of their main concerns. If you read social media and the mainstream stuff during England 2015 then you would realise how global is the support for rugby, constrained by narrow parochialism only when your team is playing, and otherwise the good of the game is the thing.

Back to Brighton. Japan were trailing 32–29 in the dying moments. Small reward for the magnificence of their play, notably in contact phases against the mighty Springboks. Then they were given a penalty within easy range to draw the match. And a draw in itself would have been a full-blown sensation.

Cameras panned to Eddie Jones, the Japan coach, sitting up in the stand. You could see the joy on his face with Japan apparently about to go for goal in the dying seconds, and therefore draw. Poor Eddie's face changed markedly shortly after. Japan, gloriously, went for a lineout and a shot at the winning try. That took courage and confidence.

The historic moment when Karne Hesketh scored to give Japan victory over South Africa in Brighton.

Even then, the wonders did not cease. We all might have expected a frantic series of charges for the line, with the defence tackling desperately against a horde of panicking dervishes. But there was nothing like it. Japan kept ice cool.

They won the lineout, drove the ball around the fringes for a while with their outstanding forwards. Then they moved it to the right and then wider to the right, battering almost to the South African line. Then, a final switch of play, the ball went zipping across to the left, Amanaki Mafi, on as replacement in the back row, contributed a check-and-go, made priceless space down the left and Karne Hesketh dived over to score, and to win the match.

The camera panned around the Brighton stadium, caught Eddie Jones with a massive beam, caught the wild celebrations of the Japanese and caught Japanese fans in the stands in floods of tears. And caught the supposedly reserved English going crackers. Unforgettable.

And yet so was the next six weeks. World Rugby and England Rugby 2015, the organising body on behalf of the Rugby Football Union, could not have dared hope that it would be as good as it was. Big numbers came rolling out across the games – the biggest crowds ever, the biggest income, the biggest impact, the highest torrents on social media. No number in any phase of it was not a record.

Yet rugby demands more than numbers and finance. Some of us felt that a few of the old behaviours on which rugby bases its ethos, had slipped. Some of the forgiving nature of the action, and the interaction between the teams had dipped. There had been a growth in appealing by players, some of the bite amongst the coaches, teams and fans had become marked.

Rugby World Cup 2015 had fans from all nations at its heart from start to finish.

There was no crisis, not really, but the World Cup clearly gave everyone in the sport an opportunity to prove their contention that rugby truly is a sport apart. And so it proved. The attendances at the games still stagger you now, months on. When 90,000 came to Wembley for the Ireland-Romania game, the announcement of the attendance strained credulity. Tens of thousands of people must have asked out loud: "How many?" But it was true. There was never a disappointing attendance at any game.

And as for the ethos, the grand old traditions of celebration and bonhomie were going strong. The fanzones installed in Trafalgar Square, in Richmond, in central Manchester and then one each in or around all the stadiums, provided the most spectacular side show. Here, people without tickets or people who simply wanted to share in the party came in their masses. At one time before the Ireland-France game, the fanzone at Cardiff Arms Park was packed, with at least 2,000 waiting outside, patiently prepared to queue for a long time for a long drink.

And the ambience of the whole thing was beyond reproach. The sight of South African fans forming a tunnel at Brighton Railway Station and applauding a long line of Japanese fans onto their train, stood out. Yet the feeling and respect between supporters of all nations, presented rugby as one world, a kind of single entity in which there was no social class or religion or age group or sexual orientation which was not welcomed as warmly as hot toast.

And what of the players? Again, and leaving aside the wonderful play for a moment, the tournament found the sport in perfect balance. There were amazingly few incidents of dirty play and bitterness, the only controversies probably surrounded an understandable urge of World Rugby to show the game in its best light and therefore, possibly, to become a little too disciplinarian, a little too anxious. This is hardly a crime, but the spirit in which the matches were played despite their hardness, was unbelievable.

There were many individual examples. When Juan Martín Fernández Lobbe limped off the field in the bronze final between Argentina and South Africa at The Stadium, Queen Elizabeth Olympic Park, having already announced his retirement after a spectacular career with the Pumas, he was waved on his way by Schalk Burger, also about to leave the field for the last time. The wave of respect between the two men who had battered each other remorselessly down the years was typical.

There were similar incidents throughout – many will remember Sonny Bill Williams jogging quite a long way on the final whistle of New Zealand's semi-final victory over South Africa, to try to console the inconsolable Jesse Kriel, the South African centre.

And we also remember the respect between New Zealand and Australia during and after the final – with everyone who was Australian or of any other nationality lording the achievements of the brilliant winning team, and not only as a collective but also through tributes to Richie McCaw, playing his last game in a staggering career in the final; and Dan Carter, man of the match in the final who also now moves away from New Zealand to play in Europe.

And yet there was also respect clean across the tiers. Steve Hansen, the All Blacks coach, curtailed a press conference after New Zealand had beaten an outgunned but valiant

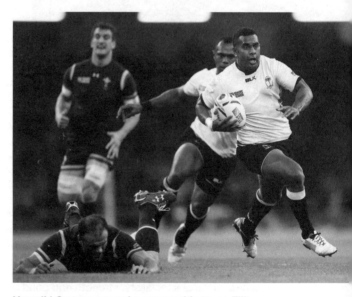

Vereniki Goneva scored a memorable try as Fiji nearly ran Wales off their feet in Cardiff.

Namibia. He expressed a wish to get away to have a drink with the Namibians and both coaching groups and the teams sat down together for some precious time in the dressing rooms. And there, Johan Deysel, the Namibian centre, could celebrate the try he had scored that evening, bursting through the defence to put Namibia on the map.

And yet like Japan, there were some of the tier two teams who did more than simply score late consolations when the match was already done. Fiji, not at their best in the opening game against England, were vastly improved and almost ran Wales off their feet in a pool match in Cardiff, which was actually lung-bursting simply to watch, let alone to take part in. Wales could easily have lost, they somehow hung on to win 23–13, but not before Fiji had broken out of defence to score a memorable try by Vereniki Goneva.

And wonder upon wonders, what about the Fijian scrum? Traditionally, it has been their weakest area. Fijians love playing with the ball, not getting down and dirty in the dark places. They love sevens, not endless locking of horns.

Yet some time ago, World Rugby's excellent development department decided to try to help Fiji gain a stage on which to conjure. The scrummage specialist Alan Muir, together with World Rugby, helped set up a scrum factory in Fiji, attracting the big men, trying to pass on all the fruits of

Georgia's Vasil Lobzhanidze became the youngest player in Rugby World Cup history and impressed with his composure.

experience and trying to make the big guys powerful and athletic, and to deem that scrummaging was sexy.

And what a success. The old building commandeered for the scrum factory was equipped, the big men rumbled in. And at the World Cup, with the likes of Campese Ma'afu and Manasa Saulo up front, Fiji hardly budged. They scrummaged superbly, and gave the rest of the team a chance to play.

This help from the central source was replicated. Remarkably, World Rugby paid for more than 100 professionals to come in amongst the tier two nations, to fill major places in terms of back-up, coaches, medical specialists, strength and conditioners, management personnel and clued-up baggage men.

And so we had the most competitive World Cup. We saw Georgia, led by the Hercules that is Mamuka Gorgodze, hammer Tonga in an early game and remain competitive. We saw Georgia bring along a teenage scrum-half in the fresh-faced Vasil Lobzhanidze. The young man maintained a fierce composure, so much so that at the end of the tournament he was named on the shortlist for Breakthrough Player of the Year, and will be back, conceivably, for the next three World Cups.

The list goes on. Romania, outstandingly led by number eight Mihai Macovei, were another team vastly improved, making their World Cup with victory against Canada. Tonga eventually managed a win against a Namibian team unrecognisable from its recent past. It seemed highly likely before the tournament that Namibia could concede 100 points easily against New Zealand, and another hatful against Argentina and Georgia. As it turned out, their final points difference deficit was only just over 100, and all the massive soakings people had predicted for the likes of Namibia, and Uruguay, never eventuated.

There was simply not a team which failed to provide something of note, especially in those heady weeks when all 20 of the competing teams were hammering away. It is now of the most vital importance that not only World Rugby but also the major individual nations themselves, keep providing the lifeline of finance, encouragement, and competition – most teams from outside the old elite have now proved that they are worth a fixture on their own grounds, and it will be a shocking waste of a legacy of England 2015 if those fixtures do not sprout like fast-growing mushrooms.

Naturally, the true technical merit of any World Cup comes in the knockout stages. For me, everything went up about five notches then. Perhaps surprisingly, previous World Cups have been a little flat at the quarter-final stages but this time, we had an epic weekend. Wales, to their horror, failed to top their pool when they could not score the try with Australia having two men in the bin, a shortcoming that will haunt them forever.

And yet so, too, will their defeat against South Africa in the quarter-final, when the genius that is Fourie du Preez escaped and scored in the dying moments – this after the teams had blasted each other toe to toe, with Wales giving at least as good as they got.

The easy game to pick was meant to be Australia v Scotland, this after the improved Scots had come through the pool ahead of Japan, Samoa and the USA – it was sheer bad luck for Japan that they had only a four-day turnaround before playing Scotland, after the draining heroism of the win over South Africa.

But as for Australia-Scotland being easy to pick, at one stage in the dying seconds it was easy to pick Scotland, who led. Then a controversial award of a penalty which even World Rugby was to cast doubt on later, gave Australia the chance to kick the winning penalty and to go through, leaving the Scots angry and devastated.

New Zealand had already hammered France with a breathtaking display in a quarter-final in Cardiff, with Julian Savea scoring a hat-trick and with all the current weaknesses in the French make-up blindingly obvious.

And the remaining quarter-final was a lovely treat. Ireland, supported in huge numbers throughout, had disposed of France in a game of mighty atmosphere and passions, but their injury toll, like that of Wales, was horrendous. For the Argentina match they were without Paul O'Connell, their talisman, and also Sean O'Brien, Peter O'Mahony and Johnny Sexton. This was the core of their team.

Juan Imhoff flies in to score Argentina's final try in their sensational quarter-final win over Ireland.

Yet would even their first choices have been able to do much about Argentina? The Pumas are famous for their excellence in the World Cup, they had taken New Zealand all the way at Wembley, brushed away the rest of the pool and against Ireland they were a sensation.

They maintained a great deal of their old forward power but by now they had added a backline brilliance. They played some sensational rugby, orchestrated by Nicolás Sánchez and Juan Martín Hernández, dominating large parts of the game, pulling clear with beautiful tries from Sánchez and Juan Imhoff and then cutting Ireland to ribbons again at the end with another try by Imhoff and a brilliant effort by Joaquín Tuculet. It was one of the finest performances of the tournament, raucously received by the massed ranks of Argentina fans and also, so the story goes, by an engaged public back at home.

Argentina were too ambitious in their semi-final against Australia, giving the galvanised Australians a start which, in fact, they may not even have needed. The final score was 29–15 to Australia although it could so easily have been so much closer. In the other semi-final, New Zealand beat South Africa by 20–18 but by more than the final score suggests, leaving the two southern hemisphere giants to provide the climax.

And it was one of the great finals. New Zealand won 34–17, although there were only seven points in it until the final minutes, and then a beautiful drop goal by Carter and a great try by Beauden Barrett sealed it, ensuring that McCaw and Carter and Hansen would be departing England with glory, and with the Webb Ellis Cup.

New Zealand were hailed by many as the greatest team ever. Certainly, they were improved on the bunch which took the World Cup for the first time in 24 years, with their home victory in Auckland in 2011. They were fit, fast, optimistic, ambitious, occasionally regal. And in England's autumn, unbeatable.

Perhaps the measure of their greatness was that they had increased their lead on the chasing pack. And this despite the fact that all the great teams had spent millions of pounds and man hours trying to catch up, trying to close the gap on the flying men from New Zealand. But they did not, New Zealand moved even faster, and they deserved every plaudit.

And what of England? The team and the nation? It is almost now an intrusion on private grief to record that England could beat Fiji and Uruguay but could not beat Australia or Wales, and therefore became the first host team not to proceed to the quarter-finals – this let loose a barrage of criticism aimed at the team, the squad, the coaches and the Rugby Football Union, much of it deserved. All these parties probably felt an awful lot worse than the critics and the fans. England at least knew that they needed radical improvements in all departments and Stuart Lancaster left his position as head coach a few weeks after the tournament.

And the country? World champion. Tens of thousands of followers came from all around the world to England. The Welsh hosted eight games, quite magnificently. The Irish came in massive numbers, and the Scots came in increasing numbers. They all joined the party.

But the foundation stone of the World Cup, its profitability but also its good humour and enormous crowds, was the decent, loyal, open and friendly sporting public of England, men and women and boys and girls, picking up on the Olympic spirit and carrying it through with style. Wondrous too, were the volunteers, The Pack, and the face of the whole thing bore a smile that lasted all seven weeks. The nation was alive with rugby.

The English may have had little to cheer from their own men in white, but they cheered everything else that happened, shrugged their shoulders and got on with

Richie McCaw and Dan Carter, two All Blacks legends who retired from test rugby with a second RWC winners' medal around their necks.

it. Rugby owes England a debt, and it will be ferociously difficult for any future hosts of the World Cup to top it all.

Or will it? In four years' time we go to Japan. There have been doubts about their ability to host such a gigantic tournament. But there were also doubts about their ability to beat South Africa. And look what happened. Glory days.

Rugby set for sea of change with Olympic Games debut

By Seb Lauzier

The date was 1 November, 2015, the occasion the World Rugby Awards the night after New Zealand had won their third Rugby World Cup, and if you listened carefully you could almost make out a collective intake of breath as the host spelled it out eloquently: "In a little over 270 days our finest athletes will be lining up on sport's grandest stage, at the Rio 2016 Olympic Games".

Excited glances scattered across the room, mixed with quizzical looks, astonished guffaws and questioning shakes of the head from the casual rugby followers. In their midst, knowing smiles broke out from those 'in the know' and necks craned to allow hundreds of pairs of eyes to search out tables full of All Blacks and scan for any hint of a let-on from the likes of Sonny Bill Williams and Nehe Milner-Skudder.

Later on, when Williams was questioned about whether he might fancy a crack at becoming the next James Bond, he gave a very short and polite two-letter answer. Had he been asked instead whether he'd be trying out for a rugby 007s role at the Olympic Games the answer would almost certainly have been different.

"As a rugby player you strive to be an All Black, win a World Cup, win a Super Rugby title and as a league player, for myself you strived to win a comp. I'm lucky enough to have achieved that, but as a sportsman, most would like to go to the Olympics and I haven't achieved that," Williams had already been on the record as saying.

"At this stage I've committed to sevens full-time. The other players have had sevens experience, but I've had nothing. I think going into such a big campaign for me to put my best foot forward I know that's the only way," he added, confirming that one of rugby's genuine superstars is set to play at least half of the 10 rounds on the HSBC World Rugby Sevens Series this season.

"I was lucky enough to have a meeting with Titch [All Blacks Sevens coach Sir Gordon Tietjens] and he explained all the training routines you have to get accustomed to."

RWC 2015 winner Sonny Bill Williams is committed to sevens and trying to become an Olympian.

This is the same coach who was parachuted in by the All Blacks camp before their World Cup campaign in 2011 to help hone the fitness of certain key players; the same coach who prides himself on the fact that his sessions are so physically and mentally gruelling that actually playing a World Series match is relatively straightforward.

Incidentally anyone who questions his methods needs only look up his resumé: 12 World Series titles, four Commonwealth Games gold medals and two Rugby World Cup Sevens titles. It is an astonishing haul probably not matched in world sport and points to the scary fact that if Williams is to reach his potential in sevens, Tietjens is the man to help him do it.

And this is where the fascination lies as the new 2015-16 sevens season gets underway with a shiny new HSBC World Rugby Sevens Series. While the very best in women's rugby are already playing sevens, in the men's game

Could defending World Sevens Series champions Fiji win the country's first ever Olympic medal?

Rugby World Cup 2015 stars like Williams, Bryan Habana, Damian de Allende, Quade Cooper, Henry Speight and Santiago Cordero are all now set to throw their hats in the ring. And those names come just from the four teams down south that make up The Rugby Championship. It will be fascinating to see how many of the 15s game's other heavyweights try their hand, and then transition successfully into sevens.

Some of them, like Cordero, Liam Messam, Julian Savea and Bernard Foley, have played the game before and would likely step back in with relative ease, while for others the emphasis on speed, endurance and fitness could take months of adjustment, weight-shedding and training. In an era of sevens specialists and a super-honed Fiji as reigning men's series champions, it could even become a chastening experience for some of the game's biggest stars.

In such a sea of uncertainty one fact does stand clear: the prospect of rugby sevens athletes – whoever they are – running out for the men's and women's competitions at the Olympic Games will bring a sea change for rugby and arguably the most thrilling and enticing leap forward for the game since it declared itself open 20 years ago.

"To be back at the Olympics is a great honour and an incredibly important moment for rugby for many reasons," said World Rugby Chief Executive Brett Gosper. "It is great to have another ground-breaking event within a year of a record-breaking Rugby World Cup that has reached over a billion people on social media, and this will continue to help the sport grow."

The day of rugby's acceptance by the International Olympic Committee was one of the sport's finest and is now all the more poignant with the passing of the great Jonah Lomu. When Jacques Rogge, then the IOC President, announced to the membership of a packed Copenhagen auditorium that rugby sevens had been accepted overwhelmingly, Lomu was one of rugby's team of seven who stood to punch the air, embrace and celebrate a triumphant success. Having such a giant of the game, rugby's first household name, there and a key part of rugby's presentation was a giant coup – especially as Lomu, like fellow lobbyist Agustín Pichot, had performed heroics for his country in sevens, as well as in 15s.

Lomu would have moved heaven and earth to be there in Rio, not so much to see the fruits of his own labour as to see a new beginning for the sport he held so dear.

"Jonah never played on the World Series for New Zealand but he certainly played in Hong Kong and almost single-handedly won the Rugby World Cup Sevens in 2001. He would have loved to see it on that stage," added Gosper.

"For the athletes, trying to win a World Sevens Series and a Sevens World Cup is obviously a huge motivation but the added interest of trying to qualify for and win an Olympics only makes sevens become even more exciting and there will be international players from the 15-man game who will want to play in the Olympics and will try their hand at sevens over the next season. I see there being a lot of crossover between 15s and sevens which will be great for the game of rugby in general.

"The aerobic fitness of the sevens guys is extraordinary and part of the sport is the nature of being able to sustain that endurance. They are some of the fittest athletes in the world, they really are, and they do the entire sport proud."

One of the biggest legacies of the Olympic acceptance has already started to bear fruit, but won't be fully realised and converted until after Rio 2016. On a participation level, being an 'Olympic sport' means that rugby boots are now finding their way into school corridors in countries like China, India, Russia and the USA. That in itself is a huge step forward from the grassroots up but in many countries National Olympic Committees and governments are now also seeing fit to complement that by investing top-down in programmes that are creating full-time, funded athletes able to live and breathe the sport of rugby without having to juggle the demands of training, work and studies.

That investment on its own is one thing and a first major step, but much of the potential will only become a reality when sevens experiences its first truly global shop window through the power of the Olympic Games' global broadcast platform in 2016. The Olympic Games is one of only a handful of sporting events – including Rugby World Cup – that can genuinely claim to have the entire world watching and Gosper is thrilled at the opportunity rugby will have to showcase itself for the first time to a whole new audience of casual sports fans for whom rugby is not yet on the radar.

Sprinter-turned-rugby player Carlin Isles is the 'fastest man in world rugby'.

"Rio will provide a fantastic introduction to rugby for so many people," he said. "Sevens is a great sport, a hidden gem in many respects, and literally millions of people will watch it for the very first time in 2016, which is hugely exciting. The Olympics gets untold television audiences in countries where rugby is not so heavily penetrated so Rio will provide fabulous exposure to the skills and values of our game. Rugby has been building for a long time, each Rugby World Cup sees us move on and Rio will be another huge leap forward."

The burning question is whether rugby's national unions will be ready for the inevitable deluge of interest and new players, and that is where much of the work is currently being focused around the world, particularly in those countries already qualified for the Olympics but still relatively new-world in rugby terms.

One case in point is the USA, who as fate would have it are the defending Olympic rugby champions, having won the last competition played in 15-man rugby back in 1924. Both the men's and women's teams are safely qualified for Rio 2016 and the men announced themselves as genuine medal contenders by winning the final round of the 2014-15 World Series at Twickenham. In an Olympics-centred nation, women's rugby is the fastest-growing team sport.

With the full backing of the US Olympic Committee, the country's finest men's and women's sevens athletes train day in and day out alongside fellow Olympians of all persuasions at the world-class Chula Vista facility outside San Diego. They do so under the guidance of one of the few men capable of rivalling Tietjens, and Fiji's coach Ben Ryan, on the world stage in Mike Friday.

"The big thing in America is: if you can't be an NFL player, an NBA player or a baseball player, you want to be an Olympian," said Friday, who was previously in charge of both England and Kenya. "The Olympics captures the imagination of the sporting public in America. If rugby can position itself and we can do well as an Olympic sport, then all of a sudden it will hit the eyes of so many more Americans."

Nothing captures the imagination in the States quite like success and it is no coincidence that sevens' latest boon has come on the back of the men's team rising to sixth in the world under Friday and the women's to fifth. And with the likes of the 'fastest man in world rugby', sprinter-turned-rugby player Carlin Isles, fast becoming a key performer, they now also have a calling card for other athletes not quite making the grade in their first chosen sport.

And that is what USA Rugby needs as it continues its daily mission to grow the game in a sporting market dominated by the behemoths of American sport. Yes, they can put structures in place to grow the game organically and that will bring success in the future, but in the short term they also need the likes of Isles, who introduced himself to USA Rugby's chief executive Nigel Melville by email and a subsequent phone call after watching sevens online.

"Sevens is a really interesting thing and it's a brand of rugby that's taken off in the States in a big way, for men and women," said Melville, who has overseen an 81 per cent rise in participation between 2008 and 2013 and also has the backing of NBC Sports as a host broadcaster for rugby.

If the period between 2009 and 2016 has seen record growth with global participation doubling, the four years between the Rio and Tokyo Olympic Games will be hugely important for rugby, and here again the USA have been handed a major trump card with the hosting of the seventh Rugby World Cup Sevens – the third for both men and women – in San Francisco. With the country already hosting HSBC World Rugby Sevens Series events for both men and women, this is seen not as a risk but as a priceless opportunity to give North America – both USA and Canada – another stepping stone on which to build the game's future.

"We were delighted to be chosen to host Rugby World Cup Sevens 2018 and are looking forward to delivering a fantastic rugby sevens experience for the players, fans, sponsors and media," added Melville.

"Hosting a Rugby World Cup is an important step forward for rugby in the USA and will bring high levels of visibility and interest for the game in the country. We will also be using the opportunity to develop Impact 2018, a national legacy programme for the whole USA Rugby community."

Canada captain Jen Kish will be hoping to inspire her side to Olympic gold in Brazil.

USA is one of 11 teams now qualified in the men's and women's competitions in Rio. Hosts Brazil were the first to ink their names onto both draws and were joined by the top four-ranked nations in the 2014-15 series – Fiji, South Africa, New Zealand and England (Team GB) in the men's and New Zealand, Canada, Australia and England (Team GB) in the women's. Since then Argentina, USA, France, Japan, Australia and Kenya have come through regional qualifiers in the men's, while Colombia, USA, France, South Africa and Fiji have sealed their places in the women's. For those who have so far missed out – some by the cruellest of margins – the remaining coveted spots will be taken by the winners of a mouth-watering global repechage tournament to be held in June 2016.

"The HSBC World Rugby Sevens Series for both men and women have gained huge interest over the last few years and that will only continue because of Rio," added Gosper, who is convinced that rugby will be one of the most popular events in Brazil after proving a huge draw card at multisport events in recent memory, most notably the 2014 Commonwealth Games in Glasgow.

"The challenge for all new sports coming into the Olympic Games is that some spectators are not always used to them so there is always a lot of curiosity.

"But rugby sevens is a perfect fit for the Olympics, delivering skill, speed and action on the pitch and a stadium packed with a young audience looking for a good time and which, crucially, is also socially engaged and looking to share their experience.

"I believe that rugby sevens will fit seamlessly into the Olympics, so much so that people will wonder why it wasn't in there earlier. It is a very natural and impactful fit. The Olympic values and rugby values are very aligned, and not by accident: Pierre de Coubertin, who founded the modern Olympics, was a first-grade rugby referee and was fascinated by the sport. He made many visits to Rugby School so the spiritual links and value links between the two go back a very long way.

"We really do want to see rugby cement itself as a top, crowd-pleasing Olympic sport and we are working very hard to help make that happen.

"We will be doing our very best to show the world and the Olympics the very best of rugby. We are confident that we can demonstrate that we are a very important Olympic sport going forward."

As the host country, Brazil's nascent rugby scene has also come under the spotlight and gained significant investment as a result of the Olympics. Rugby is one of the fastest-growing team sports in Brazil, and with more than 46,000 children introduced to the game in the past two years the Brazilian union and World Rugby are committed to ensuring that Rio 2016 provides a platform to inspire more growth. As part of Olympic Day celebrations this year, children and young people from social projects across Rio were invited to the symbolic opening of a rugby pitch on Copacabana. The city and its culture remains dominated by football, of course, but at least now somewhere among the soccer mania a rugby pitch is there as a permanent feature while Rugby Brazil targets taking the game to 1,000 schools in the city.

"It is great to see the first set of rugby posts being erected in the Olympic host city. Rugby sevens promises to be a thrilling spectacle and the sport will play a full part in the dynamic, youth focused atmosphere we will create in Deodoro," said Agberto Guimaraes, Rio 2016 Executive Director of Sport and Paralympic Integration.

"With nations qualified and the venue construction progressing well, the Olympic rugby sevens competition is now becoming an exciting reality. We look forward to welcoming rugby fans from around the world to Rio in just over one years' time to enjoy an excellent competition with memorable celebrations."

The competition will be memorable. The question on everyone's lips at the moment is: who will create rugby sevens' first Olympic memories? Who would bet against Sonny Bill Williams?

"I don't know if I'm going to be any good at sevens," he says. "That's why it's pretty scary, but all you can do is have a go and do your best. It's going to be a massive challenge, probably the biggest of my career. Time will tell."

World rankings

By Karen Bond

New Zealand's historic back-to-back Rugby World Cup successes ensured that they would celebrate six years at the top of the World Rugby Rankings, a position they have occupied since 16 November, 2009 and for an incredible 85.08 per cent of the time since the rankings were introduced in October 2003.

The All Blacks will start 2016 with a 6.77 rating point cushion over Australia, the side they overcame 34–17 in the Rugby World Cup 2015 final at Twickenham on 31 October to create another chapter in the tournament's history with their third success overall and the first outside of New Zealand.

While this is a comfortable advantage over their trans-Tasman rivals, it is not the biggest that New Zealand have enjoyed in their dominance of the rankings, the All Blacks having had a 9.21 rating point cushion over the Wallabies back in October 2010.

However, the story would have been very different had Australia lifted the Webb Ellis Cup for a third time on British soil as they would then have climbed to the summit of the rankings for the first time, joining fellow Rugby World Cup winners South Africa and England as the other sides to occupy that coveted spot.

RWC 2015 fittingly featured the top 20 sides in the rankings and with the points exchange doubled to reflect the importance of matches at the tournament there was plenty of movement over the six weeks of enthralling rugby in 13 venues across England and in Cardiff.

Argentina were one of six nations to finish the tournament in a higher position than they began it, Los Pumas' run to the semi-finals lifting them four places to fourth before defeat in the bronze final saw them slip below Wales into fifth. Had they managed to beat South Africa at The Stadium, Queen Elizabeth Olympic Park then Argentina, who had earned plaudits for their attacking style of play, would have equalled their highest ever ranking of third.

Japan would also return home three places higher than when they arrived on English shores, the Brave Blossoms returning to the top 10 after an historic campaign which saw them stun the sporting world by beating South Africa 34–32 on the opening weekend in Brighton and follow that with wins over Samoa and USA to become the first nation to win three matches and not reach the quarter-finals.

By finishing third in their pool, Japan confirmed their place at RWC 2019 as did Georgia, another nation to enjoy their best ever tournament in 2015, beating Tonga and Namibia to record two wins in a single edition for the first time. Those wins earned the Lelos a two-place climb to 14th and many new fans in the process.

Argentina had cause to celebrate often during RWC 2015, including a climb in the rankings.

While these nations had plenty to smile about after RWC 2015, the same cannot be said for hosts England and Samoa who both now occupy their lowest ever positions of eighth and 15th respectively after disappointing campaigns. England, the first hosts to fail to reach the quarter-finals, fell four places after losses to Wales and Australia in Pool A, while Samoa won only one of their four matches in Pool B – against the lower-ranked USA – to return home three places lower.

Canada are the other team who graced Rugby World Cup 2015 to find themselves in their lowest ever position of 18th after a year which saw the Canucks win only two of their 14 test matches, narrow wins over Namibia last November and Georgia in September.

England and Samoa are therefore the two biggest fallers in the top 20 over the last 12 months, sliding five and seven places respectively, while Argentina have made the biggest climb after beginning the period ranked 10th and finishing it five places higher.

Sri Lanka won Division 1 of the new-look Asia Rugby Championship to return to the top 40.

There are 102 nations now in the World Rugby Rankings but New Zealand were the only team to remain stationary for the last 12 months, although 10 others have returned to their positions after movement up or down. They are France (7), Tonga (13), Uruguay (19), Spain (21), Hong Kong (24), Korea (25), Poland (36), the Cook Islands (46), Bermuda (66) and China (67). In total, 54 nations have seen their ranking improve over the last 12 months, while 37 ended this period lower than they began it.

A number of nations have enjoyed significant gains over this period and reached new highs in the world rankings. Luxembourg are one such example, having rocketed 22 places on the back of five wins in a row over higher-ranked opponents in the European Nations Cup Division 2C, including convincing away victories over Serbia (36–0) and, most recently, Austria (34–6). They currently top the standings with three matches to play and the prize of promotion to the tier above as motivation to keep their good run going.

Switzerland have also shot up to their highest ever ranking of 34th after recording four victories from five matches in Division 2A in the last year, beating sides around them in the Czech Republic (20–14), Malta (23–20) and Israel (29–18) on the road and Croatia (40–20) at home.

Three sides have also surged up the rankings on the back of titles in the revamped Asia Rugby Championship in 2015 in Sri Lanka, Malaysia and Guam. Sri Lanka beat their hosts the Philippines (35–14) and Kazakhstan (27–14) to win Division 1 and return to the top 40, while Malaysia made the most of home advantage to claim the Division 2 title with victories over Chinese Taipei (46–13), United Arab Emirates (20–19) and Thailand (53–7) in May. Guam, meanwhile, equalled their highest ranking of 70 after beating Indonesia (17–6) and China (34–17) to lift the Division 3 East trophy.

Further up the rankings, Kenya also entered the top 30 for the first time in 2015, helped by victories in Nairobi over touring sides Portugal (41–15) and Spain (36–27) and Africa Cup rivals Tunisia (46–15). Colombia, a country where rugby continues to grow, were another to reach a new frontier, earning an early Christmas present of breaking into the top 50 of the World Rugby Rankings for the first time on the back of an impressive 62–24 victory over Mexico in Mexico City on 13 December.

Yet while these nations had plenty of reasons to celebrate, others have experienced a chastening run of results over the last 12 months which has seem them suffer falls into double figures. Thailand, for example, have lost four of their five matches across a tour by Malaysia and Division 2 of the Asia Rugby Championship, three of those losses by more than 15 points to suffer the maximum impact on their rating points in the rankings.

Sweden and Denmark are two others to have suffered significant falls, of 10 and 11 places respectively after losing all of their matches in the European Nations Cup. Sweden prop up the Division 1A standings after losing six matches in the last 12 months, five of them by more than 15 points against Ukraine (45–0), Moldova (57–8), Belgium (71–10 away and 48–20 at home) and Poland (29–11) to edge closer to their lowest ever ranking of 58th. Denmark, like their Scandinavian neighbours, are also facing the prospect of relegation as they sit bottom of Division 2C after losing four matches in this period. Their margins of defeat have been smaller than Sweden's, but three of those defeats – against Slovenia (16–10), Serbia (25–22) and Austria (31–25) – have come at home and against sides ranked around them or lower.

The World Rugby Rankings are published every Monday on **www. worldrugby.org**. They are calculated using a points exchange system in which teams take points off each other based on the match result. Whatever one team gains, the other team loses. The exchanges are determined by the match result, the relative strength of the team and the margin of victory. There is also an allowance for home advantage.

One hundred and two of World Rugby's member unions have a rating, typically between 0 and 100 with the top side in the world usually having a rating above 90 – New Zealand's was 96.10 after their RWC 2015 success. Any match that is not a full international between two countries or a test against the British and Irish Lions does not count towards the rankings. Likewise neither does a match against a country that is not a World Rugby full member union. For more details visit **www.worldrugby.org**.

WORLD RUGBY RANKINGS 13/10/14 – 02/11/15

POSITION	MEMBER UNION	RATING	MOVEMENT	HIGHEST EVER	LOWEST EVER
1	New Zealand	96.10		1	2
2	Australia	89.33	Up 2	2	6
3	South Africa	87.66	Down 1	1	6
4	Wales	83.49	Up 2	4	10
5	Argentina	82.59	Up 5	3	12
6	Ireland	81.17	Down 1	2	9
7	France	79.77		2	8
8	England	79.77	Down 5	1	8
9	Scotland	77.94	Down 1	6	12
10	Japan	77.05	Up 1	9	20
11	Fiji	76.96	Up 1	9	16
12	Italy	72.74	Up 2	8	15
13	Tonga	71.60		9	20
14	Georgia	71.45	Up 1	13	23
15	Samoa	70.36	Down 7	7	15
16	USA	67.30	Up 2	14	20
17	Romania	68.66	Down 1	13	19
18	Canada	67.77	Down 1	11	18
19	Uruguay	62.11		14	23
20	Namibia	58.39	Up 2	19	29
21	Spain	61.54		18	32
22	Russia	61.10	Down 1	16	26
23	Chile	57.34	Up 5	23	30
24	Hong Kong	57.31		22	39
25	Korea	56.70		20	33
26	Zimbabwe	56.16	Up 2	25	35
27	Kenya	55.89	Up 4	31	53
28	Portugal	55.72	Down 5	16	29
29	Belgium	55.69	Up 1	21	55
30	Ukraine	55.51	Up 3	24	40
31	Germany	54.78	Down 5	24	37
32	Moldova	53.69	Down 3	25	53
33	Netherlands	51.86	Down 1	28	48
34	Switzerland	50.95	Up 11	34	67
35	Poland	50.74		25	42
36	Paraguay	50.46	Up 1	29	42
37	Sri Lanka	49.79	Up 11	37	64
38	Czech Republic	49.61	Up 1	24	53
39	Brazil	49.26	Down 3	27	37
40	Tunisia	49.11	Down 2	27	44
41	Lithuania	48.86	Up 9	35	73
42	Madagascar	48.71	Up 1	35	56
43	Kazakhstan	48.14	Down 3	25	50
44	Malta	48.12	Down 3	39	67
45	Trinidad & Tobago	47.38	Up 8	42	60
46	Cook Islands	47.11		46	59
47	Colombia	46.37	Up 11	47	86
48	Uganda	46.35	Up 9	31	69
49	Senegal	45.96	Down 7	39	83
50	Ivory Coast	45.76	Down 3	38	48
51	Philippines	45.12	Up 1	51	72
52	Guyana	44.88	Up 2	52	79
53	Croatia	44.83	Down 4	34	56
54	Sweden	44.49	Down 10	32	58

WORLD RUGBY RANKINGS 13/10/14 – 02/11/15

POSITION	MEMBER UNION	RATING	MOVEMENT	HIGHEST EVER	LOWEST EVER
55	Israel	44.20	Down 4	46	94
56	Mexico	43.61	Up 5	56	76
57	Malaysia	43.53	Up 14	56	83
58	Singapore	42.92	Up 1	42	67
59	Andorra	42.88	Up 4	52	74
60	Cayman Islands	42.87	Down 5	57	74
61	Latvia	41.97	Up 3	35	75
62	Venezuela	41.65	Up 3	42	71
63	Luxembourg	41.62	Up 22	62	95
64	Botswana	40.99	Up 8	63	89
65	Chinese Taipei	40.27	Down 3	32	65
66	Bermuda	40.03		47	68
67	China	39.58		38	70
68	Peru	38.84	Up 7	51	79
69	Slovenia	38.80	Up 15	42	84
70	Guam	38.11	Up 18	70	90
71	Hungary	37.94	Down 3	61	89
72	Thailand	37.46	Down 11	52	74
73	Barbados	37.39	Up 5	59	81
74	India	37.12	Down 1	65	93
75	Nigeria	37.03	Up 4	73	92
76	Jamaica	36.99	Up 4	76	90
77	St Vincent & The Grenadines	36.84	Up 4	71	85
78	Serbia	36.82	Up 5	56	91
79	Pakistan	36.74	Up 3	71	81
80	Bosnia & Herzegovina	36.18	Up 10	79	95
81	Zambia	35.80	Up 8	60	89
82	Austria	35.00	Down 6	63	93
83	UAE	34.92	Up 16	83	99
84	Bahamas	34.55	Up 10	4	94
85	Denmark	34.35	Down 11	36	85
86	Norway	34.00	Up 10	78	97
87	Uzbekistan	31.94	Up 9	86	97
88	Mauritius	33.86	Up 3	83	101
89	Swaziland	32.04	Up 6	80	96
90	Bulgaria	31.57	Up 3	75	94
91	Indonesia	28.73	Up 8	90	99
92	Greece	28.55	Up 10	92	102
93	Finland	28.34	Up 5	90	102
94	Morocco	25.59	* Down 60	19	94
95	Papua New Guinea	23.14	* Down 39	46	95
96	Niue Islands	20.22	* Down 27	60	96
97	Tahiti	19.81	* Down 11	85	100
98	Cameroon	19.16	* Down 21	76	98
99	Monaco	17.59	* Down 12	76	100
100	Solomon Islands	16.82	* Down 30	67	100
101	Vanuatu	16.73	* Down 9	89	101
102	American Samoa	15.72	* Down 3	96	102

* On 1 January, 2015 any side who had not played a test match in 12 months had their rating halved

The Numbers Game

25 million

The RWC record TV audience who watched the Brave Blossoms beat Samoa back in Japan

12

The years that had passed since Uruguay last played on the RWC stage

2,439

Points were scored at RWC 2015, giving an average of 51 per match

97

271

Tries scored in the 48 matches

Points scored by the top point scorer at RWC 2015, Argentina fly-half Nicolás Sánchez

17

Number of turnovers made by Wallabies number eight David Pocock in the tournament

2,477,805

Fans attended matches at RWC 2015

1.5 billion

The total social reach of the tournament

 **34**

Points scored by Japan as they caused the biggest upset of RWC history by beating South Africa

 **2**

#RWC2015 was used twice a second throughout the tournament

 **15**

Springbok winger Bryan Habana drew level with Jonah Lomu's record of RWC tries after scoring a hat-trick against USA in Pool B

 **8,741**

Days between Japan's first and second RWC victories

Sponsored by

WORLD RUGBY™
AWARDS

Carter honoured after realising his Rugby World Cup dream

Daniel Carter, World Rugby Player of the Year 2015.

New Zealand fly-half Daniel Carter was named World Rugby Player of the Year in association with MasterCard at a star-studded awards ceremony in London on 1 November, a day after the All Blacks had beaten Australia 34–17 in the Rugby World Cup 2015 final at Twickenham to become the first nation to successfully defend the Webb Ellis Cup.

Carter joined his All Blacks captain and fellow test centurion Richie McCaw in becoming a three-time recipient of the prestigious accolade, having also been named Player of the Year in 2005 and 2012, and is the third New Zealander in a row to win the award after Kieran Read and Brodie Retallick in 2013 and 2014 respectively.

It was a fitting finale to Carter's illustrious career, the 33-year-old having been in inspired form as RWC 2015 progressed, determined to play a full part in more All Blacks success having missed much of the 2011 tournament on home soil due to injury.

That burning desire was clear for all to see as the fly-half steered the ship through tricky encounters with his trusty boot and vision, providing a calming influence in the final as Australia fought back to 21–17 at one stage to ensure victory in his 112th and final test in the famous jersey.

Carter, who bowed out of international rugby with a world record 1,598 test points to his name and one final man of the match award, beat off stiff competition from a shortlist that featured his All Blacks team-mate and RWC 2015 top try-scorer Julian Savea, Australian flanker Michael Hooper and number eight David Pocock, Wales second-row Alun Wyn Jones and Scotland captain and scrum-half Greig Laidlaw.

"It's a dream come true," Carter admitted. "It's not why you play the game, for personal accolades, but at the same time it's very pleasing and a very proud moment because I've had to work extremely hard, especially these last two to three years with the injuries that I've had and the criticism that I've had from various people questioning if I was up to it or not.

"To come out fighting on the other side and achieve what I've achieved personally but also what the team's achieved, it has been a very special moment of my career. There's been a lot of amazing moments throughout my career, right from my first day as an All Black in 2003, when the dream became a reality, and to finish it on such a high is very special."

On a special evening celebrating a remarkable 2015 at Battersea Evolution, world champions New Zealand were named Team of the Year – for the sixth year in a row – and Michael Cheika the Coach of the Year after turning around Australia's fortunes in his 12 months at the helm of the Wallabies.

Carter and the All Blacks were not the only New Zealand winners on the night, though, with Kendra Cocksedge named World Rugby Women's Player of the Year after playing a leading role in the Black Ferns' success

Kendra Cocksedge.

in the inaugural Women's Rugby Super Series in Canada in July with victories over their hosts, the USA and world champions England.

Portia Woodman's reward for becoming only the fifth player in World Sevens Series history, men's or women's, to score more than 50 tries in a season as New Zealand defended their title and qualified for the 2016 Olympic Games in Rio was to be named World Rugby Women's Sevens Player of the Year.

Portia Woodman.

Julian Savea.

Two other winners were All Black wingers Nehe Milner-Skudder and Julian Savea, the latter receiving the IRPA Try of the Year award for his second try against France in the quarter-finals when he charged through three Les Bleus' players at the Millennium Stadium. His try was selected as the winner from a shortlist of six by guests at the World Rugby Awards, who voted for their favourite try during dinner.

A panel including George Gregan and Felipe Contepomi selected Milner-Skudder as the inaugural World Rugby Breakthrough Player of the Year, an award which recognises players who have made an impact in their first year of international rugby. After an impressive debut Super Rugby campaign with the Hurricanes, Milner-Skudder made his All Blacks debut in July and went on to score six tries at RWC 2015, including his side's first in the final at Twickenham.

"I just pinch myself every day to be in this set up and be an All Black and to get recognised like this alongside the other two players (Scotland's Mark Bennett and Georgia's Vasil Lobzhanidze)," admitted the 24-year-old. "Thinking back 12 months from where I am now, I definitely didn't picture myself sitting here with a World Cup medal and having this award here next to me so I'm just really thankful for all the support I've had along the way."

Another new award in 2015 was the Rugby World Cup Best Match Moment, a partnership between World Rugby and Facebook which engaged more than five million people. The clear winner was Japan's victory over South Africa on the opening weekend which sent shockwaves through the world of rugby when Karne Hesketh's try secured a 34–32 victory in Brighton. This moment beat off competition from Jonah Lomu's try-fest against England at RWC 1995, Jonny Wilkinson's drop goal in the RWC 2003 final and France's comeback victory over New Zealand at RWC 1999.

Among the other winners was South Africa's Werner Kok, who was overcome with emotion after being named World Rugby Sevens Player of the Year in association with HSBC. He had been instrumental in the Blitzboks finishing second in the men's series and securing qualification for the 2016 Olympic Games in Rio.

Two former captains in Ireland's Brian O'Driscoll and Nathan Sharpe of Australia received the IRPA Special Merit award. O'Driscoll played 141 tests from 1999–2014, leaving a huge hole in the Ireland midfield when he retired as the most-capped player in test history. Sharpe was a RWC runner-up in 2003, just a year after making his debut and he bowed out a decade later with 116 caps to his name.

One of the biggest cheers of the night, perhaps surprisingly, was reserved for Nigel Owens when he received the World Rugby Referee Award only a day after taking charge of the RWC 2015 final. The popular Owens is only the seventh to be given the honour of refereeing the game's showpiece match, but admitted his next assignment would be in a completely different environment to Twickenham – a community match back in Wales.

"It's pretty special being awarded the World Cup final and then to be awarded this as well really is special," Owens said. "There are a lot of other referees out there who are just as worthy if not more worthy than me, not only on the international stage but the referees who give up time in the week, Saturdays and Sundays just to referee kids games, who ensure games can go ahead and who probably don't get a thank you for it."

The first two awards of the night were the Vernon Pugh Award for Distinguished Service, presented to former England international turned commentator Nigel Starmer-Smith,

Nehe Milner-Skudder.

and the Award for Character in association with Land Rover, which went to the Pakistan Rugby Union for the way the rugby community came together in a show of solidarity with a match held in Peshawar just two months after terrorist attacks had killed more than 150 people at the Army Public School in the city.

The Société Générale Dream Team, selected by a panel representing the professional and amateur games, was also unveiled on the night by Jonny Wilkinson. The team is: 1. Marcos Ayerza (Argentina) 2. Stephen Moore (Australia) 3. Ramiro Herrera (Argentina) 4. Eben Etzebeth (South Africa) 5. Leone Nakarawa (Fiji) 6. Mamuka Gorgodze (Georgia) 7. Schalk Burger (South Africa) 8. David Pocock (Australia) 9. Greig Laidlaw (Scotland) 10. Daniel Carter (New Zealand) 11. Julian Savea (New Zealand) 12. Matt Giteau (Australia) 13. Conrad Smith (New Zealand) 14. Nehe Milner-Skudder (New Zealand) 15. Ayumu Goromaru (Japan).

During RWC 2015, the World Rugby Hall of Fame also welcomed 26 new inductees, including posthumously Nelson Mandela at St James' Park in Newcastle ahead of the South Africa v Scotland match on 3 October. The former South African president provided one of the most iconic moments in RWC history when, in 1995, he presented the Webb Ellis Cup to the victorious captain Francois Pienaar wearing a Springbok jersey. Two weeks earlier, players from seven different countries and a wide array of backgrounds were inducted at Wembley Stadium ahead of the New Zealand v Argentina encounter, among them 18 captains of their country and RWC winners Tim Horan and Joost van der Westhuizen.

For more information on the World Rugby Awards and the Hall of Fame, visit **www.worldrugby.org**.

Roll of Honour

Rugby World Cup 2015: New Zealand

RBS Six Nations: Ireland

The Rugby Championship: Australia

RBS Women's Six Nations: Ireland

World Rugby Nations Cup: Romania

World Rugby Tbilisi Cup: Emerging Ireland

World Rugby Pacific Nations Cup: Fiji

World Rugby Pacific Challenge: Argentina Pampas XV

World Rugby U20 Championship: New Zealand

World Rugby U20 Trophy: Georgia

HSBC Sevens World Series: Fiji

World Rugby Women's Sevens Series: New Zealand

Aviva Premiership: Saracens

Top 14: Stade Français

Guinness PRO12: Glasgow Warriors

European Rugby Champions Cup: Toulon

European Rugby Challenge Cup: Gloucester

Super Rugby: Highlanders

International Tournaments

REVIEW OF RUGBY WORLD CUP 2015

EIGHTH TOURNAMENT IN ENGLAND

THE POOL MATCHES

POOL A

18 September, Twickenham, London

ENGLAND 35 (3G 1T 3PG) FIJI 11 (1T 2PG)

ENGLAND: M Brown; A Watson, J Joseph, B Barritt, J May; G Ford, B Youngs; J Marler, T Youngs, D Cole, G Parling, C Lawes, T Wood, C Robshaw (captain), B Morgan

SUBSTITUTIONS: R Wigglesworth, B Vunipola, J Launchbury and M Vunipola for B Youngs, Morgan, Parling and Marler (52 mins); O Farrell and S Burgess for Ford and Barritt (62 mins); K Brookes for Cole (68 mins); R Webber for T Youngs (74 mins)

SCORERS: *Tries*: Penalty Try, Brown (2), B Vunipola *Conversions*: Farrell (2), Ford *Penalty Goals*: Farrell, Ford (2)

FIJI: M Talebula; W Nayacelevu, V Goneva, G Lovobalavu, N Nadolo; B Volavola, N Matawalu; C Ma'afu, A Koto, M Saulo, A Ratuniyarawa, L Nakarawa, D Waqaniburotu, A Qera (captain), S Matadigo

SUBSTITUTIONS: T Cavubati for Ratuniyarawa (41 mins); P Yato for Waqaniburotu (60 mins); P Ravai and T Tuapati for Ma'afu and Koto (74 mins); I Colati for Saulo (76 mins)

SCORERS: *Try*: Nadolo *Penalty Goals*: Volavola, Nadolo

YELLOW CARD: Matawalu (13 mins)

REFEREE: J Peyper (South Africa)

MAN OF THE MATCH: M Brown (England)

20 September, Millennium Stadium, Cardiff

WALES 54 (7G 1T) URUGUAY 9 (3PG)

WALES: L Williams; A Cuthbert, C Allen, S Williams, H Amos; R Priestland, G Davies; P James, S Baldwin, S Lee, J Ball, L Charteris, S Warburton (captain), J Tipuric, J King

SUBSTITUTIONS: A Jarvis for James (29 mins); M Morgan for L Williams (36 mins); J King and D Day for Charteris and Moriarty (48 mins); Lloyd Williams for Allen (55 mins); D Lydiate for Warburton (59 mins); K Owens for Baldwin (63 mins); King for Lydiate (75 mins)

SCORERS: *Tries*: Lee, Allen (3), Amos, Davies (2), Tipuric *Conversions*: Priestland (7)

URUGUAY: G Mieres; S Gibernau, J Prada, A Vilaseca, R Silva; F Berchesi, A Ormaechea; A Corral, C Arboleya, M Sagario, S Vilaseca (captain), J Zerbino, JM Gaminara, M Beer, A Nieto

SUBSTITUTIONS: J de Freitas for Beer (59 mins); F Lamanna for Zerbino (62 mins); O Duran for Sagario (72 mins); A Duran, A Alonso and F Bulanti for Ormaechea, S Vilaseca and Prada (75 mins); G Kessler and M Sanguinetti for Arboleya and Corral (78 mins)

SCORER: *Penalty Goals*: Berchesi (3)

REFEREE: R Poite (France)

MAN OF THE MATCH: C Allen (Wales)

23 September, Millennium Stadium, Cardiff

AUSTRALIA 28 (2G 1T 3PG) FIJI 13 (1G 2PG)

AUSTRALIA: I Folau; A Ashley-Cooper, T Kuridrani, M Giteau, R Horne; B Foley, W Genia; S Sio, S Moore (captain), S Kepu, K Douglas, R Simmons, S Fardy, M Hooper, D Pocock

SUBSTITUTIONS: J Slipper for Sio (temp 56–67 mins); G Holmes for Kepu (56 mins); D Mumm for Simmons (62 mins); N Phipps and T Polota-Nau for Genia and Moore (67 mins);; W Skelton for Douglas (71 mins); K Beale for Giteau (72 mins); M Toomua for Foley (78 mins)

SCORERS: *Tries*: Pocock (2), Kepu *Conversions*: Foley (2) *Penalty Goals*: Foley (3)

YELLOW CARD: T Kuridrani (73 mins)

FIJI: M Talebula; W Nayacelevu, V Goneva, G Lovobalavu, N Nadolo; B Volavola, N Matawalu; C Ma'afu, T Tuapati, M Saulo, T Cavubati, L Nakarawa, P Yato, A Qera (captain), N Talei

SUBSTITUTIONS: A Tikoirotuma for Nayacelevu (5 mins); P Ravai for Yato (temp 35–40 mins); N Kenatale for Matawalu (50 mins); N Soqeta for Cavubati (62 mins); M Ravulo for Talei (67 mins); I Colati for Saulo (78 mins)

SCORERS: *Try*: Volavola *Conversion*: Nadolo *Penalty Goals*: Nadolo (2)

YELLOW CARD: Ma'afu (30 mins)

REFEREE: G Jackson (New Zealand)

MAN OF THE MATCH: D Pocock (Australia)

26 September, Twickenham, London

ENGLAND 25 (1G 5PG 1DG) WALES 28 (1G 7PG)

ENGLAND: M Brown; A Watson, B Barritt, S Burgess, J May; O Farrell, B Youngs; J Marler, T Youngs, D Cole, G Parling, C Lawes, T Wood, C Robshaw (captain), B Vunipola

SUBSTITUTIONS: J Launchbury for Lawes (40 mins); R Wigglesworth for B Youngs (49 mins); M Vunipola for Marler (61 mins); J Haskell for B Vunipola (63 mins); R Webber for T Youngs (67 mins); G Ford for Burgess (70 mins); K Brookes for Cole (72 mins)

SCORERS: *Try*: May *Conversion*: Farrell *Penalty Goals*: Farrell (5) *Drop Goal*: Farrell

WALES: L Williams; G North, S Williams, J Roberts, H Amos; D Biggar, G Davies; G Jenkins, S Baldwin, T Francis, B Davies, AW Jones, D Lydiate, S Warburton (captain), T Faletau

SUBSTITUTIONS: K Owens and S Lee for Baldwin and Francis (49 mins); A Cuthbert for S Williams (63 mins); Lloyd Williams and R Priestland for Amos and L Williams (67 mins); L Charteris and J Tipuric for B Davies and Lydiate (70 mins)

SCORERS: *Try*: G Davies *Conversion*: Biggar *Penalty Goals*: Biggar (7)

REFEREE: J Garcès (France)

MAN OF THE MATCH: D Biggar (Wales)

27 September, Villa Park, Birmingham

AUSTRALIA 65 (5G 6T) URUGUAY 3 (1PG)

AUSTRALIA: K Beale; J Tomane, H Speight, M Toomua, D Mitchell; Q Cooper, N Phipps; S Sio, T Polota-Nau, T Smith, D Mumm (captain), W Skelton, B McCalman, S McMahon, W Palu

SUBSTITUTIONS: R Simmons for Palu (40 mins); S Kepu for Sio (49 mins); K Douglas for Skelton (57 mins); T Kuridrani for Toomua (78 mins)

SCORERS: *Tries*: McMahon (2), Tomane, Mumm, Speight, McCalman (2), Mitchell (2), Toomua, Kuridrani *Conversions*: Cooper (5)

URUGUAY: G Mieres; L Leivas, J Prada, A Vilaseca, R Silva; F Berchesi, A Ormaechea; M Sanguinetti, G Kessler, M Sagario, S Vilaseca (captain), F Lamanna, J de Freitas, M Beer, JM Gaminara

SUBSTITUTIONS: C Arboleya for Kessler (41 mins); O Duran and N Klappenbach for Sanguinetti and Sagario (53 mins); A Nieto and D Magno for De Freitas and Lamanna (55 mins); F Bascou, A Duran and A Roman for Gaminara, Berchesi and A Vilaseca (70 mins)

SCORER: *Penalty Goal*: Berchesi

REFEREE: P Gaüzère (France)

MAN OF THE MATCH: S McMahon (Australia)

1 October, Millennium Stadium, Cardiff

WALES 23 (2G 3PG) FIJI 13 (1G 2PG)

WALES: M Morgan; A Cuthbert, T Morgan, J Roberts, G North; D Biggar, G Davies; G Jenkins, S Baldwin, T Francis, B Davies, AW Jones, D Lydiate, S Warburton (captain), T Faletau

SUBSTITUTIONS: L Charteris for B Davies (temp 14–27 and 64 mins); L Williams for Cuthbert (temp 20–27 mins); S Lee for Francis (50 mins); K Owens for Baldwin (55 mins); A Jarvis for Jenkins (67 mins); J Tipuric for Lydiate (69 mins); J Hook for M Morgan (71 mins); R Priestland for Biggar (73 mins)

SCORERS: *Tries*: G Davies, Baldwin *Conversions*: Biggar (2) *Penalty Goals*: Biggar (3)

FIJI: M Talebula; T Nagusa, V Goneva, L Botia, A Tikoirotuma; B Volavola, N Kenatale; C Ma'afu, S Koto, M Saulo, T Cavubati, L Nakarawa, D Waqaniburotu, A Qera (captain), N Talei

SUBSTITUTIONS: M Ravulo and N Soqeta for Waqaniburotu and Cavubati (69 mins); H Seniloli and J Matavesi for Kenatale and Goneva (71 mins); V Veikoso and K Murimurivalu for Koto and Botia (75 mins); P Revai and L Atalifo for Ma'afu and Saulo (77 mins)

SCORERS: *Try*: Goneva *Conversion*: Volavola *Penalty Goals*: Volavola (2)

REFEREE: J Lacey (Ireland)

MAN OF THE MATCH: G Davies (Wales)

3 October, Twickenham, London

ENGLAND 13 (1G 2PG) AUSTRALIA 33 (3G 4PG)

ENGLAND: M Brown; A Watson, J Joseph, B Barritt, J May; O Farrell, B Youngs; J Marler, T Youngs, D Cole, J Launchbury, G Parling, T Wood, C Robshaw (captain), B Morgan

SUBSTITUTIONS: G Ford for May (40 mins); M Vunipola and R Wigglesworth for Marler and B Youngs (50 mins); K Brookes for Cole (54 mins); N Easter for Morgan (58 mins); R Webber for T Youngs (61 mins); S Burgess for Barritt (65 mins); G Kruis for Launchbury (69 mins)

SCORERS: *Try*: Watson *Conversion*: Farrell *Penalty Goals*: Farrell (2)

YELLOW CARD: O Farrell (71 mins)

AUSTRALIA: I Folau; A Ashley-Cooper, T Kuridrani, M Giteau, R Horne; B Foley, W Genia; S Sio, S Moore (captain), S Kepu, K Douglas, R Simmons, S Fardy, M Hooper, D Pocock

SUBSTITUTIONS: K Beale for Horne (11 mins); J Slipper and G Holmes for Sio and Kepu (57 mins); N Phipps for Genia (61 mins); M Toomua, T Polota-Nau and D Mumm for Folau, Moore and Simmons (65 mins); B McCalman for Fardy (76 mins)

SCORERS: *Tries*: Foley (2), Giteau *Conversions*: Foley (3) *Penalty Goals*: Foley (4)

REFEREE: R Poite (France)

MAN OF THE MATCH: J Launchbury (England)

RUGBY WORLD CUP 2015

6 October, Stadium MK, Milton Keynes

FIJI 47 (6G 1T) URUGUAY 15 (1G 1T 1PG)

FIJI: K Murimurivalu; A Tikoirotuma, V Goneva, L Botia, N Nadolo; B Volavola, N Kenatale; C Ma'afu, S Koto, L Atalifo, A Ratuniyarawa, L Nakarawa, D Waqaniburotu, A Qera (captain), S Matadigo

SUBSTITUTIONS: N Talei and T Cavubati for Matadigo and Ratuniyarawa (56 mins); H Saniloli for Kenatale (61 mins); T Nagusa for Goneva (65 mins); P Ravai for Waqaniburotu (67 mins); J Matavesi for Volavola (69 mins); T Koroi and V Veikoso for Atalifo and Koto (75 mins); Waqaniburotu for Ma'afu (78 mins)

SCORERS: *Tries*: Penalty Try (2), Kenatale, Nakarawa, Cavubati, Murimurivalu, Nadolo*Conversions*: Nadolo (6)

YELLOW CARD: C Ma'afu (66 mins)

URUGUAY: G Mieres; S Gibernau, J Prada, A Vilaseca, R Silva; A Duran, A Ormaechea; A Corral, C Arboleya, M Sagario, S Vilaseca (captain), J Zerbino, JM Gaminara, M Beer, A Nieto

SUBSTITUTIONS: M Sanguinetti for Corral (40 mins); J Etcheverry, O Duran and M Palomeque for A Duran, Sagario and Zerbino (65 mins); F Lamanna for Beer (70 mins); J de Freitas and F Bulanti for Gaminara and Gibernau (75 mins)

SCORERS: *Tries*: Arboleya, Ormaechea *Conversion*: Ormaechea *Penalty Goal*: Duran

YELLOW CARD: Ormaechea (3 mins and 66 mins)

RED CARD: A Ormaechea (66 mins)

REFEREE: JP Doyle (England)

MAN OF THE MATCH: L Nakawara (Fiji)

10 October, Twickenham, London

AUSTRALIA 15 (5PG) WALES 6 (2PG)

AUSTRALIA: I Folau; A Ashley-Cooper, T Kuridrani, M Giteau, D Mitchell; B Foley, W Genia; S Sio, S Moore (captain), S Kepu, K Douglas, D Mumm, S Fardy, S McMahon, D Pocock

SUBSTITUTIONS: B McCalman for McMahon (49 mins); G Holmes for Kepu (56 mins); R Simmons for Pocock (60 mins); J Slipper for Sio (63 mins); K Beale, T Polota-Nau and M Toomua for Mitchell, Moore and Giteau (67 mins);; N Phipps for Genia (68 mins)

SCORER: *Penalty Goals*: Foley (5)

YELLOW CARDS: W Genia (57 mins); D Mumm (60 mins)

WALES: G Anscombe; A Cuthbert, G North, J Roberts, L Williams; D Biggar, G Davies; P James, S Baldwin, S Lee, L Charteris, AW Jones, S Warburton (captain), J Tipuric, T Faletau

SUBSTITUTIONS: T Francis for Lee (54 mins); A Jarvis, K Owens and R Moriarty for James, Baldwin and Tipuric (73 mins); J Hook and R Priestland for Williams and Biggar (74 mins); Lloyd Williams for Roberts (80 mins)

SCORER: *Penalty Goals*: Biggar (3)

YELLOW CARD: Cuthbert (77 mins)

REFEREE: C Joubert (South Africa)

MAN OF THE MATCH: G Davies (Wales)

ENGLAND 60 (5G 5T) URUGUAY 3 (1PG)

ENGLAND: A Goode; A Watson, H Slade, O Farrell, J Nowell; G Ford, D Care; M Vunipola, T Youngs, D Cole, J Launchbury, G Parling, J Haskell, C Robshaw (captain), N Easter

SUBSTITUTIONS: J George for Youngs (30 mins); D Wilson for Cole (43 mins); G Kruis for Parling (55 mins); J Joseph for Farrell (59 mins); T Wood for Haskell (61 mins); Brown for Watson (67 mins); J Marler and R Wigglesworth for Vunipola and Care (71 mins)

SCORERS: *Tries*: Watson, Easter (3), Slade, Nowell (3), Penalty Try *Conversions*: Farrell (4), Ford

URUGUAY: G Mieres; S Gibernau, J Prada, A Vilaseca, R Silva; F Berchesi, A Ormaechea; M Sanguinetti, C Arboleya, M Sagario, S Vilaseca (captain), J Zerbino, JM Gaminara, M Beer, A Nieto

SUBSTITUTIONS: A Corral, N Klappenbach and M Palomeque for Sanguinetti, Sagario and Zerbino (63 mins); D Magno and A Alonso for Beer and Nieto (69 mins); O Duran for Arboleya (71 mins); A Duran and M Blengio for Berchesi and Ormaechea (74 mins)

SCORER: *Penalty Goal*: Berchesi

YELLOW CARD: Vilaseca (40 mins)

REFEREE: C Pollock (New Zealand)

MAN OF THE MATCH: N Easter (England)

POOL A FINAL TABLE

	P	W	D	L	PF	PA	PD	TF	TA	BP	PTS
Australia	4	4	0	0	141	35	+106	17	2	1	17
Wales	4	3	0	1	111	62	+49	11	2	1	13
England	4	2	0	2	133	75	+58	16	5	3	11
Fiji	4	1	0	3	84	101	-17	10	11	1	5
Uruguay	4	0	0	4	30	226	-196	2	36	0	0

P=Played; W=Won; D=Draw; L=Lost; PF= Points For; PA=Points Against; TF=Tries For; TA=Tries Against; BP=Bonus Points; PTS=Points

POOL B

SOUTH AFRICA 32 (3G 1T 2PG) JAPAN 34 (2G 1T 5PG)

SOUTH AFRICA: Z Kirchner; B Habana, J Kriel, J de Villiers (captain), L Mvovo; P Lambie, R Pienaar; T Mtawarira, B du Plessis, J du Plessis, L de Jager, V Matfield, PS du Toit, F Louw, S Burger

SUBSTITUTIONS: T Nyakane for Mtawarira (temp 54–80 mins); A Strauss and C Oosthuizen for B du Plessis and J du Plessis (54 mins); S Kolisi for Du Toit (57 mins); H Pollard and F du Preez for Lambie and Pienaar (58 mins); E Etzebeth for De Jager (68 mins); J du Plessis for Kolisi (80 mins)

SCORERS: *Tries:* Louw, B du Plessis, De Jager, Strauss *Conversions:* Lambie (2), Pollard *Penalty Goals:* Lambie, Pollard

YELLOW CARD: C Oosthuizen (79 mins)

JAPAN: A Goromaru; A Yamada, M Sau, H Tatekawa, K Matsushima; K Ono, F Tanaka; M Mikami, S Horie, K Hatakeyama, L Thompson, H Ono, M Leitch (captain), M Broadhurst, H Tui

SUBSTITUTIONS: H Yamashita for Hatakeyama (temp 10–19 and 54 mins); A Mafi for Tui (46 mins); S Makabefor H Ono (54 mins); K Inagaki for Mikami (58 mins); A Hiwasa for Tanaka (67 mins); T Kizu for Horie (70 mins); Y Tamura for K Ono (73 mins); K Hesketh for Yamada (79 mins)

SCORERS: *Tries:* Leitch, Goromaru, Hesketh *Conversions:* Goromaru (2) *Penalty Goals:* Goromaru (5)

REFEREE: J Garcès (France)

MAN OF THE MATCH: F Tanaka (Japan)

SAMOA 25 (2T 5PG) USA 16 (2T 2PG)

SAMOA: T Nanai-Williams; K Pisi, P Perez, R Lee-Lo, A Tuilagi; T Pisi, K Fotuali'i; S Taulafo, WO Avei, A Perenise, T Paulo, I Tekori, M Faasavalu, J Lam, O Treviranus (captain)

SUBSTITUTIONS: M Stanley for Lee-Lo (temp 2–9 mins); C Johnston and A Faosiliva for Perenise and Faasavalu (51 mins); F Levave and Stanley for Tekori and T Pisi (58 mins); M Matu'u for Avei (66 mins); F Autagavaia for Tuilagi (73 mins)

SCORERS: *Tries:* Nanai-Williams, Treviranus *Penalty Goals:* T Pisi (4), Stanley

USA: B Scully; T Ngwenya, S Kelly, T Palamo, C Wyles (captain); AJ MacGinty, M Petri; E Fry, Z Fenoglio, T Lamositele, H Smith, G Peterson, A McFarland, A Durutalo, S Manoa

SUBSTITUTIONS: B Thompson and P Thiel for Scully and Fenoglio (51 mins); C Dolan for Smith (51 mins); D Barrett for Peterson (58 mins); O Kilifi and C Baumann for Fry and Lamositele (71 mins)

SCORERS: *Tries:* Wyles, Baumann *Penalty Goals:* MacGinty (2)

REFEREE: G Clancy (Ireland)

MAN OF THE MATCH: T Nanai-Williams (Samoa)

23 September, Kingsholm, Gloucester

SCOTLAND 45 (4G 1T 4PG) JAPAN 10 (1G 1PG)

SCOTLAND: S Hogg; T Seymour, M Bennett, M Scott, S Lamont; F Russell, G Laidlaw (captain); A Dickinson, R Ford, WP Nel, G Gilchrist, J Gray, R Wilson, J Hardie, D Denton

SUBSTITUTIONS: R Gray for Gilchrist (50 mins); J Strauss for Wilson (57 mins); R Grant and S Maitland for Dickinson and Hogg (66 mins); J Welsh and F Brown for Nel and Ford (70 mins); P Horne for Bennett (75 mins)

SCORERS: *Tries*: Hardie, Bennett (2), Seymour, Russell *Conversions*: Laidlaw (4) *Penalty Goals*: Laidlaw (4)

JAPAN: A Goromaru; K Matsushima, M Sau, Y Tamura, K Fukuoka; H Tatekawa, F Tanaka; K Inagaki, S Horie, H Yamashita, L Thompson, J Ives, M Leitch (captain), M Broadhurst, A Mafi

SUBSTITUTIONS: M Mikami for Inagaki (40 mins); H Tui for Mafi (45 mins); K Hatakeyama for Yamashita (53 mins); S Makabe for Ives (61 mins); S Ito and A Hiwasa for Thompson and Tanaka (65 mins); T Kizu for Horie (70 mins); K Hesketh for Tatekawa (72 mins)

SCORERS: *Try*: Mafi *Conversion*: Goromaru *Penalty Goal*: Goromaru

YELLOW CARD: Matsushima (23 mins)

REFEREE: J Lacey (Ireland)

MAN OF THE MATCH: G Laidlaw (Scotland)

26 September, Villa Park, Birmingham

SOUTH AFRICA 46 (2G 4T 4PG) SAMOA 6 (2PG)

SOUTH AFRICA: W le Roux; JP Pietersen, J de Villiers (captain), D de Allende, B Habana; H Pollard, R Pienaar; T Mtawarira, A Strauss, J du Plessis, E Etzebeth, V Matfield, F Louw, S Burger, D Vermeulen, F du Preez

SUBSTITUTIONS: J Kriel for De Allende (48 mins); F Malherbe for Du Plessis (54 mins); L de Jager for Matfield (55 mins); T Nyakane for Mtawarira (62 mins); S Kolisi and S Brits for Burger and Strauss (68 mins); P Lambie for De Villiers (72 mins); R Pienaar for Du Preez (74 mins); De Villiers for Kriel (77 mins)

SCORERS: *Tries*: Pietersen (3), Burger, Brits, Habana *Conversions*: Pollard, Lambie *Penalty Goals*: Pollard (4)

SAMOA: T Nanai-Williams; K Pisi, P Perez, R Lee-Lo, A Tuilagi; M Stanley, K Fotuali'i; S Taulafo, M Matu'u, C Johnston, T Paulo, I Tekori, TJ Ioane, J Lam, O Treviranus (captain)

SUBSTITUTIONS: F Levave for Tekori (47 mins); WO Avei and A Perenise for Matu'u and Johnston (52 mins); T Pisi for Stanley (54 mins); V Tuilagi for Treviranus (62 mins); V Afatia for Taulafo (63 mins); G Pisi for A Tuilagi (66 mins); V Afemai for Fotuali'i (77 mins)

SCORER: *Penalty Goals*: Stanley (2)

REFEREE: W Barnes (England)

MAN OF THE MATCH: H Pollard (South Africa)

27 September, Elland Road, Leeds

SCOTLAND 39 (4G 1T 2PG) USA 16 (1G 3PG)

SCOTLAND: S Hogg; S Maitland, M Bennett, P Horne, T Visser; F Russell, H Pyrgos (captain); R Grant, R Ford, J Welsh, R Gray, G Gilchrist, A Strokosch, R Wilson, J Strauss

SUBSTITUTIONS: T Swinson for Gilchrist (18 mins); A Dickinson for Grant (40 mins); WP Nel for Welsh (41 mins); F Brown for Wilson (46 mins); G Laidlaw for Pyrgos (53 mins); M Scott for Horne (55 mins); D Weir for Russell (60 mins); K Bryce for Ford (78 mins)

SCORERS: *Tries*: Visser, Maitland, Nel, Scott, Weir *Conversions*: Russell, Laidlaw (3) *Penalty Goals*: Russell, Hogg

USA: C Wyles (captain); T Ngwenya, S Kelly, T Palamo, B Scully; AJ MacGinty, M Petri; E Fry, P Thiel, T Lamositele, H Smith, G Peterson, A McFarland, A Durutalo, S Manoa

SUBSTITUTIONS: C Dolan for Smith (43 mins); D Barrett and S Suniula for Peterson and Petri (50 mins); F Niua and J Quill for Scully and Durutalo (59 mins); Z Fenoglio for Thiel (64 mins); O Kilifi for Fry (67 mins); C Baumann for Lamositele (69 mins)

SCORERS: *Try*: Lamositele *Conversion*: MacGinty *Penalty Goals*: MacGinty (3)

REFEREE: C Pollock (New Zealand)

MAN OF THE MATCH: S Hogg (Scotland)

3 October, Stadium MK, Milton Keynes

SAMOA 5 (1T) JAPAN 26 (2G 4PG)

SAMOA: T Nanai-Williams; K Pisi, P Perez, J Leota, A Tuilagi; T Pisi, K Fotuali'i; S Taulafo, WO Avei, C Johnston, T Paulo, K Thompson, O Treviranus (captain), TJ Ioane, F Levave

SUBSTITUTIONS: V Afatia for A Tuilagi (temp 22–29 mins); J Lam and R Lee-Lo for Ioane and A Tuilagi (48 mins); A Perenise for Johnston (51 mins); M Matu'u for Avei (56 mins); V Afatia for Taulafo (62 mins); V Tuilagi for Treviranus (70 mins); V Afemai for Fotuali'i (74 mins)

SCORER: *Try*: Perez

YELLOW CARDS: F Levave (16 mins); S Taulafo (19 mins); T Paulo (78 mins)

JAPAN: A Goromaru; A Yamada, M Sau, H Tatekawa, K Matsushima; K Ono, F Tanaka; K Inagaki, S Horie, K Hatakeyama, L Thompson, H Ono, M Leitch (captain), M Broadhurst, RK Holani

SUBSTITUTIONS: J Ives for H Ono (40 mins); K Hesketh for Yamada (56 mins); A Mafi for Holani (60 mins); H Tui and H Yamashita for Broadhurst and Hatakeyama (65 mins); T Kizu and A Hiwasa for Sau and Tanaka (72 mins)

SCORERS: *Tries*: Penalty Try, Yamada *Conversions*: Goromaru (2) *Penalty Goals*: Goromaru (4)

REFEREE: C Joubert (South Africa)

MAN OF THE MATCH: A Goromaru (Japan)

SOUTH AFRICA 34 (2G 1T 4PG 1DG) SCOTLAND 16 (1G 3PG)

SOUTH AFRICA: W le Roux; JP Pietersen, J Kriel, D de Allende, B Habana; H Pollard, F du Preez; T Mtawarira, B du Plessis, J du Plessis, E Etzebeth, L de Jager, F Louw, S Burger, D Vermeulen

SUBSTITUTIONS: F Malherbe for J du Plessis (50 mins); A Strauss for B du Plessis (56 mins); T Nyakane for Mtawarira (61 mins); W Alberts and P Lambie for Burger and Pietersen (70 mins); PS du Toit and J Serfontein for De Jager and De Allende (75 mins); R Pienaar for Du Preez (78 mins)

SCORERS: *Tries*: Burger, Pietersen, Habana *Conversions*: Pollard (2) *Penalty Goals*: Pollard (4) *Drop Goal*: Pollard

YELLOW CARD: J du Plessis (34 mins)

SCOTLAND: S Hogg; T Seymour, R Vernon, M Scott, T Visser; D Weir, G Laidlaw (captain); G Reid, F Brown, WP Nel, R Gray, J Gray, J Strauss, B Cowan, D Denton

SUBSTITUTIONS: R Wilson for Strauss (temp 30–34 and 55 mins); A Dickinson for Reid (51 mins); R Ford for Brown (temp 61–78 mins); S Lamont for Hogg (63 mins); J Welsh for Nel (64 mins); P Horne for Vernon (65 mins); T Swinson for J Gray (68 mins); S Hidalgo-Clyne for Laidlaw (70 mins)

SCORERS: *Try*: Seymour *Conversion*: Laidlaw *Penalty Goals*: Laidlaw (2), Weir

YELLOW CARD: Laidlaw (53 mins)

REFEREE: N Owens (Wales)

MAN OF THE MATCH: L de Jager (South Africa)

SOUTH AFRICA 64 (7G 3T) USA 0

SOUTH AFRICA: W le Roux; B Habana, J Kriel, D de Allende, L Mvovo; H Pollard, F du Preez (captain); T Mtawarira, B du Plessis, F Malherbe, E Etzebeth, L de Jager, F Louw, S Burger, D Vermeulen

SUBSTITUTIONS: J Serfontein for Habana (temp 23–26 mins); W Alberts for Burger (48 mins); S Brits, T Nyakane and M Steyn for Du Plessis, Mtawarira and Pollard (56 mins); J Serfontein and C Oosthuizen for De Allende and Malherbe (60 mins); R Piage and PS du Toit for Du Preez and De Jager (63 mins)

SCORERS: *Tries*: De Allende, Penalty Try, Habana (3), Du Plessis, Louw (2), Kriel, Mvovo *Conversions*: Pollard (4), Steyn (3)

USA: B Scully; B Thompson, F Niua, A Suniula, Z Test; S Suniula, N Kruger; O Kilifi, P Thiel, C Baumann, L Standfill, M Trouville, D Barrett, J Quill, S Manoa (captain)

SUBSTITUTIONS: C Wyles for Scully (temp 23–26 and 70 mins); C Dolan for Manoa (48 mins); A McFarland for Barrett (58 mins); M Moeakiola for Kilifi (59 mins); Z Fenoglio for Trouville (70 mins); J Taufetee for Thiel (72 mins)

REFEREE: P Gaüzère (France)

MAN OF THE MATCH: D de Allende (South Africa)

10 October, St James' Park, Newcastle

SAMOA 33 (2G 2T 3PG) SCOTLAND 36 (3G 5PG)

SAMOA: T Nanai-Williams; P Perez, G Pisi, R Lee-Lo, F Autagavaia; T Pisi, K Fotuali'i (captain); S Taulafo, M Leiataua, C Johnston, T Paulo, K Thompson, M Faasavalu, J Lam, A Faosiliva

SUBSTITUTIONS: F Levave for Thompson (29 mins); V Tuilagi, A Perenise and V Afatia for Faosiliva, Johnston and Taulafo (59 mins); K Pisi and T Pisi for Autagavaia and K Pisi (71 mins); M Matu'u for Leiataua (74 mins); V Afemai for Fotuali'i (79 mins)

SCORERS: *Tries:* T Pisi, Leiataua, Lee-Lo, Matu'u *Conversions:* T Pisi, Faapale *Penalty Goals:* T Pisi (3)

SCOTLAND: S Hogg; S Maitland, M Bennett, M Scott, T Seymour; F Russell, G Laidlaw (captain); A Dickinson, R Ford, WP Nel, R Gray, J Gray, R Wilson, J Hardie, D Denton

SUBSTITUTIONS: G Reid for Dickinson (temp 23–28 mins); J Strauss for Wilson (53 mins); T Swinson for J Gray (62 mins); F Brown for Ford (66 mins); S Lamont for Hogg (71 mins); P Horne for Scott (76 mins)

SCORERS: *Tries:* Seymour, Hardie, Laidlaw *Conversions:* Laidlaw (3) *Penalty Goals:* Laidlaw (5)

REFEREE: J Peyper (South Africa)

MAN OF THE MATCH: J Hardie (Scotland)

11 October, Kingsholm, Gloucester

USA 18 (1G 1T 2PG) JAPAN 28 (2G 1T 3PG)

USA: C Wyles (captain); T Ngwenya, S Kelly, T Palamo, Z Test; AJ MacGinty, M Petri; E Fry, Z Fenoglio, T Lamositele, H Smith, G Peterson, A McFarland, A Durutalo, S Manoa

SUBSTITUTIONS: C Dolan for Smith (31 mins); P Thiel and D Barrett for Fenoglio and McFarland (64 mins); J Quill for Peterson (77 mins)

SCORERS: *Tries:* Ngwenya, Wyles *Conversion:* MacGinty *Penalty Goals:* MacGinty (2)

YELLOW CARD: Fry (61 mins)

JAPAN: A Goromaru; Y Fujita, H Tatekawa, C Wing, K Matsushima; K Ono, F Tanaka; K Inagaki, S Horie, H Yamashita, L Thompson, J Ives, M Leitch (captain), M Broadhurst, RK Holani

SUBSTITUTIONS: K Hatakeyama and A Mafi for Yamashita and Holani (41 mins); K Hesketh for Matsushima (temp 49–57 mins); M Mikami for Inagaki (59 mins); A Hiwasa for Tanaka (62 mins); S Makabe for Ives (68 mins); K Hesketh and H Tui for Ono and Broadhurst (73 mins); T Kizu for Horie (77 mins)

SCORERS: *Tries:* Matsushima, Fujita, Mafi *Conversions:* Goromaru (2) *Penalty Goals:* Goromaru (3)

REFEREE: G Jackson (New Zealand)

MAN OF THE MATCH: A Goromaru (Japan)

POOL B FINAL TABLE

49

	P	W	D	L	PF	PA	PD	TF	TA	BP	PTS
South Africa	4	3	0	1	176	56	+120	23	4	4	16
Scotland	4	3	0	1	136	93	+43	14	9	2	14
Japan	4	3	0	1	98	100	-2	9	12	0	12
Samoa	4	1	0	3	69	124	-55	7	13	2	6
USA	4	0	0	4	50	156	-106	5	20	0	0

P=Played; W=Won; D=Draw; L=Lost; PF= Points For; PA=Points Against; TF=Tries For; TA=Tries Against; BP=Bonus Points; PTS=Points

POOL C

19 September, Kingsholm, Gloucester

TONGA 10 (1G 1PG) GEORGIA 17 (2G 1PG)

TONGA: V Lilo; T Veainu, W Helu, S Piutau, F Vainikolo; K Morath, S Takulua; T Mailau, E Taione, H 'Aulika, T Lokotui, S Mafi, S Kalamafoni, N Latu (captain), V Ma'afu

SUBSTITUTIONS: P Ngauamo, S Taumalolo and S Piukala for Taione, Mailau and Helu (52 mins); H T-Pole for Mafi (60 mins); S Puafisi for 'Aulika (65 mins); J Ram for Latu (72 mins)

SCORERS: *Try*: Vainikolo *Conversion*: Morath *Penalty Goal*: Morath

GEORGIA: M Kvirikashvili; T Mchedlidze, D Kacharava, M Sharikadze, G Aptsiauri; L Malaguradze, V Lobzhanidze; M Nariashvili, J Bregvadze, D Zirakashvili, G Nemsadze, K Mikautadze, G Tkhilaishvili, V Kolelishvili, M Gorgodze (captain)

SUBSTITUTIONS: S Mamukashvili, K Asieshvili and L Chilachava for Bregvadze, Nariashvili and Zirakashvili (61 mins); L Datunashvili for Mikautadze (64 mins); S Sutiashvili for Tkhilaishvili (66 mins); G Begadze for Lobzhanidze (79 mins)

SCORERS: *Tries*: Gorgodze, Tkhilaishvili *Conversions*: Kvirikashvili (2) *Penalty Goal*: Kvirikashvili

YELLOW CARD: Kvirikashvili (73 mins)

REFEREE: N Owens (Wales)

MAN OF THE MATCH: M Gorgodze (Georgia)

RUGBY WORLD CUP 2015

20 September, Wembley Stadium, London

NEW ZEALAND 26 (2G 4PG) ARGENTINA 16 (1G 3PG)

NEW ZEALAND: B Smith; N Milner-Skudder, C Smith, M Nonu, J Savea; D Carter, A Smith; T Woodcock, D Coles, O Franks, B Retallick, S Whitelock, J Kaino, R McCaw (captain), K Read

SUBSTITUTIONS: W Crockett and SB Williams for Woodcock and Nonu (46 mins); C Faumuina and B Barrett for O Franks and Milner-Skudder (50 mins); S Cane for Kaino (65 mins); K Mealamu for Coles (68 mins); TJ Perenara for A Smith (69 mins); V Vito for Retallick (71 mins)

SCORERS: *Tries*: A Smith, Cane *Conversions*: Carter (2) *Penalty Goals*: Carter (4)

YELLOW CARDS: McCaw (30mins), Smith (37 mins)

ARGENTINA: J Tuculet; S Cordero, M Bosch, JM Hernández, J Imhoff; N Sánchez, T Cubelli; M Ayerza, A Creevy (captain), N Tetaz Chaparro, G Petti, T Lavanini, P Matera, JM Fernández Lobbe, L Senatore

SUBSTITUTIONS: M Galarza for Petti (23 mins); R Herrera for Tetaz Chaparro (54 mins); JM Leguizamón for Matera (58 mins); M Landajo for Cubelli (62 mins); J Montoya for Senatore (65 mins); J de la Fuente for Sánchez (69 mins); L González Amorosino and L Noguera for Tuculet and Creevy (70 mins)

SCORERS: *Try*: Petti *Conversion*: Sánchez *Penalty Goals*: Sánchez (3)

YELLOW CARD: Matera (10 mins)

REFEREE: W Barnes (England)

MAN OF THE MATCH: B Retallick (New Zealand)

Getty Images

Man of the match Brodie Retallick bulldozes his way past Argentina's Juan Martín Fernández Lobbe at Wembley.

24 September, The Stadium, Queen Elizabeth Olympic Park, London

NEW ZEALAND 58 (5G 4T 1PG) NAMIBIA 14 (1T 3PG)

NEW ZEALAND: C Slade; N Milner-Skudder, M Fekitoa, SB Williams, J Savea; B Barrett, TJ Perenara; B Franks, C Taylor, C Faumuina, L Romano, S Whitelock, J Kaino, S Cane (captain), V Vito

SUBSTITUTIONS: T Kerr-Barlow for Perenara (48 mins); B Smith and K Read for Slade and Whitelock (52 mins); R McCaw and M Nonu for Kaino and Williams (62 mins); W Crockett for Faumuina (64 mins)

SCORERS: *Tries*: Vito, Milner-Skudder (2), Fekitoa, Barrett, Savea (2), Smith, Taylor *Conversions*: Barrett (4), Slade *Penalty Goal*: Barrett

NAMIBIA: J Tromp; D Philander, JC Greyling, J Deysel, C Marais; T Kotze, E Jantjies; J Engels, T van Jaarsveld, J Coetzee, PJ van Lill, T Uanivi, J Burger (captain), T du Plessis, L Damens

SUBSTITUTIONS: C Botha and R Bothma for Marais and Damens (45 mins); R Larson for Coetzee (temp 48–60 mins and 69–73 mins); Damens for Du Plessis (temp 50–53 mins); C Viviers for Philander (58 mins); R Kitshoff for Van Lill (63 mins); J Venter for Burger (65 mins); Philander for Engels (69 mins); L van der Westhuizen and E Buitendag for Van Jaarsveld and Jantjies (73 mins)

SCORERS: *Try*: Deysel *Penalty Goals*: Kotze (3)

YELLOW CARD: Engels (57 mins)

REFEREE: R Poite (France)

MAN OF THE MATCH: N Milner-Skudder (New Zealand)

Centre Johan Deysel scores Namibia's first ever try against the All Blacks and their first try of RWC 2015.

RUGBY WORLD CUP 2015

25 September, Kingsholm, Gloucester

ARGENTINA 54 (5G 2T 2PG 1DG) GEORGIA 9 (3PG)

ARGENTINA: J Tuculet; S Cordero, M Bosch, JM Hernández, J Imhoff; N Sánchez, T Cubelli; M Ayerza, A Creevy (captain), N Tetaz Chaparro, M Alemanno, T Lavanini, JM Leguizamón, JM Fernández Lobbe, F Isa

SUBSTITUTIONS: J de la Fuente for Hernández (37 mins); P Matera, M Landajo and R Herrera for Leguizamón, Cubelli and Tetaz Chaparro (58 mins); J Montoya for Creevy (63 mins); J Ortega Desio and L González Amorosino for Fernández Lobbe and Sánchez (65 mins); L Noguera for Ayerza (68 mins)

SCORERS: *Tries*: Lavanini, Cubelli, Imhoff (2), Cordero (2), Landajo *Conversions*: Sánchez (3), Bosch (2) *Penalty Goals*: Sánchez (2) *Drop Goal*: Sánchez

GEORGIA: M Kvirikashvili; T Mchedlidze, D Kacharava, M Sharikadze, G Aptsiauri; L Malaguradze, V Lobzhanidze; M Nariashvili, J Bregvadze, D Zirakashvili, G Nemsadze, K Mikautadze, G Tkhilaishvili, V Kolelishvili, M Gorgodze (captain)

SUBSTITUTIONS: L Datunashvili and S Mamukashvili for Mikautadze and Bregvadze (49 mins); K Asieshvili and L Chilachava for Nariashvili and Zirakashvili (52 mins); M Giorgadze for Kvirikashvili (54 mins); G Begadze and S Sutiashvili for Lobzhanidze and Kolelishvili (58 mins); G Pruidze for Mchedlidze (59 mins)

SCORER: *Penalty Goals*: Kvirikashvili (3)

YELLOW CARD: Gorgodze (45 mins)

REFEREE: JP Doyle (England)

MAN OF THE MATCH: S Cordero (Argentina)

Getty Images

Argentina's flying winger Santiago Cordero evades the grasp of Giorgi Tkhilaishvili during their Pool C clash at Kingsholm.

29 September, Sandy Park, Exeter

TONGA 35 (2G 3T 2PG) NAMIBIA 21 (3G)

TONGA: V Lilo; D Halaifonua, S Piutau (captain), S Piukala, T Veainu; L Fosita, S Takulua; S Tonga'uiha, A Lutui, S Puafisi, H T-Pole, J Tuineau, S Kalamafoni, J Ram, V Ma'afu

SUBSTITUTIONS: O Fonua for Kalamafoni (33 mins); T Lokotui for T-Pole (43 mins); P Ngauamo for Lutui (47 mins); S Fisilau and K Morath for Takulua and Piutau (58 mins); T Mailau, H 'Aulika and W Helu for Tonga'uiha, Puafisi and Lilo (60 mins)

SCORERS: *Tries*: Veainu (2), Ram (2), Fosita *Conversions*: Lilo (2) *Penalty Goals*: Lilo, Morath

NAMIBIA: C Botha; J Tromp, D van Wyk, J Deysel, R van Wyk; T Kotze, E Buitendag; C Viviers, T van Jaarsveld, J Coetzee, J Venter, T Uanivi, J Burger (captain), R Kitshoff, R Bothma

SUBSTITUTIONS: J Redelinghuys for Viviers (40 mins); PJ van Lill for Venter (41 mins); T du Plessis for Bothma (68 mins); D Stevens for Buitendag (71 mins); AJ de Klerk and D de la Harpe for Coetzee and Deysel (72 mins); L van der Westhuizen for Van Jaarsveld (74 mins)

SCORERS: *Tries*: Tromp, Burger (2) *Conversions*: Kotze (3)

REFEREE: G Jackson (New Zealand)

MAN OF THE MATCH: J Ram (Tonga)

2 October, Millennium Stadium, Cardiff

NEW ZEALAND 43 (4G 3T) GEORGIA 10 (1G 1PG)

NEW ZEALAND: B Smith; W Naholo, C Smith, SB Williams, J Savea; D Carter, A Smith; W Crockett, D Coles, C Faumuina, B Retallick, S Whitelock, J Kaino, R McCaw (captain), K Read

SUBSTITUTIONS: M Fekitoa for Naholo (53 mins); V Vito for Williams (56 mins); T Woodcock, O Franks and S Cane for Crockett, Faumuina and McCaw (61 mins); Williams for C Smith (63 mins); T Kerr-Barlow and K Mealamu for A Smith and Coles (71 mins)

SCORERS: *Tries*: Naholo, Savea (3), Coles, Read, Fekitoa *Conversions*: Carter (4)

GEORGIA: B Tsiklauri; G Aptsiauri, D Kacharava, T Mchedlidze, A Todua; L Malaguradze, G Begadze; K Asieshvili, S Mamukashvili, L Chilachava, G Chkhaidze, L Datunashvili, S Sutiashvili, M Gorgodze (captain), L Lomidze

SUBSTITUTIONS: V Lobzhanidze for Begadze (45 mins); K Mikautadze for Gorgodze (48 mins); M Nariashvili and A Peikrishvili for Asieshvili and Chilachava (51 mins); M Sharikadze and S Maisuradze for Todua and Mamukashvili (66 mins); V Kolelishvili for Lomidze (68 mins); M Giorgadze for Mchedlidze (76 mins)

SCORERS: *Try*: Tsiklauri *Conversion*: Malaguradze *Penalty Goals*: Malaguradze

REFEREE: P Gaüzère (France)

MAN OF THE MATCH: M Gorgodze (Georgia)

54

ARGENTINA 45 (4G 1T 4PG) TONGA 16 (2T 2PG)

ARGENTINA: J Tuculet; S Cordero, M Moroni, J de la Fuente, J Imhoff; N Sánchez, M Landajo; M Ayerza, A Creevy (captain), R Herrera, G Petti, T Lavanini, P Matera, JM Fernández Lobbe, L Senatore

SUBSTITUTIONS: F Isa for Senatore (51 mins); H Agulla for Imhoff (58 mins); L Noguera, JP Orlandi, T Cubelli, J Montoya and M Alemanno for Ayerza, Herrera, Landajo, Creevy and Petti (65 mins); S González Iglesias for Moroni (71 mins)

SCORERS: *Tries*: Tuculet, Imhoff, Sánchez, Montoya, Cordero *Conversions*: Sánchez (4) *Penalty Goals*: Sánchez (4)

TONGA: V Lilo; T Veainu, S Piutau, S Piukala, F Vainikolo; K Morath, S Takulua; S Tonga'uiha, E Taione, H 'Aulika, T Lokotui, J Tuineau, S Kalamafoni, N Latu (captain), V Ma'afu

SUBSTITUTIONS: L Fosita for Piukala (50 mins); S Taumalolo, A Lutui and O Fonua for Tonga'uiha, Taione and Ma'afu (61 mins); S Mafi for Tuineau (67 mins); S Puafisi, S Fisilau and D Halaifonua for 'Aulika, Takalua and Lilo (71 mins)

SCORERS: *Tries*: Morath, Tonga'uiha *Penalty Goals*: Morath (2)

REFEREE: J Peyper (South Africa)

MAN OF THE MATCH: N Sánchez (Argentina)

NAMIBIA 16 (1G 3PG) GEORGIA 17 (2G 1PG)

NAMIBIA: C Botha; D Philander, D van Wyk, D de la Harpe, R van Wyk; T Kotze, E Jantjies; J Redelinghuys, T van Jaarsveld, R Larson, P van Lill, T Uanivi, J Burger (captain), T du Plessis, R Bothma

SUBSTITUTIONS: R Kitshoff for Burger (10 mins); H Smit for D van Wyk (28 mins); J Coetzee for Philander (temp 40–51 mins); J Engels, J Coetzee and W Conradie for Redelinghuys, Larson and Du Plessis (60 mins); D Stevens and Du Plessis for Jantjies and Van Lill (68 mins); L van der Westhuizen for Coetzee (71 mins); J Tromp for De la Harpe (76 mins)

SCORER: *Try*: Kotze *Conversion*: Kotze *Penalty Goals*: Kotze (3)

YELLOW CARDS: R Larson (40 mins); J Coetzee (40 mins); R Bothma (51 mins)

GEORGIA: M Kvirikashvili; T Mchedlidze, D Kacharava, M Sharikadze, A Todua; L Malaguradze, V Lobzhanidze; M Nariashvili, J Bregvadze, D Zirakashvili, G Nemsadze, K Mikautadze, G Tkhilaishvili, V Kolelishvili, M Gorgodze (captain)

SUBSTITUTIONS: K Asieshvili for Nariashvili (36 mins); L Lomidze for Kolelishvili (40 mins); G Aptsiauri for Mchedlidze (43 mins); S Mamukashvili and L Datunashvili for Bregvadze and Mikautadze (57 mins); G Begadze for Lobzhanidze (66 mins); B Tsiklauri for Kvirikashvili (76 mins)

SCORERS: *Tries*: Gorgodze, Malaguradze *Conversions*: Kvirikashvili (2) *Penalty Goal*: Kvirikashvili

YELLOW CARD: Bregvadze (35 mins)

REFEREE: G Clancy (Ireland)

MAN OF THE MATCH: T du Plessis (Namibia)

9 October, St James' Park, Newcastle

NEW ZEALAND 47 (6G 1T) TONGA 9 (3PG)

NEW ZEALAND: B Smith; N Milner-Skudder, C Smith, M Nonu, W Naholo; D Carter, A Smith; T Woodcock, D Coles, O Franks, L Romano, S Whitelock, J Kaino, S Cane, K Read (captain)

SUBSTITUTIONS:W Crockett for Woodcock (43 mins); B Retallick for Romano (49 mins); B Barrett for Naholo (57 mins); SB Williams and B Franks for C Smith and O Franks (62 mins); K Mealamu and L Messam for Coles and Whitelock (66 mins); T Kerr-Barlow for A Smith (72 mins)

SCORERS: *Tries:* B Smith, Woodcock, Milner-Skudder (2), Williams, Cane, Nonu *Conversions:* Carter (6)

YELLOW CARD: Read (38 mins)

TONGA: V Lilo; T Veainu, S Piutau, L Fosita, F Vainikolo; K Morath, S Takulua; S Tonga'uiha, E Taione, H 'Aulika, T Lokotui, J Tuineau, S Kalamafoni, N Latu (captain), V Ma'afu

SUBSTITUTIONS: P Ngauamo for Taione (49 mins); S Mafi for Tuineau (54 mins); S Taumalolo for Tonga'uiha (55 mins); V Tahitua for Morath (62 mins); J Ram and W Helu for V Ma'afu and Veainu (66 mins); S Puafisa and S Fislau for 'Aulika and Takulua (70 mins)

SCORER: *Penalty Goals:* Morath (3)

YELLOW CARD: Ngauamo (70 mins)

REFEREE: J Lacey (Ireland)

MAN OF THE MATCH: N Milner-Skudder (New Zealand)

11 October, Leicester City Stadium, Leicester

ARGENTINA 64 (8G 1T 1PG) NAMIBIA 19 (2G 1T)

ARGENTINA: L González Amorosino; M Moroni, S González Iglesias, JP Socino, H Agulla; JM Hernández, M Landajo (captain); L Noguera, J Montoya, JP Orlandi, G Petti, M Alemanno, P Matera, J Ortega Desio, F Isa

SUBSTITUTIONS: L Senatore for Matera (50 mins); M Bosch for Hernández (51 mins); T Cubelli and R Herrera for Landajo and Orlandi (53 mins); JM Fernández Lobbe for Alemanno (61 mins); J Imhoff and A Creevy for González Iglesias and Montoya (70 mins)

SCORERS: *Tries:* Hernández, Moroni, Agulla, Isa, Noguera, Alemanno, Senatore, Montoya, Cubelli *Conversions:* Socino (4), González Iglesias (4) *Penalty Goal:* González Iglesias

YELLOW CARD: Bosch (53 mins)

NAMIBIA: C Botha; J Tromp, JC Greyling, J Deysel, C Marais; T Kotze, D Stevens; J Engels, T van Jaarsveld, J Coetzee, J Venter, T Uanivi, R Kitshoff (captain), W Conradie, L Damens

SUBSTITUTIONS: PJ Van Lill for Venter (6 mins); AJ de Klerk for Coetzee (47 mins); J Redelinghuys and L van der Westhuizen for Engels and Van Jaarsveld (52 mins); R van Wyk and T du Plessis for Botha and Damens (58 mins); H Smith for Greyling (temp 65–70 mins); E Jantjies for Stevens (65 mins)

SCORERS: *Tries:* Tromp, Greyling, Jantjies *Conversions:* Kotze (2)

YELLOW CARDS: Greyling (11 mins); du Plessis (76 mins)

REFEREE: P Gaüzère (France)

MAN OF THE MATCH: H Agulla (Argentina)

POOL C FINAL TABLE

	P	W	D	L	PF	PA	PD	TF	TA	BP	PTS
New Zealand	4	4	0	0	174	49	+125	25	3	3	19
Argentina	4	3	0	1	179	70	+109	22	7	3	15
Georgia	4	2	0	2	53	123	-70	5	16	0	8
Tonga	4	1	0	3	70	130	-60	8	17	2	6
Namibia	4	0	0	4	70	174	-104	8	25	1	1

P=Played; W=Won; D=Draw; L=Lost; PF= Points For; PA=Points Against; TF=Tries For; TA=Tries Against; BP=Bonus Points; PTS=Points

POOL D

19 September, Millennium Stadium, Cardiff

IRELAND 50 (6G 1T 1PG) CANADA 7 (1G)

IRELAND: R Kearney; D Kearney, J Payne, L Fitzgerald, K Earls; J Sexton, C Murray; J McGrath, R Best, M Ross, I Henderson, P O'Connell (captain), P O'Mahony, S O'Brien, J Heaslip

SUBSTITUTIONS: I Madigan for Sexton (56 mins); S Cronin, C Healy and N White for Best, McGrath and Ross (61 mins); C Henry for O'Brien (63 mins); E Reddan for Murray (66 mins); D Ryan and S Zebo for O'Connell and Fitzgerald (74 mins)

SCORERS: *Tries*: O'Brien, Henderson, Sexton, D Kearney, Cronin, R Kearney, Payne *Conversions*: Sexton (3), Madigan (3) *Penalty Goal*: Sexton

YELLOW CARD: O'Connell (42 mins)

CANADA: M Evans; J Hassler, C Hearn, N Blevins, DTH van der Merwe; N Hirayama, G McRorie; H Buydens, R Barkwill, D Wooldridge, B Beukeboom, J Cudmore (captain), K Gilmour, J Moonlight, A Carpenter

SUBSTITUTIONS: L Underwood and C Trainor for Evans and Hassler (41 mins); D Sears-Duru, J Sinclair and P Mack for Buydens, Gilmour and McRorie (48 mins); B Piffero for Barkwill (63 mins); A Tiedemann for Wooldridge (66 mins); R Thorpe for Underwood (75 mins)

SCORERS: *Try*: Van der Merwe *Conversion*: Hirayama

YELLOW CARD: Cudmore (17 mins)

REFEREE: G Jackson (New Zealand)

MAN OF THE MATCH: J Sexton (Ireland)

FRANCE 32 (2G 6PG) ITALY 10 (1G 1PG)

FRANCE: S Spedding; Y Huget, M Bastareaud, A Dumoulin, N Nakaitaci; F Michalak, S Tillous-Borde; E Ben Arous, G Guirado, R Slimani, P Papé, Y Maestri, T Dusautoir (captain), D Chouly, L Picamoles

SUBSTITUTIONS: G Fickou for Huget (55 mins); M Parra for Tillous-Borde (57 mins); B Kayser for Guirado (temp 61–67 and 75 mins); V Debaty for Ben Arous (61 mins); N Mas for Slimani (63 mins); B le Roux for Picamoles (66 mins); A Flanquart for Maestri (69 mins); R Talès for Michalak (76 mins)

SCORERS: *Tries:* Slimani, Mas *Conversions:* Michalak (2) *Penalty Goals:* Michalak (5), Spedding

ITALY: L McLean; L Sarto, M Campagnaro, A Masi, G Venditti; T Allan, E Gori; M Aguero, L Ghiraldini (captain), ML Castrogiovanni, Q Geldenhuys, J Furno, A Zanni, F Minto, S Vunisa

SUBSTITUTIONS: E Bacchin for Masi (11 mins); M Rizzo and L Cittadini for Aguero and Castrogiovanni (50 mins); S Favaro for Minto (61 mins); A Manici for Ghiraldini (63 mins); V Bernabò and G Palazzani for Furno and E Gori (72 mins); C Canna for Allan (79 mins)

SCORERS: *Try:* Venditti *Conversion:* Allan *Penalty Goal:* Allan

REFEREE: C Joubert (South Africa)

MAN OF THE MATCH: L Picamoles (France)

FRANCE 38 (5G 1PG) ROMANIA 11 (1T 2PG)

FRANCE: B Dulin; S Guitoune, G Fickou, W Fofana, N Nakaitaci; R Talès, M Parra; V Debaty, D Szarzewski (captain), U Atonio, B le Roux, A Flanquart, Y Nyanga, F Ouedraogo, L Picamoles

SUBSTITUTIONS: B Kayser for Szarzewski (temp 23–32 and 50 mins); N Mas and D Chouly for Atonio and Picamoles (50 mins); R Kockott and E Ben Arous for Parra and Debaty (68 mins)

SCORERS: *Tries:* Guitoune (2), Nyanga, Fofana, Fickou *Conversions:* Parra (3), Kockott (2) *Penalty Goal:* Parra

ROMANIA: C Fercu; M Lemnaru, P Kinikinilau, F Vlaicu, A Apostol; D Dumbrava, F Surugiu; M Lazar, O Turashvili, P Ion, V Poparlan, J van Heerden, V Ursache, V Lucaci, M Macovei (captain)

SUBSTITUTIONS: H Pungea for Ursache (temp 36–40 mins); C Gal for Dumbrava (47 mins); A Radoi for Turashvili (59 mins); O Tonita for Poparlan (68 mins); A Ursache for Lazar (71 mins); I Botezatu and S Burcea for Apostol and Lucaci (72 mins); V Calafeteanu and H Pungea for Surugiu and Ion (73 mins)

SCORERS: *Try:* Ursache *Penalty Goals:* Vlaicu (2)

YELLOW CARD: Ion (30 mins)

REFEREE: J Peyper (South Africa)

MAN OF THE MATCH: W Fofana (France)

26 September, Elland Road, Leeds

ITALY 23 (2G 3PG) CANADA 18 (1G 1T 2PG)

ITALY: L McLean; L Sarto, T Benvenuti, G Garcia, G Venditti; T Allan, E Gori; M Rizzo, L Ghiraldini (captain), L Cittadini, Q Geldenhuys, J Furno, A Zanni, F Minto, S Vunisa

SUBSTITUTIONS: C Canna for Allan (temp 32–40 mins); M Aguero and ML Castrogiovanni for Rizzo and Cittadini (47 mins); M Bergamasco for Vunisa (58 mins); D Giazzon and M Campagnaro for Ghiraldini and Benvenuti (59 mins); G Palazzani for Garcia (72 mins); M Fuser for Geldenhuys (79 mins)

SCORERS: *Tries*: Rizzo, Garcia *Conversions*: Allan (2) *Penalty Goals*: Allan (3)

CANADA: M Evans; P Mackenzie, C Hearn, C Braid, DTH van der Merwe; N Hirayama, J Mackenzie; H Buydens, R Barkwill, D Wooldridge, J Sinclair, J Cudmore, N Dala, J Moonlight, T Ardron (captain)

SUBSTITUTIONS: C Trainor for Braid (14 mins); D Sears-Duru and P Mack for Buydens and J Mackenzie (56 mins); A Carpenter for Barkwill (58 mins); K Gilmour for Dala (59 mins); E Olmstead for Cudmore (72 mins); H Jones for Hirayama (73 mins)

SCORERS: *Tries*: Van der Merwe, Evans *Conversion*: Hirayama *Penalty Goals*: Hirayama (2)

REFEREE: G Clancy (Ireland)

MAN OF THE MATCH: DTH van der Merwe (Canada)

27 September, Wembley Stadium, London

IRELAND 44 (4G 2T 2PG) ROMANIA 10 (1G 1PG)

IRELAND: S Zebo; T Bowe, J Payne, D Cave, K Earls; I Madigan, E Reddan; C Healy, R Strauss, N White, D Ryan, D Toner, J Murphy, C Henry, J Heaslip (captain)

SUBSTITUTIONS: R Kearney for Earls (temp 49–56 and 64 mins); J McGrath for Healy (54 mins); P Jackson for Payne (58 mins); S O'Brien and S Cronin for Heaslip and Strauss (60 mins); P O'Connell and T Furlong for Ryan and White (64 mins); C Murray for Kearney (71 mins)

SCORERS: *Tries*: Bowe, Earls, Kearney, Henry *Conversions*: Madigan (4) *Penalty Goals*: Madigan (2)

ROMANIA: C Fercu; A Apostol, P Kinikinilau, C Gal, I Botezatu; M Wiringi, V Calafeteanu; V Ursache, A Radoi, P Ion, V Poparlan, O Tonita, V Lucaci, M Macovei (captain), D Carp

SUBSTITUTIONS: F Ionita and A Tarus for Apostol and Ion (54 mins); O Turashvili for Radoi (56 mins); J van Heerden for Lucaci (60 mins); F Vlaicu, M Lazar, S Burcea and F Surugiu for Wiringi, Ursache, Macovei and Calafeteanu (68 mins)

SCORERS: *Try*: Tonita *Conversion*: Calafeteanu *Penalty Goal*: Calafeteanu

REFEREE: C Joubert (South Africa)

MAN OF THE MATCH: K Earls (Ireland)

1 October, Stadium MK, Milton Keynes

FRANCE 41 (5G 2PG) CANADA 18 (1G 1T 2PG)

FRANCE: S Spedding; R Grosso, M Bastareaud, W Fofana, B Dulin; F Michalak, S Tillous-Borde; E Ben Arous, G Guirado, R Slimani, P Papé, Y Maestri, T Dusautoir (captain), B le Roux, D Chouly

SUBSTITUTIONS: M Parra, V Debaty and B Kayser for Tillous-Borde, Ben Arous and Guirado (59 mins); N Mas for Slimani (63 mins); R Talès and Y Nyanga for Michalak and Le Roux (68 mins); A Dumoulin for Bastareaud (70 mins); F Ouedraogo for Chouly (73 mins)

SCORERS: *Tries*: Fofana, Guirado, Slimani, Papé, Grosso *Conversions*: Michalak (4), Parra *Penalty Goals*: Michalak (2)

CANADA: M Evans; P Mackenzie, C Hearn, N Blevins, DTH van der Merwe; N Hirayama, P Mack; H Buydens, A Carpenter, D Wooldridge, B Beukeboom, J Cudmore, K Gilmour, R Thorpe, T Ardron (captain)

SUBSTITUTIONS: N Dala for Ardron (19 mins); H Jones for Evans (37 mins); D Sears-Duru and R Barkwill for Buydens and Thorpe (48 mins); E Olmstead for Carpenter (62 mins); C Trainor for Jones (64 mins); G McRorie for Mack (66 mins); A Tiedemann and Jones for Wooldridge and Mackenzie (68 mins)

SCORERS: *Tries*: Van der Merwe, Carpenter *Conversion*: Hirayama *Penalty Goals*: Hirayama (2)

REFEREE: JP Doyle (England)

MAN OF THE MATCH: F Michalak (France)

4 October, The Stadium, Queen Elizabeth Olympic Park, London

IRELAND 16 (1G 3PG) ITALY 9 (3PG)

IRELAND: S Zebo; T Bowe, K Earls, R Henshaw, D Kearney; J Sexton, C Murray; J McGrath, R Best, M Ross, I Henderson, P O'Connell (captain), P O'Mahony, S O'Brien, J Heaslip

SUBSTITUTIONS: N White and C Healy for Ross and McGrath (59 mins); D Toner and C Henry for Henderson and O'Brien (67 mins); S Cronin for Best (70 mins); L Fitzgerald for Earls (76 mins)

SCORERS: *Try*: Earls *Conversion*: Sexton *Penalty Goals*: Sexton (3)

YELLOW CARD: O'Mahony (72 mins)

ITALY: L McLean; L Sarto, M Campagnaro, G Garcia, G Venditti; T Allan, E Gori; M Aguero, A Manici, L Cittadini, Q Geldenhuys, J Furno, F Minto, S Favaro S Parisse (captain)

SUBSTITUTIONS: T Benvenuti for Garcia (4 mins); D Giazzon for Manici (40 mins); M Rizzo for Aguero (temp 62–72 mins); D Chistolini for Cittadini (62 mins); A Zanni and C Canna for Parisse and Allan (65 mins) M Bergamasco for Favaro (67 mins); G Palazzani for Gori (76 mins)

SCORER: *Penalty Goals*: Allan (3)

REFEREE: J Garcès (France)

MAN OF THE MATCH: I Henderson (Ireland)

6 October, Leicester City Stadium, Leicester

CANADA 15 (1G 1T 1PG) ROMANIA 17 (2G 1PG)

CANADA: H Jones; J Hassler, C Hearn, N Blevins, DTH van der Merwe; N Hirayama, G McRorie; H Buydens, R Barkwill, D Wooldridge, B Beukeboom, J Cudmore (captain), J Sinclair, J Moonlight, A Carpenter

SUBSTITUTIONS: D Sears-Duru for Buydens (temp 46–54 and 62 mins); P Mack and C Trainor for McRorie and Blevins (50 mins); N Dala for Moonlight (63 mins); J Ilnicki for Wooldridge (68 mins); J Pritchard for Jones (75 mins)

SCORERS: *Tries:* Van der Merwe, Hassler *Conversion:* Hirayama *Penalty Goal:* McRorie

YELLOW CARD: Sinclair (72 mins)

ROMANIA; C Fercu; M Lemnaru, P Kinikinilau, F Vlaicu, I Botezatu; M Wiringi, F Surugiu; M Lazar, O Turashvili, P Ion, V Poparlan, J van Heerden, V Ursache, V Lucaci, M Macovei (captain)

SUBSTITUTIONS: V Calafeteanu for Surugiu (23 mins); A Ursache for Ion (46 mins); C Gal for Wiringi (52 mins); A Radoi for Turashvili (66 mins); A Tarus for Lazar (75 mins); D Carpo for Lucaci (77 mins)

SCORERS: *Tries:* Macovei (2) *Conversions:* Vlaicu (2) *Penalty Goal:* Vlaicu

YELLOW CARD: Fercu (20 mins)

REFEREE: W Barnes (England)

MAN OF THE MATCH: J Hassler (Canada)

11 October, Sandy Park, Exeter

ITALY 32 (3G 1T 2PG) ROMANIA 22 (2G 1T 1PG)

ITALY: L McLean; L Sarto, M Campagnaro, T Benvenuti, G Venditti; T Allan, E Gori; M Aguero, A Manici, L Cittadini, Q Geldenhuys (captain), J Furno, F Minto, S Favaro, A Zanni

SUBSTITUTIONS: E Bacchin for Campagnaro (35 mins); D Giazzon, D Chistolini and A de Marchi for Manici, Cittadini and Aguero (56 mins); G Palazzani and S Vunisa for McLean and Favaro (64 mins); C Canna for Gori (68 mins); V Bernabò for Furno (75 mins)

SCORERS: *Tries:* Sarto, Gori, Allan, Zanni *Conversions:* Allan (3) *Penalty Goals:* Allan (2)

ROMANIA: C Fercu; M Lemnaru, P Kinikinilau, F Vlaicu, I Botezatu; M Wiringi, V Calafeteanu; M Lazar, O Turashvili, P Ion, V Poparlan, J van Heerden, V Ursache (captain), V Lucaci, D Carpo

SUBSTITUTIONS: C Gal and A Ursache for Wiringi and Ion (41 mins); S Burcea for V Ursache (48 mins); M Antonescu for Van Heerden (55 mins); V Ursache for Lucaci (56 mins); A Radoi for Turashvili (58 mins); T Bratu for Calafeteanu (60 mins); A Apostol for Botezatu (64 mins); H Pungea for Lazar (66 mins)

SCORERS: *Tries:* Apostol (2), Poparlan *Conversions:* Vlaicu (2) *Penalty Goal:* Vlaicu

YELLOW CARD: van Heerden (16 mins)

REFEREE: R Poite (France)

MAN OF THE MATCH: E Gori (Italy)

FRANCE 9 (3PG) IRELAND 24 (1G 1T 4PG)

FRANCE: S Spedding; N Nakaitaci, M Bastareaud, W Fofona, B Dulin; F Michalak, S Tillous-Borde; E Ben Arous, G Guirado, R Slimani, P Papé, Y Maestri, T Dusautoir (captain), D Chouly, L Picamoles

SUBSTITUTIONS: V Debaty for Ben Arous (temp 43–48 and 65 mins); R Talès, M Parra and B le Roux for Michalak, Tillous-Borde and Chouly (55 mins); B Kayser for Guirado (59 mins); A Dumoulin for Bastareaud (62 mins); N Mas for Slimani (64 mins); A Flanquart for Papé (73 mins)

SCORERS: *Penalty Goals*: Spedding (2), Parra

IRELAND: R Kearney; T Bowe, K Earls, R Henshaw, D Kearney; J Sexton, C Murray; C Healy, R Best, M Ross, D Toner, P O'Connell (captain), P O'Mahony, S O'Brien, J Heaslip

SUBSTITUTIONS: I Madigan for Sexton (26 mins); I Henderson for O'Connell (40 mins); C Henry for O'Mahony (55 mins); J McGrath for Healy (57 mins); L Fitzgerald for Earls (62 mins); N White for Ross (65 mins); R Strauss for Best (73 mins); E Reddan for Murray (77 mins)

SCORERS: *Tries*: R Kearney, Murray *Conversion*: Madigan *Penalty Goals*: Sexton (2), Madigan (2)

REFEREE: N Owens (Wales)

MAN OF THE MATCH: S O'Brien (Ireland)

POOL D FINAL TABLE

	P	W	D	L	PF	PA	PD	TF	TA	BP	PTS
Ireland	4	4	0	0	134	35	+99	16	2	2	18
France	4	3	0	1	120	63	+57	12	6	2	14
Italy	4	2	0	2	74	88	-14	7	8	2	10
Romania	4	1	0	3	60	129	-69	7	17	0	4
Canada	4	0	0	4	58	131	-73	7	16	2	2

P=Played; W=Won; D=Draw; L=Lost; PF= Points For; PA=Points Against; TF=Tries For; TA=Tries Against; BP=Bonus Points; PTS=Points

RUGBY WORLD CUP 2015

THE QUARTER-FINALS

17 October, Twickenham, London

SOUTH AFRICA 23 (1T 5PG 1DG) WALES 19 (1G 3PG 1DG)

SOUTH AFRICA: W le Roux; JP Pietersen, J Kriel, D de Allende, B Habana; H Pollard, F du Preez (captain); T Mtawarira, B du Plessis, F Malherbe, E Etzebeth, L de Jager, F Louw, S Burger, D Vermeulen

SUBSTITUTIONS: A Strauss for B du Plessis (temp 12–24 and 56 mins); T Nyakane for Mtawarira (57 mins); J du Plessis for Malherbe (61 mins); J Serfontein, PS du Toit and W Alberts for Kriel, Etzebeth and Louw (68 mins); P Lambie for Pollard (77 mins)

SCORERS: *Try*: Du Preez *Penalty Goals*: Pollard (5) *Drop Goal*: Pollard

WALES: G Anscombe; A Cuthbert, T Morgan, J Roberts, G North; D Biggar, G Davies; G Jenkins, S Baldwin, S Lee, L Charteris, AW Jones, D Lydiate, S Warburton (captain), T Faletau

SUBSTITUTIONS: P James and T Francis for Jenkins and Lee (56 mins); K Owens for Baldwin (57 mins); B Davies for Charteris (64 mins); J Tipuric and J Hook for Lydiate and Morgan (68 mins); L Williams for G Davies (71 mins); R Priestland for Biggar (74 mins)

SCORERS: *Try*: G Davies *Conversion*: Biggar *Penalty Goals*: Biggar (3) *Drop Goal*: Biggar

REFEREE: W Barnes (England)

MAN OF THE MATCH: S Burger (South Africa)

Getty Images

Springbok captain Fourie du Preez breaks Welsh hearts by scoring late on in their quarter-final match at Twickenham.

17 October, Millennium Stadium, Cardiff

NEW ZEALAND 62 (7G 2T 1PG) FRANCE 13 (1G 2PG)

NEW ZEALAND: B Smith; N Milner-Skudder, C Smith, M Nonu, J Savea; D Carter, A Smith; W Crockett, D Coles, O Franks, B Retallick, S Whitelock, J Kaino, R McCaw (captain), K Read

SUBSTITUTIONS: J Moody for Crockett (28 mins); B Barrett for Milner-Skudder (40 mins); C Faumuina for Franks (51 mins); SB Williams for C Smith (52 mins); K Mealamu for Coles (60 mins); V Vito for Kaino (65 mins); T Kerr-Barlow for A Smith (65 mins); S Cane for McCaw (69 mins)

SCORERS: *Tries:* Retallick, Milner-Skudder, Savea (3), Kaino, Read, Kerr-Barlow (2) *Conversions:* Carter (7) *Penalty Goal:* Carter

FRANCE: S Spedding; N Nakaitaci, A Dumoulin, W Fofona, B Dulin; F Michalak, M Parra; E Ben Arous, G Guirado, R Slimani, P Papé, Y Maestri, T Dusautoir (captain), B le Roux, L Picamoles

SUBSTITUTIONS: R Talès for Michalak (12 mins); Y Nyanga for Papé (48 mins); D Szarzewski for Guirado (57 mins); N Mas for Slimani (61 mins); V Debaty for Ben Arous (61 mins); M Bastareaud for Dumoulin (61 mins); R Kockott for Parra (69 mins); D Chouly for Picamoles (72 mins)

SCORERS: *Try:* Picamoles *Conversion:* Parra *Penalty Goals:* Parra, Spedding

YELLOW CARD: Picamoles (47 mins)

REFEREE: N Owens (Wales)

MAN OF THE MATCH: J Savea (New Zealand)

Getty Images

All Black centre Conrad Smith used all of his experience to outwit the French in the quarter-final in Cardiff.

18 October, Millennium Stadium, Cardiff

IRELAND 20 (2G 2PG) ARGENTINA 43 (4G 5PG)

IRELAND: R Kearney; T Bowe, K Earls, R Henshaw, D Kearney; I Madigan, C Murray; C Healy, R Best, M Ross, I Henderson, D Toner, J Murphy, C Henry, J Heaslip (captain)

SUBSTITUTIONS: L Fitzgerald for Bowe (13 mins); J McGrath and N White for Healy and Ross (51 mins); R Strauss for Best (66 mins); R Ruddock and E Reddan for Murphy and Murray (70 mins); D Ryan for Henderson (71 mins)

SCORERS: *Tries:* Fitzgerald, Murphy *Conversions: Madigan (2) Penalty Goals: Madigan (2)*

ARGENTINA: J Tuculet; S Cordero, M Moroni, JM Hernández, J Imhoff; N Sánchez, M Landajo; M Ayerza, A Creevy (captain), R Herrera, G Petti, T Lavanini, P Matera, JM Fernández Lobbe, L Senatore

SUBSTITUTIONS: JP Orlandi for Senatore (temp 23–28 mins); F Isa for Senatore (51 mins); T Cubelli for Landajo (53 mins); J Montoya for Creevy (56 mins); M Alemanno for Petti (60 mins); L Noguera and J de la Fuente for Ayerza and Moroni (68 mins); Orlandi for Herrera (72 mins)

SCORERS: *Tries:* Moroni, Imhoff (2), Tuculet *Conversions:* Sánchez (4) *Penalty Goals:* Sánchez (5)

YELLOW CARD: Herrera (17 mins)

REFEREE: J Garcès (France)

MAN OF THE MATCH: N Sánchez (Argentina)

Getty Images

The Argentina players join the fans in celebrating their scintillating victory over Ireland at the Millennium Stadium.

AUSTRALIA 35 (2G 3T 2PG) SCOTLAND 34 (2G 1T 5PG)

AUSTRALIA: K Beale; A Ashley-Cooper, T Kuridrani, M Giteau, D Mitchell; B Foley, W Genia; S Sio, S Moore (captain), S Kepu, K Douglas, R Simmons, S Fardy, M Hooper, B McCalman

SUBSTITUTIONS: J Slipper for Sio (51 mins); G Holmes for Kepu (54 mins); T Polota-Nau for Moore (62 mins); D Mumm for Simmons (66 mins); N Phipps for Genia (71 mins)

SCORERS: *Tries*: Ashley-Cooper, Mitchell (2), Hooper, Kuridrani *Conversions*: Foley (2) *Penalty Goals*: Foley (2)

SCOTLAND: S Hogg; S Maitland, M Bennett, P Horne, T Seymour; F Russell, G Laidlaw (captain); A Dickinson, R Ford, WP Nel, R Gray, J Gray, B Cowan, J Hardie, D Denton

SUBSTITUTIONS: G Reid for Dickinson (47 mins); F Brown for Ford (54 mins); S Lamont for Seymour (63 mins); J Strauss and T Swinson for Cowan and J Gray (67 mins); R Vernon for Horne (71 mins); J Welsh for Nel (75 mins)

SCORERS: *Tries*: Horne, Seymour, Bennett *Conversions*: Laidlaw (2) *Penalty Goals*: Laidlaw (5)

YELLOW CARD: Maitland (42 mins)

REFEREE: C Joubert (South Africa)

MAN OF THE MATCH: M Giteau (Australia)

Australia's Bernard Foley holds his nerve to kick a match-winning penalty in the dying seconds at Twickenham.

RUGBY WORLD CUP 2015

THE SEMI-FINALS

24 October, Twickenham, London

SOUTH AFRICA 18 (6PG) NEW ZEALAND 20 (2G 1PG 1DG)

SOUTH AFRICA: W le Roux; JP Pietersen, J Kriel, D de Allende, B Habana; H Pollard, F du Preez (captain); T Mtawarira, B du Plessis, F Malherbe, E Etzebeth, L de Jager, F Louw, S Burger, D Vermeulen

SUBSTITUTIONS: W Alberts for Louw (temp 29–35 mins); A Strauss and T Nyakane for B du Plessis and Mtawarira (53 mins); J du Plessis and V Matfield for Malherbe and De Jager (60 mins); W Alberts for Burger (64 mins); P Lambie for Pollard (65 mins); K Mealamu and S Cane for Coles and Kaino (67 mins); J Serfontein for De Allende (80 mins)

SCORERS: *Penalty Goals:* Pollard (5), Lambie

YELLOW CARD: Habana (52 mins)

NEW ZEALAND: B Smith; N Milner-Skudder, C Smith, M Nonu, J Savea; D Carter, A Smith; J Moody, D Coles, O Franks, B Retallick, S Whitelock, J Kaino, R McCaw (captain), K Read

SUBSTITUTIONS: B Barrett for Milner-Skudder (49 mins); C Faumuina and SB Williams for O Franks and Nonu (52 mins); B Franks for Moody (69 mins)

SCORERS: *Tries:* Kaino, Barrett *Conversions:* Carter (2) *Penalty Goal:* Carter *Drop Goal*: Carter

YELLOW CARD: Kaino (39 mins)

REFEREE: J Garcès (France)

MAN OF THE MATCH: B Smith (New Zealand)

Getty Images

Full-back Ben Smith was imperious under the high ball in the semi-final victory over the Springboks at Twickenham.

25 October, Twickenham, London

ARGENTINA 15 (5PG) AUSTRALIA 29
(3G 1T 1PG)

ARGENTINA: J Tuculet; S Cordero, M Bosch, JM Hernández, J Imhoff; N Sánchez, M Landajo; M Ayerza, A Creevy (captain), R Herrera, G Petti, T Lavanini, P Matera, JM Fernández Lobbe, L Senatore

SUBSTITUTIONS: L González Amorosino for Imhoff (18 mins); J Montoya for Creevy (31 mins); J de la Fuente for Hernández (44 mins); F Isa for Senatore (49 mins); T Cubelli for Landajo (56 mins); M Alemanno for Petti (58 mins); J Figallo and L Noguera for Herrera and Ayerza (61 mins)

SCORER: *Penalty Goals:* Sánchez (5)

YELLOW CARD: Lavanini (26 mins)

AUSTRALIA: I Folau; A Ashley-Cooper, T Kuridrani, M Giteau, D Mitchell; B Foley, W Genia; J Slipper, S Moore (captain), S Kepu, K Douglas, R Simmons, S Fardy, M Hooper, D Pocock

SUBSTITUTIONS: K Beale for Giteau (47 mins); T Smith and G Holmes for Slipper and Kepu (53 mins); B McCalman for Fardy (temp 56–61 and 71 mins); T Polota-Nau for Moore (59 mins); M Toomua for Folau (65 mins); N Phipps and D Mumm for Genia and Simmons (67 mins)

SCORERS: *Tries:* Simmons, Ashley-Cooper (3) *Conversions:* Foley (3) *Penalty Goal:* Foley

REFEREE: W Barnes (England)

MAN OF THE MATCH: A Ashley-Cooper (Australia)

RUGBY WORLD CUP 2015

Getty Images

Wallabies wing Adam Ashley-Cooper scored a sublime hat-trick to take his team to the Rugby World Cup 2015 final.

THE BRONZE FINAL

30 October, The Stadium, Queen Elizabeth Olympic Park, London

SOUTH AFRICA 24 (1G 1T 4PG) ARGENTINA 13 (1G 1PG 1DG)

SOUTH AFRICA: W le Roux; JP Pietersen, J Kriel, D de Allende, B Habana; H Pollard, R Pienaar; T Mtawarira, B du Plessis, F Malherbe, E Etzebeth, V Matfield (captain), F Louw, S Burger, D Vermeulen

SUBSTITUTIONS: T Nyakane for Mtawarira (40 mins); A Strauss for B du Plessis (49 mins); W Alberts for Burger (53 mins); J du Plessis for Malherbe (temp 61–70 mins); S Burger for Louw (temp 61–66 mins); L de Jager for Matfield (63 mins); P Lambie for Le Roux (64 mins); J Serfontein for Habana (67 mins); R Paige for Pienaar (77 mins)

SCORERS: *Tries:* Etzebeth, Pietersen *Conversion:* Pollard *Penalty Goals:* Pollard (4)

ARGENTINA: L González Amorosino; S Cordero, M Moroni, J de la Fuente, H Agulla; N Sánchez (captain), T Cubelli; J Figallo, J Montoya, R Herrera, M Alemanno, T Lavanini, J Ortega Desio, JM Fernández Lobbe, JM Leguizamón

SUBSTITUTIONS: L Noguera for Figallo (temp 15–22, 61–64 and 71 mins); G Petti for Alemanno (47 mins); F Isa and M Landajo for Fernández Lobbe and Cubelli (53 mins); JP Orlandi for Herrera (55 mins); JP Socino for Agulla (58 mins); S González Iglesias for De la Fuente (71 mins); SG Botta for Montoya (77 mins)

SCORERS: *Try:* Orlandi *Conversion:* Sánchez *Penalty Goal:* Sánchez *Drop Goal:* Sánchez

YELLOW CARD: Cubelli (5 mins)

REFEREE: J Lacey (Ireland)

MAN OF THE MATCH: D de Allende (South Africa)

Getty Images

Veteran lock Victor Matfield earned his 127th and final cap in the bronze final victory over Argentina in London.

THE FINAL

31 October, Twickenham, London

NEW ZEALAND 34 (2G 1T 4PG 1DG) AUSTRALIA 17 (2G 1PG)

NEW ZEALAND: B Smith; N Milner-Skudder, C Smith, M Nonu, J Savea; D Carter, A Smith; J Moody, D Coles, O Franks, B Retallick, S Whitelock, J Kaino, R McCaw (captain), K Read

SUBSTITUTIONS: SB Williams for C Smith (40 mins); C Faumuina for O Franks (54 mins); B Franks for Moody (59 mins); B Barrett and K Mealamu for Milner-Skudder and Coles (65 mins); T Kerr-Barlow and V Vito for A Smith and Kaino (71 mins); S Cane for McCaw (80 mins)

SCORERS: *Tries:* Milner-Skudder, Nonu, Barrett *Conversions:* Carter (2) *Penalty Goals:* Carter (4) *Drop Goal:* Carter

YELLOW CARD: Smith (52 mins)

AUSTRALIA: I Folau; A Ashley-Cooper, T Kuridrani, M Giteau, D Mitchell; B Foley, W Genia; Sio, S Moore (captain), S Kepu, K Douglas, R Simmons, S Fardy, M Hooper, D Pocock

SUBSTITUTIONS: D Mumm for Douglas (15 mins); K Beale for Giteau (26 mins); T Polota-Nau for Moore (55 mins); J Slipper and G Holmes for Sio and Kepu (59 mins); B McCalman for Fardy (60 mins); M Toomua for Mitchell (temp 66–71 mins); N Phipps for Genia (70 mins)

SCORERS: *Tries:* Pocock, Kuridrani *Conversions:* Foley (2) *Penalty Goal:* Foley

REFEREE: N Owens (Wales)

MAN OF THE MATCH: D Carter (New Zealand)

RUGBY WORLD CUP 2015

Two of the game's greatest players, Richie McCaw and Dan Carter ended their international careers on a high.

RUGBY WORLD CUP RECORDS
1987–2015

(FINAL STAGES ONLY)

OVERALL RECORDS

MOST MATCHES WON IN FINAL STAGES

44	New Zealand
39	Australia
33	France
31	England
30	South Africa

MOST OVERALL PENALTIES IN FINAL STAGES

58	JP Wilkinson	England	1999–2011
36	AG Hastings	Scotland	1987–95
35	G Quesada	Argentina	1999–2003
33	MP Lynagh	Australia	1987–95
33	AP Mehrtens	New Zealand	1995–99

MOST OVERALL POINTS IN FINAL STAGES

277	JP Wilkinson	England	1999–2011
227	AG Hastings	Scotland	1987–95
195	MP Lynagh	Australia	1987–95
191	DW Carter	New Zealand	2003–15
170	GJ Fox	New Zealand	1987–91

MOST OVERALL DROP GOALS IN FINAL STAGES

14	JP Wilkinson	England	1999–2011
6	JH de Beer	South Africa	1999
5	CR Andrew	England	1987–95
5	GL Rees	Canada	1987–99
4	JM Hernández	Argentina	2003–15

MOST OVERALL TRIES IN FINAL STAGES

15	JT Lomu	New Zealand	1995–99
15	BG Habana	South Africa	2007–15
14	DA Mitchell	Australia	2007–15
13	DC Howlett	New Zealand	2003–07
11	R Underwood	England	1987–95
11	JT Rokocoko	New Zealand	2003–07
11	CE Latham	Australia	1999–2007
11	V Clerc	France	2007–11
11	AP Ashley-Cooper	Australia	2007–15

MOST MATCH APPEARANCES IN FINAL STAGES

22	J Leonard	England	1991–2003
22	RH McCaw	New Zealand	2003–15
20	GM Gregan	Australia	1995–2007
20	SWP Burger	South Africa	2003–15
20	KF Mealamu	New Zealand	2003–15

MOST OVERALL CONVERSIONS IN FINAL STAGES

58	DW Carter	New Zealand	2003–15
39	AG Hastings	Scotland	1987–95
37	GJ Fox	New Zealand	1987–91
36	MP Lynagh	Australia	1987–95
28	JP Wilkinson	England	1999–2011
27	PJ Grayson	England	1999–2003
27	SM Jones	Wales	1999–2011

MOST POINTS IN ONE TOURNAMENT

126	GJ Fox	New Zealand	1987
113	JP Wilkinson	England	2003
112	T Lacroix	France	1995
105	PC Montgomery	South Africa	2007
104	AG Hastings	Scotland	1995
103	F Michalak	France	2003
102	G Quesada	Argentina	1999
101	MC Burke	Australia	1999

MOST TRIES IN ONE TOURNAMENT

8	JT Lomu	New Zealand	1999
8	BG Habana	South Africa	2007
8	SJ Savea	New Zealand	2015
7	MCG Ellis	New Zealand	1995
7	JT Lomu	New Zealand	1995
7	DC Howlett	New Zealand	2003
7	JM Muliaina	New Zealand	2003
7	DA Mitchell	Australia	2007

MOST CONVERSIONS IN ONE TOURNAMENT

30	GJ Fox	New Zealand	1987
23	DW Carter	New Zealand	2015
22	PC Montgomery	South Africa	2007
20	MP Lynagh	Australia	1987
20	SD Culhane	New Zealand	1995
20	LR MacDonald	New Zealand	2003
20	NJ Evans	New Zealand	2007

MOST PENALTY GOALS IN ONE TOURNAMENT

31	G Quesada	Argentina	1999
26	T Lacroix	France	1995
23	JP Wilkinson	England	2003
23	H Pollard	South Africa	2015
21	GJ Fox	New Zealand	1987
21	EJ Flatley	Australia	2003
20	CR Andrew	England	1995
20	FN Sánchez	Argentina	2015

MOST DROP GOALS IN ONE TOURNAMENT

8	JP Wilkinson	England	2003
6	JH de Beer	South Africa	1999
5	JP Wilkinson	England	2007
4	JM Hernández	Argentina	2007

RUGBY WORLD CUP TOURNAMENTS

MATCH RECORDS

MOST POINTS IN A MATCH
BY A TEAM

145	New Zealand v Japan	1995
142	Australia v Namibia	2003
111	England v Uruguay	2003
108	New Zealand v Portugal	2007
101	New Zealand v Italy	1999
101	England v Tonga	1999

BY A PLAYER

45	SD Culhane	New Zealand v Japan	1995
44	AG Hastings	Scotland v Ivory Coast	1995
42	MS Rogers	Australia v Namibia	2003
36	TE Brown	New Zealand v Italy	1999
36	PJ Grayson	England v Tonga	1999
34	JH de Beer	South Africa v England	1999
33	NJ Evans	New Zealand v Portugal	2007
32	JP Wilkinson	England v Italy	1999

MOST TRIES IN A MATCH
BY A TEAM

22	Australia v Namibia	2003
21	New Zealand v Japan	1995
17	England v Uruguay	2003
16	New Zealand v Portugal	2007
14	New Zealand v Italy	1999

BY A PLAYER

6	MCG Ellis	New Zealand v Japan	1995
5	CE Latham	Australia v Namibia	2003
5	OJ Lewsey	England v Uruguay	2003
4	IC Evans	Wales v Canada	1987
4	CI Green	New Zealand v Fiji	1987
4	JA Gallagher	New Zealand v Fiji	1987
4	BF Robinson	Ireland v Zimbabwe	1991
4	AG Hastings	Scotland v Ivory Coast	1995
4	CM Williams	South Africa v Western Samoa	1995
4	JT Lomu	New Zealand v England	1995
4	KGM Wood	Ireland v United States	1999
4	JM Muliaina	New Zealand v Canada	2003
4	BG Habana	South Africa v Samoa	2007
4	V Goneva	Fiji v Namibia	2011
4	ZR Guildford	New Zealand v Canada	2011

MOST CONVERSIONS IN A MATCH
BY A TEAM

20	New Zealand v Japan	1995
16	Australia v Namibia	2003
14	New Zealand v Portugal	2007
13	New Zealand v Tonga	2003
13	England v Uruguay	2003

BY A PLAYER

20	SD Culhane	New Zealand v Japan	1995
16	MS Rogers	Australia v Namibia	2003
14	NJ Evans	New Zealand v Portugal	2007
12	PJ Grayson	England v Tonga	1999
12	LR MacDonald	New Zealand v Tonga	2003

MOST PENALTY GOALS IN A MATCH
BY A TEAM

8	Scotland v Tonga	1995
8	France v Ireland	1995
8	Australia v South Africa	1999
8	Argentina v Samoa	1999

BY A PLAYER

8	AG Hastings	Scotland v Tonga	1995
8	T Lacroix	France v Ireland	1995
8	MC Burke	Australia v South Africa	1999
8	G Quesada	Argentina v Samoa	1999

MOST DROP GOALS IN A MATCH
BY A TEAM

5	South Africa v England	1999
3	Fiji v Romania	1991
3	England v France	2003
3	Argentina v Ireland	2007
3	Namibia v Fiji	2011

BY A PLAYER

5	JH de Beer	South Africa v England	1999
3	JP Wilkinson	England v France	2003
3	JM Hernández	Argentina v Ireland	2007
3	TAW Kotze	Namibia v Fiji	2011

INTERNATIONAL TOURNAMENTS

FIRST TOURNAMENT: 1987
IN AUSTRALIA AND NEW ZEALAND

POOL 1

Australia	19	England	6
USA	21	Japan	18
England	60	Japan	7
Australia	47	USA	12
England	34	USA	6
Australia	42	Japan	23

	P	W	D	L	F	A	Pts
Australia	3	3	0	0	108	41	6
England	3	2	0	1	100	32	4
USA	3	1	0	2	39	99	2
Japan	3	0	0	3	48	123	0

POOL 2

Canada	37	Tonga	4
Wales	13	Ireland	6
Wales	29	Tonga	16
Ireland	46	Canada	19
Wales	40	Canada	9
Ireland	32	Tonga	9

	P	W	D	L	F	A	Pts
Wales	3	3	0	0	82	31	6
Ireland	3	2	0	1	84	41	4
Canada	3	1	0	2	65	90	2
Tonga	3	0	0	3	29	98	0

POOL 3

New Zealand	70	Italy	6
Fiji	28	Argentina	9
New Zealand	74	Fiji	13
Argentina	25	Italy	16
Italy	18	Fiji	15
New Zealand	46	Argentina	15

	P	W	D	L	F	A	Pts
New Zealand	3	3	0	0	190	34	6
Fiji	3	1	0	2	56	101	2
Argentina	3	1	0	2	49	90	2
Italy	3	1	0	2	40	110	2

POOL 4

Romania	21	Zimbabwe	20
France	20	Scotland	20
France	55	Romania	12
Scotland	60	Zimbabwe	21
France	70	Zimbabwe	12
Scotland	55	Romania	28

	P	W	D	L	F	A	Pts
France	3	2	1	0	145	44	5
Scotland	3	2	1	0	135	69	5
Romania	3	1	0	2	61	130	2
Zimbabwe	3	0	0	3	53	151	0

QUARTER-FINALS

New Zealand	30	Scotland	3
France	31	Fiji	16
Australla	33	Ireland	15
Wales	16	England	3

SEMI-FINALS

France	30	Australia	24
New Zealand	49	Wales	6

THIRD PLACE MATCH

Wales	22	Australia	21

First Rugby World Cup Final, Eden Park, Auckland, 20 June 1987

NEW ZEALAND 29 (1G 2T 4PG 1DG)
FRANCE 9 (1G 1PG)

NEW ZEALAND: JA Gallagher; JJ Kirwan, JT Stanley, WT Taylor, CI Green; GJ Fox, DE Kirk (*captain*); SC McDowell, SBT Fitzpatrick, JA Drake, MJ Pierce, GW Whetton, AJ Whetton, MN Jones, WT Shelford **SCORERS:** *Tries*: Jones, Kirk, Kirwan *Conversion*: Fox *Penalty Goals*: Fox (4) *Drop Goal*: Fox

FRANCE: S Blanco; D Camberabero, P Sella, D Charvet, P Lagisquet; F Mesnel, P Berbizier; P Ondarts, D Dubroca (*captain*), J-P Garuet, A Lorieux, J Condom, E Champ, D Erbani, L Rodriguez

SCORERS: *Try*: Berbizier *Conversion*: Camberabero *Penalty Goal*: Camberabero

REFEREE: KVJ Fitzgerald (Australia)

SECOND TOURNAMENT: 1991
IN BRITAIN, IRELAND AND FRANCE

POOL 1

New Zealand	18	England	12
Italy	30	USA	9
New Zealand	46	USA	6
England	36	Italy	6
England	37	USA	9
New Zealand	31	Italy	21

	P	W	D	L	F	A	Pts
New Zealand	3	3	0	0	95	39	6
England	3	2	0	1	85	33	4
Italy	3	1	0	2	57	76	2
USA	3	0	0	3	24	113	0

POOL 2

Scotland	47	Japan	9
Ireland	55	Zimbabwe	11
Ireland	32	Japan	16
Scotland	51	Zimbabwe	12
Scotland	24	Ireland	15
Japan	52	Zimbabwe	8

	P	W	D	L	F	A	Pts
Scotland	3	3	0	0	122	36	6
Ireland	3	2	0	1	102	51	4
Japan	3	1	0	2	77	87	2
Zimbabwe	3	0	0	3	31	158	0

POOL 3

Australia	32	Argentina	19
Western Samoa	16	Wales	13
Australia	9	Western Samoa	3
Wales	16	Argentina	7
Australia	38	Wales	3
Western Samoa	35	Argentina	12

	P	W	D	L	F	A	Pts
Australia	3	3	0	0	79	25	6
Western Samoa	3	2	0	1	54	34	4
Wales	3	1	0	2	32	61	2
Argentina	3	0	0	3	38	83	0

POOL 4

France	30	Romania	3
Canada	13	Fiji	3
France	33	Fiji	9
Canada	19	Romania	11
Romania	17	Fiji	15
France	19	Canada	13

	P	W	D	L	F	A	Pts
France	3	3	0	0	82	25	6
Canada	3	2	0	1	45	33	4
Romania	3	1	0	2	31	64	2
Fiji	3	0	0	3	27	63	0

QUARTER-FINALS

England	19	France	10
Scotland	28	Western Samoa	6
Australia	19	Ireland	18
New Zealand	29	Canada	13

SEMI-FINALS

England	9	Scotland	6
Australia	16	New Zealand	6

THIRD PLACE MATCH

New Zealand	13	Scotland	6

Second Rugby World Cup Final, Twickenham, London, 2 November 1991

AUSTRALIA 12 (1G 2PG) ENGLAND 6 (2PG)

AUSTRALIA: MC Roebuck; DI Campese, JS Little, TJ Horan, RH Egerton; MP Lynagh, NC Farr-Jones (*captain*); AJ Daly, PN Kearns, EJA McKenzie, RJ McCall, JA Eales, SP Poidevin, V Ofahengaue, T Coker

SCORERS *Try*: Daly *Conversion*: Lynagh *Penalty Goals*: Lynagh (2)

ENGLAND: JM Webb; SJ Halliday, WDC Carling (*captain*), JC Guscott, R Underwood; CR Andrew, RJ Hill; J Leonard, BC Moore, JA Probyn, PJ Ackford, WA Dooley, MG Skinner, PJ Winterbottom, MC Teague

SCORER: *Penalty Goals*: Webb (2)

REFEREE: WD Bevan (Wales)

THIRD TOURNAMENT: 1995
IN SOUTH AFRICA

POOL A

South Africa	27	Australia	18
Canada	34	Romania	3
South Africa	21	Romania	8
Australia	27	Canada	11
Australia	42	Romania	3
South Africa	20	Canada	0

	P	W	D	L	F	A	Pts
South Africa	3	3	0	0	68	26	6
Australia	3	2	0	1	87	41	4
Canada	3	1	0	2	45	50	2
Romania	3	0	0	3	14	97	0

POOL B

Western Samoa	42	Italy	18
England	24	Argentina	18
Western Samoa	32	Argentina	26
England	27	Italy	20
Italy	31	Argentina	25
England	44	Western Samoa	22

	P	W	D	L	F	A	Pts
England	3	3	0	0	95	60	6
Western Samoa	3	2	0	1	96	88	4
Italy	3	1	0	2	69	94	2
Argentina	3	0	0	3	69	87	0

POOL C

Wales	57	Japan	10
New Zealand	43	Ireland	19
Ireland	50	Japan	28
New Zealand	34	Wales	9
New Zealand	145	Japan	17
Ireland	24	Wales	23

	P	W	D	L	F	A	Pts
New Zealand	3	3	0	0	222	45	6
Ireland	3	2	0	1	93	94	4
Wales	3	1	0	2	89	68	2
Japan	3	0	0	3	55	252	0

POOL D

Scotland	89	Ivory Coast	0
France	38	Tonga	10
France	54	Ivory Coast	18
Scotland	41	Tonga	5
Tonga	29	Ivory Coast	11
France	22	Scotland	19

	P	W	D	L	F	A	Pts
France	3	3	0	0	114	47	6
Scotland	3	2	0	1	149	27	4
Tonga	3	1	0	2	44	90	2
Ivory Coast	3	0	0	3	29	172	0

QUARTER-FINALS

France	36	Ireland	12
South Africa	42	Western Samoa	14
England	25	Australia	22
New Zealand	48	Scotland	30

SEMI-FINALS

South Africa	19	France	15
New Zealand	45	England	29

THIRD PLACE MATCH

France	19	England	9

RUGBY WORLD CUP TOURNAMENTS

Third Rugby World Cup Final, Ellis Park, Johannesburg, 24 June 1995

SOUTH AFRICA 15 (3PG 2DG)
NEW ZEALAND 12 (3PG 1DG) *

SOUTH AFRICA: AJ Joubert; JT Small, JC Mulder, HP Le Roux, CM Williams; JT Stransky, JH van der Westhuizen; JP du Randt, CLC Rossouw, IS Swart, JJ Wiese, JJ Strydom, JF Pienaar (*captain*), RJ Kruger, MG Andrews

SUBSTITUTIONS: GL Pagel for Swart (68 mins); RAW Straeuli for Andrews (90 mins); B Venter for Small (97 mins)

SCORER: *Penalty Goals*: Stransky (3) *Drop Goals*: Stransky (2)

NEW ZEALAND: GM Osborne; JW Wilson, FE Bunce, WK Little, JT Lomu; AP Mehrtens, GTM Bachop; CW Dowd, SBT Fitzpatrick (*captain*), OM Brown, ID Jones, RM Brooke, MR Brewer, JA Kronfeld, ZV Brooke

SUBSTITUTIONS: JW Joseph for Brewer (40 mins); MCG Ellis for Wilson (55 mins); RW Loe for Dowd (83 mins); AD Strachan for Bachop (temp 66 to 71 mins)

SCORER: *Penalty Goals*: Mehrtens (3) *Drop Goal*: Mehrtens

REFEREE: EF Morrison (England)

* after extra time: 9–9 after normal time

Getty Images

A poignant moment in history as South Africa captain Francois Pienaar is congratulated by President Nelson Mandela.

POOL A

Spain	15	Uruguay	27
South Africa	46	Scotland	29
Scotland	43	Uruguay	12
South Africa	47	Spain	3
South Africa	39	Uruguay	3
Scotland	48	Spain	0

	P	W	D	L	F	A	Pts
South Africa	3	3	0	0	132	35	6
Scotland	3	2	0	1	120	58	4
Uruguay	3	1	0	2	42	97	2
Spain	3	0	0	3	18	122	0

POOL B

England	67	Italy	7
New Zealand	45	Tonga	9
England	16	New Zealand	30
Italy	25	Tonga	28
New Zealand	101	Italy	3
England	101	Tonga	10

	P	W	D	L	F	A	Pts
New Zealand	3	3	0	0	176	28	6
England	3	2	0	1	184	47	4
Tonga	3	1	0	2	47	171	2
Italy	3	0	0	3	35	196	0

POOL C

Fiji	67	Namibia	18
France	33	Canada	20
France	47	Namibia	13
Fiji	38	Canada	22
Canada	72	Namibia	11
France	28	Fiji	19

	P	W	D	L	F	A	Pts
France	3	3	0	0	108	52	6
Fiji	3	2	0	1	124	68	4
Canada	3	1	0	2	114	82	2
Namibia	3	0	0	3	42	186	0

POOL D

Wales	23	Argentina	18
Samoa	43	Japan	9
Wales	64	Japan	15
Argentina	32	Samoa	16
Wales	31	Samoa	38
Argentina	33	Japan	12

	P	W	D	L	F	A	Pts
Wales	3	2	0	1	118	71	4
Argentina	3	2	0	1	83	51	4
Samoa	3	2	0	1	97	72	4
Japan	3	0	0	3	36	140	0

POOL E

Ireland	53	United States	8
Australia	57	Romania	9
United States	25	Romania	27
Ireland	3	Australia	23
Australia	55	United States	19
Ireland	44	Romania	14

	P	W	D	L	F	A	Pts
Australia	3	3	0	0	135	31	6
Ireland	3	2	0	1	100	45	4
Romania	3	1	0	2	50	126	2
United States	3	0	0	3	52	135	0

QUARTER-FINAL PLAY-OFFS

England	45	Fiji	24
Scotland	35	Samoa	20
Ireland	24	Argentina	28

QUARTER-FINALS

Wales	9	Australia	24
South Africa	44	England	21
France	47	Argentina	26
Scotland	18	New Zealand	30

SEMI-FINALS

South Africa	21	Australia	27
New Zealand	31	France	43

THIRD PLACE MATCH

South Africa	22	New Zealand	18

RUGBY WORLD CUP TOURNAMENTS

Fourth Rugby World Cup Final, Millennium Stadium, Cardiff, 6 November 1999

AUSTRALIA 35 (2G 7PG) FRANCE 12 (4PG)

AUSTRALIA: M Burke; BN Tune, DJ Herbert, TJ Horan, JW Roff; SJ Larkham, GM Gregan; RLL Harry, MA Foley, AT Blades, DT Giffin, JA Eales (*captain*), MJ Cockbain, DJ Wilson, RST Kefu

SUBSTITUTIONS: JS Little for Herbert (46 mins); ODA Finegan for Cockbain (52 mins); MR Connors for Wilson (73 mins); DJ Crowley for Harry (75 mins); JA Paul for Foley (85 mins); CJ Whitaker for Gregan (86 mins); NP Grey for Horan (86 mins)

SCORERS: *Tries*: Tune, Finegan *Conversions*: Burke (2) *Penalty Goals*: Burke (7)

FRANCE: X Garbajosa; P Bernat Salles, R Dourthe, E Ntamack, C Dominici; C Lamaison, F Galthié; C Soulette, R Ibañez (*captain*), F Tournaire, A Benazzi, F Pelous, M Lièvremont, O Magne, C Juillet

SUBSTITUTIONS: O Brouzet for Juillet (HT); P de Villiers for Soulette (47 mins); A Costes for Magne (temp 19 to 22 mins) and for Lièvremont (67 mins); U Mola for Garbajosa (67 mins); S Glas for Dourthe (temp 49 to 55 mins and from 74 mins); S Castaignède for Galthié (76 mins); M Dal Maso for Ibañez (79 mins)

SCORER: *Penalty Goals*: Lamaison (4)

REFEREE: AJ Watson (South Africa)

Getty Images

At RWC 1999, Australia became the first team to lift the coveted Webb Ellis Cup twice after victory over France.

POOL A

Australia	24	Argentina	8
Ireland	45	Romania	17
Argentina	67	Namibia	14
Australia	90	Romania	8
Ireland	64	Namibia	7
Argentina	50	Romania	3
Australia	142	Namibia	0
Ireland	16	Argentina	15
Romania	37	Namibia	7
Australia	17	Ireland	16

	P	W	D	L	F	A	Pts
Australia	4	4	0	0	273	32	18
Ireland	4	3	0	1	141	56	15
Argentina	4	2	0	2	140	57	11
Romania	4	1	0	3	65	192	5
Namibia	4	0	0	4	28	310	0

POOL B

France	61	Fiji	18
Scotland	32	Japan	11
Fiji	19	United States	18
France	51	Japan	29
Scotland	39	United States	15
Fiji	41	Japan	13
France	51	Scotland	9
United States	39	Japan	26
France	41	United States	14
Scotland	22	Fiji	20

	P	W	D	L	F	A	Pts
France	4	4	0	0	204	70	20
Scotland	4	3	0	1	102	97	14
Fiji	4	2	0	2	98	114	10
United States	4	1	0	3	86	125	6
Japan	4	0	0	4	79	163	0

POOL C

South Africa	72	Uruguay	6
England	84	Georgia	6
Samoa	60	Uruguay	13
England	25	South Africa	6
Samoa	46	Georgia	9
South Africa	46	Georgia	19
England	35	Samoa	22
Uruguay	24	Georgia	12
South Africa	60	Samoa	10
England	111	Uruguay	13

	P	W	D	L	F	A	Pts
England	4	4	0	0	255	47	19
South Africa	4	3	0	1	184	60	15
Samoa	4	2	0	2	138	117	10
Uruguay	4	1	0	3	56	255	4
Georgia	4	0	0	4	46	200	0

POOL D

New Zealand	70	Italy	7
Wales	41	Canada	10
Italy	36	Tonga	12
New Zealand	68	Canada	6
Wales	27	Tonga	20
Italy	19	Canada	14
New Zealand	91	Tonga	7
Wales	27	Italy	15
Canada	24	Tonga	7
New Zealand	53	Wales	37

	P	W	D	L	F	A	Pts
New Zealand	4	4	0	0	282	57	20
Wales	4	3	0	1	132	98	14
Italy	4	2	0	2	77	123	8
Canada	4	1	0	3	54	135	5
Tonga	4	0	0	4	46	178	1

QUARTER-FINALS

New Zealand	29	South Africa	9
Australia	33	Scotland	16
France	43	Ireland	21
England	28	Wales	17

SEMI-FINALS

Australia	22	New Zealand	10
England	24	France	7

THIRD PLACE MATCH

New Zealand	40	France	13

RUGBY WORLD CUP TOURNAMENTS

ENGLAND 20 (1T 4PG 1DG)
AUSTRALIA 17 (1T 4PG) *

ENGLAND: JT Robinson; OJ Lewsey, WJH Greenwood, MJ Tindall, BC Cohen; JP Wilkinson, MJS Dawson; TJ Woodman, SG Thompson, PJ Vickery, MO Johnson (*captain*), BJ Kay, RA Hill, NA Back, LBN Dallaglio

SUBSTITUTIONS: MJ Catt for Tindall (78 mins); J Leonard for Vickery (80 mins); IR Balshaw for Lewsey (85 mins); LW Moody for Hill (93 mins)

SCORERS: *Try*: Robinson *Penalty Goals*: Wilkinson (4) *Drop Goal*: Wilkinson

AUSTRALIA: MS Rogers; WJ Sailor, SA Mortlock, EJ Flatley, L Tuqiri; SJ Larkham, GM Gregan (*captain*); WK Young, BJ Cannon, AKE Baxter, JB Harrison, NC Sharpe, GB Smith, DJ Lyons, PR Waugh

SUBSTITUTIONS: DT Giffin for Sharpe (48 mins); JA Paul for Cannon (56 mins); MJ Cockbain for Lyons (56 mins); JW Roff for Sailor (70 mins); MJ Dunning for Young (92 mins); MJ Giteau for Larkham (temp 18 to 30 mins; 55 to 63 mins; 85 to 93 mins)

SCORERS: *Try*: Tuqiri *Penalty Goals*: Flatley (4)

REFEREE: AJ Watson (South Africa)

* *after extra time: 14–14 after normal time*

Getty Images

Winger Jason Robinson scores England's only try in their victory over Australia in the RWC 2003 final in Sydney.

SIXTH TOURNAMENT: 2007
IN FRANCE, WALES AND SCOTLAND

POOL A

England	28	USA	10
South Africa	59	Samoa	7
USA	15	Tonga	25
England	0	South Africa	36
Samoa	15	Tonga	19
South Africa	30	Tonga	25
England	44	Samoa	22
Samoa	25	USA	21
England	36	Tonga	20
South Africa	64	USA	15

	P	W	D	L	F	A	Pts
South Africa	4	4	0	0	189	47	19
England	4	3	0	1	108	88	14
Tonga	4	2	0	2	89	96	9
Samoa	4	1	0	3	69	143	5
USA	4	0	0	4	61	142	1

POOL B

Australia	91	Japan	3
Wales	42	Canada	17
Japan	31	Fiji	35
Wales	20	Australia	32
Fiji	29	Canada	16
Wales	72	Japan	18
Australia	55	Fiji	12
Canada	12	Japan	12
Australia	37	Canada	6
Wales	34	Fiji	38

	P	W	D	L	F	A	Pts
Australia	4	4	0	0	215	41	20
Fiji	4	3	0	1	114	136	15
Wales	4	2	0	2	168	105	12
Japan	4	0	1	3	64	210	3
Canada	4	0	1	3	51	120	2

POOL C

New Zealand	76	Italy	14
Scotland	56	Portugal	10
Italy	24	Romania	18
New Zealand	108	Portugal	13
Scotland	42	Romania	0
Italy	31	Portugal	5
Scotland	0	New Zealand	40
Romania	14	Portugal	10
New Zealand	85	Romania	8
Scotland	18	Italy	16

	P	W	D	L	F	A	Pts
New Zealand	4	4	0	0	309	35	20
Scotland	4	3	0	1	116	66	14
Italy	4	2	0	2	85	117	9
Romania	4	1	0	3	40	161	5
Portugal	4	0	0	4	38	209	1

POOL D

France	12	Argentina	17
Ireland	32	Namibia	17
Argentina	33	Georgia	3
Ireland	14	Georgia	10
France	87	Namibia	10
France	25	Ireland	3
Argentina	63	Namibia	3
Georgia	30	Namibia	0
France	64	Georgia	7
Ireland	15	Argentina	30

	P	W	D	L	F	A	Pts
Argentina	4	4	0	0	143	33	18
France	4	3	0	1	188	37	15
Ireland	4	2	0	2	64	82	9
Georgia	4	1	0	3	50	111	5
Namibia	4	0	0	4	30	212	0

QUARTER-FINALS

Australia	10	England	12
New Zealand	18	France	20
South Africa	37	Fiji	20
Argentina	19	Scotland	13

SEMI-FINALS

France	9	England	14
South Africa	37	Argentina	13

BRONZE FINAL

France	10	Argentina	34

RUGBY WORLD CUP TOURNAMENTS

Sixth Rugby World Cup Final, Stade de France, Paris, 20 October 2007

SOUTH AFRICA 15 (5PG) ENGLAND 6 (2PG)

SOUTH AFRICA: PC Montgomery; J-PR Pietersen, J Fourie, FPL Steyn, BG Habana; AD James, PF du Preez; JP du Randt, JW Smit (*captain*), CJ van der Linde, JP Botha, V Matfield, JH Smith, SWP Burger, DJ Rossouw

SUBSTITUTIONS: JL van Heerden for Rossouw (72 mins); BW du Plessis for Smit (temp 71 to 76 mins)

SCORERS: *Penalty Goals*: Montgomery (4), Steyn

ENGLAND: JT Robinson; PH Sackey, MJM Tait, MJ Catt, MJ Cueto; JP Wilkinson, ACT Gomarsall; AJ Sheridan, MP Regan, PJ Vickery (*captain*), SD Shaw, BJ Kay, ME Corry, LW Moody, NJ Easter

SUBSTITUTIONS: MJH Stevens for Vickery (40 mins); DJ Hipkiss for Robinson (46 mins); TGAL Flood for Catt (50 mins); GS Chuter for Regan (62 mins); JPR Worsley for Moody (62 mins); LBN Dallaglio for Easter (64 mins); PC Richards for Worsley (70 mins)

SCORER: *Penalty Goals*: Wilkinson (2)

REFEREE: AC Rolland (Ireland)

Getty Images

South Africa's Francois Steyn attempts to make a break during the RWC 2007 final against England.

SEVENTH TOURNAMENT: 2011
IN NEW ZEALAND

POOL A

New Zealand	41	Tonga	10
France	47	Japan	21
Tonga	20	Canada	25
New Zealand	83	Japan	7
France	46	Canada	19
Tonga	31	Japan	18
New Zealand	37	France	17
Canada	23	Japan	23
France	14	Tonga	19
New Zealand	79	Canada	15

	P	W	D	L	F	A	Pts
New Zealand	4	4	0	0	240	49	20
France	4	2	0	2	124	96	11
Tonga	4	2	0	2	80	98	9
Canada	4	1	1	2	82	168	6
Japan	4	0	1	3	69	184	1

POOL B

Scotland	34	Romania	24
Argentina	9	England	13
Scotland	15	Georgia	6
Argentina	43	Romania	8
England	41	Georgia	10
England	67	Romania	3
Argentina	13	Scotland	12
Georgia	25	Romania	9
England	16	Scotland	12
Argentina	25	Georgia	7

	P	W	D	L	F	A	Pts
England	4	4	0	0	137	34	18
Argentina	4	3	0	1	90	40	14
Scotland	4	2	0	2	73	59	11
Georgia	4	1	0	3	48	90	4
Romania	4	0	0	4	44	169	0

POOL C

Australia	32	Italy	6
Ireland	22	USA	10
Russia	6	USA	13
Australia	6	Ireland	15
Italy	53	Russia	17
Australia	67	USA	5
Ireland	62	Russia	12
Italy	27	USA	10
Australia	68	Russia	22
Ireland	36	Italy	6

	P	W	D	L	F	A	Pts
Ireland	4	4	0	0	135	34	17
Australia	4	3	0	1	173	48	15
Italy	4	2	0	2	92	95	10
USA	4	1	0	3	38	122	4
Russia	4	0	0	4	57	196	1

POOL D

Fiji	49	Namibia	25
South Africa	17	Wales	16
Samoa	49	Namibia	12
South Africa	49	Fiji	3
Wales	17	Samoa	10
South Africa	87	Namibia	0
Fiji	7	Samoa	27
Wales	81	Namibia	7
South Africa	13	Samoa	5
Wales	66	Fiji	0

	P	W	D	L	F	A	Pts
South Africa	4	4	0	0	166	24	18
Wales	4	3	0	1	180	34	15
Samoa	4	2	0	2	91	49	10
Fiji	4	1	0	3	59	167	5
Namibia	4	0	0	4	44	266	0

QUARTER-FINALS

Ireland	10	Wales	22
England	12	France	19
South Africa	9	Australia	11
New Zealand	33	Argentina	10

SEMI-FINALS

Wales	8	France	9
Australia	6	New Zealand	20

BRONZE FINAL

Australia	21	Wales	18

RUGBY WORLD CUP TOURNAMENTS

Seventh Rugby World Cup Final, Eden Park, Auckland, 23 October 2011

NEW ZEALAND 8 (1T 1PG) FRANCE 7 (1G)

NEW ZEALAND: IJA Dagg; CS Jane, CG Smith, MA Nonu, RD Kahui; AW Cruden, PAT Weepu; TD Woodcock, KF Mealamu, OT Franks, BC Thorn, SL Whitelock, J Kaino, RH McCaw (*captain*), KJ Read

SUBSTITUTIONS: SR Donald for Cruden (33 mins); AJ Williams for Whitelock (48 mins); AK Hore for Mealamu (48 mins); AM Ellis for Weepu (49 mins); S Williams for Nonu (75 mins)

SCORERS: *Try*: Woodcock *Penalty Goal*: Donald

FRANCE: M Médard; V Clerc, A Rougerie, M Mermoz, A Palisson; M Parra, D Yachvili; J-B Poux, W Servat, N Mas, P Papé, L Nallet, T Dusautoir (*captain*), J Bonnaire, I Harinordoquy

SUBSTITUTIONS: F Trinh-Duc for Parra (temp 11 to 17 mins and 22 mins); D Traille for Clerc (45 mins); D Szarzewski for Servat (64 mins); F Barcella for Poux (64 mins); J Pierre for Papé (69 mins); J-M Doussain for Yachvili (75 mins)

SCORERS: *Try*: Dusautoir *Conversion*: Trinh-Duc

REFEREE: C Joubert (South Africa)

Getty Images

Richie McCaw holds aloft the Webb Ellis Cup after New Zealand ended a 24-year wait for a second title.

IRELAND CROWNED CHAMPIONS ON INCREDIBLE DAY OF DRAMA

By Stephen Jones, The Sunday Times

Getty Images

Ireland captain Paul O'Connell lifts the RBS 6 Nations trophy at Murrayfield after a breathtaking final day.

On 21 March, 2015 there were nearly 200,000 at the three stadiums – in Rome, London and Edinburgh – and a record television audience. But surely, not all were rugby fans. Such was the sustained drama, tens of thousands more from outside rugby's orbit were clearly drawn in. It was rugby's longest day, and one of the sport's greatest. Only at the very end, in the last act in a wondrous drama, was the RBS 6 Nations of 2015 decided.

At the start of play and provided that all three of the top teams, Wales, Ireland and England, won their games then it would all come down to points difference. Ireland's points difference was superior to Wales by 21 and England's was superior to Wales by 25. England were top of the table but with a fragile four point superiority over Ireland. As the day wore on, each of the three teams seemed to be, at different times, on their way to the trophy. In the end, Ireland squeezed out ahead to proudly retain the title they won in 2014.

If there was one breed not enamoured of this sensational series of matches then it must have been the defence coaches. An incredible 27 tries were scored in the three games and if truth be told, Ireland were probably the team that best maintained a balance between all-out attack and a vestige of pragmatism.

It started at lunchtime. Wales made wonderful attempts to make up on the points difference deficiency and also to extend their own lead beyond that which England and Ireland could later achieve. They gave a blistering performance in the 61–20 win over Italy in Rome, and they must have scared the coaches of England and Ireland stiff as the barrage of eight tries was fired at Italy. George North scored a hat-trick and the outstanding Welsh backs, at full blast, cashed in.

Towards the end, Wales launched an attack which would have taken them more than 30 points above Ireland in the differential, had they scored. But Gareth Davies, the replacement, knocked on as he was winding up for a scoring dive, Italy counter-attacked and Leonardo Sarto, the Italian wing, scored at the other end. It was a 14-point swing at a crucial time, and Sarto's touchdown kept Wales within the grasp of both Ireland and England.

Ireland now stepped up at Murrayfield, knowing that they needed to win by a margin of 20 points or more to catch Wales, although in their advantage was the fact that Scotland, after beginning the season with such optimism, had lost all their games and were runaway favourites to win the Wooden Spoon – an unwanted honour they duly achieved.

And Ireland, so full of hard-heads and hard-noses, did the job. It never really looked like they would fail either to overcome Wales or to set England a stiff task. Amongst an increasingly excitable Irish contingent in the stadium, they scored tries through Sean O'Brien (2), Jared Payne and Paul O'Connell, and rampaged along to a 40–10 scoreline.

In this game there was none of the abandon of the Welsh performance – a necessary facet in Rome given the Welsh points deficiency. Ireland were clinical, with Johnny Sexton marshalling resources and the experienced pack well on top, with O'Connell, O'Brien and Jamie Heaslip superlative.

And the final score of 40–10 meant that England needed a margin of 26 points in the last game. France were in no mood to crumble (Scotland were criticised by England players after the weekend for their lack of fire in their performance), but their deficiencies were far more likely to be caused by a lack of confidence.

Frankly, the England v France game, which ended 55–35, was frantic, crazy, compelling. What it was not, however, was structured. England's achievement in coming so close to the 26-point margin they needed was significant.

So, arguably, was their failure to go all the way. They scored seven tries against a French team which at least played with passion and energy, and yet in the season to date France had only conceded two tries – indeed, it was the French defence which saved them from complete humiliation because the rest of their game barely existed. Amazingly, France scored a brave 35 points and yet easily lost.

England tries came from Jonathan Joseph, Jack Nowell (2), George Ford, Ben Youngs and Chris Robshaw, and Ford, who emerged as an imposing figure in the England midfield, put over all seven conversions. In patches, it seemed that they might make up the 26-point margin.

Yet it also seemed as if England had become obsessed with the need to score at the expense of the need to defend. France kept on hitting back, putting up the score that England were required to achieve. England needed to steady themselves after they had put points on the board, but it often seemed to be a basketball match, with alternating scorers.

With a full 15 minutes left, England were only 10 points short of the requisite margin – a converted try and a penalty would have made them champions. This was the time to exit the helter-skelter, the time to play for territory and be clinical about those 10 points. But England lacked composure in the closing stages – a late try from Nowell with only five minutes remaining again put them within a converted try, but in the final analysis they had attacked quite beautifully but ignored a little too much of the other tasks.

So up in Murrayfield, Ireland and their followers celebrated the retention of the title and also that they had safely played through what they always assumed might be a nightmare – the first season after the end of the Brian O'Driscoll era. Two promising centres, Robbie Henshaw and Payne, emerged steadily to fill the cavernous gap and, in the end, it was another icon in O'Connell who lifted the RBS 6 Nations trophy itself.

Weeks earlier, the tournament had begun with a colossal occasion – Wales v England on a Friday evening in Cardiff, which brought the capital of Wales to a standstill, though admittedly through the transport problems of a Friday evening as well as the mass of interest. England won by 21–16, even after trailing both 10–0 and 16–8 during the clash.

Yet they bounced back splendidly. A try from Joseph, the best news of the season for England, gave them the lead and Wales were bitterly disappointing in the final quarter. The achievement of the England coaches in producing a team ready for the fray was considerable, and it was the best kick-start England could possibly have had.

Next day, Ireland won 26–3 in Rome, where Italy's problems with the lack of authoritative midfield backs continued, despite the best efforts of Kelly Haimona. Ireland were without both Sexton and Heaslip, but came through satisfactorily.

We also had the first inklings that neither France nor Scotland would be fighting for the title. In a drab match in Paris, France won with five penalties from Camille Lopez at fly-half, and although Dougie Fife scored the only try of the match for Scotland, it was a mediocre occasion enlivened for the Scots only by the promise of Alex Dunbar and Mark Bennett in the centre.

Round two at least saw the shackles fall off England with Joseph again starring in a 47–17 home win over Italy. However, Italy did manage three tries and two of them came from Luca Morisi, the new centre who had created a highly favourable impression in a team that otherwise struggled.

Significantly, Ireland saw off the challenge of France by 18–11 in Dublin with Sexton, back in the team, kicking five penalties. France did score the only try through Romain Taofifenua, but Lopez did not give France enough direction and purpose at fly-half and Ireland managed to win without really hitting their straps.

Wales then sneaked a 26–23 win away in Edinburgh, in a game the Scots had to win if they were to make anything of the season. Yet it was the sort of winnable game they have forgotten how to win.

As soon as England had won in Cardiff, it was obvious that their trip to Dublin could well decide the destination of the title. And yet on the big day, England made too many mistakes, too many odd tactical choices, and there was no doubting the clear superiority of Ireland in a 19–9 win, in which the chief component was a clever try by Henshaw, chasing and leaping up to gather a chip ahead by Conor Murray to score at a vital time. Once again England would finish a season without a Grand Slam, extending their Slam-less run to a melancholy 12 years.

And there was also melancholia in Paris. Wales won by 20–13 against a French team that was apparently slowing down and becoming less organised and passionate as the season progressed and as the coaching reign of Philippe Saint-André approached its end.

Also on this third weekend, the Wooden Spoon was all but decided. Scotland, with Bennett impressive, appeared to be pulling clear, but the Italian forwards came hammering back and were deservedly awarded a penalty try for persistent infringement in maul defence near their line. Italy won 22–19 and left Scotland staring at a bucket of whitewash.

The fourth round was marked by the continuation of the Welsh revival when, in a thunderous game at the Millennium Stadium, they beat Ireland by 23–16, helping their cause no end with an incredible goal-line stand when Ireland appeared to be encamped on their line for hours.

Scott Williams scored the Welsh try after 61 minutes, which seemed to settle the game until Ireland came back to within a score when they were awarded a penalty try after 68 minutes. Wales, with Dan Biggar inspirational, held on well and the Irish Slam aspirations went the same way as those of England.

France stirred themselves in Rome to win by 29–0, although none of the tries came from the starting backs, and England laboured to a 25–13 victory over Scotland, in what was far from a vintage display at Twickenham. After this penultimate weekend the amateur mathematicians did their calculations, giving a delicious sense of anticipation and import to what was to come. It pointed to a day that, so it seemed, could not fall flat. And it did not. It took off like a rocket, and stayed in the stratosphere.

The ribbons on the trophy may have been emerald green, but the final day was a gorgeous panoply of different colours.

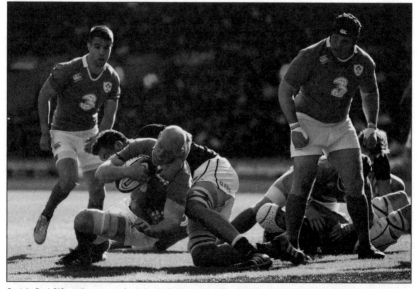

Captain Paul O'Connell goes over for Ireland's first try against Scotland on the final day of the RBS 6 Nations.

RBS 6 NATIONS

RBS 6 NATIONS 2015
FINAL TABLE

	P	W	D	L	For	Against	Pts
Ireland	5	4	0	1	119	56	8
England	5	4	0	1	157	100	8
Wales	5	4	0	1	146	93	8
France	5	2	0	3	103	101	4
Italy	5	1	0	4	62	182	2
Scotland	5	0	0	5	73	128	0

Points: Win 2; Draw 1; Defeat 0. Champions determined on superior points-difference.

There were 660 points scored at an average of 44 a match. The Championship record (803 points at an average of 53.5 a match) was set in 2000. George Ford was the leading individual points scorer with 75, 14 points shy of the Championship record Jonny Wilkinson set in 2001. Jonathan Joseph was the Championship's leading try-scorer with four, four short of the all-time record shared between England's Cyril Lowe (1914) and Scotland's Ian Smith (1925).

Getty Images

Sam Warburton powers through the Italian defence to score the seventh of Wales' eight tries at the Stadio Olimpico.

INTERNATIONAL TOURNAMENTS

WALES 16 (1G 2PG 1DG) ENGLAND 21 (1G 1T 3PG)

WALES: L Halfpenny; A Cuthbert, J Davies, J Roberts, G North; D Biggar, R Webb; G Jenkins, R Hibbard, S Lee, J Ball, AW Jones, D Lydiate, S Warburton (captain), T Faletau

SUBSTITUTIONS: L Williams for North (temp 31–39 mins); P James for Jenkins (60 mins); L Charteris for Ball (69 mins); M Phillips for Webb (69 mins); A Jarvis for Lee (72 mins)

YELLOW CARD: Cuthbert (61 mins)

SCORERS: *Tries*: Webb *Conversion*: Halfpenny *Penalty Goals*: Halfpenny (2) *Drop Goal*: Biggar

ENGLAND: A Goode; A Watson, J Joseph, L Burrell, J Nowell; G Ford, B Youngs; J Marler, D Hartley, D Cole, D Atwood, G Kruis, J Haskell, C Robshaw (captain), B Vunipola

SUBSTITUTIONS: T Youngs for Hartley (55 mins); M Vunipola for Marler (55 mins); K Brookes for Cole (62 mins); R Wigglesworth for B Youngs (69 mins); N Easter for Kruis (72 mins); B Twelvetrees for Burrell (76 mins)

SCORERS: *Tries*: Watson, Joseph *Conversion*: Ford *Penalty Goals*: Ford (3)

REFEREE: J Garcès (France)

ITALY 3 (1PG) IRELAND 26 (2G 4PG)

ITALY: A Masi; L Sarto, M Campagnaro, L Morisi, L McLean; K Haimona, E Gori; M Aguero, L Ghiraldini, ML Castrogiovanni, G Biagi, J Furno, A Zanni, F Minto, S Parisse (captain)

SUBSTITUTIONS: M Barbini for Zanni (47 mins); A de Marchi for Aguero (53 mins); T Allan for Campagnaro (63 mins); M Fuser for Barbini (68 mins); D Chistolini for Castrogiovanni (69 mins); A Manici for Minto (69 mins); M Barbini for Biagi (75 mins); F Minto for Ghiraldini (75 mins); G Venditti for Masi (77 mins)

SCORER: *Penalty Goal*: Haimona

YELLOW CARD: Ghiraldini (64 mins)

IRELAND: R Kearney; T Bowe, J Payne, R Henshaw, S Zebo; I Keatley, C Murray; J McGrath, R Best, M Ross, D Toner, P O'Connell (captain), P O'Mahony, T O'Donnell, J Murphy

SUBSTITUTIONS: S Cronin for Best (47 mins); M Moore for Ross (52 mins); I Henderson for O'Mahony (66 mins); I Madigan for Keatley (66 mins); J Cronin for McGrath (68 mins); F Jones for Payne (68 mins); I Boss for Murray (69 mins)

SCORERS: *Tries*: Murray, O'Donnell *Conversions*: Keatley, Madigan *Penalty Goals*: Keatley (4)

REFEREE: P Gaüzère (France)

7 February, Stade de France, Paris

FRANCE 15 (5PG) SCOTLAND 8 (1T 1PG)

FRANCE: S Spedding; Y Huget, M Bastareaud, W Fofana, T Thomas; C Lopez, R Kockott; A Menini, G Guirado, R Slimani, P Papè, Y Maestri, T Dusautoir (captain), B le Roux, D Chouly

SUBSTITUTIONS: E Ben Arous for Menini (40 mins); B Kayser for Guirado (48 mins); A Atonio for Slimani (55 mins); M Parra for Kockott (55 mins); R Taoififenua for Papé (61 mins); R Lamerat for Bastareaud (72 mins); L Goujon for Dusautoir (80 mins)

SCORERS: *Penalty Goals*: Lopez (5)

SCOTLAND: S Hogg; T Seymour, M Bennett, A Dunbar, T Visser; F Russell, G Laidlaw (captain); A Dickinson, R Ford, E Murray, R Gray, J Gray, R Harley, B Cowan, J Beattie

SUBSTITUTIONS: D Fife for Seymour (17 mins); A Strokosch for Harley (53 mins); R Harley for Cowan (temp 55–62 mins); G Reid for Dickinson (65 mins); G Cross for Murray (65 mins); J Hamilton for Gray (65 mins); F Brown for Ford (68 mins); P Horne for Dunbar (68 mins); S Hidalgo-Clyne for Laidlaw (79 mins)

SCORERS: *Try*: Fife *Penalty Goal*: Laidlaw

YELLOW CARD: Beattie (62 mins)

REFEREE: N Owens (Wales)

14 February, Twickenham, London

ENGLAND 47 (4G 2T 3PG) ITALY 17 (1G 2T)

ENGLAND: M Brown; A Watson, J Joseph, L Burrell, J May; G Ford, B Youngs; J Marler, D Hartley, D Cole, D Attwood, G Kruis, J Haskell, C Robshaw (captain), B Vunipola

SUBSTITUTIONS: B Twelvetrees for Brown (13 mins); N Easter for Attwood (51 mins); T Youngs for Hartley (59 mins); K Brookes for Cole (59 mins); M Vunipola for Marler (63 mins); T Croft for Haskell (63 mins); D Cipriani for Ford (63 mins); R Wigglesworth for B Youngs (67 mins)

SCORERS: *Tries*: B Vunipola, Youngs, Joseph (2), Cipriani, Easter *Conversions*: Ford (3), Cipriani *Penalty Goals*: Ford (3)

ITALY: L McLean; L Sarto, L Morisi, A Masi, G Venditti; K Haimona, E Gori; A de Marchi, L Ghiraldini, ML Castrogiovanni, G Biagi, M Bortolami, F Minto, M Bergamasco, S Parisse (captain)

SUBSTITUTIONS: S Vunisa for Minto (temp 29–38 mins); J Furno for Bortolami (46 mins); A Manici for Ghiraldini (59 mins); M Aguero for De Marchi (59 mins); D Chistolini for Castrogiovanni (59 mins); S Vunisa for Bergamasco (59 mins); G Palazzani for Gori (70 mins); T Allan for Haimona (70 mins); G Bisegni for Sarto (78 mins)

SCORERS: *Tries*: Parisse, Morisi (2) *Conversion*: Allan

REFEREE: P Gaüzère (France)

IRELAND 18 (6PG) FRANCE 11 (1T 2PG)

IRELAND: R Kearney; T Bowe, J Payne, R Henshaw, S Zebo; J Sexton, C Murray; J McGrath, R Best, M Ross, M Ross, D Toner, P O'Connell (captain), P O'Mahony, S O'Brien, J Heaslip

SUBSTITUTIONS: I Madigan for Sexton (temp 45–55 mins); J Murphy for Heaslip (60 mins); C Healy for Ross (63 mins); M Moore for McGrath (63 mins); S Cronin for O'Brien (66 mins); S O'Brien for Best (72 mins); I Henderson for Toner (75 mins)

SCORERS: *Penalty Goals*: Sexton (5), Madigan

YELLOW CARD: Best (61 mins)

FRANCE: S Spedding; Y Huget, M Bastareaud, W Fofana, T Thomas; C Lopez, R Kockott; E Ben Arous, G Guirado, R Slimani, P Papè, Y Maestri, T Dusautoir (captain), B le Roux, D Chouly

SUBSTITUTIONS: R Lamerat for Fofana (temp 16–23 mins); R Lamerat for Thomas (33 mins); R Talès for Bastareaud (45 mins); B Kayser for Guirado (50 mins); U Atonio for Ben Arous (50 mins); V Debaty for Slimani (50 mins); M Bastareaud for Spedding; R Taofifenua for Papé (64 mins); M Parra for Kockott (66 mins); L Goujon for Chouly (72 mins)

SCORERS: *Try*: Taofifenua *Penalty Goals*: Lopez (2)

YELLOW CARD: Papé (53 mins)

REFEREE: W Barnes (England)

SCOTLAND 23 (2G 3PG) WALES 26 (2G 4PG)

SCOTLAND: S Hogg; S Lamont, M Bennett, A Dunbar, T Visser; F Russell, G Laidlaw (captain); A Dickinson, R Ford, G Cross, R Gray, J Gray, R Harley, B Cowan, J Beattie

SUBSTITUTIONS: J Welsh for Cross (50 mins); J Hamilton for R Gray (57 mins); A Strokosch for Beattie (59 mins); M Scott for Dunbar (59 mins); G Reid for Dickinson (temp 62–65 mins); F Brown for Ford (72 mins); S Hidalgo-Clyne for Laidlaw (72 mins)

SCORERS: *Tries*: Hogg, Welsh *Conversions*: Laidlaw, Russell *Penalty Goals*: Laidlaw (3)

YELLOW CARD: Davies (36 mins)

WALES: L Halfpenny; A Cuthbert, J Davies, J Roberts, L Williams; D Biggar, R Webb; G Jenkins, R Hibbard, A Jarvis, J Ball, AW Jones, D Lydiate, S Warburton (captain), T Faletau

SUBSTITUTIONS: S Baldwin for Hibbard (61 mins); S Andrews for Jarvis (61 mins); L Charteris for Ball (61 mins); J Tipuric for Lydiate (62 mins); P James for Jenkins (72 mins); M Phillips for Webb (75 mins)

SCORERS: *Tries*: Webb, Davies *Conversions*: Halfpenny (2) *Penalty Goals*: Halfpenny (4)

YELLOW CARD: Russell (31 mins)

REFEREE: G Jackson (New Zealand)

28 February, Murrayfield, Edinburgh

SCOTLAND 19 (1G 4PG) ITALY 22 (2G 1T 1PG)

SCOTLAND: S Hogg; T Seymour, M Bennett, A Dunbar, S Lamont; P Horne, G Laidlaw (captain); A Dickinson, R Ford, E Murray, T Swinson, J Gray, R Harley, B Cowan, J Beattie

SUBSTITUTIONS: H Watson for Beattie (51 mins); F Brown for Ford (67 mins); R Grant for Dickinson (67 mins); M Scott for Bennett (67 mins); B Toolis for Swinson (70 mins); G Cross for Murray (75 mins); S Hidalgo-Clyne for Laidlaw (75 mins); G Tonks for Horne (79 mins)

SCORERS: *Try*: Bennett *Conversion*: Laidlaw *Penalty Goals*: Laidlaw (4)

YELLOW CARDS: Toolis (78 mins); Watson (80 mins)

ITALY: L McLean; M Visentin, L Morisi, E Bacchin, G Venditti; K Haimona, E Gori; M Aguero, L Ghiraldini, D Chistolini, G Biagi, J Furno, F Minto, S Favaro, S Parisse (captain)

SUBSTITUTIONS: T Allan for Haimona (44 mins); A de Marchi for Aguero (57 mins); L Cittadini for Chistolini (57 mins); S Vunisa for Favaro (62 mins); A Manici for Ghiraldini (67 mins); M Fuser for Biagi (67 mins); G Bisegni for Venditti (70 mins)

SCORERS: *Tries*: Furno, Venditti, Penalty Try *Conversions*: Haimona (2) *Penalty Goal*: Haimona

REFEREE: G Clancy (Ireland)

28 February, Stade de France, Paris

FRANCE 13 (1G 2PG) WALES 20 (1T 5PG)

FRANCE: B Dulin; Y Huget, R Lamerat, W Fofana, S Guitoune; C Lopez, M Parra; E Ben Arous, G Guirado, R Slimani, R Taofifenua, Y Maestri, T Dusautoir (captain), B le Roux, D Chouly

SUBSTITUTIONS: M Bastareaud for Lamerat (17 mins); B Kayser for Guirado (53 mins); U Atonio for Slimani (53 mins); V Debaty for Ben Arous (53 mins); S Tillous-Borde for Parra (53 mins); J Suta for Taofifenua (61 mins); R Talès for Fofana (69 mins); L Goujon for Chouly (74 mins)

SCORERS: *Try*: Dulin *Conversion*: Lopez *Penalty Goals*: Lopez (2)

WALES: L Halfpenny; G North, J Davies, J Roberts, L Williams; D Biggar, R Webb; G Jenkins, S Baldwin, S Lee, L Charteris, AW Jones, D Lydiate, S Warburton (captain), T Faletau

SUBSTITUTIONS: R Hibbard for Baldwin (69 mins); P James for Jenkins (69 mins); B Davies for Charteris (69 mins); J Tipuric for Warburton (69 mins); R Priestland for Biggar (75 mins); A Jarvis for Lee (80 mins)

SCORERS: *Try*: Biggar *Penalty Goals*: Halfpenny (5)

REFEREE: J Peyper (South Africa)

IRELAND 19 (1G 4PG) ENGLAND 9 (2PG 1DG)

IRELAND: R Kearney; T Bowe, J Payne, R Henshaw, S Zebo; J Sexton, C Murray; J McGrath, R Best, M Ross, D Toner, P O'Connell (captain), P O'Mahony, S O'Brien, J Murphy

SUBSTITUTIONS: T O'Donnell for O'Brien (25 mins); I Madigan for Sexton (54 mins); M Moore for Ross (58 mins); C Healy for McGrath (60 mins); I Henderson for Toner (66 mins); F Jones for Payne (71 mins); S Cronin for Best (74 mins)

SCORERS: *Try*: Henshaw *Conversion*: Sexton *Penalty Goals*: Sexton (4)

ENGLAND: A Goode; A Watson, J Joseph, L Burrell, J Nowell; G Ford, B Youngs; J Marler, D Hartley, D Cole, D Atwood, G Kruis, J Haskell, C Robshaw (captain), B Vunipola

SUBSTITUTIONS: T Youngs for Hartley (54 mins); T Croft for Haskell (62 mins); M Vunipola for Marler (66 mins); N Easter for Attwood (68 mins); R Wigglesworth for B Youngs (68 mins); B Twelvetrees for Joseph (68 mins)

SCORER: *Penalty Goals*: Ford (2) *Drop Goal*: Ford

REFEREE: C Joubert (South Africa)

WALES 23 (1T 5PG 1DG) IRELAND 16 (1G 3PG)

WALES: L Halfpenny; G North, J Davies, J Roberts, L Williams; D Biggar, R Webb; G Jenkins, S Baldwin, S Lee, L Charteris, AW Jones, D Lydiate, S Warburton (captain), T Faletau

SUBSTITUTIONS: A Jarvis for Lee (12 mins); R Evans for Jenkins (40 mins); R Hibbard for Baldwin (temp 57–79 mins); S Williams for Roberts (60 mins); J Tipuric for Lydiate (69 mins); M Phillips for Webb (69 mins); J Ball for Jones (72 mins)

YELLOW CARDS: Warburton (28 mins); Davies (78 mins)

SCORERS: *Try*: S Williams *Penalty Goals*: Halfpenny (5) *Drop Goal*: Biggar

IRELAND: R Kearney; T Bowe, J Payne, R Henshaw, S Zebo; J Sexton, C Murray; J McGrath, R Best, M Ross, D Toner, P O'Connell (captain), P O'Mahony, S O'Brien, J Heaslip

SUBSTITUTIONS: C Healy for McGrath (57 mins); S Cronin for Best (63 mins); M Moore for Ross (63 mins); I Henderson for Toner (63 mins); E Reddan for Murray (63 mins); J Murphy for Heaslip (72 mins); I Madigan for Sexton (75 mins)

SCORERS: *Try*: Penalty Try *Conversion*: Sexton *Penalty Goals*: Sexton (3)

REFEREE: W Barnes (England)

14 March, Twickenham, London

ENGLAND 25 (2G 1T 2PG) SCOTLAND 13 (1G 2PG)

ENGLAND: M Brown; A Watson, J Joseph, L Burrell, J Nowell; G Ford, B Youngs; J Marler, D Hartley, D Cole, D Attwood, C Lawes, J Haskell, C Robshaw (captain), B Vunipola

SUBSTITUTIONS: T Youngs for Hartley (51 mins); G Parling for Attwood (51 mins); M Vunipola for Marler (59 mins); R Wigglesworth for B Youngs (67 mins); K Brookes for Cole (67 mins); T Wood for Haskell (67 mins); D Cipriani for Brown (77 mins)

SCORERS: *Tries*: Joseph, Ford, Nowell *Conversions*: Ford (2) *Penalty Goals*: Ford (2)

SCOTLAND: S Hogg; D Fife, M Bennett, M Scott, T Seymour; F Russell, G Laidlaw (captain); A Dickinson, R Ford, E Murray, J Hamilton, J Gray, R Harley, B Cowan, D Denton

SUBSTITUTIONS: T Swinson for Hamilton (temp 36–40 mins and 48 mins); G Tonks for Scott (40 mins); G Cross for Murray (54 mins); A Ashe for Denton (54 mins); F Brown for Ford (59 mins); R Grant for Dickinson (59 mins); J Beattie for Harley (67 mins); S Hidalgo-Clyne for Russell (73 mins)

SCORERS: *Try*: Bennett *Conversions*: Laidlaw (2) *Penalty Goal*: Laidlaw

REFEREE: R Poite (France)

15 March, Stadio Olimpico, Rome

ITALY 0 FRANCE 29 (2G 5PG)

ITALY: L McLean; L Sarto, L Morisi, A Masi, G Venditti; T Allan, E Gori; S Parisse (captain), M Aguero, L Ghiraldini, D Chistolini, G Biagi, J Furno, F Minto, S Vunisa

SUBSTITUTIONS: L Orquera for Allan (14 mins); A de Marchi for Aguero (34 mins); E Bacchin for Morisi (38 mins); L Cittadini for Chistolini (51 mins); Q Geldenhuys for Biagi (51 mins); A Manici for Ghiraldini (59 mins); G Palazzani for Gori (73 mins); M Barbini for Parisse (75 mins)

FRANCE: S Spedding; Y Huget, G Fickou, M Mermoz, N Nakaitaci; C Lopez, S Tillous-Borde; E Ben Arous, G Guirado, N Mas, A Flanquart, Y Maestri, T Dusautoir (captain), B le Roux, L Goujon

SUBSTITUTIONS: J Plisson for Lopez (40 mins); R Slimani for Mas (51 min); B Kayser for Guirado (54 mins); V Debaty for Ben Arous (58 mins); R Kockott for Tillous-Borde (64 mins); R Taofifenua for Maestri (65 mins); M Bastareaud for Fickou (70 mins); D Chouly for Goujon (73 mins)

SCORERS: *Tries*: Maestri, Bastareaud *Conversions*: Plisson (2) *Penalty Goals*: Lopez (2), Spedding, Plisson (2)

REFEREE: JP Doyle (England)

21 March, Stadio Olimpico, Rome

ITALY 20 (2G 2PG) WALES 61 (6G 2T 3PG)

ITALY: L McLean; L Sarto, L Morisi, A Masi, G Venditti; K Haimona, E Gori; M Rizzo, L Ghiraldini (captain), ML Castrogiovanni, G Biagi, J Furno, F Minto, M Bergamasco, S Vunisa

SUBSTITUTIONS: L Orquera for Haimona (5 mins); A Manici for Ghiraldini (51 mins); A de Marchi for Rizzo (51 mins); D Chistolini for Castrogiovanni (51 mins); Q Geldenhuys for Biagi (51 mins); R Barbieri for Vunisa (70 mins); G Palazzani for Gori (74 mins); E Bacchin for Morisi (74 mins)

SCORERS: *Tries*: Venditti, Sarto *Conversions*: Orquera (2) *Penalty Goals*: Haimona, Orquera

WALES: L Halfpenny; G North, J Davies, J Roberts, L Williams; D Biggar, R Webb; R Evans, S Baldwin, A Jarvis, L Charteris, AW Jones, D Lydiate, S Warburton (captain), T Faletau

SUBSTITUTIONS: S Williams for Halfpenny (34 mins); R Gill for Evans (53 mins); K Owens for Baldwin (56 mins); J Tipuric for Lydiate (56 mins); G Davies for Webb (71 mins); R Priestland for L Williams (71 mins); S Andrews for Jarvis (74 mins); J Ball for Charteris (74 mins)

SCORERS: *Tries*: Roberts, L Williams, North (3), Webb, Warburton, S Williams *Conversions*: Biggar (6) *Penalty Goals*: Halfpenny (2), Biggar

REFEREE: C Pollock (New Zealand)

21 March, Murrayfield, Edinburgh

SCOTLAND 10 (1G 1PG) IRELAND 40 (4G 4PG)

SCOTLAND: S Hogg; D Fife, M Bennett, M Scott, T Seymour; F Russell, G Laidlaw (captain); R Grant, R Ford, E Murray, J Hamilton, J Gray, A Ashe, B Cowan, D Denton

SUBSTITUTIONS: T Visser for Fife (temp 12–22 mins); G Cross for Murray (12 mins); A Dickinson for Grant (32 mins); F Brown for Ford (53 mins); T Swinson for Hamilton (53 mins); R Harley for Ashe (56 mins); S Hidalgo-Clyne for Laidlaw (56 mins); G Tonks for Scott (70 mins); T Visser for Bennett (71 mins)

SCORERS: *Try*: Russell *Conversion*: Laidlaw *Penalty Goal*: Laidlaw

YELLOW CARD: Cross (56 mins)

IRELAND: R Kearney; T Bowe, J Payne, R Henshaw, L Fitzgerald; J Sexton, C Murray; C Healy, R Best, M Ross, D Toner, P O'Connell (captain), P O'Mahony, S O'Brien, J Heaslip

SUBSTITUTIONS: M Moore for Ross (46 mins); J McGrath for Healy (53 mins); S Cronin for Best (62 mins); I Henderson for Toner (62 mins); I Madigan for Sexton (71 mins); J Murphy for O'Brien (73 mins); E Reddan for Murray (80 mins)

SCORERS: *Tries*: O'Connell, O'Brien (2), Payne *Conversions*: Sexton (3), Madigan *Penalty Goals*: Sexton (4)

REFEREE: J Garcès (France)

21 March, Twickenham, London

ENGLAND 55 (7G 2PG) FRANCE 35 (2G 3T 2PG)

ENGLAND: M Brown; A Watson, J Joseph, L Burrell, J Nowell; G Ford, B Youngs; J Marler, D Hartley, D Cole, G Parling, C Lawes, J Haskell, C Robshaw (captain), B Vunipola

SUBSTITUTIONS: T Youngs for Hartley (53 mins); M Vunipola for Marler (63 mins); K Brookes for Cole (63 mins); D Cipriani for Watson (63 mins); N Easter for Parling (68 mins); T Wood for Haskell (68 mins); R Wigglesworth for B Youngs (72 mins); B Twelvetrees for Burrell (72 mins)

SCORERS: *Tries*: Youngs (2), Watson, Ford, Nowell (2), Vunipola *Conversions*: Ford (7) *Penalty Goals*: Ford (2)

YELLOW CARD: Haskell (57 mins)

FRANCE: S Spedding; Y Huget, G Fickou, M Mermoz, N Nakaitaci; J Plisson, S Tillous-Borde; V Debaty, G Guirado, N Mas, A Flanquart, Y Maestri, T Dusautoir (captain), B le Roux, L Goujon

SUBSTITUTIONS: B Kayser for Guirado (48 mins); R Slimani for Mas (48 mins); R Kockott for Tillous-Borde (49 mins); U Atonio for Debaty (61 mins); D Chouly for Goujon (63 mins); R Taofifenua for Maestri (68 mins); R Talès for Plisson (72 mins); M Bastareaud for Mermoz (72 mins); Debaty for Slimani (79 mins)

SCORERS: *Tries*: Tillous-Borde, Nakaitaci, Mermoz, Debaty, Kayser *Conversions*: Plisson (2) *Penalty Goals*: Plisson, Kockott

REFEREE: N Owens (Wales)

Getty Images

Pure elation for the Italian players as a last-gasp penalty try gives them victory over Scotland at Murrayfield.

RBS 6 NATIONS

PREVIOUS WINNERS:

1883 England	1884 England	1885 Not completed
1886 England & Scotland	1887 Scotland	1888 Not completed
1889 Not completed	1890 England & Scotland	1891 Scotland
1892 England	1893 Wales	1894 Ireland
1895 Scotland	1896 Ireland	1897 Not completed
1898 Not completed	1899 Ireland	1900 Wales
1901 Scotland	1902 Wales	1903 Scotland
1904 Scotland	1905 Wales	1906 Ireland & Wales
1907 Scotland	1908 Wales	1909 Wales
1910 England	1911 Wales	1912 England & Ireland
1913 England	1914 England	1920 England & Scotland & Wales
1921 England	1922 Wales	1923 England
1924 England	1925 Scotland	1926 Scotland & Ireland
1927 Scotland & Ireland	1928 England	1929 Scotland
1930 England	1931 Wales	1932 England & Ireland & Wales
1933 Scotland	1934 England	1935 Ireland
1936 Wales	1937 England	1938 Scotland
1939 England & Ireland & Wales	1947 England & Wales	1948 Ireland
1949 Ireland	1950 Wales	1951 Ireland
1952 Wales	1953 England	1954 England & Wales & France
1955 Wales & France	1956 Wales	1957 England
1958 England	1959 France	1960 England & France
1961 France	1962 France	1963 England
1964 Scotland & Wales	1965 Wales	1966 Wales
1967 France	1968 France	1969 Wales
1970 Wales & France	1971 Wales	1972 Not completed
1973 Five Nations tie	1974 Ireland	1975 Wales
1976 Wales	1977 France	1978 Wales
1979 Wales	1980 England	1981 France
1982 Ireland	1983 Ireland & France	1984 Scotland
1985 Ireland	1986 Scotland & France	1987 France
1988 Wales & France	1989 France	1990 Scotland
1991 England	1992 England	1993 France
1994 Wales	1995 England	1996 England
1997 France	1998 France	1999 Scotland
2000 England	2001 England	2002 France
2003 England	2004 France	2005 Wales
2006 France	2007 France	2008 Wales
2009 Ireland	2010 France	2011 England
2012 Wales	2013 Wales	2014 Ireland
2015 Ireland		

England and Wales have both won the title outright 26 times; France 17; Scotland 14; Ireland 13; Italy 0.

TRIPLE CROWN WINNERS:

England (24 times) 1883, 1884, 1892, 1913, 1914, 1921, 1923, 1924, 1928, 1934, 1937, 1954, 1957, 1960, 1980, 1991, 1992, 1995, 1996, 1997, 1998, 2002, 2003, 2014

Wales (20 times) 1893, 1900, 1902, 1905, 1908, 1909, 1911, 1950, 1952, 1965, 1969, 1971, 1976, 1977, 1978, 1979, 1988, 2005, 2008, 2012

Scotland (10 times) 1891, 1895, 1901, 1903, 1907, 1925, 1933, 1938, 1984, 1990

Ireland (10 times) 1894, 1899, 1948, 1949, 1982, 1985, 2004, 2006, 2007, 2009

GRAND SLAM WINNERS:

England (12 times) 1913, 1914, 1921, 1923, 1924, 1928, 1957, 1980, 1991, 1992, 1995, 2003
Wales (11 times) 1908, 1909, 1911, 1950, 1952, 1971, 1976, 1978, 2005, 2008, 2012
France (Nine times) 1968, 1977, 1981, 1987, 1997, 1998, 2002, 2004, 2010
Scotland (Three times) 1925, 1984, 1990
Ireland (Twice) 1948, 2009

THE SIX NATIONS CHAMPIONSHIP 2000–15

COMPOSITE TABLE

	P	W	D	L	Pts
England	80	55	1	24	111
Ireland	80	53	2	25	108
France	80	52	2	26	106
Wales	80	44	2	34	90
Scotland	80	19	2	59	40
Italy	80	12	1	67	25

RECORD	DETAIL		SET
Most team points in season	229 by England	in five matches	2001
Most team tries in season	29 by England	in five matches	2001
Highest team score	80 by England	80-23 v Italy	2001
Biggest team win	57 by England	80-23 v Italy	2001
Most team tries in match	12 by Scotland	v Wales	1887
Most appearances	65 for Ireland	BG O'Driscoll	2000–2014
Most points in matches	557 for Ireland	RJR O'Gara	2000–2013
Most points in season	89 for England	JP Wilkinson	2001
Most points in match	35 for England	JP Wilkinson	v Italy, 2001
Most tries in matches	26 for Ireland	BG O'Driscoll	2000–2014
Most tries in season	8 for England	CN Lowe	1914
	8 for Scotland	IS Smith	1925
Most tries in match	5 for Scotland	GC Lindsay	v Wales, 1887
Most cons in matches	89 for England	JP Wilkinson	1998–2011
Most cons in season	24 for England	JP Wilkinson	2001
Most cons in match	9 for England	JP Wilkinson	v Italy, 2001
Most pens in matches	109 for Ireland	RJR O'Gara	2000–2013
Most pens in season	19 for Wales	SL Halfpenny	2013
Most pens in match	7 for England	SD Hodgkinson	v Wales, 1991
	7 for England	CR Andrew	v Scotland, 1995
	7 for England	JP Wilkinson	v France, 1999
	7 for Wales	NR Jenkins	v Italy, 2000
	7 for France	G Merceron	v Italy, 2002
	7 for Scotland	CD Paterson	v Wales, 2007
	7 for Wales	SL Halfpenny	v Scotland, 2013
Most drops in matches	11 for England	JP Wilkinson	1998–2011
Most drops in season	5 for France	G Camberabero	1967
	5 for Italy	D Dominguez	2000
	5 for Wales	NR Jenkins	2001
	5 for England	JP Wilkinson	2003
	5 for Scotland	DA Parks	2010
Most drops in match	3 for France	P Albaladejo	v Ireland, 1960
	3 for France	J-P Lescarboura	v England, 1985
	3 for Italy	D Dominguez	v Scotland 2000
	3 for Wales	NR Jenkins	v Scotland 2001

RUGBY'S VALUES

integrity
Integrity is central to the fabric of the game and i generated through honesty and fair play.

respect
Respect for team mates, opponents, match officials and those involved in the game is paramount.

solidarity
Rugby provides a unifyin spirit that leads to life lor friendships, camaraderie teamwork and loyalty which transcends cultura geographic, political and religious differences.

passion
Rugby people have a passionate enthusiasm for the game. Rugby generates excitement, emotional attachment and a sense of belonging to the global rugby famil

discipline
Discipline is an integral part of the game both on and off the field and is reflected through adherence to the laws, the regulations and rugby's core values.

WORLD RUGBY™

WORLDRUGBY.ORG

THE RUGBY CHAMPIONSHIP

AUSTRALIA ENJOY FIRST TITLE SUCCESS

By Alex Broun

The Wallabies enjoy their first Rugby Championship title after recording victories over New Zealand, South Africa and Argentina.

The shortened Rugby Championship, the fourth since the expansion of the former Tri-Nations in 2012, was historic for a number of reasons in 2015.

For the first time New Zealand did not claim the title, with Australia remaining undefeated to win their inaugural Championship.

While for Argentina it was a year of great progress: for the first time they did not finish in last place, coming third; they won their second ever Rugby Championship match, following on from the 21–17 win over Australia in Mendoza last year; and that victory was their first ever over the mighty Springboks, winning 37–25 in Durban, their first win in 20 attempts against South Africa, stretching back to 1993.

For South Africa it was a campaign to forget as they lost all three of their matches, albeit very narrowly in tight finishes against the All Blacks and Wallabies.

It was the first Rugby Championship for new Australia coach Michael Cheika, who after clinching a Super Rugby title with the NSW Waratahs in 2014 was elevated to the Wallabies coaching job to replace Ewen McKenzie.

While the three other nation's coaches remained the same – Heyneke Meyer (South Africa) and Steve Hansen (New Zealand) on their fourth campaigns, and Daniel Hourcade (Argentina) in his second year in The Rugby Championship.

The tournament was shortened due to Rugby World Cup 2015 with just one round robin of matches taking place, in contrast to the usual home-and-away format.

The first round of matches saw New Zealand notch up a comfortable 39–18 home win over Argentina on a Friday night in Christchurch, scoring five tries to two. But those two tries for Argentina were scored by captain and hooker Agustín Creevy, back-to-back five pointers in the second half off the back of a powerful rolling maul.

Creevy's double made him the first player from Argentina to score two tries in a Rugby Championship match and the seventh forward overall, including the first front-rower since 2008 and the third overall after All Blacks Keven Mealamu (2006) and Tony Woodcock (2008).

Pleasingly for the All Blacks key players who they would rely on for their RWC 2015 campaign, such as captain and flanker Richie McCaw, fly-half Daniel Carter and number eight Kieran Read, put in impressive performances.

The next day saw the most thrilling match in the competition in Brisbane when a try after the 80-minute mark by centre Tevita Kuridrani saw Australia pull off a remarkable comeback victory over South Africa.

Trailing 20–10 with just seven minutes left the Wallabies came from nowhere to score two converted tries, the first by flanker Michael Hooper, to win 24–20.

The Australian hero was captain Stephen Moore who, in the final moments, made a bold decision to kick for the line when the Wallabies were awarded a penalty, rather than take a shot at goal. The penalty would have given his team a draw but Moore took the more risky approach to go for the win.

Moore's bravery was rewarded when Kuridrani crashed over several phases after the lineout, making Matt Giteau's successful conversion unnecessary.

For a rugby nation starved of success in recent years the nature of the victory, and Moore's brave gamble, gave Australian fans reason to hope.

That hope gathered strength the following weekend when the Wallabies shrugged off a long flight to Mendoza to record a comprehensive 34–9 victory over Los Pumas. Kurtley Beale came off the bench to notch up his 50th test cap in an all-round strong performance for the Wallabies, who brought up the bonus point through tries by Adam Ashley-Cooper, Joe Tomane, Kuridrani and a stunning solo burst by returning second-row Dean Mumm.

Australia also defended well, restricting Los Pumas to just three penalties by fly-half Nicolás Sánchez. The win took the Wallabies to the top of The Rugby Championship for the first time in the competition's history.

Earlier in the day in Johannesburg, the Springboks slumped to their third consecutive loss for the first time since 2011, when a late McCaw try from a lineout saw the All Blacks sneak home 27–20. It was tough on South Africa, who for the second week in a row led coming into the last 10 minutes, but a neatly worked move close to the Springboks' line saw McCaw go over for the decisive try, converted by fly-half Lima Sopoaga in his debut test. Another penalty by the impressive Sopoaga stretched the All Blacks' margin of victory in the 80th minute.

This set up a virtual Rugby Championship final a fortnight later in Sydney when the two undefeated teams, New Zealand and Australia, faced off in the decider.

The Wallabies had a very poor record against the All Blacks coming into the match, failing to record a victory in their last 10 matches, with their last win over New Zealand way back in 2011.

They had come close the previous year with a 12–12 draw at the same venue in The Rugby Championship, and were within a minute of recording a victory in Brisbane in the final Bledisloe Cup test of the year before a last second try to Malakai Fekitoa, converted by Colin Slade.

But with a man of the match performance by Hooper, and a powerful forward effort marshalled by captain and hooker Moore, the Wallabies scored three tries through Sekope Kepu, Ashley-Cooper and unlikely hero Nic White to get home 27–19 and inflict only New Zealand's second ever loss in The Rugby Championship – and their biggest – the first coming the previous season in a 27–25 reverse to South Africa in Johannesburg.

THE RUGBY CHAMPIONSHIP

The unlikely hero for the Wallabies was reserve scrum-half White, who was brought on for starting No.9 Nick Phipps in the 65th minute with the game hanging in the balance and Australia trailing 19–17, and quickly notched up 10 points, through a converted try and a long-range penalty, to get Australia home.

For the All Blacks the usually reliable Carter had an off night, missing two conversions, but there were still highlights for the visitors with debutant winger Nehe Milner-Skudder crossing for two well taken tries and captain McCaw bringing up his 141st cap to equal former Ireland captain Brian O'Driscoll's record for the most test appearances.

With Australia clinching their maiden title the final match was a play-off for third place in the table between South Africa and Argentina in Durban.

It was another surprise with a superb performance by Los Pumas, spearheaded by a hat-trick of tries by winger Juan Imhoff, seeing them triumph 37–25. It was Argentina's first ever win over South Africa and their first away victory since joining The Rugby Championship in 2012.

Imhoff's hat-trick was Argentina's first in The Rugby Championship and the first hat-trick by any player in the competition since Israel Folau scored three for Australia against Argentina in 2013.

The match was virtually decided at the start of the second half with Imhoff going over for his third, and Argentina's fourth, within a minute of the restart to give Los Pumas a 34–13 lead.

South Africa claimed some revenge the following weekend, as did New Zealand, both winning extra matches played as warm-ups for Rugby World Cup 2015. The Springboks defeated Argentina 26–12 in Buenos Aires, while New Zealand retained the Bledisloe Cup with a comprehensive 41–13 win over Australia in Auckland.

The win for South Africa was scant consolation for Meyer after overseeing the Boks' poorest ever Rugby Championship campaign.

"They say that sport or rugby builds character. It doesn't build character, it reveals character," he said. "When I took the job I said it's not about me, this job is bigger than the individual.

"The most important thing for me is to keep my integrity. I know there is a lot of criticism. I don't have any excuses and I know where the public comes from. There is a lot of negativity and I understand that but, like I said from the start, I'm going to keep my integrity and that's more important to me than just winning."

Hourcade, the delighted Pumas coach, said Argentina's performance was down to a new attacking philosophy they planned to take into RWC 2015.

"Given the chance, we will attack," Hourcade explained. "Not like crazy. First we need to get a chance. For that, we need to have good lineout throws, quality balls. If not, we won't try to force situations, because that can turn out really bad. If given the situation, we will do it from anywhere on the pitch."

All Blacks coach Hansen congratulated Australia on their success but was confident his team would bounce back quickly – as the case proved.

"We just got beaten by a better side on the night," he said. "We have to face up to that reality. It's an inconvenient fact, but we've been here before. We've lost games before and it doesn't mean we've all of a sudden become a bad team. We just have some things we need to tidy up and we'll get back and start that process."

Victorious coach Cheika, as has become his standard, downplayed his team's achievement, choosing to focus on contests to come.

"I don't want to be a sad sack," said Cheika. "You take a moment to congratulate the players, then you sing the national anthem loud and proud, then sit around with your mates in the dressing room like old fashioned times and talk about what happened.

"Then you get on the bus back to the hotel and think, 'what am I doing now to get ready for next week?' That's the responsible thing to do, that's what I'm going to be doing as coach."

Getty Images

Full-back Israel Folau beats Julian Savea in the air in Australia's 27–19 victory over the All Blacks.

THE RUGBY CHAMPIONSHIP
2015 FINAL STANDINGS

	P	W	D	L	F	A	BP	PTS
Australia	3	3	0	0	85	48	1	13
New Zealand	3	2	0	1	85	65	1	9
Argentina	3	1	0	2	64	98	1	5
South Africa	3	0	0	3	65	88	2	2

POINTS: WIN 4; DRAW 2; FOUR OR MORE TRIES, OR DEFEAT BY SEVEN OR FEWER POINTS 1

17 July, AMI Stadium, Christchurch

NEW ZEALAND 39 (4G 1T 2PG) ARGENTINA 18 (1G 1T 2PG)

NEW ZEALAND: I Dagg; W Naholo, M Nonu, SB Williams, C Piutau; D Carter, TJ Perenara; T Woodcock, K Mealamu, O Franks, L Romano, B Retallick, J Kaino, R McCaw (captain), K Read

SUBSTITUTIONS: C Slade for Naholo (52 mins); N Laulala for Franks (55 mins); C Taylor, W Crockett and J Thrush for Mealamu, Woodcock and Romano (60 mins); L Messam and A Ellis for Kaino and Perenara (71 mins); R Crotty for Nonu (73 mins)

SCORERS: *Tries:* McCaw, Nonu, Piutau, Read, Taylor *Conversions:* Carter (4) *Penalty Goals:* Carter (2)

ARGENTINA: J Tuculet; H Agulla, M Bosch, J de la Fuente, S Cordero; N Sánchez, T Cubelli; M Ayerza, A Creevy (captain), R Herrera, G Petti, M Carizza, JM Leguizamón, JM Fernández Lobbe, F Isa

SUBSTITUTIONS: J Ortega Desio for Leguizamón (50 mins); N Tetaz Chaparro for Herrera (55 mins); M Landajo and L González Amorosino for Cubelli and Tuculet (56 mins); J Montoya, L Noguera and B Macome for Creevy, Ayerza and Petti (63 mins) S González Iglesias for De la Fuente (69 mins)

SCORERS: *Tries:* Creevy (2) *Conversion:* Sánchez *Penalty Goals:* Sánchez (2)

REFEREE: C Joubert (South Africa)

AUSTRALIA 24 (3G 1PG) SOUTH AFRICA 20 (2G 2PG)

AUSTRALIA: I Folau; A Ashley-Cooper, T Kuridrani, M Giteau, R Horne; Q Cooper, W Genia; J Slipper, S Moore (captain), S Kepu, W Skelton, R Simmons, S Fardy, M Hooper, S Higginbotham

SUBSTITUTIONS: N Phipps for Genia (40 mins); G Holmes and D Pocock for Kepu and Higginbotham (46 mins); J Horwill for Skelton (51 mins); D Mitchell for Horne (58 mins); S Sio and M Toomua for Slipper and Cooper (66 mins); Cooper for Giteau (temp 68–75 mins)

SCORERS: *Tries:* Ashley-Cooper, Hooper, Kuridrani *Conversions:* Cooper (2), Giteau *Penalty Goal:* Cooper

SOUTH AFRICA: W le Roux; JP Pietersen, J Kriel, D de Allende, B Habana; H Pollard, R Pienaar; T Mtawarira, B du Plessis, J du Plessis, E Etzebeth, V Matfield (captain), F Louw, M Coetzee, S Burger

SUBSTITUTIONS: F Malherbe for J du Plessis (temp 14–18 mins); L de Jager for Matfield (18 mins); T Mohoje for Louw (temp 29–40 mins); Malherbe for J du Plessis (48 mins); A Strauss and H van der Merwe for B du Plessis and Mtawarira (50mins); C Reinach and P Lambie for Pienaar and Pollard (68 mins); Mohoje for Coetzee (70 mins); L Mvovo for Kriel (77 mins)

SCORERS: *Tries:* Etzebeth, Kriel *Conversions:* Pollard (2) *Penalty Goals:* Pollard (2)

REFEREE: N Owens (Wales)

Getty Images

Matt Giteau became Australia's first overseas-based player and was pivotal in his side's maiden Rugby Championship title.

THE RUGBY CHAMPIONSHIP

25 July, Ellis Park, Johannesburg

SOUTH AFRICA 20 (2G 2PG) NEW ZEALAND 27 (3G 2PG)

SOUTH AFRICA: W le Roux; C Hendricks, J Kriel, D de Allende, B Habana; H Pollard, R Pienaar; T Mtawarira, B du Plessis, J du Plessis, E Etzebeth, L de Jager, H Brussiw, F Louw, S Burger (captain)

SUBSTITUTIONS: P Lambie for Pollard (temp 40–41 mins); V Koch for J du Plessis (40 mins); W Whitely for Louw (42 mins); F van der Merwe for De Jager (60 mins); T Nyakane for Koch (62 mins); Lambie for Le Roux (63 mins); A Strauss for Mtawarira (70 mins); C Reinach for Pienaar (75 mins); L Mapoe for Kriel (78 mins)

SCORERS: *Tries:* Le Roux, Kriel *Conversions:* Pollard (2) *Penalty Goals:* Pollard (2)

NEW ZEALAND: I Dagg; B Smith, C Smith, M Nonu, C Piutau; L Sopoaga, A Smith; T Woodcock, D Coles, O Franks, B Retallick, J Broadhurst, L Messam, R McCaw (captain), K Read

SUBSTITUTIONS: S Whitelock for Broadhurst (40 mins); M Fekitoa for Nonu (47 mins); W Crockett for Woodcock (50 mins); B Barrett for Dagg (52 mins); B Franks and V Vito for O Franks and Messam (57 mins); C Taylor for Coles (63 mins); TJ Perenara for A Smith (65 mins)

SCORERS: *Tries:* B Smith, Coles, McCaw *Conversions:* Sopoaga (3) *Penalty Goals:* Sopoaga (2)

YELLOW CARD: Whitelock (59 mins)

REFEREE: J Garcès (France)

25 July, Estadio Malvinas Argentinas, Mendoza

ARGENTINA 9 (3PG) AUSTRALIA 34 (1G 3T 4PG)

ARGENTINA: S Cordero; G Camacho, M Moroni, JP Socino, J Imhoff; N Sánchez, M Landajo; M Ayerza, A Creevy (captain), R Herrera, M Carizza, T Lavanini, J Ortega Desio, JM Fernández Lobbe, F Isa

SUBSTITUTIONS: N Tetaz Chaparro for Herrera (54 mins); L González Amorosino for Camacho (56 mins); T Cubelli for Landajo (62 mins); L Senatore for Isa (64 mins); M Diaz, M Alemanno and S González Iglesias for Ayerza, Lavanini and Sánchez (67 mins); S González Iglesias for Sánchez (67 mins); S Iglesias Valdez for Creevy (73 mins)

SCORER: *Penalty Goals:* Sánchez (3)

AUSTRALIA: I Folau; A Ashley-Cooper, T Kuridrani, M Toomua, J Tomane; B Foley, N Phipps; J Slipper, S Moore (captain), G Holmes, W Skelton, R Simmons, S Fardy, D Pocock, B McCalman

SUBSTITUTIONS: Q Cooper for Toomua (10 mins); S Sio for Slipper (40 mins); M Hooper for McCalman (49 mins); D Mumm for Fardy (54 mins); S Kepu for Holmes (56 mins); T Polota-Nau for Moore (67 mins); N White and K Beale for Phipps and Cooper (76 mins)

SCORERS: *Tries:* Tomane, Mumm, Kuridrani, Ashley-Cooper *Conversion:* Foley *Penalty Goals:* Foley (4)

YELLOW CARD: Cooper (65 mins)

REFEREE: J Peyper (South Africa)

AUSTRALIA 27 (3G 2PG) NEW ZEALAND 19 (2T 3PG)

AUSTRALIA: I Folau; A Ashley-Cooper, T Kuridrani, M Giteau, D Mitchell; B Foley, N Phipps; S Sio, S Moore (captain), S Kepu, D Mumm, J Horwill, S Fardy, M Hooper, D Pocock

SUBSTITUTIONS: G Holmes for Hooper (temp 16–19 mins); M Toomua for Foley (51 mins); Holmes for Kepu (55 mins); J Slipper and W Skelton for Sio and Horwill (59 mins); B McCalman for Pocock (temp 62–66 mins); N White and K Beale for Phipps and Giteau (66 mins); T Polota-Nau for Moore (69 mins); McCalman for Fardy (77 mins)

SCORERS: *Tries:* Kepu, Ashley-Cooper, White *Conversions:* Giteau (2), White *Penalty Goals:* Giteau, White

YELLOW CARDS: Kepu (8 mins); Phipps (54 mins)

NEW ZEALAND: B Smith; N Milner-Skudder, C Smith, SB Williams, J Savea; D Carter, A Smith; T Woodcock, D Coles, O Franks, B Retallick, L Romano, J Kaino, R McCaw (captain), K Read

SUBSTITUTIONS: N Laulala for O Franks (45 mins); S Whitelock and M Fekitoa for Romano and Williams (55 mins); B Barrett for B Smith (62 mins); C Taylor for Coles (69 mins); B Franks and S Cane for Woodcock and Kaino (74 mins); S Cane for Kaino (74 mins); TJ Perenara for A Smith (78 mins)

SCORERS: *Tries:* Milner-Skudder (2) *Penalty Goals:* Carter (3)

YELLOW CARD: A Smith (54 mins)

REFEREE: W Barnes (England)

All Blacks captain Richie McCaw won his 141st cap against Australia to equal Brian O'Driscoll's test appearance record.

THE RUGBY CHAMPIONSHIP

8 August, King's Park, Durban

SOUTH AFRICA 25 (2G 1T 2PG) ARGENTINA 37 (4G 2PG 1DG)

SOUTH AFRICA: W le Roux; J Kriel, J de Villiers, D de Allende, B Habana; H Pollard, R Pienaar; T Mtawarira, B du Plessis, V Koch, E Etzebeth, L de Jager, H Brussow, M Coetzee, S Burger (captain)

SUBSTITUTIONS: M van der Merwe for Koch (40 mins); A Strauss for Du Plessis (57 mins); C Reinach, T Nyakane and PS du Toit for Pienaar, Mtawarira and Etzebeth (60 mins); S Kolisi for Brussow (63 mins); P Lambie and L Mvovo for Pollard and Coetzee (66 mins)

SCORERS: *Tries:* De Jager, Le Roux, Habana *Conversions:* Pollard (2) *Penalty Goals:* Pollard (2)

ARGENTINA: J Tuculet; H Agulla, M Bosch, J de la Fuente, J Imhoff, JM Hernández; T Cubelli; M Ayerza, A Creevy (captain), N Tetaz Chaparro, G Petti, T Lavanini, P Matera, JM Leguizamón, L Senatore

SUBSTITUTIONS: L Noguera for Ayerza (53 mins); S González Iglesias for De la Fuente (56 mins); M Alemanno for Petti (57 mins); L González Amorosino for Hernández (63 mins); T Lezana and M Landajo for Leguizamón and Cubelli (66 mins); J Montoya for Creevy (68 mins); M Diaz for Tetaz Chaparro (71 mins)

SCORERS: *Tries:* Bosch, Imhoff (3) *Conversions:* Hernández (4) *Penalty Goals:* Hernández, Bosch *Drop Goal:* Bosch

YELLOW CARD: Matera (76 mins)

REFEREE: R Poite (France)

Getty Images

Full-back Juan Imhoff scored a brilliant hat-trick in Durban to seal Argentina's first ever victory over South Africa.

RUGBY CHAMPIONSHIP (FORMERLY TRI-NATIONS) RECORDS 1996–2015

PREVIOUS WINNERS

1996 New Zealand	1997 New Zealand	1998 South Africa	1999 New Zealand
2000 Australia	2001 Australia	2002 New Zealand	2003 New Zealand
2004 South Africa	2005 New Zealand	2006 New Zealand	2007 New Zealand
2008 New Zealand	2009 South Africa	2010 New Zealand	2011 Australia
2012 New Zealand	2013 New Zealand	2014 New Zealand	2015 Australia

GRAND SLAM WINNERS

New Zealand (Six times) 1996, 1997, 2003, 2010, 2012 and 2013
South Africa (Once) 1998
Australia (Once) 2015

TEAM RECORD	DETAIL		SET
Most team points in season	203 by S Africa	in six matches	2013
Most team tries in season	24 by N Zealand	in six matches	2013
Highest team score	73 by S Africa	73–13 v Argentina (h)	2013
Biggest team win	60 by S Africa	73–13 v Argentina (h)	2013
Most team tries in match	9 by S Africa	v Argentina (h)	2013

INDIVIDUAL RECORD	DETAIL	PLAYER	SET
Most appearances	58 for N Zealand	RH McCaw	2002–2015
Most points in matches	554 for N Zealand	DW Carter	2003–2015
Most points in season	99 for N Zealand	DW Carter	2006
Most points in match	31 for S Africa	M Steyn	v N Zealand (h) 2009
Most tries in matches	19 for S Africa	BG Habana	2005–2015
Most tries in season	8 for N Zealand	BR Smith	2013
Most tries in match	4 for S Africa	JL Nokwe	v Australia (h) 2008
Most cons in matches	76 for N Zealand	DW Carter	2003–2015
Most cons in season	17 for S Africa	M Steyn	2013
Most cons in match	8 for S Africa	M Steyn	v Argentina (h) 2013
Most pens in matches	120 for N Zealand	DW Carter	2003–2015
Most pens in season	23 for S Africa	M Steyn	2009
Most pens in match	9 for N Zealand	AP Mehrtens	v Australia (h) 1999
Most drops in matches	4 for S Africa	AS Pretorius	2002–2006
	4 for S Africa	M Steyn	2009–2014
	4 for N Zealand	DW Carter	2003–2015
Most drops in season	3 for S Africa	M Steyn	2009
Most drops in match	2 for S Africa	JH de Beer	v N Zealand (h) 1997
	2 for S Africa	FPL Steyn	v Australia (h) 2007

From 1996–2015 inclusive, each nation played four matches in a season. The nations have played six matches since, except in 2007 and 2011 (Rugby World Cup years) when they reverted to four, and in 2015 when only three matches were played by each nation.

THE RUGBY CHAMPIONSHIP

Dan Biggar's accuracy with the boot helped an injury-hit Wales come from behind to beat RWC 2015 hosts England at Twickenham.

Getty Images

WORLD
RUGBY™
PACIFIC NATIONS CUP

FIJI DIG DEEP TO CLAIM TITLE

By Jon Newcombe

Fiji earned regional bragging rights after victory over Samoa in the Pacific Nations Cup 2015 final in Canada.

Fijian flair overcame Samoan physicality as a highly competitive World Rugby Pacific Nations Cup 2015 concluded with a 39–29 win for John McKee's side in a captivating final at the Swangard Stadium in Burnaby, Canada.

Fiji went into the six-team tournament intent on becoming the top side in the Pacific region and they achieved that goal by staying true to their attack-minded philosophy while also showing definite signs of improvement in the scrum.

Tonga made it a Pacific Island 1-2-3 with victory over Japan in the third place play-off and became one of the world's top 10 ranked teams as a result, while the USA got the better of North American rivals Canada to finish fifth.

With the tournament kicking off exactly two months before Rugby World Cup 2015, it served as a golden opportunity for teams to fine-tune their game plans and try out those on the fringe of the national team.

Given the proximity of the nations to one another in the World Rugby Rankings – Samoa started the tournament in ninth with Canada ranked 17th – it was perhaps entirely predictable that the 2015 edition would feature so many tight matches. Half of the 12 fixtures played ended with a score or less between the sides and one draw.

2015 saw the six nations split into two pools with fixtures played across venues in Fiji, USA and Canada in a cross-pool format. The results from the pool phase of the competition determined the line-up on finals day with Samoa and Fiji contesting the title-decider as winners of Pools A and B after two wins and a draw.

Fiji and Tonga had the honour of getting the action underway in the sweltering heat of Suva on 18 July, the only match played outside of North America. Six tries were shared equally in a typically entertaining and physical encounter, but it was the goal-kicking of Fiji debutant Ben Volavola that proved decisive.

Lepani Botia also made an early impression on the tournament after bouncing off three would-be Tongan tacklers to set up Henry Seniloli for a try that handed Fiji a narrow half-time advantage. The lead went on to change hands five times as the match remained on a knife-edge throughout, and it was only when Peni Ravai dotted down with eight minutes to go that Fiji finally put the game out of the 'Ikale Tahi's reach at 30–22.

Over in San Jose, Japan's all-time record points scorer Ayumu Goromaru kicked 15 points and Yoshikazu Fujita scored the only try of the match as the Brave Blossoms extended their unbeaten run against Canada to seven matches with a 20–6 win at the Avaya Stadium.

The USA Eagles were a side transformed after the break in the second match of the San Jose double header when 11 points from the boot of Irish-born fly-half AJ MacGinty and a late Titi Lamositele try saw them come within five points of Samoa, who'd earlier raced into a 21–3 half-time lead thanks to tries from captain and winger Alesana Tuilagi and full-back Ahsee Tuala and the kicking of fly-half Patrick Fa'apale.

While victory over Samoa had narrowly eluded them the USA made it count six days later when they faced Japan, another of their RWC 2015 Pool B opponents, at Bonney Field in Sacramento. Six MacGinty penalties and a 68th-minute try from flanker Andrew Durutalo saw the Eagles reward a partisan home crowd with a 21–16 victory. Earlier in the day Fiji and Samoa had fought out a thrilling 30–30 draw, Fa'apale stepping off the bench to level the scores with a last-minute penalty for

Samoa after team-mate Paul Perez had earlier bagged a brace of tries to cancel out Fijian second-row Leone Nakarawa's own try double.

The openness of the Pacific Nations Cup 2015 was reflected by the fact that on the eve of the final round of pool matches only Canada were unable to reach the final. BMO Field in Toronto played host to a 33–19 win for Tonga against the USA in one of the few one-sided contests on show, fly-half Kurt Morath kicking 18 points and wingers Fetu'u Vainikolo (2) and Telusa Veainu scoring the tries that gave the 'Ikale Tahi a fully deserved seventh straight victory over the Eagles.

Fiji then booked their place in the final following a hard-fought 27–22 win over Japan. Three yellow cards in the second half, including two in the last five minutes for forwards Nakarawa and Campese Ma'afu, nearly proved costly as Fiji threatened to surrender the 24–9 advantage they'd established early in the second half.

Canada thought they'd picked up a first win of the tournament – and first ever over Samoa – in the final match of pool play when Phil Mackenzie pierced the Pacific Islanders' defence with four minutes to go. But Sakaria Taulafo broke the Canucks' hearts when he pounced on a loose ball from a lineout to score his first international try in 36 outings on the stroke of full-time and send Samoa through to the final.

In the third place play-off in Burnaby, Tonga recorded a fourth straight win over Japan thanks to 16 points from the boot of Morath and tries from Halani 'Aulika, Vainikolo and Sonatane Takulua. Morath finished the tournament as top points scorer with 47 points, three more than MacGinty, while team-mates Takulua and Vainikolo were joint top try scorers alongside Fiji's Nakawara with four tries apiece.

MacGinty scored all of the Eagles' points in the North American derby that followed, ensuring a 15–13 victory for his side with a coolly taken last-minute drop goal. Captain Chris Wyles hailed the impact made by the Dubliner who'd only qualified for the USA on residential grounds in January. "He showed a lot of composure with that drop goal and his game management has been superb. He's a great kicker and a real asset. I'm really excited about him growing in this role with us," said Wyles, after his first tournament as captain.

In the final Fiji had to withstand a fierce second-half fightback from Samoa to get their hands on the trophy they'd last won in 2013. Fiji raced into a 17–3 lead when Nakawara started and finished off a free-flowing move before livewire scrum-half Niko Matawalu added a second.

However Samoa clawed their way back into the contest through the kicking of Mike Stanley and a third PNC title looked within their grasp when tries from Jack Lam and Fa'atoina Autagavaia edged them in front. But the introduction of Volavola from the bench helped to tip the balance back in Fiji's favour, the fly-half's cross-field kick setting up

Nakawara for his second and then another two tries, from full-back Kini Murimurivalu and captain Akapusi Qera, put them 36–24 in front and seemingly out of sight.

A second try for Autagavaia while Fiji were down to 14 men set up a grandstand finish but Volavola ensured local bragging rights went the way of Fiji by coolly stroking over a penalty from wide out with three minutes to go. "We knew Samoa would come out firing after the first game was drawn and we were ready for it. I think we wanted it more than them in the end," said a jubilant Qera.

WORLD RUGBY PACIFIC NATIONS CUP 2015 RESULTS

18/07/15	Fiji 30–22 Tonga	ANZ Stadium, Suva
18/07/15	Canada 6–20 Japan	Avaya Stadium, San Jose
18/07/15	USA 16–21 Samoa	Avaya Stadium, San Jose
24/07/15	Fiji 30–30 Samoa	Bonney Field, Sacramento
24/07/15	Canada 18–28 Tonga	Swangard Stadium, Burnaby
24/07/15	USA 23–18 Japan	Bonney Field, Sacramento
29/07/15	USA 19–33 Tonga	BMO Field, Toronto
29/07/15	Fiji 27–22 Japan	BMO Field, Toronto
29/07/15	Canada 20–21 Samoa	BMO Field, Toronto
03/08/15	Tonga 31–20 Japan	Swangard Stadium, Burnaby
03/08/15	USA 15–13 Canada	Swangard Stadium, Burnaby
03/08/15	Fiji 39–29 Samoa	Swangard Stadium, Burnaby

WORLD RUGBY PACIFIC NATIONS CUP 2015 FINAL STANDINGS

POOL A

	P	W	D	L	PF	PA	BP	PTS
Samoa	3	2	1	0	72	66	1	11
Tonga	3	2	0	1	83	67	0	8
Japan	3	1	0	2	60	56	2	6

POOL B

	P	W	D	L	PF	PA	BP	PTS
Fiji	3	2	1	0	87	76	1	11
USA	3	1	0	2	58	72	1	5
Canada	3	0	0	3	44	69	1	1

Note: Teams were seeded from 1–6 based on pool standings to determine final day fixtures

ROMANIA REGAIN NATIONS CUP CROWN

By Jon Newcombe

Romania were crowned World Rugby Nations Cup champions for the third time in four years after completing a clean sweep of victories with a 23–0 win against previously unbeaten Argentina Jaguars in the decisive and concluding match of the 2015 edition.

The Oaks' experience at the Nations Cup, held on home soil in Bucharest, was entirely different to that of fellow RWC 2015 qualifiers Namibia, who finished the tournament without a win and a point to their name and ultimately a change of coach, after the resignation of Danie Vermeulen.

For Spain and Argentina Jaguars the Nations Cup afforded both nations the chance to blood new players in a competitive environment and, from that perspective, many positives were gained over the nine days of competition.

To the delight of coach Lynn Howells, Romania improved visibly as the Nations Cup wore on. The errors, ill-discipline and lack of accuracy in attack that took the gloss off routine victories over Spain (35–9) and Namibia (43–3) had largely been worked out of the system by the time they confronted the Jaguars in a straight shootout for the title.

"After the Namibia match we had a long meeting when some hard truths were spelt out," explained Howells. "We discussed the plans for the World Cup build-up and analysed the shortcomings revealed by the game: the contact area, the lineout, game awareness and attention to detail. You name it! The players absorbed the criticism and produced a much better performance against the Jaguars."

Finishing the tournament without conceding a try was obviously a huge plus for Romania, but the advances made in their attacking game will have been particularly pleasing for Howells, whose decision to bring in overseas players such as New Zealand-born playmaker Michael

Wiringi appeared fully vindicated with the backs having much more purpose and direction than previously had been the case.

Romania, however, relied on one of their tried and trusted figures to see them to victory in the opening game, all-time leading point scorer Florin Vlaicu once again proving his worth with a 20-point haul in a 35–9 win over a resourceful Spanish outfit. The Felipe Contepomi coached Jaguars kicked off their campaign with a four tries to one, 30–10 victory over Namibia.

In the second round, two tries from captain Mihai Macovei helped Romania to continue their winning run against Namibia, while it took two tries inside the first 10 minutes of the second half for the Jaguars to finally see off Spain 15–6 and set up the winner-takes-all finale with Romania at the Stadionul National Arcul de Triumf.

Spain defied the terrible conditions caused by incessant rain to defeat Namibia 20–3 in the final-day wooden spoon decider. Spain's tries all came in the first half and were scored by Ignacio Contard, Anibal Bonan and Pierre Garcia.

What followed was a one-sided 'final'. Romania bossed their South American opponents in the set-piece exchanges and stifled what few opportunities the Jaguars had in open play with an aggressive defence. Mihaita Lazar's first-half try and 11 points from the boot of Vlaicu had put Romania in command at 16–0 before the *coup de grâce* was supplied by replacement scrum-half Florin Surugiu, who marked his 50th appearance by darting down the blindside to score the title-clinching try.

WORLD RUGBY NATIONS CUP 2015 RESULTS

12/06/15	Namibia 10–35 Argentina Jaguars	Stadionul National Arcul de Triumf, Bucharest
12/06/15	Romania 35–9 Spain	Stadionul National Arcul de Triumf, Bucharest
17/06/15	Argentina Jaguars 15–6 Spain	Stadionul National Arcul de Triumf, Bucharest
17/06/15	Romania 43–3 Namibia	Stadionul National Arcul de Triumf, Bucharest
21/06/15	Spain 20–3 Namibia	Stadionul National Arcul de Triumf, Bucharest
21/06/15	Romania 23–0 Argentina Jaguars	Stadionul National Arcul de Triumf, Bucharest

FINAL STANDINGS

	P	W	D	L	PF	PA	BP	Pts
Romania	3	3	0	0	101	12	1	13
Argentina Jaguars	3	2	0	1	45	39	1	9
Spain	3	1	0	2	35	53	0	4
Namibia	3	0	0	3	16	93	0	0

WORLD RUGBY™
TBILISI CUP

IRISH CLAIM TITLE IN TBILISI

By Jon Newcombe

Emerging Ireland completed an Eastern Europe one-two by adding the World Rugby Tbilisi Cup 2015 title to the Nations Cup crown they won in Bucharest 12 months earlier. And with spots in Joe Schmidt's Rugby World Cup 2015 training squad up for grabs the Emerging Ireland squad did not lack for motivation, and the three bonus-point wins achieved over Emerging Italy, Uruguay and Georgia were a fair reflection of their superiority during the eight-day competition.

As an added bonus back-row Jack Conan and centre/fly-half Noel Reid sufficiently impressed Schmidt to be included in Ireland's extended 45-man squad in preparation for RWC 2015. Sadly, the broken arm suffered by captain Rhys Ruddock against Uruguay dashed any hopes he had of making the initial squad.

"We are very satisfied to win the tournament overall, although we are a little bit frustrated with some of our play," reflected Emerging Ireland coach Allen Clarke after his side's victory against Georgia. "Over the three games we have probably put together three good halves of rugby."

The opening match against Emerging Italy was typical of the hit-and-miss performances Clarke spoke of. The Irish stormed into a 20–0 lead on the back of tries from Eoin Griffin, Andrew Conway and Stuart McClosky, however they had to wait until the final minute of the match to score their fourth try through Tiernan O'Halloran for a final scoreline of 25–0.

A match-up between two RWC 2015 competitors followed in the second match on day one and it was hosts Georgia who got the better of Uruguay, 19–10, in an error-strewn encounter that produced one try apiece for either team.

Disaster struck Tbilisi later that weekend as torrential rainfall caused the River Vere, which runs through the Georgian capital, to burst its banks leading to devastation and fatalities in the surrounding area. Prior to Wednesday's double-header a minute's silence was held at the Avchala

Stadium as a mark of respect for the people who'd been affected by the tragedy.

The first game on day two involved another Jekyll and Hyde performance from the Irish against Uruguay. Emerging Ireland scored four first-half tries – Conway finding his way onto the scoresheet once again – but only one after the break to secure a 33–7 victory. That meant Georgia needed to beat Emerging Italy in the match that followed to prevent the Irish winning the title with a round to spare.

Handicapped by the loss of key fly-half Lasha Malaguradze to an early injury, the Lelos never got into their game and two second-half tries from Simone Marinaro and Maxime Mbanda and the reliable kicking of Carlo Canna saw the Italians record a shock 26–10 victory. "It was a tough game but our players stepped up to the challenge and we are so happy with the win," said Emerging Italy manager Andrea Duodo.

First-half tries from hooker Oliviero Fabiani and winger Gabriele Di Giulio and 13 points from the boot of Canna saw Emerging Italy beat Uruguay 23–13 in the final round to claim second place. "At the start of the tournament I couldn't imagine that we could win two games," Duodo said. "We have got better and better as the tournament has progressed."

In the tournament finale, Emerging Ireland produced a clinical second-half display in front of Schmidt and his coaching team to record a comprehensive 45–12 victory over Georgia, winger Conway maintaining his record of scoring in every game as one of the five players to get their name on the scoresheet.

WORLD RUGBY TBILISI CUP 2015 RESULTS

13/06/15	Emerging Ireland 25–0 Emerging Italy	Avchala Stadium, Tbilisi
13/06/15	Georgia 19–10 Uruguay	Avchala Stadium, Tbilisi
17/06/15	Uruguay 7–33 Emerging Ireland	Avchala Stadium, Tbilisi
17/06/15	Georgia 10–26 Emerging Italy	Avchala Stadium, Tbilisi
21/06/15	Uruguay 13–23 Emerging Italy	Avchala Stadium, Tbilisi
21/06/15	Georgia 12–45 Emerging Ireland	Avchala Stadium, Tbilisi

FINAL STANDINGS

	P	W	D	L	F	A	BP	PTS
Emerging Ireland	3	3	0	0	103	19	3	15
Emerging Italy	3	2	0	1	49	48	0	8
Georgia	3	1	0	2	41	81	0	4
Uruguay	3	0	0	3	30	75	0	0

WORLD RUGBY™
U20 CHAMPIONSHIP

NEW ZEALAND INSPIRED BY ITALIAN RETURN

By Karen Bond

New Zealand celebrate their first World Rugby U20 Championship title since 2011 after defeating England in the final.

There was a sense of déjà vu as the World Rugby U20 Championship 2015 unfolded in Italy. A feeling that New Zealand would end a barren spell without the silverware that had virtually been their property in the early years of the tournament, and so it proved as they triumphed 21–16 in the final in Cremona in late June, denying England a third successive title in the process.

Four years earlier, when the tournament had first been held in another region of Italy, the outcome had been exactly the same, a New Zealand side with current All Blacks Sam Cane, Beauden Barrett, Brodie Retallick and TJ Perenara in its ranks recording a 33–22 victory over an England side featuring the likes of George Ford and Owen Farrell.

That was New Zealand's fourth title in as many years, but 2015 was only their second final appearance in the last four years and they had tasted defeat in the other, against South Africa in Cape Town in 2012. Some of those early success stories were built around a theme or philosophy that truly united and inspired the squad and this year it was honouring fallen heroes who had fought their own battles on Italian soil.

"Our theme this year was the Italian campaign of the second division, which involved the New Zealand Maori battalion as well, and we used a lot of their themes, when they were in Italy," explained coach Scott Robertson after the final. "They fought hard and had their final in Trieste. We used that tonight. We have our dog tags and we fought for the heroes and the fallen before us so it was pretty empowered and it was amazing."

New Zealand certainly had to dig deep and call upon all their reserves in the final at the Stadio Giovanni Zini as they recovered from conceding the first try – just as in 2011 – and then the early loss of centre TJ Faiane to a knee injury. His replacement Vince Tavae-Aso, though, took just 20 seconds to make his mark on the title decider, somehow escaping the clutches of two players to score in the corner, and two Otere Black penalties meant New Zealand held a slender 11–10 advantage at half-time.

That was extended when Akira Ioane dived over the line, but the inspirational number eight was sin-binned within minutes and England chipped away at the lead with two Rory Jennings penalties in his absence. It could have been worse after Piers O'Connor won the race to dot down a kick ahead, but he had been ahead of the kicker and the try was correctly ruled out by the TMO. Instead Black eased any nerves with another penalty and it was New Zealand who celebrated with not one, but two hakas either side of the trophy presentation.

"It was a test level match, both sides were great with the passion and emotion they put on the field," insisted England coach Jon Callard afterwards. "It could have gone either way, the first 20 minutes by us was sensational, but we struggled in keeping possession in the second half. I can't ask my side for more and I'm sure that we will see many of them playing at the World Cup in 2019 and 2023."

If the final had, in the words of Robertson, been a "tough arm-wrestle", the last four encounters for New Zealand and England could not have been more different. New Zealand conceded the first try against France but then the favourites cut loose, scoring six tries – three of them by Tevita Li to make the winger the leading try-scorer in U20 Championship history with 13 – amid a scintillating display of attacking rugby by their backline to triumph 45–7, the highest score in a semi-final. France manager Fabien Pelous could only state afterwards: "What went wrong? Maybe our opponents were what went wrong, they were outstanding, too quick and too technical today for us. We won against England last week, but this match was simply too difficult for our team. We tried many things but we never found solutions to the problems they gave us."

England's victory by contrast came in a battle of the forwards, South Africa ultimately paying the price for early indiscipline with two players sin-binned and then turning down several kickable penalties in the second half. It was only two tries in the final three minutes, while England had try-scorer Nick Tompkins in the sin-bin, that put some respectability into the final score of 28–20.

That defeat meant that Hanro Liebenberg, one of the yellow-carded players, would not lead South Africa to the title as his brother Wiaan had done in 2012. But the Junior Springboks put aside that disappointment and bounced back to beat France 31–18 in the third place play-off in Cremona, with four first-half tries – two by flanker Dan du Preez – ultimately enough to see off a brave fight-back by Les Bleuets after the break. France, despite the defeat, had matched their best ever placing in what was only their second appearance in the semi-finals in eight editions.

There were also wins on the final day for Australia, Ireland, Argentina and hosts Italy. Australia, who for the second tournament running had missed out on the best runner-up place in the semi-finals on point differential – this time to England, finished fifth after a hard-fought 28–23 defeat of Wales, nearly paying the price for not taking their chances and allowing their opponents back into the match late on.

Two tries by winger Stephen Fitzgerald saw Ireland battle to a 17–9 victory over Scotland in the seventh place play-off, but eighth is still the Scots' best ever ranking in the U20 Championship. Japan, returning to the U20 Championship for the first time since 2009 after winning last year's U20 Trophy, had already guaranteed their best finish too, regardless of what happened against Argentina in the ninth place play-off. They continued to impress but Los Pumitas came home 38–21.

The stakes could not have been any higher for the opening match in Cremona as Italy and Samoa battled for their U20 Championship survival and it was an encounter that went right down to the final play when

Malu Falaniko had a chance to rescue his Samoan side with a penalty just inside the Italian half. However, the winger's kick fell agonisingly short and Italian players fell to their knees in relief with the 20–19 defeat meaning Samoa will drop down into the U20 Trophy in Zimbabwe in 2016. It was a match that had ebbed one way and then the other as Italy, roared on by the home fans, avenged their 30–24 loss to Samoa in the pool stages and for the Pacific Islanders it was another missed opportunity as they knew that had they scored just one more try against the Azzurrini in that Pool B encounter then they, and not Scotland, would have been the eighth seeds and safe from the threat of relegation. Instead, Samoa's place will be taken in the 2016 edition in England by Georgia, who had won the U20 Trophy for the first time a few weeks earlier in Portugal.

Italy captain Paolo Buonfiglio has now survived two relegation play-offs in as many years and found it hard to put into words his relief afterwards. "I feel really good, we wanted to save ourselves and in the end we did it. I am very proud of my guys, we have had a difficult tournament. I can't speak right now … The crowd helped a lot, they were fantastic – not just today but in the whole tournament."

WORLD RUGBY U20 CHAMPIONSHIP 2015 RESULTS

POOL A

Round One: **France** 19–10 **Wales**, **England** 59–7 **Japan**. Round Two: **France** 47–7 **Japan**, **England** 30–16 **Wales**. Round Three: **England** 18–30 **France**, **Wales** 66–3 **Japan**.

POOL B

Round One: **Australia** 34–22 **Samoa**, **South Africa** 33–5 **Italy**. Round Two: **South Africa** 40–8 **Samoa**, **Australia** 31–15 **Italy**. Round Three: **Samoa** 30–24 **Italy**, **South Africa** 46–13 **Australia**.

POOL C

Round One: **Ireland** 18–16 **Argentina**, **New Zealand** 68–10 **Scotland**. Round Two: **Ireland** 24–20 **Scotland**, **New Zealand** 32–29 **Argentina**. Round Three: **Argentina** 6–29 **Scotland**, **New Zealand** 25–3 **Ireland**.

POOL TABLES

POOL A

	P	W	D	L	F	A	BP	PTS
France	3	3	0	0	96	35	1	13
England	3	2	0	1	107	53	2	10
Wales	3	1	0	2	92	52	1	5
Japan	3	0	0	3	17	172	0	0

POOL B

	P	W	D	L	F	A	BP	PTS
South Africa	3	3	0	0	119	26	3	15
Australia	3	2	0	1	78	83	2	10
Samoa	3	1	0	2	60	98	0	4
Italy	3	0	0	3	44	94	2	2

POOL C

	P	W	D	L	F	A	BP	PTS
New Zealand	3	3	0	0	125	42	2	14
Ireland	3	2	0	1	45	61	0	8
Scotland	3	1	0	2	59	98	1	5
Argentina	3	0	0	3	51	79	2	2

PLAY-OFFS FIRST PHASE

Ninth place semi-finals	**Argentina** 46–5 **Italy**
	Samoa 12–29 **Japan**
Fifth place semi-finals	**Australia** 31–21 **Scotland**
	Ireland 12–22 **Wales**
Semi-finals	**New Zealand** 45–7 **France**
	South Africa 20–28 **England**

U20 CHAMPIONSHIP

PLAY-OFFS SECOND PHASE

11th place play-off	**Italy** 20–19 **Samoa**
Ninth place play-off	**Argentina** 38–21 **Japan**
Seventh place play-off	**Ireland** 17–9 **Scotland**
Fifth place play-off	**Australia** 23–28 **Wales**

THIRD PLACE PLAY-OFF

20 June, 2015, Stadio Giovanni Zini, Cremona

FRANCE 18 (3T 1PG) SOUTH AFRICA 31 (4G 1PG)

FRANCE: A Pilati; A Bonneval, D Penaud, E Roudil, L Blanc; L Meret, G Doubrere; T Estorge, C Chat, C Castets, T Labouteley, M Tanguy, A Jelonch, L Bachelier (captain), F Sanconnie.

SUBSTITUTIONS: J Delannoy for Tanguy (33 mins); T Fortunel for Meret (44 mins); J Marchand for Chat (60 mins); T Paiva and P Fouyssac for Estorge and Blanc (67 mins);

SCORERS: *Tries*: Bonneval, Delannoy, Blanc *Penalty Goals*: Meret

SOUTH AFRICA: W Gelant; M Jaer, EW Viljoen, D du Plessis, L Zas; B Thomson, I van Zyl; O Nche, J van der Merwe, T du Toit, J Jenkins, RG Snyman, J Vermeulen, D du Preez, H Liebenberg (captain).

SUBSTITUTIONS: J Dweba and JL du Preez for J van der Merwe and D du Preez (55 mins); G Hermanus for Zas (70 mins); T de Beer for Thomson (74 mins); M Majola and F van Wyk for Nche and du Toit (76 mins).

SCORERS: *Tries*: Du Toit, Jenkins, D du Preez (2) *Conversions*: Thomson (4) *Penalty Goal*: Thomson

YELLOW CARD: Liebenberg (76 mins)

REFEREE: M Carley (England)

NEW ZEALAND 21 (1G 1T 3PG) ENGLAND 16 (1G 3PG)

NEW ZEALAND: M Hunt; Jack Goodhue, A Lienert-Brown, TJ Faiane, T Li; O Black, T Toiroa Tahuriorangi; R Riccitelli, L Polwart, A Moli (captain), Joshua Goodhue, H Dalzell, M Dunshea, B Gibson, A Ioane

SUBSTITUTIONS: I Tu'ungafasi for Riccitelli (temp 20–27 mins and 53 mins); V Tavae-Aso for Faiane (25 mins); S Misa for Polwart (53 mins); T Koloamatangi for Moli (72 mins); C Parker for Hill (77 mins)

YELLOW CARD: Ioane (49 mins)

SCORERS: *Tries*: Tavae-Aso, Ioane *Conversion*: Black *Penalty Goals*: Black (3)

ENGLAND: A Morris; G Perkins, N Tompkins, M Clark, H Packman; R Jennings, J Mitchell; E Genge, J Walker, P Hill, W Witty, C Ewels (captain), L Ludlam, W Owen, J Chisholm

SUBSTITUTIONS: P O'Conor for Morris (30 mins); W Homer for Mitchell (49 mins); S Adeniran-Olule and K Treadwell for Genge and Witty (50 mins); L Evans for Jennings (72 mins); S Skinner for Owen (73 mins)

SCORERS: *Try*: Clark *Conversion*: Jennings *Penalty Goals*: Jennings (3)

REFEREE: W Houston (Australia)

U20 CHAMPIONSHIP

FINAL STANDINGS

1. New Zealand	**7. Ireland**
2. England	**8. Scotland**
3. South Africa	**9. Argentina**
4. France	**10. Japan**
5. Australia	**11. Italy**
6. Wales	**12. Samoa**

Romania's inspirational captain Mihai Macovei scored two tries in his team's record-breaking 17–15 comeback win over Canada in Leicester.

GEORGIA CREATE HISTORY IN PORTUGAL

By Jon Newcombe

Georgia further enhanced its reputation as a burgeoning rugby nation by claiming the World Rugby U20 Trophy title for the first time with a convincing 49–24 victory over Canada in the final.

The Junior Lelos will now play in next year's World Rugby U20 Championship in England and judging by their performances over the course of 12 days in Lisbon in May – combining their traditional forward dominance with scintillating back play to run in 20 tries and score 148 points across four matches – they will certainly not look out of place.

In Vasil Lobzhanidze and Rezi Jintchvelashvili, Georgia have unearthed an exciting pair of young half-backs with the latter – who scored 19 points in the final to take his overall tally for the tournament to 51 – looking destined to follow Lobzhanidze onto the test stage.

While Georgia were playing in their first final Canada had been there once before, losing to Italy in 2013. However it was the Junior Lelos who raced into a 24–0 lead after scoring four tries through Mikheil Babunashvili, Giorgi Melikidze, Giorgi Kveseladze and Tomike Zoidze at the sun-lit Estadio Universitario.

Canada cut out the first-half errors to establish some semblance of parity in the second half, number eight Luke Bradley capping a fine tournament with a brace of tries, but they never got close enough to entertain hopes of a comeback. Irakli Svanidze and Kveseladze scored within minutes of each other to put the game out of reach before star man Jintchvelashvili rounded off proceedings with Georgia's seventh try.

Having kicked off their campaign with a 46–12 win against Uruguay in an ill-tempered affair at the CAR Rugby do Jamor, Georgia knew they'd have to get past pre-tournament favourites Fiji to entertain any hopes of making their first final. The Junior Lelos' power-based game and the assured goal-kicking of Jintchvelashvili, who booted five penalties and a conversion, saw them home 30–13.

Georgia then made heavy weather of beating Portugal in their final Pool A match, tries from Otar Giorgadze, Jintchvelashvili and a superb finish from winger Anzor Sichinava earning them a nervy 19–11 victory.

A straight shootout between Canada and Tonga, runners-up in 2013 and 2014 respectively, would determine who would join Georgia in the final after both teams had recorded wins over Hong Kong and Namibia in their opening two games. An evenly balanced contest went right down to the wire, Canadian centre Giuseppe du Toit kicking a last-gasp penalty to secure a 13–11 victory.

Tonga suffered further heartbreak in the third place play-off, losing 44–43 to Uruguay in a game of 12 tries. There were points aplenty too in the battles for fifth and seventh place, Fiji putting a disappointing campaign behind them to beat Namibia 36–24 while Portugal signed off with a 47–21 win over Hong Kong.

WORLD RUGBY U20 TROPHY 2015 RESULTS

POOL A

Round One: **Fiji** 34–19 **Portugal**, **Uruguay** 12–46 **Georgia**. Round Two: **Fiji** 13–30 **Georgia**, **Uruguay** 37–26 **Portugal**. Round Three: **Fiji** 26–28 **Uruguay**, **Georgia** 19–11 **Portugal**.

POOL B

Round One: **Tonga** 35–16 **Hong Kong**, **Canada** 35–20 **Namibia**. Round Two: **Tonga** 45–11 **Namibia**, **Canada** 24–15 **Hong Kong**. Round Three: **Tonga** 11–13 **Canada**, **Namibia** 36–12 **Hong Kong**.

PLAY-OFFS

Seventh place play-off	**Portugal** 47–21 **Hong Kong**
Fifth place play-off	**Fiji** 36–24 **Namibia**
Third place play-off	**Uruguay** 44–43 **Tonga**
Final	**Georgia** 49–24 **Canada**

FINAL STANDINGS

1. Georgia	5. Fiji
2. Canada	6. Namibia
3. Uruguay	7. Portugal
4. Tonga	8. Hong Kong

WORLD RUGBY

PACIFIC CHALLENGE

PAMPAS DEFEND PACIFIC CHALLENGE CROWN

By Jon Newcombe

Allan Stephen

The Argentina Pampas XV again proved too strong and retained their World Rugby Pacific Challenge crown.

The World Rugby Pacific Challenge, formerly known as the Pacific Rugby Cup, was won for the second year in a row by the Argentina Pampas XV, who defeated Fiji Warriors 17–9 in a hard-fought final at the ANZ Stadium in Suva on 23 March.

As well as a change of name, the 10th edition of this key development tournament had a more compact structure with six national representative teams playing 12 matches in one location over a two-week period.

Fixtures took on a cross-pool format with the teams in Pool A – the Pampas XV, Samoa A and Junior Japan – playing those in Pool B, namely the host nation's Fiji Warriors, Tonga A and tournament newcomers Canada A. The pool winners would meet in the final with the third and fifth place play-offs taking place as curtain-raisers.

Winger Phil Mackenzie got Canada A off to a flying start in the tournament opener with a hat-trick in a 69–17 win over Junior Japan, and points were plentiful in the second match too, with Samoa A edging Tonga A 30–28 to claim Pacific bragging rights.

The Warriors' hopes of a winning start against the Pampas XV came unstuck when scrum-half Samu Laqai was sent off and captain and number eight Nemani Nagusa sin-binned 10 minutes into the second half for their role in a scuffle. Winger Manuel Montero grabbed his second try shortly after the pair were dispatched and the Pampas XV went on to win 22–20.

In round two, the Pampas XV and Samoa A made it two from two by overcoming Tonga A and Canada A respectively. The Samoans owed their 19–17 victory to three second-half penalties from the boot of Patrick Faapale. Fiji Warriors, meanwhile, got their campaign up and running with a resounding 83–0 triumph over Junior Japan to join Canada on six points at the top of Pool B.

Tonga A kicked off the final round of pool play with a 60–24 win over the Japanese, before Canada A slipped to defeat against the Pampas XV, with Montero scoring another two tries, to mean that unless the Warriors, given their superior point difference, capitulated against their Samoan rivals they would book their place in the final. The Fijians trailed by two points at the break but turned on the style in the second half to score four tries and win 42–20.

On an emotionally charged finals day following the tragic passing of Fiji Warriors prop Bele Tabalala in his sleep 48 hours earlier, all the teams wore black armbands and the hosts their black strip in his memory.

Tonga A made it two wins against Junior Japan in the space of five days to claim fifth place, before Canada A snatched third place from Samoa A after flanker Alistair Clark scored in the last minute of a tight encounter.

In the title decider, tournament top points scorer Serupepeli Vularika kicked three penalties to hand Fiji Warriors a 9–7 half-time lead, with the Pampas' points coming from a Santiago Cordero try and Santiago González Iglesias conversion.

An error-ridden start to the second half and a string of penalties kept the score that way until Jerónimo de la Fuente latched on to his own kick to touch down on the hour mark. González Iglesias converted the try and added a late penalty to ensure the trophy would be heading back to South America for a second time.

"We're happy to get the win and the title after a tough tournament. But we came here to develop as a team and that's the most important thing we'll take out of it," said Pampas captain González Iglesias.

WORLD RUGBY PACIFIC CHALLENGE 2015 RESULTS

10/03/2015	Junior Japan 17–69 Canada A	ANZ Stadium, Suva
10/03/2015	Samoa A 30–28 Tonga A	ANZ Stadium, Suva
10/03/2015	Pampas XV 22–20 Fiji Warriors	ANZ Stadium, Suva
14/03/2015	Pampas XV 31–7 Tonga A	ANZ Stadium, Suva
14/03/2015	Samoa A 19–17 Canada A	ANZ Stadium, Suva
14/03/2015	Junior Japan 0–83 Fiji Warriors	ANZ Stadium, Suva
18/03/2015	Junior Japan 24–60 Tonga A	ANZ Stadium, Suva
18/03/2015	Pampas XV 36–15 Canada A	ANZ Stadium, Suva
18/03/2015	Samoa A 20–42 Fiji Warriors	ANZ Stadium, Suva
23/03/2015	Junior Japan 24–43 Tonga A	ANZ Stadium, Suva
23/03/2015	Samoa A 26–28 Canada A	ANZ Stadium, Suva
23/03/2015	Pampas XV 17–9 Fiji Warriors	ANZ Stadium, Suva

WORLD RUGBY PACIFIC CHALLENGE 2015 FINAL STANDINGS

POOL A

	P	W	D	L	F	A	BP	PTS
Pampas XV	3	3	0	0	89	42	2	14
Samoa A	3	2	0	1	69	87	1	9
Junior Japan	3	0	0	3	41	212	1	1

POOL B

	P	W	D	L	F	A	BP	PTS
Fiji Warriors	3	2	0	1	145	42	3	11
Canada A	3	1	0	2	101	72	2	6
Tonga A	3	1	0	2	95	85	2	6

Captain and man mountain Mamuka Gorgodze was one of Georgia's standout players at RWC 2015.

REGIONAL COMPETITIONS A VITAL PART OF RWC 2015 PREPARATION

By Jon Newcombe

Tamuna Kulumbegashvili

Georgia's teenage scrum-half Vasil Lobzhanidze would enjoy a record-breaking debut year in test rugby.

The countdown to Rugby World Cup 2015 gave added significance to international competitions featuring the nations that had made it through to the game's showpiece event in England as it handed them an ideal opportunity to fine-tune game-plans and try out new combinations in a competitive environment ahead of the challenges to come. For those teams that had missed out on qualification, there was still prized silverware and regional pride – and in some cases, promotion – at stake.

With their places at RWC 2015 already secured thanks to their top-two finishes in the 2014 European Nations Cup, champions Georgia and runners-up Romania unashamedly used the 2015 edition to assess the strength of their respective playing pools. The selection of teenager Vasil Lobzhanidze, for example, proved an inspired one by Georgia coach Milton Haig as the scrum-half was virtually an ever-present in 2015, winning a place in the Lelos' World Cup squad and becoming the youngest player in the tournament's history when he played against Tonga aged 18 years and 340 days.

The Lelos' experimental approach to the European Nations Cup meant performances often fell below their increasingly high standards, and only one try bonus-point was secured – in the 64–8 opening win against newly-promoted Germany – on their way to five straight victories. Romania had to settle for second place at the halfway stage of the competition, on points difference from Spain and Russia, after Georgia defeated them 15–6 in the concluding fixture. Portugal's only win came against Germany, who suffered a whitewash on their return to the top tier. There were positives to Germany's campaign, however, as they ran Portugal close (11–3) and in the narrow 17–12 loss to Romania, when the boot of Florin Vlaicu once again came to the Oaks' rescue, hooker Dale Garner achieved the distinction of becoming the first front-row forward in the history of test rugby to drop a goal.

Elsewhere in the European Nations Cup, Belgium, Switzerland and Lithuania remain in command of Divisions 1B, 2A and 2B respectively while, of the newly-promoted teams, Luxembourg have fared the best of all by winning all six of their matches over the last 12 months to sit top of Division 2C. Slovenia provide the biggest threat to their chances of back-to-back promotions, while Bosnia and Herzegovina lead the way in Division 2D after six wins from six and Slovakia and Estonia were the standout teams in Division 3.

A streamlined Asia Rugby Championship may have provided a new look for the region's elite international competition but it produced the same result – another title for Japan. Nothing could rain on Japan's parade – not even the torrential downpour that forced the abandonment of their final match against Hong Kong – as three teams not the previous five fought for the right to be crowned Asian champions. A 10th straight Asian title had already been sewn up by the time the deluge descended on the Aberdeen Sports Ground thanks to a 66–10 win over Korea in the penultimate round. Hong Kong held on to their number two spot in the region with Korea third. The Division 1 honours went to Sri Lanka after a 27–14 win against the Philippines in the final, while Malaysia claimed the Division 2 title despite stiff opposition from the United Arab Emirates. A 27–8 victory over Iran in the first ever 15s international between the sides handed Lebanon the Division 3 West title with Guam overcoming China to win Division 3 East.

Meanwhile in Africa, Namibia's preparations for the Africa Cup in August were hardly ideal given their disappointing showing at the World

Rugby Nations Cup two months earlier, and the subsequent resignation of head coach Danie Vermeulen. However, technical advisor Phil Davies stepped into the breach and steered the Welwitschias to their second consecutive title with victories over Kenya (46–13) and Zimbabwe (80–6) in Windhoek, following an earlier 22–14 defeat of Tunisia. Captain Rohan Kitshoff led from the front against Zimbabwe, scoring a hat-trick of tries as Namibia extended their winning run under Davies to four matches. Tunisia finished bottom and will be replaced by Division 1B champions Uganda in 2016.

In North America and the Caribbean, Trinidad and Tobago claimed their first NACRA Championship title since 2008 and only the third in their history, after a 30–16 victory over first-time finalists and North Championship League winners Mexico. The Calypso Warriors deserved their success having beaten reigning champions Guyana 22–20 in a nerve-jangling South Championship League decider, while newly-promoted Mexico booked their place in the final after dominating the Cayman Islands 24–3. Bottom-placed Barbados will play Trinidad and Tobago and Guyana again next season after they saw off the British Virgin Islands 17–15 in a tense promotion-relegation play-off in November.

The South American Championship decider once again was between Chile and Uruguay in early May after both had seen off the challenge of Brazil and Paraguay. Los Teros took an early lead through Joaquín Prada before Chile hit back to score three unanswered tries with Cristian Onetto, Juan Pablo Perrotta and Italo Zunino crossing the line. With Javier Valderrama enjoying a good day with the boot Chile were out of sight at 30–8 before Uruguay's forward dominance was rewarded with a penalty try. Paraguay secured third place in the tournament with a 20–11 win away to Brazil, who's future in the top tier of South American rugby rests on the outcome of a play-off against Colombia in São Paulo on 12 December. Inspired by captain and hat-trick scorer Sebastián Mejía Gil, Colombia followed up earlier wins over Venezuela and Ecuador to clinch their second straight B Championship title with a 28–15 win over host nation Peru on 14 November.

THE REST OF THE WORLD

International Sevens Tournaments

GO, FIJI, GO!

By Ben Ryan, Fiji Sevens coach

Getty Images

Ben Ryan's Fiji played electrifying sevens rugby to lift the HSBC World Sevens Series 2014–15 trophy in London.

This was a different year to all others. The HSBC Sevens World Series has been steadily getting more competitive as nations up the ante in a quest for success. However, the 2014–15 season also represented the first, tangible movement towards rugby's return to the Olympic Games. The top four finishers would secure automatic qualification. Golden tickets to Rio were to be the additional prizes on offer in what was the most competitive season of international sevens in its history.

For me, it was probably the biggest challenge I have had in almost a decade coaching international sevens. Fiji, a country addicted to the short version of the game, expects. The worst financial period of the union's history had just occurred and over the close season we had lost over half our team to overseas contracts. Other changes had manifested too with new coaches for Scotland, USA, Canada, Australia and a reshuffle with Kenya, although only Scotland's Calum MacRae was new to the series.

As the teams assembled on the Gold Coast for the first day of term, there is always a question mark within the teams. Have you got your pre-season right? Played enough games going in? Will the off-season adjustments have added value?

We garnered some confidence the week before in Noosa, winning the Oceania tournament with our second string side – of which half would go on to play in the series. I always have a chat with the groundsman if I can find him. Forget about anyone else at the ground – the most important person to chat to about conditions, the field and any other gems is him and he underlined what I thought – the pitch was running fast and hard . . . perfect for us.

As coaches, you also get a sense of how the team is running from the first couple of games. I am generally quiet pitch-side because I am looking for harmony; how we are moving as a team. I am not getting tied up in knots with tactics as I know the games are all likely to unfold in our favour when I see us moving as one in attack and defence. We started to flow both sides of the ball early in the tournament, culminating in a very physical performance against Australia on Saturday night.

Sunday I felt calm as we went through the gears and then put in a fantastic performance against England, who had played incredibly well to beat New Zealand in the Cup quarters. That 48–7 win put us into the final against Samoa, racing into a big lead before our Island rivals came pounding back, showing how easily momentum can swing in a final. Luckily we scored again to seal the opening title. We had scored more points in the tournament than anyone had managed since the Singapore leg of the series in 2006, where Serevi, Ryder et al ran amok.

That comparison with the only previous Fijian side to win the World Series would come up regularly across the year – a sign that this particular vintage would be talked about in the same vein.

Dubai, a simply marvellous tournament, was next. We landed back in Fiji and almost immediately lost four of our 12 players to overseas contracts in Sri Lanka. That momentum hit a serious speed bump as the consistency we so yearned for was getting affected, again from the outside. We had some excellent replacements but it was certainly not ideal when combined with half the squad having already gone the previous season.

Other teams had their noses put out of joint; New Zealand would not want another early exit, South Africa would be disappointed with their start and Australia would want to bounce back from home losses. I must be close to Dubai's number one fan. When the night begins to fall on the Saturday evening for the semi-finals and finals, you feel blanketed in noise and drama. The competitions that take place on the outside pitches have ended and the stadium is filled with a swirl of sound from the stands. Hong Kong on a Sunday is just as good. While other tournaments have had their moments over the years, finals day at these two spots are ahead of the rest. I get hairs to rise now thinking of some of the memories at these two places – what an honour to have ever been part of the proceedings.

Dubai also showed South Africa had indeed stiffened their sinews. They were to reign supreme in the next fortnight, playing some outstanding rugby. They flowed and they fought for each other – particularly in Port Elizabeth. A 33–7 win over a resurgent Australia was their final result that came after a huge morale-boosting 28–0 whitewash of the All Blacks Sevens in the semi-finals. The Australians played a terrific semi-final against us to win a thriller and get their season moving. By the end of Dubai they would occupy an automatic qualification place for Rio but it wouldn't be until their visit to Tokyo that everything changed for both them and Simon Amor's England.

Fiji's first match of the series against New Zealand in the third place play-off gave us victory in a hugely uncompromising 14 minutes. When I took the job to lead Fiji, one of the most salivating thoughts was to be pitch-side, part of a Fiji/NZ battle. There is mutual respect and reams of rich tales and battles between the two. Hits are that little harder and tries are more often than not all top drawer, as each side brings the best out in each other. It would end up an unbeaten set of results for us this time, but I have no doubt we will have some unbelievable match-ups next year as Gordon Tietjens tinkers and tweaks to get them ready for Rio. In almost nine years of head to heads with the knighted one while with England and now Fiji, its 24–17 to Titch.

We are the two head coaches with the most tournaments left on the circuit and he has been instrumental in leading the international game of sevens in the last 20 years. His name will forever be engrained in the game and no one will achieve the number of victories he has. I remember all the New Zealand games probably more than any other, such is the respect they and their coach have. Their two losses to South Africa in Dubai and PE, combined with their record against us would be their downfall this year and push them into third place come London. New Zealand Rugby's foresight to centrally contract their 15s stars and their financial backing by government plus the expertise they have either side of the white-lines, means they will be a very different animal next season. Beware all.

It is so tough to win back-to-back events and huge kudos to the Blitzbokke that they did it. It meant they took the box seat in the series that they held all the way to Glasgow and those victories almost got them over the line. Tries by the impressive quartet of Afrika, Senatla, Smith and Snyman gave them a 26–17 win over New Zealand in the final with Australia taking third, beating Argentina 34–19. Scotland was also beginning to motor and playing some lovely football, while USA were starting to make waves.

Back to the Cake Tin and a very different atmosphere as the stadium lacked the atmosphere of previous years. The Fijian support was growing tournament to tournament inside the stadiums and there was another vocal presence in Wellington. On the field, New Zealand stepped up. They beat England in the pool stage and again in the final with Rieko Ioane's brace a highlight of the final game. For England, this result and the Tokyo tournament proved to be decisive in their drive for the treasured fourth place. For Fiji, Wellington and Port Elizabeth was a blow to our series title ambitions. Two consecutive Cup quarter-final exits were scant return for a team desperate to be higher up the standings. However, after our extra-time defeat to England, the Osea Kolinisau-led side began to purr.

Las Vegas was next and it's a tournament that's been getting better and better. It has taken the US a bit of time to get to grips with the event but they are smashing it now. The crowd is getting bigger and bigger and the atmosphere was great this year. For the home nation, it also gave them a significant result in their draw with South Africa in the pool. The Blitzbokke were to gain revenge in the third place play-off but it showed the advances being made.

It wouldn't be until the final legs that the Americans would manage to hit Cup knockout stages in consecutive weeks, to hint there is still much progress to be made as a consistent threat, but more teams at the top table is a good thing full stop. The other telling moments over the weekend belonged to Fiji. New Zealand were beaten in a tight game in pool play and a scorching start in the semi-final against South Africa with Semi Kunatani giving a virtuoso display, pitted Fiji versus the All Blacks Sevens again.

The Kiwis were down on numbers through injuries and the final was a one-sided affair. Kunatani went over for a brace, as did Jerry Tuwai – World Sevens Rookie of the Year – with two typically classy and mesmerising efforts. The final score was 35–19 with a couple of late New Zealand tries after we had led 28–0 at one stage.

The standings after Vegas gave South Africa a five-point lead over

New Zealand and seven over Fiji. Four tournaments remained and any clashes now between the three sides could lead to big points swings. For Fiji, we would end up playing the two a collective six times and gain five wins. It proved to be the difference.

Hong Kong. On a personal note it has been a tournament of close but no cigar. Plenty of semi-finals and a final but failed to win the main event. I was getting to the point of thinking I might have to purchase a few of the 'Ba Gua' mirrors that are used to deflect evil spirits in Hong Kong from the ladies market in Mong Kok! Perhaps it was going to be one of those things. 2014 was the first time I was there with Fiji and I saw the passion the Fijian people had towards the event. Crazy.

It was also a tournament I learnt a lot from. We had constant distractions from those that meant well but came to knock on the players' doors in the middle of the night to share a prayer or wish them well. By the time we got to the semi-finals in 2014, we were running on vapours. This year, it wouldn't repeat. We kept guard, kept out distractions and gave the boys an even chance to do their thing.

I wonder whether other coaches ever get similar feelings but from the captains' run on the Thursday, I was certain we would deliver. In sevens, other things can trip you up and believe me, they can come from any and everywhere. Yet, there was a calmness that covered the entire squad like a blanket. A calmness that you get just before a storm, only we were to control this particular weather pattern. Playing Pacific rivals Samoa first really focused the boys and we went on to record a terrific 38–12 win. Six different try-scorers showed we were flowing and in harmony. We had a tough game against England in the quarter-final and we needed it. Our defence was tested, but even though the score-line was tight, winning 14–12, we all felt in control. Another rocket of a start against South Africa put us in the final to face New Zealand. Samoa would regroup after their loss to us and take the Kiwis to the wire in the other semi-final, but in the 40th anniversary tournament, it was fitting the two behemoths of the modern game would be facing each other again.

The anthems rang out, the players flew onto the ball and into their opposition and Fiji went into a 21–0 lead. Save Rawaca was having a brilliant debut season and stamped his mark on the final with a double. When New Zealand struck back, Fiji counter-punched again and kept the lead a healthy one. 33–19 as the whistle blew; two consecutive tournament wins for Fiji and the trio of teams at the top were a hair's breadth apart going to Tokyo.

Backing up one week to the next in the World Series is tough. I think it's even tougher after Hong Kong, the three days of competition plus the added adrenaline surge of playing at the So Kon Po Stadium. Tokyo looked a slower pace on the field and shows just how intense the series has become. The pool stages threw up some oddities. Australia beat New Zealand while Fiji handed England a big loss. So the Aussies move closer to automatic qualification, yes? No. They were to lose to an impressive Scotland and Portugal to get bundled into the Bowl, while England went from that loss to their first tournament victory under Simon Amor.

Canada took one of their greatest scalps, beating New Zealand in the quarters to face England. Sometimes the draw helps and sometimes it hinders. England would not beat a top eight side en route to the final but they still had to beat the current series leaders in a fractious, but well-timed final for England. Fiji were to lose 7–5 to South Africa, a converted Smith try from a turned over scrum proving the difference. We had our chances in that game but our 18-game winning run ended there. The last loss was in the Wellington quarter-finals and ultimately the longest run in Fijian sevens history was a huge factor in lifting the series title in London.

England won the final 21–14, a length of the field Phil Burgess score was timed to perfection and gave them that coveted fourth place they were not to give up. It can be a cruel sport. Australia had been beating England in their head to heads and out-performed them up to Tokyo. Yet over those 48 hours in Japan, the tables turned. Both sides deserve to be in Rio and Australia must now negotiate November's Oceania qualifier to take their place.

At the other end of the standings, it was too little too late for Japan. A great run saw them go to the Plate semi-final, but Portugal's consistent reaping of points put them too far ahead to be caught and it will be Japan that are replaced by Russia next year as a core team. The Japanese staff and players were a huge credit to all concerned and will be missed, but I am sure, will also be back.

So to Glasgow and London. The draw immediately threw up an early confrontation. South Africa losing 24–19 to Gordon's men meant Fiji would play the series leaders in the quarter-finals. It was a chance for us to leapfrog our great rivals and we took it with an efficient, workmanlike and clinical performance in the wet conditions to win 15–0. USA reached the semi-finals and though they were to lose to Fiji and then England to finish fourth, it was the start of an unforgettable fortnight for them. For Mike Friday and his trusty conditioner Chris Brown, another important duck was broken. With Kenya and now the USA, the pair had not quite managed to hit consecutive Cup stages in the tournament pairing. In Glasgow and London they were to change that and more.

Again in the final, New Zealand were blighted by injuries but put a game plan together that almost worked. It had not been our best first half of rugby in the final but thankfully we woke up, strung a few possessions together and powered through to take our fourth Cup of the season. My flight to London was booked that evening so I missed the boys lifting the Cup as I dashed to the airport for one final week of the season. It would hinge on one game.

London is my birthplace and my home. My family have swapped the white of England for the white of Fiji and were all proudly supporting the team in the stands. We got the simple things right in the week and went into the first day ready. After a very tough match against a terrific Argentina, we posted two further wins to complete the pool stages of the year. Played 27, won 27. A perfect day one record and another indication this was a new chapter for Fiji. A Fiji side that were consistent.

An upset happened in our crossover pool with South Africa falling to USA. That meant one solitary thing. Fiji would face the Blitzbokke in the quarter-finals. Win and the world title would be ours. Lose and all is lost. I didn't wrap it up any other way to the team. We threw all our eggs, and anything else we could find, into the basket. I told them it was all about that game and nothing more.

Before the game I had to take them to one side. There were tears in the changing room before running out and they were so emotional I knew I needed to calm them down a little. Some smiles, some deep breaths and some unravelling of frowns and we were ready. We play best with a smile on our faces and as they ran out their grins shone through. We put in a great defensive effort at the start of the game and then scored some ruthless tries to win the game and the World Series.

Back on the mainland – the nation went into hysterics. The two-hour bus journey from the airport to Suva took 10 hours as every village put up roadblocks so they could meet the team and the trophy. The capital's roads were sealed off as celebrations took hold. Songs were written and babies named after those involved. The craziest sevens mad country on the planet? Too right.

Only Fiji's second ever series title in 16 years – this group will go down in the folklore of the nation's game with plenty still to come. I couldn't have been prouder. South Africa had been a quite marvellous rival all season and with New Zealand refusing to be shaken off it was a season that had it all. The USA went on to win an historic first title and the following month underlined that with their Olympic qualification, while England grabbed the last automatic spot on behalf of Team GB. Argentina and France have now qualified too.

Without doubt, the biggest days for sevens are to come in 2016. Yet the 2014–15 season was also seminal. The "Olympic effect" brought real change across the board. Better to come? For sure. August 2016 will bring tension and drama we have never seen before. However, this year will be known as the season Fiji roared back. The team that plays like no other played like no other in breath-taking fashion. More off-loads, more line-breaks, more tackles and more tries than any other team. Pure, undiluted joyful rugby. Go, Fiji, Go!

HSBC SEVENS WORLD SERIES 2014–15 RESULTS

AUSTRALIA: 11–12 OCTOBER

Fiji (22), Samoa (19), England (17), South Africa (15), New Zealand (13), Argentina (12), Australia (10), Wales (10), USA (8), France (7), Portugal (5), Scotland (5), Canada (3), Kenya (2), Japan (1), American Samoa (1)

DUBAI: 5–6 DECEMBER

South Africa (22), Australia (19), Fiji (17), New Zealand (15), Argentina (13), Scotland (12), England (10), Wales (10), Samoa (8), France (7), USA (5), Portugal (5), Canada (3), Kenya (2), Japan (1), Brazil (1)

SOUTH AFRICA: 13–14 DECEMBER

South Africa (22), New Zealand (19), Australia (17), Argentina (15), USA (13), Fiji (12), England (10), Scotland (10), Canada (8), Kenya (7), France (5), Wales (5), Portugal (3), Samoa (2), Japan (1), Zimbabwe (1)

NEW ZEALAND: 6–7 FEBRUARY

New Zealand (22), England (19), South Africa (17), Scotland (15), Fiji (13), Australia (12), USA (10), Kenya (10), France (8), Argentina (7), Portugal (5), Wales (5), Canada (3), Samoa (2), Japan (1), Papua New Guinea (1)

USA: 13–15 FEBRUARY

Fiji (22), New Zealand (19), South Africa (17), USA (15), Australia (13), England (12), France (10), Canada (10), Kenya (8), Argentina (7), Scotland (5), Samoa (5), Portugal (3), Wales (2), Japan (1), Brazil (1)

HONG KONG: 27–29 MARCH

Fiji (22), New Zealand (19), South Africa (17), Samoa (15), Australia (13), USA (12), England (10), Argentina (10), Scotland (8), France (7), Canada (5), Wales (5), Kenya (3), Japan (2), Portugal (1), Belgium (1)

HSBC SEVENS WORLD SERIES

JAPAN: 4–5 APRIL

England (22), South Africa (19), Fiji (17), Canada (15), New Zealand (13), Scotland (12), France (10), Japan (10), USA (8), Australia (7), Samoa (5), Wales (5), Portugal (3), Argentina (2), Kenya (1), Hong Kong (1)

SCOTLAND: 9–10 MAY

Fiji (22), New Zealand (19), England (17), USA (15), South Africa (13), Scotland (12), Canada (10), Australia (10), Wales (8), Argentina (7), Kenya (5), France (5), Samoa (3), Portugal (2), Japan (1), Russia (1)

ENGLAND: 16–17 MAY

USA (22), Australia (19), Fiji (17), England (15), New Zealand (13), South Africa (12), Scotland (10), Canada (10), Kenya (8), Argentina (7), Samoa (5), Wales (5), Japan (3), France (2), Brazil (1), Portugal (1)

FINAL STANDINGS

Fiji – 164	Wales – 55
South Africa – 154	Kenya – 46
New Zealand – 152	Portugal – 28
England – 132	Japan – 21
Australia – 120	Brazil – 3
USA – 108	Hong Kong – 1
Scotland – 89	Belgium – 1
Argentina – 80	Russia – 1
Canada – 67	Papua New Guinea – 1
Samoa – 64	Zimbabwe – 1
France – 61	American Samoa – 1

PREVIOUS WINNERS

1999–00 – New Zealand	2005–06 – Fiji	2011–12 – New Zealand
2000–01 – New Zealand	2006–07 – New Zealand	2012–13 – New Zealand
2001–02 – New Zealand	2007–08 – New Zealand	2013–14 – New Zealand
2002–03 – New Zealand	2008–09 – South Africa	2014–15 – Fiji
2003–04 – New Zealand	2009–10 – Samoa	
2004–05 – New Zealand	2010–11 – New Zealand	

SEVENS

WORLD
RUGBY™
WOMEN'S SEVENS SERIES

OLYMPIC QUALIFICATION ADDS
SPICE TO WOMEN'S SERIES

By Melodie Robinson

The prolific Portia Woodman scored 52 tries as New Zealand again defended the Women's Sevens Series title.

This was the stellar sevens season we were waiting for. The rise of new powerhouses to challenge the southern hemisphere stranglehold of the World Rugby Women's Sevens Series like Canada, Russia, the United States and England. Add to that the most nail-biting, dramatic finish to a women's series yet. In particular for teams vying for Olympic qualification with the result not known until the second to last game of the season! When it comes to the question of a favourite for the 2016 Olympic gold medal, what this season has taught us is that the competition is more wide open than ever.

There were also upsets from unlikely teams. France, finally putting resources into the shorter version of the game, were quick out of the blocks. Spain, later on in the series, were the most surprising team and took the largest scalp available – world champions New Zealand. Plus one non-traditional nation made a Cup final for the first time in Langford, Canada – the superbly fit Russians with colourful coach Pavel Baranovsky and his entertaining theatrics from the sideline.

Once again New Zealand won the series title after a perfect start to the season with victories in Dubai, Brazil, the USA and Canada. But the story wasn't that clear cut, by the third tournament in Atlanta in February, Australia started to falter as injuries in their squad asked questions of their depth. Instead Russia, the USA and Canada joined New Zealand in the Cup semi-finals. A month later it was New Zealand and Russia in the final in Canada. By London and Amsterdam, New Zealand's 15-month unbeaten run was over, Australia were back in form and Canada would secure their first World Rugby event title in Amsterdam.

There were two changes to the 2014–15 World Rugby Women's Sevens Series. Firstly, the circuit was increased to a record six tournaments and secondly that 11 core teams would travel to every event. Fiji, France, South Africa and China the last sides to gain core status after going through the qualifying event in September last year.

Beginning in Dubai in late November, France were probably the biggest surprise there because for the first time they had selected their top players from the 15s national team, and had them specifically focused on sevens in the months leading up to the start of the series. Playing with typical French flair and fast moving brilliance, they beat England on the way to the Cup semi-finals but lost by just one try to the more experienced Canadian team in the play-off for third and fourth. The French had well and truly announced they were serious about Olympic qualification.

The Fijiana women's team also thrilled audiences with a crazy style of sevens in the Plate final against England where they played a rugby version of hot potato, keeping the ball in play constantly, which nearly upset the English girls who ended up winning 19–12.

New Zealand won the final against, arguably, the form team of the tournament Australia thanks to a last-minute beauty from the superbly fit Sarah Goss, the end score 19–17. The Kiwis had looked vulnerable earlier in the tournament, and in fact Russia, in an extra-time Cup quarter-final thriller, had two chances to beat New Zealand. But their usually accurate kicker Nadezda Kudinova missed two sitters in front of the posts to allow the Kiwis through.

In Brazil two months later the temperatures were challenging and the teams that handled the conditions better stood out. Being at home was great for the Brazilian team who made the Cup quarter-finals for the first time, the hard work being put in off the field paying dividends for a team that played an entertaining, passionate style.

As in Dubai it was an Australia-New Zealand final, once again it was an intense encounter, New Zealand won but only by one score, 17–10. The individual star of Brazil was Portia Woodman, the Kiwi flyer crossing for 13 tries. She was near unstoppable with the ball in hand and set a new record for points scored in a game with 25 against France, a feat she repeated against hosts USA in Atlanta a month later.

In Atlanta all that potential the Americans had been promising surfaced. Coach Ric Suggitt, one of the characters on the circuit, had been quite vocal for some time that because of the population resources available to him in America, one of his missions was to find the best athletes for his team. It didn't matter what sport they came from, he said he could turn them into rugby players. Well that plan clicked into place at their home tournament.

With players like Leyla Alev Kelter, who has represented her country in both soccer and ice hockey, getting more game time, the Americans shocked Australia 10–5 in the Cup quarter-finals, then beat Russia in the semis. Sure they got soundly beaten 50–12 by the Kiwis in the final, but revenge would come later.

Meanwhile the race for Olympic qualification was heating up. The USA's second-place finish saw them leapfrog England, who didn't have a great tournament, in the standings. The top four remained the same – New Zealand, Australia, Canada and France – but the USA were now fifth, England starting to feel the heat at the halfway point.

Next up a first visit to Canada, and there were high hopes for the host team that didn't come to fruition, instead the Russians were the next nation to put their best foot forward. Kudinova, in the middle of everything creative for her side, saw the Russians beat Australia for just the second time in Series history in the Cup quarters. Then they took down France in the semi-final by two points. Their 29–10 defeat to New Zealand in the final a respectable finish, their second place vaulting them into contention for a top four finish and Olympic qualification.

That race to Rio 2016 meant the pressure was on in May for the final two tournaments, which were back-to-back in London and Amsterdam. New Zealand had virtually already qualified thanks to a

WOMEN'S SEVENS SERIES

massive lead at the top of the standings with a perfect 80 points, but below them only 12 points separated second-placed Canada from Russia in seventh. For three European teams – Russia, England in fifth and France in fourth – there was the prospect of having to go through a very tough regional qualifier after the Women's Sevens Series if they didn't make the top four. None of the teams were keen on that prospect.

Perhaps it was desperation, more likely teams suddenly got into the groove of sevens rugby, but these two tournaments saw huge improvements across the board and New Zealand's perfect record was ended by an unlikely contender in Spain. A fitter looking Spain played confrontational sevens to shock the Kiwis 19–15 in pool play on day one. Considering New Zealand had been unbeaten for 37 games, it was arguably the biggest upset seen on the circuit so far.

The Kiwis bounced back by beating France in their next game to cement their Olympic qualification and took down a vastly improving English team 24–12 in the quarters. But Australia were on fire and smashed them out of the semis 24–5. The final at Twickenham was sensational with the Aussies coming from behind to beat Canada, in their first final of the season, by just three points.

To the final round in Amsterdam and it was all on the line. Russia, due to injuries to key players, were limping over the finish line, the French had lost some momentum also, but England, the USA and Canada had their sails up and were full steam ahead.

The USA stampeded New Zealand on day one with an historic 34–5 win. That set up England against the Kiwis in the quarters, a game they simply had to win if they had any chance of making that crucial top four to qualify Team GB for Rio 2016. Win they did, 17–13, meaning it ultimately all came down to the play-off for third and fourth between them and the USA. The game was intense with few breakouts and plenty of huge hits. In the end the English team packed with Women's Rugby World Cup 2014 winners prevailed 15–14 and they were through to the Olympics. The Americans would ultimately join them a few weeks later by winning their regional qualifier.

The final between Australia and Canada was just as spectacular. This time it was Canada who would turn the tables on the London result and take their first Women's Sevens Series title, another tense affair and victory by three points, 20–17. The four teams to qualify for the Olympics in the end were New Zealand, Canada, Australia and England in that order.

With so many teams and individuals standing out over the course of the season, it was a difficult job to select who would make the shortlist for the World Rugby Women's Sevens Player of the Year. But in the end four outstanding individuals were named, Australia's playmaker Caslick,

Kudinova.

Twenty-year-old Caslick put pressure on the opposition defensive systems every time she touched the ball and was a big part of her team's success this year. Same story for Kudinova whose influence was so pivotal, her season-ending injury in London coincided with the struggling form of the Russian side. Goss was exceptional as a leader, and there is no argument with prolific try-scorer Woodman's naming. She scored 52 tries this season which is five more than Seabelo Senatla, the top try-scorer from the men's series, in three less tournaments.

There is no doubt that this season new teams came of age, and also that women's sevens is still a sport morphing and growing into an entertainment package that amazes and thrills fans all over the world. Some teams still need to build, some need more depth, but essentially eight teams can now beat any other team on their day, after just three seasons of the World Rugby Women's Sevens Series. Next year's title is very much anyone's to win.

WORLD RUGBY WOMEN'S SEVENS SERIES 2014–15 RESULTS

DUBAI: 28–29 NOVEMBER

New Zealand (20), Australia (18), Canada (16), France (14), England (12), Fiji (10), USA (8), Russia (6), Brazil (4), South Africa (3), Spain (2), China (1)

BRAZIL: 21–22 FEBRUARY

New Zealand (20), Australia (18), Canada (16), France (14), England (12), USA (10), Russia (8), Brazil (6), Fiji (4), Spain (3), China (2), South Africa (1)

USA: 15–16 MARCH

New Zealand (20), USA (18), Canada (16), Russia (14), Australia (12), France (10), England (8), Brazil (6), Fiji (4), Spain (3), China (2), South Africa (1)

CANADA: 18–19 APRIL

New Zealand (20), Russia (18), England (16), France (14), USA (12), Canada (10), Australia (8), Fiji (6), Spain (4), Brazil (3), China (2), South Africa (1)

WOMEN'S SEVENS SERIES

SEVENS

ENGLAND: 15–16 MAY

Australia (20), **Canada** (18), **New Zealand** (16), **USA** (14), **England** (12), **France** (10), **Russia** (8), **Spain** (6), **Fiji** (4), **China** (3), **South Africa** (2), **Brazil** (1)

NETHERLANDS: 22–23 MAY

Canada (20), **Australia** (18), **England** (16), **USA** (14), **New Zealand** (12), **France** (10), **Spain** (8), **Russia** (6), **Fiji** (4), **China** (3), **Netherlands** (2), **South Africa** (1)

FINAL STANDINGS

New Zealand – 108	Fiji – 32
Canada – 96	Spain – 26
Australia – 94	Brazil – 20
England – 76	China – 13
USA – 76	South Africa – 9
France – 72	Netherlands – 2
Russia – 60	

PREVIOUS WINNERS

2012–13 – New Zealand   2013–14 – New Zealand   2014–15 – New Zealand

THE ROAD TO RIO 2016

By Karen Bond

The excitement surrounding rugby sevens reached new heights in 2014–15 as the carrot of Olympic qualification was dangled in front of teams, the chance to go for gold in Rio de Janeiro when the sport makes its debut in August 2016.

The top four ranked sides in both the men's and women's World Series would qualify with 12 further places being filled by regional qualifiers taking place between June and November 2015. Host nation Brazil were granted automatic qualification by World Rugby, leaving one place in each event at the Deodoro Olympic Park to be determined by the global repechage tournament.

Twenty-one of the 24 places at Rio 2016 have, at the time of writing, already been filled.

WORLD SERIES

The prize of Olympic qualification added a new buzz to both the men's and women's series, the dream of Rio 2016 now firmly in the sights of teams. In the HSBC Sevens World Series, Fiji and South Africa became the first to qualify by reaching the Cup quarter-finals in Glasgow in early May and were joined by New Zealand a day later. This trio won seven of the nine rounds and it was Tokyo winner England who claimed the fourth place for Team GB after a strong finish to the series, finishing 12 points ahead of Australia in the final standings.

In the women's series, New Zealand won the first four titles and wrapped up qualification in London, despite seeing a 37-match unbeaten run ended by Spain. Canada and Australia, the others to win tournaments in 2014–15, joined them on the plane to Rio by reaching the Cup quarter-finals a week later in Amsterdam. The final place went down to the last minute of a winner-takes-all third place play-off between England and USA. England won 15–14 to secure qualification for Team GB, albeit only on point differential after both sides finished the season with 76 points.

ASIA (ASIA RUGBY)

With Japanese rugby still on a high after Rugby World Cup 2015, their men's sevens team secured Olympic qualification in early November,

SEVENS

scoring four second-half tries to beat hosts Hong Kong 24–10 in the final. Japan had scored 228 points and conceded none in reaching the final of the Asian regional qualifier, but they were given a scare when Hong Kong led 10–0 at half-time.

The Asian women's qualifier is a two-legged affair, unlike the men's, and reaches its conclusion in Tokyo on 28–29 November with the winner determined by points accumulated across the two rounds. Japan top the standings after round one but Kazakhstan – the side they beat 22–0 in the Hong Kong final – as well as Hong Kong and China remain in contention.

AFRICA (RUGBY AFRICA)

Johannesburg was the venue for both of Africa's regional qualifiers, albeit nearly two months apart. South Africa's men had qualified through the World Series and their women's team won all six of their matches in the Rugby Africa Sevens in late September, scoring 265 points and conceding just five – in the final against Kenya – to secure the qualification spot.

They were later joined by Kenya's men on 15 November after they edged Zimbabwe 21–17 thanks to a final play try by Dennis Ombachi, who shrugged off several players to run in from deep in his own half at Kempton Park.

EUROPE (RUGBY EUROPE)

It was double delight for France after topping both the men's and women's Rugby Europe Grand Prix Series standings. The men were in imperious form, winning all 18 matches they played across three rounds in Moscow, Lyon and Exeter.

Russia won the first women's round in Kazan, but then lost to France in the semi-finals in Brive and the host nation lifted the title to qualify for Rio 2016. Spain's men and Russia's women booked their places in the global repechage as runners-up. They were later joined by the men's teams of Russia, Germany and Ireland and the women's teams of Spain, Ireland and Portugal who safely negotiated the European repechage event in July.

NORTH AMERICA AND CARIBBEAN (RUGBY AMERICAS NORTH)

A week after the South American qualifier, the USA's men and women booked their places at Rio 2016 in contrasting fashion. The women, having agonisingly missed out on qualification through the World Series, were a class apart on home soil in Cary, North Carolina, and claimed the title with an emphatic 88–0 victory over Mexico in the final.

Their male counterparts, who had claimed a first World Series Cup title a month before in London, raced into a 21–0 half-time lead against neighbours Canada and held firm, conceding only a try after the break to qualify and avoid the repechage.

OCEANIA (OCEANIA RUGBY)

Australia, who had occupied one of the coveted top four spots for much of the World Series before falling away in the final rounds, dominated the men's qualifier, scoring 297 points and conceding just one try in six matches, against the Cook Islands on day one. Australia beat surprise finalists Tonga 50–0 in the final to confirm their passage to Rio.

The women's event also went according to the form book with Fiji having the pace, physicality and patterns of play that were too sophisticated for their opponents to handle. Fijiana, a core team on the women's series, beat a much-improved Samoa 55–0 in the final in Auckland.

SOUTH AMERICA (SUDAMÉRICA RUGBY)

Fittingly it was South America who provided the first regional qualifiers back in June when Argentina's men and Colombia's women emerged victorious in Santa Fe. It was no surprise that Argentina's men triumphed. Having survived an early scare on day one against Chile – trailing 10–0 at half-time – they scored 308 unanswered points before seeing off Uruguay 45–0 in the final.

Colombia, though, sprung a surprise by beating Argentina 12–7 at the death in what was a de-facto final of the round-robin tournament. It was an intense match and was only settled 10 seconds from time when Guadalupe López scored the try to secure Olympic qualification.

REPECHAGE

The confirmed teams are: Uruguay, Chile, Canada, Mexico, Spain, Russia, Germany, Ireland, Hong Kong, Korea, Sri Lanka, Tonga, Samoa, Zimbabwe, Morocco and Tunisia (men) and Argentina, Venezuela, Mexico, Trinidad and Tobago, Russia, Spain, Ireland, Portugal, Kenya, Tunisia, Zimbabwe, Samoa and the Cook Islands (women). The women's event will be completed by three teams from Asia.

Italy celebrate their impressive 17–12 victory over France in the Women's Six Nations.

Getty Images

Women's Rugby

NATIONS BUILD TOWARDS WRWC 2017

By Ali Donnelly

Ireland lift the RBS Women's 6 Nations trophy for the second time in three years after a 73–3 defeat of Scotland.

The year following a World Cup is often played out against a backdrop of rebuilding as international teams go through a typical transitional phase. However, while there has been plenty of that over the last 12 months in the women's game, with the World Cup cycle having been cut by a year to avoid a clash with the sevens equivalent, there was an air of urgency this time around.

Women's Rugby World Cup 2017, which will take place in Ireland, is now firmly on the radar of the world's leading teams and while we saw a plethora of new faces on and off the pitch in 2014–15, there's no doubt that eyes are already on the ultimate prize in the game.

With an RBS Women's 6 Nations, an Asian Championship, a Super Series – featuring some of the world's leading sides – and an Elgon Cup packed in alongside numerous other senior and U20 internationals, there has also been no shortage of drama.

Following on from the hugely successful Women's Rugby World Cup 2014 in Paris was always going to be a difficult ask, but the Six Nations in 2015 gave it a run for its money in twists and turns. There was also the added spice this year with Italy, Wales and Scotland in a battle for two World Cup spots, with the two best ranked of these sides across the 2015 and 2016 Championships qualifying.

While Ireland emerged eventual and deserving champions, the fate of world champions England was fascinating to follow and with the brave-hearted Italians securing their best finish ever, there was plenty of action in all parts of the table for fans to invest in.

First to the bottom of the table and to Scotland, who took to this year's Six Nations with a raft of new faces and a new base for their home games at Broadwood Stadium. While losing every game again will be frustrating for the Scottish Rugby Union who are investing plenty into their women's game now, there were positives too with the Scots starting finally to find a way to turn pressure into points. A highlight will be the 13 points they scored against England – which gave them their best ever tally against the Auld Enemy. At the end of the competition the Scots were also handed a boost with news that experienced professional coach Shade Munro is to become the head coach of the national side from Glasgow Warriors. It is a tough job in Scotland with the development of the game hampered simply by the playing numbers in the country, but the future looks significantly brighter this year than it has in some time and there is plenty of work going on at grassroots level.

Next to Wales, who made a sensational start with only their second ever victory over England. The 13–0 win set the tone for what would be an unpredictable competition. England were a team much in transition when they took to the St Helen's field on the opening day with 14 players missing for various reasons from their World Cup squad, while Wales were changed little and it showed with a well-deserved victory, Catrin Edwards and Laurie Harries getting a try each to help the Welsh to another famous win.

Things got even better for Wales in week two with five second-half tries in a 39–3 win over Scotland seeing them shoot to the top of the table, but they came back to earth with a thud when a ruthless French display saw them lose 28–7 away from home. Hopes that their campaign could get back on track at home in the fourth round were dashed when Ireland travelled in fine form and took home a 20–0 win, and the final day defeat to Italy meant that what had been a very promising start ended in disappointment for a young Welsh outfit.

For world champions England it was also to be a disappointing competition, and it got off to a bad start when the coaches of the triumph in Paris left their roles just weeks before kick-off and the RFU's Head of Performance Nicola Ponsford took over temporarily from Gary Street and Graham Smith. From the opening day defeat in Wales, England

WOMEN'S RUGBY

did bounce back with a strong 39–7 win over Italy at The Twickenham Stoop, the likes of Hannah Gallagher impressing among a host of relatively new faces in the white jersey.

With Ireland up next in Ashbourne, victory was vital if England wanted to get a hand on the title but they stuttered and lost narrowly in poor conditions. A 42–13 win over Scotland in their first outing at the Northern Echo Arena had England back on track but the final day defeat to France at Twickenham meant they could only finish fourth. Nevertheless it was a special day for England prop Rochelle Clark, who won her 100th cap on the day – a fantastic achievement that will surely have gone in some way to make up for the disappointment of her side's final ranking.

Next to Italy, who came alive well and truly in the Championship, perhaps not surprising given they had a point to prove having missed out on the World Cup – and boy did they deliver.

The Italian game has been improving slowly but steadily over the past decade and from Biella, where they made their historic Women's 6 Nations debut against France in 2007, to Venice this year where they beat France for the second time in three years, it has been a tale of hard work and commitment.

Their third-place finish in 2015 came courtesy of two impressive wins – one over the French, who went into that match on course for the Grand Slam, and the other against Wales, where a 22–5 win in Padova left no one in any doubt that this is a team on the up. And with players like Flavia Severin, who was outstanding in all five games, Italy are well on the way to grabbing a World Cup spot for 2017.

To France, who like many others went into 2015 with a brand new coaching team and dealing with the loss of several key players to retirement post-World Cup. Like England, the French too were without most of their experienced backs due to the demands of the World Rugby Women's Sevens Series.

In winning their toughest two games on the road against Ireland and England, the loss to Italy certainly came as something of a surprise, especially as Les Bleues had promised so much after their opening day defeat of Scotland. But the victories in Twickenham and Ashbourne will have been savoured and France know there is plenty to come from a team who seem capable of coping with the loss of players through retirement and sevens commitments. They will be the team to watch next year.

Finally to Ireland, who have the French slip-up against Italy to thank for being in the mix for the title on the final day when it seemed France all but had their name on the trophy. Ireland too were all change this year with a new coaching regime and 12 new players in their squad. It hardly showed on the opening day with a 30–5 win over Italy, though the 10–5 loss to France meant the girls in green were no longer in the driving seat. A win over England kept the pressure on France and with the French losing to Italy, Ireland knew exactly what they needed to do against Scotland on the final day to win a second title in three years. The 73–3 win, shown live on Irish television, was emphatic, with Claire Molloy, Sophie Spence and captain Niamh Briggs all in superb form.

In the background to the Six Nations, France, Scotland and England all played under-20 fixtures with their commitment to the youth game surely going to bear fruit in the years ahead.

The Top 3 of the Asian Rugby Championship between Japan, Hong Kong and Kazakhstan took place in April with the Japanese emerging victorious for the first time ever. Kazakhstan have long been the kingpins in Asian women's 15s, while Hong Kong have made serious investment in their women's programmes in the last few years, not least appointing full-time coaches for both their 15s and sevens sides. Hong Kong showed signs of progress in their two losses, but it was Japan who impressed most and showed that they are targeting Women's Rugby World Cup 2017 very seriously indeed.

This year's annual Elgon Cup – a two-legged affair between Kenya and Uganda – couldn't have been closer. A 5–5 draw in game one followed by a 7–6 win for Kenya on the return leg saw them take the spoils thanks to a try from Sinaida Aura and a crucial conversion from Janet Awuor.

The test season ended with the Women's Rugby Super Series, a revamped Nations Cup. Canada have been hosting similar women's tournaments for more than 20 years, but not since 2004 had they brought together such a star-studded cast as that which gathered in Alberta at the end of June. As well as WRWC 2014 runners-up Canada and neighbours USA, the tournament also included England and their predecessors as world champions New Zealand.

In truth, almost every side fielded experimental line-ups in this competition but with just two years to go now until the next World Cup, there were fascinating sub-plots throughout.

Both the Black Ferns and England began the round robin series with new-look coaching teams and with victories in their opening matches. New Zealand's win over Canada was convincing at 40–22, while England's 39–13 defeat of the USA was equally impressive.

The Black Ferns were too good for the world champions in round two with some excellent tries and strong organisation from Kendra Cocksedge at scrum-half securing the 26–7 victory, and with the USA Women's Eagles defeating Canada in a thrilling game the scene was set for an exciting final round.

England edged Canada 15–14 to leave the hosts winless, but New

Zealand came out on top overall with a more than convincing 47–14 win over the USA to suggest that their rebuilding job is well and truly on track.

With more women playing the game than ever before, 2016 promises to be another exciting year as the world's leading teams look to lay down a marker as Women's Rugby World Cup 2017 looms larger on the horizon, not to mention players hoping to be part of history when sevens makes its debut on the Olympic stage in Rio.

2014–15 WOMEN'S INTERNATIONAL RESULTS

WOMEN'S RUGBY

02/11/2014	Switzerland 24–31 Russia	Stade du Pachy, Waterloo, Belgium
02/11/2014	Netherlands 12 –3 Belgium	Stade du Pachy, Waterloo, Belgium
23/11/2014	Italy 27–3 Scotland	Nuovo Impianto Rugby, Avezzano, Italy
06/02/2015	Italy 5–30 Ireland	Stadio Mario Lodigiani, Florence, Italy
07/02/2015	France 42–0 Scotland	Stade Henri Desgrange, La Roche-sur-Yon, France
08/02/2015	Wales 13–0 England	St Helen's, Swansea, Wales
13/02/2015	Ireland 5–10 France	Ashbourne Recreation Ground, Ashbourne, Ireland
14/02/2015	Scotland 3–39 Wales	Broadwood Stadium, Cumbernauld, Scotland
15/02/2015	England 39–7 Italy	Twickenham Stoop, Twickenham, England
27/02/2015	France 28–7 Wales	Stade de Sapiac, Montauban, France
27/02/2015	Ireland 11–8 England	Ashbourne Recreation Ground, Ashbourne, Ireland
01/03/2015	Scotland 8–31 Italy	Broadwood Stadium, Cumbernauld, Scotland
13/03/2015	England 42–13 Scotland	Northern Echo Arena, Darlington, England
14/03/2015	Italy 17–12 France	Nuovi Impianti Sportivi, Badia Polesine, Italy
15/03/2015	Wales 0–20 Ireland	St Helen's, Swansea, Wales
21/03/2015	England 15–21 France	Twickenham, London, England
21/03/2015	Italy 22–5 Wales	Stadio Plebiscito, Padova, Italy
22/03/2015	Scotland 3–73 Ireland	Broadwood Stadium, Cumbernauld, Scotland
18/04/2015	Switzerland 0–41 French Military	Stade Philippe Pottier, Monthey, Switzerland
25/04/2015	Kazakhstan 40–0 Hong Kong	National Stadium, Almaty, Kazakhstan
09/05/2015	Japan 27–12 Kazakhstan	Level 5 Stadium, Fukuoka, Japan
23/05/2015	Hong Kong 12–27 Japan	Aberdeen Sports Ground, Hong Kong, Hong Kong
13/06/2015	Kenya 5–5 Uganda	RFUEA Grounds, Nairobi, Kenya
20/06/2015	Uganda 6–7 Kenya	Kampala, Uganda
27/06/2015	Canada 22–40 New Zealand	Rugby Park, Calgary, Canada
27/06/2015	USA 13–39 England	Rugby Park, Calgary, Canada
01/07/2015	Canada 28–36 USA	Red Deer Rugby Club, Red Deer, Canada
01/07/2015	New Zealand 26–7 England	Red Deer Rugby Club, Red Deer, Canada
05/07/2015	Canada 14–15 England	Ellerslie Rugby Park, Edmonton, Canada
05/07/2015	New Zealand 47–14 USA	Ellerslie Rugby Park, Edmonton, Canada
03/10/2015	Belgium 21–38 British Army	Zonnebeke, Belgium
29/10/2015	Russia 12–27 Switzerland	Sportplatz Schönenbühl Unterägeri, Belgium
29/10/2015	Belgium 20–3 Czech Republic	Sportplatz Schönenbühl Unterägeri, Belgium
01/11/2015	Czech Republic 15–41 Russia	Sportplatz Schönenbühl Unterägeri, Belgium
01/11/2015	Belgium 50–20 Switzerland	Sportplatz Schönenbühl Unterägeri, Belgium
07/11/2015	France 11–0 England	Stade Francis Turcan, Martigues, France
14/11/2015	England 8-3 Ireland	Twickenham Stoop, Twickenham, England

International Records and Statistics

INTERNATIONAL RECORDS

RESULTS OF INTERNATIONAL MATCHES

UP TO 1 NOVEMBER, 2015

Cap matches involving senior executive council member unions only. Years for International Championship matches are for the second half of the season: eg 1972 means season 1971–72. Years for matches against touring teams from the southern hemisphere refer to the actual year of the match.

Points-scoring was first introduced in 1886, when an International Board was formed by Scotland, Ireland and Wales. Points values varied among the countries until 1890, when England agreed to join the Board, and uniform values were adopted.

Northern hemisphere seasons	Try	Conversion	Penalty goal	Drop goal	Goal from mark
1890–91	1	2	2	3	3
1891–92 to 1892–93	2	3	3	4	4
1893–94 to 1904–05	3	2	3	4	4
1905–06 to 1947–48	3	2	3	4	3
1948–49 to 1970–71	3	2	3	3	3
1971–72 to 1991–92	4	2	3	3	3*
1992–93 onwards	5	2	3	3	–

*The goal from mark ceased to exist when the free-kick clause was introduced, 1977–78.

WC indicates a fixture played during a Rugby World Cup. LC indicates a fixture played in the Latin Cup. TN indicates a fixture played in the Tri Nations. RC indicates a fixture played in The Rugby Championship. QT indicates a fixture in the Quadrangular Tournament.

ENGLAND v SCOTLAND

Played 133 England won 73, Scotland won 42, Drawn 18
Highest scores England 43–3 in 2001 and 43–22 in 2005, Scotland 33–6 in 1986
Biggest wins England 43–3 in 2001, Scotland 33–6 in 1986

1871	Raeburn Place (Edinburgh) **Scotland** 1G 1T to 1T	1911	Twickenham **England** 13–8
1872	The Oval (London) **England** 1G 1DG 2T to 1DG	1912	Inverleith **Scotland** 8–3
1873	Glasgow **Drawn** no score	1913	Twickenham **England** 3–0
1874	The Oval **England** 1DG to 1T	1914	Inverleith **England** 16–15
1875	Raeburn Place **Drawn** no score	1920	Twickenham **England** 13–4
1876	The Oval **England** 1G 1T to 0	1921	Inverleith **England** 18–0
1877	Raeburn Place **Scotland** 1 DG to 0	1922	Twickenham **England** 11–5
1878	The Oval **Drawn** no score	1923	Inverleith **England** 8–6
1879	Raeburn Place **Drawn** Scotland 1DG England 1G	1924	Twickenham **England** 19–0
1880	Manchester **England** 2G 3T to 1G	1925	Murrayfield **Scotland** 14–11
1881	Raeburn Place **Drawn** Scotland 1G 1T England 1DG 1T	1926	Twickenham **Scotland** 17–9
1882	Manchester **Scotland** 2T to 0	1927	Murrayfield **Scotland** 21–13
1883	Raeburn Place **England** 2T to 1T	1928	Twickenham **England** 6–0
1884	Blackheath (London) **England** 1G to 1T	1929	Murrayfield **Scotland** 12–6
1885	No Match	1930	Twickenham **Drawn** 0–0
1886	Raeburn Place **Drawn** no score	1931	Murrayfield **Scotland** 28–19
1887	Manchester **Drawn** 1T each	1932	Twickenham **England** 16–3
1888	No Match	1933	Murrayfield **Scotland** 3–0
1889	No Match	1934	Twickenham **England** 6–3
1890	Raeburn Place **England** 1G 1T to 0	1935	Murrayfield **Scotland** 10–7
1891	Richmond (London) **Scotland** 9–3	1936	Twickenham **England** 9–8
1892	Raeburn Place **England** 5–0	1937	Murrayfield **England** 6–3
1893	Leeds **Scotland** 8–0	1938	Twickenham **Scotland** 21–16
1894	Raeburn Place **Scotland** 6–0	1939	Murrayfield **England** 9–6
1895	Richmond **Scotland** 6–3	1947	Twickenham **England** 24–5
1896	Glasgow **Scotland** 11–0	1948	Murrayfield **Scotland** 6–3
1897	Manchester **England** 12–3	1949	Twickenham **England** 19–3
1898	Powderhall (Edinburgh) **Drawn** 3–3	1950	Murrayfield **Scotland** 13–11
1899	Blackheath **Scotland** 5–0	1951	Twickenham **England** 5–3
1900	Inverleith (Edinburgh) **Drawn** 0–0	1952	Murrayfield **England** 19–3
1901	Blackheath **Scotland** 18–3	1953	Twickenham **England** 26–8
1902	Inverleith **England** 6–3	1954	Murrayfield **England** 13–3
1903	Richmond **Scotland** 10–6	1955	Twickenham **England** 9–6
1904	Inverleith **Scotland** 6–3	1956	Murrayfield **England** 11–6
1905	Richmond **Scotland** 8–0	1957	Twickenham **England** 16–3
1906	Inverleith **England** 9–3	1958	Murrayfield **Drawn** 3–3
1907	Blackheath **Scotland** 8–3	1959	Twickenham **Drawn** 3–3
1908	Inverleith **Scotland** 16–10	1960	Murrayfield **England** 21–12
1909	Richmond **Scotland** 18–8	1961	Twickenham **England** 6–0
1910	Inverleith **England** 14–5	1962	Murrayfield **Drawn** 3–3
		1963	Twickenham **England** 10–8
		1964	Murrayfield **Scotland** 15–6
		1965	Twickenham **Drawn** 3–3
		1966	Murrayfield **Scotland** 6–3

INTERNATIONAL RESULTS

1967 Twickenham **England** 27–14	1991 Twickenham **England** 21–12
1968 Murrayfield **England** 8–6	1991 Murrayfield WC **England** 9–6
1969 Twickenham **England** 8–3	1992 Murrayfield **England** 25–7
1970 Murrayfield **Scotland** 14–5	1993 Twickenham **England** 26–12
1971 Twickenham **Scotland** 16–15	1994 Murrayfield **England** 15–14
1971 Murrayfield **Scotland** 26–6	1995 Twickenham **England** 24–12
Special centenary match –	1996 Murrayfield **England** 18–9
non-championship	1997 Twickenham **England** 41–13
1972 Murrayfield **Scotland** 23–9	1998 Murrayfield **England** 34–20
1973 Twickenham **England** 20–13	1999 Twickenham **England** 24–21
1974 Murrayfield **Scotland** 16–14	2000 Murrayfield **Scotland** 19–13
1975 Twickenham **England** 7–6	2001 Twickenham **England** 43–3
1976 Murrayfield **Scotland** 22–12	2002 Murrayfield **England** 29–3
1977 Twickenham **England** 26–6	2003 Twickenham **England** 40–9
1978 Murrayfield **England** 15–0	2004 Murrayfield **England** 35–13
1979 Twickenham **Drawn** 7–7	2005 Twickenham **England** 43–22
1980 Murrayfield **England** 30–18	2006 Murrayfield **Scotland** 18–12
1981 Twickenham **England** 23–17	2007 Twickenham **England** 42–20
1982 Murrayfield **Drawn** 9–9	2008 Murrayfield **Scotland** 15–9
1983 Twickenham **Scotland** 22–12	2009 Twickenham **England** 26–12
1984 Murrayfield **Scotland** 18–6	2010 Murrayfield **Drawn** 15–15
1985 Twickenham **England** 10–7	2011 Twickenham **England** 22–16
1986 Murrayfield **Scotland** 33–6	2011 Auckland WC **England** 16–12
1987 Twickenham **England** 21–12	2012 Murrayfield **England** 13–6
1988 Murrayfield **England** 9–6	2013 Twickenham **England** 38–18
1989 Twickenham **Drawn** 12–12	2014 Murrayfield **England** 20–0
1990 Murrayfield **Scotland** 13–7	2015 Twickenham **England** 25–13

ENGLAND v IRELAND

Played 130 England won 75, Ireland won 47, Drawn 8
Highest scores England 50–18 in 2000, Ireland 43–13 in 2007
Biggest wins England 46–6 in 1997, Ireland 43–13 in 2007

1875 The Oval (London) **England** 1G 1DG 1T to 0	1890 Blackheath (London) **England** 3T to 0
1876 Dublin **England** 1G 1T to 0	1891 Dublin **England** 9–0
1877 The Oval **England** 2G 2T to 0	1892 Manchester **England** 7–0
1878 Dublin **England** 2G 1T to 0	1893 Dublin **England** 4–0
1879 The Oval **England** 2G 1DG 2T to 0	1894 Blackheath **Ireland** 7–5
1880 Dublin **England** 1G 1T to 1T	1895 Dublin **England** 6–3
1881 Manchester **England** 2G 2T to 0	1896 Leeds **Ireland** 10–4
1882 Dublin **Drawn** 2T each	1897 Dublin **Ireland** 13–9
1883 Manchester **England** 1G 3T to 1T	1898 Richmond (London) **Ireland** 9–6
1884 Dublin **England** 1G to 0	1899 Dublin **Ireland** 6–0
1885 Manchester **England** 2T to 1T	1900 Richmond **England** 15–4
1886 Dublin **England** 1T to 0	1901 Dublin **Ireland** 10–6
1887 Dublin **Ireland** 2G to 0	1902 Leicester **England** 6–3
1888 No Match	1903 Dublin **Ireland** 6–0
1889 No Match	1904 Blackheath **England** 19–0
	1905 Cork **Ireland** 17–3

1906	Leicester	Ireland 16–6
1907	Dublin	Ireland 17–9
1908	Richmond	England 13–3
1909	Dublin	England 11–5
1910	Twickenham	Drawn 0–0
1911	Dublin	Ireland 3–0
1912	Twickenham	England 15–0
1913	Dublin	England 15–4
1914	Twickenham	England 17–12
1920	Dublin	England 14–11
1921	Twickenham	England 15–0
1922	Dublin	England 12–3
1923	Leicester	England 23–5
1924	Belfast	England 14–3
1925	Twickenham	Drawn 6–6
1926	Dublin	Ireland 19–15
1927	Twickenham	England 8–6
1928	Dublin	England 7–6
1929	Twickenham	Ireland 6–5
1930	Dublin	Ireland 4–3
1931	Twickenham	Ireland 6–5
1932	Dublin	England 11–8
1933	Twickenham	England 17–6
1934	Dublin	England 13–3
1935	Twickenham	England 14–3
1936	Dublin	Ireland 6–3
1937	Twickenham	England 9–8
1938	Dublin	England 36–14
1939	Twickenham	Ireland 5–0
1947	Dublin	Ireland 22–0
1948	Twickenham	Ireland 11–10
1949	Dublin	Ireland 14–5
1950	Twickenham	England 3–0
1951	Dublin	Ireland 3–0
1952	Twickenham	England 3–0
1953	Dublin	Drawn 9–9
1954	Twickenham	England 14–3
1955	Dublin	Drawn 6–6
1956	Twickenham	England 20–0
1957	Dublin	England 6–0
1958	Twickenham	England 6–0
1959	Dublin	England 3–0
1960	Twickenham	England 8–5
1961	Dublin	Ireland 11–8
1962	Twickenham	England 16–0
1963	Dublin	Drawn 0–0
1964	Twickenham	Ireland 18–5
1965	Dublin	Ireland 5–0
1966	Twickenham	Drawn 6–6
1967	Dublin	England 8–3
1968	Twickenham	Drawn 9–9
1969	Dublin	Ireland 17–15

1970	Twickenham	England 9–3
1971	Dublin	England 9–6
1972	Twickenham	Ireland 16–12
1973	Dublin	Ireland 18–9
1974	Twickenham	Ireland 26–21
1975	Dublin	Ireland 12–9
1976	Twickenham	Ireland 13–12
1977	Dublin	England 4–0
1978	Twickenham	England 15–9
1979	Dublin	Ireland 12–7
1980	Twickenham	England 24–9
1981	Dublin	England 10–6
1982	Twickenham	Ireland 16–15
1983	Dublin	Ireland 25–15
1984	Twickenham	England 12–9
1985	Dublin	Ireland 13–10
1986	Twickenham	England 25–20
1987	Dublin	Ireland 17–0
1988	Twickenham	England 35–3
1988	Dublin	England 21–10
		Non-championship match
1989	Dublin	England 16–3
1990	Twickenham	England 23–0
1991	Dublin	England 16–7
1992	Twickenham	England 38–9
1993	Dublin	Ireland 17–3
1994	Twickenham	Ireland 13–12
1995	Dublin	England 20–8
1996	Twickenham	England 28–15
1997	Dublin	England 46–6
1998	Twickenham	England 35–17
1999	Dublin	England 27–15
2000	Twickenham	England 50–18
2001	Dublin	Ireland 20–14
2002	Twickenham	England 45–11
2003	Dublin	England 42–6
2004	Twickenham	Ireland 19–13
2005	Dublin	Ireland 19–13
2006	Twickenham	Ireland 28–24
2007	Dublin	Ireland 43–13
2008	Twickenham	England 33–10
2009	Dublin	Ireland 14–13
2010	Twickenham	Ireland 20–16
2011	Dublin	Ireland 24–8
2011	Dublin	England 20–9
		Non-championship match
2012	Twickenham	England 30–9
2013	Dublin	England 12–6
2014	Twickenham	England 13–10
2015	Dublin	Ireland 19–9
2015	Twickenham	England 21–13
		Non-championship match

ENGLAND v WALES

Played 127 England won 58 Wales won 57, Drawn 12
Highest scores England 62–5 in 2007, Wales 34–21 in 1967
Biggest wins England 62–5 in 2007, Wales 30–3 in 2013

1881	Blackheath (London) **England** 7G 1DG 6T to 0	1929	Twickenham **England** 8–3
1882	No Match	1930	Cardiff **England** 11–3
1883	Swansea **England** 2G 4T to 0	1931	Twickenham **Drawn** 11–11
1884	Leeds **England** 1G 2T to 1G	1932	Swansea **Wales** 12–5
1885	Swansea **England** 1G 4T to 1G 1T	1933	Twickenham **Wales** 7–3
1886	Blackheath **England** 1GM 2T to 1G	1934	Cardiff **England** 9–0
1887	Llanelli **Drawn** no score	1935	Twickenham **Drawn** 3–3
1888	No Match	1936	Swansea **Drawn** 0–0
1889	No Match	1937	Twickenham **England** 4–3
1890	Dewsbury **Wales** 1T to 0	1938	Cardiff **Wales** 14–8
1891	Newport **England** 7–3	1939	Twickenham **England** 3–0
1892	Blackheath **England** 17–0	1947	Cardiff **England** 9–6
1893	Cardiff **Wales** 12–11	1948	Twickenham **Drawn** 3–3
1894	Birkenhead **England** 24–3	1949	Cardiff **Wales** 9–3
1895	Swansea **England** 14–6	1950	Twickenham **Wales** 11–5
1896	Blackheath **England** 25–0	1951	Swansea **Wales** 23–5
1897	Newport **Wales** 11–0	1952	Twickenham **Wales** 8–6
1898	Blackheath **England** 14–7	1953	Cardiff **England** 8–3
1899	Swansea **Wales** 26–3	1954	Twickenham **England** 9–6
1900	Gloucester **Wales** 13–3	1955	Cardiff **Wales** 3–0
1901	Cardiff **Wales** 13–0	1956	Twickenham **Wales** 8–3
1902	Blackheath **Wales** 9–8	1957	Cardiff **England** 3–0
1903	Swansea **Wales** 21–5	1958	Twickenham **Drawn** 3–3
1904	Leicester **Drawn** 14–14	1959	Cardiff **Wales** 5–0
1905	Cardiff **Wales** 25–0	1960	Twickenham **England** 14–6
1906	Richmond (London) **Wales** 16–3	1961	Cardiff **Wales** 6–3
1907	Swansea **Wales** 22–0	1962	Twickenham **Drawn** 0–0
1908	Bristol **Wales** 28–18	1963	Cardiff **England** 13–6
1909	Cardiff **Wales** 8–0	1964	Twickenham **Drawn** 6–6
1910	Twickenham **England** 11–6	1965	Cardiff **Wales** 14–3
1911	Swansea **Wales** 15–11	1966	Twickenham **Wales** 11–6
1912	Twickenham **England** 8–0	1967	Cardiff **Wales** 34–21
1913	Cardiff **England** 12–0	1968	Twickenham **Drawn** 11–11
1914	Twickenham **England** 10–9	1969	Cardiff **Wales** 30–9
1920	Swansea **Wales** 19–5	1970	Twickenham **Wales** 17–13
1921	Twickenham **England** 18–3	1971	Cardiff **Wales** 22–6
1922	Cardiff **Wales** 28–6	1972	Twickenham **Wales** 12–3
1923	Twickenham **England** 7–3	1973	Cardiff **Wales** 25–9
1924	Swansea **England** 17–9	1974	Twickenham **England** 16–12
1925	Twickenham **England** 12–6	1975	Cardiff **Wales** 20–4
1926	Cardiff **Drawn** 3–3	1976	Twickenham **Wales** 21–9
1927	Twickenham **England** 11–9	1977	Cardiff **Wales** 14–9
1928	Swansea **England** 10–8	1978	Twickenham **Wales** 9–6
		1979	Cardiff **Wales** 27–3

1980 Twickenham **England** 9–8	2003 Cardiff **England** 26–9
1981 Cardiff **Wales** 21–19	2003 Cardiff **England** 43–9
1982 Twickenham **England** 17–7	Non-championship match
1983 Cardiff **Drawn** 13–13	2003 Brisbane WC **England** 28–17
1984 Twickenham **Wales** 24–15	2004 Twickenham **England** 31–21
1985 Cardiff **Wales** 24–15	2005 Cardiff **Wales** 11–9
1986 Twickenham **England** 21–18	2006 Twickenham **England** 47–13
1987 Cardiff **Wales** 19–12	2007 Cardiff **Wales** 27–18
1987 Brisbane WC **Wales** 16–3	2007 Twickenham **England** 62–5
1988 Twickenham **Wales** 11–3	Non-championship match
1989 Cardiff **Wales** 12–9	2008 Twickenham **Wales** 26–19
1990 Twickenham **England** 34–6	2009 Cardiff **Wales** 23–15
1991 Cardiff **England** 25–6	2010 Twickenham **England** 30–17
1992 Twickenham **England** 24–0	2011 Cardiff **England** 26–19
1993 Cardiff **Wales** 10–9	2011 Twickenham **England** 23–19
1994 Twickenham **England** 15–8	Non-championship match
1995 Cardiff **England** 23–9	2011 Cardiff **Wales** 19–9
1996 Twickenham **England** 21–15	Non-championship match
1997 Cardiff **England** 34–13	2012 Twickenham **Wales** 19–12
1998 Twickenham **England** 60–26	2013 Cardiff **Wales** 30–3
1999 Wembley **Wales** 32–31	2014 Twickenham **England** 29–18
2000 Twickenham **England** 46–12	2015 Cardiff **England** 21–16
2001 Cardiff **England** 44–15	2015 Twickenham WC **Wales** 28–25
2002 Twickenham **England** 50–10	

ENGLAND v FRANCE

Played 101 England won 55, France won 39, Drawn 7
Highest scores England 55–35 in 2015, France 37–12 in 1972
Biggest wins England 37–0 in 1911, France 37–12 in 1972 and 31–6 in 2006

1906 Paris **England** 35–8	1931 Paris **France** 14–13
1907 Richmond (London) **England** 41–13	1947 Twickenham **England** 6–3
1908 Paris **England** 19–0	1948 Paris **France** 15–0
1909 Leicester **England** 22–0	1949 Twickenham **England** 8–3
1910 Paris **England** 11–3	1950 Paris **France** 6–3
1911 Twickenham **England** 37–0	1951 Twickenham **France** 11–3
1912 Paris **England** 18–8	1952 Paris **England** 6–3
1913 Twickenham **England** 20–0	1953 Twickenham **England** 11–0
1914 Paris **England** 39–13	1954 Paris **France** 11–3
1920 Twickenham **England** 8–3	1955 Twickenham **France** 16–9
1921 Paris **England** 10–6	1956 Paris **France** 14–9
1922 Twickenham **Drawn** 11–11	1957 Twickenham **England** 9–5
1923 Paris **England** 12–3	1958 Paris **England** 14–0
1924 Twickenham **England** 19–7	1959 Twickenham **Drawn** 3–3
1925 Paris **England** 13–11	1960 Paris **Drawn** 3–3
1926 Twickenham **England** 11–0	1961 Twickenham **Drawn** 5–5
1927 Paris **France** 3–0	1962 Paris **France** 13–0
1928 Twickenham **England** 18–8	1963 Twickenham **England** 6–5
1929 Paris **England** 16–6	1964 Paris **England** 6–3
1930 Twickenham **England** 11–5	1965 Twickenham **England** 9–6

1966	Paris **France** 13–0		1998	Paris **France** 24–17
1967	Twickenham **France** 16–12		1999	Twickenham **England** 21–10
1968	Paris **France** 14–9		2000	Paris **England** 15–9
1969	Twickenham **England** 22–8		2001	Twickenham **England** 48–19
1970	Paris **France** 35–13		2002	Paris **France** 20–15
1971	Twickenham **Drawn** 14–14		2003	Twickenham **England** 25–17
1972	Paris **France** 37–12		2003	Marseilles **France** 17–16
1973	Twickenham **England** 14–6			Non-championship match
1974	Paris **Drawn** 12–12		2003	Twickenham **England** 45–14
1975	Twickenham **France** 27–20			Non-championship match
1976	Paris **France** 30–9		2003	Sydney WC **England** 24–7
1977	Twickenham **France** 4–3		2004	Paris **France** 24–21
1978	Paris **France** 15–6		2005	Twickenham **France** 18–17
1979	Twickenham **England** 7–6		2006	Paris **France** 31–6
1980	Paris **England** 17–13		2007	Twickenham **England** 26–18
1981	Twickenham **France** 16–12		2007	Twickenham **France** 21–15
1982	Paris **England** 27–15			Non-championship match
1983	Twickenham **France** 19–15		2007	Marseilles **France** 22–9
1984	Paris **France** 32–18			Non-championship match
1985	Twickenham **Drawn** 9–9		2007	Paris WC **England** 14–9
1986	Paris **France** 29–10		2008	Paris **England** 24–13
1987	Twickenham **France** 19–15		2009	Twickenham **England** 34–10
1988	Paris **France** 10–9		2010	Paris **France** 12–10
1989	Twickenham **England** 11–0		2011	Twickenham **England** 17–9
1990	Paris **England** 26–7		2011	Auckland WC **France** 19–12
1991	Twickenham **England** 21–19		2012	Paris **England** 24–22
1991	Paris WC **England** 19–10		2013	Twickenham **England** 23–13
1992	Paris **England** 31–13		2014	Paris **France** 26–24
1993	Twickenham **England** 16–15		2015	Twickenham **England** 55–35
1994	Paris **England** 18–14		2015	Twickenham **England** 19–14
1995	Twickenham **England** 31–10			Non-championship match
1995	Pretoria WC **France** **19–9**		2015	Paris **France** 25–20
1996	Paris **France** 15–12			Non-championship match
1997	Twickenham **France** 23–20			

ENGLAND v SOUTH AFRICA

Played 37 England won 12, South Africa won 23, Drawn 2
Highest scores England 53–3 in 2002, South Africa 58–10 in 2007
Biggest wins England 53–3 in 2002, South Africa 58–10 in 2007

1906	Crystal Palace (London) **Drawn** 3–3			South Africa won series 2–0
1913	Twickenham **South Africa** 9–3		1992	Twickenham **England** 33–16
1932	Twickenham **South Africa** 7–0		1994	1 Pretoria **England** 32–15
1952	Twickenham **South Africa** 8–3			2 Cape Town **South Africa** 27–9
1961	Twickenham **South Africa** 5–0			Series drawn 1–1
1969	Twickenham **England** 11–8		1995	Twickenham **South Africa** 24–14
1972	Johannesburg **England** 18–9		1997	Twickenham **South Africa** 29–11
1984	1 Port Elizabeth **South Africa** 33–15		1998	Cape Town **South Africa** 18–0
	2 Johannesburg **South Africa** 35–9		1998	Twickenham **England** 13–7

1999	Paris WC **South Africa** 44–21
2000	1 Pretoria **South Africa** 18–13
	2 Bloemfontein **England** 27–22
	Series drawn 1–1
2000	Twickenham **England** 25–17
2001	Twickenham **England** 29–9
2002	Twickenham **England** 53–3
2003	Perth WC **England** 25–6
2004	Twickenham **England** 32–16
2006	1 Twickenham **England** 23–21
	2 Twickenham **South Africa** 25–14
	Series drawn 1–1
2007	1 Bloemfontein **South Africa** 58–10

	2 Pretoria **South Africa** 55–22
	South Africa won series 2–0
2007	Paris WC **South Africa** 36–0
2007	Paris WC **South Africa** 15–6
2008	Twickenham **South Africa** 42–6
2010	Twickenham **South Africa** 21–11
2012	1 Durban **South Africa** 22–17
	2 Johannesburg **South Africa** 36–27
	3 Port Elizabeth **Drawn** 14–14
	South Africa won series 2–0, with 1 draw
2012	Twickenham **South Africa** 16–15
2014	Twickenham **South Africa** 31–28

ENGLAND v NEW ZEALAND

Played 40 England won 7, New Zealand won 32, Drawn 1
Highest scores England 38–21 in 2012, New Zealand 64–22 in 1998
Biggest wins England 38–21 in 2012, New Zealand 64–22 in 1998

1905	Crystal Palace (London) **New Zealand** 15–0
1925	Twickenham **New Zealand** 17–11
1936	Twickenham **England** 13–0
1954	Twickenham **New Zealand** 5–0
1963	1 Auckland **New Zealand** 21–11
	2 Christchurch **New Zealand** 9–6
	New Zealand won series 2–0
1964	Twickenham **New Zealand** 14–0
1967	Twickenham **New Zealand** 23–11
1973	Twickenham **New Zealand** 9–0
1973	Auckland **England** 16–10
1978	Twickenham **New Zealand** 16–6
1979	Twickenham **New Zealand** 10–9
1983	Twickenham **England** 15–9
1985	1 Christchurch **New Zealand** 18–13
	2 Wellington **New Zealand** 42–15
	New Zealand won series 2–0
1991	Twickenham WC **New Zealand** 18–12
1993	Twickenham **England** 15–9
1995	Cape Town WC **New Zealand** **45–29**
1997	1 Manchester **New Zealand** 25–8
	2 Twickenham **Drawn** 26–26
	New Zealand won series 1–0, with 1 draw

1998	1 Dunedin **New Zealand** 64–22
	2 Auckland **New Zealand** 40–10
	New Zealand won series 2–0
1999	Twickenham WC **New Zealand** 30–16
2002	Twickenham **England** 31–28
2003	Wellington **England** 15–13
2004	1 Dunedin **New Zealand** 36–3
	2 Auckland **New Zealand** 36–12
	New Zealand won series 2–0
2005	Twickenham **New Zealand** 23–19
2006	Twickenham **New Zealand** 41–20
2008	1 Auckland **New Zealand** 37–20
	2 Christchurch **New Zealand** 44–12
	New Zealand won series 2–0
2008	Twickenham **New Zealand** 32–6
2009	Twickenham **New Zealand** 19–6
2010	Twickenham **New Zealand** 26–16
2012	Twickenham **England** 38–21
2013	Twickenham **New Zealand** 30–22
2014	1 Auckland **New Zealand** 20–15
	2 Dunedin **New Zealand** 28–27
	3 Hamilton **New Zealand** 36–13
	New Zealand won series 3–0
2014	Twickenham **New Zealand** 24–21

ENGLAND v AUSTRALIA

Played 44 England won 18, Australia won 25, Drawn 1
Highest scores England 35–18 in 2010, Australia 76–0 in 1998
Biggest wins England 20–3 in 1973, 23–6 in 1976 and 35–18 in 2010, Australia 76–0 in 1998

1909	Blackheath (London) **Australia** 9–3		1998	Twickenham **Australia** 12–11
1928	Twickenham **England** 18–11		1999	Sydney **Australia** 22–15
1948	Twickenham **Australia** 11–0		2000	Twickenham **England** 22–19
1958	Twickenham **England** 9–6		2001	Twickenham **England** 21–15
1963	Sydney **Australia** 18–9		2002	Twickenham **England** 32–31
1967	Twickenham **Australia** 23–11		2003	Melbourne **England** 25–14
1973	Twickenham **England** 20–3		2003	Sydney WC **England** 20–17 (aet)
1975	1 Sydney **Australia** 16–9		2004	Brisbane **Australia** 51–15
	2 Brisbane **Australia** 30–21		2004	Twickenham **Australia** 21–19
	Australia won series 2–0		2005	Twickenham **England** 26–16
1976	Twickenham **England** 23–6		2006	1 Sydney **Australia** 34–3
1982	Twickenham **England** 15–11			2 Melbourne **Australia** 43–18
1984	Twickenham **Australia** 19–3			Australia won series 2–0
1987	Sydney WC **Australia** 19–6		2007	Marseilles WC **England** 12–10
1988	1 Brisbane **Australia** 22–16		2008	Twickenham **Australia** 28–14
	2 Sydney **Australia** 28–8		2009	Twickenham **Australia** 18–9
	Australia won series 2–0		2010	1 Perth **Australia** 27–17
1988	Twickenham **England** 28–19			2 Sydney **England** 21–20
1991	Sydney **Australia** 40–15			Series drawn 1–1
1991	Twickenham WC **Australia** 12–6		2010	Twickenham **England** 35–18
1995	Cape Town WC **England** 25–22		2012	Twickenham **Australia** 20–14
1997	Sydney **Australia** 25–6		2013	Twickenham **England** 20–13
1997	Twickenham **Drawn** 15–15		2014	Twickenham **England** 26–17
1998	Brisbane **Australia** 76–0		2015	Twickenham WC **Australia** 33–13

ENGLAND v NEW ZEALAND NATIVES

Played 1 England won 1
Highest score England 7–0 in 1889, NZ Natives 0–7 in 1889
Biggest win England 7–0 in 1889, NZ Natives no win

1889	Blackheath **England** 1G 4T to 0

ENGLAND v RFU PRESIDENT'S XV

Played 1 President's XV won 1
Highest score England 11–28 in 1971, RFU President's XV 28–11 in 1971
Biggest win RFU President's XV 28–11 in 1971

1971	Twickenham **President's XV** 28–11

ENGLAND v ARGENTINA

Played 19 England won 14, Argentina won 4, Drawn 1
Highest scores England 51–0 in 1990 and 51–26 in 2013, Argentina 33–13 in 1997
Biggest wins England 51–0 in 1990, Argentina 33–13 in 1997

1981	1 Buenos Aires **Drawn** 19–19		2000	Twickenham **England** 19–0
	2 Buenos Aires **England** 12–6		2002	Buenos Aires **England** 26–18
	England won series 1–0, with 1 draw		2006	Twickenham **Argentina** 25–18
1990	1 Buenos Aires **England** 25–12		2009	1 Manchester **England** 37–15
	2 Buenos Aires **Argentina** 15–13			2 Salta **Argentina** 24–22
	Series drawn 1–1			Series drawn 1–1
1990	Twickenham **England** 51–0		2009	Twickenham **England** 16–9
1995	Durban WC **England** 24–18		2011	Dunedin WC **England** 13–9
1996	Twickenham **England** 20–18		2013	1 Salta **England** 32–3
1997	1 Buenos Aires **England** 46–20			2 Buenos Aires **England** 51–26
	2 Buenos Aires **Argentina** 33–13			England won series 2–0
	Series drawn 1–1		2013	Twickenham **England** 31–12

ENGLAND v ROMANIA

Played 5 England won 5
Highest scores England 134–0 in 2001, Romania 15–22 in 1985
Biggest win England 134–0 in 2001, Romania no win

1985	Twickenham **England** 22–15		2001	Twickenham **England** 134–0
1989	Bucharest **England** 58–3		2011	Dunedin WC **England** 67–3
1994	Twickenham **England** 54–3			

ENGLAND v JAPAN

Played 1 England won 1
Highest score England 60–7 in 1987, Japan 7–60 in 1987
Biggest win England 60–7 in 1987, Japan no win

1987	Sydney WC **England** 60–7

ENGLAND v UNITED STATES

Played 5 England won 5
Highest scores England 106–8 in 1999, United States 19–48 in 2001
Biggest win England 106–8 in 1999, United States no win

1987	Sydney WC **England** 34–6		2001	San Francisco **England** 48–19
1991	Twickenham WC **England** 37–9		2007	Lens WC **England** 28–10
1999	Twickenham **England** 106–8			

ENGLAND v FIJI

Played 6 England won 6
Highest scores England 58–23 in 1989, Fiji 24–45 in 1999
Biggest win England 54–12 in 2012, Fiji no win

1988	Suva **England** 25–12		1999	Twickenham WC **England** 45–24
1989	Twickenham **England** 58–23		2012	Twickenham **England** 54–12
1991	Suva **England** 28–12		2015	Twickenham WC **England** 35–11

ENGLAND v ITALY

Played 21 England won 21
Highest scores England 80–23 in 2001, Italy 23–80 in 2001
Biggest win England 67–7 in 1999, Italy no win

1991	Twickenham WC **England** 36–6		2006	Rome **England** 31–16
1995	Durban WC **England** **27–20**		2007	Twickenham **England** 20–7
1996	Twickenham **England** 54–21		2008	Rome **England** 23–19
1998	Huddersfield **England** 23–15		2009	Twickenham **England** 36–11
1999	Twickenham WC **England** 67–7		2010	Rome **England** 17–12
2000	Rome **England** 59–12		2011	Twickenham **England** 59–13
2001	Twickenham **England** 80–23		2012	Rome **England** 19–15
2002	Rome **England** 45–9		2013	Twickenham **England** 18–11
2003	Twickenham **England** 40–5		2014	Rome **England** 52–11
2004	Rome **England** 50–9		2015	Twickenham **England** 47–17
2005	Twickenham **England** 39–7			

ENGLAND v CANADA

Played 6 England won 6
Highest scores England 70–0 in 2004, Canada 20–59 in 2001
Biggest win England 70–0 in 2004, Canada no win

1992	Wembley **England** 26–13		2	Burnaby **England** 59–20
1994	Twickenham **England** 60–19			England won series 2–0
1999	Twickenham **England** 36–11		2004	Twickenham **England** 70–0
2001	1 Markham **England** 22–10			

ENGLAND v SAMOA

Played 7 England won 7
Highest scores England 44–22 in 1995 and 44–22 in 2007, Samoa 22–44 in 1995, 22–35 in 2003 and 22–44 in 2007
Biggest win England 40–3 in 2005, Samoa no win

1995	Durban WC **England** 44–22		2007	Nantes WC **England** 44–22
1995	Twickenham **England** 27–9		2010	Twickenham **England** 26–13
2003	Melbourne WC **England** 35–22		2014	Twickenham **England** 28–9
2005	Twickenham **England** 40–3			

ENGLAND v THE NETHERLANDS

Played 1 England won 1
Highest scores England 110–0 in 1998, The Netherlands 0–110 in 1998
Biggest win England 110–0 in 1998, The Netherlands no win

1998 Huddersfield **England** 110–0	

ENGLAND v TONGA

Played 2 England won 2
Highest scores England 101–10 in 1999, Tonga 20–36 in 2007
Biggest win England 101–10 in 1999, Tonga no win

1999 Twickenham WC **England** 101–10	2007 Paris WC **England** 36–20

ENGLAND v GEORGIA

Played 2 England won 2
Highest scores England 84–6 in 2003, Georgia 10–41 in 2011
Biggest win England 84–6 in 2003, Georgia no win

2003 Perth WC **England** 84–6	2011 Dunedin WC **England** 41–10

ENGLAND v URUGUAY

Played 2 England won 2
Highest scores England 111–13 in 2003, Uruguay 13–111 in 2003
Biggest win England 111–13 in 2003, Uruguay no win

2003 Brisbane WC **England** 111–13	2015 Manchester WC **England** 60–3

ENGLAND v PACIFIC ISLANDS

Played 1 England won 1
Highest scores England 39–13 in 2008, Pacific Islands 13–39 in 2008
Biggest win England 39–13 in 2008, Pacific Islands no win

2008 Twickenham **England** 39–13	

SCOTLAND v IRELAND

Played 131 Scotland won 65, Ireland won 60, Drawn 5, Abandoned 1
Highest scores Scotland 38–10 in 1997, Ireland 44–22 in 2000
Biggest wins Scotland 38–10 in 1997, Ireland 36–6 in 2003 and 40–10 in 2015

1877	Belfast **Scotland** 4G 2DG 2T to 0
1878	No Match
1879	Belfast **Scotland** 1G 1DG 1T to 0
1880	Glasgow **Scotland** 1G 2DG 2T to 0
1881	Belfast **Ireland** 1DG to 1T
1882	Glasgow **Scotland** 2T to 0
1883	Belfast **Scotland** 1G 1T to 0
1884	Raeburn Place (Edinburgh) **Scotland** 2G 2T to 1T
1885	Belfast **Abandoned** Ireland 0 Scotland 1T
1885	Raeburn Place **Scotland** 1G 2T to 0
1886	Raeburn Place **Scotland** 3G 1DG 2T to 0
1887	Belfast **Scotland** 1G 1GM 2T to 0
1888	Raeburn Place **Scotland** 1G to 0
1889	Belfast **Scotland** 1DG to 0
1890	Raeburn Place **Scotland** 1DG 1T to 0
1891	Belfast **Scotland** 14–0
1892	Raeburn Place **Scotland** 2–0
1893	Belfast **Drawn** 0–0
1894	Dublin **Ireland** 5–0
1895	Raeburn Place **Scotland** 6–0
1896	Dublin **Drawn** 0–0
1897	Powderhall (Edinburgh) **Scotland** 8–3
1898	Belfast **Scotland** 8–0
1899	Inverleith (Edinburgh) **Ireland** 9–3
1900	Dublin **Drawn** 0–0
1901	Inverleith **Scotland** 9–5
1902	Belfast **Ireland** 5–0
1903	Inverleith **Scotland** 3–0
1904	Dublin **Scotland** 19–3
1905	Inverleith **Ireland** 11–5
1906	Dublin **Scotland** 13–6
1907	Inverleith **Scotland** 15–3
1908	Dublin **Ireland** 16–11
1909	Inverleith **Scotland** 9–3
1910	Belfast **Scotland** 14–0
1911	Inverleith **Ireland** 16–10
1912	Dublin **Ireland** 10–8
1913	Inverleith **Scotland** 29–14
1914	Dublin **Ireland** 6–0
1920	Inverleith **Scotland** 19–0
1921	Dublin **Ireland** 9–8
1922	Inverleith **Scotland** 6–3
1923	Dublin **Scotland** 13–3
1924	Inverleith **Scotland** 13–8
1925	Dublin **Scotland** 14–8
1926	Murrayfield **Ireland** 3–0
1927	Dublin **Ireland** 6–0
1928	Murrayfield **Ireland** 13–5
1929	Dublin **Scotland** 16–7
1930	Murrayfield **Ireland** 14–11
1931	Dublin **Ireland** 8–5
1932	Murrayfield **Ireland** 20–8
1933	Dublin **Scotland** 8–6
1934	Murrayfield **Scotland** 16–9
1935	Dublin **Ireland** 12–5
1936	Murrayfield **Ireland** 10–4
1937	Dublin **Ireland** 11–4
1938	Murrayfield **Scotland** 23–14
1939	Dublin **Ireland** 12–3
1947	Murrayfield **Ireland** 3–0
1948	Dublin **Ireland** 6–0
1949	Murrayfield **Ireland** 13–3
1950	Dublin **Ireland** 21–0
1951	Murrayfield **Ireland** 6–5
1952	Dublin **Ireland** 12–8
1953	Murrayfield **Ireland** 26–8
1954	Belfast **Ireland** 6–0
1955	Murrayfield **Scotland** 12–3
1956	Dublin **Ireland** 14–10
1957	Murrayfield **Ireland** 5–3
1958	Dublin **Ireland** 12–6
1959	Murrayfield **Ireland** 8–3
1960	Dublin **Scotland** 6–5
1961	Murrayfield **Scotland** 16–8
1962	Dublin **Scotland** 20–6
1963	Murrayfield **Scotland** 3–0
1964	Dublin **Scotland** 6–3
1965	Murrayfield **Ireland** 16–6
1966	Dublin **Scotland** 11–3
1967	Murrayfield **Ireland** 5–3
1968	Dublin **Ireland** 14–6
1969	Murrayfield **Ireland** 16–0
1970	Dublin **Ireland** 16–11
1971	Murrayfield **Ireland** 17–5
1972	No Match

1973	Murrayfield **Scotland** 19–14	1998	Dublin **Scotland** 17–16
1974	Dublin **Ireland** 9–6	1999	Murrayfield **Scotland** 30–13
1975	Murrayfield **Scotland** 20–13	2000	Dublin **Ireland** 44–22
1976	Dublin **Scotland** 15–6	2001	Murrayfield **Scotland** 32–10
1977	Murrayfield **Scotland** 21–18	2002	Dublin **Ireland** 43–22
1978	Dublin **Ireland** 12–9	2003	Murrayfield **Ireland** 36–6
1979	Murrayfield **Drawn** 11–11	2003	Murrayfield **Ireland** 29–10
1980	Dublin **Ireland** 22–15		Non-championship match
1981	Murrayfield **Scotland** 10–9	2004	Dublin **Ireland** 37–16
1982	Dublin **Ireland** 21–12	2005	Murrayfield **Ireland** 40–13
1983	Murrayfield **Ireland** 15–13	2006	Dublin **Ireland** 15–9
1984	Dublin **Scotland** 32–9	2007	Murrayfield **Ireland** 19–18
1985	Murrayfield **Ireland** 18–15	2007	Murrayfield **Scotland** 31–21
1986	Dublin **Scotland** 10–9		Non-championship match
1987	Murrayfield **Scotland** 16–12	2008	Dublin **Ireland** 34–13
1988	Dublin **Ireland** 22–18	2009	Murrayfield **Ireland** 22–15
1989	Murrayfield **Scotland** 37–21	2010	Dublin **Scotland** 23–20
1990	Dublin **Scotland** 13–10	2011	Murrayfield **Ireland** 21–18
1991	Murrayfield **Scotland** 28–25	2011	Murrayfield **Scotland** 10–6
1991	Murrayfield WC **Scotland** 24–15		Non-championship match
1992	Dublin **Scotland** 18–10	2012	Dublin **Ireland** 32–14
1993	Murrayfield **Scotland** 15–3	2013	Murrayfield **Scotland** 12–8
1994	Dublin **Drawn** 6–6	2014	Dublin **Ireland** 28–6
1995	Murrayfield **Scotland** 26–13	2015	Murrayfield **Ireland** 40–10
1996	Dublin **Scotland** 16–10	2015	Dublin **Ireland** 28–22
1997	Murrayfield **Scotland** 38–10		Non-championship match

SCOTLAND v WALES

Played 120 Scotland won 48, Wales won 69, Drawn 3
Highest scores Scotland 35–10 in 1924, Wales 51–3 in 2014
Biggest wins Scotland 35–10 in 1924, Wales 51–3 in 2014

1883	Raeburn Place (Edinburgh) **Scotland** 3G to 1G	1898	No Match
1884	Newport **Scotland** 1DG 1T to 0	1899	Inverleith (Edinburgh) **Scotland** 21–10
1885	Glasgow **Drawn** no score	1900	Swansea **Wales** 12–3
1886	Cardiff **Scotland** 2G 1T to 0	1901	Inverleith **Scotland** 18–8
1887	Raeburn Place **Scotland** 4G 8T to 0	1902	Cardiff **Wales** 14–5
1888	Newport **Wales** 1T to 0	1903	Inverleith **Scotland** 6–0
1889	Raeburn Place **Scotland** 2T to 0	1904	Swansea **Wales** 21–3
1890	Cardiff **Scotland** 1G 2T to 1T	1905	Inverleith **Wales** 6–3
1891	Raeburn Place **Scotland** 15–0	1906	Cardiff **Wales** 9–3
1892	Swansea **Scotland** 7–2	1907	Inverleith **Scotland** 6–3
1893	Raeburn Place **Wales** 9–0	1908	Swansea **Wales** 6–5
1894	Newport **Wales** 7–0	1909	Inverleith **Wales** 5–3
1895	Raeburn Place **Scotland** 5–4	1910	Cardiff **Wales** 14–0
1896	Cardiff **Wales** 6–0	1911	Inverleith **Wales** 32–10
1897	No Match	1912	Swansea **Wales** 21–6
		1913	Inverleith **Wales** 8–0

Year	Venue	Result
1914	Cardiff	**Wales** 24–5
1920	Inverleith	**Scotland** 9–5
1921	Swansea	**Scotland** 14–8
1922	Inverleith	**Drawn** 9–9
1923	Cardiff	**Scotland** 11–8
1924	Inverleith	**Scotland** 35–10
1925	Swansea	**Scotland** 24–14
1926	Murrayfield	**Scotland** 8–5
1927	Cardiff	**Scotland** 5–0
1928	Murrayfield	**Wales** 13–0
1929	Swansea	**Wales** 14–7
1930	Murrayfield	**Scotland** 12–9
1931	Cardiff	**Wales** 13–8
1932	Murrayfield	**Wales** 6–0
1933	Swansea	**Scotland** 11–3
1934	Murrayfield	**Wales** 13–6
1935	Cardiff	**Wales** 10–6
1936	Murrayfield	**Wales** 13–3
1937	Swansea	**Scotland** 13–6
1938	Murrayfield	**Scotland** 8–6
1939	Cardiff	**Wales** 11–3
1947	Murrayfield	**Wales** 22–8
1948	Cardiff	**Wales** 14–0
1949	Murrayfield	**Scotland** 6–5
1950	Swansea	**Wales** 12–0
1951	Murrayfield	**Scotland** 19–0
1952	Cardiff	**Wales** 11–0
1953	Murrayfield	**Wales** 12–0
1954	Swansea	**Wales** 15–3
1955	Murrayfield	**Scotland** 14–8
1956	Cardiff	**Wales** 9–3
1957	Murrayfield	**Scotland** 9–6
1958	Cardiff	**Wales** 8–3
1959	Murrayfield	**Scotland** 6–5
1960	Cardiff	**Wales** 8–0
1961	Murrayfield	**Scotland** 3–0
1962	Cardiff	**Scotland** 8–3
1963	Murrayfield	**Wales** 6–0
1964	Cardiff	**Wales** 11–3
1965	Murrayfield	**Wales** 14–12
1966	Cardiff	**Wales** 8–3
1967	Murrayfield	**Scotland** 11–5
1968	Cardiff	**Wales** 5–0
1969	Murrayfield	**Wales** 17–3
1970	Cardiff	**Wales** 18–9
1971	Murrayfield	**Wales** 19–18
1972	Cardiff	**Wales** 35–12
1973	Murrayfield	**Scotland** 10–9
1974	Cardiff	**Wales** 6–0
1975	Murrayfield	**Scotland** 12–10
1976	Cardiff	**Wales** 28–6
1977	Murrayfield	**Wales** 18–9
1978	Cardiff	**Wales** 22–14
1979	Murrayfield	**Wales** 19–13
1980	Cardiff	**Wales** 17–6
1981	Murrayfield	**Scotland** 15–6
1982	Cardiff	**Scotland** 34–18
1983	Murrayfield	**Wales** 19–15
1984	Cardiff	**Scotland** 15–9
1985	Murrayfield	**Wales** 25–21
1986	Cardiff	**Wales** 22–15
1987	Murrayfield	**Scotland** 21–15
1988	Cardiff	**Wales** 25–20
1989	Murrayfield	**Scotland** 23–7
1990	Cardiff	**Scotland** 13–9
1991	Murrayfield	**Scotland** 32–12
1992	Cardiff	**Wales** 15–12
1993	Murrayfield	**Scotland** 20–0
1994	Cardiff	**Wales** 29–6
1995	Murrayfield	**Scotland** 26–13
1996	Cardiff	**Scotland** 16–14
1997	Murrayfield	**Wales** 34–19
1998	Wembley	**Wales** 19–13
1999	Murrayfield	**Scotland** 33–20
2000	Cardiff	**Wales** 26–18
2001	Murrayfield	**Drawn** 28–28
2002	Cardiff	**Scotland** 27–22
2003	Murrayfield	**Scotland** 30–22
2003	Cardiff	**Wales** 23–9
	Non-championship match	
2004	Cardiff	**Wales** 23–10
2005	Murrayfield	**Wales** 46–22
2006	Cardiff	**Wales** 28–18
2007	Murrayfield	**Scotland** 21–9
2008	Cardiff	**Wales** 30–15
2009	Murrayfield	**Wales** 26–13
2010	Cardiff	**Wales** 31–24
2011	Murrayfield	**Wales** 24–6
2012	Cardiff	**Wales** 27–13
2013	Murrayfield	**Wales** 28–18
2014	Cardiff	**Wales** 51–3
2015	Murrayfield	**Wales** 26–23

SCOTLAND v FRANCE

Played 89 Scotland won 34, France won 52, Drawn 3
Highest scores Scotland 36–22 in 1999, France 51–16 in 1998 and 51–9 in 2003
Biggest wins Scotland 31–3 in 1912, France 51–9 in 2003

1910	Inverleith (Edinburgh) **Scotland** 27–0		1976	Murrayfield **France** 13–6
1911	Paris **France** 16–15		1977	Paris **France** 23–3
1912	Inverleith **Scotland** 31–3		1978	Murrayfield **France** 19–16
1913	Paris **Scotland** 21–3		1979	Paris **France** 21–17
1914	No Match		1980	Murrayfield **Scotland** 22–14
1920	Paris **Scotland** 5–0		1981	Paris **France** 16–9
1921	Inverleith **France** 3–0		1982	Murrayfield **Scotland** 16–7
1922	Paris **Drawn** 3–3		1983	Paris **France** 19–15
1923	Inverleith **Scotland** 16–3		1984	Murrayfield **Scotland** 21–12
1924	Paris **France** 12–10		1985	Paris **France** 11–3
1925	Inverleith **Scotland** 25–4		1986	Murrayfield **Scotland** 18–17
1926	Paris **Scotland** 20–6		1987	Paris **France** 28–22
1927	Murrayfield **Scotland** 23–6		1987	Christchurch WC **Drawn** 20–20
1928	Paris **Scotland** 15–6		1988	Murrayfield **Scotland** 23–12
1929	Murrayfield **Scotland** 6–3		1989	Paris **France** 19–3
1930	Paris **France** 7–3		1990	Murrayfield **Scotland** 21–0
1931	Murrayfield **Scotland** 6–4		1991	Paris **France** 15–9
1947	Paris **France** 8–3		1992	Murrayfield **Scotland** 10–6
1948	Murrayfield **Scotland** 9–8		1993	Paris **France** 11–3
1949	Paris **Scotland** 8–0		1994	Murrayfield **France** 20–12
1950	Murrayfield **Scotland** 8–5		1995	Paris **Scotland** 23–21
1951	Paris **France** 14–12		1995	Pretoria WC **France** 22–19
1952	Murrayfield **France** 13–11		1996	Murrayfield **Scotland** 19–14
1953	Paris **France** 11–5		1997	Paris **France** 47–20
1954	Murrayfield **France** 3–0		1998	Murrayfield **France** 51–16
1955	Paris **France** 15–0		1999	Paris **Scotland** 36–22
1956	Murrayfield **Scotland** 12–0		2000	Murrayfield **France** 28–16
1957	Paris **Scotland** 6–0		2001	Paris **France** 16–6
1958	Murrayfield **Scotland** 11–9		2002	Murrayfield **France** 22–10
1959	Paris **France** 9–0		2003	Paris **France** 38–3
1960	Murrayfield **France** 13–11		2003	Sydney WC **France** 51–9
1961	Paris **France** 11–0		2004	Murrayfield **France** 31–0
1962	Murrayfield **France** 11–3		2005	Paris **France** 16–9
1963	Paris **Scotland** 11–6		2006	Murrayfield **Scotland** 20–16
1964	Murrayfield **Scotland** 10–0		2007	Paris **France** 46–19
1965	Paris **France** 16–8		2008	Murrayfield **France** 27–6
1966	Murrayfield **Drawn** 3–3		2009	Paris **France** 22–13
1967	Paris **Scotland** 9–8		2010	Murrayfield **France** 18–9
1968	Murrayfield **France** 8–6		2011	Paris **France** 34–21
1969	Paris **Scotland** 6–3		2012	Murrayfield **France** 23–17
1970	Murrayfield **France** 11–9		2013	Paris **France** 23–16
1971	Paris **France** 13–8		2014	Paris **France** 19–17
1972	Murrayfield **Scotland** 20–9		2015	Paris **France** 15–8
1973	Paris **France** 16–13		2015	Paris **France** 19–16
1974	Murrayfield **Scotland** 19–6			Non-championship match
1975	Paris **France** 10–9			

SCOTLAND v SOUTH AFRICA

Played 26 Scotland won 5, South Africa won 21, Drawn 0
Highest scores Scotland 29–46 in 1999, South Africa 68–10 in 1997
Biggest wins Scotland 21–6 in 2002, South Africa 68–10 in 1997

1906 Glasgow **Scotland** 6–0	2 Johannesburg **South Africa** 28–19
1912 Inverleith **South Africa** 16–0	South Africa won series 2–0
1932 Murrayfield **South Africa** 6–3	2004 Murrayfield **South Africa** 45–10
1951 Murrayfield **South Africa** 44–0	2006 1 Durban **South Africa** 36–16
1960 Port Elizabeth **South Africa** 18–10	2 Port Elizabeth **South Africa** 29–15
1961 Murrayfield **South Africa** 12–5	South Africa won series 2–0
1965 Murrayfield **Scotland** 8–5	2007 Murrayfield **South Africa** 27–3
1969 Murrayfield **Scotland** 6–3	2008 Murrayfield **South Africa** 14–10
1994 Murrayfield **South Africa** 34–10	2010 Murrayfield **Scotland** 21–17
1997 Murrayfield **South Africa** 68–10	2012 Murrayfield **South Africa** 21–10
1998 Murrayfield **South Africa** 35–10	2013 Nelspruit QT **South Africa** 30–17
1999 Murrayfield WC **South Africa** 46–29	2013 Murrayfield **South Africa** 28–0
2002 Murrayfield **Scotland** 21–6	2014 Port Elizabeth **South Africa** 55–6
2003 1 Durban **South Africa** 29–25	2015 Newcastle WC **South Africa** 34–16

SCOTLAND v NEW ZEALAND

Played 30 Scotland won 0, New Zealand won 28, Drawn 2
Highest scores Scotland 31–62 in 1996, New Zealand 69–20 in 2000
Biggest wins Scotland no win, New Zealand 69–20 in 2000

1905 Inverleith (Edinburgh) **New Zealand** 12–7	1991 Cardiff WC **New Zealand** 13–6
	1993 Murrayfield **New Zealand** 51–15
1935 Murrayfield **New Zealand** 18–8	1995 Pretoria WC **New Zealand** 48–30
1954 Murrayfield **New Zealand** 3–0	1996 1 Dunedin **New Zealand** 62–31
1964 Murrayfield **Drawn** 0–0	2 Auckland **New Zealand** 36–12
1967 Murrayfield **New Zealand** 14–3	New Zealand won series 2–0
1972 Murrayfield **New Zealand** 14–9	1999 Murrayfield WC **New Zealand** 30–18
1975 Auckland **New Zealand** 24–0	2000 1 Dunedin **New Zealand** 69–20
1978 Murrayfield **New Zealand** 18–9	2 Auckland **New Zealand** 48–14
1979 Murrayfield **New Zealand** 20–6	New Zealand won series 2–0
1981 1 Dunedin **New Zealand** 11–4	2001 Murrayfield **New Zealand** 37–6
2 Auckland **New Zealand** 40–15	2005 Murrayfield **New Zealand** 29–10
New Zealand won series 2–0	2007 Murrayfield WC **New Zealand** 40–0
1983 Murrayfield **Drawn** 25–25	2008 Murrayfield **New Zealand** 32–6
1987 Christchurch WC **New Zealand** 30–3	2010 Murrayfield **New Zealand** 49–3
1990 1 Dunedin **New Zealand** 31–16	2012 Murrayfield **New Zealand** 51–22
2 Auckland **New Zealand** 21–18	2014 Murrayfield **New Zealand** 24–16
New Zealand won series 2–0	

SCOTLAND v AUSTRALIA

Played 29 Scotland won 9, Australia won 20, Drawn 0
Highest scores Scotland 34–35 in 2015, Australia 45–3 in 1998
Biggest wins Scotland 24–15 in 1981, Australia 45–3 in 1998

1927	Murrayfield **Scotland** 10–8		1997	Murrayfield **Australia** 37–8
1947	Murrayfield **Australia** 16–7		1998	1 Sydney **Australia** 45–3
1958	Murrayfield **Scotland** 12–8			2 Brisbane **Australia** 33–11
1966	Murrayfield **Scotland** 11–5			Australia won series 2–0
1968	Murrayfield **Scotland** 9–3		2000	Murrayfield **Australia** 30–9
1970	Sydney **Australia** 23–3		2003	Brisbane WC **Australia** 33–16
1975	Murrayfield **Scotland** 10–3		2004	1 Melbourne **Australia** 35–15
1981	Murrayfield **Scotland** 24–15			2 Sydney **Australia** 34–13
1982	1 Brisbane **Scotland** 12–7			Australia won series 2–0
	2 Sydney **Australia** 33–9		2004	1 Murrayfield **Australia** 31–14
	Series drawn 1–1			2 Glasgow **Australia** 31–17
1984	Murrayfield **Australia** 37–12			Australia won series 2–0
1988	Murrayfield **Australia** 32–13		2006	Murrayfield **Australia** 44–15
1992	1 Sydney **Australia** 27–12		2009	Murrayfield **Scotland** 9–8
	2 Brisbane **Australia** 37–13		2012	Newcastle (Aus) **Scotland** 9–6
	Australia won series 2–0		2013	Murrayfield **Australia** 21–15
1996	Murrayfield **Australia** 29–19		2015	Twickenham WC **Australia** 35–34

SCOTLAND v SRU PRESIDENT'S XV

Played 1 Scotland won 1
Highest scores Scotland 27–16 in 1972, SRU President's XV 16–27 in 1973
Biggest win Scotland 27–16 in 1973, SRU President's XV no win

1973	Murrayfield **Scotland** 27–16

SCOTLAND v ROMANIA

Played 13 Scotland won 11 Romania won 2, Drawn 0
Highest scores Scotland 60–19 in 1999, Romania 28–55 in 1987 and 28–22 in 1984
Biggest wins Scotland 48–6 in 2006 and 42–0 in 2007, Romania 28–22 in 1984 and 18–12 in 1991

1981	Murrayfield **Scotland** 12–6		1999	Glasgow **Scotland** 60–19
1984	Bucharest **Romania** 28–22		2002	Murrayfield **Scotland** 37–10
1986	Bucharest **Scotland** 33–18		2005	Bucharest **Scotland** 39–19
1987	Dunedin WC **Scotland** 55–28		2006	Murrayfield **Scotland** 48–6
1989	Murrayfield **Scotland** 32–0		2007	Murrayfield WC **Scotland** 42–0
1991	Bucharest **Romania** 18–12		2011	Invercargill WC **Scotland** 34–24
1995	Murrayfield **Scotland** 49–16			

SCOTLAND v ZIMBABWE

Played 2 Scotland won 2
Highest scores Scotland 60–21 in 1987, Zimbabwe 21–60 in 1987
Biggest win Scotland 60–21 in 1987 and 51–12 in 1991, Zimbabwe no win

1987	Wellington WC **Scotland** 60–21	1991	Murrayfield WC **Scotland** 51–12

SCOTLAND v FIJI

Played 6 Scotland won 5, Fiji won 1
Highest scores Scotland 38–17 in 1989, Fiji 51–26 in 1998
Biggest win Scotland 38–17 in 1989, Fiji 51–26 in 1998

1989	Murrayfield **Scotland** 38–17	2003	Sydney WC **Scotland** 22–20
1998	Suva **Fiji** 51–26	2009	Murrayfield **Scotland** 23–10
2002	Murrayfield **Scotland** 36–22	2012	Lautoka **Scotland** 37–25

SCOTLAND v ARGENTINA

Played 15 Scotland won 6, Argentina won 9, Drawn 0
Highest scores Scotland 49–3 in 1990, Argentina 31–22 in 1999 and 31–41 in 2014
Biggest wins Scotland 49–3 in 1990, Argentina 31–22 in 1999 and 25–16 in 2001

1990	Murrayfield **Scotland** 49–3		2 Buenos Aires **Scotland** 26–14
1994	1 Buenos Aires **Argentina** 16–15		Series drawn 1–1
	2 Buenos Aires **Argentina** 19–17	2009	Murrayfield **Argentina** 9–6
	Argentina won series 2–0	2010	1 Tucumán **Scotland** 24–16
1999	Murrayfield **Argentina** 31–22		2 Mar del Plata **Scotland** 13–9
2001	Murrayfield **Argentina** 25–16		Scotland won series 2–0
2005	Murrayfield **Argentina** 23–19	2011	Wellington WC **Argentina** 13–12
2007	Paris WC **Argentina** 19–13	2014	Córdoba **Scotland** 21–19
2008	1 Rosario **Argentina** 21–15	2014	Murrayfield **Scotland** 41–31

SCOTLAND v JAPAN

Played 5 Scotland won 5
Highest scores Scotland 100–8 in 2004, Japan 17–42 in 2013
Biggest win Scotland 100–8 in 2004, Japan no win

1991	Murrayfield WC **Scotland** 47–9	2013	Murrayfield **Scotland** won 42–17
2003	Townsville WC **Scotland** 32–11	2015	Gloucester WC **Scotland** 45–10
2004	Perth **Scotland** 100–8		

SCOTLAND v SAMOA

Played 10 Scotland won 8, Samoa won 1, Drawn 1
Highest scores Scotland 38–3 in 2004, Samoa 33–36 in 2015
Biggest win Scotland 38–3 in 2004, Samoa 27–17 in 2013

1991	Murrayfield WC **Scotland** 28–6	
1995	Murrayfield **Drawn** 15–15	
1999	Murrayfield WC **Scotland** 35–20	
2000	Murrayfield **Scotland** 31–8	
2004	Wellington (NZ) **Scotland** 38–3	

2005	Murrayfield **Scotland** 18–11	
2010	Aberdeen **Scotland** 19–16	
2012	Apia **Scotland** 17–16	
2013	Durban QT **Samoa** 27–17	
2015	Newcastle WC **Scotland** 36–33	

SCOTLAND v CANADA

Played 4 Scotland won 3, Canada won 1
Highest scores Scotland 41–0 in 2008, Canada 26–23 in 2002
Biggest win Scotland 41–0 in 2008, Canada 26–23 in 2002

1995	Murrayfield **Scotland** 22–6
2002	Vancouver **Canada** 26–23

2008	Aberdeen **Scotland** 41–0
2014	Toronto **Scotland** 19–17

SCOTLAND v IVORY COAST

Played 1 Scotland won 1
Highest scores Scotland 89–0 in 1995, Ivory Coast 0–89 in 1995
Biggest win Scotland 89–0 in 1995, Ivory Coast no win

1995	Rustenburg WC **Scotland** 89–0

SCOTLAND v TONGA

Played 4 Scotland won 3, Tonga won 1
Highest scores Scotland 43–20 in 2001, Tonga 21–15 in 2012
Biggest win Scotland 41–5 in 1995, Tonga 21–15 in 2012

1995	Pretoria WC **Scotland** 41–5
2001	Murrayfield **Scotland** 43–20

2012	Aberdeen **Tonga** 21–15
2014	Kilmarnock **Scotland** 37–12

SCOTLAND v ITALY

Played 25 Scotland won 17, Italy won 8
Highest scores Scotland 48–7 in 2015, Italy 37–17 in 2007
Biggest wins Scotland 48–7 in 2015, Italy 37–17 in 2007

1996	Murrayfield **Scotland** 29–22
1998	Treviso **Italy** 25–21
1999	Murrayfield **Scotland** 30–12
2000	Rome **Italy** 34–20
2001	Murrayfield **Scotland** 23–19

2002	Rome **Scotland** 29–12
2003	Murrayfield **Scotland** 33–25
2003	Murrayfield **Scotland** 47–15
	Non-championship match
2004	Rome **Italy** 20–14

2005	Murrayfield **Scotland** 18–10
2006	Rome **Scotland** 13–10
2007	Murrayfield **Italy** 37–17
2007	Saint Etienne WC **Scotland** 18–16
2008	Rome **Italy** 23–20
2009	Murrayfield **Scotland** 26–6
2010	Rome **Italy** 16–12
2011	Murrayfield **Scotland** 21–8
2011	Murrayfield **Scotland** 23–12
	Non-championship match

2012	Rome **Italy** 13–6
2013	Murrayfield **Scotland** 34–10
2013	Pretoria QT **Scotland** 30–29
2014	Rome **Scotland** 21–20
2015	Murrayfield **Italy** 22–19
2015	Turin **Scotland** 16–12
	Non-championship match
2015	Murrayfield **Scotland** 48–7
	Non-championship match

SCOTLAND v URUGUAY

Played 1 Scotland won 1
Highest scores Scotland 43–12 in 1999, Uruguay 12–43 in 1999
Biggest win Scotland 43–12 in 1999, Uruguay no win

1999	Murrayfield WC **Scotland** 43–12

SCOTLAND v SPAIN

Played 1 Scotland won 1
Highest scores Scotland 48–0 in 1999, Spain 0–48 in 1999
Biggest win Scotland 48–0 in 1999, Spain no win

1999	Murrayfield WC **Scotland** 48–0

SCOTLAND v UNITED STATES

Played 5 Scotland won 5
Highest scores Scotland 65–23 in 2002, United States 23–65 in 2002
Biggest win Scotland 53–6 in 2000, United States no win

2000	Murrayfield **Scotland** 53–6		2014	Houston **Scotland** 24–6
2002	San Francisco **Scotland** 65–23		2015	Leeds WC **Scotland** 39–16
2003	Brisbane WC **Scotland** 39–15			

SCOTLAND v PACIFIC ISLANDS

Played 1 Scotland won 1
Highest scores Scotland 34–22 in 2006, Pacific Islands 22–34 in 2006
Biggest win Scotland 34–22 in 2006, Pacific Islands no win

2006	Murrayfield **Scotland** 34–22

SCOTLAND v PORTUGAL

Played 1 Scotland won 1
Highest scores Scotland 56–10 in 2007, Portugal 10–56 in 2007
Biggest win Scotland 56–10 in 2007, Portugal no win

2007	Saint Etienne WC **Scotland** 56–10

SCOTLAND v GEORGIA

Played 1 Scotland won 1
Highest scores Scotland 15–6 in 2011, Georgia 6–15 in 2011
Biggest win Scotland 15–6 in 2011, Georgia no win

2011	Invercargill WC **Scotland** 15–6	

IRELAND v WALES

Played 123 Ireland won 50, Wales won 67, Drawn 6
Highest scores Ireland 54–10 in 2002, Wales 34–9 in 1976
Biggest wins Ireland 54–10 in 2002, Wales 29–0 in 1907

1882	Dublin **Wales** 2G 2T to 0		1924	Cardiff **Ireland** 13–10
1883	No Match		1925	Belfast **Ireland** 19–3
1884	Cardiff **Wales** 1DG 2T to 0		1926	Swansea **Wales** 11–8
1885	No Match		1927	Dublin **Ireland** 19–9
1886	No Match		1928	Cardiff **Ireland** 13–10
1887	Birkenhead **Wales** 1DG 1T to 3T		1929	Belfast **Drawn** 5–5
1888	Dublin **Ireland** 1G 1DG 1T to 0		1930	Swansea **Wales** 12–7
1889	Swansea **Ireland** 2T to 0		1931	Belfast **Wales** 15–3
1890	Dublin **Drawn** 1G each		1932	Cardiff **Ireland** 12–10
1891	Llanelli **Wales** 6–4		1933	Belfast **Ireland** 10–5
1892	Dublin **Ireland** 9–0		1934	Swansea **Wales** 13–0
1893	Llanelli **Wales** 2–0		1935	Belfast **Ireland** 9–3
1894	Belfast **Ireland** 3–0		1936	Cardiff **Wales** 3–0
1895	Cardiff **Wales** 5–3		1937	Belfast **Ireland** 5–3
1896	Dublin **Ireland** 8–4		1938	Swansea **Wales** 11–5
1897	No Match		1939	Belfast **Wales** 7–0
1898	Limerick **Wales** 11–3		1947	Swansea **Wales** 6–0
1899	Cardiff **Ireland** 3–0		1948	Belfast **Ireland** 6–3
1900	Belfast **Wales** 3–0		1949	Swansea **Ireland** 5–0
1901	Swansea **Wales** 10–9		1950	Belfast **Wales** 6–3
1902	Dublin **Wales** 15–0		1951	Cardiff **Drawn** 3–3
1903	Cardiff **Wales** 18–0		1952	Dublin **Wales** 14–3
1904	Belfast **Ireland** 14–12		1953	Swansea **Wales** 5–3
1905	Swansea **Wales** 10–3		1954	Dublin **Wales** 12–9
1906	Belfast **Ireland** 11–6		1955	Cardiff **Wales** 21–3
1907	Cardiff **Wales** 29–0		1956	Dublin **Ireland** 11–3
1908	Belfast **Wales** 11–5		1957	Cardiff **Wales** 6–5
1909	Swansea **Wales** 18–5		1958	Dublin **Wales** 9–6
1910	Dublin **Wales** 19–3		1959	Cardiff **Wales** 8–6
1911	Cardiff **Wales** 16–0		1960	Dublin **Wales** 10–9
1912	Belfast **Ireland** 12–5		1961	Cardiff **Wales** 9–0
1913	Swansea **Wales** 16–13		1962	Dublin **Drawn** 3–3
1914	Belfast **Wales** 11–3		1963	Cardiff **Ireland** 14–6
1920	Cardiff **Wales** 28–4		1964	Dublin **Wales** 15–6
1921	Belfast **Wales** 6–0		1965	Cardiff **Wales** 14–8
1922	Swansea **Wales** 11–5		1966	Dublin **Ireland** 9–6
1923	Dublin **Ireland** 5–4		1967	Cardiff **Ireland** 3–0

1968	Dublin **Ireland** 9–6		1995	Cardiff **Ireland** 16–12
1969	Cardiff **Wales** 24–11		1995	Johannesburg WC **Ireland** 24–23
1970	Dublin **Ireland** 14–0		1996	Dublin **Ireland** 30–17
1971	Cardiff **Wales** 23–9		1997	Cardiff **Ireland** 26–25
1972	No Match		1998	Dublin **Wales** 30–21
1973	Cardiff **Wales** 16–12		1999	Wembley **Ireland** 29–23
1974	Dublin **Drawn** 9–9		2000	Dublin **Wales** 23–19
1975	Cardiff **Wales** 32–4		2001	Cardiff **Ireland** 36–6
1976	Dublin **Wales** 34–9		2002	Dublin **Ireland** 54–10
1977	Cardiff **Wales** 25–9		2003	Cardiff **Ireland** 25–24
1978	Dublin **Wales** 20–16		2003	Dublin **Ireland** 35–12
1979	Cardiff **Wales** 24–21		2004	Dublin **Ireland** 36–15
1980	Dublin **Ireland** 21–7		2005	Cardiff **Wales** 32–20
1981	Cardiff **Wales** 9–8		2006	Dublin **Ireland** 31–5
1982	Dublin **Ireland** 20–12		2007	Cardiff **Ireland** 19–9
1983	Cardiff **Wales** 23–9		2008	Dublin **Wales** 16–12
1984	Dublin **Wales** 18–9		2009	Cardiff **Ireland** 17–15
1985	Cardiff **Ireland** 21–9		2010	Dublin **Ireland** 27–12
1986	Dublin **Wales** 19–12		2011	Cardiff **Wales** 19–13
1987	Cardiff **Ireland** 15–11		2011	Wellington WC **Wales** 22–10
1987	Wellington WC **Wales** 13–6		2012	Dublin **Wales** 23–21
1988	Dublin **Wales** 12–9		2013	Cardiff **Ireland** 30–22
1989	Cardiff **Ireland** 19–13		2014	Dublin **Ireland** 26–3
1990	Dublin **Ireland** 14–8		2015	Cardiff **Wales** 23–16
1991	Cardiff **Drawn** 21–21		2015	Cardiff **Ireland** 35–21
1992	Dublin **Wales** 16–15			Non-championship Match
1993	Cardiff **Ireland** 19–14		2015	Dublin **Wales** 16–10
1994	Dublin **Wales** 17–15			Non-championship Match

IRELAND v FRANCE

Played 94 Ireland won 32, France won 55, Drawn 7
Highest scores Ireland 31–43 in 2006, France 45–10 in 1996
Biggest wins Ireland 24–0 in 1913, France 44–5 in 2002

1909	Dublin **Ireland** 19–8		1931	Paris **France** 3–0
1910	Paris **Ireland** 8–3		1947	Dublin **France** 12–8
1911	Cork **Ireland** 25–5		1948	Paris **Ireland** 13–6
1912	Paris **Ireland** 11–6		1949	Dublin **France** 16–9
1913	Cork **Ireland** 24–0		1950	Paris **Drawn** 3–3
1914	Paris **Ireland** 8–6		1951	Dublin **Ireland** 9–8
1920	Dublin **France** 15–7		1952	Paris **Ireland** 11–8
1921	Paris **France** 20–10		1953	Belfast **Ireland** 16–3
1922	Dublin **Ireland** 8–3		1954	Paris **France** 8–0
1923	Paris **France** 14–8		1955	Dublin **France** 5–3
1924	Dublin **Ireland** 6–0		1956	Paris **France** 14–8
1925	Paris **Ireland** 9–3		1957	Dublin **Ireland** 11–6
1926	Belfast **Ireland** 11–0		1958	Paris **France** 11–6
1927	Paris **Ireland** 8–3		1959	Dublin **Ireland** 9–5
1928	Belfast **Ireland** 12–8		1960	Paris **France** 23–6
1929	Paris **Ireland** 6–0		1961	Dublin **France** 15–3
1930	Belfast **France** 5–0		1962	Paris **France** 11–0

1963	Dublin **France** 24–5
1964	Paris **France** 27–6
1965	Dublin **Drawn** 3–3
1966	Paris **France** 11–6
1967	Dublin **France** 11–6
1968	Paris **France** 16–6
1969	Dublin **Ireland** 17–9
1970	Paris **France** 8–0
1971	Dublin **Drawn** 9–9
1972	Paris **Ireland** 14–9
1972	Dublin **Ireland** 24–14
	Non-championship match
1973	Dublin **Ireland** 6–4
1974	Paris **France** 9–6
1975	Dublin **Ireland** 25–6
1976	Paris **France** 26–3
1977	Dublin **France** 15–6
1978	Paris **France** 10–9
1979	Dublin **Drawn** 9–9
1980	Paris **France** 19–18
1981	Dublin **France** 19–13
1982	Paris **France** 22–9
1983	Dublin **Ireland** 22–16
1984	Paris **France** 25–12
1985	Dublin **Drawn** 15–15
1986	Paris **France** 29–9
1987	Dublin **France** 19–13
1988	Paris **France** 25–6
1989	Dublin **France** 26–21
1990	Paris **France** 31–12
1991	Dublin **France** 21–13
1992	Paris **France** 44–12

1993	Dublin **France** 21–6
1994	Paris **France** 35–15
1995	Dublin **France** 25–7
1995	Durban WC **France** 36–12
1996	Paris **France** 45–10
1997	Dublin **France** 32–15
1998	Paris **France** 18–16
1999	Dublin **France** 10–9
2000	Paris **Ireland** 27–25
2001	Dublin **Ireland** 22–15
2002	Paris **France** 44–5
2003	Dublin **Ireland** 15–12
2003	Melbourne WC **France** 43–21
2004	Paris **France** 35–17
2005	Dublin **France** 26–19
2006	Paris **France** 43–31
2007	Dublin **France** 20–17
2007	Paris WC **France** 25–3
2008	Paris **France** 26–21
2009	Dublin **Ireland** 30–21
2010	Paris **France** 33–10
2011	Dublin **France** 25–22
2011	Bordeaux **France** 19–12
	Non-championship match
2011	Dublin **France** 26–22
	Non-championship match
2012	Paris **Drawn** 17–17
2013	Dublin **Drawn** 13–13
2014	Paris **Ireland** 22–20
2015	Dublin **Ireland** 18–11
2015	Cardiff WC **Ireland** 24–9

IRELAND v SOUTH AFRICA

Played 22 Ireland won 5, South Africa won 16, Drawn 1
Highest scores Ireland 32–15 in 2006, South Africa 38–0 in 1912
Biggest wins Ireland 32–15 in 2006, South Africa 38–0 in 1912

1906	Belfast **South Africa** 15–12
1912	Dublin **South Africa** 38–0
1931	Dublin **South Africa** 8–3
1951	Dublin **South Africa** 17–5
1960	Dublin **South Africa** 8–3
1961	Cape Town **South Africa** 24–8
1965	Dublin **Ireland** 9–6
1970	Dublin **Drawn** 8–8
1981	1 Cape Town **South Africa** 23–15
	2 Durban **South Africa** 12–10
	South Africa won series 2–0
1998	1 Bloemfontein **South Africa** 37–13
	2 Pretoria **South Africa** 33–0

	South Africa won series 2–0
1998	Dublin **South Africa** 27–13
2000	Dublin **South Africa** 28–18
2004	1 Bloemfontein **South Africa** 31–17
	2 Cape Town **South Africa** 26–17
	South Africa won series 2–0
2004	Dublin **Ireland** 17–12
2006	Dublin **Ireland** 32–15
2009	Dublin **Ireland** 15–10
2010	Dublin **South Africa** 23–21
2012	Dublin **South Africa** 16–12
2014	Dublin **Ireland** 29–15

IRELAND v NEW ZEALAND

Played 28 Ireland won 0, New Zealand won 27, Drawn 1
Highest scores Ireland 29–40 in 2001, New Zealand 66–28 in 2010
Biggest win Ireland no win, New Zealand 60–0 in 2012

1905	Dublin **New Zealand** 15–0		2002	1 Dunedin **New Zealand** 15–6
1924	Dublin **New Zealand** 6–0			2 Auckland **New Zealand** 40–8
1935	Dublin **New Zealand** 17–9			New Zealand won series 2–0
1954	Dublin **New Zealand** 14–3		2005	Dublin **New Zealand** 45–7
1963	Dublin **New Zealand** 6–5		2006	1 Hamilton **New Zealand** 34–23
1973	Dublin **Drawn** 10–10			2 Auckland **New Zealand** 27–17
1974	Dublin **New Zealand** 15–6			New Zealand won series 2–0
1976	Wellington **New Zealand** 11–3		2008	Wellington **New Zealand** 21–11
1978	Dublin **New Zealand** 10–6		2008	Dublin **New Zealand** 22–3
1989	Dublin **New Zealand** 23–6		2010	New Plymouth **New Zealand** 66–28
1992	1 Dunedin **New Zealand** 24–21		2010	Dublin **New Zealand** 38–18
	2 Wellington **New Zealand** 59–6		2012	1 Auckland **New Zealand** 42–10
	New Zealand won series 2–0			2 Christchurch **New Zealand** 22–19
1995	Johannesburg WC **New Zealand** 43–19			3 Hamilton **New Zealand** 60–0
1997	Dublin **New Zealand** 63–15			New Zealand won series 3–0
2001	Dublin **New Zealand** 40–29		2013	Dublin **New Zealand** 24–22

IRELAND v AUSTRALIA

Played 32 Ireland won 10, Australia won 21, Drawn 1
Highest scores Ireland 27–12 in 1979, Australia 46–10 in 1999
Biggest wins Ireland 27–12 in 1979 and 21–6 in 2006, Australia 46–10 in 1999

1927	Dublin **Australia** 5–3		1996	Dublin **Australia** 22–12
1947	Dublin **Australia** 16–3		1999	1 Brisbane **Australia** 46–10
1958	Dublin **Ireland** 9–6			2 Perth **Australia** 32–26
1967	Dublin **Ireland** 15–8			Australia won series 2–0
1967	Sydney **Ireland** 11–5		1999	Dublin WC **Australia** 23–3
1968	Dublin **Ireland** 10–3		2002	Dublin **Ireland** 18–9
1976	Dublin **Australia** 20–10		2003	Perth **Australia** 45–16
1979	1 Brisbane **Ireland** 27–12		2003	Melbourne WC **Australia** 17–16
	2 Sydney **Ireland** 9–3		2005	Dublin **Australia** 30–14
	Ireland won series 2–0		2006	Perth **Australia** 37–15
1981	Dublin **Australia** 16–12		2006	Dublin **Ireland** 21–6
1984	Dublin **Australia** 16–9		2008	Melbourne **Australia** 18–12
1987	Sydney WC **Australia** 33–15		2009	Dublin **Drawn** 20–20
1991	Dublin WC **Australia** 19–18		2010	Brisbane **Australia** 22–15
1992	Dublin **Australia** 42–17		2011	Auckland WC **Ireland** 15–6
1994	1 Brisbane **Australia** 33–13		2013	Dublin **Australia** 32–15
	2 Sydney **Australia** 32–18		2014	Dublin **Ireland** 26–23
	Australia won series 2–0			

IRELAND v NEW ZEALAND NATIVES

Played 1 New Zealand Natives won 1
Highest scores Ireland 4–13 in 1888, Zew Zealand Natives 13–4 in 1888
Biggest win Ireland no win, New Zealand Natives 13–4 in 1888

1888	Dublin **New Zealand Natives** 4G 1T to 1G 1T

IRELAND v IRU PRESIDENT'S XV

Played 1 Drawn 1
Highest scores Ireland 18–18 in 1974, IRFU President's XV 18–18 in 1974

1974	Dublin **Drawn** 18–18

IRELAND v ROMANIA

Played 9 Ireland won 9
Highest scores Ireland 60–0 in 1986, Romania 35–53 in 1998
Biggest win Ireland 60–0 in 1986, Romania no win

1986	Dublin **Ireland** 60–0		2002	Limerick **Ireland** 39–8
1993	Dublin **Ireland** 25–3		2003	Gosford WC **Ireland** 45–17
1998	Dublin **Ireland** 53–35		2005	Dublin **Ireland** 43–12
1999	Dublin WC **Ireland** 44–14		2015	Wembley WC **Ireland** 44–10
2001	Bucharest **Ireland** 37–3			

IRELAND v CANADA

Played 7 Ireland won 6 Drawn 1
Highest scores Ireland 55–0 in 2008, Canada 27–27 in 2000
Biggest win Ireland 55–0 in 2008, Canada no win

1987	Dunedin WC **Ireland** 46–19		2009	Vancouver **Ireland** 25–6
1997	Dublin **Ireland** 33–11		2013	Toronto **Ireland** 40–14
2000	Markham **Drawn** 27–27		2015	Cardiff WC **Ireland** 50–7
2008	Limerick **Ireland** 55–0			

IRELAND v TONGA

Played 2 Ireland won 2
Highest scores Ireland 40–19 in 2003, Tonga 19–40 in 2003
Biggest win Ireland 32–9 in 1987, Tonga no win

1987	Brisbane WC **Ireland** 32–9	2003	Nuku'alofa **Ireland** 40–19

IRELAND v SAMOA

Played 6 Ireland won 5, Samoa won 1, Drawn 0
Highest scores Ireland 49–22 in 1988, Samoa 40–25 in 1996
Biggest wins Ireland 40–9 in 2013, Samoa 40–25 in 1996

1988	Dublin **Ireland** 49–22	2003	Apia **Ireland** 40–14
1996	Dublin **Samoa** 40–25	2010	Dublin **Ireland** 20–10
2001	Dublin **Ireland** 35–8	2013	Dublin **Ireland** 40–9

IRELAND v ITALY

Played 25 Ireland won 21, Italy won 4, Drawn 0
Highest scores Ireland 61–6 in 2003, Italy 37–29 in 1997 and 37–22 in 1997
Biggest wins Ireland 61–6 in 2003, Italy 37–22 in 1997

1988	Dublin **Ireland** 31–15	2007	Rome **Ireland** 51–24
1995	Treviso **Italy** 22–12	2007	Belfast **Ireland** 23–20
1997	Dublin **Italy** 37–29		Non-championship match
1997	Bologna **Italy** 37–22	2008	Dublin **Ireland** 16–11
1999	Dublin **Ireland** 39–30	2009	Rome **Ireland** 38–9
2000	Dublin **Ireland** 60–13	2010	Dublin **Ireland** 29–11
2001	Rome **Ireland** 41–22	2011	Rome **Ireland** 13–11
2002	Dublin **Ireland** 32–17	2011	Dunedin WC **Ireland** 36–6
2003	Rome **Ireland** 37–13	2012	Dublin **Ireland** 42–10
2003	Limerick **Ireland** 61–6	2013	Rome **Italy** 22–15
	Non-championship match	2014	Dublin **Ireland** 46–7
2004	Dublin **Ireland** 19–3	2015	Rome **Ireland** 26–3
2005	Rome **Ireland** 28–17	2015	London WC **Ireland** 16–9
2006	Dublin **Ireland** 26–16		

IRELAND v ARGENTINA

Played 16 Ireland won 10 Argentina won 6
Highest scores Ireland 46–24 in 2012, Argentina 43–20 in 2015
Biggest win Ireland 46–24 in 2012, Argentina 43–20 in 2015

1990	Dublin **Ireland** 20–18		Argentina won series 2–0
1999	Dublin **Ireland** 32–24	2007	Paris WC **Argentina** 30–15
1999	Lens WC **Argentina** 28–24	2008	Dublin **Ireland** 17–3
2000	Buenos Aires **Argentina** 34–23	2010	Dublin **Ireland** 29–9
2002	Dublin **Ireland** 16–7	2012	Dublin **Ireland** 46–24
2003	Adelaide WC **Ireland** 16–15	2014	1 Resistencia **Ireland** 29–17
2004	Dublin **Ireland** 21–19		2 Tucumán **Ireland** 23–17
2007	1 Santa Fé **Argentina** 22–20		Ireland won series 2–0
	2 Buenos Aires **Argentina** 16–0	2015	Cardiff WC **Argentina** 43–20

IRELAND v NAMIBIA

195

Played 4 Ireland won 2, Namibia won 2
Highest scores Ireland 64–7 in 2003, Namibia 26–15 in 1991
Biggest win Ireland 64–7 in 2003, Namibia 26–15 in 1991

1991	1 Windhoek **Namibia** 15–6		2003	Sydney WC **Ireland** 64–7
	2 Windhoek **Namibia** 26–15		2007	Bordeaux WC **Ireland** 32–17
	Namibia won series 2–0			

IRELAND v ZIMBABWE

Played 1 Ireland won 1
Highest scores Ireland 55–11 in 1991, Zimbabwe 11–55 in 1991
Biggest win Ireland 55–11 in 1991, Zimbabwe no win

1991	Dublin WC **Ireland** 55–11

IRELAND v JAPAN

Played 5 Ireland won 5
Highest scores Ireland 78–9 in 2000, Japan 28–50 in 1995
Biggest win Ireland 78–9 in 2000, Japan no win

1991	Dublin WC **Ireland** 32–16		2005	1 Osaka **Ireland** 44–12
1995	Bloemfontein WC **Ireland** 50–28			2 Tokyo **Ireland** 47–18
2000	Dublin **Ireland** 78–9			Ireland won series 2–0

IRELAND v UNITED STATES

Played 8 Ireland won 8
Highest scores Ireland 83–3 in 2000, United States 18–25 in 1996
Biggest win Ireland 83–3 in 2000, United States no win

1994	Dublin **Ireland** 26–15		2004	Dublin **Ireland** 55–6
1996	Atlanta **Ireland** 25–18		2009	Santa Clara **Ireland** 27–10
1999	Dublin WC **Ireland** 53–8		2011	New Plymouth WC **Ireland** 22–10
2000	Manchester (NH) **Ireland** 83–3		2013	Houston **Ireland** 15–12

IRELAND v FIJI

Played 3 Ireland won 3
Highest scores Ireland 64–17 in 2002, Fiji 17–64 in 2002
Biggest win Ireland 64–17 in 2002, Fiji no win

1995	Dublin **Ireland** 44–8		2009	Dublin **Ireland** 41–6
2002	Dublin **Ireland** 64–17			

INTERNATIONAL RESULTS

IRELAND v GEORGIA

Played 4 Ireland won 4
Highest scores Ireland 70–0 in 1998, Georgia 14–63 in 2002
Biggest win Ireland 70–0 in 1998, Georgia no win

1998	Dublin **Ireland** 70–0		2007	Bordeaux WC **Ireland** 14–10
2002	Dublin **Ireland** 63–14		2014	Dublin **Ireland** 49–7

IRELAND v RUSSIA

Played 2 Ireland won 2
Highest scores Ireland 62–12 in 2011, Russia 12–62 in 2011
Biggest win Ireland 62–12 in 2011, Russia no win

2002	Krasnoyarsk **Ireland** 35–3		2011	Rotorua WC **Ireland** 62–12

IRELAND v PACIFIC ISLANDS

Played 1 Ireland won 1
Highest scores Ireland 61–17 in 2006, Pacific Islands 17–61 in 2006
Biggest win Ireland 61–17 in 2006, Pacific Islands no win

2006	Dublin **Ireland** 61–17

WALES v FRANCE

Played 93 Wales won 47, France won 43, Drawn 3
Highest scores Wales 49–14 in 1910, France 51–0 in 1998
Biggest wins Wales 47–5 in 1909, France 51–0 in 1998

1908	Cardiff **Wales** 36–4		1948	Swansea **France** 11–3
1909	Paris **Wales** 47–5		1949	Paris **France** 5–3
1910	Swansea **Wales** 49–14		1950	Cardiff **Wales** 21–0
1911	Paris **Wales** 15–0		1951	Paris **France** 8–3
1912	Newport **Wales** 14–8		1952	Swansea **Wales** 9–5
1913	Paris **Wales** 11–8		1953	Paris **Wales** 6–3
1914	Swansea **Wales** 31–0		1954	Cardiff **Wales** 19–13
1920	Paris **Wales** 6–5		1955	Paris **Wales** 16–11
1921	Cardiff **Wales** 12–4		1956	Cardiff **Wales** 5–3
1922	Paris **Wales** 11–3		1957	Paris **Wales** 19–13
1923	Swansea **Wales** 16–8		1958	Cardiff **France** 16–6
1924	Paris **Wales** 10–6		1959	Paris **France** 11–3
1925	Cardiff **Wales** 11–5		1960	Cardiff **France** 16–8
1926	Paris **Wales** 7–5		1961	Paris **France** 8–6
1927	Swansea **Wales** 25–7		1962	Cardiff **Wales** 3–0
1928	Paris **France** 8–3		1963	Paris **France** 5–3
1929	Cardiff **Wales** 8–3		1964	Cardiff **Drawn** 11–11
1930	Paris **Wales** 11–0		1965	Paris **France** 22–13
1931	Swansea **Wales** 35–3		1966	Cardiff **Wales** 9–8
1947	Paris **Wales** 3–0		1967	Paris **France** 20–14

1968	Cardiff **France** 14–9		1995	Paris **France** 21–9
1969	Paris **Drawn** 8–8		1996	Cardiff **Wales** 16–15
1970	Cardiff **Wales** 11–6		1996	Cardiff **France** 40–33
1971	Paris **Wales** 9–5			Non-championship match
1972	Cardiff **Wales** 20–6		1997	Paris **France 27–22**
1973	Paris **France** 12–3		1998	Wembley **France** 51–0
1974	Cardiff **Drawn** 16–16		1999	Paris **Wales** 34–33
1975	Paris **Wales** 25–10		1999	Cardiff **Wales** 34–23
1976	Cardiff **Wales** 19–13			Non-championship match
1977	Paris **France** 16–9		2000	Cardiff **France** 36–3
1978	Cardiff **Wales** 16–7		2001	Paris **Wales** 43–35
1979	Paris **France** 14–13		2002	Cardiff **France** 37–33
1980	Cardiff **Wales** 18–9		2003	Paris **France** 33–5
1981	Paris **France** 19–15		2004	Cardiff **France** 29–22
1982	Cardiff **Wales** 22–12		2005	Paris **Wales** 24–18
1983	Paris **France** 16–9		2006	Cardiff **France** 21–16
1984	Cardiff **France** 21–16		2007	Paris **France** 32–21
1985	Paris **France** 14–3		2007	Cardiff **France** 34–7
1986	Cardiff **France** 23–15			Non-championship match
1987	Paris **France** 16–9		2008	Cardiff **Wales** 29–12
1988	Cardiff **France** 10–9		2009	Paris **France** 21–16
1989	Paris **France** 31–12		2010	Cardiff **France** 26–20
1990	Cardiff **France** 29–19		2011	Paris **France** 28–9
1991	Paris **France** 36–3		2011	Auckland WC **France** 9–8
1991	Cardiff **France** 22–9		2012	Cardiff **Wales** 16–9
	Non-championship match		2013	Paris **Wales** 16–6
1992	Cardiff **France** 12–9		2014	Cardiff **Wales** 27–6
1993	Paris **France** 26–10		2015	Paris **Wales** 20–13
1994	Cardiff **Wales** 24–15			

WALES v SOUTH AFRICA

Played 31 Wales won 2, South Africa won 28, Drawn 1
Highest scores Wales 36–38 in 2004, South Africa 96–13 in 1998
Biggest win Wales 29–19 in 1999, South Africa 96–13 in 1998

1906	Swansea **South Africa** 11–0		2004	Pretoria **South Africa** 53–18
1912	Cardiff **South Africa** 3–0		2004	Cardiff **South Africa** 38–36
1931	Swansea **South Africa** 8–3		2005	Cardiff **South Africa** 33–16
1951	Cardiff **South Africa** 6–3		2007	Cardiff **South Africa** 34–12
1960	Cardiff **South Africa** 3–0		2008	1 Bloemfontein **South Africa** 43–17
1964	Durban **South Africa** 24–3			2 Pretoria **South Africa** 37–21
1970	Cardiff **Drawn** 6–6			South Africa won series 2–0
1994	Cardiff **South Africa** 20–12		2008	Cardiff **South Africa** 20–15
1995	Johannesburg **South Africa** 40–11		2010	Cardiff **South Africa** 34–31
1996	Cardiff **South Africa** 37–20		2010	Cardiff **South Africa** 29–25
1998	Pretoria **South Africa** 96–13		2011	Wellington WC **South Africa** 17–16
1998	Wembley **South Africa** 28–20		2013	Cardiff **South Africa** 24–15
1999	Cardiff **Wales** 29–19		2014	1 Durban **South Africa** 38–16
2000	Cardiff **South Africa** 23–13			2 Nelspruit **South Africa** 31–30
2002	1 Bloemfontein **South Africa** 34–19			South Africa won series 2–0
	2 Cape Town **South Africa** 19–8		2014	Cardiff **Wales** 12–6
	South Africa won series 2–0		2015	Twickenham WC **South Africa** 23–19

WALES v NEW ZEALAND

Played 30 Wales won 3, New Zealand won 27, Drawn 0
Highest scores Wales 37–53 in 2003, New Zealand 55–3 in 2003
Biggest wins Wales 13–8 in 1953, New Zealand 55–3 in 2003

1905	Cardiff **Wales** 3–0	
1924	Swansea **New Zealand** 19–0	
1935	Cardiff **Wales** 13–12	
1953	Cardiff **Wales** 13–8	
1963	Cardiff **New Zealand** 6–0	
1967	Cardiff **New Zealand** 13–6	
1969	1 Christchurch **New Zealand** 19–0	
	2 Auckland **New Zealand** 33–12	
	New Zealand won series 2–0	
1972	Cardiff **New Zealand** 19–16	
1978	Cardiff **New Zealand** 13–12	
1980	Cardiff **New Zealand** 23–3	
1987	Brisbane WC **New Zealand** 49–6	
1988	1 Christchurch **New Zealand** 52–3	
	2 Auckland **New Zealand** 54–9	
	New Zealand won series 2–0	
1989	Cardiff **New Zealand** 34–9	
1995	Johannesburg WC **New Zealand 34–9**	
1997	Wembley **New Zealand** 42–7	
2002	Cardiff **New Zealand** 43–17	
2003	Hamilton **New Zealand** 55–3	
2003	Sydney WC **New Zealand** 53–37	
2004	Cardiff **New Zealand** 26–25	
2005	Cardiff **New Zealand** 41–3	
2006	Cardiff **New Zealand** 45–10	
2008	Cardiff **New Zealand** 29–9	
2009	Cardiff **New Zealand** 19–12	
2010	1 Dunedin **New Zealand** 42–9	
	2 Hamilton **New Zealand** 29–10	
	New Zealand won series 2–0	
2010	Cardiff **New Zealand** 37–25	
2012	Cardiff **New Zealand** 33–10	
2014	Cardiff **New Zealand** 34–16	

WALES v AUSTRALIA

Played 39 Wales won 10, Australia won 28, Drawn 1
Highest scores Wales 29–29 in 2006, Australia 63–6 in 1991
Biggest wins Wales 28–3 in 1975, Australia 63–6 in 1991

1908	Cardiff **Wales** 9–6	
1927	Cardiff **Australia** 18–8	
1947	Cardiff **Wales** 6–0	
1958	Cardiff **Wales** 9–3	
1966	Cardiff **Australia** 14–11	
1969	Sydney **Wales** 19–16	
1973	Cardiff **Wales** 24–0	
1975	Cardiff **Wales** 28–3	
1978	1 Brisbane **Australia** 18–8	
	2 Sydney **Australia** 19–17	
	Australia won series 2–0	
1981	Cardiff **Wales** 18–13	
1984	Cardiff **Australia** 28–9	
1987	Rotorua WC **Wales** 22–21	
1991	Brisbane **Australia** 63–6	
1991	Cardiff WC **Australia** 38–3	
1992	Cardiff **Australia** 23–6	
1996	1 Brisbane **Australia** 56–25	
	2 Sydney **Australia** 42–3	
	Australia won series 2–0	
1996	Cardiff **Australia** 28–19	
1999	Cardiff WC **Australia** 24–9	
2001	Cardiff **Australia** 21–13	
2003	Sydney **Australia** 30–10	
2005	Cardiff **Wales** 24–22	
2006	Cardiff **Drawn** 29–29	
2007	1 Sydney **Australia** 29–23	
	2 Brisbane **Australia** 31–0	
	Australia won series 2–0	
2007	Cardiff WC **Australia** 32–20	
2008	Cardiff **Wales** 21–18	
2009	Cardiff **Australia** 33–12	
2010	Cardiff **Australia** 25–16	
2011	Auckland WC **Australia** 21–18	
2011	Cardiff **Australia** 24–18	
2012	1 Brisbane **Australia** 27–19	
	2 Melbourne **Australia** 25–23	
	3 Sydney **Australia** 20–19	
	Australia won series 3–0	
2012	Cardiff **Australia** 14–12	
2013	Cardiff **Australia** 30–26	
2014	Cardiff **Australia** 33–28	
2015	Twickenham WC **Australia** 15–6	

WALES v NEW ZEALAND NATIVES

Played 1 Wales won 1
Highest scores Wales 5–0 in 1888, New Zealand Natives 0–5 in 1888
Biggest win Wales 5–0 in 1888, New Zealand Natives no win

1888	Swansea **Wales** 1G 2T to 0	

WALES v NEW ZEALAND ARMY

Played 1 New Zealand Army won 1
Highest scores Wales 3–6 in 1919, New Zealand Army 6–3 in 1919
Biggest win Wales no win, New Zealand Army 6–3 in 1919

1919	Swansea **New Zealand Army** 6–3	

WALES v ROMANIA

Played 8 Wales won 6, Romania won 2
Highest scores Wales 81–9 in 2001, Romania 24–6 in 1983
Biggest wins Wales 81–9 in 2001, Romania 24–6 in 1983

1983	Bucharest **Romania** 24–6	2001	Cardiff **Wales** 81–9
1988	Cardiff **Romania** 15–9	2002	Wrexham **Wales** 40–3
1994	Bucharest **Wales** 16–9	2003	Wrexham **Wales** 54–8
1997	Wrexham **Wales** 70–21	2004	Cardiff **Wales** 66–7

WALES v FIJI

Played 11 Wales won 9, Fiji won 1, Drawn 1
Highest scores Wales 66–0 in 2011, Fiji 38–34 in 2007
Biggest win Wales 66–0 in 2011, Fiji 38–34 in 2007

1985	Cardiff **Wales** 40–3	2007	Nantes WC **Fiji** 38–34
1986	Suva **Wales** 22–15	2010	Cardiff **Drawn** 16–16
1994	Suva **Wales** 23–8	2011	Hamilton WC **Wales** 66–0
1995	Cardiff **Wales** 19–15	2014	Cardiff **Wales** 17–13
2002	Cardiff **Wales** 58–14	2015	Cardiff WC **Wales** 23–13
2005	Cardiff **Wales** 11–10		

WALES v TONGA

Played 7 Wales won 7
Highest scores Wales 51–7 in 2001, Tonga 20–27 in 2003
Biggest win Wales 51–7 in 2001, Tonga no win

1986	Nuku'Alofa **Wales** 15–7	2001	Cardiff **Wales** 51–7
1987	Palmerston North WC **Wales** 29–16	2003	Canberra WC **Wales** 27–20
1994	Nuku'Alofa **Wales** 18–9	2013	Cardiff **Wales** 17–7
1997	Swansea **Wales** 46–12		

WALES v SAMOA

Played 9 Wales won 5, Samoa won 4, Drawn 0
Highest scores Wales 50–6 in 2000, Samoa 38–31 in 1999
Biggest wins Wales 50–6 in 2000, Samoa 34–9 in 1994

1986	Apia **Wales** 32–14		2000	Cardiff **Wales** 50–6
1988	Cardiff **Wales** 28–6		2009	Cardiff **Wales** 17–13
1991	Cardiff WC **Samoa** 16–13		2011	Hamilton WC **Wales** 17–10
1994	Moamoa **Samoa** 34–9		2012	Cardiff **Samoa** 26–19
1999	Cardiff WC **Samoa** 38–31			

WALES v CANADA

Played 12 Wales won 11, Canada won 1, Drawn 0
Highest scores Wales 61–26 in 2006, Canada 26–24 in 1993 and 26–61 in 2006
Biggest wins Wales 60–3 in 2005, Canada 26–24 in 1993

1987	Invercargill WC **Wales** 40–9		2003	Melbourne WC **Wales** 41–10
1993	Cardiff **Canada** 26–24		2005	Toronto **Wales** 60–3
1994	Toronto **Wales** 33–15		2006	Cardiff **Wales** 61–26
1997	Toronto **Wales** 28–25		2007	Nantes WC **Wales** 42–17
1999	Cardiff **Wales** 33–19		2008	Cardiff **Wales** 34–13
2002	Cardiff **Wales** 32–21		2009	Toronto **Wales** 32–23

WALES v UNITED STATES

Played 7 Wales won 7
Highest scores Wales 77–3 in 2005, United States 23–28 in 1997
Biggest win Wales 77–3 in 2005, United States no win

1987	Cardiff **Wales** 46–0			Wales won series 2–0
1997	Cardiff **Wales** 34–14		2000	Cardiff **Wales** 42–11
1997	1 Wilmington **Wales** 30–20		2005	Hartford **Wales** 77–3
	2 San Francisco **Wales** 28–23		2009	Chicago **Wales** 48–15

WALES v NAMIBIA

Played 4 Wales won 4
Highest scores Wales 81–7 in 2011, Namibia 30–34 in 1990
Biggest win Wales 81–7 in 2011, Namibia no win

1990	1 Windhoek **Wales** 18–9		1993	Windhoek **Wales** 38–23
	2 Windhoek **Wales** 34–30		2011	New Plymouth WC **Wales** 81–7
	Wales won series 2–0			

Played 4 Wales won 2, Barbarians won 2
Highest scores Wales 31–10 in 1996, Barbarians 31–24 in 1990 and 31–28 in 2011
Biggest wins Wales 31–10 in 1996, Barbarians 31–24 in 1990

1990	Cardiff **Barbarians** 31–24		2011	Cardiff **Barbarians** 31–28
1996	Cardiff **Wales** 31–10		2012	Cardiff **Wales** 30–21

WALES v ARGENTINA

Played 15 Wales won 10, Argentina won 5
Highest scores Wales 44–50 in 2004, Argentina 50–44 in 2004
Biggest wins Wales won 40–6 in 2013, Argentina 45–27 in 2006

1991	Cardiff WC **Wales** 16–7			Series drawn 1–1
1998	Llanelli **Wales** 43–30		2006	1 Puerto Madryn **Argentina** 27–25
1999	1 Buenos Aires **Wales** 36–26			2 Buenos Aires **Argentina** 45–27
	2 Buenos Aires **Wales** 23–16			Argentina won series 2–0
	Wales won series 2–0		2007	Cardiff **Wales** 27–20
1999	Cardiff WC **Wales** 23–18		2009	Cardiff **Wales** 33–16
2001	Cardiff **Argentina** 30–16		2011	Cardiff **Wales** 28–13
2004	1 Tucumán **Argentina** 50–44		2012	Cardiff **Argentina** 26–12
	2 Buenos Aires **Wales** 35–20		2013	Cardiff **Wales** 40–6

WALES v ZIMBABWE

Played 3 Wales won 3
Highest scores Wales 49–11 in 1998, Zimbabwe 14–35 in 1993
Biggest win Wales 49–11 in 1998, Zimbabwe no win

1993	1 Bulawayo **Wales** 35–14			Wales won series 2–0
	2 Harare **Wales** 42–13		1998	Harare **Wales** 49–11

WALES v JAPAN

Played 9 Wales won 8, Japan won 1
Highest scores Wales 98–0 in 2004, Japan 30–53 in 2001
Biggest win Wales 98–0 in 2004, Japan 23–8 in 2013

1993	Cardiff **Wales** 55–5		2004	Cardiff **Wales** 98–0
1995	Bloemfontein WC **Wales 57–10**		2007	Cardiff WC **Wales** 72–18
1999	Cardiff WC **Wales** 64–15		2013	1 Osaka **Wales** 22–18
2001	1 Osaka **Wales** 64–10			2 Tokyo **Japan** 23–8
	2 Tokyo **Wales** 53–30			Series drawn 1–1
	Wales won series 2–0			

INTERNATIONAL RESULTS

WALES v PORTUGAL

Played 1 Wales won 1
Highest scores Wales 102–11 in 1994, Portugal 11–102 in 1994
Biggest win Wales 102–11 in 1994, Portugal no win

1994	Lisbon **Wales** 102–11	

WALES v SPAIN

Played 1 Wales won 1
Highest scores Wales 54–0 in 1994, Spain 0–54 in 1994
Biggest win Wales 54–0 in 1994, Spain no win

1994	Madrid **Wales** 54–0	

WALES v ITALY

Played 23 Wales won 20, Italy won 2, Drawn 1
Highest scores Wales 61–20 in 2015, Italy 30–22 in 2003
Biggest win Wales 61–20 in 2015, Italy 30–22 in 2003

1994	Cardiff **Wales** 29–19	2006	Cardiff **Drawn** 18–18
1996	Cardiff **Wales** 31–26	2007	Rome **Italy** 23–20
1996	Rome **Wales** 31–22	2008	Cardiff **Wales** 47–8
1998	Llanelli **Wales** 23–20	2009	Rome **Wales** 20–15
1999	Treviso **Wales** 60–21	2010	Cardiff **Wales** 33–10
2000	Cardiff **Wales** 47–16	2011	Rome **Wales** 24–16
2001	Rome **Wales** 33–23	2012	Cardiff **Wales** 24–3
2002	Cardiff **Wales** 44–20	2013	Rome **Wales** 26–9
2003	Rome **Italy** 30–22	2014	Cardiff **Wales** 23–15
2003	Canberra WC **Wales** 27–15	2015	Rome **Wales** 61–20
2004	Cardiff **Wales** 44–10	2015	Cardiff **Wales** 23–19
2005	Rome **Wales** 38–8		Non-championship match

WALES v PACIFIC ISLANDS

Played 1 Wales won 1
Highest scores Wales 38–20 in 2006, Pacific Islands 20–38 in 2006
Biggest win Wales 38–20 in 2006, Pacific Islands no win

2006	Cardiff **Wales** 38–20	

WALES v URUGUAY

Played 1 Wales won 1
Highest scores Wales 54–9 in 2015, Uruguay 9–54 in 2015
Biggest win Wales 54–9 in 2015, Uruguay no win

2015	Cardiff WC **Wales** 54–9	

BRITISH/IRISH ISLES v SOUTH AFRICA

Played 46 British/Irish won 17, South Africa won 23, Drawn 6
Highest scores: British/Irish 28–9 in 1974 and 2009, South Africa 35–16 in 1997
Biggest wins: British/Irish 28–9 in 1974 and 2009, South Africa 34–14 in 1962

1891 1 Port Elizabeth **British/Irish** 4–0	Series drawn 2–2
2 Kimberley **British/Irish** 3–0	1962 1 Johannesburg **Drawn** 3–3
3 Cape Town **British/Irish** 4–0	2 Durban **South Africa** 3–0
British/Irish won series 3–0	3 Cape Town **South Africa** 8–3
1896 1 Port Elizabeth **British/Irish** 8–0	4 Bloemfontein **South Africa** 34–14
2 Johannesburg **British/Irish** 17–8	South Africa won series 3–0, with 1
3 Kimberley **British/Irish** 9–3	draw
4 Cape Town **South Africa** 5–0	1968 1 Pretoria **South Africa** 25–20
British/Irish won series 3–1	2 Port Elizabeth **Drawn** 6–6
1903 1 Johannesburg **Drawn** 10–10	3 Cape Town **South Africa** 11–6
2 Kimberley **Drawn** 0–0	4 Johannesburg **South Africa** 19–6
3 Cape Town **South Africa** 8–0	South Africa won series 3–0, with 1
South Africa won series 1–0 with two	draw
drawn	1974 1 Cape Town **British/Irish** 12–3
1910 1 Johannesburg **South Africa** 14–10	2 Pretoria **British/Irish** 28–9
2 Port Elizabeth **British/Irish** 8–3	3 Port Elizabeth **British/Irish** 26–9
3 Cape Town **South Africa** 21–5	4 Johannesburg **Drawn** 13–13
South Africa won series 2–1	British/Irish won series 3–0, with 1
1924 1 Durban **South Africa** 7–3	draw
2 Johannesburg **South Africa** 17–0	1980 1 Cape Town **South Africa** 26–22
3 Port Elizabeth **Drawn** 3–3	2 Bloemfontein **South Africa** 26–19
4 Cape Town **South Africa** 16–9	3 Port Elizabeth **South Africa** 12–10
South Africa won series 3–0, with 1	4 Pretoria **British/Irish** 17–13
draw	South Africa won series 3–1
1938 1 Johannesburg **South Africa** 26–12	1997 1 Cape Town **British/Irish** 25–16
2 Port Elizabeth **South Africa** 19–3	2 Durban **British/Irish** 18–15
3 Cape Town **British/Irish** 21–16	3 Johannesburg **South Africa** 35–16
South Africa won series 2–1	British/Irish won series 2–1
1955 1 Johannesburg **British/Irish** 23–22	2009 1 Durban **South Africa** 26–21
2 Cape Town **South Africa** 25–9	2 Pretoria **South Africa** 28–25
3 Pretoria **British/Irish** 9–6	3 Johannesburg **British/Irish** 28–9
4 Port Elizabeth **South Africa** 22–8	South Africa won series 2–1

BRITISH/IRISH ISLES v NEW ZEALAND

Played 35 British/Irish won 6, New Zealand won 27, Drawn 2
Highest scores: British/Irish 20–7 in 1993, New Zealand 48–18 in 2005
Biggest wins: British/Irish 20–7 in 1993, New Zealand 38–6 in 1983

1904 Wellington **New Zealand** 9–3	4 Wellington **New Zealand** 22–8
1930 1 Dunedin **British/Irish** 6–3	New Zealand won series 3–1
2 Christchurch **New Zealand** 13–10	1950 1 Dunedin **Drawn** 9–9
3 Auckland **New Zealand** 15–10	2 Christchurch **New Zealand** 8–0

3 Wellington **New Zealand** 6–3
4 Auckland **New Zealand** 11–8
New Zealand won series 3–0, with 1
draw

1959 1 Dunedin **New Zealand** 18–17
2 Wellington **New Zealand** 11–8
3 Christchurch **New Zealand** 22–8
4 Auckland **British/Irish** 9–6
New Zealand won series 3–1

1966 1 Dunedin **New Zealand** 20–3
2 Wellington **New Zealand** 16–12
3 Christchurch **New Zealand** 19–6
4 Auckland **New Zealand** 24–11
New Zealand won series 4–0

1971 1 Dunedin **British/Irish** 9–3
2 Christchurch **New Zealand** 22–12
3 Wellington **British/Irish** 13–3
4 Auckland **Drawn** 14–14
British/Irish won series 2–1, with 1 draw

1977 1 Wellington **New Zealand** 16–12
2 Christchurch **British/Irish** 13–9
3 Dunedin **New Zealand** 19–7
4 Auckland **New Zealand** 10–9
New Zealand won series 3–1

1983 1 Christchurch **New Zealand** 16–12
2 Wellington **New Zealand** 9–0
3 Dunedin **New Zealand** 15–8
4 Auckland **New Zealand** 38–6
New Zealand won series 4–0

1993 1 Christchurch **New Zealand** 20–18
2 Wellington **British/Irish** 20–7
3 Auckland **New Zealand** 30–13
New Zealand won series 2–1

2005 1 Christchurch **New Zealand** 21–3
2 Wellington **New Zealand** 48–18
3 Auckland **New Zealand** 38–19
New Zealand won series 3–0

ANGLO–WELSH v NEW ZEALAND

Played 3 New Zealand won 2, Drawn 1
Highest scores Anglo Welsh 5–32 in 1908, New Zealand 32–5 in 1908
Biggest win Anglo Welsh no win, New Zealand 29–0 in 1908

1908 1 Dunedin **New Zealand** 32–5
2 Wellington **Drawn** 3–3
3 Auckland **New Zealand** 29–0

New Zealand won series 2–0, with
1 draw

BRITISH/IRISH ISLES v AUSTRALIA

Played 23 British/Irish won 17, Australia won 6, Drawn 0
Highest scores: British/Irish 41–16 in 2013, Australia 35–14 in 2001
Biggest wins: British/Irish 31–0 in 1966, Australia 35–14 in 2001

1899 1 Sydney **Australia** 13–3
2 Brisbane **British/Irish** 11–0
3 Sydney **British/Irish** 11–10
4 Sydney **British/Irish** 13–0
British/Irish won series 3–1

1904 1 Sydney **British/Irish** 17–0
2 Brisbane **British/Irish** 17–3
3 Sydney **British/Irish** 16–0
British/Irish won series 3–0

1930 Sydney **Australia** 6–5

1950 1 Brisbane **British/Irish** 19–6

2 Sydney **British/Irish** 24–3
British/Irish won series 2–0

1959 1 Brisbane **British/Irish** 17–6
2 Sydney **British/Irish** 24–3
British/Irish won series 2–0

1966 1 Sydney **British/Irish** 11–8
2 Brisbane **British/Irish** 31–0
British/Irish won series 2–0

1989 1 Sydney **Australia** 30–12
2 Brisbane **British/Irish** 19–12
3 Sydney **British/Irish** 19–18

British/Irish won series 2–1

2001   1 Brisbane **British/Irish** 29–13
      2 Melbourne **Australia** 35–14
      3 Sydney **Australia** 29–23
      Australia won series 2–1

2013   1 Brisbane **British/Irish** 23–21
      2 Melbourne **Australia** 16–15
      3 Sydney **British/Irish** 41–16
      British/Irish won series 2–1

BRITISH/IRISH ISLES v ARGENTINA

Played 1 British/Irish won 0, Argentina won 0, Drawn 1
Highest scores: British/Irish 25–25 in 2005, Argentina 25–25 in 2005
Biggest wins: British/Irish no win to date, Argentina no win to date

2005   Cardiff **Drawn** 25–25

FRANCE v SOUTH AFRICA

Played 39 France won 11, South Africa won 22, Drawn 6
Highest scores France 36–26 in 2006, South Africa 52–10 in 1997
Biggest wins France 30–10 in 2002, South Africa 52–10 in 1997

1913   Bordeaux **South Africa** 38–5
1952   Paris **South Africa** 25–3
1958   1 Cape Town **Drawn** 3–3
      2 Johannesburg **France** 9–5
      France won series 1–0, with 1 draw
1961   Paris **Drawn** 0–0
1964   Springs (SA) **France** 8–6
1967   1 Durban **South Africa** 26–3
      2 Bloemfontein **South Africa** 16–3
      3 Johannesburg **France** 19–14
      4 Cape Town **Drawn** 6–6
      South Africa won series 2–1, with 1
      draw
1968   1 Bordeaux **South Africa** 12–9
      2 Paris **South Africa** 16–11
      South Africa won series 2–0
1971   1 Bloemfontein **South Africa** 22–9
      2 Durban **Drawn** 8–8
      South Africa won series 1–0, with 1
      draw
1974   1 Toulouse **South Africa** 13–4
      2 Paris **South Africa** 10–8
      South Africa won series 2–0
1975   1 Bloemfontein **South Africa** 38–25
      2 Pretoria **South Africa** 33–18
      South Africa won series 2–0
1980   Pretoria **South Africa** 37–15

1992   1 Lyons **South Africa** 20–15
      2 Paris **France** 29–16
      Series drawn 1–1
1993   1 Durban **Drawn** 20–20
      2 Johannesburg **France** 18–17
      France won series 1–0, with 1 draw
1995   Durban WC **South Africa** **19–15**
1996   1 Bordeaux **South Africa** 22–12
      2 Paris **South Africa** 13–12
      South Africa won series 2–0
1997   1 Lyons **South Africa** 36–32
      2 Paris **South Africa** 52–10
      South Africa won series 2–0
2001   1 Johannesburg **France** 32–23
      2 Durban **South Africa** 20–15
      Series drawn 1–1
2001   Paris **France** 20–10
2002   Marseilles **France** 30–10
2005   1 Durban **Drawn** 30–30
      2 Port Elizabeth **South Africa** 27–13
      South Africa won series 1–0, with 1
      draw
2005   Paris **France** 26–20
2006   Cape Town **France** 36–26
2009   Toulouse **France** 20–13
2010   Cape Town **South Africa** 42–17
2013   Paris **South Africa** 19–10

FRANCE v NEW ZEALAND

Played 56 France won 12, New Zealand won 43, Drawn 1
Highest scores France 43–31 in 1999, New Zealand 62–13 in 2015
Biggest wins France 22–8 in 1994, New Zealand 61–10 in 2007

1906	Paris **New Zealand** 38–8	
1925	Toulouse **New Zealand** 30–6	
1954	Paris **France** 3–0	
1961	1 Auckland **New Zealand** 13–6	
	2 Wellington **New Zealand** 5–3	
	3 Christchurch **New Zealand** 32–3	
	New Zealand won series 3–0	
1964	Paris **New Zealand** 12–3	
1967	Paris **New Zealand** 21–15	
1968	1 Christchurch **New Zealand** 12–9	
	2 Wellington **New Zealand** 9–3	
	3 Auckland **New Zealand** 19–12	
	New Zealand won series 3–0	
1973	Paris **France** 13–6	
1977	1 Toulouse **France** 18–13	
	2 Paris **New Zealand** 15–3	
	Series drawn 1–1	
1979	1 Christchurch **New Zealand** 23–9	
	2 Auckland **France** 24–19	
	Series drawn 1–1	
1981	1 Toulouse **New Zealand** 13–9	
	2 Paris **New Zealand** 18–6	
	New Zealand won series 2–0	
1984	1 Christchurch **New Zealand** 10–9	
	2 Auckland **New Zealand** 31–18	
	New Zealand won series 2–0	
1986	Christchurch **New Zealand** 18–9	
1986	1 Toulouse **New Zealand** 19–7	
	2 Nantes **France** 16–3	
	Series drawn 1–1	
1987	Auckland WC **New Zealand** 29–9	
1989	1 Christchurch **New Zealand** 25–17	
	2 Auckland **New Zealand** 34–20	
	New Zealand won series 2–0	
1990	1 Nantes **New Zealand** 24–3	
	2 Paris **New Zealand** 30–12	

	New Zealand won series 2–0	
1994	1 Christchurch **France** 22–8	
	2 Auckland **France** 23–20	
	France won series 2–0	
1995	1 Toulouse **France** 22–15	
	2 Paris **New Zealand** 37–12	
	Series drawn 1–1	
1999	Wellington **New Zealand** 54–7	
1999	Twickenham WC **France** 43–31	
2000	1 Paris **New Zealand** 39–26	
	2 Marseilles **France** 42–33	
	Series drawn 1–1	
2001	Wellington **New Zealand** 37–12	
2002	Paris **Drawn** 20–20	
2003	Christchurch **New Zealand** 31–23	
2003	Sydney WC **New Zealand** 40–13	
2004	Paris **New Zealand** 45–6	
2006	1 Lyons **New Zealand** 47–3	
	2 Paris **New Zealand** 23–11	
	New Zealand won series 2–0	
2007	1 Auckland **New Zealand** 42–11	
	2 Wellington **New Zealand** 61–10	
	New Zealand won series 2–0	
2007	Cardiff WC **France** 20–18	
2009	1 Dunedin **France** 27–22	
	2 Wellington **New Zealand** 14–10	
	Series drawn 1–1	
2009	Marseilles **New Zealand** 39–12	
2011	Auckland WC **New Zealand** 37–17	
2011	Auckland WC **New Zealand** 8–7	
2013	1 Auckland **New Zealand** 23–13	
	2 Christchurch **New Zealand** 30–0	
	3 New Plymouth **New Zealand** 24–9	
	New Zealand won series 3–0	
2013	Paris **New Zealand** 26–19	
2015	Cardiff WC **New Zealand** 62–13	

FRANCE v AUSTRALIA

Played 46 France won 18, Australia won 26, Drawn 2
Highest scores France 34–6 in 1976, Australia 59–16 in 2010
Biggest wins France 34–6 in 1976, Australia 59–16 in 2010

1928	Paris **Australia** 11–8		Australia won series 2–1
1948	Paris **France** 13–6	1993	1 Bordeaux **France** 16–13
1958	Paris **France** 19–0		2 Paris **Australia** 24–3
1961	Sydney **France** 15–8		Series drawn 1–1
1967	Paris **France** 20–14	1997	1 Sydney **Australia** 29–15
1968	Sydney **Australia** 11–10		2 Brisbane **Australia** 26–19
1971	1 Toulouse **Australia** 13–11		Australia won series 2–0
	2 Paris **France** 18–9	1998	Paris **Australia** 32–21
	Series drawn 1–1	1999	Cardiff WC **Australia** 35–12
1972	1 Sydney **Drawn** 14–14	2000	Paris **Australia** 18–13
	2 Brisbane **France** 16–15	2001	Marseilles **France** 14–13
	France won series 1–0, with 1 draw	2002	1 Melbourne **Australia** 29–17
1976	1 Bordeaux **France** 18–15		2 Sydney **Australia** 31–25
	2 Paris **France** 34–6		Australia won series 2–0
	France won series 2–0	2004	Paris **France** 27–14
1981	1 Brisbane **Australia** 17–15	2005	Brisbane **Australia** 37–31
	2 Sydney **Australia** 24–14	2005	Marseilles **France** 26–16
	Australia won series 2–0	2008	1 Sydney **Australia** 34–13
1983	1 Clermont–Ferrand **Drawn** 15–15		2 Brisbane **Australia** 40–10
	2 Paris **France** 15–6		Australia won series 2–0
	France won series 1–0, with 1 draw	2008	Paris **Australia** 18–13
1986	Sydney **Australia** 27–14	2009	Sydney **Australia** 22–6
1987	Sydney WC **France** 30–24	2010	Paris **Australia** 59–16
1989	1 Strasbourg **Australia** 32–15	2012	Paris **France** 33–6
	2 Lille **France** 25–19	2014	1 Brisbane **Australia** 50–23
	Series drawn 1–1		2 Melbourne **Australia** 6–0
1990	1 Sydney **Australia** 21–9		3 Sydney **Australia** 39–13
	2 Brisbane **Australia** 48–31		Australia won series 3–0
	3 Sydney **France** 28–19	2014	Paris **France** 29–26

FRANCE v UNITED STATES

Played 7 France won 6, United States won 1, Drawn 0
Highest scores France 41–9 in 1991 and 41–14 in 2003, United States 31–39 in 2004
Biggest wins France 41–9 in 1991, United States 17–3 in 1924

1920	Paris **France** 14–5		*Abandoned after 43 mins
1924	Paris **United States** 17–3		France won series 2–0
1976	Chicago **France** 33–14	2003	Wollongong WC **France** 41–14
1991	1 Denver **France** 41–9	2004	Hartford **France** 39–31
	2 Colorado Springs **France** 10–3*		

FRANCE v ROMANIA

Played 50 France won 40, Romania won 8, Drawn 2
Highest scores France 67–20 in 2000, Romania 21–33 in 1991
Biggest wins France 59–3 in 1924, Romania 15–0 in 1980

1924	Paris **France** 59–3	1981	Narbonne **France** 17–9
1938	Bucharest **France** 11–8	1982	Bucharest **Romania** 13–9
1957	Bucharest **France** 18–15	1983	Toulouse **France** 26–15
1957	Bordeaux **France** 39–0	1984	Bucharest **France** 18–3
1960	Bucharest **Romania** 11–5	1986	Lille **France** 25–13
1961	Bayonne **Drawn** 5–5	1986	Bucharest **France** 20–3
1962	Bucharest **Romania** 3–0	1987	Wellington WC **France** 55–12
1963	Toulouse **Drawn** 6–6	1987	Agen **France** 49–3
1964	Bucharest **France** 9–6	1988	Bucharest **France** 16–12
1965	Lyons **France** 8–3	1990	Auch **Romania** 12–6
1966	Bucharest **France** 9–3	1991	Bucharest **France** 33–21
1967	Nantes **France** 11–3	1991	Béziers WC **France** 30–3
1968	Bucharest **Romania** 15–14	1992	Le Havre **France** 25–6
1969	Tarbes **France** 14–9	1993	Bucharest **France** 37–20
1970	Bucharest **France** 14–3	1993	Brive **France** 51–0
1971	Béziers **France** 31–12	1995	Bucharest **France** 24–15
1972	Constanza **France** 15–6	1995	Tucumán LC **France** **52–8**
1973	Valence **France** 7–6	1996	Aurillac **France** 64–12
1974	Bucharest **Romania** 15–10	1997	Bucharest **France** 51–20
1975	Bordeaux **France** 36–12	1997	Lourdes LC **France** **39–3**
1976	Bucharest **Romania** 15–12	1999	Castres **France** 62–8
1977	Clermont–Ferrand **France** 9–6	2000	Bucharest **France** 67–20
1978	Bucharest **France** 9–6	2003	Lens **France** 56–8
1979	Montauban **France** 30–12	2006	Bucharest **France** 62–14
1980	Bucharest **Romania** 15–0	2015	London WC **France** 38–11

FRANCE v NEW ZEALAND MAORI

Played 1 New Zealand Maori won 1
Highest scores France 3–12 in 1926, New Zealand Maori 12–3 in 1926
Biggest win France no win, New Zealand Maori 12–3 in 1926

1926	Paris **New Zealand Maori** 12–3	

FRANCE v GERMANY

Played 15 France won 13, Germany won 2, Drawn 0
Highest scores France 38–17 in 1933, Germany 17–16 in 1927 and 17–38 in 1933
Biggest wins France 34–0 in 1931, Germany 3–0 in 1938

1927	Paris **France** 30–5		1934	Hanover **France** 13–9
1927	Frankfurt **Germany** 17–16		1935	Paris **France** 18–3
1928	Hanover **France** 14–3		1936	1 Berlin **France** 19–14
1929	Paris **France** 24–0			2 Hanover **France** 6–3
1930	Berlin **France** 31–0			France won series 2–0
1931	Paris **France** 34–0		1937	Paris **France** 27–6
1932	Frankfurt **France** 20–4		1938	Frankfurt **Germany** 3–0
1933	Paris **France** 38–17		1938	Bucharest **France** 8–5

FRANCE v ITALY

Played 37 France won 34, Italy won 3, Drawn 0
Highest scores France 60–13 in 1967, Italy 40–32 in 1997
Biggest wins France 60–13 in 1967, Italy 40–32 in 1997

1937	Paris **France** 43–5		1997	Auch LC **France 30–19**
1952	Milan **France** 17–8		2000	Paris **France** 42–31
1953	Lyons **France** 22–8		2001	Rome **France** 30–19
1954	Rome **France** 39–12		2002	Paris **France** 33–12
1955	Grenoble **France** 24–0		2003	Rome **France** 53–27
1956	Padua **France** 16–3		2004	Paris **France** 25–0
1957	Agen **France** 38–6		2005	Rome **France** 56–13
1958	Naples **France** 11–3		2006	Paris **France** 37–12
1959	Nantes **France** 22–0		2007	Rome **France** 39–3
1960	Treviso **France** 26–0		2008	Paris **France** 25–13
1961	Chambéry **France** 17–0		2009	Rome **France** 50–8
1962	Brescia **France** 6–3		2010	Paris **France** 46–20
1963	Grenoble **France** 14–12		2011	Rome **Italy** 22–21
1964	Parma **France** 12–3		2012	Paris **France** 30–12
1965	Pau **France** 21–0		2013	Rome **Italy** 23–18
1966	Naples **France** 21–0		2014	Paris **France** 30–10
1967	Toulon **France** 60–13		2015	Rome **France** 29–0
1995	Buenos Aires LC **France 34–22**		2015	Twickenham WC **France** 32–10
1997	Grenoble **Italy** 40–32			

FRANCE v BRITISH XVs

Played 5 France won 2, British XVs won 3, Drawn 0
Highest scores France 27–29 in 1989, British XV 36–3 in 1940
Biggest wins France 21–9 in 1945, British XV 36–3 in 1940

1940	Paris **British XV** 36–3		1946	Paris **France** 10–0
1945	Paris **France** 21–9		1989	Paris **British XV** 29–27
1945	Richmond **British XV** 27–6			

FRANCE v WALES XVs

Played 2 France won 1, Wales XV won 1
Highest scores France 12–0 in 1946, Wales XV 8–0 in 1945
Biggest win France 12–0 in 1946, Wales XV 8–0 in 1945

1945	Swansea **Wales XV** 8–0	1946	Paris **France** 12–0

FRANCE v IRELAND XVs

Played 1 France won 1
Highest scores France 4–3 in 1946, Ireland XV 3–4 in 1946
Biggest win France 4–3 in 1946, Ireland XV no win

1946	Dublin **France** 4–3

FRANCE v NEW ZEALAND ARMY

Played 1 New Zealand Army won 1
Highest scores France 9–14 in 1946, New Zealand Army 14–9 in 1946
Biggest win France no win, New Zealand Army 14–9 in 1946

1946	Paris **New Zealand Army** 14–9

FRANCE v ARGENTINA

Played 48 France won 34, Argentina won 13, Drawn 1
Highest scores France 49–10 in 2012, Argentina 41–13 in 2010
Biggest wins France 49–10 in 2012, Argentina 41–13 in 2010

1949	1 Buenos Aires **France** 5–0			France won series 1–0, with 1 draw
	2 Buenos Aires **France** 12–3		1982	1 Toulouse **France** 25–12
	France won series 2–0			2 Paris **France** 13–6
1954	1 Buenos Aires **France** 22–8			France won series 2–0
	2 Buenos Aires **France** 30–3		1985	1 Buenos Aires **Argentina** 24–16
	France won series 2–0			2 Buenos Aires **France** 23–15
1960	1 Buenos Aires **France** 37–3			Series drawn 1–1
	2 Buenos Aires **France** 12–3		1986	1 Buenos Aires **Argentina** 15–13
	3 Buenos Aires **France** 29–6			2 Buenos Aires **France** 22–9
	France won series 3–0			Series drawn 1–1
1974	1 Buenos Aires **France** 20–15		1988	1 Buenos Aires **France** 18–15
	2 Buenos Aires **France** 31–27			2 Buenos Aires **Argentina** 18–6
	France won series 2–0			Series drawn 1–1
1975	1 Lyons **France** 29–6		1988	1 Nantes **France** 29–9
	2 Paris **France** 36–21			2 Lille **France** 28–18
	France won series 2–0			France won series 2–0
1977	1 Buenos Aires **France** 26–3		1992	1 Buenos Aires **France** 27–12
	2 Buenos Aires **Drawn** 18–18			2 Buenos Aires **France** 33–9

France won series 2–0

1992 Nantes **Argentina** 24–20

1995 Buenos Aires LC **France** 47–12

1996 1 Buenos Aires **France** 34–27

2 Buenos Aires **France** 34–15

France won series 2–0

1997 Tarbes LC **France** 32–27

1998 1 Buenos Aires **France** 35–18

2 Buenos Aires **France** 37–12

France won series 2–0

1998 Nantes **France** 34–14

1999 Dublin WC **France** 47–26

2002 Buenos Aires **Argentina** 28–27

2003 1 Buenos Aires **Argentina** 10–6

2 Buenos Aires **Argentina** 33–32

Argentina won series 2–0

2004 Marseilles **Argentina** 24–14

2006 Paris **France** 27–26

2007 Paris WC **Argentina** 17–12

2007 Paris WC **Argentina** 34–10

2008 Marseilles **France** 12–6

2010 Buenos Aires **Argentina** 41–13

2010 Montpellier **France** 15–9

2012 1 Cordoba **Argentina** 23–20

2 Tucuman **France** 49–10

Series drawn 1–1

2012 Lille **France** 39–22

2014 Paris **Argentina** 18–13

FRANCE v CZECHOSLOVAKIA

Played 2 France won 2
Highest scores France 28–3 in 1956, Czechoslovakia 6–19 in 1968
Biggest win France 28–3 in 1956, Czechoslovakia no win

1956 Toulouse **France** 28–3

1968 Prague **France** 19–6

FRANCE v FIJI

Played 9 France won 9
Highest scores France 77–10 in 2001, Fiji 19–28 in 1999
Biggest win France 77–10 in 2001, Fiji no win

1964 Paris **France** 21–3

1987 Auckland WC **France** 31–16

1991 Grenoble WC **France** 33–9

1998 Suva **France** 34–9

1999 Toulouse WC **France** 28–19

2001 Saint Etienne **France** 77–10

2003 Brisbane WC **France** 61–18

2010 Nantes **France** 34–12

2014 Marseilles **France** 40–15

FRANCE v JAPAN

Played 3 France won 3
Highest scores France 51–29 in 2003, Japan 29–51 in 2003
Biggest win France 51–29 in 2003, Japan no win

1973 Bordeaux **France** 30–18

2003 Townsville WC **France** 51–29

2011 Albany WC **France** 47–21

FRANCE v ZIMBABWE

Played 1 France won 1
Highest scores France 70–12 in 1987, Zimbabwe 12–70 in 1987
Biggest win France 70–12 in 1987, Zimbabwe no win

1987	Auckland WC **France** 70–12	

FRANCE v CANADA

Played 9 France won 8, Canada won 1, Drawn 0
Highest scores France 50–6 in 2005, Canada 20–33 in 1999
Biggest wins France 50–6 in 2005, Canada 18–16 in 1994

1991	Agen WC **France** 19–13	2004	Toronto **France** 47–13
1994	Nepean **Canada** 18–16	2005	Nantes **France** 50–6
1994	Besançon **France** 28–9	2011	Napier WC **France** 46–19
1999	Béziers WC **France** 33–20	2015	Milton Keynes WC **France** 41–18
2002	Paris **France** 35–3		

FRANCE v TONGA

Played 5 France won 3, Tonga won 2
Highest scores France 43–8 in 2005, Tonga 20–16 in 1999
Biggest win France 43–8 in 2005, Tonga 19–14 in 2011

1995	Pretoria WC **France** 38–10	2011	Wellington WC **Tonga** 19–14
1999	Nuku'alofa **Tonga** 20–16	2013	Le Havre **France** 38–18
2005	Toulouse **France** 43–8		

FRANCE v IVORY COAST

Played 1 France won 1
Highest scores France 54–18 in 1995, Ivory Coast 18–54 in 1995
Biggest win France 54–18 in 1995, Ivory Coast no win

1995	Rustenburg WC **France** 54–18	

FRANCE v SAMOA

Played 3 France won 3
Highest scores France 43–5 in 2009, Samoa 22–39 in 1999
Biggest win France 43–5 in 2009, Samoa no win

1999	Apia **France** 39–22	2012	Paris **France** 22–14
2009	Paris **France** 43–5		

FRANCE v NAMIBIA

Played 2 France won 2
Highest scores France 87–10 in 2007, Namibia 13–47 in 1999
Biggest win France 87–10 in 2007, Namibia no win

1999　Bordeaux WC **France** 47–13	2007　Toulouse WC **France** 87–10

FRANCE v GEORGIA

Played 1 France won 1
Highest scores France 64–7 in 2007, Georgia 7–64 in 2007
Biggest win France 64–7 in 2007, Georgia no win

2007　Marseilles WC **France** 64–7

FRANCE v PACIFIC ISLANDS

Played 1 Wales won 1
Highest scores France 42–17 in 2008, Pacific Islands 17–42 in 2008
Biggest win France 42–17 in 2008, Pacific Islands no win

2008　Sochaux **France** 42–17

SOUTH AFRICA v NEW ZEALAND

Played 91 New Zealand won 53, South Africa won 35, Drawn 3
Highest scores New Zealand 55–35 in 1997, South Africa 46–40 in 2000
Biggest wins New Zealand 52–16 in 2003, South Africa 17–0 in 1928

1921　1 Dunedin **New Zealand** 13–5	South Africa won series 4–0
2 Auckland **South Africa** 9–5	1956　1 Dunedin **New Zealand** 10–6
3 Wellington **Drawn** 0–0	2 Wellington **South Africa** 8–3
Series drawn 1–1, with 1 draw	3 Christchurch **New Zealand** 17–10
1928　1 Durban **South Africa** 17–0	4 Auckland **New Zealand** 11–5
2 Johannesburg **New Zealand** 7–6	New Zealand won series 3–1
3 Port Elizabeth **South Africa** 11–6	1960　1 Johannesburg **South Africa** 13–0
4 Cape Town **New Zealand** 13–5	2 Cape Town **New Zealand** 11–3
Series drawn 2–2	3 Bloemfontein **Drawn** 11–11
1937　1 Wellington **New Zealand** 13–7	4 Port Elizabeth **South Africa** 8–3
2 Christchurch **South Africa** 13–6	South Africa won series 2–1, with 1 draw
3 Auckland **South Africa** 17–6	1965　1 Wellington **New Zealand** 6–3
South Africa won series 2–1	2 Dunedin **New Zealand** 13–0
1949　1 Cape Town **South Africa** 15–11	3 Christchurch **South Africa** 19–16
2 Johannesburg **South Africa** 12–6	4 Auckland **New Zealand** 20–3
3 Durban **South Africa** 9–3	New Zealand won series 3–1
4 Port Elizabeth **South Africa** 11–8	1970　1 Pretoria **South Africa** 17–6

2 Cape Town **New Zealand** 9–8	2001 Cape Town TN **New Zealand** 12–3
3 Port Elizabeth **South Africa** 14–3	2001 Auckland TN **New Zealand** 26–15
4 Johannesburg **South Africa** 20–17	2002 Wellington TN **New Zealand** 41–20
South Africa won series 3–1	2002 Durban TN **New Zealand** 30–23
1976 1 Durban **South Africa** 16–7	2003 Pretoria TN **New Zealand** 52–16
2 Bloemfontein **New Zealand** 15–9	2003 Dunedin TN **New Zealand** 19–11
3 Cape Town **South Africa** 15–10	2003 Melbourne WC **New Zealand** 29–9
4 Johannesburg **South Africa** 15–14	2004 Christchurch TN **New Zealand** 23–21
South Africa won series 3–1	2004 Johannesburg TN **South Africa** 40–26
1981 1 Christchurch **New Zealand** 14–9	2005 Cape Town TN **South Africa** 22–16
2 Wellington **South Africa** 24–12	2005 Dunedin TN **New Zealand** 31–27
3 Auckland **New Zealand** 25–22	2006 Wellington TN **New Zealand** 35–17
New Zealand won series 2–1	2006 Pretoria TN **New Zealand** 45–26
1992 Johannesburg **New Zealand** 27–24	2006 Rustenburg TN **South Africa** 21–20
1994 1 Dunedin **New Zealand** 22–14	2007 Durban TN **New Zealand** 26–21
2 Wellington **New Zealand** 13–9	2007 Christchurch TN **New Zealand** 33–6
3 Auckland **Drawn** 18–18	2008 Wellington TN **New Zealand** 19–8
New Zealand won series 2–0, with 1 draw	2008 Dunedin TN **South Africa** 30–28
1995 Johannesburg WC **South Africa** 15–12	2008 Cape Town TN **New Zealand** 19–0
(aet)	2009 Bloemfontein TN **South Africa** 28–19
1996 Christchurch TN **New Zealand** 15–11	2009 Durban TN **South Africa** 31–19
1996 Cape Town TN **New Zealand** 29–18	2009 Hamilton TN **South Africa** 32–29
1996 1 Durban **New Zealand** 23–19	2010 Auckland TN **New Zealand** 32–12
2 Pretoria **New Zealand** 33–26	2010 Wellington TN **New Zealand** 31–17
3 Johannesburg **South Africa** 32–22	2010 Soweto TN **New Zealand** 29–22
New Zealand won series 2–1	2011 Wellington TN **New Zealand** 40–7
1997 Johannesburg TN **New Zealand** 35–32	2011 Port Elizabeth TN **South Africa** 18–5
1997 Auckland TN **New Zealand** 55–35	2012 Dunedin RC **New Zealand** 21–11
1998 Wellington TN **South Africa** 13–3	2012 Soweto RC **New Zealand** 32–16
1998 Durban TN **South Africa** 24–23	2013 Auckland RC **New Zealand** 29–13
1999 Dunedin TN **New Zealand** 28–0	2013 Johannesburg RC **New Zealand** 38–27
1999 Pretoria TN **New Zealand** 34–18	2014 Wellington RC **New Zealand** 14–10
1999 Cardiff WC **South Africa** 22–18	2014 Johannesburg RC **South Africa** 27–25
2000 Christchurch TN **New Zealand** 25–12	2015 Johannesburg RC **New Zealand** 27–20
2000 Johannesburg TN **South Africa** 46–40	2015 Twickenham WC **New Zealand** 20–18

SOUTH AFRICA v AUSTRALIA

Played 81 South Africa won 45, Australia won 35, Drawn 1
Highest scores South Africa 61–22 in 1997, Australia 49–0 in 2006
Biggest wins South Africa 53–8 in 2008, Australia 49–0 in 2006

1933 1 Cape Town **South Africa** 17–3	South Africa won series 2–0
2 Durban **Australia** 21–6	1953 1 Johannesburg **South Africa** 25–3
3 Johannesburg **South Africa** 12–3	2 Cape Town **Australia** 18–14
4 Port Elizabeth **South Africa** 11–0	3 Durban **South Africa** 18–8
5 Bloemfontein **Australia** 15–4	4 Port Elizabeth **South Africa** 22–9
South Africa won series 3–2	South Africa won series 3–1
1937 1 Sydney **South Africa** 9–5	1956 1 Sydney **South Africa** 9–0
2 Sydney **South Africa** 26–17	2 Brisbane **South Africa** 9–0

South Africa won series 2–0
| 1961 | 1 Johannesburg **South Africa** 28–3

2 Port Elizabeth **South Africa** 23–11
South Africa won series 2–0
1963 1 Pretoria **South Africa** 14–3
2 Cape Town **Australia** 9–5
3 Johannesburg **Australia** 11–9
4 Port Elizabeth **South Africa** 22–6
Series drawn 2–2
1965 1 Sydney **Australia** 18–11
2 Brisbane **Australia** 12–8
Australia won series 2–0
1969 1 Johannesburg **South Africa** 30–11
2 Durban **South Africa** 16–9
3 Cape Town **South Africa** 11–3
4 Bloemfontein **South Africa** 19–8
South Africa won series 4–0
1971 1 Sydney **South Africa** 19–11
2 Brisbane **South Africa** 14–6
3 Sydney **South Africa** 18–6
South Africa won series 3–0
1992 Cape Town **Australia** 26–3
1993 1 Sydney **South Africa** 19–12
2 Brisbane **Australia** 28–20
3 Sydney **Australia** 19–12
Australia won series 2–1
1995 Cape Town WC **South Africa** 27–18
1996 Sydney TN **Australia** 21–16
1996 Bloemfontein TN **South Africa** 25–19
1997 Brisbane TN **Australia** 32–20
1997 Pretoria TN **South Africa** 61–22
1998 Perth TN **South Africa** 14–13
1998 Johannesburg TN **South Africa** 29–15
1999 Brisbane TN **Australia** 32–6
1999 Cape Town TN **South Africa** 10–9
1999 Twickenham WC **Australia** 27–21
2000 Melbourne **Australia** 44–23
2000 Sydney TN **Australia** 26–6

2000 Durban TN **Australia** 19–18
2001 Pretoria TN **South Africa** 20–15
2001 Perth TN **Drawn** 14–14
2002 Brisbane TN **Australia** 38–27
2002 Johannesburg TN **South Africa** 33–31
2003 Cape Town TN **South Africa** 26–22
2003 Brisbane TN **Australia** 29–9
2004 Perth TN **Australia** 30–26
2004 Durban TN **South Africa** 23–19
2005 Sydney **Australia** 30–12
2005 Johannesburg **South Africa** 33–20
2005 Pretoria TN **South Africa** 22–16
2005 Perth TN **South Africa** 22–19
2006 Brisbane TN **Australia** 49–0
2006 Sydney TN **Australia** 20–18
2006 Johannesburg TN **South Africa** 24–16
2007 Cape Town TN **South Africa** 22–19
2007 Sydney TN **Australia** 25–17
2008 Perth TN **Australia** 16–9
2008 Durban TN **Australia** 27–15
2008 Johannesburg TN **South Africa** 53–8
2009 Cape Town TN **South Africa** 29–17
2009 Perth TN **South Africa** 32–25
2009 Brisbane TN **Australia** 21–6
2010 Brisbane TN **Australia** 30–13
2010 Pretoria TN **South Africa** 44–31
2010 Bloemfontein TN **Australia** 41–39
2011 Sydney TN **Australia** 39–20
2011 Durban TN **Australia** 14–9
2011 Wellington WC **Australia** 11–9
2012 Perth RC **Australia** 26–19
2012 Pretoria RC **South Africa** 31–8
2013 Brisbane RC **South Africa** 38–12
2013 Cape Town RC **South Africa** 28–8
2014 Perth RC **Australia** 24–23
2014 Cape Town RC **South Africa** 28–10
2015 Brisbane RC **Australia** 24–20

SOUTH AFRICA v WORLD XVs

Played 3 South Africa won 3
Highest scores South Africa 45–24 in 1977, World XV 24–45 in 1977
Biggest win South Africa 45–24 in 1977, World XV no win

1977 Pretoria **South Africa** 45–24
1989 1 Cape Town **South Africa** 20–19

2 Johannesburg **South Africa** 22–16
South Africa won series 2–0

SOUTH AFRICA v SOUTH AMERICA

Played 8 South Africa won 7, South America won 1, Drawn 0
Highest scores South Africa 50–18 in 1982, South America 21–12 in 1982
Biggest wins South Africa 50–18 in 1982, South America 21–12 in 1982

1980 1 Johannesburg **South Africa** 24–9	1982 1 Pretoria **South Africa** 50–18
2 Durban **South Africa** 18–9	2 Bloemfontein **South America** 21–12
South Africa won series 2–0	Series drawn 1–1
1980 1 Montevideo **South Africa** 22–13	1984 1 Pretoria **South Africa** 32–15
2 Santiago **South Africa** 30–16	2 Cape Town **South Africa** 22–13
South Africa won series 2–0	South Africa won series 2–0

SOUTH AFRICA v UNITED STATES

Played 4 South Africa won 4
Highest scores South Africa 64–10 in 2007 and 64–0 in 2015, United States 20–43 in 2001
Biggest win South Africa 64–0 in 2015, United States no win

1981 Glenville **South Africa** 38–7	2007 Montpellier WC **South Africa** 64–10
2001 Houston **South Africa** 43–20	2015 London WC **South Africa** 64–0

SOUTH AFRICA v NEW ZEALAND CAVALIERS

Played 4 South Africa won 3, New Zealand Cavaliers won 1, Drawn 0
Highest scores South Africa 33–18 in 1986, New Zealand Cavaliers 19–18 in 1986
Biggest wins South Africa 33–18 in 1986, New Zealand Cavaliers 19–18 in 1986

1986 1 Cape Town **South Africa** 21–15	3 Pretoria **South Africa** 33–18
2 Durban **New Zealand Cavaliers**	4 Johannesburg **South Africa** 24–10
19–18	South Africa won series 3–1

SOUTH AFRICA v ARGENTINA

Played 22 South Africa won 20, Argentina won 1, Drawn 1
Highest scores South Africa 73–13 in 2013, Argentina 37–25 in 2015
Biggest wins South Africa 73–13 in 2013, Argentina 37–25 in 2015

1993 1 Buenos Aires **South Africa** 29–26	2005 Buenos Aires **South Africa** 34–23
2 Buenos Aires **South Africa** 52–23	2007 Paris WC **South Africa** 37–13
South Africa won series 2–0	2008 Johannesburg **South Africa** 63–9
1994 1 Port Elizabeth **South Africa** 42–22	2012 Cape Town RC **South Africa** 27–6
2 Johannesburg **South Africa** 46–26	2012 Mendoza RC **Drawn** 16–16
South Africa won series 2–0	2013 Soweto RC **South Africa** 73–13
1996 1 Buenos Aires **South Africa** 46–15	2013 Mendoza RC **South Africa** 22–17
2 Buenos Aires **South Africa** 44–21	2014 Pretoria RC **South Africa** 13–6
South Africa win series 2–0	2014 Salta RC **South Africa** 33–31
2000 Buenos Aires **South Africa** 37–33	2015 Durban RC **Argentina** 37–25
2002 Springs **South Africa** 49–29	2015 Buenos Aires **South Africa** 26–12
2003 Port Elizabeth **South Africa** 26–25	2015 London WC **South Africa** 24–13
2004 Buenos Aires **South Africa** 39–7	

SOUTH AFRICA v SAMOA

Played 9 South Africa won 9
Highest scores South Africa 60–8 in 1995, 60–18 in 2002 and 60–10 in 2003, Samoa 23–56 in 2013
Biggest win South Africa 60–8 in 1995 and 59–7 in 2007, Samoa no win

1995	Johannesburg **South Africa** 60–8	2007	Paris WC **South Africa** 59–7
1995	Johannesburg WC **South Africa** 42–14	2011	Albany WC **South Africa** 13–5
2002	Pretoria **South Africa** 60–18	2013	Pretoria QT **South Africa** 56–23
2003	Brisbane WC **South Africa** 60–10	2015	Birmingham WC **South Africa** 46–6
2007	Johannesburg **South Africa** 35–8		

SOUTH AFRICA v ROMANIA

Played 1 South Africa won 1
Highest score South Africa 21–8 in 1995, Romania 8–21 in 1995
Biggest win South Africa 21–8 in 1995, Romania no win

1995	Cape Town WC **South Africa** 21–8

SOUTH AFRICA v CANADA

Played 2 South Africa won 2
Highest scores South Africa 51–18 in 2000, Canada 18–51 in 2000
Biggest win South Africa 51–18 in 2000, Canada no win

1995	Port Elizabeth WC **South Africa** 20–0	2000	East London **South Africa** 51–18

SOUTH AFRICA v ITALY

Played 12 South Africa won 12
Highest scores South Africa 101–0 in 1999, Italy 31–62 in 1997
Biggest win South Africa 101–0 in 1999, Italy no win

1995	Rome **South Africa** 40–21	2008	Cape Town **South Africa** 26–0
1997	Bologna **South Africa** 62–31	2009	Udine **South Africa** 32–10
1999	1 Port Elizabeth **South Africa** 74–3	2010	1 Witbank **South Africa** 29–13
	2 Durban **South Africa** 101–0		2 East London **South Africa** 55–11
	South Africa won series 2–0		South Africa won series 2–0
2001	Port Elizabeth **South Africa** 60–14	2013	Durban QT **South Africa** 44–10
2001	Genoa **South Africa** 54–26	2014	Padua **South Africa** 22–6

SOUTH AFRICA v FIJI

Played 3 South Africa won 3
Highest scores South Africa 49–3 in 2011, Fiji 20–37 in 2007
Biggest win South Africa 49–3 in 2011, Fiji no win

1996	Pretoria **South Africa** 43–18		2011	Wellington WC **South Africa** 49–3
2007	Marseilles WC **South Africa** 37–20			

SOUTH AFRICA v TONGA

Played 2 South Africa won 2
Higest scores South Africa 74–10 in 1997, Tonga 25–30 in 2007
Biggest win South Africa 74–10 in 1997, Tonga no win

1997	Cape Town **South Africa** 74–10		2007	Lens WC **South Africa** 30–25

SOUTH AFRICA v SPAIN

Played 1 South Africa won 1
Highest scores South Africa 47–3 in 1999, Spain 3–47 in 1999
Biggest win South Africa 47–3 in 1999, Spain no win

1999	Murrayfield WC **South Africa** 47–3

SOUTH AFRICA v URUGUAY

Played 3 South Africa won 3
Highest scores South Africa 134–3 in 2005, Uruguay 6–72 in 2003
Biggest win South Africa 134–3 in 2005, Uruguay no win

1999	Glasgow WC **South Africa** 39–3		2005	East London **South Africa** 134–3
2003	Perth WC **South Africa** 72–6			

SOUTH AFRICA v GEORGIA

Played 1 South Africa won 1
Highest scores South Africa 46–19 in 2003, Georgia 19–46 in 2003
Biggest win South Africa 46–19 in 2003, Georgia no win

2003	Sydney WC **South Africa** 46–19

SOUTH AFRICA v PACIFIC ISLANDS

Played 1 South Africa won 1
Highest scores South Africa 38–24 in 2004, Pacific Islands 24–38 in 2004
Biggest win South Africa 38–24 in 2004, Pacific Islands no win

2004	Gosford (Aus) **South Africa** 38–24

SOUTH AFRICA v NAMIBIA

Played 2 South Africa won 2
Highest scores South Africa 105–13 in 2007, Namibia 13–105 in 2007
Biggest win South Africa 105–13 in 2007, Namibia no win

2007	Cape Town **South Africa** 105–13		2011	Albany WC **South Africa** 87–0

SOUTH AFRICA v JAPAN

Played 1 Japan won 1
Highest scores South Africa 32–34 in 2015, Japan 34–32 in 2015
Biggest win South Africa no win, Japan 34–32 in 2015

2015 Brighton WC **Japan** 34–32

NEW ZEALAND v AUSTRALIA

Played 155 New Zealand won 106, Australia won 42, Drawn 7
Highest scores New Zealand 51–20 in 2014, Australia 35–39 in 2000
Biggest wins New Zealand 43–6 in 1996, Australia 28–7 in 1999

1903 Sydney **New Zealand** 22–3	3 Sydney **New Zealand** 21–13
1905 Dunedin **New Zealand** 14–3	New Zealand won series 2–1
1907 1 Sydney **New Zealand** 26–6	1934 1 Sydney **Australia** 25–11
2 Brisbane **New Zealand** 14–5	2 Sydney **Drawn** 3–3
3 Sydney **Drawn** 5–5	Australia won series 1–0, with 1
New Zealand won series 2–0, with 1	draw
draw	1936 1 Wellington **New Zealand** 11–6
1910 1 Sydney **New Zealand** 6–0	2 Dunedin **New Zealand** 38–13
2 Sydney **Australia** 11–0	New Zealand won series 2–0
3 Sydney **New Zealand** 28–13	1938 1 Sydney **New Zealand** 24–9
New Zealand won series 2–1	2 Brisbane **New Zealand** 20–14
1913 1 Wellington **New Zealand** 30–5	3 Sydney **New Zealand** 14–6
2 Dunedin **New Zealand** 25–13	New Zealand won series 3–0
3 Christchurch **Australia** 16–5	1946 1 Dunedin **New Zealand** 31–8
New Zealand won series 2–1	2 Auckland **New Zealand** 14–10
1914 1 Sydney **New Zealand** 5–0	New Zealand won series 2–0
2 Brisbane **New Zealand** 17–0	1947 1 Brisbane **New Zealand** 13–5
3 Sydney **New Zealand** 22–7	2 Sydney **New Zealand** 27–14
New Zealand won series 3–0	New Zealand won series 2–0
1929 1 Sydney **Australia** 9–8	1949 1 Wellington **Australia** 11–6
2 Brisbane **Australia** 17–9	2 Auckland **Australia** 16–9
3 Sydney **Australia** 15–13	Australia won series 2–0
Australia won series 3–0	1951 1 Sydney **New Zealand** 8–0
1931 Auckland **New Zealand** 20–13	2 Sydney **New Zealand** 17–11
1932 1 Sydney **Australia** 22–17	3 Brisbane **New Zealand** 16–6
2 Brisbane **New Zealand** 21–3	New Zealand won series 3–0

1952 1 Christchurch **Australia** 14–9
2 Wellington **New Zealand** 15–8
Series drawn 1–1
1955 1 Wellington **New Zealand** 16–8
2 Dunedin **New Zealand** 8–0
3 Auckland **Australia** 8–3
New Zealand won series 2–1
1957 1 Sydney **New Zealand** 25–11
2 Brisbane **New Zealand** 22–9
New Zealand won series 2–0
1958 1 Wellington **New Zealand** 25–3
2 Christchurch **Australia** 6–3
3 Auckland **New Zealand** 17–8
New Zealand won series 2–1
1962 1 Brisbane **New Zealand** 20–6
2 Sydney **New Zealand** 14–5
New Zealand won series 2–0
1962 1 Wellington **Drawn** 9–9
2 Dunedin **New Zealand** 3–0
3 Auckland **New Zealand** 16–8
New Zealand won series 2–0, with 1
draw
1964 1 Dunedin **New Zealand** 14–9
2 Christchurch **New Zealand** 18–3
3 Wellington **Australia** 20–5
New Zealand won series 2–1
1967 Wellington **New Zealand** 29–9
1968 1 Sydney **New Zealand** 27–11
2 Brisbane **New Zealand** 19–18
New Zealand won series 2–0
1972 1 Wellington **New Zealand** 29–6
2 Christchurch **New Zealand** 30–17
3 Auckland **New Zealand** 38–3
New Zealand won series 3–0
1974 1 Sydney **New Zealand** 11–6
2 Brisbane **Drawn** 16–16
3 Sydney **New Zealand** 16–6
New Zealand won series 2–0, with 1
draw
1978 1 Wellington **New Zealand** 13–12
2 Christchurch **New Zealand** 22–6
3 Auckland **Australia** 30–16
New Zealand won series 2–1
1979 Sydney **Australia** 12–6
1980 1 Sydney **Australia** 13–9
2 Brisbane **New Zealand** 12–9
3 Sydney **Australia** 26–10
Australia won series 2–1
1982 1 Christchurch **New Zealand** 23–16
2 Wellington **Australia** 19–16

3 Auckland **New Zealand** 33–18
New Zealand won series 2–1
1983 Sydney **New Zealand** 18–8
1984 1 Sydney **Australia** 16–9
2 Brisbane **New Zealand** 19–15
3 Sydney **New Zealand** 25–24
New Zealand won series 2–1
1985 Auckland **New Zealand** 10–9
1986 1 Wellington **Australia** 13–12
2 Dunedin **New Zealand** 13–12
3 Auckland **Australia** 22–9
Australia won series 2–1
1987 Sydney **New Zealand** 30–16
1988 1 Sydney **New Zealand** 32–7
2 Brisbane **Drawn** 19–19
3 Sydney **New Zealand** 30–9
New Zealand won series 2–0, with 1 draw
1989 Auckland **New Zealand** 24–12
1990 1 Christchurch **New Zealand** 21–6
2 Auckland **New Zealand** 27–17
3 Wellington **Australia** 21–9
New Zealand won series 2–1
1991 1 Sydney **Australia** 21–12
2 Auckland **New Zealand** 6–3
1991 Dublin WC **Australia** 16–6
1992 1 Sydney **Australia** 16–15
2 Brisbane **Australia** 19–17
3 Sydney **New Zealand** 26–23
Australia won series 2–1
1993 Dunedin **New Zealand** 25–10
1994 Sydney **Australia** 20–16
1995 Auckland **New Zealand** 28–16
1995 Sydney **New Zealand** 34–23
1996 Wellington TN **New Zealand** 43–6
1996 Brisbane TN **New Zealand** 32–25
New Zealand won series 2–0
1997 Christchurch **New Zealand** 30–13
1997 Melbourne TN **New Zealand** 33–18
1997 Dunedin TN **New Zealand** 36–24
New Zealand won series 3–0
1998 Melbourne TN **Australia** 24–16
1998 Christchurch TN **Australia** 27–23
1998 Sydney Australia 19–14
Australia won series 3–0
1999 Auckland TN **New Zealand** 34–15
1999 Sydney TN **Australia** 28–7
Series drawn 1–1
2000 Sydney TN **New Zealand** 39–35
2000 Wellington TN **Australia** 24–23
Series drawn 1–1

2001	Dunedin TN **Australia** 23–15	2009	Wellington TN **New Zealand** 33–6
2001	Sydney TN **Australia** 29–26	2009	Tokyo **New Zealand** 32–19
	Australia won series 2–0		New Zealand won series 4–0
2002	Christchurch TN **New Zealand** 12–6	2010	Melbourne TN **New Zealand** 49–28
2002	Sydney TN **Australia** 16–14	2010	Christchurch TN **New Zealand** 20–10
	Series drawn 1–1	2010	Sydney TN **New Zealand** 23–22
2003	Sydney TN **New Zealand** 50–21	2010	Hong Kong **Australia** 26–24
2003	Auckland TN **New Zealand** 21–17		New Zealand won series 3–1
	New Zealand won series 2–0	2011	Auckland TN **New Zealand** 30–14
2003	Sydney WC **Australia** 22–10	2011	Brisbane TN **Australia** 25–20
2004	Wellington TN **New Zealand** 16–7	2011	Auckland WC **New Zealand** 20–6
2004	Sydney TN **Australia** 23–18	2012	Sydney RC **New Zealand** 27–19
	Series drawn 1–1	2012	Auckland RC **New Zealand** 22–0
2005	Sydney TN **New Zealand** 30–13	2012	Brisbane **Drawn** 18–18
2005	Auckland TN **New Zealand** 34–24		New Zealand won series 2–0, with
	New Zealand won series 2–0		1 draw
2006	Christchurch TN **New Zealand** 32–12	2013	Sydney RC **New Zealand** 47–29
2006	Brisbane TN **New Zealand** 13–9	2013	Wellington RC **New Zealand** 27–16
2006	Auckland TN **New Zealand** 34–27	2013	Dunedin **New Zealand** 41–33
	New Zealand won series 3–0		New Zealand won series 3–0
2007	Melbourne TN **Australia** 20–15	2014	Sydney RC **Drawn** 12–12
2007	Auckland TN **New Zealand** 26–12	2014	Auckland RC **New Zealand** 51–20
	Series drawn 1–1	2014	Brisbane **New Zealand** 29–28
2008	Sydney TN **Australia** 34–19		New Zealand won series 2–0, with 1
2008	Auckland TN **New Zealand** 39–10		draw
2008	Brisbane TN **New Zealand** 28–24	2015	Sydney RC **Australia** 27–19
2008	Hong Kong **New Zealand** 19–14	2015	Auckland **New Zealand** 41–13
	New Zealand won series 3–1		Series drawn 1-1
2009	Auckland TN **New Zealand** 22–16	2015	Twickenham WC **New Zealand** 34–17
2009	Sydney TN **New Zealand** 19–18		

NEW ZEALAND v UNITED STATES

Played 3 New Zealand won 3
Highest scores New Zealand 74–6 in 2014, United States 6–46 in 1991 and 6–74 in 2014
Biggest win New Zealand 74–6 in 2014, United States no win

1913	Berkeley **New Zealand** 51–3	2014	Chicago **New Zealand** 74–6
1991	Gloucester WC **New Zealand** 46–6		

NEW ZEALAND v ROMANIA

Played 2 New Zealand won 2
Highest score New Zealand 85–8 in 2007, Romania 8–85 in 2007
Biggest win New Zealand 85–8 in 2007, Romania no win

1981	Bucharest **New Zealand** 14–6	2007	Toulouse WC **New Zealand** 85–8

NEW ZEALAND v ARGENTINA

Played 22 New Zealand won 21, Drawn 1
Highest scores New Zealand 93–8 in 1997, Argentina 21–21 in 1985
Biggest win New Zealand 93–8 in 1997, Argentina no win

1985	1 Buenos Aires **New Zealand** 33–20		2001	Christchurch **New Zealand** 67–19
	2 Buenos Aires **Drawn** 21–21		2001	Buenos Aires **New Zealand** 24–20
	New Zealand won series 1–0, with 1 draw		2004	Hamilton **New Zealand** 41–7
1987	Wellington WC **New Zealand** 46–15		2006	Buenos Aires **New Zealand** 25–19
1989	1 Dunedin **New Zealand** 60–9		2011	Auckland WC **New Zealand** 33–10
	2 Wellington **New Zealand** 49–12		2012	Wellington RC **New Zealand** 21–5
	New Zealand won series 2–0		2012	La Plata RC **New Zealand** 54–15
1991	1 Buenos Aires **New Zealand** 28–14		2013	Hamilton RC **New Zealand** 28–13
	2 Buenos Aires **New Zealand** 36–6		2013	La Plata RC **New Zealand** 33–15
	New Zealand won series 2–0		2014	Napier RC **New Zealand** 28–9
1997	1 Wellington **New Zealand** 93–8		2014	La Plata RC **New Zealand** 34–13
	2 Hamilton **New Zealand** 62–10		2015	Christchurch RC **New Zealand** 39–18
	New Zealand won series 2–0		2015	Wembley WC **New Zealand** 26–16

NEW ZEALAND v ITALY

Played 12 New Zealand won 12
Highest scores New Zealand 101–3 in 1999, Italy 21–31 in 1991
Biggest win New Zealand 101–3 in 1999, Italy no win

1987	Auckland WC **New Zealand** 70–6		2003	Melbourne WC **New Zealand** 70–7
1991	Leicester WC **New Zealand** 31–21		2004	Rome **New Zealand** 59–10
1995	Bologna **New Zealand** 70–6		2007	Marseilles WC **New Zealand** 76–14
1999	Huddersfield WC **New Zealand** 101–3		2009	Christchurch **New Zealand** 27–6
2000	Genoa **New Zealand** 56–19		2009	Milan **New Zealand** 20–6
2002	Hamilton **New Zealand** 64–10		2012	Rome **New Zealand** 42–10

NEW ZEALAND v FIJI

Played 5 New Zealand won 5
Highest scores New Zealand 91–0 in 2005, Fiji 18–68 in 2002
Biggest win New Zealand 91–0 in 2005, Fiji no win

1987	Christchurch WC **New Zealand** 74–13		2005	Albany **New Zealand** 91–0
1997	Albany **New Zealand** 71–5		2011	Dunedin **New Zealand** 60–14
2002	Wellington **New Zealand** 68–18			

NEW ZEALAND v CANADA

Played 5 New Zealand won 5
Highest scores New Zealand 79–15 in 2011, Canada 15–79 in 2011
Biggest win New Zealand 73–7 in 1995, Canada no win

1991	Lille WC **New Zealand** 29–13		2007	Hamilton **New Zealand** 64–13
1995	Auckland **New Zealand** 73–7		2011	Wellington WC **New Zealand** 79–15
2003	Melbourne WC **New Zealand** 68–6			

NEW ZEALAND v WORLD XVs

Played 3 New Zealand won 2, World XV won 1, Drawn 0
Highest scores New Zealand 54–26 in 1992, World XV 28–14 in 1992
Biggest wins New Zealand 54–26 in 1992, World XV 28–14 in 1992

1992	1 Christchurch **World XV** 28–14		3 Auckland **New Zealand** 26–15
	2 Wellington **New Zealand** 54–26		New Zealand won series 2–1

NEW ZEALAND v SAMOA

Played 6 New Zealand won 6
Highest scores New Zealand 101–14 in 2008, Samoa 16–25 in 2015
Biggest win New Zealand 101–14 in 2008, Samoa no win

1993	Auckland **New Zealand** 35–13	2001	Albany **New Zealand** 50–6
1996	Napier **New Zealand** 51–10	2008	New Plymouth **New Zealand** 101–14
1999	Albany **New Zealand** 71–13	2015	Apia **New Zealand** 25–16

NEW ZEALAND v JAPAN

Played 3 New Zealand won 3
Highest scores New Zealand 145–17 in 1995, Japan 17–145 in 1995
Biggest win New Zealand 145–17 in 1995, Japan no win

1995	Bloemfontein WC **New Zealand** 145–17	2013	Tokyo **New Zealand** 54–6
2011	Hamilton WC **New Zealand** 83–7		

NEW ZEALAND v TONGA

Played 5 New Zealand won 5
Highest scores New Zealand 102–0 in 2000, Tonga 10–41 in 2011
Biggest win New Zealand 102–0 in 2000, Tonga no win

1999	Bristol WC **New Zealand** 45–9	2011	Auckland WC **New Zealand** 41–10
2000	Albany **New Zealand** 102–0	2015	Newcastle WC **New Zealand** 47–9
2003	Brisbane WC **New Zealand** 91–7		

NEW ZEALAND v PACIFIC ISLANDS

Played 1 New Zealand won 1
Highest scores New Zealand 41–26 in 2004, Pacific Islands 26–41 in 2004
Biggest win New Zealand 41–26 in 2004, Pacific Islands no win

2004	Albany **New Zealand 41–26**

NEW ZEALAND v PORTUGAL

Played 1 New Zealand won 1
Highest scores New Zealand 108–13 in 2007, Portugal 13–108 in 2007
Biggest win New Zealand 108–13 in 2007, Portugal no win

2007	Lyons WC **New Zealand** 108–13

NEW ZEALAND v NAMIBIA

Played 1 New Zealand won 1
Highest scores New Zealand 58–14 in 2015, Namibia 14–58 in 2015
Biggest win New Zealand 58–14 in 2015, Namibia no win

2015	London WC **New Zealand** 58–14

NEW ZEALAND v GEORGIA

Played 1 New Zealand won 1
Highest scores New Zealand 43–10 in 2015, Georgia 10–43 in 2015
Biggest win New Zealand 43–10 in 2015, Georgia no win

2015	Cardiff WC **New Zealand** 43–10

AUSTRALIA v UNITED STATES

Played 8 Australia won 8
Highest scores Australia 67–9 in 1990 and 67–5 in 2011, United States 19–55 in 1999
Biggest win Australia 67–5 in 2011, United States no win

1912	Berkeley **Australia** 12–8		1990	Brisbane **Australia** 67–9
1976	Los Angeles **Australia** 24–12		1999	Limerick WC **Australia** 55–19
1983	Sydney **Australia** 49–3		2011	Wellington WC **Australia** 67–5
1987	Brisbane WC **Australia** 47–12		2015	Chicago **Australia** 47–10

AUSTRALIA v NEW ZEALAND XVs

Played 24 Australia won 6, New Zealand XVs won 18, Drawn 0
Highest scores Australia 26–20 in 1926, New Zealand XV 38–11 in 1923 and 38–8 in 1924
Biggest win Australia 17–0 in 1921, New Zealand XV 38–8 in 1924

1920	1 Sydney **New Zealand XV** 26–15			New Zealand XV won series 3–0
	2 Sydney **New Zealand XV** 14–6		1924	1 Sydney **Australia** 20–16
	3 Sydney **New Zealand XV** 24–13			2 Sydney **New Zealand XV** 21–5
	New Zealand XV won series 3–0			3 Sydney **New Zealand XV** 38–8
1921	Christchurch **Australia** 17–0			New Zealand XV won series 2–1
1922	1 Sydney **New Zealand XV** 26–19		1925	1 Sydney **New Zealand XV** 26–3
	2 Sydney **Australia** 14–8			2 Sydney **New Zealand XV** 4–0
	3 Sydney **Australia** 8–6			3 Sydney **New Zealand XV** 11–3
	Australia won series 2–1			New Zealand XV won series 3–0
1923	1 Dunedin **New Zealand XV** 19–9		1925	Auckland **New Zealand XV** 36–10
	2 Christchurch **New Zealand XV** 34–6		1926	1 Sydney **Australia** 26–20
	3 Wellington **New Zealand XV** 38–11			2 Sydney **New Zealand XV** 11–6

3 Sydney **New Zealand XV** 14–0	2 Dunedin **New Zealand XV** 16–14
4 Sydney **New Zealand XV** 28–21	3 Christchurch **Australia** 11–8
New Zealand XV won series 3–1	New Zealand XV won series 2–1
1928 1 Wellington **New Zealand XV** 15–12	

AUSTRALIA v SOUTH AFRICA XVs

Played 3 South Africa XVs won 3
Highest scores Australia 11–16 in 1921, South Africa XV 28–9 in 1921
Biggest win Australia no win, South Africa XV 28–9 in 1921

1921 1 Sydney **South Africa XV** 25–10	3 Sydney **South Africa XV** 28–9
2 Sydney **South Africa XV** 16–11	South Africa XV won series 3–0

AUSTRALIA v NEW ZEALAND MAORIS

Played 16 Australia won 8, New Zealand Maoris won 6, Drawn 2
Highest scores Australia 31–6 in 1936, New Zealand Maoris 25–22 in 1922
Biggest wins Australia 31–6 in 1936, New Zealand Maoris 20–0 in 1946

1922 1 Sydney **New Zealand Maoris** 25–22	1946 Hamilton **New Zealand Maoris** 20–0
2 Sydney **Australia** 28–13	1949 1 Sydney **New Zealand Maoris** 12–3
3 Sydney **New Zealand Maoris** 23–22	2 Brisbane **Drawn** 8–8
New Zealand Maoris won series 2–1	3 Sydney **Australia** 18–3
1923 1 Sydney **Australia** 27–23	Series drawn 1–1, with 1 draw
2 Sydney **Australia** 21–16	1958 1 Brisbane **Australia** 15–14
3 Sydney **Australia** 14–12	2 Sydney **Drawn** 3–3
Australia won series 3–0	3 Melbourne **New Zealand Maoris**
1928 Wellington **New Zealand Maoris** 9–8	13–6
1931 Palmerston North **Australia** 14–3	Series drawn 1–1, with 1 draw
1936 Palmerston North **Australia** 31–6	

AUSTRALIA v FIJI

Played 20 Australia won 17, Fiji won 2, Drawn 1
Highest scores Australia 66–20 in 1998, Fiji 28–52 in 1985
Biggest wins Australia 49–0 in 2007, Fiji 17–15 in 1952 and 18–16 in 1954

1952 1 Sydney **Australia** 15–9	3 Sydney **Australia** 27–17
2 Sydney **Fiji** 17–15	Australia won series 3–0
Series drawn 1–1	1980 Suva **Australia** 22–9
1954 1 Brisbane **Australia** 22–19	1984 Suva **Australia** 16–3
2 Sydney **Fiji** 18–16	1985 1 Brisbane **Australia** 52–28
Series drawn 1–1	2 Sydney **Australia** 31–9
1961 1 Brisbane **Australia** 24–6	Australia won series 2–0
2 Sydney **Australia** 20–14	1998 Sydney **Australia** 66–20
3 Melbourne **Drawn** 3–3	2007 Perth **Australia** 49–0
Australia won series 2–0, with 1 draw	2007 Montpellier WC **Australia** 55–12
1972 Suva **Australia** 21–19	2010 Canberra **Australia** 49–3
1976 1 Sydney **Australia** 22–6	2015 Cardiff WC **Australia** 28–13
2 Brisbane **Australia** 21–9	

AUSTRALIA v TONGA

Played 4 Australia won 3, Tonga won 1, Drawn 0
Highest scores Australia 74–0 in 1998, Tonga 16–11 in 1973
Biggest wins Australia 74–0 in 1998, Tonga 16–11 in 1973

1973	1 Sydney **Australia** 30–12	1993	Brisbane **Australia** 52–14
	2 Brisbane **Tonga** 16–11	1998	Canberra **Australia** 74–0
	Series drawn 1–1		

AUSTRALIA v JAPAN

Played 4 Australia won 4
Highest scores Australia 91–3 in 2007, Japan 25–50 in 1973
Biggest win Australia 91–3 in 2007, Japan no win

1975	1 Sydney **Australia** 37–7	1987	Sydney WC **Australia** 42–23
	2 Brisbane **Australia** 50–25	2007	Lyons WC **Australia** 91–3
	Australia won series 2–0		

AUSTRALIA v ARGENTINA

Played 25 Australia won 19, Argentina won 5, Drawn 1
Highest scores Australia 54–17 in 2013, Argentina 27–19 in 1987
Biggest wins Australia 53–6 in 2000, Argentina 18–3 in 1983

1979	1 Buenos Aires **Argentina** 24–13	1997	1 Buenos Aires **Australia** 23–15
	2 Buenos Aires **Australia** 17–12		2 Buenos Aires **Argentina** 18–16
	Series drawn 1–1		Series drawn 1–1
1983	1 Brisbane **Argentina** 18–3	2000	1 Brisbane **Australia** 53–6
	2 Sydney **Australia** 29–13		2 Canberra **Australia** 32–25
	Series drawn 1–1		Australia won series 2–0
1986	1 Brisbane **Australia** 39–19	2002	Buenos Aires **Australia** 17–6
	2 Sydney **Australia** 26–0	2003	Sydney WC **Australia** 24–8
	Australia won series 2–0	2012	Robina RC **Australia** 23–19
1987	1 Buenos Aires **Drawn** 19–19	2012	Rosario RC **Australia** 25–19
	2 Buenos Aires **Argentina** 27–19	2013	Perth RC **Australia** 14–13
	Argentina won series 1–0, with 1 draw	2013	Rosario RC **Australia** 54–17
1991	Llanelli WC **Australia** 32–19	2014	Robina RC **Australia** 32–25
1995	1 Brisbane **Australia** 53–7	2014	Mendoza RC **Argentina** 21–17
	2 Sydney **Australia** 30–13	2015	Mendoza RC **Australia** 34–9
	Australia won series 2–0	2015	Twickenham WC **Australia** 29–15

AUSTRALIA v SAMOA

Played 5 Australia won 4, Samoa won 1
Highest scores Australia 74–7 in 2005, Samoa 32–23 in 2011
Biggest win Australia 73–3 in 1994, Samoa 32–23 in 2011

1991	Pontypool WC **Australia** 9–3		2005	Sydney **Australia** 74–7
1994	Sydney **Australia** 73–3		2011	Sydney **Samoa** 32–23
1998	Brisbane **Australia** 25–13			

AUSTRALIA v ITALY

Played 16 Australia won 16
Highest scores Australia 69–21 in 2005, Italy 21–69 in 2005
Biggest win Australia 55–6 in 1988, Italy no win

1983	Rovigo **Australia** 29–7		2006	Rome **Australia** 25–18
1986	Brisbane **Australia** 39–18		2008	Padua **Australia** 30–20
1988	Rome **Australia** 55–6		2009	1 Canberra **Australia** 31–8
1994	1 Brisbane **Australia** 23–20			2 Melbourne **Australia** 34–12
	2 Melbourne **Australia** 20–7			Australia won series 2–0
	Australia won series 2–0		2010	Florence **Australia** 32–14
1996	Padua **Australia** 40–18		2011	Albany WC **Australia** 32–6
2002	Genoa **Australia** 34–3		2012	Florence **Australia** 22–19
2005	Melbourne **Australia** 69–21		2013	Turin **Australia** 50–20

AUSTRALIA v CANADA

Played 6 Australia won 6
Highest scores Australia 74–9 in 1996, Canada 16–43 in 1993
Biggest win Australia 74–9 in 1996, Canada no win

1985	1 Sydney **Australia** 59–3		1995	Port Elizabeth WC **Australia** 27–11
	2 Brisbane **Australia** 43–15		1996	Brisbane **Australia** 74–9
	Australia won series 2–0		2007	Bordeaux WC **Australia** 37–6
1993	Calgary **Australia** 43–16			

AUSTRALIA v KOREA

Played 1 Australia won 1
Highest scores Australia 65–18 in 1987, Korea 18–65 in 1987
Biggest win Australia 65–18 in 1987, Korea no win

1987	Brisbane **Australia** 65–18

AUSTRALIA v ROMANIA

Played 3 Australia won 3
Highest scores Australia 90–8 in 2003, Romania 9–57 in 1999
Biggest win Australia 90–8 in 2003, Romania no win

1995	Stellenbosch WC **Australia** 42–3		2003	Brisbane WC **Australia** 90–8
1999	Belfast WC **Australia** 57–9			

AUSTRALIA v SPAIN

Played 1 Australia won 1
Highest scores Australia 92–10 in 2001, Spain 10–92 in 2001
Biggest win Australia 92–10 in 2001, Spain no win

2001	Madrid **Australia** 92–10

AUSTRALIA v NAMIBIA

Played 1 Australia won 1
Highest scores Australia 142–0 in 2003, Namibia 0–142 in 2003
Biggest win Australia 142–0 in 2003, Namibia no win

2003	Adelaide WC **Australia** 142–0

AUSTRALIA v PACIFIC ISLANDS

Played 1 Australia won 1
Highest scores Australia 29–14 in 2004, Pacific Islands 14–29 in 2004
Biggest win Australia 29–14 in 2004, Pacific Islands no win

2004	Adelaide **Australia** 29–14

AUSTRALIA v RUSSIA

Played 1 Australia won 1
Highest scores Australia 68–22 in 2011, Russia 22–68 in 2011
Biggest win Australia 68–22 in 2011, Russia no win

2011	Nelson WC **Australia** 68–22

AUSTRALIA v URUGUAY

Played 1 Australia won 1
Highest scores Australia 65–3 in 2015, Uruguay 3–65 in 2015
Biggest win Australia 65–3 in 2015, Uruguay no win

2015	Birmingham WC **Australia** 65–3

The match and career records cover official test matches played up to 1 November, 2015.

MATCH RECORDS

MOST CONSECUTIVE TEST WINS

18 by Lithuania 2006 *Hun, Nor, Bul* 2007 *Aus, Hun, Bul* 2008 *Lat, Aus, Hun, Nor, And, Swi* 2009 *Ser, Arm, Isr, Hol,* And 2010 *Ser*

17 by N Zealand 1965 *SA 4,* 1966 *BI 1,2,3,4,* 1967 *A, E, W, F, S,* 1968 *A 1,2, F 1,2,3,* 1969 *W 1,2*

17 by S Africa 1997 *A 2, It, F 1,2, E, S,* 1998 *I 1,2, W 1, E 1, A 1, NZ 1,2, A 2, W 2, S, I 3*

17 by N Zealand 2013 *F 1,2,3, A 1,2, Arg 1, SA 1, Arg 2, SA 2, A 3, J, F 4, E, I,* 2014 *E 1,2,3*

* Cyprus won 24 consecutive matches from 2008–14 but were not a World Rugby member union at that time

MOST CONSECUTIVE TESTS WITHOUT DEFEAT

Matches	Wins	Draws	Period
23 by N Zealand	22	1	1987 to 1990
22 by N Zealand	21	1	2013 to 2014
20 by N Zealand	19	1	2011 to 2012
18 by Lithuania	18	0	2006 to 2010
17 by N Zealand	15	2	1961 to 1964
17 by N Zealand	17	0	1965 to 1969
17 by S Africa	17	0	1997 to 1998

MOST POINTS IN A MATCH

BY A TEAM

Pts	Opponents	Venue	Year
164 by Hong Kong	Singapore	Kuala Lumpur	1994
155 by Japan	Chinese Taipei	Tokyo	2002
152 by Argentina	Paraguay	Mendoza	2002
147 by Argentina	Venezuela	Santiago	2004
145 by N Zealand	Japan	Bloemfontein	1995
144 by Argentina	Paraguay	Montevideo	2003
142 by Australia	Namibia	Adelaide	2003
135 by Korea	Malaysia	Hong Kong	1992

BY A PLAYER

Pts	Player	Opponents	Venue	Year
60 for Japan	T Kurihara	Chinese Taipei	Tainan	2002
50 for Argentina	E Morgan	Paraguay	San Pablo	1973
50 for H Kong	A Billington	Singapore	Kuala Lumpur	1994
45 for N Zealand	SD Culhane	Japan	Bloemfontein	1995
45 for Argentina	J-M Nuñez-Piossek	Paraguay	Montevideo	2003
44 for Scotland	AG Hastings	Ivory Coast	Rustenburg	1995
44 for England	CC Hodgson	Romania	Twickenham	2001
42 for Australia	MS Rogers	Namibia	Adelaide	2003
41 for Sweden	J Hagstrom	Luxembourg	Cessange	2001
40 for Argentina	GM Jorge	Brazil	Sao Paulo	1993
40 for Japan	D Ohata	Chinese Taipei	Tokyo	2002
40 for Scotland	CD Paterson	Japan	Perth	2004

MOST TRIES IN A MATCH
BY THE TEAM

Tries	Opponents	Venue	Year
26 by Hong Kong	Singapore	Kuala Lumpur	1994
25 by Fiji	Solomon Is	Port Moresby	1969
24 by Argentina	Paraguay	Mendoza	2002
24 by Argentina	Paraguay	Montevideo	2003
23 by Japan	Chinese Taipei	Tokyo	2002
23 by Argentina	Venezuela	Santiago	2004
22 by Australia	Namibia	Adelaide	2003
21 by Fiji	Niue Island	Apia	1983
21 by N Zealand	Japan	Bloemfontein	1995
21 by S Africa	Uruguay	East London	2005

BY A PLAYER

Tries	Player	Opponents	Venue	Year
11 for Argentina	U O'Farrell	Brazil	Buenos Aires	1951
10 for H Kong	A Billington	Singapore	Kuala Lumpur	1994
9 for Argentina	J-M Nuñez-Piossek	Paraguay	Montevideo	2003
8 for Argentina	GM Jorge	Brazil	Sao Paulo	1993
8 for Japan	D Ohata	Chinese Taipei	Tokyo	2002
6 for Argentina	E Morgan	Paraguay	San Pablo	1973
6 for Fiji	T Makutu	Papua New Guinea	Suva	1979
6 for Argentina	GM Jorge	Brazil	Montevideo	1989
6 for Namibia	G Mans	Portugal	Windhoek	1990
6 for N Zealand	MCG Ellis	Japan	Bloemfontein	1995
6 for Japan	T Kurihara	Chinese Taipei	Tainan	2002
6 for S Africa	T Chavhanga	Uruguay	East London	2005
6 for Japan	D Ohata	Hong Kong	Tokyo	2005
6 for Japan	Y Fujita	UAE	Fukuoka	2012
6 for Argentina	F Barrea	Brazil	Santiago	2012

MOST CONVERSIONS IN A MATCH
BY THE TEAM

Cons	Opponents	Venue	Year
20 by N Zealand	Japan	Bloemfontein	1995
20 by Japan	Chinese Taipei	Tokyo	2002
19 by Fiji	Solomon Islands	Port Moresby	1969
18 by Fiji	Niue Island	Apia	1983
17 by Hong Kong	Singapore	Kuala Lumpur	1994
17 by Japan	Chinese Taipei	Singapore	1998
17 by Tonga	Korea	Nuku'alofa	2003
16 by Argentina	Paraguay	Mendoza	2002
16 by Australia	Namibia	Adelaide	2003
16 by Argentina	Venezuela	Santiago	2004
16 by Japan	Sri Lanka	Nagoya	2014

BY A PLAYER

Cons	Player	Opponents	Venue	Year
20 for New Zealand	SD Culhane	Japan	Bloemfontein	1995
18 for Fiji	S Koroduadua	Niue Island	Apia	1983
17 for Hong Kong	J McKee	Singapore	Kuala Lumpur	1994
17 for Tonga	P Hola	Korea	Nuku'alofa	2003
16 for Argentina	J-L Cilley	Paraguay	Mendoza	2002
16 for Australia	MS Rogers	Namibia	Adelaide	2003
16 for Japan	A Goromaru	Sri Lanka	Nagoya	2014
15 for England	PJ Grayson	Netherlands	Huddersfield	1998
15 for Japan	T Kurihara	Chinese Taipei	Tainan	2002
14 for England	CC Hodgson	Romania	Twickenham	2001
14 for Wales	GL Henson	Japan	Cardiff	2004
14 for New Zealand	NJ Evans	Portugal	Lyon	2007
14 for Japan	A Goromaru	Philippines	Fukuoka	2013

MOST PENALTIES IN A MATCH
BY THE TEAM

Penalties	Opponents	Venue	Year
9 by Japan	Tonga	Tokyo	1999
9 by N Zealand	Australia	Auckland	1999
9 by Wales	France	Cardiff	1999
9 by Portugal	Georgia	Lisbon	2000
9 by N Zealand	France	Paris	2000
8 by many countries			

BY A PLAYER

Penalties	Player	Opponents	Venue	Year
9 for Japan	K Hirose	Tonga	Tokyo	1999
9 for N Zealand	AP Mehrtens	Australia	Auckland	1999
9 for Wales	NR Jenkins	France	Cardiff	1999
9 for Portugal	T Teixeira	Georgia	Lisbon	2000
9 for N Zealand	AP Mehrtens	France	Paris	2000
8 by many players				

MOST DROP GOALS IN A MATCH
BY THE TEAM

Drops	Opponents	Venue	Year
5 by South Africa	England	Paris	1999
4 by Romania	W Germany	Bucharest	1967
4 by Uruguay	Chile	Montevideo	2002
4 by South Africa	England	Twickenham	2006
4 by Argentina	France	Paris	2014
3 by several nations			

BY A PLAYER

Drops	Player	Opponents	Venue	Year
5 for S Africa	JH de Beer	England	Paris	1999
4 for Uruguay	J Menchaca	Chile	Montevideo	2002
4 for S Africa	AS Pretorius	England	Twickenham	2006
3 for several nations				

CAREER RECORDS

MOST TEST APPEARANCES

Tests	Player	Career span
148	RH McCaw (N Zealand)	2001 to 2015
141 (8)	BG O'Driscoll (Ireland/Lions)	1999 to 2014
139	GM Gregan (Australia)	1994 to 2007
132	KF Mealamu (N Zealand)	2002 to 2015
130 (2)	RJR O'Gara (Ireland/Lions)	2000 to 2013
127	V Matfield (S Africa)	2001 to 2015
124 (5)	GD Jenkins (Wales/Lions)	2002 to 2015
119 (5)	J Leonard (England/Lions)	1990 to 2004
118	F Polous (France)	1995 to 2007
118	TD Woodcock (N Zealand)	2002 to 2015
117	BG Habana (S Africa)	2004 to 2015
116	NC Sharpe (Australia)	2002 to 2012
115	M-L Castrogiovanni (Italy)	2002 to 2015
115 (7)	PJ O'Connell (Ireland/Lions)	2002 to 2015

The figures include test appearances for the British/Irish Lions which are shown in brackets. Thus 141 (8) for Brian O'Driscoll (Ireland/Lions) indicates 133 caps for Ireland and eight tests for the Lions.

MOST TESTS AS CAPTAIN

Tests	Captain	Span as captain
110*	RH McCaw (N Zealand)	2004 to 2015
84 (1)	BG O'Driscoll (Ireland/Lions)	2002 to 2012
83	JW Smit (S Africa)	2003 to 2011
66	S Parisse (Italy)	2008 to 2015
59	WDC Carling (England)	1988 to 1996
59	GM Gregan (Australia)	2001 to 2007
56	T Dusautoir (France)	2009 to 2015
55	JA Eales (Australia)	1996 to 2001
51	SBT Fitzpatrick (N Zealand)	1992 to 1997

* McCaw's figure includes the world record of 97 test wins as captain.

The figures include test captaincies of the British/Irish Lions which are shown in brackets. Thus 84 (1) for Brian O'Driscoll (Ireland/Lions) indicates 83 captaincies for Ireland and one in tests for the Lions.

MOST CONSECUTIVE TESTS

Tests	Player	Career span
63	SBT Fitzpatrick (N Zealand) .	1986 to 1995
62	JWC Roff (Australia)	1996 to 2001
58	A Zanni (Italy)	2008 to 2014
53	GO Edwards (Wales)	1967 to 1978
52	WJ McBride (Ireland)	1964 to 1975
51	CM Cullen (N Zealand)	1996 to 2000

Getty Images

All Black Richie McCaw overtook Brian O'Driscoll in 2015 to become the most capped player of all time.

MOST POINTS IN TESTS

Points	Player	Tests	Career span
1,598	DW Carter (N Zealand)	112	2003 to 2015
1,246 (67)	JP Wilkinson (England/Lions)	97 (6)	1998 to 2011
1,090 (41)	NR Jenkins (Wales/Lions)	91 (4)	1991 to 2002
1,083 (0)	RJR O'Gara (Ireland/Lions)	130 (2)	2000 to 2013
1,010 (27)	D Dominguez (Italy/Argentina)	76 (2)	1989 to 2003
970 (53)	SM Jones (Wales/Lions)	110 (6)	1998 to 2011
967	AP Mehrtens (N Zealand)	70	1995 to 2004
911	MP Lynagh (Australia)	72	1984 to 1995
893	PC Montgomery (S Africa)	102	1997 to 2008
878	MC Burke (Australia)	81	1993 to 2004
809	CD Paterson (Scotland)	109	1999 to 2011
733 (66)	AG Hastings (Scotland/Lions)	67 (6)	1986 to 1995
711	A Goromaru (Japan)	57	2005 to 2015
698	MJ Giteau (Australia)	102	2002 to 2015
694	M Steyn (S Africa)	60	2009 to 2015
670	NJ Little (Fiji)	71	1996 to 2011

The figures include test appearances for the British/Irish Lions or second nation (shown in brackets). Thus 1,246 (67) for Jonny Wilkinson (England/Lions) indicates 1,179 points for England and 67 in tests for the Lions.

MOST TRIES IN TESTS

Tries	Player	Tests	Career span
69	D Ohata (Japan)	58	1996 to 2006
64	DI Campese (Australia)	101	1982 to 1996
64	BG Habana (South Africa)	117	2004 to 2015
60 (2)	SM Williams (Wales/Lions)	91 (4)	2000 to 2011
55	H Onozawa (Japan)	81	2001 to 2013
50 (1)	R Underwood (England/Lions)	91 (6)	1984 to 1996
49	DC Howlett (N Zealand)	62	2000 to 2007
47 (1)	BG O'Driscoll (Ireland/Lions)	141 (8)	1999 to 2014
46	CM Cullen (N Zealand)	58	1996 to 2002
46	JT Rokocoko (N Zealand)	68	2003 to 2010
44	JW Wilson (N Zealand)	60	1993 to 2001
41 (1)	Gareth Thomas (Wales/Lions)	103 (3)	1995 to 2007
40	CE Latham (Australia)	78	1998 to 2007

The figures include test appearances for the British/Irish Lions which are shown in brackets. Thus 60 (2) for Shane Williams (Wales/Lions) indicates 58 tries for Wales and two in tests for the Lions.

MOST CONVERSIONS IN TESTS

Cons	Player	Tests	Career span
293	DW Carter (N Zealand)	112	2003 to 2015
176 (0)	RJR O'Gara (Ireland/Lions)	130 (2)	2000 to 2013
169	AP Mehrtens (N Zealand)	70	1995 to 2004
169 (7)	JP Wilkinson (England/Lions)	97 (6)	1998 to 2011
162	A Goromaru (Japan)	57	2005 to 2015
160 (7)	SM Jones (Wales/Lions)	110 (6)	1998 to 2011
153	PC Montgomery (S Africa)	102	1997 to 2008
140	MP Lynagh (Australia)	72	1984 to 1995
133 (6)	D Dominguez (Italy/Argentina)	76 (2)	1989 to 2003
131 (1)	NR Jenkins (Wales/Lions))	91 (4)	1991 to 2002
118	GJ Fox (N Zealand)	46	1985 to 1993

The figures include test appearances for the British/Irish Lions or a second nation which are shown in brackets. Thus 169 (7) for Jonny Wilkinson (England/Lions) indicates 162 conversions for England and seven in tests for the Lions.

MOST PENALTY GOALS IN TESTS

Penalties	Player	Tests	Career span
281	DW Carter (N Zealand)	112	2003 to 2015
255 (16)	JP Wilkinson (England/Lions)	97 (6)	1998 to 2011
248 (13)	NR Jenkins (Wales/Lions)	91 (4)	1991 to 2002
214 (5)	D Dominguez (Italy/Argentina)	76 (2)	1989 to 2003
202 (0)	RJR O'Gara (Ireland/Lions)	130 (2)	2000 to 2013
198 (12)	SM Jones (Wales/Lions)	110 (6)	1998 to 2011
188	AP Mehrtens (N Zealand)	70	1995 to 2004
177	MP Lynagh (Australia)	72	1984 to 1995
174	MC Burke (Australia)	81	1993 to 2004
170	CD Paterson (Scotland)	109	1999 to 2011
160 (20)	AG Hastings (Scotland/Lions)	67 (6)	1986 to 1995

The figures include test appearances for the British/Irish Lions or a second nation which are shown in brackets. Thus 255 (16) for Jonny Wilkinson (England/Lions) indicates 239 penalties for England and 16 in tests for the Lions.

MOST DROP GOALS IN TESTS

Drops	Player	Tests	Career span
36 (0)	JP Wilkinson (England/Lions)	97 (6)	1998 to 2011
28 (2)	H Porta (Argentina/Jaguars)	66 (8)	1971 to 1999
23 (2)	CR Andrew (England/Lions)	76 (5)	1985 to 1997
19 (0)	D Dominguez (Italy/Argentina)	76 (2)	1989 to 2003
18	HE Botha (S Africa)	28	1980 to 1992
17	S Bettarello (Italy)	55	1979 to 1988
17	DA Parks (Scotland)	67	2004 to 2012
15	J-P Lescarboura (France)	28	1982 to 1990
15 (0)	RJR O'Gara (Ireland/Lions)	130 (2)	2000 to 2013

The figures include test appearances for the British/Irish Lions, South American Jaguars or a second nation shown in brackets. Thus 28 (2) for Hugo Porta (Argentina/Jaguars) indicates 26 drop goals for Argentina and two in tests (against South Africa in the 1980s) for the South American Jaguars.

INTERNATIONAL RECORDS

The Countries

WORLD RUGBY™

Get up close to the action
Watch World Rugby magazine show

- 26 minute show, broadcast 52 weeks a year

- News, highlights, features from the global game

- Available via the World Rugby digital platform

Contact: Michaella.Snoeck@worldrugby.org

ARGENTINA

ARGENTINA'S 2014–15 TEST RECORD

OPPONENTS	DATE	VENUE	RESULT
Uruguay	16 May	A	Won 36–14
Paraguay	23 May	A	Won 71–7
New Zealand	17 Jul	A	Lost 39–18
Australia	25 Jul	H	Lost 9–34
South Africa	8 Aug	A	Won 37–25
South Africa	15 Aug	A	Lost 26–12
New Zealand	20 Sep	N	Lost 26–16
Georgia	25 Sep	N	Won 54–9
Tonga	4 Oct	N	Won 45–16
Namibia	11 Oct	N	Won 64–19
Ireland	18 Oct	N	Won 40–23
Australia	25 Oct	N	Lost 29–15
South Africa	30 Oct	N	Lost 24–13

ARGENTINA RETURN HOME AS HEROES AFTER ENTERTAINING CAMPAIGN

By Frankie Deges

Winger Juan Imhoff outpaces the opposition defence to score his second try in the quarter-final against Ireland.

What **Los Pumas** achieved in an incredible Rugby World Cup 2015, flying home beaming with pride despite no medals around their necks, was magnificent to behold. A fourth-place finish, having only lost to their regular southern hemisphere rivals, brought no shame at all. Much more than that, it was something that was lauded in Argentina as a great success and brought joy to many in times of uncertainty.

This was not Argentina's first appearance in a Rugby World Cup semi-final and the Unión Argentina de Rugby will hope that the legacy this time around is just the same as in 2007 when youngsters were inspired by the likes of Agustín Pichot and Juan Martín Hernández and the sport changed dramatically in the country. The following season saw a reported 26 per cent increase in playing numbers with many of the young stars of the 2015 squad admitting they had been inspired to take up the game or play it seriously with the dream of wearing the Pumas jersey one day because of those seminal days in 2007.

That semi-final also saw dramatic changes begin off the pitch with the support of World Rugby through funding and direction leading to a national high performance plan being devised and the already efficient production line started to produce even better players for the national teams.

The subsequent invitation to join New Zealand, Australia and South Africa in an expanded Tri-Nations competition followed and while a first win took some time in coming – at the 18th attempt, against Australia in Mendoza in October 2014 – the benefits of inclusion in The Rugby Championship have been clear for all to see, never more so than in the 2015 edition.

Argentina, in their second Rugby Championship under the guidance of Daniel Hourcade, began by rattling New Zealand for periods with captain Agustín Creevy scoring two tries from rolling mauls, while Santiago Cordero's mazy runs in the 39–18 defeat in Christchurch were also a sign of what was to come at RWC 2015.

A week later back in Mendoza, the Wallabies avenged the previous year's defeat, but it was only two tries in the final three minutes which made the 34–9 scoreline look much worse than it was and Los Pumas gave a spirited attacking performance in defeat.

Argentina's final stop in a shortened Rugby Championship was Durban, where everything went according to plan as an almost perfect opening 50 minutes of rugby gave Los Pumas their first ever win over South Africa. Winger Juan Imhoff scored a marvellous hat-trick in the 37–25 victory, one which insured that, for the first time, Argentina did not finish bottom of the standings. South Africa may have avenged the loss a week later in a non-championship match, but the Durban victory meant Argentina arrived in London for RWC 2015 with confidence high and their belief in Hourcade's desire to play a more attacking style of play, rather than rely on their renowned pack, reinforced.

They opened their campaign against defending champions New Zealand at Wembley before a then Rugby World Cup record crowd of 89,019 on 20 September and hit the ground running, Argentina producing a performance full of spirit, skill and defensive ferocity to rally from 9–0 down to lead 13–12 at half-time. Second-row Guido Petti, at only 20, had scored the only try of the first half to become Argentina's youngest ever RWC try-scorer. That became 16–12 after another Nicolás Sánchez penalty, but the introduction of Sonny Bill Williams and return of sin-binned Richie McCaw and Conrad Smith saw New Zealand begin to take control and eventually run out 26–16 winners.

That was, on paper, their hardest match of Pool C and Los Pumas were expected to easily beat Georgia, Tonga and Namibia to take their place in the quarter-finals. They did win all three, but it was the manner of the victories that raised many eyebrows and ensured that no-one would relish facing Argentina in the knockout stages. Their attacking hunger, a predatory attitude in defence, and the flamboyance and friendliness of their fans made Argentina one of the stories of the tournament.

They started slowly against Georgia in Gloucester, conceding seven penalties in the first half to only lead 14–9 at half-time thanks to a Tomás Lavanini try. But when Georgia's talisman and captain Mamuka Gorgodze was sin-binned three minutes into the second half, Los Pumas cut loose and scored three tries in his absence. Three more followed before the final whistle to wrap up an impressive 54–9 victory with Tomás Cubelli, Cordero (2), Imhoff (2) and Martín Landajo dotting down and Sánchez kicking 19 points.

Next up, at the Leicester City Stadium, was Tonga and among the Argentina fans that day was Diego Maradona, the footballing legend who lived and breathed every moment of the game, rallying supporters and twirling a jersey throughout. The team only learned of his presence afterwards, when he joined them – and for a while the Tongan players – in their dressing room, but they put on a show for him with Sánchez contributing 25 points, including a try, in a 45–16 win. It was another breathless attacking display against the typically physical and dogged Pacific Islanders, Argentina moving the ball wide quickly with their superior fitness and direct running also seeing Cordero, Joaquín Tuculet and Julián Montoya touch down.

"He [Maradona] gave us a speech," explained Creevy. "He said the whole of Argentina was dreaming with us, everyone is behind us, supporting us, that was the reason he was here, he wanted to be a part of it. I could never have imagined he would have been there with us, it was a beautiful surprise for all of us. He said if we reached the semi-finals he will be there. He has set us a very high goal."

With qualification all but wrapped up, unless they lost to Namibia and Tonga beat New Zealand, Hourcade took the opportunity to name the youngest Pumas starting XV for 16 years for their final Pool C match in Leicester. The youthful exuberance shone through as Argentina produced some of their most expansive rugby, running the ball and flipping passes wide at every opportunity to run in nine tries in a 64–19 victory.

Argentina had to wait a few hours to learn their quarter-final opponent would be Ireland, after they beat France to top Pool D. Ireland may be the Six Nations champions, but it was Los Pumas who came charging out of the blocks at the Millennium Stadium, scoring the first try after only three minutes through Matías Moroni. Ireland were missing some key figures, but an Argentina side attacking with abandon looked untouchable as they raced into a 20–3 advantage after only 25 minutes. Ireland were stunned, but gradually worked their way back into the match, only for Argentina to kick-on once again, scoring two tries within four minutes – the latter by Imhoff celebrated with a swan-dive over the line – to book their place in the semi-finals.

Australia stood between Los Pumas and a first ever Rugby World Cup final, their management featuring a legend of Argentine rugby in forwards coach Mario Ledesma. The way he was hugged by his old team-mates and fellow countrymen in the build-up to the game was proof that this was a game involving huge respect among peers.

Argentina started slowly and two early mistakes gifted Australia two tries in the opening 10 minutes. From then on the game was controlled by a poised Wallabies outfit who knew that Los Pumas would try to attack whenever possible and simply waited for their opportunities. Argentina battled bravely, refusing to buckle and spent much of the final quarter on the offensive but just couldn't find a way through, Adam Ashley-Cooper instead completing his hat-trick to seal the 29–15 win. Los Pumas, though, had made their fans – once again including Maradona – in the stadium and back home proud.

"Everyone will agree that we should be very proud of this team," said an emotional Hourcade afterwards. "They gave it their all, they left empty. The message should be that you have to give it your all in everything you do. This team has always tried. There were many problems today but I think we are on the right path. It is a learning curve; we review the mistakes we made and our legacy will be the way we play the game."

There was one challenge left, a match that no semi-finalist wants to be involved in – the bronze final. But Argentina were eager to repeat their third-place finish of 2007 with victory over the Springboks at The Stadium, Queen Elizabeth Olympic Park. Unfortunately for Hourcade, a series of injuries meant he was forced to make 10 changes, including picking a new captain in Sánchez. Despite this setback, Los Pumas worked hard throughout the game and their reward was a last-second try – to the delight of all in the stadium – for a 24–13 defeat. There was some consolation that Sánchez finished as the tournament's top point scorer with 97, but Argentina have now set the bar for future teams to aspire to better. Attention has already turned to that future to ensure that more youngsters are ready to step up to the national side in the coming years, having gained experience with the under-20s or sevens teams as many of the current crop did.

In 2016, Argentina will also enter Super Rugby with 20 of their RWC 2015 squad already signed up to play and the strength of Los Pumas will be underpinned by year-round competition for the elite players.

So, the future is as positive as it has ever been. As Argentine rugby is bracing itself for what will be exciting times, unprecedented playing numbers and at least 30 first-class matches, the rest of the rugby world should be worried as Los Pumas can only continue to improve.

THE COUNTRIES

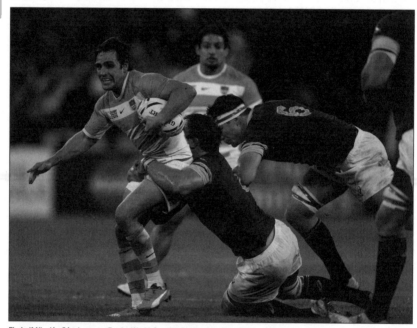

Fly-half Nicolás Sánchez was Rugby World Cup 2015's leading point scorer and captained Los Pumas in the bronze final.

MATCH RECORDS UP TO 1 NOVEMBER, 2015

WINNING MARGIN

Date	Opponent	Result	Winning Margin
01/05/2002	Paraguay	152–0	152
27/04/2003	Paraguay	144–0	144
01/05/2004	Venezuela	147–7	140
02/10/1993	Brazil	114–3	111
23/05/2012	Brazil	111–0	111

MOST POINTS IN A MATCH
BY THE TEAM

Date	Opponent	Result	Points
01/05/2002	Paraguay	152–0	152
01/05/2004	Venezuela	147–7	147
27/04/2003	Paraguay	144–0	144
02/10/1993	Brazil	114–3	114
23/05/2012	Brazil	111–0	111

BY A PLAYER

Date	Player	Opponent	Points
14/10/1973	Eduardo Morgan	Paraguay	50
27/04/2003	José María Nuñez Piossek	Paraguay	45
02/10/1993	Gustavo Jorge	Brazil	40
24/10/1977	Martin Sansot	Brazil	36
13/09/1951	Uriel O'Farrell	Brazil	33

MOST DROP GOALS IN A MATCH
BY THE TEAM

Date	Opponent	Result	DGs
22/11/2014	France	18–13	4
	3 on 6 occasions		

BY A PLAYER

Date	Player	Opponent	DGs
27/10/1979	Hugo Porta	Australia	3
02/11/1985	Hugo Porta	New Zealand	3
07/08/1971	Tomas Harris-Smith	SA Gazelles	3
26/05/2001	Juan Fernández Miranda	Canada	3
30/09/2007	Juan Martín Hernández	Ireland	3

MOST CONVERSIONS IN A MATCH
BY THE TEAM

Date	Opponent	Result	Cons
01/05/2002	Paraguay	152–0	16
01/05/2004	Venezuela	147–7	16
09/10/1979	Brazil	109–3	15
	13 on 3 occasions		

BY A PLAYER

Date	Player	Opponent	Cons
01/05/2002	Jose Cilley	Paraguay	16
21/09/1985	Hugo Porta	Paraguay	13
14/10/1973	Eduardo Morgan	Paraguay	13
25/09/1975	Eduardo de Forteza	Paraguay	11

MOST PENALTIES IN A MATCH
BY THE TEAM

Date	Opponent	Result	Pens
10/10/1999	Samoa	32–16	8
10/03/1995	Canada	29–26	8
17/06/2006	Wales	45–27	8
22/06/2013	Georgia	29–18	8

BY A PLAYER

Date	Player	Opponent	Pens
10/10/1999	Gonzalo Quesada	Samoa	8
10/03/1995	Santiago Meson	Canada	8
17/06/2006	Federico Todeschini	Wales	8
22/06/2013	Martin Bustos Moyano	Georgia	8

MOST TRIES IN A MATCH
BY THE TEAM

Date	Opponent	Result	Tries
01/05/2002	Paraguay	152–0	24
27/04/2003	Paraguay	144–0	24
01/05/2004	Venezuela	147–7	23
08/10/1989	Brazil	103–0	20

BY A PLAYER

Date	Player	Opponent	Tries
13/09/1951	Uriel O'Farrell	Brazil	11
27/04/2003	José María Nuñez Piossek	Paraguay	9
02/10/1993	Gustavo Jorge	Brazil	8
08/10/1989	Gustavo Jorge	Brazil	6
14/10/1973	Eduardo Morgan	Paraguay	6

ARGENTINA

MOST CAPPED PLAYERS	
Name	Caps
Felipe Contepomi	87
Lisandro Arbizu	86
Rolando Martin	86
Mario Ledesma	84
Pedro Sporleder	78

LEADING PENALTY SCORERS	
Name	Penalties
Felipe Contepomi	139
Gonzalo Quesada	103
Hugo Porta	101
Nicolás Sánchez	77
Santiago Meson	63

LEADING TRY SCORERS	
Name	Tries
José María Nuñez Piossek	29
Diego Cuesta Silva	28
Gustavo Jorge	24
Facundo Soler	18
Rolando Martin	18

LEADING DROP GOAL SCORERS	
Name	DGs
Hugo Porta	26
Lisandro Arbizu	11
Nicolás Sánchez	10
Juan Martín Hernández	8
Gonzalo Quesada	7

LEADING CONVERSIONS SCORERS	
Name	Conversions
Hugo Porta	84
Felipe Contepomi	74
Gonzalo Quesada	68
Santiago Meson	68
Juan Fernández Miranda	41

LEADING POINTS SCORERS	
Name	Points
Felipe Contepomi	651
Hugo Porta	590
Gonzalo Quesada	486
Santiago Meson	370
Nicolás Sánchez	356

ARGENTINA INTERNATIONAL PLAYERS
UP TO 1 NOVEMBER, 2015

A Abadie 2007 *Chl*, 2009 *E, W, S*
A Abella 1969 *Ur, Chl*
C Abud 1975 *Par, Bra, Chl*
H Achaval 1948 *OCC*
J Aguilar 1983 *Chl, Ur*
A Aguirre 1997 *Par, Chl*
ME Aguirre 1990 *E, S*, 1991 *Sa*
B Agulla 2010 *Ur, Chl*, 2011 *Chl, Ur*, 2012 *It, F*, 2013 *E, E, Geo*
H Agulla 2005 *Sa*, 2006 *Ur, E, It*, 2007 *It, F, Nm, I, S, SA, F*, 2008 *S, It, SA, F, It, I*, 2009 *E, E, E, W, S*, 2010 *Ur, Chl, S, S, F, I*, 2011 *W, E, R, S, Geo, NZ*, 2012 *SA, SA, NZ, A, NZ, A, W, F*, 2013 *SA, SA, NZ, A, NZ, A, E, W, It*, 2014 *SA, SA, NZ, NZ, A, S, It*, 2015 *NZ, SA, Tg, Nm, SA*
A Ahualli De Chazal 2014 *Ur, Chl, I, S*
L Ahualli De Chazal 2012 *Ur, Chl*, 2014 *Ur, Chl*, 2015 *Ur, Par*
P Albacete 2003 *Par, Ur, F, SA, Ur, C, A, R*, 2004 *W, W, NZ, F, I*, 2005 *It, It*, 2006 *E, It, F*, 2007 *W, F, Geo, Nm, I, S, SA, F*, 2008 *SA, F, It, I*, 2009 *E, E, E, W, S*, 2010 *S, S, F, F, I*, 2011 *W, E, R, S, Geo, NZ*, 2012 *SA, SA, NZ, A, NZ, A*, 2013 *SA, NZ, A, E, W*
DL Albanese 1995 *Ur, C, E, F*, 1996 *Ur, F, SA, E*, 1997 *NZ, Ur, R, It, F, A, A*, 1998 *F, F, R, US, C, It, F, W*, 1999 *W, W, S, I, W, Sa, J, I, F*, 2000 *I, A, SA*, 2001 *NZ, It, W, S, NZ*, 2002 *F, E, SA, A, It, I*, 2003 *F, F, SA, US, C, A, Nm, I*
F Albarracin 2007 *Chl*
G Albertario 2015 *Ur, Par*
M Albina 2001 *Ur, US*, 2003 *Par, Ur, Fj*, 2004 *Chl, Ven, W, W*, 2005 *J*
C Aidao 1961 *Chl, Bra, Ur*

MI Alemanno 2014 *Ur, Chl, I, I, S, SA, SA, NZ, A, NZ, A*, 2015 *A, SA, SA, Geo, Tg, Nm, I, A, SA*
P Alexenicer 1997 *Par, Chl*
H Alfonso 1936 *Bl, Chl*
G Allen 1977 *Par*
JG Allen 1981 *C*, 1985 *F, F, Ur, NZ, NZ*, 1986 *F, F, A, A*, 1987 *Ur, Fj, It, NZ, Sp, A, A*, 1988 *F, F, F, F*, 1989 *Bra, Chl, Par, Ur, US*
L Allen 1951 *Ur, Bra, Chl*
M Allen 1990 *C, E, S*, 1991 *NZ, Chl*
F Allogio 2011 *Chl, Ur*
A Allub 1997 *Par, Ur, It, F, A, A*, 1998 *F, F, US, C, J, It, F, W*, 1999 *W, W, S, I, W, Sa, J, I, F*, 2000 *I, A, A, SA, E*, 2001 *NZ*
M Alonso 1973 *R, R, S*, 1977 *F, F*
A Altberg 1972 *SAG, SAG*, 1973 *R, R, Par*
J Altube 1998 *Par, Chl, Ur*
C Alvarez 1958 *Ur, Per, Chl*, 1959 *JSB, JSB*, 1960 *F*
GM Alvarez 1975 *Ur, Par, Bra, Chl*, 1976 *NZ*, 1977 *Bra, Ur, Par, Chl*
S Alvarez 2013 *Ur, Chl, Bra*
R Álvarez Kairelis 1998 *Par, Chl, Ur*, 2001 *Ur, US, C, W, S, NZ*, 2002 *F, E, SA, A, It, I*, 2003 *F, SA, Fj, Ur, C, Nm, I*, 2004 *F, I*, 2006 *W, W, NZ, Chl, Ur*, 2007 *I, It, W, F, Geo, Nm, I, S, SA, F*, 2008 *SA, F, It, I*, 2009 *E*
G Alvarez 2004 *Ur, Ven*
S Ambrosio 2012 *Ur, Bra*
F Amelong 2007 *Chl*
A Amuchastegui 2002 *Ur, Par, Chl*
GP Angaut 1987 *NZ, Ur, Chl*, 1990 *S*, 1991 *NZ, Sa*

T Carrio 2013 *Ur, Chl, Bra, Geo,* 2014 *Ur,* 2015 *Par*
M Carrique 1983 *Par, Ur*
J Casanegra 1959 *JSB, JSB,* 1960 *F, F*
GF Casas 1971 *OCC,* 1973 *Par, Chl, I,* 1975 *F, F*
DM Cash 1985 *F, F, Ur, Chl, NZ, NZ,* 1986 *F, F, A, A,* 1987 *Ur, Fj, It, NZ, Sp, A, A,* 1988 *F, F, F, F,* 1989 *It, NZ, NZ, US,* 1990 *C, US, C, E, I, E, S,* 1991 *NZ, NZ, Chl, A, Sa,* 1992 *F, F*
R Castagna 1977 *F*
A Castellina 2004 *Chl, Ur, Ven*
R Castro 1971 *Chl, Bra, Par*
J Cato 1975 *Ur, Par*
R Cazenave 1965 *Rho, JSB, OCC, Chl,* 1966 *SAG, SAG*
N Centurion 2011 *Chl, Ur*
A Cerioni 1975 *F,* 1978 *E, It,* 1979 *Chl, Bra*
G Cernegoy 1938 *Chl*
H Cespedes 1997 *Ur, Chl*
M Chesta 1966 *SAG, SAG,* 1967 *Ur, Chl,* 1968 *W, W*
ML Chiappesoni 2013 *Ur, Chl, Bra*
W Chiswell 1949 *F*
V Christianson 1954 *F, F,* 1956 *OCC*
E Cilley 1932 *JSB, JSB*
J Cilley 1936 *Bl, Chl, Chl,* 1938 *Chl*
JL Cilley 1994 *SA,* 1995 *Sa, It, Par, Chl,* 1996 *Ur, F, F, SA, SA,* 1999 *W,* 2000 *A,* 2002 *Par*
J Clement 1987 *Par,* 1989 *Bra*
R Cobelo 1987 *Ur, Par, Chl*
I Comas 1951 *Bra, Chl,* 1958 *Per, Chl,* 1960 *F*
MA Comuzzi 2009 *E, W,* 2011 *Chl, Ur*
A Conen 1951 *Chl,* 1952 *I, I*
J Conrad 1927 *GBR, GBR*
CA Contepomi 1964 *Bra, Chl*
F Contepomi 1998 *Chl, Ur, F, W,* 1999 *W, S, I, J, I, F,* 2000 *I, A, A, SA, E,* 2001 *Ur, US, C, NZ, It, W, S, NZ,* 2002 *F, E, SA, A, It, I,* 2003 *F, F, SA, US, C, A, Nm, I,* 2004 *W, W, F, I,* 2005 *It, It, SA, S, It,* 2006 *W, NZ, E, F,* 2007 *I, W, F, Geo, Nm, I, S, SA, F,* 2008 *S, S, SA, F, It,* 2010 *S, S, F, It, F, I,* 2011 *W, E, S, Geo, NZ,* 2012 *It, F, F, W,* 2013 *E, E, SA, NZ, A, NZ, A*
M Contepomi 1998 *US, C, It, F, W,* 1999 *S, I, W, Sa, F,* 2003 *Ur, F, Fj, Ur, A, R,* 2004 *Chl, Ur, Ven, W, W, NZ, F, I, SA,* 2005 *SA, S,* 2006 *It, F,* 2007 *I, It, W, F, Nm, I, S, SA, F*
F Conti 1988 *F*
CEF Cooke 1997 *CBR*
KAM Cookson 1932 *JSB*
N Cooper 1936 *Bl, Chl, Chl*
R Cooper 1927 *GBR, GBR, GBR, GBR*
J Copello 1975 *Ur, Bra*
C Cordeiro 1983 *Par*
S Cordero 2013 *E, W, It,* 2014 *Ur, Chl, I, S,* 2015 *Ur, Par, NZ, A, SA, NZ, Geo, Tg, I, A, SA*
J Coria 1987 *Ur, Par, Chl,* 1989 *Bra*
I Corleto 1998 *J, F, W,* 1999 *I, J, I, F,* 2000 *I, A, SA, E,* 2001 *W, S, NZ,* 2002 *F, E, SA, A, It, I,* 2003 *F, Fj, US, Ur, C, A, I,* 2006 *It, F,* 2007 *W, F, Geo, Nm, I, S, SA, F*
ME Corral 1993 *J, Bra, Par, Ur, SA, SA,* 1994 *US, S, SA, SA,* 1995 *Ur, C, A, A, E, Sa, It*
RG Cortes 2011 *Chl, Ur,* 2012 *Ur, Chl*
M Cortese 2005 *Sa,* 2010 *Ur, Chl,* 2014 *Ur, Chl, I, I, SA, NZ, A, NZ, S, It,* 2015 *Ur, Par*
F Cortopasso 2003 *Chl, Ur*
A Costa Repetto 2005 *Sa*
JD Costante 1971 *OCC, OCC, Chl, Bra, Par, Ur,* 1976 *W, NZ,* 1977 *F*
AF Courreges 1979 *Ur, Par, Bra,* 1982 *F, F, Sp,* 1983 *WXV, A, A,* 1987 *Sp, A, A,* 1988 *F*
PH Cox 1938 *Chl*
S Craig 2012 *Bra, Chl*
A Creevy 2005 *J, Sa,* 2006 *Ur,* 2009 *S,* 2010 *S, S, F, It, F, I,* 2011 *W, E, R, S, Geo, NZ,* 2012 *A, NZ, A, W, F, I,* 2013 *SA, SA, NZ, A, NZ, A,* 2014 *SA, SA, NZ, A, NZ, A, S, F,* 2015 *NZ, A, SA, SA, NZ, Geo, Tg, Nm, I, A*
P Cremaschi 1993 *J, J,* 1995 *Par, Chl, Ur, It*
RH Crexell 1990 *I, S,* 1991 *Par,* 1992 *Sp,* 1993 *J,* 1995 *Ur, C, A, E, Sa, It, Par, Chl, Ur*
L Criscuolo 1992 *F, F,* 1993 *Bra, SA,* 1996 *Ur, F, F*
V Cruz 2012 *Ur, Bra, Chl*
J Cruz Legora 2002 *Par, Chl*
J Cruz Meabe 1997 *Par*
AG Cubelli 1977 *Bra, Ur, Chl,* 1978 *E, It,* 1979 *A, A,* 1980 *WXV,*

Fj, 1983 *Par,* 1985 *F, F, Ur, Par, NZ, NZ,* 1990 *S*
TM Cubelli 2010 *Ur, Chl,* 2011 *Chl, Ur,* 2012 *Ur, Bra, Chl, It, F, F, F,* 2013 *E, Geo, SA, SA, NZ, A, A, E, W, It,* 2014 *Ur, I, I, S, SA, SA, NZ, A, NZ, A, S, It, F,* 2015 *NZ, A, SA, SA, NZ, Geo, Tg, Nm, I, A, SA*
D Cuesta Silva 1983 *Chl, Ur,* 1985 *F, F, Ur, Chl, NZ, NZ,* 1986 *F, F, A, A,* 1987 *Ur, Fj, It, Sp, A, A,* 1988 *F, F, F, F,* 1989 *It, NZ, NZ,* 1990 *C, E, E, I, E, S,* 1991 *NZ, NZ, Chl, A, W, Sa,* 1992 *F, F, Sp, R, F,* 1993 *J, J, Bra, Par, Ur, SA, SA,* 1994 *US, S, S, US, SA,* 1995 *Ur, C, E, Sa, It, Par, R, It, F*
J Cuesta Silva 1927 *GBR, GBR, GBR, GBR*
B Cuezzo 2007 *Chl*
M Cutler 1969 *Ur,* 1971 *Chl, Bra, Par, Ur*

A Da Milano 1964 *Bra, Chl*
F D'Agnillo 1975 *Ur, Bra,* 1977 *Bra, Ur, Par, Chl*
JL Damioli 1991 *Ur, Par, Bra*
H Dande 2001 *Ur, C,* 2004 *Chl, Ven*
J Dartiguelongue 1964 *Bra, Chl,* 1968 *W, W*
S Dassen 1983 *Chl, Par, Ur*
R de Abelleyra 1932 *JSB, JSB*
M De Achaval 2010 *It, F*
L de Chazal 2001 *Ur, C,* 2004 *SA*
E de Forteza 1975 *Ur, Par, Bra, Chl*
R de la Arena 1992 *F, Sp*
J De La Fuente 2014 *Ur, Chl, I, I, SA, SA, A, A, It,* 2015 *Ur, Par, NZ, SA, NZ, Geo, Tg, I, A, SA*
T De La Vega 2011 *Chl, Ur,* 2012 *It, F, F, F,* 2013 *E, E, Geo,* 2014 *I, I, S*
JC De Pablo 1948 *OCC*
G De Robertis 2005 *A,* 2006 *Chl, Ur,* 2011 *Chl*
R de Vedia 1982 *F, Sp*
T de Vedia 2007 *I, I,* 2008 *S*
R del Busto 2007 *Chl*
F del Castillo 1994 *US, SA,* 1995 *Ur, C, A,* 1996 *Ur, F,* 1997 *Par, Ur,* 1998 *Ur*
GJ del Castillo 1991 *NZ, NZ, Chl, A, W,* 1993 *J,* 1994 *S, S, US, SA,* 1995 *C, A*
L del Chazal 1983 *Chl, Par, Ur*
G Del Prete 2015 *Ur*
R Dell'Acqua 1956 *OCC*
S Dengra 1982 *F, Sp,* 1983 *WXV, A, A,* 1986 *A,* 1987 *It, NZ, Sp, A, A,* 1988 *F, F, F, F,* 1989 *It, NZ, NZ*
C Derkheim 1927 *GBR*
M Devoto 1975 *Par, Bra,* 1977 *Par*
PM Devoto 1982 *F, F, Sp,* 1983 *WXV*
R Devoto 1960 *F*
M Diaz 1997 *Par, Chl,* 1998 *J, Par, Chl*
MD Diaz 2013 *Ur, Chl, Bra, SA, A, W,* 2014 *I, S,* 2015 *Ur, A, SA*
F Diaz Alberdi 1997 *Ur,* 1999 *S, I,* 2000 *A, A*
J Diez 1956 *OCC*
R Dillon 1956 *OCC*
P Dinisio 1989 *NZ,* 1990 *C, US*
M Dip 1979 *Par, Bra*
D Dominguez 1989 *Chl, Par*
E Dominguez 1949 *F, F,* 1952 *I, I,* 1954 *F, F*
A Donnelly 1910 *GBR*
L Dorado 1949 *F*
J Dumas 1973 *R, R, Ur, Bra, S*
M Dumas 1966 *SAG, SAG*
MA Durand 1997 *Chl,* 1998 *Par, Chl, Ur, It, F, W,* 2000 *SA,* 2001 *Ur, US, C, It, NZ,* 2002 *F, SA, A, It, I,* 2003 *Chl, Ur, Fj, US, Ur, C, A, Nm, R,* 2004 *Chl, Ur, Ven, W, W, NZ, F, I, SA,* 2005 *SA, S, It,* 2006 *W, NZ, Chl, Ur, It, F,* 2007 *I, I, It, W, F, Geo, I, F,* 2008 *S, S, It, SA, F, It, I*

C Echeverria 1932 *JSB*
G Ehrman 1948 *OCC,* 1949 *F, F,* 1951 *Ur, Bra, Chl,* 1952 *I, I,* 1954 *F*
O Elia 1954 *F*
R Elliot 1936 *Bl,* 1938 *Chl*
J Escalante 1975 *Ur, Par, Chl,* 1978 *It,* 1979 *Ur, Chl, Par, Bra*
N Escary 1927 *GBR, GBR,* 1932 *JSB, JSB*
R Espagnol 1971 *SAG*
AM Etchegaray 1964 *Ur, Bra, Chl,* 1965 *Rho, JSB, Chl,* 1967 *Ur, Chl,* 1968 *W, W,* 1969 *S, S,* 1971 *SAG, OCC, OCC,* 1972 *SAG, SAG,* 1973 *Par, Bra, I,* 1974 *F, F,* 1976 *W, NZ, NZ*
R Etchegoyen 1991 *Ur, Par, Bra*
C Ezcurra 1958 *Ur, Per, Chl*

E Ezcurra 1990 *I, E, S*
F Ezcurra 2014 *Ur, Chl*

JA Farias Cabello 2010 *F, I,* 2011 *W, E, S, Geo, NZ,* 2012 *It, F, F, SA, SA, NZ, A, NZ, A, W, F, I,* 2013 *E, E, SA, SA, NZ, A, NZ, A, E, W, It*
R Fariello 1973 *Par, Ur, Chl, S*
M Farina 1968 *W, W,* 1969 *S, S*
D Farrell 1951 *Ur*
P Felisari 1956 *OCC*
JJ Fernandez 1971 *SAG, Chl, Bra, Par, Ur,* 1972 *SAG, SAG,* 1973 *R, R, Par, Ur, Chl, I, S,* 1974 *F, F,* 1975 *F,* 1976 *W, NZ, NZ,* 1977 *F, F*
S Fernandez 2008 *It, I,* 2009 *E, E, E, W, S,* 2010 *S, S, F, It, F,* 2011 *W, E, R, S, Geo, NZ,* 2012 *SA, SA, NZ, A, NZ, A, I,* 2013 *SA, NZ, A, NZ, A, E, W*
Pablo Fernandez Bravo 1993 *SA, SA*
E Fernandez del Casal 1951 *Ur, Bra, Chl,* 1952 *I, I,* 1956 *OCC, OCC*
PF Fernandez 2013 *Chl, Bra*
CI Fernandez Lobbe 1996 *US,* 1997 *E, E,* 1998 *F, F, R, US, Ur, C, J, It, F,* 1999 *W, W, S, I, Sa, J, I, F,* 2000 *I, A, A, SA, E,* 2001 *NZ, It, W, S, NZ,* 2002 *F, E, SA, A, It, I,* 2003 *F, F, SA, US, C, A, Nm, I,* 2004 *W, W, NZ,* 2005 *SA, S, It,* 2006 *W, W, NZ, E, F,* 2007 *It, W, F, Nm, I, S, SA,* 2008 *S, S*
JM Fernandez Lobbe 2004 *Ur, Ven,* 2005 *S, It, Sa,* 2006 *W, W, NZ, E, It, F,* 2007 *I, I, It, W, F, Geo, Nm, I, S, SA, F,* 2008 *S, S, SA, F, It, I,* 2009 *E, E, E, W, S,* 2010 *S, S, F, It, F, I,* 2011 *W, E, R, S,* 2012 *SA, SA, NZ, A, NZ, A, W, F, I,* 2013 *NZ, A, NZ, A, SA, SA, NZ, A, NZ,* 2015 *NZ, A, SA, NZ, Geo, Tg, Nm, I, A, SA*
JC Fernández Miranda 1997 *Ur, R, It,* 1998 *Ur, It,* 2000 *I,* 2001 *US, C,* 2002 *Ur, Par, Chl, It, I,* 2003 *Par, Chl, Ur, Fj, US, Nm, R,* 2004 *W, NZ,* 2005 *J, Sa,* 2006 *Chl, Ur,* 2007 *It*
N Fernandez Miranda 1994 *US, S, US,* 1995 *Chl, Ur,* 1996 *F, SA, SA, E,* 1997 *E, E, NZ, NZ, Ur, R,* 1998 *R, US, C, It,* 1999 *I, F,* 2002 *Ur, Chl, It,* 2003 *Chl, Ur, F, F, SA, US, Ur, Nm, R,* 2004 *W, NZ,* 2005 *J, It,* 2006 *W, It,* 2007 *It, Geo, Nm, F*
N Ferrari 1992 *Sp, Sp*
G Fessia 2007 *I,* 2009 *E,* 2010 *S, S, F, It, F, I,* 2011 *R, S, Geo,* 2012 *It*
JG Figallo 2010 *F, It, I,* 2011 *W, E, R, S, Geo, NZ,* 2012 *SA, SA, NZ, A, NZ, A, W, F,* 2013 *SA, SA, NZ, A, NZ,* 2015 *A, SA*
A Figuerola 2008 *It, I,* 2009 *E, W, S,* 2010 *S, S*
R Follett 1948 *OCC, OCC,* 1952 *I, I,* 1954 *F*
G Foster 1971 *Chl, Bra, Par, Ur*
R Foster 1965 *Rho, JSB, OCC, OCC, Chl,* 1966 *SAG, SAG,* 1970 *I, I,* 1971 *SAG, SAG, OCC,* 1972 *SAG, SAG*
P Franchi 1987 *Ur, Par, Chl*
JL Francombe 1932 *JSB, JSB,* 1936 *BI*
J Freixas 2003 *Chl, Ur*
R Frigerio 1948 *OCC, OCC,* 1954 *F*
J Frigoli 1936 *BI, Chl, Chl*
C Fruttero 2012 *Ur, Bra, Chl,* 2013 *Ur, Chl, Bra*
P Fuselli 1998 *J, Par*

E Gahan 1954 *F, F*
M Gaitan 1998 *Ur,* 2002 *Par, Chl,* 2003 *Fj, US, Nm, R,* 2004 *W,* 2007 *It, W*
MT Galarza 2010 *S, F, It, F, I,* 2011 *W, E, R, Geo,* 2013 *E, E, Geo, SA, SA, NZ, A, E, It,* 2014 *SA, SA, NZ, A, NZ, A,* 2015 *NZ*
AM Galindo 2004 *Ur, Ven,* 2008 *S, It, SA, F, It,* 2009 *E,* 2010 *Ur, It, F,* 2012 *SA, SA*
R Gallo 1964 *Bra*
P Gambarini 2006 *W, Chl, Ur,* 2007 *I, It, Chl,* 2008 *S*
E Garbarino 1992 *Sp, Sp*
FL Garcia 1994 *SA,* 1995 *A, A, Par, Chl,* 1996 *Ur, F, F,* 1997 *NZ,* 1998 *R, Ur, J*
J Garcia 1998 *Par, Ur,* 2000 *A*
PT Garcia 1948 *OCC*
SE Garcia Botta 2013 *Ur, Chl, Bra,* 2015 *Ur, Par, SA, SA*
E Garcia Hamilton 1993 *Bra*
P Garcia Hamilton 1998 *OCC*
HM Garcia Simon 1990 *I,* 1991 *A, W, Sa,* 1992 *F*
M Garcia Veiga 2012 *Ur, Bra, Chl,* 2013 *E, E, Geo*
G Garcia-Orsetti 1992 *R, F*
PA Garreton 1987 *Sp, Ur, Chl, A, A,* 1988 *F, F, F, F,* 1989 *It, NZ, Bra, Chl, Ur, US,* 1990 *C, E, E, I, E, S,* 1991 *NZ, NZ, Chl, A, W, Sa,* 1992 *F, F,* 1993 *J, J*

P Garzon 1990 *C,* 1991 *Par, Bra*
G Gasso 1983 *Chl, Par*
JM Gauweloose 1975 *F, F,* 1976 *W, NZ, NZ,* 1977 *F, F,* 1981 *C*
E Gavina 1956 *OCC, OCC,* 1958 *Ur, Per, Chl,* 1959 *JSB, JSB,* 1960 *F, F,* 1961 *Chl, Bra, Ur*
OST Gebbie 1910 *GBR*
FA Genoud 2004 *Chl, Ur, Ven,* 2005 *J, It*
J Genoud 1952 *I, I,* 1956 *OCC, OCC*
M Gerosa 1987 *Ur, Chl*
D Giannantonio 1996 *Ur,* 1997 *Par, Ur, It, A, A,* 1998 *F, F,* 2000 *A,* 2002 *E*
MC Giargia 1973 *Par, Ur, Bra,* 1975 *Par, Chl*
T Gilardon 2013 *Ur, Chl, Bra*
R Giles 1948 *OCC,* 1949 *F, F,* 1951 *Ur,* 1952 *I, I*
C Giuliano 1959 *JSB, JSB,* 1960 *F*
L Glastra 1948 *OCC, OCC,* 1952 *I, I*
M Glastra 1979 *Ur, Chl,* 1981 *C*
FE Gomez 1985 *Ur,* 1987 *Ur, Fj, It, NZ,* 1989 *NZ,* 1990 *C, E, E*
JF Gomez 2006 *It,* 2008 *S, S, It,* 2012 *W*
N Gomez 1997 *Par, Chl*
PM Gomez Cora 2004 *NZ, SA,* 2005 *Sa,* 2006 *E*
F Gómez Kodela 2011 *Chl, Ur,* 2012 *It, F, F, I,* 2013 *E, E, Geo*
D Gonzalez 1987 *Par,* 1988 *F, F*
T Gonzalez 1979 *Ur, Chl*
LP Gonzalez Amorosino 2007 *Chl,* 2009 *E, E,* 2010 *S, S, F, It, F, I,* 2011 *R, S, Geo, NZ,* 2012 *SA, SA, NZ, A, NZ, A, F,* 2013 *SA, NZ, A, NZ, A, E, W, It,* 2014 *Chl, I, I, S, SA, SA, NZ, A, A, It, F,* 2015 *NZ, A, SA, SA, NZ, Geo, Nm, A, SA*
S Gonzalez Bonorino 2001 *Ur, US, C,* 2002 *Par,* 2003 *F, SA,* 2007 *I, I, It, W, F, Geo,* 2008 *S, S*
E Gonzalez del Solar 1960 *F,* 1961 *Chl, Bra, Ur*
N Gonzalez del Solar 1964 *Ur, Bra, Chl,* 1965 *Rho, JSB, OCC, OCC, Chl*
S Gonzalez Iglesias 2011 *Chl,* 2014 *Ur, I, I, S, SA, NZ, NZ, S, F,* 2015 *Ur, Par, NZ, A, SA, SA, Tg, Nm, SA*
AO Gosio 2011 *Geo,* 2012 *It, F*
H Goti 1961 *Chl, Bra, Ur,* 1964 *Ur, Bra, Chl,* 1965 *Rho,* 1966 *SAG*
LM Gradin 1965 *OCC, OCC, Chl,* 1966 *SAG, SAG,* 1969 *Chl,* 1970 *I, I,* 1973 *R, R, Par, Ur, Chl, S*
P Grande 1998 *Par, Chl, Ur*
RD Grau 1993 *J, Bra, Chl,* 1995 *Par, Chl,* 1996 *F, F, US, Ur, C, SA, SA, E,* 1997 *E, E, NZ, NZ, A, A,* 1998 *F, It, F,* 1999 *W, W, S, I, W, F,* 2000 *A, SA, E,* 2001 *NZ, W, S, NZ,* 2002 *F, E, SA, A, It,* 2003 *F, SA, US, Ur, C, A, I*
L Gravano 1997 *Chl,* 1998 *Chl, Ur*
LH Gribell 1910 *GBR*
B Grigolon 1948 *OCC,* 1954 *F, F*
V Grimoldi 1927 *GBR, GBR*
J Grondona 1990 *C*
R Grosse 1952 *I, I,* 1954 *F, F*
P Guarrochena 1977 *Par*
A Guastella 1956 *OCC,* 1959 *JSB, JSB,* 1960 *F*
J Guidi 1958 *Ur, Per, Chl,* 1959 *JSB,* 1960 *F,* 1961 *Chl, Bra, Ur*
MR Guidone 2011 *Chl, Ur,* 2013 *Ur, Bra, E, E, Geo*
JC Guillemaín 2014 *S*
E Guinazu 2003 *Par, Chl, Ur,* 2004 *Chl, Ur, Ven, W, W, SA,* 2005 *J, It,* 2007 *I, It, F,* 2009 *E,* 2012 *It, F, F, SA, SA, NZ, A, NZ, A, W, F, I,* 2013 *SA, SA, NZ, A, NZ, A, E, W, It*
JA Guzman 2007 *Chl,* 2010 *Ur, Chl*
SN Guzmán 2010 *S, I,* 2012 *Ur, Bra, Chl, It*

D Halle 1989 *Bra, Chl, Ur, US,* 1990 *US*
R Handley 1966 *SAG, SAG,* 1968 *W, W,* 1969 *S, S, Ur, Chl,* 1970 *I, I,* 1971 *SAG, SAG,* 1972 *SAG, SAG*
G Hardie 1948 *OCC*
TA Harris-Smith 1969 *S, S,* 1971 *SAG, OCC, OCC,* 1973 *Par, Ur*
O Hasan Jalil 1995 *Ur,* 1996 *Ur, C, SA, SA,* 1997 *E, E, NZ, R, It, F, A,* 1998 *F, F, R, US, C, It, F, W,* 1999 *W, W, S, W, Sa, J, I,* 2000 *SA, E,* 2001 *It, W, S, NZ,* 2002 *F, E, SA, A, It, I,* 2003 *US, C, A, R,* 2004 *W, W, NZ, F, I,* 2005 *It, It, SA, S, It,* 2006 *NZ, E, F,* 2007 *It, Geo, Nm, I, S, SA, F*
WM Hayman 1910 *GBR*
BH Heatlie 1910 *GBR*
P Henn 2004 *Chl, Ur, Ven,* 2005 *J, It,* 2007 *It,* 2012 *F,* 2013 *E, E*
F Henrys 1910 *GBR*
F Heriot 1910 *GBR*
JM Hernández 2003 *Par, Ur, F, F, SA, C, A, Nm, R,* 2004 *F, I, SA,* 2005 *SA, S, It,* 2006 *W, W, NZ, E, It, F,* 2007 *F, Geo, I, S, SA, F,* 2008 *It, F, It,* 2009 *E, E,* 2012 *SA, NZ, A, NZ, A,*

W, I, 2013 SA, NZ, A, NZ, A, 2014 SA, NZ, A, NZ, A, S, It, F, 2015 SA, NZ, Geo, Nm, I, A
M Hernandez 1927 GBR, GBR, GBR
L Herrera 1991 Ur, Par
R Herrera 2014 I, I, SA, SA, NZ, A, NZ, A, S, It, F, 2015 NZ, A, NZ, Geo, Tg, Nm, I, A, SA
FA Higgs 2004 Ur, Ven, 2005 J
D Hine 1938 Chl
C Hirsch 1960 F
C Hirsch 1960 F
E Hirsch 1954 F, 1956 OCC
R Hogg 1958 Ur, Per, Chl, 1959 JSB, JSB, 1961 Chl, Bra, Ur
S Hogg 1956 OCC, OCC, 1958 Ur, Per, Chl, 1959 JSB, JSB
E Holmberg 1948 OCC
B Holmes 1949 F, F
E Holmgren 1958 Ur, Per, Chl, 1959 JSB, JSB, 1960 F, F
G Holmgren 1985 NZ, NZ
E Horan 1956 OCC
L Hughes 1936 Chl
M Hughes 1954 F, F
M Hughes 1949 F, F
CA Huntley Robertson 1932 JSB, JSB

A Iachetti 1977 Bra, 1987 Chl
A Iachetti 1975 Ur, Par, 1977 Ur, Par, Chl, 1978 E, It, 1979 NZ, NZ, A, A, 1980 WXV, Fj, Fj, 1981 E, E, 1982 F, F, Sp, 1987 Ur, Par, A, A, 1988 F, F, F, F, 1989 It, NZ, 1990 C, E, E
ME Iachetti 1979 NZ, NZ, A, A
M Iglesias 1973 R, 1974 F, F
S Iglesias Valdez 2013 Ur, Chl, E, W, 2014 Ur, Chl, I, S, It, 2015 Par, A
G Illia 1965 Rho
JL Imhoff 1967 Ur, Chl
JJ Imhoff 2010 Chl, 2011 W, E, R, Geo, NZ, 2012 A, NZ, A, W, F, I, 2013 A, NZ, A, A, E, It, 2014 NZ, A, NZ, A, S, F, 2015 A, SA, SA, NZ, Geo, Tg, Nm, I, A
P Imhoff 2013 Ur, Chl, Bra
V Inchausti 1936 Bl, Chl, Chl
F Insua 1971 Chl, Bra, Par, Ur, 1972 SAG, SAG, 1973 R, R, Bra, Chl, I, S, 1974 F, F, 1976 W, NZ, NZ, 1977 F, F
R Iraneta 1974 F, 1976 W, NZ
FJ Irarrazabal 1991 Sa, 1992 Sp, Sp
S Irazoqui 1993 J, Chl, Par, Ur, 1995 E, Par
A Irigoyen 1997 Par
F Isa 2014 S, It, F, 2015 Ur, Par, NZ, A, Geo, Tg, Nm, I, A, SA
DJ Isaack 2013 Ur, Chl

C Jacobi 1979 Chl, Par
AG Jacobs 1927 GBR, GBR
AGW Jones 1948 OCC
GM Jorge 1989 Bra, Chl, Par, Ur, 1990 I, E, 1992 F, F, Sp, Sp, R, F, 1993 J, J, Bra, Chl, Ur, SA, SA, 1994 US, S, S, US
E Jurado 1995 A, A, E, Sa, It, Par, Chl, Ur, R, It, F, 1996 SA, E, 1997 E, E, NZ, NZ, Ur, R, It, F, A, A, 1998 F, Ur, C, It, 1999 W

E Karplus 1959 JSB, JSB, 1960 F, F, F
A Ker 1936 Chl, 1938 Chl
E Kossler 1960 F, F, F

EH Laborde 1991 A, W, Sa
G Laborde 1979 Chl, Bra
J Lacarra 1989 Par, Ur
R Lagarde 1956 OCC
A Lalanne 2008 SA, 2009 E, E, W, S, 2010 S, I, 2011 R, Geo, NZ
M Lamas 1998 Par, Chl
FJ Lamy 2013 Ur, Chl, Bra
M Landajo 2010 Ur, Chl, 2012 Ur, Bra, Chl, It, F, SA, NZ, A, NZ, A, W, F, I, 2013 E, SA, SA, NZ, A, NZ, A, E, W, It, 2014 Chl, I, I, S, SA, SA, NZ, A, NZ, A, S, It, F, 2015 Ur, Par, NZ, A, SA, SA, NZ, Geo, Tg, Nm, I, A, SA
TR Landajo 1977 F, Bra, Ur, Chl, 1978 E, 1979 A, A, 1980 WXV, Fj, Fj, 1981 E, E
M Lanfranco 1991 Ur, Par, Bra
AR Lanusse 1932 JSB
M Lanusse 1951 Ur, Bra, Chl
J Lanza 1985 F, Ur, Par, NZ, NZ, 1986 F, F, A, A, 1987 Ur, Fj, It, NZ
P Lanza 1983 Chl, Par, Ur, 1985 F, F, Ur, Chl, Par, NZ, NZ, 1986 F, F, A, A, 1987 It, NZ

J Lasalle 1964 Ur
TE Lavanini 2013 Ur, Bra, SA, W, It, 2014 Ur, Chl, I, I, S, SA, SA, NZ, NZ, A, S, It, F, 2015 A, SA, SA, NZ, Geo, Tg, I, A, SA
J Lavayen 1961 Chl, Bra, Ur
CG Lazcano Miranda 1998 Chl, 2004 Chl, Ur, Ven, 2005 J
RA Le Fort 1990 I, E, 1991 NZ, NZ, Chl, A, W, 1992 R, F, 1993 J, SA, SA, 1995 Ur, It
F Lecot 2003 Par, Ur, 2005 J, 2007 Chl
P Ledesma 2008 It, SA
ME Ledesma 1996 Ur, C, 1997 NZ, NZ, Ur, R, It, F, A, A, 1998 F, F, Ur, C, J, Ur, F, W, 1999 W, W, Sa, J, I, F, 2000 SA, 2001 It, W, NZ, 2002 F, E, SA, A, It, I, 2003 F, SA, Fj, US, C, A, Nm, R, 2004 W, NZ, F, I, 2005 It, It, SA, S, It, 2006 W, W, NZ, Chl, Ur, E, It, F, 2007 W, F, Geo, I, S, SA, 2008 SA, F, It, I, 2009 E, E, W, 2010 S, S, F, It, F, I, 2011 W, E, R, S, Geo, NZ
J Legora 1996 F, F, US, Ur, 1997 Chl, 1998 Par
JM Leguizamon 2005 J, It, It, SA, S, It, 2006 W, NZ, Chl, Ur, E, It, F, 2007 I, I, It, W, F, Geo, Nm, S, SA, F, 2008 S, S, It, SA, I, 2009 E, I, 2010 S, S, F, It, F, I, 2011 W, E, R, S, Geo, NZ, 2012 NZ, A, NZ, A, W, F, I, 2013 SA, SA, NZ, A, NZ, A, E, W, It, 2014 SA, SA, NZ, A, 2015 NZ, SA, NZ, Geo, SA
GP Leiros 1973 Bra, I
C Lennon 1958 Ur, Per
TC Leonardi 2009 E, W, S, 2012 It, F, F, SA, SA, NZ, A, NZ, A, W, I, 2013 E, E, Geo
FJ Leonelli Morey 2001 Ur, 2004 Ur, Ven, 2005 J, It, SA, S, It, 2006 W, W, 2007 I, I, It, 2008 F, I, 2009 E
M Lerga 1995 Par, Chl, Ur
Lesianado 1948 Ur
I Lewis 1932 JSB
TM Lezana 2014 F, 2015 Ur, Par, SA, SA
GA Llanes 1990 I, E, S, 1991 NZ, NZ, Chl, A, W, 1992 F, F, Sp, R, F, 1993 Bra, Chl, SA, SA, 1994 US, S, S, SA, SA, 1995 A, A, E, Sa, It, R, It, F, 1996 SA, SA, E, 1997 E, E, NZ, NZ, R, It, F, 1998 F, 2000 A
MA Lobato 2010 Ur, Chl
N Lobo 2012 F, I, 2013 SA, NZ, A, NZ, A, E, W, It
L Lobrauco 1996 US, 1997 Chl, 1998 J, Chl, Ur
MH Loffreda 1978 E, 1979 NZ, NZ, A, A, 1980 WXV, Fj, Fj, 1981 E, E, C, 1982 F, F, Sp, 1983 WXV, A, A, 1985 Ur, Chl, Par, 1987 Ur, Par, Chl, A, A, 1988 F, F, F, F, 1989 It, NZ, Bra, Chl, Par, Ur, US, E, E, 1994 US, S, US, SA
O Logan 1000 Bl
GM Longo Elia 1999 W, W, S, I, W, Sa, I, F, 2000 I, A, A, SA, E, 2001 US, NZ, It, W, S, NZ, 2002 F, E, SA, A, It, I, 2003 F, F, SA, Fj, C, A, I, 2004 W, W, NZ, F, I, 2005 It, It, SA, 2006 W, W, NZ, E, It, F, 2007 W, Nm, I, S, SA, F
L Lopez Fleming 2004 Ur, Ven, W, 2005 Sa
A Lopresti 1997 Par, Chl
J Loures 1954 F
R Loyola 1964 Ur, Chl, 1965 Rho, JSB, OCC, OCC, Chl, 1966 SAG, SAG, 1968 W, W, 1969 S, S, 1970 I, I, 1971 Chl, Bra, Par, Ur
E Lozada 2006 E, It, 2007 I, I, Geo, F, 2008 S, S, It, SA, F, It, I, 2009 E, E, E, 2010 It, 2012 F, F, 2013 E, E, Geo
F Lucioni 1927 GBR
R Lucke 1975 Ur, Par, Bra, Chl, 1981 C
FD Luna 2011 Ur
J Luna 1995 Par, Chl, Ur, R, It, F, 1997 Par, Chl

P Macadam 1949 F, F
AM Macome 1990 I, E, 1995 Ur, C
B Macome 2012 Ur, Bra, Chl, It, F, F, 2013 E, E, Geo, SA, NZ, NZ, A, E, It, 2014 I, A, NZ, A, 2015 NZ, SA
B Madero 2011 Chl, Ur, 2013 E, Geo
RM Madero 1978 E, It, 1979 NZ, NZ, A, A, 1980 WXV, Fj, Fj, 1981 E, E, C, 1982 F, F, Sp, 1983 WXV, A, A, 1985 F, NZ, 1986 A, A, 1987 Ur, It, NZ, Sp, Ur, Par, Chl, A, A, 1988 F, F, F, 1989 It, NZ, NZ, 1990 E, E
L Maguire 2014 Chl
M Maineri 1993 Chl, Ur
L Makin 1927 GBR
A Mamanna 1991 Par, 1997 Par
G Manso 2013 Chl, Bra
J Manuel Belgrano 1956 OCC
A Marguery 1991 Ur, Bra, 1993 Chl, Par
R Martin 1938 Chl
RA Martin 1994 US, S, S, US, SA, SA, 1995 Ur, C, A, A, E, Sa,

It, Chl, Ur, R, It, F, 1996 *Ur, F, F, Ur, C, SA, SA, E,* 1997 *E, E, NZ, NZ, It, F, A, A,* 1998 *F, F, R, US, Ur, J, Par, Chl, Ur, It, W,* 1999 *W, W, S, I, W, Sa, J, I, F,* 2000 *I, A, A, SA, E,* 2001 *Ur, US, C, NZ, It, W, S, NZ,* 2002 *Ur, Par, Chl, F, E, SA, A, It, I,* 2003 *Par, Chl, Ur, F, SA, Ur, C, A, R, I*
F Martin Aramburu 2004 *Chl, Ven, W, NZ, F, I,* 2005 *It, SA, S, It,* 2006 *NZ,* 2007 *Geo, F,* 2008 *S, SA, F, It, I,* 2009 *E, S*
J Martin Copella 1989 *Chl, Par*
C Martinez 1969 *Ur, Chl,* 1970 *I, I*
E Martinez 1971 *Chl, Bra, Ur*
O Martinez Basante 1954 *F*
M Martinez Mosquera 1971 *Chl*
RC Mastai 1975 *F,* 1976 *W, NZ, NZ,* 1977 *F, F, Bra, Ur, Par, Chl,* 1980 *WXV*
R Matarazzo 1971 *SAG, SAG, Par, Ur,* 1972 *SAG, SAG,* 1973 *R, R, Par, Ur, Chl, I, S,* 1974 *F, F*
PN Matera 2013 *Chl, Bra, SA, SA, NZ, A, NZ, A, E, W, It,* 2014 *SA, SA,* 2015 *Ur, SA, SA, NZ, Geo, Tg, Nm, I, A*
H Maurer 1932 *JSB, JSB*
L Maurette 1948 *OCC, OCC*
C Mazzini 1977 *F, F*
CJ McCarthy 1910 *GBR*
G McCormick 1964 *Bra, Chl,* 1965 *Rho, OCC, OCC, Chl,* 1966 *SAG, SAG*
M McCormick 1927 *GBR*
A Memoli 1979 *Ur, Par, Bra*
FJ Mendez 1991 *Ur, Par, Bra,* 1992 *Sp, Sp*
FE Méndez 1990 *I, E,* 1991 *NZ, NZ, Chl, A, W,* 1992 *F, F, Sp, Sp, R, F,* 1994 *S, US, SA, SA,* 1995 *Ur, C, A, A, E, Sa, It, Par, Chl, Ur, R, It, F,* 1996 *SA, SA,* 1997 *E,* 1998 *F, F, R, US, Ur, C, It, F, W,* 1999 *W, W,* 2000 *I, A, A, SA, E,* 2001 *NZ, It, W, S, NZ,* 2002 *Ur, Chl, F, E, SA, A, A,* 2003 *F, F, SA, Fj, Ur, Nm, I,* 2004 *Chl, Ur, W, W, NZ, SA*
H Mendez 1967 *Ur, Chl*
L Mendez 1958 *Ur, Per, Chl,* 1959 *JSB*
S Mendez 2013 *Ur, Chl, Bra*
CI Mendy 1987 *Ur, Par, Chl, A, A,* 1988 *F, F, F,* 1989 *It, NZ, NZ, US,* 1990 *C,* 1991 *Ur, Bra*
FJ Merello 2007 *Chl,* 2010 *Ur, Chl*
I Merlo 1993 *Bra, Chl*
P Merlo 1985 *Chl, Par*
SE Meson 1987 *Par,* 1989 *Bra, Par, Ur, US,* 1990 *US, C, S,* 1991 *NZ, Chl, Sa,* 1992 *F, F, Sp, R, F,* 1993 *J, Bra, Par, Ur, SA, SA,* 1994 *US, S, S, US,* 1995 *Ur, C, A, A,* 1996 *US, C,* 1997 *Chl*
I Mieres 2007 *Chl,* 2010 *Ur, Chl,* 2012 *It, F*
BH Miguens 1983 *WXV, A, A,* 1985 *F, F, NZ, NZ,* 1986 *F, F, A, A,* 1987 *Sp*
E Miguens 1975 *Ur, Par, Chl*
H Miguens 1969 *S, S, Ur, Chl,* 1970 *I, I,* 1971 *OCC,* 1972 *SAG, SAG,* 1973 *R, R, Par, Ur, Bra, Chl, I, S,* 1975 *F*
J Miguens 1982 *F,* 1985 *F, F,* 1986 *F, F, A, A*
GE Milano 1982 *F, F, Sp,* 1983 *WXV, A, A,* 1985 *F, F, Ur, Chl, Par, NZ, NZ,* 1986 *F, F, A, A,* 1987 *Ur, Fj, Sp, Ur, Chl, A, A,* 1988 *F, F, F,* 1989 *It, NZ, NZ*
A Mimesi 1998 *J, Par, Chl*
B Minguez 1975 *Par, Bra, Chl,* 1979 *Ur, Chl, Par,* 1983 *WXV, A, A,* 1985 *Ur, Chl*
R Miralles 2011 *Chl, F,* 2012 *Chl, F,* 2015 *Par*
B Mitchelstein 1936 *BI*
E Mitchelstein 1956 *OCC,* 1960 *F, F*
C Mold 1910 *GBR*
LE Molina 1985 *Chl,* 1987 *Ur, Fj, It, NZ,* 1989 *NZ, NZ, Bra, Chl, Par,* 1990 *C, E,* 1991 *W*
M Molina 1998 *Par, Chl, Ur*
M Montero 2012 *Ur, Bra, Chl, It, F, F, I,* 2013 *E, E,* 2014 *Ur, I, I, S, SA, SA, A, NZ, S, It, F,* 2015 *Ur*
G Montes de Oca 1961 *Chl, Bra, Ur*
JS Montoya 2014 *Ur, Chl, I, S,* 2015 *Ur, Par, NZ, SA, SA, NZ, Geo, Tg, Nm, I, A, SA*
E Montpelat 1948 *OCC, OCC*
G Morales Oliver 2001 *Ur, US, C*
C Morea 1951 *Ur, Bra, Chl*
FR Morel 1979 *A, A,* 1980 *WXV, Fj, Fj,* 1981 *E, E, C,* 1982 *F,* 1985 *F, F, Ur, Par, NZ, NZ,* 1986 *F, F, A,* 1987 *Ur, Fj*
A Moreno 1998 *Par, Chl, Ur*
D Morgan 1967 *Chl,* 1970 *I, I,* 1971 *SAG, SAG, OCC, OCC,* 1972 *SAG, SAG*
E Morgan 1969 *S, S,* 1972 *SAG, SAG,* 1973 *R, R, Par, Ur, Bra, Chl, I, S,* 1975 *F, F*

G Morgan 1977 *Bra, Ur, Par, Chl,* 1979 *Ur, Par, Bra*
M Morgan 1971 *SAG, OCC, OCC*
JS Morganti 1951 *Ur, Bra, Chl*
M Moroni 2014 *S, It,* 2015 *A, SA, Tg, Nm, I, SA*
J Mostany 1987 *Ur, Fj, NZ*
R Moyano 2011 *Chl, Ur,* 2012 *Ur, Bra,* 2014 *Ur, Chl*
E Muliero 1997 *Chl*
S Muller 1927 *GBR*
R Muniz 1975 *Par, Bra, Chl*

M Nannini 2002 *Ur, Par, Chl,* 2003 *Par, Chl*
A Navajas 1932 *JSB, JSB*
E Naveyra 1998 *Chl*
G Nazassi 1997 *Chl*
ML Negri 1979 *Chl, Bra*
E Neri 1960 *F, F,* 1961 *Chl, Bra, Ur,* 1964 *Ur, Bra, Chl,* 1965 *Rho, JSB, OCC, OCC,* 1966 *SAG, SAG*
CM Neyra 1975 *F, F,* 1976 *W, NZ, NZ,* 1983 *WXV*
A Nicholson 1979 *Ur, Par, Bra*
HM Nicola 1971 *SAG, OCC, OCC, Chl, Bra, Par, Ur,* 1975 *F, F,* 1978 *E, It,* 1979 *NZ, NZ*
L Noguera 2014 *Ur, Chl, I, I, S, SA, NZ, NZ, S, It, F,* 2015 *Ur, Par, NZ, SA, SA, NZ, Geo, Tg, Nm, I, A, SA*
EP Noriega 1991 *Par,* 1992 *Sp, Sp, R, F,* 1993 *J, J, Chl, Par, Ur, SA, SA,* 1994 *US, S, S, US, SA, SA,* 1995 *Ur, C, A, A, E, Sa, It*
JL Novillo 2015 *Ur, Par*
JM Nuñez Piossek 2001 *Ur, NZ,* 2002 *Ur, Par, Chl, A,* 2003 *Par, Ur, F, SA, Ur, C, A, R, I,* 2004 *Chl, Ur, W, W,* 2005 *It, It,* 2006 *W, W, NZ, E, F,* 2008 *S, SA*

R Ochoa 1956 *OCC*
M Odriozola 1961 *Chl, Ur*
J O'Farrell 1948 *OCC,* 1951 *Ur, Bra,* 1956 *OCC*
U O'Farrell 1951 *Ur, Bra, Chl*
C Ohanian 1998 *Par, Ur*
C Olivera 1958 *Ur, Per, Chl,* 1959 *JSB, JSB*
R Olivieri 1960 *F, F,* 1961 *Chl, Bra, Ur*
J Orengo 1996 *Ur,* 1997 *Ur, R, It,* 1998 *F, F, R, US, C, F, W,* 1999 *W,* 2000 *A, SA, E,* 2001 *Ur, US, C, NZ, W, S, NZ,* 2002 *F, E, SA, A, It, I,* 2003 *F, SA, Ur, C, A, I,* 2004 *W, W*
JP Orlandi 2008 *F, It, I,* 2009 *E, E,* 2012 *SA, NZ, A, NZ, A,* 2013 *SA, NZ, NZ, A, E,* 2015 *SA, Tg, Nm, I, SA*
M Orlando 2012 *Ur, Bra, Chl,* 2013 *E, E, Geo,* 2014 *Ur, I, S,* 2015 *Ur*
J Ortega Desio 2012 *Ur, Bra, Chl,* 2014 *Ur, Chl, I, I, S, A, S, It, F,* 2015 *Ur, Par, NZ, A, Geo, Nm, SA*
C Orti 1949 *F, F*
L Ortiz 2003 *Par, Chl, Ur*
A Orzabal 1974 *F, F*
L Ostiglia 1999 *W, W, S, I, W, J, F,* 2001 *NZ, It, W, S,* 2002 *E, SA,* 2003 *Par, Chl, It, F, F, SA, Nm, I,* 2004 *W, W, NZ, F, I, SA,* 2007 *F, Nm, I, S, SA*
B Otaño 1960 *F, F, F,* 1961 *Chl, Bra, Ur,* 1964 *Ur, Bra, Chl,* 1965 *Rho, JSB, OCC, OCC, Chl,* 1966 *SAG, SAG,* 1968 *W, W,* 1969 *S, S, Ur, Chl,* 1970 *I, I,* 1971 *SAG, OCC, OCC*
J Otaola 1970 *I,* 1971 *Chl, Bra, Par, Ur,* 1974 *F, F*

M Pacheco 1938 *Chl*
RL Pacheco 2010 *Ur, Chl*
A Palma 1949 *F, F,* 1952 *I, I,* 1954 *F, F*
D Palma 2012 *Ur, Chl*
JMC Palma 1982 *F, Sp,* 1983 *WXV, A, A*
R Palma 1985 *Chl, Par*
M Palou 1996 *US, Ur*
F Panessi 2013 *Ur, Chl*
M Parra 1975 *Ur, Bra, Chl*
A Pasalagua 1927 *GBR, GBR*
M Pascual 1965 *Rho, JSB, OCC, OCC, Chl,* 1966 *SAG, SAG,* 1967 *Ur, Chl,* 1968 *W, W,* 1969 *S, S, Ur, Chl,* 1970 *I, I,* 1971 *SAG, SAG, OCC, OCC*
HR Pascuali 1936 *BI*
H Pasman 1936 *Chl*
R Passaglia 1977 *Bra, Ur, Chl,* 1978 *E, It*
G Paz 1979 *Ur, Chl, Par, Bra,* 1983 *Chl, Par, Ur*
J Paz 2013 *Ur, Chl, Bra,* 2015 *Ur, Par*
JJ Paz 1991 *Ur, Bra*
S Peretti 1993 *Bra, Par, SA*
L Pereyra 2010 *Ur, Chl*
N Perez 1968 *W*

RN Perez 1992 *F, F, Sp, R, F*, 1993 *Bra, Par, Ur, SA*, 1995 *Ur, R, It, F*, 1996 *US, Ur, C, SA, SA*, 1998 *Ur*, 1999 *I, W*
J Perez Cobo 1979 *NZ, NZ*, 1980 *Fj*, 1981 *E, E, C*
M Peri Brusa 1998 *Chl*
R Pesce 1958 *Ur, Per, Chl*
TA Petersen 1978 *E, It*, 1979 *NZ, NZ, A, A*, 1980 *Fj, Fj*, 1981 *E, E, C*, 1982 *F*, 1983 *WXV, A, A*, 1985 *F, F, Ur, Chl, Par, NZ, NZ*, 1986 *F, F, A*
AD Petrilli 2004 *SA*, 2005 *J*
J Petrone 1949 *F, F*
R Petti 1995 *Par, Chl*
G Petti 2014 *It, F*, 2015 *Ur, Par, NZ, SA, NZ, Tg, Nm, I, A, SA*
M Pfister 1994 *SA, SA*, 1996 *F*, 1998 *R, Ur, J*
S Phelan 1997 *Ur, Chl, R, It*, 1998 *F, F, R, US, C, It*, 1999 *S, I, W, Sa, J, I, F*, 2000 *I, A, SA, E*, 2001 *NZ, It, W, S, NZ*, 2002 *Ur, Par, Chl, F, E, SA, A, It, I*, 2003 *F, SA, Fj, C, A, R*
A Phillips 1948 *OCC*, 1949 *F, F*
JP Piccardo 1981 *E*, 1983 *Chl, Par, Ur*
A Pichot 1995 *A, R, It, F*, 1996 *Ur, F, F*, 1997 *It, F, A, A*, 1998 *F, F, R, It, F, W*, 1999 *W, W, S, I, W, Sa, J, I, F*, 2000 *I, A, A, SA, E*, 2001 *Ur, US, C, NZ, It, W, S, NZ*, 2002 *F, E, SA, A, It, I*, 2003 *Ur, C, A, R, I*, 2004 *F, I, SA*, 2005 *It, SA, S, It*, 2006 *W, W, NZ, Chl, Ur, E, F*, 2007 *W, F, Nm, I, S, SA, F*
G Pimentel 1971 *Bra*
R Pineo 1954 *F*
E Pittinari 1991 *Ur, Par, Bra*
M Plaza 2015 *Par*
SA Poet 2013 *Ur, Chl, Bra*
E Poggi 1965 *JSB, OCC, OCC, Chl*, 1966 *SAG*, 1967 *Ur*, 1969 *Ur*
C Pollano 1927 *GBR*
L Ponce 2014 *Ur, Chl, S, It, F*
S Ponce 2007 *Chl*
R Pont Lezica 1951 *Ur, Bra, Chl*
H Porta 1971 *Chl, Bra, Par, Ur*, 1972 *SAG, SAG*, 1973 *R, R, Ur, Bra, Chl, I, S*, 1974 *F, F*, 1975 *F, F*, 1976 *W, NZ, NZ*, 1977 *F, F*, 1978 *E, It*, 1979 *NZ, NZ, A, A*, 1980 *WXV, Fj, Fj*, 1981 *E, E, C*, 1982 *F, F, Sp*, 1983 *A, A*, 1985 *F, F, Ur, Chl, Par, NZ, NZ*, 1986 *F, F, A*, 1987 *Fj, It, NZ, Sp, A, A*, 1990 *I, E, S*
O Portillo 1995 *Par, Chl*, 1997 *Par, Chl*
J Posse 1977 *Par*
S Posse 1991 *Par*, 1993 *Bra, Chl, Ur*
B Postiglioni 2012 *Ur, Bra, Chl, It, F, F, W*, 2013 *Geo*, 2014 *Ur, Chl, I, I, S, SA, A, A*, 2015 *Ur, Par*
C Promanzio 1995 *C*, 1996 *Ur, F, F, E*, 1997 *E, E, NZ, Ur*, 1998 *R, J*
U Propato 1956 *OCC*
L Proto 2010 *Ur, Chl*
A Puccio 1979 *Chl, Par, Bra*
M Puigdeval 1964 *Ur, Bra*
J Pulido 1960 *F*

JC Queirolo 1964 *Ur, Bra, Chl*
G Quesada 1996 *US, Ur, C, SA, E*, 1997 *E, E, NZ, NZ*, 1998 *F, R, US, C, It*, 1999 *W, S, I, W, Sa, J, I, F*, 2000 *I, SA, E*, 2001 *NZ, It, NZ*, 2002 *F, E, SA*, 2003 *F, SA, Ur, C, Nm, R, I*
E Quetglas 1965 *Chl*

R Raimundez 1959 *JSB, JSB*
C Ramallo 1979 *Ur, Chl, Par*
S Ratcliff 1936 *Chl*
F Rave 1997 *Par*
M Reggiardo 1996 *Ur, F, F, E*, 1997 *E, E, NZ, NZ, R, F, A, A*, 1998 *F, F, R, US, Ur, C, It, W*, 1999 *W, W, S, I, W, Sa, J, I, F*, 2000 *I, SA*, 2001 *NZ, It, W, S, NZ*, 2002 *F, E, SA, A, It, I*, 2003 *F, SA, Fj, US, Ur, A, Nm, I*
A Reid 1910 *GBR*
C Reyes 1927 *GBR, GBR, GBR*
M Ricci 1987 *Sp*
A Riganti 1927 *GBR, GBR, GBR*
MA Righentini 1989 *NZ*
J Rios 1960 *F, F*
G Rivero 1996 *Ur, US, Ur*
G Roan 2010 *Ur, Chl*, 2013 *E, E, Geo*
T Roan 2007 *Chl*
F Robson 1927 *GBR*
M Roby 1992 *Sp*, 1993 *J*
A Rocca 1989 *US*, 1990 *C, US, C, E*, 1991 *Ur, Bra*
S Rocchia 2013 *Ur, Chl, Bra*

O Rocha 1974 *F, F*
D Rodriguez 1998 *J, Par, Chl, Ur*
D Rodriguez 2002 *Ur, Par, Chl*
EE Rodriguez 1979 *NZ, NZ, A, A*, 1980 *WXV, Fj, Fj*, 1981 *E, E, C*, 1983 *WXV, A, A*
F Rodriguez 2007 *Chl*
M Rodriguez 2009 *E, W, S*, 2010 *S, S, F, It, F, I*, 2011 *W, E, R, S, Geo*, 2012 *SA, SA, NZ, NZ*
A Rodriguez Jurado 1965 *JSB, OCC, OCC, Chl*, 1966 *SAG, SAG*, 1968 *W, W*, 1969 *S, Chl*, 1970 *I*, 1971 *SAG*, 1973 *R, Par, Bra, Chl, I, S*, 1974 *F, F*, 1975 *F, F*
A Rodriguez Jurado 1927 *GBR, GBR, GBR, GBR*, 1932 *JSB, JSB, 1936 Chl, Chl*
M Rodriguez Jurado 1971 *SAG, OCC, Chl, Bra, Par, Ur*
J Rojas 2012 *Ur, Bra, Chl*, 2013 *It*, 2014 *Chl*
L Roldan 2001 *Ur, C*
AS Romagnoli 2004 *Chl, Ur, Ven*
R Roncero 1998 *J*, 2002 *Ur, Par, Chl*, 2003 *Fj, US, Nm, R*, 2004 *W, W, NZ, F, I*, 2005 *It, SA, S, It*, 2006 *W, W, NZ*, 2007 *W, F, Nm, I, S, SA, F*, 2008 *It, SA, F, It, I*, 2009 *E, E, E, W, S*, 2010 *S, S, F, It, F, I*, 2011 *W, E, R, S, NZ*, 2012 *It, SA, SA, NZ, A, NZ, A*
S Rondinelli 2005 *Sa*
T Rosati 2011 *Chl, Ur*
S Rosatti 1977 *Par, Chl*
M Rospide 2003 *Par, Chl, Ur*
F Rossi 1991 *Ur, Par, Bra*, 1998 *F*
D Rotondo 1997 *Par, Chl*
MA Ruiz 1997 *NZ, Chl, R, It, F, A, A*, 1998 *F, F, R, US, Ur, C, J, It, F, W*, 1999 *W, Sa, J, F*, 2002 *Ur, Par, Chl*

I Saenz Lancuba 2012 *Ur, Bra*, 2013 *Ur, Chl, Bra*
JE Saffery 1910 *GBR*
CMS Sainz Trapaga 1979 *Ur, Par, Bra*
A Salinas 1954 *F*, 1956 *OCC*, 1958 *Ur, Chl*, 1960 *F, F*
S Salvat 1987 *Ur, Fj, It*, 1988 *F*, 1989 *It, NZ*, 1990 *C, US, C, E*, 1991 *Ur, Par, Bra*, 1992 *Sp, F*, 1993 *Bra, Chl, Par, Ur, SA, SA*, 1994 *SA, SA*, 1995 *Ur, C, A, A, E, Sa, It, Par, Chl, Ur, R, It, F*
T Salzman 1936 *Bl, Chl, Chl*
M Sambucetti 2001 *Ur, US, C*, 2002 *Ur, Chl*, 2003 *Par, Chl, Fj*, 2005 *It, Sa*, 2009 *W*
HA San Martin 2009 *W, S*
FN Sanchez 2010 *Chl*, 2011 *R*, 2012 *SA, A, W, F, I*, 2013 *SA, SA, NZ, A, NZ, A, E, W, It*, 2014 *Chl, I, I, S, SA, SA, NZ, A, NZ, A, S, It, F*, 2015 *NZ, A, SA, NZ, Geo, Tg, I, A, SA*
T Sanderson 1932 *JSB*
D Sanes 1985 *Chl, Par*, 1986 *F, F*, 1987 *Ur, Par, Chl*, 1989 *Bra, Chl, Ur*
EJ Sanguinetti 1975 *Ur, Par, Chl*, 1978 *It*, 1979 *A*, 1982 *F, F, Sp*
G Sanguinetti 1979 *Ur, Chl, Par, Bra*
J Sansot 1948 *OCC*
M Sansot 1975 *F, F*, 1976 *W, NZ, NZ*, 1977 *Bra, Chl*, 1978 *E, It*, 1979 *NZ, NZ, A, A*, 1980 *WXV, Fj*, 1983 *WXV*
JM Santamarina 1991 *NZ, NZ, Chl, A, W, Sa*, 1992 *F, Sp, R, F*, 1993 *J, J*, 1994 *US, S, US*, 1995 *A, A, E, Sa, It, Ur, R, It, F*
J Santiago 1948 *OCC*, 1952 *I, I*
JR Sanz 1973 *Par, Ur, Bra, Chl*, 1974 *F, F*, 1977 *F, F*
S Sanz 2003 *US*, 2004 *Chl, Ven*, 2005 *It, Sa*, 2007 *Chl*
M Sarandon 1948 *OCC, OCC*, 1949 *F, F*, 1951 *Ur, Bra, Chl*, 1952 *I, I*, 1954 *F*
J Sartori 1979 *Chl, Par, Bra*
R Sauze 1983 *Par*
FW Saywer 1910 *GBR*
MA Scelzo 1996 *US, SA*, 1997 *R, It, F, A*, 1998 *F, US, Ur, C, Chl, F*, 1999 *I, Sa, I, F*, 2000 *I, A, A*, 2003 *F, F, Fj, Ur, C, Nm, R, I*, 2005 *SA, S, It*, 2006 *W, W, NZ, Chl, Ur, E, F*, 2007 *W, F, Nm, I, S, SA*, 2009 *E, W, S*, 2010 *S, S, F, It, F, I*, 2011 *W, E, R, S, Geo, NZ*
F Schacht 1989 *Bra, Chl, Par, Ur, US*, 1990 *C*
E Scharemberg 1961 *Chl, Bra, Ur*, 1964 *Ur, Bra*, 1965 *Rho, JSB, OCC, OCC*, 1967 *Ur, Chl*
AM Schiavio 1983 *Chl, Ur*, 1986 *A*, 1987 *Fj, It, NZ*
E Schiavio 1936 *Bl, Chl, Chl*
H Schierano 2011 *Chl, Ur*
R Schmidt 1960 *F, F, F*, 1961 *Bra*, 1964 *Ur*, 1965 *JSB*
G Schmitt 1964 *Ur, Chl*
G Schulz 2013 *Ur, Bra*
M Schusterman 2003 *Par, Fj*, 2004 *W, W, NZ, F*, 2005 *It, It, SA, S*, 2006 *W, Chl, Ur, E*, 2007 *I, It, Geo*

#KEEP RUGBY CLEAN

WORLD RUGBY™ ANTI-DOPING

Felipe Contepomi, Argentina
World Rugby Anti-Doping Ambassador

In partnership with

AUSTRALIA

AUSTRALIA'S 2014–15 TEST RECORD

OPPONENT	DATE	VENUE	RESULT
New Zealand	18 Oct	H	Lost 28–29
Wales	8 Nov	A	Won 33–28
France	15 Nov	A	Lost 29–26
Ireland	22 Nov	A	Lost 26–23
England	29 Nov	A	Lost 26–17
South Africa	18 Jul	H	Won 24–20
Argentina	25 Jul	A	Won 34–9
New Zealand	8 Aug	H	Won 27–19
New Zealand	15 Aug	A	Lost 41–13
USA	5 Sep	A	Won 47–10
Fiji	23 Sep	N	Won 28–13
Uruguay	27 Sep	N	Won 65–3
England	3 Oct	A	Won 33–13
Wales	10 Oct	N	Won 15–6
Scotland	18 Oct	N	Won 35–34
Argentina	25 Oct	N	Won 29–15
New Zealand	31 Oct	N	Lost 34–17

WALLABIES REAP REWARDS OF CHIEKA'S PHILOSOPHY

By George Gregan

Australia number eight David Pocock made the most turnovers at Rugby World Cup 2015 with 17.

When you consider the problems Australia were experiencing on and off the pitch when Michael Cheika succeeded Ewen McKenzie as head coach last October, you would have to say he enjoyed an outstanding first 12 months in the job. To turn things around so quickly and reach the final of Rugby World Cup 2015, as well as secure The Rugby Championship, was some achievement and his side achieved both with a style that was easy on the eye.

It was pretty clear when he was appointed that Cheika was going to have a different relationship with the players and the public and both responded really well to his straight up character. The players bought into what he was trying to achieve and I was delighted to see that he wanted the Wallabies to play in a way that is indicative of the way the game should be played. Cheika's side were positive, they were attacking and they backed themselves.

The other big change I think was the sense of pride that returned to the squad. Cheika reminded the players how lucky they were to be representing their country. A lot is spoken about what the All Black jumper means to the New Zealand players, but I thought he restored that same pride in the Wallaby jersey and that was reflected in the performances as the year unfolded.

Cheika also made some shrewd coaching appointments that significantly strengthened the team. His decision to bring in Mario Ledesma to work on the scrum was probably the most important and although the former Pumas hooker only linked up with the Wallabies two months before the start of the World Cup, his impact on the Australian set piece was pretty remarkable.

I was at Twickenham for the 26–17 defeat to England in November and the team was badly outscrummaged. I was talking to Martin Johnson and he predicted England would stick it up their jumper and grind the Wallabies down in the set-piece and that's exactly what they did. The scrum gave England the platform to get the win but when the two teams met in the World Cup that dominance up front was gone and Ledesma deserves a huge amount of credit for that turnaround.

The other coaches Cheika brought into the fold also produced the goods. Nathan Grey brought a new attitude to the contact area as defence coach while Stephen Larkham's role as the attack coach saw the Wallabies playing hard but with more intelligence. Stephen knows his stuff and I thought Australia looked capable of scoring points against any side in the world once he was on board.

Cheika was dropped in at the deep end with the tour of Europe just a couple of weeks before the first game and it was no big surprise the Wallabies won just one of four tests after beating Wales in Cardiff.

When The Rugby Championship came around in July he'd had the time to put his stamp on things and the win over the All Blacks in Sydney and a first title made people sit up and take notice. I'd be surprised if Cheika had genuinely sat down beforehand and targeted the silverware. I suspect he was more interested in development but their success obviously didn't do the team's confidence any harm at all.

There were good things in all three of their victories. To recover from a 13-point deficit against the Springboks in Brisbane was very impressive and definitely showed the team was on the right road while there are few tougher places to play test rugby than Mendoza but the Wallabies looked totally in control as they ran in four tries against Argentina in a 34–9 win. The prized scalp was, of course, the All Blacks. It's always great to beat New Zealand and to come out on top against the number one ranked side in the world just before the World

AUSTRALIA

Cup was evidence the Wallabies were heading in the right direction.

Cheika's squad for the World Cup didn't contain any big surprises but his masterstroke was to take advantage of the changes the ARU made to the selection criteria, allowing him to pick certain overseas-based players, and call up Matt Giteau and Drew Mitchell. With their test experience alone, they brought something to the party, but I think it was their winning mentality, their recent experience of winning domestic and European trophies with Toulon, that was a big boost to the Wallabies. Self-belief and confidence rubs off on other players and I sensed throughout the World Cup that was the case with Giteau and Mitchell. They probably thought they'd played their last test, so were also both pretty hungry to make their mark again on the international stage.

I never bought into the whole 'Pool of Death' thing at the World Cup. For me it was more a pool of opportunity because I always felt whichever side won the group would then get to the final and that's exactly how it played out.

The Wallabies were expected to beat Fiji and Uruguay in the first two games and they did. Some people were worried we didn't pick up a bonus point in the 28–13 victory over Fiji but I'm old school in that respect and believe a seven-week long knockout tournament will always take care of itself as long as you continue to produce the results.

The England game was the big one and I was so impressed by the calm and composed way the Wallabies went about their business at Twickenham. As I mentioned earlier, the English didn't get the upper hand up front this time but it was the way Australia used the ball, how relaxed they looked, how they took their points that stood out for me. Bernard Foley's second try from a lineout was incredible, the product of weeks of preparation on the training ground, and to be able to produce that when it really mattered, in front of 80,000 people, was sensational. I'd also point out that Wallabies sides of the recent past might have folded when England pulled it back to 20–13 but not Cheika's team.

Any side coached by Warren Gatland is going to be a tough nut to crack and that's exactly what Wales were the next week. The England game was all about beautiful attacking rugby but it was the Wallabies' heroic defence when they were down to 13 men that stood out in the Welsh game. The Welsh threw absolutely everything at them but they showed great spirit and heart to hold out and it was that performance which really generated a response from the people back home. The Australian public loves a team with character and they showed bags of it in the Wales match.

There's no doubt Australia enjoyed a big slice of luck in the quarter-final against Scotland with the award of a last-minute penalty. Every team needs a bit of luck and the Wallabies got theirs that day. Scotland

I think enjoyed going in as underdogs and were able to swing from the hip but Australia scored five tries and lived to fight another day.

The Pumas in the last four was always going to be tough after their amazing performance against Ireland in the quarter-finals. That was some of the best rugby I'd seen in the tournament but just when Australia needed someone to stand up and be counted Adam Ashley-Cooper showed all his class and experience with a brilliant hat-trick.

Australia had never faced the All Blacks in the final before. It was the match everyone back home wanted to see and although it was heartbreak for the Wallabies after 80 minutes, it was a great game from a neutral perspective in terms of entertainment.

The All Blacks' first half performance was irresistible. The way they controlled territory and the ball with Dan Carter dictating the tempo of the game, was very professional and they squeezed the life out of the Wallabies. They are one of the best teams in All Black history, if not the best, and they showed exactly why in the first half at Twickenham.

The way Australia came back at them and scored two tries to make it 21–17 at one stage was very impressive. It wasn't enough to lift the trophy but as Cheika plans for the future, I think he can take a lot of encouragement from the character his side displayed in the final when their backs were firmly against the wall.

In terms of individuals performances over the year I'd have to mention David Pocock because like all great players he has that uncanny knack of making his team-mates around him perform. The other back rowers Michael Hooper and Scott Fardy were also impressive and you've got to congratulate Hooper on winning his 50th cap in the semi-final against Argentina at the age of 23.

I also think Kurtley Beale consistently added a spark to the side from the bench, but the standout guy for the Wallabies for me has to be Scott Sio. The whole Australia front five made big strides under Cheika but Sio came of age as an international loose-head and the stability he brought to the team up front transformed the way the Wallabies were able to play the game. The way he battled through the pain of the dislocated elbow he suffered in the quarter-final against Scotland to play in the final spoke volumes about his character.

The Wallabies' year ended with Michael Cheika being named the World Rugby Coach of the Year and although I'm sure he was humbled by that recognition, I don't think he's going to be resting on his laurels anytime soon. Australia made great strides forward under him, and I genuinely believe the future is bright, but Cheika's a winner and the fact is his team lost in the final. He'll now be focused on how he can make further improvements and how he can take the Wallabies to the next level.

AUSTRALIA INTERNATIONAL STATISTICS
MATCH RECORDS UP TO 1 NOVEMBER, 2015

MOST CONSECUTIVE TEST WINS

10 1991 *Arg, WS, W, I, NZ, E,* 1992 *S* 1,2, *NZ* 1,2
10 1998 *NZ* 3, *Fj, Tg, Sm, F, E* 2, 1999 *I* 1,2, *E, SA* 1
10 1999 *NZ* 2, *R, I* 3, *US, W, SA* 3, *F,* 2000 *Arg* 1,2,*SA* 1

MOST CONSECUTIVE TESTS WITHOUT DEFEAT

Matches	Wins	Draws	Period
10	10	0	1991 to 1992
10	10	0	1998 to 1999
10	10	0	1999 to 2000

MOST POINTS IN A MATCH
BY THE TEAM

Pts	Opponents	Venue	Year
142	Namibia	Adelaide	2003
92	Spain	Madrid	2001
91	Japan	Lyons	2007
90	Romania	Brisbane	2003
76	England	Brisbane	1998
74	Canada	Brisbane	1996
74	Tonga	Canberra	1998
74	W Samoa	Sydney	2005
73	W Samoa	Sydney	1994
69	Italy	Melbourne	2005
68	Russia	Nelson	2011
67	United States	Brisbane	1990
67	United States	Wellington	2011

MOST POINTS IN A MATCH
BY A PLAYER

Pts	Player	Opponents	Venue	Year
42	MS Rogers	Namibia	Adelaide	2003
39	MC Burke	Canada	Brisbane	1996
30	EJ Flatley	Romania	Brisbane	2003
29	SA Mortlock	South Africa	Melbourne	2000
29	JD O'Connor	France	Paris	2010
28	MP Lynagh	Argentina	Brisbane	1995
28	BT Foley	England	Twickenham	2015
27	MJ Giteau	Fiji	Montpellier	2007
25	MC Burke	Scotland	Sydney	1998
25	MC Burke	France	Cardiff	1999
25	MC Burke	British/Irish Lions	Melbourne	2001
25	EJ Flatley*	Ireland	Perth	2003
25	CE Latham	Namibia	Adelaide	2003
24	MP Lynagh	United States	Brisbane	1990
24	MP Lynagh	France	Brisbane	1990
24	MC Burke	New Zealand	Melbourne	1998
24	MC Burke	South Africa	Twickenham	1999

* includes a penalty try

MOST TRIES IN A MATCH
BY THE TEAM

Tries	Opponents	Venue	Year
22	Namibia	Adelaide	2003
13	South Korea	Brisbane	1987
13	Spain	Madrid	2001
13	Romania	Brisbane	2003
13	Japan	Lyons	2007
12	United States	Brisbane	1990
12	Wales	Brisbane	1991
12	Tonga	Canberra	1998
12	Samoa	Sydney	2005
11	Western Samoa	Sydney	1994
11	England	Brisbane	1998
11	Italy	Melbourne	2005
11	United States	Wellington	2011
11	Uruguay	Birmingham	2015

BY A PLAYER

Tries	Player	Opponents	Venue	Year
5	CE Latham	Namibia	Adelaide	2003
4	G Cornelsen	New Zealand	Auckland	1978
4	DI Campese	United States	Sydney	1983
4	JS Little	Tonga	Canberra	1998
4	CE Latham	Argentina	Brisbane	2000
4	LD Tuqiri	Italy	Melbourne	2005

MOST CONVERSIONS IN A MATCH
BY THE TEAM

Cons	Opponents	Venue	Year
16	Namibia	Adelaide	2003
12	Spain	Madrid	2001
11	Romania	Brisbane	2003
10	Japan	Lyons	2007
9	Canada	Brisbane	1996
9	Fiji	Parramatta	1998
9	Russia	Nelson	2011
8	Italy	Rome	1988
8	United States	Brisbane	1990
7	Canada	Sydney	1985
7	Tonga	Canberra	1998
7	Samoa	Sydney	2005
7	Italy	Melbourne	2005
7	Fiji	Canberra	2010

BY A PLAYER

Cons	Player	Opponents	Venue	Year
16	MS Rogers	Namibia	Adelaide	2003
11	EJ Flatley	Romania	Brisbane	2003
10	MC Burke	Spain	Madrid	2001
9	MC Burke	Canada	Brisbane	1996
9	JA Eales	Fiji	Parramatta	1998
9	JD O'Connor	Russia	Nelson	2011
8	MP Lynagh	Italy	Rome	1988
8	MP Lynagh	United States	Brisbane	1990
7	MP Lynagh	Canada	Sydney	1985
7	SA Mortlock	Japan	Lyons	2007

MOST DROP GOALS IN A MATCH
BY THE TEAM

Drops	Opponents	Venue	Year
3	England	Twickenham	1967
3	Ireland	Dublin	1984
3	Fiji	Brisbane	1985

BY A PLAYER

Drops	Player	Opponents	Venue	Year
3	PF Hawthorne	England	Twickenham	1967
2	MG Ella	Ireland	Dublin	1984
2	DJ Knox	Fiji	Brisbane	1985

MOST PENALTIES IN A MATCH
BY THE TEAM

Penalties	Opponents	Venue	Year
8	South Africa	Twickenham	1999
7	New Zealand	Sydney	1999
7	France	Cardiff	1999
7	Wales	Cardiff	2001
7	England	Twickenham	2008
6	New Zealand	Sydney	1984
6	France	Sydney	1986
6	England	Brisbane	1988
6	Argentina	Buenos Aires	1997
6	Ireland	Perth	1999
6	France	Paris	2000
6	British/Irish Lions	Melbourne	2001
6	New Zealand	Sydney	2004
6	Italy	Padua	2008
6	New Zealand	Sydney	2009
6	South Africa	Brisbane	2010
6	Italy	Florence	2010
6	Wales	Melbourne	2012
6	Argentina	Rosario	2012
6	New Zealand	Brisbane	2012

BY A PLAYER

Pens	Player	Opponents	Venue	Year
8	MC Burke	South Africa	Twickenham	1999
7	MC Burke	New Zealand	Sydney	1999
7	MC Burke	France	Cardiff	1999
7	MC Burke	Wales	Cardiff	2001
6	MP Lynagh	France	Sydney	1986
6	MP Lynagh	England	Brisbane	1988
6	DJ Knox	Argentina	Buenos Aires	1997
6	MC Burke	France	Paris	2000
6	MC Burke	British/Irish Lions	Melbourne	2001
6	MJ Giteau	England	Twickenham	2008
6	MJ Giteau	New Zealand	Sydney	2009
6	BS Barnes	Italy	Florence	2010
6	MJ Harris	Argentina	Rosario	2012

AUSTRALIA

CAREER RECORDS

MOST CAPPED PLAYERS

Caps	Player	Career Span
139	GM Gregan	1994 to 2007
116	NC Sharpe	2002 to 2012
114	AP Ashley-Cooper	2005 to 2015
111	GB Smith	2000 to 2013
102	SJ Larkham	1996 to 2007
102	MJ Giteau	2002 to 2015
102	ST Moore	2005 to 2015
101	DI Campese	1982 to 1996
86	JA Eales	1991 to 2001
86	JWC Roff	1995 to 2004
81	MC Burke	1993 to 2004
80	TJ Horan	1989 to 2000
80	SA Mortlock	2000 to 2009
79	DJ Wilson	1992 to 2000
79	PR Waugh	2000 to 2009
78	CE Latham	1998 to 2007
75	JS Little	1989 to 2000
75	RD Elsom	2005 to 2011

MOST CONSECUTIVE TESTS

Tests	Player	Span
62	JWC Roff	1996 to 2001
46	PN Kearns	1989 to 1995
46	JA Slipper	2012 to 2015
44	GB Smith	2003 to 2006
43	MK Hooper	2012 to 2015
42	DI Campese	1990 to 1995
38	SM Kepu	2012 to 2015
37	PG Johnson	1959 to 1968

MOST TESTS AS CAPTAIN

Tests	Captain	Span
59	GM Gregan	2001 to 2007
55	JA Eales	1996 to 2001
36	NC Farr-Jones	1988 to 1992
29	SA Mortlock	2006 to 2009
24	RD Elsom	2009 to 2011
19	AG Slack	1984 to 1987
16	JE Thornett	1962 to 1967
16	GV Davis	1969 to 1972
16	JE Horwill	2011 to 2013

MOST POINTS IN TESTS

Points	Player	Tests	Career
911	MP Lynagh	72	1984 to 1995
878	MC Burke	81	1993 to 2004
698	MJ Giteau	102	2002 to 2015
489	SA Mortlock	80	2000 to 2009
315	DI Campese	101	1982 to 1996
269	BT Foley	27	2013 to 2015
260	PE McLean	30	1974 to 1982
249*	JW Roff	86	1995 to 2004
223	JD O'Connor	44	2008 to 2013
200	CE Latham	78	1998 to 2007
200	BS Barnes	51	2007 to 2013
187*	EJ Flatley	38	1997 to 2005
185	AP Ashley-Cooper	114	2005 to 2015
173	JA Eales	86	1991 to 2001

Roff and Flatley's totals include a penalty try

MOST TRIES IN TESTS

Tries	Player	Tests	Career
64	DI Campese	101	1982 to 1996
40	CE Latham	78	1998 to 2007
37	AP Ashley-Cooper	114	2005 to 2015
34	DA Mitchell	70	2005 to 2015
31*	JW Roff	86	1995 to 2004
30	TJ Horan	80	1989 to 2000
30	LD Tuqiri	67	2003 to 2008
30	MJ Giteau	102	2002 to 2015
29	MC Burke	81	1993 to 2004
29	SA Mortlock	80	2000 to 2009
25	SJ Larkham	102	1996 to 2007
24	BN Tune	47	1996 to 2006
21	JS Little	75	1989 to 2000

Roff's total includes a penalty try

MOST CONVERSIONS IN TESTS

Cons	Player	Tests	Career
140	M P Lynagh	72	1984 to 1995
106	MJ Giteau	102	2002 to 2015
104	MC Burke	81	1993 to 2004
61	SA Mortlock	80	2000 to 2009
45	BT Foley	27	2013 to 2015
39	JD O'Connor	44	2008 to 2013
31	JA Eales	86	1991 to 2001
30	EJ Flatley	38	1997 to 2005
27	PE McLean	30	1974 to 1982
27	MS Rogers	45	2002 to 2006
27	QS Cooper	58	2008 to 2015
20	JW Roff	86	1995 to 2004
19	DJ Knox	13	1985 to 1997

MOST PENALTY GOALS IN TESTS

Penalties	Player	Tests	Career
177	MP Lynagh	72	1984 to 1995
174	MC Burke	81	1993 to 2004
108	MJ Giteau	102	2002 to 2015
74	SA Mortlock	80	2000 to 2009
62	PE McLean	30	1974 to 1982
47	BT Foley	27	2013 to 2015
34	JA Eales	86	1991 to 2001
34	EJ Flatley	38	1997 to 2005
34	BS Barnes	51	2007 to 2013
31	CP Leali'ifano	16	2013 to 2014
25	JD O'Connor	44	2008 to 2013
23	MC Roebuck	23	1991 to 1993

MOST DROP GOALS IN TESTS

Drops	Player	Tests	Career
9	PF Hawthorne	21	1962 to 1967
9	MP Lynagh	72	1984 to 1995
8	MG Ella	25	1980 to 1984
8	BS Barnes	51	2007 to 2013
4	PE McLean	30	1974 to 1982
4	MJ Giteau	102	2002 to 2015

RUGBY CHAMPIONSHIP (FORMERLY TRI NATIONS) RECORDS

RECORD	DETAIL	HOLDER	SET
Most points in season	162	in six matches	2010
Most tries in season	17	in six matches	2010
Highest score	54	54–17 v Argentina (a)	2013
Biggest win	49	49–0 v S Africa (h)	2006
Highest score conceded	61	22–61 v S Africa (a)	1997
Biggest defeat	45	8–53 v S Africa (a)	2008
Most appearances	48	GM Gregan	1996 to 2007
Most points in matches	271	MC Burke	1996 to 2004
Most points in season	72	MJ Giteau	2009
Most points in match	24	MC Burke	v N Zealand (h) 1998
Most tries in matches	13	AP Ashley-Cooper	2005 to 2015
Most tries in season	5	I Folau	2013
Most tries in match	3	I Folau	v Argentina (a) 2013
Most cons in matches	39	MJ Giteau	2003 to 2015
Most cons in season	12	SA Mortlock	2006
Most cons in match	5	SA Mortlock	v S Africa (h) 2006
Most pens in matches	65	MC Burke	1996 to 2004
Most pens in season	18	CP Leali'ifano	2013
Most pens in match	7	MC Burke	v N Zealand (h) 1999

AUSTRALIA

MISCELLANEOUS RECORDS

RECORD	HOLDER	DETAIL
Longest Test Career	GM Cooke	1932–1948
Youngest Test Cap	BW Ford	18 yrs 90 days in 1957
Oldest Test Cap	AR Miller	38 yrs 113 days in 1967

CAREER RECORDS OF AUSTRALIAN INTERNATIONAL PLAYERS

UP TO 1 NOVEMBER, 2015

PLAYER BACKS:	DEBUT	CAPS	T	C	P	D	PTS
AP Ashley-Cooper	2005 v SA	114	37	0	0	0	185
KJ Beale	2009 v W	60	12	2	18	0	118
QS Cooper	2008 v It	58	8	27	18	2	154
IF Folau	2013 v BI	38	18	0	0	0	90
BT Foley	2013 v Arg	27	7	45	47	1	269
SW Genia	2009 v NZ	66	8	0	0	0	40
MJ Giteau	2002 v E	102	30	106	108	4	698
RG Horne	2010 v Fj	29	4	0	0	0	20
RTRN Kuridrani	2013 v NZ	31	9	0	0	0	45
CP Leali'ifano	2013 v BI	16	1	13	31	0	124
DA Mitchell	2005 v SA	70	34	0	0	0	170
TT Naiyaravoro	2015 v US	1	1	0	0	0	5
NJ Phipps	2011 v Sm	39	5	0	0	0	25
HV Speight	2014 v I	5	1	0	0	0	5
JM Tomane	2012 v S	17	5	0	0	0	25
MP To'omua	2013 v NZ	31	4	0	0	0	20
NW White	2013 v NZ	22	1	2	3	0	18

THE COUNTRIES

FORWARDS:

BE Alexander	2008 v F	72	4	0	0	0	20
STG Carter	2014 v F	12	0	0	0	0	0
KP Douglas	2012 v Arg	23	0	0	0	0	0
SM Fainga'a	2010 v Fj	36	0	0	0	0	0
SM Fardy	2013 v NZ	30	0	0	0	0	0
TJ Faulkner	2014 v W	2	0	0	0	0	0
LB Gill	2012 v NZ	15	0	0	0	0	0
JE Hanson	2012 v NZ	10	0	0	0	0	0
S Higginbotham	2010 v F	32	3	0	0	0	15
MJ Hodgson	2010 v Fj	11	0	0	0	0	0
GS Holmes	2005 v F	24	2	0	0	0	10
MK Hooper	2012 v S	51	9	0	0	0	45
JE Horwill	2007 v Fj	61	6	0	0	0	30
LM Jones	2014 v F	3	0	0	0	0	0
SM Kepu	2008 v It	63	2	0	0	0	10
BJ McCalman	2010 v SA	47	4	0	0	0	20
SP McMahon	2014 v W	6	3	0	0	0	15
JW Mann-Rea	2014 v Arg	2	0	0	0	0	0
ST Moore	2005 v Sm	102	5	0	0	0	25
DW Mumm	2008 v I	44	4	0	0	0	20
WL Palu	2006 v E	57	1	0	0	0	5
DW Pocock	2008 v NZ	55	7	0	0	0	35
SUT Polota-Nau	2005 v E	61	2	0	0	0	10
BA Robinson	2006 v SA	72	3	0	0	0	15
JW Schatz	2014 v Arg	2	0	0	0	0	0
RA Simmons	2010 v SA	60	2	0	0	0	10
ST Sio	2013 v NZ	16	0	0	0	0	0
WRJ Skelton	2014 v F	14	2	0	0	0	10
JA Slipper	2010 v E	74	0	0	0	0	0
TJ Smith	2015 v US	3	0	0	0	0	0

AUSTRALIA

AUSTRALIAN INTERNATIONAL PLAYERS

UP TO 1 NOVEMBER, 2015

Entries in square brackets denote matches played in RWC Finals.

Abrahams, A M F (NSW) 1967 NZ, 1968 NZ 1, 1969 W
Adams, N J (NSW) 1955 NZ 1
Adamson, R W (NSW) 1912 US
Alexander, B E (ACT) 2008 F 1(R), 2(R), It, F 3, 2009 It 1(R), 2, F(R), NZ 1(R), SA 1(R), NZ 2(t&R), SA 2, 3, NZ 3, 4, E, I, S, W, 2010 Fj, NZ 4, W, E 3, It, F, 2011 Sm, SA 1, NZ 1, SA 2, NZ 2, [It, I, US, SA, NZ, W(R)], W(R), 2012 S(R), W1(R), 2(R), 3(R), NZ2, SA1, Arg1, SA2, Arg2, E, It, W4, 2013 BI1, 2, 3, NZ1, 2, SA1(R), Arg1, SA2, Arg2, NZ3, E, It, S(R), W(R), 2014 NZ1(R), 2(R), SA1(R), Arg1(R), SA2(R), Arg2(R) , NZ 3(R), W(R), F 4(R), E(R)
Allan, T (NSW) 1946 NZ 1, M, NZ 2, 1947 NZ 2, S, I, W, 1948 E, F, 1949 M 1, 2, 3, NZ 1, 2
Anderson, R P (NSW) 1925 NZ 1
Anlezark, E A (NSW) 1905 NZ
Armstrong, A R (NSW) 1923 NZ 1, 2
Ashley-Cooper, A P (ACT, NSW) 2005 SA4(R), 2007 W1, 2, Fj, SA1(R), NZ1, SA2, NZ2, [J, Fj, C, E], 2008 F1(R), 2, SA1, NZ1, 2, SA3, NZ3, 4, It, E, F3, 2009 It1(R), 2(t&R), F, NZ1, SA1, NZ2, SA2, 3, NZ3, 4, E, I, S, W, 2010 Fj, E2(R), I, SA1, NZ1, 2, SA2, 3, NZ3, 4, W, E3, It, F, 2011 Sm, SA1, NZ1, SA2, NZ2, [It, I, US, Ru, SA, NZ, W], 2012 W1, 2, 3, NZ1, 2, SA1, Arg1, SA2, NZ3, F, E, It, I, W, 2013 BI 1, 2, 3, NZ1, 2, SA1, Arg1, SA2, Arg2, NZ3, E, It, I, W, 2014 F1, 2, 3, NZ1, 2, SA1, 2, Arg2 , NZ 3, W, F 4, I, E, 2015 SA, Arg, NZ 1, 2, [Fj, E, W, S, Arg, NZ]
Austin, L R (NSW) 1963 E

Baker, R L (NSW) 1904 BI 1, 2
Baker, W H (NSW) 1914 NZ 1, 2, 3
Ballesty, J P (NSW) 1968 NZ 1, 2, F, I, S, 1969 W, SA 2, 3, 4, 2
Bannon, D P (NSW) 1946 M
Bardsley, E J (NSW) 1928 NZ 1, 3, M (R)
Barker, H S (NSW) 1952 Fj 1, 2, NZ 1, 2, 1953 SA 4, 1954 Fj 1, 2
Barnes, B S (Q, NSW) 2007 [J(R), W, Fj, E], 2008 I, F1, 2, SA1, NZ1, 2, SA2, NZ4(R), It, 2009 It1, 2, F, SA1, NZ2, SA3, NZ3, 2010 E1, SA1(R), NZ1, SA3(R), NZ3(t&R), 4(R), W(R), E3(R), It, F, 2011 [US(R), Ru, SA(R), NZ(t&R), W], 2012 S, W1, 2, SA1, Arg1, SA2, F(R), E, It, W4, 2013 BI 1
Barnett, J T (NSW) 1907 NZ 1, 2, 3, 1908 W, 1909 E
Barry, M J (Q) 1971 SA 3
Bartholomeusz, M A (ACT) 2002 It (R)
Barton, R F D (NSW) 1899 BI 3
Batch, P G (Q) 1975 S, W, 1976 E, Fj 1, 2, 3, F 1, 2, 1978 W 1, 2, NZ 1, 2, 3, 1979 Arg 2
Batterham, R P (NSW) 1967 NZ, 1970 S
Battishall, B R (NSW) 1973 E
Baxter, A J (NSW) 1949 M 1, 2, 3, NZ 1, 2, 1951 NZ 1, 2, 1952 NZ 1, 2
Baxter, A K E (NSW) 2003 NZ 2(R), [Arg, R, I(R), S(R), NZ(R), E], 2004 S1, 2, E1, PI, NZ1, SA1, NZ2, SA2, S3, F, S4, E2, 2005 It, F1, SA1, 2, 3(R), NZ1, SA4, NZ2, F2, E, I(R), W(R), 2006 E1(R), 2(R), I1(R), NZ1(R), SA1(R), NZ3(R), SA3(R), W, It, I2, S(R), 2007 Fj, SA1(R), NZ1(R), SA2(R), NZ2(R), [J, W(R), C, E(R)], 2008 I(R), F1, 2, SA1, 2, SA2(R), 3(R), NZ3, 4, E, F3, W, 2009 It1, F, NZ1, SA1, NZ2
Baxter, T J (Q) 1958 NZ 3
Beale, K J (NSW, MR) 2009 W(R), 2010 Fj, E1(R), I(R), NZ1(R), 2, SA2, 3, NZ3, 4, W, E3, It, F, 2011 Sm(R), SA1, NZ1, SA2, NZ2, [It, I, US, SA, W], 2012 W3, NZ1, 2, SA1, Arg1(t&R), SA2, Arg2, NZ3, F, E, It, W4, 2013 BI 1(R), 2, 3, 2014 F1(R), 2(R), 3(R), NZ1, 2, SA1(R), Arg1(R), SA2(R), I(R), E(R), 2015 Arg(R), NZ 1(R), 2(t&R), US, [Fj(R), U, E(R), W(R), S, Arg(R), NZ(R)]
Beith, B McN (NSW) 1914 NZ 3, 1920 NZ 1, 2, 3
Bell, K R (Q) 1968 S

Bell, M D NSW) 1996 C
Bennett, W G (Q) 1931 M, 1933 SA 1, 2, 3,
Bermingham, J V (Q) 1934 NZ 1, 2, 1937 SA 1
Berne, J E (NSW) 1975 S
Besomo, K S (NSW) 1979 I 2
Betham, P J J (NSW) 2013 NZ3, 2014 Arg1
Betts, T N (Q) 1951 NZ2, 3, 1954 Fj 2
Biilmann, R R (NSW) 1933 SA1, 2, 3, 4
Birt, R S W (Q) 1914 NZ2
Black, J W (NSW) 1985 C1, 2, NZ, Fj1
Blackwood, J G (NSW) 1922 M 1, NZ 1, 2, 3, 1923 M 1, NZ 1, 2, 3, 1924 NZ 1, 2, 3, 1925 NZ 1, 4, 1926 NZ 1, 2, 3, 1927 I, W, S, 1928 E, F
Blades, A T (NSW) 1996 S, I, W 3, 1997 NZ 1(R), E 1(R), SA 1(R), NZ 3, SA 2, Arg 1, 2, E 2, S, 1998 E 1, S 1, 2, NZ 1, SA 1, NZ 2, SA 2, NZ 3, Fj, WS, F, E 2, 1999 I 1(R), SA 2, NZ 2, [R, I 3, W, SA 3, F]
Blades, C D (NSW) 1997 E 1
Blake, R C (Q) 2006 E1, 2, NZ2, SA2, NZ3, SA3, W
Blair, M R (NSW) 1928 F, 1931 M, NZ
Bland, G V (NSW) 1928 NZ 3, M, 1932 NZ 1, 2, 3, 1933 SA 1, 2, 4, 5
Blomley, J (NSW) 1949 M 1, 2, 3, NZ 1, 2, 1950 BI 1, 2
Boland, S B (Q) 1899 BI 3, 4, 1903 NZ
Bond, G S G (ACT) 2001 SA 2(R), Sp (R), E (R), F, W
Bond, J H (NSW) 1920 NZ 1, 2, 3, 1921 NZ
Bondfield, C (NSW) 1925 NZ 2
Bonis, E T (Q) 1929 NZ 1, 2, 3, 1930 BI, 1931 M, NZ, 1932 NZ 1, 2, 3, 1933 SA 1, 2, 3, 4, 5, 1934 NZ 1, 2, 1936 NZ 1, 2, M, 1937 SA 1, 1938 NZ 1
Bonner, J E (NSW) 1922 NZ 1, 2, 3, 1923 M 1, 2, 3, 1924 NZ 1, 2
Bosler, J M (NSW) 1953 SA 1
Bouffler, R G (NSW) 1899 BI 3
Bourke, T K (Q) 1947 NZ 2
Bowden, R (NSW) 1926 NZ 4
Bowen, S (NSW) 1993 SA 1, 2, 3, 1995 [R], NZ 1, 2, 1996 C, NZ 1, SA 2
Bowers, A J A (NSW) 1923 M 2(R), 3, NZ, 3, 1925 NZ 1, 4, 1926 NZ 1, 1927 I
Bowman, T M (NSW) 1998 E 1, S 1, 2, NZ 1, SA 1, NZ 2, SA 2, NZ 3, Fj, WS, F, E 2, 1999 I 1, 2, SA 2, [US]
Boyce, E S (NSW) 1962 NZ 1, 2, 1964 NZ 1, 2, 3, 1965 SA 1, 2, 1966 W, S, 1967 E, I 1, F, I 2
Boyce, J S (NSW) 1962 NZ 3, 4, 5, 1963 E, SA 1, 2, 3, 4, 1964 NZ 1, 3, 1965 SA 1, 2
Boyd, A (NSW) 1899 BI 3
Boyd, A F McC (Q) 1958 M 1
Brass, J E (NSW) 1966 BI 2, W, S, 1967 E, I 1, F, I 2, NZ, 1968 NZ 1, F, I, S
Breckenridge, J W (NSW) 1925 NZ 2(R), 3, 1927 I, W, S, 1928 E, F, 1929 NZ 1, 2, 3, 1930 BI
Brial, M C (NSW) 1993 F 1(R), 2, 1996 W 1(R), 2, C, NZ 1, SA 1, NZ 2, SA 2, It, I, W 3, 1997 NZ 2
Bridle, O L (V) 1931 M, 1932 NZ 1, 2, 3, 1933 SA 3, 4, 5, 1934 NZ 1, 2, 1936 NZ 1, 2, M
Broad, E G (Q) 1949 M 1
Brockhoff, J D (NSW) 1949 M 2, 3, NZ 1, 2, 1950 BI 1, 2, 1951 NZ 2, 3
Brown, B R (Q) 1972 NZ 1, 3
Brown, J V (NSW) 1956 SA 1, 2, 1957 NZ 1, 2, 1958 W, I, E, S, F
Brown, R C (NSW) 1975 E 1, 2
Brown, R N (WF) 2008 NZ3(R), 4, It, E, W, 2009 It1, F, NZ1, SA1, NZ2, SA2, SA3(R), 2010 Fj, E1, 2, I, SA1, NZ1, 2, SA2, 3(R), NZ3(R), E3(R)
Brown, S W (NSW) 1953 SA 2, 3, 4

AUSTRALIA

Cowper, D L (V) 1931 NZ, 1932 NZ 1, 2, 3, 1933 SA 1, 2, 3, 4, 5
Cox, B P (NSW) 1952 Fj 1, 2, NZ 1, 2, 1954 Fj 2, 1955 NZ 1, 1956 SA 2, 1957 NZ 1, 2
Cox, M H (NSW) 1981 W, S
Cox, P A (NSW) 1979 Arg 1, 2, 1980 Fj, NZ 1, 2, 1981 W (R), S, 1982 S 1, 2, NZ 1, 2, 3, 1984 Fj, NZ 1, 2, 3
Craig, R R (NSW) 1908 W
Crakanthorp, J S (NSW) 1923 NZ 3
Cremin, J F (NSW) 1946 NZ 1, 2, 1947 NZ 1
Crittle, C P (NSW) 1962 NZ 4, 5, 1963 SA 2, 3, 4, 1964 NZ 1, 2, 3, 1965 SA 1, 2, 1966 BI 1, 2, S, 1967 E, I
Croft, B H D (NSW) 1928 M
Croft, D N (Q) 2002 Arg (t&R), I (R), E (t&R), It (R), 2003 [Nm]
Cross, J R (NSW) 1955 NZ 1, 2, 3
Cross, K A (NSW) 1949 M 1, NZ 1, 2, 1950 BI 1, 2, 1951 NZ 2, 3, 1952 NZ 1, 1953 SA 1, 2, 3, 4, 1954 Fj 1, 2, 1955 NZ 3, 1956 SA 1, 2, 1957 NZ 1, 2
Cross, R P (WF) 2008 F1(R), 2(R), SA1(R), NZ1, 2(R), SA2(R), 3(R), NZ3, 4, E, W, 2009 It2, F(R), NZ2(R), SA2, NZ4, E(R), S
Crossman, O C (NSW) 1923 M 1(R), 2, 3, 1924, NZ 1, 2, 3, 1925 NZ 1, 3, 4, 1926 NZ 1, 2, 3, 4, 1929 NZ 2, 1930 BI
Crowe, P J (NSW) 1976 F 2, 1978 W 1, 2, 1979 I 2, NZ, Arg 1
Crowley, D J (Q) 1989 BI 1, 2, 3, 1991 [WS], 1992 I, W, 1993 C (R), 1995 Arg 1, 2, [SA, E], NZ 1, 1996 W 2(R), C, NZ 1, SA 1, 2, I, W 3, 1998 E 1(R), S 1(R), 2(R), NZ 1(R), SA 1, NZ 2, SA 2, NZ 3, Tg, WS, 1999 I 1, 2(R), E (R), SA 1, NZ 1(R), [R (R), I 3(t&R), US, F(R)]
Cummins, N M (WF) 2012 Arg2, NZ3, F, E, It, W4, 2013 SA1, Arg1, E, It, I, W, 2014 F1, 2, 3
Curley, T G P (NSW) 1957 NZ 1, 2, 1958 W, I, E, S, F, M 1, NZ 1, 2, 3
Curran, D J (NSW) 1980 NZ 3, 1981 F 1, 2, W, 1983 Arg 1
Currie, E W (Q) 1899 BI 2
Cutler, S A G (NSW) 1982 NZ 2(R), 1984 NZ 1, 2, 3, E, I, W, S, 1985 C 1, 2, NZ, Fj 1, 2, 1986 It, F, NZ 1, 2, 3, 1987 SK, [E, J, I, F, W], NZ, Arg 1, 2, 1988 E 1, 2, NZ 1, 2, 3, E, S, It, 1989 BI 1, 2, 3, NZ, 1991 [WS]

Daley, B P (Q) 2010 E1, 2, I
Daly, A J (NSW) 1989 NZ, F 1, 2, 1990 F 1, 2, 3, US, NZ 1, 2, 3, 1991 W, E, NZ 1, 2, [Arg, W, I, NZ, E], 1992 S 1, 2, NZ 1, 2, 3, SA, 1993 Tg, NZ, SA 1, 2, 3, C, F 1, 2, 1994 I 1, 2, It 1, 2, WS, NZ, 1995 [C, R]
[illegible] 2
Darveniza, P (NSW) 1969 W, SA 2, 3, 4
Darwin, B J (ACT) 2001 BI 1(R), SA 1(R), NZ 1(R), SA 2(R), NZ 2(t&R), Sp, E, F, W, 2002 NZ 1(R), SA 1(R), NZ 2(R), SA 2, Arg (R), I (R), E (R), It (R), 2003 I (R), W (t&R), E (R), SA 1(R), NZ 1(R), [Arg(R), R(R), Nm, I, S, NZ]
Davidson, R A L (NSW) 1952 Fj 1, 2, NZ 1, 2, 1953 SA 1, 1957 NZ 1, 2, 1958 W, I, E, S, F, M 1
Davies, R W (Q) 2011 Sm
Davis, C C (NSW) 1949 NZ 1, 1951 NZ 1, 2, 3
Davis, E H (V) 1947 S, W, 1949 M 1, 2
Davis, G V (NSW) 1963 E, SA 1, 2, 3, 4, 1964 NZ 1, 2, 3, 1965 SA 1, 1966 BI 1, 2, W, S, 1967 E, I 1, F, I 2, NZ, 1968 NZ 1, 2, F, I, S, 1969 W, SA 1, 2, 3, 4, 1970 S, 1971 SA 1, 2, 3, F 1, 2, 1972 F 1, 2, NZ 1, 2, 3
Davis, G W G (NSW) 1955 NZ 2, 3
Davis, R A (NSW) 1974 NZ 1, 2, 3
Davis, T S R (NSW) 1920 NZ 1, 2, 3, 1921 SA 1, 2 , 3, NZ, 1922 M 1, 2, 3, NZ 1, 2, 3, 1923 M 3, NZ 1, 2, 3, 1924 NZ 1, 2, 1925 NZ 1
Davis, W (NSW) 1899 BI 1, 3, 4
Dawson, W L (NSW) 1946 NZ 1, 2
Dennis, D A (NSW) 2012 S, W1(R), 2(R), 3(R), NZ1, 2, SA1, Arg1, SA2, Arg2(R), NZ3(R), F, E, It(R), W4(R), 2013 NZ3(R), It(R), W(R)
Diett, L J (NSW) 1959 BI 1, 2
Dix, W (NSW) 1907 NZ 1, 2, 3, 1909 E
Dixon, E J (Q) 1904 BI 3
Donald, K J (Q) 1957 NZ 1, 1958 W, I, E, S, M 2, 3, 1959 BI 1, 2
Dore, E (Q) 1904 BI 1
Dore, M J (Q) 1905 NZ
Dorr, R W (V) 1936 M, 1937 SA 1
Douglas, J A (V) 1962 NZ 3, 4, 5
Douglas, K P (NSW, Q) 2012 Arg1, SA2, Arg2, NZ3(R), F, W4, 2013 BI 1, 2, 3, NZ2(R), SA1, Arg1, E(R), W(R), 2015 NZ 2(R), US, [Fj, U(R), E, W, S, Arg, NZ]
Douglas, W A (NSW) 1922 NZ 3(R)
Dowse, J H (NSW) 1961 Fj 1, 2, SA 1, 2
Dunbar, A R (NSW) 1910 NZ 1, 2, 3, 1912 US
Duncan, J L (NSW) 1926 NZ 4
Dunlop, E E (V) 1932 NZ 3, 1934 NZ 1
Dunn, P K (NSW) 1958 NZ 1, 2, 3, 1959 BI 1, 2
Dunn, V A (NSW) 1920 NZ 1, 2, 3, 1921 SA 1, 2, 3, NZ
Dunning, M J (NSW, WF) 2003 [Nm, E(R)], 2004 S1(R), 2(R), E1(R), NZ1(R), SA1(R), NZ2(t&R), SA2(R), S3(R), F(R), S4(R), E2(R), 2005 Sm, It(R), F1(t&R), SA1(R), 2(R), 3, NZ1(t&R), SA4(t&R), NZ2(R), F2, E, W, 2007 W1, 2(R), Fj, SA1, NZ1, SA2, NZ2, [J, W, Fj, E], 2008 I, SA1(R), NZ1(R), SA2, 3, NZ4(R), It, 2009 E(R), W(R)
Dunworth, D A (Q) 1971 F 1, 2, 1972 F 1, 2, 1976 Fj 2
Dwyer, L J (NSW) 1910 NZ 1, 2, 3, 1912 US, 1913 NZ 3, 1914 NZ 1, 2, 3
Dyson, F J (Q) 2000 Arg 1, 2, SA 1, NZ 1, SA 2, NZ 2, SA 3, F, S, E

Eales, J A (Q) 1991 W, E, NZ 1, 2, [Arg, WS, W, I, NZ, E], 1992 S 1, 2, NZ 1, 2, 3, SA, I, 1994 I 1, 2, It 1, 2, WS, NZ, 1995 Arg 1, 2, [SA, C, R, E], NZ 1, 2, 1996 W 1, 2, C, NZ 1, SA 1, NZ 2, SA 2, It, S, I, 1997 F 1, 2, NZ 1, E 1, NZ 2, SA 1, Arg 1, 2, E 2, S, 1998 E 1, S 1, 2, NZ 1, SA 1, NZ 2, SA 2, NZ 3, Fj, Tg, WS, F, E 2, 1999 [R, I 3, W, SA 3, F], 2000 Arg 1, 2, SA 1, NZ 1, SA 2, NZ 2, SA 3, F, S, E, 2001 BI 1, 2, 3, SA 1, NZ 1, SA 2, NZ 2
Eastes, C C (NSW) 1946 NZ 1, 2, 1947 NZ 1, 2, 1949 M 1, 2
Edmonds, H (ACT) 2010 Fj, E1(R), 2(R), W(R)
Edmonds, M H M (NSW) 1998 Tg, 2001 SA 1(R)
Egerton, R H (NSW) 1991 W, E, NZ 1, 2, [Arg, W, I, NZ, E]
Ella, G A (NSW) 1982 NZ 1, 2, 1983 F 1, 2, 1988 E 2, NZ 1
Ella, G J (NSW) 1982 S 1, 1983 It, 1985 C 2(R), Fj 2
Ella, M G (NSW) 1980 NZ 1, 2, 3, 1981 F 2, S, 1982 E, S 1, NZ 1, 2, 3, 1983 US, Arg 1, 2, NZ, It, F 1, 2, 1984 Fj, NZ 1, 2, 3, E, I, W, S
Ellem, M A (NSW) 1976 Fj 3(R)
Elliott, F M (NSW) 1957 NZ 1
Elliott, R E (NSW) 1920 NZ 1, 1921 NZ, 1922 M 1, 2, NZ 1(R), 2, 3, 1923 M 1, 2, 3, NZ 1, 2, 3
Ellis, C S (NSW) 1899 BI 1, 2, 3, 4
Ellis, K J (NSW) 1958 NZ 1, 2, 3, 1959 BI 1, 2
Ellwood, B J (NSW) 1958 NZ 1, 2, 3, 1961 Fj 2, 3, SA 1, F, 1962 [illegible] 2, 1966 BI 1
Elsom, R D (NSW, ACT) 2005 Sm, It, F1, SA1, 2, 3(R), 4, NZ2, F2, 2006 E1, 2, I1, NZ1, SA1, NZ2, SA2, NZ3, SA3, W, It, I2, S, 2007 W1, 2, SA1, NZ1, SA2, NZ2, [J, W, Fj, E], 2008 I, F1, 2, SA1, NZ1, SA2, 3, NZ3, 2009 NZ2, SA2, 3, NZ3, 4, E, I, S, W, 2010 Fj, E1, 2, I, SA1, NZ1, 2, SA2, 3, NZ3, 4, W, E3, It, F, 2011 Sm, SA1, NZ1, SA2, NZ2, [It, I, US, Ru(R), SA, NZ]
Emanuel, D M (NSW) 1957 NZ 2, 1958 W, I, E, S, F, M 1, 2, 3
Emery, N A (NSW) 1947 NZ 2, S, I, W, 1948 E, F, 1949 M 2, 3, NZ 1, 2
Erasmus, D J (NSW) 1923 NZ 1, 2
Erby, A B (NSW) 1923 M 1, 2, NZ 2, 3, 1925 NZ 2
Evans, L J (Q) 1903 NZ, 1904 BI 1, 3
Evans, W T (Q) 1899 BI 1, 2

Fahey, E J (NSW) 1912 US, 1913 NZ 1, 2, 1914 NZ 3
Faingaa, A S (Q) 2010 NZ1(R), 2, SA3(R), NZ3(R), 2011 SA1(R), 2(R), NZ2, [It, I, US, SA(R), NZ, W(R)], W, 2012 S, W1(t&R), 2(R), 3(R), NZ1, 2(R), SA1(R), Arg1(R), SA2(t&R)
Faingaa, S M (Q) 2010 Fj(R), E1, 2, I, SA1, NZ1(R), 2, SA2, 3(R), NZ4(R), W, 2011 SA1(R), NZ1(R), 2(R), [Ru(R), W(R)], 2012 NZ2(R), SA1(R), 2013 BI 3(t&R), NZ1(R), 2(R), SA1(R), Arg1(R), SA2(R), Arg2(R), NZ3(R), E(R), It(R), S(R), 2014 SA2, Arg2, NZ 3, W, F 4, I, E
Fairfax, R L (NSW) 1971 F 1, 2, 1972 F 1, 2, NZ 1, Fj, 1973 W, E
Fardy, S M (ACT) 2013 NZ1(t&R), 2, SA1, Arg1, SA2, Arg2, E, I, S, W, 2014 F1, 2, 3, NZ1, 2, SA1, Arg1, SA2, Arg2 , NZ 3, 2015 SA, Arg, NZ 1, 2, [Fj, E, W, S, Arg, NZ]
Farmer, E H (Q) 1910 NZ 1
Farquhar, C R (NSW) 1920 NZ 2
Farr-Jones, N C (NSW) 1984 E, I, W, S, 1985 C 1, 2, NZ, Fj 1, 2, 1986 It, F, Arg 1, 2, NZ 1, 2, 3, 1987 SK, [E, I, F, W (R)], NZ, Arg 2, 1988 E 1, 2, NZ 1, 2, 3, E, S, It, 1989 BI 1, 2, 3, NZ, F 1, 2, 1990 F 1, 2, 3, US, NZ 1, 2, 3, 1991 W, E, NZ 1, 2, [Arg, WS, I, NZ, E], 1992 S 1, 2, NZ 1, 2, 3, SA, 1993 NZ, SA 1, 2, 3

Faulkner, T J (WF) 2014 W(R), I(R)

Fava, S G (ACT, WF) 2005 E(R), I(R), 2006 NZ1(R), SA1, NZ2

Fay, G (NSW) 1971 SA 2, 1972 NZ 1, 2, 3, 1973 Tg 1, 2, W, E, 1974 NZ 1, 2, 3, 1975 E 1, 2, J 1, S, W, 1976 I, US, 1978 W 1, 2, NZ 1, 2, 3, 1979 I 1

Feauai-Sautia, C (Q) 2013 SA2(R), S

Fenwicke, P T (NSW) 1957 NZ 1, 1958 W, I, E, 1959 BI 1, 2

Ferguson, R T (NSW) 1922 M 3, NZ 1, 1923 M 3, NZ 3

Fihelly, J A (Q) 1907 NZ 2

Finau, S F (NSW) 1997 NZ 3

Finegan, O D A (ACT) 1996 W 1, 2, C, NZ 1, SA 1(t), S, W 3, 1997 SA 1, NZ 3, SA 2, Arg 1, 2, E 2, S, 1998 E 1(R), S 1(t + R), 2(t + R), NZ 1(R), SA 1(t), 2(R), NZ 3(R), Fj (R), Tg, WS (t + R), F (R), E 2(R), 1999 NZ 2(R), [R, I 3(R), US, W (R), SA 3(R), F (R)], 2001 BI 1, 2, 3, SA 1, NZ 1, SA 2, NZ 2, Sp, E, F, W, 2002 F 1, 2, NZ 1, SA 1, NZ 2, SA 2, I, 2003 SA 1(t&R), NZ 1(R), SA 2(R), NZ 2(R)

Finlay, A N (NSW) 1926 NZ 1, 2, 3, 1927 I, W, S, 1928 E, F, 1929 NZ 1, 2, 3, 1930 BI

Finley, F G (NSW) 1904 BI 3

Finnane, S C (NSW) 1975 E 1, J 1, 2, 1976 E, 1978 W 1, 2

Fitter, D E S (ACT) 2005 I, W

FitzSimons, P (NSW) 1989 F 1, 2, 1990 F 1, 2, 3, US, NZ 1

Flanagan, P (Q) 1907 NZ 1, 2

Flatley, E J (Q) 1997 E 2, S, 2000 S (R), 2001 BI 1(R), 2(R), 3, SA 1, NZ 1(R), 2(R), Sp (R), F (R), W, 2002 F 1(R), 2(R), NZ 1(t+R), SA 1(R), NZ 2(t), Arg (R), I (R), E, It, 2003 I, W, SA 1, NZ 1, SA 2, NZ 2, [Arg, R, I, S, NZ, E], 2004 S3(R), F(R), S4(R), E2, 2005 NZ1(R)

Flett, J A (NSW) 1990 US, NZ 2, 3, 1991 [WS]

Flynn, J P (Q) 1914 NZ 1, 2

Fogarty, J R (Q) 1949 M 2, 3

Folau, I F (NSW) 2013 BI 1, 2, 3, NZ1, 2, SA1, Arg1, SA2, Arg2, NZ3, E, It, I, S, W, 2014 F1, 2, 3, NZ1, 2, SA1, Arg1, SA2, Arg2, NZ 3, W, F 4, I, E, 2015 SA, Arg, NZ 1, 2, [Fj, E, W, Arg, NZ]

Foley, B T (NSW) 2013 Arg2(R), NZ3(R), E(t), W(R), 2014 F1, 2, 3, NZ1(R), 2(R), SA1, Arg1, SA2, Arg2, NZ 3, W, F 4, I, E, 2015 Arg, NZ 1, US, [Fj, E, W, S, Arg, NZ]

Foley, M A (Q) 1995 [C (R), R], 1996 W 2(R), NZ 1, SA 1, NZ 2, SA 2, It, S, I, W 3, 1997 NZ 1(R), NZ 2, SA 1, NZ 3, SA 2, Arg 1, 2, E 2, S, 1998 Tg (R), F (R), E 2(R), 1999 NZ 2(R), [US, W, SA 3, F], 2000 Arg 1, 2, SA 1, NZ 1, SA 2, NZ 2, SA 3, F, S, E, 2001 BI 1(R), 2, 3, SA 1, NZ 1, SA 2, NZ 2, Sp, E, F, W

Foote, R H (NSW) 1924 NZ 2, 3, 1926 NZ 2

Forbes, C F (Q) 1953 SA 2, 3, 4, 1954 Fj 1, 1956 SA 1, 2

Ford, B (NSW) 1957 NZ 2

Ford, E E (NSW) 1927 I, W, S, 1928 E, F, 1929 NZ 1, 3

Ford, J A (NSW) 1925 NZ 4, 1926 NZ 1, 2, 1927 I, W, S, 1928 E, 1929 NZ 1, 2, 3, 1930 BI

Forman, T R (NSW) 1968 I, S, 1969 W, SA 1, 2, 3, 4

Fowles, D G (NSW) 1921 SA 1, 2, 3, 1922 M 2, 3, 1923 M 2, 3

Fox, C L (NSW) 1920 NZ 1, 2, 3, 1921 SA 1, NZ, 1922 M 1, 2, NZ 1, 1924 NZ 1, 2, 3, 1925 NZ 1, 2, 3, 1926 NZ 1, 3, 1928 F

Fox, O G (NSW) 1958 F

Francis, E (Q) 1914 NZ 1, 2

Frawley, D (Q, NSW) 1986 Arg 2(R), 1987 Arg 1, 2, 1988 E 1, 2, NZ 1, 2, 3, S, It

Freedman, J E (NSW) 1962 NZ 3, 4, 5, 1963 SA 1

Freeman, E (NSW) 1946 NZ 1(R), M

Freier, A L (NSW) 2002 Arg (R), I, E (R), It, 2003 SA 1(R), NZ 1(t), 2005 NZ2(R), 2006 E2, 2007 W1(R), 2(R), Fj, SA1(R), NZ1(R), SA2, NZ2(R), [J(R), W(R), Fj(R), C, E(R)], 2008 I(R), F1(R), 2(R), NZ3(R), W(t&R)

Freney, M E (Q) 1972 NZ 1, 2, 3, 1973 Tg 1, W, E (R)

Friend, W S (NSW) 1920 NZ 3, 1921 SA 1, 2, 3, 1922 NZ 1, 2, 3, 1923 M 1, 2, 3

Furness, D C (NSW) 1946 M

Futter, F C (NSW) 1904 BI 3

Gardner, J M (Q) 1987 Arg 2, 1988 E 1, NZ 1, E

Gardner, W C (NSW) 1950 BI 1

Garner, R L (NSW) 1949 NZ 1, 2

Gavin, K A (NSW) 1909 E

Gavin, T B (NSW) 1988 NZ 2, 3, S, It (R), 1989 NZ (R), F 1, 2, 1990 F 1, 2, 3, US, NZ 1, 2, 3, 1991 W, E, NZ 1, 2, SA, I, W, 1993 Tg, NZ, SA 1, 2, 3, C, F 1, 2, 1994 I 1, 2, It 1, 2, WS, NZ, 1995 Arg 1, 2, [SA, C, R, E], NZ 1, 2, 1996 NZ 2(R), SA 2, W 3

Gelling, A M (NSW) 1972 NZ 1, Fj

Genia, S W (Q) 2009 NZ1(R), SA1(R), NZ2(R), SA2(R), 3, NZ3, 4, E, I, S, W, 2010 E2, SA1, NZ1, 2, SA2, 3, NZ3, 4, W, E3, F, 2011 Sm(R), SA1, NZ1, SA2, NZ2, [It, I, US, SA, NZ, W], W, 2012 S, W1, 2, 3, NZ1, 2, SA1, 2013 BI 1, 2, 3, NZ1, SA1, 2(R), Arg2, NZ3, E, It, I, S, W, 2014 W(R), F 4(R), I(R), 2015 SA, US(R), [Fj], E, W, S, Arg, NZ]

George, H W (NSW) 1910 NZ 1, 2, 3, 1912 US, 1913 NZ 1, 3, 1914 NZ 1, 3

George, W G (NSW) 1923 M 1, 3, NZ 1, 2, 1924 NZ 3, 1925 NZ 2, 3, 1926 NZ 4, 1928 NZ 1, 2, 3, M

Gerrard, M A (ACT, MR) 2005 It(R), SA1(R), NZ1, 2, E, I, W, 2006 E1, 2, I1, NZ1, SA1, NZ2, SA2, NZ3(R), SA3(R), I2, S, 2007 W1, 2(R), SA2, NZ2, [J(R)], 2011 Sm

Gibbons, E de C (NSW) 1936 NZ 1, 2, M

Gibbs, P R (V) 1966 S

Giffin, D T (ACT) 1996 W 3, 1997 F 1, 2, 1999 I 1, 2, E, SA 1, NZ 1, SA 2, NZ 2, [R, I 3, US (R), W, SA 3, F], 2000 Arg 1, 2, SA 1, NZ 1, SA 2, NZ 2, SA 3, F, S, E, 2001 BI 1, 2, SA 1, NZ 2, Sp, E, F, W, 2002 Arg (R), I, E (R), It (R), 2003 I, W, E, SA 1, NZ 1, SA 2, NZ 2, [Arg, Nm(R), I, NZ(t&R), E(R)]

Gilbert, H (NSW) 1910 NZ 1, 2, 3

Gill, L B (Q) 2012 NZ2(R), SA1(R), Arg1(R), SA2(R), Arg2(R), NZ3(R), F(R), E(t&R), 2013 BI 1(R), 2(R), NZ1(R), 2(R), SA1(R), It(R), I(R)

Girvan, B (ACT) 1988 E

Giteau, M J (ACT, WF, Toulon) 2002 E (R), It (R), 2003 SA 2(R), NZ 2(R), [Arg(R), R(R), Nm, I(R), S(R), E(t)], 2004 S1, E1, PI, NZ1, SA1, NZ2, SA2, S3, F, S4, E2, 2005 Sm, It, F1, SA1, 2, 3, NZ1, SA4, F2, E(t&R), 2006 NZ1(R), SA1, NZ2, SA2, NZ3, SA3, W, It, I2, S, 2007 W1, 2, SA1, NZ1, SA2, NZ2, [J, W, Fj, E], 2008 I, F1, 2, SA1, NZ1, 2, SA2, 3, NZ3, 4, It(R), E, F3, W, 2009 It1, F, NZ1, SA1, NZ2, SA2, 3, NZ3, 4, E, I, S, W, 2010 Fj, E2, I, SA1, NZ1, 2, SA2, 3, NZ3, 4, W, E3, F(R), 2011 Sm, 2015 SA, NZ 1, 2(R), US, [Fj, E, W, S, Arg, NZ]

Gordon, G C (NSW) 1929 NZ 1

Gordon, K M (NSW) 1950 BI 1, 2

Gould, R G (Q) 1980 NZ 1, 2, 3, 1981 I, W, S, 1982 S 2, NZ 1, 2, 3, 1983 US, Arg 1, F 1, 2, 1984 NZ 1, 2, 3, E, I, W, S, 1985 NZ, 1986 It, 1987 SK, [E]

Gourley, S R (NSW) 1988 S, It, 1989 BI 1, 2, 3

Graham, C S (Q) 1899 BI 2

Graham, R (NSW) 1973 Tg 1, 2, W, E, 1974 NZ 2, 3, 1975 E 2, J 1, 2, S, W, 1976 I, US, Fj 1, 2, 3, F 1, 2

Grafton, A S I (Q) 1899 BI 1, 4, 1903 NZ

Grant, J C (NSW) 1988 E 1, NZ 2, 3, E

Graves, R H (NSW) 1907 NZ 1(R)

Greatorex, E N (NSW) 1923 M 3, NZ 3, 1924 NZ 1, 2, 3, 1925 NZ 1, 1928 E, F

Gregan, G M (ACT) 1994 It 1, 2, WS, NZ, 1995 Arg 1, 2, [SA, C (R), R, E], 1996 W 1, C (t), SA 1, NZ 2, SA 2, It, I, W 3, 1997 F 1, 2, NZ 1, E 1, NZ 2, SA 1, NZ 3, SA 2, Arg 1, 2, E 2, S, 1998 E 1, S 1, 2, NZ 1, SA 1, NZ 2, SA 2, NZ 3, Fj, WS, F, E 2, 1999 I 1, 2, E, SA 1, NZ 1, SA 2, NZ 2, [R, I 3, W, SA 3, F], 2000 Arg 1, 2, SA 1, NZ 1, SA 2, NZ 2, SA 3, 2001 BI 1, 2, 3, SA 1, NZ 1, SA 2, NZ 2, Sp, E, F, W, 2002 F 1, 2, NZ 1, SA 1, NZ 2, SA 2, Arg, I, It, 2003 I, W, E, SA 1, NZ 1, SA 2, NZ 2, [Arg, R, I, S, NZ, E], 2004 S1, 2, E1, PI, SA1, NZ2, SA2, S3, F, S4, E2, 2005 It, F1, SA1, 2, 3, NZ4, NZ2, F2, E, I, W, 2006 E1, 2(R), I1, SA1, NZ1, SA2, NZ2, SA3, 2007 W1(R), 2(R), Fj, SA1, NZ1, SA2, NZ2, [J, W, Fj, C(R), E]

Gregory, S C (Q) 1968 NZ 3, F, I, S, 1969 SA 1, 3, 1971 SA 1, 3, F 1, 2, 1972 F 1, 2, 1973 Tg 1, 2, W, E

Grey, G O (NSW) 1972 F 2(R), NZ 1, 2, 3, Fj (R)

Grey, N P (NSW) 1998 S 2(R), SA 2(R), Fj(R), Tg(R), F, E 2, 1999 I 1(R), 2(R), E, SA 1, NZ 1, SA 2, NZ 2(t&R), [R(R), I 3(R), US, SA 3(R), F(R)], 2000 S(R), E(R), 2001 BI 1, 2, 3, SA 1, NZ 1, SA 2, NZ 2, Sp, E, F, 2003 I(R), W(R), E, [Nm, NZ(t)]

Griffin, T S (NSW) 1907 NZ 1, 3, 1908 W, 1910 NZ 1, 2, 1912 US

Grigg, P C (Q) 1980 NZ 3, 1982 S2, NZ1, 2, 3, 1983 Arg2, NZ, 1984 Fj, W, S, 1985 C1, 2, NZ, Fj1, 2, 1986 Arg1, 2, NZ1, 2, 1987 SK, [E, J, I, F, W]

Grimmond, D N (NSW) 1964 NZ 2

Gudsell, K E (NSW) 1951 NZ 1, 2, 3

Guerassimoff, J (Q) 1963 SA2, 3, 4, 1964 NZ1, 2, 3, 1965 SA2, 1966 BI1, 2, 1967 E, I, F

Gunther, W J (NSW) 1957 NZ2

THE COUNTRIES

Hall, D (Q) 1980 Fj, NZ 1, 2, 3, 1981 F 1, 2, 1982 S1, 2, NZ1, 2, 1983 US, Arg1, 2, NZ, It
Hamalainen, H A (Q) 1929 NZ 1, 2, 3
Hamilton, B G (NSW) 1946 M
Hammand, C A (NSW) 1908 W, 1909 E
Hammon, J D C (V) 1937 SA 2
Handy, C B (Q) 1978 NZ 3, 1979 NZ, Arg1, 2, 1980 NZ1, 2
Hanley, R G (Q) 1983 US (R), It (R), 1985 Fj2(R)
Hanson, J E (Q) 2012 NZ3(R), 2014 NZ2(R), SA1, Arg1(R), SA2(R), W(R), F 4(R), I(R), E(R), 2015 US(R)
Hardcastle, P A (NSW) 1946 NZ 1, M, NZ 2, 1947 NZ 1, 1949 M 3
Hardcastle, W R (NSW) 1899 BI 4, 1903 NZ
Harding, M A (NSW) 1983 It
Hardman, S P (Q) 2002 F 2(R), 2006 SA1(R), 2007 SA2(t&R), [C(R)]
Hardy, M D (ACT) 1997 F 1(t), 2(R), NZ 1(R), 3(R), Arg 1(R), 2(R), 1998 Tg, WS
Harris, M J (Q) 2012 S, W2(R), SA1(R), 2(R), Arg2, NZ3, F, W4(R), 2013 S, W(R)
Harrison, J B (ACT, NSW) 2001 BI 3, NZ1, SA2, Sp, E, F, W (R), 2002 F1, 2, NZ1, SA1, NZ2, SA2, Arg, I (R), E, It, 2003 [R(R), Nm, S, NZ, E], 2004 S1, 2, E1, PI, NZ1, SA1, NZ2, SA2, S3, F, S4, E2
Harry, R L L (NSW) 1996 W1, 2, NZ 1, SA 1(t), NZ 2, It, S, 1997 F 1, 2, NZ1, 2, SA1, NZ3, SA2, Arg1, 2, E2, S, 1998 E1, S1, 2, NZ1, Fj, 1999 SA2, NZ2, [R, I3, W, SA3, F], 2000 Arg1, 2, SA1, NZ1, SA2, NZ2, SA3
Hartill, M N (NSW) 1986 NZ1, 2, 3, 1987 SK, [J], Arg1, 1988 NZ1, 2, E, It, 1989 BI 1(R), 2, 3, F1, 2, 1995 Arg1(R), 2(R), [C], NZ1, 2
Harvey, P B (Q) 1949 M1, 2
Harvey, R M (NSW) 1958 F, M3
Hatherell, W I (Q) 1952 Fj 1, 2
Hauser, R G (Q) 1975 J 1(R), 2, W (R), 1976 E, I, US, Fj1, 2, 3, F1, 2, 1978 W1, 2, 1979 I1, 2
Hawker, M J (NSW) 1980 Fj, NZ1, 2, 3, 1981 F1, 2, I, W, 1982 E, S1, 2, NZ1, 2, 3, 1983 US, Arg1, 2, NZ, It, F1, 2, 1984 NZ1, 2, 3, 1987 NZ
Hawthorne, P F (NSW) 1962 NZ3, 4, 5, 1963 E, SA1, 2, 3, 4, 1964 NZ1, 2, 3, 1965 SA1, 2, 1966 BI1, 2, W, 1967 E, I1, F, I2, NZ
Hayes, E S (Q) 1934 NZ1, 2, 1938 NZ 1, 2, 3
Heath, A (NSW) 1996 C, SA 1, NZ 2, SA 2, It, 1997 NZ 2, SA 1, E 2(R)
Heenan, D P (Q, ACT) 2003 W, 2006 E1
Heinrich, E L (NSW) 1961 Fj 1, 2, 3, SA 2, F, 1962 NZ 1, 2, 3, 1963 E, SA 1
Heinrich, V W (NSW) 1954 Fj 1, 2
Heming, R J (NSW) 1961 Fj, SA 1, 2, F, 1962 NZ 2, 3, 4, 5, 1963 SA 2, 3, 4, 1964 NZ 1, 2, 1965 SA 1, 2, 1966 BI 1, 2, W, 1967 F
Hemingway, W H (NSW) 1928 NZ 2, 3, 1931 M, NZ, 1932 NZ 3
Henderson, N J (ACT) 2004 PI(R), 2005 Sm(R), 2006 It(R)
Henjak, M T (ACT) 2004 E1(R), NZ1(R), 2005 Sm(R), I(R)
Henry, A R (Q) 1899 BI 2
Herbert, A G (Q) 1987 SK (R), [F (R)], 1990 F 1(R), US, NZ 2, 3, 1991 [WS], 1992 NZ 3(R), 1993 NZ (R), SA 2(R)
Herbert, D J (Q) 1994 I 2, It 1, 2, WS (R), 1995 Arg 1, 2, [SA, R], 1996 C, SA 2, It, S, I, 1997 NZ 1, 1998 E 1, S 1, 2, NZ 1, SA 1, NZ 2, SA 2, Fj, Tg, WS, F 2, 1999 I 1, 2, E, SA 1, NZ 1, SA 2, NZ 2, [R, I 3, W, SA 3, F], 2000 Arg 1, 2, SA 1, NZ 1, SA 2, NZ 2, SA 3, F, S, E, 2001 BI 1, 2, 3, SA 1, NZ 1, SA 2, NZ 2, Sp, E, 2002 F 1, 2, NZ 1, SA 1, NZ 2, SA 2, Arg, I, E, It
Herd, H V (NSW) 1931 M
Hickey, J (NSW) 1908 W, 1909 E
Higginbotham, S (Q, MR) 2010 F(R), 2011 Sm(R), SA1(R), NZ1(R), SA2, NZ2(R), [It(R), I(R), Ru, W], W, 2012 S, W1, 2, 3, NZ1, 2, SA1(R), Arg1(R), 2(R), NZ3, It, W4, 2014 F2(R), NZ1(R), 2(R), SA1(R), Arg1(R), Arg2, NZ 3, 2015 SA
Hill, J (NSW) 1925 NZ 1
Hillhouse, D W (Q) 1975 S, 1976 E, Fj 1, 2, 3, F 1, 2, 1978 W 1, 2, 1983 US, Arg 1, 2, NZ, It, F 1, 2
Hills, E F (V) 1950 BI 1, 2
Hindmarsh, J A (Q) 1904 BI 1
Hindmarsh, J C (NSW) 1975 J 2, S, W, 1976 US, Fj 1, 2, 3, F 1, 2
Hipwell, J N B (NSW) 1968 NZ 1(R), 2, F, I, S, 1969 W, SA 1, 2, 3, 4, 1970 S, 1971 SA 1, 2, F 1, 2, 1972 F 1, 2, 1973 Tg 1, W, E, 1974 NZ 1, 2, 3, 1975 E 1, 2, J 1, S, W, 1978 NZ 1, 2, 3, 1981 F 1, 2, I, W, 1982 E

Hirschberg, W A (NSW) 1905 NZ
Hodgins, C H (NSW) 1910 NZ 1, 2, 3
Hodgson, A J (NSW) 1933 SA 2, 3, 4, 1934 NZ 1, 1936 NZ 1, 2, M, 1937 SA 2, 1938 NZ 1, 2, 3
Hodgson, M J (WF) 2010 Fj(R), E1(R), NZ2(R), It(R), 2011 Sm, SA1(R), 2014 SA1(R), Arg1(R), NZ 3(R), W(R), F 4(R)
Hoiles, S A (NSW, ACT) 2004 S4(R), E2(R), 2006 W(R), 2007 W1(R), 2(R), Fj(R), SA1(R), NZ1(R), SA2, NZ2, [J(R), W(R), C(R), E(R)] 2006 W(R), 2007 W1(R), 2(R), Fj(R), SA1(R), NZ1(R), SA2, NZ2, [J(R), W(R), Fj(R), C(R), E(R)], 2008 F2
Holbeck, J C (ACT) 1997 NZ 1(R), E 1, NZ 2, SA 1, NZ 3, SA 2, 2001 BI 3(R)
Holdsworth, J W (NSW) 1921 SA 1, 2, 3, 1922 M 2, 3, NZ 1(R)
Holmes, G S (Q) 2005 F2(R), E(t&R), I, 2006 E1, 2, I1, NZ1, SA1, NZ2, NZ3, 2007 [Fj(R), C], 2015 SA(R), Arg, NZ 1(t&R), 2(R), US, [Fj(R), E(R), W(R), S(R), Arg(R), NZ(R)]
Holt, N C (Q) 1984 Fj
Honan, B D (Q) 1968 NZ 1(R), 2, F, I, S, 1969 SA 1, 2, 3, 4
Honan, R E (Q) 1964 NZ 1, 2
Hooper, M K (ACT, NSW) 2012 S(R), W1(R), 2(R), NZ2, SA1, Arg1, SA2, Arg2, NZ3, F, E, It, W4(R), 2013 BI 1, 2, 3 (t&R), NZ1, 2, SA1, Arg1, SA2, Arg2, NZ3, E, It, I, S, W, 2014 F1, 2, 3, NZ1, 2, SA1, Arg1, SA2, Arg2 , NZ 3, W, F 4, I, E, 2015 SA, Arg(R), NZ 1, 2, [Fj, E, S, Arg, NZ]
Horan, T J (Q) 1989 NZ, F 1, 2, 1990 F 1, NZ 1, 2, 3, 1991 W, E, NZ 1, 2, [Arg, WS, W, I, NZ, E], 1992 S 1, 2, NZ 1, 2, 3, SA, I, W, 1993 Tg, NZ, SA 1, 2, 3, C, F 1, 2, 1995 [C, R, E], NZ 1, 2, 1996 W 1, 2, C, NZ 1, SA 1, It, S, I, W 3, 1997 F 1, 2, NZ 1, E 1, NZ 2, Arg 1, 2, E 2, S, 1998 E 1, S 1, 2, NZ 1, SA 1, NZ 2, SA 2, NZ 3, Fj, Tg, WS, 1999 I 1, 2, E, SA 1, NZ 1, SA 2, NZ 2, [R, I 3, W, SA 3, F], 2000 Arg 1
Horne, R G (NSW) 2010 Fj, E1, 2, I, SA1, NZ1, 2011 [US, NZ(R), W(R)], 2012 W1, 2, 3, NZ1, 2, 2013 BI 2(R), 2014 F3(R), NZ1, 2, SA1, Arg1, SA2(R), Arg2(R), W(R), F 4(R), E, 2015 SA, US, [Fj, E]
Horodam, D J (Q) 1913 NZ 2
Horsley, G R (Q) 1954 Fj 2
Horton, P A (NSW) 1974 NZ 1, 2, 3, 1975 E 1, 2, J 1, 2, S, W, 1976 E, F 1, 2, 1978 W 1, 2, NZ 1, 2, 3, 1979 NZ, Arg 1
Horwill, J E (Q) 2007 Fj, 2008 I, F1, 2, SA1, NZ1, 2, SA2, 3, NZ3, 2009 It1, 2, F, NZ1, SA1, NZ2, SA2, SA2, NZ3, 4, E, I, S, W, 2011 SA1, NZ1, SA2, NZ2, [It, I, Ru, SA, NZ, W], W, 2013 BI 1, 2, 3, NZ1, 2, SA2, Arg2, NZ3, E, It, I, S, W, 2014 F1(R), 2, 3(R), SA1(R), Arg1(R), SA2(R), Arg2, NZ 3(R), W(R), F 4, 2015 SA(R), NZ 1, 2
Hoskins, J E (NSW) 1924 NZ 1, 2, 3
How, R A (NSW) 1967 I 2
Howard, J (Q) 1938 NZ 1, 2
Howard, J L (NSW) 1970 S, 1971 SA 1, 1972 F 1(R), NZ 2, 1973 Tg 1, 2, W
Howard, P W (Q, ACT) 1993 NZ, 1994 WS, NZ, 1995 NZ 1(R), 2(t), 1996 W 1, 2, SA 2, It, S, W 3, 1997 F 1, 2, NZ 1, Arg 1, 2, E, S
Howell, M L (NSW) 1946 NZ 1(R), 1947 NZ 1, S, I, W
Hughes, B D (NSW) 1913 NZ 2, 3
Hughes, J C (NSW) 1907 NZ 1, 3
Hughes, N McL (NSW) 1953 NZ 1, 2, 3, 4, 1955 NZ 1, 2, 3, 1956 SA 1, 2, 1958 W, I, E, S, F
Humphreys, O W (NSW) 1920 NZ 3, 1921 NZ, 1922 M 1, 2, 3, 1925 NZ 1
Hutchinson, E E (NSW) 1937 SA 1, 2
Hutchinson, F E (NSW) 1936 NZ 1, 2, 1938 NZ 1, 3
Huxley, J L (ACT) 2007 W1, 2, Fj, SA1, NZ1, SA2, [W(R), Fj(R), C]
Hynes, P J (Q) 2008 I, F1, 2, SA1, NZ1, 2, SA2, 3, NZ3, 4, E, F3, W, 2009 NZ 2, 3(R), NZ4, E, I, S, W

Ide, W P J (Q) 1938 NZ 2, 3
Ioane, D A N (WF, Q) 2007 W2, 2008 It, F3, W, 2009 NZ4, E, I, W, 2010 Fj, E1, 2, 2011 Sm, SA1, NZ1, SA2, NZ2, [It, SA, NZ, W], 2012 S, W1, 2, 3, NZ1, 2, SA1, Arg1, SA2, Arg2, E, It(R), W4(R), 2013 BI 1
Ives, W N (NSW) 1926 NZ 1, 2, 3, 4, 1929 NZ 3

James, P M (Q) 1958 M 2, 3
James, S L (NSW) 1987 SK (R), [E (R)], NZ, Arg 1, 2, 1988 NZ 2(R)
Jamieson, A E (NSW) 1925 NZ 3(R)
Jaques, T (ACT) 2000 SA 1(R), NZ 1(R)
Jessep, E M (V) 1934 NZ 1, 2
Johansson, L D T (Q) 2005 NZ2(R), F2(R), E(R)

Johnson, A P (NSW) 1946 NZ 1, M

Johnson, B B (NSW) 1952 Fj 1, 2, NZ 1, 2, 1953 SA 2, 3, 4, 1955 NZ 1, 2

Johnson, P G (NSW) 1959 BI 1, 2, 1961 Fj 1, 2, 3, SA 1, 2, F, 1962 NZ 1, 2, 3, 4, 5, 1963 E, SA 1, 2, 3, 4, 1964 NZ 1, 2, 3, 1965 SA 1, 2, 1966 BI 1, 2, W, S, 1967 E, I 1, F, I 2, NZ, 1968 NZ 1, 2, F, I, S, 1970 S, 1971 SA 1, 2, F 1, 2

Johnstone, B (Q) 1993 Tg 1(R)

Jones, G G (Q) 1952 Fj 1, 2, 1953 SA 1, 2, 3, 4, 1954 Fj 1, 2, 1955 NZ 1, 2, 3, 1956 SA 1

Jones, H (NSW) 1913 NZ 1, 2, 3

Jones, L M (MR) 2014 F2(R), I, E(R)

Jones, P A (NSW) 1963 E, SA 1

Jorgensen, P (NSW) 1992 S 1(R), 2(R)

Joyce, J E (NSW) 1903 NZ

Judd, H A (NSW) 1903 NZ, 1904 BI 1, 2, 3, 1905 NZ

Judd, P B (NSW) 1925 NZ 4, 1926 NZ 1, 2, 3, 4, 1927 I, W, S, 1928 E, 1931 M, NZ

Junee, D K (NSW) 1989 F 1(R), 2(R), 1994 WS (R), NZ (R)

Kafer, R B (ACT) 1999 NZ 2, [R, US (R)], 2000 Arg 1(R), 2, SA 1, NZ 1(t&R), SA 2(R), 3(R), F, S, E

Kahl, P R (Q) 1992 W

Kanaar, A (NSW) 2005 NZ2(R)

Kassulke, N (Q) 1985 C 1, 2

Kay, A R (V) 1958 NZ 2, 1959 BI 2

Kay, P (NSW) 1988 E 2

Kearney, K H (NSW) 1947 NZ 1, 2, S, I, W, 1948 E, F

Kearns, P N (NSW) 1989 NZ, F 1, 2, 1990 F 1, 2, 3, US, NZ 1, 2, 3, 1991 W, E, NZ 1, 2, [Arg, WS, W, I, NZ, E], 1992 S 1, 2, NZ 1, 2, 3, SA, I, W, 1993 Tg, NZ, SA, C, F 1, 2, 1994 I 1, 2, It 1, 2, WS, NZ, 1995 Arg 1, 2, [SA, C, E], NZ 1, 2, 1998 E 1, S 1, 2, NZ 1, SA 1, 2, NZ 2, SA 3, Fj, WS, F, E 2, 1999 I 2(R), SA 1(R), 2, NZ 2, [R, I 3]

Kefu, R S T (Q) 1997 SA 2(R), 1998 E 1, S 1, 2, NZ 1, SA 1, NZ 2, SA 2, NZ 3, Fj (R), Tg, WS (R), F, E 2, 1999 I 1, 2, E, SA 1, NZ 1(R), SA 2, NZ 2, [R, I 3, SA 3, F], 2000 SA 1(t&R), 1(R), SA 2(R), NZ 2, SA 3(R), F, S, E, 2001 BI 1, 2, 3, SA 1, NZ 1, SA 2, NZ 2, Sp, E, F, W, 2002 F 1, NZ 1, SA 1, NZ 2, SA 2, Arg, I, E, It, 2003 I, W, E, SA 1, SA 2, NZ 2

Kefu, S (Q) 2001 W (R), 2003 I, W, E, SA 1, NZ 1(R)

Kelaher, J D (NSW) 1933 SA 1, 2, 3, 4, 5, 1934 NZ 1, 2, 1936 NZ 1, 2, M, 1937 SA 1, 2, 1938 NZ 3

Kelaher, T P (NSW) 1992 NZ 1, I (R), 1993 NZ

Kelleher, R J (Q) 1969 SA 2, 3

Keller, D H (NSW) 1947 NZ 1, S, I, W, 1948 E, F

Kelly, A J (NSW) 1899 BI 1

Kelly, R L F (NSW) 1936 NZ 1, 2, M, 1937 SA 1, 2, 1938 NZ 1, 2

Kent, A (Q) 1912 US

Kepu, S M (NSW) 2008 It(R), F3(R), 2009 S(R), 2011 Sm, SA1, NZ1, SA2, NZ2, [It, I, US(R), Ru, SA, NZ], 2012 W1, 2, 3, NZ1, 3(R), F, E(R), It(R), W4(R), 2013 BI 1(R), 2(R), 3(t&R), NZ1(R), 2(R), SA1, Arg1(R), SA2(R), Arg2(R), NZ3(R), E(R), It(R), I, S, W, 2014 F1, 2, 3, NZ1, 2, SA1, Arg1, SA2, Arg2, NZ 3, W, F 4, I, E, 2015 SA, Arg(R), NZ 1, 2, [Fj, U(R), E, W, S, Arg, NZ]

Kerr, F R (V) 1938 NZ 1

Kimlin, P J (ACT) 2009 It1(R), 2

King, S C (NSW) 1926 NZ 1, 2, 3, 4(R), 1927 W, S, 1928 E, F, 1929 NZ 1, 2, 3, 1930 BI, 1932 NZ 1, 2

Knight, M (NSW) 1978 W 1, 2, NZ 1

Knight, S O (NSW) 1969 SA 2, 4, 1970 S, 1971 SA 1, 2, 3

Knox, D J (NSW, ACT) 1985 Fj 1, 2, 1990 US (R), 1994 WS, NZ, 1996 It, S, I, 1997 SA 1, NZ 3, SA 2, Arg 1, 2

Kraefft, D F (NSW) 1947 NZ 2, S, I, W, 1948 E, F

Kreutzer, S D (Q) 1914 NZ 2

Kuridrani, R T R N (ACT) 2013 NZ1(R), 2(R), SA2, Arg2, NZ3, E, It, I, 2014 F1, 2, 3, NZ2(R), SA1, Arg1, SA2, Arg2, NZ 3, W, F 4, I, 2015 SA, Arg, NZ 1, 2, [Fj, U(R), E, W, S, Arg, NZ]

Lamb, J S (NSW) 1928 NZ 1, 2, M

Lambie, J K (NSW) 1974 NZ 1, 2, 3, 1975 W

Lane, R E (NSW) 1921 SA 1

Lane, T A (Q) 1985 C 1, 2, NZ

Lang, C W P (V) 1938 NZ 2, 3

Langford, J F (ACT) 1997 NZ 3, SA 2, E 2, S

Larkham, S J (ACT) 1996 W 2(R), 1997 F 1, 2, NZ 1, 2(R), SA 1, NZ 3, SA 2, Arg 1, 2, E 2, S, 1998 E 1, S 1, 2, NZ 1, SA 1, NZ 2, SA 2, NZ 3, Fj, Tg (t), WS, F, E 2, 1999 [I 3, US, W, SA 3, F], 2000 Arg 1, 2, SA 1, NZ 1, SA 2, NZ 2, SA 3, 2001 BI

1, 2, NZ 1, SA 2, NZ 2, Sp, E, F, W, 2002 F 1, 2, NZ 1, SA 1, NZ 2, SA 2, Arg, I, E, 2003 SA 1(R), NZ 1, SA 2, NZ 2, [Arg, R, I, S, NZ, E], 2004S1, 2, E1, PI, NZ1, SA1, NZ2, SA2, S3, F, S4, 2005 Sm(R), It, F1, SA1, 2, 3, 2006 E1, 2, I1, NZ1, SA1, NZ2, SA2, NZ3, SA3, W, It, I2, S, 2007 W2, Fj, SA1, NZ1, SA2, NZ2, [J]

Larkin, E R (NSW) 1903 NZ

Larkin, K K (Q) 1958 M 2, 3

Latham, C E (Q) 1998 F, E 2, 1999 I 1, 2, E, [US], 2000 Arg 1, 2, SA 1, NZ 1, SA 2, NZ 2, SA 3, F, S, E, 2001 BI 1, 2(R), SA 1(R), NZ 1(R), SA 2, NZ 2, Sp, E, F, W (R), 2002 F 1, 2, NZ 1, SA 1, NZ 2, SA 2, 2003 I, W, E, NZ 1(R), SA 2, NZ 2, [Nm], 2004 S1(R), 2(R), E1(R), PI(t&R), NZ1, SA1, NZ2, SA2, S3, F, S4, E2, 2005 Sm, F1, SA2, 3, F2, E, I, W, 2006 E1, 2, I1, NZ1, SA1, NZ2, SA2, NZ3, SA3, W, It, I2, S, 2007 NZ2(R), [J, W, Fj, C, E]

Latimer, N B (NSW) 1957 NZ 2

Lawton, R (Q) 1988 E 1, NZ 2(R), 3, S

Lawton, T (NSW, Q) 1920 NZ 1, 2, 1925 NZ 4, 1927 I, W, S, 1928 E, F, 1929 NZ 1, 2, 3, 1930 BI, 1932 NZ 1, 2

Lawton, T A (Q) 1983 F 1(R), 2, 1984 Fj, NZ 1, 2, 3, E, I, W, S, 1985 C 1, 2, NZ, Fj 1, 1986 It, F, Arg 1, 2, NZ 1, 2, 3, 1987 SK, [E, US, I, F, W], NZ, Arg 1, 2, 1988 E 1, 2, NZ 1, 2, 3, E, S, It, 1989 BI 1, 2, 3

Laycock, W M B (NSW) 1925 NZ 2, 3, 4, 1926 NZ 2

Leali'ifano, C P (ACT) 2013 BI 1, 2, 3, NZ1, SA1, Arg1, SA2, Arg2, It(R), I(R), S, W, 2014 NZ 3, W, F4

Leeds, A J (NSW) 1986 NZ 3, 1987 [US, W], NZ, Arg 1, 2, 1988 E 1, 2, NZ 1, 2, 3, E, S, It

Lenehan, J K (NSW) 1958 W, E, S, F, M 1, 2, 3, 1959 BI 1, 2, 1961 SA 1, 2, F, 1962 NZ 2, 3, 4, 5, 1965 SA 1, 2, 1966 W, S, 1967 E, I 1, F, I 2

L'Estrange, R D (Q) 1971 F 1, 2, 1972 NZ 1, 2, 3, 1973 Tg 1, 2, W, E, 1974 NZ 1, 2, 3, 1975 S, W, 1976 I, US

Lewis, L S (Q) 1934 NZ 1, 2, 1936 NZ 2, 1938 NZ 1

Lidbury, S (NSW) 1987 Arg 1, 1988 E 2

Lillicrap, C P (Q) 1985 Fj 2, 1987 [US, I, F, W], 1989 BI 1, 1991 [WS]

Lindsay, R T G (Q) 1932 NZ 3

Lisle, R J (NSW) 1961 Fj 1, 2, 3, SA 1

Little, J S (Q, NSW) 1989 F 1, 2, 1990 F 1, 2, 3, US, 1991 W, E, NZ 1, 2, [Arg, W, I, NZ, E], 1992 NZ 1, 2, 3, SA, I, W, 1993 Tg, NZ, SA 1, 2, 3, C, F 1, 2, 1994 WS, NZ, 1995 Arg 1, 2, [SA, C, E], NZ 1, 2, 1996 It (R), I, W 3, 1997 F 1, 2, E 1, NZ 2, SA 1, NZ 3, SA 2, 1998 E 1(R), S 2(R), NZ 2, SA 2(R), NZ 3, Fj, Tg, WS, F, E 2, 1999 I 1(R), 2, SA 1(R), NZ 2, [R, I 3(t&R), US, W (R), SA 3(t&R, F (R)], 2000 Arg 1(R), 2(R), SA 1(R), NZ 1, SA 2, NZ 2, SA 3

Livermore, A E (Q) 1946 NZ 1, M

Loane, M E (Q) 1973 Tg 1, 2, 1974 NZ 1, 1975 E 1, 2, J 1, 1976 E, I, Fj 1, 2, 3, F 1, 2, 1978 W 1, 2, 1979 I 1, 2, NZ, Arg 1, 2, 1981 F 1, 2, I, 1982 E, S 1, 2

Logan, D L (NSW) 1958 M 1

Loudon, D B (NSW) 1921 NZ, 1922 M 1, 2, 3

Loudon, R B (NSW) 1923 NZ 1(R), 2, 3, 1928 NZ 1, 2, 3, M, 1929 NZ 2, 1933 SA 2, 3, 4, 5, 1934 NZ 2

Love, E W (NSW) 1932 NZ 1, 2, 3

Lowth, D R (NSW) 1958 NZ 1

Lucas, B C (Q) 1905 NZ

Lucas, P W (NSW) 1982 NZ 1, 2, 3

Lutge, D (NSW) 1903 NZ, 1904 BI 1, 2, 3

Lynagh, M P (Q) 1984 Fj, E, I, W, S, 1985 C 1, 2, NZ, 1986 It, F, Arg 1, 2, NZ 1, 2, 3, 1987 [E, US, J, I, F, W], Arg 1, 2, 1988 E 1, 2, NZ 1, 3(R), E, S, It, 1989 BI 1, 2, 3, NZ, F 1, 2, 1990 F 1, 2, 3, US, NZ 1, 2, 3, 1991 W, E, NZ 1, 2, [Arg, WS, W, I, NZ, E], 1992 S 1, 2, NZ 1, 2, 3, SA, I, 1993 Tg, C, F 1, 2, 1994 I 1, 2, It 1, 1995 Arg 1, 2, [SA, C, E]

Lyons, D J (NSW) 2000 Arg 1(t&R), 2(R), 2001 BI 1(R), SA 1(R), 2002 F 1(R), 2, NZ 1(R), SA 1(R), NZ 2(R), SA 2(t+R), 2003 I, W, E, SA, F, Nm, I, S, NZ, E], 2004 S1, 2, E1, PI, NZ1, SA1, NZ2, SA2, S3(R), F(R), S4, E2, 2005 Sm, It, F1, SA1, 2, NZ1, SA4, 2006 S, 2007 Fj, SA2(R), [C]

McArthur, M (NSW) 1909 E

McBain, M I (Q) 1983 It, F, 1985 Fj 2, 1986 It (R), 1987 [J], 1988 E 2(R), 1989 BI 1(R)

MacBride, J W T (NSW) 1946 NZ 1, M, NZ 2, 1947 NZ 1, 2, S, I, W, 1948 E, F

McCabe, A J M (NSW) 1909 E

McCabe, P J (ACT) 2010 It(R), 2011 Sm, SA1, NZ1, SA2, NZ2, [It,

I, US(R), SA, NZ], 2012 W1, 2, 3, Arg1, SA2, Arg2, NZ3, F, 2013 BI 1(R), 2014 F1(R), 2(R), NZ1, 2

McCall, R J (Q) 1989 F 1, 2, 1990 F 1, 2, 3, US, NZ 1, 2, 3, 1991 W, E, NZ 1, 2, [Arg, W, I, NZ, E], 1992 S 1, 2, NZ 1, 2, 3, SA, I, W, 1993 Tg, NZ, SA 1, 2, 3, C, F 1, 2, 1994 It 2, 1995 Arg 1, 2, [SA, R, E]

McCalman, B J (WF) 2010 SA1(R), 2(R), 3, NZ3, 4, W, E3, It, F, 2011 Sm, SA1, NZ1, 2(R), [It(R), I, US, Ru, SA(R), NZ(R), W], W, 2013 BI 3(R), SA1(t&R), Arg1(R), SA2(R), Arg2(R), NZ3, E(R), S(R), 2014 F1(R), 2, 3(R), Arg1, SA2, 2014 W, F 4, I, E, 2015 Arg, NZ 1(t&R), US, [U, E(R), W(R), S, Arg(t&R), NZ(R)]

McCarthy, F J C (Q) 1950 BI 1

McCowan, R H (Q) 1899 BI 1, 2, 4

McCue, P A (NSW) 1907 NZ 1, 3, 1908 W, 1909 E

McDermott, L C (Q) 1962 NZ 1, 2

McDonald, B S (NSW) 1969 SA 4, 1970 S

McDonald, J C (Q) 1938 NZ 2, 3

Macdougall, D G (NSW) 1961 Fj 1, SA 1

Macdougall, S G (NSW, ACT) 1971 SA 3, 1973 E, 1974 NZ 1, 2, 3, 1975 E 1, 2, 1976 E

McGhie, G H (Q) 1929 NZ 2, 3, 1930 BI

McGill, A N (NSW) 1968 NZ 1, 2, F, 1969 W, SA 1, 2, 3, 4, 1970 S, 1971 SA 1, 2, 3, F 1, 2, 1972 F 1, 2, NZ 1, 2, 3, 1973 Tg 1, 2

McIntyre, A J (Q) 1982 NZ 1, 2, 3, 1983 F 1, 2, 1984 Fj, NZ 1, 2, 3, E, I, W, S, 1985 C 1, 2, NZ, Fj 1, 2, 1986 It, F, Arg 1, 2, 1987 [E, US, I, F, W], NZ, Arg 2, 1988 E 1, 2, NZ 1, 2, 3, E, S, It, 1989 NZ

McIsaac, T P (WF) 2006 E1, I1, NZ1, 2(R), SA2, 3(R), W, I2

McKay, G R (NSW) 1920 NZ 2, 1921 SA 2, 3, 1922 M 1, 2, 3

MacKay, L J (NSW) 2005 NZ2(R)

McKenzie, E J A (NSW, ACT) 1990 F 1, 2, 3, US, NZ 1, 2, 3, 1991 W, E, NZ 1, 2, [Arg, W, I, NZ, E], 1992 S 1, 2, NZ 1, 2, 3, SA, I, W, 1993 Tg, NZ, SA 1, 2, 3, C, F 1, 2, 1994 I 1, 2, It 1, 2, WS, NZ, 1995 Arg 1, 2, [SA, C (R), R, E], NZ 2, 1996 W 1, 2, 1997 F 1, 2, NZ 1, E 1

McKid, W A (NSW) 1976 E, Fj 1, 1978 NZ 2, 3, 1979 I 1, 2

McKinnon, A (Q) 1904 BI 2

McKivat, C H (NSW) 1907 NZ 1, 3, 1908 W, 1909 E

McLaren, S D (NSW) 1926 NZ 4

McLaughlin, R E M (NSW) 1936 NZ 1, 2

McLean, A D (Q) 1933 SA 1, 2, 3, 4, 5, 1934 NZ 1, 2, 1936 NZ 1, 2, M

McLean, J D (Q) 1904 BI 2, 3, 1905 NZ

McLean, J J (Q) 1971 SA 2, 3, F 1, 2, 1972 F 1, 2, NZ 1, 2, 3, Fj, 1973 W, E, 1974 NZ 1

McLean, P E (Q) 1974 NZ 1, 2, 3, 1975 J 1, 2, S, W, 1976 E, I, Fj 1, 2, 3, F 1, 2, 1978 W 1, 2, NZ 2, 1979 I 1, 2, NZ, Arg 1, 2, 1980 Fj, 1981 F 1, 2, I, W, S, 1982 E, S 2

McLean, P W (Q) 1978 NZ 1, 2, 3, 1979 I 1, 2, NZ, Arg 1, 2, 1980 Fj (R), NZ 3, 1981 I, W, S, 1982 E, S 1, 2

McLean, R A (NSW) 1971 SA 1, 2, 3, F 1, 2

McLean, W M (Q) 1946 NZ 1, M, NZ 2, 1947 NZ 1, 2

McMahon, M J (Q) 1913 NZ 1

McMahon, S P (MR) 2014 W, F 4, E, 2015 US, [U, W]

McMaster, R E (Q) 1946 NZ 1, M, NZ 2, 1947 NZ 1, 2, I, W

McMeniman, H J (Q, WF) 2005 Sm(R), It(R), F2(R), E, I, W, 2007 SA2(R), NZ2(R), [J(R), Fj(R), C, E(t&R)], 2008 F2(R), SA1(t&R), NZ2(R), SA3, NZ3(R), It, E, F3, W, 2013 NZ1

MacMillan, D I (Q) 1950 BI 1, 2

McMullen, K V (NSW) 1962 NZ 3, 5, 1963 E, SA 1

McShane, J M S (NSW) 1937 SA 1, 2

Ma'afu, R S L (ACT, WF) 2010 Fj, E1, 2, I, SA1, NZ1, 2, SA2, 3, NZ3, 2011 NZ2(R), [Ru(R), W], W

Mackay, G (NSW) 1926 NZ 4

Mackney, W A R (NSW) 1933 SA 1, 5, 1934 NZ 1, 2

Magrath, E (NSW) 1961 Fj 1, SA 2, F

Maguire, D J (Q) 1989 BI 1, 2, 3

Malcolm, S J (NSW) 1927 S, 1928 E, F, NZ 1, 2, M, 1929 NZ 1, 2, 3, 1930 BI, 1931 NZ, 1932 NZ 1, 2, 3, 1933 SA 4, 5, 1934 NZ 1, 2

Malone, J H (NSW) 1936 NZ 1, 2, M, 1937 SA 2

Malouf, B P (NSW) 1982 NZ 1

Mandible, E F (NSW) 1907 NZ 2, 3, 1908 W

Manning, J (NSW) 1904 BI 2

Manning, R C S (Q) 1967 NZ

Mann-Rea, J W (ACT) 2014 Arg2(R), NZ 3(R)

Mansfield, B W (NSW) 1975 J 2

Manu, D T (NSW) 1995 [R (t)], NZ 1, 2, 1996 W 1, 2(R), SA 1, NZ 2, It, S, I, 1997 F 1, NZ 1(t), E 1, NZ 2, SA 1

Marks, H (NSW) 1899 BI 1, 2

Marks, R J P (Q) 1962 NZ 4, 5, 1963 E, SA 2, 3, 4, 1964 NZ 1, 2, 3, 1965 SA 1, 2, 1966 W, S, 1967 E, I 1, F, I 2

Marrott, R (NSW) 1920 NZ 1, 3

Marrott, W J (NSW) 1922 NZ 2, 3, 1923 M 1, 2, 3, NZ 1, 2

Marshall, J S (NSW) 1949 M 1

Martin, G J (Q) 1989 BI 1, 2, 3, NZ, F 1, 2, 1990 F 1, 3(R), NZ 1

Martin, M C (NSW) 1980 Fj, NZ 1, 2, 1981 F 1, 2, W (R)

Massey-Westropp, M (NSW) 1914 NZ 3

Mathers, M J (NSW) 1980 Fj, NZ 2(R)

Maund, J W (NSW) 1903 NZ

Mayne, A V (NSW) 1920 NZ 1, 2, 3, 1922 M 1

Meadows, J E C (V, Q) 1974 NZ 1, 1975 S, W, 1976 I, US, Fj 1, 3, F 1, 2, 1978 NZ 1, 2, 3, 1979 I 1, 2, 1981 I, S, 1982 E, NZ 2, 3, 1983 US, Arg 2, NZ

Meadows, R W (NSW) 1958 M 1, 2, 3, NZ 1, 2, 3

Meagher, F W (NSW) 1923 NZ 3, 1924 NZ 3, 1925 NZ 4, 1926 NZ 1, 2, 3, 1927 I, W

Meibusch, J H (Q) 1904 BI 3

Meibusch, L S (Q) 1912 US

Melrose, T C (NSW) 1978 NZ 3, 1979 I 1, 2, NZ, Arg 1, 2

Merrick, S (NSW) 1995 NZ 1, 2

Messenger, H H (NSW) 1907 NZ 2, 3

Middleton, S A (NSW) 1909 E, 1910 NZ 1, 2, 3

Miller, A R (NSW) 1952 Fj 1, 2, NZ 1, 2, 1953 SA 1, 2, 3, 4, 1954 Fj 1, 2, 1955 NZ 1, 2, 3, 1956 SA 1, 2, 1957 NZ 1, 2, 1958 W, E, S, F, M 1, 2, 3, 1959 BI 1, 2, 1961 Fj 1, 2, 3, SA 2, F, 1962 NZ 1, 2, 1966 BI 1, 2, W, S, 1967 I 1, F, I 2

Miller, J M (NSW) 1962 NZ 1, 1963 E, SA 1, 1966 W, S, 1967 E

Miller, J S (Q) 1986 NZ 2, 3, 1987 SK, [US, I, F], NZ, Arg 1, 2, 1988 E 1, 2, NZ 2, 3, E, S, It, 1989 BI 1, 2, 3, NZ, 1990 F 1, 3, 1991 W, [WS, W, I]

Miller, S W J (NSW) 1899 BI 3

Mingey, N (NSW) 1920 NZ 3, 1921 SA 1, 2, 3, 1923 M 1, NZ 1, 2

Mitchell, D A (Q, WF, NSW, Toulon) 2005 SA1(R), 2(R), 3(R), NZ1, SA4, NZ2, F2(R), E, I, W, 2007 W1, 2, Fj, SA1, 2(R), NZ2, [J(R), W, Fj, C, E(R)], 2008 SA1(R), NZ2(R), SA2, 3(R), NZ4, E, F3, W, 2009 It1, F, NZ1, SA1, NZ2, SA2(R), 3, NZ3, E, I, S, W, 2010 Fj(t&R), E1, 2, I, SA1, NZ1, 2, SA2, 3, NZ4, W, E3, It, F, 2011 [I(R), US, Ru], 2012 S(R), E(R), It, W4, 2015 SA(R), NZ 1, [U, W, S, Arg, NZ]

Mogg, J D (ACT) 2013 BI 3(R), NZ1, 2

Monaghan, L E (NSW) 1973 E, 1974 NZ 1, 2, 3, 1975 E 1, 2, S, W, 1976 I, US, F 1, 1978 W 1, 2, NZ 1, 1979 I 1, 2

Monti, C I A (Q) 1938 NZ 2

Moon, B J (Q) 1978 NZ 2, 3, 1979 I 1, 2, NZ, Arg 1, 2, 1980 Fj, NZ 1, 2, 3, 1981 F 1, 2, I, W, S, 1982 E, S 1, 2, 1983 US, Arg 1, 2, NZ, It, F 1, 2, 1984 Fj, NZ 1, 2, 3, E, 1986 It, F, Arg 1, 2

Mooney, T P (Q) 1954 Fj 1, 2

Moore, R C (ACT, NSW) 1999 [US], 2001 BI 2, 3, SA 1, NZ 1, SA 2, NZ 2, Sp (R), E (R), F (R), W (R), 2002 F 1(R), 2(R), SA 2(R)

Moore, S T (Q, ACT) 2005 Sm(R), It(R), F1(R), SA2(R), 3(R), F2(t&R), 2006 It(t), I2(R), S, 2007 W1, 2, Fj(R), SA1, NZ1, 2, [J, W, Fj, E], 2008 I, F1, 2, SA1, NZ1, 2, SA2, 3(R), NZ3, 4, It, E, F3, W, 2009 It1, F, NZ1, SA1, NZ2, SA2, 3(R), NZ3(R), 4, E, I, S, W, 2010 SA1(R), NZ1, SA2(t), 3, NZ3, 4, E3, It, F, 2011 Sm, SA1, NZ1, SA2, NZ2, [It, US(R), Ru, SA, NZ] , W(R), 2012 S, W1(R), 2(R), 3(R), NZ1(R), 2, F(R), E(R), It, W4(R), 2013 BI 1, 2, 3, NZ1, 2, SA1, Arg1, SA2, Arg2, NZ3, E, It, I, S, W, 2014 F1, 2015 SA, Arg, NZ 1, 2, [Fj, E, W, S, Arg, NZ]

Morahan, L J (Q) 2012 S

Moran, H M (NSW) 1908 W

Morgan, G (Q) 1992 NZ 1(R), 3(R), W, 1993 Tg, NZ, SA 1, 2, 3, C, F 1, 2, 1994 I 1, 2, It 1, WS, NZ, 1996 W 1, 2, C, NZ 1, SA 1, NZ 2, 1997 E 1, NZ 2

Morrissey, C V (NSW) 1925 NZ 2, 3, 4, 1926 NZ 2, 3

Morrissey, W (Q) 1914 NZ 2

Mortlock, S A (ACT) 2000 Arg 1, 2, SA 1, NZ 1, SA 2, NZ 2, SA 3, F, S, E, 2002 F 1, 2, NZ 1, SA 1, NZ 2, SA 2, Arg, I, E, It, 2003 IR(R), Nm, S, NZ, E], 2004 S2, E1, PI, NZ1, SA1, NZ2, SA2, S3, F, S4, 2005 Sm, It, F1, SA2, 3(R), NZ1, 2006 E1, 2, I1, NZ1, SA1, NZ2, SA2, NZ3, SA3, It, I2, S, 2007 W1, 2, Fj(R), SA1, NZ1, SA2, NZ2, [J, W, E], 2008 I, F1, 2, SA1, NZ2, SA2, 3, NZ3, 4, It, E, F3, W, 2009 It1, F, NZ1, SA1

Morton, A R (NSW) 1957 NZ 1, 2, 1958 F, M 1, 2, 3, NZ 1, 2, 3, 1959 BI 1, 2

Mossop, R P (NSW) 1949 NZ 1, 2, 1950 BI 1, 2, 1951 NZ 1

Moutray, I E (NSW) 1963 SA 2

Mowen, B S C (ACT) 2013 BI 1, 2, 3, NZ1, 2, SA1, Arg1, SA2, Arg2, NZ3, E, It, I, S, W
Mulligan, P J (NSW) 1925 NZ 1(R)
Mumm, D W (NSW) 2008 I(t&R), F1(R), 2, SA2(R), 3(R), NZ4, It, E(R), F3, W(R), 2009 It1, 2, F, NZ1(t), SA1(R), NZ2(R), 4(R), E(R), S(R), W, 2010 Fj, E1, 2, I, SA1, NZ1, 2, SA2, 3(R), NZ3(R), 4(R), W(R), E3(R), 2015 Arg(R), NZ 1, 2(R), US(R), [Fj(R), U, E(R), W, S(R), Arg(R), NZ(R)]
Munsie, A (NSW) 1928 NZ 2
Murdoch, A R (NSW) 1993 F 1, 1996 W 1
Murphy, P J (Q) 1910 NZ 1, 2, 3, 1913 NZ 1, 2, 3, 1914 NZ 1, 2, 3
Murphy, W (Q) 1912 US

Naiyaravoro, T T (NSW) 2015 US(R)
Nasser, B P (Q) 1989 F 1, 2, 1990 F 1, 2, 3, US, NZ 2, 1991 [WS]
Newman, E W (NSW) 1922 NZ 1
Nicholson, F C (Q) 1904 BI 3
Nicholson, F V (Q) 1903 NZ, 1904 BI 1
Niuqila, A S (NSW) 1988 S, It, 1989 BI 1
Noriega, E P (ACT, NSW) 1998 F, E 2, 1999 I 1, 2, E, SA 1, NZ 1, SA 2(R), NZ 2(R), 2002 F 1, 2, NZ 1, SA 1, NZ 2, Arg, I, E, It, 2003 I, W, E, SA 1, NZ 1, SA 2
Norton-Knight, S H (NSW) 2007 W1, Fj(R)
Nothling, O E (NSW) 1921 SA 1, 2, 3, NZ, 1922 M 1, 2, 3, NZ 1, 2, 3, 1923 M 1, 2, 3, 1, 2, 3, 1924 NZ 1, 2, 3
Nucifora, D V (Q) 1991 [Arg (R)], 1993 C (R)

O'Brien, F W H (NSW) 1937 SA 2, 1938 NZ 3
O'Connor, J A (NSW) 1928 NZ 1, 2, 3, M
O'Connor, J D (WF, MR) 2008 It(R), 2009 It1, 2, F(R), NZ1(R), SA1(R), NZ2, SA2, 3, NZ3, 4, I(R), S(R), W(R), 2010 E1, 2, I, SA1, NZ1, 2, SA2, 3, NZ3, 4, W, E3, F, 2011 SA1, NZ1, SA2, [It(R), I, Ru, SA, NZ, W], 2013 BI 1, 2, 3, NZ1, 2, SA1, Arg1
O'Connor, M (ACT) 1994 I 1
O'Connor, M D (ACT, Q) 1979 Arg 1, 2, 1980 Fj, NZ 1, 2, 3, 1981 F 1, 2, I, 1982 E, S 1, 2
O'Donnell, C (NSW) 1913 NZ 1, 2
O'Donnell, I C (NSW) 1899 BI 3, 4
O'Donnell, J B (NSW) 1928 NZ 1, 3, M
O'Donnell, J M (NSW) 1899 BI 4
O'Gorman, J F (NSW) 1961 Fj 1, SA 1, 2, F, 1962 NZ 2, 1963 E, SA 1, 2, 3, 4, 1965 SA 1, 2, 1966 W, S, 1967 E, I 1, F, I 2
O'Neill, D J (Q) 1964 NZ 1, 2
O'Neill, J M (Q) 1952 NZ 1, 2, 1956 SA 1, 2
Ofahengaue, V (NSW) 1990 NZ 1, 2, 3, 1991 W, E, NZ 1, 2, [Arg, W, I, NZ, E], 1992 S 1, 2, SA, I, W, 1994 WS, NZ, 1995 Arg 1, 2(R), [SA, C, E], NZ 1, 2, 1997 Arg 1(t + R), 2(R), E 2, S, 1998 E 1(R), S 1(R), 2(R), NZ 1(R), SA 1(R), NZ 2(R), SA 2(R), NZ 3(R), Fj, WS, F (R)
Ormiston, I W L (NSW) 1920 NZ 1, 2, 3
Osborne, D H (V) 1975 E 1, 2, J 1
Outterside, R (NSW) 1959 BI 1, 2
Oxenham, A McE (Q) 1904 BI 2, 1907 NZ 2
Oxlade, A M (Q) 1904 BI 2, 3, 1905 NZ, 1907 NZ 2
Oxlade, B D (Q) 1938 NZ 1, 2, 3

Palfreyman, J R L (NSW) 1929 NZ 1, 1930 BI, 1931 NZ, 1932 NZ 3
Palmer, D P (ACT) 2012 S
Palu, W L (NSW) 2006 E2(t&R), I1(R), SA2, NZ3, SA3, W, It, 2, S(R), 2007 W1, 2, SA1, NZ1, [J, W, Fj, E], 2008 I, F1, SA1, NZ1, 2, SA2, 3, NZ3, It(R), E(R), F3, 2009 NZ1, SA1, NZ3(t&R), 4, E, I, S, W, 2011 [I(R), US], 2012 W1, 2, 3, NZ3, F, E, It, W4, 2013 BI 1, 2, 3, 2014 F1, 3, NZ1, 2, SA1, 2015 NZ 2, US, [U]
Panoho, G M (Q) 1998 SA 2(R), NZ 3(R), Fj, Tg, WS (R), 1999 I 2, E, SA 1(R), NZ 1, 2000 Arg 1(R), 2(R), SA 1(R), NZ 1(R), SA 2(R), 3(R), F (R), S (R), E (R), 2001 BI 1, 2003 SA 2(R), NZ 2
Papworth, B (NSW) 1985 Fj 1, 2, 1986 It, Arg 1, 2, NZ 1, 2, 3, 1987 [E, US, J (R), I, F], NZ, Arg 1, 2
Parker, A J (Q) 1983 Arg 1(R), 2, NZ
Parkinson, C E (Q) 1907 NZ 2
Pashley, J J (NSW) 1954 Fj 1, 2, 1958 M 1, 2, 3
Paul, J A (ACT) 1998 S 1(R), NZ 1(R), SA 1(t), Fj (R), Tg, 1999 I 1, 2, E, SA 1, NZ 1, [R (R), I 3(R), W (t), F (R)], 2000 Arg 1(R), 2(R), SA 1(R), NZ 1(R), SA 2(R), NZ 2(R), SA 3(R), F (R), S (R), E (R), 2001 BI 1, 2002 F 1, NZ 1, SA 1, NZ 2, SA 2, Arg, E, 2003 I, W, E, SA 2(t&R), NZ2(R), [Arg(R), R(R), Nm, I(R), S(R),

NZ(R), E(R)], 2004 S1(R), 2(R), E1(R), PI(R), NZ1(t&R), SA1, NZ2(R), SA2(R), S3, F, S4, E2, 2005 Sm, It, F1, SA1, 2, 3, NZ1, 2006 E1(R), 2(R), I1(R), NZ1(R), SA1, NZ2, SA2(R), NZ3, SA3
Pauling, T P (NSW) 1936 NZ 1, 1937 SA 1
Payne, S J (NSW) 1996 W 2, C, NZ 1, S, 1997 F 1(t), NZ 2(R), Arg 2(t)
Pearse, G K (NSW) 1975 W (R), 1976 I, US, Fj 1, 2, 3, 1978 NZ 1, 2, 3
Penman, A P (NSW) 1905 NZ
Perrin, P D (Q) 1962 NZ 1
Perrin, T D (NSW) 1931 M, NZ
Phelps, R (NSW) 1955 NZ 2, 3, 1956 SA 1, 2, 1957 NZ 1, 2, 1958 W, I, E, S, F, M 1, NZ 1, 2, 3, 1961 Fj 1, 2, 3, SA 1, 2, F, 1962 NZ 1, 2
Phipps, J A (NSW) 1953 SA 1, 2, 3, 4, 1954 Fj 1, 2, 1955 NZ 1, 2, 3, 1956 SA 1, 2
Phipps, N J (MR, NSW) 2011 Sm, SA1(R), [Ru(R)], 2012 SA1(R), Arg1, SA2, Arg2, NZ3, F, E, It(R), W4, 2013 BI 1(R), 3(R), 2014 F1(R), 2(R), 3(R), NZ1(R), 2(R), SA1, Arg1, SA2, Arg2, NZ 3, W, F 4, I, E, 2015 SA(R), Arg, NZ 1, US, [Fj(R), U, E(R), W(R), S(R), Arg(R), NZ(R)]
Phipps, W J (NSW) 1928 NZ 2
Piggott, H R (NSW) 1922 M 3(R)
Pilecki, S J (Q) 1978 W 1, 2, NZ 1, 2, 1979 I 1, 2, NZ, Arg 1, 2, 1980 Fj, NZ 1, 2, 1982 S 1, 2, 1983 US, Arg 1, 2, NZ
Pini, M (Q) 1994 I 1, It 2, WS, NZ, 1995 Arg 1, 2, [SA, R (t)]
Piper, B J C (NSW) 1946 NZ 1, M, NZ 2, 1947 NZ 1, S, I, W, 1948 E, F, 1949 M 1, 2, 3
Pocock, D W (WF, ACT) 2008 NZ4(R), It(R), 2009 It1(R), 2, F(R), NZ1(R), SA1(R), NZ2(R), SA2(R), 3, NZ3, 4, E(R), I, W, 2010 Fj, E1, 2, I, SA1, NZ1, 2, SA2, 3, NZ3, 4, W, E3, It, F, 2011 SA1, NZ1, SA2, [It, Ru, SA, NZ, W], W, 2012 S, W1, 2, 3, NZ1, W4, 2015 SA(R), Arg, NZ 1, 2(t&R), [Fj, E, W, Arg, NZ]
Poidevin, S P (NSW) 1980 Fj, NZ 1, 2, 3, 1981 F 1, 2, I, W, S, 1982 E, NZ 1, 2, 3, 1983 US, Arg 1, 2, NZ, It, F 1, 2, 1984 Fj, NZ 1, 2, 3, E, I, W, S, 1985 C 1, 2, NZ, Fj 1, 2, 1986 It, F, Arg 1, 2, NZ 1, 2, 3, 1987 SK, [E, J, I, F, W], Arg 1, 1988 NZ 1, 2, 3, 1989 NZ 1, 1991 E, NZ 1, 2, [Arg, W, I, NZ, E]
Polota-Nau, S U T (NSW) 2005 E(R), I(R), 2006 SA(R), 2008 SA1(R), NZ2(t&R), SA2(R), 3, It(R), E(R), 2009 It1(R), 2, F(R), SA1(R), NZ2(t&R), SA2(R), 3, NZ3, 4(R), E(R), I(R), S(R), W(R), 2010 It(R), F(R), 2011 [It(R), I, US, SA(R), NZ(R)], NZ, 2012 W1, 2, 3, NZ1, SA1, Arg1, SA2, Arg2, NZ3, F, E, W4, 2013 I(R), W(R), 2014 F1(R), 2, 3, Arg1, 2015 Arg(R), NZ 1(R), 2(R), US, [Fj(R), U, E(R), W(R), S(R), Arg(R), NZ(R)]
Pope, A M (Q) 1968 NZ 2(R)
Potter, R T (Q) 1961 Fj 2
Potts, J M (NSW) 1957 NZ 1, 2, 1958 W, I, 1959 BI 1
Prentice, C W (NSW) 1914 NZ 3
Prentice, W S (NSW) 1908 W, 1909 E, 1910 NZ 1, 2, 3, 1912 US
Price, R A (NSW) 1974 NZ 1, 2, 3, 1975 E 1, 2, J 1, 2, 1976 NZ 1, 2, 3
Primmer, C J (Q) 1951 NZ 1, 3
Proctor, I J (NSW) 1967 NZ
Prosser, R B (NSW) 1967 E, I 1, 2, NZ, 1968 NZ 1, 2, F, I, S, 1969 W, SA 1, 2, 3, 4, 1971 SA 1, 2, 3, F 1, 2, 1972 F 1, 2, NZ 1, 2, 3, Fj
Pugh, G H (NSW) 1912 US
Purcell, M P (Q) 1966 W, S, 1967 I 2
Purkis, E M (NSW) 1958 S, M 1
Pym, J E (NSW) 1923 M 1

Rainbow, A E (NSW) 1925 NZ 1
Ramalli, C (NSW) 1938 NZ 2, 3
Ramsay, K M (NSW) 1936 M, 1937 SA 1, 1938 NZ 1, 3
Rankin, R (NSW) 1936 NZ 1, 2, M, 1937 SA 1, 2, 1938 NZ 1, 2
Rathbone, C (ACT) 2004 S1, 2(R), E1, PI, NZ1, SA1, NZ2, SA2, S3, F, S4, 2005 Sm, NZ1(R), SA4, NZ2, 2006E1(R), 2(R), I1(R), SA1(R), NZ2(R), SA2(R), NZ3, SA3, W, It, I2
Rathie, D S (Q) 1972 F 1, 2
Raymond, R L (NSW) 1920 NZ 1, 2, 1921 SA 2, 3, NZ, 1922 M 1, 2, 3, NZ 1, 2, 3, 1923 M 1, 2
Redwood, C (Q) 1903 NZ, 1904 BI 1, 2, 3
Reid, E J (NSW) 1925 NZ 2, 3, 4
Reid, T W (NSW) 1961 Fj 1, 2, 3, SA 1, 1962 NZ 1
Reilly, N P (Q) 1968 NZ 1, 2, F, I, S, 1969 W, SA 1, 2, 3, 4
Reynolds, L J (NSW) 1910 NZ 2(R), 3
Reynolds, R J (NSW) 1984 Fj, NZ 1, 2, 3, 1985 Fj 1, 2, 1986 Arg 1, 2, NZ 1, 1987 [J]
Richards, E W (Q) 1904 BI 1, 3, 1905 NZ, 1907 NZ 1(R), 2

271

AUSTRALIA

Richards, G (NSW) 1978 NZ 2(R), 3, 1981 F 1

Richards, T J (Q) 1908 W, 1909 E, 1912 US

Richards, V S (NSW) 1936 NZ 1, 2(R), M, 1937 SA 1, 1938 NZ 1

Richardson, G C (Q) 1971 SA 1, 2, 3, 1972 NZ 2, 3, Fj, 1973 Tg 1, 2, W

Rigney, W A (NSW) 1925 NZ 2, 4, 1926 NZ 4

Riley, S A (NSW) 1903 NZ

Ritchie, E V (NSW) 1924 NZ 1, 3, 1925 NZ 2, 3

Roberts, B T (NSW) 1956 SA 2

Roberts, H F (Q) 1961 Fj 1, 3, SA 2, F

Robertson, I J (NSW) 1975 J 1, 2

Robinson, B A (NSW) 2006 SA3, I2(R), S, 2007 W1(R), 2, Fj(R), 2008 I, F1, 2, SA1, NZ1, 2, SA2, 3, NZ3, 4, E, W, 2009 It1, F, NZ1, SA1, NZ2, SA2, 3, NZ3, 4, E, I, S, W, 2010 SA1, NZ1, 2, SA2, 3, NZ3, 4, W, E3(R), F(t&R), 2012 W1, 2, 3, NZ1, 2, SA1, Arg1, SA2, Arg2(R), NZ3, F, E, It, W4, 2013 BI 1, 2, 3, SA2(R), Arg2(R), NZ3(R), E(R), It(R), I(R), W(R), 2014 SA2(R), Arg2(R), NZ3 4(R), I(R), E(R)

Robinson, B J (ACT) 1996 It (R), S (R), I (R), 1997 F 1, 2, NZ 1 E 1, NZ 2, SA 1(R), NZ 3(R), SA 2(R), Arg 1, 2, E 2, S, 1998 Tg

Robinson, B S (Q) 2011 Sm(R)

Roche, C (Q) 1982 S 1, 2, NZ 1, 2, 3, 1983 US, Arg 1, 2, NZ, It, F 1, 2, 1984 Fj, NZ 1, 2, 3, I

Rodriguez, E E (NSW) 1984 Fj, NZ 1, 2, 3, E, I, W, S, 1985 C 1, 2, NZ, Fj 1, 1986 It, F, Arg 1, 2, NZ 1, 2, 3, 1987 SK, [E, J, W (R)], NZ, Arg 1, 2

Roe, J A (Q) 2003 [Nm(R)], 2004 E1(R), SA1(R), NZ2(R), SA2(t&R), S3, F, 2005 Sm(R), It(R), F1(R), SA1(R), 3, NZ1, SA4(t&R), NZ2(R), F2(R), E, I, W

Roebuck, M C (NSW) 1991 W, E, NZ 1, 2, [Arg, WS, W, I, NZ, E], 1992 S 1, 2, NZ 2, 3, SA, I, W, 1993 Tg, SA 1, 2, 3, C, F 2

Roff, J W (ACT) 1995 [C, R], NZ 1, 2, 1996 W 1, 2, NZ 1, SA 1, SA 2, 2 SA 2(R), S, I, W 3, 1997 F 1, 2, NZ 1, E 1, NZ 2, SA 1, NZ 3, SA 2, Arg 1, 2, E 2, S, 1998 E 1, S 1, 2, NZ 1, SA 1, NZ 2, SA 2, NZ 3, Fj, Tg, WS, F, E 2, 1999 I 1, 2, E, SA 1, NZ 1, SA 2, NZ 2(R), [R (R), I 3, US (R), W, SA 3, F], 2000 Arg 1, 2, SA 1, NZ 1, SA 2, NZ 2, SA 3, F, S, E, 2001 BI 1, 2, 3, SA 1, NZ 1, SA 2, NZ 2, Sp, E, F, W, 2003 I, W, E, SA 1, [Arg, R, I, S(R), NZ(t&R)(R)], 2004 S1, 2, E1, PI

Rogers, M S (NSW) 2002 F 1(R), 2(R), NZ 1(R), SA 1(R), NZ 2(R), SA 2(t&R), Arg, 2003 E (R), SA 1, NZ 1, SA 2, NZ 2, [Arg, R, Nm, I, S, NZ, E], 2004S3(R), F(R), S4(R), E2(R), 2005 Sm(R), It, F1(R), SA1, 4, NZ2, F2, E, I, W, 2006 E1, 2, I1, NZ1, SA1(R), NZ2(R), SA2(R), NZ3(R), W, It, I2(R), S(R)

Rose, H A (NSW), 1967 I 2, NZ, 1968 NZ 1, 2, F, I, S, 1969 W, SA 1, 2, 3, 4, 1970 S

Rosenblum, M E (NSW) 1928 NZ 1, 2, 3, M

Rosenblum, R G (NSW) 1969 SA 1, 3, 1970 S

Rosewell, J S H (NSW) 1907 NZ 1, 3

Ross, A W (NSW) 1925 NZ 1, 2, 3, 1926 NZ 1, 2, 3, 1927 I, W, S, 1928 E, F, 1929 NZ 1, 1930 BI, 1931 M, NZ, 1932 NZ 2, 3, 1933 SA 5, 1934 NZ 1, 2

Ross, W S (Q) 1979 I 1, 2, Arg 2, 1980 Fj, NZ 1, 2, 3, 1982 S 1, 2, 1983 US, Arg 1, 2, NZ

Rothwell, P R (NSW) 1951 NZ 1, 2, 3, 1952 Fj 1

Row, F L (NSW) 1899 BI 1, 3, 4

Row, N E (NSW) 1907 NZ 1, 3, 1909 E, 1910 NZ 1, 2, 3

Rowles, P G (NSW) 1972 Fj, 1973 E

Roxburgh, J R (NSW) 1968 NZ 1, 2, F, 1969 W, SA 1, 2, 3, 4, 1970 S

Ruebner, G (NSW) 1966 BI 1, 2

Russell, C J (NSW) 1907 NZ 1, 2, 3, 1908 W, 1909 E

Ryan, J R (NSW) 1975 J 2, 1976 I, US, Fj 1, 2, 3

Ryan, K J (Q) 1958 E, M 1, NZ 1, 2, 3

Ryan, P F (NSW) 1963 E, SA 1, 1966 BI 1, 2

Ryan, P J (NSW) 2012 F2(R), 2013 I(R), 2014 F1(R)

Rylance, M H (NSW) 1926 NZ 4(R)

Sailor, W J (Q) 2002 F 1, 2, Arg (R), I, E, It, 2003 I, W, E, SA 1, NZ 1, SA 2, NZ 2, [Arg, R, I, S, NZ, E], 2004 S1, 2, NZ1(R), 2(R), SA2(R), S3(R), F(R), S4(R), E2, 2005 Sm, It, F1, SA1, 2, 3, F2, I(R), W(R)

Samo, U R (ACT, Q) 2004 S1, 2, E1, PI, NZ1, S4(R), 2011 SA2(R), NZ2, [It, I, US(R), Ru, SA, NZ, W(t&R)], W(R), 2012 NZ1(R), 2(R), SA1, SA2, Arg2, F(R)

Sampson, J H (NSW) 1899 BI 4

Sayle, J L (NSW) 1967 NZ

Schatz, J W (Q) 2014 Arg2(R), I(R)

Schulte, B G (Q) 1946 NZ 1, M

Scott, P R I (NSW) 1962 NZ 1, 2

Scott-Young, S J (Q) 1990 F 2, 3(R), US, NZ 3, 1992 NZ 1, 2, 3

Shambrook, G G (Q) 1976 Fj 2, 3

Sharpe, N C (Q, WF) 2002 F 1, 2, NZ 1, SA 1, NZ 2, SA 2, 2003 I, W, E, SA 1(R), NZ 1(R), SA 2(R), NZ 2(R), [Arg, R, Nm, I, S, NZ, E], 2004 S1, 2, E1, PI, NZ1, SA1, NZ2, SA2, 2005 Sm, It, F1, SA1, 2, 3, NZ1, SA4, NZ2, F2, E, I, W, 2006 E1, 2, I1, NZ1, SA1, NZ2, SA2, NZ3, SA3, W, It, I2, S, 2007 W1, 2, SA1, NZ1, SA2, NZ2, [J, W, C, E], 2008 I, F1, SA1, NZ1, 2, 3, 4, E, F3, W, 2009 It1, F, NZ1, SA1, NZ2, 2010 Fj, E1, 2, SA1, NZ1, 2, SA2, 3, NZ3, 4, W, E3, It, F, 2011 Sm, SA1(R), 2, [US, Ru, SA(R), W], W(R), 2012 S, W1, 2, 3, NZ1, 2, SA1, Arg1, SA2, Arg2, NZ3, F, E, It, W4

Shaw, A A (Q) 1973 W, E, 1975 E 1, 2, J 2, S, W, 1976 E, I, US, Fj 1, 2, 3, F 1, 2, 1978 W 1, 2, NZ 1, 2, 3, 1979 I 1, 2, NZ, Arg 1, 2, 1980 Fj, NZ 1, 2, 3, 1981 F 1, 2, I, W, S, 1982 S 1, 2

Shaw, C (NSW) 1925 NZ 2, 3, 4(R)

Shaw, G A (NSW, Q) 1969 W, SA 1(R), 1970 S, 1971 SA 1, 2, 3, F 1, 2, 1973 W, E, 1974 NZ 1, 2, 3, 1975 E 1, 2, J 1, 2, W, 1976 E, I, US, Fj 1, 2, 3, F 1, 2, 1979 NZ

Sheehan, B R (ACT, WF) 2006 SA3(R), 2008 SA2(R), 3(R), 2012 SA2(R), Arg2(R), NZ3(R), It

Sheehan, W B J (NSW) 1921 NZ 1, 2, 3, 1922 NZ 1, 2, 3, 1923 M 1, 2, NZ 1, 2, 3, 1924 NZ 1, 2, 1926 NZ 1, 2, 3, 1927 W, S

Shehadie, N M (NSW) 1947 NZ 2, 1948 E, F, 1949 M 1, 2, 3, NZ 1, 2, 1950 BI 1, 2, 1951 NZ 1, 2, 3, 1952 Fj 1, 2, NZ 2, 1953 SA 1, 2, 3, 4, 1954 Fj 1, 2, 1955 NZ 1, 2, 3, 1956 SA 1, 2, 1957 NZ 2, 1958 W, I

Sheil, A G R (NSW) 1956 SA 1

Shepherd, C B (WF) 2006 E1(R), 2(R), I1(R), SA3, W, 2007 [C], 2008 I, F1, 2(R)

Shepherd, D J (V) 1964 NZ 3, 1965 SA 1, 2, 1966 BI 1, 2

Shepherdson, G T (ACT) 2006 I1, NZ1, SA1, NZ2(R), SA2(R), It, I2, S, 2007 W1, 2, SA1, NZ1, SA2, NZ2, [J(R), W, Fj, E]

Shipperley, D P (Q) 2012 SA1, Arg1, SA2

Shute, J L (NSW) 1920 NZ 3, 1922 M 2, 3

Simmons, R A (Q) 2010 SA1(R), NZ1(R), 2(R), SA2(R), It, F, 2011 SA1, NZ1, 2(R), [It(R), I(R), US, Ru(R), NZ(t&R), W(R)], W, 2012 S(R), W1, 2, 3(R), NZ1(t), SA2(R), F(R), 2013 BI 1(R), 2(R), 3(R), NZ1, 2, SA1, Arg1, SA2, Arg2, NZ3, It, I, S, W, 2014 F1, 2, 3, NZ1, 2, SA1, Arg1, SA2 , NZ 3, W, F 4, I, E, 2015 SA, Arg, US, [Fj, U(R), F, W(R), S, Arg, NZ]

Simpson, R J (NSW) 1913 NZ 2

Sio, S T (ACT) 2013 NZ1(R), 2(R), SA1(R), Arg1(R), 2014 F3(R), 2015 SA(R), Arg(R), NZ 1, 2, US(R), [Fj, U, E, W, S, NZ]

Skelton, W R J (NSW) 2014 F3 NZ1(R), 2(R), Arg2(R), W(R), F 4(R), I(R), E(R), 2015 SA, Arg, NZ 1(R), 2, [Fj(R), U]

Skinner, A J (NSW) 1969 W, SA 4, 1970 S

Slack, A G (Q) 1978 W 1, 2, NZ 1, 2, 1979 NZ, Arg 1, 2, 1980 Fj, 1981 I, W, S, 1982 E, S 1, NZ 3, 1983 US, Arg 1, 2 NZ, It, 1984 Fj, NZ 1, 2, 3, E, I, W, S, 1986 It, F, NZ 1, 2, 3, 1987 SK, [E, US, J, I, F, W]

Slater, S H (NSW) 1910 NZ 3

Slattery, P J (Q) 1990 US (R), 1991 W (R), E (R), [WS (R), W, I (R)], 1992 I, W, 1993 Tg, C, F 1, 2, 1994 I 1, 2, It 1(R), 1995 [C, R (R)]

Slipper, J A (Q) 2010 E1(R), 2(R), I(R), SA1(R), NZ1(R), 2(R), SA2(R), 3(R), NZ3(R), 4(R), W(R), E3(R), It, F, 2011 [It(R), I(R), US, Ru, SA(R), NZ(R), W], W, 2012 S, NZ1(R), 2(R), SA1(R), Arg1(R), SA2(R), Arg2, NZ3, F(t&R), E(R), It(R), W4(R), 2013 BI 1(R), 2(R), 3(R), NZ1, 2, SA1, Arg1, SA2, Arg2, NZ3, E, It, I, S, W, 2014 F1, 2, 3, NZ1, 2, SA1, Arg1, SA2, Arg2, NZ 3, W, F 4, I, E, 2015 SA, Arg, NZ 1(R), 2(R), US, [Fj(R), E(R), W(R), S(R), Arg, NZ(R)]

Smairl, A M (NSW) 1928 NZ 1, 2, 3

Smith, B A (Q) 1987 SK, [US, J, I (R), W], Arg 1

Smith, D P (NSW) 1993 SA 1, 2, 3, C, F 2, 1994 I 1, 2, It 1, 2, WS, NZ, 1995 Arg 1, 2, [SA, R, E], NZ 1, 2, 1998 SA 1(R), NZ 3(R), Fj

Smith, F B (NSW) 1905 NZ, 1907 NZ 1, 2, 3

Smith, G B (ACT) 2000 F, S, E, 2001 BI 1, 2, 3, SA 1, NZ 1, SA 2, NZ 2, Sp, E, F (R), W (R), 2002 F 1, 2, NZ 1, SA 1, NZ 2, SA 2, Arg, I, E, It, 2003 I, NZ 1, SA 2, NZ 2, [Arg, R, Nm, I, S, NZ, E], 2004 S1, 2(R), E1(t&R), PI(R), NZ1(R), SA1, SA2, SA2, S3, F, S4, E2, 2005 Sm, It, F1, SA1, 2, 3, NZ1, SA4(R), NZ2, F2, E, I, W, 2006 E1, 2, I1, NZ1, SA1, NZ2, SA2, NZ3(t), SA3(R), It, I2(R), S, 2007 W1(R), 2, Fj(R), SA1, NZ1, SA2, NZ2, [J, W, C, E], 2008 I, F1, 2(R), SA1, NZ1, 2, SA2, 3(R), NZ3,

4, E, F3, W(R), 2009 It1, 2, F, NZ1, SA1, NZ2, SA2, 3, NZ3, 4(R), E, I(t), S, W(R), 2013 BI 3
Smith, L M (NSW) 1905 NZ
Smith, N C (NSW) 1922 NZ 2, 3, 1923 NZ 1, 1924 NZ 1, 3(R), 1925 NZ 2, 3
Smith, P V (NSW) 1967 NZ, 1968 NZ 1, 2, F, I, S, 1969 W, SA 1
Smith, R A (NSW) 1971 SA 1, 2, 1972 F 1, 2, NZ 1, 2(R), 3, Fj, 1975 E 1, 2, J 1, 2, S, W, 1976 E, I, US, Fj 1, 2, 3, F 1, 2
Smith, T J (MR) 2015 US(R), [U, Arg(R)]
Smith, T S (NSW) 1921 SA 1, 2, 3, NZ, 1922 M 2, 3, NZ 1, 2, 3, 1925 NZ 1, 3, 4
Snell, H W (NSW) 1925 NZ 2, 3, 1928 NZ 3
Solomon, H J (NSW) 1949 M 3, NZ 2, 1950 BI 1, 2, 1951 NZ 1, 2, 1952 Fj 1, 2, NZ 1, 2, 1953 SA 1, 2, 3, 1955 NZ 1
Speight, R H V (ACT) 2014 I, E, 2015 NZ 2, US, [U]
Spooner, N R (Q) 1999 I 1, 2
Spragg, S A (NSW) 1899 BI 1, 2, 3, 4
Staniforth, S N G (NSW, WF) 1999 [US], 2002 I, It, 2006 SA3(R), I2(R), S, 2007 Fj, NZ1(R), SA2(R), NZ2(R), [W(R), Fj(R)]
Stanley, R G (NSW) 1921 NZ, 1922 M 1, 2, 3, NZ 1, 2, 3, 1923 M 2, 3, NZ 1, 2, 3, 1924 NZ 1, 3
Stapleton, E T (NSW) 1951 NZ 1, 2, 3, 1952 Fj 1, 2, NZ 1, 2, 1953 SA 1, 2, 3, 4, 1954 Fj 1, 1955 NZ 1, 2, 3, 1958 NZ 1
Steggall, J C (Q) 1931 M, NZ, 1932 NZ 1, 2, 3, 1933 SA 1, 2, 3, 4, 5
Stegman, T R (NSW) 1973 Tg 1, 2
Stephens, O G (NSW) 1973 Tg 1, 2, W, 1974 NZ 2, 3
Stewart, A A (NSW) 1979 NZ, Arg 1, 2
Stiles, N B (Q) 2001 BI 1, 2, 3, SA 1, NZ 1, SA 2, NZ 2, Sp, E, F, W, 2002 I
Stone, A H (NSW) 1937 SA 2, 1938 NZ 2, 3
Stone, C G (NSW) 1938 NZ 1
Stone, J M (NSW) 1946 M, NZ 2
Storey, G P (NSW) 1926 NZ 4, 1927 I, W, S, 1928 E, F, 1929 NZ 3(R), 1930 BI
Storey, K P (NSW) 1936 NZ 2
Storey, N J D (NSW) 1962 NZ 1
Strachan, D J (NSW) 1955 NZ 2, 3
Strauss, C P (NSW) 1999 I 1(R), 2(R), E (R), SA 1(R), NZ 1, SA 2(R), NZ 2(R), [R (R), I 3(R), US, W]
Street, N O (NSW) 1899 BI 2
Streeter, S F (NSW) 1978 NZ 1
Stuart, R (NSW) 1910 NZ 2, 3
Stumbles, B D (NSW) 1972 NZ 1(R), 2, 3, Fj
Sturtridge, G S (V) 1929 NZ 2, 1932 NZ 1, 2, 3, 1933 SA 1, 2, 3, 4, 5
Sullivan, P D (NSW) 1971 SA 1, 2, 3, F 1, 2, 1972 F 1, 2, NZ 1, 2, Fj, 1973 Tg 1, 2, W
Summons, A J (NSW) 1958 W, I, E, S, M 2, NZ 1, 2, 3, 1959 BI 1, 2
Suttor, D C (NSW) 1913 NZ 1, 2, 3
Swannell, B I (NSW) 1905 NZ
Sweeney, T L (Q) 1953 SA 1

Taafe, B S (NSW) 1969 SA 1, 1972 F 1, 2
Tabua, I (Q) 1993 SA 2, 3, C, F 1, 1994 I 1, 2, It 1, 2, 1995 [C, R]
Tahu, P J A (NSW) 2008 NZ1(R), SA2(R), 3, It
Tancred, A J (NSW) 1927 I, W, S
Tancred, H E (NSW) 1923 M 1, 2
Tancred, J L (NSW) 1926 NZ 3, 4, 1928 F
Tanner, W H (Q) 1899 BI 1, 2
Tapuai, B N L (Q) 2011 W(R), 2012 Arg2, NZ3, F, E, It, W4
Tarleton, K (NSW) 1925 NZ 2, 3
Tasker, W G (NSW) 1913 NZ 1, 2, 3, 1914 NZ 1, 2, 3
Tate, M J (NSW) 1951 NZ 3, 1952 Fj 1, 2, NZ 1, 2, 1953 SA 1, 1954 Fj 1, 2
Taylor, D A (Q) 1968 NZ 1, 2, F, I, S
Taylor, H C (NSW) 1923 NZ 1, 2, 3, 1924 NZ 4
Taylor, J I (NSW) 1971 SA 1, 1972 F 1, 2, Fj
Taylor, J M (NSW) 1922 M 1, 2
Teitzel, R G (Q) 1966 W, S, 1967 E, I 1, F, I 2, NZ
Telford, D G (NSW) 1926 NZ 3(R)
Thompson, C E (NSW) 1922 M 1, 1923 M 1, 2, NZ 1, 1924 NZ 2, 3
Thompson, E G (Q) 1929 NZ 1, 2, 3, 1930 BI
Thompson, F (NSW) 1913 NZ 1, 2, 3, 1914 NZ 1, 3
Thompson, J (Q) 1914 NZ 1, 2
Thompson, P D (Q) 1950 BI 1
Thompson, R J (WA) 1971 SA 3, F 2(R), 1972 Fj

Thorn, A M (NSW) 1921 SA 1, 2, 3, NZ, 1922 M 1, 3
Thorn, E J (NSW) 1922 NZ 1, 2, 3, 1923 NZ 1, 2, 3, 1924 NZ 1, 2, 3, 1925 NZ 1, 2, 1926 NZ 1, 2, 3, 4
Thornett, J E (NSW) 1955 NZ 1, 2, 3, 1956 SA 1, 2, 1958 W, I, S, F, M 2, 3, NZ 2, 3, 1959 BI 1, 2, 1961 Fj 2, 3, SA 1, 2, F, 1962 NZ 2, 3, 4, 5, 1963 E, SA 1, 2, 3, 4, 1964 NZ 1, 2, 3, 1965 SA 1, 2, 1966 BI 1, 2, 1967 F
Thornett, R N (NSW) 1961 Fj 1, 2, 3, SA 1, 2, F, 1962 NZ 1, 2, 3, 4, 5
Thorpe, A C (NSW) 1929 NZ 1(R)
Timani, S (NSW) 2011 Sm, 2012 S, W3, NZ1, 2, SA1, Arg2, NZ3, E, It, 2013 Arg1(R), SA2(R), Arg2(R), NZ3(R), E, It, I(R), S(R)
Timbury, F R V (Q) 1910 NZ 1, 2,
Tindall, E N (NSW) 1973 Tg 2
Toby, A E (NSW) 1925 NZ 1, 4
Tolhurst, H A (NSW) 1931 M, NZ
Tomane, J M (ACT) 2012 S, 2013 BI 2, 3, SA2, Arg2, It(R), I(R), S, W, 2014 SA2, Arg2, NZ 3, W, F 4, 2015 Arg, US, [U]
Tombs, R C (NSW) 1992 S 1, 2, 1994 I 2, It 1, 1996 NZ 2
Tonkin, A E J (NSW) 1947 S, I, W, 1948 E, F, 1950 BI 2
To'omua, M P (ACT) 2013 NZ1, 2, SA1(R), Arg1(R), SA2(R), Arg2(R), NZ3, E, It, I, 2014 F1, 2, 3, NZ1, 2, SA1, Arg1, SA2, Arg2, I, E, 2015 SA(R), Arg, NZ 1(R), 2,[Fj(R), U, E(R), W(R), Arg(R), NZ(t)]
Tooth, R M (NSW) 1951 NZ 1, 2, 3, 1954 Fj 1, 2, 1955 NZ 1, 2, 3, 1957 NZ 1, 2
Towers, C H T (NSW) 1926 NZ 1, 3(R), 4, 1927 I, 1928 E, F, NZ 1, 2, 3, M, 1929 NZ 1, 3, 1930 BI, 1931 M, NZ, 1934 NZ 1, 2, 1937 SA 1, 2
Trivett, R K (Q) 1966 BI 1, 2
Tune, B N (Q) 1996 W 2, C, NZ 1, SA 1, NZ 2, SA 2, 1997 F 1, 2, NZ 1, E 1, NZ 2, SA 1, NZ 3, SA 2, Arg, 1, 2, E 2, S, 1998 E 1, S, 1, 2, NZ 1, SA 1, 2, NZ 3, 1999 I 1, SA 1, SA 2, NZ 2, [R, I 3, W, SA 3, F], 2000 SA 2(R), NZ 2(t&R), SA 3(R), 2001 F (R), W, 2002 NZ 1, SA 1, NZ 2, SA 2, Arg, 2006 NZ1(R)
Tuqiri, L D (NSW) 2003 I (R), W (R), E (R), SA 1(R), NZ 1, SA 2, NZ 2, [Arg(R), R(R), Nm, I(R), S, NZ, E], 2004 S1, 2, E1, PI, NZ1, SA1, NZ2, SA2, S3, F, S4, E2, 2005 It, F1, SA1, 2, 3, NZ1, SA4, NZ2, F2, E, I, W, 2006 E1, 2, I1, NZ1, SA1, NZ2, SA2, NZ3, W, It, I2, S, 2007 Fj, SA1, NZ1, [J, W, Fj, C, E], 2008 I, F1, SA1, NZ1, 2, SA2, 3, NZ3, W(R)
Turinui, M P (NSW) 2003 I, W, E, 2003 [Nm(R)], 2004 S1(R), 2, E2, 2005 Sm, It(R), F1(R), SA1, 2(t&R), 3, NZ1, SA4, NZ2, F2, E, I, W
Turnbull, A (V) 1961 Fj 3
Turnbull, R V (NSW) 1968 I
Turner, L D (NSW) 2008 F2, It, 2009 It1, 2, F, NZ1, SA1, NZ2, SA2, 3, NZ3, 2010 NZ3, It, F(R), 2011 W
Tuynman, S N (NSW) 1983 F 1, 2, 1984 E, I, W, S, 1985 C 1, 2, NZ, Fj 1, 2, 1986 It, F, Arg 1, 2, NZ 1, 2, 3, 1987 SK, [E, US, J, I, W], NZ, Arg 1(R), 2, 1988 E, It, 1989 BI 1, 2, 3, NZ, 1990 NZ 1
Tweedale, E (NSW) 1946 NZ 1, 2, 1947 NZ 2, S, I, 1948 E, F, 1949 M 1, 2, 3

Valentine, J J (Q, WF) 2006 E1(R), W(R), I2(R), S(R), 2009 It2(R), F(R)
Vaughan, D (NSW) 1983 US, Arg 1, It, F 1, 2
Vaughan, G N (V) 1958 E, S, F, M 1, 2, 3
Verge, A (NSW) 1904 BI 1, 2
Vickerman, D J (ACT, NSW) 2002 F 2(R), Arg, E, It, 2003 I (R), W (R), E (R), SA 1, NZ 1, SA 2, NZ 2, [Arg(R), R, I(R), S(R)], 2004 S1(t&R), 2(R), E1(R), PI(R), NZ1(R), SA1(R), NZ2(R), SA2(R), S3, F, S4, E2, 2005 SA2(R), 3, NZ1, SA4, 2006 E1, 2, I1, NZ1, SA1, NZ2, SA2, NZ3, SA3, W, 2007 W1(R), 2, Fj, SA1, NZ1, SA2, NZ2, [J, W, Fj, E], 2008 NZ1(R), 2(t&R), SA2, 2011 Sm(R), NZ1(R), 2, [It, I, US(R), SA, NZ]
Vuna, K C (MR) 2012 W1, 2

Walden, R J (NSW) 1934 NZ 2, 1936 NZ 1, 2, M
Walker, A K (NSW) 1947 NZ 1, 1948 E, F, 1950 BI 1, 2
Walker, A M (ACT) 2000 NZ 1(R), 2001 BI 1, 2, 3, SA 1, NZ 1, 2(R)
Walker, A S B (NSW) 1912 US, 1920 NZ 1, 1921 SA 1, 2, 3, NZ, 1922 M 1, 3, NZ 1, 2, 3, 1923 M 2, 3, 1924 NZ 1, 2
Walker, L F (NSW) 1988 NZ 2, 3, S, It, 1989 BI 1, 2, 3, NZ
Walker, L R (NSW) 1982 NZ 2, 3
Wallace, A C (NSW) 1921 NZ, 1926 NZ 3, 4, 1927 I, W, S, 1928 E, F

Wallace, T M (NSW) 1994 It 1(R), 2
Wallach, C (NSW) 1913 NZ 1, 3, 1914 NZ 1, 2, 3
Walsh, J J (NSW) 1953 SA 1, 2, 3, 4
Walsh, P B (NSW) 1904 BI 1, 2, 3
Walsham, K P (NSW) 1962 NZ 3, 1963 E
Ward, P G (NSW) 1899 BI 1, 2, 3, 4
Ward, T (Q) 1899 BI 2
Watson, G W (Q) 1907 NZ 1
Watson, W T (NSW) 1912 US, 1913 NZ 1, 2, 3, 1914 NZ 1, 1920 NZ 1, 2, 3
Waugh, P R (NSW) 2000 E (R), 2001 NZ 1(R), SA 2(R), NZ 2(R), Sp (R), E (R), F, W, 2003 I (R), W, E, SA 1, NZ 1, SA 2, NZ2, [Arg, R, I, S, NZ, E], 2004 S1(R), 2, E1, PI, NZ1, SA1, NZ2, SA2, S3, F, S4, E2, 2005 SA1(R), 2(R), 3, NZ1(R), SA4, NZ2, F2, E, I, W, 2006 E1(R), I1(R), NZ1(R), SA1(R), NZ2(R), SA2(R), NZ3, SA3, W, I2, S(R), 2007 W1, 2(R), Fj, SA1(R), NZ1(R), SA2(R), NZ2(R), [W(R), Fj, C(R), E(R)], 2008 I(R), F1(R), 2, SA1(R), NZ1(R), 2, SA2(t&R), 3, NZ4(R), It, W, 2009 It2(R), F(R)
Waugh, W W (NSW, ACT) 1993 SA 1, 1995 [C], NZ 1, 2, 1996 S, I, 1997 Arg 1, 2
Weatherstone, L J (ACT) 1975 E 1, 2, J 1, 2, S (R), 1976 E, I
Webb, W (NSW) 1899 BI 3, 4
Welborn J P (NSW) 1996 SA 2, It, 1998 Tg, 1999 E, SA 1, NZ 1
Wells, B G (NSW) 1958 M 1
Weeks, L S (MR) 2014 F2(R), 3(R)
Westfield, R E (NSW) 1928 NZ 1, 2, 3, M, 1929 NZ 2, 3
Whitaker, C J (NSW) 1998 SA 2(R), Fj (R), Tg, 1999 NZ 2(R), [R (R), US, F (R)], 2000 S (R), 2001 Sp (R), W (R), 2002 Arg (R), It (R), 2003 I (R), W (R), SA 2(R), [Arg(R), Nm, S(R)], 2004 PI(R), NZ1, 2005 Sm, It(R), F1(R), SA1(R), 2(R), NZ1(t&R), SA4(R), NZ2(R), F2(R), E(R), W(R)
White, C J B (NSW) 1899 BI 1, 1903 NZ, 1904 BI 1
White, J M (NSW) 1904 BI 3
White, J P L (NSW) 1958 NZ 1, 2, 3, 1961 Fj 1, 2, 3, SA 1, 2, F, 1962 NZ 1, 2, 3, 4, 5, 1963 E, SA 1, 2, 3, 4, 1964 NZ 1, 2, 3, 1965 SA 1, 2
White, M C (Q) 1931 M, NZ 1932 NZ 1, 2, 1933 SA 1, 2, 3, 4, 5
White, N W (ACT) 2013 NZ1(R), 2(R), SA1(R), Arg1, SA2, Arg2(R), E(R), It(R), I(R), S(R), 2014 F1, 2, 3, NZ1, 2, Arg1(R), 2(R), NZ 3(R), E(R), 2015 Arg(R), NZ 1(R), 2
White, S W (NSW) 1956 SA 1, 2, 1958 I, E, S, M 2, 3
White, W G S (Q) 1933 SA 1, 2, 3, 4, 5, 1934 NZ 1, 2, 1936 NZ 1, 2, M
White, W J (NSW) 1928 NZ 1, M, 1932 NZ 1

Wickham, S M (NSW) 1903 NZ, 1904 BI 1, 2, 3, 1905 NZ
Williams, D (Q) 1913 NZ 3, 1914 NZ 1, 2, 3
Williams, I M (NSW) 1987 Arg 1, 2, 1988 E 1, 2, NZ 1, 2, 3, 1989 BI 2, 3, NZ, F 1, 2, 1990 F 1, 2, 3, US, NZ 1
Williams, J L (NSW) 1963 SA 1, 3, 4
Williams, R W (ACT) 1999 I 1(t&R), 2(t&R), E (R), [US], 2000 Arg 1, 2, SA 1, NZ 1, SA 2, NZ 2, SA 3, F (R), S (R), E
Williams, S A (NSW) 1980 Fj, NZ 1, 2, 1981 F 1, 2, 1982 E, NZ 1, 2, 3, 1983 US, Arg 1(R), 2, NZ, It, F 1, 2, 1984 NZ 1, 2, 3, E, I, W, S, 1985 C 1, 2, NZ, Fj 1, 2
Wilson, B J (NSW) 1949 NZ 1, 2
Wilson, C R (Q) 1957 NZ 1, 1958 NZ 1, 2, 3
Wilson, D J (Q) 1992 S 1, 2, NZ 1, 2, 3, SA, I, W, 1993 Tg, NZ, SA 1, 2, 3, C, F 1, 2, 1994 I 1, 2, It 1, 2, WS, NZ, 1995 Arg 1, 2, [SA, R, E], 1996 W 1, 2, C, NZ 1, SA 1, NZ 2, SA 2, It, S, I, W 3, 1997 F 1, 2, NZ 1, E 1(t + R), NZ 2(R), SA 1, NZ 3, SA 2, E 2(R), S (R), 1998 E 1, S 1, 2, NZ 1, SA 1, NZ 2, SA 2, NZ 3, Fj, WS, F, E 2, 1999 I 1, 2, E, SA 1, NZ 1, SA 2, NZ 2, [R, I 3, W, SA 3, F], 2000 Arg 1, 2, SA 1, NZ 1, SA 2, NZ 2, SA 3
Wilson, V W (Q) 1937 SA 1, 2, 1938 NZ 1, 2, 3
Windon, C J (NSW) 1946 NZ 1, 2, 1947 NZ 1, S, I, W, 1948 E, F, 1949 M 1, 2, 3, NZ 1, 2, 1951 NZ 1, 2, 3, 1952 Fj 1, 2, NZ 1, 2
Windon, K S (NSW) 1937 SA 1, 2, 1946 M
Windsor, J C (Q) 1947 NZ 2
Winning, K C (Q) 1951 NZ 1
Wogan, L W (NSW) 1913 NZ 1, 2, 3, 1914 NZ 1, 2, 3, 1920 NZ 1, 2, 3, 1921 SA 1, 2, 3, NZ, 1922 M 3, NZ 1, 2, 3, 1923 M 1, 2, 1924 NZ 1, 2, 3
Wood, F (NSW) 1907 NZ 1, 2, 3, 1910 NZ 1, 2, 3, 1913 NZ 1, 2, 3, 1914 NZ 1, 2, 3
Wood, R N (Q) 1972 Fj
Woods, H F (NSW) 1925 NZ 4, 1926 NZ 1, 2, 3, 1927 I, W, S, 1928 E
Wright, K J (NSW) 1975 E 1, 2, J 1, 1976 US, F 1, 1978 NZ 1, 2, 3
Wyld, G (NSW) 1920 NZ 2

Yanz, K (NSW) 1958 F

Young, W K (ACT, NSW) 2000 F, S, E, 2002 F 1, 2, NZ 1, SA 1, NZ 2, SA 2, Arg, E, It, 2003 I, W, E, SA 1, NZ 1, SA 2, NZ 2, [Arg, R, I, S, NZ, E], 2004 S1, 2, E1, PI, NZ1, SA1, NZ2, SA2, S3, F, S4, E2, 2005 Sm, It, F1, SA1, 2, 3, NZ1, SA4, NZ2

CANADA

CANADA'S 2014–15 TEST RECORD

OPPONENT	DATE	VENUE	RESULT
Namibia	7 Nov	N	Won 17–13
Samoa	14 Nov	N	Lost 23–13
Romania	22 Nov	A	Lost 18–9
Japan	18 Jul	N	Lost 20–6
Tonga	24 Jul	H	Lost 18–28
Samoa	29 Jul	H	Lost 20–21
USA	3 Aug	H	Lost 13–15
USA	22 Aug	H	Lost 23–41
Georgia	2 Sep	N	Won 16–15
Fiji	6 Sep	N	Lost 47–18
Ireland	19 Sep	N	Lost 50–7
Italy	26 Sep	N	Lost 23–18
France	1 Oct	N	Lost 41–18
Romania	6 Oct	N	Lost 17–15

CANADA RUE MISSED CHANCES AT RWC 2015

By Ian Gilbert

Flying winger DTH van der Merwe scored a try in every one of Canada's pool matches at Rugby World Cup 2015.

The look on captain Jamie Cudmore's face said it all as the full-time whistle blew for the end of Canada's Rugby World Cup 2015 match against Romania. The North Americans had just played their part in the biggest comeback in the tournament's history, but that's scarcely any consolation when you're on the losing side.

Canada led 15–0 as the final quarter loomed at Leicester City Stadium, but two tries by Romania captain Mihai Macovei and the kicking of centre Florin Vlaicu inflicted a crushing 17–15 defeat on the Canucks.

"The guys have worked extremely hard for the last three or four months, even years," Cudmore said afterwards. "We came up second best against a team we honestly thought we were better than."

Romania had offered Canada's seemingly best chance of victory in a Pool D campaign that will ultimately go down as a failure – played four, lost four – but nonetheless contained plenty of bright moments.

Canada opened their RWC 2015 campaign against Ireland at Cardiff's Millennium Stadium on 19 September, but suffered a 50–7 loss to the

World Rugby Rankings

Ireland were clinical in their seven-try victory, and coach Joe Schmidt acknowledged they had been wary of the Canadians' commitment. "I think we showed some respect for Canada and they deserved that," Schmidt said. "They're a combative side and difficult to out-muscle. However, we built the scoreboard pressure on them and that was satisfying."

DTH van der Merwe, whose slick finishing and shock of blond hair made him so noticeable at RWC 2011 in New Zealand, advanced his World Cup pedigree by racing 40 metres to score Canada's consolation try.

Cudmore and Ireland's Paul O'Connell – stalwart second-rows and respective captains that day – each spent a stint in the sin-bin but with tellingly different results, indicating the nous needed against nations such as Ireland.

"We conceded 19 points when we were a man down and when they were down to 14, we failed to score," Canada coach Kieran Crowley reasoned. "I was pleased with the way we played, but we have got to take our chances in the red zone."

If Canada lacked finishing precision, they were certainly not overawed by the intensity. "It was what I am used to week in, week out in France with the European Cup," Cudmore said.

While Ireland were too great an obstacle to overcome, their next opponents Italy were probably a more accurate yardstick of Canada's international progress.

A real upset was on the cards but Canada's lack of big-match control proved their undoing as the Six Nations side ran out 23–18 victors in an entertaining match at Elland Road in Leeds a week later.

The Canadians shot out to a 10–0 lead, were reeled in by Italy, but edged ahead again in the second half, 15–13 – and had a try from Phil Mackenzie ruled out. However, the final quarter proved their undoing.

Canada captain Tyler Ardron said the answer was more game time. "If we had 23 guys who played 30 or 40 games a year, I don't think things like that would happen," the Ospreys number eight said. "Eighty minutes is a long time and it's too easy to switch off."

Crowley also pointed to the lack of consistency. "We've got players out there in key positions who are only having five or six games at 15s in the last three years, and we're getting on to the big stage and having teams who play 40-odd games a year," he said of a match which saw winger Van der Merwe score another scintillating try to edge closer to Winston Stanley's Canadian try-scoring record.

CANADA

Next up were France and an inspired Frédéric Michalak, the fly-half choosing this match to become the highest points scorer in French RWC history as Les Bleus ran out 41–18 winners in Milton Keynes.

Canada nonetheless showed a French-like zeal for open rugby through the likes of Van der Merwe, fly-half Nathan Hirayama and full-back Matt Evans. Falling 17–0 behind, they pulled back to 17–12 courtesy of two tries in four minutes from Van der Merwe and Aaron Carpenter before the French moved up a gear at Stadium MK.

And so to the Romania game, which both sides entered looking for their first win of the tournament. Once again, though, the Canadians were made to pay for their failure to close down the game in the latter stages, allowing the Romanians the chance to stage their remarkable comeback.

Van der Merwe completed his record of scoring a try in each match, but was in no mood for celebration after seeing a chance to finish RWC 2015 on a winning note slip through Canada's grasp.

"We didn't win a game so it doesn't mean anything to me, scoring those tries," he said.

Canada's form line had been disappointing in the run-up to Rugby World Cup 2015, with only one win from nine matches in the calendar year and including two defeats against their neighbours the USA. But they clearly came into the tournament with high expectations.

"We put in so much effort into this World Cup," said Van der Merwe. "We've been together since July 7. I'm kind of lost for words, just disappointed. We've only got ourselves to blame."

Canada will, without doubt, learn from their RWC 2015 experiences and Cudmore, speaking after their narrow loss to Italy, believes they are already taking steps forward in development terms.

"I thought we played a good brand of rugby but we couldn't punch it over in the end. I think we've shown over the last few weeks and months that we can play with the big teams. With a few more balls going our way last week (v Ireland) we would have had three or four more tries and the scoreline (50–7) would have been much more different."

On the domestic front, UBC Thunderbirds of Vancouver claimed the Premier League title for 2015, while the provincial tournament went to the Alberta-based Wolf Pack after finishing runners-up for the past three seasons, winning 33–25 against the Ontario Blues at Calgary Rugby Park.

CANADA INTERNATIONAL STATISTICS

MATCH RECORDS UP TO 1 NOVEMBER, 2015

WINNING MARGIN

Date	Opponent	Result	Winning Margin
24/06/2006	Barbados	69–3	66
14/10/1999	Namibia	72–11	61
12/08/2006	USA	56–7	49
06/07/1996	Hong Kong	57–9	48

MOST POINTS IN A MATCH
BY THE TEAM

Date	Opponent	Result	Points
14/10/1999	Namibia	72–11	72
24/06/2006	Barbados	69–3	69
15/07/2000	Japan	62–18	62
13/11/2010	Spain	60–22	60
06/07/1996	Hong Kong	57–9	57

BY A PLAYER

Date	Player	Opponent	Points
12/08/2006	James Pritchard	USA	36
24/06/2006	James Pritchard	Barbados	29
14/10/1999	Gareth Rees	Namibia	27
23/11/2013	James Pritchard	Portugal	27
13/07/1996	Bobby Ross	Japan	26

MOST TRIES IN A MATCH
BY THE TEAM

Date	Opponent	Result	Tries
24/06/2006	Barbados	69–3	11
14/10/1999	Namibia	72–11	9
11/05/1991	Japan	49–26	8
15/07/2000	Japan	62–18	8
13/11/2010	Spain	60–22	8

BY A PLAYER

Date	Player	Opponent	Tries
15/07/2000	Kyle Nichols	Japan	4
24/06/2006	James Pritchard	Barbados	3
12/08/2006	James Pritchard	USA	3
10/05/1987	Steve Gray	USA	3

MOST CONVERSIONS IN A MATCH
BY THE TEAM

Date	Opponent	Result	Cons
14/10/1999	Namibia	72–11	9
15/07/2000	Japan	62–18	8
7 on 4 occasions			

BY A PLAYER

Date	Player	Opponent	Cons
14/10/1999	Gareth Rees	Namibia	9
15/07/2000	Jared Barker	Japan	8
7 on 4 occasions			

MOST PENALTIES IN A MATCH
BY THE TEAM

Date	Opponent	Result	Pens
25/05/1991	Scotland	24–19	8
22/08/1998	Argentina	28–54	7
6 on 6 occasions			

BY A PLAYER

Date	Player	Opponent	Pens
25/05/1991	Mark Wyatt	Scotland	8
22/08/1998	Gareth Rees	Argentina	7
6 on 5 occasions			

MOST DROP GOALS IN A MATCH
BY THE TEAM

Date	Opponent	Result	DGs
08/11/1986	USA	27–16	2
04/07/2001	Fiji	23–52	2
08/06/1980	USA	16–0	2
24/05/1997	Hong Kong	35–27	2
18/09/2011	France	19–46	2

BY A PLAYER

Date	Player	Opponent	DGs
04/07/2001	Bobby Ross	Fiji	2
24/05/1997	Bobby Ross	Hong Kong	2
18/09/2011	Ander Monro	France	2

CANADA

MOST CAPPED PLAYERS

Name	Caps
Al Charron	76
Aaron Carpenter	71
Winston Stanley	66
Scott Stewart	64
Rod Snow	62
James Pritchard	62

LEADING TRY SCORERS

Name	Tries
Winston Stanley	24
DTH van der Merwe	20
James Pritchard	18
Aaron Carpenter	15
Morgan Williams	13

LEADING CONVERSIONS SCORERS

Name	Conversions
James Pritchard	104
Bobby Ross	52
Gareth Rees	51
Jared Barker	24
Mark Wyatt	24

LEADING PENALTY SCORERS

Name	Penalties
Gareth Rees	110
James Pritchard	103
Bobby Ross	84
Mark Wyatt	64
Jared Barker	55

LEADING DROP GOAL SCORERS

Name	DGs
Bobby Ross	10
Gareth Rees	9
Mark Wyatt	5

LEADING POINTS SCORERS

Name	Points
James Pritchard	607
Gareth Rees	491
Bobby Ross	421
Mark Wyatt	263
Jared Barker	226

CANADA INTERNATIONAL PLAYERS
UP TO 1 NOVEMBER, 2015

AD Abrams 2003 *US, NZ, Tg,* 2004 *US, J, EngA, US, F, It, E,* 2005 *US, J, W, EngA, US, Ar, F, R,* 2006 *S, E, US, It*
MJ Alder 1976 *Bb*
P Aldous 1971 *W*
TJ Ardron 2012 *US, It, Geo, Sa, Rus,* 2013 *US, Fj, Tg, I, J, US, Geo, R,* 2014 *J, S, US, R,* 2015 *J, Tg, Sa, It, F*
AS Arthurs 1988 *US*
M Ashton 1971 *W*
F Asselin 1999 *Fj,* 2000 *Tg, US, SA,* 2001 *Ur, Ar, Fj,* 2002 *S, US, US, Ur, Chl, W, F*
O Atkinson 2005 *J, Ar,* 2006 *E, US, It*
S Ault 2006 *W, It,* 2008 *US, Pt,* 2009 *Geo, US, US*

JC Bain 1932 *J*
RG Banks 1999 *J, Fj, Sa, US, Tg, W, E, F, Nm,* 2000 *US, SA, I, J, It,* 2001 *US, Ur, Ar, E, Fj, J,* 2002 *S, US, US, Ur, Chl, Ur, Chl, W, F,* 2003 *EngA, US, M, M, Ur, NZ, It*
S Barber 1973 *W,* 1976 *Bb*
M Barbieri 2006 *E, US*
B Barker 1966 *BI,* 1971 *W*
J Barker 2000 *Tg, J, It,* 2002 *S, US, US, Ur, Chl, Ur, Chl, W,* 2003 *US, NZ, It,* 2004 *US, J, F, It*
R Barkwill 2012 *Sa, Rus,* 2013 *US, Fj, Tg, I, J, US, US, Geo, Pt,* 2014 *J, S, US, Nm, Sa, R,* 2015 *J, Sa, US, US, Geo, I, It, F, R*
T Bauer 1977 *US, E,* 1978 *US, F,* 1979 *US*
DR Baugh 1998 *J, HK, US, HK, J, Ur, Ar,* 1999 *J, Fj, Sa, US, Tg, W, E, F, Fj, Nm,* 2000 *US, SA, I, It,* 2001 *E, E,* 2002 *S, US, Ur, Chl*
BG Beukeboom 2012 *US, Geo, Sa,* 2013 *US, Tg, J, Geo, R, Pt,* 2014 *Nm, Sa,* 2015 *J, Tg, US, Geo, I, F, R*

A Bianco 1966 *BI*
AJ Bibby 1979 *US, F,* 1980 *W, US, NZ,* 1981 *US, Ar*
R Bice 1996 *US, A,* 1997 *US, J, HK, US, W, I,* 1998 *US, HK, J, Ur, US, Ar,* 1999 *J, Fj, Sa, US, Tg, W, F*
P Bickerton 2004 *US, J*
D Biddle 2006 *S, E, Bar,* 2007 *W, Fj, A*
JM Billingsley 1974 *Tg,* 1977 *US,* 1978 *F,* 1979 *US,* 1980 *W,* 1983 *US, It, It,* 1984 *US*
WG Bjarneson 1962 *Bb*
TJH Blackwell 1973 *W*
N Blevins 2009 *J, J,* 2010 *Bel, Sp, Geo, Pt,* 2012 *Sa, Rus,* 2013 *US, Fj, Tg, J, US, US, Geo, R, Pt,* 2014 *J, S, R,* 2015 *Sa, US, US, Geo, Fj, I, F, R*
B Bonenberg 1983 *US, It, It*
J Boone 1932 *J, J*
T Bourne 1967 *E*
CJ Braid 2010 *Bel, Geo,* 2012 *Sa, Rus,* 2013 *US, Fj, I, J, Pt,* 2014 *J, S, US, Nm, Sa,* 2015 *J, Tg, US, Fj, It*
R Breen 1986 *US,* 1987 *W,* 1990 *US,* 1991 *J, S, US, R,* 1993 *E, US*
R Breen 1983 *E,* 1987 *US*
R Brewer 1967 *E*
STT Brown 1989 *I, US*
N Browne 1973 *W,* 1974 *Tg*
S Bryan 1996 *Ur, US, Ar,* 1997 *HK, J, US, W,* 1998 *HK, J, US, Ar,* 1999 *Fj, Sa, US, Tg, W, E, F, Fj, Nm*
M Burak 2004 *US, J, EngA, US, F, It, E,* 2005 *EngA, US, Ar, F, R,* 2006 *US, Bar, W,* 2007 *NZ, Pt, W, Fj, J, A,* 2008 *I, W, S,* 2009 *I, W, Geo, US, US ·*

1991 *J, S, Fj, F, NZ*, 1992 *US, E*, 1993 *E, E, US, A, W*, 1994 *US, F, W, E, F*, 1995 *S, Ar, Fj, NZ, R, A, SA, US*, 1996 *US, US, HK, J, A, HK, J, US, Ar*, 1997 *US, J, HK, J, US*
GR Greig 1973 *W*
JR Greig 1977 *US, E*, 1978 *US*, 1979 *US, F*, 1980 *W, US, NZ*, 1981 *Ar*
J Grout 1995 *Ur*
MR Gudgeon 2010 *Bel*, 2011 *Rus*
G Gudmundseth 1973 *W*

N Hadley 1987 *US*, 1989 *I, US*, 1990 *Ar*, 1991 *S, US, Fj, R, F, NZ*, 1992 *US, E*, 1993 *E*, 1994 *E, F*
J Haley 1996 *Ur*
J Hall 1996 *US*, 1997 *HK*, 1998 *J, HK, J, US, Ar*
GRO Hamilton 2010 *Ur*, 2011 *Rus, US, US, Tg, F, J, NZ*, 2012 *US, Sa, Rus*, 2013 *US, Fj, Tg, I, J, US*
WT Handson 1985 *A, A, US*, 1986 *J, US*, 1987 *US, Tg, I, W*
J Hassler 2012 *US, Geo, Sa, Rus*, 2013 *Geo, R*, 2014 *J, S, US, Sa, R*, 2015 *J, Tg, US, Geo, I, R*
JP Hawthorn 1982 *J, J, E*, 1983 *US, It, It*
A Healy 1996 *HK, J, HK, J, Ur, US, Ar*, 1997 *US, HK, HK, I*, 1998 *HK, J, Ur*, 1999 *J*
AR Heaman 1988 *US*
C Hearn 2008 *I, W, S*, 2009 *I, W, Geo, US, US, J, J*, 2010 *Ur, Bel, Sp, Geo, Pt*, 2011 *US, US, Tg, F*, 2012 *US, It, Geo, Sa, Rus*, 2013 *US, Fj, Tg, I, J, US, US, R, Pt*, 2014 *J, S, US, Nm, Sa, R*, 2015 *J, Tg, US, US, Geo, Fj, I, It, F, R*
B Henderson 2005 *J, F, R*
S Hendry 1996 *Ur, US, Ar*
G Henrikson 1971 *W*
L Hillier 1973 *W*
RE Hindson 1973 *W*, 1974 *Tg*, 1976 *Bb*, 1977 *US, E, E*, 1978 *US, F*, 1979 *US, F*, 1980 *W, US, NZ*, 1981 *US, Ar*, 1982 *J, J, E, US*, 1983 *US, It, It*, 1984 *US*, 1985 *A, A, US*, 1986 *J*, 1987 *US, I, W*, 1990 *Ar*
G Hirayama 1977 *E, E*, 1978 *US*, 1979 *US, F*, 1980 *W, US, NZ*, 1981 *US*, 1982 *J, E, US*
NS Hirayama 2008 *Pt, S*, 2009 *J, J, Rus*, 2010 *Bel*, 2011 *US, F, NZ*, 2013 *Tg, I, US, US*, 2014 *US*, 2015 *J, Tg, Sa, US, Geo, I, It, F, R*
M Holmes 1987 *US*
TN Hotson 2008 *US, Pt, I, W, S*, 2009 *I, W, Geo, US, US, J, J, Rus*, 2010 *Ur, Sp, Geo, Pt*, 2011 *Rus, US, US, Tg, F, J, NZ*, 2012 *US, It, Geo, Sa, Rus*, 2013 *US, Fj, Tg, I, US, US, Geo, R, Pt*, 2014 *J, S, US, Nm*, 2015 *J, Sa, US*
P Howlett 1974 *Tg*
BM Hunnings 1932 *J, J*
E Hunt 1966 *Bl*, 1967 *E*
S Hunter 2005 *R*
J Hutchinson 1993 *E, A, W*, 1995 *S, Ar, Fj, A, SA, US*, 1996 *US, US, HK, J, A, HK, J, Ur, US, Ar*, 1997 *US, J, HK, HK, J, US, W, I*, 1998 *J, HK, US, US, HK, J, Ur, US, Ar*, 1999 *J, Fj, Sa, US, Tg, US, W, E, F, Fj, Nm*, 2000 *US, Sa, Fj, J*
I Hyde-Lay 1986 *J*, 1987 *US*, 1988 *US*

J Ilnicki 2013 *Geo, Pt*, 2014 *J, S, US, Sa*, 2015 *US, Fj, R*
M Irvine 2000 *Tg, SA, I, Sa, Fj, J*, 2001 *US, Ar*

DC Jackart 1991 *J, S, US, Fj, R, F*, 1992 *US, E*, 1993 *E, E, US, A, W*, 1994 *US, F, W, E, F*, 1995 *S, Ar, Fj*
RO Jackson 1970 *Fj*, 1971 *W*
J Jackson 2003 *Ur, US, Ar, W, It, Tg*, 2004 *EngA, US, It, E*, 2005 *W, US, Ar, R*, 2006 *S*, 2007 *US, NZ, J*, 2008 *I, W, S*, 2009 *J*, 2010 *Sp, Geo*
MB James 1994 *US, F, W, E, F*, 1995 *S, Ur, Ar, Fj, NZ, R, A, US*, 1996 *US, US, HK, J, A, HK, J*, 1997 *J, US, W, I*, 1998 *US, US, Ur, US, Ar*, 1999 *Sa, W, E, F, Fj, Nm*, 2000 *US*, 2002 *S, US, US, Ur, Chl, W, F*, 2003 *M, M, Ur, US, Ar, W, Tg*, 2005 *F*, 2006 *US*, 2007 *Pt, W, Fj, J, A*
G Jennings 1981 *Ar*, 1983 *US, It, It, E*
O Johnson 1970 *Fj*
G Johnston 1978 *F*
RR Johnstone 2001 *Ur, Fj, J*, 2002 *Chl, Ur, Chl*, 2003 *EngA*
CWB Jones 1987 *US*
C Jones 1983 *E*
EL Jones 1982 *J*, 1983 *US*
HA Jones 2012 *Rus*, 2013 *US, Fj, I, US, US, Geo, R, Pt*, 2014 *J, S, US*, 2015 *Sa, US, US, Geo, Fj, It, F, R*

TK Kariya 1967 *E*, 1970 *Fj*, 1971 *W*

A Kennedy 1985 *A, A*
I Kennedy 1993 *A, W*
ED Kettleson 1985 *US*
B Keys 2008 *US, Pt, I, W, S*, 2009 *Geo, US, J*
MMG King 2002 *US, Ur*, 2003 *M, US, Ar, NZ*, 2005 *US, J, W, EngA, US, Ar*
A Kingham 1974 *Tg*
A Kleeberger 2005 *F, R*, 2006 *S, E, US, Bar, It*, 2007 *US, NZ, Pt, J*, 2008 *US, Pt, I, W, S*, 2009 *I, W, Geo, US, US, J, J, Rus*, 2010 *Ur, Bel, Sp, Geo, Pt*, 2011 *US, US, Tg, F, J, NZ*, 2013 *R, Pt*, 2014 *J*
ERP Knaggs 2000 *Tg, US, SA, I, Sa, Fj, J*, 2001 *US, Ur, Ar, E, E, Fj, J*, 2002 *S*, 2003 *EngA, Ur, Ar, NZ*
JD Knauer 1992 *E*, 1993 *E, E, US, W*
MJ Kokan 1984 *US*, 1985 *US*
P Kyle 1984 *US*
JA Kyne 2010 *Bel*, 2011 *J*

A La Carte 2004 *US, J*
M Langley 2004 *EngA*, 2005 *Ar*
MJ Lawson 2002 *US, Ur, Chl, Ur, Chl, F*, 2003 *EngA, US, M, M, Ur, US, Ar, W, It, Tg*, 2004 *F, It, E*, 2005 *US, J, F, R*, 2006 *Bar, US, W*
P le Blanc 1994 *F*, 1995 *Ur, Fj, NZ*
CE le Fevre 1976 *Bb*
JL Lecky 1982 *J, US*, 1983 *US, It, It*, 1984 *US*, 1985 *A, US*, 1986 *J, US*, 1987 *I, W, US*, 1991 *J, S, Fj, R*
J Lecky 1962 *Bb, W23*
GB Legh 1973 *W*, 1974 *Tg*, 1976 *Bb*
LSF Leroy 1932 *J*
DC Lougheed 1990 *Ar*, 1991 *J, US*, 1992 *US, E*, 1993 *E, E, US*, 1994 *F, W, E, F*, 1995 *Fj, NZ, R, A, SA*, 1996 *A, HK*, 1997 *J, W, I*, 1998 *US, Ar*, 1999 *US, Tg, W, E, F, Fj, Nm*, 2003 *W, It*
J Loveday 1993 *E, E, US, A*, 1996 *HK, J*, 1998 *J, Ur*, 1999 *Sa, US*
B Luke 2004 *US, J*
M Luke 1974 *Tg*, 1976 *Bb*, 1977 *US, E, E*, 1978 *US, F*, 1979 *US, F*, 1980 *W, US, NZ*, 1981 *US*, 1982 *J, US*
S Lytton 1995 *Ur, Ar, US*, 1996 *US, HK, J, J, US, Ar*

G MacDonald 1970 *Fj*
GDT MacDonald 1998 *HK*
PM Mack 2009 *I, W, Geo, US, US, J, J, Rus*, 2012 *Rus*, 2013 *US, Fj, Tg, I, US, US, Geo, R, Pt*, 2014 *J, S, US, 2015 *J, Tg, Sa, US, US, Fj, I, It, F, R*
I MacKay 1993 *A, W*
JL Mackenzie 2010 *Bel, Sp*, 2011 *US*, 2013 *Geo, Pt*, 2015 *US, Geo, It*
PW Mackenzie 2008 *Pt, I*, 2010 *Ur, Sp, Geo, Pt*, 2011 *Rus, US, US, Tg, F, J, NZ*, 2012 *US, It, Geo, Sa*, 2013 *US, US, Geo, R*, 2015 *J, Tg, Sa, US, Geo, Fj, It, F*
GI MacKinnon 1985 *US*, 1986 *J*, 1988 *US*, 1989 *I, US*, 1990 *Ar, Ar*, 1991 *J, S, Fj, R, F, NZ*, 1992 *US, E*, 1993 *E, US, W, E, F*, 1995 *S, Ur, Ar, Fj, NZ, A, SA*
S MacKinnon 1992 *US*, 1995 *Ur, Ar, Fj*
C MacLachlan 1981 *Ar*, 1982 *J, E*
P Maclean 1983 *US, It, It, E*
I Macmillan 1981 *Ar*, 1982 *J, J, E, US*
M MacSween 2009 *Rus*
B Major 2001 *Fj, J*
D Major 1999 *E, Fj, Nm*, 2000 *Tg, US, SA, I, Fj, J*, 2001 *Ur, E, E*
A Marshall 1997 *J*, 1998 *Ur*
JA Marshall 2008 *S*, 2010 *Ur, Bel, Sp, Geo, Pt*, 2011 *US, US, Tg, F, J, NZ*, 2012 *US, It, Geo, Sa, Rus*, 2013 *US, Fj, Tg, I, J, US, US*, 2014 *J, S, US, Nm, Sa, R*, 2015 *Fj*
P Mason 1974 *Tg*
B McCarthy 1996 *US, Ar*, 1998 *J, HK, J*
J McDonald 1974 *Tg*
RN McDonald 1966 *Bl*, 1967 *E*, 1970 *Fj*
AG McGann 1985 *A, A*
R McGeein 1973 *W*
RI McInnes 1979 *F*, 1980 *NZ*, 1981 *US, Ar*, 1982 *J, J, E, US*, 1983 *US, It, It*, 1984 *US*, 1985 *US*
B McKee 1962 *Bb, W23*
B Mckee 1966 *Bl*, 1970 *Fj*
SS McKeen 2004 *US, J, EngA, US, F, It, E*, 2005 *US, J, W, EngA, F, R*, 2006 *S, US, W, It*, 2007 *US, NZ*
JR McKellar 1985 *A, A*, 1986 *J*, 1987 *W*
JH McKenna 1967 *E*
C McKenzie 1992 *US, E*, 1993 *E, US, A, W*, 1994 *US, F, W, E,*

F, 1995 *S, Ur, Ar, Fj, NZ, R, SA,* 1996 *US, HK, J, J,* 1997 *J, HK, I*

G McRorie 2014 *J, S, US, Nm, Sa, R,* 2015 *J, Tg, Sa, US, Geo, Fj, I, F, R*

SG McTavish 1970 *Fj,* 1971 *W,* 1976 *Bb,* 1977 *US, E, E,* 1978 *US, F,* 1979 *US, F,* 1980 *W, US,* 1981 *US, Ar,* 1982 *J, J, E, US,* 1985 *US,* 1987 *US, Tg, I*

R McWhinney 2005 *F, R*

J Mensah-Coker 2006 *S, E, US, Bar, US, W, It,* 2007 *US, NZ, Pt, J, A,* 2008 *US, I, W, S,* 2009 *US, US, J, J, Rus,* 2010 *Ur, Sp, Geo, Pt,* 2011 *Rus*

C Michaluk 1995 *SA,* 1996 *US, J,* 1997 *US, HK*

N Milau 2000 *US, J*

DRW Milne 1966 *BI,* 1967 *E*

AB Mitchell 1932 *J, J*

P Monaghan 1982 *J*

AHB Monro 2006 *E, US, Bar, US, W, It,* 2007 *W, A,* 2008 *US, Pt, I, W,* 2009 *I, W, Geo, US, US, J, J, Rus,* 2010 *Ur, Bel, Pt,* 2011 *Rus, US, US, Tg, F, J, NZ*

D Moonlight 2003 *EngA,* 2004 *EngA, E,* 2005 *US*

JI Moonlight 2009 *Geo,* 2012 *Sa, Rus,* 2013 *US, Fj, Tg, I, US, US, Geo, Pt,* 2014 *J, S, US, Nm,* 2015 *Tg, Sa, US, US, Geo, I, It, R*

DL Moore 1962 *Bb, W23*

K Morgan 1997 *HK, HK, J, W*

VJP Moroney 1962 *Bb*

CR Morrison 2015 *J, Tg, Sa*

B Mosychuk 1996 *Ur,* 1997 *J*

J Moyes 1981 *Ar,* 1982 *J, J, E, US*

PT Murphy 2000 *Tg, US, SA, I, Sa, Fj, J,* 2001 *Fj, J,* 2002 *S, US, US, Ur, Chl, W, F,* 2003 *US, M, M,* 2004 *F*

WA Murray 1932 *J*

K Myhre 1970 *Fj*

J Newton 1962 *W23*

GN Niblo 1932 *J, J*

K Nichols 1996 *Ur,* 1998 *J, HK, US, US, Ur,* 1999 *J, Fj, Sa, US, Tg, Fj, Nm,* 2000 *Tg, US, SA, I, Sa, Fj, J, It,* 2001 *Ur, E, Fj, J,* 2002 *S*

D Nikas 1995 *Ur, Ar*

S O'Leary 2004 *US, J, EngA, E,* 2005 *US, J*

ED Olmstead 2015 *Sa, US, US, Geo, Fj, It, F*

C O'Toole 2009 *I, US, J, J, Rus,* 2010 *Ur, Bel, Sp, Geo, Pt,* 2011 *Rus, US, US, Tg, F, J, NZ,* 2012 *US, It, Sa, Rus*

S Pacey 2005 *W*

C Pack 2006 *S, US*

J Pagano 1997 *I,* 1998 *J, HK, US, HK, J, US,* 1999 *J, Fj, Nm*

DV Pahl 1971 *W*

P Palmer 1983 *E,* 1984 *US,* 1985 *A,* 1986 *J, US,* 1987 *Tg, I, W,* 1988 *US,* 1990 *Ar, US,* 1991 *J, US, Fj, R, F,* 1992 *US*

K Parfrey 2005 *J*

PB Parfrey 2013 *US, Tg, I, J, Pt,* 2014 *Sa, R*

TF Paris 2010 *Bel, Sp, Pt,* 2012 *Sa, Rus,* 2013 *US, Fj, I, J, Pt,* 2014 *J, S,* 2015 *US*

A Pasutto 2004 *US, J*

K Peace 1978 *F,* 1979 *US, F,* 1980 *W, US*

J Penaluna 1996 *Ur*

DN Penney 1995 *US,* 1996 *US, A, US, Ar,* 1997 *HK,* 1999 *E*

JM Phelan 1980 *NZ,* 1981 *Ar,* 1982 *J, J,* 1985 *A, A*

J Phelan 2010 *Bel, Sp, Pt,* 2012 *It, Geo, Sa, Rus,* 2013 *US, Fj, I, J, US, Geo, R, Pt,* 2014 *J, US, Sa, R,* 2015 *J, Tg, US, US*

M Phinney 2006 *S, E*

CD Pierce 2013 *J*

B Piffero 2013 *Geo, R, Pt,* 2014 *J,* 2015 *Tg, Sa, US, Geo, Fj, I*

EC Pinkham 1932 *J*

C Plater 2003 *EngA*

D Pletch 2004 *US, J, EngA, It, E,* 2005 *US, J, W, EngA,* 2006 *S, E, US, Bar, US, W, It,* 2007 *US, NZ, Pt, W, Fj, J, A,* 2009 *US, US, J, J, Rus,* 2010 *Bel, Sp, Pt*

MT Pletch 2005 *Ar,* 2006 *S, E, US, Bar, W, It,* 2007 *US, NZ, Pt, W, J, A,* 2008 *US, Pt, I, W, S,* 2009 *W, Geo, US, US, J, Rus,* 2012 *It, Geo*

JG Pritchard 2003 *M, M, Ur, US, Ar, W, Tg,* 2006 *S, US, Bar, US, W,* 2007 *US, NZ, Pt, W, Fj, J, A,* 2008 *US, Pt, I, W, S,* 2009 *I, W, Geo, US, US, J, J, Rus,* 2010 *Ur, Sp, Geo, Pt,* 2011 *Rus, US, US, Tg, F, J,* 2012 *US, It, Geo, Sa, Rus,* 2013 *Tg, I, J, US, US, R, Pt,* 2014 *J, S, US, Sa, R,* 2015 *Sa, US, R*

G Puil 1962 *Bb, W23*

M Pyke 2004 *US, J, US, It,* 2005 *US, F, R,* 2006 *S, E, US, Bar, US, W, It,* 2007 *US, NZ, Pt, W, Fj, J, A,* 2008 *US*

DLJ Quigley 1976 *Bb,* 1979 *F*

RE Radu 1985 *A,* 1986 *US,* 1987 *US, Tg, I, US,* 1988 *US,* 1989 *I, US,* 1990 *Ar, Ar,* 1991 *US*

D Ramsey 2005 *US*

GL Rees 1986 *US,* 1987 *US, Tg, I, W, US,* 1989 *I, US,* 1990 *Ar, Ar,* 1991 *J, S, US, Fj, R, F, NZ,* 1992 *US, E,* 1993 *E, E, US, W,* 1994 *US, F, W, E, F,* 1995 *S, Fj, NZ, R, A, SA,* 1996 *HK, J,* 1997 *US, J, HK, J, US, W, I,* 1998 *US, US, Ur, US, Ar,* 1999 *Sa, Tg, W, E, F, Fj, Nm*

J Reid 2003 *M, US, Ar, NZ, Tg*

G Relph 1974 *Tg*

S Richmond 2004 *EngA, US, F, It, E,* 2005 *US, W, EngA, US*

PD Riordan 2003 *EngA,* 2004 *US, J, EngA, US,* 2006 *S, E, US, Bar, US, W, It,* 2007 *US, NZ, Pt, W, Fj, J, A,* 2008 *US, Pt, I, W,* 2009 *I, W, Geo, US, US, J, J, Rus,* 2010 *Ur, Bel, Sp, Geo, Pt,* 2011 *Rus, US, US, Tg, F, J, NZ*

JR Robertsen 1985 *A, A, US,* 1986 *US,* 1987 *US,* 1989 *I, US,* 1990 *Ar, US, Ar,* 1991 *Fj, F*

C Robertson 1997 *HK,* 1998 *US, US, HK, J, Ur,* 2001 *Ur*

AK Robinson 1998 *HK*

G Robinson 1966 *BI*

R Robson 1998 *HK, US,* 1999 *J, Tg*

S Rodgers 2005 *US*

RP Ross 1989 *I,* 1990 *US,* 1995 *Ar, NZ,* 1996 *US, US, HK, J, A, HK, J, Ur, US, Ar,* 1997 *US, J, HK, HK, J, US, W,* 1998 *J, HK, US, US, HK, J, Ur, US,* 1999 *J, Fj, Sa, US, W, E, F, Nm,* 2001 *Ur, E, E, Fj, J,* 2002 *US, US, Ur, Chl, Ur, Chl, F,* 2003 *EngA, US, M, Ur, Ar, W, Tg*

JG Rowland 1932 *J, J*

G Rowlands 1995 *Ar, NZ, A, US,* 1996 *US, US*

RJ Russell 1979 *US,* 1983 *E,* 1985 *A, A*

JB Ryan 1966 *BI,* 1967 *E*

IH Saundry 1932 *J, J*

MD Schiefler 1980 *US, NZ,* 1981 *US, Ar,* 1982 *J, E, US,* 1983 *US,* 1984 *US*

M Schmid 1996 *Ur, US, Ar,* 1997 *US, J, US, W, I,* 1998 *US, HK, J, Ur, Ar,* 1999 *Sa, US, W, E, F, Fj, Nm,* 2001 *US, Ur, E, E*

MA Scholz 2009 *Rus,* 2011 *Rus, US, US,* 2012 *US, It*

T Scott 1976 *Bb*

DUQ Sears-Duru 2013 *Pt,* 2015 *J, Tg, Sa, US, US, Geo, Fj, I, It, F, R*

S Selkirk 1932 *J*

JD Shaw 1978 *F*

CJ Shergold 1980 *US, NZ,* 1981 *US*

DM Shick 1970 *Fj,* 1971 *W*

JL Sinclair 2008 *Pt, I, W, S,* 2009 *I, US, US, J, J, Rus,* 2010 *Bel, Sp, Geo, Pt,* 2011 *Rus, US, US, Tg, F, J, NZ,* 2012 *US, It, Geo, Rus,* 2013 *Fj, Tg, I, US, US, Geo, R,* 2014 *S, US, Nm, Sa, R,* 2015 *Geo, Fj, I, It, R*

DC Sinnott 1979 *F,* 1981 *US, Ar*

FG Skillings 1932 *J, J*

DM Slater 1971 *W*

C Smith 1995 *Ur, US,* 1996 *HK, J, Ur, US, Ar,* 1997 *US,* 1998 *J, HK, US, HK, Ur,* 1999 *J, Fj, Sa, US, Tg, W, E, F*

RJ Smith 2003 *EngA, M, M, Ur, US, Ar, W, NZ, Tg,* 2004 *US, J, EngA, US, F, It, E,* 2005 *US, J, W, EngA, US, Ar, F, R,* 2006 *S, Bar, US, W, It,* 2007 *US, NZ, Pt, W, Fj, J,* 2008 *US, Pt, I, W, S,* 2009 *I, W, US, US,* 2010 *Bel,* 2011 *US, US, Tg, F, J, NZ*

C Smythe 1997 *J, HK*

RGA Snow 1995 *Ar, NZ, R, A, SA, US,* 1996 *HK, J, A, HK, J,* 1997 *US, HK, J, W, I,* 1998 *US, US, US, Ar,* 1999 *J, Fj, Sa, US, W, E, F, Fj, Nm,* 2000 *I, J, It,* 2001 *US, Ar, E, E, Fj, J,* 2002 *S, US, US, Ur, Chl, Ur, Chl, W, F,* 2003 *Ur, US, Ar, W, NZ, It, Tg,* 2006 *US, Bar, US,* 2007 *Pt, W, Fj, J, A*

D Spicer 2004 *E,* 2005 *R,* 2006 *S, E, US, Bar, US, W,* 2007 *US, NZ, Pt, W, Fj, J,* 2008 *US,* 2009 *I, W*

DA Speirs 1988 *US,* 1989 *I, US,* 1991 *Fj, NZ*

WE Spofford 1981 *Ar*

W Stanley 1994 *US, F,* 1995 *S, Ur, Ar, R, A, SA, US,* 1996 *US, US, A, HK, J,* 1997 *US, J, HK, HK, US, W, I,* 1998 *US, US, HK, Ur, US, Ar,* 1999 *J, Fj, Sa, US, Tg, W, E, F, Fj, Nm,* 2000 *Tg, US, SA, I, Sa, Fj, J, It,* 2001 *E, E, 2002 S, US, W, F,* 2003 *EngA, US, M, M, Ur, US, Ar, W, It, Tg*

AI Stanton 1971 *W,* 1973 *W,* 1974 *Tg*

E Stapleton 1978 *US, F*

D Steen 1966 *Bl*
SM Stephen 2005 *EngA, US*, 2006 *S, E, US, Bar, US, W*, 2007 *US, NZ, Pt, W, Fj, A*, 2008 *I, W, S*, 2009 *I, W*, 2010 *Sp, Geo, Pt*
C Stewart 1991 *S, US, Fj, R, F, NZ*, 1994 *E, F*, 1995 *S, Fj, NZ, R, A, SA*
R Stewart 2005 *R*
DS Stewart 1989 *US*, 1990 *Ar*, 1991 *US, Fj, R, F, NZ*, 1992 *E*, 1993 *E, E, US, A, W*, 1994 *US, F, W, E, F*, 1995 *S, Fj, NZ, R, A, SA, US*, 1996 *US, US, A, HK, J, Ur, US, Ar*, 1997 *US, J, HK, HK, J, US, W, I*, 1998 *US, J, Ur, Ar*, 1999 *Sa, US, Tg, W, E, F, Fj, Nm*, 2000 *US, SA, I, Sa, Fj, It*, 2001 *US, Ur, Ar, E, E*
B Stoikos 2001 *Ur*
G Stover 1962 *Bb*
R Strang 1983 *E*
C Strubin 2004 *EngA, E*
IC Stuart 1984 *US*, 1985 *A, A*, 1986 *J*, 1987 *US, Tg, I, W, US*, 1988 *US*, 1989 *US*, 1990 *Ar, US, Ar*, 1992 *E*, 1993 *A, W*, 1994 *US, F, W, E*
JD Stubbs 1962 *Bb, W23*
FJ Sturrock 1971 *W*
CW Suter 1932 *J*
KF Svoboda 1985 *A, A, US*, 1986 *J, US*, 1987 *W*, 1990 *Ar, US, Ar*, 1991 *J, US, R, F*, 1992 *US, E*, 1993 *E, E, US*, 1994 *F, W, F*, 1995 *Fj, A, US*
P Szabo 1989 *I, US*, 1990 *Ar, US, Ar*, 1991 *NZ*, 1993 *US, A, W*

JN Tait 1997 *US, J, HK, HK, J, US, W, I*, 1998 *US, Ur, Ar*, 1999 *J, Fj, Sa, US, Tg, W, E, F, Fj, Nm*, 2000 *Tg, US, SA, I, Sa, Fj, J, It*, 2001 *US, Ur, Ar, E, E*, 2002 *US, W, F*
L Tait 2005 *US, J, W, EngA*, 2006 *S, E, US, Bar, US, W, It*, 2007 *US, NZ, Pt, W, Fj, A*, 2009 *I, W*, 2010 *Ur*
WG Taylor 1978 *F*, 1979 *US, F*, 1980 *W, US, NZ*, 1981 *US, Ar*, 1983 *US, It*
J Thiel 1998 *HK, J, Ur*, 1999 *J, Fj, Sa, US, Tg, W, E, F, Fj, Nm*, 2000 *SA, I, Sa, Fj, J*, 2001 *US, Ar, E, E*, 2002 *S, US, US, Ur, Chl, Ur, W, F*, 2003 *Ur, US, Ar, W, It*, 2004 *F*, 2007 *Pt, W, Fj, J, A*, 2008 *I, W*
S Thompson 2001 *Fj, J*, 2004 *US*
W Thomson 1970 *Fj*
R Thorpe 2014 *Sa, R*, 2015 *J, Tg, US, Fj, I, F*
AA Tiedemann 2009 *W, Geo, US, US*, 2010 *Ur, Bel, Geo, Pt*, 2011 *Rus, NZ, US, NZ*, 2012 *US, It, Geo, Sa, Rus*, 2013 *US, Fj, I, J, US, US, Geo, R, Pt*, 2014 *J, S, US, Sa, R*, 2015 *J, Tg, Sa, US, Geo, I, It, F*
K Tkachuk 2000 *Tg, US, SA, Sa, Fj, It*, 2001 *Fj, J*, 2002 *Chl, J, Chl, W, F*, 2003 *EngA, US, M, M, Ur, US, Ar, W, NZ, It, Tg*, 2004 *EngA, US, F, It, E*, 2005 *US, J, W, Ar, F, R*, 2006 *US, W, It*, 2007 *US, NZ*, 2008 *US, Pt, I, W, S*, 2009 *I, W, Geo, US, US, J, J, Rus*, 2010 *Sp, Geo*
H Toews 1998 *J, HK, HK, Ur*, 1999 *Tg*, 2000 *US, Sa, J, It*, 2001 *Fj, J*
R Toews 1993 *W*, 1994 *US, F, W, E*, 1995 *S, Ur, Ar, Fj*, 1996 *US, HK, J, A*, 1997 *HK, US, I*
J Tomlinson 1996 *A*, 2001 *Ur*
CA Trainor 2011 *Rus, Tg, F, J, NZ*, 2012 *It, Geo*, 2013 *Geo, R, Pt*, 2014 *Nm, Sa, R*, 2015 *Sa, US, US, Geo, Fj, I, It, F, R*
N Trenkel 2007 *A*
DM Tucker 1985 *A, A, US*, 1986 *US*, 1987 *US, W*
A Tyler 2005 *Ar*
A Tynan 1995 *Ur, Ar, NZ, US*, 1997 *J*
CJ Tynan 1987 *US*, 1988 *US*, 1990 *Ar, US, Ar*, 1991 *J, US, Fj, F, NZ*, 1992 *US*, 1993 *E, E, US, W*, 1996 *US, J*, 1997 *HK, J*, 1998 *US*

LD Underwood 2013 *US, Fj, Tg, I, J, Geo*, 2015 *J, Tg, US, Fj, I*
DN Ure 1962 *Bb, W23*

PC Vaesen 1985 *US*, 1986 *J*, 1987 *US, Tg, US*
D van Camp 2005 *J, R*, 2006 *It*, 2007 *US, NZ*, 2008 *Pt, W*, 2009 *I, Geo*
R van den Brink 1986 *US*, 1987 *Tg*, 1988 *US*, 1991 *J, US, R, F, NZ*

D Van Der Merwe 2006 *Bar, It*, 2007 *Pt, W, Fj, J, A*, 2009 *I, W, Geo, US, US*, 2010 *Ur, Sp, Geo*, 2011 *US, US, Tg, F, J, NZ*, 2012 *US, It, Geo*, 2013 *US, US*, 2014 *J, S, US, Nm, Sa, R*, 2015 *J, Tg, Fj, I, I, It, F, R*
D Van Eeuwen 1978 *F*, 1979 *US*
A van Staveren 2000 *Tg, Sa, Fj*, 2002 *US, US, Ur, Chl, Ur, Chl, W, F*, 2003 *EngA, US, M, M, Ur, US, W, NZ, Tg*
J Verstraten 2000 *US, SA, Fj, J*
J Vivian 1983 *E*, 1984 *US*

FG Walsh 2008 *I, W, S*, 2009 *US*
KC Walt 1976 *Bb*, 1977 *US, E, E*, 1978 *US, F*
JM Ward 1962 *W23*
M Webb 2004 *US, J, US, F, It*, 2005 *US, J, W, EngA, US, Ar, F*, 2006 *US, W, It*, 2007 *J, A*, 2008 *US*
M Weingart 2004 *J*, 2005 *J, EngA, US, F, R*, 2007 *Pt*
GJM Wessels 1962 *W23*
WR Wharton 1932 *J, J*
ST White 2009 *J, J, Rus*, 2010 *Ur, Bel, Sp, Geo, Pt*, 2011 *Rus, US, F, J, NZ*, 2012 *US, It, Geo, Sa*, 2013 *US, Fj, Tg, I, J, US, US*, 2014 *Nm, Sa, R*
K Whitley 1995 *S*
C Whittaker 1993 *US, A*, 1995 *Ur*, 1996 *A*, 1997 *J*, 1998 *J, HK, US, US, HK, J, US, Ar*, 1999 *J, Fj, US*
LW Whitty 1967 *E*
DW Whyte 1974 *Tg*, 1977 *US, E, E*
RR Wickland 1966 *Bl*, 1967 *E*
JP Wiley 1977 *US, E, E*, 1978 *US, F*, 1979 *US*, 1980 *W, US, NZ*, 1981 *US*
K Wilkie 1971 *W*, 1973 *W*, 1976 *Bb*, 1978 *US*
K Wilkinson 1976 *Bb*, 1978 *F*, 1979 *F*
BN Williams 1962 *W23*
JM Williams 2001 *US, Ur, Ar, Fj, J*
M Williams 1992 *E*, 1993 *A, W*
MH Williams 1978 *US, F*, 1980 *US*, 1982 *J*
M Williams 1999 *Tg, W, E, F, Fj, Nm*, 2000 *Tg, SA, I, Sa, Fj, J, It*, 2001 *E, E, Fj, J*, 2002 *S, US, US, Ur, Chl, W, F*, 2003 *EngA, US, M, M, Ur, US, Ar, W, It, Tg*, 2004 *EngA, US, F*, 2005 *W, Ar, F, R*, 2006 *E, US, Bar, US, W, It*, 2007 *US, NZ, W, Fj, J, A*, 2008 *Pt, W, S*
A Wilson 2008 *US*
EA Wilson 2012 *Sa, Rus*
PG Wilson 1932 *J, J*
RS Wilson 1962 *Bb*
J Wilson-Ross 2014 *Nm, Sa, R*
K Wirachowski 1992 *E*, 1993 *US*, 1996 *US, HK, Ur, US, Ar*, 1997 *US, HK*, 2000 *It*, 2001 *Ur, E, Fj, J*, 2002 *S, Chl*, 2003 *EngA, US, M*
T Wish 2004 *US, J*
K Witkowski 2005 *EngA, Ar*, 2006 *E*
N Witkowski 1998 *US, J*, 2000 *Tg, US, SA, I, Sa, Fj, J, It*, 2001 *US, E, E*, 2002 *S, US, US, Ur, Chl, Ur, Chl, W, F*, 2003 *EngA, US, M, M, Ur, Ar, W, NZ, Tg*, 2005 *EngA, US*, 2006 *E*
AH Woller 1967 *E*
S Wood 1977 *E*
TA Woods 1984 *US*, 1986 *J, US*, 1987 *US, Tg, I, W*, 1988 *US*, 1989 *I, US*, 1990 *Ar, US*, 1991 *S, F, NZ*, 1996 *US, US*, 1997 *US, J*
DP Wooldridge 2009 *I, Geo, J, J, Rus*, 2010 *Ur*, 2012 *Geo, Sa, Rus*, 2013 *Fj, J, US, US*, 2014 *R*, 2015 *J, Tg, Sa, US, US, I, It, F, R*
MA Wyatt 1982 *J, J, E, US*, 1983 *US, It, It, E*, 1985 *A, A, US*, 1986 *J, US*, 1987 *Tg, I, W, US*, 1988 *US*, 1989 *I, US*, 1990 *Ar, US, Ar*, 1991 *J, S, US, R, F, NZ*
H Wyndham 1973 *W*

JJ Yeganegi 1996 *US*, 1998 *J*
C Yukes 2001 *Ur, Fj, J*, 2002 *S, US, Ur, Ur*, 2003 *EngA, US, M, M, US, Ar, W, NZ, It, Tg*, 2004 *US, J, EngA, US, F, It, E*, 2005 *W, EngA, US*, 2006 *Bar, US*, 2007 *US, NZ, Pt, W, Fj, J, A*

ENGLAND

ENGLAND'S 2014–15 TEST RECORD

OPPONENTS	DATE	VENUE	RESULT
New Zealand	8 Nov	H	Lost 21–24
South Africa	15 Nov	H	Lost 28–31
Samoa	22 Nov	H	Won 28–9
Australia	29 Nov	H	Won 26–17
Wales	6 Feb	A	Won 21–16
Italy	14 Feb	H	Won 47–17
Ireland	1 Mar	A	Lost 19–9
Scotland	14 Mar	H	Won 25–13
France	21 Mar	H	Won 55–35
France	15 Aug	H	Won 19–14
France	22 Aug	A	Lost 25–20
Ireland	5 Sep	H	Won 21–13
Fiji	18 Sep	H	Won 35–11
Wales	26 Sep	H	Lost 25–28
Australia	3 Oct	H	Lost 13–33
Uruguay	10 Oct	H	Won 60–3

LANCASTER ERA ENDS AFTER PREMATURE WORLD CUP EXIT

By Iain Spragg

England captain Chris Robshaw shows the pain of his team's early Rugby World Cup exit after defeat to Australia.

A **tournament on home** soil after a 24-year hiatus, embraced by an expectant nation but one which culminated in the team's untimely and unprecedented exit after the pool stage, Rugby World Cup 2015 was a profoundly painful experience for those connected with England and one which ultimately cost Stuart Lancaster his job as head coach.

From the moment the draw for the tournament had been made in December 2012, depositing the hosts in the same pool as both Australia and Wales, the England camp were under no illusions that qualification for the quarter-finals was far from a fait accompli, but with both pivotal matches to be played in the familiar confines of Twickenham, Lancaster, the players and the country were confident the side could get the job done.

Their late surrender to Wales was not initially fatal but when they were outplayed and outscored by the Wallabies seven days later, England's world came crashing down as they bid a premature farewell to their own tournament. It was both the first time in Rugby World Cup history the hosts had failed to reach the last eight and the first time England had not progressed safely through to the knockout stages.

The recriminations in the wake of England's humiliation were as rapid as they were vociferous and a month after his side's chastening elimination, the Rugby Football Union confirmed they had parted company with their head coach after nearly four years and 28 victories in his 46 tests at the helm.

"I am obviously extremely saddened to finish the way we did in this World Cup and to step down from the role," Lancaster said in the statement. "As I have always said, I ultimately accept and take responsibility for the team's performance. I took on the role in difficult circumstances and it has been a huge challenge to transition the team with many hurdles along the way. However, I am immensely proud of the development of this team and I know that there is an incredibly strong foundation for them to progress to great things in the future.

"We have played some excellent rugby and it was always going to be tough to get the right level of experience into them in time for 2015. It is a young group of players with the huge majority available for the World Cup in Japan in 2019, where I believe their recent experience will make them genuine contenders."

In truth there were few warning signs of the woes that would afflict England in the protracted build-up to the World Cup. Narrow defeats in November to New Zealand (24–21) and South Africa (31–28) were undeniably frustrating for a side desperate to claim coveted southern hemisphere scalps on a more regular basis, but when England toppled Australia 26–17 at Twickenham at the end of the series, less than a year before their Pool A encounter, there was a growing sense of optimism for the challenges that lay ahead.

That optimism was only amplified when England kicked off the Six Nations with a rousing 21–16 victory over Wales at the Millennium Stadium. Lancaster's side trailed 16–8 at the break in Cardiff but the urgency and verve of their second-half fight-back saw England installed as firm favourites to overcome the Principality when the two sides renewed acquaintances at Twickenham later in the year.

An attritional 19–9 reverse to Ireland in Dublin in March put paid to England's Grand Slam dreams, and ultimately their hopes of a first title since 2011, but they signed off in the Championship with a breathless and record-breaking 55–35 defeat of France at Twickenham.

England ran in seven eye-catching tries against Les Bleus on the final weekend and although a record score against the French was not enough to prevent Ireland retaining their Six Nations title on points difference,

ENGLAND

once again Lancaster's side had displayed a cutting edge and attacking ambition that seemed to augur well for the World Cup.

"I said to the boys at the end of the game, I've never seen such a courageous performance from a group of players," Lancaster said. "I'm hugely proud of what that England team has shown today and throughout the Championship. We've come up short in the end, but the mindset to play and the ability to go and keep going at a high-quality French team and score the tries that we did was a testament to the spirit and character that we've got.

"What we've got to be is more consistent over the full 80 to win a tournament like this or to win a World Cup. There's a long time to go between now and September. We'll work hard in June when we meet in camp and we'll be ready when September comes around."

The build-up to RWC 2015 was dominated by the perennial debate over the selection of the final 31-man squad but Lancaster's options were significantly narrowed in May when hooker Dylan Hartley and centre Manu Tuilagi were ruled out of contention after on and off the field disciplinary issues respectively.

When the head coach did unveil his squad in late August there were two standout decisions to discuss. The first was Lancaster's refusal to infringe on England's self-imposed policy of not selecting players from outside the Premiership, meaning Toulon flanker Steffon Armitage and Clermont Auvergne full-back Nick Abendanon, the European Player of the Year, were both overlooked, while the coach opted to bring in Sam Burgess at the expense of centre Luther Burrell only 10 months after the former had made a high-profile switch from league to union.

Unsurprisingly Lancaster's critics would revisit his controversial choices when the chastening World Cup post-mortem began after the Australia game but as RWC 2015 drew closer, England fans remained bullish and there was much talk of the significance of home advantage and 'Fortress Twickenham'.

Between the World Cup draw in late 2012 and the start of the tournament, England had played 17 tests at Twickenham and won 14 times. Only the All Blacks and the Springboks had come away from London victorious and when England finally kicked a ball in anger in the opening game of RWC 2015, beating a stubborn and physical Fiji side 35–11, their record stood at 15 wins in 18 internationals.

The fortress, however, was ransacked by Wales on 26 September. England appeared to be on course for a comfortable victory after a first-half Jonny May try and when Owen Farrell was on target with a 51st-minute penalty, the hosts had eased into a 22–12 lead and were seemingly in consummate control of proceedings.

The majority of the Twickenham crowd then sat in stunned disbelief as the Welsh fight-back unfolded. Two Dan Biggar penalties cut the arrears and when Gareth Davies went over for a converted try 10 minutes from time, the game was deadlocked at 25–25 apiece. Another Biggar penalty in the 74th minute put the Welsh in front but despite the exhortations of the England faithful and a late penalty which they opted to kick to touch rather than the uprights, the men in white were unable to rescue themselves and lost 28–25.

It was a body blow for the hosts but hope sprang eternal in the shape of the following weekend's clash with the Wallabies. The bonus point England had secured in victory over Fiji and with a fixture against the amateurs of Uruguay to conclude proceedings in Pool A, Lancaster knew victory against Australia would all but guarantee his side a place in the quarter-finals. Conversely, England were acutely aware that defeat would mean they suffered the ignominy of elimination from the tournament.

To the dismay of supporters their side rarely threatened to serve up the result the country craved. The Wallabies took the lead as early as the third minute when fly-half Bernard Foley knocked over the first of his four penalties at Twickenham and it was an advantage Australia never surrendered.

Two stunning tries from Foley ensured his side were 17–3 to the good at the break and although England briefly rallied after the restart with an Anthony Watson score, the closest they got to the Wallabies was 20–13 when Farrell was on target with a 64th-minute penalty. From that point, Australia dominated once again and eventually ran out emphatic 33–13 winners.

England dispatched Uruguay 60–3 in their final assignment but the damage had already been done and as the four Rugby Championship sides prepared to square off against a quartet of teams from the Six Nations in the knockout stages, England found themselves in the unprecedented situation of watching forlornly from the sidelines.

"We feel we let the country down today," said captain Chris Robshaw after the Australian defeat. "We apologise to them. They put us under a lot of pressure. We had a spell in the second half where we built a bit of momentum but to come back from a 17–3 half-time deficit against a quality side like that was always going to be difficult. A lot of hard work has gone into it but, for whatever reason, we haven't got the results we wanted."

Four weeks later, after an internal review of the failings of the World Cup campaign, Lancaster's fate was sealed and former Japan and Australia coach Eddie Jones was duly appointed to take the team into the Six Nations in 2016 and beyond.

ENGLAND

ENGLAND INTERNATIONAL STATISTICS

MATCH RECORDS UP TO 1 NOVEMBER, 2015

MOST CONSECUTIVE TESTS WITHOUT DEFEAT

Matches	Wins	Draws	Period
14	14	0	2002 to 2003
12	10	2	1882 to 1887
11	10	1	1922 to 1924
11	11	0	2000 to 2001

MOST CONSECUTIVE TEST WINS

14	2002 W, It, Arg, NZ, A, SA, 2003 F1, W1, It, S, I, NZ, A, W2
11	2000 SA 2, A, Arg, SA3, 2001 W, It, S, F, C1, 2, US
10	1882 W, 1883 I, S, 1884 W, I, S, 1885 W, I, 1886 W, I
10	1994 R, C, 1995 I, F, W, S, Arg, It, WS, A
10	2003 F, Gg, SA, Sm, U, W, F, A, 2004 It, S

MOST POINTS IN A MATCH
BY THE TEAM

Pts	Opponents	Venue	Year
134	Romania	Twickenham	2001
111	Uruguay	Brisbane	2003
110	Netherlands	Huddersfield	1998
106	United States	Twickenham	1999
101	Tonga	Twickenham	1999
84	Georgia	Perth	2003
80	Italy	Twickenham	2001

BY A PLAYER

Pts	Player	Opponents	Venue	Year
44	C Hodgson	Romania	Twickenham	2001
36	PJ Grayson	Tonga	Twickenham	1999
35	JP Wilkinson	Italy	Twickenham	2001
32	JP Wilkinson	Italy	Twickenham	1999
30	CR Andrew	Canada	Twickenham	1994
30	PJ Grayson	Netherlands	Huddersfield	1998
30	JP Wilkinson	Wales	Twickenham	2002
29	DJH Walder	Canada	Burnaby	2001
27	CR Andrew	South Africa	Pretoria	1994
27	JP Wilkinson	South Africa	Bloemfontein	2000
27	CC Hodgson	South Africa	Twickenham	2004
27	JP Wilkinson	Scotland	Twickenham	2007
26	JP Wilkinson	United States	Twickenham	1999

MOST TRIES IN A MATCH
BY THE TEAM

Tries	Opponents	Venue	Year
20	Romania	Twickenham	2001
17	Uruguay	Brisbane	2003
16	Netherlands	Huddersfield	1998
16	United States	Twickenham	1999
13	Wales	Blackheath	1881
13	Tonga	Twickenham	1999
12	Georgia	Perth	2003
12	Canada	Twickenham	2004
10	Japan	Sydney	1987
10	Fiji	Twickenham	1989
10	Italy	Twickenham	2001
10	Romania	Dunedin	2011
10	Uruguay	Manchester	2015

BY A PLAYER

Tries	Player	Opponents	Venue	Year
5	D Lambert	France	Richmond	1907
5	R Underwood	Fiji	Twickenham	1989
5	OJ Lewsey	Uruguay	Brisbane	2003
4	GW Burton	Wales	Blackheath	1881
4	A Hudson	France	Paris	1906
4	RW Poulton	France	Paris	1914
4	C Oti	Romania	Bucharest	1989
4	JC Guscott	Netherlands	Huddersfield	1998
4	NA Back	Netherlands	Huddersfield	1998
4	JC Guscott	United States	Twickenham	1999
4	J Robinson	Romania	Twickenham	2001
4	N Easter	Wales	Twickenham	2007
4	CJ Ashton	Italy	Twickenham	2011

MOST CONVERSIONS IN A MATCH
BY THE TEAM

Cons	Opponents	Venue	Year
15	Netherlands	Huddersfield	1998
14	Romania	Twickenham	2001
13	United States	Twickenham	1999
13	Uruguay	Brisbane	2003
12	Tonga	Twickenham	1999
9	Italy	Twickenham	2001
9	Georgia	Perth	2003
8	Romania	Bucharest	1989
8	Italy	Twickenham	2011

BY A PLAYER

Cons	Player	Opponents	Venue	Year
15	PJ Grayson	Netherlands	Huddersfield	1998
14	C Hodgson	Romania	Twickenham	2001
13	JP Wilkinson	United States	Twickenham	1999
12	PJ Grayson	Tonga	Twickenham	1999
11	PJ Grayson	Uruguay	Brisbane	2003
9	JP Wilkinson	Italy	Twickenham	2001
8	SD Hodgkinson	Romania	Bucharest	1989
7	JM Webb	Japan	Sydney	1987
7	SD Hodgkinson	Argentina	Twickenham	1990
7	PJ Grayson	Wales	Twickenham	1998
7	JP Wilkinson	Wales	Twickenham	2007
7	OA Farrell	Italy	Rome	2014
7	GT Ford	France	Twickenham	2015

MOST DROP GOALS IN A MATCH
BY THE TEAM

Drops	Opponents	Venue	Year
3	France	Sydney	2003
2	Ireland	Twickenham	1970
2	France	Paris	1978
2	France	Paris	1980
2	Romania	Twickenham	1985
2	Fiji	Suva	1991
2	Argentina	Durban	1995
2	France	Paris	1996
2	Australia	Twickenham	2001
2	Wales	Cardiff	2003
2	Ireland	Dublin	2003
2	South Africa	Perth	2003
2	Samoa	Nantes	2007
2	Tonga	Paris	2007
2	Wales	Twickenham	2011
2	Argentina	Manchester	2009

BY A PLAYER

Drops	Player	Opponents	Venue	Year
3	JP Wilkinson	France	Sydney	2003
2	R Hiller	Ireland	Twickenham	1970
2	AGB Old	France	Paris	1978
2	JP Horton	France	Paris	1980
2	CR Andrew	Romania	Twickenham	1985
2	CR Andrew	Fiji	Suva	1991
2	CR Andrew	Argentina	Durban	1995
2	PJ Grayson	France	Paris	1996
2	JP Wilkinson	Australia	Twickenham	2001
2	JP Wilkinson	Wales	Cardiff	2003
2	JP Wilkinson	Ireland	Dublin	2003
2	JP Wilkinson	South Africa	Perth	2003
2	JP Wilkinson	Samoa	Nantes	2007
2	JP Wilkinson	Tonga	Paris	2007
2	AJ Goode	Argentina	Manchester	2009
2	JP Wilkinson	Wales	Twickenham	2011

MOST PENALTIES IN A MATCH
BY THE TEAM

Penalties	Opponents	Venue	Year
8	South Africa	Bloemfontein	2000
7	Wales	Cardiff	1991
7	Scotland	Twickenham	1995
7	France	Twickenham	1999
7	Fiji	Twickenham	1999
7	South Africa	Paris	1999
7	South Africa	Twickenham	2001
7	Australia	Twickenham	2010

BY A PLAYER

Pens	Player	Opponents	Venue	Year
8	JP Wilkinson	South Africa	Bloemfontein	2000
7	SD Hodgkinson	Wales	Cardiff	1991
7	CR Andrew	Scotland	Twickenham	1995
7	JP Wilkinson	France	Twickenham	1999
7	JP Wilkinson	Fiji	Twickenham	1999
7	JP Wilkinson	South Africa	Twickenham	2001
7	TGAL Flood	Australia	Twickenham	2010

ENGLAND

CAREER RECORDS

MOST CAPPED PLAYERS

Caps	Player	Career Span
114	J Leonard	1990 to 2004
91	JP Wilkinson	1998 to 2011
85	R Underwood	1984 to 1996
85	LBN Dallaglio	1995 to 2007
84	MO Johnson	1993 to 2003
78	JPR Worsley	1999 to 2011
77	MJS Dawson	1995 to 2006
75	MJ Catt	1994 to 2007
75	MJ Tindall	2000 to 2011
73	PJ Vickery	1998 to 2009
73	SG Thompson	2002 to 2011
72	WDC Carling	1988 to 1997
71	CR Andrew	1985 to 1997
71	RA Hill	1997 to 2004
71	LW Moody	2001 to 2011
71	SD Shaw	1996 to 2011
69	DJ Grewcock	1997 to 2007
66	NA Back	1994 to 2003
66	DM Hartley	2008 to 2015
65	JC Guscott	1989 to 1999

MOST CONSECUTIVE TESTS

Tests	Player	Span
44	WDC Carling	1989 to 1995
40	J Leonard	1990 to 1995
36	JV Pullin	1968 to 1975
33	WB Beaumont	1975 to 1982
30	R Underwood	1992 to 1996

MOST TESTS AS CAPTAIN

Tests	Captain	Span
59	WDC Carling	1988 to 1996
42	CDC Robshaw	2012 to 2015
39	MO Johnson	1998 to 2003
22	LBN Dallaglio	1997 to 2004
21	WB Beaumont	1978 to 1982
21	SW Borthwick	2008 to 2010
17	ME Corry	2005 to 2007
15	PJ Vickery	2002 to 2008
13	WW Wakefield	1924 to 1926
13	NM Hall	1949 to 1955
13	E Evans	1956 to 1958
13	REG Jeeps	1960 to 1962
13	JV Pullin	1972 to 1975

MOST POINTS IN TESTS

Points	Player	Tests	Career
1179	JP Wilkinson	91	1998 to 2011
400	PJ Grayson	32	1995 to 2004
396	CR Andrew	71	1985 to 1997
343	OA Farrell	35	2012 to 2015
301	TGAL Flood	60	2006 to 2013
296	J M Webb	33	1987 to 1993
269	CC Hodgson	38	2001 to 2012
240	WH Hare	25	1974 to 1984
210	R Underwood	85	1984 to 1996

MOST TRIES IN TESTS

Tries	Player	Tests	Career
49	R Underwood	85	1984 to 1996
31	WJH Greenwood	55	1997 to 2004
31	BC Cohen	57	2000 to 2006
30	JC Guscott	65	1989 to 1999
28	JT Robinson	51	2001 to 2007
24	DD Luger	38	1998 to 2003
22	OJ Lewsey	55	1998 to 2007
20	MJ Cueto	55	2004 to 2011
19	CJ Ashton	39	2010 to 2014
18	CN Lowe	25	1913 to 1923
17	LBN Dallaglio	85	1995 to 2007

MOST CONVERSIONS IN TESTS

Cons	Player	Tests	Career
162	JP Wilkinson	91	1998 to 2011
78	PJ Grayson	32	1995 to 2004
45	OA Farrell	35	2012 to 2015
44	CC Hodgson	38	2001 to 2012
41	JM Webb	33	1987 to 1993
40	TGAL Flood	60	2006 to 2013
35	SD Hodgkinson	14	1989 to 1991
33	CR Andrew	71	1985 to 1997
23	GT Ford	17	2014 to 2015
17	L Stokes	12	1875 to 1881

MOST PENALTY GOALS IN TESTS

Penalties	Player	Tests	Career
239	JP Wilkinson	91	1998 to 2011
86	CR Andrew	71	1985 to 1997
79	OA Farrell	35	2012 to 2015
72	PJ Grayson	32	1995 to 2004
67	WH Hare	25	1974 to 1984
66	JM Webb	33	1987 to 1993
66	TGAL Flood	60	2006 to 2013
44	CC Hodgson	38	2001 to 2012
43	SD Hodgkinson	14	1989 to 1991

MOST DROP GOALS IN TESTS

Drops	Player	Tests	Career
36	JP Wilkinson	91	1998 to 2011
21	CR Andrew	71	1985 to 1997
6	PJ Grayson	32	1995 to 2004
4	JP Horton	13	1978 to 1984
4	L Cusworth	12	1979 to 1988
4	AJ Goode	17	2005 to 2009

Getty Images

Full-back Mike Brown celebrates his try against Fiji in the opening match of Rugby World Cup 2015 at Twickenham.

ENGLAND

INTERNATIONAL CHAMPIONSHIP RECORDS

RECORD	DETAIL		SET
Most points in season	229	in five matches	2001
Most tries in season	29	in five matches	2001
Highest score	80	80–23 v Italy	2001
Biggest win	57	80–23 v Italy	2001
Highest score conceded	43	13–43 v Ireland	2007
Biggest defeat	30	13–43 v Ireland	2007
Most appearances	54	J Leonard	1991–2004
Most points in matches	546	JP Wilkinson	1998–2011
Most points in season	89	JP Wilkinson	2001
Most points in match	35	JP Wilkinson	v Italy, 2001
Most tries in matches	18	CN Lowe	1913–1923
	18	R Underwood	1984–1996
Most tries in season	8	CN Lowe	1914
Most tries in match	4	RW Poulton	v France, 1914
	4	CJ Ashton	v Italy, 2011
Most cons in matches	89	JP Wilkinson	1998–2011
Most cons in season	24	JP Wilkinson	2001
Most cons in match	9	JP Wilkinson	v Italy, 2001
Most pens in matches	105	JP Wilkinson	1998–2011
Most pens in season	18	SD Hodgkinson	1991
	18	JP Wilkinson	2000
Most pens in match	7	SD Hodgkinson	v Wales, 1991
	7	CR Andrew	v Scotland, 1995
	7	JP Wilkinson	v France, 1999
Most drops in matches	11	JP Wilkinson	1998–2011
Most drops in season	5	JP Wilkinson	2003
Most drops in match	2	R Hiller	v Ireland, 1970
	2	AGB Old	v France, 1978
	2	JP Horton	v France, 1980
	2	PJ Grayson	v France, 1996
	2	JP Wilkinson	v Wales, 2003
	2	JP Wilkinson	v Ireland, 2003

MISCELLANEOUS RECORDS

RECORD	HOLDER	DETAIL
Longest Test Career	SD Shaw	1996 to 2011
Youngest Test Cap	HCC Laird	18 yrs 134 days in 1927
Oldest Test Cap	FG Gilbert	39 yrs 42 days in 1923

UP TO 1 NOVEMBER, 2015

PLAYER BACKS :	DEBUT	CAPS	T	C	P	D	PTS
BM Barritt	2012 v S	26	2	0	0	0	10
MN Brown	2007 v SA	43	8	0	0	0	40
S Burgess	2015 v F	5	0	0	0	0	0
LD Burrell	2014 v F	13	3	0	0	0	15
DS Care	2008 v NZ	53	7	0	0	3	44
DJ Cipriani	2008 v W	14	3	8	11	0	64
KO Eastmond	2013 v Arg	6	1	0	0	0	5
OA Farrell	2012 v S	35	2	45	79	2	343
GT Ford	2014 v W	17	2	23	25	1	134
DA Goode	2012 v SA	19	0	0	1	0	3
JBA Joseph	2012 v SA	16	5	0	0	0	25
JJ May	2013 v Arg	19	6	0	0	0	30
SJ Myler	2013 v Arg	1	0	1	0	0	2
JT Nowell	2014 v F	10	7	0	0	0	35
S Rokoduguni	2014 v NZ	1	0	0	0	0	0
HJH Slade	2015 v F	2	1	0	0	0	5
EM Tuilagi	2011 v W	25	11	0	0	0	55
WWF Twelvetrees	2013 v S	22	3	0	0	0	15
AKC Watson	2014 v NZ	15	8	0	0	0	40
REP Wigglesworth	2008 v It	27	1	0	0	0	5
M Yarde	2013 v Arg	7	4	0	0	0	20
BR Youngs	2010 v S	52	9	0	0	0	45

ENGLAND

FORWARDS :

DMJ Attwood	2010 v NZ	22	0	0	0	0	0
K Brookes	2014 v NZ	15	0	0	0	0	0
CT Clark	2015 v F	1	0	0	0	0	0
DR Cole	2010 v W	56	1	0	0	0	5
AR Corbisiero	2011 v It	20	0	0	0	0	0
LA Cowan-Dickie	2015 v F	1	0	0	0	0	0
TR Croft	2008 v F	40	4	0	0	0	20
NJ Easter	2007 v It	54	9	0	0	0	45
JE George	2015 v F	3	0	0	0	0	0
DM Hartley	2008 v PI	66	1	0	0	0	5
JAW Haskell	2007 v W	62	4	0	0	0	20
GEJ Kruis	2014 v NZ	10	0	0	0	0	0
JO Launchbury	2012 v Fj	28	2	0	0	0	10
CL Lawes	2009 v A	42	0	0	0	0	0
JWG Marler	2012 v SA	37	0	0	0	0	0
BJ Morgan	2012 v S	31	5	0	0	0	25
MJ Mullan	2010 v It	9	0	0	0	0	0
GMW Parling	2012 v S	29	1	0	0	0	5
CDC Robshaw	2009 v Arg	43	2	0	0	0	10
MWIN Vunipola	2012 v Fj	27	1	0	0	0	5
VML Vunipola	2013 v Arg	21	4	0	0	0	20
RW Webber	2012 v It	16	1	0	0	0	5
DG Wilson	2009 v Arg	44	1	0	0	0	5
TA Wood	2011 v W	42	0	0	0	0	0
TN Youngs	2012 v Fj	28	0	0	0	0	0

Nick Easter scored a hat-trick of tries and put in a man of the match performance against Uruguay in Manchester.

ENGLAND INTERNATIONAL PLAYERS
UP TO 1 NOVEMBER, 2015

Note: Years given for International Championship matches are for second half of season; eg 1972 means season 1971–72. Years for all other matches refer to the actual year of the match. Entries in square brackets denote matches played in RWC Finals.

Aarvold, C D (Cambridge U, W Hartlepool, Headingley, Blackheath) 1928 A, W, I, F, S, 1929 W, I, F, 1931 W, S, F, 1932 SA, W, I, S, 1933 W

Abbott, S R (Wasps, Harlequins) 2003 W2, F3, [Sm, U, W(R)], 2004 NZ1(t&R), 2, 2006 I, A2(R)

Abendanon, N A (Bath) 2007 SA2(R), F2

Ackford, P J (Harlequins) 1988 A, 1989 S, I, F, W, R, Fj, 1990 I, F, W, S, Arg 3, 1991 W, S, I, F, A, [NZ, It, F, S, A]

Adams, A A (London Hospital) 1910 F

Adams, F R (Richmond) 1875 I, S, 1876 S, 1877 I, 1878 S, 1879 S, I

Adebayo, A A (Bath) 1996, It, 1997 Arg 1, 2, A 2, NZ 1, 1998 S

Adey, G J (Leicester) 1976 I, F

Adkins, S J (Coventry) 1950 I, F, S, 1953 W, I, F, S

Agar, A E (Harlequins) 1952 SA, W, S, I, F, 1953 W, I

Alcock, A (Guy's Hospital) 1906 SA

Alderson, F H R (Hartlepool R) 1891 W, I, S, 1892 W, S, 1893 W

Alexander, H (Richmond) 1900 I, S, 1901 W, I, S, 1902 W, I

Alexander, W (Northern) 1927 F

Allen, A O (Gloucester) 2006 NZ, Arg

Allison, D F (Coventry) 1956 W, I, S, F, 1957 W, 1958 W, S

Allport, A (Blackheath) 1892 W, 1893 I, 1894 W, I, S

Anderson, S (Rockcliff) 1899 I

Anderson, W F (Orrell) 1973 NZ 1

Anderton, C (Manchester FW) 1889 M

Andrew, C R (Cambridge U, Nottingham, Wasps, Toulouse, Newcastle) 1985 R, F, S, I, W, 1986 W, S, I, F, 1987 I, F, W, [J (R), US], 1988 S, I 1, 2, A 1, 2, Fj, A, 1989 S, I, F, W, R, Fj, 1990 I, F, W, S, Arg 3, 1991 W, S, I, F, Fj, A, [NZ, It, US, F, S, A], 1992 S, I, F, W, C, S, [Arg, It, A, NZ, F], 1993 F, W, NZ, 1994 S, I, F, W, SA 1, 2, R, C, 1995 I, F, W, S, [Arg, It, A, NZ, F], 1997 W (R)

Appleford, G N (London Irish) 2002 Arg

Archer, G S (Bristol, Army, Newcastle) 1996 S, I, 1997 A 2, NZ 1, SA, NZ 2, 1998 F, W, S, I, A 1, NZ 1, H, It, 1999 Tg, Fj, 2000 I, F, W, It, S

Archer, H (Bridgwater A) 1909 W, F, I

Armitage, D A (London Irish) 2008 PI, A, SA, NZ3, 2009 It, W, I, F, S, Arg 1, 2, 2010 W, It, I, S, A2(R), NZ(R), A3(R), Sm(R), 2011 W2, 3(t&R), I2(R), [Arg, Gg, R(R), S]

Armitage, S E (London Irish) 2009 It, Arg 1, 2, 2010 W(R), It(R)

Armstrong, R (Northern) 1925 W

Arthur, T G (Wasps) 1966 W, I

Ashby, R C (Wasps) 1966 I, F, 1967 A

Ashcroft, A (Waterloo) 1956 W, I, S, F, 1957 W, I, F, S, 1958 W, A, I, F, S, 1959 I, F, S

Ashcroft, A H (Birkenhead Park) 1909 A

Ashford, W (Richmond) 1897 W, I, 1898 S, W

Ashton, C J (Northampton, Saracens) 2010 F, A1, 2, NZ, A3, Sm, SA, 2011 W1, It, F, S, I1, 2, [Arg, Gg, R, S, F], 2012 S, It, W, F, I, SA 1, 2, 3, A, SA4, NZ, 2013 S, I, F, It, W, A, Arg3, NZ, 2014 NZ2(R), 3

Ashworth, A (Oldham) 1892 I

Askew, J G (Cambridge U) 1930 W, I, F

Aslett, A R (Richmond) 1926 W, I, F, S, 1929 S, F

Assinder, E W (O Edwardians) 1909 A, W

Aston, R L (Blackheath) 1890 S, I

Attwood, D M J (Gloucester, Bath) 2010 NZ(R), Sm(R), 2013 Arg1, 2, A(R), 2014 F(R), S(R), I(R), W(R), It(R), NZ1(R), 3(t&R), 4, SA, Sm, A, 2015 W, It, I 1, S, F 2(R), 3(R)

Auty, J R (Headingley) 1935 S

Back, N A (Leicester) 1994 S, I, 1995 [Arg (t), It, WS], 1997 NZ 1(R), SA, NZ 2, 1998 F, W, S, I, H, It, A 2, SA 2, 1999 S, I, F,

W, A, US, C, [It, NZ, Fj, SA], 2000 I, F, W, It, S, SA 1, 2, A, Arg, SA 3, 2001 W, It, S, F, I, A, R, SA, 2002 S, I, F, W, It, NZ (t + R), A, SA, 2003 F 1, W 1, S, I, NZ, A, F 3, [Gg, SA, Sm, W, F, A]

Bailey, M D (Cambridge U, Wasps) 1984 SA 1, 2, 1987 [US], 1989 Fj, 1990 I, F, S (R)

Bainbridge, S (Gosforth, Fylde) 1982 F, W, 1983 F, W, S, I, NZ, 1984 S, I, F, W, 1985 NZ 1, 2, 1987 F, W, S, [J, US]

Baker, D G S (OMTs) 1955 W, I, F, S

Baker, E M (Moseley) 1895 W, I, S, 1896 W, I, S, 1897 W

Baker, H C (Clifton) 1887 W

Balshaw, I R (Bath, Leeds, Gloucester) 2000 I (R), F (R), It (R), S (R), A (R), Arg, SA 3(R), 2001 W, It, S, F, I, 2002 S (R), I (R), 2003 F2, 3, [Sm, U, A(R)], 2004 It, S, I, 2005 It, S, 2006 A1, 2, NZ, Arg, 2007 It, SA1, 2008 W, It, F, S, I

Banahan, M A (Bath) 2009 Arg 1, 2, A, Arg 3, NZ, 2010 Sm, SA(R), 2011 It(R), F(R), S(R), I1, W2, 3, [Gg(R), S(R), F(R)]

Bance, J F (Bedford) 1954 S

Barkley, O J (Bath) 2001 US (R), 2004 It(R), I(t), W, F, NZ2(R), A1(R), 2005 W(R), F, I, It, S, A(R), Sm(R), 2006 A1, 2(R), 2007 F2, 3(R), [US, Sm, Tg], 2008 NZ1, 2(R)

Barley, B (Wakefield) 1984 I, F, W, A, 1988 A 1, 2, Fj

Barnes, S (Bristol, Bath) 1984 A, 1985 R (R), NZ 1, 2, 1986 S (R), F (R), 1987 I (R), 1988 Fj, 1993 S, I

Barr, R J (Leicester) 1932 SA, W, I

Barrett, E I M (Lennox) 1903 S

Barrington, T J M (Bristol) 1931 W, I

Barrington-Ward, L E (Edinburgh U) 1910 W, I, F, S

Barritt, B M (Saracens) 2012 S, It, W, F, I, SA 1, 3(t&R), Fj, A, SA4, NZ, 2013 S, I, F, It, W, 2014 F(R), S(R), NZ 4, SA, Sm, A, 2015 I 2, [Fj, W, A]

Barron, J H (Bingley) 1896 S, 1897 W, I

Bartlett, J T (Waterloo) 1951 W

Bartlett, R M (Harlequins) 1957 W, I, F, S, 1958 I, F, S

Barton, J (Coventry) 1967 I, F, W, 1972 F

Batchelor, T B (Oxford U) 1907 F

Bates, S M (Wasps) 1989 R

Bateson, A H (Otley) 1930 W, I, F, S

Bateson, H D (Liverpool) 1879 I

Batson, T (Blackheath) 1872 S, 1874 S, 1875 I

Batten, J M (Cambridge U) 1874 S

Baume, J L (Northern) 1950 S

Baxendell, J J N (Sale) 1998 NZ 2, SA 1

Baxter, J (Birkenhead Park) 1900 W, I, S

Bayfield, M C (Northampton) 1991 Fj, A, 1992 S, I, F, W, C, SA, 1993 F, W, S, I, 1994 S, I, SA 1, 2, R, C, 1995 I, F, W, S, [Arg, It, A, NZ, Fj], SA, WS, 1996 F, W

Bazley, R C (Waterloo) 1952 I, F, 1953 W, I, F, S, 1955 W, I, F, S

Beal, N D (Northampton) 1996 Arg, 1997 A 1, 1998 NZ 1, 2, SA 1, H (R), SA 2, 1999 S, F (R), A (t), C (R), [It (R), Tg (R), Fj, SA]

Beaumont, W B (Fylde) 1975 I, A 1(R), 2, 1976 A, W, S, I, F, 1977 S, I, F, W, 1978 F, W, S, I, NZ, 1979 S, I, F, W, NZ, 1980 I, F, W, S, 1981 W, S, I, F, Arg 1, 2, 1982 A, S

Bedford, H (Morley) 1889 M, 1890 S, I

Bedford, L L (Headingley) 1931 W, I

Beer, I D S (Harlequins) 1955 F, S

Beese, M C (Liverpool) 1972 W, I, F

Beim, T D (Sale) 1998 NZ 1(R), 2

Bell, D S C (Bath) 2005 It(R), S, 2009 A(R), Arg 3, NZ

Bell, F J (Northern) 1900 W

Bell, H (New Brighton) 1884 I

Bell, J L (Darlington) 1878 I

Bell, P J (Blackheath) 1968 W, I, F, S

Bell, R W (Northern) 1900 W, I, S

Bendon, G J (Wasps) 1959 W, I, F, S

Bennett, N O (St Mary's Hospital, Waterloo) 1947 W, S, F, 1948 A, W, I, S

Bennett, W N (Bedford, London Welsh) 1975 S, A1, 1976 S (R), 1979 S, I, F, W

Bennetts, B B (Penzance) 1909 A, W

Bentley, J (Sale, Newcastle) 1988 I 2, A 1, 1997 A 1, SA

Bentley, J E (Gipsies) 1871 S, 1872 S

Benton, S (Gloucester) 1998 A 1

Berridge, M J (Northampton) 1949 W, I

Berry, H (Gloucester) 1910 W, I, F, S

Berry, J (Tyldesley) 1891 W, I, S

Berry, J T W (Leicester) 1939 W, I, S

Beswick, E (Swinton) 1882 I, S

Biggs, J M (UCH) 1878 S, 1879 I

Birkett, J G G (Harlequins) 1906 S, F, SA, 1907 F, W, S, 1908 F, W, I , S, 1910 W, I, S, 1911 W, F, I , S, 1912 W, I , S, F

Birkett L (Clapham R) 1875 S, 1877 I, S

Birkett, R H (Clapham R) 1871 S, 1875 S, 1876 S, 1877 I

Bishop, C C (Blackheath) 1927 F

Black, B H (Blackheath) 1930 W, I, F, S, 1931 W, I, S, F, 1932 S, 1933 W

Blacklock, J H (Aspatria) 1898 I, 1899 I

Blakeway, P J (Gloucester) 1980 I, F, W, S, 1981 W, S, I, F, 1982 I, F, W, 1984 I, F, W, SA 1, 1985 R, F, S, I

Blakiston, A F (Northampton) 1920 S, 1921 W, I, S, F, 1922 W, 1923 S, F, 1924 W, I, F, S, 1925 NZ, W, I, S, F

Blatherwick, T (Manchester) 1878 I

Body, J A (Gipsies) 1872 S, 1873 S

Bolton, C A (United Services) 1909 F

Bolton, R (Harlequins) 1933 W, 1936 S, 1937 S, 1938 W, I

Bolton, W N (Blackheath) 1882 I, S, 1883 W, I, S, 1884 W, I, S, 1885 I, 1887 I, S

Bonaventura, M S (Blackheath) 1931 W

Bond, A M (Sale) 1978 NZ, 1979 S, I, NZ, 1980 I, 1982 I

Bonham-Carter, E (Oxford U) 1891 S

Bonsor, F F (Bradford) 1886 W, I, S, 1887 W, S, 1889 M

Boobbyer, B (Rosslyn Park) 1950 W, I, F, S, 1951 W, F, 1952 S, I, F

Booth, L A (Headingley) 1933 W, I, S, 1934 S, 1935 W, I, S

Borthwick, S W (Bath, Saracens) 2001 F, C 1, 2(R), US, R, 2003 A(t), W 2(t), F 2, 2004 I, F(R), NZ1(R), 2, A1, C, SA, A2, 2005 W(R), It(R), S(R), A, NZ, Sm, 2006 W, It, S, F, I, 2007 W2, F3, [SA1(t&R), Sm(R), Tg], 2008 W, It, F, S, I, NZ1, 2, PI, A, SA, NZ3, 2009 It, W, I, F, S, Arg 1, 2, A, Arg 3, NZ, 2010 W, It, I, S

Botha, M J (Saracens) 2011 W2(R), 2012 S, It, W, F, I, SA 1, 2, 3(R), 4(R)

Botting, I J (Oxford U) 1950 W, I

Boughton, H J (Gloucester) 1935 W, I, S

Boyle, C W (Oxford U) 1873 S

Boyle, S B (Gloucester) 1983 W, S, I

Boylen, F (Hartlepool R) 1908 F, W, I, S

Bracken, K P P (Bristol, Saracens) 1993 NZ, 1994 S, I, C, 1995 I, F, W, S, [It, WS (t)], SA, 1996 It (R), 1997 Arg 1, 2, A 2, NZ 1, 2, 1998 F, W, 1999 S(R), I, F, A, 2000 SA 1, 2, A, 2001 It (R), S (R), F (R), C 1, 2, US, I (R), A, R (R), SA, 2002 S, I, F, W, It, 2003 W 1, It(R), I(t), NZ, A, F3, [SA, U(R), W(R), F(t&R)]

Bradby, M S (United Services) 1922 I, F

Bradley, R (W Hartlepool) 1903 W

Bradshaw, H (Bramley) 1892 S, 1893 W, I, S, 1894 W, I, S

Brain, S E (Coventry) 1984 SA 2, A (R), 1985 R, F, S, I, W, NZ 1, 2, 1986 W, S, I, F

Braithwaite, J (Leicester) 1905 NZ

Braithwaite-Exley, B (Headingley) 1949 W

Brettargh, A T (Liverpool OB) 1900 W, 1903 I, S, 1904 W, I, S, 1905 I, S

Brewer, J V (Gipsies) 1876 I

Briggs, A (Bradford) 1892 W, I, S

Brinn, A (Gloucester) 1972 W, I, S

Broadley, T (Bingley) 1893 W, S, 1894 W, I, S, 1896 S

Bromet, W E (Richmond) 1891 W, I, 1892 W, I, S, 1893 W, I, S, 1895 W, I, S, 1896 I

Brook, P W P (Harlequins) 1930 S, 1931 F, 1936 S

Brooke, T J (Richmond) 1968 F, S

Brookes, K (Newcastle, Northampton) 2014 NZ2(R), 3(R), 4(R), SA(R), Sm(R), A(R), 2015 W(R), It(R), S(R), F 1(R), 2, I 2(R), [Fj(R), W(R), A(R)]

Brooks, F G (Bedford) 1906 SA

Brooks, M J (Oxford U) 1874 S

Brophy, T J (Liverpool) 1964 I, F, S, 1965 W, I, 1966 W, I, F

Brough, J W (Silloth) 1925 NZ, W

Brougham, H (Harlequins) 1912 W, I, S, F

Brown, A A (Exeter) 1938 S

Brown A T (Gloucester) 2006 A1, 2007 SA1, 2

Brown, L G (Oxford U, Blackheath) 1911 W, F, I, S, 1913 SA, W, F, I, S, 1914 W, I, S, F, 1921 W, I, S, F, 1922 W

Brown, M N (Harlequins) 2007 SA1, 2, 2008 NZ1, 2012 S(R), W(R), I(R), SA 1, Fj(R), A(R), SA4, NZ, 2013 S, I, F, It, W, Arg1, 2, A, Arg3, NZ, 2014 F, S, I, W, It, NZ1, 2, 3, 4, SA, Sm, A, 2015 W, It, S, F 1, 3, I 2, [Fj, W, A, U(R)]

Brown S P (Richmond) 1998 A 1, SA 1

Brown, T W (Bristol) 1928 S, 1929 W, I, S, F, 1932 S, 1933 W, I, S

Brunton, J (N Durham) 1914 W, I, S

Brutton, E B (Cambridge U) 1886 S

Bryden, C C (Clapham R) 1876 I, 1877 S

Bryden, H A (Clapham R) 1874 S

Buckingham, R A (Leicester) 1927 F

Bucknall, A L (Richmond) 1969 SA, 1970 I, W, S, F, 1971 W, I, F, S (2[1C])

Buckton, J R D (Saracens) 1988 A (R), 1990 Arg 1, 2

Budd, A J (Blackheath) 1878 I, 1879 S, I, 1881 W, S

Budworth, R T D (Blackheath) 1890 W, 1891 W, S

Bull, A G (Northampton) 1914 W

Bullough, E (Wigan) 1892 W, I, S

Bulpitt, M P (Blackheath) 1970 S

Bulteel, A M (Manchester) 1876 I

Bunting, W L (Moseley) 1897 I, S, 1898 I, S, W, 1899 S, 1900 S, 1901 I, S

Burgess, S (Bath) 2015 F 2, I 2(R), [Fj(R), W, A(R)]

Burland, D W (Bristol) 1931 W, I, F, 1932 I, S, 1933 W, I, S

Burns, B H (Blackheath) 1871 S

Burns, F S (Gloucester, Leicester) 2012 NZ(R), 2013 Arg1, 2, 2014 NZ1, 3

Burrell, L D (Northampton) 2014 F, S, I, W, It, NZ2, 3(R), 2015 W, It, I 1, S, F1, 3

Burton, G W (Blackheath) 1879 S, I, 1880 S, 1881 I, W, S

Burton, H C (Richmond) 1926 W

Burton, M A (Gloucester) 1972 W, I, F, S, SA, 1974 F, W, 1975 S, A 1, 2, 1976 A, W, S, I, F, 1978 F, W

Bush, J A (Clifton) 1872 S, 1873 S, 1875 S, 1876 I, S

Butcher, C J S (Harlequins) 1984 SA 1, 2, A

Butcher, W V (Streatham) 1903 S, 1904 W, I, S, 1905 W, I, S

Butler, A G (Harlequins) 1937 W, I

Butler, P E (Gloucester) 1975 A 1, 1976 F

Butterfield, J (Northampton) 1953 F, S, 1954 W, NZ, I, S, F, 1955 W, I, F, S, 1956 W, I, S, F, 1957 W, I, F, S, 1958 W, A, I, F, S, 1959 W, I, F, S

Byrne, F A (Moseley) 1897 W

Byrne, J F (Moseley) 1894 W, I, S, 1895 I, S, 1896 I, 1897 W, I, S, 1898 I, S, W, 1899 I

Cain, J J (Waterloo) 1950 W

Cairns, M I (Saracens) 2007 SA1(R)

Callard, J E B (Bath) 1993 NZ, 1994 S, I, 1995 [WS], SA

Campbell, D A (Cambridge U) 1937 W, I

Candler, P L (St Bart's Hospital) 1935 W, 1936 NZ, W, I, S, 1937 W, I, S, 1938 W, S

Cannell, L B (Oxford U, St Mary's Hospital) 1948 F, 1949 W, I, F, S, 1950 W, I, F, S, 1952 SA, W, 1953 W, I, F, 1956 I, S, F, 1957 W, I

Caplan, D W N (Headingley) 1978 S, I

Cardus, R M (Roundhay) 1979 F, W

Care, D S (Harlequins) 2008 NZ1(R), 2, PI, A, SA, NZ3, 2009 I(R), F(R), S(R), Arg 1, 2, A, Arg 3(R), NZ(R), 2010 W, It, I, S, F, A1, 2(R), NZ2(R), A3(R), Sm(R), SA(R), 2011 W1(R), It(R), F(R), S(R), I1(R), W2, 3(R), 2012 S, It, W, F(R), It, W(R), Arg3(R), 2014 F, S, I, W, It, NZ2, 4, SA, 2015 F 2(R), 3(R), [U]

Carey, G M (Blackheath) 1895 W, I, S, 1896 W, I

Carleton, J (Orrell) 1979 NZ, 1980 I, F, W, S, 1981 W, S, I, F, Arg 1, 2, 1982 A, S, I, F, W, 1983 F, W, S, I, NZ, 1984 S, I, F, W, A

Carling, W D C (Durham U, Harlequins) 1988 F, W, S, I 1, 2, A2, Fj, A, 1989 S, I, F, W, Fj, 1990 I, F, W, S, Arg 1, 2, 3, 1991 W, S, I, F, Fj, A, [NZ, It, US, F, S, A], 1992 S, I, F, W, C, SA, 1993 F, W, S, I, 1994 S, I, F, W, SA 1, 2, R, C, 1995 I, F, W, S, [Arg, WS, A, NZ, F], SA, WS, 1996 F, W, S, I, It, Arg, 1997 S, I, F, W

Carpenter, A D (Gloucester) 1932 SA

Carr, R S L (Manchester) 1939 W, I, S

Cartwright, V H (Nottingham) 1903 W, I, S, 1904 W, S, 1905 W, I, S, NZ, 1906 W, I, S, F, SA

Catcheside, H C (Percy Park) 1924 W, I, F, S, 1926 W, I, 1927 I, S

Catt, M J (Bath, London Irish) 1994 W (R), C (R), 1995 I, F, W, S, [Arg, It, WS, A, NZ, F], SA, WS, 1996 F, W, S, I, It, Arg, 1997 W, Arg 1, A 1, 2, NZ 1, SA, 1998 F, W (R), I, A 2(R), SA 2, 1999 S, F, W, A, C (R), [Tg (R), Fj, SA (R)], 2000 I, F, W, It, S, SA 1, 2, A, Arg, 2001 W, It, S, F, I, A, R (R), SA, 2003 [Sm(R), U, W(R), F, A(R)], 2004 W(R), F(R), NZ1, A1, 2006 A1, 2, 2007 F1, W1, F2, [US, SA1, A, F, SA2]

Cattell, R H B (Blackheath) 1895 W, I, S, 1896 W, I, S, 1900 W

Cave, J W (Richmond) 1889 M

Cave, W T C (Blackheath) 1905 W

Challis, R (Bristol) 1957 I, F, S

Chambers, E L (Bedford) 1908 F, 1910 W, I

Chantrill, B S (Bristol) 1924 W, I, F, S

Chapman, C E (Cambridge U) 1884 W

Chapman, D E (Richmond) 1998 A 1(R)

Chapman, F E (Hartlepool) 1910 W, I, F, S, 1912 W, 1914 W, I

Cheesman, W I (OMTs) 1913 SA, W, F, I

Cheston, E C (Richmond) 1873 S, 1874 S, 1875 I, S, 1876 S

Chilcott, G J (Bath) 1984 A, 1986 I, F, 1987 F (R), W, [J, US, W (R)], 1988 I 2(R), Fj, 1989 I (R), F, W, R

Christophers, P D (Bristol) 2002 Arg, SA, 2003 W 1 (R)

Christopherson, P (Blackheath) 1891 W, S

Chuter, G S (Leicester) 2006 A1(R), 2, NZ, Arg, SA1, 2(R), 2007 S, It, I, F1, W1, 2(R), [US(R), SA1(R), Sm, Tg, A(R), F(R), SA2(R)], 2008 S(R), I(R), 2009 Arg 2(R), 2010 A1(R), 2(R)

Cipriani, D J (Wasps, Sale) 2008 W(R), It(R), I, Pl, A, SA, NZ3(R), 2014 NZ1(R), 3(R), 2015 It(R), S(R), F 1(R), 2(R), 3(R)

Clark, C T (Northampton) 2015 F 2

Clark, C W H (Liverpool) 1876 I

Clarke, A J (Coventry) 1935 W, I, S, 1936 NZ, W, I

Clarke, B B (Bath, Richmond) 1992 SA, 1993 F, W, S, I, NZ, 1994 S, F, W, SA 1, 2, R, C, 1995 I, F, W, S, [Arg, It, A, NZ, F], SA, WS, 1996 F, W, S, I, Arg (R), 1997 W, Arg 1, 2, A 1(R), 1998 A 1(t), NZ 1, 2, SA 1, H, It, 1999 A (R)

Clarke, S J S (Cambridge U, Blackheath) 1963 W, I, F, S, NZ 1, 2, A, 1964 NZ, W, I, 1965 I, F, S

Clayton, J H (Liverpool) 1871 S

Clements, J W (O Cranleighans) 1959 I, F, S

Cleveland, C R (Blackheath) 1887 W, S

Clibborn, W G (Richmond) 1886 W, I, S, 1887 W, I, S

Clough, P J (Cambridge U, Orrell) 1986 I, F, 1987 [J (R), US]

Coates, C H (Yorkshire W) 1880 S, 1881 S, 1882 S

Coates, V H M (Bath) 1913 SA, W, F, I, S

Cobby, W (Hull) 1900 W

Cockerham, A (Bradford Olicana) 1900 W

Cockerill, R (Leicester) 1997 Arg 1(R), 2, A 2(t+R), NZ 1, SA, NZ 2, 1998 W, S, I, A 1, NZ 1, 2, SA 1, H, It, A 2, 1999 S, I, F, W, A, C (R), [It, NZ, Tg (R), Fj (R)]

Codling, A J (Harlequins) 2002 Arg

Cohen, B C (Northampton) 2000 I, F, W, It, S, SA 2, Arg, SA 3, 2001 W, It, S, F, R, 2002 S, I, F, W, It, NZ, A, SA, 2003 F 1, W 1, S, I, NZ, A, F2, 3, [Gg, SA, Sm, W, F, A], 2004 It, S, I, W, F, NZ1, 2, A1, C(R), A2(R), 2005 F(R), A, NZ, 2006 W, It, S, F, I, NZ, Arg, SA1, 2

Colclough, M J (Angoulême, Wasps, Swansea) 1978 S, I, 1979 NZ, 1980 F, W, S, 1981 W, S, I, F, 1982 A, S, I, F, W, 1983 F, NZ, 1984 S, I, F, W, 1986 W, S, I, F

Cole, D R (Leicester) 2010 W(R), It, I, S, F, A1, 2, NZ, A3, Sm(R), SA, 2011 W1, It, F, S, I1, W3, I2, [Arg, Gg, R, S, F], 2012 S, It, W, F, I, SA 1, 2, 3, Fj, A, SA4, NZ, 2013 S, I, F, It, W, A, Arg3(R), NZ, 2014 F, S , 2015 W, It, I 1, S, F 1, 3, I 2, [Fj, W, A, U]

Coley, E (Northampton) 1929 F, 1932 W

Collins, P J (Camborne) 1952 S, I, F

Collins, W E (O Cheltonians) 1874 S, 1875 I, S, 1876 I, S

Considine, S G U (Bath) 1925 F

Conway, G S (Cambridge U, Rugby, Manchester) 1920 F, I, S, 1921 F, 1922 W, I, F, S, 1923 W, I, S, F, 1924 W, I, F, S, 1925 NZ, 1927 W

Cook, J G (Bedford) 1937 S

Cook, P W (Richmond) 1965 I, F

Cooke, D A (Harlequins) 1976 W, S, I, F

Cooke, D H (Harlequins) 1981 W, S, I, F, 1984 I, 1985 R, F, S, I, W, NZ 1, 2

Cooke, P (Richmond) 1939 W, I

Coop, T (Leigh) 1892 S

Cooper, J G (Moseley) 1909 A, W

Cooper, M J (Moseley) 1973 F, S, NZ 2(R), 1975 F, W, 1976 A, W, 1977 S, I, F, W

Coopper, S F (Blackheath) 1900 W, 1902 W, I, 1905 W, I, S, 1907 W

Corbett, L J (Bristol) 1921 F, 1923 W, I, 1924 W, I, F, S, 1925 NZ, W, I, S, F, 1927 W, I, S, F

Corbisiero, A R (London Irish, Northampton) 2011 It, F(R), S, I1, W2, 3, [Gg(R), R, S(R), F(R)], 2012 S, It, W, F, I, SA 2(t&R), 4, NZ, 2013 Arg3(R)), 2015 F 2(R)

Corless, B J (Coventry, Moseley) 1976 A, I (R), 1977 S, I, F, W, 1978 F, W, S, I

Corry, M E (Bristol, Leicester) 1997 Arg 1, 2, 1998 H, It, SA 2(t), 1999 F(R), A, C (t), [It (R), NZ (t+R), SA (R)], 2000 I (R), F (R), W (R), It (R), S (R), Arg (R), SA 3(t), 2001 W (R), It (R), F (t), C 1, I, 2002 F (t+R), W (t), 2003 W 2, F 2, 3, [U], 2004 A1(R), C, SA, A2, 2005 F, I, It, S, A, NZ, Sm, 2006 W, It, S, F, I, NZ, Arg, SA1, 2, 2007 S, It, I, F1, W1, 2, F2(R), 3, [US(R), SA1, Sm, Tg, A, F, SA2]

Cotton, F E (Loughborough Colls, Coventry, Sale) 1971 S 2[1C]), P, 1973 W, I, F, S, NZ 2, A, 1974 S, I, 1975 I, F, W, 1976 A, W, S, I, F, 1977 S, I, F, W, 1978 S, I, F, 1979 NZ, 1980 I, F, W, S, 1981 W

Coulman, M J (Moseley) 1967 A, I, F, S, W, 1968 W, I, F, S

Coulson, T J (Coventry) 1927 W, 1928 A, W

Court, E D (Blackheath) 1885 W

Coverdale, H (Blackheath) 1910 F, 1912 I, F, 1920 W

Cove-Smith, R (OMTs) 1921 S, F, 1922 I, F, S, 1923 W, I, S, F, 1924 W, I, S, F, 1925 NZ, W, I, S, F, 1927 W, I, S, F, 1928 A, W, I, F, S, 1929 W, I

Cowan-Dickie, L A (Exeter) 2015 F 2(R)

Cowling, R J (Leicester) 1977 S, I, F, W, 1978 F, NZ, 1979 S, I

Cowman, A R (Loughborough Colls, Coventry) 1971 S (2[1C]), P, 1973 W, I

Cox, N S (Sunderland) 1901 S

Crane, J S (Leicester) 2008 SA(R), 2009 Arg 1(R), A

Cranmer, P (Richmond, Moseley) 1934 W, I, S, 1935 W, I, S, 1936 NZ, W, I, S, 1937 W, I, S, 1938 W, I, S

Creed, R N (Coventry) 1971 P

Cridlan, A G (Blackheath) 1935 W, I, S

Croft, T R (Leicester) 2008 F(R), S, I, NZ2(R), Pl, A, SA(R), NZ3(R), 2009 It(R), W(R), I(R), F, S, A, Arg 3, NZ(R), 2010 A1, 2, NZ, A3, Sm(R), SA, 2011 S(R), I1(R), W2, I2, [Arg, Gg(R), R, S, F], 2012 S, It, W, F, I, 2013 It(R), W, 2015 It(R), I (R)

Crompton, C A (Blackheath) 1871 S

Crompton, D E (Bristol) 2007 SA1(R)

Crosse, C W (Oxford U) 1874 S, 1875 I

Cueto, M J (Sale) 2004 C, SA, A2, 2005 W, F, I, It, S, A, NZ, Sm, 2006 W, It, S, F, I, SA1, 2, 2007 W1, F3, [US, Sm, Tg, SA2], 2009 It, W, I, F, S, A, Arg 1, 2, A, Arg 3, NZ, 2010 W, It, I, S, F, A1, 2, NZ, A3, Sm, SA, 2011 W1, It, F, S, I1, W2, 3, I2, [R, F]

Cumberlege, B S (Blackheath) 1920 W, I, S, 1921 W, I, S, F, 1922 W

Cumming, D C (Blackheath) 1925 S, F

Cunliffe, F L (RMA) 1874 S

Currey, F I (Marlborough N) 1872 S

Currie, J D (Oxford U, Harlequins, Bristol) 1956 W, I, S, F, 1957 W, I, F, S, 1958 W, A, I, F, S, 1959 W, I, F, S, 1960 W, I, F, S, 1961 SA, 1962 W, I, F

Cusani, D A (Orrell) 1987 I

Cusworth, L (Leicester) 1979 NZ, 1982 F, W, 1983 F, W, NZ, 1984 S, I, F, W, 1988 F, W

D'Aguilar, F B G (Royal Engineers) 1872 S

Dallaglio, L B N (Wasps) 1995 SA (R), WS, 1996 F, W, S, I, It, Arg, 1997 S, I, F, A 1, 2, NZ 1, SA, NZ 2, 1998 F, W, S, I, A 2, SA 2, 1999 S, I, F, W, US, C, [It, NZ, Tg, Fj, SA], 2000 I, F, W, It, S, SA 1, 2, A, Arg, SA 3, 2001 W, It, S, F, 2002 It (R), NZ, A (t), SA(R), 2003 F 1 (R), W 1, It, S, I, NZ, A, [Gg, SA, Sm, U, W, F, A], 2004 It, S, I, W, F, NZ1, 2, A1, 2006 W(t&R), It(R), S(R), F(R), 2007 W2(R), F2, 3(R), [US, Tg(R), A(R), F(R), SA2(R)]

Dalton, T J (Coventry) 1969 S(R)

Danby, T (Harlequins) 1949 W

Daniell, J (Richmond) 1899 W, 1900 I, S, 1902 I, S, 1904 I, S

Darby, A J L (Birkenhead Park) 1899 I

Davenport, A (Ravenscourt Park) 1871 S

Davey, J (Redruth) 1908 S, 1909 W

Davey, R F (Teignmouth) 1931 W
Davidson, Jas (Aspatria) 1897 S, 1898 S, W, 1899 I, S
Davidson, Jos (Aspatria) 1899 W, S
Davies, G H (Cambridge U, Coventry, Wasps) 1981 S, I, F, Arg 1, 2, 1982 A, S, I, 1983 F, W, S, 1984 S, SA 1, 2, 1985 R (R), NZ 1, 2, 1986 W, S, I, F
Davies, P H (Sale) 1927 I
Davies, V G (Harlequins) 1922 W, 1925 NZ
Davies, W J A (United Services, RN) 1913 SA, W, F, I, S, 1914 I, S, F, 1920 F, I, S, 1921 W, I, S, F, 1922 I, F, S, 1923 W, I, S, F
Davies, W P C (Harlequins) 1953 S, 1954 NZ, I, 1955 W, I, F, S, 1956 W, 1957 F, S, 1958 W
Davis, A M (Torquay Ath, Harlequins) 1963 W, I, S, NZ 1, 2, 1964 NZ, W, I, F, S, 1966 W, 1967 A, 1969 SA, 1970 I, W, S
Dawe, R G R (Bath) 1987 I, F, W, [US], 1995 [WS]
Dawson, E F (RIEC) 1878 I
Dawson, M J S (Northampton, Wasps) 1995 WS, 1996 F, W, S, I, 1997 A 1, SA, NZ 2(R), 1998 W (R), S, I, NZ 1, 2, SA 1, H, It, A 2, SA 2, 1999 S, F(R), W, A(R), US, C, [It, NZ, Tg, Fj (R), SA], 2000 I, F, W, It, S, A (R), Arg, SA 3, 2001 W, It, S, F, I, 2002 W (R), It (R), NZ, A, SA, 2003 It, S, I, A(R), F3(R), [Gg, Sm, W, F, A], 2004It(R), S(R), I, W, F, NZ1, 2(R), A1(R), 2005 W, F(R), I(R), It(R), S(R), A, NZ, 2006 W(R), It(R), S(t&R), F, I(R)
Day, H L V (Leicester) 1920 W, 1922 W, F, 1926 S
Deacon, L P (Leicester) 2005 Sm, 2006 A1, 2(R), 2007 S, It, I, F1(R), W1(R), 2009 Arg 1, 2, A, Arg 3, NZ(R), 2010 W(R), It(R), I(R), S, F, 2011 W1, It, F, S, I1, W3, I2, [Arg, R, S, F]
Dean, G J (Harlequins) 1931 I
Dee, J M (Hartlepool R) 1962 S, 1963 NZ 1
Devitt, Sir T G (Blackheath) 1926 I, F, 1928 A, W
Dewhurst, J H (Richmond) 1887 W, I, S, 1890 W
De Glanville, P R (Bath) 1992 SA (R), 1993 W (R), NZ, 1994 S, I, F, W, SA 1, 2, C (R), 1995 [Arg (R), It, WS], SA (R), 1996 W (R), I (R), It, 1997 S, I, F, W, Arg 1, 2, A 1, 2, NZ 1, 2, 1998 W (R), S (R), I (R), A 2, SA 2, 1999 A (R), US, [It, NZ, Fj (R), SA]
De Winton, R F C (Marlborough N) 1893 W
Dibble, R (Bridgwater A) 1906 S, F, SA, 1908 F, W, I, S, 1909 A, W, F, I, S, 1910 S, 1911 W, F, I, S, 1912 W, I, S
Dicks, J (Northampton) 1934 W, I, S, 1935 W, I, S, 1936 S, 1937 I
Dickson, L A W (Northampton) 2012 S(R), It(R), W, F, I, SA 1(R), 2(R), 2013 Arg1, 2, A, Arg3, NZ, 2014 F(R), S(R), W(R), It(R), NZ1(R), 3(R)
Dillon, E W (Blackheath) 1904 W, I, S, 1905 W
Dingle, A J (Hartlepool R) 1913 I, 1914 S, F
Diprose, A J (Saracens) 1997 Arg 1, 2, A 2, NZ 1, 1998 W (R), S (R), I, A 1, NZ 2, SA 1
Dixon, P J (Harlequins, Gosforth) 1971 P, 1972 W, I, F, S, 1973 I, F, S, 1974 S, I, F, W, 1975 I, 1976 F, 1977 S, I, F, W, 1978 F, S, I, NZ
Dobbs, G E B (Plymouth Albion) 1906 W, I
Doble, S A (Moseley) 1972 SA, 1973 NZ 1, W
Dobson, D D (Newton Abbot) 1902 W, I, S, 1903 W, I, S
Dobson, T H (Bradford) 1895 S
Dodge, P W (Leicester) 1978 W, S, I, NZ, 1979 S, I, F, W, 1980 W, S, 1981 W, S, I, F, Arg 1, 2, 1982 A, S, F, W, 1983 F, W, S, I, NZ, 1985 R, F, S, I, W, NZ 1, 2
Donnelly, M P (Oxford U) 1947 I
Dooley, W A (Preston Grasshoppers, Fylde) 1985 R, F, S, I, W, NZ 2(R), 1986 W, S, I, F, 1987 F, W, S, [A, US, W], 1988 F, W, S, I 1, 2, A 1, 2, Fj, A, 1989 S, I, F, W, R, Fj, 1990 I, F, W, S, Arg 1, 2, 3, 1991 W, S, I, F, [NZ, US, F, S, A], 1992 S, I, F, W, C, SA, 1993 W, S, I
Doran-Jones, P P L (Gloucester, Northampton) 2009 Arg 3(R), 2011 S(R), I1(R), 2012 SA 1(R), 2013 Arg1(R), 2(R)
Dovey, B A (Rosslyn Park) 1963 W, I
Down, P J (Bristol) 1909 A
Dowson, A O (Moseley) 1899 S
Dowson, P D A (Northampton) 2012 S, It, W(R), F(R), I(R), SA 1(R), 3(R)
Drake-Lee, N J (Cambridge U, Leicester) 1963 W, I, F, S, 1964 NZ, W, I, 1965 W
Duckett, H (Bradford) 1893 I, S
Duckham, D J (Coventry) 1969 I, F, S, W, SA, 1970 I, W, S, F, 1971 W, I, F, S, 2[1C], P, 1972 W, I, F, S, 1973 NZ 1, W, I, F, S, NZ 2, A, 1974 S, I, F, W, 1975 I, F, W, 1976 A, W, S
Dudgeon, H W (Richmond) 1897 S, 1898 I, S, W, 1899 W, I, S
Dugdale, J M (Ravenscourt Park) 1871 S

Dun, A F (Wasps) 1984 W
Duncan, R F H (Guy's Hospital) 1922 I, F, S
Duncombe, N S (Harlequins) 2002 S (R), I (R)
Dunkley, P E (Harlequins) 1931 I, S, 1936 NZ, W, I, S
Duthie, J (W Hartlepool) 1903 W
Dyson, J W (Huddersfield) 1890 S, 1892 S, 1893 I, S

Easter, N J (Harlequins) 2007 It, F1, SA1, 2, W2, F3, [SA1, Sm, Tg, A, F, SA2], 2008 It, F, S, I, PI, A, SA, NZ3, 2009 It, W, I, F, S, Arg 1, 2, 2010 W, It, I, S, F, A1, 2, NZ, A3, Sm, SA, 2011 W1, It, F, S, I1, W3, [Arg, S(t&R), F], 2015 W(R), It(R), I1(R), F 1(R), 3(R), [A (R), U]
Eastmond, K O (Bath) 2013 Arg1(R), 2, 2014 NZ1, 3 , 4, SA
Ebdon, P J (Wellington) 1897 W, I
Eddison, J H (Headingley) 1912 W, I, S, F
Edgar, C S (Birkenhead Park) 1901 S
Edwards, R (Newport) 1921 W, I, S, F, 1922 W, F, 1923 W, 1924 W, F, S, 1925 NZ
Egerton, D W (Bath) 1988 I 2, A 1, Fj (R), A, 1989 Fj, 1990 I, Arg 2(R)
Elliot, C H (Sunderland) 1886 W
Elliot, E W (Sunderland) 1901 W, I, S, 1904 W
Elliot, W (United Services, RN) 1932 I, S, 1933 W, I, S, 1934 W, I
Elliott, A E (St Thomas's Hospital) 1894 S
Ellis, H A (Leicester) 2004 SA(R), A2(R), 2005 W(R), F, I, It, S, Sm, 2006 W, It, S, F(R), I, 2007 S, It, I, F1, W1, 2008 PI(R), A(R), SA(R), NZ3(R), 2009 It, W, I, F, S
Ellis, J (Wakefield) 1939 S
Ellis, S S (Queen's House) 1880 I
Emmott, C (Bradford) 1892 W
Enthoven, H J (Richmond) 1878 I
Erinle, A O (Biarritz) 2009 A(R), NZ
Estcourt, N S D (Blackheath) 1955 S
Evans, B J (Leicester) 1988 A 2, Fj
Evans, E (Sale) 1948 A, 1950 W, 1951 I, F, S, 1952 SA, W, S, I, F, 1953 I, F, S, 1954 W, NZ, I, F, 1956 W, I, S, F, 1957 W, I, F, S, 1958 W, A, I, F, S
Evans, G W (Coventry) 1972 S, 1973 W (R), F, S, NZ 2, 1974 S, I, F, W
Evans, N L (RNEC) 1932 W, I, S, 1933 W, I
Evanson, A M (Richmond) 1883 W, I, S, 1884 S
Evanson, W A D (Richmond) 1875 S, 1877 S, 1878 S, 1879 S, I, 1893 W, I, S
Evershed, F (Blackheath) 1889 M, 1890 W, S, I, 1892 W, I, S, 1893 W, I, S
Eyres, W C T (Richmond) 1927 I

Fagan, A R St L (Richmond) 1887 I
Fairbrother, K E (Coventry) 1969 I, F, S, W, SA, 1970 I, W, S, F, 1971 W, I, F
Faithfull, C K T (Harlequins) 1924 I, 1926 F, S
Fallas, H (Wakefield T) 1884 I
Farrell, A D (Saracens) 2007 S, It, I, W2, F3, [US(R), SA1, Tg(R)]
Farrell, O A (Saracens) 2012 S, It, W, F, I, SA 1, 2(R), 3(R), Fj(R), A(R), SA4(t&R), NZ, 2013 S, I, F, W, A, Arg3, NZ, 2014 F, S, I, W, It, NZ2, 4, SA, Sm, A(t&R), 2015 F 2, I 2(R), [F(R), W, A, U]
Fegan, J H C (Blackheath) 1895 W, I, S
Fernandes, C W L (Leeds) 1881 I, W, S
Fidler, J H (Gloucester) 1981 Arg 1, 2, 1984 SA 1, 2
Fidler, R J (Gloucester) 1998 NZ 2, SA 1
Field, E (Middlesex W) 1893 W, I
Fielding, K J (Moseley, Loughborough Colls) 1969 I, F, S, SA, 1970 I, F, 1972 W, I, F, S
Finch, R T (Cambridge U) 1880 S
Finlan, J F (Moseley) 1967 I, F, S, W, NZ, 1968 W, I, 1969 I, F, S, W, 1970 F, 1973 NZ 1
Finlinson, H W (Blackheath) 1895 W, I, S
Finney, S (RIE Coll) 1872 S, 1873 S
Firth, F (Halifax) 1894 W, I, S
Flatman, D L (Saracens) 2000 SA 1(t), 2(t+R), A (t), Arg (t+R), 2001 F (t), C 2(t+R), US (t+R), 2002 Arg
Fletcher, N C (OMTs) 1901 W, I, S, 1903 S
Fletcher, T (Seaton) 1897 W
Fletcher, W R B (Marlborough N) 1873 S, 1875 S
Flood, T G A L (Newcastle, Leicester) 2006 Arg(R), SA2(R), 2007 S(R), It(R), F1, W1, SA1, 2, W2(t), [A(R), F(R), SA2(R)], 2008 W, It, F, S, I, NZ2, PI(R), A(R), SA(R), NZ3, 2009 W(R), I, F, S, 2010 W, F, A1, 2, NZ, A3, Sm, SA, 2011 W1, It, F, S, I1, W3, I2(R), [Gg, R(R), S(R), F], 2012 W(R), SA 1(R), 2, 3, Fj, A, SA4, 2013 S(R), F(R), It, W(R), A(R), Arg3(R), NZ(R)

Hancock, P S (Richmond) 1904 W, I, S
Handford, F G (Manchester) 1909 W, F, I, S
Hands, R H M (Blackheath) 1910 F, S
Hanley, J (Plymouth A) 1927 W, S, F, 1928 W, I, F, S
Hanley, S M (Sale) 1999 W
Hannaford, R C (Bristol) 1971 W, I, F
Hanvey, R J (Aspatria) 1926 W, I, F, S
Hape, S E (Bath, London Irish) 2010 A1, 2, NZ, A3, Sm, SA, 2011 W1, It, F, S, I1, W3, [Gg]
Harding, E H (Devonport Services) 1931 I
Harding, R M (Bristol) 1985 R, F, S, 1987 S, [A, J, W], 1988 I 1(R), 2, A 1, 2, Fj
Harding, V S J (Saracens) 1961 F, S, 1962 W, I, F, S
Hardwick, P F (Percy Park) 1902 I, S, 1903 W, I, S, 1904 W, I, S
Hardwick, R J K (Coventry) 1996 It (R)
Hardy, E M P (Blackheath) 1951 I, F, S
Hare, W H (Nottingham, Leicester) 1974 W, 1978 F, NZ, 1979 NZ, 1980 I, F, W, S, 1981 W, S, Arg 1, 2, 1982 F, W, 1983 F, W, S, I, NZ, 1984 S, I, F, W, SA 1, 2
Harper, C H (Exeter) 1899 W
Harriman, A T (Harlequins) 1988 A
Harris, S W (Blackheath) 1920 I, S
Harris, T W (Northampton) 1929 S, 1932 I
Harrison, A C (Hartlepool R) 1931 I, S
Harrison, A L (United Services, RN) 1914 I, F
Harrison, G (Hull) 1877 I, S, 1879 S, I, 1880 S, 1885 W, I
Harrison, H C (United Services, RN) 1909 S, 1914 I, S, F
Harrison, M E (Wakefield) 1985 NZ 1, 2, 1986 S, I, F, 1987 I, F, W, S, [A, J, US, W], 1988 F, W
Hartley, B C (Blackheath) 1901 S, 1902 S
Hartley, D M (Northampton) 2008 PI(R), A(R), SA(R), NZ3(R), 2009 It, I, S, F, NZ(R), A3, Sm, SA, 2011 W1, It, F, S, I1, W2, I2(R), [Arg(R), Gg, S(R), F(R)], 2012 S, It, W, F, I, SA 1, 2, 3, 2013 S(R), I(R), F, It(R), W(R), A(R), Arg3, NZ, 2014 F, S, I, W, It, NZ2(R), 3, 4, SA, Sm(R), A, 2015 W, It, I 1, S, F 1
Haskell, J A W (Wasps, Stade Français, Ricoh Black Rams, Otago Highlanders) 2007 W1, F2, 2008 W, It, F, I(R), NZ1, 2, PI(t&R), A(R), SA, NZ3, 2009 It, W, I, F(R), S(R), Arg 1, 2(R), A(R), Arg 3, NZ, 2010 W, It, I, S, F(R), A1(R), Sm, 2011 W1, It, F, S, I1, W2, 3(R), I2, [Arg, Gg, R, S, F(R)], 2012 SA 3, 4(R), NZ(R), 2013 S(R), I, F(R), It, W(R), A(R), 2014 NZ1, Sm, A(R), 2015 W, It, I 1, S, F 1, 2(R), 3, [W(R), U]
Haslett, L W (Birkenhead Park) 1926 I, F
Hastings, G W D (Gloucester) 1955 W, I, F, S, 1957 W, I, F, S, 1958 W, A, I, F, S
Havelock, H (Hartlepool R) 1908 F, W, I
Hawcridge, J J (Bradford) 1885 W, I
Hayward, L W (Cheltenham) 1910 I
Hazell, A R (Gloucester) 2004 C, SA(t&R), 2005 W, F(t), It(R), S(R), 2007 SA1
Hazell, D St G (Leicester) 1955 W, I, F, S
Healey, A S (Leicester) 1997 I (R), W, A 1(R), 2(R), NZ 1(R), SA (R), NZ 2, 1998 F, W, S, I, A 1, NZ 1, 2, H, It, A 2, SA 2(R), 1999 US, C, [It, NZ, Tg, Fj], SA (R)], 2000 I, F, W, It, S, SA 1, 2, A, SA 3(R), 2001 W (R), It, S, F, I (R), A, R, SA, 2002 S, I, F, W, It (R), NZ (R), A (R), SA(R), 2003 F2
Hearn, R D (Bedford) 1966 F, S, 1967 I, F, S, W
Heath, A H (Oxford U) 1876 S
Heaton, J (Waterloo) 1935 W, I, S, 1939 W, I, S, 1947 I, S, F
Henderson, A P (Edinburgh Wands) 1947 W, I, S, F, 1948 I, S, F, 1949 W, I
Henderson, R S F (Blackheath) 1883 W, S, 1884 W, S, 1885 W
Heppell, W G (Devonport A) 1903 I
Herbert, A J (Wasps) 1958 F, S, 1959 W, I, F, S
Hesford, R (Bristol) 1981 S (R), 1982 A, S, F (R), 1983 F (R), 1985 R, F, S, I, W
Heslop, N J (Orrell) 1990 Arg 1, 2, 3, 1991 W, S, I, F, [US, F], 1992 W (R)
Hetherington, J G G (Northampton) 1958 A, I, 1959 W, I, F, S
Hewitt, E N (Coventry) 1951 W, I, F
Hewitt, W W (Queen's House) 1881 I, W, S, 1882 I
Hickson, J L (Bradford) 1887 W, I, S, 1890 W, S, I
Higgins, R (Liverpool) 1954 W, NZ, I, S, 1955 W, I, F, S, 1957 W, I, F, S, 1959 W
Hignell, A J (Cambridge U, Bristol) 1975 A 2, 1976 A, W, S, I, 1977 S, I, F, W, 1978 W, 1979 S, I, F, W
Hill, B A (Blackheath) 1903 I, S, 1904 W, I, 1905 W, NZ, 1906 SA, 1907 F, W
Hill, R A (Saracens) 1997 S, I, F, W, A 1, 2, NZ 1, SA, NZ 2, 1998

F, W, H (R), It (R), A 2, SA 2, 1999 S, I, F, W, A, US, C, [It, NZ, Tg, Fj (R), SA], 2000 I, F, W, It, S, SA 1, 2, A, Arg, SA 3, 2001 W, It, S, F, I, A, SA, 2002 S, I, F, W, It, NZ, A, SA, 2003 F 1, W 1, It, S, I, NZ, A, F 3, [Gg, F, A], 2004 It, S, I, W, F, NZ1, 2, A1
Hill, R J (Bath) 1984 SA 1, 2, 1985 I (R), NZ 2(R), 1986 F (R), 1987 I, F, W, [US], 1989 Fj, 1990 I, F, W, S, Arg 1, 2, 3, 1991 W, S, I, F, Fj, A, [NZ, It, US, F, S, A]
Hillard, R J (Oxford U) 1925 NZ
Hiller, R (Harlequins) 1968 W, I, F, S, 1969 I, F, S, W, SA, 1970 I, W, S, 1971 I, F, S (2[1C]), P, 1972 W, I
Hind, A E (Leicester) 1905 NZ, 1906 W
Hind, G R (Blackheath) 1910 S, 1911 I
Hipkiss, D J (Leicester) 2007 W2, F3, [Sm(R), Tg(R), F(R), SA2(R)], 2008 NZ3(R), 2009 Arg 1, 2, A, Arg 3, NZ, 2010 W(R)
Hobbs, R F A (Blackheath) 1899 S, 1903 W
Hobbs, R G S (Richmond) 1932 SA, W, I, S
Hobson, J D (Bristol) 2008 NZ2(R)
Hodges, H A (Nottingham) 1906 W, I
Hodgkinson, S D (Nottingham) 1989 R, Fj, 1990 I, F, W, S, Arg 1, 2, 3, 1991 W, S, I, F, [US]
Hodgson, C C (Sale, Saracens) 2001 R, 2002 S (R), I (R), It (R), Arg, 2003 F 1, W 1, It (R), 2004 NZ1, 2, A1, C, SA, A2, 2005 W, F, I, It, S, A, NZ, Sm, 2006 W, It, S, F, NZ, Arg, SA1, 2008 S(R), NZ1, 2010 A3(R), Sm(R), SA(R), 2011 W2(R), 3(R), 2012 S, It
Hodgson, J McD (Northern) 1932 SA, W, I, S, 1934 W, I, 1936 I
Hodgson, P K (London Irish) 2008 I(R), 2009 Arg 1(R), 2(R), A(R), Arg 3, NZ, 2010 W(R), It(R), I(R)
Hodgson, S A M (Durham City) 1960 W, I, F, S, 1961 SA, W, 1962 W, I, F, S, 1964 W
Hofmeyr, M B (Oxford U) 1950 W, F, S
Hogarth, T B (Hartlepool R) 1906 F
Holland, D (Devonport A) 1912 W, I, S
Holliday, T E (Aspatria) 1923 S, F, 1925 I, S, F, 1926 F, S
Holmes, C B (Manchester) 1947 S, 1948 I, F
Holmes, E (Manningham) 1890 S, I
Holmes, W A (Nuneaton) 1950 W, I, F, S, 1951 W, I, F, S, 1952 SA, S, I, F, 1953 W, I, F, S
Holmes, W B (Cambridge U) 1949 W, I, F, S
Hook, W G (Gloucester) 1951 S, 1952 SA, W
Hooper, C A (Middlesex W) 1894 W, I, S
Hopley, D P (Wasps) 1995 [WS (R)], SA, WS
Hopley, F J V (Blackheath) 1907 F, W, 1908 I
Horak, M J (London Irish) 2002 Arg
Hordern, P C (Gloucester) 1931 I, S, F, 1934 W
Horley, C H (Swinton) 1885 I
Hornby, A N (Manchester) 1877 I, S, 1878 S, I, 1880 I, 1881 I, S, 1882 I, S
Horrocks-Taylor, J P (Cambridge U, Leicester, Middlesbrough) 1958 W, A, 1961 S, 1962 S, 1963 NZ 1, 2, A, 1964 NZ, W
Horsfall, E L (Harlequins) 1949 W
Horton, A L (Blackheath) 1965 W, I, F, S, 1966 F, S, 1967 NZ
Horton, J P (Bath) 1978 W, S, I, NZ, 1980 I, F, W, S, 1981 W, 1983 S, I, 1984 SA 1, 2
Horton, N E (Moseley, Toulouse) 1969 I, F, S, W, 1971 I, F, S, 1974 S, 1975 W, 1977 S, I, F, W, 1978 F, W, 1979 S, I, F, W, 1980 I
Hosen, R W (Bristol, Northampton) 1963 NZ 1, 2, A, 1964 F, S, 1967 A, I, F, S, W
Hosking, G R d'A (Devonport Services) 1949 W, I, F, S, 1950 W
Houghton, S (Runcorn) 1892 I, 1896 W
Howard, P D (O Millhillians) 1930 W, I, F, S, 1931 W, I, S, F
Hubbard, G C (Blackheath) 1892 W, I
Hubbard, J C (Harlequins) 1930 S
Hudson, A (Gloucester) 1906 W, I, F, 1908 F, W, I, S, 1910 F
Hughes, G E (Barrow) 1896 S
Hull, P A (Bristol, RAF) 1994 SA 1, 2, R, C
Hulme, F C (Birkenhead Park) 1903 W, I, 1905 W, I
Hunt, J T (Manchester) 1882 I, S, 1884 W
Hunt, R (Manchester) 1880 I, 1881 W, S, 1882 I
Hunt, W H (Manchester) 1876 S, 1877 I, S, 1878 I
Hunter, I (Northampton) 1992 C, 1993 F, W, 1994 F, W, 1995 [WS, F]
Huntsman, R P (Headingley) 1985 NZ 1, 2
Hurst, A C B (Wasps) 1962 S
Huskisson, T F (OMTs) 1937 W, I, S, 1938 W, I, 1939 W, I, S
Hutchinson, F (Headingley) 1909 F, I, S
Hutchinson, J E (Durham City) 1906 I
Hutchinson, W C (RIE Coll) 1876 S, 1877 I
Hutchinson, W H H (Hull) 1875 I, 1876 I

Leyland, R (Waterloo) 1935 W, I, S
Linnett, M S (Moseley) 1989 Fj
Lipman, M R (Bath) 2004 NZ2(R), A1(R), 2006 A2, 2008 It, F, S, I, PI(R), A(R), NZ3
Livesay, R O'H (Blackheath) 1898 W, 1899 W
Lloyd, L D (Leicester) 2000 SA 1(R), 2(R), 2001 C 1, 2, US
Lloyd, R H (Harlequins) 1967 NZ, 1968 W, I, F, S
Locke, H M (Birkenhead Park) 1923 S, F, 1924 W, F, S, 1925 W, I, S, F, 1927 W, I, S
Lockwood, R E (Heckmondwike) 1887 W, I, S, 1889 M, 1891 W, I, S, 1892 W, I, S, 1893 W, I, 1894 W, I
Login, S H M (RN Coll) 1876 I
Lohden, F C (Blackheath) 1893 W
Long, A E (Bath) 1997 A 2, 2001 US (R)
Longland, R J (Northampton) 1932 S, 1933 W, S, 1934 W, I, S, 1935 W, I, S, 1936 NZ, W, I, S, 1937 W, I, S, 1938 W, I, S
Lowe, C N (Cambridge U, Blackheath) 1913 SA, W, F, I, S, 1914 W, I, S, F, 1920 W, F, I, S, 1921 W, I, S, F, 1922 W, I, F, S, 1923 W, I, S, F
Lowrie, F W (Wakefield T) 1889 M, 1890 W
Lowry, W M (Birkenhead Park) 1920 F
Lozowski, R A P (Wasps) 1984 A
Luddington, W G E (Devonport Services) 1923 W, I, S, F, 1924 W, I, F, S, 1925 W, I, S, F, 1926 W
Luger, D D (Harlequins, Saracens) 1998 H, It, SA 2, 1999 S, I, F, W, A, US, C, [It, NZ, Tg, Fj, SA], 2000 SA 1, A, Arg, SA 3, 2001 W, I, A, R, SA, 2002 F (R), W, It, 2003 F 1, W 1, It, S (R), I (R), NZ(R), W 2, [Gg(R), SA(R), U, W]
Lund, M B (Sale) 2006 A1, 2(R), NZ(R), Arg(t&R), 2007 S, It, I, F1(R), W1(R), SA2
Luscombe, F (Gipsies) 1872 S, 1873 S, 1875 I, S, 1876 I, S
Luscombe, J H (Gipsies) 1871 S
Luxmoore, A F C C (Richmond) 1900 S, 1901 W
Luya, H F (Waterloo, Headingley) 1948 W, I, S, F, 1949 W
Lyon, A (Liverpool) 1871 S
Lyon, G H d'O (United Services, RN) 1908 S, 1909 A

McCanlis, M A (Gloucester) 1931 W, I
McCarthy, N (Gloucester) 1999 I (t), US (R), 2000 It (R)
McFadyean, C W (Moseley) 1966 I, F, S, 1967 A, I, F, S, W, NZ, 1968 W, I
MacIlwaine, A H (United Services, Hull & E Riding) 1912 W, I, S, F, 1920 I
Mackie, O G (Wakefield T, Cambridge U) 1897 S, 1898 I
Mackinlay, J E H (St George's Hospital) 1872 S, 1873 S, 1875 I
MacLaren, W (Manchester) 1871 S
MacLennan, R R F (OMTs) 1925 I, S, F
McLeod, N F (RIE Coll) 1879 S, I
Madge, R J P (Exeter) 1948 A, W, I, S
Malir, F W S (Otley) 1930 W, I, S
Mallett, J A (Bath) 1995 [WS (R)]
Mallinder, J (Sale) 1997 Arg 1, 2
Mangles, R H (Richmond) 1897 W, I
Manley, D C (Exeter) 1963 W, I, F, S
Mann, W E (United Services, Army) 1911 W, F, I
Mantell, N D (Rosslyn Park) 1975 A 1
Mapletoft, M S (Gloucester) 1997 Arg 2
Markendale, E T (Manchester R) 1880 I
Marler, J W G (Harlequins) 2012 SA 1, 2, 3, Fj, A, 2013 S, I, F, It(R), W, Arg1, 2, A(R), Arg3, NZ, 2014 F, S, I, W, NZ1, 2, 3, 4, SA, Sm, A, 2015 It, I 1, S, F 1, 3, I 2, [Fj, W, A, U(R)]
Marques, R W D (Cambridge U, Harlequins) 1956 W, I, S, F, 1957 W, I, F, S, 1958 W, A, I, F, S, 1959 W, I, F, S, 1960 W, I, F, S, 1961 SA, W
Marquis, J C (Birkenhead Park) 1900 I, S
Marriott, C J B (Blackheath) 1884 W, I, S, 1886 W, I, S, 1887 I
Marriott, E E (Manchester) 1876 I
Marriott, V R (Harlequins) 1963 NZ 1, 2, A, 1964 NZ
Marsden, G H (Morley) 1900 W, I, S
Marsh, H (RIE Coll) 1873 S
Marsh, J (Swinton) 1892 I
Marshall, H (Blackheath) 1893 W
Marshall, M W (Blackheath) 1873 S, 1874 S, 1875 I, S, 1876 I, S, 1877 I, S, 1878 S, I
Marshall, R M (Oxford U) 1938 I, S, 1939 W, I, S
Martin, C R (Bath) 1985 I, S, F, W
Martin, N O (Harlequins) 1972 F (R)
Martindale, S A (Kendal) 1929 F
Massey, E J (Leicester) 1925 W, I, S

Mather, B-J (Sale) 1999 W
Mathias, J L (Bristol) 1905 W, I, S, NZ
Matters, J C (RNE Coll) 1899 S
Matthews, J R C (Harlequins) 1949 F, S, 1950 I, F, S, 1952 SA, W, S, I, F
Maud, P (Blackheath) 1893 W, I
Maxwell, A W (New Brighton, Headingley) 1975 A 1, 1976 A, W, S, I, F, 1978 F
Maxwell-Hyslop, J E (Oxford U) 1922 I, F, S
May, J J (Gloucester) 2013 Arg 2, 2014 F, S, I, W, It, NZ1, 4, SA, Sm, A, 2015 W, It, F 2, 3, I 2, [Fj, W, A]
May, T A (Newcastle) 2009 Arg 1, 2
Maynard, A F (Cambridge U) 1914 W, I, S
Mears, L A (Bath) 2005 Sm(R), 2006 W(R), It(R), F(R), I, A1, 2(R), NZ(R), Arg(R), SA1(R), 2, 2007 S(R), It(R), I(R), W1(R), F2(R), 3(R), [Tg(R)], 2008 W(R), It(R), F(R), S, I, NZ1, 2, PI, A, SA, NZ3, 2009 It, W, I, F, S, 2010 I(R), 2011 W2(R), 3(R), [R(R)], 2012 I(R), SA 1(R), 2(R), 3(t)
Meikle, G W C (Waterloo) 1934 W, I, S
Meikle, S S C (Waterloo) 1929 S
Mellish, F W (Blackheath) 1920 W, F, I, S, 1921 W, I
Melville, N D (Wasps) 1984 A, 1985 I, W, NZ 1, 2, 1986 W, S, I, F, 1988 F, W, S, I 1
Merriam, L P B (Blackheath) 1920 W, F
Michell, A T (Oxford U) 1875 I, S, 1876 I
Middleton, B B (Birkenhead Park) 1882 I, 1883 I
Middleton, J A (Richmond) 1922 S
Miles, J H (Leicester) 1903 W
Millett, H (Richmond) 1920 F
Mills, F W (Marlborough N) 1872 S, 1873 S
Mills, S G F (Gloucester) 1981 Arg 1, 2, 1983 W, 1984 SA 1, A
Mills, W A (Devonport A) 1906 W, I, S, F, SA, 1907 F, W, I, S, 1908 F, W
Milman, D L K (Bedford) 1937 W, 1938 W, I, S
Milton, C H (Camborne S of M) 1906 I
Milton, J G (Camborne S of M) 1904 W, I, S, 1905 S, 1907 I
Milton, W H (Marlborough N) 1874 S, 1875 I
Mitchell, F (Blackheath) 1895 W, I, S, 1896 W, I, S
Mitchell, W G (Richmond) 1890 W, S, I, 1891 W, I, S, 1893 S
Mobbs, E R (Northampton) 1909 A, W, F, I, S, 1910 I, F
Moberley, W O (Ravenscourt Park) 1872 S
Monye, Y C C (Harlequins) 2008 PI, A, SA, NZ3, 2009 F, S, A, Arg 3, NZ, 2010 W, It, I, S, 2012 Fj
Moody, L W (Leicester, Bath) 2001 C 1, 2, US, I (R), R, SA (R), 2002 I (R), W, It, Arg, NZ, A, SA, 2003 F 1, W 2, F 2, 3(R), [Gg(R), SA, Sm(R), U, W, F(R), A(R)], 2004 C, SA, A2, 2005 F, I, It, S, A, NZ, Sm, 2006 W, It, S, F, I, A1, NZ, Arg, SA1(R), 2(R), W2(R), 2007 [US(R), SA1(R), Sm(R), Tg, A, F, SA2], 2008 W, 2009 A, Arg 3, NZ, 2010 W, It, I, S(R), F, A1, 2, NZ, A3, SA, 2011 W2, [Gg, R, S, F]
Moore, B C (Nottingham, Harlequins) 1987 S, [A, J, W], 1988 F, W, S, I 1, 2, A 1, 2, Fj, A, 1989 S, I, F, W, R, Fj, 1990 I, F, W, S, Arg 1, 2, 1991 W, S, I, F, Fj, A, [NZ, It, F, S, A], 1992 S, I, F, W, SA, 1993 F, W, S, I, NZ, 1994 S, I, F, W, SA 1, 2, R, C, 1995 I, F, W, S, [Arg, It, WS (R), A, NZ, F]
Moore, E J (Blackheath) 1883 I, S
Moore, N J N H (Bristol) 1904 W, I, S
Moore, P B C (Blackheath) 1951 W
Moore, W K T (Leicester) 1947 W, I, 1949 F, S, 1950 I, F, S
Mordell, R J (Rosslyn Park) 1978 W
Morfitt, S (W Hartlepool) 1894 W, I, S, 1896 W, I, S
Morgan, B J (Scarlets, Gloucester) 2012 S(R), It(R), W, F, I, SA 1, 2, 4, NZ, 2013 S, Arg1, 2, A(R), Arg3(R), NZ(R), 2014 F(R), S(R), I(R), W, It, NZ1, 2, 3(R), 4(R), SA(R), Sm, A, 2015 F 2, I 2, [Fj, A]
Morgan, J R (Hawick) 1920 W
Morgan, O C (Gloucester) 2007 S, I
Morgan, W G D (Medicals, Newcastle) 1960 W, I, F, S, 1961 SA, W, I, F, S
Morley, A J (Bristol) 1972 SA, 1973 NZ 1, W, I, 1975 S, A 1, 2
Morris, A D W (United Services, RN) 1909 A, W, F
Morris, C D (Liverpool St Helens, Orrell) 1988 A, 1989 S, I, F, W, 1992 S, I, F, W, C, SA, 1993 S, W, I, 1994 F, W, SA 1, 2, R, 1995 S (t), [Arg, WS, A, NZ, F]
Morris, R (Northampton) 2003 W 1, It
Morrison, P H (Cambridge U) 1890 W, S, I, 1891 I
Morse, S (Marlborough N) 1873 S, 1874 S, 1875 S
Mortimer, W (Marlborough N) 1899 W
Morton, H J S (Blackheath) 1909 I, S, 1910 W, I
Moss, F J S (Broughton Rangers) 1885 W, I, 1886 W

Mullan, M J (Worcester, Wasps) 2010 It(R), 2013 NZ(R), 2014 It(R), NZ2(R), 3(R), 4(R), SA(R), Sm(R), A(R)
Mullins, A R (Harlequins) 1989 Fj
Mycock, J (Sale) 1947 W, I, S, F, 1948 A
Myers, E (Bradford) 1920 I, S, 1921 W, I, 1922 W, I, F, S, 1923 W, I, S, F, 1924 W, I, F, S, 1925 S, F
Myers, H (Keighley) 1898 I
Myler, S J (Northampton) 2013 Arg 2(R)

Nanson, W M B (Carlisle) 1907 F, W
Narraway, L J W (Gloucester) 2008 W, It(R), S(R), NZ1, 2, 2009 W(R), I(R)
Nash, E H (Richmond) 1875 I
Neale, B A (Rosslyn Park) 1951 I, F, S
Neale, M E (Blackheath) 1912 F
Neame, S (O Cheltonians) 1879 S, I, 1880 I, S
Neary, A (Broughton Park) 1971 W, I, F, S (2[1C]), P, 1972 W, I, F, S, SA, 1973 NZ 1, W, I, F, S, NZ 2, A, 1974 S, I, F, W, 1975 I, F, W, S, A 1, 1976 A, W, S, I, F, 1977 I, 1978 F (R), 1979 S, I, F, W, NZ, 1980 I, F, W, S
Nelmes, B G (Cardiff) 1975 A 1, 2, 1978 W, S, I, NZ
Newbold, C J (Blackheath) 1904 W, I, S, 1905 W, I, S
Newman, S C (Oxford U) 1947 F, 1948 A, W
Newton, A W (Blackheath) 1907 S
Newton, P A (Blackheath) 1882 S
Newton-Thompson, J O (Oxford U) 1947 S, F
Nicholl, W (Brighouse R) 1892 W, S
Nicholas, P L (Exeter) 1902 W
Nicholson, B E (Harlequins) 1938 W, I
Nicholson, E S (Leicester) 1935 W, I, S, 1936 NZ, W
Nicholson, E T (Birkenhead Park) 1900 W, I
Nicholson, T (Rockcliff) 1893 I
Ninnes, B F (Coventry) 1971 W
Noon, J D (Newcastle) 2001 C 1, 2, US, 2003 W 2, F 2(t+R), 2005 W, F, I, It, S, A, NZ, 2006 W, It, S, F, I, 2006 A1(R), 2, NZ, Arg, SA1, 2, 2007 SA2, F2, [US, SA1], 2008 It, F, S, I, NZ1(R), 2, PI, A, SA, NZ3, 2009 It
Norman, D J (Leicester) 1932 SA, W
North, E H G (Blackheath) 1891 W, I, S
Northmore, S (Millom) 1897 I
Novak, M J (Harlequins) 1970 W, S, F
Novis, A L (Blackheath) 1929 S, F, 1930 W, I, F, 1933 I, S
Nowell, J T (Exeter) 2014 F, S, I, W, It, 2015 I 1, S, F 1, 3, [U]

Oakeley, F E (United Services, RN) 1913 S, 1914 I, S, F
Oakes, R F (Hartlepool R) 1897 W, I, S, 1898 I, S, W, 1899 W, S
Oakley, L F L (Bedford) 1951 W
Obolensky, A (Oxford U) 1936 NZ, W, I, S
Ojo, T O (London Irish) 2008 NZ1, 2
Ojomoh, S O (Bath, Gloucester) 1994 I, F, SA 1(R), 2, R, 1995 S (R), [Arg, WS, A (t), F], 1996 F, 1998 NZ 1
Old, A G B (Middlesbrough, Leicester, Sheffield) 1972 W, I, F, S, SA, 1973 NZ 2, A, 1974 S, I, F, W, 1975 I, A 2, 1976 S, I, 1978 F
Oldham, W L (Coventry) 1908 S, 1909 A
Olver, C J (Northampton) 1990 Arg 3, 1991 [US], 1992 C
O'Neill, A (Teignmouth, Torquay A) 1901 W, I, S
Openshaw, W E (Manchester) 1879 I
Orwin, J (Gloucester, RAF, Bedford) 1985 R, F, S, I, W, NZ 1, 2, 1988 F, W, S, I 1, 2, A 1, 2
Osborne, R R (Manchester) 1871 S
Osborne, S H (Oxford U) 1905 S
Oti, C (Cambridge U, Nottingham, Wasps) 1988 S, I 1, 1989 S, I, F, W, R, 1990 Arg 1, 2, 1991 Fj, A, [NZ, It]
Oughtred, B (Hartlepool R) 1901 S, 1902 W, I, S, 1903 W, I
Owen, J E (Coventry) 1963 W, I, F, S, A, 1964 NZ, 1965 W, I, F, S, 1966 I, F, S, 1967 NZ
Owen-Smith, H G O (St Mary's Hospital) 1934 W, I, S, 1936 NZ, W, I, S, 1937 W, I, S

Page, J J (Bedford, Northampton) 1971 W, I, F, S, 1975 S
Paice, D J (London Irish) 2008 NZ1(R), 2(R), 2012 Fj(R), A(R), SA4(R), NZ(R), 2013 Arg1(R), 2(R)
Pallant, J N (Notts) 1967 I, F, S
Palmer, A C (London Hospital) 1909 I, S
Palmer, F H (Richmond) 1905 W
Palmer, G V (Richmond) 1928 I, F, S
Palmer, J A (Bath) 1984 SA 1, 2, 1986 I (R)
Palmer, T P (Leeds, Wasps, Stade Français) 2001 US (R), 2006 Arg(R), SA1, 2, 2007 It(R), I(R), F1, W1, 2008 NZ1, 2, PI(R),

A, SA, 2010 F(R), A1, 2, NZ, A3, Sm, SA, 2011 W1, It, F, S, I1, W2, 3(R), I2(R), [Arg(R), Gg, R, S(R), F], 2012 S, It, F(R), I(R), SA 1(R), 2(R), 3, Fj, A
Pargetter, T A (Coventry) 1962 S, 1963 F, NZ 1
Parker, G W (Gloucester) 1938 I, S
Parker, Hon S (Liverpool) 1874 S, 1875 S
Parling, G M W (Leicester, Exeter) 2012 S(R), It(R), W, F, I, SA 1, 2, 3, Fj, A, SA4, NZ, 2013 S, I, F, It, W, Arg3(R), NZ(R), 2014 NZ1, 2, 2015 S(R), F 1, 2, I 2, [Fj, W, A, U]
Parsons, E I (RAF) 1939 S
Parsons, M J (Northampton) 1968 W, I, F, S
Patterson, W M (Sale) 1961 SA, S
Pattisson, R M (Blackheath) 1883 I, S
Paul, H R (Gloucester) 2002 F(R), 2004 It(t&R), S(R), C, SA, A2
Paul, J E (RIE Coll) 1875 S
Payne, A T (Bristol) 1935 I, S
Payne, C M (Harlequins) 1964 I, F, S, 1965 I, F, S, 1966 W, I, F, S
Payne, J H (Broughton) 1882 S, 1883 W, I, S, 1884 I, 1885 W, I
Payne, T A N (Wasps) 2004 A1, 2006 A1(R), 2(R), 2007 F1, W1, 2008 It, NZ1(R), 2, SA, NZ3, 2009 Arg 1, 2, A, Arg 3, NZ, 2010 W, It, I, S, F, A1, 2
Pearce, G S (Northampton) 1979 S, I, F, W, 1981 Arg 1, 2, 1982 A, S, 1983 F, W, S, I, NZ, 1984 I, SA 2, A, 1985 R, F, S, I, W, NZ 1, 2, 1986 W, S, I, F, 1987 I, F, W, S, [A, US, W], 1988 Fj, 1991 [US]
Pears, D (Harlequins) 1990 Arg 1, 2, 1992 F (R), 1994 F
Pearson, A W (Blackheath) 1875 I, S, 1876 I, S, 1877 S, 1878 S, I
Peart, T G A H (Hartlepool R) 1964 F, S
Pease, F E (Hartlepool R) 1887 I
Pennell, C J (Worcester) 2014 NZ1(R)
Penny, S H (Leicester) 1909 A
Penny, W J (United Hospitals) 1878 I, 1879 S, I
Percival, L J (Rugby) 1891 I, 1892 I, 1893 S
Periton, H G (Waterloo) 1925 W, 1926 W, I, F, S, 1927 W, I, S, F, 1928 A, I, F, S, 1929 W, I, S, F, 1930 W, I, F, S
Perrott, E S (O Cheltonians) 1875 I
Perry, D G (Bedford) 1963 F, S, NZ 1, 2, A 1964 NZ, W, I, 1965 W, I, F, S, 1966 W, I, F
Perry, M B (Bath) 1997 A 2, NZ 1, SA, NZ 2, 1998 W, S, I, A 1, NZ 1, 2, SA 1, H, It, A 2, 1999 I, F, W, A US, C, [It, NZ, Tg, Fj, SA], 2000 I, F, W, It, S, SA 1, 2, A, SA 3, 2001 W (R), F, A
Perry, S A (Bristol) 2006 NZ, Arg, SA1(R), 2(R), 2007 I(R), F1(R), W1(R), SA1(R), 2(R), W2, F2, 3, [US, SA1]
Perry, S V (Cambridge U, Waterloo) 1947 W, I, 1948 A, W, I, S, F
Peters, J (Plymouth) 1906 S, F, 1907 I, S, 1908 W
Phillips, C (Birkenhead Park) 1880 S, 1881 I, S
Phillips, M S (Fylde) 1958 A, I, F, S, 1959 W, I, F, S, 1960 W, I, S, 1961 W, 1963 W, I, F, S, NZ 1, 2, A, 1964 NZ, W, I, F, S
Pickering, A S (Harrogate) 1907 I
Pickering, R D A (Bradford) 1967 I, F, S, W, 1968 F, S
Pickles, R C W (Bristol) 1922 I, F
Pierce, R (Liverpool) 1898 I, 1903 S
Pilkington, W N (Cambridge U) 1898 S
Pillman, C H (Blackheath) 1910 W, I, F, S, 1911 W, F, I, S, 1912 W, F, 1913 SA, W, F, I, S, 1914 W, I, S
Pillman, R L (Blackheath) 1914 F
Pinch, J (Lancaster) 1896 W, I, 1897 S
Pinching, W W (Guy's Hospital) 1872 S
Pitman, I J (Oxford U) 1922 S
Plummer, K C (Bristol) 1969 W, 1976 S, I, F
Pool-Jones, R J (Stade Francais) 1998 A 1
Poole, F O (Oxford U) 1895 W, I, S
Poole, R W (Hartlepool R) 1896 S
Pope, E B (Blackheath) 1931 W, S, F
Portus, G V (Blackheath) 1908 F, I
Potter, S (Leicester) 1998 A 1(t)
Poulton, R W (later Poulton Palmer) (Oxford U, Harlequins, Liverpool) 1909 F, I, S, 1910 W, 1911 S, 1912 W, I, S, 1913 SA, W, F, I, S, 1914 W, I, S, F
Powell, D L (Northampton) 1966 W, I, 1969 I, F, S, W, 1971 W, I, F, S (2[1C])
Pratten, W E (Blackheath) 1927 S, F
Preece, I (Coventry) 1948 I, S, F, 1949 F, S, 1950 W, I, F, S, 1951 W, I, F
Preece, P S (Coventry) 1972 SA, 1973 NZ 1, W, I, F, S, NZ 2, 1975 I, F, W, A 2, 1976 W (R)
Preedy, M (Gloucester) 1984 SA 1

Prentice, F D (Leicester) 1928 I, F, S
Prescott, R E (Harlequins) 1937 W, I, 1938 I, 1939 W, I, S
Preston, N J (Richmond) 1979 NZ, 1980 I, F
Price, H L (Harlequins) 1922 I, S, 1923 W, I
Price, J (Coventry) 1961 I
Price, P L A (RIE Coll) 1877 I, S, 1878 S
Price, T W (Cheltenham) 1948 S, F, 1949 W, I, F, S
Probyn, J A (Wasps, Askeans) 1988 F, W, S, I 1, 2, A 1, 2, A, 1989 S, I, R (R), 1990 I, F, W, S, Arg 1, 2, 3, 1991 W, S, I, F, Fj, A, [NZ, It, F, S, A], 1992 S, I, F, W, 1993 F, W, S, I
Prout, D H (Northampton) 1968 W, I
Pullin, J V (Bristol) 1966 W, 1968 W, I, F, S, 1969 I, F, S, W, SA, 1970 I, W, S, F, 1971 W, I, F, S (2[1C]), P, 1972 W, I, F, S, SA, 1973 NZ 1, W, I, F, S, NZ 2, A, 1974 S, I, F, W, 1975 I, W (R), S, A 1, 2, 1976 F
Purdy, S J (Rugby) 1962 S
Pyke, J (St Helens Recreation) 1892 W
Pym, J A (Blackheath) 1912 W, I, S, F

Quinn, J P (New Brighton) 1954 W, NZ, I, S, F

Rafter, M (Bristol) 1977 S, F, W, 1978 F, W, S, I, 1979 S, I, F, W, NZ, 1980 W(R), 1981 W, Arg 1, 2
Ralston, C W (Richmond) 1971 S (C), P, 1972 W, I, F, S, SA, 1973 NZ 1, W, I, F, S, NZ 2, A, 1974 S, I, F, W, 1975 I, F, W, S
Ramsden, H E (Bingley) 1898 S, W
Ranson, J M (Rosslyn Park) 1963 NZ 1, 2, A, 1964 W, I, F, S
Raphael, J E (OMTs) 1902 W, I, S, 1905 W, S, NZ, 1906 W, S, F
Ravenscroft, J (Birkenhead Park) 1881 I
Ravenscroft, S C W (Saracens) 1998 A 1, NZ 2(R)
Rawlinson, W C W (Blackheath) 1876 S
Redfern, S P (Leicester) 1984 I (R)
Redman, N C (Bath) 1984 A, 1986 S (R), 1987 I, S, [A, J, W], 1988 Fj, 1990 Arg 1, 2, 1991 Fj, [It, US], 1993 NZ, 1994 F, W, SA 1, 2, 1997 Arg 1, A 1
Redmond, G F (Cambridge U) 1970 F
Redwood, B W (Bristol) 1968 W, I
Rees, D L (Sale) 1997 A 2, NZ 1, SA, NZ 2, 1998 F, W, SA 2(R), 1999 S, I, F, A
Rees, G W (Nottingham) 1984 SA 2(R), A, 1986 I, F, 1987 F, W, S, [A, J, US, W], 1988 S (R), I 1, 2, A 1, 2, Fj, 1989 W (R), R (R), Fj (R), 1990 Arg 3(R), 1991 Fj, [US]
Rendall, P A G (Wasps, Askeans) 1984 W, SA 2, 1986 W, S, 1987 I, F, S, [A, J, W], 1988 F, W, S, I 1, 2, A 1, 2, A, 1989 S, I, F, W, R, 1990 I, F, W, S, 1991 [It (R)]
Rew, H (Blackheath) 1929 S, F, 1930 F, S, 1931 W, S, F, 1934 W, I, S
Reynolds, F J (O Cranleighans) 1937 S, 1938 I, S
Reynolds, S (Richmond) 1900 W, I, S, 1901 I
Rhodes, J (Castleford) 1896 W, I, S
Richards, D (Leicester) 1986 I, F, 1987 S, [A, J, US, W], 1988 F, W, S, I 1, A 1, 2, Fj, A, 1989 S, I, F, W, R, 1990 Arg 3, 1991 W, S, I, F, Fj, A, [NZ, It, US], 1992 S (R), F, W, C, 1993 NZ, 1994 W, SA 1, C, 1995 I, F, W, S, [WS, A, NZ], 1996 F (t), S, I
Richards, E E (Plymouth A) 1929 S, F
Richards, J J (Bradford) 1891 W, I, S
Richards, P C (Gloucester, London Irish) 2006 A1, 2, NZ(R), Arg(R), SA1, 2, 2007 [US(R), SA1(R), Tg(R), A(t), F(R)], 2008 NZ2(R)
Richards, S B (Richmond) 1965 W, I, F, S, 1967 A, I, F, S, W
Richardson, J V (Birkenhead Park) 1928 A, W, I, F, S
Richardson, W R (Manchester) 1881 I
Rickards, C H (Gipsies) 1873 S
Rimmer, G (Waterloo) 1949 W, I, 1950 W, 1951 W, I, F, 1952 SA, W, 1954 W, NZ, I, S
Rimmer, L I (Bath) 1961 SA, W, I, F, S
Ripley, A G (Rosslyn Park) 1972 W, I, F, S, SA, 1973 NZ 1, W, I, F, S, NZ 2, A, 1974 S, I, F, W, 1975 I, F, S, A 1, 2, 1976 A, W, S

Risman, A B W (Loughborough Coll) 1959 W, I, F, S, 1961 SA, W, I, F
Ritson, J A S (Northern) 1910 F, S, 1912 F, 1913 SA, W, F, I, S
Rittson-Thomas, G C (Oxford U) 1951 W, I, F
Robbins, G L (Coventry) 1986 W, S
Robbins, P G D (Oxford U, Moseley, Coventry) 1956 W, I, S, F, 1957 W, I, F, S, 1958 W, A, I, S, 1960 W, I, F, S, 1961 SA, W, 1962 S
Roberts, A D (Northern) 1911 W, F, I, S, 1912 I, S, F, 1914 I
Roberts, E W (RNE Coll) 1901 W, I, 1905 NZ, 1906 W, I, 1907 S
Roberts, G D (Harlequins) 1907 S, 1908 F, W
Roberts, J (Sale) 1960 W, I, F, S, 1961 SA, W, I, F, S, 1962 W, I, F, S, 1963 W, I, F, S, 1964 NZ
Roberts, R S (Coventry) 1932 I
Roberts, S (Swinton) 1887 W, I
Roberts, V G (Penryn, Harlequins) 1947 F, 1949 W, I, F, S, 1950 I, F, S, 1951 W, I, F, S, 1956 W, I, S, F
Robertshaw, A R (Bradford) 1886 W, I, S, 1887 W, S
Robinson, A (Blackheath) 1889 M, 1890 W, S, I
Robinson, E T (Coventry) 1954 S, 1961 I, F, S
Robinson, G C (Percy Park) 1897 I, S, 1898 I, 1899 W, 1900 I, S, 1901 I, S
Robinson, J T (Sale) 2001 It (R), S (R), F (R), I, A, R, SA, 2002 S, I, F, It, A, SA, 2003 F 1, W 1, S, I, NZ, A F 3, [Gg, SA, Sm, U(R), W, F, A], 2004 It, S, I, W, F, C, SA, A2, 2005 W, F, I, 2007 S, It, F1, W1, SA1, W2, F3, [US, SA1, A, F, SA2]
Robinson, J J (Headingley) 1893 S, 1902 W, I, S
Robinson, R A (Bath) 1988 A 2, Fj, A, 1989 S, I, F, W, 1995 SA
Robshaw, C D C (Harlequins) 2009 Arg 2, 2012 S, It, W, F, I, SA 1, 2, Fj, A, SA4, NZ, 2013 S, I, F, It, W, A, Arg3, NZ, 2014 F, S, I, W, It, NZ1, 2, 3, 4, SA, Sm, A, 2015 W, It, I 1, S, F 1, 3, I 2, [Fj, W, A, U]
Robson, A (Northern) 1924 W, I, F, S, 1926 W
Robson, M (Oxford U) 1930 W, I, F, S
Rodber, T A K (Army, Northampton) 1992 S, I, 1993 NZ, 1994 I, F, W, SA 1, 2, R, C, 1995 I, F, W, S, [Arg, It, WS (R), A, NZ, F], SA, WS, 1996 W, S (R), I (t), It, Arg, 1997 S, I, F, W, A 1, 1998 H (R), It (R), A 2, SA 2, 1999 S, I, F, W, A, US (R), [NZ (R), Fj (R)]
Rogers, D P (Bedford) 1961 I, F, S, 1962 W, I, F, 1963 W, I, F, S, NZ 1, 2, A, 1964 NZ, W, I, F, S, 1965 W, I, F, S, 1966 W, I, F, S, 1967 A, S, W, NZ, 1969 I, F, S, W
Rogers, J H (Moseley) 1890 W, S, I, 1891 S
Rokoduguni, S (Bath) 2014 NZ 4
Rogers, W L Y (Blackheath) 1905 W, I
Rollitt, D M (Bristol) 1967 I, F, S, W, 1969 I, F, S, W, 1975 S, A, I, 2
Roncoroni, A D S (West Herts, Richmond) 1933 W, I, S
Rose, W M H (Cambridge U, Coventry, Harlequins) 1981 I, F, 1982 A, S, I, 1987 I, F, W, S, [A]
Rossborough, P A (Coventry) 1971 W, 1973 NZ 2, A, 1974 S, I, 1975 I, F
Rosser, D W A (Wasps) 1965 W, I, F, S, 1966 W
Rotherham, Alan (Richmond) 1883 W, S, 1884 W, S, 1885 W, I, 1886 W, I, S, 1887 W, I, S
Rotherham, Arthur (Richmond) 1898 S, W, 1899 W, I, S
Roughley, D (Liverpool) 1973 A, 1974 S, I
Rowell, R E (Leicester) 1964 W, 1965 W
Rowley, A J (Coventry) 1932 SA
Rowley, H C (Manchester) 1879 S, I, 1880 I, S, 1881 I, W, S, 1882 I, S
Rowntree, G C (Leicester) 1995 S (t), [It, WS], WS, 1996 F, W, S, I, It, Arg, 1997 S, I, F, W, A 1, 1998 A 1, NZ 1, 2, SA 1, H (R), It (R), 1999 US, C, [It (R), Tg, Fj (R)], 2001 C 1, 2, US, I(R), A, R, SA, 2002 S, I, F, It, 2003 F 1(R), W 1, It, S, I, NZ, F 2, 2004 C, SA, A2, 2005 W, F, I, It, 2006 A1, 2
Royds, P M R (Blackheath) 1898 S, W, 1899 W
Royle, A V (Broughton R) 1889 M
Rudd, E L (Liverpool) 1965 W, I, S, 1966 W, I, S
Russell, R F (Leicester) 1905 NZ
Rutherford, D (Percy Park, Gloucester) 1960 W, I, F, S, 1961 SA, 1965 W, I, F, S, 1966 W, I, F, S, 1967 NZ
Ryalls, H J (New Brighton) 1885 W, I
Ryan, D (Wasps, Newcastle) 1990 Arg 1, 2, 1992 C, 1998 S
Ryan, P H (Richmond) 1955 W, I

Sackey, P H (Wasps) 2006 NZ, Arg, 2007 F2, 3(R), [SA1, Sm, Tg, A, F, SA2], 2008 W, It, F, S, I, PI, A, SA, NZ3, 2009 It, W, I
Sadler, E H (Army) 1933 I, S
Sagar, J W (Cambridge U) 1901 W, I

ENGLAND

Stokes, F (Blackheath) 1871 S, 1872 S, 1873 S
Stokes, L (Blackheath) 1875 I, 1876 S, 1877 I, S, 1878 S, 1879 S, I, 1880 I, S, 1881 I, W, S
Stone, F Ie S (Blackheath) 1914 F
Stoop, A D (Harlequins) 1905 S, 1906 S, F, SA, 1907 F, W, 1910 W, I, S, 1911 W, F, I, S, 1912 W, S
Stoop, F M (Harlequins) 1910 S, 1911 F, I, 1913 SA
Stout, F M (Richmond) 1897 W, I, 1898 I, S, W, 1899 I, S, 1903 S, 1904 W, I, S, 1905 W, I, S
Stout, P W (Richmond) 1898 S, W, 1899 W, I, S
Strettle, D (Harlequins, Saracens) 2007 I, F1, W1, 2, 2008 W, NZ1, 2011 I1(R), 2012 S, It, W, I, SA2, 2013 S(R), Arg1
Stringer, N C (Wasps) 1982 A (R), 1983 NZ (R), 1984 SA 1(R), A, 1985 R
Strong, E L (Oxford U) 1884 W, I, S
Sturnham B (Saracens) 1998 A 1, NZ 1(t), 2(t)
Summerscales, G E (Durham City) 1905 NZ
Sutcliffe, J W (Heckmondwike) 1889 M
Swarbrick, D W (Oxford U) 1947 W, I, F, 1948 A, W, 1949 I
Swayne, D H (Oxford U) 1931 W
Swayne, J W R (Bridgwater) 1929 W
Swift, A H (Swansea) 1981 Arg 1, 2, 1983 F, W, S, 1984 SA 2
Syddall, J P (Waterloo) 1982 I, 1984 A
Sykes, A R V (Blackheath) 1914 F
Sykes, F D (Northampton) 1955 F, S, 1963 NZ 2, A
Sykes, P W (Wasps) 1948 F, 1952 S, I, F, 1953 W, I, F
Syrett, R E (Wasps) 1958 W, A, I, F, 1960 W, I, F, S, 1962 W, I, F

Tait, M J M (Newcastle, Sale) 2005 W, 2006 A1, 2, SA1, 2, 2007 It(R), I(R), F1(R), W1, SA1, 2, W2, [US(R), SA1(R), Sm, Tg, A, F, SA2], 2008 It(t), F(R), S(R), It(t&R), NZ2, 2009 It(R), W(R), I(R), F(R), S(R), Arg 1(R), 2(R), NZ(R), 2010 W, It, I, S, F(R), A1(R)
Tallent, J A (Cambridge U, Blackheath) 1931 S, F, 1932 SA, W, 1935 I
Tanner, C C (Cambridge U, Gloucester) 1930 S, 1932 SA, W, I, S
Tarr, F N (Leicester) 1909 A, W, F, 1913 S
Tatham, W M (Oxford U) 1882 S, 1883 W, I, S, 1884 W, I, S
Taylor, A S (Blackheath) 1883 W, I, 1886 W, I
Taylor, E W (Rockcliff) 1892 I, 1893 I, 1894 W, I, S, 1895 W, I, S, 1896 W, I, 1897 W, I, S, 1899 I
Taylor, F (Leicester) 1920 F, I
Taylor, F M (Leicester) 1914 W
Taylor, H H (Blackheath) 1879 S, 1880 S, 1881 W, 1882 S
Taylor, J T (W Hartlepool) 1897 I, 1899 I, 1900 I, 1901 W, I, 1902 W, I, S, 1903 W, I, 1905 S
Taylor, P J (Northampton) 1955 W, I, 1962 W, I, F, S
Taylor, R B (Northampton) 1966 W, 1967 I, F, S, W, NZ, 1969 F, S, W, SA, 1970 I, W, S, F, 1971 S (2[1C])
Taylor, W J (Blackheath) 1928 A, W, I, F, S
Teague, M C (Gloucester, Moseley) 1985 F (R), NZ 1, 2, 1989 S, I, F, W, 1990 F, W, S, 1991 W, S, I, F, Fj, A, [NZ, It, F, S, A], 1992 SA, 1993 F, W, S, I
Teden, D E (Richmond) 1939 W, I, S
Teggin, A (Broughton R) 1884 I, 1885 W, 1886 I, S, 1887 I, S
Tetley, T S (Bradford) 1876 S
Thomas, C (Barnstaple) 1895 W, I, S, 1899 I
Thomas, H M (Sale) 2013 Arg 1(R), 2(R), 2014 S(R), I(R), W(R), It(R), NZ1(R)
Thompson, P H (Headingley, Waterloo) 1956 W, I, S, F, 1957 W, I, F, S, 1958 W, A, I, F, S, 1959 W, I, F, S
Thompson, S G (Northampton, Brive, Leeds, Wasps) 2002 S, I, F, W, It, Arg, NZ, A, SA, 2003 F 1, W 1, It, S, I, NZ, A, F 2(R), 3, [Gg, SA, Sm(R), W, F, A], 2004 It, S, I, W, F, NZ1, A1(R), C, SA, A2, 2005 W, F, I, It, S, A, NZ, Sm, 2006 W, It, S, F, I(R), 2009 Arg 1(R), A, Arg 3(R), NZ(R), 2010 W(R), It(R), S(R), F(R), A1, 2, NZ, A3(R), Sm(R), SA(R), 2011 W1(R), It(R), F(R), S(R), I1(R), W3, I2, [Arg, Gg(t&R), R, S, F]
Thomson, G T (Halifax) 1878 S, 1882 I, S, 1883 W, I, S, 1884 I, S, 1885 I
Thomson, W B (Blackheath) 1892 W, 1895 W, I, S
Thorne, J D (Bristol) 1963 W, I, F
Tindall, M J (Bath, Gloucester) 2000 I, F, W, It, S, SA 1, 2, A, Arg, SA 3, 2001 W (R), R, SA (R), 2002 S, I, F, W, It, NZ, A, SA, 2003 It, S, I, NZ, A, F 2, [Gg, SA, Sm, W, F(R), A], 2004 W, F, NZ1, 2, A1, C, SA, A2, 2005 A, NZ, Sm, 2006 W, It, S, F, I(t&R), 2007 S, It, I, F1, 2008 W, NZ1, 2, 2009 W, I, F, S, 2010 F, A1, 2, NZ, A3, SA, 2011 W1, It, F, S, W3, I2, [Arg, R, S]
Tindall, V R (Liverpool U) 1951 W, I, F, S
Titterrell, A J (Sale) 2004 NZ2(R), C(R), 2005 It(R), S(R), 2007 SA2(R)

Tobin, F (Liverpool) 1871 S
Todd, A F (Blackheath) 1900 I, S
Todd, R (Manchester) 1877 S
Toft, H B (Waterloo) 1936 S, 1937 W, I, S, 1938 W, I, S, 1939 W, I, S
Tomkins, J A (Saracens) 2013 A, Arg3, NZ
Toothill, J T (Bradford) 1890 S, I, 1891 W, I, 1892 W, I, S, 1893 W, I, S, 1894 W, I
Tosswill, L R (Exeter) 1902 W, I, S
Touzel, C J C (Liverpool) 1877 I, S
Towell, A C (Bedford) 1948 F, 1951 S
Travers, B H (Harlequins) 1947 W, I, 1948 A, W, 1949 F, S
Treadwell, W T (Wasps) 1966 I, F, S
Trick, D M (Bath) 1983 I, 1984 SA 1
Tristram, H B (Oxford U) 1883 S, 1884 W, S, 1885 W, 1887 S
Troop, C L (Aldershot S) 1933 I, S
Tucker, J S (Bristol) 1922 W, 1925 NZ, W, I, S, F, 1926 W, I, F, S, 1927 W, I, S, F, 1928 A, W, I, F, S, 1929 W, I, F, 1930 W, I, F, S, 1931 F
Tucker, W E (Blackheath) 1894 W, I, 1895 W, I, S
Tucker, W E (Blackheath) 1926 I, 1930 W, I
Tuilagi, E M (Leicester) 2011 W2, I2, [Arg, Gg, R, S, F], 2012 W, F, I, SA 1, 2, 3, Fj, A, SA4, NZ, 2013 I(R), F, It, W, 2014 It(R), NZ1, 2, 3
Turner, D P (Richmond) 1871 S, 1872 S, 1873 S, 1874 S, 1875 I, S
Turner, E B (St George's Hospital) 1876 I, 1877 I, 1878 I
Turner, G R (St George's Hospital) 1876 S
Turner, H J C (Manchester) 1871 S
Turner, M F (Blackheath) 1948 S, F
Turner, S C (Sale) 2007 W1(R), SA1, 2(R)
Turner-Hall, J (Harlequins) 2012 S(R), It(R)
Turquand-Young, D (Richmond) 1928 A, W, 1929 I, S, F
Twelvetrees, W W F (Gloucester) 2013 S, I, It(R), W(R), Arg1, A, Arg3, NZ, 2014 F, S, I, W, It, NZ2, Sm(R), A, 2015 W(R), It(R), I 1(R), F 1(R), 2(R), 3(R)
Twynam, H T (Richmond) 1879 I, 1880 I, 1881 W, 1882 I, 1883 I, 1884 W, I, S

Ubogu, V E (Bath) 1992 C, SA, 1993 NZ, 1994 S, I, F, W, SA 1, 2, R, C, 1995 I, F, W, S, [Arg, WS, A, NZ, F], SA, 1999 F (R), W (R), A (R)
Underwood, A M (Exeter) 1962 W, I, F, S, 1964 I
Underwood, R (Leicester, RAF) 1984 I, F, W, A, 1985 R, F, S, I, W, 1986 W, I, F, 1987 I, F, W, S, [A, J, W], 1988 F, W, S, I, 1, 2, A 1, 2, Fj, A, 1989 S, I, F, W, R, Fj, 1990 I, F, W, S, Arg 3, 1991 W, S, I, F, Fj, A, [NZ, It, US, F, S, A], 1992 S, I, F, W, SA, 1993 F, W, S, I, NZ, 1994 S, I, F, W, SA 1, 2, R, C, 1995 I, F, W, S, [Arg, It, WS, A, NZ, F], SA, WS, 1996 F, W, S, I
Underwood, T (Leicester, Newcastle) 1992 C, SA, 1993 S, I, NZ, 1994 S, I, W, SA 1, 2, R, C, 1995 I, F, W, S, [Arg, It, A, NZ], 1996 Arg, 1997 S, I, F, W, 1998 A 2, SA 2
Unwin, E J (Rosslyn Park, Army) 1937 S, 1938 W, I, S
Unwin, G T (Blackheath) 1898 S
Uren, R (Waterloo) 1948 I, S, F, 1950 I
Uttley, R M (Gosforth) 1973 I, F, S, NZ 2, A, 1974 I, F, W, 1975 F, W, S, A, 1, 2, 1977 S, I, F, W, 1978 NZ, 1979 S, 1980 I, F, W, S

Vainikolo, L P I (Gloucester) 2008 W(R), It, F, S, I
Valentine J (Swinton) 1890 W, 1896 W, I, S
Vanderspar, C H R (Richmond) 1873 S
Van Gisbergen, M C (Wasps) 2005 A(t)
Van Ryneveld, C B (Oxford U) 1949 W, I, F, S
Varley, H (Liversedge) 1892 S
Varndell, T W (Leicester) 2005 Sm(R), 2006 A1, 2, 2008 NZ2
Vassall, H (Blackheath) 1881 W, S, 1882 I, S, 1883 W
Vassall, H H (Blackheath) 1908 I
Vaughan, D B (Headingley) 1948 A, W, I, S, 1949 I, F, S, 1950 W
Vaughan-Jones, A (Army) 1932 I, S, 1933 W
Verelst, C L (Liverpool) 1876 I, 1878 I
Vernon, G F (Blackheath) 1878 S, I, 1880 I, S, 1881 I
Vesty, S B (Leicester) 2009 Arg 1(R), 2(R)
Vickery, G (Aberavon) 1905 I
Vickery, P J (Gloucester, Wasps) 1998 W, A 1, NZ 1, 2, SA 1, 1999 US, C, [It, NZ, Tg, SA], 2000 I, F, W, S, A, Arg (R), SA 3(R), 2001 W, It, S, A, SA, 2002 I, F, Arg, NZ, A, SA, 2003 NZ(R), A, [Gg, SA, Sm(R), U, W, F, A], 2004 It, S, I, W, F, 2005 W(R), F, A, NZ, 2006 SA1(R), 2, 2007 S, It, I, W2, F2(R), 3, [US, Tg(R), A, F, SA2], 2008 W, F, S, I, PI(R), A, SA, NZ3, 2009 It, W, I, F, S

Vivyan, E J (Devonport A) 1901 W, 1904 W, I, S

Voyce, A T (Gloucester) 1920 I, S, 1921 W, I, S, F, 1922 W, I, F, S, 1923 W, I, S, F, 1924 W, I, F, S, 1925 NZ, W, I, S, F, 1926 W, I, F, S

Voyce, T M D (Bath, Wasps) 2001 US (R), 2004 NZ2, A1, 2005 Sm, 2006 W(R), It, F(R), I, A1

Vunipola, M W I N (Saracens) 2012 Fj(R), A(R), SA4(R), NZ(R), 2013 S(R), I(R), F(R), It, W(R), A, 2014 F(R), S(R), I(R), W(R), It, 2015 W(R), It(R), I1(R), S(R), F 1(R), 2, 3(R), I 2(R), [Fj(R), W(R), A(R), U]

Vunipola, V M L (Wasps, Saracens) 2013 Arg1(R), 2(R), A, Arg3, NZ, 2014 F, S, I, NZ2(R), 3, 4, SA, 2015 W, It, I 1, S, F 1, 3, I 2(R), [Fj(R), W]

Vyvyan, H D (Saracens) 2004 C(R)

Wackett, J A S (Rosslyn Park) 1959 W, I

Wade, C (Wasps) 2013 Arg 1

Wade, C G (Richmond) 1883 W, I, S, 1884 W, S, 1885 W, 1886 W, I

Wade, M R (Cambridge U) 1962 W, I, F

Wakefield, W W (Harlequins) 1920 W, F, I, S, 1921 W, I, S, F, 1922 W, I, F, S, 1923 W, I, S, F, 1924 W, I, F, S, 1925 NZ, W, I, S, F, 1926 W, I, F, S, 1927 S, F

Walder, D J H (Newcastle) 2001 C 1, 2, US, 2003 W 2(R)

Waldrom, T R (Leicester) 2012 SA 2(R), 3, Fj, A, 2013 I(R)

Walker, G A (Blackheath) 1939 W, I

Walker, H W (Coventry) 1947 W, I, S, F, 1948 A, W, I, S, F

Walker, R (Manchester) 1874 S, 1875 I, 1876 S, 1879 S, 1880 S

Wallens, J N S (Waterloo) 1927 F

Walshe, N P J (Bath) 2006 A1(R), 2(R)

Walton, E J (Castleford) 1901 W, I, 1902 I, S

Walton, W (Castleford) 1894 S

Ward, H (Bradford) 1895 W

Ward, J A G (Leicester) 1913 W, F, S, 1914 W, I, S

Ward, J I (Richmond) 1881 I, 1882 I

Ward, J W (Castleford) 1896 W, I, S

Wardlow, C S (Northampton) 1969 SA (R), 1971 W, I, F, S (2[1C])

Warfield, P J (Rosslyn Park, Durham U) 1973 NZ 1, W, I, 1975 I, F, S

Warr, A L (Oxford U) 1934 W, I

Waters, F H H (Wasps) 2001 US, 2004 NZ2(R), A1(R)

Watkins, J A (Gloucester) 1972 SA, 1973 NZ 1, W, NZ 2, A, 1975 F, W

Watkins, J K (United Services, RN) 1939 W, I, S

Watson, A K C (Bath) 2014 NZ 4(R), SA, Sm, A, 2015 W, It, I 1, S, F 1, 2, I 2, [Fj, W, A, U]

Watson, F B (United Services, RN) 1908 S, 1909 S

Watson, J H D (Blackheath) 1914 W, S, F

Watt, D E J (Bristol) 1967 I, F, S, W

Webb, C S H (Devonport Services, RN) 1932 SA, W, I, S, 1933 W, I, S, 1935 S, 1936 NZ, W, I, S

Webb, J M (Bristol, Bath) 1987 [A (R), J, US, W], 1988 F, W, S, I 1, 2, A 1, 2, A, 1989 S, I, F, W, 1991 Fj, A, [NZ, It, F, S, A], 1992 S, I, F, W, C, SA, 1993 F, W, S, I

Webb, J W G (Northampton) 1926 S, 1929 S

Webb, R E (Coventry) 1967 S, W, NZ, 1968 I, F, S, 1969 I, F, S, W, 1972 I, F

Webb, St L H (Bedford) 1959 W, I, F, S

Webber, R W (Wasps, Bath) 2012 It(R), W(R), F(R), 2013 Arg1, 2, 2014 NZ1, 2, 3(R), 4(R), SA(t&R), Sm , A(R), 2015 F 2, [Fj(R), W(R), A(R)]

Webster, J G (Moseley) 1972 W, I, SA, 1973 NZ 1, W, NZ 2, 1974 S, W, 1975 I, F, W

Wedge, T G (St Ives) 1907 F, 1909 W

Weighill, R H G (RAF, Harlequins) 1947 S, F, 1948 S, F

Wells, C M (Cambridge U, Harlequins) 1893 S, 1894 W, S, 1896 S, 1897 W, S

West, B R (Loughborough Colls, Northampton) 1968 W, I, F, S, 1969 SA, 1970 I, W, S

West, D E (Leicester) 1998 F (R), S (R), 2000 Arg (R), 2001 W, It, S, F (t), C 1, 2, US, I (R), A, SA, 2002 F (R), W (R), It (R), 2003 W 2(R), F 2, 3(t+R), [U, F(R)]

West, R (Gloucester) 1995 [WS]

Weston, H T F (Northampton) 1901 S

Weston, L E (W of Scotland) 1972 F, S

Weston, M P (Richmond, Durham City) 1960 W, I, F, S, 1961 SA, W, I, F, S, 1962 W, I, F, 1963 W, I, F, S, NZ 1, 2, A, 1964 NZ, W, I, F, S, 1965 F, S, 1966 S, 1968 F, S

Weston, W H (Northampton) 1933 I, S, 1934 I, S, 1935 W, I, S, 1936 NZ, W, S, 1937 W, I, S, 1938 W, I, S

Wheatley, A A (Coventry) 1937 W, I, S, 1938 W, S

Wheatley, H F (Coventry) 1936 I, 1937 S, 1938 W, S, 1939 W, I, S

Wheeler, P J (Leicester) 1975 F, W, 1976 A, W, S, I, 1977 S, I, F, W, 1978 F, W, S, I, NZ, 1979 S, I, F, W, NZ, 1980 I, F, W, S, 1981 W, S, I, F, 1982 A, S, I, F, W, 1983 F, S, I, NZ, 1984 S, I, F, W

White, C (Gosforth) 1983 NZ, 1984 S, I, F

White, D F (Northampton) 1947 W, I, S, 1948 I, F, 1951 S, 1952 SA, W, S, I, F, 1953 W, I, S

White, J M (Saracens, Bristol, Leicester) 2000 SA 1, 2, Arg, SA 3, 2001 F, C 1, 2, US, I, R (R), 2002 S, W, It, 2003 F 1(R), W 2, F 2, 3, [Sm, U(R)], 2004 W(R), F(R), NZ1, 2, A1, C, SA, A2, 2005 W, 2006 W(R), It(R), S, F, I, A1, 2, NZ, Arg, SA1, 2, 2007 S(R), It(R), I(R), F1, W1, 2009 It(R), W(R), It(t&R), F(t&R), S(R), Arg 1(R), 2

White-Cooper, W R S (Harlequins) 2001 C 2, US

Whiteley, E C P (O Alleynians) 1931 S, F

Whiteley, W (Bramley) 1896 W

Whitely, H (Northern) 1929 W

Wightman, B J (Moseley, Coventry) 1959 W, 1963 W, I, NZ 2, A

Wigglesworth, H J (Thornes) 1884 I

Wigglesworth, R E P (Sale, Saracens) 2008 It(R), F, S, I, NZ1, 2011 W2(R), 3, I2, [Arg, R(R), S(R), F(R)], 2013 Arg1(R), 2(R), 2014 Sm(R), A(R), 2015 W(R), It(R), I 1(R), S(R), F 1(R), 2, I 2(R), [Fj(R), W(R), A(R), U(R)]

Wilkins, D T (United Services, RN, Roundhay) 1951 W, I, F, S, 1952 SA, W, S, I, F, 1953 W, I, F, S

Wilkinson, E (Bradford) 1886 W, I, S, 1887 W, S

Wilkinson, H (Halifax) 1929 W, I, S, 1930 F

Wilkinson, H J (Halifax) 1889 M

Wilkinson, J P (Newcastle, Toulon) 1998 I (R), A 1, NZ 1, 1999 S, I, F, W, A, US, C, [It, NZ, Fj, SA (R)], 2000 I, F, W, It, S, SA 2, A, Arg, SA 3, 2001 W, It, S, F, I, A, SA, 2002 S, I, F, W, It, NZ, A, SA, 2003 F 1, W 1, It, S, I, NZ, A, F 3, [Gg, SA, Sm, W, F, A], 2007 S, It, I, SA1, 2, W2, F2(R), F3, [Sm, Tg, A, F, SA2], 2008 W, It, F, S, I(R), 2009 A, Arg 3, NZ, 2010 W, It, I, S, F(R), A1(R), 2(R), 2011 W1(R), It(R), F(R), S(R), I1(R), W2, I2, [Arg, R, S, F]

Wilkinson, P (Law Club) 1872 S

Wilkinson, R M (Bedford) 1975 A 2, 1976 A, W, S, I, F

Willcocks, T H (Plymouth Albion) 1902 W

Willcox, J G (Oxford U, Harlequins) 1961 I, F, S, 1962 W, I, F, S, 1963 W, I, F, S, 1964 W, I, F, S

William-Powlett, P B R W (United Services, RN) 1922 S

Williams, C G (Gloucester, RAF) 1976 F

Williams, C S (Manchester) 1910 F

Williams, J E (O Millhillians, Sale) 1954 F, 1955 W, I, F, S, 1956 I, S, F, 1965 W

Williams, J M (Penzance-Newlyn) 1951 I, S

Williams, P N (Orrell) 1987 S, [A, J, W]

Williams, S G (Devonport A) 1902 W, I, S, 1903 I, S, 1907 I, S

Williams, S H (Newport) 1911 W, F, I, S

Williamson, R H (Oxford U) 1908 W, I, S, 1909 A, F

Wilson, A J (Camborne S of M) 1909 I

Wilson, C E (Blackheath) 1898 I

Wilson, C P (Cambridge U, Marlborough N) 1881 W

Wilson, D G (Newcastle, Bath) 2009 Arg 1, 2(R), A, NZ(R), 2010 W, It(R), I(R), S(R), F(R), A1(R), 2(t&R), NZ2(R), A3(R), Sm, SA(R), 2011 W1(R), It(R), W2(R), [R(R)], 2012 Fj(R), SA4(R), NZ(R), 2013 S(R), It(R), W(R), Arg1, 2, A(R), Arg3, NZ(R), 2014 I, W, It, NZ1, 2, 3, 4, SA, Sm, A, 2015 F2(R), 3(R), [U(R)]

Wilson, D S (Met Police, Harlequins) 1953 F, 1954 W, NZ, I, S, F, 1955 F, S

Wilson, G S (Tyldesley) 1929 W, I

Wilson, K J (Gloucester) 1963 F

Wilson, R P (Liverpool OB) 1891 W, I, S

Wilson, W C (Richmond) 1907 I, S

Winn, C E (Rosslyn Park) 1952 SA, W, S, I, F, 1954 W, S, F

Winterbottom, P J (Headingley, Harlequins) 1982 A, S, I, F, W, 1983 F, W, S, I, NZ, 1984 S, F, W, SA 1, 2, 1986 W, S, I, F, 1987 I, F, W, [A, J, US, W], 1988 F, W, S, 1989 R, Fj, 1990 I, F, W, S, Arg 1, 2, 3, 1991 W, S, I, F, A, [NZ, It, F, S, A], 1992 S, I, F, W, C, SA, 1993 F, W, S, I

Winters, R A (Bristol) 2007 SA1(R), 2

Wintle, T C (Northampton) 1966 S, 1969 I, F, S, W

Wodehouse, N A (United Services, RN) 1910 F, 1911 W, F, I, S, 1912 W, I, S, F, 1913 SA, W, F, I, S

Wood, A (Halifax) 1884 I

Wood, A E (Gloucester, Cheltenham) 1908 F, W, I

Wood, G W (Leicester) 1914 W

Wood, M B (Wasps) 2001 C 2(R), US (R)
Wood, R (Liversedge) 1894 I
Wood, R D (Liverpool OB) 1901 I, 1903 W, I
Wood, T A (Northampton) 2011 W1, It, F, S, I1, W2(R), 3, [Gg, R(R)], 2012 Fj(R), A(R), SA4, NZ, 2013 S, I, F, It, W, Arg1, 2, A, Arg3, NZ, 2014 F, S, I, W, It, NZ2, 3, 4, SA, Sm(R), A, 2015 S(R), F 1(R), 2, I 2, [Fj, W, A, U(R)]
Woodgate, E E (Paignton) 1952 W
Woodhead, E (Huddersfield) 1880 I
Woodman, T J (Gloucester) 1999 US (R), 2000 I (R), It (R), 2001 W (R), It (R), 2002 NZ, 2003 S (R), I(t + R), A, F 3, [Gg, SA, W(R), F, A], 2004 It, S, I, W, F, NZ1, 2
Woodruff, C G (Harlequins) 1951 W, I, F, S
Woods, S M J (Cambridge U, Wellington) 1890 W, S, I, 1891 W, I, S, 1892 I, S, 1893 W, I, 1895 W, I, S
Woods, T (Bridgwater) 1908 S
Woods, T (United Services, RN, Pontypool) 1920 S, 1921 W, I, S, F
Woodward, C R (Leicester) 1980 I (R), F, W, S, 1981 W, S, I, F, Arg 1, 2, 1982 A, S, I, F, W, 1983 I, NZ, 1984 S, I, F, W
Woodward, J E (Wasps) 1952 SA, W, S, 1953 W, I, F, S, 1954 W, NZ, I, S, F, 1955 W, I, 1956 S
Wooldridge, C S (Oxford U, Blackheath) 1883 W, I, S, 1884 W, I, S, 1885 I
Wordsworth, A J (Cambridge U) 1975 A 1(R)
Worsley, J P R (Wasps) 1999 [Tg, Fj], 2000 It (R), S (R), SA 1(R), 2(R), 2001 It (R), S (R), F (R), C 1, 2, US, A, R, SA, 2002 S, I, F, W (t+R), Arg, 2003 W 1(R), It, S(R), I(t), NZ(R), A(R), W 2, [SA(t), Sm, U], 2004 It, I, W(R), F, NZ1(R), 2, A1, SA, A2, 2005 W, F, I, It, S, 2006 W, It, S, F, I, A1(R), 2, SA1, 2, 2007 S, I, F1, W1, 2, F2, 3(R), [US, Sm, A(R), F(R), SA2(R)], 2008 NZ1(R), 2(R), 2009 It(R), W, I, F, S, Arg 3(R), NZ, 2010 I(R), S, F, 2011 W1(R)
Worsley, M A (London Irish, Harlequins) 2003 It(R), 2004 A1(R), 2005 S(R)

Worton, J R B (Harlequins, Army) 1926 W, 1927 W
Wrench, D F B (Harlequins) 1964 F, S
Wright, C C G (Cambridge U, Blackheath) 1909 I, S
Wright, F T (Edinburgh Acady, Manchester) 1881 S
Wright, I D (Northampton) 1971 W, I, F, S (R)
Wright, J C (Met Police) 1934 W
Wright, J F (Bradford) 1890 W
Wright, T P (Blackheath) 1960 W, I, F, S, 1961 SA, W, I, F, S, 1962 W, I, F, S
Wright, W H G (Plymouth) 1920 W, F
Wyatt, D M (Bedford) 1976 S (R)

Yarde, M (London Irish, Harlequins) 2013 Arg 2, A, 2014 NZ1, 2, 3, Sm(t&R), A(R)
Yarranton, P G (RAF, Wasps) 1954 W, NZ, I, 1955 F, S
Yates, K P (Bath, Saracens) 1997 Arg 1, 2, 2007 SA1, 2
Yiend, W (Hartlepool R, Gloucester) 1889 M, 1892 W, I, S, 1893 I, S
Young, A T (Cambridge U, Blackheath, Army) 1924 W, I, F, S, 1925 NZ, F, 1926 I, F, S, 1927 I, S, F, 1928 A, W, I, F, S, 1929 I
Young, J R C (Oxford U, Harlequins) 1958 I, 1960 W, I, F, S, 1961 SA, W, I, F
Young, M (Gosforth) 1977 S, I, F, W, 1978 F, W, S, I, NZ, 1979 S
Young, P D (Dublin Wands) 1954 W, NZ, I, S, F, 1955 W, I, F, S
Youngs, N G (Leicester) 1983 I, NZ, 1984 S, I, F, W
Youngs, B R (Leicester) 2010 S(R), A1(R), 2, NZ, A3, Sm, SA, 2011 W1, It, F, S, I1, [Arg(R), Gg, R, S, F], 2012 It, W(R), F(R), I(R), SA 1, 2, Fj(R), A(R), SA4, NZ, 2013 S, I, F, It(R), W, A(R), NZ(R), 2014 NZ1, 2(R), 3, 4(R), SA(R), Sm, A, 2015 W, It, I 1, S, F 1, 3, I 2, [Fj, W, A]
Youngs, T N (Leicester) 2012 Fj, A, SA4, NZ, 2013 S, I, F(R), It, W, A, Arg3(R), NZ(R), 2014 F(R), S(R), I(R), W(R), It(R)), 2015 W(R), It(R), I 1(R), S(R), F 1(R), 3, I 2, [Fj, W, A, U]

Wing Anthony Watson leaps on the loose ball to score England's opening try in their 60–3 victory over Uruguay.

FIJI

FIJI'S 2014–15 TEST RECORD

OPPONENT	DATE	VENUE	RESULT
France	8 Nov	A	Lost 40–15
Wales	15 Nov	A	Lost 17–13
USA	21 Nov	N	Won 20–14
Tonga	18 Jul	H	Won 30–22
Samoa	24 Jul	N	Drew 30–30
Japan	29 Jul	N	Won 27–22
Samoa	3 Aug	N	Won 39–29
Canada	6 Sep	N	Won 47–18
England	18 Sep	N	Lost 35–11
Australia	23 Sep	N	Lost 28–13
Wales	1 Oct	N	Lost 23–13
Uruguay	6 Oct	N	Won 47–15

FIJI IMPRESS WITH SOLID RUGBY WORLD CUP

By Alex Broun

Powerful centre Nemani Nadolo was Fiji's stand-out player at Rugby World Cup 2015, scoring 33 points in three matches.

The **Flying Fijians** enjoyed a positive year, putting in a solid display at Rugby World Cup 2015 on the back of celebrating their second World Rugby Pacific Nations Cup title in August. In all they played 12 matches, winning six, drawing one and losing five and scored 305 points while conceding 293.

In terms of the World Rugby Rankings the year saw them climb from 12th to equal their highest ever position of ninth before settling back to 11th at the end of RWC 2015.

The team showed the hallmarks of new structures put in place by head coach John McKee, in his first full year in charge, and were markedly more stable at the set-piece with their scrum one of the best at RWC 2015. With a solid platform laid in the forwards this gave Fiji the opportunity to unleash their always dangerous backline.

Fiji's preparations for RWC 2015 began in November 2014 when

RUGBY WORLD CUP 2015 IN PICTURES

Try, try again: Of the 271 tries scored at Rugby World Cup 2015, Johan Deysel's for Namibia against New Zealand (above, left), Bryan Habana's spectacular dive against the USA (above) to equal Jonah Lomu's record of 15 Rugby World Cup tries, Juan Imhoff's flying leap in Argentina's quarter-final win over Ireland (left) and Karne Hesketh's dramatic and historic last-minute score to give Japan victory against South Africa (below), were among the most notable.

Action men: From Twickenham to Exeter and Cardiff to Newcastle, Rugby World Cup 2015 was characterised by the passion, commitment and skill of the players who performed, without exception, in front of thrilled and enthusiastic crowds in packed-out stadiums.

Rivals and friends:
Epitomised in the moment (above) when All Blacks star Sonny Bill Williams consoled defeated opponent, Jesse Kriel, at the end of the semi-final between New Zealand and South Africa, from the pitch to the stands – and even the Royal Box – RWC 2015 was played out in the sporting spirit of friendly rivalry that has become synonymous with the game.

Emotions abound: Argentina's Tomás Cubelli (above, right) struggles to hold back the tears during the national anthems before the quarter-final with Ireland, summing up the passion and emotion that characterised the whole tournament – from the pitches to the stands as young and old celebrated an unforgettable few weeks.

History-makers:
Among the historic moments were Italy's Mauro Bergamasco becoming only the second man to play in five tournaments (above), Japan beating South Africa (above, right), Romania recording the biggest comeback in Rugby World Cup history, recovering from 15-0 down to beat Canada (right), and Georgia beating Tonga (below).

Celebrate good times: The All Blacks congratulate Julian Savea after scoring what was later named the IRPA Try of the Year against France (above) and South Africa enjoy the moment of victory after the final whistle of their titanic battle against Wales.

Wonderful Wallabies: Australia put up an almighty fight in a thrilling final against New Zealand, with Tevita Kuridrani's converted try bringing them to within four points of the All Blacks, which had seemed unlikely after Ma'a Nonu's electric burst through to score early in the second half.

Victory dance: But in the end there can only be one winner, and New Zealand – becoming the first team to win back-to-back Rugby World Cups – were more than worthy of that accolade. After the trophy presentation the All Blacks serenaded the Webb Ellis Cup with the final haka of Rugby World Cup 2015.

McKee, the New Zealander who was appointed in May that year, led a strong team on tour to Europe.

In their first match they were well beaten 40–15 by France in Marseille, but just as at RWC 2015 the team got stronger the more time they stayed together, narrowly going down to Wales 17–13 in Cardiff the following week. They finished their tour with a hard-fought three tries to two 20–14 win over USA in Vannes, France.

Fiji launched their 2015 campaign in July with a match against the Maori All Blacks in Suva. They led 26–10 at half-time but 17 unanswered points in the second half saw the Maori sneak home 27–26.

But they put that disappointment behind them with a solid 30–22 victory over Tonga at the same venue seven days later, in the first round of this year's Pacific Nations Cup. This was followed up with a thrilling 30–30 draw with Samoa in Sacramento, as the tournament moved to North America, followed by a 29–22 win over Japan in Toronto, Canada.

This meant Fiji qualified for the final in Burnaby, Canada, with ranging second-row Leone Nakarawa scoring two of his side's five tries to inspire them to a 39–29 victory over Samoa. This was Fiji's penultimate match before RWC 2015 and meant they arrived in England with some confidence. This was only enhanced by an emphatic 47–18 victory over Canada in Gloucester.

Fiji had been drawn in the 'Pool of Death' at RWC 2015, faced with the challenging assignment of matches against hosts England, Wales and Australia as well as Uruguay, but McKee was able to announce an experienced squad with four players appearing at their third Rugby World Cup in Netani Talei, captain Akapusi Qera, Gabiriele Lovobalavu and Sunia Koto.

It was a great honour for Fiji to open RWC 2015, taking on the host nation in front of a packed Twickenham on 18 September. After an impressive opening ceremony it was down to business and the Flying Fijians soon found themselves behind the eight ball, going down 15–0 after 23 minutes.

The scoreline was compounded when scrum-half Nikola Matawalu was yellow-carded for pulling down a maul trying to prevent the first England try. But no sooner was Matawalu back on the field than out of nowhere he skipped down the right touchline to almost score a stunning solo try.

A few minutes later giant winger Nemani Nadolo did get over after soaring into the night sky to take a well-judged cross-field kick from Fiji's impressive fly-half Ben Volavola. At half-time the match was finely poised at 18–8, but two further tries for England in the second half saw them home 35–11 to the delight of many at Twickenham.

For their next match against Australia in Cardiff McKee stuck closely

FIJI

to the team that performed so well at Twickenham, making just three changes, and his faith was rewarded as they held the Wallabies to 28–13, with the highlight coming from an Volavola solo try on 60 minutes.

The Fijian scrum was again impressive, against a pack that ended up being one of the best performing in the tournament.

After the match Nadolo, up to that point Fiji's best player at RWC 2015, was suspended for the next match against Wales due to a dangerous tackle. In all McKee was forced to make six changes to his starting XV for the Millennium Stadium encounter, but in one positive captain Qera became the third player to win 50 caps for Fiji, following Nicky Little (71) and Seremaia Bai (50).

Fiji were down 17–3 but fought back well early in the second half after centre Vereniki Goneva capped off one of the tries of the tournament to narrow the gap to four points by the 50-minute mark.

They continued to throw everything at the Welsh line in the final 30 minutes but just couldn't find the final pass to unlock some determined defence, and two further penalties to Wales made the final score 23–13.

But with Nadolo returning Fiji were buoyant and determined to finish RWC 2015 on a high in their final match against Uruguay in Milton Keynes.

They did just that with two penalty tries, the first the fastest in Rugby World Cup history, and further tries by scrum-half Nemia Kenatale, Nakarawa, second-row Tevita Cavubati, full-back Kini Murimurivalu and Nadolo making the final score 47–15.

"We came with high ambitions and we believed we could roll over one or two of the bigger teams, but it didn't happen so it was important to get a good win tonight," said a relieved McKee after the match at Stadium MK.

"For Fijian rugby it's been a very positive tournament, we have shown we can compete. There was a lot of talk before the tournament on our set plays and our fitness and whether we would cope, but we have proved that we are a competitive nation."

McKee said he was committed to Fiji going forward and was already thinking about Japan 2019.

"We have got about 27, maybe 28, tests between now and Japan 2019 so we really need to be smart in our cycle and see it as a four-year cycle rather than on a yearly basis," he insisted.

"I have only had 18 months with these guys so it was tough to build a squad for this tournament. We need to get younger players into the squad and develop them as much as we can so game-plans and combinations can be installed in them early."

With the improvements already shown at RWC 2015, and clearly more to come, the future is looking brighter for the Flying Fijians.

MATCH RECORDS UP TO 1 NOVEMBER, 2015

WINNING MARGIN

Date	Opponent	Result	Winning Margin
10/09/1983	Niue Island	120–4	116
28/06/2014	Cook Islands	108–6	102
21/08/1969	Solomon Islands	113–13	100
08/09/1983	Solomon Islands	86–0	86
30/08/1979	Papua New Guinea	86–0	86

MOST POINTS IN A MATCH
BY THE TEAM

Date	Opponent	Result	Points
10/09/1983	Niue Island	120–4	120
21/08/1969	Solomon Islands	113–13	113
28/06/2014	Cook Islands	108–6	108
23/08/1969	Papua New Guinea	88–3	88

BY A PLAYER

Date	Player	Opponent	Points
10/09/1983	Severo Koroduadua	Niue Island	36
21/08/1969	Semesa Sikivou	Solomon Islands	27
28/08/1999	Nicky Little	Italy	25
30/08/1979	Tevita Makutu	Papua New Guinea	24
29/09/1996	Nicky Little	Hong Kong	24

MOST TRIES IN A MATCH
BY THE TEAM

Date	Opponent	Result	Tries
21/08/1969	Solomon Islands	113–13	25
10/09/1983	Niue Island	120–4	21
23/08/1969	Papua New Guinea	88–3	20
18/08/1969	Papua New Guinea	79–0	19
30/08/1979	Papua New Guinea	86–0	18

BY A PLAYER

Date	Player	Opponent	Tries
30/08/1979	Tevita Makutu	Papua New Guinea	6
18/08/1969	George Sailosi	Papua New Guinea	5
	4 on 10 occasions		

MOST CONVERSIONS IN A MATCH
BY THE TEAM

Date	Opponent	Result	Cons
21/08/1969	Solomon Islands	113–13	19
10/09/1983	Niue Island	120–4	18
23/08/1969	Papua New Guinea	88–3	14
18/08/1969	Papua New Guinea	79–0	11

BY A PLAYER

Date	Player	Opponent	Cons
10/09/1983	Severo Koroduadua	Niue Island	18
21/08/1969	Semesa Sikivou	Solomon Islands	12
07/10/1989	Severo Koroduadua	Belgium	10
23/08/1969	Semesa Sikivou	Papua New Guinea	9
08/09/1983	Ilai Musanamasi	Solomon Islands	9

MOST PENALTIES IN A MATCH
BY THE TEAM

Date	Opponent	Result	Pens
08/07/2001	Samoa	28–17	7
	6 on 4 occasions		

BY A PLAYER

Date	Player	Opponent	Pens
08/07/2001	Nicky Little	Samoa	7
26/05/2000	Nicky Little	Tonga	6
25/05/2001	Nicky Little	Tonga	6
05/10/1996	Nicky Little	Hong Kong	6
08/07/1967	Inoke Tabualevu	Tonga	6

MOST DROP GOALS IN A MATCH
BY THE TEAM

Date	Opponent	Result	DGs
02/07/1994	Samoa	20–13	3
12/10/1991	Romania	15–17	3

BY A PLAYER

Date	Player	Opponent	Pens
02/07/1994	Opeti Turuva	Samoa	3
12/10/1991	Tomasi Rabaka	Romania	2

FIJI

MOST CAPPED PLAYERS

Name	Caps
Nicky Little	71
Akapusi Qera	51
Jacob Rauluni	50
Joeli Veitayaki	49
Sisa Koyamaibole	48
Seremaia Baikeinuku	48

LEADING TRY SCORERS

Name	Tries
Senivalati Laulau	18
Fero Lasagavibau	17
Nemani Nadolo	17
Norman Ligairi	16
Viliame Satala	16
Fero Lasagavibau	16

LEADING CONVERSIONS SCORERS

Name	Cons
Nicky Little	117
Severo Koroduadua	56
Seremaia Baikeinuku	56
Waisale Serevi	40

LEADING PENALTY SCORERS

Name	Pens
Nicky Little	140
Seremaia Baikeinuku	53
Severo Koroduadua	47
Waisale Serevi	27
Nemani Nadolo	19

LEADING DROP GOAL SCORERS

Name	DGs
Opeti Turuva	5
Severo Koroduadua	5
Waisale Serevi	3

LEADING POINTS SCORERS

Name	Points
Nicky Little	670
Seremaia Baikeinuku	299
Severo Koroduadua	268
Waisale Serevi	221
Nemani Nadolo	192

FIJI INTERNATIONAL PLAYERS
UP TO 1 NOVEMBER, 2015

A Apimeleki 1924 *Sa, Tg, Tg, Tg, Sa*, 1926 *Tg, Tg*
S Aria 1986 *W*, 1988 *Tg, Sa, E, Tg*, 1991 *C, F*, 1993 *Sa, Tg*, 1994 *J*
LE Atalifo 2014 *Coo*, 2015 *C, W, Ur*

S Baikeinuku 2000 *J, US, C, It*, 2001 *Tg, Sa, Tg*, 2002 *W, I, S*, 2004 *Tg, Sa*, 2005 *M, NZ, Tg, Sa, Tg, Sa, W, It*, 2006 *Tg, It, Sa, J*, 2007 *J, C, A, W, SA*, 2009 *Sa, J, S, I*, 2010 *F, W, It*, 2011 *J, NZ, Tg, Nm, SA, Sa, W*, 2013 *CAB, US, Tg, Pt, It, R, Bb*
J Bale 2004 *Tg, Sa*, 2005 *M, NZ, Tg, Sa, Tg, Sa, W, It*, 2006 *Tg, It, Sa, J*
P Bale 1995 *C, Sa, Tg, W, I*
S Baleca 1951 *M*, 1952 *A, A*, 1954 *A, A*
DV Baleinadogo 2001 *Tg, Sa, Tg, Sa, C, Sa*, 2002 *Sa, Tg*, 2007 *Sa, J*
K Baleisawani 2004 *Tg, Sa*
N Baleiverata 1988 *Tg, Sa, E*, 1990 *J*
D Baleiwai 1990 *J, HK*, 1991 *Tg, C, F, R*
J Balewai 1926 *Tg, Tg*, 1928 *Tg, Tg, Tg, Sa*, 1932 *Tg, Tg, Tg*
S Banuve 1990 *Tg*
S Baravilala 1934 *Tg, Tg*, 1947 *Tg, Tg*, 1948 *M, M*
M Bari 1995 *Sa, Tg, W, I*, 1996 *Sa, Tg, HK, HK, M*, 1997 *NZ, Coo, Sa*, 1998 *S, US, A, Tg*, 1999 *Ur, F*
G Barley 1964 *W, F*, 1970 *M, C*
I Basiyalo 1994 *J*
S Basiyalo 1976 *I*
A Batibasaga 1967 *Tg*, 1968 *Tg, Tg*, 1969 *W, PNG, SI, PNG*
I Batibasaga 1974 *M*
I Batibasaga 1970 *C*, 1972 *Tg, Tg, Tg, A*, 1973 *Tg, E*, 1974 *M, M*, 1976 *I*, 1977 *Tg, Tg*, 1979 *M*
A Batikaciwa 1932 *Tg, Tg*, 1934 *Tg, Tg*
E Batimala 1994 *J, J, M, W, Sa, Tg*, 1995 *C, Sa, Tg*, 1996 *HK*, 1998 *S*
J Bibi 1928 *Tg, Tg, Tg, Sa*

TM Biumaiwai 1954 *A, A, M, M*
PTQ Biu 1999 *Sp, Ur*, 2000 *J, Tg, Sa*, 2001 *It, F*, 2002 *Sa, Tg, Sa, NZ, Tg*, 2003 *Chl*
M Black 1996 *SA, Sa, Tg, HK*
S Bobo 2004 *Tg, Sa*, 2005 *M, NZ, Tg, W, Pt*, 2007 *W, SA*, 2010 *A*, 2013 *J, CAB, US, Tg*, 2014 *Tg, Sa*
R Bogisa 1994 *J, W*, 1995 *C, W*
K Bogiwalu 1924 *Sa, Tg, Tg, Tg, Sa*, 1926 *Tg, Tg*
A Boko 2009 *S, I, R*
A Bola 1934 *Tg*
D Bola 1983 *Sa, Niu, Tg*, 1984 *A, Sa, NZ*
E Bola 1939 *M*
IC Bolakoro 2009 *Sa*, 2011 *Sa*
K Bola 2009 *R*, 2010 *Tg, Sa*, 2012 *J, Sa, Tg, E, Geo*
FV Bolavucu 2009 *Tg, J*
E Bolawaqatabu 1963 *Sa, Tg, Sa, Tg*, 1969 *W, PNG, SI, PNG*, 1970 *M, M*, 1972 *Tg, Tg, Tg, A*, 1973 *M, M*
P Bolea 2001 *Sa*
A Bose 1932 *Tg, Tg, Tg*, 1934 *Tg, Tg, Tg*
E Bose 1998 *Sa*
K Bose 1958 *Tg, Tg*, 1959 *Tg, Tg*, 1961 *A, A, A*
V Bose 1980 *A*
I Buadromo 1970 *C*
VT Buatava 2007 *Sa, J, A*, 2010 *A*, 2011 *Tg, Sa, J, NZ, Tg, Tg, Nm, SA, Sa, W*
T Bucaonadi 1983 *Tg, Sa*
S Bueta 1986 *Tg*
V Bueta 1982 *Sa, Sa, E*
V Buli 1963 *Tg, Sa, Tg*
A Burogolevu 1954 *A, A*
A Buto 2012 *J, Sa, S*

I Cagilaba 1974 *M*, 1976 *I*, 1977 *Tg, Tg*, 1979 *M, E, F, PNG, Sa*
GK Cakobau 1939 *M*
J Cama 1987 *NZ*

FIJI

A Kunawave 1957 *M, M*, 1958 *Tg, Tg, Tg*, 1959 *Tg*
M Kurisaru 1968 *Tg, Tg*, 1969 *PNG, SI, PNG*, 1970 *M, C, 1972 Tg, Tg, Tg*, 1973 *M, Tg, E*, 1976 *A*
A Kuruisaqila 1957 *M*, 1959 *Tg*
R Kuruisiga 1926 *Tg, Tg, Tg*

M Labaibure 1948 *M, M, M*, 1952 *A*, 1954 *A, M, M, M*
E Labalaba 1979 *E, F, PNG, Sa, Tg*, 1980 *M*, 1981 *Tg, Tg, Tg*
P Lagilagi 1939 *M*
S Lala Ragata 1999 *Ur*, 2000 *J, Tg, Sa, US*
A Laqeretabua 1924 *Sa, Tg, Sa*, 1926 *Tg, Tg, Tg*, 1928 *Tg, Tg, Tg, Sa*, 1932 *Tg, Tg, Tg*, 1934 *Tg, Tg, Tg*, 1938 *M, M*
F Lasagavibau 1997 *NZ, Tg, Coo, Sa*, 1998 *S, F, US, Sa, Tg*, 1999 *C, US, Tg, Sa, M, Sp, Nm, C, F*, 2001 *It, F*, 2002 *W, I, S*
T Latianara 2002 *Sa, Tg*
T Latianara 1976 *I*
R Latilevu 1970 *C*, 1972 *Tg, Tg*, 1973 *E*, 1974 *NZ*, 1976 *A, A*
S Laulau 1980 *A, It, M, NZ, Ar, Ar*, 1981 *Sa, Sa, Tg, Tg, Tg*, 1982 *Sa, Sa, Sa, Tg*, 1983 *Tg, Sa, SI, Niu, Tg, Sa*, 1984 *A, Sa, Tg, Tg, NZ*, 1985 *Sa, Tg, A, A, I, W*
S Leawere 2003 *Tg, Ar, Chl*, 2006 *Tg, J*
SK Leawere 2002 *S*, 2003 *Tg, Tg, Ar, Chl, F, J*, 2004 *Tg, Sa*, 2005 *W, Pt, It*, 2007 *Sa, A, Tg, J, C, W, SA*, 2008 *Sa, M, J, Tg*, 2009 *Tg, Sa, J*
I Ledua 2009 *Tg, Sa, J, S, I, R*
P Lese 1951 *M*
J Levula 1951 *M*, 1952 *A*, 1954 *A, A, M, M, M*, 1957 *M, M*, 1958 *Tg, Tg, Tg*, 1959 *Tg*, 1961 *A, A, A*
RWG Lewaravu 2007 *Sa, J, A, J, A, SA*, 2008 *Sa, M*, 2009 *S, I*, 2010 *F, It*, 2011 *Tg, Tg, Nm, SA, W*, 2013 *J, C, CAB, Tg, Pt, It, R*, 2014 *It, Sa*
I Leweniqila 1984 *Tg*
NAS Ligairi 2000 *Tg, Sa, US, C, It*, 2001 *Sa, Tg, Sa, C, Sa*, 2002 *Sa, Tg, Sa, NZ, Tg, W, I, S*, 2003 *Ar, Chl, F, J, S*, 2004 *Tg, Sa*, 2005 *M, NZ, Tg, Sa, Tg, Sa, W, It*, 2006 *Tg, It, Sa, J*, 2007 *Tg, J, C, A, W, SA*, 2009 *I, R*, 2010 *F, It*
S Ligamamada 1970 *C*, 1977 *Tg*
V Lilidamu 1986 *Tg*, 1988 *Tg*
L Little 1995 *C, Sa, Tg, W, I*, 1996 *SA, M*, 1997 *Tg, Coo, Sa*, 1998 *S*, 1999 *US, Tg, Sp*
N Little 1996 *SA, Sa, Tg, HK, HK, M*, 1997 *NZ, Tg, Coo, Sa*, 1998 *S, F, US, Sa*, 1999 *C, US, J, Tg, Sa, Sp, It, Nm, C, F, E*, 2000 *J, Tg, Sa, US, C, It*, 2001 *Tg, Sa, Sa, It, F*, 2002 *Tg, Sa, NZ, W, I*, 2003 *Tg, Ar, Chl, F, US, J, S*, 2005 *M, NZ, Sa, Tg, Sa, It*, 2007 *J, C, W*, 2009 *S, I*, 2011 *Tg, Sa, Tg, SA, Sa, W*
Livai 1926 *Tg*
V Loba 1939 *M*
D Lobendhan 1973 *M, Tg*, 1976 *A*
IM Male 1998 *A*, 1999 *Ur, E*, 2000 *J, Tg, Sa, US, C, It*, 2001 *Tg, Sa, Tg, Sa, C, S*
J Lotawa 2004 *Tg, Sa*, 2006 *Tg, J*
T Lovo 1989 *S, E*, 1990 *HK*, 1991 *Tg, C, F*, 1993 *S, Sa, Tg*
GV Lovobalavu 2007 *J, A, Tg, A, SA*, 2009 *S, I, R*, 2010 *F, W, It*, 2011 *Tg, Nm, SA, Sa, W*, 2015 *MAB, Sa, Sa, C, E, A*
E Lovodua 1958 *Tg, Tg, Tg*, 1961 *A, A, A*, 1963 *Sa, Tg, Sa, Tg*, 1964 *M*
S Lovokuru 1986 *W, Sa, Tg*, 1987 *NZ*
I Lutumailagi 1979 *F, PNG*, 1980 *It, NZ, M, Ar, Ar*, 1982 *Tg*
JB Lutumailagi 2013 *J, C, CAB*
WS Luveniyali 2007 *Tg, A*, 2008 *Sa, M, J, Tg*, 2009 *Sa, J*, 2010 *A*, 2011 *Sa, J, Tg, Tg, Nm, SA, Sa*, 2013 *Pt, Bb*

GDC Ma'afu 2010 *A, J, Tg, Sa, W, It*, 2011 *Sa, NZ, Tg, Tg, Nm, SA, Sa, W*, 2013 *J, C, CAB, US, Tg, Pt, It, R, Bb*, 2014 *It, Tg, Sa, Coo, F, W*, 2015 *MAB, Tg, Sa, J, Sa, C, E, A, W, Ur*
V Maimuri 2003 *Ar, US, J, S*
I Makutu 1976 *A, A, A*
RPN Makutu 2011 *Tg, Sa, J*, 2012 *E*
T Makutu 1979 *PNG, Sa, Tg*, 1980 *NZ, M, NZ, Ar, Ar*, 1981 *Sa, Sa, Tg, Tg, Tg*, 1982 *Sa, Sa*
K Malai 1988 *Tg, Sa, Tg*
E Malele 1973 *Tg*, 1976 *I*
D Manaseitava 1981 *Sa*, 1983 *Niu, Sa*, 1985 *Sa, Tg*
DT Manu 2009 *S*, 2010 *A, F, W, It*, 2011 *Tg, Sa, NZ, Tg, Nm, SA, Sa*, 2012 *E*
A Mara 1928 *Tg, Tg, Tg, Sa*
RT Rawaqa 2007 *Sa, J, A*, 2008 *Sa, M, J*, 2009 *Tg, Sa, J*, 2010 *A, Tg, Sa, W*, 2011 *Sa, J, NZ*

B Masilevu 2015 *MAB*
W Masirewa 1995 *Sa, W, I*, 1998 *A*
M Masitabua 1974 *M*
MS Matadigo 2006 *Tg*, 2009 *Tg*, 2011 *Sa, NZ, Tg, Tg, SA, W*, 2013 *CAB, US, It, R*, 2014 *F, W, US*, 2015 *MAB, Tg, Sa, Sa, C, E, Ur*
E Matalau 1976 *A, A*
S Matalulu 1994 *M, W, Sa*
RDT Tonawai 2007 *Tg*, 2010 *Tg, Sa*
J Matanatabu 1993 *Sa, Tg*
A Matanibuka 1932 *Tg, Tg, Tg*, 1934 *Tg, Tg, Tg*
A Matanibukaca 2005 *M, NZ, Tg, Tg*
S Matasarasara 1928 *Tg, Tg*
JL Matavesi 2009 *S, I, R*, 2010 *F, W*, 2012 *E*, 2014 *W, US*, 2015 *MAB, Tg, Sa, J, Sa, C, W, Ur*
S Matavesi 2013 *C, R, Bb*
NL Matawalu 2010 *J, Tg, Sa*, 2012 *J, S, Tg, E, Geo*, 2013 *J, CAB, US, Tg, Pt, It, Bb*, 2014 *It, Tg, Sa, Coo, F, W*, 2015 *MAB, Tg, J, Sa, C, E, A*
L Matea 1924 *Sa, Tg, Tg, Tg, Sa*
W Mateiwai 1993 *Sa, Tg, Tg*
N Matirawa 1984 *Tg*, 1989 *Tg, Tg, E*
JTF Matson 1999 *M, Ur*
J McLennan 1994 *M, W, Sa, Tg*, 1995 *C*, 1996 *HK*
T Mitchell 1986 *Tg, Tg*, 1987 *It, F, Sa, Tg*, 1988 *Tg, Sa, E, Tg, Tg*
V Mocelutu 1974 *NZ, M, M*
M Mocetadra 2012 *Tg*
S Morrell 2009 *J*
I Mow 2002 *Sa, Tg, Sa, Tg*, 2003 *Tg*
A Mucunabita 1994 *J, J*
J Mucunabitu 1957 *M, M*, 1959 *Tg*, 1964 *M, W, F*, 1968 *NZ, Tg, Tg*
K Murimurivalu 2011 *Tg, Tg, Tg, Nm, SA, Sa*, 2015 *MAB, Tg, J, Sa, C, W, Ur*
I Musanamasi 1982 *Sa, Sa, E*, 1983 *SI*
K Musunamasi 1977 *Tg, Tg, Tg, BI*, 1979 *M, E, PNG, Sa*

L Nabaro 1976 *I*
N Nabaro 1957 *M, M*, 1959 *Tg*, 1961 *A, A, A*, 1964 *M*
M Nabati 1985 *A, A, W*
O Nabavu 1926 *Tg, Tg*
K Nabili 1926 *Tg*, 1928 *Tg, Tg, Tg, Sa*
K Nabili 1985 *Tg*
I Nabobo 1976 *I*
G Naborisi 1992 *Tg*
G Naborisi 1954 *A*
I Nabou 1961 *A, A, A*
M Nabuta 1967 *Tg, Tg*, 1968 *NZ, Tg, Tg, Tg*, 1969 *PNG, SI, PNG*
S Nacaka 1981 *Tg*, 1982 *Sa, Tg, S*
F Naceba 1924 *Sa, Tg, Tg, Tg, Sa*
S Nacolai 1968 *NZ, Tg, Tg*, 1969 *W, SI, PNG*
V Nadaku 1934 *Tg, Tg*, 1938 *M, M, M*
A Nadolo 1987 *It, F, Sa, Tg*, 1988 *E, Tg, Tg*, 1989 *Tg, Tg*, 1991 *Sa, Tg, Tg, R*, 1992 *Sa, Tg*, 1993 *S, Sa, Tg, Tg*, 1995 *C, Sa, Tg, I*
J Nadolo 2000 *Tg, Sa, US, C, It*
A Nadredre 1964 *F, C*, 1968 *Tg*
M Nadridri 2004 *Sa*, 2005 *Sa, Tg*
N Nadruku 1988 *Tg, Sa, E, Tg, Tg*, 1989 *Tg, Bel, S, E*, 1990 *J, HK*, 1991 *C, R*
S Nadruku 1981 *Sa, Sa, Tg, Tg*, 1982 *Sa, Sa, Sa, Tg, S, E*, 1983 *SI, Tg*, 1984 *Sa, Tg, NZ*
A Naevo 1996 *HK, HK, M*, 1997 *NZ, Tg, Sa*, 1998 *S, F, US, Sa, Tg*, 1999 *J, Tg, Sa, M, Sp, Ur, It, Nm, C*, 2001 *Tg, Sa, Sa, C, Sa*, 2002 *W, I, S*, 2003 *Tg, F, US, S*
I Nagatalevu 1939 *M*
A Nagi 2001 *It, F*, 2004 *Tg, Sa*, 2005 *W, Pt, It*, 2006 *Tg, It, Sa, J*
A Nagicu 1996 *HK*
N Nagusa 2012 *Geo*, 2013 *R, Bb*, 2014 *It, Tg, Sa*
T Nagusa 2008 *Sa, M, J*, 2009 *Tg, I, R*, 2010 *A, J*, 2011 *Tg, J, NZ*, 2013 *CAB, US, Pt, It, R*, 2014 *It, Tg, Coo, F, W, US*, 2015 *W, Ur*
Naibuka 1968 *Tg*
T Naidole 1954 *M*, 1957 *M, M*, 1958 *Tg, Tg, Tg*, 1959 *Tg*
S Naiduki 1979 *PNG, Sa, Tg*
J Naikadawa 2009 *R*, 2010 *A, J, It*, 2011 *J*
AN Naikatini 2012 *J, Sa, S, Tg, E, Geo*, 2013 *J, C, CAB, US, Tg, Pt, It, R, Bb*, 2014 *It, Tg, Coo*

S Ralawa 1934 *Tg, Tg, Tg,* 1938 *M, M, M,* 1939 *M*
J Ralulu 2008 *Sa, Tg,* 2010 *J, Tg, Sa,* 2012 *S, Tg, Geo,* 2014 *It, Tg, Sa, Coo, F, US*
TD Ralumu 1979 *E, F*
T Ranavue 1947 *Tg, Tg,* 1952 *A, A,* 1954 *A, A, M, M, M*
NS Kenatale 2008 *J, Tg,* 2009 *Tg, Sa, J,* 2010 *F, W, It,* 2011 *Tg, Sa, NZ, Tg, Nm, SA, Sa, W,* 2012 *Sa, S,* 2013 *J, C, CAB, US, Tg, Pt, It, R, Bb,* 2014 *It, Tg, Coo, US,* 2015 *MAB, Sa, C, A, W, Ur*
S Rarasea 1961 *A*
V Rarawa 2010 *It*
L Rasala 1994 *J, J*
M Rasari 1988 *Tg, Sa, E, Tg,* 1989 *Bel, S, E,* 1990 *Sa,* 1991 *Sa, Tg*
I Rasila 1992 *Sa, M,* 1998 *S, F, A,* 1999 *C, US, Sp, Ur, E,* 2000 *J, Tg, Sa, US, C, It,* 2001 *Tg, Sa, Tg, Sa, C, Sa, It,* 2002 *Sa, Tg, Sa, NZ, S,* 2003 *Tg, Tg, Ar, Chl, J, S*
P Rasiosateki 1963 *Sa, Tg,* 1964 *M, W, F, C*
S Rasolea 1984 *Tg, NZ,* 1985 *Sa, Tg, A*
S Rasua 1961 *A, A, A*
RA Ratini 2014 *F*
J Ratu 1980 *NZ, Ar, Ar,* 1981 *Sa, Tg, Tg, Tg,* 1982 *Sa, Tg, S, E*
Q Ratu 1976 *I,* 1977 *Tg, Tg, Tg, Bl*
R Ratu 2009 *Sa, J,* 2010 *A, J, Tg, Sa, W*
S Ratu 1968 *Tg*
J Ratu 2009 *S, R*
N Ratudina 1972 *Tg, Tg,* 1973 *M, M, E,* 1974 *NZ, M, M,* 1977 *Tg, Tg, Tg, Bl,* 1979 *M, F*
E Ratudradra 1980 *A, M, NZ, Ar, Ar,* 1981 *Tg, Tg, Tg*
V Ratudradra 1976 *A, A,* 1977 *Tg, Bl,* 1979 *M, E,* 1980 *NZ, M,* 1981 *Sa, Sa,* 1982 *Sa,* 1984 *Tg*
S Ratumaiyali 1947 *Tg*
K Ratumuri 1980 *M,* 1981 *Sa, Sa*
E Ratuniata 2001 *Sa, Tg,* 2002 *Sa, Sa*
A Ratuniyarawa 2012 *E, Geo,* 2013 *J, C, CAB, US, Tg, Pt,* 2014 *It, Tg, Sa, Coo, F,* 2015 *MAB, Sa, C, E, Ur*
RARG Ratuva 2005 *M, NZ, Tg, Tg, Sa, W, It,* 2006 *Sa, J,* 2007 *Tg, J, A, W, SA,* 2008 *Sa, M, J, Tg*
I Ratuva 2012 *J, Sa, S, Tg, E, Geo,* 2013 *C, US*
N Ratuveilawa 1961 *A,* 1963 *Sa, Tg, Sa, Tg,* 1964 *C*
K Ratuvou 2005 *Sa, W, Pt, It,* 2006 *Tg, It, Sa, J,* 2007 *Tg, J, C, W, SA,* 2008 *Sa, M, J,* 2012 *Sa, S*
SD Raulini 1997 *Sa*
T Raulumi 1973 *M*
J Rauluni 1995 *C, Sa, Tg, W, I,* 1996 *SA, Sa, Tg,* 1997 *NZ, Tg,* 1998 *S, F, US, Sa, Tg,* 1999 *J, M, Ur, It, Nm, C, F, E,* 2000 *Sa, C, It,* 2001 *Sa, Tg, Sa, C, Sa,* 2002 *Sa, Tg, Sa, NZ, Tg, W, I, S,* 2003 *Tg, S,* 2005 *M, NZ, Tg, Sa, Tg,* 2006 *It, Sa, J*
MN Rauluni 1996 *M,* 1997 *Tg, Coo, Sa,* 1998 *A,* 1999 *Sp, It, C, E,* 2000 *J, Tg, US, C, It,* 2001 *Tg,* 2003 *Ar, Chl, F, US, J, S,* 2004 *Tg, Sa,* 2005 *M, NZ, Tg, Sa, Tg, Sa, W, Pt, It,* 2007 *A, Tg, J, C, A, W, SA,* 2008 *Sa, M,* 2009 *S, I*
P Rauluni 1984 *A, Sa, Tg,* 1986 *Sa, Tg*
T Rauluni 1968 *Tg,* 1972 *Tg,* 1974 *NZ, M*
V Rauluni 1990 *Sa,* 1991 *Sa, Tg, E*
V Rauluni 2004 *NZ, J, A*
V Rauluni 1992 *Sa,* 1993 *S, Tg*
J Rauto 1976 *A, A, A,* 1977 *Tg, Tg, Bl,* 1979 *M, E,* 1980 *Ar, Ar,* 1981 *Sa, Sa, Tg, Tg, Tg,* 1982 *Sa, Sa, Tg, E,* 1984 *Tg, NZ*
P Ravaga 1926 *Tg, Tg,* 1928 *Tg, Tg, Sa*
J Ravai 1928 *Tg, Tg, Tg, Sa*
M Ravai 1928 *Tg, Tg*
E Ravi 1961 *A, A, A*
E Ravouvou 1928 *Tg, Tg, Tg, Sa*
I Ravouvou 1958 *Tg, Tg, Tg,* 1959 *Tg*
I Ravouvou 1986 *Sa, Tg,* 1987 *Sa, Tg*
J Ravouvou 1979 *PNG, Sa, Tg,* 1980 *NZ, M, NZ, Ar, Ar*
N Ravouvou 1967 *Tg, Tg, Tg,* 1968 *NZ, Tg, Tg,* 1969 *W, PNG, Sl, PNG,* 1970 *M, M, C,* 1972 *A,* 1973 *M, M, Tg, E*
T Ravouvou 1948 *M*
J Ravu 1948 *M, M,* 1954 *M, M, M*
T Ravualala 1976 *I*
L Tabuarua 2013 *J, C, US*
M Ravula 1958 *Tg, Tg, Tg*
RMM Ravulo 2010 *F, W,* 2011 *Tg, Sa, NZ, Tg, Nm, Sa, W,* 2012 *J, Sa, S, E, Geo,* 2013 *J, C, CAB, US, Tg, Pt, It, R, Bb,* 2014 *It, Tg, Sa, Coo, F, W, US,* 2015 *MAB, Tg, Sa, J, A, W*
AQ Qiodravu 2000 *US, Tg, It,* 2001 *Tg, Sa, Tg, Sa, C, Sa, It, F,* 2007 *A, Tg, J, C, A, W, SA*

I Rawaqa 2002 *Sa, Tg, Sa, NZ, Tg, I,* 2003 *Ar, Chl, F, US, S,* 2004 *Tg, Sa,* 2005 *M, NZ, Tg, Sa, Tg, Sa, W, Pt, It,* 2006 *Tg, It,* 2007 *J, A, Tg, C, A, W, SA,* 2008 *Sa, M, J,* 2009 *Sa, S, I,* 2010 *W,* 2011 *J*
F Rayasi 1994 *M, W, Sa, Tg,* 1995 *C, Sa, Tg, W, I,* 1996 *SA, HK, HK,* 1997 *NZ*
E Rayawa 1961 *A*
J Rayawa 1979 *F, PNG, Sa, Tg*
P Rika 1958 *Tg, Tg*
A Rinakama 2001 *Sa, C, Sa*
A Robe 1964 *W, F, C*
S Rokini 2000 *J, Tg, Sa, US,* 2001 *Sa, Tg, Sa, C, Sa, It,* 2003 *Chl*
AV Rokobaro 2013 *Pt, R, Bb*
S Rokobaro 2004 *Tg, Sa,* 2005 *M, NZ*
N Rokobiau 2009 *I, R*
E Rokowailoa 1982 *Sa, Tg, S,* 1983 *Tg, Niu, Tg, Sa,* 1987 *Ar, NZ, It,* 1990 *J, Tg, Sa,* 1992 *M,* 1993 *S, Sa, Tg, Tg*
RMS Saulo 2012 *E, Geo,* 2013 *J, C, CAB, US, Tg, Pt, It, R, Bb,* 2014 *It, Tg, Sa, Coo, F, W, US,* 2015 *MAB, Tg, Sa, J, Sa, C, E, A, W*
D Rouse 1995 *C, Tg, W,* 1996 *SA, Tg, HK, HK, M,* 1997 *NZ, Tg, Coo, Sa,* 1998 *US, A, Sa, Tg,* 1999 *US, J, Tg, Sa, M, Ur, It, Nm, C, F, E*
S Rovuaka 1947 *Tg, Tg*
E Ruivadra 2002 *Tg, Tg, W, S,* 2003 *Tg, J, S,* 2005 *M, NZ, Tg, Sa, Tg, W, Pt, It,* 2006 *Tg, J,* 2010 *J, Sa*

S Sacere 1968 *Tg*
S Sadria 1991 *Sa, Tg, Tg,* 1993 *Sa, Tg,* 1994 *J, J, M*
P Sailasa 1934 *Tg*
G Sailosi 1969 *W, PNG, PNG*
K Salabogi 2005 *W, Pt, It,* 2006 *It*
W Salabogi 1951 *M,* 1952 *A, A,* 1954 *A, A*
L Saladoka 1947 *Tg*
K Salawa 2003 *Tg, Tg, Ar, Chl, F, S*
I Salusalu 2012 *Sa,* 2013 *C*
K Salusalu 1982 *Tg, S, E,* 1983 *Tg, Sa, Sl, Niu, Tg, Sa,* 1987 *It, F, Sa, Tg,* 1990 *Sa*
R Samo 2005 *Tg, Tg,* 2006 *Tg, It, Sa, J*
R Samuels 1973 *M, M, Tg, E,* 1974 *NZ, M, M*
J Sanday 1987 *Ar, It*
K Sarai 1988 *Tg, Sa, Tg*
M Sarasau 1976 *I*
A Sassen 1993 *Tg*
A Satala 2005 *Tg, Sa, Tg,* 2007 *A,* 2009 *I, R*
V Satala 1999 *C, US, J, Tg, Sa, M, Sp, It, Nm, C, F, E,* 2000 *C, It,* 2001 *Tg, Sa, Tg, C, Sa, It, F,* 2002 *Tg, Sa, NZ, Tg, I, S,* 2005 *M, NZ*
RMS Naevo 2006 *Sa, J,* 2007 *J, C, W, SA,* 2008 *Sa, M, J,* 2009 *Tg, Sa,* 2010 *F, W, It*
I Saukuru 1994 *J, J, W*
J Saukuru 1954 *A, A, M, M, M,* 1957 *M, M,* 1958 *Tg, Tg, Tg,* 1959 *Tg,* 1963 *Sa, Tg, Sa, Tg*
WR Saukuru 2010 *Tg, Sa*
S Saumaisue 1998 *S, F, US*
M Saunaki 1984 *NZ*
S Sautu 1957 *M, M,* 1958 *Tg, Tg, Tg*
V Sauturaga 2007 *Tg, C, A, W,* 2008 *Sa, M, J,* 2009 *R*
I Savai 1984 *A, Sa, Tg, Tg, NZ,* 1985 *Sa, Tg, A,* 1987 *Ar, NZ, It, F,* 1989 *Tg, Bel, S, E,* 1990 *J, Tg, Sa, HK,* 1991 *Sa, Tg, E, C, F, R,* 1992 *Sa, Tg, M,* 1993 *Tg,* 1994 *J, J, M, W, Sa, Tg,* 1995 *C*
M Seavula 1988 *Sa,* 1989 *Tg, Bel*
A Secake 1957 *M,* 1958 *Tg,* 1959 *Tg*
N Senilagakali 1980 *NZ, Ar, Ar*
RHW Senliloli 2013 *R, Bb,* 2014 *F, W, US,* 2015 *Tg, Sa, J, W, Ur*
M Seniloli 1926 *Tg, Tg,* 1928 *Tg, Sa*
R Seniloli 1934 *Tg, Tg, Tg*
T Seniloli 1926 *Tg,* 1928 *Sa*
I Senivau 1968 *NZ*
W Serevi 1989 *Bel, S,* 1990 *J, Sa,* 1991 *Tg, E, C, F,* 1992 *Sa,* 1993 *S,* 1996 *SA, Tg, M,* 1998 *S, F, US, A, Sa, Tg,* 1999 *Tg, Sa, M, Sp, Ur, It, Nm, C, E,* 2001 *It, F,* 2002 *W, I, S,* 2003 *Tg, Ar, Chl, F, J*
F Seru 1990 *Tg, Sa, HK,* 1991 *Tg, E, C, F, R,* 1992 *Sa,* 1993 *Tg*
N Seru 2003 *Ar, Chl, F, US, S*
S Seru 1980 *M, NZ*
S Seruvakula 2002 *Sa*
SG Seruvatu 1952 *A, A,* 1954 *A, M, M, M,* 1959 *Tg*

FIJI

V Seuseu 2008 *Sa, M, J, Tg*, 2009 *Tg, Sa, I, R*
S Sevu 2001 *Sa*
K Sewabu 1999 *C, US, J, Tg, Sa, M, Sp, It, Nm, C, F, E*, 2000 *US, C, It*, 2002 *Sa, NZ, Tg*, 2003 *Tg, Ar, US, J, S*
S Sikivou 1968 *Tg*, 1969 *W, PNG, SI, PNG*, 1970 *M, M*, 1973 *M*
R Silotolu 1954 *M, M, M*
M Sisiwa 1994 *J*
G Smith 1995 *W, I*, 1996 *SA, Sa, Tg, HK, HK, M*, 1997 *NZ, Tg, Coo, Sa*, 1998 *US, Sa, Tg*, 1999 *J, Tg, Sa, M, It, Nm, C, F, E*, 2000 *US, C, It*, 2001 *Tg, Sa, Tg, Sa, C, Sa*, 2002 *Sa, Tg, Sa, NZ, Tg, W, I, S*, 2003 *F, US, J, S*
J Sokovata 1963 *Sa, Tg, Tg*, 1964 *M*
S Somoca 2011 *J, NZ, Tg, Sa, W*, 2012 *J, Sa, S, Tg, E, Geo*, 2013 *J, C, CAB, US, Tg, Pt, It, R, Bb*
NR Soqeta 2014 *F, W, US*, 2015 *MAB, Tg, Sa, Sa, A, W*
TN Soqeta 2007 *Sa, J, A*
A Soqosoqo 1964 *M, W, F, C*
SC Sorovaki 1995 *C, Sa, Tg, W, I*, 1996 *SA, Sa, Tg, HK, HK, M*, 1997 *NZ, Tg, Coo, Sa*, 1998 *S, F, US, A, Sa, Tg*
W Sotutu 1999 *C, US, J, Tg, M, Sp, Ur, It, Nm, C, F, E*
V Sovalevu 1992 *Sa, Tg*
J Sovau 1970 *M, M, C*, 1972 *A*, 1973 *M*, 1974 *M*, 1976 *A, A*, 1979 *PNG, Sa, Tg*
Sovu 1928 *Sa*
S Speight 2013 *Bb*
W Suka 1990 *HK*, 1993 *Sa, Tg*
WS Sukanaveita 2009 *Tg, J*
J Suluaqalo 1932 *Tg, Tg*
A Suluoqalo 1964 *M*
J Susu 1948 *M, M, M*, 1951 *M*, 1952 *A, A*

J Tabaiwalu 1957 *M, M*, 1958 *Tg, Tg, Tg*, 1959 *Tg*, 1961 *A, A, A*, 1963 *Sa, Sa*
S Tabua 2005 *M, NZ*
I Tabualevu 1984 *Sa, Tg*
I Tabualevu 1958 *Tg, Tg, Tg*, 1967 *Tg, Tg*
S Tabualevu 1983 *Sa*
M Tabukaci 1947 *Tg, Tg*
P Tabulutu 1986 *Tg, Sa, Tg*, 1987 *Ar, Sa, Tg*, 1988 *Tg, E, Tg, Tg*, 1990 *J, Sa*, 1991 *Sa, Tg, E, C, F, R*
S Tadulala 2009 *R*
MV Taga 1987 *NZ*, 1988 *Tg, Sa, E, Tg*, 1989 *Tg, Tg, Bel, S, E*, 1990 *J, Tg, HK*, 1991 *Sa, Tg, E, C, F*, 1992 *Sa, Tg, M*, 1993 *S, Sa, Tg, Tg*, 1996 *HK, M*, 1997 *NZ, Coo*, 1998 *S, F, A*
N Taga 1952 *A*
N Tagi 2004 *Tg, Sa*
ML Tagicakibau 2007 *Tg*, 2008 *J*, 2010 *W*, 2011 *Tg, W*
JR Railomo 2005 *NZ*, 2007 *J, C, A, W, SA*, 2008 *Sa, M, J, Tg*
MS Tagivetaua 1981 *Tg, Tg*, 1982 *Sa, Sa*, 1983 *Tg, Sa*
S Taka 2006 *Tg*, 2007 *Sa, J*, 2010 *F, W*
S Talawadua 1985 *A*
M Talebula 2012 *S, Tg, E, Geo*, 2013 *It, R*, 2014 *It, Tg, Sa, Coo, F, W*, 2015 *Sa, J, Sa, C, E, A, W*
NE Talei 2006 *Tg, It, Sa, J*, 2007 *Sa, J, J, C, A*, 2008 *Sa, M, J, Tg*, 2009 *Tg, Sa, J*, 2011 *Tg, Nm, SA, Sa, W*, 2012 *J, Sa, S*, 2013 *J, CAB, US, Tg, Bb*, 2015 *C, A, W, Ur*
V Taliga 1928 *Tg, Sa*
S Tamanibeka 1924 *Sa, Tg, Tg, Tg, Sa*, 1926 *Tg*, 1928 *Tg, Tg, Tg, Sa*
M Tamanitoakula 1998 *S, F, A*
I Tabua 1990 *J, Tg*, 1995 *W*, 1998 *F, A, Sa, Tg*, 1999 *C, US, J, Tg, Sa, M, Sp, It, C, F*
S Tamanivalu 1967 *Tg, Tg*
T Tamanivalu 1995 *I*, 1996 *SA, Sa, Tg, HK, HK, M*
M Tamata 1981 *Sa, Tg, Tg, Tg*, 1982 *Tg, S, E*
N Tamaya 1981 *Sa*
B Tanivukavu 1957 *M*
I Taoba 1974 *M*, 1976 *A, A, A*, 1977 *Tg, Tg, Tg, Bl*, 1980 *A, It, NZ*, 1981 *Sa, Tg, Tg, Tg*, 1982 *Tg, S, E*
J Taqaiwai 1991 *Tg, E*
J Taqiri 1976 *A*
A Tarogi 2009 *J, I, R*
I Tasere 1974 *NZ, M, M*
E Tatawaqa 1981 *Tg, Tg, Tg*, 1982 *Sa, Sa, Sa, Tg, S*
P Tatukivei 1958 *Tg*
E Tauga 1994 *Tg*
I Taukei 1924 *Sa, Tg, Tg, Tg, Sa*, 1926 *Tg*
I Tawake 1986 *W*, 1987 *Sa, Tg*, 1988 *Tg, Tg*, 1990 *J*, 1991 *Tg, E, C, F, R*, 1992 *Sa, Tg, M*, 1993 *S, Sa, Tg*, 1994 *J, J, M, W, Sa, Tg*, 1995 *C, Sa, Tg, W, I*, 1996 *SA, Sa, Tg, HK, M*,

1997 *NZ, Coo, Sa*, 1998 *S, F, US, A*, 1999 *C, US, Tg, Sp, Ur, E*
S Tawake 1992 *Sa, M*, 1998 *Sa, Tg*, 1999 *C, US, J, M, It, Nm, C, F, E*, 2002 *Sa, NZ, Tg, W, I, S*, 2003 *Chl*
S Tawase 1961 *A, A*
E Teleni 1982 *Sa, Sa, S, E*, 1983 *Tg, Sa, Niu, Tg, Sa*, 1984 *A, Sa, Tg*, 1985 *A, A, I, W*, 1986 *W*, 1988 *Tg*, 1989 *Tg, Tg, Bel, S, E*
L Temani 1924 *Sa, Tg, Tg, Tg, Sa*
DD Thomas 2007 *Tg*, 2008 *M, Tg*
I Tikoduadua 1982 *S, E*, 1983 *Sa*
T Matawalu 2005 *Pt*, 2007 *Sa, J*
E Tikoidraubuta 1992 *Tg*
A Tikoirotuma 2013 *Pt, It, R, Bb*, 2014 *It, Sa, Coo, F, W, US*, 2015 *Tg, Sa, Sa, C, A, W, Ur*
P Bosco 1968 *Tg, Tg*, 1970 *M, M*, 1972 *Tg, Tg, Tg, A*, 1973 *M, M, Tg, E*, 1977 *Tg, Tg, Tg, Bl*, 1979 *M, E*
I Tikomaimakogai 1999 *US, J, Tg, Sa, M, Ur, It, Nm, E*, 2000 *J, Tg*
K Tilalati 2000 *J, Sa*
A Toga 1963 *Tg, Sa, Tg*
S Toga 1964 *W, C*, 1967 *Tg, Tg, Tg*, 1968 *NZ, Tg*, 1969 *W, PNG, SI, PNG*, 1970 *C*
A Tokairavua 1967 *Tg*, 1970 *M, C*, 1972 *Tg, Tg, Tg, A*, 1973 *M, Tg*, 1977 *Tg, Tg*
J Toloi 1994 *M, W, Sa, Tg*
S Tolotu 1964 *F*
J Tora 2005 *Tg, Sa, Tg, Sa, Pt*, 2006 *Tg, J*
P Tora 1986 *Sa, Tg*
P Tove 1951 *M*
TD Tuapati 2010 *A, J, Tg, Sa, F, W, It*, 2011 *Tg, Sa, Tg, SA, Sa*, 2012 *Sa, S, Tg, Geo*, 2013 *J, C, CAB, US, Tg*, 2014 *It, Tg, Sa, US*, 2015 *MAB, Tg, J, Sa, E, A*
T Tubananitu 1980 *A, It, NZ*, 1981 *Sa, Sa, Tg, Tg, Tg*, 1982 *Sa, Sa, Sa, S*, 1983 *Niu, Tg, Sa*, 1984 *Tg, NZ*, 1985 *A*
W Tubu 1967 *Tg*
P Tubui 1981 *Sa, Sa*
S Tubuna 1932 *Tg, Tg, Tg*
N Tubutubu 1924 *Sa, Tg, Tg, Tg, Sa*
E Tudia 1974 *Tg*
P Tuidraki 1994 *J, J, M, W, Sa, Tg*
P Tuidraki 1932 *Tg, Tg, Tg*
J Tuikabe 1999 *US, Sa, Ur*, 2000 *J, Tg, Sa, US, C, It*, 2001 *Tg, Sa, Tg, Sa, C, Sa, It, F*
A Tuilevu 1996 *SA, Sa, Tg, HK*, 1997 *Tg, Coo, Sa*, 1998 *S, F, A, Sa*, 2003 *Tg, Tg, Ar, F, US, J, S*, 2004 *Tg*
J Tuilevu 2008 *Tg*
W Tuinagiagia 1968 *Tg*, 1976 *I*
E Tuisese 2001 *F*
I Tuisese 1969 *W, SI*, 1970 *M, M, C*, 1972 *Tg, Tg*, 1973 *E*, 1974 *NZ, M, M*, 1976 *A, A*, 1977 *Tg, Tg, Bl*
I Tuisese 2000 *J, Sa*
S Tuisese 1958 *Tg*, 1963 *Sa, Tg, Sa, Tg*, 1964 *M, W, F*
W Tuisese 1947 *Tg*, 1948 *M, M, M*
A Tuitavua 1938 *M, M, M*, 1939 *M*, 1947 *Tg, Tg*, 1948 *M, M, M*, 1952 *A, A*, 1954 *A, A, M, M, M*
E Tuivunivono 1993 *Tg*
N Tuiyau 1948 *M, M, M*
T Tukaitabua 1968 *NZ, Tg, Tg, Tg*, 1972 *Tg*
U Tukana 1963 *Sa, Sa, Tg*, 1964 *M, W, F, C*
T Tukunia 1984 *Tg*
AV Vata 2005 *It*, 2008 *Sa, J, Tg*
W Turaga 1986 *Tg*
A Turagacoko 1968 *NZ, Tg, Tg*, 1969 *W*
A Turukawa 2004 *Sa*, 2005 *Pt*, 2007 *Sa, J, A, Tg*
E Turuva 1984 *A*, 1985 *A, I*
O Turuva 1990 *HK*, 1991 *E, R*, 1994 *Sa, Tg*, 1995 *C, Sa, Tg*, 1998 *A*, 1999 *C, US*
S Tuva 1959 *Tg*, 1961 *A, A, A*
M Tuvoli 1951 *M*
S Tuvula 1985 *A, I, W*, 1986 *W*, 1987 *Ar, NZ, It*
E Tuvunivono 1992 *M*, 1993 *S, Tg*, 1997 *NZ*

T Uliuviti 1926 *Tg, Tg, Tg*, 1928 *Tg*
A Uluinayau 1996 *SA, Sa, Tg, HK, HK, M*, 1997 *NZ, Tg, Coo, Sa*, 1998 *F, Sa, Tg*, 1999 *C, J, Tg, Sa, Nm, C, F, E*, 2001 *Tg, C, Sa*, 2002 *Sa, Sa, NZ*, 2003 *Tg, US*
N Uluiviti 1957 *M, M*, 1959 *Tg*
N Uluvula 1976 *I*, 1979 *M, E, F, PNG, Tg*, 1980 *Ar, Ar*, 1982 *Sa, Sa*, 1983 *Tg, Sa, SI, Sa*, 1984 *A, Tg, NZ*, 1986 *Tg*

FRANCE

FRANCE'S 2014–15 TEST RECORD

OPPONENTS	DATE	VENUE	RESULT
Fiji	8 Nov	H	Won 40–15
Australia	15 Nov	H	Won 29–26
Argentina	22 Nov	H	Lost 13–18
Scotland	7 Feb	H	Won 15–8
Ireland	14 Feb	A	Lost 18–11
Wales	28 Feb	H	Lost 13–20
Italy	15 Mar	A	Won 29–0
England	21 Mar	A	Lost 55–35
England	15 Aug	A	Lost 19–14
England	22 Aug	H	Won 25–20
Scotland	6 Sep	H	Won 19–16
Italy	19 Sep	N	Won 32–10
Romania	23 Sep	N	Won 38–11
Canada	1 Oct	N	Won 41–18
Ireland	11 Oct	N	Lost 24–9
New Zealand	17 Oct	N	Lost 62–13

SOMBRE EXIT FOR FRANCE AND SAINT-ANDRÉ

By Iain Spragg

France got their Rugby World Cup 2015 campaign off to a winning start by beating Italy 32–10 at Twickenham.

The fourth and final year of Philippe Saint-André's inauspicious reign as head coach climaxed in depressingly familiar fashion for beleaguered supporters of Les Bleus as their side stumbled once again in the RBS 6 Nations before they were ripped apart by the All Blacks in Cardiff in the quarter-finals of Rugby World Cup 2015.

France's tepid displays in the Six Nations, finishing a distant fourth and culminating in conceding 55 points to England on the final weekend, came as little surprise given their failure to finish in the top three under Saint-André, but his team's 62–13 savaging by New Zealand on the game's greatest stage was a new nadir for a national coach on whose head the crown had never rested comfortably.

Saint-André already knew that irrespective of Les Bleus' results or performances Rugby World Cup 2015 would be his last hurrah before making way for his preordained successor Guy Novès and he departed

in the most ignominious manner imaginable, France surrendering more
points against New Zealand than they had ever done in any of their
721 previous test matches.

A meagre return of 20 victories in 45 internationals told the sad story
of Saint-André's reign. Novès will face the same challenges as he bids
to revive French fortunes going forward and while in 2014 Saint-André
had bemoaned the lack of homegrown players in the Top 14, he used
his final interviews as head coach a year later to expand on what he
perceived as the major problems facing Gallic rugby.

"We need to realise at a high level that French rugby needs to bring
something different to its organisation," he said. "It's not my job to tell
them [the FFR] what to do, that is their job. Our players play 40 games
a year but New Zealand players play 25 games a year.

"I accept my responsibilities. I've taken a lot of blows over the past
four years, but I'm ready to take more. I think in our sport we have to
show dignity in victory and in defeat. We have to congratulate New
Zealand for its exceptional performance. We knew that we would have
to put a great doubt in them to be close to their score."

The countdown to what would prove a chastening World Cup experience began with three tests in November 2014. A comfortable victory
over Fiji (40–15) in Marseille was followed by an eye-catching defeat
of the Wallabies (29–26) in Paris, but French hopes of registering a clean
sweep for the first time since 2012 were dashed when Argentina came
away from the Stade de France with a deserved 18–13 triumph.

The more serious business of the Six Nations began in early February
but their failure to score a try in a difficult 15–8 win against Scotland
in Paris in their opening fixture was a portent of their struggles to come
and there was precious little to celebrate from a French perspective as
the tournament unfolded. There was certainly no disgrace in their 18–11
reverse against defending champions Ireland in Dublin but a 20–13
defeat to Wales in Paris a fortnight later was a body blow to a side
desperately looking to build momentum and confidence.

The result inevitably intensified the already considerable pressure on
Saint-André and not for the first time during his tenure he was forced
to mount an impassioned defence of his regime, if not his players.

"I've never abandoned ship, whether as a player, as a captain or as
a manager," he said. "I've been given a role, to prepare this team for
the World Cup and I'll fight every day to do that. International rugby
is about combat, humility but above all it's a collective sport. We don't
need starlets. In rugby, the team is the star and we need champions.
Yesterday [against Wales], I didn't see any champions."

His displeasure with the performance was evidenced by the eight changes for France's penultimate fixture against Italy and his new-look side responded with a much-improved performance in Rome, Yoann Maestri and Mathieu Bastareaud going over for the tries in a 29–0 success.

The result gave France an outside chance of the Six Nations title going into the final game at Twickenham but lingering hope was cruelly replaced by a scene of devastation as England ran in seven tries to register a 55–35 victory, the first time they had surpassed the half century against Les Bleus. Five well-worked tries from France in London were scant consolation and it was another Six Nations campaign in which Saint-André's side had failed to justify their reputation as one of the game's heavyweights.

The confirmation in May that Novès was to be the next man in the hot seat put pay to speculation that Saint-André might not survive long enough to take the side to the World Cup and he was able to instil a degree of calm if not burgeoning confidence in the squad after leading Les Bleus to warm-up victories in Paris over Scotland and England. They were narrowly beaten by England at Twickenham in the reverse fixture but it was a period of preparation mercifully free of alarm or disharmony and Saint-André's final 31-man RWC 2015 squad featured no seismic shocks, his decision to name the resurgent Frédéric Michalak ahead of François Trinh-Duc as one of his two fly-halves the headline call.

France began the tournament in September against familiar foes in the shape of Italy at Twickenham. The boot of Michalak was Les Bleus' only source of points in the opening 40 minutes but second-half tries from props Rabah Slimani and Nicolas Mas – his first in 81 tests for his country – ensured they began RWC 2015 on the front foot with a 32–10 win.

The challenges of Romania (38–11) and Canada (41–18) were met and overcome to make it three from three and a clash with Ireland at the Millennium Stadium to determine the Pool D winners lay ahead. More significantly the victors in Cardiff knew they would face Argentina rather than the All Blacks in the quarter-finals.

France promised to throw down a physical gauntlet to the Irish and they delivered on that but were unable to trouble Joe Schmidt's side defensively for prolonged periods and two penalties from full-back Scott Spedding and a third from Morgan Parra were all they had to show for their efforts as they crashed to a 24–9 defeat in the Welsh capital.

"We didn't perform well today but Ireland were quite exceptional and disciplined in all the phases of play," conceded Saint-André. "But we have no time to think about the defeat now because we enter another competition, it is the knockout phase now. We will prepare with enthusiasm and appetite.

"The history of the World Cup says everything can happen. When you're French, it's not good when you're favourite. We must not think, we must play rugby. New Zealand are favourites, but in a game of rugby you never know. It's important for us to stick together."

If the media reports which emanated from the French camp in the week before the New Zealand game were to be believed however, the exact opposite occurred and Saint-André was forced to fend off questions about an alleged player revolt as the quarter-final loomed. The encounter with the world champions proved to be a brutal dissection of every facet of the French team. It all began to spectacularly unravel when the All Blacks scored the first of their nine tries in the 10th minute at the Millennium Stadium at the same time as France lost Michalak to injury, and although number eight Louis Picamoles did score Les Bleus were already 29–13 adrift at half-time.

An early yellow card for Picamoles after the restart only compounded France's woes and five further New Zealand tries, including the completion of Julian Savea's hat-trick, turned defeat into a rout and Saint-André's final game in charge into a devastating disappointment for the man himself and French rugby in general.

The post-mortems began immediately and while the rumours persisted that Saint-André had lost the dressing room, at least one of the squad was prepared to support the departing head coach and his assertion that the team's failings could not be laid exclusively at the door of the current management.

"We believed we could do it with our preparation, that we would be able to make up for the lost time," said second-row Pascal Papé after his 65th and final cap for France. "But I think the problem is much deeper. We're in a system with a championship where you have to play 40 games a year. What happened tonight shows that when you play against a team whose players have played 20 games in the year, you can't compete. The national team comes last. It is time that everyone in French rugby sit around a table and make the France team a priority. If this does not happen the next coach will face the same problems."

FRANCE INTERNATIONAL STATISTICS

MATCH RECORDS UP TO 1 NOVEMBER, 2015

MOST CONSECUTIVE TEST WINS

10	1931 E,G, 1932 G, 1933 G, 1934 G, 1935 G, 1936 G1,2, 1937 G,It
8	1998 E, S, I, W, Arg 1,2, Fj, Arg 3
8	2001 SA3, A, Fj 2002 It, W, E, S, I
8	2004 I, It, W, S, E, US, C, A

MOST CONSECUTIVE TESTS WITHOUT DEFEAT

Matches	Wins	Draws	Period
10	10	0	1931 to 1938
10	8	2	1958 to 1959
10	9	1	1986 to 1987

MOST POINTS IN A MATCH
BY THE TEAM

Pts	Opponents	Venue	Year
87	Namibia	Toulouse	2007
77	Fiji	Saint Etienne	2001
70	Zimbabwe	Auckland	1987
67	Romania	Bucharest	2000
64	Romania	Aurillac	1996
64	Georgia	Marseilles	2007
62	Romania	Castres	1999
62	Romania	Bucharest	2006
61	Fiji	Brisbane	2003
60	Italy	Toulon	1967

BY A PLAYER

Pts	Player	Opponents	Venue	Year
30	D Camberabero	Zimbabwe	Auckland	1987
28	C Lamaison	New Zealand	Twickenham	1999
28	F Michalak	Scotland	Sydney	2003
27	G Camberabero	Italy	Toulon	1967
27	C Lamaison	New Zealand	Marseilles	2000
27	G Merceron	South Africa	Johannesburg	2001
27	J-B Elissalde	Namibia	Toulouse	2007
26	T Lacroix	Ireland	Durban	1995
26	F Michalak	Fiji	Brisbane	2003
25	J-P Romeu	United States	Chicago	1976
25	P Berot	Romania	Agen	1987
25	T Lacroix	Tonga	Pretoria	1995

MOST TRIES IN A MATCH
BY THE TEAM

Tries	Opponents	Venue	Year
13	Romania	Paris	1924
13	Zimbabwe	Auckland	1987
13	Namibia	Toulouse	2007
12	Fiji	Saint Etienne	2001
11	Italy	Toulon	1967
10	Romania	Aurillac	1996
10	Romania	Bucharest	2000

BY A PLAYER

Tries	Player	Opponents	Venue	Year
4	A Jauréguy	Romania	Paris	1924
4	M Celhay	Italy	Paris	1937

MOST CONVERSIONS IN A MATCH
BY THE TEAM

Cons	Opponents	Venue	Year
11	Namibia	Toulouse	2007
9	Italy	Toulon	1967
9	Zimbabwe	Auckland	1987
8	Romania	Wellington	1987
8	Romania	Lens	2003

BY A PLAYER

Cons	Player	Opponents	Venue	Year
11	J-B Elissalde	Namibia	Toulouse	2007
9	G Camberabero	Italy	Toulon	1967
9	D Camberabero	Zimbabwe	Auckland	1987
8	G Laporte	Romania	Wellington	1987

MOST PENALTIES IN A MATCH
BY THE TEAM

Penalties	Opponents	Venue	Year
8	Ireland	Durban	1995
7	Wales	Paris	2001
7	Italy	Paris	2002
6	Argentina	Buenos Aires	1977
6	Scotland	Paris	1997
6	Italy	Auch	1997
6	Ireland	Paris	2000
6	South Africa	Johannesburg	2001
6	Argentina	Buenos Aires	2003
6	Fiji	Brisbane	2003
6	England	Twickenham	2005
6	Wales	Paris	2007
6	England	Twickenham	2007
6	Ireland	Dublin	2011
6	England	Paris	2015
6	Italy	Twickenham	2015

BY A PLAYER

Pens	Player	Opponents	Venue	Year
8	T Lacroix	Ireland	Durban	1995
7	G Merceron	Italy	Paris	2002
6	J-M Aguirre	Argentina	Buenos Aires	1977
6	C Lamaison	Scotland	Paris	1997
6	C Lamaison	Italy	Auch	1997
6	G Merceron	Ireland	Paris	2000
6	G Merceron	South Africa	Johannesburg	2001
6	F Michalak	Fiji	Brisbane	2003
6	D Yachvili	England	Twickenham	2005

MOST DROP GOALS IN A MATCH
BY THE TEAM

Drops	Opponents	Venue	Year
3	Ireland	Paris	1960
3	England	Twickenham	1985
3	New Zealand	Christchurch	1986
3	Australia	Sydney	1990
3	Scotland	Paris	1991
3	New Zealand	Christchurch	1994

BY A PLAYER

Drops	Player	Opponents	Venue	Year
3	P Albaladejo	Ireland	Paris	1960
3	J-P Lescarboura	England	Twickenham	1985
3	J-P Lescarboura	New Zealand	Christchurch	1986
3	D Camberabero	Australia	Sydney	1990

FRANCE

CAREER RECORDS

MOST CAPPED PLAYERS

Caps	Player	Career Span
118	F Pelous	1995 to 2007
111	P Sella	1982 to 1995
98	R Ibañez	1996 to 2007
93	S Blanco	1980 to 1991
89	O Magne	1997 to 2007
86	D Traille	2001 to 2011
85	N Mas	2003 to 2015
84	S Marconnet	1998 to 2011
83	D Szarzewski	2004 to 2015
82	I Harinordoquy	2002 to 2012
80	T Dusautoir	2006 to 2015
78	A Benazzi	1990 to 2001
77	F Michalak	2001 to 2015
76	A Rougerie	2001 to 2012
75	J Bonnaire	2004 to 2012

MOST CONSECUTIVE TESTS

Tests	Player	Span
46	R Bertranne	1973 to 1979
45	P Sella	1982 to 1987
44	M Crauste	1960 to 1966
42	M Parra	2009 to 2013
35	B Dauga	1964 to 1968

MOST TESTS AS CAPTAIN

Tests	Captain	Span
56	T Dusautoir	2009 to 2015
42	F Pelous	1997 to 2006
41	R Ibanez	1998 to 2007
34	J-P Rives	1978 to 1984
34	P Saint-André	1994 to 1997
25	D Dubroca	1986 to 1988
25	F Galthié	1999 to 2003
24	G Basquet	1948 to 1952
22	M Crauste	1961 to 1966

MOST POINTS IN TESTS

Points	Player	Tests	Career
436	F Michalak	77	2001 to 2015
380	C Lamaison	37	1996 to 2001
373	D Yachvili	61	2002 to 2012
367	T Lacroix	43	1989 to 1997
355	M Parra	66	2008 to 2015
354	D Camberabero	36	1982 to 1993
267	G Merceron	32	1999 to 2003
265	J-P Romeu	34	1972 to 1977
247	T Castaignède	54	1995 to 2007
233	S Blanco	93	1980 to 1991
214	J-B Elissalde	35	2000 to 2008
200	J-P Lescarboura	28	1982 to 1990

MOST CONVERSIONS IN TESTS

Cons	Player	Tests	Career
61	F Michalak	77	2001 to 2015
59	C Lamaison	37	1996 to 2001
51	D Yachvili	61	2002 to 2012
48	D Camberabero	36	1982 to 1993
47	M Parra	66	2008 to 2015
45	M Vannier	43	1953 to 1961
42	T Castaignède	54	1995 to 2007
40	J-B Elissalde	35	2000 to 2008
36	R Dourthe	31	1995 to 2001
36	G Merceron	32	1999 to 2003
32	T Lacroix	43	1989 to 1997
29	P Villepreux	34	1967 to 1972

MOST TRIES IN TESTS

Tries	Player	Tests	Career
38	S Blanco	93	1980 to 1991
34	V Clerc	67	2002 to 2013
33*	P Saint-André	69	1990 to 1997
30	P Sella	111	1982 to 1995
26	E Ntamack	46	1994 to 2000
26	P Bernat Salles	41	1992 to 2001
25	C Dominici	67	1998 to 2007
23	C Darrouy	40	1957 to 1967
23	A Rougerie	76	2001 to 2012

* Saint-André's total includes a penalty try against Romania in 1992

MOST PENALTY GOALS IN TESTS

Penalties	Player	Tests	Career
89	T Lacroix	43	1989 to 1997
85	D Yachvili	61	2002 to 2012
81	M Parra	66	2008 to 2015
79	F Michalak	77	2001 to 2015
78	C Lamaison	37	1996 to 2001
59	D Camberabero	36	1982 to 1993
57	G Merceron	32	1999 to 2003
56	J-P Romeu	34	1972 to 1977
38	J-B Elissalde	35	2000 to 2008
33	P Villepreux	34	1967 to 1972
33	P Bérot	19	1986 to 1989

MOST DROP GOALS IN TESTS

Drops	Player	Tests	Career
15	J-P Lescarboura	28	1982 to 1990
12	P Albaladejo	30	1954 to 1964
11	G Camberabero	14	1961 to 1968
11	D Camberabero	36	1982 to 1993
9	J-P Romeu	34	1972 to 1977
9	F Michalak	77	2001 to 2015

THE COUNTRIES

RECORD	DETAIL	HOLDER	SET
Most points in season	156	in five matches	2002
Most tries in season	18	in four matches	1998
	18	in five matches	2006
Highest score	56	56–13 v Italy	2005
Biggest win	51	51–0 v Wales	1998
Highest score conceded	55	35–55 v England	2015
Biggest defeat	37	0–37 v England	1911
Most appearances	50	P Sella	1983–1995
Most points in matches	217	D Yachvili	2003–2012
Most points in season	80	G Merceron	2002
Most points in match	24	S Viars	v Ireland, 1992
	24	C Lamaison	v Scotland, 1997
	24	J-B Elissalde	v Wales, 2004
Most tries in matches	14	S Blanco	1981–1991
	14	P Sella	1983–1995
Most tries in season	5	P Estève	1983
	5	E Bonneval	1987
	5	E Ntamack	1999
	5	P Bernat Salles	2001
	5	V Clerc	2008
Most tries in match	3	M Crauste	v England, 1962
	3	C Darrouy	v Ireland, 1963
	3	E Bonneval	v Scotland, 1987
	3	D Venditti	v Ireland, 1997
	3	E Ntamack	v Wales, 1999
	3	V Clerc	v Ireland, 2008
Most cons in matches	30	D Yachvili	2003–2012
Most cons in season	11	M Parra	2010
Most cons in match	6	D Yachvili	v Italy, 2003
Most pens in matches	49	D Yachvili	2003–2012
Most pens in season	18	G Merceron	2002
Most pens in match	7	G Merceron	v Italy, 2002
Most drops in matches	9	J-P Lescarboura	1982–1988
Most drops in season	5	G Camberabero	1967
Most drops in match	3	P Albaladejo	v Ireland, 1960
	3	J-P Lescarboura	v England, 1985

FRANCE

MISCELLANEOUS RECORDS

RECORD	HOLDER	DETAIL
Longest Test Career	F Michalak	2001 to 2015
Youngest Test Cap	C Dourthe	18 yrs 7 days in 1966
Oldest Test Cap	A Roques	37 yrs 329 days in 1963

CAREER RECORDS OF FRANCE INTERNATIONAL PLAYERS

UP TO 1 NOVEMBER, 2015

PLAYER BACKS :	DEBUT	CAPS	T	C	P	D	PTS
M Bastareaud	2009 v W	39	3	0	0	0	15
H Bonneval	2014 v It	4	1	0	0	0	5
B Dulin	2012 v Arg	24	4	0	1	0	23
A Dumoulin	2014 v Fj	8	0	0	0	0	0
G Fickou	2013 v S	15	2	0	0	0	10
W Fofana	2012 v It	39	13	0	0	0	65
R Grosso	2015 v C	1	1	0	0	0	5
S Guitoune	2013 v Tg	5	3	0	0	0	15
Y Huget	2010 v Arg	41	7	0	0	0	35
R Kockott	2014 v Fj	11	0	3	3	0	15
R Lamerat	2014 v A	7	0	0	0	0	0
C Lopez	2013 v NZ	9	0	6	20	0	72
M Médard	2008 v Arg	41	11	0	0	1	58
M Mermoz	2008 v A	30	3	0	0	0	15
F Michalak	2001 v SA	77	10	61	79	9	436
N Nakaitaci	2015 v It	8	2	0	0	0	10
M Parra	2008 v S	66	3	47	81	1	355
J Pélissié	2013 v Tg	1	0	0	0	0	0
J Plisson	2014 v E	6	0	4	4	0	20
S Spedding	2014 v Fj	14	0	0	7	0	21
R Talès	2013 v NZ	24	0	0	0	0	0
T Thomas	2014 v Fj	4	4	0	0	0	20
S Tillous-Borde	2008 v A	19	3	0	0	0	15
F Trinh-Duc	2008 v S	50	9	2	1	6	70

THE COUNTRIES

U Atonio	2014 v Fj	10	0	0	0	0	0
E Ben Arous	2013 v NZ	12	0	0	0	0	0
X Chiocci	2014 v Fj	4	0	0	0	0	0
D Chouly	2007 v NZ	36	1	0	0	0	5
V Debaty	2006 v R	37	1	0	0	0	5
T Dusautoir	2006 v R	80	6	0	0	0	30
A Flanquart	2013 v NZ	17	0	0	0	0	0
L Goujon	2015 v S	6	0	0	0	0	0
G Guirado	2008 v It	38	2	0	0	0	10
B Kayser	2008 v A	37	2	0	0	0	10
B Le Roux	2013 v NZ	23	0	0	0	0	0
Y Maestri	2012 v It	42	1	0	0	0	5
N Mas	2003 v NZ	85	1	0	0	0	5
A Menini	2014 v A	6	0	0	0	0	0
Y Nyanga	2004 v US	46	6	0	0	0	30
C Ollivon	2014 v Fj	2	0	0	0	0	0
F Ouedraogo	2007 v NZ	39	2	0	0	0	10
P Papé	2004 v I	65	5	0	0	0	25
L Picamoles	2008 v I	51	7	0	0	0	35
R Slimani	2013 v NZ	21	2	0	0	0	10
J Suta	2012 v A	6	0	0	0	0	0
D Szarzewski	2004 v C	83	7	0	0	0	35
R Taofifenua	2012 v Arg	8	1	0	0	0	5
S Vahaamahina	2012 v A	17	0	0	0	0	0

FRANCE

Getty Images

France centre Wesley Fofana dives to score a try in their 41–18 defeat of Pool D rivals Canada at Stadium MK.

FRANCE INTERNATIONAL PLAYERS

UP TO 1 NOVEMBER, 2015

Note: Years given for International Championship matches are for second half of season; eg 1972 means season 1971–72. Years for all other matches refer to the actual year of the match. Entries in square brackets denote matches played in RWC Finals.

Abadie, A (Pau) 1964 I
Abadie, A (Graulhet) 1965 R, 1967 SA 1, 3, 4, NZ, 1968 S, I
Abadie, L (Tarbes) 1963 R
Accoceberry, G (Bègles) 1994 NZ 1, 2, C 2, 1995 W, E, S, I, R 1, [Iv, S], It, 1996 I, W 1, R, Arg 1, W 2(R), SA 2, 1997 S, It 1
Aguerre, R (Biarritz O) 1979 S
Aguilar, D (Pau) 1937 G
Aguirre, J-M (Bagnères) 1971 A 2, 1972 S, 1973 W, I, J, R, 1974 I, W, Arg 2, R, SA 1, 1976 W (R), E, US, A 2, R, 1977 W, E, S, I, Arg 1, 2, NZ 1, 2, R, 1978 E, S, I, W, R, 1979 I, W, E, S, NZ 1, 2, R, 1980 W, I
Ainciart, E (Bayonne) 1933 G, 1934 G, 1935 G, 1937 G, It, 1938 G 1
Albaladéjo, P (Dax) 1954 E, It, 1960 W, I, It, R, 1961 S, SA, E, W, I, NZ 1, 2, A, 1962 S, E, W, I, 1963 S, I, E, W, It, 1964 S, NZ, W, It, I, SA, Fj
Albouy, A (Castres) 2002 It (R)
Alvarez, A-J (Tyrosse) 1945 B2, 1946 B, I, K, W, 1947 S, I, W, E, 1948 I, A, S, W, E, 1949 I, E, W, 1951 S, E, W
Amand, H (SF) 1906 NZ
Ambert, A (Toulouse) 1930 S, I, E, G, W
Amestoy, J-B (Mont-de-Marsan) 1964 NZ, E
André, G (RCF) 1913 SA, E, W, I, 1914 I, W, E
Andreu, M (Castres) 2010 W(R), It, E, SA(R), Arg2, A(R), 2013 NZ3
Andrieu, M (Nîmes) 1986 Arg 2, NZ 1, R 2, NZ 2, 1987 [R, Z], R, 1988 E, S, I, W, Arg 1, 2, 3, 4, R, 1989 I, W, E, S, NZ 2, B, A 2, 1990 W, E, I (R)
Anduran, J (SCUF) 1910 W
Aqua, J-L (Toulon) 1999 R, Tg, NZ 1(R)
Araou, R (Narbonne) 1924 R
Arcalis, R (Brive) 1950 S, I, 1951 I, E, W
Arias, J (SF) 2009 A(R), 2010 Fj
Arino, M (Agen) 1962 R
Aristouy, P (Pau) 1948 S, 1949 Arg 2, 1950 S, I, E, W
Arlettaz, P (Perpignan) 1995 R 2
Armary, L (Lourdes) 1987 [R], R, 1988 S, I, W, Arg 3, 4, R, 1989 W, S, A 1, 2, 1990 W, E, S, I, A 1, 2, 3, NZ 1, 1991 W 2, 1992 S, I, R, Arg 1, 2, SA 1, 2, Arg, , 1993 E, S, I, W, SA 1, 2, R 2, A 1, 2, 1994 I, W, NZ 1(t), 2(t), 1995 I, R 1 [Tg, I, SA]
Arnal, J-M (RCF) 1914 I, W
Arnaudet, M (Lourdes) 1964 I, 1967 It, W
Arotca, R (Bayonne) 1938 R
Arrieta, J (SF) 1953 E, W
Arthapignet, P (see Harislur-Arthapignet)
Artiguste, E (Castres) 1999 WS
Astre, R (Béziers) 1971 R, 1972 I 1, 1973 E (R), 1975 E, S, I, SA 1, 2, Arg 2, 1976 A 2, R
Atonio, U (La Rochelle) 2014 Fj(R), A 4(R), Arg(R), 2015 S 1(R), I(R), W(R), E 1(R), 2(R), 3(R), [R]
Attoub, D (Castres, SF) 2006 R, 2012 W, Arg 1, 2
Aucagne, D (Pau) 1997 W (R), S, It 1, R 1(R), A 1, R 2(R), SA 2(R), 1998 S (R), W (R), Arg 2(R), Fj (R), Arg 3, A, 1999 W 1(R), S (R)
Audebert, A (Montferrand) 2000 R, 2002 W (R)
Aué, J-M (Castres) 1998 W (R)
Augé, J (Dax) 1929 S, W

Augras-Fabre, L (Agen) 1931 I, S, W
August, B (Biarritz) 2007 W1(R)
Auradou, D (SF) 1999 E (R), S (R), WS (R), Tg, NZ 1, W 2(R), [Arg (R)], 2000 A (R), NZ 1, 2, 2001 S, I, It, W, E (R), SA 1, 2, NZ (R), SA 3, A, Fj, 2002 It, E, I (R), C (R), 2003 S (R), It (R), W (R), Arg, 1, 2, NZ (R), R (R), E 2(R), 3, [J(R), US, NZ] , 2004 I(R), It(R), S(R), E(R)
Averous, J-L (La Voulte) 1975 S, I, SA 1, 2, 1976 I, W, E, US, A 1, 2, R, 1977 W, E, S, I, Arg 1, R, 1978 E, S, I, 1979 NZ 1, 2, 1980 E, S, 1981 A 2
Avril, D (Biarritz) 2005 A1
Azam, O (Montferrand, Gloucester) 1995 R 2, Arg (R), 2000 A (R), NZ 2(R), 2001 SA 2(R), NZ, 2002 E (R), I (R), Arg (R), A 1
Azarete, J-L (Dax, St Jean-de-Luz) 1969 W, R, 1970 S, I, W, R, 1971 S, I, E, SA 1, 2, A 1, 1972 E, W, I 2, A 1, R, 1973 NZ, W, I, R, 1974 I, R, SA 1, 2, 1975 W

Baby, B (Toulouse, Clermont-Auvergne) 2005 I, SA2(R), A1, 2008 Arg, PI, A3, 2009 I(R), S, W
Bacqué, N (Pau) 1997 R 2
Bader, E (Primevères) 1926 M, 1927 I, S
Badin, C (Chalon) 1973 W, I, 1975 Arg 1
Baillette, M (Perpignan) 1925 I, NZ, S, 1926 W, M, 1927 I, W, G 2, 1929 G, 1930 S, I, E, G, 1931 I, S, E, 1932 G
Baladie, G (Agen) 1945 B 1, 2, W, 1946 B, I, K
Ballarin, J (Tarbes) 1924 E, 1925 NZ, S
Baquey, J (Toulouse) 1921 I
Barbazanges, A (Roanne) 1932 G, 1933 G
Barcella, F (Auch, Biarritz) 2008 It, W, Arg, 2009 S, W, It, NZ1, 2, A, SA, NZ3, 2010 Arg1, 2011 I3(R), [J, C(t&R), NZ1(R), Tg(R), E(R), W(R), NZ2(R)]
Barrau, M (Beaumont, Toulouse) 1971 S, E, W, 1972 E, W, A 1, 2, 1973 S, NZ, E, I, J, R, 1974 I, S
Barrau, M (Agen) 2004 US, C(R), NZ2(R)
Barrère, P (Toulon) 1929 G, 1931 W
Barrière, R (Béziers) 1960 R
Barthe, F (SBUC) 1925 W, E
Barthe, J (Lourdes) 1954 Arg 1, 2, 1955 S, 1956 I, W, It, E, Cz, 1957 S, I, E, W, R 1, 2, 1958 S, E, A, W, It, I, SA 1, 2, 1959 S, E, It, W
Basauri, R (Albi) 1954 Arg 1
Bascou, P (Bayonne) 1914 E
Basquet, G (Agen) 1945 W, 1946 B, I, K, W, 1947 S, I, W, E, 1948 I, A, S, W, E, 1949 S, I, E, W, Arg 1, 1950 S, I, E, W, 1951 S, I, E, W, Arg 1, 2, 1952 S, I, SA, W, E, It
Bastareaud, M (SF, Toulon) 2009 W, E, It(R), NZ1, 2010 S, I, W, It(R), E, 2013 It(R), W, E, I(t&R), S, NZ2(R), 3(t&R), Tg(t&R), SA(R), 2014 E, It, W, S, I, A2, 3, Fj, Arg(t&R), 2015 S1, I, W(R), It(R), E 1(R), 3, S 2, [It, C, I, NZ(R)]
Bastiat, J-P (Dax) 1969 R, 1970 S, I, W, 1971 S, I, SA 2, 1972 S A 1, 1973 E, 1974 Arg 1, 2, SA 1, 2, 1975 W, Arg 1, 2, R, 1976 S, I, W, E, A 1, 2, R, 1977 W, E, S, I, 1978 E, S, I, W
Baudry, N (Montferrand) 1949 S, I, W, Arg 1, 2
Baulon, R (Vienne, Bayonne) 1954 S, NZ, W, E, It, 1955 I, E, W, It, 1956 S, I, W, It, E, Cz, 1957 S, I, It
Baux, J-P (Lannemezan) 1968 NZ 1, 2, SA 1, 2

Bavozet, J (Lyon) 1911 S, E, W

Bayard, J (Toulouse) 1923 S, W, E, 1924 W, R, US

Bayardon, J (Chalon) 1964 S, NZ, E

Beaurin-Gressier, C (SF) 1907 E, 1908 E

Beauxis, L (SF, Toulouse) 2007 It(R), I(R), W1(R), E1(R), S, W2, [Nm(R), I(R), Gg, NZ, E, Arg 2(R)], 2009 I, S, A, 2012 It(R), S(R), I(R), E, W

Bégu, J (Dax) 1982 Arg 2(R), 1984 E, S

Béguerie, C (Agen) 1979 NZ 1

Béguet, L (RCF) 1922 I, 1923 S, W, E, I, 1924 S, I, E, R, US

Béhotéguy, A (Bayonne, Cognac) 1923 E, 1924 S, I, E, W, R, US, 1926 E, 1927 E, G, 1, 2, 1928 A, I, E, G, W, 1929 S, W, E

Béhotéguy, H (RCF, Cognac) 1923 W, 1928 A, I, E, G, W

Bélascain, C (Bayonne) 1977 R, 1978 E, S, I, W, R, 1979 I, W, E, S, 1982 W, E, S, I, 1983 E, S, I, W

Belletante, G (Nantes) 1951 I, E, W

Belot, F (Toulouse) 2000 I (R)

Ben Arous, E (Racing Métro) 2013 NZ3(R), 2015 S1(R), I, W, It, E 3, S 2, [It, R(R), C, I, NZ]

Benazzi, A (Agen) 1990 A 1, 2, 3, NZ 1, 2, 1991 E, US 1(R), 2, [R, Fj, C], 1992 SA 1(R), 2, Arg, 1993 E, S, I, W, A 1, 2, 1994 I, W, E, S, C 1, NZ 1, 2, C 2, 1995 W, E, S, I, [Tg, Iv, S, I, SA, E], NZ 1, 2, 1996 E, S, I, W 1, Arg 1, 2, W 2, SA 1, 2, 1997 I, W, E, S, R 1, A 1, 2, It 2, R 2(R), Arg, SA 1, 2, 1999 R, WS, W 2, [C, Nm (R), Fj, Arg, NZ 2, A], 2000 W, E, I, It (R), R, 2001 S, F(R), I (t&R), E

Bénésis, R (Narbonne) 1969 W, R, 1970 S, I, W, E, R, 1971 S, I, E, W, A 2, R, 1972 S, I 1, E, W, I 2, A 1, R, 1973 NZ, E, W, I, J, R, 1974 I, W, E, S

Benetière, J (Roanne) 1954 It, Arg 1

Benetton, P (Agen) 1989 B, 1990 NZ 2, 1991 US 2, 1992 Arg 1, 2(R), SA 1(R), 2, Arg, 1993 E, S, I, W, SA 1, 2, R 2, A 1, 2, 1994 I, W, E, S, C 1, NZ 1, 2, C 2, 1995 W, E, S, I, [Tg, Iv (R), S], It, R 2(R), Arg, NZ 1, 2, 1996 Arg 1, 2, W 2, SA 1, 2, 1997 I, It 1, 2(R), R 2, Arg, SA 1 2 1998 E, S (R), I (R), W (R), Arg 1(R), 2(R), Fj (R), 1999 I, W 1, S (R)

Benezech, L (RCF) 1994 E, S, C 1, NZ 1, 2, C 2, 1995 W, E, [Iv, S, E], R 2, Arg, NZ 1, 2

Berbizier, P (Lourdes, Agen) 1981 S, I, W, E, NZ 1, 2, 1982 I, R, 1983 S, I, 1984 S (R), NZ 1, 2, 1985 Arg 1, 2, 1986 S, I, W, E, R 1, Arg 1, A, NZ 1, R 2, NZ 2 3, 1987 W, E, S, I, [S, R, Fj, A, NZ], R, 1988 E, S, I, W, Arg 1, 2, 1989 I, W, E, S, NZ 1, 2, B, A 1, 1990 W, E, 1991 S, I, W 1, E

Berejnoï, J-C (Tulle) 1963 R, 1964 S, W, It, I, SA, Fj, R, 1965 S, I, E, W, It, R, 1966 S, I, E, W, It, R, 1967 S, A, E, It, W, I, R

Bergès, B (Toulouse) 1926 I

Berges-Cau, R (Lourdes) 1976 E (R)

Bergese, F (Bayonne) 1936 G 2, 1937 G, It, 1938 G 1, R, G 2

Bergougnan, Y (Toulouse) 1945 B 1, W, 1946 B, I, K, W, 1947 S, I, W, E, 1948 S, W, E, 1949 S, E, Arg 1, 2

Bernard, R (Bergerac) 1951 S, I, E, W

Bernat-Salles, P (Pau, Bègles-Bordeaux, Biarritz) 1992 Arg, 1993 R 1, SA 1, 2, R 2, A 1, 2, 1994 I, 1995 E, S, 1996 E (R), 1997 R 1, A 1, 2, 1998 E, S, I, W, Arg 1, 2, Fj, Arg 3(R), A 1999 I, W 1, R, Tg, [Nm, Fj, Arg, NZ 2, A], 2000 I, It, NZ 1(R), 2, 2001 S, I, E, W

Bernon, J (Lourdes) 1922 I, 1923 S

Bérot, J-L (Toulouse) 1968 NZ 3, A, 1969 S, I, 1970 E, R, 1971 S, I, E, W, SA 1, 2, A 1, 2, R, 1972 S, I 1, E, W, A 1, 1974 I

Bérot, P (Agen) 1986 R 2, NZ 2, 3, 1987 W, E, S, I, R, 1988 E, S, I, Arg 1, 2, 3, 4, R, 1989 S, NZ 1, 2

Bertrand, P (Bourg) 1951 I, E, W, 1953 S, I, E, W, It

Bertranne, R (Bagnères) 1971 E, W, SA 2, A 1, 2, 1972 S, I 1, 1973 NZ, E, J, R, 1974 I, W, E, S, Arg 1, 2, R, SA 1, 2, 1975 W, E, S, I, SA 1, 2, Arg 1, 2, R, 1976 S, I, W, E, US, A 1, 2, R, 1977 W, E, S, I, Arg 1, 2, NZ 1, 2, R, 1978 E, S, I, W, R, 1979 I, W, E, S, R, 1980 W, E, S, I, SA, R, 1981 S, I, W, E, R, NZ 1, 2

Berty, D (Toulouse) 1990 NZ 2, 1992 R (R), 1993 R 2, 1995 NZ 1(R), 1996 W 2(R), SA 1

Besset, E (Grenoble) 1924 S

Besset, L (SCUF) 1914 W, E

Besson, M (CASG) 1924 I, 1925 I, E, 1926 S, W, 1927 I

Besson, P (Brive) 1963 S, I, E, 1965 R, 1968 SA 1

Betsen, S (Biarritz) 1997 It 1(R), 2000 W (R), E (R), A (R), NZ 1(R), 2(R), 2001 S (R), I (R), It (R), W (R), SA 3(R), A, Fj, 2002 It, W, E, S, I, Arg, A 1, 2, SA, NZ, C, 2003 E 1, S, I, It, W, R, E 2, [Fj, J, S, I, E], 2004 I, It, W, S, E, A, Arg, NZ, 2005 E, W, I, It, 2006 SA, NZ2(R), Arg(R), 2007 It, I, W1, E1, S, E2, W2, [Arg 1, I, Gg, NZ, E]

Bianchi, J (Toulon) 1986 Arg 1

Bichindaritz, J (Biarritz O) 1954 It, Arg 1, 2

Bidabé, P (Biarritz) 2004 C, 2006 R

Bidart, L (La Rochelle) 1953 W

Biémouret, P (Agen) 1969 E, W, 1970 I, W, E, 1971 W, SA 1, 2, A 1, 1972 E, W, I 2, A 2, R, 1973 S, NZ, E, W, I

Biénès, R (Cognac) 1950 S, I, E, W, 1951 S, I, E, W, 1952 S, I, SA, W, E, It, 1953 S, I, E, 1954 S, I, NZ, W, E, Arg 1, 2, 1956 S, I, W, It, E

Bigot, C (Quillan) 1930 S, 1931 I, S

Bilbao, L (St Jean-de-Luz) 1978 I, 1979 I

Billac, E (Bayonne) 1920 S, E, W, I, US, 1921 S, W, 1922 W, 1923 E

Billière, M (Toulouse) 1968 NZ 3

Bioussa, A (Toulouse) 1924 W, US, 1925 I, NZ, S, E, 1926 S, I, E, 1928 E, G, W, 1929 I, S, W, E, 1930 S, I, E, G, W

Bioussa, C (Toulouse) 1913 W, I, 1914 I

Biraben, M (Dax) 1920 W, I, US, 1921 S, W, E, I, 1922 S, E, I

Blain, A (Carcassonne) 1934 G

Blanco, S (Biarritz O) 1980 SA, 1981 S, W, E, A 1, 2, R, NZ 1, 2, 1982 W, E, S, I, R, Arg 1, 2, 1983 E, S, I, W, 1984 I, W, E, S, NZ 1, 2, R, 1985 E, S, I, W, Arg 1, 2, 1986 S, I, W, E, R 1, Arg 2, A, NZ 1, R 2, NZ 2, 3, 1987 W, E, S, I, [S, R, Fj, A, NZ], R, 1988 E, S, I, W, Arg 1, 2, 3, 4, R, 1989 I, W, E, S, NZ 1, 2, 1990 I, E, S, I, A 1, 2, 3, NZ 1, 2, 1991 S, I, W 1, E, R, US 1, 2, W 2, [R, Fj, C, E]

Blond, J (SF) 1935 G, 1936 G 2, 1937 G, 1938 G 1, R, G 2

Blond, X (RCF) 1990 A 3, 1991 S, I, W 1, E, 1994 NZ 2(R)

Boffelli, V (Aurillac) 1971 A 2, R, 1972 S, I 1, 1973 J, R, 1974 I, W, E, S, Arg 1, 2, R, SA 1, 2, 1975 W, S, I

Bonal, J-M (Toulouse) 1968 E, W, Cz, NZ 2, 3, SA 1, 2, R, 1969 S, I, E, R, 1970 W, E

Bonamy, R (SB) 1928 A, I

Bondouy, P (Narbonne, Toulouse) 1997 S (R), It 1, A 2(R), R 2, 2000 R (R)

Bonetti, S (Biarritz) 2001 It, W, NZ (R)

Boniface, A (Mont-de-Marsan) 1954 I, NZ, W, E, It, Arg 1, 2, 1955 S, I, 1956 S, I, W, It, Cz, 1957 S, I, W, R 2, 1958 S, E, 1959 E, 1961 NZ 1, 3, A, R, 1962 E, W, I, It, R, 1963 S, I, E, W, It, R, 1964 S, NZ, E, W, It, R, 1965 S, I, E, W

Boniface, G (Mont-de-Marsan) 1960 W, I, It, R, Arg 1, 2, 3, 1961 S, SA, E, W, It, I, NZ 1, 2, 3, R, 1962 R, 1963 S, I, E, W, It, R, 1964 S, 1965 S, I, E, W, It, R, 1966 S, I, E, W

Bonnaire, J (Bourgoin, Clermont-Auvergne) 2004 S(t&R), A(R), NZ(R), 2005 S, E, W, I, It, SA1, 2, A1, C, Tg, SA3, 2006 S, I, It(R), E(R), W, R, SA(R), NZ1, 2, Arg, 2007 It, I(R), W1, E1, S, E2, 3(R), [Arg1(R), Nm, I, Gg, NZ, E], 2008 S(R), I, E, It(R), W, I, SA(R), Sm, NZ3, 2010 S(R), I(R), W, It, E, SA, Arg1, 2, A(R), 2011 S, I1, E(R), It, W, I2(R), 3, [J(R), C, NZ1, Tg, E, W, NZ2], 2012 It, S(R), I, E, W

Bonnes, E (Narbonne) 1924 W, R, US

Bonneval, E (Toulouse) 1984 NZ 2(R), 1985 W, Arg 1, 1986 W, E, R 1, Arg 1, 2, A, R 2, NZ 2, 3, 1987 W, E, S, I, [Z], 1988 E

Bonneval, H (SF) 2014 It, W, A1, 3

Bonnus, F (Toulon) 1950 S, I, E, W

Bonnus, M (Toulon) 1937 It, 1938 G 1, R, G 2, 1940 B

Bontemps, D (La Rochelle) 1968 SA 2

Borchard, G (RCF) 1908 E, 1909 E, W, I, 1911 I

Borde, F (RCF) 1920 I, US, 1921 S, W, E, 1922 S, W, 1923 S, I, 1924 E, 1925 I, 1926 E

Bordenave, L (Toulon) 1948 A, S, W, E, 1949 S

Bory, D (Montferrand) 2000 I, It, A, NZ 1, 2001 S, I, SA 1, 2, 3, A, Fj, 2002 It, E, S, I, C, 2003 [US, NZ]

Boubée, J (Tarbes) 1921 S, E, I, 1922 E, W, 1923 E, I, 1925 NZ, S

Boudreaux, R (SCUF) 1910 W, S

Bouet, D (Dax) 1989 NZ 1, 2, B, A 2, 1990 A 3

Bouguyon, G (Grenoble) 1961 SA, E, W, It, I, NZ 1, 2, 3, A

Bouic, G (Agen) 1996 SA 1

Bouilhou, J (Toulouse) 2001 NZ, 2003 Arg 1

Boujet, C (Grenoble) 1968 NZ 2, A (R), SA 1

Bouquet, J (Bourgoin, Vienne) 1954 S, 1955 E, 1956 S, I, W, It, E, Cz, 1957 S, E, W, R 2, 1958 S, E, 1959 S, It, W, I, 1960 S, E, W, I, R, 1961 S, SA, E, W, It, I, R, 1962 S, E, W, I
Bourdeu, J-R (Lourdes) 1952 S, I, SA, W, E, It, 1953 S, I, E
Bourgarel, R (Toulouse) 1969 R, 1970 S, I, E, R, 1971 W, SA 1, 2, 1973 S
Bourguignon, G (Narbonne) 1988 Arg 3, 1989 I, E, B, A 1, 1990 R
Bousquet, A (Béziers) 1921 E, I, 1924 R
Bousquet, R (Albi) 1926 M, 1927 I, S, W, E, G 1, 1929 W, E, 1930 W
Bousses, G (Bourgoin) 2006 S(R)
Boyau, M (SBUC) 1912 I, S, W, E, 1913 W, I
Boyer, P (Toulon) 1935 G
Boyet, B (Bourgoin) 2006 I(R), 2007 NZ1, 2, 2008 A1, 2(R)
Boyoud, Π (Dax) 2008 A1(R), 2, 2009 S(R)
Branca, G (SF) 1928 S, 1929 I, S
Branlat, A (RCF) 1906 NZ, E, 1908 W
Bréjassou, R (Tarbes) 1952 S, I, SA, W, E, 1953 W, E, 1954 S, I, NZ, 1955 S, I, E, W, It
Brèthes, R (St Séver) 1960 Arg 2
Bringeon, A (Biarritz O) 1925 W
Brouzet, O (Grenoble, Bègles, Northampton, Montferrand) 1994 S, NZ 2(R), 1995 E, S, I, R 1, [Tg, Iv, E (t)], It, Arg (R), 1996 W 1(R), 1997 R 1, A 1, 2, It 2, Arg, SA 1, 2, 1998 E, S, I, W, Arg 1, 2, Fj, Arg 3, A, 1999 I, W 1, E, S, R, [C (R), Nm, Fj (R), Arg, NZ 2(R), A (R)], 2000 W, E, S, I, It, A, NZ 1(R), 2(R), 2001 SA 1, 2, NZ, 2002 W, E, S, I, Arg, A 1(R), 2, SA, NZ, C, 2003 E 1, S, I, It, W, E 3, [Fj(R), J, S(R), US, I(R)]
Bru, Y (Toulouse) 2001 A (R), Fj (R), 2002 It, 2003 Arg 2, NZ, R, E 2, 3(R), [J, S(R), US, I(t&R), NZ], 2004 I(R), It(R), W(R), S(R), E(R)
Brugnaut, J (Dax) 2008 S, I(R)
Brun, G (Vienne) 1950 E, W, 1951 S, E, W, 1952 S, I, SA, W, E, It, 1953 E, W, It
Bruneau, M (SBUC) 1910 W, E, 1913 SA, E
Brunet, Y (Perpignan) 1975 SA 1, 1977 Arg 1
Bruno, S (Béziers, Sale) 2002 W (R), 2004 A(R), NZ(t&R), 2005 S(R), E, W, I, It, SA1, 2(R), A1(R), 2(R), C, SA3(R), 2006 S(R), I(R), 2007 I(R), E1(R), NZ1, 2, E3(R), W2(R), [Gg, Arg 2(t&R)], 2008 A1, 2
Brusque, N (Pau, Biarritz) 1997 R 2(R), 2002 W, E, S, I, Arg, A 2, SA, NZ, C, 2003 E 2, [Fj, S, I, E, NZ(R)], 2004 I, It, W, S, E, A, Arg, 2005 SA1(R), 2, A1, 2006 S
Buchet, E (Nice) 1980 R, 1982 E, R (R), Arg 1, 2
Buisson, H (see Empereur-Buisson)
Buonomo, Y (Béziers) 1971 A 2, R, 1972 I 1
Burban, A (SF) 2014 E(R), A1(R), 2(R)
Burgun, M (RCF) 1909 I, 1910 W, S, I, 1911 S, E, 1912 I, S, 1913 S, E, 1914 E
Bustaffa, D (Carcassonne) 1977 Arg 1, 2, NZ 1, 2, 1978 W, R, 1980 W, E, S, SA, R
Buttin, J-M (Clermont-Auvergne) 2012 W(R), Arg 1
Buzy, C-E (Lourdes) 1946 K, W, 1947 S, I, W, E, 1948 I, A, S, W, E, 1949 S, I, E, W, Arg 1, 2

Caballero, Y (Montauban) 2008 A2(R)
Cabanier, J-M (Montauban) 1963 R, 1964 S, Fj, 1965 S, I, W, It, R, 1966 S, I, E, W, It, R, 1967 S, A, E, It, W, I, SA 1, 3, NZ, R, 1968 S, I
Cabannes, L (RCF, Harlequins) 1990 NZ 2(R), 1991 S, I, W 1, E, US 2, W 2, [R, Fj, C, E], 1992 W, E, S, I, R, Arg 2, SA 1, 2, 1993 E, S, I, W, R 1, SA 1, 2, 1994 E, S, C 1, NZ 1, 2, 1995 W, E, S, R 1, [Tg (R), Iv, S, I, SA, E], 1996 E, S, I, W 1, 1997 It 2, Arg, SA 1, 2
Cabrol, H (Béziers) 1972 A 1(R), 2, 1973 J, 1974 SA 2
Cadenat, JP (SCUF) 1910 S, E, 1911 W, I, 1912 W, E, 1913 I
Cadieu, J-M (Toulouse) 1991 R, US 1, [R, Fj, C, E], 1992 W, I, R, Arg 1, 2, SA 1
Cahuc, F (St Girons) 1922 S
Califano, C (Toulouse, Saracens, Gloucester) 1994 NZ 1, 2, C 2, 1995 W, E, S, I, [Iv, S, I, SA, E], It, Arg, NZ 1, 2, 1996 E, S, I, W 1, R, Arg 1, 2, SA 1, 2, 1997 I, W, E, A 1, 2, It 2, R 2(R), Arg, SA 1, 2, 1998 E, S, I, W, 1999 I, W 1, E (R), S, WS, Tg (R), NZ 1, W 2, [C, Nm, Fj], 2000 W, E, S, I, It,

R, A, NZ 1, 2(R), 2001 S (R), I (R), It, W, SA 1(R), 2(R), NZ, 2003 E 1, S (R), I (R), 2007 NZ1, 2
Cals, R (RCF) 1938 G 1
Calvo, G (Lourdes) 1961 NZ 1, 3
Camberabero, D (La Voulte, Béziers) 1982 R, Arg 1, 2, 1983 E, W, 1987 [R (R), Z, Fj (R), A, NZ], 1988 I, 1989 B, A 1, 1990 W, S, I, R A 1, 2, 3, NZ 1, 2, 1991 S, I, W 1, E, R, US 1, 2, W 2, [R, Fj, C], 1993 E, S, I
Camberabero, G (La Voulte) 1961 NZ 3, 1962 R, 1964 R, 1967 A, E, It, W, I, SA 1, 3, 4, 1968 S, E, W
Camberabero, L (La Voulte) 1964 R, 1965 S, I, 1966 E, W, 1967 A, E, It, W, I, 1968 S, E, W
Cambré, T (Oloron) 1920 E, W, I, US
Camel, A (Toulouse) 1928 S, A, I, E, G, W, 1929 W, E, G, 1930 S, I, E, G, W, 1935 G
Camel, M (Toulouse) 1929 S, W, E
Camicas, F (Tarbes) 1927 G 2, 1928 S, I, E, G, W, 1929 I, S, W, E
Camo, E (Villeneuve) 1931 I, S, W, E, G, 1932 G
Campaès, A (Lourdes) 1965 W, 1967 NZ, 1968 S, I, E, W, Cz, NZ 1, 2, A, 1969 S, W, 1972 R, 1973 NZ
Campan, O (Agen) 1993 SA 1(R), 2(R), R 2(R), 1996 I, W 1, R
Candelon, J (Narbonne) 2005 SA1, A1(R)
Cantoni, J (Béziers) 1970 W, R, 1971 S, I, E, W, SA 1, 2, R, 1972 S, I 1, 1973 S, NZ, W, I, 1975 W (R)
Capdouze, J (Pau) 1964 SA, Fj, R, 1965 S, I, E
Capendeguy, J-M (Bègles) 1967 NZ, R
Capitani, P (Toulon) 1954 Arg 1, 2
Capmau, J-L (Toulouse) 1914 E
Carabignac, G (Agen) 1951 S, I, 1952 SA, W, E, 1953 S, I
Carbonne, J (Perpignan) 1927 W
Carbonneau, P (Toulouse, Brive, Pau) 1995 R 2, Arg, NZ 1, 2, 1996 E, S, R, Arg 2, W 2, SA 1, 1997 I (R), W, E, S (R), R 1(R), A 1, 2, 1998 E, S, I, W, Arg 1, 2, Fj, Arg 3, A, 1999 I, W 1, E, S, 2000 NZ 2(R), 2001 I
Carminati, A (Béziers, Brive) 1986 R 2, NZ 2, 1987 [R, Z], 1988 I, W, Arg 1, 2, 1989 I, W, S, NZ 1(R), 2, A 2, 1990 S, 1995 It, R 2, Arg, NZ 1, 2
Caron, L (Lyon O, Castres) 1947 E, 1948 I, A, W, E, 1949 S, I, E, W, Arg 1
Carpentier, M (Lourdes) 1980 E, SA, R, 1981 S, I, A 1, 1982 E, S
Carrère, C (Toulon) 1966 R, 1967 S, A, E, W, I, SA 1, 3, 4, NZ, R, 1968 S, I, E, W, Cz, NZ 3, A, R, 1969 S, I, 1970 S, I, W, E, 1971 E, W
Carrère, J (Vichy, Toulon) 1956 S, 1957 E, W, R 2, 1958 S, SA 1, 2, 1959 I
Carrère, R (Mont-de-Marsan) 1953 E, It
Casadei, D (Brive) 1997 S, R 1, SA 2(R)
Casaux, L (Tarbes) 1959 I, It, 1962 S
Cassagne, P (Pau) 1957 It
Cassayet-Armagnac, A (Tarbes, Narbonne) 1920 S, E, W, US, 1921 W, E, I, 1922 S, E, W, 1923 S, W, E, I, 1924 S, E, W, R, US, 1925 I, NZ, S, W, 1926 S, I, E, W, M, 1927 I, S, W
Cassiède, M (Dax) 1961 NZ 3, A, R
Castaignède, S (Mont-de-Marsan) 1999 W 2, [C (R), Nm (R), Fj, Arg (R), NZ 2(R), A (R)]
Castaignède, T (Toulouse, Castres, Saracens) 1995 R 2, Arg, NZ 1, 2, 1996 E, S, I, W 1, Arg 1, 2, 1997 I, A 1, 2, It 2, 1998 E, S, I, W, Arg 1, 2, Fj, 1999 I, W 1, E, S, R, WS, Tg (R), NZ 1, W 2, [C], 2000 W, E, S, It, 2002 SA, NZ, C, 2003 E 1(R), S (R), It, W, Arg 1, 2005 A2(R), C, Tg, SA3, 2006 It, E, W, R, SA(R), 2007 NZ1, 2
Castel, R (Toulouse, Béziers) 1996 I, W 1, W 2, SA 1(R), 2, 1997 I (R), W, E (R), S (R), A 1(R), 1998 Arg 3(R), A (R), 1999 W 1(R), E, S
Castets, J (Toulon) 1923 W, E, I
Caujolle, J (Tarbes) 1909 E, 1913 SA, E, 1914 W, E
Caunègre, R (SB) 1938 R, G 2
Caussade, A (Lourdes) 1978 R, 1979 I, W, E, NZ 1, 2, R, 1980 W, E, S, 1981 S, I
Caussarieu, G (Pau) 1929 I
Cayrefourcq, E (Tarbes) 1921 E
Cazalbou, J (Toulouse) 1997 It 2(R), R 2, Arg, SA 2(R)
Cazals, P (Mont-de-Marsan) 1961 NZ 1, A, R
Cazenave, A (Pau) 1927 E, G 1, 1928 S, A, G
Cazenave, F (RCF) 1950 E, 1952 S, 1954 I, NZ, W, E

Cécillon, M (Bourgoin) 1988 I, W, Arg 2, 3, 4, R, 1989 I, E, NZ 1, 2, A 1, 1991 S, I, E (R), R, US 1, W 2, [E], 1992 W, E, S, I, R, Arg 1, 2, SA 1, 2, 1993 E, S, I, W, R 1, SA 1, 2, R 2, A 1, 2, 1994 I, W, NZ 1(R), 1995 I, R 1, [Tg, S (R), I, SA]

Celaya, M (Biarritz O, SBUC) 1953 E, W, It, 1954 I, E, It, Arg 1, 2, 1955 S, I, E, W, It, 1956 S, I, W, It, E, Cz 1957 S, I, E, W, R 2, 1958 S, E, A, W, It, 1959 S, E, 1960 S, E, W, I, R, Arg 1, 2, 3, 1961 S, SA, E, W, It, I, NZ 1, 2, 3, A, R

Celhay, M (Bayonne) 1935 G, 1936 G 1, 1937 G, It, 1938 G 1, 1940 B

Cermeno, F (Perpignan) 2000 R

Cessieux, N (Lyon) 1906 NZ

Cester, E (TOEC, Valence) 1966 S, I, E, 1967 W, 1968 S, I, E, W, Cz, NZ 1, 3, A, SA 1, 2, R, 1969 S, I, E, W, 1970 S, I, W, E, 1971 A 1, 1972 R, 1973 S, NZ, W, I, J, R, 1974 I, W, E, S

Chabal, S (Bourgoin, Sale, Racing-Metro) 2000 S, 2001 SA 1, 2, NZ (R), Fj (R), 2002 Arg (R), A 2, SA (R), NZ (t), C (R), 2003 E 1(R), S (R), I (R), Arg 2, NZ (R), 3, [J(R), US, NZ], 2005 S, E, A2(R), Tg, 2007 It, I, E1, NZ1, 2, E2(R), W2, [Arg1(R), Nm, I, NZ(R), E(R), Arg 2(R)], 2008 A1, 2, Arg(R), PI(R), A3, 2009 I, S(R), W, E, It, NZ1(R), 2, SA(R), Sm, NZ3, 2010 W(R), It(R), E(R), Fj(R), Arg2, 4, 2011 S(R), I1(R), E, It

Chaban-Delmas, J (CASG) 1945 B 2

Chabowski, H (Nice, Bourgoin) 1985 Arg 2, 1986 R 2, NZ 2, 1989 B (R)

Chadebech, P (Brive) 1982 R, Arg 1, 2, 1986 S, I

Champ, E (Toulon) 1985 Arg 1, 2, 1986 I, W, E, R 1, Arg 1, 2, A, NZ 1, R 2, NZ 2, 3, 1987 W, E, S, I, [S, R, Fj, A, NZ], R, 1988 E, S, Arg 1, A, R, 1989 W, S, A 1, 2, 1990 W, E, NZ 1, 1991 R, US 1, [R, Fj, C, E]

Chapuy, L (SF) 1926 S

Charpentier, G (SF) 1911 E, 1912 W, E

Charton, P (Montferrand) 1940 B

Charvet, D (Toulouse) 1986 W, E, R 1, Arg 1, A, NZ 1, 3, 1987 W, E, S, I, [S, R, Z, Fj, A, NZ], R, 1989 E (R), 1990 W, E, 1991 S, I

Chassagne, J (Montferrand) 1938 G 1

Chatau, A (Bayonne) 1913 SA

Chaud, E (Toulon) 1932 G, 1934 G, 1935 G

Chazalet, A (Bourgoin) 1999 Tg

Chenevay, C (Grenoble) 1968 SA 1

Chevallier, B (Montferrand) 1952 S, I, SA, W, E, It, 1953 E, W, It, 1954 S, I, NZ, W, Arg 1, 1955 S, I, E, W, It, 1956 S, I, W, It, E, Cz, 1957 S

Chiberry, J (Chambéry) 1955 It

Chilo, A (RCF) 1920 S, W, 1925 I, NZ

Chiocci, X (Toulon) 2014 NZ1(R), A 4(R), Arg, 2015 E 2(R)

Cholley, G (Castres) 1975 E, S, I, SA 1, 2, Arg 1, 2, R, 1976 S, I, W, E, A 1, 2, R, 1977 W, E, S, I, Arg 1, 2, NZ 1, 2, R, 1978 E, S, I, W, R, 1979 I, S

Chouly, D (Brive, Perpignan, Clermont-Auvergne) 2007 NZ1(R), 2, 2009 NZ2(R), A(R), 2012 A(R), Arg3(R), Sm(R), 2013 It(R), W(R), NZ3, 4, Tg, SA, 2014 E(R), It(R), W(R), S, I, A1, 2, 3, Fj, A 4, Arg, 2015 S 1, I, W, It(R), E 1(R), 3, S 2, [It, R(R), C, I, NZ(R)]

Choy J (Narbonne) 1930 S, I, E, G, W, 1931 I, 1933 G, 1934 G, 1935 G, 1936 G 2

Cigagna, A (Toulouse) 1995 [E]

Cimarosti, J (Castres) 1976 US (R)

Cistacq, J-C (Agen) 2000 R (R)

Claassen, A D (Castres) 2013 E(R), I(R), S, NZ3, 4(R), 2014 S(R)

Clady, A (Lezignan) 1929 G, 1931 I, S, E, G

Clarac, H (St Girons) 1938 G 1

Claudel, R (Lyon) 1932 G, 1934 G

Clauzel, F (Béziers) 1924 E, W, 1925 W

Clavé, J (Agen) 1936 G 2, 1938 R, G 2

Claverie, H (Lourdes) 1954 NZ, W

Cléda, T (Pau) 1998 E (R), S (R), I (R), W (R), Arg 1(R), Fj (R), Arg 3(R), 1999 I (R), S

Clément, G (RCF) 1931 W

Clément, J (RCF) 1921 S, W, E, 1922 S, E, W, I, 1923 S, W, I

Clemente, M (Oloron) 1978 R, 1980 S, I

Clerc, V (Toulouse) 2002 SA, NZ, C, 2003 E 1, S, I, It (R), W (R), Arg 2, NZ, 2004 I, It, W, 2005 SA2, Tg, 2006 SA, 2007 I, W1, E1, S, E2, W2, [Nm, I, Gg(R), NZ, E, Arg 2(R)], 2008 S, I, E, It(t), W, 2009 NZ1, 2, A(R), SA, Sm, NZ3, 2010 S(R),

I, SA, Arg1, 2011 S(R), I1(R), E, It, W, I2, 3(R), [J, C, NZ1, Tg, E, W, NZ2], 2012 It, S, I, E, A, Arg3, Sm, 2013 E, I, S

Cluchague, L (Biarritz O) 1924 S, 1925 E

Coderc, J (Chalon) 1932 G, 1933 G, 1934 G, 1935 G, 1936 G 1

Codorniou, D (Narbonne) 1979 NZ 1, 2, R, 1980 W, E, S, I, 1981 S, W, E, A 2, 1983 E, S, I, W, A 1, 2, R, 1984 I, W, E, S, NZ 1, 2, R, 1985 E, S, I, W, Arg 1, 2

Coeurveille, C (Agen) 1992 Arg 1(R), 2

Cognet, L (Montferrand) 1932 G, 1936 G 1, 2, 1937 G, It

Collazo, P (Bègles) 2000 R

Colombier, J (St Junien) 1952 SA, W, E

Colomine, G (Narbonne) 1979 NZ 1

Comba, F (SF) 1998 Arg 1, 2, Fj, Arg 3, 1999 I, W 1, E, S, 2000 A, NZ 1, 2, 2001 S, I

Combe, J (SF) 1910 S, E, I, 1911 S

Combes, G (Fumel) 1945 B 2

Communeau, M (SF) 1906 NZ, E, 1907 E, 1908 E, W, 1909 E, W, I, 1910 S, E, I, 1911 S, E, I, 1912 I, S, W, E, 1913 SA, E, W

Condom, J (Boucau, Biarritz O) 1982 R, 1983 E, S, I, W, A 1, 2, R, 1984 I, W, E, S, NZ 1, 2, R, 1985 E, S, I, W, Arg 1, 2, 1986 S, I, W, E, R 1, Arg 1, 2, NZ 1, R 2, NZ 2, 3, 1987 W, E, S, I, [S, R, Z, A, NZ], R, 1988 E, S, W, Arg 1, 2, 3, 4, R, 1989 I, W, E, S, NZ 1, 2, A 1, 1990 I, R, A 2, 3(R)

Conilh de Beyssac, J-J (SBUC) 1912 I, S, 1914 I, W, E

Constant, G (Perpignan) 1920 W

Correia, P (Albi) 2008 A2

Coscolla, G (Béziers) 1921 S, W

Costantino, J (Montferrand) 1973 R

Costes, A (Montferrand) 1994 C 2, 1995 R 1, [Iv], 1997 It 1, 1999 WS, Tg (R), NZ 1, [Nm (R), Fj (R), Arg (R), NZ 2(R), A (t&R)], 2000 S (R), I

Costes, F (Montferrand) 1979 E, S, NZ 1, 2, R, 1980 W, I

Couffignal, H (Colomiers) 1993 R 1

Coulon, E (Grenoble) 1928 S

Courtiols, M (Bègles) 1991 R, US 1, W 2

Coux, J-F (Bourgoin) 2007 NZ1, 2

Couzinet, D (Biarritz) 2004 US, C(R), 2008 A1(R)

Crabos, R (RCF) 1920 S, E, W, I, US, 1921 S, W, E, I, 1922 S, E, W, I, 1923 S, I, 1924 S, I

Crampagne, J (Bègles) 1967 SA 4

Crancée, R (Lourdes) 1960 Arg 3, 1961 S

Crauste, M (RCF, Lourdes) 1957 R 1, 2, 1958 S, E, A, W, It, I, 1959 E, It, W, I, 1960 S, E, W, I, It, R, Arg 1, 3, 1961 S, SA, E, W, It, I, NZ 1, 2, 3, A, R, 1962 S, E, W, I, It, R, 1963 S, I, E, W, It, R, 1964 S, NZ, E, W, It, I, SA, Fj, 1965 S, I, E, W, It, R, 1966 S, I, E, W, It

Cremaschi, M (Lourdes) 1980 R, 1981 R, NZ 1, 2, 1982 W, S, 1983 A 1, 2, R, 1984 I, W

Crenca, J-J (Agen) 1996 SA 2(R), 1999 R, Tg, WS (R), NZ 1(R), 2001 SA 1, 2, NZ (R), SA 3, A, Fj, 2002 It, W, E, S, I, Arg, A 2, SA, NZ, C, 2003 E 1, S, I, It, W, R E 2, [Fj, J(t&R), S, I, E, NZ(R)], 2004 I(R), It(R), W(R), S(R), E(R)

Crichton, W H (Le Havre) 1906 NZ, E

Cristina, J (Montferrand) 1979 R

Cussac, P (Biarritz O) 1934 G

Cutzach, A (Quillan) 1929 G

Daguerre, F (Biarritz O) 1936 G 1

Daguerre, J (CASG) 1933 G

Dal Maso, M (Mont-de-Marsan, Agen, Colomiers) 1988 R (R), 1990 NZ 2, R(R), 1992 I, 1997 I, W, E, S, It 1, R 1(R), A 1, 2, It 2, Arg, SA 1, 2, 1998 W (R), Arg 1(t), Fj (R), 1999 R (R), WS (R), Tg, NZ 1(R), W 2(R), [Nm (R), Fj (R), Arg (R), A (R)], 2000 W, E, S, I, It

Danion, J (Toulon) 1924 I

Danos, P (Toulon, Béziers) 1954 Arg 1, 2, 1957 R 2, 1958 S, E, W, It, I, SA 1, 2, 1959 S, E, It, W, I, 1960 S, E

Dantiacq, D (Pau) 1997 R 1

Darbos, P (Dax) 1969 R

Darracq, R (Dax) 1957 It

Darrieussecq, A (Biarritz O) 1973 E

Darrieussecq, J (Mont-de-Marsan) 1953 It

Darrouy, C (Mont-de-Marsan) 1957 I, E, W, It, R 1, 1959 E, 1961 R, 1963 S, I, E, W, It, 1964 NZ, E, W, It, I, SA, Fj, R,

1965 S, I, E, It, R, 1966 S, I, E, W, It, R, 1967 S, A, E, It, W, I, SA 1, 2, 4

Daudé, J (Bourgoin) 2000 S

Daudignon, G (SF) 1928 S

Dauga, B (Mont-de-Marsan) 1964 S, NZ, E, W, It, I, SA, Fj, R, 1965 S, I, E, W, It, R, 1966 S, I, E, W, It, R, 1967 S, A, E, It, W, I, SA 1, 2, 3, 4, NZ, R, 1968 S, I, NZ 1, 2, 3, A, SA 1, 2, R, 1969 S, I, E, R, 1970 S, I, W, E, R, 1971 S, I, E, W, SA 1, 2, A 1, 2, R, 1972 S, I 1, W

Dauger, J (Bayonne) 1945 B 1, 2, 1953 S

Daulouède, P (Tyrosse) 1937 G, It, 1938 G 1, 1940 B

David, Y (Bourgoin, Toulouse) 2008 It, 2009 SA, Sm(R), NZ3(R)

Debaty, V (Perpignan, Clermont-Auvergne) 2006 R(R), 2012 It, S(R), I(R), E(R), W(R), Arg 1(R), 2, 2, A(R), Arg3(R), Sm(R), 2013 It(R), W(R), E(R), I(R), S(R), NZ1(R), 2(R), 4(R), Tg(R), 2014 W(t), S(R), I(R), A1(R), 3(R), 2015 I(R), W(R), It(R), E 1, 2, 3(R), S 2(R), [It(R), R, C(R), I(R), NZ(R)]

De Besombes, S (Perpignan) 1998 Arg 1(R), Fj (R)

Decamps, P (RCF) 1911 S

Dedet, J (SF) 1910 S, E, I, 1911 W, I, 1912 S, 1913 E, I

Dedeyn, P (RCF) 1906 NZ

Dedieu, P (Béziers) 1963 E, It, 1964 W, It, I, SA, Fj, R, 1965 S, I, E, W

De Gregorio, J (Grenoble) 1960 S, E, W, I, It, R, Arg 1, 2, 1961 S, SA, E, W, I, 1962 S, E, W, 1963 S, W, It, 1964 NZ, E

Dehez, J-L (Agen) 1967 SA 2, 1969 R

De Jouvencel, E (SF) 1909 W, I

De Laborderie, M (RCF) 1921 I, 1922 I, 1925 W, E

Delage, C (Agen) 1983 S, I

De Malherbe, H (CASG) 1932 G, 1933 G

De Malmann, R (RCF) 1908 E, W, 1909 E, W, I, 1910 E, I

De Muizon, J J (SF) 1910 I

Delaigue, G (Toulon) 1973 J, R

Delaigue, Y (Toulon, Toulouse, Castres) 1994 S, NZ 2(R), C 2, 1995 I, R 1, [Tg, Iv], It, R 2(R), 1997 It 1, 2003 Arg 1, 2, 2005 S, E, W, I, It, A2(R), Tg, SA3(R)

Delmotte, G (Toulon) 1999 R, Tg

Delque, A (Toulouse) 1937 It, 1938 G 1, R, G 2

De Rougemont, M (Toulon) 1995 E (t), R 1(t), [Iv], NZ 1, 2, 1996 I (R), Arg 1, 2, W 2, SA 1, 1997 E (R), S (R), It 1

Desbrosse, C (Toulouse) 1999 [Nm (R)], 2000 I

Descamps, P (SB) 1927 G 2

Desclaux, F (RCF) 1949 Arg 1, 2, 1953 It

Desclaux, J (Perpignan) 1934 G, 1935 G, 1936 G 1, 2, 1937 G, It, 1938 G 1, R, G 2, 1945 B 1

Deslandes, C (RCF) 1990 A 1, NZ 2, 1991 W 1, 1992 R, Arg 1, 2

Desnoyer, L (Brive) 1974 R

Destarac, L (Tarbes) 1926 S, I, E, W, M, 1927 W, E, G 1, 2

Desvouges, R (SF) 1914 W

Detrez, P-E (Nîmes) 1983 A 2(R), 1986 Arg 1(R), 2, A (R), NZ1

Devergie, T (Nîmes) 1988 R, 1989 NZ 1, 2, B, A 2, 1990 W, E, S, I, R, A 1, 2, 3, 1991 US 2, W 2, 1992 R (R), Arg 2(R)

De Villiers, P (SF) 1999 W 2, [Arg (R), NZ 2(R), A (R)], 2000 W (R), E (R), S (R), I (R), It R, NZ 1(R), 2, 2001 S, I, It, W, E, SA 1, 2, NZ (R), SA 3, A, Fj, 2002 It, W, E, I, SA, NZ, C, 2003 Arg 1, 2, NZ (R), 2004 I, It, W, S, E, US, C, NZ, 2005 S, I(R), It(R), SA1(R), 2, A1(R), 2, C, Tg(R), SA3, 2006 S, I, It, E, W, SA, NZ1, 2, Arg, 2007 It, I, E1, S, W2, [Arg1, Nm, I, NZ, E]

Deygas, M (Vienne) 1937 It

Deylaud, C (Toulouse) 1992 R, Arg 1, 2, SA 1, 1994 C 1, NZ 1, 2, 1995 W, E, S, [Iv (R), S, I, SA], It, Arg

Diarra, I (Montauban) 2008 It

Dintrans, P (Tarbes) 1979 NZ 1, 2, R, 1980 E, S, I, SA, R, 1981 S, I, W, E, A 1, 2, R, 1982 W, E, S, I, R, Arg 1, 2, 1983 A 1, 2, R, 1984 I, W, E, S, NZ 1, 2, R, 1985 E, S, I, W, Arg 1, 2, 1987 [R], 1988 Arg 1, 2, 3, 1989 W, E, S, 1990 R

Dispagne, S (Toulouse) 1996 I (R), W 1

Dizabo, P (Tyrosse) 1948 A, S, E, 1949 S, I, E, W, Arg 2, 1950 S, I, 1960 Arg 1, 2, 3

Domec, A (Carcassonne) 1929 W

Domec, H (Lourdes) 1953 W, It, 1954 S, I, NZ, W, E, It, 1955 S, I, E, W, 1956 I, W, It, 1958 E, A, W, It, I

Domenech, A (Vichy, Brive) 1954 W, E, It, 1955 S, I, E, W, 1956 S, I, W, It, E, Cz, 1957 S, I, E, W, It, R 1 2, 1958 S, E, It,

1959 It, 1960 S, E, W, I, It, R, Arg 1, 2, 3, 1961 S, SA, E, W, It, I, NZ 1, 2, 3, A, R, 1962 S, E, W, I, It, R, 1963 W, It

Domercq, J (Bayonne) 1912 I, S

Domingo, T (Clermont-Auvergne) 2009 W(R), E(R), It(R), NZ2(R), Sm, 2010 S, I, W, It, E, SA, Arg2, A, 2011 S, I1, E, W, 2012 Arg 2(R), A(R), Arg3(R), Sm, 2013 E, I, S, NZ1, 2, 3, SA(R), 2014 E, It, W, S, I, A1, 2(R), 3(R)

Dominici, C (SF) 1998 E, S, Arg 1, 2, 1999 E, S, WS, NZ 1, W 2, [C, Fj, Arg, NZ, A 2, A], 2000 W, E, S, R, 2001 I (R), It, W, E, SA 1, 2, NZ, Fj, 2003 Arg 1, R, E 2, 3, [Fj, J, S, I, E], 2004 I, It, W, S, E, A(R), NZ(R), 2005 S, E, W, I, It, 2006 S, I, It, E, W, NZ1, 2(R), Arg, 2007 It, I, W1, E1, S(R), E3, W2(R), [Arg 1, Gg, NZ(R), E(R), Arg 2]

Dorot, J (RCF) 1935 G

Dospital, P (Bayonne) 1977 R, 1980 I, 1981 S, I, W, E, 1982 I, R, Arg 1, 2, 1983 E, S, I, W, 1984 E, S, NZ 1, 2, R, 1985 E, S, I, W, Arg 1

Dourthe, C (Dax) 1966 R, 1967 S, A, E, W, I, SA 1, 2, 3, NZ, 1968 W, NZ 3, SA 1, 2, 1969 W, 1971 SA 2(R), R, 1972 I 1, 2, A 1, 2, R, 1973 S, NZ, E, 1974 I, Arg 1, 2, SA 1, 2, 1975 W, E, S

Dourthe, M (Dax) 2000 NZ 2(t)

Dourthe, R (Dax, SF, Béziers) 1995 R 2, Arg, NZ 1, 2, 1996 E, R, 1996 Arg 1, 2, SA 1, 2, 1997 W, A 1, 1999 I, W 1, 2, [C, Nm, Fj, Arg, NZ 2, A], 2000 W, E, It, R, A, NZ 1, 2, 2001 S, I

Doussain, J-M (Toulouse) 2011 [NZ2(R)], 2013 NZ1(R), 3, 4(R), SA(R), 2014 E, It, W, S(R), I(R)

Doussau, E (Angoulême) 1938 R

Droitecourt, M (Montferrand) 1972 R, 1973 NZ (R), E, 1974 E, S, Arg 1, 2, 1975 SA 1, 2, Arg 1, 2, R, 1976 S, I, W, A 1, 1977 Arg 2

Dubertrand, A (Montferrand) 1971 A 1, 2, R, 1972 I 2, 1974 I, W, E, SA 2, 1975 Arg 1, 2, R, 1976 S, US

Dubois, D (Bègles) 1971 S

Dubroca, D (Agen) 1979 NZ 2, 1981 NZ 2(R), 1982 E, S, 1984 W, E, S, 1985 Arg 2, 1986 S, I, W, E, R 1, Arg 2, A, NZ 1, R 2, NZ 2, 3, 1987 W, E, S, I, [S, Z, Fj, A, NZ], R, 1988 E, S, I, W

Ducalcon, L (Castres, Racing Métro) 2010 S(R), Fj, Arg2(R), 2011 S(R), It(R), W(R), I2, [C, NZ1, Tg], 2013 It(R), W(R), E(R), S(R), NZ1, 2(R), 3(R)

Duché, A (Limoges) 1929 G

Duclos, A (Lourdes) 1931 S

Ducousso, J (Tarbes) 1925 S, W, E

Dufau, G (RCF) 1948 I, A, 1949 I, W, 1950 S, E, W, 1951 S, I, E, W, 1952 SA, W, 1953 S, I, E, W, 1954 S, I, NZ, W, E, It, 1955 S, I, E, W, It, 1956 S, I, W, It, 1957 S, I, E, W, It, R 1

Dufau, J (Biarritz) 1912 I, S, W, E

Duffaut, Y (Agen) 1954 Arg 1, 2

Duffour, R (Tarbes) 1911 W

Dufourcq, J (SBUC) 1906 NZ, E, 1907 E, 1908 W

Duhard, Y (Bagnères) 1980 E

Duhau, J (SF) 1928 I, 1930 I, G, 1931 I, S, W, 1933 G

Dulaurens, C (Toulouse) 1926 I, 1928 S, 1929 W

Dulin, B (Agen, Castres, Racing Métro) 2012 Arg 1, 2, A, Arg3, Sm, 2013 NZ2(R), 3, 4, Tg, SA, 2014 E, It, W, S, I, A1(R), 2, 3, 2015 W, E 2, [R, C, I, NZ]

Duluc, A (Béziers) 1934 G, 2015 W, E 2, [R, C, I, NZ]

Du Manoir, Y le P (RCF) 1925 I, NZ, S, W, E, 1926 S, 1927 I, S

Dumoulin, A (Racing Métro) 2014 Fj, A 4, 2015 E 2, S 2(R), [It, C(R), I(R), NZ]

Dupont, C (Lourdes) 1923 S, W, I, 1924 S, I, W, R, US, 1925 S, 1927 E, G 1, 2, 1928 A, G, W, 1929 I

Dupont, J-L (Agen) 1983 S

Dupont, L (RCF) 1934 G, 1935 G, 1936 G 1, 2, 1938 R, G 2

Dupouy, A (SB) 1924 W, R

Duprat, B (Bayonne) 1966 E, W, It, R, 1967 S, A, E, SA 2, 3, 1968 S, I, 1972 E, W, I 2, A 1

Dupré, P (RCF) 1909 W

Dupuy, J (Leicester, SF) 2009 NZ1, 2, A(R), SA, Sm(R), NZ3, 2012 S(R), E

Dupuy, J-V (Tarbes) 1956 S, I, W, It, E, Cz, 1957 S, I, E, W, It, R 2, 1958 S, E, SA 1, 2, 1959 S, E, It, W, I, 1960 W, I, It, Arg 1, 3, 1961 S, SA, E, NZ 2, R, 1962 S, E, W, I, It, 1963 W, It, R, 1964 S

Durand, N (Perpignan) 2007 NZ1, 2

Dusautoir, T (Biarritz, Toulouse) 2006 R, SA, NZ1, 2007 E3, W2(R), [Nm, I, NZ, E, Arg 2], 2008 S, I, E, W, Arg, PI, A3, 2009 I, S, W, E, It, NZ1, 2, A, SA, Sm, NZ3, 2010 S, I, W, It, E, SA, Arg1, 2, A, 2011 S, I1, E, W, I2, [J, NZ1, Tg, E, W, NZ2], 2012 It, S, I, E, W, 2013 It, W, E, I, S, NZ1, 2, 3, 4, Tg, SA, 2014 A2, 3, Fj, A 4, Arg, 2015 S 1, I, W, It, E 1, S 2, [It, C, I, NZ]

Du Souich, C J (see Judas du Souich)

Dutin, B (Mont-de-Marsan) 1968 NZ 2, A, SA 2, R

Dutour, F X (Toulouse) 1911 E, I, 1912 S, W, E, 1913 S

Dutrain, H (Toulouse) 1945 W, 1946 B, I, 1947 E, 1949 I, E, W, Arg 1

Dutrey, J (Lourdes) 1940 B

Duval, R (SF) 1908 E, W, 1909 E, 1911 E, W, I

Echavé, L (Agen) 1961 S

Elhorga, P (Agen) 2001 NZ, 2002 A 1, 2, 2003 Arg 2, NZ (R), R, [Fj(R), US, I(R), NZ], 2004 I(R), S, E, 2005 S, E, 2006 NZ2, Arg, 2008 A1

Elissalde, E (Bayonne) 1936 G 2, 1940 B

Elissalde, J-B (La Rochelle, Toulouse) 2000 S (R), R (R), 2003 It (R), W (R), 2004 I, It, W, A, Arg, 2005 SA1, 2(R), A1, 2, SA3, 2006 S, I, It, W(R), NZ1(R), 2, 2007 E2(R), 3, W2(R), [Arg 1(R), Nm, I, Gg(R), NZ, E, Arg 2], 2008 S, I, W, Arg, PI

Elissalde, J-P (La Rochelle) 1980 SA, R, 1981 A 1, 2, R

Empereur-Buisson, H (Béziers) 1931 E, G

Erbani, D (Agen) 1981 A 1, 2, NZ 1, 2, 1982 Arg 1, 2, 1983 S (R), I, W, A 1, 2, R, 1984 W, E, R, 1985 E, W (R), Arg 2, 1986 S, I, W, E, R 1, Arg 2, NZ 1, 2(R), 3, 1987 W, E, S, I, [S, R, Fj, A, NZ], 1988 E, S, 1989 I (R), W, E, S, NZ 1, A 2, 1990 W, E

Escaffre, P (Narbonne) 1933 G, 1934 G

Escommier, M (Montelimar) 1955 It

Esponda, J-M (RCF) 1967 SA 1, 2, R, 1968 NZ 1, 2, SA 2, R, 1969 S, I (R), E

Estebanez, F (Brive, Racing Metro) 2010 Fj, Arg2(R), A(R), 2011 W(R), I3, [J, NZ1(R), Tg(R)]

Estève, A (Béziers) 1971 SA 1, 1972 I 1, E, W, I 2, A 2, R, 1973 S, NZ, E, I, 1974 I, W, E, S, R, SA 1, 2, 1975 W, E

Estève, A P (Narbonne, Lavelanet) 1982 R, Arg 1, 2, 1983 E, S, I, W, A 1, 2, R, 1984 I, W, E, S, NZ 1, 2, R, 1985 E, S, I, W, 1986 S, I, 1987 [S, Z]

Etcheberry, J (Rochefort, Cognac) 1923 W, I, 1924 S, I, E, W, R, US, 1926 S, I, E, M, 1927 I, S, W, G 2

Etchenique, J-M (Biarritz O) 1974 R, SA 1, 1975 E, Arg 2

Etchepare, A (Bayonne) 1922 I

Etcheverry, M (Pau) 1971 S, I

Eutrope, A (SCUF) 1913 I

Fabre, E (Toulouse) 1937 It, 1938 G 1, 2

Fabre, J (Toulouse) 1963 S, I, E, W, It, 1964 S, NZ, E

Fabre, L (Lezignan) 1930 G

Fabre, M (Béziers) 1981 A 1, R, NZ 1, 2, 1982 I, R

Failliot, P (RCF) 1911 S, W, I, 1912 I, S, E, 1913 E, W

Fall, B (Bayonne, Racing Métro) 2009 Sm, 2010 S, 2012 Arg 2, 2013 It, W, E

Fargues, G (Dax) 1923 I

Fauré, P (Tarbes) 1914 I, W, E

Faure, L (Sale) 2008 S, I, E, A1, PI, A3, 2009 I, E

Fauvel, J-P (Tulle) 1980 R

Favre, M (Lyon) 1913 E, W

Ferrand, L (Chalon) 1940 B

Ferrien, R (Tarbes) 1950 S, I, E, W

Fickou, G (Toulouse) 2013 S(R), NZ4(R), Tg, 2014 E(R), It(R), W(R), S(R), I, A1, 2015 It, E 1, 2(t&R), 3(R), [It(R), R]

Finat, R (CASG) 1932 G, 1933 G

Fite, R (Brive) 1963 W, It

Flanquart, A (SF) 2013 NZ1(R), 3, 2014 E, S(R), I(R), A1(R), 2, 3, Fj(R), 2015 It, E 1, 2, 3(R), S 2, [It(R), R, I(R)]

Floch, A (Clermont-Auvergne) 2008 E(R), It, W

Fofana, W (Clermont-Auvergne) 2012 It, S, I, E, W, Arg 1, 2(R), A, Arg3, Sm, 2013 It, W, E, I, S, NZ1, 2, 3, 4, Tg, SA, 2014 E, It, W, A1, 2, 3, Fj, A 4, Arg, 2015 S 1, I, W, E 3, S 2, [R, C, I, NZ]

Forest, M (Bourgoin) 2007 NZ1(R), 2(R)

Forestier, J (SCUF) 1912 W

Forestier, Y (Castres) 2012 A, Arg3, Sm(R), 2013 It, W, NZ4, Tg, SA, 2014 E(R), It(R), W(R)

Forgues, F (Bayonne) 1911 S, E, W, 1912 I, W, E, 1913 S, SA, W, 1914 I, E

Fort, J (Agen) 1967 It, W, I, SA 1, 2, 3, 4

Fourcade, G (BEC) 1909 E, W

Foures, H (Toulouse) 1951 S, I, E, W

Fournet, F (Montferrand) 1950 W

Fouroux, J (La Voulte) 1972 I 2, R, 1974 W, E, Arg 1, 2, R, SA 1, 2, 1975 W, Arg 1, R, 1976 S, I, W, E, US, A 1, 1977 W, E, S, I, Arg 1, 2, NZ 1, 2, R

Francquenelle, A (Vaugirard) 1911 S, 1913 W, I

Fritz, F (Toulouse) 2005 SA1, A2, SA3, 2006 S, I, It, E, W, SA, NZ1, 2, Arg, 2007 It, 2009 I, E(R), It, NZ2(R), A, 2010 Arg1, 2012 W, Arg 1, 2, A, Arg3, Sm, 2013 It, W(R), E(R), I, NZ1, 2, 3, 4, SA

Froment, R (Castres) 2004 US(R)

Furcade, R (Perpignan) 1952 S

Gabernet, S (Toulouse) 1980 E, S, 1981 S, I, W, E, A 1, 2, R, NZ 1, 2, 1982 I, 1983 A 2, R

Gachassin, J (Lourdes) 1961 S, I, 1963 R, 1964 S, NZ, E, W, It, I, SA, Fj, R, 1965 S, I, E, W, It, R, 1966 S, I, E, W, 1967 S, A, It, W, I, NZ, 1968 I, E, 1969 S, I

Galasso, A (Toulon, Montferrand) 2000 R (R), 2001 E (R)

Galau, H (Toulouse) 1924 S, I, E, W, US

Galia, J (Quillan) 1927 E, G 1, 2, 1928 S, A, I, E, W, 1929 I, E, G, 1930 S, I, E, G, W, 1931 S, W, E, G

Gallart, P (Béziers) 1990 R, A 1, 2(R), 3, 1992 S, I, R, Arg 1, 2, SA 1, 2, Arg, 1994 I, W, E, 1995 I (t), R 1, [Tg]

Gallion, J (Toulon) 1978 E, S, I, W, 1979 I, W, E, S, NZ 2, R, 1980 W, E, S, I, 1983 A 1, 2, R, 1984 I, W, E, S, R, 1985 E, S, I, W, 1986 Arg 2

Galthié, F (Colomiers, SF) 1991 R, US 1, [R, Fj, C, E], 1992 W, E, S, R, 1994 I, W, E, 1995 [SA, E], 1996 W 1(R), 1997 I, It 2, SA 1, 2, 1998 W (R), Fj (R), 1999 R, WS (R), Tg, NZ 1(R), [Fj (R), Arg, NZ 2, A], 2000 W, E, A, NZ 1, 2, 2001 S, It, W, E, SA 1, 2, NZ, SA 3, A, Fj, 2002 E, S, I, SA, NZ, C, 2003 E 1, S, Arg 1, 2, NZ, R, E 2, [Fj, J, S, I, E]

Galy, J (Perpignan) 1953 W

Garbajosa, X (Toulouse) 1998 I, W, Arg 2(R), Fj, 1999 W 1(R), E, S, WS, NZ 1, W 2, [C, Nm (R), Fj (R), Arg, NZ 2, A], 2000 A, NZ 1, 2, 2001 S, I, E, 2002 It (R), W, SA (R), C (R), 2003 E 1, S, I, It, W, E 3

Garuet-Lempirou, J-P (Lourdes) 1983 A 1, 2, R, 1984 I, NZ 1, 2, R, 1985 E, S, I, W, Arg 1, 1986 S, I, W, E, R 1, Arg 1, NZ 1, R 2, NZ 2, 3, 1987 W, E, S, I, [S, R, Fj, A, NZ], 1988 E, S, Arg 2, R, 1989 E (R), S, NZ 1, 2, 1990 W, E

Gasc, J (Graulhet) 1977 NZ 2

Gasparotto, G (Montferrand) 1976 A 2, R

Gauby, G (Perpignan) 1956 Cz

Gaudermen, P (RCF) 1906 E

Gayraud, W (Toulouse) 1920 I

Gelez, F (Agen) 2001 SA 3, 2002 I (R), A 1, SA, NZ, C (R), 2003 S, I

Geneste, R (BEC) 1945 B 1, 1949 Arg 2

Genet, J-P (RCF) 1992 S, I, R

Gensane, R (Béziers) 1962 S, E, W, I, It, R, 1963 S

Gérald, G (RCF) 1927 E, G 2, 1928 S, 1929 I, S, W, E, G, 1930 S, I, E, G, W, 1931 I, S, E, G

Gérard, D (Bègles) 1999 Tg

Gérintes, G (CASG) 1924 W, 1925 I, 1926 W

Geschwind, P (RCF) 1936 G 1, 2

Giacardy, M (SBUC) 1907 E

Gimbert, P (Bègles) 1991 R, US 1, 1992 W, E

Giordani, P (Dax) 1999 E, S

Glas, S (Bourgoin) 1996 S (t), I (R), W 1, R, Arg 2(R), W 2, SA 1, 2, 1997 I, W, E, S, It 2(R), R 2, Arg, SA 1, 2, 1998 E, S, I, W, Arg 1, 2, Fj, Arg 3, A, 1999 W 2, [C, Nm, Arg (R), NZ 2(R), A (t&R)], 2000 I, 2001 E, SA 1, 2, NZ

Gomès, A (SF) 1998 Arg 1, 2, Fj, Arg 3, A, 1999 I (R)

Gommes, J (RCF) 1909 I

Gonnet, C-A (Albi) 1921 E, I, 1922 E, W, 1924 S, E, 1926 S, I, E, W, M, 1927 I, S, W, E, G 1

Gonzalez, J-M (Bayonne) 1992 Arg 1, 2, SA 1, 2, Arg, 1993 R

1, SA 1, 2, R 2, A 1, 2, 1994 I, W, E, S, C 1, NZ 1, 2, C 2, 1995 W, E, S, I, R 1, [Tg, S, I, SA, E], It, Arg, 1996 E, S, I, W 1

Got, R (Perpignan) 1920 I, US, 1921 S, W, 1922 S, E, W, I, 1924 I, E, W, R, US

Goujon, L (Bordeaux-Bègles) 2015 S 1(R), I(R), W(R), It, E 1, 2(R)

Gourdon, J-F (RCF, Bagnères) 1974 S, Arg 1, 2, R, SA 1, 2, 1975 W, E, S, I, R, 1976 S, I, W, E, 1978 E, S, 1979 W, E, S, R, 1980 I

Gourragne, J-F (Béziers) 1990 NZ 2, 1991 W 1

Goutta, B (Perpignan) 2004 C

Goyard, A (Lyon U) 1936 G 1, 2, 1937 G, It, 1938 G 1, R, G 2

Graciet, R (SBUC) 1926 I, W, 1927 S, G 1, 1929 E, 1930 W

Grandclaude, J-P (Perpignan) 2005 E(R), W(R), 2007 NZ1

Graou, S (Auch, Colomiers) 1992 Arg (R), 1993 SA 1, 2, R 2, A 2(R), 1995 R 2, Arg (t), NZ 2(R)

Gratton, J (Agen) 1984 NZ 2, R, 1985 E, S, I, W, Arg 1, 2, 1986 S, NZ 1

Graule, V (Arl Perpignan) 1926 I, E, W, 1927 S, W, 1931 G

Greffe, M (Grenoble) 1968 W, Cz, NZ 1, 2, SA 1

Griffard, J (Lyon U) 1932 G, 1933 G, 1934 G

Grosso, R (Castres) 2015 [C]

Gruarin, A (Toulon) 1964 W, It, I, SA, Fj, R, 1965 S, I, E, W, It, 1966 S, I, E, W, It, R, 1967 S, A, E, It, W, I, NZ, 1968 S, I

Guélorget, P (RCF) 1931 E, G

Guichemerre, A (Dax) 1920 E, 1921 E, I, 1923 S

Guilbert, A (Toulon) 1975 E, S, I, SA 1, 2, 1976 A 1, 1977 Arg 1, 2, NZ 1, 2, R, 1979 I, W, E

Guillemin, P (RCF) 1908 E, W, 1909 E, I, 1910 W, S, E, I, 1911 S, E, W

Guilleux, P (Agen) 1952 SA, It

Guirado, G (Perpignan, Toulon) 2008 It(R), 2009 A(R), Sm(R), 2010 SA(R), Arg1(R), Fj, Arg2(R), A(R), 2011 S(R), E(R), It(R), W(R), I2(R), 3(R), [C(R)], 2013 I(R), S(R), NZ1(R) , 2014 S(R), I(R), A1, 2, 3, Fj, A 4, Arg(R), 2015 S 1, I, W, It, E 1, 2(R), 3, S 2, [It, C, I, NZ]

Guiral, M (Agen) 1931 G, 1932 G, 1933 G

Guiraud, H (Nîmes) 1996 R

Guitoune, S (Perpignan, Bordeaux-Bègles) 2013 Tg, SA, 2015 W, E 2, [R]

Haget, A (PUC) 1953 E, 1954 I, NZ, E, Arg 2, 1955 E, W, It, 1957 I, E, It, R 1, 1958 It, SA 2

Haget, F (Agen, Biarritz O) 1974 Arg 1, 2, 1975 SA 2, Arg 1, 2, R, 1976 S, 1978 S, I, W, R, 1979 I, W, E, S, NZ 1, 2, R, 1980 W, S, I, 1984 S, NZ 1, 2, R, 1985 E, S, I, 1986 S, I, W, E, R 1, Arg 1, A, NZ 1, 1987 S, I, [R, Fj]

Haget, H (CASG) 1928 S, 1930 G

Halet, R (Strasbourg) 1925 NZ, S, W

Hall, S (Béziers) 2002 It, W

Harinordoquy, I (Pau, Biarritz)) 2002 W, E, S, I, A 1, 2, SA, NZ, C, 2003 E 1, S, I, It, W, Arg 1(R), 2, NZ, R, E 2, 3(R), [Fj, S, I, E], 2004 I, It, W, E, A, Arg, NZ, 2005 W(R), 2006 R(R), SA, 2007 It(R), I, W1(R), E1(R), S, E3, W2, [Arg 1, Nm(R), NZ(R), E(R), Arg 2], 2008 A1, 2, Arg, PI, A3, 2009 I, S, W, E, It, SA, 2010 S, I, W, It, E, Fj, Arg2(R), 2011 S, I1, E, It(R), W, I2, [J, C(R), NZ1(R), Tg(R), E, W, NZ2], 2012 It(R), S, I, E, W

Harislur-Arthapignet, P (Tarbes) 1988 Arg 4(R)

Harize, D (Cahors, Toulouse) 1975 SA 1, 2, 1976 A 1, 2, R, 1977 W, E, S, I

Hauc, J (Toulon) 1928 E, G, 1929 I, S, G

Hauser, M (Lourdes) 1969 E

Hedembaigt, M (Bayonne) 1913 S, SA, 1914 W

Hericé, D (Bègles) 1950 I

Herrero, A (Toulon) 1963 R, 1964 NZ, E, W, It, I, SA, Fj, R, 1965 S, I, E, W, 1966 W, It, R, 1967 S, A, E, It, I, R

Herrero, B (Nice) 1983 I, 1986 Arg 1

Heyer, F (Montferrand) 1990 A 2

Heymans, C (Agen, Toulouse, Bayonne) 2000 It (R) R, 2002 A 2(R), SA, NZ, 2004 W(R), US, C(R), A, Arg, NZ, 2005 I, It, SA1, 2, A1, 2, C, SA3, 2006 S, I, W(R), R, SA, NZ2, Arg, 2007 It, I(R), E1(R), S, E3, W2, [Arg 1, Nm, I, NZ, E], 2008 S, I, E, W(R), Arg, PI, A3, 2009 I(R), S, W, E, It, NZ1, 2, A, SA, NZ3(R), 2011 I3, [J, NZ1(R), Tg(R), E(R)]

Hiquet, J-C (Agen) 1964 E

Hoche, M (PUC) 1957 I, E, W, It, R 1

Hondagné-Monge, M (Tarbes) 1988 Arg 2(R)

Hontas, P (Biarritz) 1990 S, I, R, 1991 R, 1992 Arg, 1993 E, S, I, W

Hortoland, J-P (Béziers) 1971 A 2

Houblain, H (SCUF) 1909 E, 1910 W

Houdet, J (SF) 1927 S, W, G 1, 1928 G, W, 1929 I, S, E, 1930 S, E

Hourdebaigt, A (SBUC) 1909 I, 1910 W, S, E, I

Hubert, A (ASF) 1906 E, 1907 E, 1908 E, W, 1909 E, W, I

Hueber, A (Lourdes, Toulon) 1990 A 3, NZ 1, 1991 US 2, 1992 I, Arg 1, 2, SA 1, 2, 1993 E, S, I, W, R 1, SA 1, 2, R 2, A 1, 2, 1995 [Tg, S (R), I], 2000 It, R

Huget, Y (Bayonne, Toulouse) 2010 Arg2, A, 2011 S, I1, E, It, W(R), 2012 Arg 1, 2, A(R), Arg3(R), Sm(R), 2013 It, W, E, I, S, NZ1, 2, 3, 4, SA, 2014 E, It, W, S, I, A1, 2, 3, Fj, A 4, Arg, 2015 S 1, I, W, It, E 1, 3, S 2, [It]

Hutin, R (CASG) 1927 I, S, W

Hyardet, A (Castres) 1995 It, Arg (R)

Ibañez, R (Dax, Perpignan, Castres, Saracens, Wasps) 1996 W 1(R), 1997 It 1(R), R 1, It 2(R), R 2, SA 2(R), 1998 E, S, I, W, Arg 1, 2, Fj, Arg 3, A, 1999 I, W 1, E, S, R, WS, Tg (R), NZ 1, W 2, [C, Nm, Fj, Arg, NZ 2, A], 2000 W (R), E (R), S (R), I (R), It (R), R, 2001 S, I, It, W, E, SA 1, 2, NZ (R), SA 3, A, Fj, 2002 It (R), W, E, S, I, Arg, A 1(R), 2, SA, NZ, C, 2003 E 1, S, I, It, W, R(R), E 2(R), 3, [Fj, J(R), S, I, E, NZ(R)], 2005 C(R), Tg, 2006 I, It, E, W, R, SA(R), NZ1(R), 2, Arg, 2007 It, I, W1, E1, S, NZ1(R), 2(R), E2, 3, [Arg 1, Nm(R), I, NZ, E, Arg 2]

Icard, J (SF) 1909 E, W

Iguiniz, E (Bayonne) 1914 E

Ihingoué, D (BEC) 1912 I, S

Imbernon, J-F (Perpignan) 1976 I, W, E, US, A 1, 1977 W, E, S, I, Arg 1, 2, 1978 E, R, 1979 I, 1981 S, I, W, E, 1982 I, 1983 I, W

Iraçabal, J (Bayonne) 1968 NZ 1, 2, SA 1, 1969 S, I, W, R, 1970 S, I, W, E, R, 1971 W, SA 1, 2, A 1, 1972 E, W, I 2, A 2, R, 1973 S, NZ, E, W, I, J, 1974 I, W, E, S, Arg 1, 2, SA 2(R)

Isaac, H (RCF) 1907 E, 1908 E

Ithurra, E (Biarritz O) 1936 G 1, 2, 1937 G

Jacquet, L (Clermont-Auvergne) 2006 NZ2(R), Arg, 2008 S, I(t&R)

Janeczek, T (Tarbes) 1982 Arg 1, 2, 1990 R

Janik, K (Toulouse) 1987 R

Janin, D (Bourgoin) 2008 A1(R), 2

Jarasse, A (Brive) 1945 B 1

Jardel, J (SB) 1928 I, E

Jauréguy, A (RCF, Toulouse, SF) 1920 S, E, W, I, US, 1922 S, W, 1923 S, W, E, I, 1924 S, W, R, US, 1925 I, NZ, 1926 S, E, W, M, 1927 I, E, 1928 S, A, E, G, W, 1929 I, S, E

Jauréguy, P (Toulouse) 1913 S, SA, W, I

Jauzion, Y (Colomiers, Toulouse) 2001 SA 1, 2, NZ, 2002 A 1(R), 2(R), 2003 Arg 2, NZ, R, E 2, 3, [Fj, S, I, E], 2004 I, It, W, S, E, A, Arg, NZ(t), 2005 W, I, It, SA1, 2, A1, 2, C, Tg(R), SA3, 2006 R, SA, NZ1, 2, Arg, 2007 It, I, W1, E1, S, E3, W2, [Arg 1, Nm(R), I(R), Gg, NZ, E], 2008 It, W, Arg, PI, A3, 2009 I, S, W, E, It, NZ1(R), Sm, NZ3, 2010 S, I, W, It, E, Arg2, A, 2011 I1(R), E, It

Jeangrand, M-H (Tarbes) 1921 I

Jeanjean, N (Toulouse) 2001 SA 1, 2, NZ, SA 3(R), A (R), Fj (R), 2002 It, Arg, A 1

Jeanjean, P (Toulon) 1948 I

Jérôme, G (SF) 1906 NZ, E

Joinel, J-L (Brive) 1977 NZ 1, 1978 R, 1979 I, W, E, S, NZ 1, 2, R, 1980 W, E, S, I, SA, 1981 S, I, W, E, R, NZ 1, 2, 1982 E, S, I, R, 1983 E, S, I, W, A 1, 2, 1984 I, W, E, S, NZ 1, 2, 1985 S, I, W, Arg 1, 1986 S, I, W, E, R 1, Arg 1, 2, A, 1987 [Z]

Jol, M (Biarritz O) 1947 S, I, W, E, 1949 S, I, E, W, Arg 1, 2

Jordana, J-L (Pau, Toulouse) 1996 R (R), Arg 1(t), 2, W 2, 1997 I (t), W, S (R)

Judas du Souich, C (SCUF) 1911 W, I

Juillet, C (Montferrand, SF) 1995 R 2, Arg, 1999 E, S, WS, NZ 1, [C, Fj, Arg, NZ 2, A], 2000 A, NZ 1, 2, 2001 S, I, It, W

Mermoz, M (Toulouse, Perpignan, Toulon) 2008 A2, 2009 S(R), NZ2, A, SA, 2010 SA, Arg1(R), 2011 S, I2, [C, NZ1, Tg, E, W, NZ2], 2012 It(R), E(R), Arg 1(R), 2, A, Arg3, Sm, 2013 It, W, NZ1(R), 2014 S, I(R), Arg, 2015 It, E 1

Merquey, J (Toulon) 1950 S, I, E, W

Mesnel, F (RCF) 1986 NZ 2(R), 3, 1987 W, E, S, I, [S, Z, Fj, A, NZ], R, 1988 E, Arg 1, 2, 3, 4, R, 1989 I, W, E, S, NZ 1, A 1, 2, 1990 E, S, I, A 2, 3, NZ 1, 2, 1991 S, I, W 1, E, R, US 1, 2, W 2, [R, Fj, C, E], 1992 W, E, S, I, SA 1, 2, 1993 E (R), W, 1995 I, R 1, [Iv, E]

Mesny, P (RCF, Grenoble) 1979 NZ 1, 2, 1980 SA, R, 1981 I, W (R), A 1, 2, R, NZ 1, 2, 1982 I, Arg 1, 2

Meyer, G-S (Périgueux) 1960 S, E, It, R, Arg 2

Meynard, J (Cognac) 1954 Arg 1, 1956 Cz

Mias, L (Mazamet) 1951 S, I, E, W, 1952 I, SA, W, E, It, 1953 S, I, W, It, 1954 S, I, NZ, W, 1957 R 2, 1958 S, E, A, W, I, SA 1, 2, 1959 S, It, W, I

Michalak, F (Toulouse, Natal Sharks, Toulon) 2001 SA 3(R), A, Fj (R), 2002 It, A 1, 2, 2003 It, W, Arg 2(R), NZ, R, E 2, [Fj, J, S, I, E, NZ(R)], 2004 I, W, S, E, A, Arg, NZ, 2005 S(R), E(R), W(R), I(R), It(R), SA1, 2, A1, 2, C, Tg(R), SA3, 2006 S, I, It, E, W, 2007 E2(R), 3, [Arg1(t&R), Nm, I, NZ(R), E(R), Arg 2], 2009 It(R), 2010 S(R), I(R), W(R), 2012 Arg 1(R), 2, A, Arg3, Sm, 2013 It, W, E(R), I, S, NZ1(R), 2, Tg(R), SA(R), 2014 A1, 2(R), 3(R), 2015 E 3, S 2, [It, C, I, NZ]

Mignardi, A (Agen) 2007 NZ1, 2

Mignoni, P (Béziers, Clermont-Auvergne)) 1997 R 2(R), Arg (t), 1999 R (RS), NZ 1, W 2(R), [C, Nm], 2002 W, E (R), I (R), Arg, A 2(R), 2005 S, It(R), C(R), 2006 R, 2007 It, I, W1, E1(R), S, E2, 3(R), W2, [Arg 1, Gg, Arg 2(R)]

Milhères, C (Biarritz) 2001 E

Milliand, P (Grenoble) 1936 G 2, 1937 G, It

Millo-Chluski, R (Toulouse) 2005 SA1, 2008 Arg, PI, A3(R), 2009 I(R), S, W(R), NZ1, 2, A, SA, Sm(R), NZ3, 2010 SA, Fj, A(R), 2011 I2, [C]

Milloud, O (Bourgoin) 2000 R (R), 2001 NZ, 2002 W (R), E (R), 2003 It (R), W (R), Arg 1, R (R), E 2(t+R), 3, [J, S(R), US, I(R), E(R)], 2004 US, C(R), A, Arg, NZ(R), 2005 S(R), E(R), W(R), SA1, 2(R), A1, 2, C(R), Tg, SA3, 2006 S(R), I, It, E(R), W(R), NZ1(R), 2, Arg, 2007 It, I(R), W1, E1, S, E2, 3, [Arg 1, I, Gg, NZ, E]

Minjat, R (Lyon) 1945 B 1

Miorin, H (Toulouse) 1996 R, SA 1, 1997 I, W, E, S, It 1, 2000 It (R), R (R)

Mir, J-H (Lourdes) 1967 R, 1968 I

Mir, J-P (Lourdes) 1967 A

Modin, R (Brive) 1987 [Z]

Moga, A-M-A (Bègles) 1945 B 1, 2, W, 1946 B, I, K, W, 1947 S, I, W, E, 1948 I, A, S, W, E, 1949 S, I, E, W, Arg 1, 2

Mola, U (Dax, Castres) 1997 S (R), 1999 R (R), WS, Tg (R), NZ 1, W 2, [C, Nm, Fj, Arg (R), NZ 2(R), A (R)]

Momméjat, B (Cahors, Albi) 1958 It, I, SA 1, 2, 1959 S, E, It, W, I, 1960 S, E, I, R, 1962 S, E, W, I, It, R, 1963 S, I, W

Moncla, F (RCF, Pau) 1956 Cz, 1957 I, E, W, It, R 1, 1958 SA 1, 2, 1959 S, E, It, W, I, 1960 S, E, W, I, It, R, Arg 1, 2, 3, 1961 S, SA, E, W, It, I, NZ 1, 2, 3

Moni, C (Nice, SF) 1996 R, 2000 A, NZ 1, 2, 2001 S, I, It, A (R)

Monié, R (Perpignan) 1956 Cz, 1957 E

Monier, R (SBUC) 1911 I, 1912 S

Monniot, M (RCF) 1912 W, E

Montade, A (Perpignan) 1925 I, NZ, S, W, 1926 W

Montanella, F (Auch) 2007 NZ1(R)

Montlaur, P (Agen) 1992 E (R), 1994 S (R)

Moraitis, B (Toulon) 1969 E, W

Morel, A (Grenoble) 1954 Arg 2

Morère, J (Toulouse) 1927 E, G 1, 1928 S, A

Moscato, V (Bègles) 1991 R, US 1, 1992 W, E

Mougeot, C (Bègles) 1992 W, E, Arg

Mouniq, P (Toulouse) 1911 S, E, W, I, 1912 I, E, 1913 S, SA, E

Moure, H (SCUF) 1908 E

Moureu, P (Béziers) 1920 I, US, 1921 W, E, I, 1922 S, W, I, 1923 S, W, E, I, 1924 S, I, E, W, 1925 E

Mournet, A (Bagnères) 1981 A 1(R)

Mouronval, F (SF) 1909 I

Muhr, A H (RCF) 1906 NZ, E, 1907 E

Murillo, G (Dijon) 1954 It, Arg 1

Nakaitaci, N (Clermont-Auvergne) 2015 It, E 1, 3, S 2, [It, R, I, NZ]

Nallet, L (Bourgoin, Castres, Racing-Métro) 2000 R, 2001 E, SA 1(R), 2(R), NZ, SA3(R), A (R), Fj (R), 2003 NZ, 2005 A2(R), C, Tg(R), SA3, 2006 I(R), It(R), E(R), W(R), R, SA(R), NZ1(R), 2, Arg, 2007 It, I, W1, E1, S, E3(R), [Nm, I(R), Gg, Arg 2], 2008 S, I, E, It, W, A1, 2, Arg, PI, A3, 2009 I, S, W, E, It, SA, NZ3(R), 2010 S, I, W, It, E, SA, Arg1, 2, 2011 S, I1, E, It, W, I2(R), 3, [J, NZ1, Tg, E, W, NZ2], 2012 It, S(R), I(R), E(R)

Namur, R (Toulon) 1931 E, G

Noble, J-C (La Voulte) 1968 E, W, Cz, NZ 3, A, R

Noirot, B (Racing Metro) 2010 Fj(R)

Normand, A (Toulouse) 1957 R 1

Novès, G (Toulouse) 1977 NZ 1, 2, R, 1978 W, R, 1979 I, W

Ntamack, E (Toulouse) 1994 W, C 1, NZ 1, 2, C 2, 1995 W, I, R 1, [Tg, S, I, SA, E], It, R 2, Arg, NZ 1, 2, 1996 E, S, I, W 1, R (R), Arg 1, 2, W 2, 1997 I, 1998 Arg 3, 1999 I, W 1, E, S, WS, NZ 1, W 2(R), [C (R), Nm, Fj, Arg, NZ 2, A], 2000 W, E, S, I, It

Ntamack F (Colomiers) 2001 SA 3

Nyanga, Y (Béziers, Toulouse , Racing Métro) 2004 US, C, 2005 S(R), E(R), W, I, It, SA1, 2, A1(R), 2, C(t&R), Tg, SA3, 2006 S, I, E, W, 2007 E2(R), 3, [Nm, I(R), Gg, Arg 2], 2012 A, Arg3, Sm, 2013 E, I, S(t&R), NZ1(R), 2(R), SA(R), 2014 E, It, W, A2, 3(R), A 4(R), 2015 E 2, 3(R), S 2(R), [R, C(R), NZ(R)]

Olibeau, O (Perpignan) 2007 NZ1(R), 2(R)

Olive, D (Montferrand) 1951 I, 1952 I

Ollivon, C (Bayonne) 2014 Fj(R), Arg(R)

Ondarts, P (Biarritz O) 1986 NZ 3, 1987 W, E, S, I, [S, Z, Fj, A, NZ], R, 1988 E, I, W, Arg 1, 2, 3, 4, R, 1989 I, W, E, NZ 1, 2, A 2, 1990 W, E, S, I, R (R), NZ 1, 2, 1991 S, I, W 1, E, US 2, W 2, [R, Fj, C, E]

Orso, J-C (Nice, Toulon) 1982 Arg 1, 2, 1983 E, S, A 1, 1984 E (R), S, NZ 1, 1985 I (R), W, 1988 I

Othats, J (Dax) 1960 Arg 2, 3

Ouedraogo, F (Montpellier) 2007 NZ2(R), 2008 S, I, E(R), It, W, A1, 2, Arg(R), PI, A3, 2009 I, S, W, NZ1, 2, A, NZ3, 2010 S, I, Fj, A, 2011 I3, [C, W(R)], 2012 Arg 1, 2, A, Arg3, Sm, 2013 It, W, NZ1, Tg, 2014 A1, 3, 2015 E 2, [R, C(R)]

Ougier, S (Toulouse) 1992 R, Arg 1, 1993 E (R), 1997 It 1

Paco, A (Béziers) 1974 Arg 1, 2, R, SA 1, 2, 1975 W, E, Arg 1, 2, 1976 S, I, W, E, US, A 1, 2, R, 1977 W, E, S, I, NZ 1, 2, R, 1978 E, S, I, W, R, 1979 I, W, E, S, 1980 W

Palat, J (Perpignan) 1938 G 2

Palisson, A (Brive, Toulon) 2008 A1, 2, Arg(R), PI(R), A3(R), 2010 I, W, It, E, Fj(R), Arg2, A, 2011 E(R), W, I2, 3, [Tg, E, W, NZ2], 2012 W

Palmié, M (Béziers) 1975 SA 1, 2, Arg 1, 2, R, 1976 S, I, W, E, US, 1977 W, E, S, I, Arg 1, 2, NZ 1, 2, R, 1978 E, S, I, W

Paoli, R (see Simonpaoli)

Paparemborde, R (Pau) 1975 SA 1, 2, Arg 1, 2, R, 1976 S, I, W, E, US, A 1, 2, R, 1977 W, E, S, I, Arg 1, NZ 1, 2, 1978 E, S, I, W, R, 1979 I, W, E, S, NZ 1, 2, R, 1980 W, E, S, SA, R, 1981 S, I, W, E, A 1, 2, R, NZ 1, 2, 1982 W, I, R, Arg 1, 2 1983 E, S, I, W

Papé, P (Bourgoin, Castres, SF) 2004 I, It, W, S, E, C, NZ(R), 2005 I(R), It(R), SA1, 2, A1, 2006 NZ1, 2, 2007 It(R), I, S(R), NZ1, 2, 2008 E, 2009 NZ1, A, Sm, 2010 S, I, Arg1, 2011 W(R), I3, [J(R), C, NZ1, Tg, E, W, NZ2], 2012 It, S, I, E, W, Arg 1, 2, A, Arg3, Sm, 2013 It, NZ4, Tg(R), SA, 2014 E, It, W, S, I, Fj, A 4, Arg, 2015 S 1, I, E, S 2, [It, C, I, NZ]

Pardo, L (Hendaye) 1924 I, E

Pardo, L (Bayonne) 1980 SA, R, 1981 S, I, W, E, A 1, 1982 W, E, S, 1983 A 1(R), 1985 S, I, Arg 2

Pargade, J-H (Lyon U) 1953 It

Pariès, L (Biarritz O) 1968 SA 2, R, 1970 S, I, W, 1975 E, S, I

Parra, M (Bourgoin, Clermont-Auvergne) 2008 S(R), I(R), E, Arg(R), 2009 I(R), S(R), W, E, It, SA(R), Sm, NZ3(R), 2010 S, I, W, It, E, SA, Arg1, Fj(R), Arg2, A, 2011 S, I1, E(R), It,

W, I2(R), 3, [J(R), C, NZ1, Tg, E, W, NZ2], 2012 It(R), S, I, E(R), W(R), Arg 1, 2(R), A(R), Arg3(R), Sm, 2013 It(R), W(R), E, I, S, NZ4, Tg, SA, 2014 A1(R), 2, 2015 S 1(R), I(R), W, E 2, S 2(R), [It(R), R, C(R), I(R), NZ]

Pascalin, P (Mont-de-Marsan) 1950 I, E, W, 1951 S, I, E, W

Pascarel, J-R (TOEC) 1912 W, E, 1913 S, SA, E, I

Pascot, J (Perpignan) 1922 S, E, I, 1923 S, 1926 I, 1927 G 2

Paul, R (Montferrand) 1940 B

Pauthe, G (Graulhet) 1956 E

Pebeyre, E-J (Fumel, Brive) 1945 W, 1946 I, K, W, 1947 S, I, W, E

Pebeyre, M (Vichy, Montferrand) 1970 E, R, 1971 I, SA 1, 2, A 1, 1973 W

Péclier, A (Bourgoin) 2004 US, C

Pécune, J (Tarbes) 1974 W, E, S, 1975 Arg 1, 2, R, 1976 I, W, E, US

Pédeutour, P (Bègles) 1980 I

Pélissié, J (Montpellier) 2013 Tg(R)

Pellissier, L (RCF) 1928 A, I, E, G, W

Pelous, F (Dax, Toulouse) 1995 R 2, Arg, NZ 1, 2, 1996 E, S, I, R (R), Arg 1, 2, W 2, SA 1, 2, 1997 I, W, E, S, It 1, R 1, A 1, 2, It 2, R 2, Arg, SA 1, 2(R), 1998 E, S, I, W, Arg 1, 2, Fj, Arg 3, A, 1999 I, W 1, E, R (R), WS, Tg (R), NZ 1, W 2, [C, Nm, Fj, NZ 2, A], 2000 W, E, S, I, It, A, NZ 1, 2, 2001 S, I, It, W, E, 2002 It (R), W (R), E (R), S, I, Arg, A 1, 2, SA, NZ, C, 2003 E 1, S, I, It, W, R, E 2, 3(R), [Fj, J, S, I, E, NZ(R)], 2004 I, It, W, S, E, US, C, A, Arg, NZ, 2005 S, E, W, I, It, A2, 2006 S, I, It, E, W, R, SA, NZ1, 2007 E2, 3, W2(R), [Arg1, Nm(R), Gg(R), NZ, E]

Penaud, A (Brive, Toulouse) 1992 W, E, S, I, R, Arg 1, 2, SA 1, 2, Arg, 1993 R 1, SA 1, 2, R 2, A 1, 2, 1994 I, W, E, 1995 NZ 1, 2, 1996 S, R, Arg 1, 2, W 2, 1997 I, E, R 1, A 2, 2000 W (R), It

Périé, M (Toulon) 1996 E, S, I (R)

Péron, P (RCF) 1975 SA 1, 2

Perrier, P (Bayonne) 1982 W, E, S, I (R)

Pesteil, J-P (Béziers) 1975 SA 1, 1976 A 2, R

Petit, C (Lorrain) 1931 W

Peyras, J-B (Bayonne) 2008 A2(R)

Peyrelade, H (Tarbes) 1940 B

Peyrelongue, J (Biarritz) 2004 It, S(R), C(R), A(R), Arg(R), NZ

Peyroutou, G (Périgueux) 1911 S, E

Phliponeau, J-F (Montferrand) 1973 W, I

Piazza, A (Montauban) 1968 NZ 1, A

Picamoles, L (Montpellier, Toulouse) 2008 I(R), E, It, A1, 2(t&R), Arg, PI(R), A3(R), 2009 I(R), S(R), E(R), It(R), NZ1, 2, SA 2010 SA(R), Arg1, 2011 I3, [C, NZ1, E(R)], 2012 It, S, I(R), E(R), W(R), Arg 1, 2, A, Arg3, Sm, 2013 It, W, E, I, S, NZ1, 2, 2014 E, It, W, I, A2(R), 3(R), 2015 E 2, 3, S 2, [It, R, I, NZ]

Picard, T (Montferrand) 1985 Arg 2, 1986 R 1(R), Arg 2

Pierre, J (Bourgoin, Clermont-Auvergne) 2007 NZ1, 2, 2010 S(R), I(R), W, It, E, SA(R), Arg1(R), Fj(R), Arg2, A, 2011 S, I1, E, It, W, I2, 3(R), [J, C(R), NZ1(R), Tg(R), E(R), W(R), NZ2(R)], 2012 W(R)

Pierrot, G (Pau) 1914 I, W, E

Pilon, J (Périgueux) 1949 E, 1950 E

Piqué, J (Pau) 1961 NZ 2, 3, A, 1962 S, It, 1964 NZ, E, W, It, I, SA, Fj, R, 1965 S, I, E, W, It

Piquemal, M (Tarbes) 1927 I, S, 1929 I, G, 1930 S, I, E, G, W

Piquiral, E (RCF) 1924 S, I, E, W, R, US, 1925 E, 1926 S, I, E, W, M, 1927 I, S, W, E, G 1, 2, 1928 E

Piteu, R (Pau) 1921 S, W, E, I, 1922 S, E, W, I, 1923 E, 1924 E, 1925 I, NZ, W, E, 1926 E

Plante, A (Perpignan) 2013 NZ1, 2

Plantefol, A (RCF) 1967 SA 2, 3, 4, NZ, R, 1968 E, W, Cz, NZ 2, 1969 E, W

Plantey, S (RCF) 1961 A, 1962 It

Plisson, J (SF) 2014 E, It, W, S, 2015 It(R), E 1

Podevin, G (SF) 1913 W, I

Poeydebasque, F (Bayonne) 1914 I, W

Poirier, A (SCUF) 1907 W

Poitrenaud, C (Toulouse) 2001 SA 3, A, Fj, 2003 E 1, S, I, It, W, Arg 1, NZ, E 3, [J, US, E(R), NZ], 2004 E(R), US, C, Arg(R), NZ, 2006 R, 2007 It, I, W1, E1, S, E2, 3, [Nm, I, Gg, Arg 2], 2009 I, S, 2010 S, I, W, It, E, SA, Arg1(R), 2011 S(R), I1, 2012 I, E, W

Pomathios, M (Agen, Lyon U, Bourg) 1948 I, A, S, W, E, 1949 S, I, E, W, Arg 1, 2, 1950 S, I, W, 1951 S, I, E, W, 1952 W, E, 1953 S, I, W, 1954 S

Pons, P (Toulouse) 1920 S, E, W, 1921 S, W, 1922 S

Porcu, C (Agen) 2002 Arg (R), A 1, 2(R)

Porical, J (Perpignan) 2010 Arg1, Fj, Arg2(R), A

Porra, M (Lyon) 1931 I

Porthault, A (RCF) 1951 S, E, W, 1952 I, 1953 S, I, It

Portolan, C (Toulouse) 1986 A, 1989 I, E

Potel, A (Begles) 1932 G

Poux, J-B (Narbonne, Toulouse) 2001 Fj (R), 2002 S, I (R), Arg, A 1(R), 2(R), 2003 E 3, [Fj, J, US, NZ], 2007 E2, 3, W2(R), [Nm, I(R), Gg, NZ(R), E(R), Arg 2], 2008 E(R), It(R), W(R), 2010 W(R), It(R), E(R), SA(R), Arg1(R), 2011 I2(R), 3, [J(R), C, NZ1, Tg, E, W, NZ2], 2012 It(R), S, I, E, W

Prat, J (Lourdes) 1945 B 1, 2, W, 1946 B, I, K, W, 1947 S, I, W, E, 1948 I, A, S, W, E, 1949 S, I, E, W, Arg 1, 2, 1950 S, I, E, W, 1951 S, E, W, 1952 S, I, SA, W, E, It, 1953 S, I, E, W, It, 1954 S, I, NZ, W, E, It, 1955 S, I, E, W, It

Prat, M (Lourdes) 1951 I, 1952 S, I, SA, W, E, 1953 S, I, E, 1954 I, NZ, W, E, It, 1955 S, I, E, W, It, 1956 I, W, It, Cz, 1957 S, I, W, It, R 1, 1958 A, W, I

Prévost, A (Albi) 1926 M, 1927 I, S, W

Prin-Clary, J (Cavaillon, Brive) 1945 B 1, 2, W, 1946 B, I, K, W, 1947 S, I, W

Privat, T (Béziers, Clermont-Auvergne) 2001 SA 3, A, Fj, 2002 It, W, S (R), SA (R), 2003 [NZ], 2005 SA2, A1(R)

Puech, L (Toulouse) 1920 S, E, I, 1921 E, I

Puget, M (Toulouse) 1961 It, 1966 S, I, It, 1967 SA 1, 3, 4, NZ, 1968 Cz, NZ 1, 2, SA 1, 2, R, 1969 E, R, 1970 W

Puig, A (Perpignan) 1926 S, E

Pujol, A (SOE Toulouse) 1906 NZ

Pujolle, M (Nice) 1989 B, A 1, 1990 S, I, R, A 1, 2, NZ 2

Puricelli, J (Bayonne) 2009 NZ1(R), A, Sm(R), NZ3(R)

Quaglio, A (Mazamet) 1957 R 2, 1958 S, E, A, W, I, SA 1, 2, 1959 S, E, It, W, I

Quilis, A (Narbonne) 1967 SA 1, 4, NZ, 1970 R, 1971 I

Rabadan, P (SF) 2004 US(R), C(R)

Ramis, R (Perpignan) 1922 E, I, 1923 W

Rancoule, H (Lourdes, Toulon, Tarbes) 1955 E, W, It, 1958 A, W, It, I, SA 1, 1959 S, It, W, 1960 I, It, R, Arg 1, 2, 1961 SA, E, W, It, NZ 1, 2, 1962 S, E, W, I, It

Rapin, A (SBUC) 1938 R

Raymond, F (Toulouse) 1925 S, 1927 W, 1928 I

Raynal, F (Perpignan) 1935 G, 1936 G 1, 2, 1937 G, It

Raynaud, F (Carcassonne) 1933 G

Raynaud, M (Narbonne) 1999 W 1, E (R)

Razat, J-P (Agen) 1962 R, 1963 S, I, R

Rebujent, R (RCF) 1963 E

Revailler, D (Graulhet) 1981 S, I, W, E, A 1, 2, R, NZ 1, 2, 1982 W, S, I, R, Arg 1

Revillon, R (RCF) 1926 I, E, 1927 S

Ribère, E (Perpignan, Quillan) 1924 I, 1925, I, NZ, S, 1926 S, I, W, M, 1927 I, S, W, E, G 1, 2, 1928 S, A, I, E, G, W, 1929 I, E, G, 1930 S, I, E, W, 1931 I, S, W, E, G, 1932 G, 1933 G

Rives, J-P (Toulouse, RCF) 1975 E, S, I, Arg 1, 2, R, 1976 S, I, W, E, US, A 1, 2, R, 1977 W, E, S, I, Arg 1, 2, R, 1978 E, S, I, W, R, 1979 I, W, E, S, NZ 1, 2, R, 1980 W, E, S, I, SA, 1981 S, I, W, E, A 1, 2, 1982 W, E, S, I, R, 1983 E, S, I, W, A 1, 2, R, 1984 I, W, E, S

Rochon, A (Montferrand) 1936 G 1

Rodrigo, M (Mauléon) 1931 I, W

Rodriguez, L (Mont-de-Marsan, Montferrand, Dax) 1981 A 1, 2, R, NZ 1, 2, 1982 W, E, S, I, R, 1983 E, S, 1984 I, NZ 1, 2, R, 1985 E, S, I, W, 1986 Arg 1, A, R 2, NZ 2, 3, 1987 W, E, S, I, [S, Z, Fj, A, NZ], R, 1988 E, S, I, W, Arg 1, 2, 3, 4, 1989 I, E, S, NZ 1, 2, B, A 1, 1990 W, E, S, I, NZ 1

Rogé, L (Béziers) 1952 It, 1953 E, W, It, 1954 S, Arg 1, 2, 1955 S, I, 1956 W, It, 1957 S, 1960 S, E

Rollet, J (Bayonne) 1960 Arg 3, 1961 NZ 3, A, 1962 It, 1963 I

Romero, H (Montauban) 1962 S, E, W, I, It, R, 1963 E

Romeu, J-P (Montferrand) 1972 R, 1973 S, NZ, E, W, I, R, 1974 W, E, S, Arg 1, 2, R, SA 1, 2(R), 1975 W, SA 2, Arg 1, 2, R, 1976 S, I, W, E, US, 1977 W, E, S, I, Arg 1, 2, NZ 1, 2, R

Roques, A (Cahors) 1958 A, W, It, I, SA 1, 2, 1959 S, E, W, I, 1960 S, E, W, I, It, Arg 1, 2, 3, 1961 S, SA, E, W, It, I, 1962 S, E, W, I, It, 1963 S

Roques, J-C (Brive) 1966 S, I, It, R

Rossignol, J-C (Brive) 1972 A 2

Rouan, J (Narbonne) 1953 S, I

Roucariès, G (Perpignan) 1956 S

Rouffia, L (Narbonne) 1945 B 2, W, 1946 W, 1948 I

Rougerie, A (Montferrand, Clermont-Auvergne) 2001 SA 3, A, Fj (R), 2002 It, W, E, S, I, Arg, A 1, 2, 2003 E 1, S, I, It, W, Arg 1, 2, NZ, R, E 2, 3(R), [Fj, J, S, I, E], 2004 US, C, A, Arg, NZ, 2005 S, W, A2, C, Tg, SA3, 2006 I, It, E, W, NZ1, 2, 2007 E2, W2, [Arg1, Nm(R), I(R), Gg, Arg 2], 2008 S(R), I, E, It, 2010 S, SA, Arg2, A, 2011 S, I1, E, It, I3, [J, C, NZ1, Tg, E, W, NZ2], 2012 It, S, I, E, W

Rougerie, J (Montferrand) 1973 J

Rougé-Thomas, P (Toulouse) 1989 NZ 1, 2

Roujas, F (Tarbes) 1910 I

Roumat, O (Dax) 1989 NZ 2(R), B, 1990 W, E, S, I, R, A 1, 2, 3, NZ 1, 2, 1991 S, I, W 1, E, R, US 1, W 2, [R, Fj, C, E], 1992 W (R), E (R), S, I, SA 1, 2, Arg, 1993 E, S, I, W, R 1, SA 1, 2, R 2, A 1, 2, 1994 I, W, E, C 1, NZ 1, 2, C 2, 1995 W, E, S, [Iv, S, I, SA, E], 1996 E, S, I, W 1, Arg 1, 2

Rousie, M (Villeneuve) 1931 S, G, 1932 G, 1933 G

Rousset, G (Béziers) 1975 SA 1, 1976 US

Rué, J-B (Agen) 2002 SA (R), C (R), 2003 E 1(R), S (R), It (R), W (R), Arg 1, 2(R)

Ruiz, A (Tarbes) 1968 SA 2, R

Rupert, J-J (Tyrosse) 1963 R, 1964 S, Fj, 1965 E, W, It, 1966 S, I, E, W, It, 1967 It, R, 1968 S

Sadourny, J-L (Colomiers) 1991 W 2(R), [C (R)], 1992 E (R), S, I, Arg 1(R), 2, SA 1, 2, 1993 R 1, SA 1, 2, R 2, A 1, 2, 1994 I, W, E, S, C 1, NZ 1, 2, C 2, 1995 W, E, S, I, R 1, [Tg, S, I, SA, E], It, R 2, Arg, NZ 1, 2, 1996 E, S, I, W 1, Arg 1, 2, W 2, SA 1, 2, 1997 I, W, E, S, It 1, R 1, A 1, 2, It 2, R 2, Arg, SA 1, 2, 1998 E, S, I, W, 1999 R, Tg, NZ 1(R), 2000 NZ 2, 2001 It, W, E

Sagot, P (SF) 1906 NZ, 1908 E, 1909 W

Sahuc, A (Métro) 1945 B 1, 2

Sahuc, F (Toulouse) 1936 G 2

Saint-André, P (Montferrand, Gloucester) 1990 R, A 3, NZ 1, 2, 1991 I (R), W 1, E, US 1, 2, W 2, [R, Fj, C, E], 1992 W, E, S, I, R, Arg 1, 2, SA 1, 2, 1993 E, S, I, W, SA 1, 2, A 1, 2, 1994 I, W, E, S, C 1, NZ 1, 2, C 2, 1995 W, E, S, I, R 1, [Tg, Iv, S, I, SA, E], It, R 2, Arg, NZ 1, 2, 1996 E, S, I, W 1, R, Arg, NZ 1, 2, W 2, 1997 It 1, R 2, Arg, SA 1, 2

Saisset, O (Béziers) 1971 R, 1972 S, I 1, A 1, 2, 1973 S, NZ, E, W, I, J, R, 1974 I, Arg 2, SA 1, 2, 1975 W

Salas, P (Narbonne) 1979 NZ 1, 2, R, 1980 W, E, 1981 A 1, 1982 Arg 2

Salinié, R (Perpignan) 1923 E

Sallefranque, M (Dax) 1981 A 2, 1982 W, E, S

Salut, J (TOEC) 1966 R, 1967 S, 1968 I, E, Cz, NZ 1, 1969 I

Samatan, A (Agen) 1930 S, I, E, G, W, 1931 I, S, W, E, G

Samson, C (Toulon, Castres) 2012 Arg 2(R), 2013 E, I, S(R), NZ2

Sanac, A (Perpignan) 1952 It, 1953 S, I, 1954 E, 1956 Cz, 1957 S, I, E, W, It

Sangalli, F (Narbonne) 1975 I, SA 1, 2, 1976 S, A 1, 2, R, 1977 W, E, S, I, Arg 1, 2, NZ 1, 2

Sanz, H (Narbonne) 1988 Arg 3, 4, R, 1989 A 2, 1990 S, I, R, A 1, 2, NZ 2, 1991 W 2

Sappa, M (Nice) 1973 J, R, 1977 R

Sarrade, R (Pau) 1929 I

Sarraméa, O (Castres) 1999 R, WS (R), Tg, NZ 1

Saux, J-P (Pau) 1960 W, It, Arg 1, 2, 1961 SA, E, W, It, I, NZ 1, 2, 3, A, 1962 S, E, W, I, It, 1963 S, I, E, It

Savitsky, M (La Voulte) 1969 R

Savy, M (Montferrand) 1931 I, S, W, E, 1936 G 1

Sayrou, J (Perpignan) 1926 W, M, 1928 E, G, W, 1929 S, W, E, G

Schuster, J (Perpignan) 2010 Fj, A(R)

Scohy, R (BEC) 1931 S, W, E, G

Sébedio, J (Tarbes) 1913 S, E, 1914 I, 1920 S, I, US, 1922 S, E, 1923 S

Séguier, R (Béziers) 1973 J, R

Seigne, L (Agen, Merignac) 1989 B, A 1, 1990 NZ 1, 1993 E, S, I, W, R 1, A 1, 2, 1994 S, C 1, 1995 E (R), S

Sella, P (Agen) 1982 R, Arg 1, 2, 1983 E, S, I, W, A 1, 2, R, 1984 I, W, E, S, NZ 1, 2, R, 1985 E, S, I, W, Arg 1, 2, 1986 S, I, W, E, R 1, Arg 1, 2, A, NZ 1, R 2, NZ 2, 3, 1987 W, E, S, I, [S, R, Z (R), Fj, A, NZ], 1988 E, S, I, W, Arg 1, 2, 3, 4, R, 1989 I, W, E, S, NZ 1, 2, B, A 1, 2, 1990 W, E, S, I, A 1, 2, 3, 1991 W 1, E, R, US 1, 2, W 2, [Fj, C, E], 1992 W, E, S, I, Arg, 1993 E, S, I, W, R 1, SA 1, 2, R 2, A 1, 2, 1994 I, W, E, S, C 1, NZ 1, 2, C 2, 1995 W, E, S, I, [Tg, S, I, SA, E]

Semmartin, J (SCUF) 1913 W, I

Sénal, G (Béziers) 1974 Arg 1, 2, R, SA 1, 2, 1975 W

Sentilles, J (Tarbes) 1912 W, E, 1913 S, SA

Serin, L (Béziers) 1928 E, 1929 W, E, G, 1930 S, I, E, G, W, 1931 I, W, E

Serre, P (Perpignan) 1920 S, E

Serrière, P (RCF) 1986 A, 1987 R, 1988 E

Servat, W (Toulouse) 2004 I, It, W, S, E, US, C, A, Arg, NZ 2005 S, E(R), W(R), It(R), SA1(R), 2, 2008 S, I(R), E(R), W(R), 2009 It(R), NZ1, 2, SA, NZ3, 2010 S, I, W, It, E, Arg2, A, 2011 S, I, E, It, W, [J, C, NZ1(R), Tg, E, W, NZ2], 2012 It, S(R), I(R), E(R), W

Servole, L (Toulon) 1931 I, S, W, E, G, 1934 G, 1935 G

Sicart, N (Perpignan) 1922 I

Sillières, J (Tarbes) 1968 R, 1970 S, I, 1971 S, I, E, 1972 E, W

Siman, M (Montferrand) 1948 E, 1949 S, 1950 S, I, E, W

Simon, S (Bègles) 1991 R, US 1

Simonpaoli, R (SF) 1911 I, 1912 I, S

Sitjar, M (Agen) 1964 W, It, I, R, 1965 It, R, 1967 A, E, It, W, I, SA 1, 2

Skrela, D (Colomiers, SF, Toulouse) 2001 NZ, 2007 It, I, W1, E1, (R), W2, [Arg 1, Gg(R), Arg 2], 2008 S(R), I, E(R), W, Arg, PI, A3, 2010 SA(R), Fj(R), 2011 I2(R), 3, [J(R)]

Skrela, J-C (Toulouse) 1971 SA 2, A 1, 2, 1972 I 1(R), E, W, I 2, A 1, 1973 W, J, R, 1974 W, E, S, Arg 1, R, 1975 W (R), E, S, I, SA 1, 2, R, 1976 S, I, W, E, US, A 1, 2, R, 1977 W, E, S, I, Arg 1, 2, NZ 1, 2, R, 1978 E, S, I, W

Slimani, R (SF) 2013 NZ4(R), Tg(R), SA(R), 2014 E(R), It(R), S(R), I(R), A1(R), 2, 3, 2015 S 1, I, W, It(R), E 1(R), 3, S 2, [It, C, I, NZ]

Soler, M (Quillan) 1929 G

Soro, R (Lourdes, Romans) 1945 B 1, 2, W, 1946 B, I, K, 1947 S, I, W, E, 1948 I, A, S, W, E, 1949 S, I, E, W, Arg 1, 2

Sorondo, L-M (Montauban) 1946 K, 1947 S, I, W, E, 1948 I

Soulette, C (Béziers, Toulouse) 1997 R 2, 1998 S (R), I (R), W (R), Arg 1, 2, Fj, 1999 W 2(R), [C (R), Nm (R), Arg, NZ 2, A]

Soulié, E (CASG) 1920 E, I, US, 1921 S, E, I, 1922 E, W, I

Sourgens, J (Bègles) 1926 M

Sourgens, O (Bourgoin) 2007 NZ2

Souverbie, J-M (Bègles) 2000 R

Spanghero, C (Narbonne) 1971 E, W, SA 1, 2, A 1, 2, R, 1972 S, E, W, I 2, A 1, 2, 1974 I, W, E, S, R, SA 1, 1975 E, S, I

Spanghero, W (Narbonne) 1964 SA, Fj, R, 1965 S, I, E, W, It, R, 1966 S, I, E, W, It, R, 1967 S, A, E, SA 1, 2, 3, 4, NZ, 1968 S, I, E, W, NZ 1, 2, 3, A, SA 1, 2, R, 1969 S, I, W, 1970 R, 1971 W, SA 1, 1972 E, I 2, A 1, 2, R, 1973 S, NZ, E, W, I

Spedding, S L (Bayonne, Clermont-Auvergne) 2014 Fj, A 4, Arg, 2015 S 1, I, It, E 1, 2, 3, S 2, [It, C, I, NZ]

Stener, G (PUC) 1956 S, I, E, 1958 S, I

Struxiano, P (Toulouse) 1913 W, I, 1920 S, E, W, I, US

Suta, J (Toulon) 2012 A, Arg3(R), Sm(R), 2013 W, E(R), 2015 W(R)

Sutra, G (Narbonne) 1967 SA 2, 1969 W, 1970 S, I

Swierczinski, C (Bègles) 1969 E, 1977 Arg 2

Szarzewski, D (Béziers, SF, Racing Métro) 2004 C(R), 2005 I(R), A1, 2, SA3, 2006 S, E(R), W(t&R), R(R), SA, NZ1, 2(R), Arg(R), 2007 It(R), E2(R), W2, [Arg1(R), Nm, I(R), Gg(R), NZ(R), E(R)], 2008 S(R), I, E, It, W, Arg, PI, A3, 2009 I, S,

GEORGIA

GEORGIA'S 2014–15 TEST RECORD

OPPONENT	DATE	VENUE	RESULT
Tonga	8 Nov	H	Lost 9–23
Ireland	16 Nov	A	Lost 49–7
Japan	23 Nov	H	Won 35–24
Germany	7 Feb	A	Won 64–8
Portugal	14 Feb	H	Won 20–15
Spain	28 Feb	A	Won 26–13
Russia	14 Mar	H	Won 33–0
Romania	21 Mar	A	Won 15–6
Uruguay	13 Jun	H	Won 19–10
Canada	2 Sep	N	Lost 16–15
Japan	5 Sep	N	Lost 13–10
Tonga	19 Sep	N	Won 17–10
Argentina	25 Sep	N	Lost 54–9
New Zealand	2 Oct	N	Lost 43–10
Namibia	7 Oct	N	Won 17–16

GEORGIA CREATE RUGBY WORLD CUP HISTORY

By Lúcás Ó'Ceallacháin

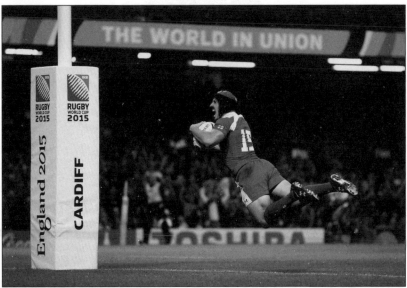

Full-back Beka Tsiklauri dives over the line to score Georgia's first ever try against the All Blacks.

When head coach Milton Haig described Georgia's best performance at a Rugby World Cup as the culmination of four years of hard work, he may well have been underselling the achievements of the Lelos and himself as head coach. Since their debut at RWC 2003 they have improved dramatically from tournament to tournament, while continuing to dominate the European Nations Cup and develop domestically. Their place in Pool C was confirmed almost 18 months in advance and the Lelos management knew that two victories would likely secure them automatic qualification for RWC 2019. The planning started early.

Another undefeated campaign in 2015 in the European Nations Cup seems almost routine for Georgia but, given the impressive performance of Romania at Rugby World Cup 2015, it would do a disservice to the competitiveness of the tournament. Victories against Germany (64–8), Portugal (20–15), Spain (26–13), Russia (33–0) and

Romania (15–6) set the squad up nicely for their World Cup goals.

The long-term professional structures put in place by the Georgian Rugby Union with strong government support are starting to reap rewards. The academy system has seen more domestic players graduate to the senior squad, while the World Rugby U20 Trophy, the World Rugby Tbilisi Cup and regular test matches at international level have provided the coaches with plenty of opportunity to blood players.

The U20 Trophy, which Georgia won for the first time in May, saw youngster Vasil Lobzhanidze make this season his own, but also saw the emergence of a more expansive style of play. Defeating Uruguay (46–12), top seeds Fiji (30–13) and hosts Portugal (19–11) saw Georgia reach the final against Canada where they powered to a 49–24 victory. Georgia will now make their bow in the World Rugby U20 Championship for the first time in 2016 before hosting the event the following year.

The Tbilisi Cup provided more competitive action for Georgia's mainly home-based players. Victory against Uruguay (19–10) saw them off to a good start, but ultimately Emerging Italy and champions Emerging Ireland had too much, winning 26–10 and 45–12 respectively.

The prodigious Lobzhanidze had made his senior debut against Germany in the European Nations Cup opener in February and went on to be nominated for World Rugby's Breakthrough Player of the Year award alongside All Black Nehe Milner-Skudder and Scotland's Mark Bennett – a clear indication of the scrum-half's talent. Another key element to the continued success has been the retention of experienced heads to guide these young starlets – record point scorer Merab Kvirikashvili and second-row Giorgi Chkhaidze were heading into their fourth Rugby World Cup and would prove key.

Haig aimed to make this the best prepared side Georgia had ever sent to a Rugby World Cup with training camps at the Shevardeni high performance base in Tbilisi and cryotherapy camps in Poland, as well as additional warm-up matches. But despite losses to the Newcastle Falcons (27–7), Canada (16–15) and Japan (13–10), the matches were used as part of the team's preparation in the UK before the tournament.

Georgia's professional preparation was clear for all to see as they got their campaign underway against a physical Tongan side who had beaten them 23–9 in Tbilisi last November. In front of a packed Kingsholm, the Georgian pack laid the platform for a powerful performance. Lobzhanidze became the youngest player in Rugby World Cup history at the age of 18 years and 340 days and linked well with his back row. Man of the match Mamuka Gorgodze's pick and go try at the base of the posts got the scoreboard moving, before fellow back-row Giorgi Tkhilaishvili sealed the victory in the second half. It finished 17–10 in

Georgia's favour after an heroic defensive effort kept the Tongans at bay, sparking wild celebrations back home.

Next up at Kingsholm were Argentina six days later. Despite a tight first 20 minutes, the sin-binning of the totemic Gorgodze led to the scintillating Los Pumas scoring 21 points. Gorgodze was a nuisance at the breakdown throughout the tournament, poaching nine turnovers, but found himself on the wrong side of the law on this occasion. With the advantage, Argentina simply had too much class and gas, romping away to a 54–9 victory.

The reality check of the Argentina game focused Georgian minds for the biggest of rugby challenges – world champions New Zealand. Georgia knew their dream of qualification for RWC 2019 was still alive and the match represented a first ever test against New Zealand. With one eye on Namibia, head coach Milton Haig made several changes to his starting line-up and it was one of those who gave Georgia something to cheer about early on as full-back Beka Tsiklauri hacked on to score an historic try that raised the roof of the Millennium Stadium. Georgia's defence put the All Blacks under severe pressure, forcing uncharacteristic errors and ensuring the Lelos remained in touch, trailing 22–10 at half-time.

All Blacks winger Julian Savea put in a powerful performance, making 106 metres and running in a hat-trick of tries, and it would take something special to overshadow that kind of performance. But Gorgodze obliged with another man of the match showing – four turnovers, a lineout steal and some destructive tackling to boot. It was indicative of the workmanlike performance that when Gorgodze was announced as man of the match he looked bemused and humbled despite the raucous cheers of the packed stadium.

It finished 43–10 to the All Blacks, but captain Richie McCaw and his team were left with questions. "We've seen through this tournament, compared to other tournaments that I've played in, that the so-called 'easy' games aren't easy anymore," he said.

Knowing the prize at stake and fully aware it would be a final farewell for several senior players, Georgia held their nerve against a Namibian side who were just as determined to leave their mark on RWC 2015. The game was framed in terms of two inspirational captains, man mountain Gorgodze and the blockbusting Jacques Burger of Namibia. In what was a nervy affair, Burger left the field due to an injury after putting his body on the line yet again, but rather than weakening Namibia, it only cemented their resolve.

This was epitomised by what must surely be one of the longest halves of rugby ever when Georgia camped on the Namibian five-metre line with scrum after scrum until eventually a forward pass enabled the referee to call a halt after almost 64 minutes of real time. Ultimately it was Georgia and Gorgodze who came up trumps, delighting the Sandy Park crowd as he ploughed through Namibian defenders to secure the 17–16 win.

The prize of automatic qualification was secured and celebrated along with the final curtain call of some of the Lelos' top performers. When players with the calibre of Clermont Auvergne prop Davit Zirakashvili, a stalwart of the front row with 54 tests, can afford to step away you know the team is in good hands. "In my position, Georgia is not lacking in players to take my place," he said. "I wouldn't abandon my country if that was the case. Of course it's sad for me to leave, but everything must come to an end."

The Lelos can now focus on bringing through their talented young under-20 squad to senior level and ensuring that they are battle-hardened and ready to push for a first qualification to the knockout stages of a Rugby World Cup. If the Georgians can add more discipline to their game in the lead up to Japan 2019 – they conceded almost 13 penalties per match in England and poached nine turnovers per game, seven of those coming from captain Gorgodze – then there is no telling how far they can go.

GEORGIA

Getty Images

Georgia held on to beat Namibia 17–16 and confirm their qualification for Rugby World Cup 2019 in Japan.

GEORGIA INTERNATIONAL STATISTICS

MATCH RECORDS UP TO 1 NOVEMBER, 2015

WINNING MARGIN

Date	Opponent	Result	Winning Margin
07/04/2007	Czech Republic	98–3	95
03/02/2002	Netherlands	88–0	88
06/02/2010	Germany	77–3	74
26/02/2005	Ukraine	65–0	65
12/06/2005	Czech Republic	75–10	65

MOST CONVERSIONS IN A MATCH
BY THE TEAM

Date	Opponent	Result	Cons
06/02/2010	Germany	77–3	11
03/02/2002	Netherlands	88–0	9
07/04/2007	Czech Republic	98–3	9
12/06/2005	Czech Republic	75–10	7
07/02/2015	Germany	64–8	7

BY A PLAYER

Date	Player	Opponent	Cons
06/02/2010	Merab Kvirikashvili	Germany	11
03/02/2002	Pavle Jimsheladze	Netherlands	9
07/04/2007	Merab Kvirikashvili	Czech Republic	9
12/06/2005	Malkhaz Urjukashvili	Czech Republic	7
	6 on 2 occasions		

MOST DROP GOALS IN A MATCH
BY THE TEAM

Date	Opponent	Result	DGs
20/10/1996	Russia	29–20	2
21/11/1991	Ukraine	19–15	2
15/07/1992	Ukraine	15–0	2
04/06/1994	Switzerland	22–21	2

BY A PLAYER

Date	Player	Opponent	DGs
15/07/1992	Davit Chavleishvili	Ukraine	2

MOST POINTS IN A MATCH
BY THE TEAM

Date	Opponent	Result	Points
07/04/2007	Czech Republic	98–3	98
03/02/2002	Netherlands	88–0	88
06/02/2010	Germany	77–3	77
12/06/2005	Czech Republic	75–10	75
23/03/1995	Bulgaria	70–8	70

BY A PLAYER

Date	Player	Opponent	Points
06/02/2010	Merab Kvirikashvili	Germany	32
08/02/2014	Merab Kvirikashvili	Portugal	24
08/03/2003	Pavle Jimsheladze	Russia	23
07/04/2007	Merab Kvirikashvili	Czech Republic	23
17/11/2012	Merab Kvirikashvili	Japan	22

MOST TRIES IN A MATCH
BY THE TEAM

Date	Opponent	Result	Tries
07/04/2007	Czech Republic	98–3	16
03/02/2002	Netherlands	88–0	14
	11 on 4 occasions		

BY A PLAYER

Date	Player	Opponent	Tries
	3 on 7 occasions		

MOST PENALTIES IN A MATCH
BY THE TEAM

Date	Opponent	Result	Pens
08/03/2003	Russia	23–17	6
28/09/2011	Romania	25–9	6
	5 on 7 occasions		

BY A PLAYER

Date	Player	Opponent	Pens
08/03/2003	Pavle Jimsheladze	Russia	6
	5 on 4 occasions		

MOST CAPPED PLAYERS

Player	Caps
Merab Kvirikashvili	88
Davit Kacharava	87
Giorgi Chkhaidze	86
Irakli Abuseridze	85
Tedo Zibzibadze	77

LEADING TRY SCORERS

Player	Tries
Mamuka Gorgodze	25
Irakli Machkhaneli	23
Tedo Zibzibadze	21
Malkhaz Urjukashvili	18
Davit Kacharava	17

LEADING CONVERSIONS SCORERS

Player	Cons
Merab Kvirikashvili	113
Pavle Jimsheladze	61
Malkhaz Urjukashvili	47
Lasha Malaguradze	29
Beka Tsiklauri	11

LEADING PENALTY SCORERS

Player	Pens
Merab Kvirikashvili	124
Pavle Jimsheladze	48
Malkhaz Urjukashvili	46
Lasha Malaguradze	25
Nugzar Dzagnidze	22

LEADING DROP GOAL SCORERS

Player	DGs
Kakha Machitidze	4
3 by 4 players	

LEADING POINTS SCORERS

Player	Points
Merab Kvirikashvili	667
Malkhaz Urjukashvili	325
Pavle Jimsheladze	320
Lasha Malaguradze	162
Mamuka Gorgodze	125

GEORGIA

GEORGIA INTERNATIONAL PLAYERS

UP TO 1 NOVEMBER, 2015

V Abashidze 1998 *It, Ukr, I,* 1999 *Tg, Tg,* 2000 *It, Mor, Sp,* 2001 *H, Pt, Rus, Sp, R,* 2006 *J*

N Abdaladze 1997 *Cro, De*

I Abuseridze 2000 *It, Pt, Mor, Sp, H, R,* 2001 *H, Pt, Rus, Sp, R,* 2002 *Pt, Rus, Sp, R, I, Rus,* 2003 *Pt, Rus, Cze, R, It, E, Sa, SA,* 2004 *Rus,* 2005 *Pt, Ukr, R,* 2006 *Rus, R, Pt, Ukr, J, R, Sp, Pt, Pt,* 2007 *R, Rus, Cze, Nm, ESA, ItA, Ar, I, Nm, F,* 2008 *Pt, R, Pt, Rus, Sp, S,* 2009 *Ger, Pt, Sp, R, Rus, ArJ, ItA,* 2010 *Pt, Sp, R, Rus, C, US,* 2011 *Ukr, Sp, Pt, R, Rus, S, E, R, Ar,* 2012 *Sp, R, Rus, Ukr, US, C, J, Fj,* 2013 *Sp*

V Akhvlediani 2007 *Cze*

K Alania 1994 *Lux,* 1996 *Swi,* 1996 *Cze, Cze, Rus,* 1997 *Pt, Pol, Cro, De,* 1998 *It,* 2001 *H, Pt, Sp, F, SA,* 2002 *H, Pt, Rus, Sp, R, I, Rus,* 2003 *Rus,* 2004 *Pt, Sp*

N Andghuladze 1997 *Pol,* 2000 *It, Pt, Mor, Sp, H, R,* 2004 *Sp, Rus, Cze, R*

G Aptsiauri 2014 *J,* 2015 *Ger, Pt, Sp, Rus, R, Ur, Elt, C, J, Tg, Ar, NZ, Nm*

D Ashvetia 1998 *Ukr,* 2005 *Pt,* 2006 *R,* 2007 *Sp*

K Asieshvili 2008 *ItA,* 2010 *S, ItA, Nm,* 2012 *Sp,* 2014 *Sp,* 2015 *Pt, Sp, Rus, R, C, J, Tg, Ar, NZ, Nm*

G Babunashvili 1992 *Ukr, Ukr, Lat,* 1993 *Rus, Pol, Lux,* 1996 *Cze*

Z Bakuradze 1989 *Z,* 1990 *Z,* 1991 *Ukr, Ukr,* 1993 *Rus, Pol*

D Baramidze 2000 *H*

O Barkalaia 2002 *I,* 2004 *Sp, Rus, Cze, R, Ur, Chl, Rus,* 2005 *Pt, Ukr, R, Cze, Chl,* 2006 *Rus, R, Pt, Ukr, J, Bb, R, Sp,* 2007 *Nm, ItA, I, F,* 2008 *Pt, R, Pt, Rus, Sp, ESA, Ur, ItA, S,* 2009 *Ger, Sp, R*

D Basilaia 2008 *Pt, R, Pt, Cze, Rus, Sp, S,* 2009 *Ger, Sp, R, C, US, ItA,* 2011 *SAK, ArJ, Nm, S, E, R,* 2012 *Sp, Pt, R, Rus, I,* 2015 *Ger, Pt*

G Begadze 2011 *ArJ,* 2012 *Pt, R, Rus, Ukr, US, J,* 2013 *Bel, Pt, Rus, R, Elr, Ur, Ar, C, US, Sa,* 2014 *Bel, Pt, Rus, Sp, R, Sp, ArJ, Elt, Tg, I, J,* 2015 *Ger, Pt, R, Ur, Elt, Elr, C, J, Tg, Ar, NZ, Nm*

R Belkania 2004 *Sp,* 2005 *Chl,* 2007 *Sp, Rus,* 2012 *Pt, R, Rus, Ukr, US,* 2013 *Bel, Pt, Sp, Elr, Ur, SAP, Ar*

G Beriashvili 1993 *Rus, Pol,* 1995 *Ger*

G Berishvili 2011 *SAK, ArJ, Nm, E, R,* 2012 *Sp, Pt, R, Rus, US, C,* 2013 *Elr, Ur, SAP,* 2014 *Sp, ArJ, Elt*

M Besselia 1991 *Ukr,* 1993 *Rus, Pol,* 1996 *Rus,* 1997 *Pt*

A Bezhashvili 2015 *Ur, Elt*

B Bitsadze 2012 *Ukr, US, C, Fj,* 2013 *Pt, Ur, SAP, Ar,* 2014 *ArJ, Elt,* 2015 *Ger, Rus, R, Ur, Elt, Elr*

D Bolgashvili 2000 *It, Pt, H, R,* 2001 *H, Pt, Rus, Sp, R, F, SA,* 2002 *H, Pt, Rus, I,* 2003 *Pt, Sp, Rus, Cze, R, E, Sa, SA,* 2004 *Rus, Ur, Chl, Rus,* 2005 *Cze,* 2007 *Sp,* 2010 *ItA*

J Bregvadze 2008 *ESA, ItA,* 2009 *C, IrA,* 2010 *Sp, R, S, Nm,*

2011 *Ukr, Sp, R, Rus, Nm, S, E, R, Ar*, 2013 *R, Ar*, 2014 *Bel, Pt, Rus, Sp, R*, 2015 *Ur, Elt, Elr, C, J, Tg, Ar, Nm*

G Buguianishvili 1996 *Cze, Rus*, 1997 *Pol*, 1998 *It, Rus, I, R*, 2000 *Sp, H, R*, 2001 *H, F, SA*, 2002 *Rus*

D Chavleishvili 1990 *Z, Z*, 1992 *Ukr, Ukr, Lat*, 1993 *Pol, Lux*

D Chichua 2008 *Cze*

I Chikava 1993 *Pol, Lux*, 1994 *Swi*, 1995 *Bul, Mol, H*, 1996 *Cze, Cze*, 1997 *Pol*, 1998 *I*

R Chikvaidze 2004 *Ur, Chl*

L Chikvinidze 1994 *Swi*, 1995 *Bul, Mol, Ger, H*, 1996 *Cze, Rus*

L Chilachava 2012 *Sp, C*, 2013 *Bel, Elr, Ur, SAP, Ar, C, US, Sa*, 2014 *Bel, Pt, Rus, Sp, R, Tg, I, J*, 2015 *Ger, Pt, Sp, Rus, R, C, Tg, Ar, NZ*

G Chkhaidze 2002 *H, R, I, Rus*, 2003 *Pt, Cze, It, E, SA, Ur*, 2004 *Cze, R*, 2006 *Pt, Ukr*, 2007 *R, Rus, Cze, Nm, ESA, ItA, Ar, I, Nm, F*, 2008 *R, Pt, Cze, Rus, Sp*, 2009 *Ger, Pt, Sp, R, Rus, ArJ, ItA*, 2010 *Ger, Pt, Sp, R, Rus, C, US*, 2011 *Ukr, Sp, Pt, R, Rus, S, E, R, Ar*, 2012 *Sp, Pt, R, Rus, Ukr, US, C*, 2013 *Bel, Pt, Rus, Sp, R, Elr, Ur, Ar, C, US, Sa*, 2014 *Bel, Pt, Rus, Sp, R, Tg, I, J*, 2015 *Pt, Sp, Ur, Elt, Elr, C, J, NZ*

S Chkhenkeli 1997 *Pol*

I Chkhikvadze 2005 *Chl*, 2007 *Sp*, 2008 *Pt, R, Pt, Cze, Rus, ESA, Ur, ItA, S*, 2009 *Ger, Sp, ItA*, 2010 *Sp, Rus, S, ItA, Nm, C, US*, 2011 *Pt, SAK, ArJ, Nm, R*, 2012 *Pt*

I Chkonia 2007 *ESA, ItA*

D Dadunashvili 2003 *It, E, SA, Ur*, 2004 *Sp, Rus, Cze, R*, 2005 *Chl*, 2007 *Sp, Rus, Cze, Nm, ItA*, 2008 *Pt, R, Pt, Cze, Rus, Sp, S*, 2009 *C, IrA, US, ItA*, 2010 *Sp, S, ItA, Nm*

L Datunashvili 2004 *Sp*, 2005 *Pt, Ukr, R, Cze*, 2006 *Rus, R, Pt, Ukr, J, Bb, Cze, Pt, Pt*, 2007 *R, Rus, Nm, ESA, ItA, I, Nm, F*, 2008 *Pt, Pt*, 2009 *Sp, R, Rus, C, US, ArJ*, 2010 *Ger, Pt, Sp, R, Rus, C, US*, 2011 *Ukr, Sp, Pt, R, Rus, S, E, R, Ar*, 2012 *Sp, Pt, Rus, J, Fj*, 2013 *Sp, R, Ar, C, US, Sa*, 2014 *Bel, Pt, Rus, R, Tg, I, J*, 2015 *Sp, R, Ur, Elt, Elr, C, J, Tg, Ar, NZ, Nm*

V Didebulidze 1991 *Ukr*, 1994 *Kaz*, 1995 *Bul, Mol*, 1996 *Cze*, 1997 *De*, 1999 *Tg*, 2000 *H*, 2001 *H, Pt, Rus, Sp, R, F, SA*, 2002 *H, Pt, Rus, Sp, R, I, Rus*, 2003 *Pt, Sp, Rus, Cze, R, It, E, Sa, SA*, 2004 *Rus*, 2005 *Pt*, 2006 *R, R*, 2007 *R, Sp, Rus, Cze, Nm, ESA, ItA, Ar, Nm, F*

E Dzagnidze 1992 *Ukr, Ukr, Lat*, 1993 *Rus, Pol*, 1995 *Bul, Mol, Ger, H*, 1998 *I*

N Dzagnidze 1989 *Z*, 1990 *Z, Z*, 1991 *Ukr*, 1992 *Ukr, Ukr, Lat*, 1993 *Rus, Pol*, 1994 *Swi*, 1995 *Ger, H*

T Dzagnidze 2008 *ESA*

D Dzneladze 1992 *Ukr, Lat*, 1993 *Lux*, 1994 *Kaz*

Z Dzneladze 2013 *SAP*

P Dzotsenidze 1995 *Ger, H*, 1997 *Pt, Pol*

G Elizbarashvili 2002 *Rus*, 2003 *Sp*, 2004 *Chl*, 2005 *Cze*, 2006 *Pt, Ukr, J, Bb, Cze, Sp, Pt*, 2007 *R, Sp, Rus, I, F*, 2009 *C, IrA*

O Eloshvili 2002 *H*, 2003 *SA*, 2006 *Bb, Cze*, 2007 *Sp, Cze, Nm, ESA, ItA, I, F*

S Essakia 1999 *Tg*, 2000 *It, Mor, Sp, H*, 2004 *Cze, R*

M Gagnidze 1991 *Ukr, Ukr*

D Gasviani 2004 *Sp, Rus*, 2005 *Cze, Chl*, 2006 *Ukr, J*, 2007 *Rus, Cze*, 2008 *ESA, Ur, ItA, S*

A Ghibradze 1992 *Ukr, Ukr, Lat*, 1994 *Swi*, 1995 *Bul, Mol, Ger*, 1996 *Cze*

D Ghudushauri 1989 *Z*, 1991 *Ukr, Ukr*

L Ghvaberidze 2004 *Pt*

R Gigauri 2006 *Ukr, J, Bb, Cze, Sp, Pt, Pt*, 2007 *R, Nm, ESA, ItA, Ar, Nm, F*, 2008 *Pt, R, Pt, Rus, Sp, ESA, Ur*, 2009 *C, IrA, US, ArJ, ItA*, 2010 *S, ItA, Nm*, 2011 *ArJ, Nm, S, E, R*, 2012 *Sp*, 2014 *Sp, Elt*, 2015 *Ur, Elr*

A Giorgadze 1996 *Cze*, 1998 *It, Ukr, Rus, R*, 1999 *Tg, Tg*, 2000 *It, Pt, Mor, H, R*, 2001 *H, Pt, Rus, Sp, R, F, SA*, 2002 *H, Pt, Rus, Sp, R, I, Rus*, 2003 *Sp, Rus, R, It, E, Sa, SA, Ur*, 2005 *Pt, Ukr, R, Cze*, 2006 *Rus, R, Pt, Bb, Cze, Sp, Pt*, 2007 *R, Ar, I, Nm, F*, 2009 *Ger, Pt, Sp, ArJ*, 2010 *Ger, Pt, C, US*, 2011 *Pt, SAK, ArJ, S, Ar*

I Giorgadze 2001 *F, SA*, 2003 *Pt, Sp, Rus, R, It, E, Sa, Ur*, 2004 *Rus*, 2005 *Pt, Cze*, 2006 *Rus, R, Pt, Bb, Cze, R, Sp, Pt, Pt*, 2007 *R, Sp, Rus, Cze, Ar, Nm, F*, 2008 *R*, 2009 *Ger, Pt, Sp, Rus*, 2010 *Ger, Pt, C, US*, 2011 *Pt, SAK*

M Giorgadze 2014 *Sp, Elt, I*, 2015 *Pt, Rus, Elt, J, Ar, NZ*

O Giorgadze 2015 *Elt, Elr*

B Gorgadze 2015 *Ur, Elt*

M Gorgodze 2003 *Sp, Rus*, 2004 *Pt, Sp, Rus, Cze, R, Ur, Chl, Rus*, 2005 *Pt, Ukr, R, Cze, Chl*, 2006 *Rus, Pt, Bb, Cze, R, Sp, Pt, Pt*, 2007 *Ar, I, Nm*, 2008 *R, Rus, Sp*, 2009 *Ger, Pt, Sp, R, Rus, ArJ*, 2011 *R, Rus, S, E, R, Ar*, 2012 *Pt, R, Rus, J, Fj*, 2013 *Bel, Pt, Rus, Sp, R, C, US, Sa*, 2014 *Rus, Sp, R*, 2015 *Rus, R, C, J, Tg, Ar, NZ, Nm*

E Gueguchadze 1990 *Z, Z*

L Gugava 2004 *Sp, Rus, Cze, Ur, Chl, Rus*, 2005 *Pt, Ukr*, 2006 *Bb, Cze*, 2009 *C, IrA, US*, 2010 *C, US*, 2011 *Ukr, Sp, Pt, R, Rus, ArJ, Nm, Ar*, 2012 *Ukr, C*

I Guiorkhelidze 1998 *R*, 1999 *Tg, Tg*

G Guiunashvili 1989 *Z*, 1990 *Z*, 1991 *Ukr, Ukr*, 1992 *Ukr, Ukr, Lat*, 1993 *Rus, Pol, Lux*, 1994 *Swi*, 1996 *Rus*, 1997 *Pt*

K Guiunashvili 1990 *Z, Z*, 1991 *Ukr, Ukr*, 1992 *Ukr, Ukr, Lat*

B Gujaraidze 2008 *ESA*, 2012 *Ukr*

I Gundishvili 2002 *I*, 2003 *Pt, Sp, Rus, Cze*, 2008 *ESA, Ur, ItA*, 2009 *C, US*

D Gurgenidze 2007 *Sp, ItA*

A Gusharashvili 1998 *Ukr*

D Iobidze 1993 *Rus, Pol*

E Iovadze 1992 *Ukr*, 1994 *Kaz*, 1995 *Bul, Mol, Ger, H*, 2001 *Sp, F, SA*, 2002 *H, Rus, Sp, R, I*

A Issakadze 1989 *Z*

N Iurini 1991 *Ukr*, 1994 *Swi*, 1995 *Ger, H*, 1996 *Cze, Cze, Rus*, 1997 *Pt, Pol, Cro, De*, 1998 *Ukr, Rus*, 2000 *It, Sp, H, R*

S Janelidze 1991 *Ukr, Ukr*, 1993 *Rus*, 1994 *Kaz*, 1995 *Ger*, 1997 *Pt*, 1998 *Ukr, I, R*, 1999 *Tg*, 2000 *R*

R Japarashvili 1992 *Ukr, Lat*, 1993 *Pol, Lux*, 1996 *Cze*, 1997 *Pt*

L Javelidze 1997 *Cro*, 1998 *I*, 2001 *H, R, F, SA*, 2002 *H, R*, 2004 *R*, 2005 *Ukr*, 2007 *Sp*

G Jgenti 2004 *Ur*, 2005 *Chl*, 2007 *Sp, Cze, Nm, ESA, ItA*, 2009 *C, IrA, US*, 2011 *R*

D Jghenti 2004 *Cze, R*

D Jhamutashvili 2005 *Chl*

G Jimsheladze 2011 *SAK*

P Jimsheladze 1995 *Bul, Mol, H*, 1996 *Cze, Cze, Rus*, 1997 *De*, 1998 *It, Ukr, Rus, I, R*, 1999 *Tg, Tg*, 2000 *Pt, Mor, Sp, H, R*, 2001 *H, Pt, Rus, Sp, R, F, SA*, 2002 *H, Pt, Rus, Sp, I, Rus*, 2003 *Pt, Sp, Rus, Cze, R, It, E, Sa, SA, Ur*, 2004 *Rus*, 2005 *R*, 2006 *Rus, R, Pt, Ukr, J, Bb, Cze, Pt, Pt*, 2007 *R, Rus, Cze, Ar*

R Jinchvelashvili 2013 *SAP*

K Jintcharadze 1993 *Rus, Pol*, 2000 *It, Mor*

D Kacharava 2006 *Ukr, J, R, Sp, Pt*, 2007 *R, Sp, Rus, Cze, Nm, ESA, ItA, I, Nm*, 2008 *Pt, R, Pt, Cze, Rus, Sp, S*, 2009 *Ger, Pt, Sp, R, Rus, C, IrA, US, ArJ, ItA*, 2010 *Ger, Pt, Sp, R, Rus, C, US*, 2011 *Ukr, Sp, Pt, R, Rus, S, E, R, Ar*, 2012 *Sp, Pt, R, Rus, Ukr, US, C, J, Fj*, 2013 *Bel, Pt, Rus, Sp, R, Elr, Ur, SAP, Ar, C, US, Sa*, 2014 *Bel, Pt, Rus, R, Sp, Tg, I, J*, 2015 *Ger, Pt, Sp, Rus, R, C, J, Tg, Ar, NZ, Nm*

G Kacharava 2005 *Ukr*, 2006 *J, Bb, Cze, R*, 2007 *Sp*, 2008 *Cze*

G Kakhiani 1995 *Bul, Mol*

V Kakovin 2008 *S*, 2009 *C, IrA, US, ItA*, 2010 *S, ItA, Nm*, 2011 *Ukr, Sp, Pt, R, Rus, SAK, ArJ, Nm, R, Ar*, 2012 *Pt, R, Rus*, 2013 *Rus, Sp, R, Ar*

G Kalmakhelidze 2012 *Sp, Ukr*

V Katsadze 1997 *Pol*, 1998 *It, Ukr, Rus, I, R*, 1999 *Tg, Tg*, 2000 *Pt, Mor, Sp, H, R*, 2001 *H, Pt, Rus, Sp, R*, 2002 *Pt, Rus, Sp, R, I, Rus*, 2003 *Pt, Sp, Cze, R, E, Sa, SA, Ur*, 2004 *Sp*, 2005 *Ukr*

A Kavtarashvili 1994 *Swi*, 1995 *Bul, Mol, Ger*, 1996 *Cze, Rus*, 1997 *Pt, Cro, De*, 1998 *It, Rus, I, R*, 1999 *Tg, Tg*, 2000 *It, H, R*, 2001 *H*, 2003 *SA, Ur*

G Kavtidze 2008 *S*, 2014 *ArJ, Elt*

I Kerauli 1991 *Ukr, Ukr*, 1992 *Ukr, Ukr*

L Khachirashvili 2005 *Ukr*

T Khakhaleishili 1994 *Kaz*

B Khamashuridze 1989 *Z*

B Khamashuridze 1998 *It, Ukr, Rus, I, R*, 1999 *Tg, Tg*, 2000 *It, Pt, Sp, H, R*, 2001 *Pt, Rus, Sp, R, F, SA*, 2002 *H, Pt, Rus, Sp, R, I, Rus*, 2003 *Pt, Cze, R, It, E, Sa, SA, Ur*, 2004 *Pt, Rus, Rus*, 2005 *Pt, Ukr, Chl*, 2006 *Rus, R, Pt, R, Sp, Pt, Pt*, 2007 *Rus, Cze, ESA, Ar, Nm, F*, 2008 *Pt*, 2010 *US*, 2011 *Ukr, Sp, R, Rus, SAK, ArJ, Nm*

M Kharshiladze 1991 *Ukr*

N **Khatiashvili** 2015 *Ur, Elt*
B **Khekhelashvili** 1999 *Tg, Tg,* 2000 *It, Pt, Mor, Sp, H, R,* 2001 *H, Pt, R, F, SA,* 2002 *H, Pt, Rus, Sp, R, I,* 2003 *Sp, Rus, Cze, R, E, Sa,* 2004 *Sp*
D **Khinchagishvili** 2003 *Sp, Cze,* 2004 *Pt, Sp, Rus,* 2006 *Bb, Cze, Sp, Pt, Pt,* 2007 *R, Rus, Nm, ESA, ItA, Ar, I, Nm,* 2009 *Ger, Pt, Sp, R, Rus, ArJ, ItA,* 2010 *Ger, Pt, R, Rus, C,* 2011 *Ukr, Pt, R, Rus, S, E, R,* 2012 *Rus, J, Fj,* 2013 *Bel, Pt, C, US*
L **Khmaladze** 2008 *ESA, ItA,* 2009 *ItA,* 2010 *S, ItA, Nm,* 2011 *SAK, ArJ, Nm, E, R, Ar,* 2012 *Ukr, US, J, Fj,* 2013 *Bel, Pt, Rus, R, Ur, Ar, C, US, Sa,* 2014 *Bel, Pt, Rus, Sp, R, Tg, I, J,* 2015 *Ger, Pt, Sp, Rus, C*
G **Khonelidze** 2003 *SA*
G **Khositashvili** 2008 *ESA, Ur, ItA*
N **Khuade** 1989 *Z,* 1990 *Z, Z,* 1991 *Ukr, Ukr,* 1993 *Rus, Pol, Lux,* 1994 *Swi,* 1995 *Ger*
A **Khutsishvili** 2015 *Ger, Sp, Rus, Elt, Elr*
V **Khutsishvili** 2013 *Rus, Sp, R, Ur, SAP, Ar,* 2014 *Bel, Pt, Rus, Sp, R, Tg, I, J,* 2015 *Sp, Rus, Ur, Elt, Elr, C*
Z **Khutsishvili** 1993 *Lux,* 1994 *Kaz, Swi,* 1995 *Bul,* 1996 *Cze*
A **Khvedelidze** 1989 *Z,* 1990 *Z, Z,* 1991 *Ukr, Ukr,* 1992 *Ukr, Ukr, Lat,* 1993 *Rus, Pol*
I **Kiasashvili** 2008 *Pt, Cze, Ur,* 2010 *S, Nm,* 2012 *Rus, Ukr, US, C, J, Fj,* 2013 *Pt, SAP, Ar,* 2014 *ArJ*
D **Kiknadze** 2004 *Rus,* 2005 *Pt, Ukr*
A **Kobakhidze** 1997 *Cro,* 1998 *I*
K **Kobakhidze** 1995 *Ger, H,* 1996 *Rus,* 1997 *Pt,* 1998 *It, Ukr, Rus, I, R,* 1999 *Tg,* 2000 *It*
Z **Koberidze** 2004 *Ur*
V **Kolelishvili** 2008 *ItA,* 2010 *S, ItA, Nm, US,* 2011 *Pt, Rus, SAK, ArJ, Nm, S, Ar,* 2012 *Pt, R, J, Fj,* 2013 *Bel, Rus, Sp, R, Elr, Ur, Ar, C,* 2014 *Bel, Pt, Rus, R, Tg, I, J,* 2015 *J, Tg, Ar, NZ, Nm*
A **Kopaleishvili** 2004 *Ur*
A **Kopaliani** 2003 *It, SA, Ur,* 2004 *Pt,* 2005 *Ukr, R,* 2006 *Rus, R, Ukr, J, Bb, Cze, R, Sp, Pt,* 2007 *R, Sp, Rus, Cze, Ar, I, Nm, F*
G **Korkelia** 2010 *S, ItA*
D **Kubriashvili** 2008 *Pt, R, Pt, Rus, Sp,* 2009 *Pt, Sp, R, Rus, ArJ, ItA,* 2010 *Ger, Pt, Sp, US,* 2011 *ArJ, Nm, S, E, Ar,* 2012 *Pt, R, Rus, J, Fj,* 2013 *Bel, Rus, Sp, R, C, US, Sa,* 2014 *Bel, Sp, Elt, Tg, I, J,* 2015 *Ger, J*
E **Kuparadze** 2007 *ESA,* 2014 *ArJ, Elt*
G **Kutarashvili** 2004 *Pt, Sp, Cze, R,* 2005 *Chl,* 2006 *Rus, R, Pt, Ukr, J, R*
B **Kvinikhidze** 2002 *R,* 2004 *Pt, Sp, Cze, R,* 2005 *Chl*
M **Kvirikashvili** 2003 *Pt, Sp, Cze, E, Sa, SA, Ur,* 2004 *Rus, Cze, R, Chl,* 2005 *Cze, Chl,* 2007 *R, Sp, Rus, Cze, Nm, ESA, ItA, Ar, I, Nm, F,* 2008 *Pt, Cze, Rus, Sp, S,* 2009 *Ger, Pt, R, Rus, C, IrA, US, ArJ, ItA,* 2010 *Ger, Pt, Sp, R, Rus, ItA, Nm, C, US,* 2011 *Ukr, Sp, Pt, R, Rus, S, E, R, Ar,* 2012 *Sp, Pt, R, Rus, US, C, J, Fj,* 2013 *Bel, Pt, Rus, Sp, R, C, US, Sa,* 2014 *Bel, Pt, Rus, Sp, R, J, Tg, Ar, Nm*

G **Labadze** 1996 *Cze, Rus,* 1997 *Pt, Pol, Cro, De,* 1998 *It, Ukr, Rus, I, R,* 1999 *Tg, Tg,* 2000 *It, Pt, Sp, H, R,* 2001 *H, Pt, Rus, Sp, F, SA,* 2002 *Pt, Rus, Sp, R, Rus,* 2003 *Rus, Cze, R, It, E, Sa,* 2004 *Rus,* 2005 *R,* 2006 *Rus, R, Pt, J, R, Pt, Pt,* 2007 *Rus, Ar, Nm,* 2009 *Ger, Pt, Sp, R, Rus, C, IrA, US, ArJ,* 2010 *Ger, Pt, Sp, R, Rus, C,* 2011 *Ukr, Sp, R,* 2012 *US, C*
I **Lezhava** 1991 *Ukr, Ukr,* 1992 *Ukr,* 1995 *Bul*
Z **Lezhava** 1991 *Ukr,* 1995 *Ger,* 1996 *Cze, Rus,* 1997 *Pt, Cro, De,* 1998 *It, Rus, R,* 1999 *Tg*
L **Liluashvili** 1997 *Pt*
V **Liluashvili** 1989 *Z,* 1990 *Z, Z*
O **Liparteliani** 1989 *Z,* 1990 *Z, Z*
S **Liparteliani** 1991 *Ukr,* 1994 *Kaz, Swi,* 1996 *Cze*
Z **Liparteliani** 1994 *Kaz, Swi,* 1995 *Bul, Mol, Ger, H*
V **Lobzhanidze** 2015 *Ger, Pt, Sp, Rus, R, J, Tg, Ar, NZ, Nm*
G **Lomgadze** 2009 *US*
L **Lomidze** 2013 *Rus,* 2014 *Sp, ArJ, Elt, Tg, J,* 2015 *Pt, Sp, Rus, R, Ur, Elr, C, NZ, Nm*
D **Losaberidze** 2009 *IrA*
M **Lossaberidze** 1989 *Z*

K **Machitidze** 1989 *Z,* 1993 *Rus,* 1995 *Bul, Mol, Ger, H,* 1996 *Cze, Cze, Rus,* 1997 *Pt, Pol, Cro, De,* 1998 *It, Ukr, Rus, I,* 1999 *Tg*
I **Machkhaneli** 2002 *H, R,* 2003 *It, E, Sa, SA, Ur,* 2004 *Pt, Ur,*

Chl, Rus, 2005 *Pt, Ukr, R, Cze, Chl,* 2006 *Rus, R, Pt, Bb, Cze, R, Pt,* 2007 *R, Ar, I, Nm,* 2008 *S,* 2009 *Ger, Pt, Sp, R, Rus, US, ArJ, ItA,* 2010 *Ger, Pt, Sp, R, Rus, C, US,* 2011 *Ukr, Sp, Pt, R, Rus, S, E,* 2012 *Sp, Pt, R, Rus, Ukr, US, C, J, Fj,* 2013 *Pt, Rus, Sp, R, Elr, Ur, Ar, C,* 2014 *Bel, Pt, Rus, Sp, R, Tg,* 2015 *Elr*
M **Magrakvelidze** 1998 *Ukr,* 2000 *Mor,* 2001 *F,* 2002 *Pt, Sp, R,* 2004 *Rus,* 2005 *Pt, R,* 2006 *Bb, Cze, Pt, Pt,* 2007 *R, Cze, Nm, ESA, ItA, I, F*
I **Maisuradze** 1997 *Cro,* 1998 *It, Ukr,* 1999 *Tg, Tg,* 2004 *Rus, R,* 2005 *Cze,* 2006 *Bb, Cze, R, Pt, Pt,* 2007 *R, Sp, Rus, Cze, ESA, ItA, I, F*
S **Maisuradze** 2008 *Pt, Cze, Rus, Sp, ESA, Ur, ItA, S,* 2009 *IrA, US, ItA,* 2010 *S, Nm, C, US,* 2011 *Pt, ArJ,* 2013 *Elr, Ur, SAP, C, US, Sa,* 2014 *Sp, ArJ, Tg, I, J,* 2015 *Sp, Rus, Elt, Elr, NZ*
V **Maisuradze** 2011 *Ukr, Sp, Pt, R, Rus, SAK, ArJ, Nm, S, E, R, Ar,* 2012 *Ukr, US, C, J, Fj,* 2013 *Pt, Elr, Ur, SAP, Ar,* 2015 *Ger, Rus*
Z **Maisuradze** 2004 *Pt, Sp, Cze, Ur, Chl, Rus,* 2005 *Ukr, R,* 2006 *Rus, R, Pt, Ukr, J, Bb, Cze, Sp,* 2007 *Nm, ESA, ItA, Ar, I, F,* 2008 *Pt,* 2009 *C, IrA, US,* 2011 *Ukr, Sp, SAK, Nm,* 2012 *Ukr, US*
L **Malaguradze** 2008 *Pt, R, Pt, Cze, Rus, Sp, ESA, Ur, ItA, S,* 2009 *Ger, Pt, Sp, R, Rus, C, IrA, US, ArJ, ItA,* 2010 *Ger, Pt, Sp, R, Rus, C, US,* 2011 *Ukr, Sp, Pt, Rus, Ar,* 2012 *R, Rus, Ukr, US, C,* 2013 *Elr, Ur, SAP, Ar,* 2014 *Bel, Pt, Rus, Sp, R, Sp, ArJ, Elt, Tg, I,* 2015 *Ger, Pt, R, Ur, Elt, C, J, Tg, Ar, NZ, Nm*
S **Mamukashvili** 2011 *SAK, ArJ,* 2012 *Sp, Pt, Ukr, US, C, J, Fj,* 2013 *Bel, Pt, Rus, SAP, C, US, Sa,* 2014 *Bel, Pt, Rus, Sp, R, Sp, ArJ, Elt, Tg, I, J,* 2015 *Ger, Pt, C, J, Tg, Ar, NZ, Nm*
K **Margvelashvili** 2003 *It, E, Sa, SA*
M **Marjanishvili** 1990 *Z, Z,* 1992 *Ukr, Ukr, Lat,* 1993 *Rus, Pol, Lux*
A **Matchutadze** 1993 *Lux,* 1994 *Kaz,* 1995 *Bul, Mol,* 1997 *Pt, Pol, Cro, De*
Z **Matiashvili** 2003 *Sp,* 2005 *Chl*
T **Mchedlidze** 2013 *Bel, Pt, Rus, Sp, R, Elr, SAP, Ar, C, US, Sa,* 2014 *Pt, Rus, Sp, R, Sp, ArJ, Elt, Tg, I, J,* 2015 *Ger, Pt, Sp, Rus, R, Ur, Elt, Elr, C, J, Tg, Ar, NZ, Nm*
G **Mchedlishvili** 2008 *Cze,* 2014 *Sp, ArJ*
S **Melikidze** 2008 *Cze, Sp, ESA, ItA*
L **Mgueladze** 1992 *Ukr, Ukr*
N **Mgueladze** 1995 *Bul, Mol, H,* 1997 *Pol*
K **Mikautadze** 2010 *S, ItA, Nm,* 2012 *Sp, Fj,* 2013 *Bel, Pt, Rus, Sp, R, Elr, SAP, C, US, Sa,* 2014 *Bel, Pt, Rus, Sp, R, Sp, ArJ, Elt, Tg, I, J,* 2015 *Ger, Pt, Sp, Rus, R, Ur, Elt, Elr, C, J, Tg, Ar, NZ, Nm*
I **Mirtskhulava** 2012 *Ukr, US,* 2013 *Pt, Elr, Ur,* 2015 *Ur, Elt*
I **Modebadze** 2003 *SA, Ur,* 2004 *Sp*
S **Modebadze** 1994 *Kaz,* 1995 *Mol,* 1996 *Cze, Cze, Rus,* 1997 *Pt, Pol, Cro, De,* 1998 *It, Ukr, Rus,* 1999 *Tg,* 2000 *It, Pt,* 2001 *Sp, F, SA,* 2002 *H, Pt, Rus, Sp, R*
A **Mtchedlishvili** 2004 *Ur, Chl,* 2008 *Cze*
S **Mtchedlishvili** 2000 *It,* 2007 *Sp*
Z **Mtchedlishvili** 1995 *Mol,* 1996 *Cze,* 1997 *Cro, De,* 1998 *It, Ukr, Rus, I, R,* 1999 *Tg, Tg,* 2000 *Pt, Mor, Sp, H, R,* 2001 *Rus, Sp, R, F, SA,* 2002 *H, Pt, Rus, I, Rus,* 2003 *Pt, Sp, Rus, Cze, R, It, E, Sa, Ur,* 2004 *Pt, Rus,* 2005 *Pt,* 2006 *J,* 2007 *Rus, Cze, Nm, ESA, ItA, F*
M **Mtiulishvili** 1991 *Ukr,* 1994 *Kaz,* 1996 *Cze, Cze, Rus,* 1997 *Pt, Pol, Cro, De,* 1998 *It, Ukr, Rus, R,* 2001 *H, Pt, Rus, Sp, R,* 2002 *H, Pt, Rus, Sp, R, I,* 2003 *Rus, Cze, R,* 2004 *Rus, Cze, R*
V **Nadiradze** 1994 *Kaz, Swi,* 1995 *H,* 1996 *Rus,* 1997 *Pt, De,* 1998 *I, R,* 1999 *Tg,* 2000 *Pt, Mor, Sp, H, R,* 2001 *H, Pt, Rus, Sp, R, F, SA,* 2002 *H, Pt, Rus, Sp, R, I, Rus,* 2003 *Pt, Sp, Rus, Cze, R, It, E, Sa*
M **Nariashvili** 2012 *Sp, Pt, R, Ukr, US, C, J, Fj,* 2013 *Bel, Pt, Sp, C, US, Sa,* 2014 *Bel, Pt, Rus, R, Tg, I, J,* 2015 *Ger, Pt, Sp, Rus, R, C, J, Tg, Ar, NZ, Nm*
A **Natchqebia** 1990 *Z, Z*
I **Natriashvili** 2006 *Ukr, J,* 2007 *ItA,* 2008 *Pt, R, Pt, Rus, Sp, ESA, Ur, ItA, S,* 2009 *Ger, Pt, Sp, R, Rus, C, IrA, US, ArJ, ItA,* 2010 *Ger, R, Rus, ItA, Nm, US,* 2011 *Ukr, Sp, Pt, R,* 2012 *R, Rus, J, Fj,* 2013 *Rus, Sp, R,* 2015 *R*
N **Natroshvili** 1992 *Ukr, Ukr, Lat*
G **Nemsadze** 2005 *Chl,* 2006 *Ukr,* 2007 *Sp,* 2008 *Cze, Sp, ESA, Ur, ItA,* 2009 *IrA, US, ArJ, ItA,* 2010 *Ger, Pt, R, Rus, US,* 2011 *R, Rus, SAK, ArJ, Nm, Ar,* 2012 *Sp, R, Rus, J,* 2013 *Elr, Ur, SAP, Ar, US, Sa,* 2014 *Bel, Pt, Rus, Sp, R, Sp, ArJ, Elt, Tg,*

GEORGIA

I, J, 2015 *Ger, Pt, Sp, Rus, R, C, J, Tg, Ar, Nm*
A Nijaradze 2008 *Cze*
I Nikolaenko 1999 *Tg, Tg,* 2000 *It, Mor, Sp, H, R,* 2001 *R, F,* 2003 *Pt, Sp, E, Sa, SA, Ur*
I Ninidze 2004 *Ur, Chl*
M Ninidze 2010 *S, Nm,* 2015 *Elr*

D Oboladze 1993 *Rus, Pol, Lux,* 1994 *Swi,* 1995 *Bul, Mol, Ger, H,* 1996 *Cze, Cze, Rus,* 1997 *Pt, Pol,* 1998 *It, Ukr*
T Odisharia 1989 *Z,* 1994 *Kaz*

S Papashvili 2001 *SA,* 2004 *Cze, R,* 2006 *Bb, Cze,* 2007 *Sp*
S Partsikanashvili 1994 *Kaz,* 1996 *Cze, Rus,* 1997 *Pol,* 1999 *Tg, Tg,* 2000 *It, Pt, Mor*
A Peikrishvili 2008 *Pt, Pt,* 2009 *R,* 2010 *Pt, R, Rus,* 2011 *Sp,* 2013 *SAP, Ar,* 2014 *Pt, Sp, R,* 2015 *Sp, Elt, Elr, NZ*
G Peradze 1991 *Ukr*
Z Peradze 1997 *Pol,* 1998 *Rus*
Z Petriashvili 2009 *C*
D Pinchukovi 2004 *Cze*
L Pirpilashvili 2004 *Rus, Cze, R, Ur, Chl,* 2005 *Ukr, R, Cze*
G Pirtskhalava 1989 *Z,* 1995 *Ger,* 1996 *Cze, Rus,* 1997 *Pt, Pol*
T Pkhakadze 1989 *Z,* 1990 *Z, Z,* 1993 *Rus, Pol, Lux,* 1994 *Kaz,* 1996 *Cze*
G Pruidze 2015 *Ur, Elt, Elr, C, Ar*

G Rapava-Ruskini 1990 *Z,* 1992 *Ukr, Lat,* 1994 *Kaz,* 1996 *Rus,* 1997 *Pt, Cro, De,* 1998 *It, Ukr, Rus, R,* 1999 *Tg*
T Ratianidze 2000 *It,* 2001 *H, Pt, Sp, R, SA,* 2002 *Pt, Rus, Sp, R, I, Rus,* 2003 *Pt, Sp, Rus, Cze, R*
Z Rekhviashvili 1995 *H,* 1997 *Pt, Pol*
G Rokhvadze 2008 *ItA,* 2009 *C, IrA, US,* 2010 *S, ItA,* 2013 *SAP,* 2014 *Sp, ArJ, Elt*

S Sakandelidze 1996 *Cze,* 1998 *Ukr*
S Sakvarelidze 2010 *S, ItA*
B Samkharadze 2004 *Pt, Sp, Rus, Cze, R, Ur, Chl,* 2005 *Cze, Chl,* 2006 *Rus, R, Pt, Ukr, Bb, Cze, R, Sp, Pt, Pt,* 2007 *R, Sp, Rus, Cze, Nm, ESA, Ar, I, Nm, F,* 2008 *Pt, R, Pt, Sp, ESA, Ur, ItA, S,* 2009 *Ger, Sp, Pt, ArJ, ItA,* 2010 *Ger, Pt, Sp, R, S, ItA, Nm, C,* 2011 *Ukr, Sp, Pt, SAK, Nm, E, R, Ar,* 2012 *Pt, C*
A Sanadze 2004 *Chl*
P Saneblidze 1994 *Kaz*
G Sonikidze 2004 *Ur, Chl*
B Sardanashvili 2004 *Chl*
V Satseradze 1989 *Z,* 1990 *Z,* 1991 *Ukr,* 1992 *Ukr, Ukr, Lat*
E Shanidze 1994 *Swi*
M Sharikadze 2012 *Sp, Pt, R, Rus, Ukr, US, J, Fj,* 2013 *Bel, Pt, Rus, Sp, R, Elr, Ur, Ar, C, US, Sa,* 2014 *Bel, Rus, Sp, R, ArJ, Elt, Tg, I, J,* 2015 *Ger, Pt, Sp, Rus, R, Ur, C, J, Tg, Ar, NZ, Nm*
B Sheklashvili 2010 *S, ItA, Nm,* 2011 *Sp,* 2012 *Sp*
G Shkinin 2004 *Cze, R, Chl,* 2005 *Chl,* 2006 *Rus, R, Ukr, J, R, Sp, Pt, Pt,* 2007 *R, Sp, Rus, Cze, Nm, ESA, ItA, Ar, I, Nm,* 2008 *R, Pt, Cze, Rus, Sp, ESA, Ur, ItA, S,* 2009 *Pt,* 2012 *Sp, Pt, R,* 2013 *Sa,* 2014 *Bel, Pt*
S Shubitidze 2015 *Ur, Elt, Elr*
B Shvanguiradze 1990 *Z, Z,* 1992 *Ukr, Ukr, Lat,* 1993 *Rus, Pol, Lux*
G Shvelidze 1998 *I, R,* 1999 *Tg, Tg,* 2000 *It, Pt, Sp, H, R,* 2001 *H, Pt, Sp, F, SA,* 2002 *H, Rus, I, Rus,* 2003 *Pt, Sp, Rus, Cze, R, It, E, Sa, Ur,* 2004 *Rus,* 2005 *Pt, Cze,* 2006 *Rus, R, Pt, R, Sp, Pt, Pt,* 2007 *Ar, I, Nm, F,* 2008 *Pt, R, Pt, Cze, Rus,* 2009 *Ger, Pt, Sp, R, Rus, ArJ,* 2010 *Sp, R, Rus, C, US,* 2011 *Pt, SAK, ArJ, Nm, E, R, Ar*
I Sikharulidze 1994 *Kaz*
T Sokhadze 2005 *Cze,* 2006 *Rus, R, Pt, Ukr, J, Pt, Pt,* 2009 *C, IrA*
M Sujashvili 2004 *Pt, Rus,* 2005 *Pt, Ukr, R, Cze,* 2006 *Pt, Ukr, J, Bb, Cze*
S Sultanishvili 1998 *Ukr*
S Sutiashvili 2005 *Chl,* 2006 *Ukr,* 2007 *Cze, Nm, ESA,* 2008 *Pt, R, Cze, Rus, S,* 2010 *S, ItA, Nm, C, US,* 2011 *Ukr, Sp, Pt, R, Rus, S, E,* 2012 *Pt, R, Rus, C, J, Fj,* 2013 *Pt, Rus, Sp, R, Elr, Ur, Ar, C, US, Sa,* 2014 *Pt, Sp, Sp, Elt,* 2015 *Ger, Pt, Sp, Rus, R, J, Tg, Ar, NZ*
I Svanidze 2015 *Elr*
P Svanidze 1992 *Ukr*

G Talakhadze 2015 *Ur, Elt*
T Tavadze 1991 *Ukr, Ukr*
L Tavartkiladze 2009 *ItA,* 2010 *Ger, Sp, R, Rus, S, ItA, Nm,* 2011 *Sp*
N Tchavtchavadze 1998 *It, Ukr,* 2004 *Cze, R, Ur, Chl*
M Tcheishvili 1989 *Z,* 1990 *Z, Z,* 1995 *H*
G Tedoradze 2015 *Ur*
B Tepnadze 1995 *H,* 1996 *Cze,* 1997 *Cro,* 1998 *I, R,* 1999 *Tg*
G Tetrashvili 2013 *Elr, SAP,* 2015 *Ur, Elr*
G Tkhilaishvili 2012 *Ukr, US, C, J,* 2013 *SAP, C, US, Sa,* 2014 *Bel, Sp, Sp, ArJ, Elt, Tg, I, J,* 2015 *Ger, Pt, Sp, R, C, Tg, Ar, Nm*
A Todua 2008 *Cze, Rus, Sp, ESA, Ur, ItA, S,* 2009 *Sp, R, C, IrA, US, ArJ, ItA,* 2010 *Ger, Pt, R, Rus, S, ItA, Nm,* 2011 *SAK, ArJ, Nm, S, E, R, Ar,* 2012 *Sp, Pt, R, Rus, US, C, J, Fj,* 2013 *Bel, Ur, SAP,* 2014 *Sp, ArJ, Elt, Tg, I, J,* 2015 *Ger, Sp, R, NZ, Nm*
P Tqabladze 1993 *Lux,* 1995 *Bul*
L Tsabadze 1994 *Kaz, Swi,* 1995 *Bul, Ger, H,* 1996 *Cze, Rus,* 1997 *Cro, De,* 1998 *It, Rus, I, R,* 1999 *Tg, Tg,* 2000 *Pt, Mor, Sp, R,* 2001 *H, Pt, Rus, Sp, R, F, SA,* 2002 *H, Pt, Rus, Sp, R, I, Rus*
B Tsiklauri 2008 *ItA,* 2012 *Pt, Ukr,* 2013 *Bel, Rus, Sp, Elr, Ur, SAP, Ar, US, Sa,* 2014 *Bel, Sp, Sp, Elt, J,* 2015 *Ur, Elt, Elr, C, NZ, Nm*
G Tsiklauri 2003 *SA, Ur*
D Tskhvediani 1998 *Ukr*
V Tskitishvili 1994 *Swi,* 1995 *Bul, Mol*
T Turdzeladze 1989 *Z,* 1990 *Z, Z,* 1991 *Ukr,* 1995 *Ger, H*

K Uchava 2002 *Sp,* 2004 *Sp,* 2008 *Pt, R, Pt, Rus, Sp, ESA, Ur, ItA, S,* 2009 *Ger, Pt, R, C, IrA,* 2010 *S, ItA, Nm*
B Udesiani 2001 *Sp, F,* 2002 *H,* 2004 *Pt, Sp, Cze, R, Rus,* 2005 *Pt, Ukr, R, Cze, Chl,* 2006 *Rus, R, Ukr, J, Bb, Cze, R, Sp, Pt, Pt,* 2007 *R, Rus, Cze, Ar, Nm,* 2008 *Cze, Sp, ESA, Ur, ItA, S,* 2010 *Ger, Pt, Sp, R, Rus, C, US,* 2011 *Ukr*
B Urjukashvili 2011 *Ukr, Sp, Pt, Rus, SAK, ArJ, Nm*
M Urjukashvili 1997 *Cro, De,* 1998 *Ukr, Rus, R,* 1999 *Tg, Tg,* 2000 *It, Pt, Mor, Sp,* 2001 *Pt, Rus, Sp, R, F, SA,* 2002 *H, Pt, Sp, R, I, Rus,* 2003 *Pt, Sp, Rus, R, It, E, Sa, Ur,* 2004 *Pt, Rus, Ur, Chl, Rus,* 2005 *Pt, R, Cze,* 2006 *Rus, R, Pt, Ukr, J, R, Sp,* 2007 *Rus, Cze, Nm, ESA, ItA, Ar, I, Nm, F,* 2008 *Sp,* 2009 *R, Rus,* 2010 *Ger, Sp, R, Rus, ItA, Nm, C,* 2011 *SAK, Nm, S, R, Ar*
R Urushadze 1997 *Pol,* 2002 *R,* 2004 *Pt, Rus, Rus,* 2005 *Pt, Ukr, R, Cze, Chl,* 2006 *Rus, R, Pt, Bb, Cze, R, Sp, Pt, Pt,* 2007 *Nm, ESA, ItA, I, Nm, F,* 2008 *Pt, R, Pt, Rus, Sp, S,* 2009 *Ger, Pt, Sp, R, Rus, C, IrA, US, ArJ, ItA*

Z Valishvili 2004 *Chl*
D Vartaniani 1991 *Ukr, Ukr,* 1992 *Ukr, Ukr, Lat,* 1997 *Pol,* 2000 *Sp, H, R*
L Vashadze 1991 *Ukr,* 1992 *Ukr, Ukr, Lat*
G Yachvili 2001 *H, Pt, R,* 2003 *Pt, Sp, Rus, Cze, R, It, E, Sa, Ur*

I Zedginidze 1998 *I,* 2000 *It, Pt, Mor, Sp, H, R,* 2001 *H, Pt, Rus, Sp, R,* 2002 *H, Rus, Sp, I, Rus,* 2003 *Pt, Sp, Rus, Cze, R, It, Sa, SA, Ur,* 2004 *Pt, Sp, Rus, Cze, R, Rus,* 2005 *Pt, Ukr, R, Cze,* 2006 *Rus, R, Pt, Ukr, Cze, R, Sp, Pt, Pt,* 2007 *R, Ar, I,* 2008 *S,* 2009 *Ger, Pt, Sp, Rus, ArJ, ItA,* 2010 *Ger, Pt, Sp, R, Rus,* 2011 *SAK, ArJ, Nm, E, R, Ar*
Z Zhvania 2013 *Sp, R, Sa,* 2014 *Bel, Pt, Rus, Sp, Sp, ArJ, Elt, Tg, I, J,* 2015 *Ger, Pt, Sp, Rus, R, Elr*
T Zibzibadze 2000 *It, Pt, Mor, Sp,* 2001 *H, Pt, Rus, Sp, R, F, SA,* 2002 *H, Pt, Rus, Sp, R, I, Rus,* 2003 *Pt, Sp, Rus, Cze, R, Rus,* 2005 *Pt, Ukr, R, Cze,* 2006 *Pt, Ukr, R,* 2009 *Ar, ArJ,* 2010 *Ger, Pt, Sp, R, Rus, S, ItA, Nm, C, US,* 2011 *Sp, Pt, R, Rus, S, E, R, Ar,* 2012 *R, Rus, C, J,* 2013 *Pt, Rus, R, Elr, Ur, C, US, Sa,* 2014 *Pt, Rus, Sp, R, ArJ*
D Zirakashvili 2004 *Ur, Chl, Rus,* 2005 *Ukr, R, Cze,* 2006 *Rus, R, Pt, R, Sp, Pt,* 2007 *R, Ar, Nm, F,* 2008 *R,* 2009 *Ger,* 2010 *Ger, Pt, Sp, Rus, C, US,* 2011 *Ukr, US, C, J, Fj,* 2013 *Pt, Rus, Sp, R, Ur, Ar,* 2014 *Rus, R,* 2015 *Ger, Pt, Rus, R, C, J, Tg, Ar, Nm*

IRELAND

IRELAND'S 2014–15 TEST RECORD

OPPONENTS	DATE	VENUE	RESULT
South Africa	8 Nov	H	Won 29–15
Georgia	16 Nov	H	Won 49–7
Australia	23 Nov	H	Won 26–23
Italy	7 Feb	A	Won 26–3
France	14 Feb	H	Won 18–11
England	1 Mar	H	Won 19–9
Wales	14 Mar	A	Lost 23–16
Scotland	21 Mar	A	Won 40–10
Wales	8 Aug	A	Won 35–21
Scotland	15 Aug	H	Won 28–22
Wales	29 Aug	H	Lost 10–16
England	5 Sep	H	Lost 13–21
Canada	19 Sep	N	Won 50–7
Romania	27 Sep	N	Won 44–10
Italy	4 Oct	N	Won 16–9
France	11 Oct	N	Won 24–9
Argentina	18 Oct	N	Lost 43–20

IRELAND FALL AT THE QUARTER-FINAL HURDLE AGAIN

By Ruaidhri O'Connor

Getty Images

Ireland beat France in a titanic clash in Cardiff, but it turned out to be a pyrrhic victory as the injuries mounted.

There was a familiar hollowness for Ireland's fans at the Millennium Stadium on 18 October as they watched the Argentinian players' tears flow and their fans bounce up and down with joy.

Another Rugby World Cup, another quarter-final exit. This campaign had promised so much more, built on the back of successive RBS 6 Nations titles and victories over Australia and South Africa in November 2014 there was real confidence that history was within the grasp of an experienced bunch of players.

It began so well and, for the second time in a row, Ireland topped their pool, though it came at a price that proved too high to pay. Injuries to Jared Payne, Peter O'Mahony, Johnny Sexton and captain Paul O'Connell combined with a one-week suspension for inspirational flanker Sean O'Brien ripped the heart from the team for the last eight meeting with Los Pumas.

Still, there was hope that the guiding hand of coach Joe Schmidt could find a way to beat Argentina in Cardiff, but that lasted just two minutes as Matías Moroni crossed for a try that set Daniel Hourcade's team on a path to the final four for the second time in their history.

So, another group of Irish players so successful in every other facet of their rugby careers must reconcile their achievements with the fact that no team from their side of the Irish Sea has ever won a Rugby World Cup knockout game.

For O'Connell, it was his final chance as he departs for Toulon and international retirement after a stellar career in green. Others might get another chance in Japan in four years' time, but given the age profile of the squad there is plenty of rebuilding to do.

Yet Schmidt, who is contracted until 2017, believes the glass ceiling can be broken if Ireland can sustain their levels of consistency.

"I'm sure it can be broken, I'm sure it will be broken," he said. "I think the fact that we've topped our pool the last two World Cups in a row. I think the fact that we got to the ranking we did [second], and the fact that we've won the last two Six Nations.

"If you get lucky, you win a game or you might win two but you've got to work really hard to win a championship or to get to a sustained level of success. So I think for us, the degree of depth we select from four teams, they have a number of players who aren't available to us to select and that's obviously going to give you a reasonably small group to select from.

"We're probably more reliant than some teams [on certain players] . . . We've sustained injuries before but if you picked out five guys you couldn't have picked out five much worse ones from a leadership and experience perspective. We lost 250-odd caps in the space of 80 minutes."

Ireland's campaign had looked so promising up until that point.

Schmidt's men opened in Cardiff, where an inspired Sexton helped put Canada to the sword in front of a vocal Irish support in the Millennium Stadium. Tries from Sexton, Payne, Rob Kearney, Sean Cronin, O'Brien, Dave Kearney and Iain Henderson led to an impressive 50–7 victory.

Eight days later, they dismissed Romania in front of a RWC record crowd of 89,267 at Wembley who watched Tommy Bowe and Keith Earls grab a pair of tries each in a 44–10 win.

Italy were next up for the Six Nations champions, but their familiar foe caused a lot more problems and after taking the lead through Earls' first-half try, they needed a superb Peter O'Mahony try-saving tackle on Josh Furno to qualify for the quarter-finals with a 16–9 victory.

A week later, top spot in Pool D came down to the meeting with another Six Nations rival, France. After a visit from five legends of Irish sport – footballer Niall Quinn, boxer Barry McGuigan, jockey AP McCoy, athlete Sonia O'Sullivan and hurler Henry Shefflin – the team were inspired to put in a defining performance despite losing O'Connell, Sexton and O'Mahony to injury. Tries from Rob Kearney and Conor Murray did the damage and all eyes turned to Argentina in the quarter-finals.

However, the injuries and loss of O'Brien due to a one-week suspension for striking France's Pascal Papé took the wind out of Ireland's sails and they were undone early on by Los Pumas' brilliant attacking flair.

Tries from Moroni and Juan Imhoff combined with the accuracy from the kicking tee of Nicolás Sánchez gave an inexperienced line-up a tough task, but led by replacement Luke Fitzgerald, who scored one try and created another for Jordi Murphy, they came back at Argentina and, had Ian Madigan landed his 58th-minute penalty, would have entered the final quarter on level terms.

Instead, Argentina kicked on and scored two more tries through Imhoff and Joaquín Tuculet as Ireland conceded their record number of points in a quarter-final, losing 43–20.

It was a devastating way to end what had been an excellent year for Ireland. Rarely have they gone into a World Cup on the back of such good results.

It began with an injury-ravaged team overcoming the Springboks in Dublin on 4 November. The 29–15 win was delivered despite the fact that flanker Chris Henry, who had been named to start at openside flanker, came down with a mystery illness on the morning of the match.

Rhys Ruddock stepped in at the 11th hour and scored Ireland's first try. Tommy Bowe also crossed as the touring South Africans dominated possession and territory but couldn't break Ireland down.

Henry was later diagnosed to have suffered a mini-stroke and his career lay in the balance. Slowly but surely, he worked his way back to fitness and played a full part in Ireland's World Cup campaign. He would miss the rest of the 2014–15 international season, however, but despite another missing player the squad overcame Georgia and Australia to finish the November series ranked third in the World Rugby Rankings.

The Wallabies win was a different kind of victory as Ireland raced into a lead through tries by Bowe and Simon Zebo, but were pegged back by Michael Cheika's men who played some sensational rugby. With the game in the balance, Sexton delivered a pressure kick and O'Connell led a successful rear-guard action; all seemed well for the Six Nations.

Certainly, Schmidt was picking from a stronger hand for that Championship, but a series of concussions suffered by Sexton meant he was stood down for 12 weeks by his neurosurgeon and missed the opener against Italy in Rome.

Ireland also lost the recently returned O'Brien as he injured his hamstring in the warm-up, but they managed to win despite a stifled performance with tries from Murray and Tommy O'Donnell breaking it open in the second half.

A week later on St Valentine's Day, Sexton made his return against France with the suggestion he could be targeted after a long absence from the game.

But when he met Mathieu Bastareaud head-on in the early stages and stood tall, the Aviva Stadium erupted and he managed to guide his team to a bruising 18–11 win.

Despite the conservative nature of Ireland's game-plan drawing criticism from some quarters, the champions securing two wins from their first two games meant the words 'Grand' and 'Slam' entered the discussion, and when new centre Robbie Henshaw rose above Alex Goode to score a brilliant try in the win over England, the Irish fans couldn't help but get excited.

That 19–9 triumph in Dublin meant wins over Wales and Scotland would secure just a third clean sweep in Irish history, but an epic defensive performance from Warren Gatland's team repelled Ireland and denied them that chance at history.

That set up a Super Saturday in which four teams could win the Six Nations title on points difference depending on results and Ireland, set a target of 20 points to chase by Wales after a big win in Rome, duly delivered their most complete attacking performance of the tournament as they ran in four tries to defeat the Scots 40–10.

Then came the wait as the team and management watched on from Murrayfield as England chased their tally brilliantly, running in seven tries against France and just coming up short to leave Ireland the back-to-back champions for the first time since 1949.

It was a moment to savour for the coach and his players, but thoughts soon turned to the World Cup as the provinces failed to deliver silverware of any kind for the first time since 2010.

Leinster came closest in Europe, but Matt O'Connor's men came up short in extra-time as they exited at the semi-final stage. The Australian lost his job as a result of the province's poor league season as they failed to make the play-offs for the first time, while Ulster and Munster both suffered at the hands of champions Glasgow Warriors.

That was long forgotten when the players returned to the start line for pre-World Cup training and Ireland won two of their four warm-ups against Wales and Scotland, losing to England and the Welsh in Dublin.

That left them in good stead for their World Cup assault, but ultimately they would end up where they almost always do, watching the semi-finals from home.

IRELAND INTERNATIONAL STATISTICS

MATCH RECORDS UP TO 1 NOVEMBER, 2015

MOST CONSECUTIVE TEST WINS

10	2002 R, Ru, Gg, A, Fj, Arg, 2003 S 1, It 1, F, W 1
10	2014 It, F, Arg 1, 2, SA, Gg, A, 2015 It, F, E 1
8	2003 Tg, Sm, W 2 , It 2, S 2, R , Nm, Arg
8	2008 Arg, 2009 F, It , E, S, W ,C, US
6	1968 S, W, A, 1969 F, E, S
6	2004 SA, US, Arg, 2005 It, S, E

MOST CONSECUTIVE TESTS WITHOUT DEFEAT

Matches	Wins	Draws	Period
12	11	1	2008 to 2010
10	10	0	2002 to 2003
10	10	0	2014 to 2015
8	8	0	2003
7	6	1	1968 to 1969
6	6	0	2004 to 2005

MOST POINTS IN A MATCH
BY THE TEAM

Pts	Opponents	Venue	Year
83	United States	Manchester (NH)	2000
78	Japan	Dublin	2000
70	Georgia	Dublin	1998
64	Fiji	Dublin	2002
64	Namibia	Sydney	2003
63	Georgia	Dublin	2002
62	Russia	Rotorua	2011
61	Italy	Limerick	2003
61	Pacific Islands	Dublin	2006
60	Romania	Dublin	1986
60	Italy	Dublin	2000

BY A PLAYER

Pts	Player	Opponents	Venue	Year
32	RJR O'Gara	Samoa	Apia	2003
30	RJR O'Gara	Italy	Dublin	2000
26	DG Humphreys	Scotland	Murrayfield	2003
26	DG Humphreys	Italy	Limerick	2003
26	P Wallace	Pacific Islands	Dublin	2006
24	PA Burke	Italy	Dublin	1997
24	DG Humphreys	Argentina	Lens	1999
23	RP Keyes	Zimbabwe	Dublin	1991
23	RJR O'Gara	Japan	Dublin	2000
22	DG Humphreys	Wales	Dublin	2002

MOST TRIES IN A MATCH
BY THE TEAM

Tries	Opponents	Venue	Year
13	United States	Manchester (NH)	2000
11	Japan	Dublin	2000
10	Romania	Dublin	1986
10	Georgia	Dublin	1998
10	Namibia	Sydney	2003
9	Fiji	Dublin	2003
9	Russia	Rotorua	2011
8	Western Samoa	Dublin	1988
8	Zimbabwe	Dublin	1991
8	Georgia	Dublin	2002
8	Italy	Limerick	2003
8	Pacific Islands	Dublin	2006
8	Italy	Rome	2007
8	Canada	Limerick	2008

BY A PLAYER

Tries	Player	Opponents	Venue	Year
4	BF Robinson	Zimbabwe	Dublin	1991
4	KGM Wood	United States	Dublin	1999
4	DA Hickie	Italy	Limerick	2003
3	R Montgomery	Wales	Birkenhead	1887
3	JP Quinn	France	Cork	1913
3	E O'D Davy	Scotland	Murrayfield	1930
3	SJ Byrne	Scotland	Murrayfield	1953
3	KD Crossan	Romania	Dublin	1986
3	BJ Mullin	Tonga	Brisbane	1987
3	MR Mostyn	Argentina	Dublin	1999
3	BG O'Driscoll	France	Paris	2000
3	MJ Mullins	United States	Manchester (NH)	2000
3	DA Hickie	Japan	Dublin	2000
3	RAJ Henderson	Italy	Rome	2001
3	BG O'Driscoll	Scotland	Dublin	2002
3	KM Maggs	Fiji	Dublin	2002
3	FL McFadden	Canada	Toronto	2013

MOST CONVERSIONS IN A MATCH
BY THE TEAM

Cons	Opponents	Venue	Year
10	Georgia	Dublin	1998
10	Japan	Dublin	2000
9	United States	Manchester (NH)	2000
7	Romania	Dublin	1986
7	Georgia	Dublin	2002
7	Namibia	Sydney	2003
7	United States	Dublin	2004
7	Russia	Rotorua	2011
6	Japan	Bloemfontein	1995
6	Romania	Dublin	1998
6	United States	Dublin	1999
6	Italy	Dublin	2000
6	Italy	Limerick	2003
6	Japan	Tokyo	2005
6	Pacific Islands	Dublin	2006
6	Canada	Limerick	2008
6	Canada	Cardiff	2015

BY A PLAYER

Cons	Player	Opponents	Venue	Year
10	EP Elwood	Georgia	Dublin	1998
10	RJR O'Gara	Japan	Dublin	2000
8	RJR O'Gara	United States	Manchester (NH)	2000
7	MJ Kiernan	Romania	Dublin	1986
7	RJR O'Gara	Namibia	Sydney	2003
7	DG Humphreys	United States	Dublin	2004
6	PA Burke	Japan	Bloemfontein	1995
6	RJR O'Gara	Italy	Dublin	2000
6	DG Humphreys	Italy	Limerick	2003
6	DG Humphreys	Japan	Tokyo	2005
6	P Wallace	Pacific Islands	Dublin	2006
6	RJR O'Gara	Russia	Rotorua	2011

MOST PENALTIES IN A MATCH
BY THE TEAM

Penalties	Opponents	Venue	Year
8	Italy	Dublin	1997
7	Argentina	Lens	1999
6	Scotland	Dublin	1982
6	Romania	Dublin	1993
6	United States	Atlanta	1996
6	Western Samoa	Dublin	1996
6	Italy	Dublin	2000
6	Wales	Dublin	2002
6	Australia	Dublin	2002
6	Samoa	Apia	2003
6	Japan	Osaka	2005
6	France	Dublin	2015

BY A PLAYER

Pens	Player	Opponents	Venue	Year
8	P A Burke	Italy	Dublin	1997
7	D G Humphreys	Argentina	Lens	1999
6	S O Campbell	Scotland	Dublin	1982
6	E P Elwood	Romania	Dublin	1993
6	S J P Mason	Western Samoa	Dublin	1996
6	R J R O'Gara	Italy	Dublin	2000
6	D G Humphreys	Wales	Dublin	2002
6	R J R O'Gara	Australia	Dublin	2002

MOST DROP GOALS IN A MATCH
BY THE TEAM

Drops	Opponents	Venue	Year
2	Australia	Dublin	1967
2	France	Dublin	1975
2	Australia	Sydney	1979
2	England	Dublin	1981
2	Canada	Dunedin	1987
2	England	Dublin	1993
2	Wales	Wembley	1999
2	New Zealand	Dublin	2001
2	Argentina	Dublin	2004
2	England	Dublin	2005

BY A PLAYER

Drops	Player	Opponents	Venue	Year
2	C M H Gibson	Australia	Dublin	1967
2	W M McCombe	France	Dublin	1975
2	S O Campbell	Australia	Sydney	1979
2	E P Elwood	England	Dublin	1993
2	D G Humphreys	Wales	Wembley	1999
2	D G Humphreys	New Zealand	Dublin	2001
2	R J R O'Gara	Argentina	Dublin	2004
2	R J R O'Gara	England	Dublin	2005

IRELAND

CAREER RECORDS

MOST CAPPED PLAYERS

Caps	Player	Career Span
133	BG O'Driscoll	1999 to 2014
128	RJR O'Gara	2000 to 2013
108	PJ O'Connell	2002 to 2015
105	JJ Hayes	2000 to 2011
98	PA Stringer	2000 to 2011
94	DP O'Callaghan	2003 to 2013
92	ME O'Kelly	1997 to 2009
89	RD Best	2005 to 2015
82	GT Dempsey	1998 to 2008
82	GW D'Arcy	1999 to 2015
80	JPR Heaslip	2006 to 2015
72	DG Humphreys	1996 to 2005
72	DP Wallace	2000 to 2011
72	GEA Murphy	2000 to 2011
70	KM Maggs	1997 to 2005
69	CMH Gibson	1964 to 1979

MOST CONSECUTIVE TESTS

Tests	Player	Span
52	WJ McBride	1964 to 1975
49	PA Orr	1976 to 1986
43	DG Lenihan	1981 to 1989
39	MI Keane	1974 to 1981
38	PA Stringer	2003 to 2007
37	GV Stephenson	1920 to 1929

MOST TESTS AS CAPTAIN

Tests	Captain	Span
83	BG O'Driscoll	2002 to 2012
36	KGM Wood	1996 to 2003
28	PJ O'Connell	2004 to 2015
24	TJ Kiernan	1963 to 1973
19	CF Fitzgerald	1982 to 1986
17	JF Slattery	1979 to 1981
17	DG Lenihan	1986 to 1990

MOST POINTS IN TESTS

Points	Player	Tests	Career
1083	RJR O'Gara	128	2000 to 2013
565*	DG Humphreys	72	1996 to 2005
525	JJ Sexton	56	2009 to 2015
308	MJ Kiernan	43	1982 to 1991
296	EP Elwood	35	1993 to 1999
245	BG O'Driscoll	133	1999 to 2014
217	SO Campbell	22	1976 to 1984
158	TJ Kiernan	54	1960 to 1973
150	TJ Bowe	67	2004 to 2015
145	DA Hickie	62	1997 to 2007
113	AJP Ward	19	1978 to 1987

*Humphreys's total includes a penalty try against Scotland in 1999

MOST TRIES IN TESTS

Tries	Player	Tests	Career
46	BG O'Driscoll	133	1999 to 2014
30	TJ Bowe	67	2004 to 2015
29	DA Hickie	62	1997 to 2007
21	SP Horgan	65	2000 to 2009
19	GT Dempsey	82	1998 to 2008
18	GEA Murphy	72	2000 to 2011
17	BJ Mullin	55	1984 to 1995
16	RJR O'Gara	128	2000 to 2013
16	A D Trimble	58	2005 to 2015
16	KG Earls	46	2008 to 2015
15	KGM Wood	58	1994 to 2003
15	KM Maggs	70	1997 to 2005
14	GV Stephenson	42	1920 to 1930

MOST CONVERSIONS IN TESTS

Cons	Player	Tests	Career
176	RJR O'Gara	128	2000 to 2013
88	DG Humphreys	72	1996 to 2005
60	JJ Sexton	56	2009 to 2015
43	EP Elwood	35	1993 to 1999
40	MJ Kiernan	43	1982 to 1991
26	TJ Kiernan	54	1960 to 1973
25	IL Madigan	25	2013 to 2015
16	RA Lloyd	19	1910 to 1920
15	SO Campbell	22	1976 to 1984

MOST PENALTY GOALS IN TESTS

Penalties	Player	Tests	Career
202	RJR O'Gara	128	2000 to 2013
118	JJ Sexton	56	2009 to 2015
110	DG Humphreys	72	1996 to 2005
68	EP Elwood	35	1993 to 1999
62	MJ Kiernan	43	1982 to 1991
54	SO Campbell	22	1976 to 1984
31	TJ Kiernan	54	1960 to 1973
29	AJP Ward	19	1978 to 1987

MOST DROP GOALS IN TESTS

Drops	Player	Tests	Career
15	RJR O'Gara	128	2000 to 2013
8	DG Humphreys	72	1996 to 2005
7	RA Lloyd	19	1910 to 1920
7	SO Campbell	22	1976 to 1984
6	CMH Gibson	69	1964 to 1979
6	BJ McGann	25	1969 to 1976
6	MJ Kiernan	43	1982 to 1991

THE COUNTRIES

INTERNATIONAL CHAMPIONSHIP RECORDS

RECORD	DETAIL	HOLDER	SET
Most points in season	168	In five matches	2000
Most tries in season	17	In five matches	2000
	17	in five matches	2004
	17	in five matches	2007
Highest score	60	60–13 v Italy	2000
Biggest win	47	60–13 v Italy	2000
Highest score conceded	50	18–50 v England	2000
Biggest defeat	40	6–46 v England	1997
Most appearances	66	BG O'Driscoll	2000–2014
Most points in matches	557	RJR O'Gara	2000–2013
Most points in season	82	RJR O'Gara	2007
Most points in match	30	RJR O'Gara	v Italy, 2000
Most tries in matches	26	BG O'Driscoll	2000–2014
Most tries in season	5	JE Arigho	1928
	5	BG O'Driscoll	2000
	5	TJ Bowe	2012
Most tries in match	3	R Montgomery	v Wales, 1887
	3	JP Quinn	v France, 1913
	3	EO'D Davy	v Scotland, 1930
	3	SJ Byrne	v Scotland, 1953
	3	BG O'Driscoll	v France, 2000
	3	RA J Henderson	v Italy, 2001
	3	BG O'Driscoll	v Scotland, 2002
Most cons in matches	81	RJR O'Gara	2000–2013
Most cons in season	11	RJR O'Gara	2000
	11	RJR O'Gara	2004
Most cons in match	6	RJR O'Gara	v Italy, 2000
Most pens in matches	109	RJR O'Gara	2000–2013
Most pens in season	17	RJR O'Gara	2006
Most pens in match	6	SO Campbell	v Scotland, 1982
	6	RJR O'Gara	v Italy, 2000
	6	DG Humphreys	v Wales, 2002
Most drops in matches	7	RA Lloyd	1910–1920
Most drops in season	2	on several occasions	
Most drops in match	2	WM McCombe	v France, 1975
	2	EP Elwood	v England, 1993
	2	DG Humphreys	v Wales, 1999
	2	RJR O'Gara	v England, 2005

IRELAND

MISCELLANEOUS RECORDS

RECORD	HOLDER	DETAIL
Longest Test Career	GW D'Arcy	1999 to 2015
Youngest Test Cap	FS Hewitt	17 yrs 157 days in 1924
Oldest Test Cap	JJ Hayes	37 yrs 277 days in 2011

CAREER RECORDS OF IRELAND INTERNATIONAL PLAYERS

UP TO 1 NOVEMBER, 2015

PLAYER BACKS :	DEBUT	CAPS	T	C	P	D	PTS
IJ Boss	2006 v NZ	22	3	0	0	0	15
TJ Bowe	2004 v US	67	30	0	0	0	150
DM Cave	2009 v C	11	2	0	0	0	10
GW D'Arcy	1999 v R	82	7	0	0	0	35
KG Earls	2008 v C	46	16	0	0	0	80
LM Fitzgerald	2006 v PI	34	4	0	0	0	20
CJH Gilroy	2012 v Arg	6	2	0	0	0	10
RA Henshaw	2013 v US	15	1	0	0	0	5
DP Jackson	2013 v S	13	1	11	13	0	66
FA Jones	2011 v S	13	3	0	0	0	15
DR Kearney	2013 v Sm	14	3	0	0	0	15
RDJ Kearney	2007 v Arg	67	13	1	0	0	67
IJ Keatley	2009 v C	4	0	5	7	0	31
IL Madigan	2013 v F	25	1	25	19	0	112
KD Marmion	2014 v Arg	4	0	0	0	0	0
LD Marshall	2013 v S	6	0	0	0	0	0
P Marshall	2013 v It	3	0	0	0	0	0
FL McFadden	2011 v It	29	9	0	0	0	45
CG Murray	2011 v F	42	4	0	0	0	20
S Olding	2013 v US	2	1	0	0	0	5
JB Payne	2014 v SA	10	2	0	0	0	10
EG Reddan	2006 v F	68	2	0	0	0	10
N Reid	2014 v Arg	1	0	0	0	0	0
JJ Sexton	2009 v Fj	56	9	60	118	2	525
AD Trimble	2005 v A	58	16	0	0	0	80
SR Zebo	2012 v NZ	21	7	0	0	0	35

RL Ah You	2014 v Arg	3	0	0	0	0	0
MR Bent	2012 v SA	4	0	0	0	0	0
RD Best	2005 v NZ	89	8	0	0	0	40
JE Conan	2015 v S	1	0	0	0	0	0
R Copeland	2014 v Gg	1	0	0	0	0	0
J Cronin	2014 v Arg	2	0	0	0	0	0
SM Cronin	2009 v Fj	48	3	0	0	0	15
RJE Diack	2014 v Arg	2	0	0	0	0	0
D Foley	2014 v Gg	2	0	0	0	0	0
TV Furlong	2015 v W	3	0	0	0	0	0
CE Healy	2009 v A	56	3	0	0	0	15
JPR Heaslip	2006 v PI	80	10	0	0	0	50
WI Henderson	2012 v SA	23	2	0	0	0	10
CG Henry	2010 v A	24	4	0	0	0	20
RW Herring	2014 v Arg	1	0	0	0	0	0
D Kilcoyne	2012 v SA	15	1	0	0	0	5
MP McCarthy	2011 v S	17	0	0	0	0	0
JC McGrath	2013 v Sm	25	1	0	0	0	5
MJ Moore	2014 v S	10	0	0	0	0	0
J Murphy	2014 v E	14	1	0	0	0	5
SK O'Brien	2009 v Fj	41	6	0	0	0	30
PJ O'Connell	2002 v W	108	8	0	0	0	40
T O'Donnell	2013 v US	9	2	0	0	0	10
PJ O'Mahony	2012 v It	35	1	0	0	0	5
MR Ross	2009 v C	56	0	0	0	0	0
RJ Ruddock	2010 v A	6	1	0	0	0	5
Dominic Ryan	2014 v Gg	1	0	0	0	0	0
DC Ryan	2008 v Arg	34	0	0	0	0	0
M Sherry	2013 v US	1	0	0	0	0	0
CR Strauss	2012 v SA	13	2	0	0	0	10
DA Toner	2010 v Sm	31	0	0	0	0	0
DM Tuohy	2010 v NZ	11	1	0	0	0	5
NJ White	2015 v S	8	0	0	0	0	0

IRELAND

IRELAND INTERNATIONAL PLAYERS
UP TO 1 NOVEMBER, 2015

Note: Years given for International Championship matches are for second half of season; eg 1972 means season 1971–72. Years for all other matches refer to the actual year of the match. Entries in square brackets denote matches played in RWC Finals.

THE COUNTRIES

Abraham, M (Bective Rangers) 1912 E, S, W, SA, 1914 W

Adams, C (Old Wesley), 1908 E, 1909 E, F, 1910 F, 1911 E, S, W, F, 1912 S, W, SA, 1913 W, F, 1914 F, E, S

Agar, R D (Malone) 1947 F, E, S, W, 1948 F, 1949 S, W, 1950 F, E, W

Agnew, P J (CIYMS) 1974 F (R), 1976 A

Ahern, T J (Queen's Coll, Cork) 1899 E

Aherne, L F P (Dolphin, Lansdowne) 1988 E 2, WS, It, 1989 F, W, E, S, NZ, 1990 E, S, F, W (R), 1992 E, S, F, A

Ah You, R (Connacht) 2014 Arg 1(R), SA(R), Gg(R)

Alexander, R (NIFC, Police Union) 1936 E, S, W, 1937 E, S, W, 1938 E, S, 1939 E, S, W

Allen, C E (Derry, Liverpool) 1900 E, S, W, 1901 E, S, W, 1903 S, W, 1904 E, S, W, 1905 E, S, W, NZ, 1906 E, S, W, SA, 1907 S, W

Allen, G G (Derry, Liverpool) 1896 E, S, W, 1897 E, S, 1898 E, S, 1899 E, W

Allen, T C (NIFC) 1885 E, S 1

Allen, W S (Wanderers) 1875 E

Allison, J B (Edinburgh U) 1899 E, S, 1900 E, S, W, 1901 E, S, W, 1902 E, S, W, 1903 S

Anderson, F E (Queen's U, Belfast, NIFC) 1953 F, E, S, W, 1954 NZ, F, E, S, W, 1955 F, E, S, W

Anderson, H J (Old Wesley) 1903 E, S, 1906 E, S

Anderson, W A (Dungannon) 1984 A, 1985 S, F, W, E, 1986 F, S, R, 1987 E, S, F, W, [W, C, Tg, A], 1988 S, F, W, E 1, 2, 1989 F, W, E, NZ, 1990 E, S

Andrews, G (NIFC) 1875 E, 1876 E

Andrews, H W (NIFC) 1888 M, 1889 S, W

Archer, A M (Dublin U, NIFC) 1879 S

Archer, S (Munster) 2013 It(R), A(R)

Arigho, J E (Lansdowne) 1928 F, E, W, 1929 F, E, S, W, 1930 F, E, S, W, 1931 F, E, S, W, SA

Armstrong, W K (NIFC) 1960 SA, 1961 E

Arnott, D T (Lansdowne) 1876 E

Ash, W H (NIFC) 1875 E, 1876 E, 1877 S

Aston, H R (Dublin U) 1908 E, W

Atkins, A P (Bective Rangers) 1924 F

Atkinson, J M (NIFC) 1927 F, A

Atkinson, J R (Dublin U) 1882 W, S

Bagot, J C (Dublin U, Lansdowne) 1879 S E, 1880 E, S, 1881 S

Bailey, A H (UC Dublin, Lansdowne) 1934 W, 1935 E, S, W, NZ, 1936 E, S, W, 1937 E, S, W, 1938 E, S

Bailey, N (Northampton) 1952 E

Bardon, M E (Bohemians) 1934 E

Barlow, M (Wanderers) 1875 E

Barnes, R J (Dublin U, Armagh) 1933 W

Barr, A (Belfast Collegians) 1898 W, 1899 S, 1901 E, S

Barry, N J (Garryowen) 1991 Nm 2(R)

Beamish, C E St J (RAF, Leicester) 1933 W, S, 1934 S, W, 1935 E, S, W, NZ, 1936 E, S, W, 1938 W

Beamish, G R (RAF, Leicester) 1925 E, S, W, 1928 F, E, S, W, 1929 F, E, S, W, 1930 F, S, W, 1931 F, E, S, W, SA, 1932 E, S, W, 1933 E, W, S

Beatty, W J (NIFC, Richmond) 1910 F, 1912 F, W

Becker, V A (Lansdowne) 1974 F, W

Beckett, G G P (Dublin U) 1908 E, S, W

Bell, J C (Ballymena, Northampton, Dungannon) 1994 A 1, 2, US, 1995 S, It, [NZ, W, F], Fj, 1996 US, S, F, W, E, WS, A, 1997 It 1, F, W, E, S, 1998 Gg, R, SA 3, 1999 F, W, S It (R), A 2, [US (R), A 3(R), R], 2001 R (R), 2003 Tg, Sm, It 2(R)

Bell, R J (NIFC) 1875 E, 1876 E

Bell, W E (Belfast Collegians) 1953 F, E, S, W

Bennett, F (Belfast Collegians) 1913 S

Bent, G C (Dublin U) 1882 W, E

Bent, M R (Leinster) 2012 SA(R), Arg(R), 2015 W 2(R), S 2(R)

Berkery, P J (Lansdowne) 1954 W, 1955 W, 1956 S, W, 1957 F, E, S, W, 1958 A, E, S

Bermingham, J J C (Blackrock Coll) 1921 E, S, W, F

Best, N A (Ulster) 2005 NZ(R), R, 2006 NZ1, 2, A1, SA, A2, 2007 F(R), E(R), S1(R), Arg1, 2(R), S2, It2, [Nm(R), Gg(R), F(R), Arg(t&R]

Best, R D (Ulster) 2005 NZ(R), A(t), 2006 W(R), A1(R), SA, A2, PI(R), 2007 W, F, E, S1, It1, S2(R), It2, [Nm, Gg, Arg(R)], 2008 It, F(R), S(R), W, E, NZ1(R), A, C(R), NZ2, Arg(R), 2009 F(R), It(R), E(R), S, W(R), C, US, 2010 It(R), F(R), E, W, S, SA, Sm(R), NZ2, 2011 It, F1, S1, W, E1, F2, 3, E2(R), [US, A, It, W], 2012 W, It, F, S, E, NZ 1, 2, 3, 2013 W, E, S, F, It, Sm, A, NZ, 2014 S, W, E, F, Arg 1, 2, A, 2015 It, F, E 1, W 1, S 1, W 2(t&R) E 2, [C, It, F, Arg]

Best, S J (Belfast Harlequins, Ulster) 2003 Tg (R), W 2, S 2(R), 2003 [Nm(R)], 2004 W(R), US(R), 2005 J1, 2, NZ(R), R(R), W(R), PI(R), 2007 E(R), S1, It1(R), Arg1, 2, S2, It2(R), [Nm(R), Gg(R), F(R)]

Bishop, J P (London Irish) 1998 SA, 1, 2, Gg, R, SA 3, 1999 F, W, E, S, It, A 1, 2, Arg 1, [US, A 3, Arg 2], 2000 E, Arg, C, 2002 NZ 1, 2, Fj, Arg, 2003 W 1, E

Blackham, J C (Queen's Coll, Cork) 1909 S, W, F, 1910 E, S, W

Blake-Knox, S E F (NIFC) 1976 E, S, 1977 F (R)

Blayney, J J (Wanderers) 1950 S

Bond, A T W (Derry) 1894 S, W

Bornemann, W W (Wanderers) 1960 E, S, W, SA

Boss, I J (Ulster, Leinster) 2006 NZ2(R), A1(R), SA(R), A2, PI(R), 2007 F, E(R), Arg1, S2, It2(R), [Gg(R), Arg(R)], 2010 Sm(R), 2011 S2(R), [Ru], 2013 US, C, 2014 S(R), W(R), E(R), 2015 It(R), S 2

Bowe, T J (Ulster, Ospreys) 2004 US, 2005 J1, 2, NZ, A, R, 2006 It, F, 2007 Arg1, S2, 2008 S, W, E, NZ1, A, C, NZ2, Arg, 2009 F, It, E, S, W, A, SA, 2010 It, F, E, W, S, NZ1, A, SA, Sm, NZ2, Arg, 2011 S1, W, E1, 2, [US, A, It, W], 2012 W, It, F, S, E, SA, Arg, 2013 Sm, A, NZ, 2014 SA, A, 2015 It, F, E 1, W 1, S 1, 2, E 2, [R, It, F, Arg]

Bowen, D St J (Cork Const) 1977 W, E, S

Boyd, C A (Dublin U) 1900 S, 1901 S, W

Boyle, C V (Dublin U) 1935 NZ, 1936 E, S, W, 1937 E, S, W, 1938 W, 1939 W

Brabazon, H M (Dublin U) 1884 E, 1885 S 1, 1886 E

Bradley, M J (Dolphin) 1920 W, F, 1922 E, S, W, F, 1923 E, S, W, F, 1925 F, S, W, 1926 F, E, S, W, 1927 F, W

Bradley, M T (Cork Constitution) 1984 A, 1985 S, F, W, E, 1986 F, W, E, S, R, 1987 E, S, F, W, [W, C, Tg, A], 1988 S, F, W, E 1, 1990 W, 1992 NZ 1, 2, 1993 S, F, W, E, R, 1994 F, W, E, S, A 1, 2, US, 1995 S, F, [NZ]

Bradshaw, G (Belfast Collegians) 1903 W

Bradshaw, R M (Wanderers) 1885 E, S 1, 2

Brady, A M (UC Dublin, Malone) 1966 S, 1968 E, S, W

IRELAND

Downing, A J (Dublin U) 1882 W
Dowse, J C A (Monkstown) 1914 F, S, W
Doyle, J A P (Greystones) 1984 E, S
Doyle, J T (Bective Rangers) 1935 W
Doyle, M G (Blackrock Coll, UC Dublin, Cambridge U, Edinburgh Wands) 1965 F, E, S, W, SA, 1966 F, E, S, W, 1967 A 1, E, S, W, F, A 2, 1968 F, E, S, W, A
Doyle, T J (Wanderers) 1968 E, S, W
Duffy, G W (Harlequins, Connacht) 2004 SA 2(R), 2005 S(R), J1, 2, 2007 Arg1, 2, S2, [Arg(R)], 2009 C, US
Duggan, A T A (Lansdowne) 1963 NZ, 1964 F, 1966 W, 1967 A 1, S, W, A 2, 1968 F, E, S, W, 1969 F, E, S, W, 1970 SA, F, E, S, W, 1971 F, E, S, W, 1972 F 2
Duggan, W (UC Cork) 1920 S, W
Duggan, W P (Blackrock Coll) 1975 E, S, F, W, 1976 A, F, W, S, NZ, 1977 W, E, S, F, 1978 S, F, W, E, NZ, 1979 E, S, A 1, 2, 1980 E, 1981 F, W, E, S, SA 1, 2, A, 1982 W, E, S, 1983 S, F, W, E, 1984 F, W, E, S
Duignan, P (Galwegians) 1998 Gg, R
Duncan, W R (Malone) 1984 W, E
Dunlea, F J (Lansdowne) 1989 W, E, S
Dunlop, R (Dublin U) 1889 W, 1890 S, W, E, 1891 E, S, W, 1892 E, S, 1893 W, 1894 W
Dunn, P E F (Bective Rangers) 1923 S
Dunn, T B (NIFC) 1935 NZ
Dunne, M J (Lansdowne) 1929 F, E, S, 1930 F, E, S, W, 1932 E, S, W, 1933 E, W, S, 1934 E, S, W
Dwyer, P J (UC Dublin) 1962 W, 1963 F, NZ, 1964 S, W

Earls, K G (Munster) 2008 C, NZ2(R), 2009 A(R), Fj, SA, 2010 It(R), F, E, W, S, SA(R), NZ2(R), Arg(R), 2011 It, F1, S1, W, E1, F2, 3, E2, [US, A, Ru, It, W], 2012 It, F, S, E, NZ 1, 3, SA, Arg, 2013 W(R), E(R), S, F, It, 2015 W 2, 3, [C, R, It, F, Arg]
Easterby, S H (Llanelli Scarlets) 2000 S, It, F, W, Arg, US, C, 2001 S, Sm (R), 2002 W, E (R), S (R), It, F, NZ 1, 2, R, Ru, Gg, 2003 Tg, Sm, It 2, S 2(t+R), [Nm, Arg, A, F], 2004 F, W, E, It, S, SA1, 2, 3, US, Arg, 2005 It, S, E, F, W, NZ, A, 2006 It, F, W, S, E, SA(R), A2(R), PI, 2007 W, F, E, S1, It1, 2, [Nm, Gg, F, Arg], 2008 It, S(R), E(R)
Easterby, W G (Ebbw Vale, Ballynahinch, Llanelli, Leinster) 2000 US, C (R), 2001 R (R), S, W (R), Sm (R), 2002 W (R), S (R), R (R), Ru (R), Gg (R), Fj, 2003 S 1(R), It (R), Tg, Sm, W 2(R), It 2, S 2(R), [R(R), Nm(R), F(R)], 2004 W(R), It(R), S(R), SA2(R), US, 2005 S(R)
Edwards, H G (Dublin U) 1877 E, 1878 E
Edwards, R W (Malone) 1904 W
Edwards, T (Lansdowne) 1888 M, 1890 S, W, E, 1892 W, 1893 E
Edwards, W V (Malone) 1912 F, E
Egan, J D (Bective Rangers) 1922 S
Egan, J T (Cork Constitution) 1931 F, E, SA
Egan, M S (Garryowen) 1893 E, 1895 S
Ekin, W (Queen's Coll, Belfast) 1888 W, S
Elliott, W R J (Bangor) 1979 S
Elwood, E P (Lansdowne, Galwegians) 1993 W, E, R, 1994 F, W, E, S, A 1, 2, 1995 F, W, [NZ, W, F], 1996 US, S, 1997 F, W, E, NZ, C, It 2(R), 1998 F, W, E, SA 1, 2, Gg, R, SA 3, 1999 It, Arg 1(R), [US (R), A 3(R), R]
English, M A F (Lansdowne, Limerick Bohemians) 1958 W, F, 1959 E, S, F, 1960 E, S, 1961 S, W, F, 1962 F, W, 1963 E, S, W, NZ
Ennis, F N G (Wanderers) 1979 A 1(R)
Ensor, A H (Wanderers) 1973 W, F, 1974 F, W, E, S, P, NZ, 1975 E, S, F, W, 1976 A, F, W, E, NZ, 1977 E, 1978 S, F, W, E
Entrican, J C (Queen's U, Belfast) 1931 S
Erskine, D J (Sale) 1997 NZ (R), C, It 2

Fagan, G L (Kingstown School) 1878 E
Fagan, W B C (Wanderers) 1956 F, E, S
Farrell, J L (Bective Rangers) 1926 F, E, S, W, 1927 F, E, S, W, A, 1928 F, E, S, W, 1929 F, E, S, W, 1930 F, E, S, W, 1931 F, E, S, W, SA, 1932 E, S, W
Feddis, N (Lansdowne) 1956 E
Feighery, C F P (Lansdowne) 1972 F 1, E, F 2
Feighery, T A O (St Mary's Coll) 1977 W, E
Ferris, H H (Queen's Coll, Belfast) 1901 W
Ferris, J H (Queen's Coll, Belfast) 1900 E, S, W

Ferris, S (Ulster) 2006 PI, 2007 Arg1(R), 2, S2, 2008 A(R), C, NZ2(R), Arg, 2009 F, It, E, S, W, A, Fj, SA, 2010 F, E, W, S, SA, Sm(R), NZ2, Arg, 2011 F3(R), E2, [US, A, It, W], 2012 W, It, F, S, E
Field, M J (Malone) 1994 E, S, A 1(R), 1995 F (R), W (t), It (R), [NZ(t + R)], J, Fj, 1996 F (R), W, E, A (R), 1997 F, W, E, S
Finlay, J E (Queen's Coll, Belfast) 1913 E, S, W, 1920 E, S, W
Finlay, W (NIFC) 1876 E, 1877 E, S, 1878 E, 1879 S, E, 1880 S, 1882 S
Finn, M C (UC Cork, Cork Constitution) 1979 E, 1982 W, E, S, F, 1983 S, F, W, E, 1984 E, S, A, 1986 F, W
Finn, R G A (UC Dublin) 1977 F
Fitzgerald, C C (Glasgow U, Dungannon) 1902 E, 1903 E, S
Fitzgerald, C F (St Mary's Coll) 1979 A 1, 2, 1980 E, S, F, W, 1982 W, E, S, F, 1983 S, F, W, E, 1984 F, W, A, 1985 S, F, W, E, 1986 F, W, E, S
Fitzgerald, D C (Lansdowne, De La Salle Palmerston) 1984 E, S, 1986 W, E, S, R, 1987 E, S, F, W, [W, C, A], 1988 S, F, W, E 1, 1989 NZ 2(R), 1990 E, S, F, W, Arg, 1991 F, W, E, S, Nm 1, 2, [Z, S, A], 1992 W, S (R)
Fitzgerald, J (Wanderers) 1884 W
Fitzgerald, J J (Young Munster) 1988 S, F, 1990 S, F, W, 1991 F, W, E, S, [J], 1994 A 1, 2
Fitzgerald, L M (Leinster) 2006 PI, 2007 Arg2(R), 2008 W(R), E(R), C, NZ2, Arg, 2009 F, It, E, S, W, A, 2010 SA, Sm, NZ2, 2011 It, F1, S1, W, S2, F2, 3(R), 2013 S(R), F(R), It(R), NZ(R), 2015 S 1, 2, W 3, [C, It(R), F(R), Arg(R)]
Fitzgibbon, M J J (Shannon) 1992 W, E, S, F, NZ 1, 2
Fitzpatrick, D J (Ulster) 2012 NZ 1, 3(R), 2013 W(R), E(R), C(R), Sm(R), NZ(R)
Fitzpatrick, J M (Dungannon) 1998 SA 1, 2 Gg (R), R (R), SA 3, 1999 F (R), W (R), E (R), It, Arg 1(R), [US (R), A 3, R, Arg 2(t&R)], 2000 S (R), It (R), Arg (R), US, C, SA (t&R), 2001 R (R), 2003 W 1(R), E (R), Tg, W 2(R), It 2(R)
Fitzpatrick, M P (Wanderers) 1978 S, 1980 S, F, W, 1981 F, W, E, S, A, 1985 F (R)
Flannery, J P (Munster) 2005 R(R), 2006 It, F, W, S, E, NZ1, 2, A1, 2007 W(R), F(R), E(R), S1(R), It1(R), Arg1, S2, It2(R), [Nm(R), Gg(R), F, Arg], 2008 NZ1, A(R), C, NZ2(R), Arg, 2009 F, It, E, S(R), W, A, Fj, SA, 2010 It, F, 2011 S2(R), F2(R), 3(R), E2, [US(R)]
Flavin, P (Blackrock Coll) 1997 F (R), S
Fletcher, W W (Kingstown) 1882 W, S, 1883 E
Flood, R S (Dublin U) 1925 W
Flynn, M K (Wanderers) 1959 F, 1960 F, 1962 E, S, F, W, 1964 E, S, W, F, 1965 F, E, S, W, SA, 1966 F, E, S, 1972 F 1, E, F 2, 1973 NZ
Fogarty, J (Leinster) 2010 NZ1(R)
Fogarty, T (Garryowen) 1891 W
Foley, A G (Shannon, Munster) 1995 E, S, F, W, It, [J(t + R)], 1996 A, 1997 It 1, E (R), 2000 E, S, It, F, W, Arg, C, J, SA, 2001 It, F, R, S, W, E, Sm, NZ, 2002 W, E, S, It, F, NZ 1, 2, R, Ru, Gg, A, Fj, Arg, 2003 S 1, It 1, F, W 1, E, W 2, [R, A], 2004 F, W, E, It, S, SA1, 2, 3, US(R), Arg, 2005 It, S, E, F, W
Foley, B O (Shannon) 1976 F, C, 1977 W (R), 1980 F, W, 1981 F, E, S, SA 1, 2, A
Foley, D (Munster) 2014 Gg, A(R)
Forbes, R E (Malone) 1907 E
Forrest, A J (Wanderers) 1880 E, S, 1881 E, S, 1882 W, E, 1883 E, 1885 S 2
Forrest, E G (Wanderers) 1888 M, 1889 S, W, 1890 S, E, 1891 E, 1893 S, W, 1894 E, S, W, 1895 W, 1897 E, S
Forrest, H (Wanderers) 1893 S, W
Fortune, J J (Clontarf) 1963 NZ, 1964 E
Foster, A R (Derry) 1910 E, S, F, 1911 E, S, W, F, 1912 F, E, S, W, 1914 E, S, W, 1921 E, S, W
Francis, N P J (Blackrock Coll, London Irish, Old Belvedere) 1987 [Tg, A], 1988 WS, It, 1989 S, 1990 E, F, W, 1991 E, S, Nm 1, 2, [Z, J, S, A], 1992 W, E, S, 1993 F, R, 1994 F, W, E, S, A 1, 2, US, 1995 E, [NZ, J, W, F], Fj, 1996 US, S
Franks, J G (Dublin U) 1898 E, S, W
Frazer, E F (Bective Rangers) 1891 S, 1892 S
Freer, A E (Lansdowne) 1901 E, S, W
Fulcher, G M (Cork Constitution, London Irish) 1994 A 2, US, 1995 E (R), S, F, W, It, [NZ, W, F], Fj, 1996 US, S, F, W, E, A, 1997 It 1, W (R), 1998 SA 1(R)

Fulton, J (NIFC) 1895 S, W, 1896 E, 1897 E, 1898 W, 1899 E, 1900 W, 1901 E, 1902 E, S, W, 1903 E, S, W, 1904 E, S
Furlong, J N (UC Galway) 1992 NZ 1, 2
Furlong, T V (Leinster) 2015 W 3(R), E 2(R), [R(R)]

Gaffikin, W (Windsor) 1875 E
Gage, J H (Queen's U, Belfast) 1926 S, W, 1927 S, W
Galbraith, E (Dublin U) 1875 E
Galbraith, H T (Belfast Acad) 1890 W
Galbraith, R (Dublin U) 1875 E, 1876 E, 1877 E
Galwey, M J (Shannon) 1991 F, W, Nm 2(R), [J], 1992 E, S, F, NZ 1, 2, A, 1993 F, W, E, R, 1994 F, W, E, S, A 1, US (R), 1995 E, 1996 WS, 1998 F (R), 1999 W (R), 2000 E (R), S, It, F, W, Arg, C, 2001 It, F, R, W, E, Sm, NZ, 2002 W, E, S
Ganly, J B (Monkstown) 1927 F, E, S, W, A, 1928 F, E, S, W, 1929 F, S, 1930 F
Gardiner, F (NIFC) 1900 E, S, 1901 E, W, 1902 E, S, W, 1903 E, W, 1904 E, S, W, 1906 E, S, W, 1907 S, W, 1908 S, W, 1909 E, S, F
Gardiner, J B (NIFC) 1923 E, S, W, F, 1924 F, E, S, W, NZ, 1925 F, E, S, W
Gardiner, S (Belfast Albion) 1893 E, S
Gardiner, W (NIFC) 1892 E, S, 1893 E, S, W, 1894 E, S, W, 1895 E, S, W, 1896 E, S, W, 1897 E, S, 1898 W
Garry, M G (Bective Rangers) 1909 E, S, W, F, 1911 E, S, W
Gaston, J T (Dublin U) 1954 NZ, F, E, S, W, 1955 W 1956 F, E
Gavin, T J (Moseley, London Irish) 1949 F, E
Geoghegan, S P (London Irish, Bath) 1991 F, W, E, S, Nm 1, [Z, S, A], 1992 E, S, F, A, 1993 S, F, W, E, R, 1994 F, W, E, S, A 1, 2, US, 1995 E, S, F, W, [NZ, J, W, F], Fj, 1996 US, S, W, E
Gibson, C M H (Cambridge U, NIFC) 1964 E, S, W, F, 1965 F, E, S, W, SA, 1966 F, E, S, W, 1967 A 1, E, S, W, F, A 2, 1968 E, S, W, A, 1969 E, S, W, 1970 SA, F, E, S, W, 1971 F, E, S, W, 1972 F 1, E, F 2, 1973 NZ, E, S, W, F, 1974 F, W, E, S, P, 1975 E, S, F, W, 1976 A, F, W, E, S, NZ, 1977 W, E, S, F, 1978 F, W, E, NZ, 1979 S, A 1, 2
Gibson, M E (Lansdowne, London Irish) 1979 F, W, E, S, 1981 W (R), 1986 R, 1988 S, F, W, E 2
Gifford, H P (Wanderers) 1890 S
Gillespie, J C (Dublin U) 1922 W, F
Gilpin, F G (Queen's U, Belfast) 1962 E, S, F
Gilroy, C J H (Ulster) 2012 Arg, 2013 W, E, S, It, 2014 Gg
Glass, D C (Belfast Collegians) 1958 F, 1960 W, 1961 W, SA
Gleeson, K D (St Mary's Coll, Leinster) 2002 W (R), F, NZ 1, 2, R, Ru, Gg, A, Arg, 2003 S 1, It 1, F, W 1, E, A, W 2, [R, A, F], 2004 F, W, E, It, 2006 NZ1(R), A1(R), 2007 Arg1, S2(R)
Glennon, B T (Lansdowne) 1993 F (R)
Glennon, J J (Skerries) 1980 E, S, 1987 E, S, F, [W (R)]
Godfrey, R P (UC Dublin) 1954 S, W
Goodall, K G (City of Derry, Newcastle U) 1967 A 1, E, S, W, F, A 2, 1968 F, E, S, W, A, 1969 F, E, S, 1970 SA, F, E, S, W
Gordon, A (Dublin U) 1884 S
Gordon, T G (NIFC) 1877 E, S, 1878 E
Gotto, R P C (NIFC) 1906 SA
Goulding, W J (Cork) 1879 S
Grace, T O (UC Dublin, St Mary's Coll) 1972 F 1, E, 1973 NZ, E, S, W, 1974 E, S, P, NZ, 1975 E, S, F, W, 1976 A, F, W, E, S, NZ, 1977 W, E, S, F, 1978 S
Graham, R I (Dublin U) 1911 F
Grant, E L (CIYMS) 1971 F, E, S, W
Grant, P J (Bective Rangers) 1894 S, W
Graves, C R A (Wanderers) 1934 E, S, W, 1935 E, S, W, NZ, 1936 E, S, W, 1937 E, S, 1938 E, S, W
Gray, R D (Old Wesley) 1923 E, S, 1925 F, 1926 F
Greene, E H (Dublin U, Kingstown) 1882 W, 1884 W, 1885 E, S 2, 1886 E
Greer, R (Kingstown) 1876 E
Greeves, T J (NIFC) 1907 E, S, W, 1909 W, F
Gregg, R J (Queen's U, Belfast) 1953 F, E, S, W, 1954 F, E, S
Griffin, C S (London Irish) 1951 F, E
Griffin, J L (Wanderers) 1949 S, W
Griffiths, W (Limerick) 1878 E
Grimshaw, C (Queen's U, Belfast) 1969 E (R)
Guerin, B N (Galwegians) 1956 S
Gwynn, A P (Dublin U) 1895 W

Gwynn, L H (Dublin U) 1893 S, 1894 E, S, W, 1897 S, 1898 E, S

Hagan, J R (Leinster) 2013 US(R)
Hakin, R F (CIYMS) 1976 W, S, NZ, 1977 W, E, F
Hall, R O N (Dublin U) 1884 W
Hall, W H (Instonians) 1923 E, S, W, F, 1924 F, S
Hallaran, C F G T (Royal Navy) 1921 E, S, W, 1922 E, S, W, 1923 E, F, 1924 F, E, S, W, 1925 F, 1926 F, E
Halpin, G F (Wanderers, London Irish) 1990 E, 1991 [J], 1992 E, S, F, 1993 R, 1994 F (R), 1995 It, [NZ, W, F]
Halpin, T (Garryowen) 1909 S, W, F, 1910 E, S, W, 1911 E, S, W, F, 1912 F, E, S
Halvey, E O (Shannon) 1995 F, W, It, [J, W (t), F (R)], 1997 NZ, C (R)
Hamilton, A J (Lansdowne) 1884 W
Hamilton, G F (NIFC) 1991 F, W, E, S, Nm 2, [Z, J, S, A], 1992 A
Hamilton, R L (NIFC) 1926 F
Hamilton, R W (Wanderers) 1893 W
Hamilton, W J (Dublin U) 1877 E
Hamlet, G T (Old Wesley) 1902 E, S, W, 1903 E, S, W, 1904 S, W, 1905 E, S, W, NZ, 1906 SA, 1907 E, S, W, 1908 E, S, W, 1909 E, S, W, F, 1910 E, S, F, 1911 E, S, W, F
Hanrahan, C J (Dolphin) 1926 S, W, 1927 E, S, W, 1928 F, E, S, 1929 F, E, S, W, 1930 F, E, S, W, 1931 F, 1932 S, W
Harbison, H T (Bective Rangers) 1984 W (R), E, S, 1986 R, 1987 E, S, F, W
Hardy, G G (Bective Rangers) 1962 S
Harman, G R A (Dublin U) 1899 E, W
Harper, J (Instonians) 1947 F, E, S
Harpur, T G (Dublin U) 1908 E, S, W
Harrison, T (Cork) 1879 S, 1880 S, 1881 S
Harvey, F M W (Wanderers) 1907 W, 1911 F
Harvey, G A D (Wanderers) 1903 E, S, 1904 W, 1905 E, S
Harvey, T A (Dublin U) 1900 W, 1901 S, W, 1902 E, S, W, 1903 E, W
Haycock, P P (Terenure Coll) 1989 E
Hayes, J J (Shannon, Munster) 2000 S, It, F, W, Arg, C, J, SA, 2001 It, F, R, S, W, E, Sm, NZ, 2002 W, E, S, It, F, NZ 1, 2, R, Ru, Gg, A, Fj, Arg, 2003 S 1, It 1, F, W 1, E, [R(R), Nm, Arg, A, F], 2004 F, W, E, It, S, SA1, 2, 3, US, Arg, 2005 It, S, E, F, W, NZ, A, R(R), 2006 It, F, W, S, E, NZ1, 2, A1, SA, A2, PI, 2007 W, F, E, S1, It1, S2(R), It2, [Nm, Gg, F, Arg], 2008 It, F, S, W, E, NZ1, A, C(R), NZ2, Arg, 2009 F, It, E, S, W, A, Fj, SA, 2010 It, F, E, W, S, Sm, NZ2(R), 2011 S2(R)
Headon, T A (UC Dublin) 1939 S, W
Healey, P (Limerick) 1901 E, S, W, 1902 E, S, W, 1903 E, S, W, 1904 S
Healy, C E (Leinster) 2009 A, SA, 2010 It, F, E, W, S, NZ1, A, SA, Sm(R), NZ2, Arg, 2011 It, F1, S1, W, E1, F2, 3, E2, [A, Ru, It, W], 2012 W, It, F, S, E, NZ 1, 2, 3, SA, Arg, 2013 W, E, F, It, Sm(R), A, NZ, 2014 S, W, E, It, F, Arg, 2015 F(R), E 1(R), W 1(R), S 1, [C(R), R, It(R), F, Arg]
Heaslip, J P R (Leinster) 2006 PI, 2007 Arg1, S2, 2008 It(R), F, S, W, E, NZ1, A, C, NZ2, Arg, 2009 F, It, E, S(R), W, A, Fj, SA, 2010 It, F, E, W, S, NZ1, A, SA, Sm, NZ2, Arg, 2011 F1, S1, W, E1, F2(R), 3, E2, [US, A, Ru, It, W], 2012 W, It, F, S, E, NZ 1, 2, SA, Arg, 2013 W, E, S, F, It, Sm, A, NZ, 2014 S, W, E, It, F, Arg 1(R), 2, SA, A, 2015 F, W 1, S 1, W 2, 3, E 2, [C, R, It, F, Arg]
Heffernan, M R (Cork Constitution) 1911 E, S, W, F
Hemphill, R (Dublin U) 1912 F, E, S, W
Henderson, N J (Queen's U, Belfast, NIFC) 1949 S, W, 1950 F, 1951 F, E, S, W, SA, 1952 F, S, W, E, 1953 F, E, S, W, 1954 NZ, F, E, S, W, 1955 F, S, W, 1956 S, W, 1957 F, E, S, W, 1958 A, E, S, W, F, 1959 E, S, W, F
Henderson R A J (London Irish, Wasps, Young Munster) 1996 WS, 1997 NZ, C, 1998 F, W, SA 1(R), 2(R), 1999 F (R), E, S (R), It, 2000 S (R), It (R), F, W, Arg, US, J (R), SA, 2001 It, F, 2002 W (R), E (R), F, R (R), Ru (t), Gg (R), 2003 It 1(R), 2
Henderson, W I (Ulster) 2012 SA(R), Arg(R), 2013 S(R), F(R), It(R), US, 2014 S(R), E(R), It, F(R), Arg 1, 2(R), 2015 It(R), F(R), E 1(R), W 1(R), S 1(R), W 2, 3, [C, It, F(R), Arg]
Henebrey, G J (Garryowen) 1906 E, S, W, SA, 1909 W, F

Kelly, H C (NIFC) 1877 E, S, 1878 E, 1879 S, 1880 E, S
Kelly, J C (UC Dublin) 1962 F, W, 1963 F, E, S, W, NZ, 1964 E, S, W, F
Kelly, J P (Cork Constitution) 2002 It, NZ 1, 2, R, Ru, Gg, A (R), 2003 It 1, F, A, Tg, Sm, It 2, [R(R), Nm(R), A(R), F]
Kelly, S (Lansdowne) 1954 S, W, 1955 S, 1960 W, F
Kelly, W (Wanderers) 1884 S
Kennedy, A G (Belfast Collegians) 1956 F
Kennedy, A P (London Irish) 1986 W, E
Kennedy, F (Wanderers) 1880 E, 1881 E, 1882 W
Kennedy, F A (Wanderers) 1904 E, W
Kennedy, H (Bradford) 1938 S, W
Kennedy, J M (Wanderers) 1882 W, 1884 W
Kennedy, K W (Queen's U, Belfast, London Irish) 1965 F, E, S, W, SA, 1966 F, E, W, 1967 A 1, E, S, W, F, A 2, 1968 F, A, 1969 F, E, S, W, 1970 SA, F, E, S, W, 1971 F, E, S, W, 1972 F 1, E, F 2, 1973 NZ, E, S, W, F, 1974 F, W, E, S, P, NZ, 1975 F, W
Kennedy, T J (St Mary's Coll) 1978 NZ, 1979 F, W, E (R), A 1, 2, 1980 E, S, F, W, 1981 SA 1, 2, A
Kenny, P (Wanderers) 1992 NZ 2(R)
Keogh, F S (Bective Rangers) 1964 W, F
Keon, J J (Limerick) 1879 E
Keyes, R P (Cork Constitution) 1986 E, 1991 [Z, J, S, A], 1992 W, E, S
Kidd, H (Dublin U, Lansdowne) 1877 E, S, 1878 E
Kiely, M D (Lansdowne) 1962 W, 1963 F, E, S, W
Kiernan, M J (Dolphin, Lansdowne) 1982 W (R), E, S, F, 1983 S, F, W, E, 1984 E, S, A, 1985 S, F, W, E, 1986 F, W, E, S, R, 1987 E, S, F, W, [W, C, A], 1988 S, F, W, E 1, 2, WS, 1989 F, W, E, S, 1990 E, S, F, W, Arg, 1991 F
Kiernan, T J (UC Cork, Cork Const) 1960 E, S, W, F, SA, 1961 E, S, W, F, SA, 1962 E, W, 1963 F, E, S, W, NZ, 1964 E, S, 1965 F, E, S, W, SA, 1966 F, E, S, W, 1967 A 1, E, S, W, F, A 2, 1968 F, E, S, W, A, 1969 F, E, S, W, 1970 SA, F, E, S, W, 1971 F, 1972 F 1, E, F 2, 1973 NZ, E, S
Kilcoyne, D (Munster) 2012 SA(t), Arg(R), 2013 W(R), E(R), S(R), It(R), US, C(R), 2014 Arg 1(R), 2, SA(R), Gg, 2015 W 2(R), S 2, W 3(R)
Killeen, G V (Garryowen) 1912 E, S, W, 1913 E, S, W, F, 1914 E, S, W
King, H (Dublin U) 1883 E, S
Kingston, T J (Dolphin) 1987 [W, Tg, A], 1988 S, F, W, E 1, 1990 F, W, 1991 [J], 1993 F, W, E, R, 1994 F, W, E, S, 1995 F, W, It, [NZ, J (R), W, F], Fj, 1996 US, S, F
Knox, J H (Dublin U, Lansdowne) 1904 W, 1905 E, S, W, NZ, 1906 E, S, W, 1907 W, 1908 S
Kyle, J W (Queen's U, Belfast, NIFC) 1947 F, E, S, W, A, 1948 F, E, S, W, 1949 F, E, S, W, 1950 F, E, S, W, 1951 F, E, S, W, SA, 1952 F, S, W, E, 1953 F, E, S, W, 1954 NZ, F, 1955 F, E, W, 1956 F, E, S, W, 1957 F, E, S, W, 1958 A, E, S

Lambert, N H (Lansdowne) 1934 S, W
Lamont, R A (Instonians) 1965 F, E, SA, 1966 F, E, S, W, 1970 SA, F, E, S, W
Landers, M F (Cork Const) 1904 W, 1905 E, S, W, NZ
Lane, D J (UC Cork) 1934 S, W, 1935 E, S
Lane, M F (UC Cork) 1947 W, 1949 F, E, S, W, 1950 F, E, S, W, 1951 F, S, W, SA, 1952 F, S, 1953 F, E
Lane, P (Old Crescent) 1964 W
Langan, D J (Clontarf) 1934 W
Langbroek, J A (Blackrock Coll) 1987 [Tg]
Lavery, P (London Irish) 1974 W, 1976 W
Lawlor, P J (Clontarf) 1951 S, SA, 1952 F, S, W, E, 1953 F, 1954 NZ, E, S, 1956 F, E
Lawlor, P J (Bective Rangers) 1935 E, S, W, 1937 E, S, W
Lawlor, P J (Bective Rangers) 1990 Arg, 1992 A, 1993 S
Leahy, K T (Wanderers) 1992 NZ 1
Leahy, M W (UC Cork) 1964 W
Leamy, D P (Munster) 2004 US, 2005 It, J2, NZ, A, R, 2006 It, F, W, S, E, NZ1, 2, A1, SA, A2, PI(R), 2007 W, F, E, S1, It1, 2, [Nm, Gg, F, Arg], 2008 It, F, S, W, E, NZ1, A, 2009 F(R), It(t&R), E(R), S, W(R), C, US, A(t&R), Fj, 2010 Sm, NZ2(R), Arg(R), 2011 It, S1(R), W(R), E1(R), S2, F2, E2(R), [US(R), Ru(R), It(R), W(R)]
Lee, S (NIFC) 1891 E, S, W, 1892 E, S, W, 1893 E, S, W, 1894 E, S, W, 1895 E, W, 1896 E, S, W, 1897 E, 1898 E

Le Fanu, V C (Cambridge U, Lansdowne) 1886 E, S, 1887 E, W, 1888 S, 1889 W, 1890 E, 1891 E, 1892 E, S, W
Lenihan, D G (UC Cork, Cork Const) 1981 A, 1982 W, E, S, F, 1983 S, F, W, E, 1984 F, W, E, S, A, 1985 S, F, W, E, 1986 F, W, E, S, R, 1987 E, S, F, W, [W, C, Tg, A], 1988 S, F, W, E 1, 2, WS, It, 1989 F, W, E, S, NZ, 1990 S, F, W, Arg, 1991 Nm 2, [Z, S, A], 1992 W
L'Estrange, L P F (Dublin U) 1962 E
Levis, F H (Wanderers) 1884 E
Lewis, K P (Leinster) 2005 J2(R), 2007 Arg1, 2(R)
Lightfoot, E J (Lansdowne) 1931 F, E, S, W, SA, 1932 E, S, W, 1933 E, W, S
Lindsay, H (Dublin U, Armagh) 1893 E, S, W, 1894 E, S, W, 1895 E, 1896 E, S, W, 1898 E, S, W
Little, T J (Bective Rangers) 1898 W, 1899 S, W, 1900 S, W, 1901 E, S
Lloyd, R A (Dublin U, Liverpool) 1910 E, S, 1911 E, S, W, F, 1912 F, E, S, W, SA, 1913 E, S, W, F, 1914 F, E, 1920 E, F
Longwell, G W (Ballymena) 2000 J (R), SA, 2001 F (R), R, S (R), Sm, NZ (R), 2002 W (R), E (R), S (R), It, F, NZ 1, 2, R, Ru, Gg, A, Arg, 2003 S 1, It 1, F, E, A, It 2, 2004 It(R)
Loughney, R (Connacht) 2012 NZ 1(R)
Lydon, C T J (Galwegians) 1956 S
Lyle, R K (Dublin U) 1910 W, F
Lyle, T R (Dublin U) 1885 E, S 1, 2, 1886 E, 1887 E, S
Lynch, J F (St Mary's Coll) 1971 F, E, S, W, 1972 F 1, E, F 2, 1973 NZ, E, S, W, 1974 F, W, E, S, P, NZ
Lynch, L M (Lansdowne) 1956 S
Lytle, J H (NIFC) 1894 E, S, W, 1895 W, 1896 E, S, W, 1897 E, S, 1898 E, S, 1899 S
Lytle, J N (NIFC) 1888 M, 1889 W, 1890 E, 1891 E, S, 1894 E, S, W
Lyttle, V J (Collegians, Bedford) 1938 E, 1939 E, S

McAleese, D R (Ballymena) 1992 F
McAllan, G H (Dungannon) 1896 S, W
Macauley, J (Limerick) 1887 E, S
McBride, W D (Malone) 1988 W, E 1, WS, It, 1989 S, 1990 F, W, Arg, 1993 S, F, W, E, R, 1994 W, E, S, A 1(R), 1995 S, F, [NZ, W, F], Fj (R), 1996 W, E, WS, A, 1997 It 1(R), F, W, E, S
McBride, W J (Ballymena) 1962 E, S, F, W, 1963 F, E, S, W, NZ, 1964 E, S, F, 1965 F, E, S, W, SA, 1966 F, E, S, W, 1967 A 1, E, S, W, F, A 2, 1968 F, E, S, W, A, 1969 F, E, S, W, 1970 SA, F, E, S, W, 1971 F, E, S, W, 1972 F 1, E, F 2, 1973 NZ, E, S, W, F, 1974 F, W, E, S, P, NZ, 1975 E, S, F, W
McCahill, S A (Sunday's Well) 1995 Fj (t)
McCall, B W (London Irish) 1985 F (R), 1986 E, S
McCall, M C (Bangor, Dungannon, London Irish) 1992 NZ 1(R), 2, 1994 W, 1996 E (R), A, 1997 It 1, NZ, C, It 2, 1998 S, E, SA 1, 2
McCallan, B (Ballymena) 1960 E, S
McCarten, R J (London Irish) 1961 E, W, F
McCarthy, E A (Kingstown) 1882 W
McCarthy, J S (Dolphin) 1948 F, E, S, W, 1949 F, E, S, W, 1950 W, 1951 F, E, S, W, SA, 1952 F, S, W, E, 1953 F, E, S, 1954 NZ, F, E, S, W, 1955 F, E
McCarthy, M P (Connacht, Leinster) 2011 S2, F3(R), 2012 S(R), E(R), SA, Arg, 2013 W, E, F, It, US, C(R), Sm, A(R), NZ(R), 2014 SA(R), Gg
McCarthy, P (Cork Const) 1992 NZ 1, 2, A, 1993 S, R (R)
MacCarthy, St G (Dublin U) 1882 W
McCarthy, T (Cork) 1898 W
McClelland, T A (Queen's U, Belfast) 1921 E, S, W, F, 1922 E, W, F, 1923 E, S, W, F, 1924 F, E, S, W, NZ
McClenahan, R O (Instonians) 1923 E, S, W
McClinton, A N (NIFC) 1910 W, F
McCombe, W McM (Dublin U, Bangor) 1968 F, 1975 E, S, F, W
McConnell, A A (Collegians) 1947 A, 1948 F, E, S, W, 1949 F, E
McConnell, G (Derry, Edinburgh U) 1912 F, E, 1913 W, F
McConnell, J W (Lansdowne) 1913 S
McCormac, F M (Wanderers) 1909 W, 1910 W, F
McCormick, W J (Wanderers) 1930 E
McCoull, H C (Belfast Albion) 1895 E, S, W, 1899 E

McCourt, D (Queen's U, Belfast) 1947 A
McCoy, J J (Dungannon, Bangor, Ballymena) 1984 W, A, 1985 S, F, W, E, 1986 F, 1987 [Tg], 1988 E 2, WS, It, 1989 F, W, E, S, NZ
McCracken, H (NIFC) 1954 W
McCullen, A (Lansdowne) 2003 Sm
McCullough, M T (Ulster) 2005 J1, 2, NZ(R), A(R)
McDermott, S J (London Irish) 1955 S, W
McDonald, J A (Methodist Coll, Belfast) 1875 E, 1876 E, 1877 S, 1878 E, 1879 S, 1880 E, 1881 S, 1882 E, S, 1883 E, S, 1884 E, S
McDonald, J P (Malone) 1987 [C], 1990 E (R), S, Arg
McDonnell, A C (Dublin U) 1889 W, 1890 S, W, 1891 E
McDowell, J C (Instonians) 1924 F, NZ
McFadden, F L (Leinster) 2011 It, F1, S2, F2(R), E2(R), [Ru], 2012 W, It(R), F(R), S(R), E(R), NZ 1, 2, 3, SA(R), Arg(R), 2013 F, US, C, Sm, A, 2014 S(R), W(R), E(R), It(R), F(R), Arg 1(R), 2, 2015 W 2
McFarland, B A T (Derry) 1920 S, W, F, 1922 W
McGann, B J (Lansdowne) 1969 F, E, S, W, 1970 SA, F, E, S, W, 1971 F, E, S, W, 1972 F 1, E, F 2, 1973 NZ, E, S, W, 1976 F, W, E, S, NZ
McGowan, A N (Blackrock Coll) 1994 US
McGown, T M W (NIFC) 1899 E, S, 1901 S
McGrath, D G (UC Dublin, Cork Const) 1984 S, 1987 [W, C, Tg, A]
McGrath, J C (Leinster) 2013 Sm, A(R), NZ(R), 2014 S(R), W(R), E(R), It(R), F(R), Arg 1, 2(R), SA, A, 2015 It, F, E 1, W 1, S 1(R), W 2, 3, E 2, [C, R(R), It, F(R), Arg(R)]
McGrath, N F (Oxford U, London Irish) 1934 W
McGrath, P J (UC Cork) 1965 E, S, W, SA, 1966 F, E, S, W, 1967 A 1, A 2
McGrath, R J M (Wanderers) 1977 W, E, F (R), 1981 SA 1, 2, A, 1982 W, E, S, F, 1983 S, F, W, E, 1984 F, W
McGrath, T (Garryowen) 1956 W, 1958 F, 1960 E, S, W, F, 1961 SA
McGuinness, C D (St Mary's Coll) 1997 NZ, C, 1998 F, W, E, SA 1, 2, Gg, R (R), SA 3, 1999 F, W, E, S
McGuire, E P (UC Galway) 1963 E, S, W, NZ, 1964 E, S, W, F
MacHale, S (Lansdowne) 1965 F, E, S, W, SA, 1966 F, E, S, W, 1967 S, W, F
McHugh, M (St Mary's Coll) 2003 Tg
McIldowie, G (Malone) 1906 SA, 1910 E, S, W
McIlrath, J A (Ballymena) 1976 A, F, NZ, 1977 W, E
MacIlwaine, E H (NIFC) 1895 S, W
MacIlwaine, E N (NIFC) 1875 E, 1876 E
MacIlwaine, J E (NIFC) 1897 E, S, 1898 E, S, W, 1899 E, W
McIntosh, L M (Dublin U) 1884 S
MacIvor, C V (Dublin U) 1912 F, E, S, W, 1913 E, S, F
McIvor, S C (Garryowen) 1996 A, 1997 It 1, S (R)
McKay, J W (Queen's U, Belfast) 1947 F, E, S, W, A, 1948 F, E, S, W, 1949 F, E, S, W, 1950 F, E, S, W, 1951 F, E, S, W, SA, 1952 F
McKee, W D (NIFC) 1947 A, 1948 F, E, S, W, 1949 F, E, S, W, 1950 F, E, 1951 SA
McKeen, A J W (Lansdowne) 1999 [R (R)]
McKelvey, J M (Queen's U, Belfast) 1956 F, E
McKenna, P (St Mary's Coll) 2000 Arg
McKibbin, A R (Instonians, London Irish) 1977 W, E, S, 1978 S, F, W, E, NZ, 1979 F, W, E, S, 1980 E, S
McKibbin, C H (Instonians) 1976 S (R)
McKibbin, D (Instonians) 1950 F, E, S, W, 1951 F, E, S, W
McKibbin, H R (Queen's U, Belfast) 1938 W, 1939 E, S, W
McKinney, S A (Dungannon) 1972 F 1, E, F 2, 1973 W, F, 1974 F, E, S, P, NZ, 1975 E, S, 1976 A, F, W, E, S, NZ, 1977 W, E, S, 1978 S (R), F, W, E
McLaughlin, J H (Derry) 1887 E, S, 1888 W, S
McLaughlin, K R (Leinster) 2010 It, 2011 S2(R), 2012 NZ 1(R), 2, 3, 2013 C, A(R), NZ(R)
McLean, R E (Dublin U) 1881 S, 1882 W, E, S, 1883 E, S, 1884 E, S, 1885 E, S 1
Maclear, B (Cork County, Monkstown) 1905 E, S, W, NZ, 1906 E, S, W, SA, 1907 E, S, W
McLennan, A C (Wanderers) 1977 F, 1978 S, F, W, E, NZ, 1979 F, W, E, S, 1980 E, F, 1981 F, W, E, S, SA 1, 2
McLoughlin, F M (Northern) 1976 A
McLoughlin, G A J (Shannon) 1979 F, W, E, S, A 1, 2, 1980

E, 1981 SA 1, 2, 1982 W, E, S, F, 1983 S, F, W, E, 1984 F
McLoughlin, R J (UC Dublin, Blackrock Coll, Gosforth) 1962 E, S, F, 1963 E, S, W, NZ, 1964 E, S, 1965 F, E, S, W, SA, 1966 F, E, S, W, 1971 F, E, S, W, 1972 F 1, E, F 2, 1973 NZ, E, S, W, F, 1974 W, E, S, P, NZ, 1975 E, S, F, W
McMahon, L B (Blackrock Coll, UC Dublin) 1931 E, SA, 1933 E, 1934 E, 1936 E, S, W, 1937 E, S, W, 1938 E, S
McMaster, A W (Ballymena) 1972 F 1, E, F 2, 1973 NZ, E, S, W, F, 1974 F, E, S, P, 1975 F, W, 1976 A, F, W, NZ
McMordie, J (Queen's Coll, Belfast) 1886 S
McMorrow, A (Garryowen) 1951 W
McMullen, A R (Cork) 1881 E, S
McNamara, V (UC Cork) 1914 E, S, W
McNaughton, P P (Greystones) 1978 S, F, W, E, 1979 F, W, E, S, A 1, 2, 1980 E, S, F, W, 1981 F
MacNeill, H P (Dublin U, Oxford U, Blackrock Coll, London Irish) 1981 F, W, E, S, A, 1982 W, E, S, F, 1983 S, F, W, E, 1984 F, W, E, A, 1985 S, F, W, E, 1986 F, W, E, S, R, 1987 E, S, F, W, [W, C, Tg, A], 1988 S (R), E 1, 2
McQuilkin, K P (Bective Rangers, Lansdowne) 1996 US, S, F, 1997 F (t & R), S
MacSweeney, D A (Blackrock Coll) 1955 S
McVicker, H (Army, Richmond) 1927 E, S, W, A, 1928 F
McVicker, J (Collegians) 1924 F, E, S, W, NZ, 1925 F, E, S, W, 1926 F, E, S, W, 1927 F, E, S, W, A, 1928 W, 1930 F
McVicker, S (Queen's U, Belfast) 1922 E, S, W, F
McWeeney, J P J (St Mary's Coll) 1997 NZ
Madden, M N (Sunday's Well) 1955 E, S, W
Madigan, I L (Leinster) 2013 F(R), It(R), US, C, Sm(R), A(R), NZ(R), 2014 F(R), Arg 1(R), 2(R), SA(R), Gg, A(R), 2015 It(R), F(t), E 1(R), W 1(R), S 1(R), W 2(R), S 2, E 2(t&R), [C(R), R, F(R), Arg]
Magee, A M (Louis) (Bective Rangers, London Irish) 1895 E, S, W, 1896 E, S, W, 1897 E, S, 1898 E, S, W, 1899 E, S, W, 1900 E, S, W, 1901 E, S, W, 1902 E, S, W, 1903 E, S, W, 1904 W
Magee, J T (Bective Rangers) 1895 E, S
Maggs, K M (Bristol, Bath, Ulster) 1997 NZ (R), C, It 2, 1998 S, F, W, E, SA 1, 2, Gg, R (R), SA 3, 1999 F, W, E, S, It, A 1, 2, Arg 1, [US, A 3, Arg 2], 2000 E, F, Arg, US (R), C, 2001 It (R), F (R), R, S (R), W, E, Sm, NZ, 2002 W, E, S, R, Ru, Gg, A, Fj, Arg, 2003 S 1, It 1, F, W 1, E, A, W 2, S 2, [R, Nm, Arg, A, F], 2004 F(R), E(R), It(R), S(R), SA1(R), 2, US, 2005 S, F, W, J1
Maginiss, R M (Dublin U) 1875 E, 1876 E
Magrath, R M (Cork Constitution) 1909 S
Maguire, J F (Cork) 1884 S
Mahoney, J (Dolphin) 1923 E
Malcomson, G L (RAF, NIFC) 1935 NZ, 1936 E, S, W, 1937 E, S, W
Malone, N G (Oxford U, Leicester) 1993 S, F, 1994 US (R)
Mannion, N P (Corinthians, Lansdowne, Wanderers) 1988 WS, It, 1989 F, W, E, S, NZ, 1990 E, S, F, W, Arg, 1991 Nm 1(R), 2, [J], 1993 S
Marmion, K D (Connacht) 2014 Arg 1(R), 2(R), Gg(R), 2015 W 2(R)
Marshall, B D E (Queen's U, Belfast) 1963 E
Marshall, L D (Ulster) 2013 S, F, It, A, 2014 S, Arg 1
Marshall, P (Ulster) 2013 It(R), US(R), C(R)
Mason, S J P (Orrell, Richmond) 1996 W, E, WS
Massey-Westropp, R H (Limerick, Monkstown) 1886 E
Matier, R N (NIFC) 1878 E, 1879 S
Matthews, P M (Ards, Wanderers) 1984 A, 1985 S, F, W, E, 1986 R, 1987 E, S, F, W, [W, Tg, A], 1988 S, F, W, E 1, 2, WS, It, 1989 F, W, E, S, NZ, 1990 E, S, 1991 F, W, E, S, Nm 1 [Z, S, A], 1992 W, E, S
Mattsson, J (Wanderers) 1948 E
Mayne, R B (Queen's U, Belfast) 1937 W, 1938 E, W, 1939 E, S, W
Mayne, R H (Belfast Academy) 1888 W, S
Mayne, T (NIFC) 1921 E, S, F
Mays, K M A (UC Dublin) 1973 NZ, E, S, W
Meares, A W D (Dublin U) 1899 S, W, 1900 E, W
Megaw, J (Richmond, Instonians) 1934 W, 1938 W
Millar, H J (Monkstown) 1904 W, 1905 E, S, W
Millar, S (Ballymena) 1958 F, 1959 E, S, W, F, 1960 E, S, W,

F, SA, 1961 E, S, W, F, SA, 1962 E, S, F, 1963 F, E, S, W, 1964 F, 1968 F, E, S, W, A, 1969 F, E, S, W, 1970 SA, F, E, S, W

Millar, W H J (Queen's U, Belfast) 1951 E, S, W, 1952 S, W

Miller, A (Kingstown) 1880 E, S, 1883 E

Miller, E R P (Leicester, Tererure Coll, Leinster) 1997 It 1, F, W, E, NZ, It 2, 1998 S, W (R), Gg, R, 1999 F, W, E (R), S, Arg 1(R), [US (R), A 3(t&R), Arg 2(R)], 2000 US, C (R), SA, 2001 R, W, E, Sm, NZ, 2002 E, S, It (R), Fj (R), 2003 W 1(t+R), Tg, Sm, It 2, S 2, [Nm, Arg(R), A(t&R), F(R)], 2004 SA3(R), US, Arg(R), 2005 It(R), S(R), F(R), W(R), J1(R), 2

Miller, F H (Wanderers) 1886 S

Milliken, R A (Bangor) 1973 E, S, W, F, 1974 F, W, E, S, P, NZ, 1975 E, S, F, W

Millin, T J (Dublin U) 1925 W

Minch, J B (Bective Rangers) 1912 SA, 1913 E, S, 1914 E, S

Moffat, J (Belfast Academy) 1888 W, S, M, 1889 S, 1890 S, W, 1891 S

Moffatt, J E (Old Wesley) 1904 S, 1905 E, S, W

Moffett, J W (Ballymena) 1961 E, S

Molloy, M G (UC Galway, London Irish) 1966 F, E, 1967 A 1, E, S, W, F, A 2, 1968 F, E, S, W, A, 1969 F, E, S, W, 1970 F, E, S, W, 1971 F, E, S, W, 1973 F, 1976 A

Moloney, J J (St Mary's Coll) 1972 F 1, E, F 2, 1973 NZ, E, S, W, F, 1974 F, W, E, S, P, NZ, 1975 E, S, F, W, 1976 S, 1978 S, F, W, E, 1979 A 1, 2, 1980 S, W

Moloney, L A (Garryowen) 1976 W (R), S, 1978 S (R), NZ

Molony, J U (UC Dublin) 1950 S

Monteith, J D E (Queen's U, Belfast) 1947 E, S, W

Montgomery, A (NIFC) 1895 S

Montgomery, F P (Queen's U, Belfast) 1914 E, S, W

Montgomery, R (Cambridge U) 1887 E, S, W, 1891 E, 1892 W

Moore, A H (Windsor) 1876 E, 1877 S

Moore, C M (Dublin U) 1887 S, 1888 W, S

Moore, D F (Wanderers) 1883 E, S, 1884 E, W

Moore, F W (Wanderers) 1884 W, 1885 E, S 2, 1886 S

Moore, H (Queen's U, Belfast) 1910 S, 1911 W, F, 1912 F, E, S, W, SA

Moore, M J (Leinster) 2014 S(R), W(R), E(R), It(R), F(R), 2015 It(R), F(R), E 1(R), W 1(R), S 1(R)

Moore, T A P (Highfield) 1967 A 2, 1973 NZ, E, S, W, F, 1974 F, W, E, S, P, NZ

Moore, W D (Queen's Coll, Belfast) 1878 E

Moran, F G (Clontarf) 1936 E, 1937 E, S, W, 1938 S, W, 1939 E, S, W

Morell, H B (Dublin U) 1881 E, S, 1882 W, E

Morgan, G J (Clontarf) 1934 E, S, W, 1935 E, S, W, NZ, 1936 E, S, W, 1937 E, S, W, 1938 E, S, W, 1939 E, S, W

Moriarty, C C H (Monkstown) 1899 W

Moroney, J C M (Garryowen) 1968 W, A, 1969 F, E, S, W

Moroney, R J M (Lansdowne) 1984 F, W, 1985 F

Moroney, T A (UC Dublin) 1964 W, 1967 A 1, E

Morphy, E McG (Dublin U) 1908 E

Morris, D P (Bective Rangers) 1931 W, 1932 E, 1935 E, S, W, NZ

Morrow, J W R (Queen's Coll, Belfast) 1882 S, 1883 E, S, 1884 E, W, 1885 S 1, 2, 1886 E, S, 1888 S

Morrow, R D (Bangor) 1986 F, E, S

Mortell, M (Bective Rangers, Dolphin) 1953 F, E, S, W, 1954 NZ, F, E, S, W

Morton, W A (Dublin U) 1888 S

Mostyn, M R (Galwegians) 1999 A 1, Arg 1, [US, A 3, R, Arg 2]

Moyers, L W (Dublin U) 1884 W

Moylett, M M F (Shannon) 1988 E 1

Mulcahy, W A (UC Dublin, Bective Rangers, Bohemians) 1958 A, E, S, W, F, 1959 E, S, W, F, 1960 E, S, W, SA, 1961 E, S, W, SA, 1962 E, S, W, 1963 F, E, S, W, NZ, 1964 E, S, W, F, 1965 F, E, S, W, SA

Muldoon, J (Connacht) 2009 C, US, 2010 NZ1

Mullan, B (Clontarf) 1947 F, E, S, W, 1948 F, E, S, W

Mullane, J P (Limerick Bohemians) 1928 W, 1929 F

Mullen, K D (Old Belvedere) 1947 F, E, S, W, A, 1948 F, E, S, W, 1949 F, E, S, W, 1950 F, E, S, W, 1951 F, E, S, W, SA, 1952 F, S, W

Mulligan, A A (Wanderers) 1956 F, E, 1957 F, E, S, W, 1958 A, E, S, F, 1959 E, S, W, F, 1960 E, S, W, F, SA, 1961 W, F, SA

Mullin, B J (Dublin U, Oxford U, Blackrock Coll, London Irish) 1984 A, 1985 S, W, E, 1986 F, W, E, S, R, 1987 E, S, F, W, [W, C, Tg, A], 1988 S, F, W, E 1, 2, WS, It, 1989 F, W, E, S, NZ, 1990 E, S, W, Arg, 1991 F, W, E, S, Nm 1, 2, [J, S, A], 1992 W, E, S, 1994 US, 1995 E, S, F, W, It, [NZ, J, W, F]

Mullins, M J (Young Munster, Old Crescent) 1999 Arg 1(R), [R], 2000 E, S, It, Arg (t&R), US, C, 2001 It, R, W (R), E (R), Sm, NZ (R), 2003 Tg, Sm

Murphy, B J (Munster) 2007 Arg 1(R), 2, 2009 C, US

Murphy, C J (Lansdowne) 1939 E, S, W, 1947 F, E

Murphy, G E A (Leicester) 2000 US, C (R), J, 2001 R, S, Sm, 2002 W, E, NZ 1, 2, Fj, 2003 S 1(R), It 1, F, W 1, E, A, W 2, It 2(R), S 2, 2004 It, S, SA1, 3, US, Arg, 2005 It, S, E, F, W, NZ, A, R, 2006 It, F, W, S, E, NZ1, 2, A1(R), SA(R), A2, 2007 W(t&R), F, Arg1(t&R), 2, S2, It2, [Nm(R), Arg], 2008 It, F, S, E, NZ1(R), A(R), Arg, 2009 F(R), It(R), S(R), W(R), 2010 E, W, S, NZ1(R), A(R), Arg, 2011 E2, [US, Ru(R)]

Murphy, J (Leinster) 2014 E(R), It(R), Arg 1, 2(R), 2015 It, F(R), E 1, W 1(R), S 1(R), W 2, S 2(R), W 3, [R, Arg]

Murphy, J G M W (London Irish) 1951 SA, 1952 S, W, E, 1954 NZ, 1958 W

Murphy, J J (Greystones) 1981 SA 1, 1982 W (R), 1984 S

Murphy, J N (Greystones) 1992 A

Murphy, K J (Cork Constitution) 1990 E, S, F, W, Arg, 1991 F, W (R), S (R), 1992 S, F, NZ 2(R)

Murphy, N A A (Cork Constitution) 1958 A, E, S, W, F, 1959 F, S, W, F, 1960 E, S, W, F, SA, 1961 E, S, W, 1962 E, 1963 NZ, 1964 E, S, W, F, 1965 F, E, S, W, SA, 1966 F, E, S, W, 1967 A 1, E, S, W, F, 1969 F, E, S, W

Murphy, N F (Cork Constitution) 1930 E, W, 1931 F, E, S, W, SA, 1932 E, S, W, 1933 E

Murphy-O'Connor, J (Bective Rangers) 1954 E

Murray, C G (Munster) 2011 F2(R), E2(R), [US, A(R), It, W], 2012 W, It, F, NZ 1, 2, 3, SA, Arg, 2013 W, E, S, F, It, Sm, A(R), NZ, 2014 S, W, E, It, F, Arg 1, SA, A, 2015 It, F, E 1, W 1, S 1, W 3, E 2, [C, R(R), It, F, Arg]

Murray, H W (Dublin U) 1877 S, 1878 E, 1879 E

Murray, J B (UC Dublin) 1963 F

Murray, P F (Wanderers) 1927 F, 1929 F, E, S, 1930 F, E, S, W, 1931 F, E, S, W, SA, 1932 E, S, W, 1933 E, W, S

Murtagh, C W (Portadown) 1977 S

Myles, J (Dublin U) 1875 E

Nash, L C (Queen's Coll, Cork) 1889 S, 1890 W, E, 1891 E, S, W

Neely, M R (Collegians) 1947 F, E, S, W

Neill, H J (NIFC) 1885 E, S 1, 2, 1886 S, 1887 E, S, W, 1888 W, S

Neill, J McF (Instonians) 1926 F

Nelson, J E (Malone) 1947 A, 1948 E, S, W, 1949 F, E, S, W, 1950 F, E, S, W, 1951 F, E, W, 1954 F

Nelson, R (Queen's Coll, Belfast) 1882 E, S, 1883 S, 1886 S

Nesdale, R P (Newcastle) 1997 W, E, S, NZ (R), C, 1998 F (R), W (R), Gg, SA 3(R), 1999 It, A 2(R), [US (R), R]

Nesdale, T J (Garryowen) 1961 F

Neville, W C (Dublin U) 1879 S, E

Nicholson, P C (Dublin U) 1900 E, S, W

Norton, G W (Bective Rangers) 1949 F, E, S, W, 1950 F, E, S, W, 1951 F, E, S

Notley, J R (Wanderers) 1952 F, S

Nowlan, K W (St Mary's Coll) 1997 NZ, C, It 2

O'Brien, B (Derry) 1893 S, W

O'Brien, B A P (Shannon) 1968 F, E, S

O'Brien, D J (London Irish, Cardiff, Old Belvedere) 1948 E, S, W, 1949 F, E, S, W, 1950 F, E, S, W, 1951 F, E, S, W, SA, 1952 F, S, W, E

O'Brien, K A (Broughton Park) 1980 E, 1981 SA 1(R), 2

O'Brien, S K (Leinster) 2009 Fj(R), SA(R), 2010 It(R), Sm, 2011 It, F1, S1, W, E1, F2, 3, [A, Ru, It, W], 2012 W, It, F, E, NZ 1, 2, 3, 2013 W, E, S, F, It, Sm(R), A, NZ, 2015 F, E 1, W 1, S 1, 2, W 3(R), E 2, [C, R(R), It, F]

O'Brien-Butler, P E (Monkstown) 1897 S, 1898 E, S, 1899 S, W, 1900 E

O'Callaghan, C T (Carlow) 1910 W, F, 1911 E, S, W, F, 1912 F

O'Callaghan, D P (Cork Const, Munster) 2003 W 1(R), Tg (R), Sm (R), W 2(R), It2(R), [R(R), A(t&R)], 2004 F(t&R), W, It,

S(t&R), SA2(R), US, 2005 It(R), S(R), W(R), NZ, A, R, 2006 It(R), F(R), W, S(R), E(R), NZ1, 2, A1, SA, A2, PI(R), 2007 W, F, E, S1, It1, 2, [Nm, Gg, F, Arg], 2008 It, F, S, W, E, NZ1, A, C, NZ2, Arg, 2009 F, It, E, S, W, A, Fj(R), SA, 2010 E, W, S, NZ1, A, SA, Sm, NZ2, Arg, 2011 It, F1, S1, W, E1, F2, 3, E2, [US, A, Ru, It, W], 2012 W, It, F, S, E, NZ 1(R), 2(R), 3(R), SA(t&R), Arg(R), 2013 W(R), E(R), S, F(R)

O'Callaghan, M P (Sunday's Well) 1962 W, 1964 E, F

O'Callaghan, P (Dolphin) 1967 A 1, E, A 2, 1968 F, E, S, W, 1969 F, E, S, W, 1970 SA, F, E, S, W, 1976 F, W, E, S, NZ

O'Connell, K D (Sunday's Well) 1994 F, E (t)

O'Connell, P (Bective Rangers) 1913 W, F, 1914 F, E, S, W

O'Connell, P J (Young Munster, Munster, Toulon) 2002 W, It (R), F (R), NZ 1, 2003 E (R), A (R), Tg, Sm, W 2, S 2, [R, Nm, Arg, A, F], 2004 F, W, E, S, SA1, 2, 3, US, Arg, 2005 It, S, E, F, W, 2006 It, F, S, E, NZ1, 2, A1, SA, A2, PI, 2007 W, F, E, S1, 2, It2, [Nm, Gg, F, Arg], 2008 S(R), W, E, NZ1, A, C, NZ2, Arg, 2009 F, It, E, S, W, A, Fj, SA, 2010 It, F, E, W, S, 2011 It, F1, S1, W, E1, F2(R), 3, E2, [US, A, It, W], 2012 W, It, F, 2013 Sm(t&R), A, NZ, 2014 W, E, It, F, Arg 1, 2, SA, A, 2015 It, F, E 1, W 1, S 1, 2(R), W 3, E 2, [C, R(R), It, F]

O'Connell, W J (Lansdowne) 1955 F

O'Connor, H S (Dublin U) 1957 F, E, S, W

O'Connor, J (Garryowen) 1895 S

O'Connor, J H (Bective Rangers) 1888 M, 1890 S, W, E, 1891 E, S, 1892 E, W, 1893 E, S, 1894 E, S, W, 1895 E, 1896 E, S, W

O'Connor, J H (Wasps) 2004 SA3, Arg, 2005 S, E, F, W, J1, NZ, A, R, 2006 W(R), E(t&R)

O'Connor, J J (Garryowen) 1909 F

O'Connor, J J (UC Cork) 1933 S, 1934 E, S, W, 1935 E, S, W, NZ, 1936 S, W, 1938 S

O'Connor, P J (Lansdowne) 1887 W

O'Cuinneagain, D (Sale, Ballymena) 1998 SA 1, 2, Gg (R), R (R), SA 3, 1999 F, W, E, S, It, A 1, 2, Arg 1, [US, A 3, R, Arg 2], 2000 E, It (R)

Odbert, R V M (RAF) 1928 F

O'Donnell, R C (St Mary's Coll) 1979 A 1, 2, 1980 S, F, W

O'Donnell, T (Munster) 2013 US(t&R), C, 2014 S(R), W(R), SA(R), Gg, 2015 It, E 1(R), W 2

O'Donoghue, P J (Bective Rangers) 1955 F, E, S, W, 1956 W, 1957 F, E, 1958 A, E, S, W

O'Driscoll, B G (Blackrock Coll, Leinster) 1999 A 1, 2, Arg 1, [US, A 3, R (R), Arg 2], 2000 E, S, It, F, W, J, SA, 2001 F, S, W, E, Sm, NZ, 2002 W, E, S, It, F, NZ 1, 2, R, Ru, Gg, A, Fj, Arg, 2003 S 1, It 1, F, W 1, E, W 2, S 2, [R, Nm, Arg, A, F], 2004 W, E, It, S, SA1, 2, 3, US, Arg, 2005 It, E, F, W, 2006 It, F, W, S, E, NZ1, 2, A1, SA, A2, PI, 2007 W, E, S1, It1, S2, [Nm, Gg, F, Arg], 2008 It, F, S, W, NZ1, A, C, NZ2, Arg, 2009 F, It, E, S, W, A, Fj, SA, 2010 It, F, E(R), W(R), S(R), NZ1, A, SA, Sm, NZ2(R), Arg(R), 2011 It(R), F1(R), S1, W, E1(R), F2, 3(R), E2, [US(R), A(R), Ru, It, W], 2012 W(R), It(R), F(R), S(R), E(R), NZ 1(R), 2(R), 3(R), SA(R), Arg(R), 2013 E(R), S(R)

O'Grady, D (Sale) 1997 It 2

O'Driscoll, B J (Manchester) 1971 F (R), E, S, W

O'Driscoll, J B (London Irish, Manchester) 1978 S, 1979 A 1, 2, 1980 E, S, F, W, 1981 F, W, E, S, SA 1, 2, A, 1982 W, E, S, F, 1983 S, F, W, E, 1984 F, W, E, S

O'Driscoll, M R (Cork Const, Munster) 2001 R (R), 2002 Fj (R), 2005 R(R), 2006 W(R), NZ1(R), 2(R), A1(R), 2007 E(R), It1, Arg1(t&R), 2, 2008 It(R), F(R), S, E(R), 2009 C, US, 2010 NZ1, A, SA, NZ2, Arg, 2011 S2(R)

O'Flanagan, K P (London Irish) 1947 A

O'Flanagan, M (Lansdowne) 1948 S

O'Gara, R J R (Cork Const, Munster) 2000 S, It, F, W, Arg (R), US, C (R), J, SA, 2001 It, F, S, W (R), E (R), Sm, 2002 W (R), E (R), S (R), It (t), F (R), NZ 1, 2, R, Ru, Gg, A, Arg, 2003 W 1(R), E (R), A (t+R), Tg, Sm, S 2, [R(R), Nm, Arg(R), A, F], 2004 F, W, E, It, S, SA1, 2, 3, Arg, 2005 It, S, E, F, W, NZ, A, R(R), 2006 It, F, W, S, E, NZ1, 2, A1, SA, A2, PI(R), 2007 W, F, E, S1, It1, S2(R), It2, [Nm, Gg, F, Arg], 2008 It, F, S, W, E, NZ1, A, C, NZ2, Arg, 2009 F, It, E, S, W, A, 2010 It, F, E(R), W(R), S(R), NZ1, A, SA, NZ2(R), Arg(R), 2011 It(R), F1(R), S1, W, E1(R), F2, 3(R), E2, [US(R), A(R), Ru, It, W], 2012 W(R), It(R), F(R), S(R), E(R), NZ 1(R), 2(R), 3(R), SA(R), Arg(R), 2013 E(R), S(R)

O'Hanlon, B (Dolphin) 1947 E, S, W, 1948 F, E, S, W, 1949 F, E, S, W, 1950 F

O'Hara, P T J (Sunday's Well, Cork Const) 1988 WS (R), 1989 F, W, E, NZ, 1990 E, S, F, W, 1991 Nm 1, [J], 1993 F, W, E, 1994 US

O'Kelly, M E (London Irish, St Mary's Coll, Leinster) 1997 NZ, C, It 2, 1998 S, F, W, E, SA 1, 2, Gg, R, SA 3, 1999 A 1(R), 2, Arg 1(R), [US (R, A 3, R, Arg 2], 2000 E, S, It, F, W, Arg, US, J, SA, 2001 It, F, S, W, E, NZ, 2002 E, S, It, F, NZ 1(R), 2, R, Ru, Gg, A, Fj, Arg, 2003 S 1, It 1, F, W 1, E, A, W 2 S 2, [R, Nm, Arg, A, F], 2004 F, W(R), E, It, S, SA1, 2, 3, Arg, 2005 It, S, E, F, W, NZ, A, 2006 It, F, W, S, E, SA(R), A2(R), PI, 2007 Arg1, 2(R), S2, It2(R), [F(R), Arg(R)], 2008 It, F, 2009 It(R)

Olding, S (Ulster) 2013 US, 2014 Gg(R)

O'Leary, A (Cork Constitution) 1952 S, W, E

O'Leary, T G (Munster) 2007 Arg1(R), 2008 NZ2, Arg, 2009 F, It, E, S(R), W, A, Fj(R), SA, 2010 It, F, E, W, S, NZ1, A, 2011 It, F1, S2, F3, 2012 S(R), E(R)

O'Loughlin, D B (UC Cork) 1938 E, S, W, 1939 E, S, W

O'Mahony, David (Cork Constitution) 1995 It

O'Mahony, D W (UC Dublin, Moseley, Bedford) 1995 It, [F], 1997 It 2, 1998 R

O'Mahony, P J (Munster) 2012 It(R), F(R), S, E(R), NZ 1, 2(R), 3, SA, Arg, 2013 W, E, S, F, It, US, C, Sm, A, NZ, 2014 S, W, E, F, SA, A, 2015 It, F, E 1, W 1, S 1, W 3, E 2, [C, It, F]

O'Meara, B T (Cork Constitution) 1997 E (R), S, NZ (R), 1998 S, 1999 [US (R), A (R)], 2001 It (R), 2003 Sm (R), It 2(R)

O'Meara, J A (UC Cork, Dolphin) 1951 F, E, S, W, SA, 1952 F, S, W, E, 1953 F, E, S, W, 1954 NZ, F, E, S, 1955 F, E, 1956 S, W, 1958 W

O'Neill, H O'H (Queen's U, Belfast, UC Cork) 1930 E, S, W, 1933 E, S, W

O'Neill, J B (Queen's U, Belfast) 1920 S

O'Neill, W A (UC Dublin, Wanderers) 1952 E, 1953 F, E, S, W, 1954 NZ

O'Reilly, A J F (Old Belvedere, Leicester) 1955 F, E, S, W, 1956 F, E, S, W, 1957 F, E, S, W, 1958 A, E, S, W, F, 1959 E, S, W, F, 1960 E, 1961 E, F, SA, 1963 F, S, W, 1970 E

Orr, P A (Old Wesley) 1976 F, W, E, S, NZ, 1977 W, E, S, F, 1978 S, F, W, E, NZ, 1979 F, W, E, S, A 1, 2, 1980 E, S, F, W, 1981 F, W, E, S, SA 1, 2, A, 1982 W, E, S, F, 1983 S, F, W, E, 1984 F, W, E, S, A, 1985 S, F, W, E, 1986 F, S, R, 1987 E, S, F, W, [W, C, A]

O'Shea, C M P (Lansdowne, London Irish) 1993 R, 1994 F, W, E, S, A 1, 2, US, 1995 E, S, [J, W, F], 1997 It 1, F, S (R), 1998 S, F, SA 1, 2, Gg, R, SA 3, 1999 F, W, E, S, It, A 1, Arg 1, [US, A 3, R, Arg 2], 2000 E

O'Sullivan, A C (Dublin U) 1882 S

O'Sullivan, J M (Limerick) 1884 S, 1887 S

O'Sullivan, P J A (Galwegians) 1957 F, E, S, W, 1959 E, S, W, F, 1960 SA, 1961 E, S, 1962 F, W, 1963 F, NZ

O'Sullivan, W (Queen's Coll, Cork) 1895 S

Owens, R H (Dublin U) 1922 E, S

Parfrey, P (UC Cork) 1974 NZ

Parke, J C (Monkstown) 1903 W, 1904 E, S, W, 1905 W, NZ, 1906 E, S, W, SA, 1907 E, S, W, 1908 E, S, W, 1909 E, S, W, F

Parr, J S (Wanderers) 1914 F, E, S, W

Patterson, C S (Instonians) 1978 NZ, 1979 F, W, E, S, A 1, 2, 1980 E, S, F, W

Patterson, R d'A (Wanderers) 1912 F, S, W, SA, 1913 E, S, W, F

Payne, C T (NIFC) 1926 F, 1927 F, E, S, A, 1928 F, E, S, W, 1929 F, E, W, 1930 F, E, S, W

Payne, J B (Ulster) 2014 SA, 2015 It, F, E 1, W 1, S 1, 2, E 2, [C, R]

Pedlow, A C (CIYMS) 1953 W, 1954 NZ, F, E, 1955 F, E, S, W, 1956 F, E, S, W, 1957 F, E, S, W, 1958 A, E, S, W, F, 1959 F, E, S, W, 1960 F, E, S, W, 1961 SA, W, 1962 W, 1963 F

Pedlow, J (Bessbrook) 1882 S, 1884 W

Pedlow, R (Bessbrook) 1891 W

Pedlow, T B (Queen's Coll, Belfast) 1889 S, W

Peel, T (Limerick) 1892 E, S, W

Peirce, W (Cork) 1881 E

Phipps, G C (Army) 1950 E, W, 1952 F, W, E

Pike, T O (Lansdowne) 1927 E, S, W, A, 1928 F, E, S, W
Pike, V J (Lansdowne) 1931 E, S, W, SA, 1932 E, S, W, 1933 E, W, S, 1934 E, S, W
Pike, W W (Kingstown) 1879 E, 1881 E, S, 1882 E, 1883 S
Pinion, G (Belfast Collegians) 1909 E, S, W, F
Piper, O J S (Cork Constitution) 1909 E, S, W, F, 1910 E, S, W, F
Polden, S E (Clontarf) 1913 W, F, 1914 F, 1920 F
Popham, I (Cork Constitution) 1922 S, W, F, 1923 F
Popplewell, N J (Greystones, Wasps, Newcastle) 1989 NZ, 1990 Arg, 1991 Nm 1, 2, [Z, S, A], 1992 W, E, S, F, NZ 1, 2, A, 1993 S, F, W, E, R, 1994 F, W, E, S, US, 1995 E, S, F, W, It, [NZ, J, W, F], Fj, 1996 US, S, F, W, E, A, 1997 It 1, F, W, E, NZ, C, 1998 S (t), F (R)
Potterton, H N (Wanderers) 1920 W
Pratt, R H (Dublin U) 1933 E, W, S, 1934 E, S
Price, A H (Dublin U) 1920 S, F
Pringle, J C (NIFC) 1902 S, W
Purcell, N M (Lansdowne) 1921 E, S, W, F
Purdon, H (NIFC) 1879 S, E, 1880 E, 1881 E, S
Purdon, W B (Queen's Coll, Belfast) 1906 E, S, W
Purser, F C (Dublin U) 1898 E, S, W

Quinlan, A N (Shannon, Munster) 1999 [R (R)], 2001 It, F, 2002 NZ 2(R), Ru (R), Gg (R), A (R), Fj, Arg (R), 2003 S 1(R), It 1(R), F (R), W 1, E (R), A, W 2, [R(R), Nm, Arg], 2004 SA1(R), 2(R), 2005 J1, 2(t&R), 2007 Arg2, S2(t&R), 2008 C(R), NZ2
Quinlan, D P (Northampton) 2005 J1(R), 2
Quinlan, S V J (Blackrock Coll) 1956 F, E, W, 1958 W
Quinn, B T (Old Belvedere) 1947 F
Quinn, F P (Old Belvedere) 1981 F, W, E
Quinn, J P (Dublin U) 1910 E, S, 1911 E, S, W, F, 1912 E, S, W, 1913 E, W, F, 1914 F, E, S
Quinn, K (Old Belvedere) 1947 F, A, 1953 F, E, S
Quinn, M A M (Lansdowne) 1973 F, 1974 F, W, E, S, P, NZ, 1977 S, F, 1981 SA 2
Quirke, J M T (Blackrock Coll) 1962 E, S, 1968 S

Rainey, P I (Ballymena) 1989 NZ
Rambaut, D F (Dublin U) 1887 E, S, W, 1888 W
Rea, H H (Edinburgh U) 1967 A 1, 1969 F
Read, H M (Dublin U) 1910 E, S, 1911 E, S, W, F, 1912 F, E, S, W, SA, 1913 E, S
Reardon, J V (Cork Constitution) 1934 E, S
Reddan, E G (Wasps, Leinster) 2006 F(R), 2007 Arg2, S2(R), [F, Arg], 2008 It, F, S, W, E, NZ1, A(R), C, NZ2(R), 2009 C(R), US(R), Fj, 2010 It(R), F(R), W(R), NZ1(R), SA, NZ2, Arg(R), 2011 It(R), F1(R), S1, W, E1, F2, 3(R), E2, [US(R), A, Ru(R), It(R), W(R)], 2012 W(R), It(R), F(R), S, E, NZ 1(R), 2(R), 3(R), SA(R), Arg(R), 2013 W(R), S(R), F(R), Sm(R), A, 2014 It(R), F(R), Arg 2, SA(R), Gg, A(t&R), 2015 W 1(R), W 2, S 2(R), W 3(R), E 2(R), [C(R), It, F(R), Arg(R)]
Reid, C (NIFC) 1899 S, W, 1900 E, 1903 W
Reid, J L (Richmond) 1934 S, W
Reid, N (Leinster) 2014 Arg 2(R)
Reid, P J (Garryowen) 1947 A, 1948 F, E, W
Reid, T E (Garryowen) 1953 E, S, W, 1954 NZ, 1955 E, S, 1956 F, E, 1957 F, E, S, W
Reidy, C J (London Irish) 1937 W
Reidy, G F (Dolphin, Lansdowne) 1953 W, 1954 F, E, S, W
Richey, H A (Dublin U) 1889 W, 1890 S
Ridgeway, E C (Wanderers) 1932 S, W, 1935 E, S, W
Rigney, B J (Greystones) 1991 F, W, E, S, Nm 1, 1992 F, NZ 1(R), 2
Ringland, T M (Queen's U, Belfast, Ballymena) 1981 A, 1982 W, E, F, 1983 S, F, W, E, 1984 F, W, E, S, A, 1985 S, F, W, E, 1986 F, W, E, S, R, 1987 E, S, F, W, [W, C, Tg, A], 1988 S, F, W, E 1
Riordan, W F (Cork Constitution) 1910 E
Ritchie, J S (London Irish) 1956 F, E
Robb, C G (Queen's Coll, Belfast) 1904 E, S, W, 1905 NZ, 1906 S
Robbie, J C (Dublin U, Greystones) 1976 A, F, NZ, 1977 S, F, 1981 W, E, S
Robinson, B F (Ballymena, London Irish) 1991 F, W, E, S, Nm 1, 2, [Z, S, A], 1992 W, E, S, F, NZ 1, 2, A, 1993 W, E, R, 1994 F, W, E, S, A 1, 2

Robinson, T T H (Wanderers) 1904 E, S, 1905 E, S, W, NZ, 1906 SA, 1907 E, S, W
Roche, J (Wanderers) 1890 S, W, E, 1891 E, S, W, 1892 W
Roche, R E (UC Galway) 1955 E, S, 1957 S, W
Roche, W J (UC Cork) 1920 E, S, F
Roddy, P J (Bective Rangers) 1920 S, F
Roe, R (Lansdowne) 1952 E, 1953 F, E, S, W, 1954 F, E, S, W, 1955 F, E, S, W, 1956 F, E, S, W, 1957 F, E, S, W
Rolland, A C (Blackrock Coll) 1990 Arg, 1994 US (R), 1995 It (R)
Ronan, N (Munster) 2009 C, US, 2010 A, 2011 S2
Rooke, C V (Dublin U) 1891 E, W, 1892 E, S, W, 1893 E, S, W, 1894 E, S, W, 1895 E, S, W, 1896 E, S, W, 1897 E, S
Ross, D J (Belfast Albion) 1884 E, 1885 S 1, 2, 1886 E, S
Ross, G R P (CIYMS) 1955 W
Ross, J F (NIFC) 1886 S
Ross, J P (Lansdowne, NIFC) 1885 E, S 1, 2, 1886 E, S
Ross, M R (Harlequins, Leinster) 2009 C(R), US, 2011 It, F1, S1, W, E1, F2, 3, E2, [US, A, Ru(R), It, W], 2012 W, It, F, S, E, NZ 2, 3, SA, Arg, 2013 W, E, S, F, It, US, C, Sm, A, NZ, 2014 S, W, E, It, F, Arg 1, 2, SA, Gg, A, 2015 It, F, E 1, W 1, S 1, W 2, S 2, E 2, [C, It, F, Arg]
Ross, N G (Malone) 1927 F, E
Ross, W McC (Queen's U, Belfast) 1932 E, S, W, 1933 E, W, S, 1934 E, S, 1935 NZ
Ruddock, R J (Leinster) 2010 A(R), 2014 It(R), Arg 2 , SA, A, 2015 [Arg(R)]
Russell, J (UC Cork) 1931 F, E, S, W, SA, 1933 E, W, S, 1934 E, S, W, 1935 E, S, W, 1936 E, S, W, 1937 E, S
Russell, P (Instonians) 1990 E, 1992 NZ 1, 2, A
Rutherford, W G (Tipperary, Lansdowne) 1884 E, S, 1885 E, S 1, 1886 E, 1888 W
Ryan, D C (Leinster) 2014 Gg
Ryan, D C (Munster) 2008 Arg(R), 2009 C(R), US(R), 2010 It(R), F(R), SA(R), Sm(R), 2011 S2, F2, E2(R), [Ru, It(R), W(R)], 2012 W(R), It(R), F(R), S, E, NZ 1, 2, 3, SA, Arg, 2013 W, E, S, F, It, 2015 W 2, 3(R), E 2(R), [C(R), R, Arg(R)]
Ryan, E (Dolphin) 1937 W, 1938 E, S
Ryan, J (Rockwell Coll) 1897 E, 1898 E, S, W, 1899 E, S, W, 1900 S, W, 1901 E, S, W, 1902 E, 1904 E
Ryan, J G (UC Dublin) 1939 E, S, W
Ryan, M (Rockwell Coll) 1897 E, S, 1898 F, S, W, 1899 F, S, W, 1900 E, S, W, 1901 E, S, W, 1903 E, 1904 E, S

Saunders, R (London Irish) 1991 F, W, E, S, Nm 1, 2, [Z, J, S, A], 1992 W, 1994 F (t)
Saverimutto, C (Sale) 1995 Fj, 1996 US, S
Sayers, H J M (Lansdowne) 1935 E, S, W, 1936 E, S, W, 1938 W, 1939 E, S, W
Scally, C J (U C Dublin) 1998 Gg (R), R, 1999 S (R), It
Schute, F (Wanderers) 1878 E, 1879 E
Schute, F G (Dublin U) 1912 SA, 1913 E, S
Scott, D (Malone) 1961 F, SA, 1962 S
Scott, R D (Queen's U, Belfast) 1967 E, F, 1968 F, E, S
Scovell, R H (Kingstown) 1883 E, 1884 E
Scriven, G (Dublin U) 1879 S, E, 1880 E, S, 1881 E, 1882 S, 1883 E, S
Sealy, J (Dublin U) 1896 E, S, W, 1897 S, 1899 E, S, W, 1900 E, S
Sexton, J F (Dublin U, Lansdowne) 1988 E 2, WS, It, 1989 F
Sexton, J J (Leinster, Racing Métro) 2009 Fj, SA, 2010 F(R), E, W, S, NZ1(R), A, SA, NZ2, Arg, 2011 It, F1, S1(R), W(R), E1, S2, F3, E2(R), [US, A, Ru(R), It(R), W(R)], 2012 W, It, F, S, E, NZ 1, 2, 3, SA, Arg, 2013 W, E, A, NZ, 2014 S, W, E, It, F, Arg 1, 2, SA, A, 2015 F E 1, W 1, S 1, W 3, E 2, [C, It, F]
Sexton, W J (Garryowen) 1984 A, 1988 S, E 2
Shanahan, T (Lansdowne) 1885 E, S 1, 2, 1886 E, 1888 S, W
Shaw, G M (Windsor) 1877 S
Sheahan, F J (Cork Const, Munster) 2000 US (R), 2001 It (R), R, W (R), Sm, 2002 W, E, S, Gg (R), A (t+R), Fj, 2003 S 1(R), It 1(R), 2004 F(R), W(R), It(R), S(R), SA1(R), US, 2005 It(R), S(R), W(R), J1, 2, 2006 SA(R), A2(R), PI, 2007 Arg2, [F(t&R)]
Sheehan, M D (London Irish) 1932 E
Sherry, B F (Terenure Coll) 1967 A 1, E, S, A 2, 1968 F, E
Sherry, M (Munster) 2013 US(R)

Sherry, M J A (Lansdowne) 1975 F, W

Shields, P M (Ballymena) 2003 Sm (R), It 2(R)

Siggins, J A E (Belfast Collegians) 1931 F, E, S, W, SA, 1932 E, S, W, 1933 E, W, S, 1934 E, S, W, 1935 E, S, W, NZ, 1936 E, S, W, 1937 E, S, W

Slattery, J F (UC Dublin, Blackrock Coll) 1970 SA, F, E, S, W, 1971 F, E, S, W, 1972 F 1, E, F 2, 1973 NZ, E, S, W, F, 1974 F, W, E, S, P, NZ, 1975 E, S, F, W, 1976 A, 1977 S, F, 1978 S, F, W, E, NZ, 1979 F, W, E, S, A 1, 2, 1980 E, S, F, W, 1981 F, W, E, S, SA 1, 2, A, 1982 W, E, S, F, 1983 S, F, W, E, 1984 F

Smartt, F N B (Dublin U) 1908 E, S, 1909 E

Smith, B A (Oxford U, Leicester) 1989 NZ, 1990 S, F, W, Arg, 1991 F, W, E, S

Smith, J H (London Irish) 1951 F, E, S, W, SA, 1952 F, S, W, E, 1954 NZ, W, F

Smith, R E (Lansdowne) 1892 E

Smith, S J (Ballymena) 1988 E 2, WS, It, 1989 F, W, E, S, NZ, 1990 E, 1991 F, W, E, S, Nm 1, 2, [Z, S, A], 1992 W, E, S, F, NZ 1, 2, 1993 S

Smithwick, F F S (Monkstown) 1898 S, W

Smyth, J T (Queen's U, Belfast) 1920 F

Smyth, P J (Belfast Collegians) 1911 E, S, F

Smyth, R S (Dublin U) 1903 E, S, 1904 E

Smyth, T (Malone, Newport) 1908 E, S, W, 1909 E, S, W, 1910 E, S, W, F, 1911 E, S, W, 1912 E

Smyth, W S (Belfast Collegians) 1910 W, F, 1920 E

Solomons, B A H (Dublin U) 1908 E, S, W, 1909 E, S, W, F, 1910 E, S, W

Spain, A W (UC Dublin) 1924 NZ

Sparrow, W (Dublin U) 1893 W, 1894 E

Spillane, B J (Bohemians) 1985 S, F, W, E, 1986 F, W, E, 1987 F, W, [W, C, A (R)], 1989 E (R)

Spring, D E (Dublin U) 1978 S, NZ, 1979 S, 1980 S, F, W, 1981 W

Spring, R M (Lansdowne) 1979 F, W, E

Spunner, H F (Wanderers) 1881 E, S, 1884 W

Stack, C R R (Dublin U) 1889 S

Stack, G H (Dublin U) 1875 E

Staples, J E (London Irish, Harlequins) 1991 W, E, S, Nm 1, 2, [Z, J, S, A], 1992 W, E, NZ 1, 2, A, 1995 F, W, It, [NZ], Fj, 1996 US, S, F, A, 1997 W, E, S

Staunton, J W (Garryowen, Wasps) 2001 Sm, 2005 J1(R), 2(R), 2006 A1(R), 2007 Arg2

Steele, H W (Ballymena) 1976 E, 1977 F, 1978 F, W, E, 1979 F, W, E, A 1, 2

Stephenson, G V (Queen's U, Belfast, London Hosp) 1920 F, 1921 E, S, W, F, 1922 E, S, W, F, 1923 E, S, W, F, 1924 F, E, S, W, NZ, 1925 F, E, S, W, 1926 F, E, S, W, 1927 F, E, S, W, A, 1928 F, E, S, W, 1929 F, E, W, 1930 F, E, S, W

Stephenson, H W V (United Services) 1922 S, W, F, 1924 F, E, S, W, NZ, 1925 F, E, S, W, 1927 A, 1928 E

Stevenson, J (Dungannon) 1888 M, 1889 S

Stevenson, J B (Instonians) 1958 A, E, S, W, F

Stevenson, R (Dungannon) 1887 E, S, W, 1888 M, 1889 S, W, 1890 S, W, E, 1891 W, 1892 W, 1893 E, S, W

Stevenson, T H (Belfast Acad) 1895 E, 1896 E, S, W, 1897 E, S

Stewart, A L (NIFC) 1913 W, F, 1914 F

Stewart, J W (Queen's U, Belfast, NIFC) 1922 F, 1924 S, 1928 F, E, S, W, 1929 F, E, S, W

Stoker, E W (Wanderers) 1888 W, S

Stoker, F O (Wanderers) 1886 S, 1888 W, M, 1889 S, 1891 W

Stokes, O S (Cork Bankers) 1882 E, 1884 E

Stokes, P (Garryowen) 1913 E, S, 1914 F, 1920 E, S, W, F, 1921 E, S, F, 1922 W, F

Stokes, R D (Queen's Coll, Cork) 1891 S, W

Strathdee, E (Queen's U, Belfast) 1947 E, S, W, A, 1948 W, F, 1949 E, S, W

Strauss, C R (Leinster) 2012 SA, Arg, 2013 US, C , 2014 SA(R), Gg, 2015 W 2, S 2(R), W 3, E 2(R), [R, F(R), Arg(R)]

Stringer, P A (Shannon, Munster) 2000 S, It, F, W, Arg, C, J, SA, 2001 It, F, R, S (R), W, E, Sm, NZ, 2002 W, E, S, It, F, NZ 1, 2, R, Ru, Gg, A, Arg, 2003 S 1, It 1, F, W 1, E, A, W 2, S 2, [R, Nm, Arg, A, F], 2004 F, W, E, It, S, SA1, 2, 3, US(R), Arg, 2005 It, S, E, F, W, J1, 2, NZ, A, R(R), 2006 It, F, W, S, E, NZ1, 2, A1, SA, A2(R), PI, 2007 W, E, S1,

It1, 2, [Nm, Gg], 2008 It(R), S(R), E(R), NZ1(R), A, C(R), 2009 It(t&R), E(R), S, W(R), C, US, 2010 SA(R), Sm, NZ2(R), Arg, 2011 S1(R), W(R), E1(R)

Stuart, C P (Clontarf) 1912 SA

Stuart, I M B (Dublin U) 1924 E, S

Sugars, H S (Dublin U) 1905 NZ, 1906 SA, 1907 S

Sugden, M (Wanderers) 1925 F, E, S, W, 1926 F, E, S, W, 1927 E, S, W, A, 1928 F, E, S, W, 1929 F, E, S, W, 1930 F, E, S, W, 1931 F, E, S, W

Sullivan, D B (UC Dublin) 1922 E, S, W, F

Sweeney, J A (Blackrock Coll) 1907 E, S, W

Symes, G R (Monkstown) 1895 E

Synge, J S (Lansdowne) 1929 S

Taggart, T (Dublin U) 1887 W

Taylor, A S (Queen's Coll, Belfast) 1910 E, S, W, 1912 F

Taylor, D R (Queen's Coll, Belfast) 1903 E

Taylor, J (Belfast Collegians) 1914 E, S, W

Taylor, J W (NIFC) 1879 S, 1880 E, S, 1881 S, 1882 E, S, 1883 E, S

Tector, W R (Wanderers) 1955 F, E, S

Tedford, A (Malone) 1902 E, S, W, 1903 E, S, W, 1904 E, S, W, 1905 E, S, W, NZ, 1906 E, S, W, SA, 1907 E, S, W, 1908 E, S, W

Teehan, C (UC Cork) 1939 E, S, W

Thompson, C (Belfast Collegians) 1907 E, S, 1908 E, S, W, 1909 E, S, W, F, 1910 E, S, W, F

Thompson, J A (Queen's Coll, Belfast) 1885 S 1, 2

Thompson, J K S (Dublin U) 1921 W, 1922 E, S, F, 1923 E, S, W, F

Thompson, R G (Lansdowne) 1882 W

Thompson, R H (Instonians) 1951 SA, 1952 F, 1954 NZ, F, E, S, W, 1955 F, S, W, 1956 W

Thornhill, T (Wanderers) 1892 E, S, W, 1893 E

Thrift, H (Dublin U) 1904 W, 1905 E, S, W, NZ, 1906 E, W, SA, 1907 E, S, W, 1908 E, S, W, 1909 E, S, W, F

Tierney, D (UC Cork) 1938 S, W, 1939 E

Tierney, T A (Garryowen) 1999 A 1, 2, Arg 1, [US, A 3, R, Arg 2], 2000 E

Tillie, C R (Dublin U) 1887 E, S, 1888 W, S

Todd, A W P (Dublin U) 1913 W, F, 1914 F

Toner, D A (Leinster) 2010 Sm, NZ2(R), Arg(R), 2013 S(R), It(R), US, C, Sm, A, NZ, 2014 S, W, E, It, F, Arg 1(R), 2, SA, Gg(R), A, 2015 It, F, E 1, W 1, S 1, 2, E 2, [R, It(R), F, Arg]

Topping, J A (Ballymena) 1996 WS, A, 1997 It 1, F, E, 1999 [R], 2000 US, 2003 A

Torrens, J D (Bohemians) 1938 W, 1939 E, S, W

Trimble, A D (Ulster) 2005 A, R, 2006 F(R), W, S, E, NZ1, 2, A1, SA, 2007 W, F(R), E(R), It1(R), Arg1, S2(R), It2, [Nm, F], 2008 It, F, S, W, E, 2009 Fj(R), 2010 It, E(R), NZ1, A, Sm, Arg, 2011 E1, S2, F2, 3, E2, [US(R), A(t&R), Ru, It(R), , W(R)], 2012 W, It, F, S, E, NZ 2, 3(t&R), SA, 2013 C, 2014 S, W, E, It, F, Arg 1, 2 , 2015 W 2

Tucker, C C (Shannon) 1979 F, W, 1980 F (R)

Tuke, B B (Bective Rangers) 1890 E, 1891 F, S, 1892 E, 1894 E, S, W, 1895 E, S

Tuohy, D M (Ulster) 2010 NZ1(R), A(t&R), 2012 NZ 1, 2, 3, 2013 US(R), C, 2014 S, W(R), 2015 W 2(R), S 2

Turley, N (Blackrock Coll) 1962 E

Tweed, D A (Ballymena) 1995 F, W, It, [J]

Tydings, J J (Young Munster) 1968 A

Tyrrell, W (Queen's U, Belfast) 1910 F, 1913 E, S, W, F, 1914 F, E, S, W

Uprichard, R J H (Harlequins, RAF) 1950 S, W

Varley, D A (Munster) 2010 A(R), Arg(R), 2014 Arg 1(R)

Waide, S L (Oxford U, NIFC) 1932 E, S, W, 1933 E, W

Waites, J (Bective Rangers) 1886 S, 1888 M, 1889 W, 1890 S, W, E, 1891 E

Waldron, O C (Oxford U, London Irish) 1966 S, W, 1968 A

Walker, S (Instonians) 1934 S, W, 1935 E, S, W, NZ, 1936 E, S, W, 1937 E, S, W, 1938 E, S, W

Walkington, D B (NIFC) 1887 E, W, 1888 W, 1890 W, E, 1891 E, S, W

Walkington, R B (NIFC) 1875 E, 1876 E, 1877 E, S, 1878 E, 1879 S, 1880 E, S, 1882 E, S

Wall, H (Dolphin) 1965 S, W

Wallace, D P (Garryowen, Munster) 2000 Arg, US, 2001 It, F, R (R), S (R), W, E, NZ, 2002 W, E, S, It, F, 2003 Tg (R), Sm (R), W 2(t+R), S 2, 2004 S, SA1, 2, 2005 J2, 2006 It, F, W, S, E, NZ1, 2, A1, SA, A2, 2007 W, F, E, S1, It1, [Nm, Gg, F, Arg], 2008 It, F, S, W, E, NZ1, C(R), NZ2, Arg, 2009 F, It, E, S, W, A, SA, 2010 It, F, E, W, S, NZ1, SA, NZ2, Arg, 2011 It, F1, S1, W, E1, 2

Wallace, Jas (Wanderers) 1904 E, S

Wallace, Jos (Wanderers) 1903 S, W, 1904 E, S, W, 1905 E, S, W, NZ, 1906 W

Wallace, P R (Ulster) 2006 SA(R), PI, 2007 E(R), Arg1, S2, [Nm(R)], 2008 S(R), E(R), NZ1, A, C(R), NZ2(R), 2009 F, It, E, W(R), A, FJ(R), SA, 2010 It(R), F(t&R), A, Sm, 2011 It(R), W(R), E1(R), S2, F2, [Ru], 2012 NZ 3

Wallace, P S (Blackrock Coll, Saracens) 1995 [J], Fj, 1996 US, W, E, WS, A, 1997 It 1, F, W, E, S, NZ, C, 1998 S, F, W, E, SA 1, 2, Gg, R, 1999 F, W, E, S, It (R), 1999 A 1, 2, Arg 1, [US, A 3, R, Arg 2], 2000 E, US, C (R), 2002 W (R), E (R), S (R), It (R), F (R), NZ 2(R), Ru (R), Gg (R)

Wallace, R M (Garryowen, Saracens) 1991 Nm 1(R), 1992 W, E, S, F, A, 1993 S, F, W, E, R, 1994 F, W, E, S, 1995 W, It, [NZ, J, W], Fj, 1996 US, S, F, WS, 1998 S, F, W, E

Wallace, T H (Cardiff) 1920 E, S, W

Wallis, A K (Wanderers) 1892 E, S, W, 1893 E, W

Wallis, C O'N (Old Cranleighans, Wanderers) 1935 NZ

Wallis, T G (Wanderers) 1921 F, 1922 E, S, W, F

Wallis, W A (Wanderers) 1880 S, 1881 E, S, 1882 W, 1883 S

Walmsley, G (Bective Rangers) 1894 E

Walpole, A (Dublin U) 1888 S, M

Walsh, E J (Lansdowne) 1887 E, S, W, 1892 E, S, W, 1893 E

Walsh, H D (Dublin U) 1875 E, 1876 E

Walsh, J C (UC Cork, Sunday's Well) 1960 S, SA, 1961 E, S, F, SA, 1963 E, S, W, NZ, 1964 E, S, W, F, 1965 F, S, W, SA, 1966 F, S, W, 1967 E, S, W, F, A 2

Ward, A J (Ballynahinch) 1998 F, W, E, SA 1, 2, Gg, R, SA 3, 1999 W, E, S, It (R), A 1, 2, Arg 1, [US, A 3, R, Arg] 2000 F (R), W (t&R), Arg (R), US (R), C, J, SA (R), 2001 It (R), F (R)

Ward, A J P (Garryowen, St Mary's Coll, Greystones) 1978 S, F, W, E, NZ, 1979 F, W, E, S, 1981 W, E, S, A, 1983 E (R), 1984 E, S, 1986 S, 1987 [C, Tg]

Warren, J P (Kingstown) 1883 E

Warren, R G (Lansdowne) 1884 W, 1885 E, S 1, 2, 1886 E, 1887 E, S, W, 1888 W, S, M, 1889 S, W, 1890 S, W, E

Watson, R (Wanderers) 1912 SA

Wells, H G (Bective Rangers) 1891 S, W, 1894 E, S

Westby, A J (Dublin U) 1876 E

Wheeler, G H (Queen's Coll, Belfast) 1884 S, 1885 E

Wheeler, J R (Queen's U, Belfast) 1922 E, S, W, F, 1924 E

Whelan, P C (Garryowen) 1975 E, S, 1976 NZ, 1977 W, E, S, F, 1978 S, F, W, E, NZ, 1979 F, W, E, S, 1981 F, W, E

White, M (Queen's Coll, Cork) 1906 E, S, W, SA, 1907 E, W

White, N J (Connacht) 2015 S 2(R), W3, E 2(R), [C(R), R, It(R), F(R)]

Whitestone, A M (Dublin U) 1877 E, 1879 S, E, 1880 E, 1883 S

Whitten, I W (Ulster) 2009 C, US

Whittle, D (Bangor) 1988 F

Wilkinson, C R (Malone) 1993 S

Wilkinson, R W (Wanderers) 1947 A

Williamson, F W (Dolphin) 1930 E, S, W

Willis, J W W (Lansdowne) 1879 E

Wilson, F (CIYMS) 1977 W, E, S

Wilson, H G (Glasgow U, Malone) 1905 E, S, W, NZ, 1906 E, S, W, SA, 1907 E, S, W, 1908 E, S, W, 1909 E, S, W, 1910 W

Wilson, R G (Ulster) 2005 J1

Wilson, W H (Bray) 1877 E, S

Withers, H H C (Army, Blackheath) 1931 F, E, S, W, SA

Wolfe, E J (Armagh) 1882 E

Wood, G H (Dublin U) 1913 W, 1914 F

Wood, B G M (Garryowen) 1954 E, S, 1956 F, E, S, W, 1957 F, E, S, W, 1958 A, E, S, W, F, 1959 E, S, W, F, 1960 E, S, W, F, SA, 1961 E, S, W, F, SA

Wood, K G M (Garryowen, Harlequins) 1994 A 1, 2, US, 1995 E, S, [J], 1996 A, 1997 It 1, F, 1997 NZ, It 2, 1998 S, F, W, E, SA 1, 2, R (R), SA 3, 1999 F, W, E, S, It (R), A 1, 2, Arg 1, [US, A 3, R (R), Arg 2], 2000 E, S, It, F, W, Arg, US, C, J, SA, 2001 It, F, S, W, E, NZ, 2002 F NZ 1, 2, Ru, 2003 W 2, S 2, [R, Nm, Arg, A, F]

Woods, D C (Bessbrook) 1888 M, 1889 S

Woods, N K P J (Blackrock Coll, London Irish) 1994 A 1, 2, 1995 E, F, 1996 F, W, E, 1999 W

Wright, R A (Monkstown) 1912 S

Yeates, R A (Dublin U) 1889 S, W

Young, B G (Ulster) 2006 NZ2(R), A1(R), SA(R), A2, PI, 2007 Arg1, 2, S2

Young, G (UC Cork) 1913 E

Young, R M (Collegians) 1965 F, E, S, W, SA, 1966 F, E, S, W, 1967 W, F, 1968 W, A, 1969 F, E, S, W, 1970 SA, F, E, S, W, 1971 F, E, S, W

Zebo, S R (Munster) 2012 NZ 1, SA, Arg, 2013 W, E, US, 2014 Arg 1, 2, SA, Gg, A, 2015 It, F, E 1, W 1, 2(R), S 2, E 2, [C(R), R, It]

ITALY

ITALY'S 2014–15 TEST RECORD

OPPONENT	DATE	VENUE	RESULT
Samoa	8 Nov	H	Won 24–13
Argentina	14 Nov	H	Lost 18–20
South Africa	22 Nov	H	Lost 6–22
Ireland	7 Feb	H	Lost 3–26
England	14 Feb	A	Lost 47–17
Scotland	28 Feb	A	Won 22–19
France	15 Mar	H	Lost 0–29
Wales	21 Mar	H	Lost 20–61
Scotland	22 Aug	H	Lost 16–21
Scotland	29 Aug	A	Lost 48–7
Wales	5 Sep	A	Lost 23–19
France	19 Sep	N	Lost 32–10
Canada	26 Sep	N	Won 23–18
Ireland	4 Oct	N	Lost 16–9
Romania	11 Oct	N	Won 32–22

ITALY MISS A MASSIVE TARGET BUT WILL BOUNCE BACK

With Mauro Bergamasco

Getty Images

Italy flanker Mauro Bergamasco (right) played in his fifth and final Rugby World Cup in 2015 before retiring.

Italy had made no secret of their target for Rugby World Cup 2015 – reaching the quarter-finals for the first time. That would be no easy feat, given they would face Ireland and France in Pool D, but they had beaten both sides in the last two years and for a number of the players in the Italy squad it was now or never as they graced the stage for the last time.

One such player was Mauro Bergamasco, the flanker due to hang up his boots after playing in a record-equalling fifth Rugby World Cup. The 36-year-old played his first RWC match in England in 1999, so described 2015 as "a circle coming to its end" and believed it was "almost mystic, like giving real sense to the end of such an important chapter of my life."

Sadly for Bergamasco, it was not the fairy-tale ending that he had hoped for as Italy again fell short of their goal, having to settle for third place in Pool D after losing to both Ireland and France and beating the lower-ranked Canada and Romania, the only consolation being that they had secured automatic qualification for RWC 2019 in Japan.

Italy arrived in England with a record of seven defeats in eight matches in 2015, their only win being the last-gasp success against Scotland in the Six Nations. Two of those losses in the warm-up matches – against Scotland in Turin and Wales in Cardiff – had been by a single score, but a more painful pill to swallow was the loss of their talisman and captain Sergio Parisse after he underwent surgery for a haematoma in his calf and was ruled out of at least their opening match of RWC 2015 – against France at Twickenham on 19 September.

"There is no doubt that Sergio is an important player for us and his absence was obviously influential," admitted Bergamasco, who played for more than a decade alongside Parisse in the Italy back-row. "But we knew right from the start of the campaign that he was going to miss the France game and we worked even harder to face his absence."

Italy shaded possession and territory against France, but failed to turn that into points on the scoreboard as the boot of Frédéric Michalak and prop Rabah Slimani's try gave Les Bleus a commanding 25–3 lead early in the second half. Italy had not been helped by the loss of another key player early on, Andrea Masi suffering an Achilles tendon injury that would end his involvement in the tournament, but finally got on the board when winger Giovanbattista Venditti dotted down with 30 minutes to go. That was as close as Italy got though with France running out 32–10 winners to put a huge dent in the Azzurri's quarter-final aspirations.

"The first match against France was crucial, and it went wrong," said Bergamasco, who watched the defeat from the Twickenham stands. "We weren't at our best, we allowed our opponents to take the lead early in the game and when we realised that, it was too late.

"Lineouts and scrums didn't go as we expected and we paid for the lack of discipline. We gave away too many penalties and they were good enough in putting points on the board, creating a gap that was hard to fill."

A week later, Italy ran out against Canada at Elland Road desperate to bounce back to winning ways against a side ranked three places below them in the World Rugby Rankings. Canada, though, had other ideas and raced into a 10–0 lead early on. Italy fought back on that occasion, and again when Canada edged ahead 15–13, to hold firm and grind out a 23–18 victory, much to the relief of Bergamasco who had come off the bench and played a part in Gonzalo Garcia's try that gave the Azzurri a lead they would not relinquish.

"Canada played a clever, consistent game," admitted Bergamasco.

ITALY

"They are a physical side, with huge, skilled backs and their game-plan was brilliant. For almost an hour, we were in real trouble and full credit to them. Fortunately when our replacements came on things turned on the right side for us."

A welcome sight in the Italy camp in the build-up to the do-or-die match with Ireland was Parisse, proving a "huge boost to the team morale" as the squad sought to "push away all the negatives from the first two rounds and take our destiny in our own hands." The two old hands knew it was now or never if their quarter-final dreams were to remain a possibility, but despite an improved performance Italy slipped to a 16–9 loss in the cauldron of noise that was The Stadium, Queen Elizabeth Olympic Park on 4 October, three penalties by fly-half Tommaso Allan all they could manage. It may have been a different story had it not been for a superb try-saving tackle by Peter O'Mahony that denied Josh Furno in the second half, but Italy's quarter-final aspirations were nonetheless over.

"We made a good performance against Ireland, despite the final result, but it was not enough. At the highest level details count and Ireland were capable of building on the few mistakes that we made," said Bergamasco, a veteran of 106 tests between 1998 and 2015. "The atmosphere was great, though, the ideal stage for such a great clash."

That defeat would be Bergamasco's final appearance in the Azzurri blue as he was not selected against Romania, a decision he admits made him "angry and disappointed" but one he had to put to one side so as "to avoid distracting the team and having a bad influence on our preparation."

With Bergamasco and Parisse watching on from the stands in Exeter, Italy overcame a frustrating start and being pushed back 10 metres at the first scrum to gradually exert their dominance on their Romanian opponents with tries by winger Leonardo Sarto, scrum-half Edoardo Gori and his half-back partner Allan giving the Azzurri a commanding 22–3 lead at half-time. The try bonus point – Italy's first of the tournament – was wrapped up within minutes of the restart when number eight Alessandro Zanni powered over off the back of the scrum, the Azzurri's high-tempo play reaping the rewards after man of the match Gori and Francesco Minto had gone close to scoring. Romania gained a second wind with the introduction of their replacements and while they scored three tries in the final 15 minutes there was never a feeling that Italy would relinquish the victory and that qualification spot for RWC 2019.

As the retiring Bergamasco was thrown into the air by his team-mates afterwards and then carried shoulder-high around Sandy Park, attention was already turning to the next generation of players who will have to carry Italy forward and try to realise that first quarter-final in Japan. Italy may be losing some wise old heads like Bergamasco, but in the likes of Gori, Sarto, Furno, centre Michele Campagnaro and Luca Morisi – who missed RWC 2015 after damaging knee ligaments in their final warm-up match against Wales – they have a new generation of players who have already shown they can compete at the highest level.

"There are many interesting young players, some of them have already proved to be ready to compete on the international arena," admitted Bergmasco. "All of them must keep on improving and the ones who are currently playing overseas will have a further stimulus in competing in the best European championships. My suggestion to them is to keep working hard with the highest possible attention to detail."

With coach Jacques Brunel's contract coming to an end, a new man will be at the helm to guide these young players in the coming years and realise the potential that Bergamasco sees in Italian rugby.

"A generation of players is coming to an end, partially at least, so facing it will be the first challenge for the new coach. Whoever that new coach will be, knowing Italian rugby in depth, from the grassroots to the elite level, will be the first step to be successful. Italian rugby has qualities and chances to keep on growing, for me there is no doubt about that and I think that a long-term vision and strategy and more focus and spending on youth rugby will be crucial approaching Japan 2019.

"Rugby is now a totally different sport in Italy, both on and off the field, to what it was when I made my test debut. The Six Nations legacy is huge, competing on a yearly basis in such a big championship with great media exposure has brought huge benefits to the game in our country."

Bergamasco, though, will be in front of the television set when Italy play their next match, against France in Paris on 6 February, an excited fan happy to have realised one of his targets in England.

"I reflected a lot on all the steps which brought me to play in my fifth Rugby World Cup. It wasn't about setting a record, it was about reaching a personal goal, having fun on a rugby field once again which was probably something I missed during the 2011 edition. I'll always be thankful to my family, my closest friends and Zebre for helping me play high level rugby until I turned 36.

"To play in my fifth Rugby World Cup was one of the last goals I had from a personal point of view. It would have been great to be lined-up more frequently but that's not up to me. As a team, we missed a massive target and there will certainly be a review. But that part doesn't belong to me anymore, I'll be in front of the TV the next time Italy play."

ITALY

ITALY INTERNATIONAL STATISTICS

MATCH RECORDS UP TO 1 NOVEMBER, 2015

WINNING MARGIN

Date	Opponent	Result	Winning Margin
18/05/1994	Czech Republic	104–8	96
07/10/2006	Portugal	83–0	83
17/06/1993	Croatia	76–11	65
19/06/1993	Morocco	70–9	61
02/03/1996	Portugal	64–3	61

MOST POINTS IN A MATCH
BY THE TEAM

Date	Opponent	Result	Points
18/05/1994	Czech Republic	104–8	104
07/10/2006	Portugal	83–0	83
17/06/1993	Croatia	76–11	76
19/06/1993	Morocco	70–9	70
	67 on 2 occasions		

BY A PLAYER

Date	Player	Opponent	Points
10/11/2001	Diego Dominguez	Fiji	29
05/02/2000	Diego Dominguez	Scotland	29
01/07/1983	Stefano Bettarello	Canada	29
21/05/1994	Diego Dominguez	Netherlands	28
20/12/1997	Diego Dominguez	Ireland	27

MOST TRIES IN A MATCH
BY THE TEAM

Date	Opponent	Result	Tries
18/05/1994	Czech Republic	104–8	16
07/10/2006	Portugal	83–0	13
18/11/1998	Netherlands	67–7	11
17/06/1993	Croatia	76–11	11
	10 on 4 occasions		

BY A PLAYER

Date	Player	Opponent	Tries
19/06/1993	Ivan Francescato	Morocco	4
10/10/1937	Renzo Cova	Belgium	4
	3 on 14 occasions		

MOST CONVERSIONS IN A MATCH
BY THE TEAM

Date	Opponent	Result	Cons
18/05/1994	Czech Republic	104–8	12
19/06/1993	Morocco	70–9	10
17/06/1993	Croatia	76–11	9
07/10/2006	Portugal	83–0	9
	8 on 2 occasions		

BY A PLAYER

Date	Player	Opponent	Cons
18/05/1994	Luigi Troiani	Czech Republic	12
19/06/1993	Gabriel Filizzola	Morocco	10
17/06/1993	Luigi Troiani	Croatia	9
	8 on 3 occasions		

MOST PENALTIES IN A MATCH
BY THE TEAM

Date	Opponent	Result	Pens
01/10/1994	Romania	24–6	8
27/11/2010	Fiji	24–16	8
10/11/2001	Fiji	66–10	7
	6 on 11 occasions		

BY A PLAYER

Date	Player	Opponent	Pens
01/10/1994	Diego Dominguez	Romania	8
27/11/2010	Mirco Bergamasco	Fiji	8
10/11/2001	Diego Dominguez	Fiji	7
	6 on 10 occasions		

MOST DROP GOALS IN A MATCH
BY THE TEAM

Date	Opponent	Result	DGs
07/10/1990	Romania	29–21	3
05/02/2000	Scotland	34–20	3
11/07/1973	Transvaal	24–28	3

BY A PLAYER

Date	Player	Opponent	DGs
05/02/2000	Diego Dominguez	Scotland	3
11/07/1973	Rocco Caligiuri	Transvaal	3
	2 on 7 occasions		

THE COUNTRIES

MOST CAPPED PLAYERS	
Player	Caps
Martin Castrogiovanni	115
Sergio Parisse	114
Marco Bortolami	112
Mauro Bergamasco	106
Andrea Lo Cicero	103

LEADING PENALTY SCORERS	
Player	Pens
Diego Dominguez	209
Stefano Bettarello	106
Luigi Troiani	57
Ramiro Pez	52
Mirco Bergamasco	49

LEADING TRY SCORERS	
Player	Tries
Marcello Cuttitta	25
Paolo Vaccari	22
Manrico Marchetto	21
Carlo Checchinato	21
Alessandro Troncon	19

LEADING DROP GOAL SCORERS	
Player	DGs
Diego Dominguez	19
Stefano Bettarello	15
Ramiro Pez	6

LEADING POINTS SCORERS	
Player	Points
Diego Dominguez	983
Stefano Bettarello	483
Luigi Troiani	294
Ramiro Pez	260
Mirco Bergamasco	256

LEADING CONVERSIONS SCORERS	
Player	Cons
Diego Dominguez	127
Luigi Troiani	57
Stefano Bettarello	46
David Bortolussi	35
Ramiro Pez	33

ITALY

ITALY INTERNATIONAL PLAYERS
UP TO 1 NOVEMBER, 2015

E Abbiati 1968 *WGe*, 1970 *R*, 1971 *Mor, F*, 1972 *Pt, Sp, Sp, Yug*, 1973 *Pt, ETv*, 1974 *Leo*
A Agosti 1933 *Cze*
M Aguero 2005 *Tg, Ar, Fj*, 2006 *Fj*, 2007 *Ur, Ar, I, Pt*, 2008 *A, Ar, PI*, 2009 *A*, 2010 *I, E, S, F, W*, 2013 *SA, S, A, Fj, Ar*, 2014 *S, E, Fj, Sa, Sa, Ar, SA*, 2015 *I, E, S, F, S, S, W, F, C, I, R*
A Agujari 1967 *Pt*
E Aio 1974 *WGe*
G Aiolfi 1952 *Sp, Ger, F*, 1953 *F*, 1955 *Ger, F*
A Alacevich 1939 *R*
A Albonico 1934 *R*, 1935 *F*, 1936 *Ger, R*, 1937 *Ger, R, Bel, Ger, F*, 1938 *Cze*
N Aldorvandi 1994 *Sp, Cze, H*
M Alfonsetti 1994 *F*
T Allan 2013 *A, Fj, Ar*, 2014 *W, F, S, I, E, Sa, J*, 2015 *I, E, S, F, S, S, W, F, C, I, R*
E Allevi 1929 *Sp*, 1933 *Cze*
I Aloisio 1933 *Cze, Cze*, 1934 *Cat, R*, 1935 *Cat*, 1936 *Ger, R*
A Altigeri 1973 *Rho, WTv, Bor, NEC, Nat, Leo, FS, Tva, Cze, Yug, A*, 1974 *Pt, WGe*, 1975 *F, E, Pol, H, Sp*, 1976 *F, R, J*, 1978 *Ar, USS, Sp*, 1979 *F, Pol, R*
T Altissimi 1929 *Sp*
V Ambron 1962 *Ger, R*, 1963 *F*, 1964 *Ger, F*, 1965 *F, Cze*, 1966 *F, Ger, R*, 1967 *Pt, R*, 1968 *Pt, WGe, Yug*, 1969 *Bul, Sp, Bel*, 1970 *Mad, Mad, R*, 1971 *Mor*, 1972 *Sp, Sp*
R Ambrosio 1987 *NZ, USS, Sp*, 1988 *F, R, A, I*, 1989 *R, Sp, Ar, Z, USS*
B Ancillotti 1978 *Sp*, 1979 *F, Pol, R*
E Andina 1952 *F*, 1955 *F*

C Angelozzi 1979 *E, Mor*, 1980 *Coo*
A Angioli 1960 *Ger, F*, 1961 *Ger, F*, 1962 *F, Ger, R*, 1963 *F*
A Angrisiani 1979 *Mor, F, Pol, USS, Mor*, 1980 *Coo*, 1984 *Tun*
S Annibal 1980 *Fj, Coo, Pol, Sp*, 1981 *F, WGe*, 1982 *R, E, WGe*, 1983 *F, USS, Sp, Mor, F, A*, 1984 *F*, 1985 *F, Z, Z*, 1986 *Tun, F, Pt*, 1990 *F*
JM Antoni 2001 *Nm, SA*
C Appiani 1976 *Sp*, 1977 *Mor, Pol, Sp*, 1978 *USS*
S Appiani 1985 *R*, 1986 *Pt*, 1988 *A*, 1989 *F*
O Arancio 1993 *Rus*, 1994 *Cze, H, A, A, R, W, F*, 1995 *S, I, Sa, E, Ar, F, R, NZ, SA*, 1996 *W, Pt, W, A, E, S*, 1997 *I, I*, 1998 *S, Ar, E*, 1999 *F, W, I, SA, E, NZ*
D Armellin 1965 *Cze*, 1966 *Ger*, 1968 *Pt, WGe, Yug*, 1969 *Bul, Sp, Bel, F*
A Arrigoni 1949 *Cze*
G Artuso 1977 *Pol, R*, 1978 *Sp*, 1979 *F, E, NZ, Mor*, 1980 *F, R, JAB*, 1981 *F*, 1982 *F, E, Mor*, 1983 *F, R, USS, C, C*, 1984 *USS*, 1985 *R, EngB, USS, R*, 1986 *Tun, F, Tun*, 1987 *Pt, F, R, NZ*
E Augeri 1962 *F, Ger, R*, 1963 *F*
A Autore 1961 *Ger, F*, 1962 *F*, 1964 *Ger*, 1968 *Pt, WGe, Yug*, 1969 *Bul, Sp, Bel, F*
L Avigo 1959 *F*, 1962 *F, Ger, R*, 1963 *F*, 1964 *Ger, F*, 1965 *F, Cze*, 1966 *Ger, R*
R Aymonod 1933 *Cze*, 1934 *Cat, R*, 1935 *F*
A Azzali 1981 *WGe*, 1982 *F, R, WGe*, 1983 *F, R, USS, Sp, Mor, F*, 1984 *F, Mor, R*, 1985 *R, EngB, Sp*

S Babbo 1996 *Pt*
A Bacchetti 2009 *I, S*

FS, Tva, 1975 E, Pol, H, Sp, 1976 F, R, J, A, Sp, 1978 F,
  Ar, USS, Sp, 1979 F, Pol, R
A Caluzzi 1970 R, 1971 Mor, F, 1972 Pt, Pt, Sp, Sp, 1973 Pt,
  1974 Oxo, WGe, Leo
P Camiscioni 1975 E, 1976 R, J, A, Sp, 1977 F, 1978 F
M Campagna 1933 Cze, 1934 Cat, 1936 Ger, R, 1937 Ger, R,
  Bel, 1938 Ger
M Campagnaro 2013 Fj, Ar, 2014 W, F, S, I, E, Fj, J, Sa, Ar,
  SA, 2015 I, S, F, C, I, R
GJ Canale 2003 S, Geo, NZ, Tg, C, W, 2004 S, I, W, R, J, C,
  2005 I, Ar, Ar, A, Tg, Ar, Fj, 2006 I, E, F, W, S, A, Ar, C,
  2007 F, E, S, W, J, I, R, Pt, S, 2008 I, E, W, F, S, A, 2009
  E, I, S, W, F, A, NZ, NZ, Sa, 2010 I, E, S, F, W, SA, SA,
  Ar, A, Fj, 2011 I, E, W, F, S, J, S, A, Rus, US, I, 2012 F,
  E, I, W, S, 2013 F, S, W, E, I, Sa, S, Fj, Ar
PL Canavosio 2005 A, Tg, Fj, 2006 I, E, F, W, S, Fj, Pt, Rus,
  A, Ar, 2007 Ar, J, I, Pt, 2008 I, SA, Ar, A, Ar, 2009 S, W,
  F, A, 2010 E, S, F, W, Ar, A, 2011 I, E, W, S, J, Rus
C Canna 2015 S, S, W, F, C, I, R
C Cantoni 1956 Ger, F, Cze, 1957 Ger
L Capitani 1989 F, R, Sp, Ar, Z, USS
M Capuzzoni 1993 Cro, 1995 I
A Caranci 1989 R
M Carli 1955 Sp, Cze
C Carloni 1935 F
D Carpente 2004 R, J
T Carraro 1937 R
T Casagrande 1977 R
U Casellato 1990 Sp, 1992 R, S, 1993 Sp, F, Pt, Cro, Mor, F,
  S
R Cassina 1992 R, S
A Castellani 1994 Cze, 1995 Ar, R, 1996 W, S, 1997 Ar, R, I,
  1998 S, W, Rus, H, E, 1999 F, W, Ur, Sp, Fj, Tg, NZ
ML Castrogiovanni 2002 NZ, Sp, R, Ar, A, 2003 I, E, F, S, I,
  Geo, NZ, Tg, C, W, 2004 E, F, S, I, W, J, 2005 I, W, S, E,
  F, Ar, A, Ar, Fj, 2006 I, E, F, W, S, Pt, Rus, A, Ar, C, 2007
  F, E, S, J, I, NZ, R, Pt, S, 2008 I, E, W, F, S, 2009 E, I, S,
  W, F, NZ, SA, Sa, 2010 I, E, S, F, W, SA, Ar, A, Fj, 2011
  I, E, W, F, S, J, S, A, Rus, US, I, 2012 F, E, S, Ar, C, US,
  Tg, NZ, A, 2013 F, S, W, E, Sa, Sa, S, A, Fj, Ar, 2014 W,
  F, S, I, Ar, SA, 2015 I, E, W, S, S, W, F, C
L Catotti 1979 Pol, E
A Cazzini 1933 Cze, Cze, 1934 Cat, R, 1935 Cat, F, 1936 Ger,
  R, 1937 Ger, R, Bel, Ger, F, 1939 R, 1942 R
G Cecchetto 1955 F
A Cecchetto-Milani 1952 Sp, Ger, F
G Cecchin 1970 Cze, R, 1971 F, R, 1972 Pt
G Ceccotti 1972 Pt, Sp
LL Cedaro 2013 S
A Centinari 1930 Sp
R Centinari 1935 F, 1936 Ger, R, 1937 Bel, F, 1939 Ger
A Cepolino 1999 Ur, Sp, Fj, Tg, NZ
L Cesani 1929 Sp, 1930 Sp, 1935 Cat, F
F Ceselin 1989 F, R
C Checchinato 1990 Sp, 1991 Nm, Nm, US, NZ, USS, 1992
  Sp, F, R, S, 1993 Pt, Cro, Sp, F, Rus, F, S, 1994 Sp, R,
  Cze, A, A, R, W, F, 1995 Sa, F, Ar, R, NZ, 1996 W, E, 1997
  I, F, Ar, R, SA, I, 1998 Rus, A, R, E, 1999 F, S, SA, San,
  Ur, Fj, E, Tg, NZ, 2000 S, W, I, E, F, Sa, Fj, 2001 I, E, F,
  S, W, Nm, SA, Ur, Ar, Fj, SA, Sa, 2002 F, S, W, Sp, R,
  2003 Geo, NZ, Tg, C, W, 2004 E, F, I
G Chechinato 1973 Cze, Yug, A, 1974 WGe, Leo
G Cherubini 1949 Cze, 1951 Sp
A Chillon 2013 S
D Chistolini 2014 Sa, J, Sa, Ar, SA, 2015 I, E, S, F, W, S, I,
  R
T Ciccio 1992 R, 1993 Sp, F, Mor, F
E Cicognani 1940 Ger
R Cinelli 1968 Pt, 1969 Sp
G Cinti 1973 Rho, WTv, ETv
F Cioni 1967 Pt, R, 1968 Pt, 1969 Bul, Sp, Bel, 1970 Cze,
  Mad, Mad, R
L Cittadini 2008 I, 2010 SA, SA, A, 2011 J, S, A, Rus, 2012
  F, E, I, W, S, Tg, NZ, A, 2013 F, S, W, E, I, SA, Sa, S, A,
  Fj, Ar, 2014 W, F, S, I, E, Fj, Sa, J, Sa, 2015 S, F, S, W,
  F, C, I, R
L Clerici 1939 Ger

A Colella 1983 R, USS, C, C, Sp, Mor, F, A, USS, 1984 R,
  Tun, USS, 1985 F, R, EngB, Sp, Z, Z, USS, R, 1986 Tun,
  F, Pt, E, A, Tun, USS, 1987 Pt, F, Ar, Fj, USS, Sp, 1988
  F, R, USS, 1989 R, Sp, Ar, 1990 Pol, R
O Collodo 1977 Pol, Cze, R, Sp, 1978 F, 1986 Pt, E, A, USS,
  1987 Pt, F, R, NZ, Ar, Fj
S Colombini 1971 R
F Colombo 1933 Cze
G Colussi 1957 F, 1958 F, 1964 Ger, F, 1965 F, Cze, 1968 Pt
C Colusso 1982 F
U Conforto 1965 Cze, 1966 Ger, R, 1967 F, R, 1968 Pt, WGe,
  Yug, 1969 Bul, Sp, Bel, F, 1970 Cze, 1971 Mor, F, 1972
  Yug, 1973 Pt
F Coppio 1993 F, Pt, Cro, Mor, Sp
L Cornella 1999 Sp
R Corvo 1985 F, Sp, Z
U Cossara 1971 Mor, F, R, 1972 Pt, Sp, 1973 Pt, Rho, NEC,
  Nat, Leo, FS, Tva, 1975 F, Sp, R, Cze, E, Pol, H, 1976
  F, J, A, 1977 Pol
A Costa 1940 F, Ger, 1942 R
S Costanzo 2004 R, C, NZ, US
E Cottafava 1973 Pt
R Cova 1937 Bel, Ger, F, 1938 Ger, 1939 Ger, R, 1942 R
C Covi 1988 F, R, USS, A, I, 1989 F, R, Sp, Ar, Z, USS, 1990
  F, Pol, R, 1991 F, R, Nm, Nm, 1996 E
F Crepaz 1972 Pt
M Crescenzo 1984 R
U Crespi 1933 Cze, Cze, 1934 Cat, R, 1935 Cat, 1937 Ger
W Cristofoletto 1992 R, 1993 Mor, Sp, F, 1996 Pt, A, E, S,
  1997 I, F, F, Ar, SA, I, 1998 S, W, Rus, Ar, E, 1999 F, S,
  W, I, SA, SA, Sp, Fj, E, NZ, 2000 E, F
G Croci 1990 Sp, H, R, USS, 1991 F, R, Nm, US, E, NZ, USS,
  1992 Sp, F, 1993 S, 1996 S, 1997 I, F, F, Ar, R, SA, I,
  1998 S, W
R Crotti 1993 S, 1995 SA
L Cucchiarelli 1966 R, 1967 R
G Cucchiella 1973 A, 1974 Sus, 1979 Sp, F, Pol, USS, NZ,
  Mor, 1980 F, R, Fj, JAB, Coo, 1985 USS, R, 1986 Tun, F,
  Pt, E, 1987 Pt, F, Fj
M Cuttitta 1987 Pt, F, R, NZ, Ar, Fj, USS, Sp, 1988 F, R, 1989
  Z, USS, 1990 Pol, R, 1991 F, R, Nm, US, E, NZ, USS,
  1992 Sp, F, R, R, S, 1993 Sp, F, Mor, Sp, F, F, 1994 Sp,
  R, H, A, A, F, 1995 S, I, Sa, 1996 S, 1997 I, F, F, Ar, R,
  SA, I, 1998 S, W, Rus, Ar, 1999 F
M Cuttitta 1990 Pol, R, Sp, H, R, USS, 1991 F, Nm, Nm, US,
  E, NZ, USS, 1992 Sp, F, R, R, S, 1993 Sp, F, Pt, Cro, Mor,
  Sp, F, Rus, F, S, 1994 Sp, R, Cze, H, A, A, W, F, 1995 S,
  I, Sa, E, Ar, F, Ar, R, NZ, SA, 1996 W, Pt, W, E, S, 1997
  I, F, F, Ar, SA, I, 1998 W, Rus, Ar, H, E, 1999 F, S, W,
  2000 S, W, I, E

G Dagnini 1949 F
D Dal Maso 2000 Sa, Fj, 2001 I, E, 2004 J, C, NZ, US, 2005
  I, W, S, E, F, A
M Dal Sie 1993 Pt, 1994 R, W, F, 1995 F, Ar, 1996 A
A D'Alberton 1966 F, Ger, R, 1967 F, R
D Daldoss 1979 Pol, R, E, Sp, Mor
C D'Alessio 1937 R, Bel, F, 1938 Ger, 1939 Ger
D Dallan 1999 F, S, W, 2000 S, W, I, E, F, C, R, NZ, 2001 I,
  E, F, W, Fj, SA, Sa, 2002 F, S, W, Sp, R, 2003 W, I,
  E, F, S, Tg, C, W, 2004 E, F, S, I, W, C, 2006 J, 2007 F,
  E
M Dallan 1997 Ar, R, I, 1998 Ar, H, E, 1999 SA, SA, 2000 S,
  Sa, C, 2001 F, S, 2003 Tg, C, 2004 E, F, S
A Danieli 1955 Ger, F, Sp, F, Cze
V D'Anna 1993 Rus
T D'Apice 2011 J, S, Rus, 2012 F, E, I, W, S, C, US
P Dari 1951 Sp, 1952 Sp, Ger, F, 1953 Ger, R, 1954 Sp, F
G De Angelis 1934 Cat, R, 1935 Cat, F, 1937 R
E De Anna 1972 Yug, 1973 Cze, A, 1975 F, Sp, R, Cze, E, Pol,
  H, Sp, 1976 F, R, 1978 Ar, USS, 1979 F, Sp, Mor,
  F, USS, NZ, 1980 F, R, Fj, JAB
R De Bernardo 1980 USS, Sp, 1981 F, R, USS, WGe, 1982 R,
  E, 1983 USS, C, C, Sp, Mor, F, A, USS, 1984 F, USS,
  1985 R, EngB, 1988 I, 1989 Ar, Z
CF De Biase 1987 Sp, 1988 F, A

389

ITALY

G De Carli 1996 W, 1997 R, 1998 S, Rus, Ar, H, E, 1999 F, I, SA, SA, Ur, Fj, 2000 S, Sa, Fj, 2001 I, E, W, SA, Ur, Fj, SA, Sa, 2002 F, S, W, I, E, 2003 W, I, E
B de Jager 2006 J
L De Joanni 1983 C, Mor, F, A, USS, 1984 R, Tun, USS, 1985 F, R, EngB, Sp, Z, 1986 A, Tun, 1989 F, R, Sp, Ar, Z, 1990 R
A De Marchi 2012 Ar, US, Tg, NZ, 2013 F, S, W, E, I, SA, Sa, S, 2014 W, F, S, I, E, Fj, Sa, J, Sa, Ar, SA, 2015 I, E, S, F, W, R
A De Marchi 2014 Fj, J
R De Marchis 1935 F
H De Marco 1993 Pt
JR de Marigny 2004 E, F, S, I, W, US, 2005 I, W, S, 2007 F, E, S, W, I, Ur, J, I, NZ, Pt
A de Rossi 1999 Ur, Sp, E, 2000 I, E, F, Sa, C, R, NZ, 2001 SA, Ur, Ar, 2002 I, E, NZ, Sp, R, 2003 W, I, E, F, S, I, Geo, Tg, C, W, 2004 E, F, S, I, W, R
C De Rossi 1994 Sp, H, R
L De Santis 1952 Sp
M De Stefani 1989 Z
C De Vecchi 1948 F
G Degli Antoni 1963 F, 1965 F, 1966 F, Ger, R, 1967 F
M Del Bono 1960 Ger, F, 1961 Ger, F, 1962 F, Ger, R, 1963 F, 1964 Ger, F
G Del Bono 1951 Sp
CA Del Fava 2004 W, R, J, 2005 I, W, S, E, F, Tg, Ar, Fj, 2006 I, E, F, W, S, J, Fj, Pt, 2007 Ur, Ar, Pt, S, 2008 I, E, W, F, S, SA, Ar, A, Ar, 2009 I, S, W, F, A, NZ, NZ, SA, Sa, 2010 I, S, F, SA, Ar, A, Fj, 2011 I, E, F, S, S, A
C Della Valle 1968 WGe, Yug, 1969 F, 1970 Mad, Mad, 1971 F
S Dellapè 2002 F, S, I, E, NZ, Sp, Ar, 2003 F, S, S, Geo, Tg, C, W, 2004 E, F, S, I, W, C, NZ, 2005 I, W, S, E, F, Ar, 2006 I, E, W, S, J, Fj, Pt, Rus, A, Ar, C, 2007 F, E, S, W, I, J, NZ, R, S, 2008 I, E, W, SA, Ar, 2009 E, I, S, W, F, 2010 Ar, A, Fj, 2011 I, E, W, F
G Delli Ficorilli 1969 F
PE Derbyshire 2009 A, 2010 E, F, SA, SA, Ar, A, Fj, 2011 F, S, J, S, A, Rus, US, I, 2013 F, S, W, I, 2014 S, I, E, Fj
A Di Bello 1930 Sp, 1933 Cze, Cze, 1934 Cat
A Di Bernardo 2013 SA, Sa, S, A
F Di Carlo 1975 Sp, R, Cze, Sp, 1976 F, Sp, 1977 Pol, R, Pol, 1978 Ar, USS
B Di Cola 1973 A
G Di Cola 1972 Sp, Sp, 1973 A
F Di Maura 1971 Mor
A Di Zitti 1958 R, 1960 Ger, 1961 Ger, F, 1962 F, Ger, R, 1964 Ger, F, 1965 F, Cze, 1966 F, Ger, R, 1967 F, Pt, R, 1969 Bul, Sp, Bel, 1972 Pt, Sp
R Dolfato 1985 F, 1986 A, 1987 Pt, Fj, USS, Sp, 1988 F, R, USS
D Dominguez 1991 F, R, Nm, Nm, US, E, NZ, USS, 1992 Sp, F, R, S, 1993 Sp, F, Rus, F, S, 1994 R, H, R, W, 1995 S, I, Sa, E, Ar, SA, 1996 W, Pt, W, A, E, S, 1997 I, F, F, Ar, R, SA, I, 1998 S, W, Rus, Ar, H, E, 1999 F, S, W, I, Ur, Sp, Fj, E, Tg, NZ, 2000 S, W, I, E, F, 2001 F, S, W, Fj, SA, Sa, 2002 F, S, I, E, Ar, 2003 W, I
D Dondana 1929 Sp, 1930 Sp
G Dora 1929 Sp
R D'Orazio 1969 Bul
M Dotti IV 1939 R, 1940 R, Ger
F Dotto 1971 Mor, F, 1972 Pt, Pt, Sp
P Dotto 1993 Sp, Cro, 1994 Sp, R

J Erasmus 2008 F, S, SA
A Esposito 2014 W, S, I, E, Sa, 2015 S

U Faccioli 1948 F
A Falancia 1975 E, Pol
G Faliva 1999 SA, 2002 NZ, Ar, A
G Faltiba 1993 Pt
G Fanton 1979 Pol
P Farina 1987 F, NZ, Fj
P Farinelli 1940 R, 1949 F, Cze, 1951 Sp, 1952 Sp
T Fattori 1936 Ger, R, 1937 R, Ger, F, 1938 Ger, 1939 Ger, R, 1940 R, Ger

E Fava 1948 F, Cze
P Favaretto 1951 Sp
R Favaro 1988 F, USS, A, I, 1989 F, R, Sp, Ar, Z, USS, 1990 F, Pol, R, H, R, USS, 1991 F, R, Nm, Nm, US, E, NZ, USS, 1992 Sp, F, R, 1993 Sp, F, Cro, Sp, F, 1994 Cze, A, A, R, W, F, 1995 S, I, Sa, 1996 Pt
S Favaro 2009 A, NZ, NZ, SA, Sa, 2010 SA, 2012 F, I, W, S, Ar, C, US, Tg, NZ, A, 2013 F, S, W, E, I, 2014 Sa, Ar, 2015 S, F, I, R
G Favretto 1948 Cze, 1949 Cze
A Fedrigo 1972 Yug, 1973 Pt, Rho, WTv, Bor, NEC, Nat, ETv, Leo, FS, Cze, Yug, A, 1974 Pt, Mid, Sus, Oxo, WGe, Leo, 1975 F, Sp, R, Cze, E, Pol, H, Sp, 1976 F, J, A, Sp, 1977 F, Pol, R, Cze, R, Sp, 1978 F, Ar, 1979 Pol, R
P Fedrigo 1973 Pt
I Fernandez- Rouyet 2008 SA, Ar, 2009 A, NZ, NZ, SA, Sa
P Ferracin 1975 R, Cze, E, Pol, H, Sp, 1976 F, 1977 Mor, Pol, 1978 USS
C Festuccia 2003 W, I, E, F, S, S, I, Geo, NZ, Tg, C, W, 2004 E, F, S, I, 2005 F, Ar, Ar, A, Tg, Ar, 2006 E, F, W, S, Pt, Rus, A, Ar, C, 2007 F, E, S, W, I, Ur, Ar, J, NZ, R, S, 2008 I, E, W, 2009 E, I, 2010 A, Fj, 2011 F, S, 2012 Ar, C, US
G Figari 1940 R, Ger, 1942 R
EG Filizzola 1993 Pt, Mor, Sp, F, Rus, F, S, 1994 Sp, Cze, A, 1995 R, NZ
M Finocchi 1968 Yug, 1969 F, 1970 Cze, Mad, Mad, R, 1971 Mor, R
G Fornari 1952 Sp, Ger, F, 1953 F, Ger, R, 1954 Sp, F, 1955 Ger, F, Sp, F, Cze, 1956 Ger, F, Cze
B Francescato 1977 Cze, R, Sp, 1978 F, Sp, 1979 F, Sp, 1981 R
I Francescato 1990 R, USS, 1991 F, R, US, E, NZ, USS, 1992 R, S, 1993 Mor, F, 1994 Sp, H, R, W, F, 1995 S, I, Sa, E, Ar, F, Ar, R, NZ, SA, 1996 W, Pt, W, A, E, S, 1997 F, F, Ar, R, SA
N Francescato 1972 Yug, 1973 Rho, WTv, Bor, NEC, Nat, ETv, Leo, 1974 Pt, 1976 J, A, Sp, 1977 F, Mor, Pol, R, R, Sp, 1978 F, Ar, USS, Sp, 1979 F, R, E, Sp, Mor, F, Pol, USS, NZ, 1980 F, R, Fj, JAB, Coo, Pol, USS, Sp, 1981 F, R, 1982 Mor
R Francescato 1976 Sp, 1978 Ar, USS, 1979 Sp, F, Pol, USS, NZ, Mor, 1980 F, R, Fj, JAB, Coo, Pol, USS, Sp, 1981 F, R, 1982 WGe, 1983 F, R, USS, C, C, Sp, Mor, F, A, 1984 Mor, R, Tun, 1985 F, Sp, Z, USS, 1986 Tun, F
G Franceschini 1975 H, 1976 F, J, 1977 F, Pol, Pol, Cze, R, Sp
A Francese 1939 R, 1940 R
J Francesio 2000 W, I, Sa, 2001 Ur
F Frati 2000 C, NZ, 2001 I, S
F Frelich 1955 Cze, 1957 F, Ger, 1958 F, R
M Fumei 1984 F
JR Furno 2011 S, 2012 S, Ar, C, US, Tg, 2013 E, I, SA, S, A, Fj, 2014 W, F, S, I, E, Fj, Sa, J, Sa, Ar, SA, 2015 I, E, S, F, W, S, W, F, C, I, R
A Fusco 1982 E, 1985 R, 1986 Tun, F, Tun
E Fusco 1960 Ger, F, 1961 F, 1962 F, Ger, R, 1963 F, 1964 Ger, F, 1965 F, 1966 F
M Fuser 2012 C, 2014 J, 2015 I, S, S, C

R Gabanella 1951 Sp, 1952 Sp
P Gabrielli 1948 Cze, 1949 F, Cze, 1951 Sp, 1954 F
F Gaetaniello 1980 Sp, 1982 E, 1984 USS, 1985 R, Sp, Z, Z, USS, R, 1986 Pt, E, A, Tun, USS, 1987 Pt, F, NZ, Ar, Fj, USS, Sp, 1988 F, 1990 F, R, Sp, H, 1991 Nm, US, E, NZ
F Gaetaniello 1975 H, 1976 R, A, Sp, 1977 F, Pol, R, Pol, R, Sp, 1978 Sp, 1979 Pol, R, E, Sp, Mor, F, Pol, USS, NZ, Mor, 1980 Fj, JAB, Sp, 1981 F, R, USS, WGe, 1982 F, R, E, WGe, Mor, 1983 F, R, USS, C, C, Sp
A Galante 2007 Ur, Ar
A Galeazzo 1985 Sp, 1987 Pt, R, Ar, USS
M Galletto 1972 Pt, Sp, Yug
E Galon 2001 I, 2005 Tg, Ar, Fj, 2006 W, S, Rus, 2007 I, Ur, Ar, I, NZ, R, S, 2008 I, E, W, F, S
R Ganzerla 1973 Bor, NEC
G Garcia 2008 SA, Ar, A, Ar, Pl, 2009 E, I, S, A, NZ, NZ, SA, Sa, 2010 I, E, S, F, W, 2011 I, E, F, S, A, US, I, 2013 W, E, I, Sa, 2014 F, S, I, E, Sa, J, 2015 S, W, C, I
M Gardin 1981 USS, WGe, 1982 Mor, 1983 F, R, 1984 Mor,

R, USS, 1985 EngB, USS, R, 1986 Tun, F, Pt, Tun, USS, 1987 Pt, F, R, NZ, Ar, Fj, USS, Sp, 1988 R
JM Gardner 1992 R, S, 1993 Rus, F, 1994 Sp, R, H, F, 1995 S, I, Sa, E, Ar, 1996 W, 1997 I, F, SA, I, 1998 S, W
P Gargiullo 1973 FS, 1974 Mid, Sus, Oxo
F Garguillo 1972 Yug
F Garguilo 1967 F, Pt, 1968 Yug, 1974 Sus
S Garozzo 2001 Ur, Ar, 2002 Ar
M Gatto 1967 Pt, R
G Gattoni 1933 Cze, Cze
Q Geldenhuys 2009 A, A, NZ, NZ, SA, Sa, 2010 I, E, S, F, W, SA, SA, Ar, A, Fj, 2011 I, E, W, F, S, J, Rus, US, I, 2012 F, E, I, W, S, Tg, NZ, A, 2013 F, S, W, E, I, A, Fj, Ar, 2014 W, F, S, I, E, Fj, Sa, J, Sa, Ar, SA, 2015 F, W, S, S, W, F, C, I, R
A Gerardo 1968 Yug, 1969 Sp, 1970 Cze, Mad, 1971 R, 1972 Sp
F Geremia 1980 JAB, Pol
G Geremia 1956 Cze
E Gerosa 1952 Sp, Ger, F, 1953 F, Ger, R, 1954 Sp
M Gerosa 1994 Cze, A, A, R, W, 1995 E, Ar
C Ghezzi 1938 Ger, 1939 Ger, R, 1940 R, Ger
A Ghini 1981 USS, WGe, 1982 F, R, E, Mor, 1983 F, R, C, Mor, F, A, USS, 1984 F, Mor, R, USS, 1985 F, R, EngB, Z, Z, USS, 1987 Fj, 1988 R, USS
L Ghiraldini 2006 J, Fj, 2007 I, J, Pt, 2008 I, E, W, F, S, SA, Ar, A, Ar, Pl, 2009 S, W, F, A, A, NZ, NZ, SA, Sa, 2010 I, E, S, F, W, SA, SA, Ar, 2011 I, E, W, F, S, J, A, US, I, 2012 F, E, I, W, Tg, NZ, A, 2013 F, S, W, E, I, SA, Sa, S, A, Fj, Ar, 2014 W, F, S, I, E, Fj, Sa, J, Sa, Ar, SA, 2015 I, E, S, F, W, S, S, W, F, C
S Ghizzoni 1977 F, Mor, Pol, R, Pol, Cze, R, Sp, 1978 F, Ar, USS, 1979 F, Pol, Sp, Mor, F, Pol, 1980 R, Fj, JAB, Coo, Pol, USS, Sp, 1981 F, 1982 F, R, E, WGe, Mor, 1983 F, USS, C, C, Sp, Mor, F, A, USS, 1984 F, Mor, R, Tun, USS, 1985 F, R, EngB, Z, Z, USS, R, 1986 F, E, A, Tun, USS, 1987 Pt, F, R, NZ
M Giacheri 1992 R, 1993 Sp, F, Pt, Rus, F, S, 1994 Sp, R, Cze, H, A, A, F, 1995 S, I, E, Ar, F, Ar, R, NZ, SA, 1996 W, 1999 S, W, I, Ur, Fj, E, Tg, NZ, 2001 Nm, SA, Ur, Ar, SA, 2002 F, S, W, I, E, NZ, A, 2003 E, F, S, I
G Giani 1966 Ger, R, 1967 F, Pt, R
D Giazzon 2012 Ar, US, Tg, NZ, A, 2013 F, S, W, E, I, SA, S, A, Fj, Ar, 2014 W, F, S, I, Fj, 2015 S, C, I, R
G Gini 1968 Pt, WGe, Yug, 1969 Bul, Sp, Bel, F, 1970 Cze, Mad, Mad, R, 1971 Mor, F, 1972 Pt, Pt, 1974 Mid, Oxo
G Giorgio 1968 Pt, WGe
M Giovanelli 1989 Z, USS, 1990 Pol, Sp, H, R, USS, 1991 F, R, Nm, E, NZ, USS, 1992 Sp, F, S, 1993 Sp, F, Pt, Cro, Mor, Sp, F, 1994 R, Cze, H, A, A, 1995 F, Ar, R, NZ, SA, 1996 A, E, S, 1997 F, F, Ar, R, SA, I, 1998 S, W, Rus, Ar, H, E, 1999 S, W, I, SA, SA, Ur, Sp, Fj, E, Tg, NZ, 2000 S
E Giugovaz 1965 Cze, 1966 F
R Giuliani 1951 Sp
E Gori 2010 A, Fj, 2011 I, J, S, A, Rus, US, I, 2012 F, E, I, S, Ar, C, US, Tg, NZ, A, 2013 F, S, W, E, I, SA, Sa, A, Fj, Ar, 2014 W, F, S, I, E, Sa, Ar, SA, 2015 I, E, S, F, W, W, F, C, I, R
M Gorni 1939 R, 1940 R, Ger
M Goti 1990 H
C Gower 2009 A, A, NZ, NZ, SA, Sa, 2010 I, E, S, F, W, SA, SA, Ar
G Grasselli 1952 Ger
G Grespan 1989 F, Sp, USS, 1990 F, R, 1991 R, NZ, USS, 1992 R, S, 1993 Sp, F, Cro, Sp, F, Rus, 1994 Sp, Cze, R, W
PR Griffen 2004 E, F, S, I, W, R, J, C, NZ, US, 2005 W, S, F, Ar, Ar, A, Tg, Ar, Fj, 2006 I, E, F, W, S, J, Fj, Rus, A, Ar, C, 2007 F, I, Ur, Ar, I, NZ, R, Pt, 2009 I, S, W, F
A Gritti 1996 Pt, 2000 S, W, I, E, F, Sa, Fj, C, R, NZ, 2001 E, F, S, W
G Guidi 1996 Pt, E, 1997 F, Ar, R

KH Haimona 2014 Sa, Ar, SA, 2015 I, E, S, W

T Iannone 2012 Tg, 2013 SA, Sa, A, Fj, Ar, 2014 W, F, Sa, J
M Innocenti 1981 WGe, 1982 F, R, E, WGe, Mor, 1983 F, USS,

C, C, Mor, F, A, USS, 1984 F, Mor, Tun, USS, 1985 F, R, EngB, Sp, USS, R, 1986 Tun, F, Pt, E, A, Tun, USS, 1987 Pt, F, R, NZ, Ar, Fj, USS, Sp, 1988 F, R, A
G Intoppa 2004 R, J, C, NZ, 2005 I, W, E

C Jannone 1981 USS, 1982 F, R

S Lanfranchi 1949 F, Cze, 1953 F, Ger, R, 1954 Sp, F, 1955 F, 1956 Ger, Cze, 1957 F, 1958 F, 1959 F, 1960 F, 1961 F, 1962 F, Ger, R, 1963 F, 1964 Ger, F
G Lanzi 1998 Ar, H, E, 1999 Sp, 2000 S, W, I, 2001 I
G Lari 1972 Yug, 1973 Yug, A, 1974 Pt, Mid, Sus, Oxo, Leo
E Lazzarini 1970 Cze, 1971 Mor, F, R, 1972 Pt, Pt, Sp, Sp, 1973 Pt, Rho, WTv, Bor, NEC, Leo, FS, Tva, Cze, Yug, A, 1974 Pt, Mid, Sus, Oxo, WGe
U Levorato 1956 Ger, F, 1957 F, 1958 F, R, 1959 F, 1961 Ger, F, 1962 F, Ger, R, 1963 F, 1964 Ger, F, 1965 F
A Lijoi 1977 Pol, R, 1978 Sp, 1979 R, Mor
G Limone 1979 E, Mor, USS, Mor, 1980 JAB, Sp, 1981 USS, WGe, 1982 E, 1983 USS
A Lo Cicero 2000 E, F, Sa, Fj, C, R, NZ, 2001 I, E, F, S, W, Fj, SA, Sa, 2002 F, S, W, Sp, R, A, 2003 F, S, S, I, Geo, Tg, C, W, 2004 E, F, S, I, W, R, J, C, NZ, US, 2005 I, W, S, E, F, Ar, Ar, A, Tg, Ar, 2006 E, F, W, S, J, Fj, Pt, Rus, A, Ar, C, 2007 F, E, S, W, Ur, Ar, J, NZ, R, Pt, S, 2008 I, E, W, F, S, Ar, Pl, 2010 Ar, A, Fj, 2011 I, E, W, F, S, J, S, A, US, I, 2012 F, E, W, S, Tg, NZ, A, 2013 F, S, W, E, I
C Loranzi 1973 Nat, ETv, Leo, FS, Tva
F Lorigiola 1979 Sp, F, Pol, USS, NZ, Mor, 1980 F, R, Fj, JAB, Pol, USS, Sp, 1981 F, R, USS, 1982 WGe, 1983 R, USS, C, Sp, 1984 Tun, 1985 Sp, 1986 Pt, E, A, Tun, USS, 1987 Pt, F, R, NZ, Ar, 1988 F
G Luchini 1973 Rho, Nat
L Luise 1955 Ger, F, Sp, F, Cze, 1956 Ger, F, Cze, 1957 Ger, 1958 F
R Luise III 1959 F, 1960 Ger, F, 1961 Ger, F, 1962 F, Ger, R, 1965 F, Cze, 1966 F, 1971 R, 1972 Pt, Sp, Sp
T Lupini 1987 R, NZ, Ar, Fj, USS, Sp, 1988 F, R, USS, A, 1989 R

O Maestri 1935 Cat, F, 1937 Ger
R Maffioli 1933 Cze, Cze, 1934 Cat, R, 1935 Cat, 1936 Ger, R, 1937 Ger, R, Bel, Ger
R Maini 1948 F, Cze
G Malosti 1953 F, 1954 Sp, 1955 F, 1956 Ger, F, 1957 F, 1958 F
G Mancini 1952 Ger, F, 1953 F, Ger, R, 1954 Sp, F, 1955 Cze, 1956 Ger, F, Cze, 1957 F
R Mandelli 2004 I, W, R, J, US, 2007 F, E, Ur, Ar
A Manici 2013 Sa, 2014 Sa, J, Sa, Ar, SA, 2015 I, E, S, F, W, S, W, F, I, R
A Mannato 2004 US, 2005 Ar, A
E Manni 1976 J, A, Sp, 1977 Mor
L Manteri 1996 W, A, E, S
A Marcato 2004 J, Pt, 2008 I, E, W, F, S, SA, Ar, A, Ar, Pl, 2009 E, S, W, F
M Marchetto 1972 Yug, 1973 Pt, Cze, Yug, 1974 Pt, Mid, Sus, WGe, Leo, 1975 F, Sp, R, Cze, E, Pol, H, Sp, 1976 F, R, J, A, Sp, 1977 F, Mor, Pol, R, Cze, R, Sp, 1978 F, USS, Sp, 1979 F, Pol, R, E, Pol, USS, NZ, Mor, 1980 F, Coo, 1981 USS
A Marescalchi 1933 Cze, 1935 F, 1937 R
P Mariani 1976 R, A, Sp, 1977 F, Pol, 1978 F, Ar, USS, Sp, 1979 F, Pol, R, Sp, F, Pol, USS, NZ, Mor, 1980 F, R, Fj, JAB
P Marini 1949 F, Cze, 1951 Sp, 1953 F, Ger, R, 1955 Ger
L Martin 1997 F, R, 1998 S, W, Rus, H, E, 1999 F, S, W, I, SA, SA, Ur, Sp, Fj, E, 2000 S, W, I, E, F, Sa, Fj, C, R, NZ, 2001 I, E, S, W, SA, Ar, Fj, SA, Sa, 2002 F, S
F Martinenghi 1952 Sp, Ger
R Martinez-Frugoni 2002 NZ, Sp, R, 2003 W, I, E, F, S, S, NZ
G Martini 1965 F, 1967 F, 1968 Pt
R Martini 1959 F, 1960 Ger, F, 1961 Ger, F, 1964 Ger, F, 1965 F, 1966 WGe, Yug
P Masci 1948 Cze, 1949 F, Cze, 1952 Sp, Ger, F, 1953 F, 1954 Sp, 1955 F
M Mascioletti 1977 Mor, Pol, 1978 Ar, USS, Sp, 1979 Pol, E,

Sp, Mor, F, Pol, USS, NZ, Mor, 1980 F, R, Fj, 1981 WGe, 1982 F, R, WGe, 1983 F, R, USS, C, C, Sp, Mor, F, A, USS, 1984 F, Mor, Tun, 1985 F, R, Z, Z, USS, R, 1986 Tun, F, Pt, E, Tun, USS, 1987 NZ, Ar, Fj, 1989 Sp, Ar, Z, USS, 1990 Pol

A Masi 1999 Sp, 2003 E, F, S, S, I, NZ, Tg, C, W, 2004 E, I, W, R, J, C, 2005 I, W, S, E, F, Ar, Ar, A, 2006 J, Fj, Pt, Rus, 2007 F, S, J, NZ, R, Pt, S, 2008 I, E, W, F, S, SA, A, Ar, Pl, 2009 E, I, 2010 I, E, S, F, SA, SA, Ar, A, Fj, 2011 I, E, W, F, S, S, A, Rus, I, 2012 F, E, I, W, S, Tg, NZ, A, 2013 F, S, W, E, I, SA, Sa, S, 2014 I, E, Fj, Sa, Sa, Ar, SA, 2015 I, E, F, W, S, S, W, F

L Mastrodomenico 2000 Sa, C, NZ, 2001 Nm, Ar

I Matacchini 1948 F, Cze, 1949 F, Cze, 1954 Sp, 1955 Ger, F, Sp, F

L Mattarolo 1973 Bor, Nat, ETv, Leo, FS, Tva, Cze

M Mattei 1967 R

R Mattei 1978 F, USS

F Mazzantini 1965 Cze, 1966 F, 1967 F

M Mazzantini 2000 S, 2001 S, W, 2002 E, NZ, 2003 E, F, Geo, NZ, C

F Mazzariol 1995 F, Ar, R, NZ, 1996 Pt, 1997 F, R, SA, 1998 Ar, H, 1999 F, SA, SA, Sp, E, NZ, 2000 Fj, C, 2001 Nm, SA, Ur, Ar, Fj, SA, 2002 W, NZ, Sp, 2003 S, I, NZ, C, W, 2004 R

G Mazzi 1998 H, 1999 SA, SA, Ur, Sp

N Mazzucato 1995 SA, 1996 Pt, S, 1997 I, 1999 Sp, E, Tg, NZ, 2000 F, Sa, Fj, R, 2001 Nm, SA, Ur, Ar, 2002 W, I, E, NZ, Sp, R, Ar, A, 2003 E, F, S, I, NZ, Tg, W, 2004 E, F, S, I, W, R, J

I Mazzucchelli 1965 F, Cze, 1966 F, Ger, R, 1967 F, 1968 Pt, WGe, 1969 Bul, F, 1971 F, 1972 Pt, Sp, 1974 WGe, 1975 F, R, Cze, Pol, 1976 F, R

LJ McLean 2008 SA, Ar, Pl, 2009 E, I, S, W, F, A, A, NZ, NZ, SA, Sa, 2010 I, E, S, F, W, SA, SA, Ar, A, Fj, 2011 I, E, W, S, J, A, Rus, US, I, 2012 F, E, I, W, US, Tg, NZ, A, 2013 F, S, W, E, I, SA, Sa, S, A, Fj, Ar, 2014 W, F, S, I, E, Fj, Sa, J, Sa, Ar, SA, 2015 I, E, S, F, W, S, S, W, F, C, I, R

P Menapace 1996 Pt

E Michelon 1969 Bel, F, 1970 Cze, Mad, Mad, R, 1971 R

A Miele 1968 Yug, 1970 Mad, 1971 R, 1972 Pt, Sp

GE Milano 1990 USS

F Minto 2012 NZ, A, 2013 F, S, W, E, I, 2014 W, F, Ar, SA, 2015 I, E, S, F, W, S, S, W, F, C, I, R

A Mioni 1955 Ger, F, F, 1957 F

A Modonesi 1929 Sp

L Modonesi 1966 Ger, R, 1967 F, Pt, R, 1968 Pt, WGe, 1970 Cze, Mad, Mad, R, 1971 F, 1974 Leo, 1975 R, Cze

N Molari 1957 F, 1958 R

F Molinari 1973 NEC

G Molinari 1948 F

P Monfeli 1970 R, 1971 Mor, F, 1972 Pt, 1976 J, A, Sp, 1977 F, R, Cze, R, Sp, 1978 F

JF Montauriol 2009 E, A

G Morelli 1981 WGe, 1982 R, E, Mor, 1983 USS, 1984 F

G Morelli 1976 F, 1982 F, R, Mor, 1983 R, C, Sp, A, USS, 1984 Mor, R, USS, 1985 R, EngB, Z, Z, USS, R, 1986 Tun, F, E, A, Tun, USS, 1987 F, NZ

G Morelli 1988 I, 1989 F, R

A Moreno 1999 Tg, NZ, 2002 F, S, 2008 Ar

A Moretti 1997 R, 1998 Rus, 1999 Ur, Sp, Tg, NZ, 2002 E, NZ, Sp, R, Ar, A, 2005 Ar

U Moretti 1933 Cze, 1934 R, 1935 Cat, 1937 R, Ger, F, 1942 R

A Morimondi 1930 Sp, 1933 Cze, 1934 Cat, 1935 Cat

LE Morisi 2012 E, US, 2013 SA, S, A, Fj, 2014 Sa, Ar, SA, 2015 I, E, S, F, W, S, W

A Moscardi 1993 Pt, 1995 R, 1996 S, 1998 Ar, H, E, 1999 F, S, W, I, SA, SA, Ur, Fj, E, Tg, NZ, 2000 S, W, I, E, F, Sa, Fj, C, R, NZ, 2001 I, E, F, S, W, Nm, SA, Ur, Ar, Fj, SA, Sa, 2002 F, S, W, I, E

A Muraro 2000 C, R, NZ, 2001 I, E, Nm, SA, Ur, Ar, Fj, SA, Sa, 2002 F

E Nathan 1930 Sp

G Navarini 1957 Ger, 1958 R

M Nicolosi 1982 R

C Nieto 2002 E, 2005 Ar, Ar, A, Tg, Ar, Fj, 2006 I, E, F, W, J, Fj, A, Ar, C, 2007 F, S, W, I, Ar, 2008 E, F, S, SA, Ar, A, Ar, Pl, 2009 E, I, S, W, F

A Nisti 1929 Sp, 1930 Sp

L Nitoglia 2004 C, NZ, US, 2005 I, W, S, E, F, Ar, Tg, Ar, Fj, 2006 I, E, F, W, S

F Ongaro 2000 C, 2001 Nm, SA, Ur, Ar, 2002 Ar, A, 2003 E, F, S, I, Geo, NZ, Tg, C, W, 2004 E, F, S, I, W, R, J, C, NZ, US, 2005 I, W, S, E, F, Tg, Ar, Fj, 2006 I, E, F, W, S, J, Fj, Pt, Rus, Ar, C, 2007 F, S, Ur, Ar, I, NZ, S, 2008 F, S, SA, Ar, A, Ar, Pl, 2009 E, I, NZ, SA, Sa, 2010 I, E, S, F, W, SA, SA, A, Fj, 2011 I, E, S, Rus, US, I, 2012 S

C Orlandi 1992 S, 1993 Sp, F, Mor, F, Rus, F, S, 1994 Sp, Cze, H, A, A, R, W, 1995 S, I, Sa, E, Ar, F, Ar, R, NZ, SA, 1996 W, Pt, W, A, E, S, 1997 I, F, F, Ar, R, SA, I, 1998 S, W, 2000 W, F

S Oriando 2004 E, S, W, C, NZ, US, 2005 E, F, Ar, A, 2006 J, 2007 Ur, Ar, Pt

L Orquera 2004 C, NZ, US, 2005 I, W, S, E, F, Ar, Tg, 2008 A, Ar, 2009 W, F, 2010 Ar, A, Fj, 2011 I, E, W, F, S, J, S, A, US, I, 2012 NZ, A, 2013 F, S, E, I, SA, Sa, Fj, Ar, 2014 F, S, I, E, Fj, Sa, J, Ar, SA, 2015 F, W

A Osti 1981 F, R, USS, 1982 E, Mor, 1983 R, C, A, USS, 1984 R, USS, 1985 F, 1986 Tun, 1988 R

S Pace 1977 Mor, 1984 R, Tun

S Pace 2001 SA, Sa, 2005 Fj

P Pacifici 1969 Bul, Sp, F, 1970 Cze, Mad, Mad, R, 1971 Mor, F

R Paciucci 1937 R, Ger, F

F Paganelli 1972 Sp

G Palazzani 2014 Fj, Sa, J, Ar, SA, 2015 E, F, W, S, S, W, F, C, I, R

S Palmer 2002 Ar, A, 2003 I, E, F, S, S, NZ, C, W, 2004 I, R

P Paoletti 1972 Pt, Sp, Yug, 1973 Pt, Rho, WTv, Bor, NEC, Nat, ETv, Leo, FS, Tva, 1974 Mid, Oxo, WGe, Leo, 1975 F, Sp, 1976 R

T Paoletti 2000 S, W, I, E, F, Sa, C, R, NZ, 2001 F, Nm, Ur, Ar, Fj, SA

G Paolin 1929 Sp

S Parisse 2002 NZ, Sp, R, Ar, A, 2003 S, I, Geo, NZ, Tg, C, W, 2004 E, F, S, 2005 I, W, S, E, F, Ar, Ar, A, Tg, Ar, Fj, 2006 I, E, F, W, S, Fj, Pt, Rus, A, Ar, C, 2007 F, E, S, W, I, J, I, NZ, R, Pt, S, 2008 I, E, W, F, S, Ar, A, Ar, Pl, 2009 E, I, S, W, F, A, A, NZ, NZ, SA, 2010 SA, SA, Ar, A, Fj, 2011 I, E, W, F, S, J, S, A, Rus, US, I, 2012 F, E, I, W, S, Tg, NZ, A, 2013 F, S, E, I, SA, Sa, S, A, Fj, Ar, 2014 W, F, S, E, Sa, Ar, SA, 2015 I, E, S, F, W, I

E Parmiggiani 1942 R, 1948 Cze

P Paselli 1929 Sp, 1930 Sp, 1933 Cze

E Passarotto 1975 Sp

E Patrizio 2007 Ur, 2008 F, S, SA

R Pavan 2008 SA

A Pavanello 2007 Ar, 2009 SA, Sa, 2012 E, I, Ar, C, US, Tg, NZ, A, 2013 F, S, W, E, I, SA, Sa, S, A, 2014 I

E Pavanello 2002 R, Ar, A, 2004 R, J, C, NZ, US, 2005 Ar, A

P Pavesi 1977 Pol, 1979 Mor, 1980 USS

M Pavin 1980 USS, 1986 F, Pt, E, A, Tun, USS, 1987 Ar

R Pedrazzi 2001 Nm, Ar, 2002 F, S, W, 2005 S, E, F

P Pedroni 1989 Z, USS, 1990 F, Pol, R, 1991 F, R, Nm, 1993 Rus, F, 1994 Sp, R, Cze, H, 1995 I, Sa, E, Ar, F, Ar, R, NZ, SA, 1996 W, W

G Peens 2002 W, I, E, NZ, Sp, R, Ar, A, 2003 E, F, S, S, I, Geo, NZ, 2004 NZ, 2005 E, F, Ar, Ar, A, 2006 Pt, A

L Pelliccione 1983 Sp, Mor, F

L Pelliccione 1977 Pol

M Percudani 1952 F, 1954 F, 1955 Ger, Sp, F, Cze, 1956 Cze, 1957 F, 1958 R

F Perrini 1955 Sp, F, Cze, 1956 Ger, F, Cze, 1957 F, 1958 F, 1959 F, 1962 R, 1963 F

F Perrone 1951 Sp

AR Persico 2000 S, W, E, F, Sa, Fj, 2001 F, S, W, Nm, SA, Ur, Ar, Fj, SA, Sa, 2002 F, S, W, I, E, NZ, Sp, R, Ar, A, 2003 W, I, E, F, S, I, Geo, Tg, C, W, 2004 E, F, S, I, W, R, J, C, NZ, 2005 I, W, S, E, F, Ar, Ar, Tg, Ar, 2006 I, E

J Pertile 1994 *R*, 1995 *Ar*, 1996 *W, A, E, S*, 1997 *I, F, SA*, 1998 *Rus*, 1999 *S, W, I, SA, SA*

S Perugini 2000 *I, F, Sa, Fj*, 2001 *S, W, Nm, SA, Ur, Ar*, 2002 *W, I*, 2003 *W, S, Geo, NZ, Tg, W*, 2004 *E, F, I, W, C, NZ, US*, 2005 *I, W, S, E, F*, 2006 *I, E, F, W, S, Pt, Rus*, 2007 *F, E, S, W, I, J, I, NZ, Pt, S*, 2008 *I, E, W, F, S, A, Ar, PI*, 2009 *E, I, S, W, F, A, A, NZ, NZ, SA, Sa*, 2010 *I, E, S, F, W, SA, SA, Ar, Fj*, 2011 *I, E, W, F, S, Rus, US, I*

L Perziano 1993 *Pt*

M Perziano 2000 *NZ*, 2001 *F, S, W, Nm, SA, Ur, Ar, Fj, SA*

V Pesce 1988 *I*, 1989 *R*

P Pescetto 1956 *Ger, Cze*, 1957 *F*

G Petralia 1984 *F*

R Pez 2000 *Sa, Fj, C, R, NZ*, 2001 *I*, 2002 *S, W, E, A*, 2003 *I, E, F, S, S, Geo*, 2005 *Ar, A, Tg, Ar, Fj*, 2006 *I, E, F, W, S, J, Fj, Pt, Rus, A, Ar*, 2007 *F, E, S, W, I, J, R, S*

M Phillips 2002 *F, S, W, I, E*, 2003 *W, I, E, F, S, S, I, NZ, W*

G Pianna 1934 *R*, 1935 *Cat, F*, 1936 *Ger, R*, 1938 *Ger*

A Piazza 1990 *USS*

F Piccini 1963 *F*, 1964 *Ger*, 1966 *F*

S Picone 2004 *I, W*, 2005 *F*, 2006 *E, F, S, J, Pt, Rus, Ar, C*, 2008 *E, W, F, S, SA, Ar*, 2009 *NZ, SA, Sa*, 2010 *I, SA, SA*

F Pietroscanti 1987 *USS, Sp*, 1988 *A, I*, 1989 *F, R, Sp, Ar, Z, USS*, 1990 *F, Pol, R, H*, 1991 *Nm, Nm*, 1992 *Sp, F, R*, 1993 *Sp, Mor, Sp, F, Rus, F*

F Pignotti 1968 *WGe, Yug*, 1969 *Bul, Sp, Bel*

C Pilat 1997 *I*, 1998 *S, W*, 2000 *E, Sa*, 2001 *I, W*

MJ Pini 1998 *H, E*, 1999 *F, Ur, Fj, E, Tg, NZ*, 2000 *S, W, I, F*

M Piovan 1973 *Pt*, 1974 *Pt, Mid, Sus, Oxo*, 1976 *A*, 1977 *F, Mor, R*, 1979 *F*

R Piovan 1996 *Pt*, 1997 *R*, 2000 *R, NZ*

M Piovene 1995 *NZ*

E Piras 1971 *R*

M Pisaneschi 1948 *Cze*, 1949 *Cze*, 1953 *F, Ger, R*, 1954 *Sp, F*, 1955 *Ger, F, Sp, F, Cze*

F Pitorri 1948 *Cze*, 1949 *F*

M Pitorri 1973 *NEC*

G Pivetta 1979 *R, E, Mor*, 1980 *Coo, USS*, 1981 *R, USS, WGe*, 1982 *F, R, WGe, Mor*, 1983 *F, USS, C, Sp, Mor, F, USS*, 1984 *F, Mor, R, Tun*, 1985 *F, R, Sp, Z, Z*, 1986 *Pt*, 1987 *Sp*, 1989 *Sp*, 1990 *F, Pol, R, Sp, R, USS*, 1991 *F, R, Nm, Nm, US, E, NZ, USS*, 1992 *Sp, F, R*, 1993 *Cro, Mor, Sp*

M Platania 1994 *F*, 1995 *F, R*, 1996 *Pt*

I Ponchia 1955 *F, Sp, F, Cze*, 1956 *F*, 1957 *Ger*, 1958 *F*

E Ponzi 1973 *Cze, A*, 1974 *WGe*, 1975 *F, Sp, R, Cze, E, Pol, H, Sp*, 1976 *F, R, J, A, Sp*, 1977 *F, Mor, Pol, R*

G Porcellato 1989 *R*

G Porzio 1970 *Cze, Mad, Mad*

C Possamai 1970 *Cze, Mad, Mad*

W Pozzebon 2001 *I, E, F, S, W, Nm, SA, Ur, Ar, Fj, SA, Sa*, 2002 *NZ, Sp*, 2004 *R, J, C, NZ, US*, 2005 *W, E*, 2006 *C*

A Pratichetti 2012 *C*

C Pratichetti 1988 *R*, 1990 *Pol*

M Pratichetti 2004 *NZ*, 2007 *E, W, I, Ur, Ar, I, Pt*, 2008 *SA, Ar, Ar, PI*, 2009 *E, I, S, W, F, A, NZ, SA*, 2010 *W, SA*, 2011 *J, Rus*

G Preo 1999 *I*, 2000 *I, E, Sa, Fj, R, NZ*

P Presutti 1974 *Mid, Sus, Oxo*, 1977 *Pol, Cze, R, Sp*, 1978 *F*

FP Properzi-Curti 1990 *Pol, Sp, H, R*, 1991 *F, Nm, Nm, US, E, NZ*, 1992 *Sp, F, R*, 1993 *Cro, Mor, F, Rus, F, S*, 1994 *Sp, R, H, A, A*, 1995 *S, I, Sa, E, Ar, NZ, SA*, 1996 *W, Pt, W, A, E*, 1997 *I, F, F, Ar, SA*, 1998 *Ar*, 1999 *S, W, I, SA, SA, Ur, E, Tg, NZ*, 2001 *F, S, W*

C Prosperini 1966 *R*, 1967 *F, Pt, R*

F Pucciarello 1999 *Sp, Fj, E*, 2002 *S, W, I, E, Ar*

G Puglisi 1971 *F*, 1972 *Yug*, 1973 *Cze*

M Pulli 1968 *F*, 1972 *Pt, Pt*

A Puppo 1972 *Pt, Pt, Sp, Sp*, 1973 *Pt, Rho, WTv, Bor, NEC, Nat, ETv, Leo, FS, Tva*, 1974 *Mid, Sus, Oxo, WGe, Leo*, 1977 *R*

I Quaglio 1970 *R*, 1971 *R*, 1972 *Pt, Sp*, 1973 *WTv, Bor, NEC, Nat, Leo, FS, Tva*, 1975 *H, Sp*, 1976 *F, R*

M Quaglio 1984 *Tun*, 1988 *F, R*

R Quartaroli 2009 *W, F, A*, 2012 *Ar, US*

JM Queirolo 2000 *Sa, Fj*, 2001 *E, F, Fj*, 2002 *NZ, Sp, A*, 2003 *Geo*

P Quintavala 1958 *R*

C Raffo 1929 *Sp*, 1930 *Sp*, 1933 *Cze, Cze*, 1937 *R, Bel*

G Raineri 1998 *H*, 2000 *Fj, R, NZ*, 2001 *I, E, S, W, Nm, SA, Ur, Ar*, 2002 *W, I, E, NZ*, 2003 *W, I, E, F, S, Geo*

G Raisi 1956 *Ger, F*, 1957 *F, Ger*, 1960 *Ger*, 1964 *Ger, F*

R Rampazzo 1996 *W*, 1999 *I*

M Ravazzolo 1993 *Cro, Sp, F, F, S*, 1994 *Sp, R, Cze, H*, 1995 *S, I, Sa, F, Ar, NZ*, 1996 *W, Pt, W, A*, 1997 *F, Ar, R, SA*

A Re Garbagnati 1936 *Ger, R*, 1937 *Ger, Bel, Ger, F*, 1938 *Ger*, 1939 *Ger, R*, 1940 *R, Ger*, 1942 *R*

P Reale 1987 *USS, Sp*, 1988 *USS, A, I*, 1989 *Z*, 1992 *S*

T Reato 2008 *I, SA, Ar, A, Ar, PI*, 2009 *E, I, A*

G Riccardi 1955 *Ger, F, Sp, F, Cze*, 1956 *F, Cze*

G Ricci 1967 *Pt*, 1969 *Bul, Sp, Bel, F*

G Ricciarelli 1962 *Ger*

L Riccioni 1951 *Sp*, 1952 *Sp, Ger, F*, 1953 *F, Ger, F*, 1954 *F*

S Rigo 1992 *S*, 1993 *Sp, F, Pt*

A Rinaldo 1977 *Mor, Pol, R, Cze*

W Rista 1968 *Yug*, 1969 *Bul, Sp, Bel, F*

M Rivaro 2000 *S, W, I*, 2001 *E*

M Rizzo 2005 *A*, 2008 *SA*, 2012 *I, C, US, A*, 2013 *I, Sa, A, Fj, Ar*, 2014 *W, F, I, E*, 2015 *W, S, S, W, F, C, I*

G Rizzoli 1935 *F*, 1936 *Ger, R*

C Robazza 1978 *Ar, Sp*, 1979 *F, Pol, R, E, Sp, F, Pol, USS, NZ, Mor*, 1980 *F, R, Fj, JAB, Coo, Pol, Sp*, 1981 *F, R, USS, WGe*, 1982 *E, WGe*, 1983 *F, USS, C, Mor, F*, 1984 *F, Tun*, 1985 *F*

KP Robertson 2004 *R, J, C, NZ, US*, 2005 *I, W, S, F, Ar, Ar, A*, 2006 *Pt, Rus*, 2007 *F, E, S, W, I, Ur, Ar, J, I, NZ, R, S*, 2008 *I, E, F, S, SA, Ar, A, Ar, PI*, 2009 *E, I, A, NZ, NZ, Sa*, 2010 *I, E, S, F, W, SA*

A Rocca 1973 *WTv, Bor, NEC*, 1977 *R*

G Romagnoli 1965 *F, Cze*, 1967 *Pt, R*

S Romagnoli 1982 *Mor*, 1984 *R, Tun, USS*, 1985 *F, Z, Z*, 1986 *Tun, Pt, A, Tun, USS*, 1987 *Pt, F, Fj*

G Romano 1942 *R*

L Romano 2012 *Ar, C*

P Romano 1942 *R*

F Roselli 1995 *F, R*, 1996 *W*, 1998 *Rus, Ar, H, E*, 1999 *F, S, W, I, SA, SA, Ur, Fj, Tg*

P Rosi 1948 *F, Cze*, 1949 *F, Cze*, 1951 *Sp*, 1952 *Ger, F*, 1953 *F, Ger, R*, 1954 *Sp, F*

G Rossi 1981 *USS, WGe*, 1982 *E, WGe, Mor*, 1983 *F, R, USS, C, C, Mor, F, A, USS*, 1984 *Mor*, 1985 *F, R, EngB, Sp, Z, USS, R*, 1986 *Tun, F, E, A, Tun, USS*, 1987 *R, NZ, Ar, USS, Sp*, 1988 *USS, A, I*, 1989 *F, R, Sp, Ar, Z, USS*, 1990 *F, R*, 1991 *R*

N Rossi 1973 *Yug*, 1974 *Pt, Mid, Sus, Oxo, WGe, Leo*, 1975 *Sp, Cze, E, H*, 1976 *J, A, Sp*, 1977 *Cze*, 1980 *USS*

Z Rossi 1959 *F*, 1961 *Ger, F*, 1962 *F, Ger, R*

E Rossini 1948 *F, Cze*, 1949 *F, Cze*, 1951 *Sp*, 1952 *Ger*

B Rovelli 1960 *Ger, F*, 1961 *Ger, F*

G Rubini 2009 *S, W, F, A*

A Russo 1986 *E*

D Sacca 2003 *I*

R Saetti 1957 *Ger*, 1958 *F, R*, 1959 *F*, 1960 *F*, 1961 *Ger, F*, 1964 *Ger, F*

R Saetti 1988 *USS, I*, 1989 *F, R, Sp, Ar, Z, USS*, 1990 *F, Sp, H, R, USS*, 1991 *R, Nm, Nm, US, E*, 1992 *R*

A Sagramora 1970 *Mad, Mad*, 1971 *R*

E Saibene 1957 *F, Ger*

C Salmasso 1966 *F*, 1967 *F*

L Salsi 1971 *Mor*, 1972 *Pt, Sp, Yug*, 1973 *Pt, Rho, WTv, Nat, ETv, Leo, FS, Tva, Cze, Yug, A*, 1974 *Pt, Oxo, WGe, Leo*, 1975 *Sp, R, Sp*, 1977 *R, Pol, Cze, R, Sp*, 1978 *F*

F Salvadego 1985 *Z*

R Salvan 1973 *Yug*, 1974 *F*

L Salvati 1987 *USS*, 1988 *USS, I*

R Santofadre 1952 *Sp, Ger, F*, 1954 *Sp, F*

Sarto 2013 *A*, 2014 *W, F, S, I, E, Fj, J, Sa, Ar, SA*, 2015 *I, E, F, W, S, S, W, F, C, I, R*

F Sartorato 1956 *Ger, F*, 1957 *F*

M Savi 2004 *R, J*, 2005 *E*

S Saviozzi 1998 *Rus, H*, 1999 *W, I, SA, SA, Ur, Fj, Tg, NZ*, 2000 *C, NZ*, 2002 *NZ, Sp*
F Sbaraglini 2009 *S, F, A, NZ*, 2010 *SA*
D Scaglia 1994 *R, W*, 1995 *S*, 1996 *W, A*, 1999 *W*
E Scalzotto 1974 *Mid, Sus, Oxo*
A Scanavacca 1999 *Ur*, 2001 *E*, 2002 *Sp, R*, 2004 *US*, 2006 *Ar, C*, 2007 *F, E, S, I*
R Sciacol 1965 *Cze*
I Scodavolpe 1954 *Sp*
F Screnci 1977 *Cze, R, Sp*, 1978 *F*, 1979 *Pol, R, E*, 1982 *F*, 1984 *Mor*
A Selvaggio 1973 *Rho, WTv, ETv, Leo, FS, Tva*
F Semenzato 2011 *E, W, F, S, S, A, US, I*, 2012 *F, E, I, W*
M Sepe 2006 *J, Fj*, 2010 *SA*
D Sesenna 1992 *R*, 1993 *Cro, Mor, F*, 1994 *R*
G Sessa 1930 *Sp*
G Sessi 1942 *R*
A Sgarbi 2008 *E, W*, 2009 *A, A, SA*, 2010 *Ar, A, Fj*, 2011 *I, E, W, S, J, Rus*, 2012 *F, I, W, Ar, C, US, Tg, NZ, A*, 2013 *F, SA, S, A*, 2014 *W, Fj*
E Sgorbati 1933 *Cze*, 1934 *Cat, R*, 1935 *Cat, F*, 1936 *Ger*, 1937 *Ger*, 1938 *Ger*, 1939 *Ger*, 1940 *R, Ger*, 1942 *R*
E Sgorbati 1968 *WGe, Yug*
A Sgorlon 1993 *Pt, Mor, Sp, F, Rus, F, S*, 1994 *Cze, R, W*, 1995 *S, E, Ar, F, Ar, R, NZ, SA*, 1996 *W, Pt, W, A, E, S*, 1997 *I, F, F, Ar, R, SA, I*, 1998 *S, W, Rus*, 1999 *F, S, W*
P Sguario 1958 *R*, 1959 *F*, 1960 *Ger, F*, 1961 *Ger*, 1962 *R*
M Silini 1955 *Ger, Sp, F, Cze*, 1956 *Cze*, 1957 *Ger*, 1958 *F*, 1959 *F*
S Silvestri 1954 *F*
U Silvestri 1949 *F, Cze*
U Silvestri 1967 *Pt, R*, 1968 *Pt, WGe*
L Simonelli 1956 *Ger, F, Cze*, 1958 *F*, 1960 *Ger, F*
F Sinitich 1980 *Fj, Coo, Pol, Sp*, 1981 *R*, 1983 *USS*
JW Sole 2005 *Ar, Tg, Ar*, 2006 *I, E, W, S, J, Fj, Rus, A, Ar, C*, 2007 *F, E, I, Ur, Ar, J, I, R, S*, 2008 *I, E, W, F, S, SA, Ar, A, Ar, Pl*, 2009 *E, I, S, W, F, NZ, SA, Sa*, 2010 *I, E, S, F, W*, 2011 *I*
F Soro 1965 *Cze*, 1966 *F, Ger, R*
A Spagnoli 1973 *Rho*
E Speziali 1965 *Cze*
W Spragg 2006 *C*
F Staibano 2006 *J, Fj*, 2007 *W, I, Ur, Ar*, 2009 *A, A, NZ*, 2012 *I, W*
MP Stanojevic 2006 *Pt, Rus, A, Ar, C*, 2007 *J, NZ*
U Stenta 1937 *Bel, Ger, F*, 1938 *Ger, F*, 1939 *Ger, R*, 1940 *R, Ger*, 1942 *R*
P Stievano 1948 *F*, 1952 *F*, 1953 *F, Ger, R*, 1954 *Sp, F*, 1955 *Ger*
S Stocco 1998 *H*, 1999 *S, I*, 2000 *Fj*
CA Stoica 1997 *I, F, SA, I*, 1998 *S, W, Rus, Ar, H, E*, 1999 *S, W, SA, SA, Ur, Sp, Fj, E, Tg, NZ*, 2000 *S, W, I, E, F, Sa, Fj, C, R, NZ*, 2001 *I, E, F, S, W, Fj, SA, Sa*, 2002 *F, S, W, I, E, Sp, R, Ar, A*, 2003 *W, I, S, I, Geo, Tg, C, W*, 2004 *E, F, S, I, W, US*, 2005 *S, Tg, Ar*, 2006 *I, E, F, W, S*, 2007 *Ur, Ar*

L Tagliabue 1930 *Sp*, 1933 *Cze, Cze*, 1934 *Cat, R*, 1935 *F*, 1937 *Ger*
S Tartaglini 1948 *Cze*, 1949 *F, Cze*, 1951 *Sp*, 1952 *Sp, Ger, F*, 1953 *F*
A Tassin 1973 *A*
A Taveggia 1954 *F*, 1955 *Ger, F, Sp, F*, 1956 *Ger, F, Cze*, 1957 *F, Ger*, 1958 *F, R*, 1959 *F*, 1960 *Ger, F*, 1967 *Pt*
D Tebaldi 1985 *Z, Z*, 1987 *R, Ar, Fj, USS, Sp*, 1988 *F, A, I*, 1989 *F*, 1990 *F, Pol, R*, 1991 *Nm*
T Tebaldi 2009 *A, A, NZ, NZ, SA, Sa*, 2010 *I, E, S, F, W, SA, SA, Ar*, 2012 *C, US*, 2014 *I, E, Sa, J*
T Tedeschi 1948 *F*
G Testoni 1937 *Bel*, 1938 *Ger*, 1942 *R*
C Tinari 1980 *JAB, Coo, Pol, USS, Sp*, 1981 *USS, WGe*, 1982 *F, WGe*, 1983 *R, USS, C, C, Sp, Mor, A, USS*, 1984 *Mor, R*
M Tommasi 1990 *Pol*, 1992 *R, S*, 1993 *Pt, Cro, Sp, F*
G Toniolatti 2008 *A*, 2009 *E, I, A, NZ*, 2011 *J, Rus, US*, 2012 *W, S, Ar, C*, 2014 *Sa, Ar, SA*
C Torresan 1980 *F, R, Fj, Coo, Pol, USS*, 1981 *R, USS*, 1982

R, Mor, 1983 *C, F, A, USS*, 1984 *F, Mor, Tun, USS*, 1985 *Z, Z, USS*
F Tozzi 1933 *Cze*
P Travagli 2004 *C, NZ*, 2008 *I, E, W, F, S, Ar, Pl*
L Travini 1999 *SA, Ur, Sp, Fj*, 2000 *I*
F Trebbi 1933 *Cze, Cze*
F Trentin 1979 *Mor, F, Pol, USS*, 1981 *R*
M Trevisiol 1988 *F, USS, A, I*, 1989 *F, Ar, USS*, 1994 *R*
M Trippiteli 1979 *Pol*, 1980 *Pol, Sp*, 1981 *F, R*, 1982 *F, E, WGe*, 1984 *Tun*
LR Troiani 1985 *R*, 1986 *Tun, F, Pt, A, USS*, 1987 *Pt, F*, 1988 *R, USS, A, I*, 1989 *Sp, Ar, Z, USS*, 1990 *F, Pol, R, Sp, H, R, USS*, 1991 *F, R, Nm, Nm, US, E*, 1992 *Sp, F, R, R, S*, 1993 *Sp, F, Cro, Rus, F*, 1994 *Sp, Cze, A, A, F*, 1995 *S, E, Ar*
A Troncon 1994 *Sp, R, Cze, H, A, A, R, W, F*, 1995 *S, I, Sa, E, A, F, A, R, NZ, SA*, 1996 *W, W, A, A, E, S*, 1997 *I, F, F, Ar, SA, I*, 1998 *S, W, Rus, Ar, H, E*, 1999 *F, S, W, I, Ur, Sp, Fj, E, Tg, NZ*, 2000 *S, W, I, E, F, R, NZ*, 2001 *I, F, Nm, SA, Ur, Ar, Fj, SA, Sa*, 2002 *F, S, W, I, E, Sp, R, Ar, A*, 2003 *W, I, E, F, S, S, I, Geo, NZ, Tg, C, W*, 2004 *R, J*, 2005 *I, W, S, E, F*, 2007 *F, E, S, W, I, J, I, NZ, R, Pt, S*
G Troncon 1962 *F, Ger, R*, 1963 *F*, 1964 *Ger, F*, 1965 *Cze*, 1966 *F, R*, 1967 *F*, 1968 *Yug*, 1972 *Pt*
L Turcato 1952 *Sp, Ger, F*, 1953 *Ger, R*
M Turcato 1949 *F*, 1951 *Sp*

P Vaccari 1991 *Nm, Nm, US, E, NZ, USS*, 1992 *Sp, F, R, R, S*, 1993 *Mor, Sp, F, Rus, F, S*, 1994 *Sp, R, Cze, H, A, A, R, W, F*, 1995 *I, Sa, E, Ar, F, A, R, NZ, SA*, 1996 *W, W, E, S*, 1997 *I, F, F, Ar, R, SA, I*, 1998 *S, W, Ar*, 1999 *Ur, Sp, E, Tg, NZ*, 2001 *Fj*, 2002 *F, S, Ar, A*, 2003 *W, I, E, F, S*
V Vagnetti 1939 *R*, 1940 *R*
F Valier 1968 *Yug*, 1969 *F*, 1970 *Cze, R*, 1971 *Mor, R*, 1972 *Pt*
L Valtorta 1957 *Ger*, 1958 *F*
C Van Zyl 2011 *J, S, A, Rus, US, I*, 2012 *F, W*
G Venditti 2012 *F, E, I, S, Ar, C, US, NZ, A*, 2013 *F, S, W, E, I, SA, Sa, S, Fj, Ar*, 2014 *Fj, Sa, J*, 2015 *I, E, S, F, W, S, W, F, C, I, R*
O Vene 1966 *F*
E Venturi 1983 *C*, 1985 *EngB, Sp*, 1986 *Tun, Pt*, 1988 *USS, A*, 1989 *F, R, Sp, Ar, USS*, 1990 *F, Pol, R, Sp, H, R, USS*, 1991 *F, R, NZ, USS*, 1992 *Sp, F, R*, 1993 *Sp, F*
P Vezzani 1973 *Yug*, 1975 *F, Sp, R, Cze, E, Pol, H, Sp*, 1976 *F*
P Vialetto 1972 *Yug*
V Viccariotto 1948 *F*
S Vigliano 1937 *R, Bel, Ger, F*, 1939 *R*, 1942 *R*
L Villagra 2000 *Sa, Fj*
E Vinci I 1929 *Sp*
P Vinci II 1929 *Sp*, 1930 *Sp*, 1933 *Cze*
F Vinci III 1929 *Sp*, 1930 *Sp*, 1934 *Cat, R*, 1935 *Cat, F*, 1936 *Ger, R*, 1937 *Ger, R, Ger, F*, 1939 *Ger, R*, 1940 *Ger*
P Vinci IV 1929 *Sp*, 1930 *Sp*, 1933 *Cze, Cze*, 1934 *Cat, R*, 1935 *Cat, F*, 1937 *Ger, Bel, Ger, F*, 1939 *Ger*
M Violi 2015 *S, S*
A Visentin 1970 *R*, 1972 *Pt, Sp*, 1973 *Rho, WTv, Bor, NEC, Nat, ETv, Leo, FS, Tva, Cze, Yug, A*, 1974 *Pt, Leo*, 1975 *F, Sp, R, Cze*, 1976 *R*, 1978 *Ar*
G Visentin 1935 *Cat, F*, 1936 *R*, 1937 *Ger, Bel, Ger, F*, 1938 *Ger*, 1939 *Ger*
M Visentin 2015 *S*
T Visentin 1996 *W*
W Visser 1999 *I, SA, SA*, 2000 *S, W, I, F, C, R, NZ*, 2001 *I, E, F, S, W, Nm, SA, Ur, Ar, Fj, SA, Sa*
F Vitadello 1985 *Sp*, 1987 *Pt*
C Vitelli 1973 *Cze, Yug*, 1974 *Pt, Sus*
I Vittorini 1969 *Sp*
RMS Vosawai 2007 *J, I, NZ, R, Pt*, 2010 *W, SA*, 2011 *W*, 2012 *S, A*, 2013 *W, Sa, Fj*, 2014 *I, Fj, Sa, J*
SN Vunisa 2014 *SA*, 2015 *E, S, F, W, S, S, W, F, C, R*

RS Wakarua 2003 *Tg, C, W*, 2004 *E, F, S, W, J, C, NZ*, 2005 *Fj*
F Williams 1995 *SA*

M Zaffiri 2000 *Fj, R, NZ,* 2001 *W,* 2003 *S,* 2005 *Tg, Fj,* 2006 *W, S, C,* 2007 *E, S, W, I*

R Zanatta 1954 *Sp, F*

G Zanchi 1953 *Ger, R,* 1955 *Sp, Cze,* 1957 *Ger*

A Zanella 1977 *Mor*

M Zanella 1976 *J, Sp,* 1977 *R, Pol, Cze,* 1978 *Ar,* 1980 *Pol, USS*

E Zanetti 1942 *R*

F Zani 1960 *Ger, F,* 1961 *Ger, F,* 1962 *F, R,* 1963 *F,* 1964 *F,* 1965 *F,* 1966 *Ger, R*

G Zani 1934 *R*

A Zanni 2005 *Tg, Ar, Fj,* 2006 *F, W, S, Pt, Rus, A, Ar, C,* 2007 *S, W, I, Ur, I, NZ,* 2008 *I, E, W, F, S, SA, Ar, A, PI,* 2009 *E, I, S, W, F, A, A, NZ, NZ, SA, Sa,* 2010 *I, E, S, F, W, SA, SA, Ar, A, Fj,* 2011 *I, E, W, F, S, J, S, A, Rus, US, I,* 2012 *F, E, I, W, S, Ar, C, US, Tg, NZ, A,* 2013 *F, S, W, E, I, SA, Sa, S, A, Fj, Ar,* 2014 *W, F, S, Sa, Ar, SA,* 2015 *I, S, S, W, F, C, I, R*

C Zanoletti 2001 *Sa,* 2002 *E, NZ, R, Ar, A,* 2005 *A*

G Zanon 1981 *F, R, USS, WGe,* 1982 *R, E, WGe, Mor,* 1983 *F, R, USS, C, C, Sp, Mor, F, A, USS,* 1984 *F, Mor, R, USS,* 1985 *F, R, EngB, Sp, Z, Z, USS,* 1986 *USS,* 1987 *R, Ar, USS,* 1989 *Sp, Ar,* 1990 *F, Pol, R, Sp, H, R, USS,* 1991 *Nm, US, E*

M Zingarelli 1973 *A*

N Zisti 1999 *E, NZ,* 2000 *E, F*

G Zoffoli 1936 *Ger, R,* 1937 *Ger, R, Ger,* 1938 *Ger,* 1939 *R*

S Zorzi 1985 *R,* 1986 *Tun, F,* 1988 *F, R, USS,* 1992 *R*

A Zucchelo 1956 *Ger, F*

C Zucchi 1952 *Sp,* 1953 *F*

L Zuin 1977 *Cze,* 1978 *Ar, USS, Sp,* 1979 *F, Pol, R*

Getty Images

Number eight Alessandro Zanni scores Italy's fourth try in their final Pool D match against Romania in Exeter.

ITALY

JAPAN

JAPAN'S 2014–15 TEST RECORD

OPPONENTS	DATE	VENUE	RESULT
Romania	16 Nov	A	Won 18–13
Georgia	24 Nov	A	Lost 34–25
Korea	13 Apr	A	Won 56–30
Hong Kong	2 May	H	Won 41–0
Korea	9 May	H	Won 66–10
Hong Kong	23 May	A	Drew 0–0*
Canada	19 Jul	A	Won 20–6
USA	24 Jul	A	Lost 23–18
Fiji	29 Jul	N	Lost 27–22
Tonga	3 Aug	N	Lost 31–20
Uruguay	22 Aug	H	Won 30–8
Uruguay	29 Aug	H	Won 40–0
Georgia	5 Sep	N	Won 13–10
South Africa	19 Sep	N	Won 34–32
Scotland	23 Sep	N	Lost 45–10
Samoa	3 Oct	N	Won 26–5
USA	11 Oct	N	Won 28–18

* Match abandoned as a draw due to heavy rain

BRAVE BLOSSOMS MAKE RUGBY WORLD CUP HISTORY

By Rich Freeman

Japan shocked the sporting world by beating the Springboks 34–32 at the Brighton Community Stadium.

Japan came to Rugby World Cup 2015 with two goals – to make it to the quarter-finals and to be remembered as the team of the tournament.

They may not have achieved the former, but in beating South Africa and becoming the first side to win three games and not progress to the knockout stages, they certainly did the latter.

"Let's be honest, before this tournament Japan were one of the joke teams," departing head coach Eddie Jones said. "Teams would put out their B team against them and win by 80–90 points. To come here and win three out of four games is a super effort from the team."

And the victories were no flukes.

Against the Springboks they showed incredible bravery and resilience; against Samoa great discipline, and against the USA they dug deep into their physical and mental reserves to grind out a win.

"They have changed Japanese rugby," said Jones. "They have worked hard but, more importantly, they have played with courage – not only physical courage but mental courage."

Japan's preparations for the World Cup began in April and the team underwent some gruelling training sessions as Jones sought to implement what he called the 'Japan Way'.

"The Japan Way encompasses the style of play, the philosophy, the preparation and selection of players," said Jones. "The whole point about the Japan Way is not having excuses and finding ways to have a competitive edge. Japanese players are small so we have to find a style of play and a way to prepare that makes that disadvantage an advantage."

That meant being the fittest team and making sure the players realised that the long-term goal – Rugby World Cup 2015 – was more important than the short term.

"This really is a special group of players and coaches," said captain Michael Leitch. "It's going to be flipping hard to get the same quality of coaches into the environment. Eddie gave us the structure and how we got the result was down to the hard work of the players."

Japan's World Rugby Pacific Nations Cup campaign saw them lose three of four games, but Jones had said all along that everything he was doing was to ensure the team peaked on 19 September.

And peak they did.

In front of a superb crowd and under ideal conditions, the Brave Blossoms shocked not just international rugby but the whole sporting world.

The two-time world champions may not have been at the top of their game, but they were stifled by a Japan side that collectively played the match of their lives.

Trailing 32–29 with just minutes left on the clock, the self-belief in the team reached new limits when Leitch opted against a kick at goal and a draw.

The social media clips from around the world of fans watching what happened next have become the thing of legend as the Brave Blossoms kept the ball alive for a number of phases, before Amanaki Mafi put Karne Hesketh in the clear and the wing evaded the tackle of JP Pietersen to go over in the corner.

Japanese rugby, and indeed world rugby, had never experienced anything like it, and the noise and atmosphere in the Brighton Community Stadium will be forever remembered by those fortunate enough to be there.

"We've been going through the toughest training in the world for this past four years to make history," said full-back Ayumu Goromaru. "I'm glad we've managed to not only surprise our own fans back in Japan but also fans across the world."

However, any chance the players had of celebrating was short-lived as a quick turnaround meant they faced Scotland just four days later.

Leitch and his team-mates battled valiantly against a side playing their first game of the tournament, but the legs started to go at the 60-minute mark, allowing the Scots to seal the 45–10 win.

Scotland captain Greig Laidlaw admitted the Brave Blossoms had struggled in the second stanza, but Jones was not making any excuses.

"At half-time we had a realistic chance of winning the game. They got in our 22 and took opportunities and we gave them a number of opportunities to score from. They scored at least two tries from our mistakes, intercepted passes and things. When we got into their 22 we weren't clinical enough, so that was the difference."

A week later Japan were back to winning ways as they beat Samoa 26–5, thanks to one of the most disciplined 40 minutes of rugby they have ever played.

"Our forwards were fantastic today," said Jones. "They shut Samoa down, gave us set-piece dominance and their work rate around the ruck in attack and defence was first-rate."

Japan went into their final Pool B game against the Eagles knowing a quarter-final spot was beyond them after Scotland had edged Samoa the day before. But they put aside their disappointment to produce what Jones called one of their best ever wins.

"The players were fantastic. We were 15 to 20 per cent off our best and kept battling away. It shows they have grown up. To win when you are not at your best. Full credit to them."

It all seemed a long way from November 2014 when Japan had lost twice to the Maori All Blacks, defeated Romania and lost to Georgia.

Of the other games played, the new Asia Rugby Championship had been duly won but had ended in bizarre circumstances when the encounter with Hong Kong was abandoned due to heavy rain; the Pacific Nations Cup was, in Jones' words, nothing more than a training exercise, while the warm-up games with Uruguay and Georgia had produced good, if unspectacular, wins.

Following Rugby World Cup 2015 the team returned home heroes, although there was not much time off for the players with the Top League starting a few weeks later and then Japan's new Super Rugby side kicking off in February 2016.

In the domestic season, Panasonic Wild Knights were the defending Top League champions after they beat Yamaha Jubilo 30–12 in the final, though Yamaha ended the season by winning the All-Japan Championship thanks to a 15–3 win over Suntory Sungoliath.

MATCH RECORDS UP TO 1 NOVEMBER, 2015

WINNING MARGIN

Date	Opponent	Result	Winning Margin
06/07/2002	Chinese Taipei	155–3	152
27/10/1998	Chinese Taipei	134–6	128
10/05/2014	Sri Lanka	132–10	122
20/04/2013	Philippines	121–0	121
21/07/2002	Chinese Taipei	120–3	117

MOST POINTS IN A MATCH
BY THE TEAM

Date	Opponent	Result	Points
06/07/2002	Chinese Taipei	155–3	155
27/10/1998	Chinese Taipei	134–6	134
10/05/2014	Sri Lanka	132–10	132
20/04/2013	Philippines	121–0	121
21/07/2002	Chinese Taipei	120–3	120

BY A PLAYER

Date	Player	Opponent	Points
21/07/2002	Toru Kurihara	Chinese Taipei	60
06/07/2002	Daisuke Ohata	Chinese Taipei	40
10/05/2014	Ayumu Goromaru	Sri Lanka	37
20/04/2013	Ayumu Goromaru	Philippines	36
16/06/2002	Toru Kurihara	Korea	35

MOST TRIES IN A MATCH
BY THE TEAM

Date	Opponent	Result	Tries
06/07/2002	Chinese Taipei	155–3	23
27/10/1998	Chinese Taipei	134–6	20
10/05/2014	Sri Lanka	132–10	20
	18 on 3 occasions		

BY A PLAYER

Date	Player	Opponent	Tries
06/07/2002	Daisuke Ohata	Chinese Taipei	8
21/07/2002	Toru Kurihara	Chinese Taipei	6
08/05/2005	Daisuke Ohata	Hong Kong	6
05/05/2012	Yoshikazu Fujita	United Arab Emirates	6

MOST CONVERSIONS IN A MATCH
BY THE TEAM

Date	Opponent	Result	Cons
06/07/2002	Chinese Taipei	155–3	20
27/10/1998	Chinese Taipei	134–6	17
10/05/2014	Sri Lanka	132–10	16
21/07/2002	Chinese Taipei	120–3	15
20/04/2013	Philippines	121–0	14

BY A PLAYER

Date	Player	Opponent	Cons
10/05/2014	Ayumu Goromaru	Sri Lanka	16
21/07/2002	Toru Kurihara	Chinese Taipei	15
20/04/2013	Ayumu Goromaru	Philippines	14
	12 on 3 occasions		

MOST PENALTIES IN A MATCH
BY THE TEAM

Date	Opponent	Result	Pens
08/05/1999	Tonga	44–17	9
08/04/1990	Tonga	28–16	6
23/11/2013	Spain	40–7	6
15/11/2014	Romania	18–13	6

BY A PLAYER

Date	Player	Opponent	Pens
08/05/1999	Keiji Hirose	Tonga	9
08/04/1990	Takahiro Hosokawa	Tonga	6
23/11/2013	Ayumu Goromaru	Spain	6
15/11/2014	Ayumu Goromaru	Romania	6

MOST DROP GOALS IN A MATCH
BY THE TEAM

Date	Opponent	Result	DGs
15/09/1998	Argentina	44–29	2

BY A PLAYER

Date	Player	Opponent	DGs
15/09/1998	Kensuke Iwabuchi	Argentina	2

JAPAN

MOST CAPPED PLAYERS	
Name	Caps
Hitoshi Ono	96
Hirotoki Onozawa	81
Yukio Motoki	79
Kensuke Hatakeyama	72
Takashi Kikutani	68

LEADING PENALTY SCORERS	
Name	Pens
Ayumu Goromaru	99
Keiji Hirose	76
Toru Kurihara	35
James Arlidge	28
Takahiro Hosokawa	24

LEADING TRY SCORERS	
Name	Tries
Daisuke Ohata	69
Hirotoki Onozawa	55
Takashi Kikutani	32
Terunori Masuho	28
Yoshikazu Fujita	26

LEADING DROP GOAL SCORERS	
Name	DGs
Kyohei Morita	5

LEADING POINTS SCORERS	
Name	Points
Ayumu Goromaru	711
Keiji Hirose	413
Toru Kurihara	347
Daisuke Ohata	345
James Arlidge	286
Hirotoki Onozawa	275

LEADING CONVERSIONS SCORERS	
Name	Cons
Ayumu Goromaru	162
James Arlidge	78
Keiji Hirose	77
Toru Kurihara	71
Ryan Nicholas	53

JAPAN INTERNATIONAL PLAYERS
UP TO 1 NOVEMBER, 2015

T Adachi 1932 *C, C*
M Aizawa 1984 *Kor*, 1986 *US, C, S, E, Kor*, 1987 *A, NZ, NZ*, 1988 *OU, Kor*
H Akama 1973 *F*, 1975 *A, W*, 1976 *S, E, It, Kor*, 1977 *S*
T Akatsuka 1994 *Fj*, 1995 *Tg, NZ*, 1996 *Kor*, 2005 *Sp*, 2006 *HK, Kor*
J Akune 2001 *W, C*
M Amino 2000 *Kor, C*, 2003 *Rus, AuA, Kor, E, E, S, Fj, US*
E Ando 2006 *AG, Kor, Geo, Tg, Sa, JAB, Fj*, 2007 *HK, Fj, Tg, Sa, JAB, It*
D Anglesey 2002 *Tg, Tai, Tai*
T Aoi 1959 *BCo, BCo, OCC*, 1963 *BCo*
S Aoki 1989 *S*, 1990 *Fj*, 1991 *US, C*, 1993 *W*
Y Aoki 2007 *Kor, AuA, JAB*, 2008 *Kor, Kaz, HK, AuA, Tg, Fj, Sa, US, US*, 2009 *Kaz, Sin, Sa, JAB, Tg, Fj*, 2011 *Sa, Tg, US, NZ*, 2013 *Phl, HK, Kor, UAE, Tg, Fj, NZ, S*
S Arai 1959 *BCo, BCo*
R Arita 2012 *Kaz, UAE, Kor, HK, Fj, Tg, Sa*, 2015 *HK, HK*
JA Arlidge 2007 *Kor*, 2008 *Kor, AG, Kaz, HK, AuA, Tg, Fj, M, Sa*, 2009 *Sa, JAB, Tg, Fj, C, C*, 2010 *Kor, AG, Kaz, HK, Fj, Sa, Tg, Sa, Rus*, 2011 *Kaz, UAE, Tg, It, F, Tg, C*
G Aruga 2006 *HK, Kor*, 2007 *Kor, HK, AuA, Sa, JAB, It, Fj, C*, 2008 *Kor, HK*, 2009 *C, C*, 2011 *UAE, Fj*, 2012 *R, Geo*
K Aruga 1974 *NZU*, 1975 *A, A, W, W*, 1976 *S, E, It, Kor*
T Asahara 2013 *Phl, HK, Kor, UAE, Fj*

R Asano 2003 *AuA, AuA, F, Fj*, 2005 *Ar, HK, Kor, R, C, I, I, Sp*, 2006 *Kor, Geo, Tg, It, HK, Kor*, 2007 *Kor, It, W*
M Atokawa 1969 *HK*, 1970 *Tha, BCo*, 1971 *E, E*
H Atou 1976 *BCo*

T Baba 1932 *C*
GTM Bachop 1999 *C, Tg, Sa, Fj, Sp, Sa, W, Ar*
I Basiyalo 1997 *HK, US, US, C, HK*
J Bennetts 2015 *C, Tg*
D Bickle 1996 *HK, HK, C, US, US, C*
M Broadhurst 2012 *R, Geo*, 2013 *Phl, HK, Kor, UAE, Tg, Fj, W, W, C, US, NZ, S, Rus, Sp*, 2015 *C, US, Fj, Tg, Ur, Geo, SA, S, Sa, US*

KCC Chang 1930 *BCo*, 1932 *C, C*
T Chiba 1930 *BCo*
M Chida 1980 *Kor*, 1982 *HK, C, C, Kor*, 1983 *W*, 1984 *F, F, Kor*, 1985 *US, I, I, F, F*, 1986 *US, C, S, E, Kor*, 1987 *US, E*

H Daimon 2004 *S, W*

K Endo 2004 *It*, 2006 *AG, Kor, Geo, Tg, It, JAB, Fj*, 2007 *HK, Fj, Tg, AuA, Sa, It, Fj, W, C*, 2008 *AuA, Tg, Fj, M, US, US*, 2009 *C, C*, 2010 *Kor, AG, Kaz, HK, Fj, Sa, Tg, Sa, Rus*, 2011 *UAE, Sa, Tg, It, F, Tg, C*

JAPAN

T Madea 1991 *US, C, HK*, 1995 *Tg*
AL Mafi 2014 *R, Geo*, 2015 *Geo, SA, S, Sa, US*
P Mafileo 2008 *US*
S Makabe 2009 *C*, 2010 *Kaz*, 2012 *Kaz, UAE, Kor, HK, Fj, Tg, Sa*, 2013 *Phl, HK, Kor, UAE, Tg, W, C, US, S, Rus, Sp*, 2014 *SL, Kor, HK, Sa, C, US, It, R, Geo*, 2015 *Ur, Geo, SA, S, US*
HAW Makiri 2005 *Ur, Ar, HK, Kor, R, I, I*, 2006 *AG, Tg, Sa, JAB*, 2007 *Kor, Tg, AuA, Sa, JAB, It, A, Fj, W, C*, 2008 *AuA, Tg, Fj, M, Sa*
M Mantani 1969 *HK*, 1970 *Tha, BCo*, 1971 *E, E*, 1972 *HK*
G Marsh 2007 *AuA, Sa, JAB*
T Masuho 1991 *US, C, HK, S, I, Z*, 1993 *Ar, Ar*, 1994 *Fj, Fj, Kor*, 1995 *Tg, W*, 1996 *HK, C, US, US, C*, 1997 *HK, C, US, C, HK*, 1998 *C, US, HK, HK, US, C, Ar, Kor, Tai, HK*, 1999 *C, US, Sp, Sa*, 2000 *Fj, US, Tg, Sa, Kor, C*, 2001 *Kor, W, Sa, C*
Y Masutome 1986 *Kor*
K Matsubara 1930 *BCo*
T Matsubara 1932 *C, C*
Y Matsubara 2004 *Kor, Rus, C, It*, 2005 *Sp*, 2006 *AG, Kor, Geo, Tg, It, Sa, JAB, Fj, Kor*, 2007 *Kor, Fj, Tg, Sa, JAB, It, Fj, W, C*
T Matsuda 1992 *HK*, 1993 *W*, 1994 *Fj, HK, Kor*, 1995 *Tg, R, W, I, NZ*, 1996 *HK, HK, C, US, US, C, Kor*, 1998 *US, HK, HK, US, C, Ar, Kor, Tai, HK, Kor*, 1999 *C, Fj, US, Sp, Sa, Ar*, 2001 *Kor, Tai, W*, 2003 *US, AuA, Kor, E, S, Fj, US*
C Matsui 2015 *Kor, HK*
J Matsumoto 1977 *S*, 1978 *F*, 1980 *H*, 1982 *C, C*
T Matsunaga 1985 *F, F*
Y Matsunobu 1963 *BCo*
H Matsuo 2003 *AuA, AuA, Kor, E, E*
K Matsuo 1986 *US, C, S, E, Kor*, 1987 *E, NZ*, 1988 *Kor*, 1990 *Tg, Kor, Sa, US*, 1991 *US, HK, S, I, Z*, 1993 *Ar, Ar*, 1994 *Fj, Fj, HK*, 1995 *Tg*
Y Matsuo 1974 *SL*, 1976 *BCo, E, It, Kor*, 1977 *S*, 1979 *HK, E, E*, 1982 *HK, C, C*, 1983 *OCC, W*, 1984 *F, F, Kor*
S Matsuoka 1963 *BCo*, 1970 *Tha*
K Matsushima 2014 *Phl, SL, Kor, Sa, R, Geo*, 2015 *C, US, Fj, Tg, Ur, Geo, SA, S, Sa, US*
K Matsushita 2008 *US, US*, 2010 *AG, HK, Fj, Sa, Tg*
F Mau 2004 *Rus, C, It, S, R, W*
AF McCormick 1996 *HK, HK, US*, 1997 *HK, C, US, US, C, HK*, 1998 *C, US, HK, Ar, Kor, Tai, HK*, 1999 *C, Tg, Sa, Fj, US, Sp, Sa, W, Ar*
M Mikami 2013 *Phl, HK, UAE, Tg, Fj, W, W, C, US, NZ, S, Rus, Sp*, 2014 *Phl, SL, Kor, HK, Sa, C, US, It, R, Geo*, 2015 *Kor, HK, Kor, Ur, Ur, Geo, SA, S, US*
R Miki 1999 *Sp*, 2002 *Tg, Tai, Kor, Tai, Kor*, 2004 *S, R, W*
A Miller 2002 *Rus, Kor, Tai, Kor, Tai*, 2003 *Kor, S, F, Fj, US*
S Miln 1998 *C, US, HK, HK, US*
Y Minamikawa 1976 *BCo*, 1978 *F, Kor*, 1979 *HK, E, E*, 1980 *H, F, Kor*, 1982 *HK, C, C, Kor*
M Mishima 1930 *BCo*, 1932 *C, C*
T Miuchi 2002 *Rus, Kor, Kor, Tai, Kor*, 2003 *US, Rus, AuA, Kor, E, E, S, F, Fj, US*, 2004 *Rus, C, It, S, R, W*, 2005 *Ur, Ar, HK, Kor, R, C, I, I*, 2006 *HK, Kor*, 2007 *Kor, HK, Fj, Tg, Sa, It, Fj, W, C*, 2008 *Kor, AG, Kaz, HK, AuA, Tg, Fj, Sa*
S Miura 1963 *BCo*
K Miyai 1959 *BCo, BCo*, 1963 *BCo*
K Miyaji 1969 *HK*
K Miyajima 1959 *BCo, BCo*
H Miyaji-Yoshizawa 1930 *BCo*
T Miyake 2005 *Sp*, 2006 *Sa, JAB, Fj*
K Miyamoto 1986 *S, E*, 1987 *US, E, A*, 1988 *Kor*, 1991 *I*
K Miyata 1971 *E, E*, 1972 *HK*
M Miyauchi 1975 *W*, 1976 *It, Kor*
K Mizobe 1997 *C*
K Mizoguchi 1997 *C*
K Mizobe 1997 *HK*
H Mizuno 2004 *R*, 2005 *HK, Kor, R, C, I*, 2006 *AG, Geo, Tg, It, Sa, JAB*
M Mizutani 1970 *Tha*, 1971 *E*
N Mizuyama 2008 *Tg, M, Sa, US*
Y Mochizuki 2012 *Kaz, UAE, Kor, HK, Fj, Tg, Sa*
S Mori 1974 *NZU, SL*, 1975 *A, A, W, W*, 1976 *BCo, S, E, It,*

Kor, 1977 *S*, 1978 *F*, 1979 *HK, E, E, CU*, 1980 *NZU, H, F, Kor*, 1981 *AuUn*
K Morikawa 2012 *UAE*
K Morioka 1982 *Kor*
K Morita 2004 *C, It*, 2005 *Ur, Ar, Kor, R, C, I*
A Moriya 2006 *Tg, It, Sa, JAB, Fj*, 2008 *AG, Kaz*
Y Motoki 1991 *US, US, C*, 1992 *HK*, 1993 *Ar, Ar*, 1994 *Fj, Fj, Kor*, 1995 *Tg, Tg, R, W, I, NZ*, 1996 *HK, HK, C, US, US, C, Kor*, 1997 *HK, C, US, US, C, HK*, 1998 *C, US, HK, HK, US, C, Ar, Kor, HK, Kor*, 1999 *C, Tg, Sa, Fj, US, Sp, Sa, W, Ar*, 2001 *W, W, Sa, C*, 2002 *Rus, Tg, Kor, Tai, Kor, Tai, Kor*, 2003 *Kor, E, E, S, Fj, US*, 2004 *Kor, Rus, C, It, S, R, W*, 2005 *Ur, Ar, HK, Kor, R, C, I, I*
K Motoyoshi 2001 *Tai*
S Mukai 1985 *I, I, F*, 1986 *US, C, E, Kor*, 1987 *US, A, NZ, NZ*
M Mukoyama 2004 *Kor, C, It, S, R, W*
K Muraguchi 1976 *S, Kor*
D Murai 1985 *I, I, F, F*, 1987 *E*
D Murata 2014 *Phl, SL*
K Murata 1963 *BCo*
T Murata 2015 *Kor, HK, Kor, US, Ur*
W Murata 1991 *US, S*, 1995 *Tg, NZ*, 1996 *HK, HK, C, US, US, C, Kor*, 1997 *HK, C, US, US, HK*, 1998 *HK, HK, US, C, Ar, Kor, Kor*, 1999 *US, W*, 2001 *W, W, Sa*, 2002 *Rus, Tg, Kor, Tai, Kor, Tai*, 2003 *US, AuA, E*, 2005 *Ur, Ar, Kor, I, I*
Y Murata 1971 *E, E*, 1972 *HK*, 1973 *W*, 1974 *NZU, SL*

Y Nagae 2012 *Kaz, UAE, Kor, HK, Fj, Tg, Sa, R, Geo*, 2013 *W, W, C, US, NZ, S*, 2014 *Phl, SL*, 2015 *HK*
M Nagai 1988 *Kor*
Y Nagatomo 2010 *Kor, AG, Kaz*, 2012 *Kaz, UAE, Kor, HK, Fj, Sa*
Y Nagatomo 1993 *W*, 1994 *Fj, HK*, 1995 *Tg*, 1996 *US, US*, 1997 *C*
T Naito 1934 *AuUn*
M Nakabayashi 2005 *HK, Kor, R, I*
T Nakai 2005 *Ur, HK, C, I, I, Sp*, 2006 *AG, Kor, Geo, Tg, It, Fj*
T Nakamichi 1996 *HK, HK, US, US, C*, 1998 *Ar, Kor*, 1999 *C, Sa, Fj, Sp, W, Ar*, 2000 *Fj, US, Tg*
N Nakamura 1996 *HK, HK, US, C, Ar, Kor, Tai, HK, Kor*, 1999 *C, Tg, Sa, Fj, US, Sp, W, Ar*, 2000 *I*
R Nakamura 2013 *UAE*, 2014 *Phl, Kor, Sa*
S Nakamura 2009 *Kaz, Sin*, 2010 *AG, Kaz, HK, Fj*
S Nakashima 1989 *S*, 1990 *Fj, Tg, Kor, Sa, US*, 1991 *US, US, C, HK, S*
T Nakayama 1976 *BCo*, 1978 *F*, 1979 *E*, 1980 *H*, 1982 *C, C*
Y Nakayama 2008 *Kor, AG, Kaz, HK, Tg, M*, 2009 *HK, Kor, Sin, Tg, Fj*
H Namba 2000 *Fj, US, Tg, Sa, Kor, C, I*, 2001 *Tai, W, W, C*, 2002 *Rus, Tg, Kor, Tai, Kor*, 2003 *US, Rus, AuA, AuA, Kor, E, E, F*
RT Nicholas 2008 *Kor, Kaz, HK, AuA, Tg, Fj, Sa, US, US*, 2009 *HK, Kor, Sa, JAB, Tg, Fj, C, C*, 2010 *Kor, Kaz, HK, Fj, Sa, Tg, Sa, Rus*, 2011 *HK, UAE, Sa, Tg, Fj, It, US, F, Tg, C*, 2012 *Fj, Tg, Sa*
H Nishida 1994 *Fj*
S Nishigaki 1932 *C, C*
T Nishiura 2004 *W*, 2006 *HK, Kor*, 2007 *Kor, Fj, Tg, Sa, It, Fj, W, C*, 2008 *Kor, HK, AuA, Tg, Fj, Sa*
H Nishizumi 1963 *BCo*
M Niwa 1932 *C*
I Nogami 1932 *C*, 1936 *NZU*
T Nozawa 2000 *Tg, Sa, Kor, C*

M Oda 2000 *US, Tg, Sa, Kor, I*
H Ogasawara 1969 *HK*, 1970 *Tha, BCo*, 1971 *E, E*, 1973 *F*, 1974 *NZU*, 1975 *A, A, W, W*, 1976 *NZU*, 1977 *S*
K Oguchi 1997 *US, C, HK*, 1998 *Tai*, 1999 *Sa, Ar*, 2000 *Fj, Tg, Sa, Kor*
K Ohara 1998 *Kor, Tai*, 2000 *Kor, C, I*
D Ohata 1996 *Kor*, 1997 *HK, C, US*, 1998 *HK, C, Ar, Kor, HK*, 1999 *C, Tg, Sa, Fj, US, Sp, Sa, W, Ar*, 2000 *Fj, US, Kor, C, I*, 2002 *Rus, Kor, Tai, Kor, Tai, Kor*, 2003 *US, Rus, AuA, AuA, Kor, E, E, S, F, Fj, US*, 2004 *Kor, Rus, C, It*, 2005 *Ur, Ar, HK, Kor, R, C, I, I*, 2006 *AG, Kor, Geo, Tg, HK, Kor*

Fj, W, W, C, US, NZ, S, Rus, Sp, 2014 Phl, SL, Kor, HK, Sa, C, US, It, Geo, 2015 Kor, HK, Kor, HK, C, Fj, Ur, SA, S

A Tanabe 2010 Rus, 2011 Kaz, SL
F Tanaka 2008 AG, HK, AuA, Tg, Fj, Sa, US, US, 2009 Kaz, HK, Sin, Sa, Tg, Fj, 2010 Kor, Kaz, HK, Fj, Sa, Tg, Sa, Rus, 2011 Kaz, UAE, SL, Sa, Tg, It, F, Tg, C, 2012 R, Geo, 2013 W, W, C, US, NZ, S, Rus, Sp, 2014 C, US, It, 2015 Fj, Tg, Ur, Ur, Geo, SA, S, Sa, US
K Tanaka 2004 S, R, W
N Tanaka 1974 SL, 1975 A, W, 1976 BCo, S, E, 1977 S, 1980 F, Kor, 1982 HK, Kor
S Tanaka 1959 BCo, BCo
N Tanifuji 1979 HK, E, E, 1982 C, C, 1983 W, 1984 F, Kor, 1985 US
Y Tanigawa 1969 HK
I Taniguchi 2010 Rus, 2011 Kaz, SL, Sa, Tg, Fj, US, F, NZ, Tg
T Taniguchi 2006 Tg, It, JAB, 2008 Kor, Kaz, HK, AuA, Tg, Fj, M, Sa, US
H Tanuma 1996 Kor, 1997 HK, C, US, US, HK, 1998 C, US, HK, 1999 Sa, Fj, US, Sp, Sa, W, Ar, 2000 Fj, US, Tg, Sa, Kor, C, I, 2001 Kor, Tai, W, W, Sa, C, 2002 Kor, 2003 AuA, E, F
J Tarrant 2009 Kaz, HK, Kor, Sa, JAB, Tg, Fj
H Tatekawa 2012 Kaz, UAE, Kor, HK, Fj, Tg, Sa, R, Geo, 2013 Phl, HK, Kor, UAE, Tg, Fj, W, W, C, US, NZ, 2014 Kor, HK, Sa, C, US, It, R, Geo, 2015 Kor, HK, Kor, HK, C, US, Fj, Tg, Ur, Ur, Geo, SA, S, Sa, US
M Tatsukawa 2000 Sa
T Taufa 2009 Kaz, Kor, Sin, Sa, JAB, Tg, Fj, C, C, 2010 Kor, AG, Kaz, HK, Fj, Sa, Tg, Sa, 2011 HK, Kaz, UAE, SL, C
N Taumoefolau 1985 F, F, 1986 US, C, S, E, Kor, 1987 US, E, A, NZ, 1988 Kor, 1989 S, 1990 Fj
T Terai 1969 HK, 1970 Tha, 1971 E, E, 1972 HK, 1973 W, F, 1974 NZU, 1975 A, W, W, 1976 S, E, It, Kor
S Teramura 1930 BCo
LM Thompson 2007 HK, Fj, Tg, Sa, JAB, It, Fj, W, C, 2008 M, Sa, US, US, 2009 Kaz, Kor, Sa, Tg, Fj, 2010 Kor, AG, Kaz, HK, Fj, Sa, Tg, Sa, Rus, 2011 HK, Kaz, SL, Sa, Tg, It, US, F, Tg, C, 2012 R, Geo, 2013 NZ, S, Rus, Sp, 2014 HK, Sa, C, US, It, Geo, 2015 Kor, HK, Kor, HK, C, US, Fj, Ur, Ur, Geo, SA, S, Sa, US
R Thompson 1998 C, US, HK, HK, US, C
Z Toba-Nakajima 1930 BCo, 1932 C
K Todd 2000 Fj, Sa, I
H Tominaga 1959 BCo, BCo
K Tomioka 2008 US, US, 2009 Kor, Sin, Sa, JAB
T Tomioka 2005 I, I
T Toshi 1932 C, C
H Toshima 1980 H, F, 1982 HK, C, C, 1984 F, F, Kor
M Toyoda 2008 US
N Toyoda 1982 HK
S Toyoda 1974 SL
T Toyoda 1978 Kor
M Toyota 2009 Sin, Sa, Tg, Fj, 2010 Kor, AG, Kaz, HK
K Toyoyama 1976 BCo, 1979 E, E, 1980 H
M Toyoyama 2000 Fj, US, Sa, C, 2001 Kor, W, W, Sa, C, 2002 Rus, Kor, Tai, Kor, Tai, 2003 US, Rus, AuA, Kor, E, E, S, Fj, US
H Tsuboi 2012 Kaz, UAE
M Tsuchida 1985 F
T Tsuchiya 1956 AuUn, 1959 BCo, BCo
E Tsuji 1980 Kor, 1982 Kor
T Tsuji 2003 S, Fj, US, 2005 HK, R, C, 2006 Kor
Y Tsujimoto 2001 Kor
K Tsukagoshi 2002 Kor, 2005 Ur, Ar, HK, Kor, R, C, I, I
S Tsukda 2001 Kor, C, 2002 Tg, Tai, Kor, Tai, Kor, 2003 AuA, E
T Tsuyama 1976 BCo, Kor
H Tui 2012 Tg, Sa, R, Geo, 2013 Phl, HK, Kor, UAE, Tg, Fj, W, W, C, US, NZ, S, Rus, Sp, 2014 Phl, SL, HK, Sa, C, US, It, R, Geo, 2015 Fj, Tg, Ur, Ur, Geo, SA, S, Sa, US
P Tuidraki 1997 HK, C, 1998 C, US, HK, HK, US, C, Tai, 1999 Tg, Sa, Tg, Sa, W, Ar, 2000 I, 2001 Tai, W, W
A Tupuailai 2009 C, C, 2010 Kor, AG, Kaz, HK, Fj, Sa, Tg, Sa, Rus, 2011 HK, Kaz, SL, It, US, F, NZ, Tg, C

K Uchida 2012 Kaz, UAE, 2013 UAE, Fj, 2014 Phl, SL, Kor, HK, 2015 Kor, HK, US, Ur
M Uchida 1969 HK
A Ueda 1975 W, 1978 Kor, 1979 E, E
T Ueda 2011 HK, Kaz, UAE, SL, US, NZ
S Ueki 1963 BCo
R Ueno 2011 SL
N Ueyama 1973 F, 1974 NZU, SL, 1975 A, A, W, W, 1976 BCo, E, It, Kor, 1978 F, 1980 Kor
H Ujino 1976 BCo, 1977 S, 1978 F, Kor, 1979 HK, E, E, 1980 H, Kor, 1982 HK, Kor
R Umei 1958 NZ23, NZ23, NZ23
Y Uryu 2000 Sa, 2001 Kor
K Usami 2015 Kor, HK, Kor, C
T Usuzuki 2011 UAE, SL, Sa, Fj, It, US, NZ
S Vatuvei 2010 Kor, AG, Kaz, Sa, 2011 US, NZ, Tg, C

K Wada 1997 HK, US, US, C, HK
K Wada 2010 AG, Kaz, Fj, Tg, Rus
S Wada 1930 BCo
T Wada 1975 A, 1976 S, 1979 E, E
J Washington 2005 Ur, Ar, HK, Kor, R, C, I
M Washiya 2000 Kor, C
H Watanabe 1990 Sa
T Watanabe 2015 Ur, Ur
T Watanabe 2002 Kor
Y Watanabe 1996 HK, HK, 1998 C, US, HK, HK, Ar, Kor, Tai, HK, 1999 C, Tg, US, Sp, Sa, 2000 Fj, US, I, 2003 Rus, AuA, AuA, E, S, 2004 Kor, 2005 HK, R, C, 2007 HK, Fj, Tg, Sa, JAB, A, W
SJ Webb 2008 AG, Kaz, HK, AuA, Tg, Fj, M, US, US, 2009 Kaz, Kor, Sa, Tg, Fj, C, C, 2010 Kor, Kaz, HK, Fj, Sa, Tg, 2011 HK, Kaz, UAE, SL, Sa, Tg, Fj, It, US, F, NZ, Tg, C
IM Williams 1993 W
MC Williams 2011 Sa, Fj, US, F, NZ, C
C Wing 2013 UAE, Fj, W, W, US, NZ, S, 2015 Tg, Ur, Geo, US
T Yagai 1930 BCo
T Yajima 1978 Kor, 1979 E
A Yamada 2013 Rus, Sp, 2014 SL, Kor, HK, Sa, C, US, It, R, 2015 HK, US, Fj, SA, Sa
K Yamada 1963 BCo
K Yamaguchi 1936 NZU
T Yamaguchi 2004 S, R, W
Y Yamaguchi 1970 Tha, BCo, 1971 E, E, 1972 HK
E Yamamoto 2001 Kor, W, 2002 Tg, Kor
I Yamamoto 1973 W
M Yamamoto 2002 Rus, Kor, Tai, Kor, 2003 Rus, AuA, AuA, Kor, E, E, Fj, US, 2004 Kor, Rus, C, S, R, W, 2006 Sa, JAB, Fj, 2007 HK, Fj, AuA, JAB, A
M Yamamoto 2004 C, S, W, 2006 HK, Kor, 2007 HK, Fj, Tg, AuA, Sa
T Yamamoto 1988 Kor, 1989 S, 1990 Fj
R Yamamura 2001 W, 2002 Tg, Tai, Tai, 2003 AuA, F, 2004 Kor, Rus, C, It, S, R, W, 2005 Ur, Ar, HK, Kor, R, C, I, I, Sp, 2006 Kor, Geo, It, Sa, JAB, Fj, HK, Kor, 2007 Kor, Tg, AuA, Sa, JAB, It, A, Fj, W, C
R Yamanaka 2002 AG, 2015 Kor, Kor, US
T Yamaoka 2004 It, S, R, W, 2005 Sp, 2006 AG, Kor, Geo, Tg, It, Sa, JAB, Fj
H Yamashita 2009 Kaz, HK, Kor, Sin, Sa, JAB, Tg, Fj, 2012 Kor, HK, Fj, Tg, Sa, R, Geo, 2013 Phl, HK, Kor, UAE, Tg, Fj, W, W, C, US, NZ, S, Rus, Sp, 2014 Phl, SL, Kor, HK, Sa, C, It, R, 2015 Kor, Kor, C, Fj, Tg, Ur, Ur, Geo, SA, S, Sa, US
O Yamashita 1974 SL
M Yasuda 1984 F
N Yasuda 2000 Kor, I
Y Yasue 2009 HK, Kor
R Yasui 2013 UAE, W
T Yasui 1976 S, E, 1977 S, 1978 F, Kor, 1979 HK, E
K Yasumi 1986 C, 1987 US, NZ
Y Yatomi 2006 Kor, 2007 HK, Fj, Tg, AuA, Sa, JAB, A, Fj, 2009 Kaz, Kor, JAB, C, 2014 Geo, 2015 Kor, HK
O Yatsuhashi 1996 US, C, 1998 US, HK, HK, US, C, Ar, Tai, Kor, 2000 Kor, C
A Yokoi 1969 HK, 1970 Tha, NZU, BCo, 1971 E, 1972 AuUn, AuUn, HK, 1973 W, E, F, 1974 NZU

A Yoshida 1995 *R, W, I, NZ,* 1996 *C, US, C, Kor,* 1997 *US, HK,* 1999 *Sa,* 2000 *Fj, US, Tg, Sa, Kor, C*
H Yoshida 2001 *Sa, C,* 2002 *Tg, Tai,* 2004 *R, W,* 2006 *AG, Kor, Geo, Tg, Sa, JAB, Fj, HK, Kor*
H Yoshida 2008 *Kor, AG, Kaz, M,* 2009 *Kaz, HK, Sin*
J Yoshida 1973 *W, F*
M Yoshida 1974 *NZU,* 1975 *A, A, W,* 1976 *BCo, S, E, It, Kor,* 1977 *S,* 1978 *F, Kor*
T Yoshida 2002 *Tg, Tai, Kor,* 2003 *E*
T Yoshida 2007 *Kor, Fj, Tg, Sa, It, Fj, W, C,* 2008 *Kor, Kaz, AuA, Tg, M, Sa, US,* 2009 *Kor, Sa, JAB, C, C,* 2010 *AG,*
HK, Sa, 2011 *US, NZ*
Y Yoshida 1988 *Kor,* 1989 *S,* 1990 *Fj, Tg, Kor, Sa, US, Kor,* 1991 *US, US, C, HK, S, I, Z,* 1992 *HK,* 1993 *Ar, Ar, W,* 1994 *Fj, Fj, HK, Kor,* 1995 *Tg, Tg, R, I, NZ,* 1996 *HK*
K Yoshinaga 1986 *Kor,* 1987 *US, A, NZ,* 1990 *Sa*
K Yoshino 1973 *W*
T Yoshino 1985 *US, I, I, F, F,* 1986 *Kor,* 1987 *NZ*
H Yuhara 2010 *Kor, AG, HK, Fj, Rus,* 2011 *HK, UAE, SL, NZ,* 2013 *Phl, Kor, Rus, Sp,* 2014 *Phl, SL, Sa, R, Geo,* 2015 *Kor, Kor, US, Ur*

THE COUNTRIES

Getty Images

Japan's all-time leading points scorer Ayumu Goromaru was named at full-back in the Société Générale Dream Team for RWC 2015.

NAMIBIA

NAMIBIA'S 2014–15 TEST RECORD

OPPONENT	DATE	VENUE	RESULT
Germany	29 Oct	H	Won 58–20
Canada	7 Nov	N	Lost 17–13
Portugal	22 Nov	A	Lost 29–20
Tunisia	6 Jun	A	Won 22–14
Romania	17 Jun	A	Lost 43–3
Spain	21 Jun	N	Lost 20–3
Russia	11 Jul	H	Won 39–19
Russia	18 Jul	H	Won 45–5
Kenya	8 Aug	H	Won 46–13
Zimbabwe	15 Aug	H	Won 80–6
New Zealand	24 Sep	N	Lost 58–14
Tonga	29 Sep	N	Lost 35–21
Georgia	7 Oct	N	Lost 17–16
Argentina	11 Oct	N	Lost 64–19

PROUD NAMIBIA MAKE BIG STRIDES FORWARD

By Jon Newcombe

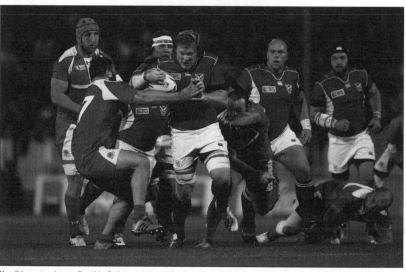

Namibian powerhouse Renaldo Bothma takes on the Georgian defence in their Pool C clash at Sandy Park, Exeter.

Ranked the lowest of the 20 participating nations at Rugby World Cup 2015, Namibia were expected by many to just make up the numbers. But the Welwitschias' fighting spirit, typified by captain Jacques Burger, shone through to ensure the one-sided scorelines that had haunted them in the past were not repeated.

Once the fall-out from Danie Vermeulen's shock resignation in June had subsided, preparations for the tournament had gone well under new head coach Phil Davies, who'd been promoted from his World Rugby-funded technical advisor role.

After a 2–0 comfortable series win over Russia, Africa Cup victories against Kenya and Zimbabwe and a successful training camp with the Springboks, a first tournament win appeared to more attainable at RWC 2015 than in any of their four previous appearances on the world's biggest stage.

Paired with reigning champions New Zealand, Argentina, Georgia and Tonga in Pool C, it was still clear from the get-go that Namibia would have their work cut out, and a tackle count averaging 129 per match indicates much of their campaign was spent on the back foot.

While they were unable to break their losing run at World Cups, Namibia certainly had their moments in the sun. Holding New Zealand to a 58–14 scoreline in their opening match at The Stadium, Queen Elizabeth Olympic Park was a remarkable achievement for a nation that had once been blown away 142–0 by Australia. For centre Johan Deysel to score against the All Blacks was a dream come true, and the celebratory scenes that marked his 52nd-minute try will live long in the memory. Theuns Kotze kicked the rest of Namibia's points, his third penalty seeing him become only the second player from his country after Jaco Coetzee to pass a century of points in a calendar year.

Five days after facing the might of New Zealand, Namibia found themselves up against Tonga at Sandy Park in Exeter. With half the preparation time of their opponents due to the tight turnaround, a slow start was perhaps understandable and Tonga raced into a 12–0 lead in as many minutes before Namibia finally picked up the relentless pace of the game to score through Johan Tromp. Tries from Latiume Fosita, Jack Ram and Telusa Veainu saw Tonga stretch out in front again but there was still time for Burger to score a brace of tries in a defiant 35–21 defeat.

For Namibia, RWC 2015 was all about gaining small victories, and scoring three tries in a match – something they had never managed at this level before – was another one to tick off the list.

Burger's brace, both from the back of a rolling maul, was just reward for another display where he showed scant regard for his own safety, and which would have won him the man of the match award had it not been for the brilliance of opposite number Ram. Such is his bravery, it would be reasonable to think the Saracens man has a screw loose. In fact he has several – with a few bolts thrown in for good measure – at the bottom of his kit bag: all reminders of the countless operations he's had to endure in a career where he constantly put his body on the line for club and country.

If anyone deserved to bow out a winner, it was Burger, and to do so against Georgia would have been sweetly ironic as the Lelos achieved their maiden World Cup victory against Namibia in 2007.

Having struggled in the scrum against Tonga, Namibia beefed up their pack by recalling their most-capped player, loose-head prop Johnny Redelinghuys, and first-choice tight-head Raoul Larson, who missed the defeat by Tonga with a strained hamstring. However, when the first scrum went according to script and the Namibian eight were forced to pedal backwards it looked like a long night was in store.

Worse was to come for Namibia when Burger – making a Namibian record-equalling 11th World Cup appearance – had to go off after just nine minutes following a blow to the head, never to return to international rugby.

While Burger's game, and career, had been cut short, those left on the pitch must have experienced the longest first half in Rugby World Cup history, all of 64 minutes in real time, after countless re-set scrums and TMO referrals. Somehow, in the face of a forward onslaught, Namibia held on to lead 6–0 at the break thanks to Kotze's two penalties. But their valiant effort had come at a price. As well as losing Burger to injury, the repeated scrum offences, five metres from their own line, saw Larson and Johannes Coetzee dispatched to the sin-bin as the first half finally drew to a close.

Georgia made their numerical advantage count 10 minutes after the re-start when their own inspirational captain Mamuka Gorgodze barged his way over from close range. The loss of barn-storming number eight Renaldo Bothma to a third yellow card was another bitter blow for Namibia to take and the concession of two penalties and a converted try left them trailing 17–6 and with a mountain to climb.

But Namibia weren't done yet. Kotze kicked a third penalty and converted his own try on 74 minutes, after a blindside break, to set things up for a grandstand finish. In the end, though, Namibia had to settle for the consolation of a losing bonus point, the first of their 18-match World Cup history.

"We said before the game that we wanted the players to play with emotion and a real performance from the heart and I thought they were magnificent. To come back like we did towards the end and nearly snatch a win was amazing," said Davies.

In scoring all his side's points in the 17–16 defeat, Kotze established a new points scoring record of 345 for Namibia, a figure he increased to 349 with two conversions in the final game against Argentina.

Unsurprisingly, Redelinghuys was denied a winning send-off on his 50th and final cap as Argentina stormed to a 64–19 victory at the Leicester City Stadium. JC Greyling and Eugene Jantjies scored their first World Cup tries while Tromp bagged his second before Namibia exited stage left with their heads held high.

Namibia's 19 points in the match took them to 70 for the tournament, meaning they scored 50+ points at a Rugby World Cup for the first time. Their previous best total was 44 in 2011. RWC 2015 is also the first time in the five-team pool format that Namibia have conceded fewer than 200 points (174).

"It's been a progressive World Cup for us," said Davies. "We have hit milestones during this World Cup. Our scores [conceded] against tier one nations have gone down and also against tier two, and we have achieved our first World Cup point."

MATCH RECORDS UP TO 1 NOVEMBER, 2015

Winning Margin

Date	Opponent	Result	Winning Margin
15/06/2002	Madagascar	112–0	112
06/07/2014	Madagascar	89–10	79
21/04/1990	Portugal	86–9	77
15/08/2015	Zimbabwe	80–6	74

MOST POINTS IN A MATCH
BY THE TEAM

Date	Opponent	Result	Points
15/06/2002	Madagascar	112–0	112
06/07/2014	Madagascar	89–10	89
21/04/1990	Portugal	86–9	86
31/08/2003	Uganda	82–13	82
27/05/2006	Kenya	82–12	82

BY A PLAYER

Date	Player	Opponent	Points
06/07/1993	Jaco Coetzee	Kenya	35
26/05/2007	Justinus van der Westhuizen	Zambia	33
27/06/2009	Chrysander Botha	Cote D'Ivoire	29
06/07/2014	Theuns Kotze	Madagascar	29
21/04/1990	Moolman Olivier	Portugal	26

MOST TRIES IN A MATCH
BY THE TEAM

Date	Opponent	Result	Tries
15/06/2002	Madagascar	112–0	18
21/04/1990	Portugal	86–9	16
17/10/1999	Germany	79–13	13
06/07/2014	Madagascar	89–10	13

BY A PLAYER

Date	Player	Opponent	Tries
21/04/1990	Gerhard Mans	Portugal	6
15/06/2002	Riaan van Wyk	Madagascar	5
16/05/1992	Eden Meyer	Zimbabwe	4
16/08/2003	Melrick Africa	Kenya	4

MOST CONVERSIONS IN A MATCH
BY THE TEAM

Date	Opponent	Result	Cons
06/07/2014	Madagascar	89–10	12
21/04/1990	Portugal	86–9	11
15/06/2002	Madagascar	112–0	11
31/08/2003	Uganda	82–13	11
27/05/2006	Kenya	82–12	11

BY A PLAYER

Date	Player	Opponent	Cons
06/07/2014	Theuns Kotze	Madagascar	12
21/04/1990	Moolman Olivier	Portugal	11
27/05/2006	Morne Schreuder	Kenya	11
15/08/2015	Theuns Kotze	Zimbabwe	10
26/05/2007	Justinus van der Westhuizen	Zambia	9

MOST PENALTIES IN A MATCH
BY THE TEAM

Date	Opponent	Result	Pens
17/11/2012	Spain	37–38	6
	5 on 6 occasions		

BY A PLAYER

Date	Player	Opponent	Pens
17/11/2012	Theuns Kotze	Spain	6
	5 on 6 occasions		

MOST DROP GOALS IN A MATCH
BY THE TEAM

Date	Opponent	Result	DGs
10/09/2011	Fiji	25–49	3

BY A PLAYER

Date	Player	Opponent	DGs
10/09/2011	Theuns Kotze	Fiji	3

NAMIBIA

MOST CAPPED PLAYERS

Name	Caps
Johnny Redelinghuys	49
Tinus Du Plessis	47
Eugene Jantjies	46
PJ Van Lill	40
Chrysander Botha	37

LEADING PENALTY SCORERS

Name	Pens
Theuns Kotze	52
Jaco Coetzee	46
Emile Wessels	21
Morne Schreuder	18
Rudi van Vuuren	14

LEADING TRY SCORERS

Name	Tries
Gerhard Mans	27
Eden Meyer	21
Chrysander Botha	16
Melrick Africa	12

LEADING DROP GOAL SCORERS

Name	DGs
Theuns Kotze	4
Jaco Coetzee	3
Eugene Jantjies	2

LEADING CONVERSIONS SCORERS

Name	Cons
Jaco Coetzee	82
Theuns Kotze	78
Morne Schreuder	36
Rudi van Vuuren	26

LEADING POINTS SCORERS

Name	Points
Theuns Kotze	349
Jaco Coetzee	340
Chrysander Botha	147
Morne Schreuder	146
Gerhard Mans	118

NAMIBIA INTERNATIONAL PLAYERS
UP TO 1 NOVEMBER, 2015

MJ Africa 2003 *Sa, Ken, Uga, Ar, I, A*, 2005 *Mad, Mor*, 2006 *Ken, Tun, Ken, Tun, Mor, Mor*, 2007 *Za, Geo, R, Uga, SA, I, F, Ar, Geo*

W Alberts 1991 *Sp, Pt, It, It, Z, Z, I, I, Z, Z, Z*, 1995 *Z*, 1996 *Z, Z*

H Amakali 2005 *Mad*

CT Arries 2013 *Ken*

J Augustyn 1991 *Z*, 1998 *Iv, Mor, Z*

RS Bardenhorst 2007 *Geo, R*

J Barnard 1990 *Z, Pt, W, W, F, F*, 1991 *Sp, Pt, It, It, Z, Z, I, I, Z, Z, Z*, 1992 *Z, Z*

RR Becker 2012 *Z, Sp*, 2013 *Sen, Z, Ken*, 2014 *Ken, Z, Mad, Ger, Pt*, 2015 *Tun, Z*

F Bertholini 2014 *C, Pt*

D Beukes 2000 *Z, Ur*, 2001 *Z, Z*

E Beukes 1990 *Z, F, WGe*

J Beukes 1994 *Z, Mor*, 1995 *Z*

AJ Blaauw 1996 *Z, Z*, 1997 *Tg*, 1998 *Pt, Tun, Z, Iv, Mor, Z*, 1999 *Z, Fj, F, C, Ger*, 2000 *Z, Z, Ur*, 2001 *It*, 2003 *Ar, I, A, R*, 2004 *Mor*

ML Blom 2010 *Sp*, 2011 *Pt, Geo*, 2012 *Sen, Mad*, 2013 *Sen, Tun, Z, Ken*, 2014 *Ken, Z, Mad, Ger, C, Pt*

JH Bock 2005 *Mad, Mor*, 2006 *Ken, Tun, Ken, Tun, Mor, Mor*, 2007 *Za, R, SA, I, F, Ar, Geo*, 2009 *Pt, Tun*, 2010 *R, Geo*, 2011 *R, Pt, Geo, SA*

J Bock 2005 *Mad, Mor*, 2009 *Iv, Iv*, 2010 *R, Geo, Pt*

J Booysen 2003 *Sa, Ken, Ar, A*, 2007 *Uga*

M Booysen 1993 *W, AG, Z*, 1994 *Rus, Z, HK*, 1996 *Z, Z*

LW Botes 2006 *Ken, Mor*, 2007 *Za, Geo, R, Uga, SA, F*

R Botes 2015 *Rus*

CA Botha 2008 *Z*, 2009 *Iv, Iv, Pt, Tun, Tun*, 2010 *Rus, R, Geo, Pt, Sp*, 2011 *R, Pt, Geo, Fj, Sa, SA, W*, 2012 *Sen, Mad, Z*, 2013 *Sen, Tun, Z, Ken*, 2014 *Ken, Z, Mad, C*, 2015 *Rus, Rus, Ken, Z, NZ, Tg, Geo, Ar*

HP Botha 2000 *Z, Z, Ur*

H Botha 2012 *Z, Sp*

R Bothma 2014 *Ken, Z, Mad*, 2015 *Rus, Rus, Ken, Z, NZ, Tg, Geo*

AC Bouwer 2012 *Sen, Mad, Sp*, 2013 *Sen, Tun, Ken*, 2014 *Ken, Z, Mad*, 2015 *Rus, Rus, Z*

H Breedt 1998 *Tun, Z*

H Brink 1992 *Z, Z*, 1993 *W, Ken, Z*, 1994 *Rus, Z, Iv, Mor, HK*

J Britz 1996 *Z*

B Buitendag 1990 *W, W, F, F, WGe*, 1991 *Sp, Pt, It, It, Z, Z, I, I, Z, Z, Z*, 1992 *Z, Z*, 1993 *W, AG, Ken, Z*

E Buitendag 2010 *Rus*, 2013 *Sen, Tun, Z*, 2014 *Ken, Z, Mad, Ger, C, Pt*, 2015 *Tun, Sp, Z, NZ, Tg*

J Burger 2004 *Za, Ken, Z, Mor*, 2006 *Tun, Tun, Mor, Mor*, 2007 *Za, Geo, R, SA, I, F, Ar, Geo*, 2008 *Z*, 2009 *Iv, Iv, Pt, Tun, Tun*, 2010 *R, Geo, Pt*, 2011 *Fj, Sa, SA, W*, 2014 *C*, 2015 *Rus, Rus, Ken, NZ, Tg, Geo*

B Calitz 1995 *Z*

C Campbell 2008 *Z*

DJ Coetzee 1990 *Pt, W, F, F, WGe*, 1991 *Sp, Pt, It, It, Z, Z, I, I, Z, Z, Z*, 1992 *Z, Z*, 1993 *W, AG, Ken, Z*, 1994 *Z, Iv, Mor, HK*, 1995 *Z, Z*

JC Coetzee 1990 *W*
JV Coetzee 2015 *Tun, Sp, Ken, Z, NZ, Tg, Geo, Ar*
W Conradie 2015 *Ken, Geo, Ar*
M Couw 2006 *Ken*
B Cronjé 1994 *Rus*

L Damens 2015 *Tun, R, Ken, NZ, Ar*
HDP Dames 2011 *Fj, Sa, SA, W*, 2012 *Sen, Mad*, 2013 *Sen, Tun*, 2014 *Ger, C, Pt*, 2015 *Z*
J Dames 1998 *Tun, Z*
D de Beer 2000 *Z*
S de Beer 1995 *Z*, 1997 *Tg*, 1998 *Tun, Z, Iv, Mor, Z*, 1999 *Ger*
AJ De Klerk 2015 *R, Sp, Rus, Rus, Ken, Tg, Ar*
AD de Klerk 2009 *Iv, Iv*
CJ De Koe 2010 *Geo, Pt, Sp*
DP De La Harpe 2010 *Rus, R, Geo, Pt, Sp*, 2011 *R, Pt, Geo, Fj, Sa, SA, W*, 2012 *Z, Sp*, 2013 *Sen, Tun, Z, Ken*, 2014 *Ken, Z, Mad, Ger, C, Pt*, 2015 *Rus, Ken, Tg, Geo*
RCA De La Harpe 2011 *R, Pt, Geo, Fj, SA, W*, 2014 *Ger, C, Pt*
SC De La Harpe 2010 *Sp*, 2012 *Z, Sp*, 2013 *Z, Ken*
H de Waal 1990 *Z, Pt*
N de Wet 2000 *Ur*
R Dedig 2004 *Mor, Za, Ken, Z, Mor*
CJH Derks 1990 *Z, Pt, W, W, F, F, WGe*, 1991 *Sp, Pt, It, It, Z, Z, I, I, Z, Z, Z*, 1992 *Z, Z*, 1993 *W, AG, Z*, 1994 *Rus, Z, Iv, Mor, HK*
J Deysel 1990 *Z, Pt, W, W*, 1991 *Sp, Pt, It, It, Z, Z, I, I, Z, Z, Z*, 1992 *Z*
J Deysel 2013 *Ken*, 2014 *Ken, Z, Mad, Ger, C, Pt*, 2015 *Rus, Z, NZ, Tg, Ar*
VA Dreyer 2002 *Z*, 2003 *I, R*
J Drotsky 2006 *Ken*, 2008 *Sen*
AJ Du Plessis 2010 *Pt, Sp*
I du Plessis 2005 *Mor*, 2009 *Tun*
M du Plessis 2001 *Z*, 2005 *Mor*
N du Plessis 1993 *Ken*, 1994 *Rus*, 1995 *Z*
O Du Plessis 2008 *Sen*
T Du Plessis 2006 *Ken, Tun, Mor, Mor*, 2007 *Geo, R, Uga, I, F, Ar, Geo*, 2008 *Sen, Z*, 2009 *Iv, Iv, Pt, Tun, Tun*, 2010 *R, Geo, Pt, Sp*, 2011 *R, Pt, Geo, Fj, Sa, SA, W*, 2012 *Sen, Sp*, 2013 *Sen, Tun, Z, Ken*, 2014 *Ken, Z, Mad, Ger*, 2015 *Sp, Rus, Rus, Z, NZ, Tg, Geo, Ar*
P du Plooy 1992 *Z, Z*, 1994 *Z, Mor, HK*
S Du Preez 2013 *Ken*, 2014 *Mad, Pt*
S du Rand 2007 *Geo, R, Uga*
JA Du Toit 2007 *Za, Geo, R, Uga, SA, I, F, Geo*, 2008 *Sen, Z*, 2009 *Pt, Tun, Tun*, 2010 *Rus, R, Geo, Pt, Sp*, 2011 *R, Pt, Geo, Sa, SA, W*
N du Toit 2002 *Tun*, 2003 *Sa, Ar, I, A, R*
V du Toit 1990 *Pt, W, W, F*
JH Duvenhage 2000 *Z, Z*, 2001 *It, Z, Z*, 2002 *Mad*, 2003 *Sa, Uga, Ar, I, R*, 2007 *Za, R, Uga*

A Engelbrecht 2000 *Z*
J Engelbrecht 1990 *WGe*, 1994 *Rus, Iv, Mor, HK*, 1995 *Z, Z*
N Engelbrecht 1996 *Z*
H Engels 1990 *F, WGe*
JB Engels 2013 *Sen, Tun, Z, Ken*, 2014 *Ken, Z, Mad, Ger*, 2015 *Tun, Rus, Rus, Ken, NZ, Geo, Ar*
E Erasmus 1997 *Tg*
G Esterhuizen 2008 *Sen, Z*
N Esterhuyse 2006 *Ken, Tun, Mor*, 2007 *Za, Geo, R, Uga, SA, I, F, Ar, Geo*, 2008 *Z*, 2009 *Iv, Iv, Pt, Tun, Tun*, 2010 *Rus, R, Geo, Pt, Sp*, 2011 *R, Pt, Geo, Fj, Sa, SA, W*, 2014 *Ger*, 2015 *Tun, R*
SF Esterhuysen 2008 *Z*, 2009 *Iv, Iv, Pt, Tun, Tun*, 2010 *Rus, R, Geo, Pt, Sp*, 2011 *R, Pt*, 2012 *Sen, Mad*

D Farmer 1997 *Tg*, 1998 *Pt, Iv, Mor, Z*, 1999 *Z, Fj, Ger*
F Fisch 1999 *Z, Ger*
TR Forbes 2014 *Mad, Ger, Pt*, 2015 *R, Sp, Rus, Z*
HH Franken 2011 *Sa*, 2012 *Sen, Mad*
S Furter 1999 *Z, Fj, F, C, Ger*, 2001 *It*, 2002 *Mad, Z, Tun, Tun*, 2003 *Sa, Ken, Uga, Ar, I, A, R*, 2004 *Mor*, 2006 *Ken, Tun, Ken*

E Gaoab 2005 *Mad, Mor*
I Gaya 2004 *Za, Ken*
J Genis 2000 *Z, Z, Ur*, 2001 *Z*
N Genis 2006 *Mor*
R Gentz 2001 *It*
R Glundeung 2006 *Ken*
CJ Goosen 1991 *Sp, Pt, It, It*, 1993 *W*
D Gouws 2000 *Z, Z, Ur*, 2001 *It, Z, Z*
T Gouws 2003 *Ken, Uga*, 2004 *Za, Ken*, 2006 *Ken, Tun*
A Graham 2001 *It, Z, Z*, 2002 *Mad, Tun*, 2003 *Ken, Uga, I*, 2004 *Mor*
A Greeff 1997 *Tg*
JC Greyling 2014 *Ger, Pt*, 2015 *Tun, R, Sp, Rus, Rus, Z, NZ, Ar*
D Grobelaar 2008 *Z*
DP Grobler 2001 *Z*, 2002 *Mad, Tun, Tun*, 2003 *Sa, Ken, Uga, Ar, I, A, R*, 2004 *Mor, Za, Ken, Z, Mor*, 2006 *Ken, Tun, Ken*, 2007 *Za, Geo, R, SA, Ar*
HJ Grobler 1990 *Z, Pt, W, W, F, F, WGe*, 1991 *Sp, Pt, It, It, Z, Z, I, I, Z, Z, Z*, 1992 *Z, Z*
T Grünewald 1990 *Z*
D Grunschloss 2003 *A*

F Hartung 1996 *Z, Z*
RJ Herridge 2009 *Pt, Tun, Tun*
L Holtzhausen 1997 *Tg*, 1998 *Pt, Tun, Z, Iv, Mor, Z*, 1999 *Ger*
F Horn 2005 *Mad, Mor*, 2006 *Ken*
H Horn 1997 *Tg*, 1998 *Pt, Iv, Mor, Z*, 1999 *Z, Fj, F, C, Ger*, 2001 *It*, 2002 *Mad, Z, Tun, Tun*, 2003 *Sa*, 2007 *Za, Geo, R, Uga, SA, I, F, Ar, Geo*, 2008 *Sen, Z*, 2009 *Iv, Iv, Tun, Tun*, 2010 *Rus*, 2011 *Fj, Sa, SA, W*
K Horn 1997 *Tg*, 1998 *Pt*
Q Hough 1995 *Z, Z*, 1998 *Pt, Tun, Z, Iv, Mor, Z*, 1999 *Z, Fj, F, C*
P Human 2012 *Sen, Mad*
D Husselman 1993 *AG*, 1994 *Z, Mor*, 2002 *Mad, Z, Tun*, 2003 *Sa, Ar, I, A*
JJ Husselman 2004 *Za, Ken*

E Isaacs 1993 *Ken*, 1994 *Iv*
P Isaacs 2000 *Z, Z, Ur*, 2001 *Z, Z*, 2005 *Mad, Mor*
E Izaacs 1998 *Pt*, 1999 *Z, Ger*, 2000 *Z, Z, Ur*, 2001 *It, Z, Z*, 2002 *Mad, Z, Tun, Tun*, 2003 *Sa, Ken, Ar, A, R*

M Jacobs 1999 *Z, Fj, F, Ger*
E Jansen 2006 *Ken*
EA Jantjies 2006 *Ken, Tun, Ken, Tun*, 2007 *Za, Geo, R, Uga, SA, I, F, Ar, Geo*, 2008 *Sen, Z*, 2009 *Iv, Iv, Pt, Tun, Tun*, 2010 *Rus, R, Geo, Pt, Sp*, 2011 *R, Pt, Geo, Fj, Sa, SA, W*, 2012 *Sen, Mad, Z, Sp*, 2013 *Z, Ken*, 2015 *R, Sp, Rus, Rus, Ken, NZ, Geo, Ar*
R Jantjies 1994 *HK*, 1995 *Z, Z*, 1996 *Z*, 1998 *Pt, Tun, Iv, Mor, Z*, 1999 *Z, Fj, F, C*, 2000 *Z, Z*
M Jeary 2003 *Uga*, 2004 *Ken, Z, Mor*
R Jeary 2000 *Z, Ur*
D Jeffrey 1990 *F*
J Jenkins 2002 *Mad, Tun*, 2003 *Ken*
AJ Jevu 2012 *Sen*

SM Kaizemi 2012 *Sp*, 2014 *Ger, Pt*, 2015 *R*
D Kamonga 2004 *Mor, Za, Ken, Z, Mor*, 2007 *Uga, Geo*
M Kapitako 2000 *Z, Z*, 2001 *It, Z, Z*, 2003 *Uga*, 2004 *Za*, 2006 *Tun*
HI Kasera 2012 *Mad*
M Kasiringwa 2012 *Z, Sp*
M Katjiuanjo 2005 *Mad, Mor*
M Kazombiaze 2006 *Ken, Tun*
U Kazombiaze 2006 *Ken, Tun, Mor, Mor*, 2007 *Za, Uga, SA, I, F, Ar, Geo*, 2008 *Sen, Z*, 2009 *Iv, Iv, Pt, Tun, Tun*, 2010 *Rus, Geo*, 2011 *W*
R Kitshoff 2010 *Pt, Sp*, 2011 *R, Pt, Geo, Fj, Sa, SA, W*, 2013 *Sen, Tun, Z, Ken*, 2014 *Ken, Z, Mad, Ger, C, Pt*, 2015 *Rus, Z, NZ, Tg, Geo, Ar*
DPW Koen 2005 *Z*
HVW Koll 2009 *Pt, Tun*, 2010 *Rus, R, Geo, Pt, Sp*, 2011 *R, Pt, Geo, Fj, Sa, SA, W*, 2012 *Sen, Mad*
A Kotze 1991 *Sp, Z, Z, I, I*, 1993 *W, AG, Z*

NAMIBIA

D Kotze 1993 *W, AG, Ken, Z,* 1994 *Rus, HK*
J Kotze 1995 *Z, Z,* 1996 *Z, Z,* 2000 *Z, Z,* 2001 *It, Z, Z,* 2002 *Mad, Z, Tun, Tun,* 2004 *Za, Ken, Z, Mor*
P Kotze 2001 *It*
P Kotze 1996 *Z*
TAW Kotze 2011 *Pt, Fj, Sa, SA, W,* 2012 *Sen, Mad, Z, Sp,* 2013 *Sen, Tun, Z, Ken,* 2014 *Ken, Z, Mad, Ger, C, Pt,* 2015 *Tun, Sp, Rus, Rus, Ken, Z, NZ, Tg, Geo, Ar*
L Kotzee 2008 *Z*
JL Kruger 2001 *It, Z, Z*
R Kruger 2003 *Ken, Uga,* 2005 *Mad, Mor*
R Kruger 2004 *Mor, Za, Ken, Mor*

SO Lambert 2000 *Z, Ur,* 2001 *It, Z, Z,* 2003 *Ken, Uga,* 2004 *Mor,* 2005 *Mad,* 2006 *Ken, Tun, Ken*
B Langenhoven 2007 *SA, I, F, Ar, Geo,* 2008 *Sen, Z,* 2009 *Pt, Tun, Tun,* 2010 *Rus*
R Larson 2011 *Fj, Sa, W,* 2015 *Rus, Rus, Z, NZ, Geo*
G Lensing 2002 *Mad, Z, Tun, Tun,* 2003 *Sa, Ar, I, A, R,* 2004 *Mor,* 2006 *Ken, Mor, Mor,* 2007 *R, SA, I, F, Ar, Geo,* 2009 *Iv, Iv, Tun, Tun*
C Lesch 2005 *Mad, Mor*
HD Lindvelt 1998 *Iv, Z,* 1999 *F, C, Ger,* 2001 *It, Z, Z,* 2002 *Mad, Z, Tun, Tun,* 2003 *Sa, Ken, Uga, Ar, I, A,* 2004 *Mor, Za, Ken, Z, Mor,* 2006 *Ken, Tun, Ken, Mor, Mor,* 2007 *Za, Geo, SA, F, Ar*
J Lombaard 1996 *Z*
H Loots 1990 *Z*
J Losper 2005 *Mor*
SJ Losper 1990 *Z, Pt, W, W, F, F, WGe,* 1991 *Sp, Pt, It, It, Z, Z, I, I, Z, Z, Z*
TC Losper 2007 *Za, Geo, R, Uga, SA, I, F,* 2008 *Sen,* 2011 *Geo, W*
W Lötter 1990 *Z*
RC Loubser 1999 *F,* 2005 *Mad, Mor*
O Louw 1993 *Ken, Z,* 1994 *Z, Iv,* 1996 *Z*

M MacKenzie 2004 *Mor,* 2006 *Ken, Tun,* 2007 *Uga, I, F, Ar*
B Malgas 1991 *Z, Z, Z,* 1993 *W, AG, Ken, Z,* 1994 *Rus, Z, Iv, Mor, HK,* 1995 *Z, Z,* 1996 *Z*
G Mans 1990 *Z, Pt, W, W, F,* 1991 *Sp, Pt, It, It, Z, Z, I, I, Z, Z, Z,* 1992 *Z, Z,* 1993 *W, AG, Ken, Z,* 1994 *Rus, Z, Iv, Mor, HK*
C Marais 2010 *Pt, Sp,* 2011 *Fj, SA,* 2015 *Tun, R, Rus, Ken, NZ, Ar*
M Marais 1992 *Z,* 1993 *W, AG, Z*
W Maritz 1990 *Z,* 1991 *Z, Z, I, I, Z, Z, Z*
S McCulley 1990 *W, W, F, WGe*
E Meyer 1991 *Sp, Pt, It, It, Z, Z, I, I, Z, Z, Z,* 1992 *Z, Z,* 1993 *W,* 1994 *Z, Iv, Mor, HK,* 1995 *Z, Z,* 1996 *Z*
H Meyer 2004 *Za, Ken, Z, Mor*
JM Meyer 2003 *Ken, Uga, Ar, I, R,* 2006 *Ken, Tun, Tun, Mor, Mor,* 2007 *Uga, SA, I, F, Ar, Geo*
P Meyer 2005 *Mad*
M Moore 2013 *Tun,* 2014 *Ger*
DA Mouton 1999 *Z, Fj, Ger,* 2000 *Z, Z, Ur,* 2002 *Mad, Z, Tun,* 2003 *Sa, Ken, Uga, Ar, I, A, R,* 2004 *Mor,* 2005 *Mad, Mor,* 2006 *Tun, Ken, Tun, Mor,* 2007 *Ar,* 2008 *Sen*
H Mouton 2000 *Z*
P Mouton 2005 *Mad, Mor*

H Neethling 1993 *Ken*
G Nel 2006 *Mor, Mor*
JA Nel 2012 *Sen, Mad, Z, Sp,* 2013 *Tun, Z, Ken,* 2014 *Z, Mad*
S Nell 2000 *Z, Z*
S Neustadt 2012 *Z, Sp,* 2013 *Sen, Tun, Ken,* 2014 *Ger, C, Pt*
J Nienaber 1998 *Pt, Tun, Z, Mor, Z*
J Nieuwenhuis 2007 *Za, Geo, R, Uga, SA, I, F, Geo,* 2008 *Sen, Z,* 2009 *Iv, Iv, Tun, Tun,* 2010 *R, Geo, Sp,* 2011 *R, Pt, Geo, Fj, SA, W*

EB O'Callaghan 2010 *R, Geo, Pt, Sp,* 2011 *R, Pt, Geo, Fj, Sa, SA, W*
J Olivier 1999 *Z, Fj, Ger,* 2000 *Z, Z, Ur*
M Olivier 1990 *Pt, F*
LT Oosthuizen 1990 *Z, Pt, W, W, F, F, WGe*
GJ Opperman 1999 *Z, Fj, F, C, Ger*

T Opperman 2002 *Mad, Z*
WJ Otto 1993 *AG, Z,* 1994 *Rus*

R Pedro 1998 *Z,* 1999 *Ger,* 2000 *Ur,* 2001 *It, Z, Z,* 2003 *Sa, Ken, Uga, Ar, I, A, R,* 2004 *Mor*
DG Philander 2008 *Sen,* 2009 *Iv, Iv, Pt, Tun, Tun,* 2010 *Rus,* 2011 *R, Pt, Geo, W,* 2013 *Sen, Tun,* 2014 *Ken, Z, Mad, C, Pt,* 2015 *Tun, R, Sp, Rus, Ken, NZ, Tg, Geo*
F Pienaar 2006 *Ken*
D Pieters 2008 *Sen*
L Plaath 2001 *It, Z, Z*
CJ Powell 2001 *It, Z, Z,* 2002 *Mad, Z, Tun, Tun,* 2003 *Sa, Ken, Uga, Ar, I, R,* 2004 *Mor, Ken, Z, Mor,* 2006 *Ken, Tun, Tun, Mor, Mor,* 2007 *Za, Geo, R, Ar, Geo*

JH Redelinghuys 2006 *Ken, Tun, Mor,* 2007 *Za, Geo, R, Uga, SA, I, F, Ar, Geo,* 2008 *Sen, Z,* 2009 *Iv, Iv, Pt, Tun,* 2010 *Rus, R, Geo, Pt, Sp,* 2011 *R, Pt, Geo, Fj, Sa, SA, W,* 2012 *Sen, Mad, Z, Sp,* 2013 *Sen, Tun, Z, Ken,* 2014 *Z, Mad, Ger, C,* 2015 *R, Sp, Ken, Z, Tg, Geo, Ar*
C Redlinghaus 2001 *It*
H Reinders 1996 *Z*
G Rich 1993 *W*
V Rodrigues 2012 *Z, Sp*
C Roets 1995 *Z*
P Rossouw 2004 *Za, Ken, Z, Mor,* 2005 *Mad, Mor,* 2006 *Mor, Mor,* 2007 *Za, Geo, R*

A Samuelson 1995 *Z,* 1996 *Z, Z,* 1997 *Tg,* 1998 *Pt, Tun, Z, Iv, Mor, Z,* 1999 *Z, Fj, F, C, Ger*
A Schlechter 2012 *Z, Sp,* 2013 *Sen, Tun, Z, Ken,* 2014 *Ken, Z, Mad, Ger, C*
M Schreuder 2002 *Mad, Z, Tun, Tun,* 2003 *Sa, Ken, Uga, I, A, R,* 2004 *Mor, Za, Ken, Z, Mor,* 2006 *Ken, Ken,* 2007 *Ar, Geo*
C Schumacher 1995 *Z*
JH Senekal 1998 *Iv, Mor, Z,* 1999 *Z, Fj, F, C, Ger,* 2002 *Mad, Z,* 2003 *Sa, Ken, Uga, Ar, I, A, R,* 2005 *Mad,* 2006 *Ken, Mor, Mor,* 2007 *Geo, R, Uga, I, Ar, Geo*
A Skinner 1990 *Z, Pt, W, W, F, F, WGe*
G Smit 1990 *F*
H Smit 2013 *Sen, Tun, Z,* 2014 *Ken, Z, Mad,* 2015 *Tun, R, Sp, Rus, Ken, Geo, Ar*
C Smith 2012 *Sen, Mad, Z, Sp*
E Smith 1998 *Tun, Iv, Mor, Z,* 1999 *Fj, F, C,* 2002 *Mad*
P Smith 1993 *Ken,* 1994 *Iv,* 1995 *Z, Z*
S Smith 1990 *Pt, W, W, F,* 1992 *Z, Z,* 1993 *W, AG, Ken, Z,* 1994 *Rus, Z, Iv, Mor, HK,* 1996 *Z*
W Smith 2002 *Mad, Z, Tun*
D Snyders 2003 *Uga,* 2005 *Mad,* 2012 *Z*
H Snyman 1990 *F, F,* 1991 *Sp, Pt, It, It, Z, Z, I, I, Z, Z, Z,* 1992 *Z, Z,* 1993 *W, AG, Ken, Z,* 1994 *Z, Iv, Mor, HK,* 1995 *Z, Z,* 1996 *Z, Z*
M Snyman 1994 *Rus, Z, Iv, Mor, HK*
D Spangenberg 2005 *Mad, Mor*
A Steenkamp 1994 *Iv, Mor*
C Steenkamp 2007 *Uga*
T Steenkamp 1992 *Z, Z,* 1993 *Ken,* 1994 *Rus, Iv,* 1995 *Z,* 1996 *Z,* 1998 *Pt, Tun, Z*
DL Stevens 2015 *Ken, Tg, Geo, Ar*
P Steyn 1996 *Z, Z,* 1997 *Tg,* 1998 *Pt, Tun, Z, Iv, Mor,* 1999 *Z, Fj, F, C*
A Stoop 1990 *Z, Pt, W,* 1991 *Sp, Pt, It, It, Z, I, I, Z*
L Stoop 1992 *Sen, Mad*
L Stoop 1994 *Iv*
H Stroh 2012 *Mad*
G Suze 2005 *Mad*
CI Swanepoel 2012 *Sen, Mad,* 2013 *Sen, Tun,* 2015 *R, Sp*
JC Swanepoel 2013 *Sen, Tun*
N Swanepoel 2003 *Ken, Ar, I, A, R,* 2004 *Mor, Za, Ken, Z, Mor*
H Swart 1995 *Z,* 1996 *Z,* 1997 *Tg,* 1998 *Pt, Tun, Z*
JL Swart 1990 *F, WGe*
BM Swartz 1990 *W, W, F, F, WGe*

R Theart 1998 *Pt*
J Theron 1998 *Iv, Mor, Z,* 1999 *Fj, F, C, Ger,* 2004 *Mor*
A Thompson 2013 *Sen, Tun*

RHR Thompson 2004 *Za, Ken, Mor*, 2005 *Mad*, 2006 *Ken, Tun, Ken, Tun, Mor, Mor*
M Tjiueza 2012 *Z, Sp*, 2013 *Sen, Tun, Z, Ken*, 2014 *Ken, Z, Mad*
D Tredoux 2001 *Z*
JA Tromp 2012 *Z, Sp*, 2013 *Sen, Z, Ken*, 2014 *Ken, Z, Mad, Ger, C, Pt*, 2015 *Tun, R, Sp, Rus, Rus, Ken, Z, NZ, Tg, Geo, Ar*

T Uanivi 2014 *Ger, C, Pt*, 2015 *Tun, R, Sp, Rus, Rus, Ken, Z, NZ, Tg, Geo, Ar*

L van Coller 1993 *AG, Ken*, 1994 *Rus, Iv*
GE van der Berg 2005 *Mor*, 2006 *Ken, Tun, Tun, Mor*
L van der Linde 2006 *Tun*
A van der Merwe 1990 *Pt, W, W, F, F, WGe*, 1991 *Sp, Pt, It, It, Z, Z, I, I, Z, Z, Z*, 1992 *Z, Z*
D van der Merwe 1990 *WGe*
S van der Merwe 1997 *Tg*, 1998 *Iv, Mor, Z*, 1999 *Z, Fj, F, C, 2002 Z, Tun, Tun*, 2003 *Sa, Ken, Ar, I, A, R*, 2004 *Za, Ken, Z, Mor*, 2006 *Tun, Mor*
J van der Westhuizen 2007 *Za, Geo*
L van der Westhuizen 2013 *Z*, 2015 *Rus, NZ, Tg, Geo, Ar*
L van Dyk 1998 *Tun, Z, Iv, Mor, Z*, 1999 *Fj, F, C, Ger*, 2002 *Mad*
TG Van Jaarsveld 2014 *Ger, C, Pt*, 2015 *Rus, Rus, Ken, Z, NZ, Tg, Geo, Ar*
JA van Lill 2002 *Mad, Tun, Tun*, 2003 *Sa, Ar, I, A, R*, 2004 *Mor*, 2006 *Tun*, 2007 *Za*
PJ Van Lill 2006 *Ken*, 2008 *Sen, Z*, 2009 *Iv, Pt, Tun, Tun*, 2010 *Rus, R, Geo, Pt, Sp*, 2011 *R, Pt, Geo, Fj, Sa, SA*, 2012 *Sen, Mad, Z, Sp*, 2013 *Sen, Tun, Z, Ken*, 2014 *Ken, Z, Mad, C, Pt*, 2015 *Tun, R, Sp, Ken, Z, NZ, Tg, Geo, Ar*
RE Van Neel 2010 *Rus*, 2011 *Sa*, 2012 *Z*
F van Rensburg 1995 *Z*, 1996 *Z, Z*, 1997 *Tg*, 1998 *Tun, Z*, 1999 *Z, Fj, F, C, Ger*, 2000 *Z*, 2001 *It, Z, Z*
SJ van Rensburg 1998 *Z, Iv, Mor, Z*, 1999 *Z, Fj, F, Ger*, 2000 *Z, Ur*
SL Van Rooi 2003 *Uga, A*, 2004 *Mor*, 2005 *Mor*
A van Rooyen 1991 *Sp, Pt, It, It, I*, 1992 *Z, Z*
M van Rooyen 1996 *Z*, 1998 *Pt, Tun, Z, Mor, Z*, 1999 *Z, F, C*
C van Schalkwyk 1993 *AG, Z*
A Van Tonder 1995 *Z*
CJ van Tonder 2002 *Tun*, 2003 *Sa, Ken, Uga, I, A, R*, 2004 *Mor, Za, Ken, Z, Mor*, 2006 *Ken, Ken*, 2007 *Za*, 2012 *Sp*
JH Van Tonder 2004 *Mor, Ken, Z, Mor*, 2006 *Ken, Tun*, 2007 *Uga, SA, I, F, Ar, Geo*, 2008 *Z*, 2009 *Iv, Iv, Pt, Tun*
N van Vuuren 1993 *AG*

RJ van Vuuren 1997 *Tg*, 1998 *Pt, Tun, Z*, 1999 *Z, Ger*, 2000 *Z, Z, Ur*, 2002 *Mad, Z*, 2003 *Ken, Uga*
A van Wyk 1993 *W, Ken*, 1994 *Iv, HK*
DN Van Wyk 2011 *R, Pt, Geo, Fj, Sa, SA, W*, 2012 *Z, Sp*, 2015 *Tun, R, Sp, Rus, Tg, Geo*
G van Wyk 1999 *Z, Fj, F, C*, 2000 *Z, Z, Ur*, 2001 *It*
L van Wyk 2004 *Mor*
M Van Wyk 2009 *Iv, Iv, Pt*, 2010 *Rus, Geo, Pt*, 2011 *R, Pt, Geo*, 2012 *Sp*
R van Wyk 2004 *Za, Ken, Z, Mor*
R van Wyk 2002 *Mad, Z, Tun, Tun*, 2003 *Sa*, 2004 *Mor, Za, Ken, Z, Mor*
RS Van Wyk 2015 *Sp, Rus, Rus, Z, Tg, Geo, Ar*
J van Zyl 2008 *Sen*
WP Van Zyl 2007 *SA, I, F, Ar, Geo*, 2008 *Z*, 2009 *Iv, Iv, Pt, Tun, Tun*, 2010 *R, Geo, Pt, Sp*, 2011 *Fj, Sa, SA, W*
R van Zyl 1997 *Tg*, 1998 *Tun, Z, Iv, Mor, Z*
J Venter 2013 *Z, Ken*, 2015 *R, Sp, Rus, Rus, Ken, Z, NZ, Tg, Ar*
M Venter 2003 *Uga*, 2004 *Mor*, 2008 *Z*, 2009 *Iv, Iv, Pt, Tun, Tun*, 2010 *Rus*
D Vermaak 1998 *Z*
JJ Vermaak 1990 *Pt*, 1994 *Rus*, 1996 *Z*
A Vermeulen 2010 *Rus*
B Vermeulen 1995 *Z*
DF Vermeulen 1996 *Z, Z*, 1997 *Tg*, 1998 *Pt*
G Vermeulen 1991 *Z*
RAG Victor 2015 *Tun*
M Visser 2007 *Za, Geo, R, Uga, SA, Ar, Geo*, 2009 *Iv, Iv, Pt, Tun, Tun*, 2010 *Rus, R, Geo, Pt, Sp*, 2011 *SA*
CW Viviers 2010 *Sp*, 2011 *R, Pt, Geo*, 2014 *Ger, C, Pt*, 2015 *Tun, R, Sp, Rus, Rus, Z, NZ, Tg*

P von Wielligh 1991 *It, Z*, 1992 *Z*, 1993 *AG, Z*, 1994 *Iv, Mor*, 1995 *Z*, 1996 *Z*
B Walters 2009 *Pt*
GAE Walters 2008 *Z*, 2009 *Iv*, 2010 *R, Geo, Pt, Sp*
W Wentzel 1991 *Sp, Z, Z*
E Wessels 2002 *Tun, Tun*, 2003 *Sa, Ar, I, A, R*, 2006 *Tun, Mor, Mor*, 2007 *SA, I, F*, 2009 *Iv, Pt, Tun, Tun*, 2010 *Rus*
DG Wiese 2014 *Z*, 2015 *Tun, R, Sp, Rus, Ken*
LP Winkler 2008 *Z*, 2009 *Iv, Iv*, 2010 *Rus, R, Geo*, 2011 *R, Pt, Geo, Fj, Sa*
RC Witbooi 2004 *Za, Z*, 2005 *Mor*, 2006 *Ken, Tun, Ken*, 2007 *Za, Geo, R, Uga, I, F, Geo*, 2008 *Sen*
J Wohler 2005 *Mad, Mor*

J Zaayman 1997 *Tg*, 1998 *Pt, Tun, Z, Iv, Mor, Z*, 1999 *Z, Fj, F, C, Ger*

Flanker Tinus du Plessis played a huge part in Namibia achieving their first ever Rugby World Cup point against Georgia.

NEW ZEALAND

NEW ZEALAND'S 2014–15 TEST RECORD

OPPONENTS	DATE	VENUE	RESULT
Australia	18 Oct	A	Won 29–28
USA	1 Nov	A	Won 74–6
England	8 Nov	A	Won 24–21
Scotland	15 Nov	A	Won 24–16
Wales	22 Nov	A	Won 34–16
Samoa	8 Jul	A	Won 25–16
Argentina	17 Jul	H	Won 39–18
South Africa	25 Jul	A	Won 27–20
Australia	8 Aug	A	Lost 27–19
Australia	15 Aug	H	Won 41–13
Argentina	20 Sep	N	Won 26–16
Namibia	24 Sep	N	Won 58–14
Georgia	2 Oct	N	Won 43–10
Tonga	9 Oct	N	Won 47–9
France	17 Oct	N	Won 62–13
South Africa	24 Oct	N	Won 20–18
Australia	31 Oct	N	Won 34–17

ALL BLACKS MAKE NATION PROUD

By Ian Jones

All Blacks captain Richie McCaw holds aloft the coveted Webb Ellis Cup as rugby history is made at Twickenham.

THE COUNTRIES

Like many millions of other New Zealanders, I was immensely proud of the way the All Blacks both played and conducted themselves at Rugby World Cup 2015. How an All Black represents the country off the pitch, what the shirt stands for, is as important as how he plays on it and Steve Hansen and his squad were superb in both departments as they became the first team to successfully retain the Webb Ellis Cup.

I was thrilled with the style of rugby they played in the tournament and that fearless approach, the team's phenomenal work ethic and almost desperate desire to keep improving, as well as their humility and integrity, is what ultimately separated New Zealand from what were in my opinion some other very strong teams over in England and what saw the All Blacks crowned champions.

The squad were under no illusions that they'd have to play very well to win the World Cup again in 2015 and when they were tested, particularly by Argentina in the pool stages and by both the Springboks and the Wallabies in the knockout phase, their collective self belief and stubborn will to win kicked in and they were able to get over the line when it really mattered. You could almost feel the sense of unity and purpose coming out of the camp over the course of the tournament.

Despite finishing unbeaten and top of Pool C, New Zealand were under a bit of pressure because they hadn't posted the cricket scores some had predicted against Georgia, Tonga and Namibia but there was no sense of panic and as a supporter watching proceedings from the outside, I found that very reassuring.

The team deserved all the plaudits that came their way after they beat Australia in what was a superb final at Twickenham. They've been hailed as the best team in the history of the game but I'm not one for comparisons between different eras and I'll leave those kind of statements to others. What I would certainly say though is Hansen and his players took the game to a new level in 2015.

There's a deceptive simplicity about how Hansen's team manage to produce such stunning rugby and for me a lot of it comes down to their aerobic conditioning. The boys work relentlessly on their conditioning and the fruits of their labour is the ability to go deeper than the opposition in the big matches. You could see it in the shape of the All Black players, they looked different to the other guys. They looked like they could run longer and harder than the other teams and when South Africa in the semi-final and Australia in the final asked questions, New Zealand were crucially able to find the answers.

It's not simply about physical fitness. It's about having the energy, but just as importantly the mental clarity, to make the right decisions when other teams are starting to succumb to fatigue. It's about the skills they practise religiously on the training ground not being compromised after 70 minutes of hard test rugby. In my opinion, that was a huge factor in the All Blacks' success.

New Zealand also owned the tramlines in a way other teams were not able to emulate. The All Blacks were able to move the ball the width of the pitch, from the left to right and back, without skipping a beat and it didn't matter whether it was Dan Carter or one of the forwards making the pass. When they attacked in open play, the numbers on the guys' backs seemed to be irrelevant.

There were, of course, so many outstanding performances in England but there were for me two players who revolutionised the way their position should be played – Dane Coles at hooker and Aaron Smith at scrum-half. Coles was outstanding and the positions he took up in the wide spaces, his skills set and his impact on the tournament were

NEW ZEALAND

sensational. Smith was also incredible and going back to aerobic conditioning, the pace at which he was able to arrive at the breakdown, the straight lines he ran to get there and the speed of his distribution was amazing. The momentum the All Blacks were so often able to maintain, which opposition teams found so difficult to counter, was a testament to Smith's amazing contribution.

It was a great tournament for Julian Savea, who top scored with eight tries. His performances drew comparisons with my old All Black team-mate Jonah Lomu but, again, I loathe talking about players or teams from different eras in that way. Jonah was a force of nature but Savea should be celebrated in his own right and whenever he is finished, his legacy will be his own.

As an old lock, I was amazed at some of the skills displayed by Brodie Retallick and the technical ability of a player like Owen Franks and it speaks volumes about the dedication of the squad and how well resourced the All Blacks are in terms of coaching that the tight-head is one of the best passers in the group. Every single one of the players in the New Zealand squad is a great athlete but it's the other work they do, the hours they put in working on their skill sets, that really earned them the World Cup.

Another key to their success is playing in exactly the style the rules are designed to encourage. It sounds simple but the All Blacks react instinctively to every nuance of the law, they understand how the administrators are trying to encourage a fast style of rugby, and they are invariably ahead of the opposition when it comes to exploiting the opportunities the modern laws of the game offer.

The squad returned to New Zealand four days after the final and the reception they got when they touched down in Auckland spoke volumes about the relationship between the players and the public. There were thousands at the airport and there were thousands more for the official parade through the city and the ones that followed in Wellington and Christchurch.

Steve Hansen is without question a brilliant coach but I also think the way he and Richie McCaw connected with the rugby public during the World Cup was fantastic. Their ability to communicate with All Black supporters in the way they spoke was extremely important and I really got the sense throughout the tournament that the coach and the skipper were trying and succeeding in bringing the fans along with them.

It was a very different experience watching the team become world champions in England in 2015 in comparison to their triumph on home soil four years earlier. In 2011 we breathed every second of it but there was also an anxiety because we hadn't won the World Cup for so long and also, as the host nation, the country wanted the world to enjoy itself. There was no less interest in 2015 but the team was off shore, there was the time difference and it was probably a less stressful experience.

The World Cup was the end of the line for the careers of many truly great All Black players and we won't see Carter, Ma'a Nonu, Conrad Smith, Keven Mealamu, Tony Woodcock or Ben Franks in the shirt again. What those guys achieved for their country is incredible and the international game will be poorer without them.

After missing out on the final in 2011 with injury, you got the over-powering feeling with Carter that the last two years of his career had really been all about the three weeks of knockout rugby in England. Nothing else mattered and he delivered when it mattered to earn the send-off he craved.

It's undoubtedly going to be a very different looking All Black XV in 2016 but whether McCaw is part of the side is, as I write this, unclear. Everyone assumed he was going to retire from test rugby at the end of the tournament but if he wants to carry on, I think he should. People argue you should go out on a high but you are a long time retired and if he's still enjoying playing, why quit? Whatever his decision, the only thing I can add to all the other plaudits that have come the skipper's way is that it has been a privilege for New Zealand to have had him in the team.

The future of the All Blacks will be fascinating. There's no argument, the guys leaving the side will create a huge hole but that's the reality of professional sport. I'm pretty sure Hansen, his assistant Ian Foster and the rest of the coaching team will be looking forward and be enthused at the prospect of working with a new group of players rather than dwelling on the big names they've parted company with.

It's the nature of All Black rugby. No-one, absolutely no-one is irre-placeable and although the team has lost some great talent, it simply means an opportunity for a new guy to come in and make an interna-tional career for himself. After all, that's exactly how a player like McCaw got into the team in the first place.

The important thing is not to compare the new players who force their way into Hansen's thinking to the ones who have just said goodbye. The Conrad Smith of 2015 for example was not the same Conrad Smith that made his test debut back in 2004 and it's vital new players are given the time to develop and improve. There's huge pressure every time you pull on the shirt but I've no doubt Hansen is capable of building another great side.

NEW ZEALAND

NEW ZEALAND INTERNATIONAL STATISTICS

MATCH RECORDS UP TO 1 NOVEMBER, 2015

MOST CONSECUTIVE TEST WINS

17	1965 SA 4, 1966 BI 1, 2, 3, 4, 1967 A, E, W, F, S, 1968 A 1,2, F 1, 2, 3, 1969 W 1, 2
17	2013 F 1, 2, 3, A 1, Arg 1, SA 1, Arg 2, SA 2, A 3, J, F 4, E, I, 2014 E 1,2,3
16	2011 Tg, J, F, C, Arg, A, F, 2012 I 1, 2, 3, A1,2, Arg1, SA1, Arg2, SA2
15	2005 A 1, SA 2, A 2, W, I E, S, 2006 I 1, 2, Arg, A 1, SA 1, A 2, 3, SA 2
15	2009 A 3, 4, W,It E,F 3, 2010 I 1, W 1,2, SA 1, 2, A 1, 2, SA 3, A 3
12	1988 A 3, 1989 F 1, 2, Arg 1,2, A, W, I, 1990 S 1,2, A 1,2

MOST CONSECUTIVE TESTS WITHOUT DEFEAT

Matches	Wins	Draws	Period
23	22	1	1987 to 1990
22	21	1	2013 to 2014
20	19	1	2011 to 2012
17	17	0	1965 to 1969
17	15	2	1961 to 1964
15	15	0	2005 to 2006
15	15	0	2009 to 2010

MOST POINTS IN A MATCH

BY THE TEAM

Pts	Opponents	Venue	Year
145	Japan	Bloemfontein	1995
108	Portugal	Lyons	2007
102	Tonga	Albany	2000
101	Italy	Huddersfield	1999
101	Samoa	N Plymouth	2008
93	Argentina	Wellington	1997
91	Tonga	Brisbane	2003
91	Fiji	Albany	2005
85	Romania	Toulouse	2007
83	Japan	Hamilton	2011
79	Canada	Wellington	2011
76	Italy	Marseilles	2007
74	Fiji	Christchurch	1987
74	USA	Chicago	2014
73	Canada	Auckland	1995
71	Fiji	Albany	1997
71	Samoa	Albany	1999

BY A PLAYER

Pts	Player	Opponents	Venue	Year
45	SD Culhane	Japan	Bloemfontein	1995
36	TE Brown	Italy	Huddersfield	1999
33	CJ Spencer	Argentina	Wellington	1997
33	AP Mehrtens	Ireland	Dublin	1997
33	DW Carter	British/Irish	Wellington	2005
33	NJ Evans	Portugal	Lyons	2007
32	TE Brown	Tonga	Albany	2000
30	MCG Ellis	Japan	Bloemfontein	1995
30	TE Brown	Samoa	Albany	2001
29	AP Mehrtens	Australia	Auckland	1999
29	AP Mehrtens	France	Paris	2000
29	LR MacDonald	Tonga	Brisbane	2003
29	DW Carter	Canada	Hamilton	2007

MOST TRIES IN A MATCH

BY THE TEAM

Tries	Opponents	Venue	Year
21	Japan	Bloemfontein	1995
16	Portugal	Lyons	2007
15	Tonga	Albany	2000
15	Fiji	Albany	2005
15	Samoa	N Plymouth	2008
14	Argentina	Wellington	1997
14	Italy	Huddersfield	1999
13	USA	Berkeley	1913
13	Tonga	Brisbane	2003
13	Romania	Toulouse	2007
13	Japan	Hamilton	2011
12	Italy	Auckland	1987
12	Fiji	Christchurch	1987
12	Canada	Wellington	2011
12	USA	Chicago	2014

BY A PLAYER

Tries	Player	Opponents	Venue	Year
6	MCG Ellis	Japan	Bloemfontein	1995
5	JW Wilson	Fiji	Albany	1997
4	D McGregor	England	Crystal Palace	1905
4	CI Green	Fiji	Christchurch	1987
4	JA Gallagher	Fiji	Christchurch	1987
4	JJ Kirwan	Wales	Christchurch	1988
4	JT Lomu	England	Cape Town	1995
4	CM Cullen	Scotland	Dunedin	1996
4	JW Wilson	Samoa	Albany	1999
4	JM Muliaina	Canada	Melbourne	2003
4	SW Sivivatu	Fiji	Albany	2005
4	ZR Guildford	Canada	Wellington	2011

MOST CONVERSIONS IN A MATCH
BY THE TEAM

Cons	Opponents	Venue	Year
20	Japan	Bloemfontein	1995
14	Portugal	Lyons	2007
13	Tonga	Brisbane	2003
13	Samoa	N Plymouth	2008
12	Tonga	Albany	2000
11	Italy	Huddersfield	1999
10	Fiji	Christchurch	1987
10	Argentina	Wellington	1997
10	Romania	Toulouse	2007
9	Canada	Melbourne	2003
9	Italy	Marseilles	2007
9	Ireland	N Plymouth	2010
9	Japan	Hamilton	2011
8	Italy	Auckland	1987
8	Wales	Auckland	1988
8	Fiji	Albany	1997
8	Italy	Hamilton	2003
8	Fiji	Albany	2005
8	Canada	Wellington	2011

BY A PLAYER

Cons	Player	Opponents	Venue	Year
20	SD Culhane	Japan	Bloemfontein	1995
14	NJ Evans	Portugal	Lyons	2007
12	TE Brown	Tonga	Albany	2000
12	LR MacDonald	Tonga	Brisbane	2003
11	TE Brown	Italy	Huddersfield	1999
10	GJ Fox	Fiji	Christchurch	1987
10	CJ Spencer	Argentina	Wellington	1997
9	DW Carter	Canada	Melbourne	2003
9	CR Slade	Japan	Hamilton	2011
8	GJ Fox	Italy	Auckland	1987
8	GJ Fox	Wales	Auckland	1988
8	AP Mehrtens	Italy	Hamilton	2002

MOST DROP GOALS IN A MATCH
BY THE TEAM

Drops	Opponents	Venue	Year
3	France	Christchurch	1986

BY A PLAYER

Drops	Player	Opponents	Venue	Year
2	OD Bruce	Ireland	Dublin	1978
2	FM Botica	France	Christchurch	1986
2	AP Mehrtens	Australia	Auckland	1995

MOST PENALTIES IN A MATCH
BY THE TEAM

Penalties	Opponents	Venue	Year
9	Australia	Auckland	1999
9	France	Paris	2000
7	Western Samoa	Auckland	1993
7	South Africa	Pretoria	1999
7	South Africa	Wellington	2006
7	Australia	Auckland	2007
7	Argentina	Auckland	2011
6	British/Irish Lions	Dunedin	1959
6	England	Christchurch	1985
6	Argentina	Wellington	1987
6	Scotland	Christchurch	1987
6	France	Paris	1990
6	South Africa	Auckland	1994
6	Australia	Brisbane	1996
6	Ireland	Dublin	1997
6	South Africa	Cardiff	1999
6	Scotland	Murrayfield	2001
6	South Africa	Christchurch	2004
6	Australia	Sydney	2004
6	South Africa	Dunedin	2008
6	Australia	Tokyo	2009
6	Australia	Brisbane	2012
6	Samoa	Apia	2015

BY A PLAYER

Pens	Player	Opponents	Venue	Year
9	AP Mehrtens	Australia	Auckland	1999
9	AP Mehrtens	France	Paris	2000
7	GJ Fox	Western Samoa	Auckland	1993
7	AP Mehrtens	South Africa	Pretoria	1999
7	DW Carter	South Africa	Wellington	2006
7	DW Carter	Australia	Auckland	2007
7	PAT Weepu	Argentina	Auckland	2011
6	DB Clarke	British/Irish Lions	Dunedin	1959
6	KJ Crowley	England	Christchurch	1985
6	GJ Fox	Argentina	Wellington	1987
6	GJ Fox	Scotland	Christchurch	1987
6	GJ Fox	France	Paris	1990
6	SP Howarth	South Africa	Auckland	1994
6	AP Mehrtens	Australia	Brisbane	1996
6	AP Mehrtens	Ireland	Dublin	1997
6	AP Mehrtens	South Africa	Cardiff	1999
6	AP Mehrtens	Scotland	Murrayfield	2001
6	DW Carter	South Africa	Dunedin	2008
6	DW Carter	Australia	Tokyo	2009
6	DW Carter	Australia	Brisbane	2012
6	DW Carter	Samoa	Apia	2015

NEW ZEALAND

CAREER RECORDS

MOST CAPPED PLAYERS

Caps	Player	Career Span
148	RH McCaw	2001 to 2015
132	KF Mealamu	2002 to 2015
118	TD Woodcock	2002 to 2015
112	DW Carter	2003 to 2015
103	MA Nonu	2003 to 2015
100	JM Muliaina	2003 to 2011
94	CG Smith	2004 to 2015
92	SBT Fitzpatrick	1986 to 1997
84	KJ Read	2008 to 2015
83	AK Hore	2002 to 2013
81	JW Marshall	1995 to 2005
79	ID Jones	1990 to 1999
78	OT Franks	2009 to 2015
77	AJ Williams	2002 to 2012
74	JF Umaga	1997 to 2005
73	SL Whitelock	2010 to 2015
71	PAT Weepu	2004 to 2013
70	AP Mehrtens	1995 to 2004

MOST TRIES IN TESTS

Tries	Player	Tests	Career
49	DC Howlett	62	2000 to 2007
46	CM Cullen	58	1996 to 2002
46	JT Rokocoko	68	2003 to 2010
44	JW Wilson	60	1993 to 2001
38	SJ Savea	41	2012 to 2015
37	JT Lomu	63	1994 to 2002
37*	JF Umaga	74	1997 to 2005
35	JJ Kirwan	63	1984 to 1994
34	JM Muliaina	100	2003 to 2011
31	MA Nonu	103	2003 to 2015
29	DW Carter	112	2003 to 2015
29	SW Sivivatu	45	2005 to 2011
28*	RH McCaw	148	2001 to 2015
26	CG Smith	94	2004 to 2015
24	JW Marshall	81	1995 to 2005
20	FE Bunce	55	1992 to 1997
20	KJ Read	84	2008 to 2015

Umaga and McCaw's hauls each include a penalty try

MOST CONSECUTIVE TESTS

Tests	Player	Span
63	SBT Fitzpatrick	1986 to 1995
51	CM Cullen	1996 to 2000
49	RM Brooke	1995 to 1999
41	JW Wilson	1996 to 1999
40	GW Whetton	1986 to 1991

MOST CONVERSIONS IN TESTS

Cons	Player	Tests	Career
293	DW Carter	112	2003 to 2015
169	AP Mehrtens	70	1995 to 2004
118	GJ Fox	46	1985 to 1993
49	CJ Spencer	35	1997 to 2004
48	AW Cruden	37	2010 to 2014
43	TE Brown	18	1999 to 2001
33	DB Clarke	31	1956 to 1964
32	SD Culhane	6	1995 to 1996

MOST TESTS AS CAPTAIN

Tests	Captain	Span
110	RH McCaw	2004 to 2015
51	SBT Fitzpatrick	1992 to 1997
30	WJ Whineray	1958 to 1965
23	RD Thorne	2002 to 2007
22	TC Randell	1998 to 2002
21	JF Umaga	2004 to 2005
19	GNK Mourie	1977 to 1982
18	BJ Lochore	1966 to 1970
17	AG Dalton	1981 to 1985

MOST PENALTY GOALS IN TESTS

Pens	Player	Tests	Career
281	DW Carter	112	2003 to 2015
188	AP Mehrtens	70	1995 to 2004
128	GJ Fox	46	1985 to 1993
52	AW Cruden	37	2010 to 2014
43	AR Hewson	19	1981 to 1984
41	CJ Spencer	35	1997 to 2004
38	DB Clarke	31	1956 to 1964
24	WF McCormick	16	1965 to 1971

MOST POINTS IN TESTS

Points	Player	Tests	Career
1598	DW Carter	112	2003 to 2015
967	AP Mehrtens	70	1995 to 2004
645	GJ Fox	46	1985 to 1993
291	CJ Spencer	35	1997 to 2004
280	AW Cruden	37	2010 to 2014
245	DC Howlett	62	2000 to 2007
236	CM Cullen	58	1996 to 2002
234	JW Wilson	60	1993 to 2001
230	JT Rokocoko	68	2003 to 2010
207	DB Clarke	31	1956 to 1964
201	AR Hewson	19	1981 to 1984

MOST DROP GOALS IN TESTS

Drops	Player	Tests	Career
10	AP Mehrtens	70	1995 to 2004
8	DW Carter	112	2003 to 2015
7	GJ Fox	46	1985 to 1993
5	DB Clarke	31	1956 to 1964
5	MA Herewini	10	1962 to 1967
5	OD Bruce	14	1976 to 1978

RUGBY CHAMPIONSHIP (FORMERLY TRI NATIONS) RECORDS

RECORD	DETAIL	HOLDER	SET
Most points in season	202	in six matches	2013
Most tries in season	24	in six matches	2013
Highest score	55	55–35 v S Africa (h)	1997
Biggest win	39	54–15 v Argentina (a)	2012
Highest score conceded	46	40–46 v S Africa (a)	2000
Biggest defeat	21	7–28 v Australia (a)	1999
Most appearances	58	RH McCaw	2002 to 2015
Most points in matches	554	DW Carter	2003 to 2015
Most points in season	99	DW Carter	2006
Most points in match	29	AP Mehrtens	v Australia (h) 1999
Most tries in matches	17	RH McCaw	2002 to 2015
Most tries in season	8	BR Smith	2013
Most tries in match	3	JT Rokocoko	v Australia (a) 2003
	3	DC Howlett	v Australia (h) 2005
	3	CS Jane	v Argentina (a) 2012
	3	BR Smith	v Australia (a) 2013
Most cons in matches	76	DW Carter	2003 to 2015
Most cons in season	14	DW Carter	2006
Most cons in match	5	AW Cruden	v Australia (h) 2014
Most pens in matches	120	DW Carter	2003 to 2015
Most pens in season	21	DW Carter	2006
Most pens in match	9	AP Mehrtens	v Australia (h) 1999

NEW ZEALAND

MISCELLANEOUS RECORDS

RECORD	HOLDER	DETAIL
Longest Test Career	E Hughes/CE Meads/RH McCaw	1907–21/1957–71/2001–15
Youngest Test Cap	JT Lomu	19 yrs 45 days in 1994
Oldest Test Cap	E Hughes	40 yrs 123 days in 1921

CAREER RECORDS OF NEW ZEALAND INTERNATIONAL PLAYERS

UP TO 1 NOVEMBER, 2015

BACKS :	DEBUT:	CAPS	T	C	P	D	PTS
BJ Barrett	2012 v I	36	9	26	16	0	145
DW Carter	2003 v W	112	29	293	281	8	1598
RS Crotty	2013 v A	15	1	0	0	0	5
AW Cruden	2010 v I	37	5	48	52	1	280
IJA Dagg	2010 v I	49	14	1	1	0	75
AM Ellis	2006 v E	28	4	0	0	0	20
MF Fekitoa	2014 v E	13	4	0	0	0	20
CS Jane	2008 v A	53	18	0	0	0	90
TNJ Kerr-Barlow	2012 v S	20	2	0	0	0	10
NR Milner-Skudder	2015 v A	8	8	0	0	0	40
G Moala	2015 v Sm	1	1	0	0	0	5
WR Naholo	2015 v Arg	3	1	0	0	0	5
CJ Ngatai	2015 v Sm	1	0	0	0	0	0
MA Nonu	2003 v E	103	31	0	0	0	155
TTR Perenara	2014 v E	17	1	0	0	0	5
ST Piutau	2013 v F	17	5	0	0	0	25
AW Pulu	2014 v US	2	0	0	0	0	0
SJ Savea	2012 v I	41	38	0	0	0	190
CR Slade	2010 v A	21	3	24	5	0	78
AL Smith	2012 v I	47	13*	1	0	0	67
BR Smith	2009 v It	48	19	0	0	0	95
CG Smith	2004 v It	94	26	0	0	0	130
LZ Sopoaga	2015 v SA	1	0	3	2	0	12
BM Weber	2015 v Sm	1	0	0	0	0	0
S Williams	2010 v E	33	9	0	0	0	45

FORWARDS :							
DJ Bird	2013 v J	2	0	0	0	0	0
JP Broadhurst	2015 v SA	1	0	0	0	0	0
SJ Cane	2012 v I	31	10	0	0	0	50
DS Coles	2012 v S	36	5	0	0	0	25
WWV Crockett	2009 v It	45	1	0	0	0	5
HTP Elliot	2010 v S	4	0	0	0	0	0
CC Faumuina	2012 v Arg	33	1	0	0	0	5
BJ Franks	2010 v I	47	2	0	0	0	10
OT Franks	2009 v It	78	0	0	0	0	0
NP Harris	2014 v Arg	2	1	0	0	0	5
J Kaino	2006 v I	67	11	0	0	0	55
NE Laulala	2015 v Sm	4	0	0	0	0	0

THE COUNTRIES

RH McCaw	2001 v I	148	28*	0	0	0	140
KF Mealamu	2002 v W	132	12	0	0	0	60
LJ Messam	2008 v S	43	6	0	0	0	30
JPT Moody	2014 v A	11	1	0	0	0	5
JW Parsons	2014 v S	1	0	0	0	0	0
KJ Read	2008 v S	84	20	0	0	0	100
BA Retallick	2012 v I	47	2	0	0	0	10
L Romano	2012 v I	22	1	0	0	0	5
CJD Taylor	2015 v Arg	4	2	0	0	0	10
JI Thrush	2013 v F	12	2	0	0	0	10
MB Todd	2013 v F	3	0	0	0	0	0
PT Tuipulotu	2014 v E	7	1	0	0	0	5
VVJ Vito	2010 v I	33	4	0	0	0	20
SL Whitelock	2010 v I	73	4	0	0	0	20
TD Woodcock	2002 v W	118	10	0	0	0	50

NB McCaw's figures include a penalty try awarded against Ireland in 2008 and AL Smith's figures include one awarded against Australia at Auckland in 2015.

NEW ZEALAND INTERNATIONAL PLAYERS
UP TO 1 NOVEMBER, 2015

Entries in square brackets denote matches played in RWC Finals.

Abbott, H L (Taranaki) 1906 F
Afeaki, B T P (North Harbour) 2013 F1(R)
Afoa, I F (Auckland) 2005 I, S, 2006 E(R), 2008 I1, SA2, A1(R), 2(R), SA3(R), A3(R), S, I2(t&R), W(R), E3(R), 2009 F1(R), 2(R), It1, SA2(R), A2(R), SA3(R), A3(R), 4(R), It2(R), E(R), 2010 SA3(R), A3(R), 4(R), E(R), S(R), I2(R), W3(R), 2011 Fj(R), SA1(R), 2, A2(R), [J(R), Arg(R)]
Aitken, G G (Wellington) 1921 SA 1, 2
Alatini, P F (Otago) 1999 F 1(R), [It, SA 3(R)], 2000 Tg, S 1, A 1, SA 1, A 2, SA 2, It, 2001 Sm, Arg 1, F, SA 1, A 1, SA 2, A 2
Allen, F R (Auckland) 1946 A 1, 2, 1947 A 1, 2, 1949 SA 1, 2
Allen, M R (Taranaki, Manawatu) 1993 WS (t), 1996 S 2 (t), 1997 Arg 1(R), 2(R), SA 2(R), A 3(R), E 2, W (R)
Allen, N H (Counties) 1980 A 3, W
Alley, G T (Canterbury) 1928 SA 1, 2, 3
Anderson, A (Canterbury) 1983 S, E, 1984 A 1, 2, 3, 1987 [Fj]
Anderson, B L (Wairarapa-Bush) 1986 A 1
Anesi, S R (Waikato) 2005 Fj(R)
Archer, W R (Otago, Southland) 1955 A 1, 2, 1956 SA 1, 3
Argus, W G (Canterbury) 1946 A 1, 2, 1947 A 1, 2
Arnold, D A (Canterbury) 1963 I, W, 1964 E, F
Arnold, K D (Waikato) 1947 A 1, 2
Ashby, D L (Southland) 1958 A 2
Asher, A A (Auckland) 1903 A
Ashworth, B G (Auckland) 1978 A 1, 2
Ashworth, J C (Canterbury, Hawke's Bay) 1978 A 1, 2, 3, 1980 A 1, 2, 3, 1981 SA 1, 2, 3, 1982 A 1, 2, 1983 Bl 1, 2, 3, 4, A, 1984 F 1, 2, A 1, 2, 3, 1985 E 1, 2, A
Atiga, B A C (Auckland) 2003 [Tg(R)]
Atkinson, H (West Coast) 1913 A 1
Avery, H E (Wellington) 1910 A 1, 2, 3

Bachop, G T M (Canterbury) 1989 W, I, 1990 S 1, 2, A 1, 2, 3, F 1, 2, 1991 Arg 1, 2, A 1, 2, [E, US, C, A, S], 1992 Wld 1, 1994 SA 1, 2, 3, A, 1995 C, [I, W, S, E, SA], A 1, 2

Bachop, S J (Otago) 1994 F 2, SA 1, 2, 3, A
Badeley, C E O (Auckland) 1921 SA 1, 2
Baird, J A S (Otago) 1913 A 2
Ball, N (Wellington) 1931 A, 1932 A 2, 3, 1935 W, 1936 E
Barrett, B J (Taranaki) 2012 I 3(R), Arg1(R), S(R), It, W(R), 2013 F1(R), 2(R), 3(R), A1(R), Arg1(R), SA1(R), Arg2(R), SA2(R), A3(R), J, I(R), 2014 E1(R), 2(R), 3(R), A1(R), 2(R), Arg1, SA1(R), Arg2, SA2, A 3, E 4(R), W, 2015 SA(R), A 1(R), [Arg(R), Nm, Tg(R), F(R), SA(R), A(R)]
Barrett, J (Auckland) 1913 A 2, 3
Barry, E F (Wellington) 1934 A 2
Barry, L J (North Harbour) 1995 F 2
Bates, S P (Waikato) 2004 It(R)
Batty, G B (Wellington, Bay of Plenty) 1972 W, S, 1973 E 1, I, F, E 2, 1974 A 1, 3, I, 1975 S, 1976 SA 1, 2, 3, 4, 1977 Bl 1
Batty, W (Auckland) 1930 Bl 1, 3, 4, 1931 A
Beatty, G E (Taranaki) 1950 Bl 1
Bell, R H (Otago) 1951 A 3, 1952 A 1, 2
Bellis, E A (Wanganui) 1921 SA 1, 2, 3
Bennet, R (Otago) 1905 A
Berghan, T (Otago) 1938 A 1, 2, 3
Berry, M J (Wairarapa-Bush) 1986 A 3(R)
Berryman, N R (Northland) 1998 SA 2(R)
Bevan, V D (Wellington) 1949 A 1, 2, 1950 Bl 1, 2, 3, 4
Bird, D J (Canterbury) 2013 J, 2014 S
Birtwistle, W M (Canterbury) 1965 SA 1, 2, 3, 4, 1967 E, W, S
Black, J E (Canterbury) 1977 F 1, 1979 A, 1980 A 3
Black, N W (Auckland) 1949 SA 3
Black, R S (Otago) 1914 A 1
Blackadder, T J (Canterbury) 1998 E 1(R), 2, 2000 Tg, S 1, 2, A 1, SA 1, A 2, SA 2, F 1, 2, It
Blair, B A (Canterbury) 2001 S (R), Arg 2, 2002 E, W
Blake, A W (Wairarapa) 1949 A 1
Blowers, A F (Auckland) 1996 SA 2(R), 4(R), 1997 I, E 1(R), W (R), 1999 F 1(R), SA 1, A 1(R), SA 2, A 2(R), [It]

Boggs, E G (Auckland) 1946 A 2, 1949 SA 1
Bond, J G (Canterbury) 1949 A 2
Booth, E E (Otago) 1906 F, 1907 A 1, 3
Boric, A F (North Harbour) 2008 E1(R), 2(R), SA2, A2(R), SA3(R), Sm, A3(R), 4(R), S, E3(R), 2009 It2, E(R), F3(R), 2010 I1, W1, A3(R), E(R), S(R), I2, W3(R), 2011 [Tg(R), J(R), F1(R), C(R)]
Boroevich, K G (Wellington) 1986 F 1, A 1, F 3(R)
Botica, F M (North Harbour) 1986 F 1, A 1, 2, 3, F 2, 3, 1989 Arg 1(R)
Bowden, N J G (Taranaki) 1952 A 2
Bowers, R G (Wellington) 1954 I, F
Bowman, A W (Hawke's Bay) 1938 A 1, 2, 3
Braid, D J (Auckland) 2002 W, 2003 [C(R), Tg], 2008 A1, 2010 S(R), W3(R)
Braid, G J (Bay of Plenty) 1983 S, E
Bremner, S G (Auckland, Canterbury) 1952 A 2, 1956 SA 2
Brewer, M R (Otago, Canterbury) 1986 F 1, A 1, 2, 3, F 2, 3, 1988 A 1, 1989 A, W, I, 1990 S 1, 2, A 1, 2, 3, F 1, 2, 1992 I 2, A 1, 1994 F 1, 2, SA 1, 2, 3, A, 1995 C, [I, W, E, SA], A 1, 2
Briscoe, K C (Taranaki) 1959 BI 2, 1960 SA 1, 2, 3, 4, 1963 I, W, 1964 E, S
Broadhurst, J P (Taranaki) 2015 SA
Brooke, R M (Auckland) 1992 I 2, A 1, 2, 3, SA, 1993 BI 1, 2, 3, A, WS, 1994 SA 2, 3, 1995 C, [J, S, E, SA], A 1, 2, It, F 1, 2, 1996 WS, S 1, 2, A 1, SA 1, A 2, SA 2, 3, 4, 5, 1997 Fj, Arg 1, 2, A 1, SA 1, A 2, SA 2, A 3, I, E 1, W, E 2, 1998 E 1, 2, A 1, SA 1, A 2, SA 2, A 3, 1999 WS, F 1, SA 1, A 1, SA 2, A 2, [Tg, E, It (R), S, F 2]
Brooke, Z V (Auckland) 1987 [Arg], 1989 Arg 2(R), 1990 A 1, 2, 3, F 1(R), 1991 Arg 2, A 1, 2, [E, It, C, A, S], 1992 A 2, 3, SA, 1993 BI 1, 2, 3(R), WS (R), S, E, 1994 F 2, SA 1, 2, 3, A, 1995 [J, S, E, SA], A 2, It, F 1, 2, 1996 WS, S 1, 2, A 1, SA 1, A 2, SA 2, 3, 4, 5, 1997 Arg 1, 2, A 1, SA 1, A 2, SA 2, A 3, I, E 1, W, E 2
Brooke-Cowden, M (Auckland) 1986 F 1, A 1, 1987 [W]
Broomhall, S R (Canterbury) 2002 SA 1(R), 2(R), E, F
Brown, C (Taranaki) 1913 A 2, 3
Brown, O M (Auckland) 1992 I 2, A 1, 2, 3, SA, 1993 BI 1, 2, 3, A, S, E, 1994 F 1, 2, SA 1, 2, 3, A, 1995 C, [I, W, S, E, SA], A 1, 2, It, F 1, 2, 1996 WS, S 1, 2, A1, SA 1, A 2, SA 2, 3, 4, 5, 1997 Fj, Arg 1, 2, A 1, SA 1, A 2, SA 2, A 3, I, E 1, W, E 2, 1998 E 1, 2, A 1, SA 1, A 2, SA 2
Brown, R H (Taranaki) 1955 A 3, 1956 SA 1, 2, 3, 4, 1957 A 1, 2, 1958 A 1, 2, 3, 1959 BI 1, 3, 1961 F 1, 2, 3, 1962 A 1
Brown, T E (Otago) 1999 WS, F 1(R), SA 1(R), A 1(R), 2(R), [E (R), It, S (R)], 2000 Tg, S 2(R), A 1(R), SA 1(R), A 2(R), 2001 Sm, Arg 1(R), F, SA 1, A 1
Brownlie, C J (Hawke's Bay) 1924 W, 1925 E, F
Brownlie, M J (Hawke's Bay) 1924 I, W, 1925 E, F, 1928 SA 1, 2, 3, 4
Bruce, J A (Auckland) 1914 A 1, 2
Bruce, O D (Canterbury) 1976 SA 1, 2, 4, 1977 BI 2, 3, 4, F 1, 2, 1978 A 1, 2, I, W, E, S
Bryers, R F (King Country) 1949 A 1
Budd, T A (Southland) 1946 A 2, 1949 A 2
Bullock-Douglas, G A H (Wanganui) 1932 A 1, 2, 3, 1934 A 1, 2
Bunce, F E (North Harbour) 1992 Wld 1, 2, 3, I 1, 2, A 1, 2, 3, SA, 1993 BI 1, 2, 3, A, WS, S, E, 1994 F 1, 2, SA 1, 2, 3, A, 1995 C, [I, W, S, E, SA], A 1, 2, It, F 1, 2, 1996 WS, S 1, 2, A1, SA 1, A 2, SA 2, 3, 4, 5, 1997 Fj, Arg 1, 2, A 1, SA 1, A 2, SA 2, A 3, I, E 1, W, E 2
Burgess, G A J (Auckland) 1981 SA 2
Burgess, G F (Southland) 1905 A
Burgess, R E (Manawatu) 1971 BI 1, 2, 3, 1972 A 3, W, 1973 I, F
Burke, P S (Taranaki) 1955 A 1, 1957 A 1, 2
Burns, P J (Canterbury) 1908 AW 2, 1910 A 1, 2, 3, 1913 A 3
Bush, R G (Otago) 1931 A
Bush, W K (Canterbury) 1974 A 1, 2, 1975 S, 1976 I, SA, 2, 4, 1977 BI 2, 3, 4(R), 1978 I, W, 1979 A
Buxton, J B (Canterbury) 1955 A 3, 1956 SA 1

Cain, M J (Taranaki) 1913 US, 1914 A 1, 2, 3

Callesen, J A (Manawatu) 1974 A 1, 2, 3, 1975 S
Cameron, D (Taranaki) 1908 AW 1, 2, 3
Cameron, L M (Manawatu) 1980 A 3, 1981 SA 1(R), 2, 3, R
Cane, S J (Bay of Plenty) 2012 I 2(R), 3, Arg2(R), It, 2013 F1, 2, 3, A1(R), Arg1(R), SA1, Arg2, SA2(R), A3, J, 2014 A1(R), 2(R), Arg1(R), SA1(R), Arg2(R), A 3(R), US, S, 2015 A 1(R), 2(R), [Arg(R), Nm, Gg(R), Tg, F(R), SA(R), A(R)]
Carleton, S R (Canterbury) 1928 SA 1, 2, 3, 1929 A 1, 2, 3
Carrington, K R (Auckland) 1971 BI 1, 3, 4
Carter, D W (Canterbury) 2003 W, F, A 1(R), [It, C, Tg, SA(R), F(R)], 2004 E1, 2, PI, A1, SA1, A2, It, W, F, 2005 Fj, BI1, 2, SA1, A1, W, E, 2006 Arg, A1, SA1, A2, 3, SA2, 3, E, F1, 2, W, 2007 F1, C, SA1, A1, SA2, A2, [It, S, F], 2008 I1, E1, 2, SA1, 2, A1, 2, SA3, Sm, A3, 4, S(R), I2, W, E3, 2009 A2, SA3, A3, 4, W, E, F3, 2010 I1, W1, 2, SA1, 2, A1, 2, SA3, A4, E, S, I2, W3, 2011 Fj(R), SA1, A1, 2, [Tg, F1], 2012 I 1, 2, A1, 2, Arg2, SA2, A3, S, E, 2013 F3, Arg1, SA1, J, F4, E, 2014 US(R), S, 2015 Sm, Arg, A, 1, 2,[Arg, Gg, Tg, F, SA, A]
Carter, M P (Auckland) 1991 A 2, [It, A], 1997 Fj (R), A 1(R), 1998 E 2(R), A 2
Casey, S T (Otago) 1905 S, I, E, W, 1907 A 1, 2, 3, 1908 AW 1
Cashmore, A R (Auckland) 1996 S 2(R), 1997 A 2(R)
Catley, E H (Waikato) 1946 A 1, 1947 A 1, 2, 1949 SA 1, 2, 3, 4
Caughey, T H C (Auckland) 1932 A 1, 3, 1934 A 1, 2, 1935 S, I, 1936 E, A 1, 1937 SA 3
Caulton, R W (Wellington) 1959 BI 2, 3, 4, 1960 SA 1, 1961 F 2, 1963 E 1, 2, I, W, 1964 E, S, F, A 1, 2, 3
Cherrington, N P (North Auckland) 1950 BI 1
Christian, D L (Auckland) 1949 SA 4
Clamp, M (Wellington) 1984 A 2, 3
Clark, D W (Otago) 1964 A 1, 2
Clark, W H (Wellington) 1953 W, 1954 I, E, S, 1955 A 1, 2, 1956 SA 2, 3, 4
Clarke, A H (Auckland) 1958 A 3, 1959 BI 4, 1960 SA 1
Clarke, D B (Waikato) 1956 SA 3, 4, 1957 A 1, 2, 1958 A 1, 3, 1959 BI 1, 2, 3, 4, 1960 SA 1, 2, 3, 4, 1961 F 1, 2, 3, 1962 A 1, 2, 3, 4, 5, 1963 E 1, 2, I, W, 1964 E, S, F, A 2, 3
Clarke, E (Auckland) 1992 Wld 2, 3, I 1, 2, 1993 BI 1, 2, S (R), E, 1998 SA 2, A 3
Clarke, I J (Waikato) 1953 W, 1955 A 1, 2, 3, 1956 SA 1, 2, 3, 4, 1957 A 1, 2, 1958 A 1, 3, 1959 BI 1, 2, 1960 SA 2, 4, 1961 F 1, 2, 3, 1962 A 1, 2, 3, 1963 E 1, 2
Clarke, R L (Taranaki) 1932 A 2, 3
Cobden, D G (Canterbury) 1937 SA 1
Cockerill, M S (Taranaki) 1951 A 1, 2, 3
Cockroft, E A P (South Canterbury) 1913 A 3, 1914 A 2, 3
Codlin, B W (Counties) 1980 A 1, 2, 3
Coles, D S (Wellington) 2012 S(R), It(R), W(R), E(R), 2013 F1, 2, A2(R), Arg1(R), SA1, 2(R), A3(R), J, F4(R), E(R), I(R), 2014 E1, 2, A1, 2, Arg1, SA1, 2(R), A 3, 4, S(R), W, 2015 SA, A 1, 2, [Arg, Gg, Tg, F, SA, A]
Collins, A H (Taranaki) 1932 A 2, 3, 1934 A 1
Collins, J (Wellington) 2001 Arg 1, 2003 E (R), W, F, SA 1, A 1, SA 2, A 2, [It, W, SA, A, F], 2004 E2(R), Arg, PI(R), A1(R), SA1, It, F, 2005 Fj, BI1, 2, 3, SA1, A1, SA2, W, E, 2006 Arg, A1, 2, 3, SA2(R), 3, F1, 2, W, 2007 F2, C, SA1, A1, SA2(R), A2, [It, Pt, R, F]
Collins, J L (Poverty Bay) 1964 A 1, 1965 SA 1, 4
Colman, J T H (Taranaki) 1907 A 1, 2, 1908 AW 1, 3
Connor, D M (Auckland) 1961 F 1, 2, 3, 1962 A 1, 2, 3, 4, 5, 1963 E 1, 2, 1964 A 2, 3
Conway, R J (Otago, Bay of Plenty) 1959 BI 2, 3, 4, 1960 SA 1, 3, 4, 1965 SA 1, 2, 3, 4
Cooke, A E (Auckland, Wellington) 1924 I, W, 1925 E, F, 1930 BI 1, 2, 3, 4
Cooke, R J (Canterbury) 1903 A
Cooksley, M S B (Counties, Waikato) 1992 Wld 1, 1993 BI 2, 3(R), A, 1994 F 1, 2, SA 1, 2, A, 2001 A 1(R), SA 2(t&R)
Cooper, G J L (Auckland, Otago) 1986 F 1, A 1, 2, 1992 Wld 1, 2, 3, I 1
Cooper, M J A (Waikato) 1992 I 2, SA (R), 1993 BI 1(R), 3(t), WS (t), S, 1994 F 1, 2
Corner, M M N (Auckland) 1930 BI 2, 3, 4, 1931 A, 1934 A 1, 1936 E
Cossey, R R (Counties) 1958 A 1

Cottrell, **A I** (Canterbury) 1929 A 1, 2, 3, 1930 BI 1, 2, 3, 4, 1931 A, 1932 A 1, 2, 3
Cottrell, **W D** (Canterbury) 1968 A 1, 2, F 2, 3, 1970 SA 1, 1971 BI 1, 2, 3, 4
Couch, **M B R** (Wairarapa) 1947 A 1, 1949 A 1, 2
Coughlan, **T D** (South Canterbury) 1958 A 1
Cowan, **Q J** (Southland) 2004 It(R), 2005 W(R), I(R), S(R), 2006 I1(R), SA1(R), A2(R), SA2(R), 3, 2008 E1(R), 2(R), SA1(R), A1(t&R), 2, SA3, Sm, A3, 4, I2, W, E3, 2009 F1, 2, A1, SA2, A2, SA3, A3, 4, W(R), It2(R), E, F3, 2010 I1, W1, 2, SA1, 2(R), A1, SA3, A3(R), 4, S, W3, 2011 Fj, SA1, 2, [Tg, J(R), C, Arg(R)]
Creighton, **J N** (Canterbury) 1962 A 4
Cribb, **R T** (North Harbour) 2000 S 1, 2, A 1, SA 1, A 2, SA 2, F 1, 2, It, 2001 Sm, F, SA 1, A 1, SA 2, A 2
Crichton, **S** (Wellington) 1983 S, E
Crockett, **W W V** (Canterbury) 2009 It1, W, It2, 2011 Fj, SA1, A1, 2012 A2, S, It(R), W(R), E(R), 2013 F1, 2, 3, A2(R), Arg1(R), SA1(R), Arg2(R), SA2(R), A3(R), J, F4(R), E(R), I, 2014 E1(R), 2(R), 3(R), A1, 2, Arg1, SA1, Arg2, A 3, E 4, S(R), W, 2015 Sm(R), Arg(R), SA(R), A 2(R),[Arg(R), Nm(R), Gg, Tg(R), F]
Cross, **T** (Canterbury) 1904 BI, 1905 A
Crotty, **R S** (Canterbury) 2013 A1(R), J(R), F4(R), E(R), I(R) 2014 E3(R), A1(R), 2, SA2(R), US, E 4(R), S, W(R), 2015 Sm, Arg(R)
Crowley, **K J** (Taranaki) 1985 E 1, 2, A, Arg 1, 2, 1986 A 3, F 2, 3, 1987 [Arg], 1990 S 1, 2, A 1, 2, 3, F 1, 2, 1991 Arg 1, 2, [A]
Crowley, **P J B** (Auckland) 1949 SA 3, 4, 1950 BI 1, 2, 3, 4
Cruden, **A W** (Manawatu) 2010 I1(R), W1(R), 2(R), SA2(R), A1(R), 3, 2011 [Arg(R), A, F2], 2012 I 1(R), 3, A2(R), Arg1, SA1, Arg2(R), SA2(R), A3(R), It, W, E(R), 2013 F1, 2, A1, Arg2, SA2, A3, F4(R), E(R), I, 2014 E1, 2, 3, A1, 2, SA1, US, E 4
Culhane, **S D** (Southland) 1995 [J], It, F 1, 2, 1996 SA 3, 4
Cullen **C M** (Manawatu, Central Vikings, Wellington) 1996 WS, S 1, 2, A 1, SA 1, A 2, SA 2, 3, 4, 5, 1997 Fj, Arg 1, 2, A 1, SA 1, A 2, SA 2, A 3, I, E 1, W, E 2, 1998 E 1, 2, A 1, SA 1, A 2, SA 2, A 3, 1999 WS, F 1, SA 1, A 1, SA 2, A 2, [Tg, E, It (R), S, F 2, SA 3], 2000 Tg, S 1, 2, A 1, SA 1, A 2, SA 2, F 1, 2, It, 2001 A 2(R), 2002 It, Fj, A 1, SA 1, A 2, F
Cummings, **W** (Canterbury) 1913 A 2, 3
Cundy, **R T** (Wairarapa) 1929 A 2(R)
Cunningham, **G R** (Auckland) 1979 S, E, 1980 A 1, 2
Cunningham, **W** (Auckland) 1905 S, I, 1906 F, 1907 A 1, 2, 3, 1908 AW 1, 2, 3
Cupples, **L F** (Bay of Plenty) 1924 I, W
Currie, **C J** (Canterbury) 1978 I, W
Cuthill, **J E** (Otago) 1913 A 1, US

Dagg, **I J A** (Hawke's Bay) 2010 I1, W1, SA2(R), A1(R), SA3(R), A3, 2011 SA2, [Tg, F1, C, A, F2], 2012 I 1, 2, 3, A1, 2, Arg1, SA1, Arg2, SA2, A3, S, W, E, 2013 F1, 2, 3, A1, 2, Arg1, SA1, Arg2, SA2, A3, F4, E, I, 2014 E1, Arg1, SA1, Arg2, SA2, A 3, US, E 4, 2015 Sm, Arg, SA
Dalley, **W C** (Canterbury) 1924 I, 1928 SA 1, 2, 3, 4
Dalton, **A G** (Counties) 1977 F 2, 1978 A 1, 2, 3, I, W, E, S, 1979 F 1, 2, S, 1981 S 1, 2, SA 1, 2, 3, R, F 1, 2, 1982 A 1, 2, 3, 1983 BI 1, 2, 3, 4, A, 1984 F 1, 2, A 1, 2, 3, 1985 E 1, 2, A
Dalton, **D** (Hawke's Bay) 1935 I, W, 1936 A 1, 2, 1937 SA 1, 2, 3, 1938 A 1, 2
Dalton, **R A** (Wellington) 1947 A 1, 2
Dalzell, **G N** (Canterbury) 1953 W, 1954 I, E, S, F
Davie, **M G** (Canterbury) 1983 E (R)
Davies, **W A** (Auckland, Otago) 1960 SA 4, 1962 A 4, 5
Davis, **K** (Auckland) 1952 A 2, 1953 W, 1954 I, E, S, F, 1955 A 2, 1958 A 1, 2, 3
Davis, **L J** (Canterbury) 1976 I, 1977 BI 3, 4
Davis, **W L** (Hawke's Bay) 1967 A, E, W, F, S, 1968 A 1, 2, F 1, 1969 W 1, 2, 1970 SA 2
Deans, **I B** (Canterbury) 1988 W 1, 2, A 1, 2, 3, 1989 F 1, 2, Arg 1, 2, A
Deans, **R G** (Canterbury) 1905 S, I, E, W, 1908 AW 3
Deans, **R M** (Canterbury) 1983 S, E, 1984 A 1(R), 2, 3

Delamore, **G W** (Wellington) 1949 SA 4
Delany, **M P** (Bay of Plenty) 2009 It 2
De Malmanche, **A P** (Waikato) 2009 It1(R), A3(R), 2010 I1(R), W1(R), 2(R)
Dermody, **C** (Southland) 2006 I1, 2, E(R)
Devine, **S J** (Auckland) 2002 E, W 2003 E (R), W, F, SA 1, A 1(R), [C, SA(R), F]
Dewar, **H** (Taranaki) 1913 A 1, US
Diack, **E S** (Otago) 1959 BI 2
Dick, **J** (Auckland) 1937 SA 1, 2, 1938 A 3
Dick, **M J** (Auckland) 1963 I, W, 1964 E, S, F, 1965 SA 3, 1966 BI 4, 1967 A, E, W, F, 1969 W 1, 2, 1970 SA 1, 4
Dixon, **M J** (Canterbury) 1954 I, E, S, F, 1956 SA 1, 2, 3, 4, 1957 A 1, 3
Dobson, **R L** (Auckland) 1949 A 1
Dodd, **E H** (Wellington) 1905 A
Donald, **A J** (Wanganui) 1983 S, E, 1984 F 1, 2, A 1, 2, 3
Donald, **J G** (Wairarapa) 1921 SA 1, 2
Donald, **Q** (Wairarapa) 1924 I, W, 1925 E, F
Donald, **S R** (Waikato) 2008 E1(R), 2(R), A2(R), SA3(R), Sm(R), A3(R), 4, S, I2(R), 2009 F1, 2, A1, SA1, 2, A2(R), SA3, A4(R), It2(R), F3(R), 2010 A4(R), S(R), W3(R), 2011[F2(R)]
Donaldson, **M W** (Manawatu) 1977 F 1, 2, 1978 A 1, 2, 3, I, E, S, 1979 F 1, 2, A, S (R), 1981 SA 3(R)
Donnelly, **T J S** (Otago) 2009 A3, 4, W(R), It2, E, F3, 2010 W2, SA1, 2, A1, 2, SA3, A3, 4, I2
Dougan, **J P** (Wellington) 1972 A 1, 1973 E 2
Dowd, **C W** (Auckland) 1993 BI 1, 2, 3, A, WS, S, E, 1994 SA 1(R), 1995 C, [I, W, J, E, SA], A 1, 2, It, F 1, 2, 1996 WS, S 1, 2, A 1, SA 1, A 2, SA 2, 3, 4, 5, 1997 Fj, Arg 1, 2, A 1, SA 1, A 2, SA 2, A 3, I, E 1, W, 1998 E 1, SA 1, A 2, 1999 SA 2(R), A 2(R), [Tg (R), E, It, S, F 2, SA 3], 2000 Tg, S 1(R), 2(R), A 1(R), SA 1(R), A 2(R)
Dowd, **G W** (North Harbour) 1992 I 1(R)
Downing, **A J** (Auckland) 1913 A 1, US, 1914 A 1, 2, 3
Drake, **J A** (Auckland) 1986 F 2, 3, 1987 [Fj, Arg, S, W, F], A
Duff, **R H** (Canterbury) 1951 A 1, 2, 3, 1952 A 1, 2, 1955 A 2, 3, 1956 SA 1, 2, 3, 4
Duggan, **R J L** (Waikato) 1999 [It (R)]
Duncan, **J** (Otago) 1903 A
Duncan, **M G** (Hawke's Bay) 1971 BI 3(R), 4
Duncan, **W D** (Otago) 1921 SA 1, 2, 3
Dunn, **E J** (North Auckland) 1979 S, 1981 S 1
Dunn, **I T W** (North Auckland) 1983 BI 1, 4, A
Dunn, **J M** (Auckland) 1946 A 1

Earl, **A T** (Canterbury) 1986 F 1, A 1, F 3(R), 1987 [Arg], 1989 W, I, 1991 Arg 1(R), 2, A 1, [E (R), US, S], 1992 A 2, 3(R)
Eastgate, **B P** (Canterbury) 1952 A 1, 2, 1954 S
Eaton, **J J** (Taranaki) 2005 I, E(t), S(R), 2006 Arg, A1, 2(R), 3, SA3(R), F1(R), 2(R), 2009 A1(R), SA1(R), A3(R), 4(R), W
Elliot, **H T P** (Hawke's Bay, Poverty Bay) 2010 S, I 2, 2012 I 1(R), 2015 Sm(R)
Elliott, **K G** (Wellington) 1946 A 1, 2
Ellis, **A M** (Canterbury) 2006 E(R), F2(R), 2007 [Pt(R), R], 2008 I1, E1, 2, SA1, 2, A1, S(R), 2009 It2, E(R), F3(R), 2010 E1(R), S(R), I2, W3(R), 2011 A1(R), SA2(R), A2(R), [J, F1(R), C(R), A(R), F2(R)], 2015 Sm, Arg(R)
Ellis, **M C G** (Otago) 1993 S, E, 1995 C, [I (R), W, J, S, SA (R)]
Ellison, **T E** (Wellington, Otago) 2009 It 2, 2012 I 3(R), SA2(R), S
Elsom, **A E G** (Canterbury) 1952 A 1, 2, 1953 W, 1955 A 1, 2, 3
Elvidge, **R R** (Otago) 1946 A 1, 2, 1949 SA 1, 2, 3, 4, 1950 BI 1, 2, 3
Erceg, **C P** (Auckland) 1951 A 1, 2, 3, 1952 A 1
Evans, **B R** (Hawke's Bay) 2009 F1(R), 2(R)
Evans, **D A** (Hawke's Bay) 1910 A 2
Evans, **N J** (North Harbour, Otago) 2004 E1(R), 2, Arg, PI(R), 2005 I, S, 2006 F2(R), W(R), 2007 F1(R), 2, SA2(R), A2(R), [Pt, S(R), R, F(R)]
Eveleigh, **K A** (Manawatu) 1976 SA 2, 4, 1977 BI 1, 2

Fanning, **A H N** (Canterbury) 1913 A 3
Fanning, **B J** (Canterbury) 1903 A, 1904 BI
Farrell, **C P** (Auckland) 1977 BI 1, 2
Faumuina, **C C** (Auckland) 2012 Arg1(R), SA1(R), Arg2(R), A3, It, W(R), E(R), 2013 A1(R), 2(R), Arg1, SA1(R), Arg2(R), SA2,

A3, F4(R), E(R), I, 2014 E1(R), 2(R), 3(R), A2(R), SA2(R), A 3(R), US, E 4(R), S, W(R), [Arg(R), Nm, Gg, F(R), SA(R), A(R)]

Fawcett, C L (Auckland) 1976 SA 2, 3

Fea, W R (Otago) 1921 SA 3

Feek, G E (Canterbury) 1999 WS (R), A 1(R), SA 2, [E (t), It], 2000 F 1, 2, It, 2001 I, S

Fekitoa, M F (Auckland) 2014 E1(R), 3, A1, 2(R), Arg2, SA2, A 3, S, 2015 SA(R), A 1(R), 2(R), [Nm, Gg(R)]

Filipo, R A (Wellington) 2007 C, SA1(R), A1(R), 2008 S(R)

Finlay, B E L (Manawatu) 1959 BI 1

Finlay, J (Manawatu) 1946 A 1

Finlayson, I (North Auckland) 1928 SA 1, 2, 3, 4, 1930 BI 1, 2

Fitzgerald, J T (Wellington) 1952 A 1

Fitzpatrick, B B J (Wellington) 1953 W, 1954 I, F

Fitzpatrick, S B T (Auckland) 1986 F 1, A 1, F 2, 3, 1987 [It, Fj, Arg, S, W, F], A, 1988 W 1, 2, A 1, 2, 3, 1989 F 1, 2, Arg 1, 2, A, W, I, 1990 S 1, 2, A 1, 2, 3, F 1, 2, 1991 Arg 1, 2, A 1, 2, [E, US, It, C, A, S], 1992 Wld 1, 2, 3, I 1, 2, A 1, 2, 3, SA, 1993 BI 1, 2, 3, A, WS, S, E, 1994 F 1, 2, SA 1, 2, 3, A, 1995 C, [I, W, S, E, SA], A 1, 2, It, F 1, 2, 1996 WS, S 1, 2, A 1, SA 1, A 2, SA 2, 3, 4, 5, 1997 Fj, Arg 1, 2, A 1, SA 1, A 2, SA 2, A 3, W (R)

Flavell, T V (North Harbour, Auckland) 2000 Tg, S 1(R), A 1(R), SA 1, 2(t), F 1(R), 2(R), It, 2001 Sm, Arg 1, F, SA 1, A 1, SA 2, A 2, 2006 I1(R), 2, 2007 F1(R), 2(R), C, SA1, A1

Fleming, J K (Wellington) 1979 S, E, 1980 A 1, 2, 3

Fletcher, C J C (North Auckland) 1921 SA 3

Flynn, C R (Canterbury) 2003 [C(R), Tg], 2004 It(R), 2008 S(R), I2(R), 2009 It2, F3(R), 2010 SA1(R), 2(R), A1(R), 2(R), 3(R), 2011 Fj(R), SA1(R), [Tg(R)]

Fogarty, R (Taranaki) 1921 SA 1, 3

Ford, B R (Marlborough) 1977 BI 3, 4, 1978 I, 1979 E

Forster, S T (Otago) 1993 S, E, 1994 F 1, 2, 1995 It, F 1

Fox, G J (Auckland) 1985 Arg 1, 1987 [It, Fj, Arg, S, W, F], A, 1988 W 1, 2, A 1, 2, 3, 1989 F 1, 2, Arg 1, 2, A, W, I, 1990 S 1, 2, A 1, 2, 3, F 1, 2, 1991 Arg 1, 2, A 1, 2, [E, It, C, A], 1992 Wld 1, 2(R), A 1, 2, 3, SA, 1993 BI 1, 2, 3, A, WS

Francis, A R H (Auckland) 1905 A, 1907 A 1, 2, 3, 1908 AW 1, 2, 3, 1910 A 1, 2, 3

Francis, W C (Wellington) 1913 A 2, 3, 1914 A 1, 2, 3

Franks, B J (Tasman, Canterbury, Hawkes' Bay) 2010 I1, W1, SA1(R), 2(R), A1(R), 2(R), SA3, 2011 Fj, SA1, A1(R), SA2(R), [Tg(R), F1(R), C(R), A(R)], 2012 I1(R), 2(R), 3(R), A1(R), 2(R), SA2(R), S(R), It(R), 2013 F1(R), 2(R), A1(R), Arg1(R), Arg2(R), SA2(R), A 3(R), US(R), E 4(R), S(R), 2015 SA(R), A 1(R), [Nm, Tg(R), SA(R), A(R)]

Franks, O T (Canterbury) 2009 It1(R), A1(R), SA1(R), 2, A2, SA3, W(R), E, F3(R) , 2010 I1, W1, 2(t&R), SA1, 2, A1, 2, 3, 4, E, S, I2, W3, 2011 A1, 2, [Tg, J, F1, C, Arg, A, F2], 2012 I 1, 2, 3, A1, 2, Arg1, SA1, Arg2, SA2, A3(t&R), S, W, E, 2013 F1, 2, 3, A1, 2, SA1, Arg2, F4, E, I(R), 2014 E1, 2, 3, A1, 2, Arg1, SA1, Arg2, SA2, A 3, US(R), E 4, W, 2015 Sm, Arg, SA, A 1, 2, [Arg, Gg(R), Tg, F, SA, A]

Fraser, B G (Wellington) 1979 S, E, 1980 A 3, W, 1981 S 1, 2, SA 1, 2, 3, R, F 1, 2, 1982 A 1, 2, 3, 1983 BI 1, 2, 3, 4, A, S, E, 1984 A 1

Frazer, H F (Hawke's Bay) 1946 A 1, 2, 1947 A 1, 2, 1949 SA 2

Fryer, F C (Canterbury) 1907 A 1, 2, 3, 1908 AW 2

Fuller, W B (Canterbury) 1910 A 1, 2

Furlong, B D M (Hawke's Bay) 1970 SA 4

Gallagher, J A (Wellington) 1987 [It, Fj, S, W, F], A, 1988 W 1, 2, A 1, 2, 3, 1989 F 1, 2, Arg 1, 2, A, W, I

Gallaher, D (Auckland) 1903 A, 1904 BI, 1905 S, E, W, 1906 F

Gard, P C (North Otago) 1971 BI 4

Gardiner, A J (Taranaki) 1974 A 3

Gear, H E (Wellington) 2008 A4, 2009 A3(R), 2010 E, S, I2, W3, 2011 A1, SA2, 2012 I 3, A1, 2, SA2, A3, It

Gear, R L (North Harbour, Nelson Bays, Tasman) 2004 PI, It, 2005 BI1(R), 2, 3, SA1, A1, SA2, W, S, 2006 Arg, A1, 2, SA2, 3(R), E, W, 2007 C(R), A1

Geddes, J H (Southland) 1929 A 1

Geddes, W McK (Auckland) 1913 A 2

Gemmell, B McL (Auckland) 1974 A 1, 2

George, V L (Southland) 1938 A 1, 2, 3

Gibbes, J B (Waikato) 2004 E1, 2, Arg(R), PI, A1, 2, SA2, 2005 BI2(R)

Gibson, D P E (Canterbury) 1999 WS, F 1, SA 1, A 1, SA 2, A 2, [Tg (R), E (R), It, S (R), F 2(R)], 2000 F 1, 2, 2002 It, I 1(R), 2(R), Fj, A 2(R), SA 2(R)

Gilbert, G D M (West Coast) 1935 S, I, W, 1936 E

Gillespie, C T (Wellington) 1913 A 2

Gillespie, W D (Otago) 1958 A 3

Gillett, G A (Canterbury, Auckland) 1905 S, I, E, W, 1907 A 2, 3, 1908 AW 1, 3

Gillies, C C (Otago) 1936 A 2

Gilray, C M (Otago) 1905 A

Glasgow, F T (Taranaki, Southland) 1905 S, I, E, W, 1906 F, 1908 AW 3

Glenn, W S (Taranaki) 1904 BI, 1906 F

Goddard, M P (South Canterbury) 1946 A 2, 1947 A 1, 2, 1949 SA 3, 4

Going, S M (North Auckland) 1967 A, F, 1968 F 3, 1969 W 1, 2, 1970 SA 1(R), 4, 1971 BI 1, 2, 3, 4, 1972 A 1, 2, 3, W, S, 1973 E 1, I, F, E 2, 1974 I, 1975 S, 1976 I (R), SA 1, 2, 3, 4, 1977 BI 1, 2

Gordon, S B (Waikato) 1993 S, E

Graham, D J (Canterbury) 1958 A 1, 2, 1960 SA 2, 3, 1961 F 1, 2, 3, 1962 A 1, 2, 3, 4, 5, 1963 E 1, 2, I, W, 1964 E, S, F, A 1, 2, 3

Graham, J B (Otago) 1913 US, 1914 A 1, 3

Graham, W G (Otago) 1979 F 1(R)

Grant, L A (South Canterbury) 1947 A 1, 2, 1949 SA 1, 2

Gray, G D (Canterbury) 1908 AW 2, 1913 A 1, US

Gray, K F (Wellington) 1963 I, W, 1964 E, S, F, A 1, 2, 3, 1965 S, 2, 3, 4, 1966 BI 1, 2, 3, 4, 1967 W, F, S, 1968 A 1, F 2, 3, 1969 W 1, 2

Gray, W N (Bay of Plenty) 1955 A 2, 3, 1956 SA 1, 2, 3, 4

Green, C I (Canterbury) 1983 S (R), E, 1984 A 1, 2, 3, 1985 E 1, 2, A, Arg 1, 2, 1986 A 2, 3, F 2, 3, 1987 [It, Fj, S, W, F], A

Grenside, B A (Hawke's Bay) 1928 SA 1, 2, 3, 4, 1929 A 2, 3

Griffiths, J L (Wellington) 1934 A 2, 1935 S, I, W, 1936 A 1, 2, 1938 A 3

Guildford, Z R (Hawke's Bay) 2009 W, E, 2010 I1(R), W2, 2011 Fj, SA1, A2, [C], 2012 I 1, 2

Guy, R A (North Auckland) 1971 BI 1, 2, 3, 4

Haden, A M (Auckland) 1977 BI 1, 2, 3, 4, F 1, 2, 1978 A 1, 2, 3, I, W, E, S, 1979 F 1, 2, A, S, E, 1980 A 1, 2, 3, W, 1981 S 2, SA 1, 2, 3, R, F 1, 2, 1982 A 1, 2, 3, 1983 BI 1, 2, 3, 4, A, 1984 F 1, 2, 1985 Arg 1, 2

Hadley, S (Auckland) 1928 SA 1, 2, 3, 4

Hadley, W E (Auckland) 1934 A 1, 2, 1935 S, I, W, 1936 E, A 1, 2

Haig, J S (Otago) 1946 A 1, 2

Haig, L S (Otago) 1950 BI 2, 3, 4, 1951 A 1, 2, 3, 1953 W, 1954 E, S

Halai, F (Counties-Manukau) 2013 J

Hales, D A (Canterbury) 1972 A 1, 2, 3, W

Hamilton, D C (Southland) 1908 AW 2

Hamilton, S E (Canterbury) 2006 Arg, SA1

Hammett, M G (Canterbury) 1999 F 1(R), SA 2(R), [It, S (R), SA 3], 2000 Tg, S 1(R), 2(t&R), A 1(R), SA 1(R), A 2(R), SA 2(R), F 2(R), It (R), 2001 Arg 1(t), 2002 It (R), I 1, 2, A 1, SA 1, 2(R), 2003 SA 1(R), A 1(R), SA 2, [It(R), C, W(R), SA(R), F(R)]

Hammond, I A (Marlborough) 1952 A 2

Harper, E T (Canterbury) 1904 BI, 1906 F

Harding, S (Otago) 2002 Fj

Harris, N P (Bay of Plenty) 2014 Arg2(R), US

Harris, P C (Manawatu) 1976 SA 3

Hart, A H (Taranaki) 1924 I

Hart, G F (Canterbury) 1930 BI 1, 2, 3, 4, 1931 A, 1934 A 1, 1935 S, I, W, 1936 A 1, 2

Harvey, B A (Wairarapa-Bush) 1986 F 1

Harvey, I H (Wairarapa) 1928 SA 4

Harvey, L R (Otago) 1949 SA 1, 2, 3, 4, 1950 BI 1, 2, 3, 4

Harvey, P (Canterbury) 1904 BI

Hasell, E W (Canterbury) 1913 A 2, 3

Hayman, C J (Otago) 2001 Sm (R), Arg 1, F (R), A 1(R), SA 2(R), A 2(R), 2002 F (t), W, 2004 E1, 2, PI, A1, 2, SA2, It,

W(R), F, 2005 BI1, SA1, A1, SA2, A2, W, E, 2006 I1, 2, A1, SA1, A2, 3, SA3, E, F1, 2, W, 2007 F1, 2, SA1, A1, SA2, A2, [It, Pt(R), S, F]

Hayward, H 0 (Auckland) 1908 AW 3

Hazlett, E J (Southland) 1966 BI 1, 2, 3, 4, 1967 A, E

Hazlett, W E (Southland) 1928 SA 1, 2, 3, 4, 1930 BI 1, 2, 3, 4

Heeps, T R (Wellington) 1962 A 1, 2, 3, 4, 5

Heke, W R (North Auckland) 1929 A 1, 2, 3

Hemi, R C (Waikato) 1953 W, 1954 I, E, S, F, 1955 A 1, 2, 3, 1956 SA 1, 3, 4, 1957 A 1, 2, 1959 BI 1, 3, 4

Henderson, P (Wanganui) 1949 SA 1, 2, 3, 4, 1950 BI 2, 3, 4

Henderson, P W (Otago) 1991 Arg 1, [C], 1992 Wld 1, 2, 3, I 1, 1995 [J]

Herewini, M A (Auckland) 1962 A 5, 1963 I, 1964 S, F, 1965 SA 4, 1966 BI 1, 2, 3, 4, 1967 A

Hewett, D N (Canterbury) 2001 I (R), S (R), Arg 2, 2002 It (R), I 1, 2, A 1, SA 1, A 2, SA 2, 2003 E, F, SA 1, A 1, SA 2, A 2, [It, Tg(R), W, SA, A, F]

Hewett, J A (Auckland) 1991 [It]

Hewitt, N J (Southland) 1995 [I (t), J], 1996 A 1(R), 1997 SA 1(R), I, E 1, W, E 2, 1998 E 2(t&R)

Hewson, A R (Wellington) 1981 S 1, 2, SA 1, 2, 3, R, F 1, 2, 1982 A 1, 2, 3, 1983 BI 1, 2, 3, 4, A, 1984 F 1, 2, A 1

Higginson, G (Canterbury, Hawke's Bay) 1980 W, 1981 S 1, SA 1, 1982 A 1, 2, 1983 A

Hill, D W (Waikato) 2006 I2(R)

Hill, S F (Canterbury) 1955 A 3, 1956 SA 1, 3, 4, 1957 A 1, 2, 1958 A 3, 1959 BI 1, 2, 3, 4

Hines, G R (Waikato) 1980 A 3

Hobbs, M J B (Canterbury) 1983 BI 1, 2, 3, 4, A, S, E, 1984 F 1, 2, A 1, 2, 3, 1985 E 1, 2, A, Arg 1, 2, 1986 A 2, 3, F 2, 3

Hoeata, J M R A (Taranaki) 2011 Fj, SA1(R), 2(R)

Hoeft, C H (Otago) 1998 E 2(t&R), A 2(R), SA 2, A 3, 1999 WS, F 1, SA 1, A 1, 2, [Tg, E, S, F 2, SA 3(R)], 2000 S 1, 2, A 1, SA 1, A 2, SA 2, 2001 Sm, Arg 1, F, SA 1, A 1, SA 2, A 2, 2003 W, [C, F(R)]

Holah, M R (Waikato) 2001 Sm, Arg 1(t&R), F (R), SA 1(R), A 1(R), SA 2(R), A 2(R), 2002 It, I 2(R), A 2(t), E, F, W (R), 2003 W, F (R), A 1(R), SA 2, [It(R), C, Tg(R), W(R), SA(t&R), A(R), F(t&R)], 2004 E1(R), 2, Arg(R), PI, A1, SA1, A2, SA2, 2005 BI3(R), A1(R), 2006 I1, SA3(R)

Holder, E C (Buller) 1934 A 2

Hook, L S (Auckland) 1929 A 1, 2, 3

Hooper, J A (Canterbury) 1937 SA 1, 2, 3

Hopkinson, A E (Canterbury) 1967 S, 1968 A 2, F 1, 2, 3, 1969 W 2, 1970 SA 1, 2, 3

Hore, A K (Taranaki) 2002 E, F, 2004 E1(t), 2(R), Arg, A1(t), 2005 W(R), I(R), S(R), 2006 I2(R), Arg(R), A1(R), SA1(R), A2(R), SA3, E(R), F2(R), W(R), 2007 F1(R), C, SA2(R), [Pt, S(R), R(R), F(R)], 2008 I1, E1, 2, SA1, 2, A1, 2, SA3, Sm, A3, 4, 2009 F1, A1, SA1, 2, A2, SA3, A3, 4, W, E, F3, 2010 S(R), I2(R), W3(R), 2011 Fj, SA1, A1(R), SA2(R), A2(R), [Tg, J(R), F1(R), C, Arg(R), A(R), F2(R)], 2012 I1, 2, 3, A1(R), 2(R), Arg1(R), SA1, Arg2, SA2, A3(R), S, W, 2013 F2(R), 3, A1, 2, Arg1, 2, SA2, J(R), I

Hore, J (Otago) 1930 BI 2, 3, 4, 1932 A 1, 2, 3, 1934 A 1, 2, 1935 S, 1936 E

Horsley, R H (Wellington) 1960 SA 2, 3, 4

Hotop, J (Canterbury) 1952 A 1, 2, 1955 A 3

Howarth, S P (Auckland) 1994 SA 1, 2, 3, A

Howlett, D C (Auckland) 2000 Tg (R), F 1, 2, It, 2001 Sm, Arg 1(R), F (R), SA 1, A 1, 2, I, S, Arg 2, 2002 It, I 1, 2(R), Fj, A 1, SA 1, A 2, SA 2, E, F, W, 2003 E, W, F, SA 1, A 1, SA 2, A 2, [It, C(R), Tg, W, SA, A, F], 2004 E1, SA1, A2, SA2, W, F, 2005 Fj, BI1, A2, I, E, 2006 I1, 2, SA1, A3, SA3, 2007 F2(R), C, SA2, A2, [It, S, R(R)]

Hughes, A M (Auckland) 1949 A 1, 2, 1950 BI 1, 2, 3, 4

Hughes, E (Southland, Wellington) 1907 A 1, 2, 3, 1908 AW 1, 1921 SA 1, 2

Hunter, B A (Otago) 1971 BI 1, 2, 3

Hunter, J (Taranaki) 1905 S, I, E, W, 1906 F, 1907 A 1, 2, 3, 1908 AW 1, 2, 3

Hurst, I A (Canterbury) 1973 I, F, E 2, 1974 A 1, 2

Ieremia, A (Wellington) 1994 SA 1, 2, 3, 1995 [J], 1996 SA 2, 5(R), 1997 A 1(R), SA 1(R), A 2, SA 2, A 3, I, E 1,

1999 WS, F 1, SA 1, A 1, SA 2, A 2, [Tg, E, S, F 2, SA 3], 2000 Tg, S 1, 2, A 1, 2, SA 2

Ifwersen, K D (Auckland) 1921 SA 3

Innes, C R (Auckland) 1989 W, I, 1990 A 1, 2, 3, F 1, 2, 1991 Arg 1, 2, A 1, 2, [E, US, It, C, A, S]

Innes, G D (Canterbury) 1932 A 2

Irvine, I B (Canterbury) 1952 A 1

Irvine, J G (Otago) 1914 A 1, 2, 3

Irvine, W R (Hawke's Bay, Wairarapa) 1924 I, W, 1925 E, F, 1930 BI 1

Irwin, M W (Otago) 1955 A 1, 2, 1956 SA 1, 1958 A 2, 1959 BI 3, 4, 1960 SA 1

Jack, C R (Canterbury, Tasman) 2001 Arg 1(R), SA 1(R), 2, A 2, I, S, Arg 2, 2002 I 1, 2, A 1, SA 1, A 2, SA 2, 2003 E, W, F, SA 1, A 1, SA 2(R), A 2, [It, C, SA, A, F], 2004 E1, 2, Arg, PI, A1, SA1, A2, SA2, It, W, F, 2005 Fj(R), BI1, 2, 3, SA1, A1, SA2, A2, W, E, S, 2006 I1, 2, A1, SA1, A2, 3, SA2(R), 3, E, F2, 2007 F1, 2, A1, SA2, A2, [It, Pt, S(R), R(R), F(R)]

Jackson, E S (Hawke's Bay) 1936 A 1, 2, 1937 SA 1, 2, 3, 1938 A 3

Jaffray, J L (Otago, South Canterbury) 1972 A 2, 1975 S, 1976 I, SA 1, 1977 BI 2, 1979 F 1, 2

Jane, C S (Wellington) 2008 A4(R), S(R), 2009 F1, 2, It1(R), A1, SA3(R), A3, 4, W, It2, F3, 2010 I1, W1, 2, SA1, 2, A1, 2, SA3, A3, 4, I2, 2011 SA1, 2(R), A2, [Tg(R), J, F1, Arg, A, F2], 2012 A1, 2, Arg1, SA1, Arg2, SA2, A3, S, It(R), W, E, 2013 F4, I, 2014 E1, 2, 3, A1, 2, SA1(R), A 3, US

Jarden, R A (Wellington) 1951 A 1, 2, 1952 A 1, 2, 1953 W, 1954 I, E, S, F, 1955 A 1, 2, 3, 1956 SA 1, 2, 3, 4

Jefferd, A C R (East Coast) 1981 S 1, 2, SA 1

Jessep, E M (Wellington) 1931 A, 1932 A 1

Johnson, L M (Wellington) 1928 SA 1, 2, 3, 4

Johnston, W (Otago) 1907 A 1, 2, 3

Johnstone, B R (Auckland) 1976 SA 2, 1977 BI 1, 2, F 1, 2, 1978 I, W, E, S, 1979 F 1, 2, S, E

Johnstone, C R (Canterbury) 2005 Fj(R), BI2(R), 3(R)

Johnstone, P (Otago) 1949 SA 2, 4, 1950 BI 1, 2, 3, 4, 1951 A 1, 2, 3

Jones, I D (North Auckland, North Harbour) 1990 S 1, 2, A 1, 2, 3, F 1, 2, 1991 Arg 1, 2, A 1, 2, [E, US, It, C, A, S], 1992 Wld 1, 2, 3, I 1, 2, A 1, 2, 3, SA 1, 1993 BI 1, 2(R), 3, WS, S, E, 1994 F 1, 2, SA 1, 3, A, 1995 C, [I, W, S, E, SA], A 1, 2, It, F 1, 2, 1996 WS, S 1, 2, A 1, SA 1, A 2, SA 2, 3, 4, 5, 1997 Fj, Arg 1, 2, A 1, SA 1, A 2, SA 2, A 3, I, E 1, W, E 2, 1998 E 1, 2, A 1, SA 1, A 2, 3(R), 1999 F 1(R), [It, S (R)]

Jones, M G (North Auckland) 1973 E 2

Jones, M N (Auckland) 1987 [It, Fj, S, F], A, 1988 W 1, 2, A 2, 3, 1989 F 1, 2, Arg 1, 2, 1990 F 1, 2, 1991 Arg 1, 2, A 1, 2, [E, US, S], 1992 Wld 1, 3, I 2, A 1, 3, SA, 1993 BI 1, 2, 3, A, WS, 1994 SA 3(R), A, 1995 A 1(R), 2, It, F 1, 2, 1996 WS, S 1, 2, A 1, SA 1, A 2, SA 2, 3, 4, 5, 1997 Fj, 1998 E 1, A 1, SA 1, A 2

Jones, P F H (North Auckland) 1954 E, S, 1955 A 1, 2, 1956 SA 3, 4, 1958 A 1, 2, 3, 1959 BI 1, 1960 SA 1

Joseph, H T (Canterbury) 1971 BI 2, 3

Joseph, J W (Otago) 1992 Wld 2, 3(R), I 1, A 1(R), 3, SA, 1993 BI 1, 2, 3, A, WS, S, E, 1994 SA 2(t), 1995 C, [I, W, J (R), S, SA (R)]

Kahui, R D (Waikato) 2008 E2, A1, 2, SA3, Sm, A3, S, W, 2010 W1(R), 2, SA1(R), 2011 SA2, [Tg, J, F1, A, F2]

Kaino, J (Auckland) 2006 I1(R), 2, 2008 I1, E1, SA1, 2, A1, 2, SA3, Sm, A3, 4, I2, W, E3, 2009 F2, It1, SA1, 2, A2, SA3, W, E(R), F3, 2010 I1, W2, SA1, 2, A1, 2, SA3, A3(R), 4, E, I2, W3, 2011 Fj(R), SA1, A1, SA2, [Tg, J, F1, C, Arg, A, F2], 2014 E1, 2, 3, A1, Arg2, SA2, E 4, W, 2015 Sm, Arg, A 1, 2(R), [Arg, Nm, Gg, Tg, F, SA, A]

Karam, J F (Wellington, Horowhenua) 1972 W, S, 1973 E 1, I, F, 1974 A 1, 2, 3, I, 1975 S

Katene, T (Wellington) 1955 A 2

Kearney, J C (Otago) 1947 A 2, 1949 SA 1, 2, 3

Kelleher, B T (Otago, Waikato) 1999 WS (R), SA 1(R), A 2(R), [Tg (R), E (R), It, F 2], 2000 S 1, A 1(R), 2(R), It (R), 2001 Sm, F (R), A 1(R), SA 2, A 2, I, S, 2002 It, I 2(R), Fj, SA

1(R), 2(R), 2003 F (R), [A(R)], 2004 Arg, PI(R), SA1(R), 2(R), It, W(R), F, 2005 Fj, BI1(R), 2, 3, SA1, W, E, 2006 I1, 2, A1, 2, 3, SA3(R), E, F1(R), 2, W, 2007 F2, C, SA1, A1, 2, [It, S, F]

Kelly, J W (Auckland) 1949 A 1, 2

Kember, G F (Wellington) 1970 SA 4

Kerr-Barlow, T N J (Waikato) 2012 S(R), It(R), 2013 F1(R), 3(R), A1(R), 2(R), Arg1(R), SA1(R), Arg2(R), SA2(R), A3(R), J, F4(R), E(R), 2014 SA2(R), 2015 [Nm(R), Gg(R), Tg(R), F(R), A(R)]

Ketels, R C (Counties) 1980 W, 1981 S 1, 2, R, F 1

Kiernan, H A D (Auckland) 1903 A

Kilby, F D (Wellington) 1932 A 1, 2, 3, 1934 A 2

Killeen, B A (Auckland) 1936 A 1

King, R M (Waikato) 2002 W

King, R R (West Coast) 1934 A 2, 1935 S, I, W, 1936 E, A 1, 2, 1937 SA 1, 2, 3, 1938 A 1, 2, 3

Kingstone, C N (Taranaki) 1921 SA 1, 2, 3

Kirk, D E (Auckland) 1985 E 1, 2, A, Arg 1, 1986 F 1, A 1, 2, 3, F 2, 3, 1987 [It, Fj, Arg, S, W, F], A

Kirkpatrick, I A (Canterbury, Poverty Bay) 1967 F, 1968 A 1(R), 2, F 1, 2, 3, 1969 W 1, 2, 1970 SA 1, 2, 3, 4, 1971 BI 1, 2, 3, 4, 1972 A 1, 2, 3, W, S, 1973 E 1, I, F, E 2, 1974 A 1, 2, 3, I 1975 S, 1976 I, SA 1, 2, 3, 4, 1977 BI 1, 2, 3, 4

Kirton, E W (Otago) 1967 E, W, F, S, 1968 A 1, 2, F 1, 2, 3, 1969 W 1, 2, 1970 SA 2, 3

Kirwan, J J (Auckland) 1984 F 1, 2, 1985 E 1, 2, A, Arg 1, 2, 1986 F 1, A 1, 2, 3, F 2, 3, 1987 [It, Fj, Arg, S, W, F], A, 1988 W 1, 2, A 1, 2, 3, 1989 F 1, 2, Arg 1, 2, A, 1990 S 1, 2, A 1, 2, 3, F 1, 2, 1991 Arg 2, A 1, 2, [E, It, C, A, S], 1992 Wld 1, 2(R), 3, I 1, 2, A 1, 2, 3, SA, 1993 BI 2, 3, A, WS, 1994 F 1, 2, SA 1, 2, 3

Kivell, A L (Taranaki) 1929 A 2, 3

Knight, A (Auckland) 1934 A 1

Knight, G A (Manawatu) 1977 F 1, 2, 1978 A 1, 2, 3, E, S, 1979 F 1, 2, A, 1980 A 1, 2, 3, W, 1981 S 1, 2, SA 1, 3, 1982 A 1, 2, 3, 1983 BI 1, 2, 3, 4, A, 1984 F 1, 2, A 1, 2, 3, 1985 E 1, 2, A, 1986 A 2, 3

Knight, L G (Poverty Bay) 1977 BI 1, 2, 3, 4, F 1, 2

Koteka, T T (Waikato) 1981 F 2, 1982 A 3

Kreft, A J (Otago) 1968 A 2

Kronfeld, S J (Otago) 1995 C, [I, W, S, E, SA], A 1, 2(R) 1996 WS, S 1, 2, A 1, SA 1, A 2, SA 2, 3, 4, 5, 1997 Fj, Arg 1, 2, A 1, SA 1, A 2, SA 2, A 3, I (R), E 1, W, E 2, 1998 E 1, 2, A 1, SA 1, 2 A 3, 1999 WS, F 1, SA 1, A 1, SA 2, A 2, [Tg, E, S, F 2, SA 3], 2000 Tg, S 1(R), 2, A 1(R), SA 1, A 2, SA 2

Laidlaw, C R (Otago, Canterbury) 1964 F, A 1, 1965 SA 1, 2, 3, 4, 1966 BI 1, 2, 3, 4, 1967 E, W, S, 1968 A 1, 2, F 1, 2, 1970 SA 1, 2, 3

Laidlaw, K F (Southland) 1960 SA 2, 3, 4

Lambert, K K (Manawatu) 1972 S (R), 1973 E 1, I, F, E 2, 1974 I, 1976 SA 1, 3, 4, 1977 BI 1, 4

Lambourn, A (Wellington) 1934 A 1, 2, 1935 S, I, W, 1936 E, 1937 A 1, 2, 3, 1938 A 3

Larsen, B P (North Harbour) 1992 Wld 2, 3, I 1, 1994 F 1, 2, SA 1, 2, A (t), 1995 [I, W, J, E(R)], It, F 1, 1996 S 2(t), SA 4(R)

Latimer, T D (Bay of Plenty) 2009 F1(R), 2, It1, 2, F3(R)

Lauaki, S T (Waikato) 2005 Fj(R), BI1(R), 2(R), 3, A2, I, S, 2007 [It(R), Pt, S(R), R], 2008 E1(R), 2(R), SA1(R), 2(R), A1(R), Sm(R)

Laulala, C D E (Canterbury) 2004 W, 2006 I2

Laulala, N E (Canterbury) 2015 Sm(R), Arg(R), A 1(R), 2(R)

Le Lievre, J M (Canterbury) 1962 A 4

Lee, D D (Otago) 2002 E (R), F

Lendrum, R N (Counties) 1973 E 2

Leonard, B G (Waikato) 2007 F1(R), 2(R), SA2(R), A2(R), [It(R), Pt, S(R), R(R), F(R)], 2009 It1, SA1, A3(R), W

Leslie, A R (Wellington) 1974 A 1, 2, 3, I, 1975 S, 1976 I, SA 1, 2, 3, 4

Leys, E T (Wellington) 1929 A 3

Lilburne, H T (Canterbury, Wellington) 1928 SA 3, 4, 1929 A 1, 2, 3, 1930 BI 1, 4, 1931 A, 1932 A 1, 1934 A 2

Lindsay, D F (Otago) 1928 SA 1, 2, 3

Lineen, T R (Auckland) 1957 A 1, 2, 1958 A 1, 2, 3, 1959 BI 1, 2, 3, 4, 1960 SA 1, 2, 3

Lister, T N (South Canterbury) 1968 A 1, 2, F 1, 1969 W 1, 2, 1970 SA 1, 4, 1971 BI 4

Little, P F (Auckland) 1961 F 2, 3, 1962 A 2, 3, 5, 1963 I, W, 1964 E, S, F

Little, W K (North Harbour) 1990 S 1, 2, A 1, 2, 3, F 1, 2, 1991 Arg 1, 2, A 1, [It, S], 1992 Wld 1, 2, 3, I 1, 2, A 1, 2, 3, SA, 1993 BI 1, WS (R), 1994 SA 2(R), A, 1995 C, [I, W, S, E, SA], A 1, 2, It, F 1, 2, 1996 S 2, A 1, SA 1, A 2, SA 2, 3, 4, 5, 1997 W, E 2, 1998 E 1, A 1, SA 1, A 2

Loader, C J (Wellington) 1954 I, E, S, F

Lochore, B J (Wairarapa) 1964 E, S, 1965 SA 1, 2, 3, 4, 1966 BI 1, 2, 3, 4, 1967 A, E, W, F, S, 1968 A 1, F 2, 3, 1969 W 1, 2, 1970 SA 1, 2, 3, 4, 1971 BI 3

Loe, R W (Waikato, Canterbury) 1987 [It, Arg], 1988 W 1, 2, A 1, 2, 3, 1989 F 1, 2, Arg 1, 2, A, W, I, 1990 S 1, 2, A 1, 2, 3, F 1, 2, 1991 Arg 1, 2, A 1, 2, [E, It, C, A, S], 1992 Wld 1, 2, 3, I 1, 2, A 1, 2, 3, SA, 1994 F 1, 2, SA 1, 2, 3, A, 1995 [J, S, SA (R)], A 2(t), F 2(R)

Lomu, J T (Counties Manukau, Wellington) 1994 F 1, 2, 1995 [I, W, S, E, SA], A 1, 2, It, F 1, 2, 1996 WS, S 1, A 1, SA 1, A 2, 1997 E 1, W, E 2, 1998 E 1, 2, A 1(R), SA 1, A 2, SA 2, A 3, 1999 WS (R), SA 1, A 1(R), SA 2(R), A 2(R), [Tg, E, It, S, F, SA 3], 2000 Tg, S 1, 2, A 1, SA 1, A 2, SA 2, F 1, 2001 Arg 1, F, SA 1, A 1, SA 2, A 2, I, S, Arg 2, 2002 It, I 1(R), 2, Fj, SA 1(R), E, F, W

Long, A J (Auckland) 1903 A

Loveridge, D S (Taranaki) 1978 W, 1979 S, E, 1980 A 1, 2, 3, W, 1981 S 1, 2, SA 1, 2, 3, R, F 1, 2, 1982 A 1, 2, 3, 1983 BI 1, 2, 3, 4, A, 1985 Arg 2

Lowen, K R (Waikato) 2002 E

Luatua, D S (Auckland) 2013 F3(R), A1, 2, Arg1, SA1(R), Arg2(R), SA2(R), A3(R), J, E(R), I, 2014 A2(R), SA1, 2(R)

Lucas, F W (Auckland) 1924 I, 1925 F, 1928 SA 4, 1930 BI 1, 2, 3, 4

Lunn, W A (Otago) 1949 A 1, 2

Lynch, T W (South Canterbury) 1913 A 1, 1914 A 1, 2, 3

Lynch, T W (Canterbury) 1951 A 1, 2, 3

McAlister, C L (North Harbour) 2005 BI3, SA1(R), A1(R), SA2(R), A2(R), 2006 I1, 2, SA1(R), A3, SA2, F1, W, 2007 F2, C, SA1(R), A1, SA2, A2, [It, S, R, F], 2009 F1(R), 2(R), It1, SA1(R), 2(R), A2, It2, F3(R)

McAtamney, F S (Otago) 1956 SA 2

McCahill, B J (Auckland) 1987 [Arg, S (R), W (R)], 1989 Arg 1(R), 2(R), 1991 A 2, [E, US, C, A]

McCaw, R H (Canterbury) 2001 I, S, Arg 2, 2002 I 1, 2, A 1, SA 1, A 2, 2003 E, F, SA 1, A 1, 2, [It, C(R), Tg(R), W, SA, A, F], 2004 E1, Arg, It, W, F, 2005 Fj, BI1, 2, SA1, A1, SA2, A2, W(R), I, S, 2006 I1, 2, A1, SA1, A2, 3, SA2, 3, E, F1, 2, W, 2007 F1, 2, C(R), SA1, A1, SA2, A2, [It, S, R(R), F], 2008 I1, E1, 2, A2, SA3, A3, 4, S(R), I2, W, E3, 2009 A1, SA1, 2, A2, SA3, A3, 4, W, E, F3, 2010 I1, W1, 2, SA1, 2, A1, 2, SA3, A3, 4, E, S, I2, W3, 2011 Fj, SA1, A1, 2, [Tg, F1, Arg, A, F2], 2012 I 1, 2, 3, A1, 2, Arg1, SA1, Arg2, SA2, A3, S, W, E, 2013 A1, 2, Arg1, SA2, J, F4, E, I, 2014 E1, 2, 3, A1, 2, Arg1, SA1, Arg2, SA2, A 3, E 4, S, W, 2015 Sm, Arg, SA, A 1, 2, [Arg, Nm(R), Gg, F, SA, A]

McCaw, W A (Southland) 1951 A 1, 2, 3, 1953 W, 1954 F

McCool, M J (Wairarapa-Bush) 1979 A

McCormick, W F (Canterbury) 1965 SA 4, 1967 E, W, F, S, 1968 A 1, 2, F 1, 2, 3, 1969 W 1, 2, 1970 SA 1, 2, 3, 1971 BI 1

McCullough, J F (Taranaki) 1959 BI 2, 3, 4

McDonald, A (Otago) 1905 S, I, E, W, 1907 A 1, 1908 AW 1, 1913 A 1, US

Macdonald, A J (Auckland) 2005 W(R), S

Macdonald, H H (Canterbury, North Auckland) 1972 W, S, 1973 E 1, I, F, E 2, 1974 I, 1975 S, 1976 I, SA 1, 2, 3

MacDonald, L R (Canterbury) 2000 S 1(R), 2(R), SA 1(t), 2(R), 2001 Sm, Arg 1, F, SA 1(R), A 1(R), SA 2, A 2, I, S, 2002 I 1, 2, Fj, A 2(R), SA 2, 2003 A 2(R), [It(R), C, Tg, W, SA, A, F], 2005 BI1, 2(R), SA1, 2, A2, W(R), I, E(R), S(R), 2006 Arg, A1, SA1, A2, 3(R), SA2, F1, 2, 2007 F1, 2, C(R), SA1(R), [It, Pt(R), S, F], 2008 I1(R), E1(R), 2, SA1(R), 2(R)

McDonnell, J M (Otago) 2002 It, I 1(R), 2(R), Fj, SA 1(R), A 2(R), E, F

McDowell, S C (Auckland, Bay of Plenty) 1985 Arg 1, 2, 1986 A 2, 3, F 2, 3, 1987 [It, Fj, S, W, F], A, 1988 W 1, 2, A 1,

2, 3, 1989 F 1, 2, Arg 1, 2, A, W, I, 1990 S 1, 2, A 1, 2, 3, F 1, 2, 1991 Arg 1, 2, A 1, 2, [E, US, It, C, A, S], 1992 Wld 1, 2, 3, I 1, 2

McEldowney, J T (Taranaki) 1977 BI 3, 4

MacEwan, I N (Wellington) 1956 SA 2, 1957 A 1, 2, 1958 A 1, 2, 3, 1959 BI 1, 2, 3, 1960 SA 1, 2, 3, 4, 1961 F 1, 2, 3, 1962 A 1, 2, 3, 4

McGrattan, B (Wellington) 1983 S, E, 1985 Arg 1, 2, 1986 F 1, A 1

McGregor, A J (Auckland) 1913 A 1, US

McGregor, D (Canterbury, Southland) 1903 A, 1904 BI, 1905 E, W

McGregor, N P (Canterbury) 1924 W, 1925 E

McGregor, R W (Auckland) 1903 A, 1904 BI

McHugh, M J (Auckland) 1946 A 1, 2, 1949 SA 3

McIntosh, D N (Wellington) 1956 SA 1, 2, 1957 A 1, 2

McKay, D W (Auckland) 1961 F 1, 2, 3, 1963 E 1, 2

McKechnie, B J (Southland) 1977 F 1, 2, 1978 A 2(R), 3, W (R), E, S, 1979 A, 1981 SA 1(R), F 1

McKellar, G F (Wellington) 1910 A 1, 2, 3

McKenzie, R J (Wellington) 1913 A 1, US, 1914 A 2, 3

McKenzie, R McC (Manawatu) 1934 A 1, 1935 S, 1936 A 1, 1937 SA 1, 2, 3, 1938 A 1, 2, 3

McLachlan, J S (Auckland) 1974 A 2

McLaren, H C (Waikato) 1952 A 1

McLean, A L (Bay of Plenty) 1921 SA 2, 3

McLean, H F (Wellington, Auckland) 1930 BI 3, 4, 1932 A 1, 2, 3, 1934 A 1, 1935 I, W, 1936 E

McLean, J K (King Country, Auckland) 1947 A 1, 1949 A 2

McLeod, B E (Counties) 1964 A 1, 2, 3, 1965 SA 1, 2, 3, 4, 1966 BI 1, 2, 3, 4, 1967 E, W, F, S, 1968 A 1, 2, F 1, 2, 3, 1969 W 1, 2, 1970 SA 1, 2

McLeod, S J (Waikato) 1996 WS, S 1, 1997 Fj (R), Arg 2(t&R), I (R), E 1(R), W (t), E 2(R), 1998 A 1, SA 1(R)

McMinn, A F (Wairarapa, Manawatu) 1903 A, 1905 A

McMinn, F A (Manawatu) 1904 BI

McMullen, R F (Auckland) 1957 A 1, 2, 1958 A 1, 2, 3, 1959 BI 1, 2, 3, 1960 SA 2, 3, 4

McNab, J R (Otago) 1949 SA 1, 2, 3, 1950 BI 1, 2, 3

McNaughton, A M (Bay of Plenty) 1971 BI 1, 2, 3

McNeece, J (Southland) 1913 A 2, 3, 1914 A 1, 2, 3

McPhail, B E (Canterbury) 1959 BI 1, 4

Macpherson, D G (Otago) 1905 A

MacPherson, G L (Otago) 1986 F 1

MacRae, I R (Hawke's Bay) 1966 BI 1, 2, 3, 4, 1967 A, E, W, F, S, 1968 F 1, 2, 1969 W 1, 2, 1970 SA 1, 2, 3, 4

McRae, J A (Southland) 1946 A 1(R), 2

McWilliams, R G (Auckland) 1928 SA 2, 3, 4, 1929 A 1, 2, 3, 1930 BI 1, 2, 3, 4

Mackintosh, J L (Southland) 2008 S

Mackrell, W H C (Auckland) 1906 F

Macky, J V (Auckland) 1913 A 2

Maguire, J R (Auckland) 1910 A 1, 2, 3

Mahoney, A (Bush) 1935 S, I, W, 1936 E

Mains, L W (Otago) 1971 BI 2, 3, 4, 1976 I

Major, J (Taranaki) 1967 A

Maka, I (Otago) 1998 E 2(R), A 1(R), SA 1(R), 2

Maling, T S (Otago) 2002 It, I 2(R), Fj, A 1, SA 1, A 2, SA 2, 2004 Arg, A1, SA1, 2

Manchester, J E (Canterbury) 1932 A 1, 2, 3, 1934 A 1, 2, 1935 S, I, W, 1936 E

Mannix, S J (Wellington) 1994 F 1

Marshall, J W (Southland, Canterbury) 1995 F 2, 1996 WS, S 1, 2, A 1, SA 1, A 2, SA 2, 3, 4, 5, 1997 Fj, Arg 1, 2, A 1, SA 1, A 2, SA 2, A 3, I, E 1, W, E 2, 1998 A 1, SA 1, A 2, SA 2, A 3, 1999 WS, F 1, SA 1, A 1, SA 2, A 2, [Tg, E, S, F 2(R), SA 3], 2000 Tg, S 2, A 1, SA 1, A 2, SA 2, F 1, 2, It, 2001 Arg 1, F, SA 1, A 1, 2(R), 2002 I 1, 2, Fj (R), A 1, SA 1, A 2, SA 2, 2003 E, SA 1, A 1, SA 2, A 2, [It, Tg, W, SA, A], 2004 E1, 2, PI, A1, SA1, A2, SA2, 2005 Fj(R), BI1, 2(R), 3(R)

Masaga, L T C (Counties Manukau) 2009 It1

Masoe, M C (Taranaki, Wellington) 2005 W, E, 2006Arg, A1(R), SA1(R), A2(R), 3(R), SA2, E, F2(R), 2007 F1, 2(R), C, A1(R), SA2(R), [It(R), Pt, S, R, F(R)]

Mason, D F (Wellington) 1947 A 2(R)

Masters, R R (Canterbury) 1924 I, W, 1925 E, F

Mataira, H K (Hawke's Bay) 1934 A 2

Matheson, J D (Otago) 1972 A 1, 2, 3, W, S

Mathewson, A S (Wellington) 2010 A2(R), 4(R), I2(R)

Mauger, A J D (Canterbury) 2001 I, S, Arg 2, 2002 It (R), I 1, 2, Fj, A 1, SA 1, A 2, SA 2, 2003 SA 1, A 1, SA 2, A 2, [W, SA, A, F], 2004 SA2(R), It(R), W, F(R), 2005 Fj, BI1, 2, SA1, A1, SA2, A2, I, E, 2006 I1, 2, A1, 2, SA3, E, 2007 F1, C, SA1, A1, [It(R), Pt, R]

Max, D S (Nelson) 1931 A, 1934 A 1, 2

Maxwell, N M C (Canterbury) 1999 WS, F 1, SA 1, A 1, SA 2, A 2, [Tg, E, S, F 2, SA 3], 2000 S 1, 2, A 1, SA 1(R), A 2, SA 2 F 1, 2, It (R), 2001 Sm, Arg 1, F, SA 1, A 1, SA 2, A2, I, S, Arg 2, 2002 It, I 1, 2, Fj, 2004 It, F

Mayerhofler, M A (Canterbury) 1998 E 1, 2, SA 1, A 2, SA 2, A 3

Meads, C E (King Country) 1957 A 1, 2, 1958 A 1, 2, 3, 1959 BI 2, 3, 4, 1960 SA 1, 2, 3, 4, 1961 F 1, 2, 3, 1962 A 1, 2, 3, 5, 1963 E 1, 2, I, W, 1964 E, S, F, A 1, 2, 3, 1965 SA 1, 2, 3, 4, 1966 BI 1, 2, 3, 4, 1967 A, E, W, F, S, 1968 A 1, 2, F 1, 2, 3, 1969 W 1, 2, 1970 SA 3, 4, 1971 BI 1, 2, 3, 4

Meads, S T (King Country) 1961 F 1, 1962 A 4, 5, 1963 I 1964 A 1, 2, 3, 1965 SA 1, 2, 3, 4, 1966 BI 1, 2, 3, 4

Mealamu, K F (Auckland) 2002 W, 2003 E (R), W, F (R), SA 1, A 1, SA 2(R), A 2, [It, W, SA, A, F], 2004 E1, 2, PI, A1, SA1, A2, SA2, W, F(R), 2005 Fj(R), BI1, 2, 3, SA1, A1, SA2, A2, I, E, 2006 I1, 2, A1, 2, 3, SA2(R), E, F1(R), 2, 2007 F1, 2(R), SA1(R), A1(R), SA2, A2(R), [It, Pt(R), R], 2008 I1(R), E1(t&R), 2(t&R), SA1(R), 2(R), A1(R), 2(R), SA3(R), Sm(R), A3(R), 4(R), S, I2, W, E3, 2009 F1(R), 2, It1, A1(R), SA1(R), 2(R), 2010 I1, W1, 2, SA1, 2, A1, 2, SA3, A3, 4, 6, W3, 2011 A1, SA2, A2, [J, F1, C(R), Arg, A, F2], 2012 I 3(R), A1, 2, Arg1, SA1(R), Arg2(R), SA2(R), A3, It, E, 2013 F1(R), 3(R), A1(R), SA1(R), Arg2(R), A3, F4, E, 2014 F1(R), 3(R), A1(R), 2(R), Arg1(R), SA1(R), Arg2, SA2, A 3(R), US(R), E 4(t&R), W(R), 2015 Sm, Arg, A 2(R), [Arg(R), Gg(R), Tg(R), F(R), SA(R), A(R)]

Meates, K F (Canterbury) 1952 A 1, 2

Meates, W A (Otago) 1949 SA 2, 3, 4, 1950 BI 1, 2, 3, 4

Meeuws, K J (Otago, Auckland) 1998 A 3, 1999 WS, F 1, SA 1, A 1, SA 2, A 2, [Tg, It (R), S (R), F 2(R), SA 3], 2000 Tg (R), S 2, A 1, SA 1, A 2, SA 2, 2001 Arg 2, 2002 It, Fj, E, F, W (R), 2003 W, F (R), SA 1(R), A 1(R), SA 2, [It(R), C, Tg, W(R), SA(R), A(R)], 2004 E1, 2, PI, A1, SA1, A2, SA2

Mehrtens, A P (Canterbury) 1995 C, [I, W, S, E, SA], A 1, 2, 1996 WS, S 1, 2, A 1, SA 1, A 2, SA 2, 5, 1997 Fj, SA 2(R), I, E 1, W, E 2, 1998 E 1, 2, SA 1, A 1(R), A 2, SA 2, A 3, 1999 F 1, SA 1, A 1, SA 2, A 2, [Tg, E, S, F 2, SA 3], 2000 S 1, 2, A 1, SA 1, A 2, SA 2, F 1, 2, It (R), 2001 Arg 1, A 1(R), SA 2, A 2, I, S, Arg 2, 2002 It, I 1, 2, Fj (R), A 1, SA 1, A 2, SA 2, E (R), F, W, 2004 E2(R), Arg, A2(R), SA2

Messam, L J (Waikato) 2008 S, 2009 F1, It2, 2010 SA1(R), 2(R), S, 2011 Fj, SA1(R), 2, 2012 I 3, A1, 2, Arg1(R), SA1, Arg2, SA2, A3, It, W, E, 2013 F1, 2, SA1, Arg2, SA2, A3, F4, E, I(R), 2014 E1, 2(R), A2, Arg1, SA2(R), A 3, US(R), E 4(R), S(R), W(R), 2015 Arg(R), SA, [Tg(R)]

Metcalfe, T C (Southland) 1931 A, 1932 A 1

Mexted, G G (Wellington) 1950 BI 4

Mexted, M G (Wellington) 1979 S, E, 1980 A 1, 2, 3, W, 1981 S 1, 2, SA 1, 2, 3, R, F 1, 2, 1982 A 1, 2, 3, 1983 BI 1, 2, 3, 4, A, S, E, 1984 F 1, 2, A 1, 2, 3, 1985 E 1, 2, A, Arg 1, 2

Mika, B M (Auckland) 2002 E (R), F, W (R)

Mika, D G (Auckland) 1999 WS, F 1, SA 1(R), A 1, 2, [It, SA 3(R)]

Mill, J J (Hawke's Bay, Wairarapa) 1924 W, 1925 E, F, 1930 BI 1

Milliken, H M (Canterbury) 1938 A 1, 2, 3

Milner, H P (Wanganui) 1970 SA 3

Milner-Skudder, N R (Manawatu) 2015 A 1, 2, [Arg, Nm, Tg, F, SA, A]

Mitchell, N A (Southland, Otago) 1935 S, I, W, 1936 E, A 2, 1937 SA 3, 1938 A 1, 2

Mitchell, T W (Canterbury) 1976 SA 4(R)

Mitchell, W J (Canterbury) 1910 A 2, 3

Mitchinson, F E (Wellington) 1907 A 1, 2, 3, 1908 AW 1, 2, 3, 1910 A 1, 2, 3, 1913 A 1(R), US

Moala, G (Auckland) 2015 Sm

Moffitt, J E (Wellington) 1921 SA 1, 2, 3
Moody, J P T (Canterbury) 2014 A1(R), Arg1(R), SA1(R), Arg2(t&R), SA2, US, S, W(R), 2015 [F(R), SA, A]
Moore, G J T (Otago) 1949 A 1
Moreton, R C (Canterbury) 1962 A 3, 4, 1964 A 1, 2, 3, 1965 SA 2, 3
Morgan, J E (North Auckland) 1974 A 3, I, 1976 SA 2, 3, 4
Morris, T J (Nelson Bays) 1972 A 1, 2, 3
Morrison, T C (South Canterbury) 1938 A 1, 2, 3
Morrison, T G (Otago) 1973 E 2(R)
Morrissey, P J (Canterbury) 1962 A 3, 4, 5
Mourie, G N K (Taranaki) 1977 BI 3, 4, F 1, 2, 1978 I, W, E, S, 1979 F 1, 2, A, S, E, 1980 W, 1981 S 1, 2, F 1, 2, 1982 A 1, 2, 3
Muliaina, J M (Auckland, Waikato) 2003 E (R), W, F, SA 1, A 1, SA 2, A 2, [It, C, Tg, W, SA, A, F], 2004 E1, 2, Arg, PI, A1, SA1, A2, SA2, It, W, F, 2005 Fj, BI1(R), 2, 3, SA1, A1, SA2, A2, W, E, 2006 I1, 2, A1, SA1, A2, 3, SA2, 3, E, F1(R), 2, W, 2007 C, SA1, A1, SA2, A2, [It, Pt, F], 2008 I1, E1, 2(t), SA1, 2, A1, 2, SA3, Sm, A3, I2, W, E3, 2009 F1, 2, It1, A1, SA1, 2, A2, SA3, A3, 4, W, It2(R), E, F3, 2010 W2, SA1, 2, A1, 2, SA3, A3, 4, E, S, I2, W3, 2011 Fj, SA1, A1, 2, [C, Arg]
Muller, B L (Taranaki) 1967 A, E, W, F, 1968 A 1, F 1, 1969 W 1, 1970 SA 1, 2, 4, 1971 BI 1, 2, 3, 4
Mumm, W J (Buller) 1949 A 1
Murdoch, K (Otago) 1970 SA 4, 1972 A 3, W
Murdoch, P H (Auckland) 1964 A 2, 3, 1965 SA 1, 2, 3
Murray, H V (Canterbury) 1913 A 1, US, 1914 A 2, 3
Murray, P C (Wanganui) 1908 AW 2
Myers, R G (Waikato) 1978 A 3
Mynott, H J (Taranaki) 1905 I, W, 1906 F, 1907 A 1, 2, 3, 1910 A 1, 3

Naholo, W R (Taranaki) 2015 Arg, [Gg, Tg]
Nathan, W J (Auckland) 1962 A 1, 2, 3, 4, 5, 1963 E 1, 2, W, 1964 F, 1966 BI 1, 2, 3, 4, 1967 A
Nelson, K A (Otago) 1962 A 4, 5
Nepia, G (Hawke's Bay, East Coast) 1924 I, W, 1925 E, F, 1929 A 1, 1930 BI 1, 2, 3, 4
Nesbit, S R (Auckland) 1960 SA 2, 3
Newby, C A (North Harbour) 2004 E2(t), SA2(R), 2006 I2(R)
Newton, F (Canterbury) 1905 E, W, 1906 F
Ngatai, C J (Taranaki) 2015 Sm(R)
Nicholls, H E (Wellington) 1921 SA 1
Nicholls, M F (Wellington) 1921 SA 1, 2, 3, 1924 I, W, 1925 E, F, 1928 SA 4, 1930 BI 2, 3
Nicholson, G W (Auckland) 1903 A, 1904 BI, 1907 A 2, 3
Nonu, M A (Wellington) 2003 E, [It(R), C, Tg(R)], 2004 It(R), W(R), F(R), 2005 BI2(R), W(R), I, S(R), 2006 I1, E, F1(R), 2, W(R), 2007 F1(R), 2(R), 2008 I1, E 2, SA1, 2, A1, 2, SA3, Sm, A3, 4(R), S, I2, W, E3, 2009 F1, 2, It1, A1, SA1, 2, A2(t&R), SA3, A3, 4, W, E, F3, 2010 SA1, 2, A1, 2, SA3, A3, 4, E, I2, W3(R), 2011 Fj, SA1, A1, 2, [Tg, J, F, Arg, A, F2], 2012 A1, 2, Arg1, SA1, Arg2, SA2, A3, It, W, E, 2013 F1, 2, 3, A1, 2, SA1, Arg2, SA2, A3, F4, E, I, 2014 E1, 2, 3, A1, Arg1, SA1, 2015 Arg, SA, A 2, [Arg, Nm(R), Tg, F, SA, A]
Norton, R W (Canterbury) 1971 BI 1, 2, 3, 4, 1972 A 1, 2, 3, W, S, 1973 E 1, I, F, E 2, 1974 A 1, 2, 3, I, 1975 S, 1976 I, SA 1, 2, 3, 4, 1977 BI 1, 2, 3, 4

O'Brien, J G (Auckland) 1914 A 1
O'Callaghan, M W (Manawatu) 1968 F 1, 2, 3
O'Callaghan, T R (Wellington) 1949 A 2
O'Donnell, D H (Wellington) 1949 A 2
O'Halloran, J D (Wellington) 2000 It (R)
Old, G H (Manawatu) 1981 SA 3, R (R), 1982 A 1(R)
O'Leary, M J (Auckland) 1910 A 1, 3, 1913 A 2, 3
Oliver, A D (Otago) 1997 Fj (t), 1998 E 1, 2, A 1, SA 1, A 2, SA 2, A 3, 1999 WS, F 1, SA 1, A 1, SA 2, A 2, [Tg, E, S, F 2, SA 3(R)], 2000 Tg, F(R), S 1, 2, A 1, SA 1, A 2, SA 2, F 1, 2, It, 2001 Sm, Arg 1, F, SA 1, A 1, SA 2, A 2, I, S, Arg 2, 2003 E, F, 2004 It, F, 2005 W, S, 2006 Arg, SA1, 2, 3(R), F1, W, 2007 F2, SA1, A1, 2, [It(R), Pt(R), S, F]
Oliver, C J (Canterbury) 1929 A 1, 2, 1934 A 1, 1935 S, I, W, 1936 E

Oliver, D J (Wellington) 1930 BI 1, 2
Oliver, D O (Otago) 1954 I, F
Oliver, F J (Southland, Otago, Manawatu) 1976 SA 4, 1977 BI 1, 2, 3, 4, F 1, 2, 1978 A 1, 2, 3, I, W, E, S, 1979 F 1, 2, 1981 SA 2
O'Neill, J A (Canterbury) 2008 SA2(R)
Orr, R W (Otago) 1949 A 1
Osborne, G M (North Harbour) 1995 C, [I, W, J, E, SA], A 1, 2, F I(R), 2, 1996 SA 2, 3, 4, 5, 1997 Arg 1(R), A 2, 3, I, 1999 [It]
Osborne, W M (Wanganui) 1975 S, 1976 SA 2(R), 4(R), 1977 BI 1, 2, 3, 4, F 1(R), 2, 1978 I, W, E, S, 1980 W, 1982 A 1, 3
O'Sullivan, J M (Taranaki) 1905 S, I, E, W, 1907 A 3
O'Sullivan, T P A (Taranaki) 1960 SA 1, 1961 F 1, 1962 A 1, 2

Page, J R (Wellington) 1931 A, 1932 A 1, 2, 3, 1934 A 1, 2
Palmer, B P (Auckland) 1929 A 2, 1932 A 2, 3
Parker, J H (Canterbury) 1924 I, W, 1925 E
Parkhill, A A (Otago) 1937 SA 1, 2, 3, 1938 A 1, 2, 3
Parkinson, R M (Poverty Bay) 1972 A 1, 2, 3, W, S, 1973 E 1, 2
Parsons, J W (North Harbour) 2014 S
Paterson, A M (Otago) 1908 AW 2, 3, 1910 A 1, 2, 3
Paton, H (Otago) 1910 A 1, 3
Pene, A R B (Otago) 1992 Wld 1(R), 2, 3, I 1, 2, A 1, 2(R), 1993 BI 3, A, WS, S, E, 1994 F 1, 2(R), SA 1(R)
Perenara, T T R (Wellington) 2014 E1(R), 2(R), 3(R), A2(R), Arg1(R), 2(R), US, E 4(R), S, W(R), 2015 Arg, SA(R), A 1(R), 2(R), [Arg(R), Nm]
Phillips, W J (King Country) 1937 SA 2, 1938 A 1, 2
Philpott, S (Canterbury) 1991 [It (R), S (R)]
Pickering, E A R (Waikato) 1958 A 2, 1959 BI 1, 4
Pierce, M J (Wellington) 1985 E 1, 2, A, Arg 1, 1986 A 2, 3, F 2, 3, 1987 [It, Arg, S, W, F], A, 1988 W 1, 2, A 1, 2, 3, 1989 F 1, 2, Arg 1, 2, A, W, I
Piutau, S T (Auckland) 2013 F3(R), A2(t&R), Arg1(R), SA1(R), Arg2(R), SA2(R), A3, J, F4, E, 2014 A 3(R), US, S, W, 2015 Sm, Arg, SA
Pokere, S T (Southland, Auckland) 1981 SA 3, 1982 A 1, 2, 3, 1983 BI 1, 2, 3, 4, A, S, E, 1984 F 1, 2, A 2, 3, 1985 E 1, 2, A
Pollock, H R (Wellington) 1932 A 1, 2, 3, 1936 A 1, 2
Porter, C G (Wellington) 1925 F, 1929 A 2, 3, 1930 BI 1, 2, 3, 4
Preston, J P (Canterbury, Wellington) 1991 [US, S], 1992 SA (R), 1993 BI 2, 3, A, WS, 1996 SA 4(R), 1997 I (R), E 1(R)
Procter, A C (Otago) 1932 A 1
Pulu, A W (Counties Manukau) 2014 US(R), S(R)
Purdue, C A (Southland) 1905 A
Purdue, E (Southland) 1905 A
Purdue, G B (Southland) 1931 A, 1932 A 1, 2, 3
Purvis, G H (Waikato) 1991 [US], 1993 WS
Purvis, N A (Otago) 1976 I

Quaid, C E (Otago) 1938 A 1, 2

Ralph, C S (Auckland, Canterbury) 1998 E 2, 2002 It, I 1, 2, A 1, SA 1, A 2, SA 2, 2003 E, A 1(R), [C, Tg, SA(R), F(t&R)]
Ranby, R M (Waikato) 2001 Sm (R)
Randell, T C (Otago) 1997 Fj, Arg 1, 2, A 1, SA 1, A 2, SA 2, A 3, I, E 1, W, E 2, 1998 E 1, 2, A 1, SA 1, A 2, SA 2, A 3, 1999 WS, F 1, SA 1, A 1, SA 2, A 2, [Tg, E, It, S, F 2, SA 3], 2000 Tg, S 1, 2(R), A 1, SA 1, A 2, SA 2, F 2(R), It (R), 2001 Arg 1, F, SA 1, A 1, SA 2, A 2, 2002 It, Fj, E, F, W
Ranger, R M N (Northland) 2010 W2(R), SA2, A3(R), 2013 F1(R), 2(R), 3
Rangi, R E (Auckland) 1964 A 2, 3, 1965 SA 1, 2, 3, 4, 1966 BI 1, 2, 3, 4
Rankin, J G (Canterbury) 1936 A 1, 2, 1937 SA 2
Rawlinson, G P (North Harbour) 2006 I1, 2(R), SA2, 2007 SA1
Read, K J (Canterbury) 2008 S, I2(R), E3(R), 2009 F1, 2, It1, A1(R), SA1(R), 2(R), A2, SA3, A3, 4(R), W, E, F3, 2010 I1, W1, 2, SA1, 2, A1, 2, SA3, A3, 4, E, S, I2, W3, 2011 A1, 2, [C, Arg, A, F2], 2012 I 1, 2, A1, 2, Arg1, SA1, Arg2, SA2, A3, It, W, E, 2013 F1, 2, 3, A1, 2, Arg1, SA1, Arg2, SA2, A3, F4, E, I, 2014 E3, A1, 2, Arg1, SA1, Arg2, SA2, A 3,

US, E 4, W, 2015 Sm, Arg, SA, A 1, 2, [Arg, Nm(R), Gg, Tg, F, SA, A]

Reedy, W J (Wellington) 1908 AW 2, 3

Reid, A R (Waikato) 1952 A 1, 1956 SA 3, 4, 1957 A 1, 2

Reid, H R (Bay of Plenty) 1980 A 1, 2, W, 1983 S, E, 1985 Arg 1, 2, 1986 A 2, 3

Reid, K H (Wairarapa) 1929 A 1, 3

Reid, S T (Hawke's Bay) 1935 S, I, W, 1936 E, A 1, 2, 1937 SA 1, 2, 3

Reihana, B T (Waikato) 2000 F 2, It

Reside, W B (Wairarapa) 1929 A 1

Retallick, B A (Bay of Plenty) 2012 I1, 2, 3(R), A1(R), 2(R), Arg1, SA1(R), Arg2(t&R), SA2, A3, It, W(R), E, 2013 F1, A1(R), 2, Arg1, SA1, Arg2, SA2, A3(R), F4, E, I, 2014 E1, 2, 3, A1, 2, Arg1, SA1, Arg2, A 3, US(R), E 4, W, 2015 Sm(t&R), Arg, SA, A 1, 2, [Arg, Gg, Tg(R), F, SA, A]

Rhind, P K (Canterbury) 1946 A 1, 2

Richardson, J (Otago, Southland) 1921 SA 1, 2, 3, 1924 I, W, 1925 E, F

Rickit, H (Waikato) 1981 S 1, 2

Riechelmann, C C (Auckland) 1997 Fj (R), Arg 1(R), A 1(R), SA 2(t), I (R), E 2(t)

Ridland, A J (Southland) 1910 A 1, 2, 3

Roberts, E J (Wellington) 1914 A 1, 2, 3, 1921 SA 2, 3

Roberts, F (Wellington) 1905 S, I, E, W, 1907 A 1, 2, 3, 1908 AW 1, 3, 1910 A 1, 2, 3

Roberts, R W (Taranaki) 1913 A 1, US, 1914 A 1, 2, 3

Robertson, B J (Counties) 1972 A 1, 3, S, 1973 E 1, I, F, 1974 A 1, 2, 3, I, 1976 I, SA 1, 2, 3, 4, 1977 BI 1, 3, 4, F 1, 2, 1978 A 1, 2, 3, W, E, S, 1979 F 1, 2, A, 1980 A 2, 3, W, 1981 S 1, 2

Robertson, D J (Otago) 1974 A 1, 2, 3, I, 1975 S, 1976 I, SA 1, 3, 4, 1977 BI 1

Robertson, S M (Canterbury) 1998 A 2(R), SA 2(R), A 3(R), 1999 [It (R)], 2000 Tg (R), S 1, 2(R), A 1, SA 1(R), 2(R), F 1, 2, It, 2001 I, S, Arg 2, 2002 I 1, 2, Fj (R), A 1, SA 1, A 2, SA 2

Robilliard, A C C (Canterbury) 1928 SA 1, 2, 3, 4

Robinson, C E (Southland) 1951 A 1, 2, 3, 1952 A 1, 2

Robinson, K J (Waikato) 2002 E, F (R), W, 2004 E1, 2, PI, 2006 E, W, 2007 SA2, A2, [R, F]

Robinson, M D (North Harbour) 1998 E 1(R), 2001 S (R), Arg 2

Robinson, M P (Canterbury) 2000 S 2, 2002 It, I 2, A 1, SA 1, E (t&R), F, W (R)

Rokocoko, J T (Auckland) 2003 E, W, F, SA 1, A 1, SA 2, A 2, [It, W, SA, A, F], 2004 E1, 2, Arg, PI, A1, SA1, A2, SA2, It, W, F, 2005 SA1(R), A1, SA2, A2, W, E(R), S, 2006 I1, 2, A1, 2, 3, SA3, E, F1, 2, 2007 F1, 2, SA1, A1, SA2, A2, [Pt, R, F], 2008 S, I2, W, E3, 2009 F1, 2, It1, SA1, 2, A2, SA3, A3, 2010 I1, W1, SA1, A1, 2, SA3, A4, E

Rollerson, D L (Manawatu) 1980 W, 1981 S 2, SA 1, 2, 3, R, F 1(R), 2

Romano, L (Canterbury) 2012 I 3, A1, 2, Arg1, SA1, Arg2, SA2(R), A3(R), S, W, E(R), 2013 F1, 2, 3, A1, E(R), 2014 S(R), 2015 Sm, Arg, A 1, [Nm, Tg]

Roper, R A (Taranaki) 1949 A 2, 1950 BI 1, 2, 3, 4

Ross, I B (Canterbury) 2009 F1, 2, It1, A1, SA1, 2, A2, SA3

Rowley, H C B (Wanganui) 1949 A 2

Rush, E J (North Harbour) 1995 [W (R), J], It, F 1, 2, 1996 S 1(R), 2, A 1(t), SA 1(R)

Rush, X J (Auckland) 1998 A 3, 2004 E1, 2, PI, A1, SA1, A2, SA2

Rutledge, L M (Southland) 1978 A 1, 2, 3, I, W, E, S, 1979 F 1, 2, A, 1980 A 1, 2, 3

Ryan, J (Wellington) 1910 A 2, 1914 A 1, 2, 3

Ryan, J A C (Otago) 2005 Fj, BI3(R), A1(R), SA2(R), A2(R), W, S, 2006 F1, W(R)

Sadler, B S (Wellington) 1935 S, I, W, 1936 A 1, 2

Saili, F (North Harbour) 2013 Arg1, J

Salmon, J L B (Wellington) 1981 R, F 1, 2(R)

Savage, L T (Canterbury) 1949 SA 1, 2, 4

Savea, S J (Wellington) 2012 I 2, Arg1, SA1, Arg2, S, It, W, E, 2013 F1, 2, A1, 2, Arg1, SA1, Arg2, SA2, A3, E, I, 2014 E2, 3, A1, 2, Arg1, SA1, Arg2, SA2, A 3, US(R), E 4, S(R), W, 2015 A 1, 2, [Arg, Nm, Gg, F, SA, A]

Saxton, C K (South Canterbury) 1938 A 1, 2, 3

Schuler, K J (Manawatu, North Harbour) 1990 A 2(R), 1992 A 2, 1995 [I (R), J]

Schuster, N J (Wellington) 1988 A 1, 2, 3, 1989 F 1, 2, Arg 1, 2, A, W, I

Schwalger, J E (Wellington) 2007 C, 2008 I1(R)

Scott, R W H (Auckland) 1946 A 1, 2, 1947 A 1, 2, 1949 SA 1, 2, 3, 4, 1950 BI 1, 2, 3, 4, 1953 W, 1954 I, E, S, F

Scown, A I (Taranaki) 1972 A 1, 2, 3, W (R), S

Scrimshaw, G (Canterbury) 1928 SA 1

Seear, G A (Otago) 1977 F 1, 2, 1978 A 1, 2, 3, I, W, E, S, 1979 F 1, 2, A

Seeling, C E (Auckland) 1904 BI, 1905 S, I, E, W, 1906 F, 1907 A 1, 2, 1908 AW 1, 2, 3

Sellars, G M V (Auckland) 1913 A 1, US

Senio, K (Bay of Plenty) 2005 A2(R)

Shaw, M W (Manawatu, Hawke's Bay) 1980 A 1, 2, 3(R), W, 1981 S 1, SA 1, 2, R, F 1, 2, 1982 A 1, 2, 3, 1983 BI 1, 2, 3, 4, A, S, E, 1984 F 1, 2, A 1, 1985 E 1, 2, A, Arg 1, 2, 1986 A 3

Shelford, F N K (Bay of Plenty) 1981 SA 3, R, 1984 A 2, 3

Shelford, W T (North Harbour) 1986 F 2, 3, 1987 [It, Fj, S, W, F], A, 1988 W 1, 2, A 1, 2, 3, 1989 F 1, 2, Arg 1, 2, A, W, I, 1990 S 1, 2

Siddells, S J (Wellington) 1921 SA 3

Simon, H J (Otago) 1937 SA 1, 2, 3

Simpson, J G (Auckland) 1947 A 1, 2, 1949 SA 1, 2, 3, 4, 1950 BI 1, 2, 3

Simpson, V L J (Canterbury) 1985 Arg 1, 2

Sims, G S (Otago) 1972 A 2

Sivivatu, S W (Waikato) 2005 Fj, BI1, 2, 3, I, E, 2006 SA2, 3, E(R), F1, 2, W, 2007 F1, 2, C, SA1, A1(R), [It, S, R, F], 2008 I1, E1, 2, SA1, A1, 2, SA3, A3, 4, I2, W, E3, 2009 A1, SA1, 2, A2, SA3, A4, It2, E, F3, 2011 Fj, A1

Skeen, J R (Auckland) 1952 A 2

Skinner, K L (Otago, Counties) 1949 SA 1, 2, 3, 4, 1950 BI 1, 2, 3, 4, 1951 A 1, 2, 3, 1952 A 1, 2, 1953 W, 1954 I, E, S, F, 1956 SA 3, 4

Skudder, G R (Waikato) 1969 W 2

Slade, C R (Canterbury) 2010 A3(R), 2011 Fj, SA1(R), A1(R), SA2, [Tg(R), J, F1(R), C, Arg], 2013 A2(R), 2014 Arg1(R), 2(R), SA2(R), A 3, S, W(R), 2015 Sm(R), Arg(R), A 2(R), [Nm]

Slater, G L (Taranaki) 2000 F 1(R), 2(R), It (R)

Sloane, P H (North Auckland) 1979 E

Smith, A E (Taranaki) 1969 W 1, 2, 1970 SA 1

Smith, A L (Manawatu) 2012 I 1, 2, 3, A1, 2, Arg1, SA1(R), Arg2, SA2, A3, It, W, E, 2013 F1, 2, A1, 2, Arg1, SA1, Arg2, SA2, A3, J(R), F4, E, I, 2014 E1, 2, 3, A1, 2, Arg1, SA1, Arg2, SA2, A 3, E 4, W, 2015 SA, A 1, 2, [Arg, Gg, Tg, F, SA, A]

Smith, B R (Otago) 2009 It 2, 2011 Fj(R), 2012 I 1(R), 2(R), 3, A2(R), Arg1(R), 2(R), A3(R), S, W(R), E(R), 2013 F1, 2, 3, A1, 2, Arg1, SA1, Arg2, SA2, A3, J, F4, E, I, 2014 E1, 2, 3, A1, 2, Arg1, SA1, Arg2, SA2, E 4, S, W, 2015 SA, A 1, 2, [Arg, Nm(R), Gg, Tg, F, SA, A]

Smith, B W (Auckland) 1984 F 1, 2, A 1

Smith, C G (Wellington) 2004 It, F, 2005 Fj(R), BI3, W, S, 2006 F1, W, 2007 SA2(R), [Pt, S, R(R)], 2008 I1, E1, SA1, 2, A1(R), 2, SA3, Sm, A3, 4, I2, E3, 2009 F2, A1, SA1, 2, A2, 4, W, E, F3, 2010 I1, W1, SA1, 2, A1, 2, SA3, A3, 4, S, I2, W3, 2011 Fj, SA1, A1, 2, [J, F1, C, Arg, A, F2], 2012 I 1, 2, 3, Arg1, SA1, Arg2, SA2, A3, It, W, E, 2013 F1, 2, 3, A1, 2, Arg1, SA1, Arg2, SA2, 2014 E1, 2, A2, Arg1, SA1, Arg2, SA2, A 3, E 4, W, 2015 SA, A 1, 2, [Arg, Gg, Tg, F, SA, A]

Smith, G W (Auckland) 1905 S, I

Smith, I S T (Otago, North Otago) 1964 A 1, 2, 3, 1965 SA 1, 2, 4, 1966 BI 1, 2, 3

Smith, J B (North Auckland) 1946 A 1, 1947 A 2, 1949 A 1, 2

Smith, R M (Canterbury) 1955 A 1

Smith, W E (Nelson) 1905 A

Smith, W R (Canterbury) 1980 A 1, 1982 A 1, 2, 3, 1983 BI 2, 3, S, E, 1984 F 1, 2, A 1, 2, 3, 1985 E 1, 2, A, Arg 2

Snow, E M (Nelson) 1929 A 1, 2, 3

Solomon, F (Auckland) 1931 A, 1932 A 2, 3

Somerville, G M (Canterbury) 2000 Tg, S 1, SA 2(R), F 1, 2, It, 2001 Sm, Arg 1(R), F, SA 1, A 1, SA 2, A 2, I, S, Arg 2(t&R), 2002 I 1, 2, A 1, SA 1, A 2, SA 2, 2003 E, F, SA 1, A 1,

SA 2(R), A 2, [It, Tg, W, SA, A, F], 2004 Arg, SA1, A2(R), SA2(R), It(R), W, F(R), 2005 Fj, Bl1(R)2, 3, SA1(R), A1(R), SA2(R), A2(R), 2006 Arg, A1(R), SA1(R), A2(R), 3(R), SA2, 2007 [Pt, R], 2008 E1, 2, SA1, A1, 2, SA3, Sm, A3, 4(R)

Sonntag, W T C (Otago) 1929 A 1, 2, 3

So'oialo, R (Wellington) 2002 W, 2003 E, SA 1(R), [It(R), C, Tg, W(t)], 2004 W, F, 2005 Fj, Bl1, 2, 3, SA1, A1, SA2, A2, W, I(R), E, 2006 I1, 2, A1, SA1, A2, 3, SA3, E(R), F1, 2, W, 2007 F1(R), 2, SA1, A1, SA2, A2, [It, Pt(R), S, F], 2008 I1, E1, 2, SA1, 2, A1, SA2, SA3, Sm, A3, 4, I2, W, E3, 2009 A1, SA1, 2, A2(R), 3(R), 4, It2

Sopoaga, L Z (Wellington) 2015 SA

Speight, M W (Waikato) 1986 A 1

Spencer, C J (Auckland) 1997 Arg 1, 2, A 1, SA 1, A 2, SA 2, A 3, E 2(R), 1998 E 2(R), A 1(R), SA 1, A 3(R), 2000 F 1(t&R), It, 2002 E, 2003 E, W, F, SA 1, A 1, SA 2, A 2, [It, C, Tg, W, SA, A, F], 2004 E1, 2, PI, A1, SA1, A2

Spencer, J C (Wellington) 1905 A, 1907 A 1(R)

Spiers, J E (Counties) 1979 S, E, 1981 R, F, 1, 2

Spillane, A P (South Canterbury) 1913 A 2, 3

Stanley, B J (Auckland) 2010 I1, W1, 2

Stanley, J T (Auckland) 1986 F 1, A 1, 2, 3, F 2, 3, 1987 [It, Fj, Arg, S, W, F], A, 1988 W 1, 2, A 1, 2, 3, 1989 F 1, 2, Arg 1, 2, A, W, I, 1990 S 1, 2

Stead, J W (Southland) 1904 Bl, 1905 S, I, E, 1906 F, 1908 AW 1, 3

Steel, A G (Canterbury) 1966 Bl 1, 2, 3, 4, 1967 A, F, S, 1968 A 1, 2

Steel, J (West Coast) 1921 SA 1, 2, 3, 1924 W, 1925 E, F

Steele, L B (Wellington) 1951 A 1, 2, 3

Steere, E R G (Hawke's Bay) 1930 Bl 1, 2, 3, 4, 1931 A, 1932 A 1

Steinmetz, P C (Wellington) 2002 W (R)

Stensness, L (Auckland) 1993 Bl 3, A, WS, 1997 Fj, Arg 1, 2, A 1, SA 1

Stephens, O G (Wellington) 1968 F 3

Stevens, I N (Wellington) 1972 S, 1973 E 1, 1974 A 3

Stewart, A J (Canterbury, South Canterbury) 1963 E 1, 2, I, W, 1964 E, S, F, A 3

Stewart, J D (Auckland) 1913 A 2, 3

Stewart, K W (Southland) 1973 E 2, 1974 A 1, 2, 3, I, 1975 S, 1976 I, SA 1, 3, 1979 S, E, 1981 SA 1, 2

Stewart, R T (South Canterbury, Canterbury) 1928 SA 1, 2, 3, 4, 1930 Bl 2

Stohr, L B (Taranaki) 1910 A 1, 2, 3

Stone, A M (Waikato, Bay of Plenty) 1981 F 1, 2, 1983 Bl 3(R), 1984 A 3, 1986 F 1, A 1, 3, F 2, 3

Storey, P W (South Canterbury) 1921 SA 1, 2

Strachan, A D (Auckland, North Harbour) 1992 Wld 2, 3, I 1, 2, A 1, 2, 3, SA, 1993 Bl 1, 1995 [J, SA (t)]

Strahan, S C (Manawatu) 1967 A, E, W, F, S, 1968 A 1, 2, F 1, 2, 3, 1970 SA 1, 2, 3, 1972 A 1, 2, 3, 1973 E 2

Strang, W A (South Canterbury) 1928 SA 1, 2, 1930 Bl 3, 4, 1931 A 1

Stringfellow, J C (Wairarapa) 1929 A 1(R), 3

Stuart, K C (Canterbury) 1955 A 1

Stuart, R C (Canterbury) 1949 A 1, 2, 1953 W, 1954 I, E, S, F

Stuart, R L (Hawke's Bay) 1977 F 1(R)

Sullivan, J L (Taranaki) 1937 SA 1, 2, 3, 1938 A 1, 2, 3

Sutherland, A R (Marlborough) 1970 SA 2, 4, 1971 Bl 1, 1972 A 1, 2, 3, W, 1973 E 1, I, F

Svenson, K S (Wellington) 1924 I, W, 1925 E, F

Swain, J P (Hawke's Bay) 1928 SA 1, 2, 3, 4

Tanner, J M (Auckland) 1950 Bl 4, 1951 A 1, 2, 3, 1953 W

Tanner, K J (Canterbury) 1974 A 1, 2, 3, I, 1975 S, 1976 I, SA 1

Taumoepeau, S (Auckland) 2004 It, 2005 I(R), S

Taylor, C J D (Canterbury) 2015 Arg(R), SA(R), A 1(R), [Nm]

Taylor, G L (Northland) 1996 SA 5(R)

Taylor, H M (Canterbury) 1913 A 1, US, 1914 A 1, 2, 3

Taylor, J M (Otago) 1937 SA 1, 2, 3, 1938 A 1, 2, 3

Taylor, M B (Waikato) 1979 F 1, 2, A, S, E, 1980 A 1, 2

Taylor, N M (Bay of Plenty, Hawke's Bay) 1977 Bl 2, 4(R), F 1, 2, 1978 A 1, 2, 3, I, 1982 A 2

Taylor, R (Taranaki) 1913 A 2, 3

Taylor, T J (Canterbury) 2013 A2, 3(R), J(R)

Taylor, W T (Canterbury) 1983 Bl 1, 2, 3, 4, A, S, 1984 F 1, 2, A 1, 2, 1985 E 1, 2, A, Arg 1, 2, 1986 A 2, 1987 [It, Fj, S, W, F], A, 1988 W 1, 2

Tetzlaff, P L (Auckland) 1947 A 1, 2

Thimbleby, N W (Hawke's Bay) 1970 SA 3

Thomas, B T (Auckland, Wellington) 1962 A 5, 1964 A 1, 2, 3

Thomson, A J (Otago) 2008 I1(t&R), E2, SA1, 2, A2(R), SA3(R), Sm, A4(t&R), S, 2009 F1, SA3(R), A3, 4, W(R), E, 2010 W1(R), 2(R), 2011 Fj, SA1, A1(R), SA2, A2, [J, F1], 2012 I1(R), 2, 3(R), SA2(R), S

Thomson, H D (Wellington) 1908 AW 1

Thorn, B C (Canterbury, Tasman) 2003 W (R), F (R), SA 1(R), A 1(R), SA 2, [It, C, Tg, W, SA(R), A(R), F(R)], 2008 I1, E1, 2, SA1, A1, 2, SA3, A3, 4, W, E, F3, 2010 I1, W1, 2, SA1, 2, A1, 2, SA3, A3, 4, E, S, W3, 2011 A1, 2, [Tg, J, F1, C(R), Arg, A, F2]

Thorne, G S (Auckland) 1968 A 1, 2, F 1, 2, 3, 1969 W 1, 1970 SA 1, 2, 3, 4

Thorne, R D (Canterbury) 1999 SA 2(R), [Tg, E, S, F 2, SA 3], 2000 Tg, S 2, A 2(R), F 1, 2, 2001 Sm, Arg 1, F, SA 1, A 1, I, S, Arg 2, 2002 It, I 1, 2, Fj, A 1, SA 1, A2, SA 2, 2003 E, W, F, SA 1, A 1, SA 2, A 2, [It, C, Tg, W, SA, A, F], 2006 SA1, 2, E, W(R), 2007 F1, 2, SA2, [S, R]

Thornton, N H (Auckland) 1947 A 1, 2, 1949 SA 1

Thrush, J I (Wellington) 2013 F2(R), Arg1(R), 2(R), A3, J, 2014 Arg1(R), SA1, Arg2(R), SA2, US, S, 2015 Arg(R)

Tialata, N S (Wellington) 2005 W, E(t), S(R), 2006 I1(R), 2(R), Arg(R), SA1, 2, 3(R), F1(R), 2(R), W, 2007 F1(R), 2(R), C, A1(R), SA2(R), [It(t&R), Pt, S(R), R], 2008 I1, E1, 2, SA1(R), 2(R), Sm(R), A4, S(R), I2, W, E3, 2009 F1, 2, A1, SA1, A3, 4, W, It2, F3, 2010 I1(R), W2

Tiatia, F I (Wellington) 2000 Tg (R), It

Tilyard, J T (Wellington) 1913 A 3

Timu, J K R (Otago) 1991 Arg 1, A 1, 2, [E, US, C, A], 1992 Wld 2, I 2, A 1, 2, 3, SA, 1993 Bl 1, 2, 3, A, WS, S, E, 1994 F 1, 2, SA 1, 2, 3, A

Tindill, E W T (Wellington) 1936 E

Todd, M B (Canterbury) 2013 F3(R), SA1(t), 2015 Sm(R)

Toeava, I (Auckland) 2005 S, 2006 Arg, A1(t&R), A3, SA2(R), 2007 F1, 2, SA1, 2, A2, [It(R), Pt, S(R), R, F(R)], 2008 SA3(R), Sm(R), A4, S, I2(R), E3(R), 2009 F1, 2(R), It1, SA3(R), A3, 2010 A4(R), E(R), S, W3, 2011 SA2, A2(R), [Tg, J, C(R), Arg(R)]

Tonu'u, O F J (Auckland) 1997 Fj (R), A 3(R), 1998 F 1, 2, SA 1(R)

To'omaga-Allen, J L (Wellington) 2013 J(R)

Townsend, L J (Otago) 1955 A 1, 3

Tremain, K R (Canterbury, Hawke's Bay) 1959 Bl 2, 3, 4, 1960 SA 1, 2, 3, 4, 1961 F 2, 3, 1962 A 1, 2, 3, 1963 E 1, 2, I, W, 1964 E, S, F, A 1, 2, 3, 1965 SA 1, 2, 3, 4, 1966 Bl 1, 2, 3, 4, 1967 A, E, W, S, 1968 A 1, F 1, 2, 3

Trevathan, D (Otago) 1937 SA 1, 2, 3

Tuck, J M (Waikato) 1929 A 1, 2, 3

Tuiali'i, M M (Auckland) 2004 Arg, A2(R), SA2(R), It, W, 2005 I, E(R), S(R), 2006 Arg

Tuigamala, V L (Auckland) 1991 [US, It, C, S], 1992 Wld 1, 2, 3, I 1, A 1, 2, 3, SA, 1993 Bl 1, 2, 3, A, WS, S, E

Tuipulotu, P T (Auckland) 2014 E2(R), 3(R), SA1(R), A 3(R), US, E 4(R), W(R)

Tuitavake, A S M (North Harbour) 2008 I1, E1, A1, 2(R), Sm, S

Tuitupou, S (Auckland) 2004 E1(R), 2(R), Arg, SA1(R), A2(R), SA2, 2006 Arg, SA1, 2(R)

Turner, R S (North Harbour) 1992 Wld 1, 2(R)

Turtill, H S (Canterbury) 1905 A

Twigden, T M (Auckland) 1980 A 2, 3

Tyler, G A (Auckland) 1903 A, 1904 Bl, 1905 S, I, E, W, 1906 F

Udy, D K (Wairarapa) 1903 A

Umaga, J F (Wellington) 1997 Fj, Arg 1, 2, A 1, SA 1, 2, 1999 WS, F 1, SA 1, A 1, SA 2, A 2, [Tg, E, S, F 2, SA 3], 2000 Tg, S 1, 2, A 1, SA 1, A 2, SA 2, 1, 2, It, 2001 Sm, Arg 1, F, SA 1, A 1, SA 2, A 2, I, S, Arg 2, 2002 I 1, Fj, SA 1(R), A 2, SA 2, E, F, W, 2003 E, W, F, SA 1, A 1, SA 2, A 2, [It], 2004 E1, 2, Arg, PI, A1, SA1, A2, SA2, It, F, 2005 Fj, Bl1, 2, 3, SA1, A1, SA2, A2, W, E, S

Urbahn, R J (Taranaki) 1959 Bl 1, 3, 4

Urlich, R A (Auckland) 1970 SA 3, 4
Uttley, I N (Wellington) 1963 E 1, 2

Vidiri, J (Counties Manukau) 1998 E 2(R), A 1
Vincent, P B (Canterbury) 1956 SA 1, 2
Vito, V V J (Wellington) 2010 I1(R), W1, A1(R), 2(R), SA3(R), A3, 2011 SA2(R), A2(R), [Tg, J, C, Arg(R), A(R)], 2012 I 1, A2(R), Arg1, A3(R), S, W(R), E(R), 2013 F2(R), 3, 2014 E1(R), 2(R), US, S, 2015 SA(R), A 2, [Arg(R), Nm, Gg(t&R), F(R), A(R)]
Vodanovich, I M H (Wellington) 1955 A 1, 2, 3

Wallace, W J (Wellington) 1903 A, 1904 BI, 1905 S, I, E, W, 1906 F, 1907 A 1, 2, 3, 1908 AW 2
Waller, D A G (Wellington) 2001 Arg 2(t)
Walsh, P T (Counties) 1955 A 1, 2, 3, 1956 SA 1, 2, 4, 1957 A 1, 2, 1958 A 1, 2, 3, 1959 BI 1, 1963 E 2
Ward, R H (Southland) 1936 A 2, 1937 SA 1, 3
Waterman, A C (North Auckland) 1929 A 1, 2
Watkins, E L (Wellington) 1905 A
Watt, B A (Canterbury) 1962 A 1, 4, 1963 E 1, 2, W, 1964 E, S, A 1
Watt, J M (Otago) 1936 A 1, 2
Watt, J R (Wellington) 1958 A 2, 1960 SA 1, 2, 3, 4, 1961 F 1, 3, 1962 A 1, 2
Watts, M G (Taranaki) 1979 F 1, 2, 1980 A 1, 2, 3(R)
Webb, D S (North Auckland) 1959 BI 2
Weber, B M (Waikato) 2015 Sm(R)
Weepu, P A T (Wellington, Auckland) 2004 W, 2005 SA1(R), A1, SA2, A2, I, E(R), S, 2006 Arg, A1(R), SA1, A3(R), SA2, F1, W(R), 2007 F1, C(R), SA1(R), A1(R), SA2, 2008 A2(R), SA3(R), Sm(R), A3(R), 4(R), S, I2(R), W(R), E3(R), 2009 F1(R), 2(R), It1(R), A1(R), SA1(R), 2(R), 2010 I1(R), W1(R), 2(R), SA1(R), 2, A1(R), 2, SA3(R), A3, 2011 Fj(R), SA1(R), A1, SA2(R), A2, [Tg(R), J(R)], F1, C(R), Arg, A, F2], 2012 I 1(R), 2(R), 3(R), A1(R), 2(R), Arg1(R), SA1, Arg2(R), SA2(R), A3(R), S, W(R), E(R), 2013 F2(R), 3
Wells, J (Wellington) 1936 A 1, 2
West, A H (Taranaki) 1921 SA 2, 3
Whetton, A J (Auckland) 1984 A 1(R), 3(R), 1985 A (R), Arg 1(R), 1986 A 2, 1987 [It, Fj, Arg, S, W, F], A 1988 W 1, 2, A 1, 2, 3, 1989 F 1, 2, Arg 1, 2, A, 1990 S 1, 2, A 1, 2, 3, F 1, 2, 1991 Arg 1, [E, US, It, C, A]
Whetton, G W (Auckland) 1981 SA 3, R, F 1, 2, 1982 A 3, 1983 BI 1, 2, 3, 4, 1984 F 1, 2, A 1, 2, 3, 1985 E 1, 2, A, Arg 2, 1986 A 2, 3, F 2, 3, 1987 [It, Fj, Arg, S, W, F], A 1988 W 1, 2, A 1, 2, 3, 1989 F 1, 2, Arg 1, 2, A, W, I, 1990 S 1, 2, A 1, 2, 3, F 1, 2, 1991 Arg 1, 2, A 1, 2, [E, US, It, C, A, S]
Whineray, W J (Canterbury, Waikato, Auckland) 1957 A 1, 2, 1958 A 1, 2, 3, 1959 BI 1, 2, 3, 4, 1960 SA 1, 2, 3, 4, 1961 F 1, 2, 3, 1962 A 1, 2, 3, 4, 5, 1963 E 1, 2, I, W, 1964 E, S, F, 1965 SA 1, 2, 3, 4
White, A (Southland) 1921 SA 1, 1924 I, 1925 E, F
White, H L (Auckland) 1954 I, E, F, 1955 A 3
White, R A (Poverty Bay) 1949 A 1, 2, 1950 BI 1, 2, 3, 4, 1951 A 1, 2, 3, 1952 A 1, 2, 1953 W, 1954 I, E, S, F, 1955 A 1, 2, 3, 1956 SA 1, 2, 3, 4
White, R M (Wellington) 1946 A 1, 2, 1947 A 1, 2
Whitelock, G B (Canterbury) 2009 It1(R)
Whitelock, L C (Canterbury) 2013 J(R)
Whitelock, S L (Canterbury) 2010 I1(R), W1(R), 2(R), SA1(R), 2(R), A1(R), 2(R), SA3(R), A4(R), E, S, I2(R), W3, 2011 Fj(R), SA1, A1(R), SA2, A2, [Tg(R), J, F1, C, Arg, A, F2], 2012 I 1, 2, 3, A1, 2, Arg1(R), SA1, Arg2, SA2, A3, S, It(R), W, E, 2013 F2, 3, A1, 2, Arg1, SA1, Arg2, SA2, A3, F4, E, I, 2014 E1, 2, 3, A1, 2, Arg1, 2, SA2, A 3, E 4,W, 2015 Sm, SA(R), A 1(R), 2, [Arg, Nm, Gg, Tg, F, SA, A]
Whiting, G J (King Country) 1972 A 1, 2, S, 1973 E 1, I, F
Whiting, P J (Auckland) 1971 BI 1, 2, 4, 1972 A 1, 2, 3, W, S, 1973 E 1, I, F, 1974 A 1, 2, 3, I, 1976 I, SA 1, 2, 3, 4

Williams, A J (Auckland, Tasman) 2002 E, F, W, 2003 E, W, F, SA 1, A 1, SA 2, A 2, [Tg, W, SA, A, F], 2004 SA1(R), A2, It(R), W, F(R), 2005 Fj, BI1, 2, 3, SA1, A1, SA2, A2, I, E, 2006 Arg, A1(R), SA1, A2, 3(R), SA2, 3, F1, 2, W, 2007 F1, 2, [It, Pt, S, F], 2008 I1, E1, 2, SA1, 2, A1, 2, SA3, Sm, A3, 4, S, I2, W, E3, 2011 Fj, SA1, A1, SA2, A2(R), [Tg, J(R), F1(R), C, Arg(R), A(R), F2(R)], 2012 I 1(R), 2(R), S(R), It
Williams, B G (Auckland) 1970 SA 1, 2, 3, 4, 1971 BI 1, 2, 4, 1972 A 1, 2, 3, W, S, 1973 E 1, I, F, E 2, 1974 A 1, 2, 3, I, 1975 S, 1976 I, SA 1, 2, 3, 4, 1977 BI 1, 2, 3, 4, F 1, 1978 A 1, 2, 3, I (R), W, E, S
Williams, G C (Wellington) 1967 E, W, F, S, 1968 A 2
Williams, P (Otago) 1913 A 1
Williams, S (Canterbury, Counties Manukau) 2010 E, S, I2(R), W3, 2011 SA1(R), A1(R), SA2, [Tg, J(R), F1(R), C, Arg, A(R), F2(R)], 2012 I 1, 2, 3, A1, 2, 2014 US, E 4, S(R), W, 2015 Sm, Arg, A 1, [Arg(R), Nm, Gg, Tg(R), F(R), SA(R), A(R)]
Williment, M (Wellington) 1964 A 1, 1965 SA 1, 2, 3, 1966 BI 1, 2, 3, 4, 1967 A
Willis, R K (Waikato) 1998 SA 2, A 3, 1999 SA 1(R), A 1(R), SA 2(R), A 2(R), [Tg (R), E (R), It, F 2(R), SA 3], 2002 SA 1(R)
Willis, T E (Otago) 2002 It, Fj, SA 2(R), A 2, SA 2
Willocks, C (Otago) 1946 A 1, 2, 1949 SA 1, 3, 4
Wilson, B W (Otago) 1977 BI 3, 4, 1978 A 1, 2, 3, 1979 F 1, 2, A
Wilson, D D (Canterbury) 1954 E, S
Wilson, H W (Otago) 1949 A 1, 1950 BI 4, 1951 A 1, 2, 3
Wilson, J W (Otago) 1993 S, E, 1994 A, 1995 C, [I, J, S, E, SA], A 1, 2, It, F 1, 1996 WS, S 1, 2, A 1, SA 1, A 2, SA 2, 3, 4, 5, 1997 Fj, Arg 1, 2, A 1, SA 1, A 2, SA 2, A 3, I, E 1, W, E 2, 1998 E 1, 2, A 1, SA 1, A 2, SA 2, A 3, 1999 WS, F 1, SA 1, A 1, SA 2, A 2, [Tg, E, It, S, F 2, SA 3], 2001 Sm, Arg 1, F, SA 1, A 1, SA 2
Wilson, N A (Wellington) 1908 AW 1, 2, 1910 A 1, 2, 3, 1913 A 2, 3, 1914 A 1, 2, 3
Wilson, N L (Otago) 1951 A 1, 2, 3
Wilson, R G (Canterbury) 1979 S, E
Wilson, S S (Wellington) 1977 F 1, 2, 1978 A 1, 2, 3, I, W, E, S, 1979 F 1, 2, A, S, E, 1980 A 1, W, 1981 S 1, 2, SA 1, 2, 3, R, F 1, 2, 1982 A 1, 2, 3, 1983 BI 1, 2, 3, 4, A, S, E
Witcombe, D J C (Auckland) 2005 Fj, BI1(R), 2(R), SA1(R), A1(R)
Wolfe, T N (Wellington, Taranaki) 1961 F 1, 2, 3, 1962 A 2, 3, 1963 E 1
Wood, M E (Canterbury, Auckland) 1903 A, 1904 BI
Woodcock, T D (North Harbour) 2002 W, 2004 E1(t&R), 2(t&R), Arg, W, F, 2005 Fj, BI1, 2, 3, SA1, A1, SA2, A2, W(R), I, E, 2006 Arg, A1, 2, 3, SA2(R), 3, E, F1, 2, W(R), 2007 F1, 2, SA1, A1, SA2, A2, [It, Pt(R), S, F], 2008 E2(R), SA1, 2, A1, 2, SA3, Sm, A3, 4, I2, W, E3, 2009 F1, 2, It1(R), A1, SA1, 2, A2, SA3, A3, 4, E, F3, 2010 W1(R), 2, SA1, 2, A1, 2, SA3, A3, 4, E, S, I2, W3, 2011 SA2, A2, [Tg, J, F1, C, Arg, A, F2], 2012 I 1, 2, 3, A1, Arg1, SA1, Arg2, SA2, A3, S(R), It, W, E, 2013 F2(R), 3(R), A1, 2, Arg1, SA1, Arg2, SA2, A3, F4, E, 2014 E1, 2, 3, 2015 Sm, Arg, SA, A 1, 2, [Arg, Gg(R), Tg]
Woodman, F A (North Auckland) 1981 SA 1, 2, F 2
Wrigley, E (Wairarapa) 1905 A
Wright, T J (Auckland) 1986 F 1, A 1, 1987 [Arg], 1988 W 1, 2, A 1, 2, 3, 1989 F 1, 2, Arg 1, 2, A, W, I, 1990 S 1, 2, A 1, 2, 3, F 1, 2, 1991 Arg 1, 2, A 1, 2, [E, US, It, S]
Wulf, R N (North Harbour) 2008 E2, SA1, 2, Sm(R)
Wylie, J T (Auckland) 1913 A 1, US
Wyllie, A J (Canterbury) 1970 SA 2, 3, 1971 BI 2, 3, 4, 1972 W, S, 1973 E 1, I, F, E 2

Yates, V M (North Auckland) 1961 F 1, 2, 3
Young, D (Canterbury) 1956 SA 2, 1958 A 1, 2, 3, 1960 SA 1, 2, 3, 4, 1961 F 1, 2, 3, 1962 A 1, 2, 3, 5, 1963 E 1, 2, I, W, 1964 E, S, F

World Rugby Breakthrough Player of the Year 2015 Nehe Milner-Skudder had a fantastic RWC 2015, scoring six tries to help his team retain the Webb Ellis Cup.

ROMANIA

ROMANIA'S 2014–15 TEST RECORD

OPPONENTS	DATE	VENUE	RESULT
USA	8 Nov	H	Lost 17–27
Japan	15 Nov	H	Lost 13–18
Canada	22 Nov	H	Won 18–9
Portugal	7 Feb	A	Won 37–10
Spain	14 Feb	H	Won 29–8
Russia	28 Feb	A	Lost 16–13
Germany	14 Mar	A	Won 17–12
Georgia	21 Mar	H	Lost 6–15
Spain	12 Jun	H	Won 35–9
Namibia	17 Jun	H	Won 43–9
Tonga	5 Sep	H	Lost 16–21
France	23 Sep	N	Lost 38–11
Ireland	27 Sep	N	Lost 44–10
Canada	6 Oct	N	Won 17–15
Italy	11 Oct	N	Lost 32–22

HOWELLS' REGIME REAPS REWARDS

By Chris Thau

The Oaks celebrate their remarkable 17–15 victory against Canada, the biggest comeback in Rugby World Cup history.

Romania came tantalisingly close to fulfilling their pre-Rugby World Cup objective of winning two matches for the first time. The first win had seemed unlikely when the Oaks trailed Canada 15–0 at half-time in Leicester, but they mounted the biggest comeback in RWC history to triumph 17–15 in the dying minutes.

Two tries from inspirational captain Mihai Macovei and the nerveless boot of Florin Vlaicu sparked the celebrations and set up what coach Lynn Howells referred to as "Romania's Rugby World Cup final" against Italy five days later at Sandy Park in Exeter.

However, the suspension of Macovei for that match and the comparatively short recovery time had blunted Romania's attacking edge and, to an extent, their confidence. Add to this Italy's superior pedigree and big match experience and the magnitude of the task that lay ahead for Romania was clear.

Unfortunately for the Oaks the script went according to most predictions with the Italians storming Romanian territory from the outset in an attempt to pre-empt the expected forward onslaught, which looked imminent after the first scrum when the Azzurri pack were unceremoniously shunted backwards.

After that, Italy regrouped and laid siege to the Romanian 22, scoring two spectacular tries, the second during the sin-binning of Romania's influential second-row Johannes van Heerden. When he returned, the Romanian pack moved back into top gear and severely tested their opponent's defence, which held firm before a third try made it 22–3 in Italy's favour at half-time.

That advantage grew to 29–3 after Alessandro Zanni's try within six minutes of the restart, but this only spurred the Romanians on and their fight-back was rewarded when replacement Adrian Apostol dotted down with 15 minutes to go. Second-row Valentin Poparlan, who started all four matches at RWC 2015, and Apostol touched down in the final six minutes to give the score a more respectful look to it at 32–22.

That meant Italy, and not Romania, finished third in Pool D to claim the automatic qualification spot for RWC 2019 in Japan, leaving the Oaks to return to the drawing board and the challenge of qualifying through the Rugby Europe competition. The news, on the eve of the Canada match, that Howells' contract had been extended until 2017 bodes well for the future with the coach admitting he was "pleased to take Romania to the next level, which will be exciting".

Romania's final build-up to RWC 2015 started with the World Rugby Nations Cup in Bucharest in June, a good opportunity for Howells to see his players in action. Romania won the title with comparative ease, beating Spain (35–9), Namibia (43–3) and the Argentina Jaguars (23–0), improving with every match they played.

The most pleasing aspect of the campaign for Howells, and for defence coach Neil Kelly in particular, was the fact that the Oaks did not concede a try in the tournament, with the front row of Mihaita Lazar, Otar Turashvili and Paulica Ion showing glimpses of the form that made them regulars at RWC 2015.

The return to action and form of Vlaicu, Romania's top points scorer, was another significant piece in Howells' jigsaw and he confirmed his worth at RWC 2015 when his last gasp penalty secured Romania the unexpected win over Canada.

After a break the squad reconvened for a 10-day camp at Caile Gradistei in the mountains, the first of several camps where the French fitness coach Olivier Rieg was given free rein to get the team in top physical form. The Romanian surges in the final quarters against both Canada and Italy validate the success of the Frenchman's approach.

A short two-match tour to the north of England and Scotland in

August, followed by a 21–16 loss to Tonga in Bucharest, helped Howells and his coaching team of Marius Tincu (forwards), Eugen Apjoc (backs) and Kelly fine-tune preparations. Romania continued their improved form against Tonga, but paid the price for failing to convert pressure into points.

In their first RWC 2015 match against France, the 50th encounter with Romania's oldest opponent, Howells' secret hope of an upset failed to materialise, although the Oaks played their hearts out at The Stadium, Queen Elizabeth Olympic Park. For periods it looked as if the Oaks could disrupt their former mentors, such was the fierce intensity of their forwards at the breakdown. But although Romania controlled possession and won eight turnovers in the first half, they again failed to put the points on the board.

Romania came close when Vlaicu had a try ruled out by the TMO, but Ion's yellow card proved costly as in his absence France scored two quick tries. Three further tries in the second half wrapped up the win but flanker Valentin Ursache's try was reward for the forwards' efforts and confirmed, according to Tincu, that "we can hold our own and compete against big nations."

Their next match, against Ireland before a RWC record crowd of 89,267 at Wembley Stadium, severely tested the strength in depth of Romania as they tried to rest key players for their targeted matches against Canada and Italy. The forwards again showed their class, but the shortcomings of their backs were exposed by a rampant Irish backline with Romania's only answer in the 44–10 defeat a try by veteran Ovidiu Tonita.

These losses, though, did confirm that Howells' regime of hard work, respect and discipline, seasoned with a fine understanding of Romania's rugby culture and traditions, was working. This belief may have made the difference between winning and losing against Canada, when Romania's warrior spirit kept them going until they snatched an unlikely win at the death. Their fitness levels, which kept them going at a time when Canada seemed to wilt, must have played a part, but ultimately it was their hearts and minds that took them to Howells' "promised land".

All four RWC 2015 matches, particularly those against Canada and Italy, provided clear evidence that the work of Howells and his team is yielding results. Add to this the talent and the multicultural ethos and expertise injected by the three foreign players – Michael Wiringi, Van Heerden and Paula Kinikinilau – and the progress of the Romanian team is easier to comprehend. This is not the end of Romania's journey and they are definitely back on the path to respectability.

ROMANIA INTERNATIONAL STATISTICS

MATCH RECORDS UP TO 1 NOVEMBER, 2015

WINNING MARGIN

Date	Opponent	Result	Winning Margin
21/09/1976	Bulgaria	100–0	100
19/03/2005	Ukraine	97–0	97
13/04/1996	Portugal	92–0	92
17/11/1976	Morocco	89–0	89
19/04/1996	Belgium	83–5	78

MOST POINTS IN A MATCH
BY THE TEAM

Date	Opponent	Result	Points
21/09/1976	Bulgaria	100–0	100
19/03/2005	Ukraine	97–0	97
13/04/1996	Portugal	92–0	92
17/11/1976	Morocco	89–0	89

BY A PLAYER

Date	Player	Opponent	Points
05/10/2002	Ionut Tofan	Spain	30
13/04/1996	Virgil Popisteanu	Portugal	27
04/02/2001	Petre Mitu	Portugal	27
13/04/1996	Ionel Rotaru	Portugal	25

MOST TRIES IN A MATCH
BY THE TEAM

Date	Opponent	Result	Tries
17/11/1976	Morocco	89–0	17
21/10/1951	East Germany	64–26	16
19/03/2005	Ukraine	97–0	15
16/04/1978	Spain	74–3	14
	13 on 3 occasions		

BY A PLAYER

Date	Player	Opponent	Tries
30/04/1972	Gheorghe Rascanu	Morocco	5
18/10/1986	Cornel Popescu	Portugal	5
13/04/1996	Ionel Rotaru	Portugal	5

MOST CONVERSIONS IN A MATCH
BY THE TEAM

Date	Opponent	Result	Cons
13/04/1996	Portugal	92–0	12
19/03/2005	Ukraine	97–0	11
04/10/1997	Belgium	83–13	10
	9 on 4 occasions		

BY A PLAYER

Date	Player	Opponent	Cons
13/04/1996	Virgil Popisteanu	Portugal	12
04/10/1997	Serban Guranescu	Belgium	10
19/03/2005	Danut Dumbrava	Ukraine	8
22/03/2008	Florin Vlaicu	Czech Republic	8

MOST PENALTIES IN A MATCH
BY THE TEAM

Date	Opponent	Result	Pens
15/06/2010	Argentina Jaguars	24–8	7
16/11/2013	Canada	21–20	7
12/06/2015	Spain	35–9	7
	6 on 4 occasions		

BY A PLAYER

Date	Player	Opponent	Pens
16/11/2013	Florin Vlaicu	Canada	7
	6 on 5 occasions		

MOST DROP GOALS IN A MATCH
BY THE TEAM

Date	Opponent	Result	DGs
29/10/1967	West Germany	27–5	4
14/11/1965	West Germany	9–8	3
17/10/1976	Poland	38–8	3
03/10/1990	Spain	19–6	3

BY A PLAYER

Date	Player	Opponent	DGs
29/10/1967	Valeriu Irimescu	West Germany	3
17/10/1976	Alexandru Dumitru	Poland	3

ROMANIA

MOST CAPPED PLAYERS

Player	Caps
Cristian Petre	93
Csaba Gal	88
Florin Vlaicu	85
Catalin Fercu	84
77 by 4 players	

LEADING PENALTY SCORERS

Player	Pens
Florin Vlaicu	128
Danut Dumbrava	71
Neculai Nichitean	53
Petre Mitu	53
Ionut Tofan	46

LEADING TRY SCORERS

Player	Tries
Petre Motrescu	33
Gabriel Brezoianu	28
Catalin Fercu	28
Florica Murariu	27
Mihai Vusec	22

LEADING DROP GOAL SCORERS

Player	DGs
Alexandru Dumitru	14
Neculai Nichitean	10
Valeriu Irimescu	10
Gelu Ignat	8

LEADING CONVERSIONS SCORERS

Player	Cons
Florin Vlaicu	105
Danut Dumbrava	73
Petre Mitu	53
Ionut Tofan	52
Ion Constantin	34

LEADING POINTS SCORERS

Player	Points
Florin Vlaicu	641
Danut Dumbrava	380
Petre Mitu	335
Ionut Tofan	322
Neculai Nichitean	257

ROMANIA INTERNATIONAL PLAYERS
UP TO 1 NOVEMBER, 2015

A Achim 1974 *Pol*, 1976 *Pol, Mor*
M Adascalitei 2007 *Rus*, 2009 *Pt, Ur, F, ItA*, 2012 *Ukr, Ur, ArJ*
Ailenei 2012 *Ukr*
M Aldea 1979 *USS, W, Pol, F*, 1980 *It, USS, I, F*, 1981 *It, Sp, USS, S, NZ, F*, 1982 *WGe, It, USS, Z, Z, F*, 1983 *Mor, WGe, It, USS, Pol, W, USS, F*, 1984 *It, S, F*, 1985 *E, USS*
C Alexandrescu 1934 *It*
N Anastasiade 1927 *Cze*, 1934 *It*
V Anastasiade 1939 *It*
I Andrei 2003 *W, I, Ar, Nm*, 2004 *Cze, Pt, Sp, Rus, Geo, It, W, J, Cze*, 2005 *Rus, US, S, Pt*, 2006 *Cze*, 2007 *Pt*, 2008 *Sp, Pt, Rus*
I Andriesi 1937 *It, H, Ger*, 1938 *F, Ger*, 1939 *It*, 1940 *It*
MC Antonescu 2014 *Elr, C*, 2015 *Pt, Sp, Rus, Sp, Nm, ArJ, Tg, It*
E Apjok 1996 *Bel*, 2000 *It*, 2001 *Pt*
AM Apostol 2011 *Nm, E*, 2012 *Rus, Geo, Sp*, 2013 *Pt, Rus, Sp, Bel, Geo*, 2014 *US*, 2015 *Pt, Sp, Rus, Ger, Geo, Sp, ArJ, Tg, F, I, It*
D Armasel 1924 *F, US*
A Atanasiu 1970 *It, F*, 1971 *It, Mor, F*, 1972 *Mor, Cze, WGe*, 1973 *Sp, Mor, Ar, Ar, WGe*, 1974 *Pol*

I Bacioiu 1976 *USS, Bul, Pol, F, Mor*
N Baciu 1964 *Cze, EGe*, 1967 *It, F*, 1968 *Cze, Cze, F*, 1969 *Pol, WGe, F*, 1970 *It*, 1971 *It, Mor, F*, 1972 *Mor, Cze, WGe*, 1973 *Ar, Ar*, 1974 *Cze, EGe*
VC Badalicescu 2012 *Pt, Elt, J*, 2015 *Sp, Nm, ArJ*
I Badiu 2014 *Rus*

B Balan 2003 *Pt, Sp, Geo*, 2004 *W*, 2005 *Rus, Ukr, J, US, S, Pt*, 2006 *Geo, Pt, Ukr, Rus, F, Geo, Sp, S*, 2007 *Sp, ESA, ItA, Nm, It, S, Pt, NZ*, 2009 *Fj*, 2010 *Ger, Rus, Ur, Ur*, 2011 *Pt*
D Balan 1983 *F*
PV Balan 1998 *H, Pol, Ukr, Ar, Geo, I*, 1999 *F, S, A, US, I*, 2000 *Mor, H, Pt, Sp, Geo, F, It*, 2001 *Pt, Sp, H, Rus, Geo, I, E*, 2002 *Pt, Sp, H, Rus, Geo, Sp, S, S*, 2003 *Cze, F, W, I, Nm*, 2004 *It, W, J, Cze*, 2005 *Geo, C, I*, 2006 *Geo, Pt, F, Geo, Sp, S*, 2007 *Geo*, 2009 *Ur, F*
L Balcan 1963 *Bul, EGe, Cze*
F Balmus 2000 *Mor, H, Pt*
S Bals 1927 *F, Ger, Cze*
G Baltaretu 1965 *WGe, F*
C Barascu 1957 *F*
M Baraulea 2004 *Cze, Pt, Geo*
A Barbu 1958 *WGe, It*, 1959 *EGe, Pol, Cze, EGe*, 1960 *F*
A Barbuliceanu 2008 *Rus, ESA*, 2009 *Sp, Ger, Rus, Geo, Pt*
S Bargaunas 1971 *It, Mor*, 1972 *F*, 1974 *Cze*, 1975 *It*
S Barsan 1934 *It*, 1936 *F, It*, 1937 *It, H, F, Ger*, 1938 *F, Ger*, 1939 *It*, 1940 *F*, 1942 *It*
RC Basalau 2007 *Pt*, 2008 *Geo, Pt, Rus, Cze, Ur, Rus, ESA*, 2010 *ItA, Tun*
CD Beca 2009 *Sp, Ger, Rus, Geo, Pt*, 2011 *Pt*
E Beches 1979 *It, Sp, USS*, 1982 *WGe, It*, 1983 *Pol*
M Bejan 2001 *I, W*, 2002 *Pt*, 2003 *Geo, Cze*, 2004 *It*
C Beju 1936 *F, It, Ger*
G Bentia 1919 *US, FAr*, 1924 *F, US*
V Bezarau 1995 *Ar, F, It*

G Corneliu 1980 *Mor*, *USS*, 1982 *WGe*, *It*, *Z*, *Z*, 1986 *Tun*, *Pt*, *F*, 1993 *I*, 1994 *W*
M Corneliu 1979 *USS*
G Corneliu 1976 *USS*, *Bul*, 1977 *F*, 1979 *It*, 1981 *S*, 1982 *Z*
F Corodeanu 1997 *WalA*, *F*, *W*, 1998 *H*, *Pol*, *Ar*, *Geo*, 1999 *F*, *S*, *A*, *US*, *I*, 2000 *H*, *Sp*, *Geo*, *F*, *It*, 2001 *Pt*, *Sp*, *H*, *Rus*, *Geo*, *I*, *E*, 2002 *Pt*, *Sp*, *Rus*, *Geo*, *It*, *Sp*, *W*, *S*, *S*, 2003 *Sp*, 2005 *Geo*, *J*, *US*, *S*, *Pt*, *C*, *I*, 2006 *Geo*, *Cze*, *Pt*, *Geo*, *Sp*, *S*, 2007 *Geo*, *ESA*, *ItA*, *Nm*, *It*, *S*, *Pt*, *NZ*, 2008 *Ur*, *Rus*, *ESA*, 2009 *Sp*, *Ger*, *Rus*, *Pt*
Coste 2007 *Pt*, 2008 *Geo*, *Sp*, *Pt*, *Rus*, *Cze*, *Ur*, 2009 *Sp*, *Rus*, *Geo*, *Pt*, *F*, 2010 *Ukr*, 2012 *Pt*, *Rus*, *Geo*, *Ur*, *ArJ*, *Elt*, *J*, *US*, 2013 *Rus*, *Bel*, *Geo*, *Tg*, *C*, *Fj*, 2014 *US*, *J*, *C*, 2015 *Geo*
L Costea 1994 *E*, 1995 *S*, *J*, *J*, *Ar*, *F*, 1997 *WalA*, *F*
L Coter 1957 *F*, *Cze*, 1959 *EGe*, *Pol*, *Cze*, 1960 *F*
F Covaci 1936 *Ger*, 1937 *H*, *F*, *Ger*, 1940 *It*, 1942 *It*
C Cratunescu 1919 *US*, *FAr*
N Crissoveloni 1936 *F*, *It*, 1937 *H*, *F*, *Ger*, 1938 *F*, *Ger*
S Cristea 1973 *Mor*
C Cristoloveanu 1952 *EGe*
G Crivat 1938 *F*, *Ger*
V Csoma 1983 *WGe*
D Curea 2005 *Rus*, *Ukr*, *J*, *US*, *S*, *Pt*

V Daiciulescu 1966 *Cze*, *F*, 1967 *It*, *Pol*, 1968 *F*, 1969 *Pol*
A Damian 1934 *It*, 1936 *F*, *It*, *Ger*, 1937 *It*, 1938 *F*, *Ger*, 1939 *It*, 1949 *Cze*
M Danila 2012 *Ukr*
G Daraban 1969 *Cze*, 1972 *Mor*, *Cze*, *WGe*, *F*, 1973 *Sp*, *Mor*, *Ar*, *Ar*, 1974 *Cze*, *EGe*, *F*, *Cze*, 1975 *It*, *Sp*, *JAB*, *Pol*, *F*, 1976 *H*, *It*, *Sp*, *USS*, *Bul*, *Pol*, *F*, *Mor*, 1977 *Sp*, *It*, *F*, 1978 *Cze*, *Sp*, *Pol*, *F*, 1982 *F*, 1983 *Mor*, *WGe*, *It*, *USS*, *W*
CR Dascalu 2006 *Ukr*, *F*, *Geo*, *Sp*, *S*, 2007 *Sp*, *Cze*, *ESA*, *NZ*, *Rus*, *Pt*, 2008 *Geo*, *Rus*, *Ur*, *Rus*, *ESA*, 2009 *Sp*, *Rus*, *Geo*, *Ur*, *ItA*, *ItA*, 2010 *Ger*, *Rus*, *Geo*, *Sp*, *Ukr*, *Ukr*, *Nm*, 2011 *Pt*, *Rus*, *Geo*, 2013 *Pt*, *Rus*, *Sp*, *Bel*, *Geo*, *Tg*, *C*, *Fj*, 2014 *Geo*, *Ur*, *Rus*, *Elr*, *J*, *C*, 2015 *Pt*, *Sp*, *Rus*, *Geo*, *Nm*
V David 1984 *Sp*, 1986 *Pt*, *S*, *F*, *Tun*, 1987 *USS*, *Z*, *F*, 1992 *USS*
S Demci 1998 *Ar*, 2001 *H*, *Rus*, *Geo*, *I*, *W*
R Demian 1959 *EGe*, 1960 *F*, 1961 *Pol*, *EGe*, *Cze*, *EGe*, *F*, 1962 *Cze*, *Pol*, *It*, *F*, 1963 *Bul*, *EGe*, *Cze*, *F*, 1964 *WGe*, *F*, 1965 *WGe*, *F*, 1966 *Cze*, *It*, *F*, 1967 *It*, *Pt*, *Pol*, *WGe*, *F*, 1968 *Cze*, *F*, 1969 *Pol*, *WGe*, *F*, 1971 *It*, *Mor*
E Denischi 1949 *Cze*, 1952 *EGe*, *EGe*
G Diaconescu 2015 *Pt*
I Diaconu 1942 *It*
C Diamandi-Telu 1938 *Ger*, 1939 *It*
Dico 2015 *Ger*
ND Dima 1999 *A*, *US*, *I*, 2000 *H*, *Pt*, *Geo*, *F*, *It*, 2001 *Sp*, *H*, *Rus*, *Geo*, *W*, *E*, 2002 *Pt*, *Sp*, *Rus*, *W*, *S*, *S*, 2004 *Cze*, *Pt*, *Sp*, *Rus*, *Geo*, 2009 *ItA*, *ItA*, 2010 *Ger*, *Geo*, *Pt*, *Sp*, *Nm*, *ArJ*, *Ur*, *Ur*, 2011 *Geo*, *Sp*, *Nm*, *Ukr*
TI Dimofte 2004 *It*, *W*, *Cze*, 2005 *C*, *I*, 2006 *Geo*, *Cze*, *Pt*, *Ukr*, *Rus*, *F*, *Geo*, *Sp*, *S*, 2007 *ESA*, *ItA*, *Nm*, *It*, *S*, *Pt*, *NZ*, *Rus*, *Pt*, 2008 *Geo*, *Sp*, *Pt*, *Rus*, *Cze*, *Ur*, *ESA*, 2009 *Sp*, *Ger*, *Rus*, *Geo*, *Pt*, *Ur*, *F*, *ItA*, *Fj*, 2010 *Ger*, *Rus*, *Geo*, *Pt*, *Sp*, *Ukr*, *Ukr*, *Nm*, *ItA*, *Tun*, *Ur*, *Ur*, 2011 *Sp*, *Nm*, *ArJ*, *Ukr*, *S*, *Ar*, *Geo*, 2013 *Bel*, *Geo*, *Rus*, *ArJ*, *Elt*
C Dinescu 1934 *It*, 1936 *F*, *It*, *Ger*, 1937 *It*, *H*, *F*, *Ger*, 1938 *F*, *Ger*, 1940 *It*, 1942 *It*
IC Dinis 2012 *Pt*, *Rus*, *Geo*, *Sp*, *Ukr*, *Ur*, *ArJ*, *Elt*, 2013 *Fj*, 2014 *Pt*, *Rus*, *Sp*, *Bel*, *Geo*
C Dinu 1965 *WGe*, *F*, 1966 *Cze*, *It*, *F*, 1967 *It*, *Pt*, *Pol*, *WGe*, 1968 *F*, 1969 *Pol*, *WGe*, *Cze*, *F*, 1970 *It*, *F*, 1971 *Mor*, *F*, 1972 *Mor*, *Cze*, *WGe*, *F*, 1973 *Sp*, *Mor*, *Ar*, *Ar*, *WGe*, *F*, 1974 *Mor*, *Pol*, *Sp*, *Cze*, *F*, *Cze*, 1975 *It*, *Sp*, 1976 *H*, *It*, *Sp*, *Pol*, *F*, *Mor*, 1977 *Sp*, *It*, *Pol*, *It*, *F*, 1978 *Sp*, *Pol*, *F*, 1979 *Sp*, *USS*, *W*, *Pol*, 1980 *I*, *Pol*, *F*, 1981 *It*, *Sp*, *USS*, *NZ*, *F*, 1982 *F*, 1983 *Mor*, *WGe*, *It*, *USS*
F Dinu 2000 *Mor*, *H*
G Dinu 1975 *Pol*, 1979 *It*, *Sp*, 1983 *Pol*, *USS*
G Dinu 1990 *It*, *F*, *H*, *Sp*, *It*, *USS*, 1991 *It*, *S*, *F*, *C*, *Fj*, 1992 *Sp*, *It*, *USS*, *F*, *It*, 1993 *F*
F Dobre 2001 *E*, 2004 *W*, *Cze*, 2007 *Pt*, 2008 *Cze*, 2012 *Rus*, *Ukr*, *Ur*, *ArJ*, *Elt*

I Dobre 1951 *EGe*, 1952 *EGe*, 1953 *It*, 1955 *Cze*, 1957 *Cze*, *Bel*, *F*, 1958 *Sp*
I Doja 1986 *Tun*, *Pt*, *F*, *I*, 1988 *F*, *W*, 1989 *Sp*, *Z*, *Sa*, *S*, 1990 *It*, 1991 *It*, *NZ*, *F*, *C*, 1992 *Sp*
V Doja 1997 *Bel*, 1998 *Pol*, *Geo*, *I*
A Domocos 1989 *Z*, *Sa*, *USS*
I Dorutiu 1957 *Cze*, *Bel*, *F*, 1958 *Sp*, *WGe*
A Draghici 1919 *US*
C Dragnea 1995 *F*, 1996 *Pol*, 1997 *WalA*, *F*, *Bel*, *Ar*, *F*, *It*, 1998 *H*, *Pol*, 1999 *F*, 2000 *F*
I Dragnea 1985 *Tun*
S Dragnea 2002 *S*
M Dragomir 2001 *H*, *Geo*, 2002 *I*
M Dragomir 1996 *Bel*, 1997 *Bel*, 1998 *H*, *Pol*, *Ukr*, *Geo*, *I*, 2001 *I*, *W*, *E*
V Dragomir 1964 *Cze*, *EGe*, 1966 *It*, 1967 *Pol*, *WGe*
G Dragomirescu 1919 *FAr*
G Dragomirescu-Rahtopol 1963 *Bul*, *EGe*, *Cze*, *F*, 1964 *Cze*, *EGe*, *WGe*, *F*, 1965 *WGe*, *F*, 1966 *Cze*, 1967 *It*, *Pt*, *Pol*, *WGe*, *F*, 1968 *Cze*, *F*, 1969 *Pol*, *WGe*, *Cze*, *F*, 1970 *It*, *F*, 1971 *It*, *Mor*, 1972 *Mor*, *Cze*, *WGe*, *F*, 1973 *WGe*, *F*
N Dragos 1995 *Ar*, *It*, 1997 *WalA*, *F*, *Ar*, *F*, *It*, 1998 *H*, *Pol*, *Ukr*, *Ar*, *Geo*, *I*, 1999 *F*, *S*, 2000 *Sp*, *Geo*, *F*
CS Draguceanu 1994 *Sp*, *Ger*, *Rus*, *It*, *W*, *It*, *E*, 1995 *S*, *J*, *Ar*, *F*, *It*, 1996 *Bel*, 1997 *W*, *Bel*, *Ar*, *F*, *It*, 1998 *H*, *Pol*, *Ukr*, *Ar*, *Geo*, *I*, 1999 *S*, *A*, *US*, *I*, 2000 *Mor*, *H*, *Pt*, *Sp*, *Geo*, *F*, *It*
C Dragulescu 1969 *Cze*, 1970 *F*, 1971 *It*, 1972 *Cze*
M Drenceanu 2014 *Rus*, 2015 *Sp*, *Nm*, *ArJ*
G Drobota 1960 *Pol*, *Cze*, 1961 *EGe*, *EGe*, *F*, 1962 *Cze*, *EGe*, *Pol*, *F*, 1964 *Cze*, *EGe*, *F*
MD Dumbrava 2002 *W*, *S*, 2003 *Sp*, *Rus*, *Geo*, *Cze*, *F*, *W*, *I*, *A*, *Nm*, 2004 *Cze*, *Pt*, *Sp*, *Rus*, *Geo*, *It*, *J*, *Cze*, 2005 *Rus*, *Geo*, *Ukr*, *J*, *US*, *S*, *Pt*, *C*, 2006 *Geo*, *Pt*, *Rus*, 2007 *Sp*, *Cze*, *Pt*, *Rus*, *Pt*, 2008 *Sp*, *Pt*, *Rus*, *Cze*, *Ur*, *Rus*, *ESA*, 2009 *Fj*, 2010 *Sp*, *Pt*, *Ukr*, *Ukr*, *Nm*, *ArJ*, *ItA*, *Tun*, *Ur*, 2011 *Pt*, *Rus*, *Geo*, *Sp*, *Nm*, *Ukr*, *S*, *E*, *Geo*, 2012 *Pt*, 2015 *Pt*, *Sp*, *Rus*, *Ger*, *Geo*, *Sp*, *Nm*, *ArJ*, *Tg*, *F*
H Dumitras 1984 *It*, 1985 *E*, *It*, *USS*, 1986 *Pt*, *F*, *I*, 1987 *It*, *USS*, *Z*, *S*, *USS*, *F*, 1988 *It*, *Sp*, *US*, *USS*, *USS*, *F*, *W*, 1989 *It*, *E*, *Z*, *Sa*, *USS*, *S*, 1990 *It*, *F*, *H*, *Sp*, *USS*, 1991 *It*, *NZ*, *F*, *S*, *F*, *C*, *Fj*, 1992 *Sp*, *USS*, *F*, *Ar*, 1993 *Pt*, *Tun*, *F*, *Sp*, *F*, *I*
I Dumitras 2002 *H*, 2006 *Geo*, *Cze*, *Ukr*, *Rus*, *F*, 2007 *Geo*, *Sp*, *Cze*, *ESA*, *ItA*, *Nm*, *It*, *S*, *Pt*, *NZ*, 2009 *Ur*, *F*, *ItA*, *ItA*, *Fj*, 2010 *Ger*, *Rus*, *Geo*, *Pt*, *Sp*, *Ur*, *Ur*, 2011 *Pt*, *Rus*, *Geo*, *Sp*, *ArJ*, *Ukr*, *S*, *Ar*, *E*, *Geo*, 2012 *Pt*, *Rus*, *Geo*, *Sp*, *Ur*, *ArJ*, *Elt*
E Dumitrescu 1953 *It*, 1958 *Sp*, *WGe*
G Dumitrescu 1988 *It*, *Sp*, *F*, *W*, 1989 *It*, *E*, *Sp*, *Z*, *Sa*, *USS*, *S*, 1990 *It*, *F*, *H*, *Sp*, *It*, *USS*, 1991 *It*, *NZ*, *F*, 1997 *It*
L Dumitrescu 1997 *Bel*, *Ar*, 2001 *W*
G Dumitriu 1937 *H*, *F*, *Ger*
A Dumitru 1974 *F*, 1975 *Sp*, *JAB*, 1976 *Sp*, *USS*, *Bul*, *Pol*, *F*, *Mor*, 1977 *Sp*, *It*, *F*, *Pol*, *F*, 1978 *Cze*, *Sp*, 1979 *It*, *Sp*, *USS*, *W*, *F*, 1980 *It*, *I*, *Pol*, *F*, 1981 *Sp*, *USS*, *S*, *NZ*, *F*, 1982 *Z*, 1983 *It*, *USS*, *Pol*, *W*, 1984 *It*, *S*, *F*, *Sp*, 1985 *E*, 1987 *It*, *USS*, *Z*, *S*, *USS*, *F*, 1988 *USS*
D Dumitru 2002 *S*, 2009 *Ur*, *F*, *ItA*, *ItA*, *Fj*
G Dumitru 1973 *Sp*, *Mor*, *Ar*, *Ar*, *WGe*, *F*, 1974 *Mor*, *Sp*, *Cze*, *EGe*, *F*, 1975 *JAB*, *Pol*, *F*, 1976 *H*, *It*, *Sp*, 1977 *Sp*, *Pol*, *F*, 1978 *Cze*, *Sp*, *Pol*, *F*, 1979 *It*, *Sp*, *USS*, *W*, *Pol*, *F*, 1980 *It*, *Mor*, *USS*, *I*, *Pol*, *F*, 1981 *It*, *Sp*, *USS*, *S*, *NZ*, *F*, 1982 *WGe*, *It*, *USS*, *Z*, *Z*, *F*, 1983 *Mor*, *WGe*, *It*, *USS*, *Pol*, *USS*, *F*, 1984 *It*, *S*, *F*, 1985 *E*, *It*, *Tun*, *USS*, 1986 *F*, *I*, 1987 *USS*, *F*, *S*, *USS*, *F*
I Dumitru 2013 *Rus*, *ArJ*, *Elt*, *Tg*, *C*, *Fj*, 2014 *Pt*, *Rus*, *Sp*, *Bel*, *Geo*, *Ur*, *Rus*, *Elr*, 2015 *Pt*
M Dumitru 1990 *F*, *H*, *Sp*, *It*, *USS*, 1991 *NZ*, *F*, *F*, *C*, 1992 *F*, 1993 *F*, *Sp*, *F*
M Dumitru 1997 *WalA*, 1998 *Ar*, 1999 *F*, 2000 *Mor*, *H*, *Pt*, *Sp*, *Geo*, *F*, 2002 *I*, 2003 *Sp*
M Dumitru 2002 *Pt*, *Sp*, *H*, *I*
S Dumitru 2004 *It*, 2005 *Rus*, *Ukr*, *US*, *S*, *Pt*
R Durbac 1968 *Cze*, 1969 *WGe*, *Cze*, 1970 *It*, *F*, 1971 *It*, *Mor*, *F*, 1972 *WGe*, *F*, 1973 *Ar*, *Ar*, *WGe*, *F*, 1974 *Mor*, *Pol*, *Sp*, *Cze*, *EGe*, *F*, *Cze*, 1975 *It*, *Sp*, *JAB*, *Pol*, *F*

A Duta 1973 *Ar*

R Eckert 1927 *F, Ger, Cze*
I Enache 1977 *It*
M Ezaru 2000 *Pt, Geo, F*

V Falcusanu 1974 *Sp, Cze*
G Fantaneanu 1934 *It,* 1936 *F, It, Ger,* 1937 *It, H, F, Ger*
C Fercu 2005 *C, I,* 2006 *Geo, Cze, Pt, Ukr, Rus, F, Geo, Sp,* 2007 *Geo, Sp, Cze, ESA, ItA, Nm, It, S, Pt,* 2008 *Sp, Pt, Rus, Cze, Ur, Rus, ESA,* 2009 *Sp, Ger, Rus, Pt, Ur, F,* 2010 *Ger, Rus, Geo, Pt, Sp, Ukr, Nm, ArJ, ItA, Tun, Ur, Ur,* 2011 *Rus, Geo, Sp, Nm, ArJ, Ukr,* 2012 *Ur, ArJ, Elt, J, US,* 2013 *Pt, Rus, Sp, Bel, Geo, Rus, ArJ, Elt, Tg, C, Fj,* 2014 *Pt, Rus, Sp, Bel, Geo, US, J, C,* 2015 *Sp, Sp, Nm, ArJ, Tg, F, I, C, It*
Filip 2012 *J, US*
C Florea 1937 *It, F, Ger*
G Florea 1981 *S, NZ, It,* 1982 *WGe, It, USS, Z, Z,* 1984 *Sp,* 1985 *USS,* 1986 *Pt, F*
IM Florea 2012 *J, US*
S Florea 2000 *It,* 2001 *Sp, Geo, I, E,* 2002 *It, Sp, W,* 2003 *Sp, Rus, Geo, Cze, A, Ar, Nm,* 2007 *Sp, Cze, S, NZ,* 2009 *Sp, Ger,* 2010 *Rus, Ukr, Ukr, Nm,* 2011 *S, Ar, E, Geo*
I Florescu 1957 *F, Cze*
M Florescu 1995 *F*
P Florescu 1967 *It, Pt, Pol, WGe, F,* 1968 *Cze, Cze, F,* 1969 *Pol, WGe, Cze, F,* 1971 *Mor,* 1973 *Sp, Mor, Ar, Ar,* 1974 *Cze, EGe, F*
P Florian 1927 *F,* 1934 *It*
T Florian 1927 *F, Ger*
V Flutur 1994 *Ger,* 1995 *J, J, C, SA, A, Ar, F, It,* 1996 *Bel, Pol,* 1997 *WalA, F*
M Foca 1992 *It, USS, It, Ar,* 1993 *Pt, Tun, F*
C Fugigi 1992 *Ar*
C Fugigi 1964 *Cze,* 1969 *Cze,* 1972 *Mor, Cze, WGe, F,* 1973 *Sp, Ar, Ar, WGe, F,* 1974 *Mor, Sp, Cze, EGe,* 1975 *It, Sp, JAB*
R Fugigi 1995 *It,* 1996 *Pt, F, Pol,* 1998 *Ukr, Ar, I,* 1999 *S, I*
S Fuicu 1976 *H,* 1980 *USS, I, Pol, F,* 1981 *It, Sp, USS, S, NZ, F,* 1982 *Z, Z, F,* 1983 *Mor, WGe, It, USS, W,* 1984 *It*
N Fulina 1988 *F, W,* 1989 *It, E, Sp, Sa, USS,* 1990 *It, F, H, Sp, USS,* 1991 *NZ, C, Fj,* 1992 *It, It,* 1993 *Pt, F, Sp, F, I,* 1994 *Sp, Ger, Rus, It, W, It*

S Galan 1985 *It, It*
CM Gal 2005 *I,* 2006 *Geo, Cze, Pt, S,* 2007 *Geo, Cze, ESA, ItA, Nm, It, S, NZ, Rus,* 2008 *Geo, Sp, Pt, Rus,* 2009 *Ger, Pt, ItA, ItA, Fj,* 2010 *Geo, Pt, Sp, Ukr, Ukr, Nm, ArJ, ItA, Tun, Ur, Ur,* 2011 *Pt, Geo, Sp, Nm, ArJ, S, Ar, E, Geo,* 2012 *Pt, Rus, Geo, Sp, Ukr, Ur, ArJ, Elt, J, US,* 2013 *Rus, Sp, Bel, Geo, Rus, ArJ, Elt, Tg, C, Fj,* 2014 *Pt, Rus, Bel, Geo, Ur, Rus, Elr, US, J, C,* 2015 *Pt, Sp, Rus, Ger, Geo, Sp, Nm, ArJ, Tg, F, I, C, It*
I Garlesteanu 1924 *F, US,* 1927 *F, Cze*
A Gealapu 1994 *It, E,* 1995 *F, S, J, J, C, SA, A, Ar, F, It,* 1996 *Pt, F, Pol*
C Gheara 2004 *Cze, Sp, Rus, Geo,* 2010 *Ger,* 2011 *Rus, Ukr, Ar, Geo,* 2012 *Pt, Rus, Geo, Ukr, Ur, ArJ, Elt, J, US*
C Gheorghe 1992 *It,* 1993 *Tun, F, Sp,* 1994 *Sp, Ger, E*
D Gherasim 1959 *Cze*
V Ghiata 1951 *EGe*
S Ghica 1937 *H, F,* 1942 *It*
V Ghioc 2000 *It,* 2001 *Pt, Sp, Rus, Geo, I, W, E,* 2002 *Pt, Sp, H, W, S, S,* 2003 *Cze, Ar,* 2004 *It, W, Cze,* 2005 *Ukr, J, S,* 2008 *Pt*
N Ghiondea 1949 *Cze,* 1951 *EGe*
D Ghiuzelea 1951 *EGe,* 1952 *EGe, EGe,* 1953 *It,* 1955 *Cze,* 1957 *Cze*
A Girbu 1992 *Ar,* 1993 *Tun, Sp, F, I,* 1994 *Sp,* 1995 *Ar, F, It,* 1996 *Pt, F, Pol,* 1997 *WalA, F, Ar, F, It,* 1998 *H, Pol, Geo, I*
L Giucal 2009 *Sp, Ger*
M Giucal 1985 *It, Tun, USS, It,* 1986 *Pt, F, Tun*
A Giugiuc 1963 *Bul, EGe, Cze,* 1964 *Cze, EGe,* 1966 *Cze*
V Giuglea 1986 *S, Tun*
I Glavan 1942 *It*

RS Gontineac 1995 *F, S, J, J, C, SA, A,* 1996 *Pt, F, Pol,* 1997 *F, W, Ar, F, It,* 1998 *H, Pol, Ukr, Ar, Geo, I,* 1999 *F, S, A, US, I,* 2000 *H, Sp, Geo, F,* 2001 *Rus, Geo,* 2002 *Pt, Sp, Rus, Geo, I, It, Sp, W, S, S,* 2003 *Pt, Sp, Geo, Cze, F, W, I, A, Ar, Nm,* 2004 *Cze, Pt, Rus, Geo, It, W, J, Cze,* 2005 *Geo, C,* 2006 *Geo, Pt, Ukr, Rus, F, Geo, Sp, S,* 2007 *Geo, Sp, It, S, Pt, NZ,* 2008 *ESA*
A Gorcioaia 2009 *Geo,* 2012 *Rus, Geo, Sp*
M Gorcioaia 2012 *Ukr*
AG Gordas 2015 *ArJ*
G Graur 1958 *It,* 1959 *EGe, Pol, Cze, EGe,* 1960 *Pol, EGe, Cze,* 1961 *EGe,* 1962 *EGe, It*
E Grigore 1982 *WGe,* 1984 *Sp,* 1985 *E, Tun,* 1987 *It, USS, Z, F, S*
V Grigorescu 1936 *F, It, Ger,* 1939 *It*
M Guramare 1982 *WGe, It,* 1983 *Mor, WGe,* 1988 *Sp*
A Guranescu 1991 *S, F,* 1992 *USS, It,* 1993 *Pt, Tun, I,* 1994 *Ger, Rus, It, W, E,* 1995 *SA, A, Ar, F, It*
S Guranescu 1997 *W, Bel, Ar,* 2001 *Sp, H, Rus, I*

A Hariton 1973 *Mor, Ar, Ar,* 1978 *Cze, Sp*
T Hell 1958 *EGe*
S Hihetah 2013 *Elt, Tg, Fj,* 2014 *Rus, Elr,* 2015 *Nm*
CN Hildan 1998 *H, Pol, Geo,* 1999 *S*
L Hodorca 1984 *It,* 1985 *Tun,* 1986 *Pt, S, F, Tun, Tun, I,* 1987 *It, Z,* 1988 *F*
M Holban 1980 *Mor,* 1982 *F,* 1985 *It, USS,* 1986 *Pt, I*
J Hussar 1919 *US*

D Iacob 1996 *Bel,* 2001 *Pt, Sp, H, Geo, W*
ML Iacob 1997 *W, Bel, Ar, F, It,* 1999 *S*
DG Ianus 2009 *Sp,* 2010 *Ukr, Nm, ItA, Tun,* 2011 *Rus, Geo, Sp, Nm, Ar, E, Geo,* 2015 *Ger*
P Ianusevici 1974 *Pol, Cze, EGe, Cze,* 1975 *It,* 1976 *USS, Bul, Pol, F, Mor,* 1977 *Sp, Pol, It, F,* 1978 *F*
I Iconomu 1919 *US, FAr*
M Iconomu 1919 *US, FAr*
N Ifrim 1937 *F, Ger*
G Ignat 1986 *Pt, S, F, Tun,* 1988 *It, Sp, US, USS, USS, F, W,* 1989 *It, E, Sp, S,* 1990 *It, F, H, Sp,* 1991 *It, NZ, F, S, F, C, Fj,* 1992 *Sp, It, USS, F, Ar,* 1993 *Pt, F, Sp, F,* 1994 *Sp, Rus, It, W, It,* 1997 *WalA*
V Ilca 1987 *F*
A Ilie 2014 *Elr*
I Ilie 1952 *EGe, EGe,* 1953 *It,* 1955 *Cze,* 1957 *F, Cze, Bel, F,* 1958 *It,* 1959 *EGe*
M Iliescu 1961 *EGe,* 1963 *Bul, EGe, Cze, F,* 1965 *WGe, F,* 1967 *WGe*
T Ioan 1937 *H, F, Ger*
V Ioan 1927 *Ger, Cze,* 1937 *It*
A Ion 2012 *Sp, Ukr*
F Ion 1991 *S,* 1992 *Sp,* 1993 *F*
G Ion 1984 *Sp,* 1986 *F, I,* 1988 *USS, F, W,* 1989 *It, E, Sp, Sa, USS, S,* 1990 *It, F, H, Sp, It, USS,* 1991 *It, NZ, F, S, F, C, Fj,* 1992 *Sp, It, USS, F, Ar,* 1993 *Pt, F, Sp, F,* 1994 *Sp, Rus, It, W, It,* 1997 *WalA*
P Ion 2003 *Ar,* 2004 *It,* 2005 *Rus, Ukr, J, US, S,* 2006 *Geo, Cze, Pt, Ukr, Rus, F, Geo, S,* 2007 *Geo, Sp, Cze, ESA, ItA, Pt, NZ, Rus,* 2008 *Geo, Sp, Rus, Ur, Rus, ESA,* 2009 *Sp, Ger, Rus, Geo, Pt, Ur, F, ItA, ItA, Fj,* 2010 *Ger, Rus, Geo, Pt,* 2011 *ArJ, Ukr, S, Ar, E, Geo,* 2012 *Geo, Sp,* 2013 *Pt, Rus, Sp, Bel, Geo, Rus, Tg, C, Fj,* 2014 *Pt, Rus, Sp, Bel, Geo, US, J, C,* 2015 *Ger, Tg, F, I, C, It*
V Ion 1980 *Mor, USS,* 1982 *Z, Z, F,* 1983 *Mor, It, USS, W, USS, F,* 1984 *S,* 1985 *It,* 1987 *It, USS, Z, F, S*
A Ionescu 1958 *EGe, It,* 1959 *EGe, Pol, Cze,* 1960 *Pol, EGe, Cze,* 1961 *Pol, Cze, EGe, F,* 1962 *EGe, It, F,* 1963 *F,* 1964 *Cze, EGe, F,* 1965 *WGe,* 1966 *Cze, It, F*
D Ionescu 1949 *Cze,* 1951 *EGe,* 1952 *EGe, EGe,* 1953 *It,* 1955 *Cze,* 1957 *F, Cze, F,* 1958 *Sp, It*
G Ionescu 1949 *Cze*
G Ionescu 1934 *It,* 1936 *F, It, Ger,* 1937 *It, F,* 1938 *F, Ger,* 1940 *It,* 1942 *It*
M Ionescu 1972 *Mor,* 1976 *USS, Bul, Pol, F,* 1977 *It, F, Pol, It, F,* 1978 *Cze, Sp, Pol, F,* 1979 *It, Sp, USS, W, Pol, F,* 1980 *I,* 1981 *NZ,* 1983 *USS*
R Ionescu 1968 *Cze, Cze,* 1971 *F*
S Ionescu 1936 *It, Ger,* 1937 *It*

Pt, Sp, Rus, Geo, J, Cze, 2005 Rus, S, Pt, C, 2006 Cze, Ukr, Rus, F, Geo, Sp, S, 2007 Geo, Sp, Cze, ESA, ItA, Nm, It, Pt, 2009 Ur, F, ItA, 2010 Geo, Pt, Sp, Ukr, Ukr, ArJ, ItA, Tun, Ur, Ur, 2011 Pt, Rus, ArJ
C Popescu 1986 Tun, Pt, F
I Popescu 1958 EGe
I Popescu 2001 Pt, Sp, H, Rus, Geo
C Popescu-Colibasi 1934 It
V Popisteanu 1996 Pt, F, Pol
F Popovici 1973 Sp, Mor
N Postolache 1972 WGe, F, 1973 Sp, Mor, WGe, F, 1974 Mor, Pol, Sp, EGe, F, Cze, 1975 It, Sp, Pol, F, 1976 H, It
C Preda 1961 Pol, Cze, 1962 EGe, F, 1963 Bul, EGe, Cze, F, 1964 Cze, EGe, WGe, F
C Pristavita 2013 Rus, Elt, Tg, C, Fj, 2014 Sp, Bel, Ur, Elr, 2015 Pt, Sp, Rus, Ger, Sp, Nrn, ArJ
H Pungea 2012 J, US, 2013 Sp, Bel, Geo, Rus, ArJ, Elt, Tg, C, Fj, 2014 Pt, Rus, Sp, Bel, Geo, Ur, Rus, Elr, J, C, 2015 Pt, Sp, Rus, Geo, Tg, F, It

NF Racean 1988 USS, USS, F, W, 1989 It, E, Z, Sa, USS, 1990 H, It, USS, 1991 NZ, F, F, C, Fj, 1992 Sp, It, USS, F, It, Ar, 1993 Pt, Tun, F, Sp, 1994 Ger, Rus, It, W, 1995 F, S, J, J, C, SA, A
A Radoi 2008 Cze, 2009 ItA, Fj, 2010 Sp, Ukr, Ukr, Nm, ArJ, ItA, Tun, 2011 Geo, Sp, ArJ, Ukr, 2012 Rus, Sp, Ukr, Ur, Elt, US, 2013 Pt, Rus, Sp, Bel, Geo, Rus, ArJ, Elt, C, Fj, 2014 Pt, Rus, Sp, Geo, US, J, C, 2015 Pt, Sp, Rus, Ger, Geo, Sp, Nm, ArJ, Tg, F, I, C, It
M Radoi 1995 F, 1996 It, Pt, Pol, 1997 WalA, F, W, Bel, Ar, F, It, 1998 H, Pol, Ukr
P Radoi 1980 Mor
T Radu 1991 NZ
C Raducanu 1985 It, 1987 It, USS, Z, F, S, 1989 It, E, Sp, Z
A Radulescu 1980 USS, Pol, 1981 It, Sp, USS, S, F, 1982 WGe, It, USS, Z, Z, 1983 Pol, W, USS, F, 1984 It, S, F, Sp, 1985 E, USS, 1988 It, Sp, US, USS, USS, F, W, 1989 It, E, Sa, USS, 1990 It, F, H, Sp, It, USS
T Radulescu 1958 Sp, WGe, 1959 EGe, Pol, Cze, EGe, 1963 Bul, Cze, F, 1964 F, 1965 WGe, F, 1966 Cze
D Rascanu 1972 WGe, F
G Rascanu 1966 It, F, 1967 It, Pt, Pol, WGe, F, 1968 Cze, Cze, F, 1969 Pol, WGe, Cze, F, 1970 It, F, 1971 It, Mor, F, 1972 Mor, Cze, WGe, F, 1974 Sp
CA Ratiu 2003 Cze, 2005 J, US, S, Pt, C, I, 2006 Cze, Pt, Ukr, Rus, F, Geo, Sp, S, 2007 Sp, Cze, ESA, It, S, Pt, NZ, Rus, Pt, 2009 Geo, Pt, 2010 Sp, 2011 Nm, ArJ, Ukr, E, 2012 Ur, ArJ, Elt, US
I Ratiu 1992 It
S Rentea 2000 Mor
I Roman 1976 Bul
M Rosca 2012 Ukr, 2013 Pt, Rus, Sp
JG Rose 2015 Sp
C Rosu 1993 I
I Rotaru 1995 J, J, C, Ar, It, 1996 Pt, F, Pol, 1997 W, Bel, Ar, F
L Rotaru 1999 F, A, I
N Rus 2007 Rus
VS Rus 2007 Rus, Pt, 2008 Geo, Pt, Rus, 2009 F, ItA, Fj, 2012 Ur, ArJ, Elt, J, US
M Rusu 1959 EGe, 1960 F, 1961 Pol, Cze, 1962 Cze, EGe, Pol, It, F, 1963 Bul, EGe, Cze, F, 1964 WGe, F, 1965 WGe, F, 1966 Cze, It, F, 1967 It, Pt, Pol
V Rusu 1960 Pol, EGe, Cze, 1961 EGe, F, 1962 Cze, EGe, Pol, It, F, 1964 Cze, EGe, WGe, F, 1965 WGe, 1966 It, F, 1967 WGe, 1968 Cze

I Sadoveanu 1939 It, 1942 It
AA Salageanu 1995 Ar, F, It, 1996 Pt, F, Pol, 1997 W, Bel, F
V Samuil 2000 It, 2001 Pt, E, 2002 Pt, Sp, Geo
C Sasu 1989 Z, 1991 It, NZ, F, S, F, C, Fj, 1993 I
C Sauan 1999 S, A, US, I, 2000 It, 2002 Geo, I, It, Sp, 2003 Pt, Rus, Geo, Cze, F, W, I, A, Ar, Nm, 2004 Cze, Pt, Sp, Rus, Geo, It, W, J, Cze, 2005 Rus, Geo, Ukr, J, US, S, Pt, 2006 Rus, 2007 Geo
G Sava 1989 Z, S, 1990 H, Sp, It, USS, 1991 It, F, S, F, C, 1992 Sp

I Sava 1959 EGe, Pol, Cze, EGe, 1960 F, 1961 Pol, EGe, Cze, EGe, F, 1962 Cze, Pol, It, F
C Scarlat 1976 H, Sp, 1977 F, 1978 Cze, Sp, 1979 It, Sp, USS, W, Pol, F, 1980 It, USS, 1982 USS
R Schmettau 1919 US, FAr
V Sebe 1960 Pol, EGe, Cze
I Seceleanu 1992 It, USS, F, It, Ar, 1993 Pt, Tun, F, Sp, F
S Seceleanu 1986 Pt, F, I, 1990 It
E Septar 1996 Bel, Pol, 1997 WalA, W, 1998 Pol, Ukr, I, 1999 F, S, A, US, I, 2000 It
B Serban 1989 Sa, USS, S, 1990 It, 1992 It, USS
C Serban 1964 Cze, EGe, WGe, 1967 Pol, 1968 Cze, F, 1969 Pol, WGe, Cze, F, 1970 It, F, 1971 It, Mor, F, 1972 F, 1973 WGe, F, 1974 Mor
M Serbu 1967 It
E Sfetescu 1924 F, US, 1927 Cze
E Sfetescu 1934 It, 1936 F, Ger, 1937 It
G Sfetescu 1927 F, Ger
M Sfetescu 1924 F, US, 1927 Ger, Cze
N Sfetescu 1927 F, Ger, Cze
G Simion 1998 H
G Simion 1919 US
I Simion 1976 H, It, Sp, 1979 Pol, F, 1980 F
ML Sirbe 2008 Cze, 2010 Ukr, Ukr, Nm, ArJ, Tun, 2011 Pt, Nrn, 2012 Ur, ArJ, Elt, J, 2013 Pt, Rus, Sp, Bel, Geo, Rus, ArJ, Elt, Tg, C, Fj, 2014 Pt, Rus, Sp, Bel, Geo, Ur, Rus, Elr, US, J, 2015 Pt, Sp, Rus, Ger, Geo
L Sirbu 1996 Pt, 2000 Mor, H, Pt, Geo, F, 2001 H, Rus, Geo, I, W, E, 2002 Pt, Sp, H, Rus, I, It, S, S, 2003 Pt, Sp, Cze, F, W, I, A, Ar, Nm, 2004 Pt, Sp, Rus, Geo, It, W, Cze, 2005 Rus, Geo, Ukr, J, US, S, Pt, C, 2006 Geo, Pt, Ukr, Rus, F, Geo, Sp, 2007 Geo, ItA, It, S, Pt, NZ, 2009 Ur, F, ItA, ItA, Fj, 2010 Rus, Geo, Pt, Sp, Nm, ArJ, ItA, Ur, Ur, 2011 Rus, Nm, Ukr, S, E
M Slobozeanu 1936 F, 1937 H, F, Ger, 1938 F, Ger
OS Slusariuc 1993 Tun, 1995 J, J, C, 1996 Pt, F, 1997 Bel, Ar, F, 1998 H, Ar, Geo, I, 1999 F, S, A
S Soare 2001 I, W, 2002 Geo
S Soare 1924 F, US
M Socaciu 2000 It, 2001 I, W, E, 2002 It, W, S, S, 2003 Pt, Sp, Rus, Geo, Cze, F, W, I, A, Nm, 2004 Cze, Pt, Sp, Rus, Geo, It, W, J, Cze, 2005 Rus, Geo, Ukr, J, US, Pt, C, I, 2006 Cze
S Socol 2001 Sp, H, Rus, Geo, 2002 It, Sp, W, 2003 Sp, Rus, Geo, F, W, I, A, Ar, Nm, 2004 Cze, Pt, Sp, Rus, Geo, 2005 Rus, Geo, Ukr, C, I, 2006 Geo, Cze, Pt, Ukr, Rus, F, Geo, Sp, S, 2007 Geo, Sp, Cze, It, S, Pt, NZ, 2009 Ur, F, ItA, Fj, 2010 Ger, Rus, Geo, Pt, Sp, Ukr, Ukr, Nm, ArJ, ItA, Ur, Ur, 2011 Rus, Geo
N Soculescu 1949 Cze, 1951 EGe, 1952 EGe, EGe, 1953 It, 1955 Cze
N Soculescu 1927 Ger
V Soculescu 1927 Cze
GL Solomie 1992 Sp, F, It, Ar, 1993 Pt, Tun, F, Sp, F, I, 1994 Sp, Ger, W, It, E, 1995 F, S, J, J, C, SA, A, Ar, F, It, 1996 Pt, F, Pol, 1997 WalA, F, W, Bel, Ar, F, It, 1998 H, Pol, Ukr, Ar, Geo, I, 1999 S, A, US, I, 2000 Sp, F, It, 2001 Sp, H, Rus
C Stan 1990 H, USS, 1991 It, F, S, F, C, Fj, 1992 Sp, It, It, Ar, 1996 Pt, Bel, F, Pol, 1997 WalA, F, W, Bel, 1998 Ar, Geo, 1999 F, S, A, US, I
A Stanca 1996 Pt, Pol
R Stanca 1997 F, 2003 Sp, Rus, 2009 Geo, Pt
A Stanciu 1958 EGe, It
G Stanciu 1958 EGe, It
C Stanescu 1957 Bel, 1958 WGe, 1959 EGe, 1960 F, 1961 Pol, EGe, Cze, 1962 Cze, It, F, 1963 Bul, EGe, Cze, F, 1964 WGe, F, 1966 Cze, It
C Stefan 1951 EGe, 1952 EGe
E Stoian 1927 Cze
E Stoica 1973 Ar, Ar, 1974 Cze, 1975 Sp, Pol, F, 1976 Sp, USS, Bul, F, Mor, 1977 Sp, It, F, Pol, It, F, 1978 Cze, Sp, Pol, F, 1979 It, Sp, USS, W, Pol, F, 1980 It, USS, I, Pol, F, 1981 It, Sp, USS, S, NZ, F, 1982 WGe, It, USS, Z, Z, F
G Stoica 1963 Bul, Cze, 1964 WGe, 1966 It, F, 1967 Pt, F, 1968 Cze, Cze, F, 1969 Pol
S Stratila 2015 Ger
I Stroe 1986 Pt

E Suciu 1976 *Bul, Pol*, 1977 *It, F, It*, 1979 *USS, Pol, F*, 1981 *Sp*
M Suciu 1968 *F*, 1969 *Pol, WGe, Cze*, 1970 *It, F*, 1971 *It, Mor, F*, 1972 *Mor, F*
SS Suciu 2013 *ArJ*
O Sugar 1983 *It*, 1989 *Z, Sa, USS, S*, 1991 *NZ, F*
K Suiogan 1996 *Bel*
F Surugiu 2008 *Ur, Rus*, 2010 *Ukr, Ukr, Nm, ArJ, ItA*, 2011 *Pt, Rus, Geo, Sp, ArJ, Ukr, S, Ar, Geo*, 2012 *Pt, Rus, Geo, Ukr, Ur, ArJ, Elt, J, US*, 2013 *Pt, Rus, Sp, Bel, Geo, ArJ, Elt, Tg, C, Fj*, 2014 *Pt, Rus, Sp, Bel, Geo, Ur, Rus, Elr, C*, 2015 *Ger, Geo, Sp, Nm, ArJ, Tg, F, I, C*

D Talaba 1996 *Bel*, 1997 *F, It*
P Tamba 2012 *J, US*, 2013 *Bel*
C Tanase 1938 *F, Ger*, 1939 *It*, 1940 *It*
A Tanasescu 1919 *FAr*, 1924 *F, US*
N Tanoviceanu 1937 *It, H, F*, 1939 *It*
I Tarabega 1934 *It*, 1936 *It*
A Tarus 2013 *ArJ*, 2014 *Ur, Rus, Elr*, 2015 *Pt, Rus, Geo, I, C*
F Tasca 2008 *Ur, Rus, ESA*, 2009 *Sp, Ger, Rus, Geo, Pt*
V Tata 1971 *F*, 1973 *Ar, Ar*
CF Tatu 2003 *Ar*, 2004 *Cze, Pt, Sp, Rus, Geo, It, W*, 2005 *Ukr, J*, 2013 *Rus, Sp*
I Tatucu 1973 *Sp, Mor*, 1974 *Cze, F*
D Teleasa 1971 *It*, 1973 *Sp, Ar, Ar*
D Tenescu 1951 *EGe*
I Teodorescu 2001 *I, W, E*, 2002 *Pt, Sp, S, S*, 2003 *Pt, Sp, Rus, W, I, A, Ar, Nm*, 2004 *Cze, Pt, Sp, Rus, Geo, W, J, Cze*, 2005 *Rus, Geo, Ukr, J, US, S, Pt, C, I*, 2006 *Geo, Cze, Pt, Ukr, F, Geo, S*, 2007 *ESA, ItA*
I Teodorescu 1958 *Sp, WGe, EGe, It*, 1960 *Pol, EGe, Cze*, 1963 *Bul, EGe, Cze*, 1965 *WGe, F*
A Teofilovici 1957 *F, Cze, Bel, F*, 1958 *Sp, WGe*, 1959 *EGe*, 1960 *F*, 1961 *Pol, EGe, Cze, EGe, F*, 1962 *Cze, Pol, It, F*, 1963 *Bul, EGe, Cze, F*, 1964 *WGe*
O Tepurica 1985 *USS*
M Tibuleac 1957 *Bel, F*, 1959 *Pol, Cze*, 1966 *It, Pt, Pol, WGe*, 1968 *Cze, Cze*
G Ticleanu 1919 *FAr*
M Tigora 2004 *Cze*
A Tinca 1987 *USS, F*
MV Tincu 2002 *Pt, Sp, H, Rus, Geo, I, It, Sp, S, S*, 2003 *Pt, Sp, Rus, Geo, F, W*, 2004 *Sp*, 2005 *Geo, Ukr, C, I*, 2006 *Geo, Cze, F, S*, 2007 *Geo, Sp, Cze, ESA, ItA, Nm, It, S, Pt, NZ*, 2008 *Geo*, 2009 *F, ItA, ItA*, 2010 *Ger, Rus, Geo, Pt, Ur, Ur*, 2011 *Nm, S, Ar, E, Geo*, 2012 *Pt, Rus, Geo, Sp*
M Toader 1982 *WGe*, 1984 *Sp*, 1985 *E, It, Tun, USS*, 1986 *S, F, Tun, Tun, Pt, F, I*, 1987 *It, USS, Z, F, S, USS, F*, 1988 *F, W*, 1989 *It, E, Sp, Sa, USS, S*, 1990 *It, F, F*
P Toderasc 2000 *It*, 2001 *Pt, Rus, Geo, W, E*, 2002 *H, Rus, Geo, I, It, Sp, W, S, S*, 2003 *Sp, Rus, Geo, Cze, F, W, I, A, Ar, Nm*, 2004 *Cze, Pt, Sp, Rus, Geo, It, J, Cze*, 2005 *J, US, S, Pt, C, I*, 2006 *Geo, Pt, Ukr, Sp*, 2007 *Geo, ESA, ItA, Nm, It, S*, 2009 *ItA, Fj*
IR Tofan 1997 *Bel, Ar, F, It*, 1998 *H, Ar*, 1999 *I*, 2000 *Mor, Sp, Geo*, 2001 *Pt, Sp, H, Geo, I, W, E*, 2002 *Pt, Sp, H, Rus, Geo, I, It, Sp, W, S, S*, 2003 *Pt, Sp, Rus, Geo, Cze, F, W, I, A, Ar, Nm*, 2004 *Sp, Geo, It, W, J*, 2005 *Rus, Geo, Ukr, J, US, I*, 2006 *Geo, Cze, Pt, Geo, Sp, S*, 2007 *Geo, ESA, ItA, Nm, S*
S Tofan 1985 *USS, It*, 1986 *Tun, Pt, F, I*, 1987 *It, USS, Z, F, S, USS, F*, 1988 *It, Sp, US, USS*, 1991 *NZ*, 1992 *Ar*, 1993 *Pt*, 1994 *It, E*
O Tonita 2000 *Mor, H, Pt, Sp, Geo, F*, 2001 *Pt, Sp, H, Rus, Geo, I*, 2002 *Sp, It, Sp, W*, 2003 *Rus, Geo, F, W, I, A, Ar, Nm*, 2004 *Sp, Rus, Geo, It*, 2005 *Rus, Pt, C, I*, 2006 *Pt, Geo, Sp, S*, 2007 *Sp, Cze, It, S, Pt, NZ*, 2009 *Ur, F, ItA, ItA, Fj*, 2010 *Ger, Rus, Geo, Pt, Nm, ArJ, ItA, Ur, Ur*, 2011 *Pt, Rus, ArJ, Ukr, S, Ar, E, Geo*, 2012 *US*, 2013 *Pt, Rus, 2014 US, J*, 2015 *F, I*
Traian 1942 *It*
N Tranca 1992 *Sp*
B Tudor 2003 *Cze*
F Tudor 1924 *F, US*
M Tudor 1924 *F, US*
AM Tudori 2003 *F, W, I, A, Ar, Nm*, 2004 *Sp, Rus, Geo, W, J,*

Cze, 2005 *Rus, Geo, Ukr, J, US, S, Pt*, 2006 *Geo, Cze, Ukr, Rus, F*, 2007 *Sp, Cze, ESA, ItA, Nm, It, S, Pt*, 2009 *Geo, Ur, ItA*
D Tudosa 1999 *S*, 2002 *Geo, I, It*, 2003 *Pt, W*
T Tudose 1977 *It*, 1978 *Cze, Sp, Pol, F*, 1979 *It, Sp, USS*, 1980 *USS*
V Tufa 1985 *USS*, 1986 *Pt, S*, 1990 *It*, 1991 *F, S, J, J, SA, A*, 1996 *Pt, F, Pol*
D Tunaru 1985 *It*
O Turashvili 2012 *Ur, ArJ, Elt, J, US*, 2013 *Tg, C, Fj*, 2014 *Ur, Rus, US, J, C*, 2015 *Pt, Sp, Rus, Ger, Geo, Sp, ArJ, Tg, F, I, C, It*
V Turlea 1974 *Sp*, 1975 *JAB, Pol, F*, 1977 *Pol*
C Turut 1937 *H*, 1938 *F*
I Tutuianu 1960 *Pol, EGe*, 1963 *Bul, EGe, Cze*, 1964 *Cze, EGe, WGe*, 1965 *WGe, F*, 1966 *Cze, It, F*, 1967 *Pt, Pol, WGe, F*, 1968 *Cze, Cze, F*, 1969 *Pol, WGe, Cze, F*, 1970 *It, F, 1971 F*
G Tutunea 1992 *Sp*

M Ungur 1996 *Bel*
V Ungureanu 1979 *It*
V Urdea 1979 *F*
A Ursache 2012 *Pt, Rus, Geo, Sp, Ukr, Ur, ArJ, Elt*, 2013 *Pt, Sp, Geo*, 2014 *Pt, Rus, Geo, US, J, C*, 2015 *Sp, Geo, Sp, Nm, Tg, F, I, C, It*
SF Ursache 2009 *ItA*, 2010 *Ukr, Nm*
VN Ursache 2004 *It, W, Cze*, 2005 *S, C*, 2006 *Geo, Ukr, Rus, F, S*, 2007 *Geo, Sp, Cze, ESA, ItA, Nm, Pt, NZ, Rus*, 2008 *Pt, Rus, Cze, Rus*, 2009 *ItA, Fj*, 2010 *Ger, Rus, Pt, Sp, Ukr, Ukr, Nm, ArJ, ItA, Tun, Ur, Ur*, 2011 *Geo, Sp, Nm, ArJ, S, Ar, Geo*, 2012 *Pt, Rus, Geo, Sp, J*, 2013 *Pt, Sp, Bel, Geo, Tg*, 2014 *C*, 2015 *Pt, Sp, Geo, Tg, F, C, It*

R Vacioiu 1977 *It, F, It*
E Valeriu 1949 *Cze*, 1952 *EGe*
JP van Heerden 2015 *Tg, F, I, C, It*
M Vardala 1924 *F, US*
N Vardela 1927 *F, Ger*
G Varga 1976 *It, USS, Bul, Pol, F, Mor*, 1977 *Sp, It, F, Pol, 1978 Sp*
N Varta 1958 *EGe*
G Varzaru 1980 *Mor, I, Pol, F*, 1981 *It, Sp, USS, F*, 1983 *Mor, WGe, It, USS, F*, 1984 *S, F*, 1985 *Tun, USS*, 1986 *F*, 1988 *It, Sp, US, USS, USS*
Z Vasluianu 1989 *Sp, Z, Sa*
P Veluda 1967 *It, Pt, Pol, WGe, F*
R Veluda 1949 *Cze*, 1952 *EGe*
R Veluda 1968 *Cze, Cze*
N Veres 1986 *Tun, Pt*, 1987 *F, USS, F*, 1988 *It, Sp, USS*
M Vidrascu 1919 *US, FAr*
P Vidrascu 1924 *F, US*, 1927 *Cze*
M Vioreanu 1994 *E*, 1998 *H, Pol, Ukr, Ar, Geo, I*, 1999 *F, S, A, US, I*, 2000 *Mor, Pt, Sp, Geo, F*, 2001 *Geo*, 2002 *Rus, Geo, I, It, Sp*, 2003 *Sp, Rus, F, I, A, Ar, Nm*
A Visan 1949 *Cze*
D Vlad 2005 *US, S, C, I*, 2006 *Rus*, 2007 *Sp, Cze, It, Rus, Pt*, 2008 *Sp, Cze*
G Vlad 1991 *C, Fj*, 1992 *Sp, It, USS, F, It, Ar*, 1993 *Pt, F, I*, 1994 *Sp, Ger, Rus, It, W, It, E*, 1995 *F, C, SA, A, Ar, It*, 1996 *Pt, F*, 1997 *W, Ar, F, It*, 1998 *Ar*
V Vlad 1980 *Mor*
FA Vlaicu 2006 *Ukr, F, Geo, Sp, S*, 2007 *Geo, Sp, Cze, ESA, ItA, Nm, S, NZ, Pt*, 2008 *Geo, Pt, Rus, Cze, Ur*, 2009 *Sp, Ger, Rus, Geo, Pt, Ur, F, ItA, ItA, Fj*, 2010 *Ger, Rus, Geo, Sp, Ukr, Ukr, ArJ, ItA, Tun, Ur*, 2011 *Pt, Rus, Geo, Sp, Nm, ArJ, Ukr, S, Ar, E, Geo*, 2012 *Pt, Rus, Geo, Ukr*, 2013 *Pt, Rus, Sp, Bel, Geo, Rus, ArJ, Elt, Tg, C, Fj*, 2014 *Pt, Rus, Sp, Bel, Geo, Ur, Rus, Elr, US, J, C*, 2015 *Ger, Sp, Nm, ArJ, Tg, F, I, C, It*
C Vlasceanu 2000 *Mor, Pt, Sp, Geo, F*
B Voicu 2003 *Cze*, 2004 *Cze, Pt, Sp, Rus, It, J*, 2005 *J, Pt*
M Voicu 1979 *Pol*
M Voicu 2002 *Pt*
V Voicu 1951 *EGe*, 1952 *EGe, EGe*, 1953 *It*, 1955 *Cze*
R Voinov 1985 *It*, 1986 *Pt, S, F, Tun*
P Volvoreanu 1924 *US*

G Vraca 1919 *US, FAr*
M Vusec 1959 *EGe, Pol, Cze, EGe*, 1960 *F*, 1961 *Pol, EGe, Cze, EGe, F*, 1962 *Cze, EGe, Pol, It, F*, 1963 *Bul, EGe, Cze, F*, 1964 *WGe, F*, 1965 *WGe, F*, 1966 *It, F*, 1967 *It, Pt, Pol, WGe, F*, 1968 *Cze, Cze, F*, 1969 *Pol, F*
RL Vusec 1998 *Geo, I*, 1999 *F, S, A, US, I*, 2000 *Mor, H, Pt, Sp, F*, 2002 *H, Rus, I*

M Wiringi 2015 *ArJ, I, C, It*
F Wirth 1934 *It*

I Zafiescu 1979 *W, Pol, F*
M Zafiescu 1980 *Mor*, 1986 *I*
D Zamfir 1949 *Cze*
B Zebega Suman 2004 *Cze, Pt, Rus, Geo, It, W, Cze*, 2005 *Rus, Ukr, US, S*, 2006 *Ukr, Sp*, 2007 *Rus, Pt*, 2008 *Geo, Pt, Rus, Cze, Ur*, 2010 *Ger, Sp, Ukr, Ukr, Nm, ArJ*, 2011 *Pt, Rus, Geo, Sp, Nm, ArJ, Ukr, S, E*
D Zlatoianu 1958 *Sp, WGe, EGe, It*, 1959 *EGe*, 1960 *Pol, EGe, Cze*, 1961 *EGe, EGe, F*, 1964 *Cze, EGe*, 1966 *Cze*

Getty Images

The moment that Florin Vlaicu kicks the match-winning penalty in the 78th minute against Canada at the Leicester City Stadium.

SAMOA

SAMOA'S 2014–15 TEST RECORD

OPPONENTS	DATE	VENUE	RESULT
Italy	8 Nov	A	Lost 24–13
Canada	14 Nov	N	Won 23–13
England	22 Nov	A	Lost 28–9
New Zealand	8 Jul	H	Lost 16–25
USA	18 Jul	A	Won 21–16
Fiji	24 Jul	N	Drew 30–30
Canada	29 Jul	A	Won 21–20
Fiji	3 Aug	N	Lost 39–29
USA	20 Sep	N	Won 25–16
South Africa	26 Sep	N	Lost 46–6
Japan	3 Oct	N	Lost 26–5
Scotland	10 Oct	N	Lost 36–33

NEW ERA BECKONS FOR SAMOA AFTER DISAPPOINTING CAMPAIGN

By Jon Newcombe

Tusi Pisi scores in the corner during Samoa's thrilling encounter with Scotland at St James' Park.

There was a certain inevitability about Stephen Betham's decision to stand down as Samoa head coach in mid-October after a Rugby World Cup 2015 campaign that fell short of expectations.

Despite fielding the oldest and most capped team in their Rugby World Cup history, Samoa's experience counted for little as they fell to consecutive defeats against South Africa (46–6), Japan (26–5) and Scotland (36–33) following a 25–16 win over USA to finish fourth in Pool B.

Few would have predicted such a meagre return from the Pacific Islands' most successful Rugby World Cup team in win-loss terms, especially after they'd given the All Blacks a stiff examination on home soil in Apia and enjoyed an unbeaten run to the final of the

A 27–24 defeat to the Barbarians, in the first-ever rugby international to be played at The Stadium, Queen Elizabeth Olympic Park, would have passed most people by had second-row Kane Thompson not been sent off for punching hooker Saia Fainga'a and subsequently banned for Samoa's opening match against the USA in Brighton. That dismissal – and the stadium's malfunctioning sprinklers – may have temporarily rained on Samoa's parade as the tournament drew ever closer, but most pundits still had them neck and neck with Scotland as principal contenders for the runners-up spot behind South Africa.

Even without three-time Rugby World Cup veteran Thompson, Samoa's run-on team for their opening match had an average age of 31 years and four days, the oldest in RWC history by three days. Age did not come before beauty in this instance though, Japan's shock 34–32 win over two-time champions South Africa had Brighton rocking by the time Samoa and the Eagles joined the south coast carnival.

USA captain Chris Wyles' superb try aside, the match failed to scale the same heights as what had come the day before. Never behind, Samoa were well directed by Tusi Pisi at fly-half and both of their tries, scored by the impressive Tim Nanai-Williams and captain Ofisa Treviranus, came from his neat grubber kicks. Pisi contributed 12 points himself from the kicking tee to close in on Earl Va'a's all-time Samoan points scoring record of 174 points as Samoa made a solid if not spectacular start to RWC 2015.

Having won their fifth tournament opener from seven attempts, and seen South Africa succumb to Japan, Samoa had every reason to believe they could build on the win against the Eagles with victory over the Springboks in Birmingham six days later. Vavae Tuilagi became the fifth of the six rugby-playing brothers to compete at a Rugby World Cup while Tusi, George and Ken Pisi made history too after appearing on the same pitch together. But Samoa's band of brothers were powerless to prevent the Springboks rampaging to a 46–6 victory at Villa Park.

For a nation renowned for its tough-tackling, Samoa's midfield defence had so far been found wanting. Only two-thirds of the 43 tackles made by centre pairing Rey Lee-Lo and Paul Perez had been successfully completed in the first two matches. The introduction of Johnny Leota shored things up in their next outing against Japan, however Samoa were their own worst enemy in other areas, a penalty count of 17 and three yellow cards giving them the worst disciplinary record in the tournament. By contrast, Japan managed to prevent Samoa having a single kick at goal until Tusi Pisi stepped up – and failed – to convert Perez's 64th-minute consolation try. By that stage Japan had racked up 26 points without reply.

Over the course of the tournament Pisi, Mike Stanley and Patrick

Fa'apale managed just 12 kicks from 21 for a success rate of 57 per cent: a poor return in normal circumstances but more so in a tournament where fair weather conditions and pristine playing surfaces were a feature.

All four of Samoa's pool matches were played in football stadia, the last at St James' Park on 10 October where a sky-high, second-half penalty count rather than missed shots at goal cost them dear in the thrill-a-minute finale against Scotland.

Samoa vice-captain and Newcastle winger Alesana Tuilagi's suspension for foul play against Japan meant he missed out on one last hurrah on the international stage in front of his 'home' fans. Fa'atoina Autagavaia took over on the left wing as one of seven changes to the starting line-up, while Treviranus was dropped from the match-day 23 altogether. He was replaced as captain by Northampton Saints scrum-half Kahn Fotuali'i, who immediately vowed to restore some national pride even if the chance to qualify for the knockout stages for the first time in two decades had gone. "Samoans are religious and church is very important to them. It has to be said, though, that rugby is up there with religion . . . we want to put a smile on their faces with a win over Scotland," he said.

Samoa hit the front four times in a pulsating first half that brought tries for Tusi Pisi, which he converted, Ma'atulimanu Leiataua and Lee-Lo. In kicking his third penalty of the half, Pisi handed Samoa a 26–23 interval lead.

Scotland rallied after the break to score 13 unanswered points, all from talisman and captain Greig Laidlaw. Even then, there were some fretful moments for the Scots, with Motu Matu'u bustling over soon after. Patrick Fa'apale added the extras but the gap remained at three at the final whistle. The defeat to Scotland was Samoa's fifth test defeat of the calendar year. The only other time this has happened was in two previous Rugby World Cup years: 1995 and 1999.

With Betham gone and the core of the team on the wrong side of 30, Samoa face a rebuilding and having to qualify for RWC 2019 in Japan. The good news is that, at 26 years of age, Samoa's new kid on the block, Tim Nanai-Williams, is young enough to still be considered for the next tournament. On the evidence of RWC 2015, Nanai-Williams will be a shoo-in. At times the New Zealand-born full-back single-handedly carried the fight to the opposition, making more metres (277) and carrying the ball more often (42) than any of his team-mates. He and centre Perez were the only players not to miss a single minute of Samoa's World Cup campaign, and while disappointed with the overall outcome the former New Zealand Sevens flyer enjoyed the experience. "I've loved playing for my country, I'm a very proud man," he said. "We've been unlucky in a few games but that's the way rugby is."

SAMOA INTERNATIONAL STATISTICS

MATCH RECORDS UP TO 1 NOVEMBER, 2015

WINNING MARGIN

Date	Opponent	Result	Winning Margin
11/07/2009	PNG	115–7	108
08/04/1990	Korea	74–7	67
18/07/2009	PNG	73–12	61
10/06/2000	Japan	68–9	59
29/06/1997	Tonga	62–13	49

MOST POINTS IN A MATCH
BY THE TEAM

Date	Opponent	Result	Points
11/07/2009	PNG	115–7	115
08/04/1990	Korea	74–7	74
18/07/2009	PNG	73–12	73
10/06/2000	Japan	68–9	68
29/06/1997	Tonga	62–13	62

BY A PLAYER

Date	Player	Opponent	Points
11/07/2009	Gavin Williams	PNG	30
29/05/2004	Roger Warren	Tonga	24
08/04/1990	Andy Aiolupo	Korea	23
03/10/1999	Silao Leaega	Japan	23
08/07/2000	Toa Samania	Italy	23

MOST TRIES IN A MATCH
BY THE TEAM

Date	Opponent	Result	Tries
11/07/2009	PNG	115–7	17
08/04/1990	Korea	74–7	13
18/07/2009	PNG	73–12	11
	10 on 4 occasions		

BY A PLAYER

Date	Player	Opponent	Tries
28/05/1991	Tupo Fa'amasino	Tonga	4
10/06/2000	Elvis Seveali'i	Japan	4
02/07/2005	Alesana Tuilagi	Tonga	4
11/07/2009	Esera Lauina	PNG	4
09/11/2012	Robert Lilomaiava	Canada	4

MOST CONVERSIONS IN A MATCH
BY THE TEAM

Date	Opponent	Result	Cons
11/07/2009	PNG	115–7	15
18/07/2009	PNG	73–12	9
08/04/1990	Korea	74–7	8
	6 on 5 occasions		

BY A PLAYER

Date	Player	Opponent	Cons
11/07/2009	Gavin Williams	PNG	10
18/07/2009	Titi Jnr Esau	PNG	9
08/04/1990	Andy Aiolupo	Korea	8
10/06/2000	Tanner Vili	Japan	6
04/07/2001	Earl Va'a	Japan	6

MOST PENALTIES IN A MATCH
BY THE TEAM

Date	Opponent	Result	Pens
29/05/2004	Tonga	24–14	8
21/06/2014	Fiji	18–13	6
	5 on 11 occasions		

BY A PLAYER

Date	Player	Opponent	Pens
29/05/2004	Roger Warren	Tonga	8
21/06/2014	Tusi Pisi	Tonga	6

MOST DROP GOALS IN A MATCH
BY THE TEAM

1 on 11 occasions

BY A PLAYER

1 on 11 occasions

SAMOA

MOST CAPPED PLAYERS

Name	Caps
Brian Lima	65
To'o Vaega	60
Semo Sititi	59
Census Johnston	52
Opeta Palepoi	42

LEADING PENALTY SCORERS

Name	Pens
Tusi Pisi	44
Darren Kellett	35
Earl Va'a	31
Silao Leaega	31
Roger Warren	29

LEADING TRY SCORERS

Name	Tries
Brian Lima	31
Alesana Tuilagi	18
Semo Sititi	17
Afato So'oialo	15
To'o Vaega	15

LEADING DROP GOAL SCORERS

Name	DGs
Darren Kellet	2
Roger Warren	2
Steve Bachop	2
Tusi Pisi	2

LEADING CONVERSIONS SCORERS

Name	Cons
Andy Aiolupo	35
Earl Va'a	33
Silao Leaega	26
Tanner Vili	21
Gavin Williams	18

LEADING POINTS SCORERS

Name	Points
Earl Va'a	184
Andy Aiolupo	178
Tusi Pisi	174
Silao Leaega	160
Darren Kellett	155

SAMOA INTERNATIONAL PLAYERS
UP TO 1 NOVEMBER, 2015

A'ati 1932 *Tg*
F Afamasaga 2015 *NZ, US, C, Fj*
V Afatia 2012 *Tg, C, 2013 I, 2014 It, C, E, 2015 NZ, US, Fj, C, Fj, SA, J, S*
V Afemai 2014 *J, It, 2015 US, C, Fj, SA, J, S*
JT Afoa 2010 *Tg, J*
Agnew 1924 *Fj, Fj*
S Ah Fook 1947 *Tg*
F Ah Long 1955 *Fj*
Ah Mu 1932 *Tg*
F Aima'asu 1981 *Fj, 1982 Fj, Fj, Fj, Tg, 1988 Tg, Fj*
AA Aiolupo 1983 *Tg, 1984 Fj, Tg, 1985 Fj, Tg, Tg, 1986 W, Fj, Tg, 1987 Fj, Tg, 1988 Tg, Fj, I, W, 1989 Fj, WGe, Bel, R, 1990 Kor, Tg, J, Tg, Fj, 1991 W, A, Ar, S, 1992 Fj, Fj, 1993 Tg, Fj, NZ, 1994 Tg, W, Fj, A*
A Aiono 2009 *PNG, 2010 J, I, E, S, 2011 Tg, 2012 Tg, S*
Aitofele 1924 *Fj, Fj*
P Alalatoa 1986 *W*
V Alalatoa 1988 *I, W, 1989 Fj, 1991 Tg, W, A, Ar, S, 1992 Tg, Fj*
P Alauni 2009 *PNG*
R Ale 1997 *Tg, Fj, 1999 J, Ar, W, S*
T Aleni 1982 *Tg, 1983 Tg, 1985 Tg, 1986 W, Fj, Tg, 1987 Fj*
S Alesana 1979 *Fj, 1980 Tg, 1981 Fj, Fj, 1982 Fj, Tg, 1983 Tg, Fj, 1984 Fj, Tg, 1985 Fj, Tg*
T Allen 1924 *Fj, Fj*
A Alofa 2014 *C, 2015 NZ, Fj*
K Anufe 2009 *Tg, 2012 Tg, Fj, J, F, 2013 It*

L Aoelua 2008 *NZ*
T Aoese 1981 *Fj, Fj, 1982 Fj, Fj, Fj, Tg, 1983 Tg*
J Apelu 1985 *Tg*
F Asi 1975 *Tg*
F Asi 1963 *Fj, Fj, Tg*
SP Asi 1999 *S, 2000 Fj, J, Tg, C, It, US, W, S, 2001 Tg, Fj, NZ, Fj, Tg, Fj*
L Asi 2010 *J*
Atiga 1924 *Fj*
S Ati'ifale 1979 *Tg, 1980 Tg, 1981 Fj, Fj*
J Atoa 1975 *Tg, 1981 Fj*
F Autagavaia 2012 *Tg, Fj, J, S, C, W, 2013 I, Geo, 2014 Tg, It, Fj, It, C, 2015 US, Fj, Fj, US, S*
WO Avei 2011 *J, Tg, SA, 2012 Tg, Fj, J, S, C, W, F, 2013 S, It, SA, I, Geo, 2014 Tg, It, Fj, It, C, 2015 NZ, US, SA, J*

SJ Bachop 1991 *Tg, Fj, W, A, Ar, S, 1998 Tg, Fj, 1999 J, C, F, NZ, US, Fj, J, Ar, W, S*
C Betham 1955 *Fj*
ML Birtwistle 1991 *Fj, W, A, Ar, S, 1993 Fj, NZ, 1994 Tg, W, Fj, A, 1996 I*
W Brame 2009 *J, Fj*
FE Bunce 1991 *W, A, Ar, S*

CH Capper 1924 *Fj*
J Cavanagh 1955 *Fj, Fj, Fj*
J Clarke 1997 *Tg, 1998 A, 1999 US, Fj, J*

Tg, SA, 2003 I, Nm, Ur, Geo, E, SA, 2004 Tg, S, 2005 A, Tg, Fj, Tg, Fj
Panapa 1932 Tg
P Papali'l 1924 Fj, Fj
M Papali'l 1955 Fj, Fj
PJ Paramore 1991 Tg, Fj, A, 1992 Fj, 1994 Tg, 1995 SA, It, Ar, SA, Fj, Tg, 1996 I, 1997 Tg, Fj, 1998 Tg, Fj, A, 1999 J, Ar, W, 2001 Tg, Fj, NZ, Fj, Tg, J, Fj
J Parkinson 2005 A, Tg
T Pati 1997 Tg
M Patolo 1986 W, Fj, Tg
T Patu 1979 Tg, Fj, 1980 Tg, 1981 Fj, Fj
O Patu 1980 Tg
HV Patu 1995 S, E, 1996 I, 2000 W, S
P Paul 1955 Fj, Fj
M Paulino 2008 NZ, 2010 J, 2012 Tg, Fj, 2014 J, 2015 US, C
P Paulo 1989 Bel, 1990 Tg, Fj
T Paulo 2012 C, W, F, 2013 S, It, SA, I, Geo, 2014 Tg, Fj, It, C, E, 2015 NZ, US, Fj, C, Fj, US, SA, J, S
T Paulo 2010 E, S, 2011 J, Fj, Tg, A, Nm, W, Fj, 2012 J, S, W, F, 2013 It, SA, I, Geo, 2014 Tg, It, Fj, It, E
A Perelini 1991 Tg, Fj, W, A, Ar, S, 1992 Tg, Fj, 1993 NZ
AI Perenise 2010 Tg, J, Fj, J, I, E, S, 2011 J, Fj, A, Nm, W, Fj, SA, 2013 Geo, 2014 Tg, It, C, E, 2015 NZ, US, Fj, C, Fj, US, SA, J, S
PL Perez 2012 Tg, Fj, J, S, C, W, F, 2015 NZ, US, Fj, C, US, SA, J, S
S Perez 1963 Fj, Fj, Tg
MS Pesamino 2009 PNG, PNG, 2010 Tg, J, Fj, J
N Petaia 1963 Fj
Petelo 1932 Tg
T Petelo 1985 Fj
P Petia 2003 Nm
O Pifeleti 1987 Fj
K Pisi 2012 Tg, Fj, 2013 Geo, 2014 It, E, 2015 NZ, US, SA, J, S
TG Pisi 2010 Tg, Fj, I, E, S, 2011 J, A, Nm, W, Fj, 2012 C, W, F, 2013 I, 2014 Tg, It, Fj, It, 2015 SA, S
T Pisi 2011 J, Fj, A, Nm, Fj, SA, 2012 S, C, W, F, 2013 S, It, SA, I, Geo, 2014 Tg, It, Fj, It, E, 2015 NZ, US, SA, J, S
S Po Ching 1990 Kor, Tg, 1991 Tg
S Poching 2000 W, S, 2001 Tg
AJ Poluleuligaga 2007 SA, J, Tg, SA, Tg, E, US, 2008 NZ, 2009 J, Tg, Fj, W, F, It, 2010 Tg, J, I, E, 2011 Nm, 2013 It, SA
HA Porter 2011 Tg
P Poulos 2003 Ur, Geo, E, SA
E Puleitu 1995 SA, E
S Punivalu 1981 Fj, 1982 Fj, Fj, 1983 Tg, Fj
JEP Purdie 2007 Fj, SA, J, Tg, SA, Tg, E, US

I Railey 1924 Fj, Fj
D Rasmussen 2003 I, Ur, Geo, E, SA, 2004 Tg, S, Fj
R Rasmussen 1997 Tg
B Reidy 1995 SA, Fj, Tg, 1996 NZ, Tg, Fj, I, 1998 Fj, A, 1999 Tg, F, NZ, US, Fj, J, Ar, W, S
K Roberts 1972 Tg
F Ropati 1982 Fj, Fj, Fj, 1984 Fj, Tg
R Ropati 2003 SA, 2008 NZ
W Ryan 1983 Fj, 1985 Tg

S Sa 2012 C
E Sa'aga 1924 Fj, Fj, 1932 Tg
PD Saena 1988 Tg, Fj, I, 1989 Fj, Bel, R, 1990 Kor, Tg, J, Tg, Fj, 1991 Tg, Fj, 1992 Tg, Fj, 1993 Tg, Fj
L Sagaga 1963 Fj, Tg
K Saifoloi 1979 Tg, Fj, 1980 Tg, 1982 Fj, Fj, 1984 Fj, Tg
P Saili 1957 Tg, Tg
M Salanoa 2005 Tg, Fj, 2006 J, Fj, Tg, 2007 Fj, SA, J, Tg, Tg
M Salavea 2010 Tg, Fj, I, E, S, 2011 J, Tg, A, W, Fj
T Salesa 1979 Tg, Fj, 1980 Tg, 1981 Fj, Fj, 1982 Fj, Fj, Fj, Tg, 1983 Tg, Fj, Fj, 1984 Tg, 1985 Fj, Tg, 1986 Tg, 1987 Fj, Tg, 1988 Tg, Fj, I, 1989 Fj, WGe, R
G Salima 2008 Fj
T Samania 1994 W, Fj, A, 1996 NZ, 2000 Fj, J, C, It, 2001 Tg
D Sanft 2006 J
Q Sanft 2000 W, S
L Sasi 1982 Fj, Tg, 1983 Tg, Fj, 1984 Fj, Tg, 1985 Tg, 1986 W, Fj, Tg, 1987 Fj, Tg, 1988 Tg, Fj
B Sasulu 2008 Fj
FI Saufoi 2015 C
S Sauila 1989 Bel
L Savai'inaea 1957 Tg, Tg

J Schaafhausen 1947 Tg
W Schaafhausen 1947 Tg
P Schmidt 1980 Tg, 1985 Tg
P Schmidt 1989 Fj, WGe
R Schmidt 1979 Tg, 1980 Tg
D Schuster 1982 Tg, 1983 Tg, Fj, Fj
H Schuster 1989 Fj, 1990 Kor, Tg, J
J Schuster 1985 Fj, Fj, Tg
NSJ Schuster 1999 Tg, F, US
M Schuster 2000 S, 2004 Tg, S, Fj
P Schuster 1975 Tg
M Schwalger 2000 W, S, 2001 It, 2003 Nm, Ur, Geo, E, 2005 S, E, Ar, 2006 J, Tg, 2007 Fj, SA, Tg, SA, Tg, E, US, 2008 Fj, 2009 J, Tg, Fj, PNG, W, F, It, 2010 Tg, J, Fj, I, E, S, 2011 Fj, A, Nm, W, Fj, SA
Sefo 1932 Tg
E Sefo 1984 Fj
T Sefo 1987 Tg, 1988 I
P Segi 2001 Fj, NZ, Fj, Tg, J, I, It, 2002 Tg, Fj, Fj, Tg
K Seinafo 1992 Tg
F Seselele 2010 Tg, J, J, 2014 J
S Semeane 2009 It
J Senio 2004 Tg, S, Fj, 2005 Tg, Fj, Tg, Fj, 2006 J, Fj, Tg
U Setu 2010 Tg, J
T Seumanutafa 1981 Fj
E Seveali'i 2000 Fj, J, Tg, C, 2001 Tg, NZ, J, Fj, It, 2002 Fj, Tg, Fj, Tg, SA, 2005 E, 2007 SA, J, Tg, SA, Tg, US
F Sililoto 1980 Tg, 1981 Fj, Fj, 1982 Fj, Fj, Fj
Simanu 1932 Tg
A Simanu 1975 Tg, 1981 Fj
V Simanu 2014 J
Sinaumea 1924 Tg
F Sini 1995 SA, Ar, E, SA
S Sinoti 2010 J, 2013 Geo, 2015 US, C, Fj
A Sio 2014 J
T Sio 1990 Tg, 1992 Fj
K Sio 1988 Tg, Fj, I, W, 1989 Fj, WGe, R, 1990 J, Tg, Fj, 1992 Tg, Fj, 1993 NZ, 1994 Tg
P Sioa 1981 Fj, Fj
S Sititi 1999 J, C, F, J, W, S, 2000 Fj, J, Tg, C, US, 2001 Tg, Fj, NZ, Fj, Tg, J, Fj, I, It, 2002 Fj, Tg, Fj, Tg, SA, 2003 I, Nm, Ur, Geo, E, SA, 2004 Tg, S, Fj, 2005 A, Tg, Fj, S, E, Ar, 2006 J, Fj, Tg, 2007 Fj, SA, J, Tg, SA, Tg, E, US, 2008 Fj, Tg, J, NZ, 2009 J, PNG, PNG
F Siu 1975 Tg
P Siu 1963 Fj, Fj, Tg
S Skelton 1982 Fj
E Skelton 2009 J, Tg, PNG, PNG
R Slade 1972 Tg
C Slade 2006 J, Fj, Tg, 2008 Fj, Tg, NZ
S Smith 1995 S, E, 1996 Tg, Fj, 1999 C, Tg, F, NZ
P Solia 1955 Fj, Fj
I Solipo 1981 Fj
F Solomona 1985 Tg
JS Sooialo 2011 J, Fj, Tg, W, 2012 C, 2013 S, SA
A So'oialo 1996 I, 1997 Tg, Fj, 1998 Tg, 1999 Tg, F, NZ, US, Fj, J, Ar, 2000 Tg, It, 2001 Tg, Fj, NZ, Fj, Tg, J, I
S So'oialo 1998 Tg, Fj, 1999 NZ, US, Fj, J, Ar, W, S, 2000 W, S, 2001 Tg, Fj, NZ, Fj, J, Fj, I, 2002 Tg, Fj, Tg, SA, 2003 I, Nm, Ur, Geo, E, SA, 2004 Tg, S, Fj, 2005 E, 2007 Fj, SA, J, Tg, E, US
F So'olefai 1999 C, Tg, 2000 W, S, 2001 Tg, Fj, NZ, Fj, J
MJ Stanley 2014 It, C, E, 2015 Fj, C, Fj, US, SA
WTN Stanley 2014 It, C
V Stet 1963 Fj
A Stewart 2005 A, Tg
G Stowers 2001 I, 2008 Fj, Tg, J, NZ, 2009 J, Tg, Fj, PNG, W, It, 2010 Fj, J, I, E, S, 2011 Fj, A, Nm, W, Fj, SA
R Stowers 2008 Fj
F Sua 1982 Fj, Fj, Tg, 1983 Tg, Fj, 1984 Fj, 1985 Fj, Tg, Tg, 1986 Fj, Tg, 1987 Fj
JI Sua 2011 W, Fj, 2012 Tg, Fj, J, S, C, W, F, 2013 S, It, SA, I, Geo, 2014 Tg
P Swepson 1957 Tg

S Ta'ala 1996 Tg, Fj, I, 1997 Tg, Fj, 1998 Tg, Fj, A, 1999 J, C, Tg, US, Fj, J, Ar, W, S, 2001 J
T Taega 1997 Fj
PI Taele 2005 Tg, Fj, E, Ar, 2006 J, Fj, Tg, 2010 J
D Tafeamalii 2000 W, S

SCOTLAND

SCOTLAND'S 2014–15 TEST RECORD

OPPONENTS	DATE	VENUE	RESULT
Argentina	8 Nov	H	Won 41–31
New Zealand	15 Nov	H	Lost 16–24
Tonga	22 Nov	H	Won 37–12
France	7 Feb	A	Lost 15–8
Wales	15 Feb	H	Lost 23–26
Italy	28 Feb	H	Lost 19–22
England	14 Mar	A	Lost 25–13
Ireland	21 Mar	H	Lost 10–40
Ireland	15 Aug	A	Lost 28–22
Italy	22 Aug	A	Won 16–12
Italy	29 Aug	H	Won 48–7
France	5 Sep	A	Lost 19–16
Japan	23 Sep	N	Won 45–10
USA	27 Sep	N	Won 39–16
South Africa	3 Oct	N	Lost 34–16
Samoa	10 Oct	N	Won 36–33
Australia	18 Oct	N	Lost 35–34

BRAVE SCOTS SUFFER QUARTER-FINAL HEARTBREAK

By Iain Spragg

Winger Tommy Seymour holds off Australia's Michael Hooper to score a try in the quarter-final at Twickenham.

A **record of** two wins in 10 matches in 2015 would not have had many Scotland fans predicting a Rugby World Cup semi-final appearance before the tournament began, even if the squad had started to show some positive signs in their warm-up matches with two victories over Italy and narrow losses away to Ireland and France.

However, having safely negotiated a tough Pool B to qualify for the quarter-finals as runners-up behind South Africa, Scotland arrived at Twickenham in confident mood, determined to prove the encounter with Australia was not going to be the one-sided procession into the last four for the Wallabies that many people expected.

Twenty-four years had passed since Scotland's only previous appearance in a Rugby World Cup semi-final – when they lost to England in 1991 – and they looked on course to end that long wait when they hit the front in the dying minutes after Mark Bennett's intercept and run in for a try in the driving rain.

There was, however, to be one final twist to Scotland's dismay as Australia were awarded a 79th-minute penalty by referee Craig Joubert after he adjudged that replacement prop Jon Welsh had played the ball in an offside position from a knock-on by team-mate John Hardie. While replays showed that Wallaby scrum-half Nick Phipps had touched the ball, a contact that would have meant a scrum to Australia and not a penalty, the laws of the game meant that Joubert was unable to refer the matter to the television match official and his decision stood.

Foley stepped forward to kick the penalty and seal a dramatic 35–34 triumph for Australia to end Scotland's World Cup adventure. World Rugby later confirmed the decision to award the penalty had been incorrect, but that was scant consolation for Cotter after the way his side had performed against the Wallabies. "It's a tough one to take and I feel sorry for the group of players that have come off the field," Cotter said. "They came very close, put in a great performance, so I feel for them and, when the emotion's gone, we'll sit back and analyse it. They never let go and fought the whole way and it's fine margins, isn't it? They put this team, who were favourites for the tournament, under pressure.

"This will make them better and more confident. They did believe throughout the game and we nearly got there. They threw everything at it, absolutely. It was a brave performance. They showed courage, character and, most of all, they showed belief. That'll get lodged into the hard drives and hopefully that'll prepare us for the next time we have to put the jersey on."

Scotland's 12-month build-up to RWC 2015 did not in truth offer extravagant evidence that, in Cotter's first full season at the helm, they would be genuine semi-final contenders.

A 41–31 success against Argentina at the start of the November series, Cotter's first game at Murrayfield, was certainly a notable result while his side were nothing if not pugnacious in their narrow 24–16 defeat to the All Blacks in Edinburgh a week later, but it was Scotland's ultimately disappointing displays in the RBS 6 Nations which suggested a World Cup semi-final appearance was beyond the team and a more realistic prospect was another exit in the pool stages as in 2011.

Scotland began the Six Nations against France in Paris in February and the match would follow a pattern that repeated itself throughout much of the Championship as the side gained parity for long phases only to ultimately find themselves on the wrong end of a close final scoreline.

Cotter's side scored the only try of the match in the Stade de France through replacement winger Dougie Fife but were beaten 15–8 by Les Bleus and it was a similar tale of what might have been eight days later when Wales were the visitors to Murrayfield and Scotland slipped to a frustrating 26–23 defeat.

That frustration began to border on dismay in round three when Italy emerged 22–19 winners in Edinburgh after the award of a 79th-minute penalty try and although Cotter's troops were admirably combative against England at Twickenham in March, they could not deny their hosts a 25–13 win.

Scotland's only heavy defeat came in their final fixture as defending champions Ireland cut loose at Murrayfield to secure the title on points difference, the visitors outscoring the Scots four tries to one in a 40–10 triumph which condemned Cotter's team to the Wooden Spoon for a fourth time since the inception of the Six Nations in 2000.

"We've got to address a fair few things in our game before we make ourselves a true threat," Cotter said afterwards. "We need a mindset change and we'll have to work towards that and become more efficient. We've got to take silly errors out of our game, learn to keep ball and apply pressure. These are things that were brought home with brutal clarity today. We know we can do it, so let's develop that, that's our building programme, our process of applying pressure. Let's continue it. Take away unforced errors, possessions lost – those are things we need to look at."

Scotland exacted a degree of revenge for their Six Nations woes by defeating Italy home and away in warm-up games in August but defeats on the road to Ireland and France suggested the team was still very much a work in progress and as the World Cup approached, the mood which pervaded the camp was one more of hope than serious expectation.

The team began the tournament against a Japanese side buoyed by their remarkable victory over South Africa in their own Pool B opener, the greatest upset in RWC history, but the Scots ensured there was not to be a second famous scalp for the Brave Blossoms, centre Bennett going over for two of five tries in Gloucester to secure a convincing 45–10 win.

Four days later they backed up what was an encouraging start with a 39–16 success against the USA in Leeds and although Cotter's team were eventually outmuscled by the Springboks in Newcastle, succumbing to a 34–16 defeat, their fate still lay in their own hands and victory over Samoa in their last Pool B assignment would send them through to the quarter-finals.

It proved to be a titanic tussle with the Pacific Islanders at St James'

Park and it was the contribution of captain Greig Laidlaw that was decisive, the scrum-half scoring a crucial 73rd-minute try to complement his five penalties and three conversions and wrap up a 36–33 success.

The build-up to their quarter-final with the Wallabies was somewhat overshadowed by the three-week suspensions handed to hooker Ross Ford and second-row Jonny Gray but Scotland appealed, they were reprieved on the eve of the match and Cotter was able to include both players in his starting XV.

The match began at a breakneck pace at Twickenham and it was Australia who struck first when Adam Ashley-Cooper went over in the eighth minute but Scotland responded in the 17th minute with a Peter Horne try and although the Wallabies were the next to cross the whitewash, Drew Mitchell scoring on the half hour followed by Michael Hooper for a third, Scotland went in at half-time with a precarious 16–15 advantage.

The tries continued to flow in the second period. Mitchell got his second of the contest just two minutes after the restart, only for Tommy Seymour to drag Scotland back to within a point of the Australians. But when Tevita Kuridrani crashed over in the 63rd minute to make it 32–24 to the Wallabies, Scotland's brave resistance appeared to have been overcome.

Cotter's side had other ideas, as did the weather as the rain fell, and when Bennett intercepted a wayward pass with only seven minutes to play it was suddenly 34–32 in the Scots' favour and a semi-final spot was in sight.

In the end, however, Scotland paid the ultimate price for a scrappy lineout just outside their own 22 in the dying seconds, an uncontrolled tap down creating panic in the ranks which led to Hardie's touch and Welsh's involuntary, instinctive take. Joubert's subsequent whistle was greeted by despair from the Scotland players and Foley proceeded to deliver the cruellest of finales.

"That is probably the toughest defeat I have ever had to take," Laidlaw admitted after the match. "We put so much into the game for 80 minutes. I am gutted to lose and to lose in that manner as well. It's a very upset dressing room as you can imagine. We've made big strides since the Six Nations. We were one kick away from being in the semi-finals and arguably we should have been there.

"Now is not the time to move forward, we need to get over this disappointment first but we've got the makings of a strong team. The spirit of our side is unbreakable at times and that's the spirit we've had throughout the tournament. We're a tight-knit group and there are no egos. Every man works as hard as the next."

SCOTLAND INTERNATIONAL STATISTICS

MATCH RECORDS UP TO 1 NOVEMBER, 2015

MOST CONSECUTIVE TEST WINS

6	1925 F, W, I, E, 1926 F, W
6	1989 Fj ,R, 1990 I, F, W, E

MOST CONSECUTIVE TESTS WITHOUT DEFEAT

Matches	Wins	Draws	Period
9	6*	3	1885 to 1887
6	6	0	1925 to 1926
6	6	0	1989 to 1990
6	4	2	1877 to 1880
6	5	1	1983 to 1984

* includes an abandoned match

MOST POINTS IN A MATCH
BY THE TEAM

Pts	Opponents	Venue	Year
100	Japan	Perth	2004
89	Ivory Coast	Rustenburg	1995
65	United States	San Francisco	2002
60	Zimbabwe	Wellington	1987
60	Romania	Hampden Park	1999
56	Portugal	Saint Etienne	2007
55	Romania	Dunedin	1987
53	United States	Murrayfield	2000
51	Zimbabwe	Murrayfield	1991
49	Argentina	Murrayfield	1990
49	Romania	Murrayfield	1995

BY A PLAYER

Pts	Player	Opponents	Venue	Year
44	AG Hastings	Ivory Coast	Rustenburg	1995
40	CD Paterson	Japan	Perth	2004
33	GPJ Townsend	United States	Murrayfield	2000
31	AG Hastings	Tonga	Pretoria	1995
27	AG Hastings	Romania	Dunedin	1987
26	KM Logan	Romania	Hampden Park	1999
26	GD Laidlaw	Samoa	Newcastle	2015
24	BJ Laney	Italy	Rome	2002
24	DA Parks	Argentina	Tucumán	2010
23	G Ross	Tonga	Murrayfield	2001
22	GD Laidlaw	Fiji	Lautoka	2012
21	AG Hastings	England	Murrayfield	1986
21	AG Hastings	Romania	Bucharest	1986
21	CD Paterson	Wales	Murrayfield	2007
21	DA Parks	South Africa	Murrayfield	2010

MOST TRIES IN A MATCH
BY THE TEAM

Tries	Opponents	Venue	Year
15	Japan	Perth	2004
13	Ivory Coast	Rustenburg	1995
12	Wales	Raeburn Place	1887
11	Zimbabwe	Wellington	1987
10	United States	San Francisco	2002
9	Romania	Dunedin	1987
9	Argentina	Murrayfield	1990

BY A PLAYER

Tries	Player	Opponents	Venue	Year
5	GC Lindsay	Wales	Raeburn Place	1887
4	WA Stewart	Ireland	Inverleith	1913
4	IS Smith	France	Inverleith	1925
4	IS Smith	Wales	Swansea	1925
4	AG Hastings	Ivory Coast	Rustenburg	1995

MOST CONVERSIONS IN A MATCH
BY THE TEAM

Cons	Opponents	Venue	Year
11	Japan	Perth	2004
9	Ivory Coast	Rustenburg	1995
8	Zimbabwe	Wellington	1987
8	Romania	Dunedin	1987
8	Portugal	Saint Etienne	2007

BY A PLAYER

Cons	Player	Opponents	Venue	Year
11	CD Paterson	Japan	Perth	2004
9	AG Hastings	Ivory Coast	Rustenburg	1995
8	AG Hastings	Zimbabwe	Wellington	1987
8	AG Hastings	Romania	Dunedin	1987

MOST PENALTIES IN A MATCH
BY THE TEAM

Penalties	Opponents	Venue	Year
8	Tonga	Pretoria	1995
7	Wales	Murrayfield	2007
6	France	Murrayfield	1986
6	Italy	Murrayfield	2005
6	Ireland	Murrayfield	2007
6	Italy	Saint Etienne	2007
6	Argentina	Tucumán	2010
6	South Africa	Murrayfield	2010
6	Wales	Murrayfield	2013

BY A PLAYER

Pens	Player	Opponents	Venue	Year
8	AG Hastings	Tonga	Pretoria	1995
7	CD Paterson	Wales	Murrayfield	2007
6	AG Hastings	France	Murrayfield	1986
6	CD Paterson	Italy	Murrayfield	2005
6	CD Paterson	Ireland	Murrayfield	2007
6	CD Paterson	Italy	Saint Etienne	2007
6	DA Parks	Argentina	Tucumán	2010
6	DA Parks	South Africa	Murrayfield	2010
6	GD Laidlaw	Wales	Murrayfield	2013

MOST DROP GOALS IN A MATCH
BY THE TEAM

Drops	Opponents	Venue	Year
3	Ireland	Murrayfield	1973
	2 on several occasions		

BY A PLAYER

Drops	Player	Opponents	Venue	Year
2	RC MacKenzie	Ireland	Belfast	1877
2	NJ Finlay	Ireland	Glasgow	1880
2	BM Simmers	Wales	Murrayfield	1965
2	DW Morgan	Ireland	Murrayfield	1973
2	BM Gossman	France	Parc des Princes	1983
2	JY Rutherford	New Zealand	Murrayfield	1983
2	JY Rutherford	Wales	Murrayfield	1985
2	JY Rutherford	Ireland	Murrayfield	1987
2	CM Chalmers	England	Twickenham	1995
2	DA Parks	Wales	Cardiff	2010
2	DA Parks	Argentina	Tucumán	2010

CAREER RECORDS

MOST CAPPED PLAYERS

Caps	Player	Career Span
109	CD Paterson	1999 to 2011
101	SF Lamont	2004 to 2015
94	RW Ford	2004 to 2015
87	S Murray	1997 to 2007
85	MRL Blair	2002 to 2012
82	GPJ Townsend	1993 to 2003
77	JPR White	2000 to 2009
77	NJ Hines	2000 to 2011
75	GC Bulloch	1997 to 2005
71	SB Grimes	1997 to 2005
70	KM Logan	1992 to 2003
70	CP Cusiter	2004 to 2014
67	DA Parks	2004 to 2012
66	SM Taylor	2000 to 2009
66	EA Murray	2005 to 2015
65	S Hastings	1986 to 1997
65	AF Jacobsen	2002 to 2012

MOST CONSECUTIVE TESTS

Tests	Player	Span
49	AB Carmichael	1967 to 1978
44	CD Paterson	2004 to 2008
40	HF McLeod	1954 to 1962
37	JM Bannerman	1921 to 1929
35	AG Stanger	1989 to 1994

MOST TESTS AS CAPTAIN

Tests	Captain	Span
25	DMB Sole	1989 to 1992
21	BW Redpath	1998 to 2003
21	GD Laidlaw	2013 to 2015
20	AG Hastings	1993 to 1995
19	J McLauchlan	1973 to 1979
19	JPR White	2005 to 2008
16	RI Wainwright	1995 to 1998
15	MC Morrison	1899 to 1904
15	AR Smith	1957 to 1962
15	AR Irvine	1980 to 1982

MOST POINTS IN TESTS

Points	Player	Tests	Career
809	CD Paterson	109	1999 to 2011
667	AG Hastings	61	1986 to 1995
446	GD Laidlaw	46	2010 to 2015
273	AR Irvine	51	1972 to 1982
266	DA Parks	67	2004 to 2012
220	KM Logan	70	1992 to 2003
210	PW Dods	23	1983 to 1991
166	CM Chalmers	60	1989 to 1999
164	GPJ Townsend	82	1993 to 2003
141	BJ Laney	20	2001 to 2004
123	DW Hodge	26	1997 to 2002
106	AG Stanger	52	1989 to 1998

SCOTLAND

MOST TRIES IN TESTS

Tries	Player	Tests	Career
24	IS Smith	32	1924 to 1933
24	AG Stanger	52	1989 to 1998
22	CD Paterson	109	1999 to 2011
17	AG Hastings	61	1986 to 1995
17	AV Tait	27	1987 to 1999
17	GPJ Townsend	82	1993 to 2003
15	I Tukalo	37	1985 to 1992
14	SF Lamont	101	2004 to 2015
13	KM Logan	70	1992 to 2003
12	AR Smith	33	1955 to 1962

MOST PENALTY GOALS IN TESTS

Penalties	Player	Tests	Career
170	CD Paterson	109	1999 to 2011
140	AG Hastings	61	1986 to 1995
104	GD Laidlaw	46	2010 to 2015
61	AR Irvine	51	1972 to 1982
55	DA Parks	67	2004 to 2012
50	PW Dods	23	1983 to 1991
32	CM Chalmers	60	1989 to 1999
29	KM Logan	70	1992 to 2003
29	BJ Laney	20	2001 to 2004
21	M Dods	8	1994 to 1996
21	RJS Shepherd	20	1995 to 1998

MOST CONVERSIONS IN TESTS

Cons	Player	Tests	Career
90	CD Paterson	109	1999 to 2011
86	AG Hastings	61	1986 to 1995
57	GD Laidlaw	46	2010 to 2015
34	KM Logan	70	1992 to 2003
26	PW Dods	23	1983 to 1991
25	AR Irvine	51	1972 to 1982
19	D Drysdale	26	1923 to 1929
17	BJ Laney	20	2001 to 2004
15	DW Hodge	26	1997 to 2002
15	DA Parks	67	2004 to 2012
14	FH Turner	15	1911 to 1914
14	RJS Shepherd	20	1995 to 1998

MOST DROP GOALS IN TESTS

Drops	Player	Tests	Career
17	DA Parks	67	2004 to 2012
12	JY Rutherford	42	1979 to 1987
9	CM Chalmers	60	1989 to 1999
7	IR McGeechan	32	1972 to 1979
7	GPJ Townsend	82	1993 to 2003
6	DW Morgan	21	1973 to 1978
5	H Waddell	15	1924 to 1930

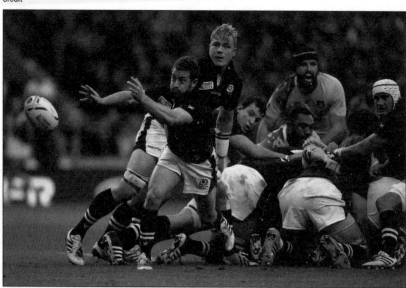

Scotland captain and scrum-half Greig Laidlaw was nominated for the World Rugby Player of the Year 2015 award.

RECORD	DETAIL	HOLDER	SET
Most points in season	120	in four matches	1999
Most tries in season	17	in four matches	1925
Highest score	38	38–10 v Ireland	1997
Biggest win	28	31–3 v France	1912
	28	38–10 v Ireland	1997
Highest score conceded	51	16–51 v France	1998
	51	3–51 v Wales	2014
Biggest defeat	48	3–51 v Wales	2014
Most appearances	53	CD Paterson	2000–2011
Most points in matches	403	CD Paterson	2000–2011
Most points in season	65	CD Paterson	2007
Most points in match	24	BJ Laney	v Italy, 2002
Most tries in matches	24	IS Smith	1924–1933
Most tries in season	8	IS Smith	1925
Most tries in match	5	GC Lindsay	v Wales, 1887
Most cons in matches	34	CD Paterson	2000–2011
Most cons in season	11	KM Logan	1999
Most cons in match	5	FH Turner	v France, 1912
	5	JW Allan	v England, 1931
	5	RJS Shepherd	v Ireland, 1997
Most pens in matches	99	CD Paterson	2000–2011
Most pens in season	17	GD Laidlaw	2013
Most pens in match	7	CD Paterson	v Wales, 2007
Most drops in matches	9	DA Parks	2004–2012
Most drops in season	5	DA Parks	2010
Most drops in match	2	on several occasions	

MISCELLANEOUS RECORDS

RECORD	HOLDER	DETAIL
Longest Test Career	WCW Murdoch	1935 to 1948
Youngest Test Cap	NJ Finlay	17 yrs 36 days in 1875*
Oldest Test Cap	J McLauchlan	37 yrs 210 days in 1979

* C Reid, also 17 yrs 36 days on debut in 1881, was a day older than Finlay, having lived through an extra leap-year day.

CAREER RECORDS OF SCOTLAND INTERNATIONAL PLAYERS

UP TO 1 NOVEMBER, 2015

PLAYER	DEBUT	CAPS	T	C	P	D	PTS
BACKS :							
MS Bennett	2014 v Arg	13	6	0	0	0	30
CP Cusiter	2004 v W	70	3	0	0	0	15
AJ Dunbar	2013 v Sm	14	4	0	0	0	20
DJ Fife	2014 v W	6	1	0	0	0	5
SP Hidalgo-Clyne	2015 v F	8	0	0	0	0	0
SW Hogg	2012 v W	38	9	0	2	0	51
P Horne	2013 v Sm	15	2	1	1	0	15
DN Hoyland	2015 v It	1	0	0	0	0	0
RC Hughes	2015 v It	1	0	0	0	0	0
RJH Jackson	2010 v NZ	27	0	4	2	2	20
GD Laidlaw	2010 v NZ	46	4	57	104	0	446
SF Lamont	2004 v Sm	101	14	0	0	0	70
SD Maitland	2013 v E	20	3	0	0	0	15
HB Pyrgos	2012 v NZ	17	4	0	0	0	20
FA Russell	2014 v US	15	2	3	1	0	19
MCM Scott	2012 v I	33	4	0	0	0	20
TSF Seymour	2013 v SA	22	11	0	0	0	55
DM Taylor	2013 v Sm	12	0	0	0	0	0
GA Tonks	2013 v Sm	6	0	0	0	0	0
RJ Vernon	2009 v Fj	24	0	0	0	0	0
TJW Visser	2012 v Fj	23	10	0	0	0	50
D Weir	2012 v F	21	2	6	10	1	55
FORWARDS :							
A Ashe	2014 v SA	6	0	0	0	0	0
JA Barclay	2007 v NZ	45	3	0	0	0	15
JW Beattie	2006 v R	38	3	0	0	0	15
HP Blake	2015 v I	1	0	0	0	0	0
FJM Brown	2013 v It	15	0	0	0	0	0
K Bryce	2014 v C	3	0	0	0	0	0
BA Cowan	2014 v US	15	2	0	0	0	10
GDS Cross	2009 v W	40	2	0	0	0	10
MPT Cusack	2015 v I	2	0	0	0	0	0
DK Denton	2011 v I	32	0	0	0	0	0

AG Dickinson	2007 v NZ	52	2	0	0	0	10
RW Ford	2004 v A	94	2	0	0	0	10
GS Gilchrist	2013 v F	12	1	0	0	0	5
R Grant	2012 v A	25	0	0	0	0	0
JD Gray	2013 v SA	19	1	0	0	0	5
RJ Gray	2010 v F	51	2	0	0	0	10
JL Hamilton	2006 v R	63	1	0	0	0	5
JI Hardie	2015 v It	5	2	0	0	0	10
RJ Harley	2012 v Sm	17	1	0	0	0	5
S Lawson	2005 v R	46	2	0	0	0	10
K Low	2013 v A	5	0	0	0	0	0
S McInally	2015 v It	2	0	0	0	0	0
EA Murray	2005 v R	66	2	0	0	0	10
WP Nel	2015 v It	8	1	0	0	0	5
GJ Reid	2014 v US	15	0	0	0	0	0
JZ Strauss	2015 v J	5	0	0	0	0	0
AK Strokosch	2006 v A	47	2	0	0	0	10
TJM Swinson	2013 v SA	17	0	0	0	0	0
B Toolis	2015 v It	1	0	0	0	0	0
HFW Watson	2015 v It	2	0	0	0	0	0
JS Welsh	2012 v It	11	1	0	0	0	5
R Wilson	2013 v W	15	0	0	0	0	0

SCOTLAND INTERNATIONAL PLAYERS
UP TO 1 NOVEMBER, 2015

Note: Years given for International Championship matches are for second half of season; eg 1972 means season 1971–72. Years for all other matches refer to the actual year of the match. Entries in square brackets denote matches played in RWC Finals.

Abercrombie, C H (United Services) 1910 I, E, 1911 F, W, 1913 F, W

Abercrombie, J G (Edinburgh U) 1949 F, W, I, 1950 F, W, I, E

Agnew, W C (Stewart's Coll FP) 1930 W, I

Ainslie, R (Edinburgh Inst FP) 1879 I, E, 1880 I, E, 1881 E, 1882 I, E

Ainslie, T (Edinburgh Inst FP) 1881 E, 1882 I, E, 1883 W, I, E, 1884 W, I, E, 1885 W, I 1, 2

Aitchison, G R (Edinburgh Wands) 1883 I

Aitchison, T G (Gala) 1929 W, I, E

Aitken, A I (Edinburgh Inst FP) 1889 I

Aitken, G G (Oxford U) 1924 W, I, E, 1925 F, W, I, E, 1929 F

Aitken, J (Gala) 1977 E, I, F, 1981 F, W, E, I, NZ 1, 2, R, A, 1982 E, I, F, W, 1983 F, W, E, NZ, 1984 W, E, I, F, R

Aitken, R (London Scottish) 1947 W

Allan, A G Glasgow Warriors) 2014 US(R)

Allan, B (Glasgow Acads) 1881 I

Allan, J (Edinburgh Acads) 1990 NZ 1, 1991, W, I, R, [J, I, WS, E, NZ]

Allan, J L (Melrose) 1952 F, W, I, 1953 W

Allan, J L F (Cambridge U) 1957 I, E

Allan, J W (Melrose) 1927 F, 1928 I, 1929 F, W, I, E, 1930 F, E, 1931 F, W, I, E, 1932 SA, W, I, 1934 I, E

Allan, R C (Hutchesons' GSFP) 1969 I

Allardice, W D (Aberdeen GSFP) 1947 A, 1948 F, W, I, 1949 F, W, I, E

Allen, H W (Glasgow Acads) 1873 E

Anderson, A H (Glasgow Acads) 1894 I

Anderson, D G (London Scottish) 1889 I, 1890 W, I, E, 1891 W, E, 1892 W, E

Anderson, E (Stewart's Coll FP) 1947 I, E

Anderson, J W (W of Scotland) 1872 E

Anderson, T (Merchiston Castle School) 1882 I

Angus, A W (Watsonians) 1909 W, 1910 F, W, E, 1911 W, I, 1912 F, W, I, E, SA, 1913 F, W, 1914 E, 1920 F, W, I, E

Ansbro, J A (Northampton, London Irish) 2010 SA, Sm, 2011 F, W, E, It1, I2, [R, E], 2012 A, Sm

Anton, P A (St Andrew's U) 1873 E

Armstrong, G (Jedforest, Newcastle) 1988 A, 1989 W, E, I, F, Fj, R, 1990 I, F, W, E, NZ 1, 2, Arg, 1991 F, W, E, I, R, [J, I, WS, E, NZ], 1993 I, F, W, E, 1994 E, I, 1996 NZ, 1, 2, A, 1997 W, SA (R), 1998 It, I, F, W, E, SA (R), 1999 W, E, I, F, Arg, R, [SA, U, Sm, NZ]

Arneil, R J (Edinburgh Acads, Leicester and Northampton) 1968 I, E, A, 1969 F, W, I, E, SA, 1970 F, W, I, E, A, 1971 F, W, I, E (2[1C]), 1972 F, W, E, NZ

Arthur, A (Glasgow Acads) 1875 E, 1876 E

Arthur, J W (Glasgow Acads) 1871 E, 1872 E

Ashe, A (Glasgow Warriors) 2014 SA, Arg 2, NZ, 2015 E(R), I 1, It 2

Asher, A G G (Oxford U) 1882 I, 1884 W, I, E, 1885 W, 1886 I, E

Auld, W (W of Scotland) 1889 W, 1890 W

Auldjo, L J (Abertay) 1878 E

Bain, D McL (Oxford U) 1911 E, 1912 F, W, E, SA, 1913 F, W, I, E, 1914 W, I

Baird, G R T (Kelso) 1981 A, 1982 E, I, F, W, A 1, 2, 1983 I, F, W, E, NZ, 1984 W, E, I, F, A, 1985 I, W, E, 1986 F, W, E, I, R, 1987 E, 1988 I

Balfour, A (Watsonians) 1896 W, I, E, 1897 E

Balfour, L M (Edinburgh Acads) 1872 E

Bannerman, E M (Edinburgh Acads) 1872 E, 1873 E

Bannerman, J M (Glasgow HSFP) 1921 F, W, I, E, 1922 F, W, I, E, 1923 F, W, I, E, 1924 F, W, I, E, 1925 F, W, I, E, 1926 F, W, I, E, 1927 F, W, I, E, A, 1928 F, W, I, E, 1929 F, W, I, E

Barclay, J A (Glasgow Warriors, Scarlets) 2007 [NZ], 2008 F, W, Arg 2, NZ, SA, C, 2009 W, F, It 1, Fj, A, 2010 F, W, It, E, I, Arg 1, 2, NZ, SA, Sm, 2011 F, W, I1, E, It1, 2, [R, Arg, E], 2012 E(R), W(R), F, I, It, A, Fj, SA, Tg(R), 2013 J(R), SA2, 2015 I 2(R), It 3

Barnes, I A (Hawick) 1972 W, 1974 E (R), 1975 E (R), NZ, 1977 I, F, W

Barrie, R W (Hawick) 1936 E

Bearne, K R F (Cambridge U, London Scottish) 1960 F, W

Beattie, J A (Hawick) 1929 F, 1930 W, 1931 F, W, I, E, 1932 SA, W, I, E, 1933 W, E, I, 1934 I, E, 1935 W, I, E, NZ, 1936 W, I, E

Beattie, J R (Glasgow Acads) 1980 I, F, W, E, 1981 F, W, E, I, 1983 F, W, E, NZ, 1984 E (R), A, 1985 I, 1986 F, W, E, I, R, 1987 I, F, W, E

Beattie, J W (Glasgow Warriors, Montpellier, Castres) 2006 R, PI, 2007 F, 2008 Arg 1, 2009 Fj, A, Arg, 2010 F, W, It, E, I, Arg 1, 2, 2011 I1, 2, 2013 It1, I, W, F, Sm, SA1, It2, SA2(R), A, 2014 I(R), E(R), It, F, US, C, NZ(R), Tg, 2015 F 1, W, It 1, E(R)

Beattie, R S (Newcastle, Bristol) 2000 NZ 1, 2(R), Sm (R), 2003 E(R), It(R), I 2, [J(R), US, Fj]

Bedell-Sivright, D R (Cambridge U, Edinburgh U) 1900 W, 1901 W, I, E, 1902 W, I, E, 1903 W, I, 1904 W, I, E, 1905 NZ, 1906 W, I, E, SA, 1907 W, I, E, 1908 W, I

Bedell-Sivright, J V (Cambridge U) 1902 W

Begbie, T A (Edinburgh Wands) 1881 I, E

Bell, D L (Watsonians) 1975 I, F, W, E

Bell, J A (Clydesdale) 1901 W, I, E, 1902 W, I, E

Bell, L H I (Edinburgh Acads) 1900 E, 1904 W, I

Bennett, M S (Glasgow Warriors) 2014 Arg 2, NZ, 2015 F 1, W, It 1, E, I 1, It 3, F 2, [J, US, Sm, A]

Berkeley, W V (Oxford U) 1926 F, 1929 F, W, I

Berry, C W (Fettesian-Lorettonians) 1884 I, E, 1885 W, I 1, 1887 I, W, E, 1888 W, I

Bertram, D M (Watsonians) 1922 F, W, I, E, 1923 F, W, I, E, 1924 W, I, E

Beveridge, G (Glasgow) 2000 NZ 2(R), US (R), Sm (R), 2002 Fj(R), 2003 W 2, 2005 R(R)

Biggar, A G (London Scottish) 1969 SA, 1970 F, I, E, A, 1971 F, W, I, E (2[1C]), 1972 F, W

Biggar, M A (London Scottish) 1975 I, F, W, E, 1976 W, E, I, 1977 I, F, W, 1978 I, F, W, E, NZ, 1979 W, E, I, F, NZ, 1980 I, F, W, E

Birkett, G A (Harlequins, London Scottish) 1975 NZ

Bishop, J M (Glasgow Acads) 1893 I

Bisset, A A (RIE Coll) 1904 W

Black, A W (Edinburgh U) 1947 F, W, 1948 E, 1950 W, I, E

Black, W P (Glasgow HSFP) 1948 F, W, I, E, 1951 E

Blackadder, W F (W of Scotland) 1938 E

Blaikie, C F (Heriot's FP) 1963 I, E, 1966 E, 1968 A, 1969 F, W, I, E

Blair, M R L (Edinburgh, Brive) 2002 C, US, 2003 F(t+R), W 1(R), SA 2(R), It 2, I 2, [US], 2004 W(R), E(R), It(R), F(R), I(R), Sm(R), A1(R), 3(R), J(R), A4(R), SA(R), 2005 I(t&R), It(R), W(R), E, R, Arg, Sm(R), NZ(R), 2006 F, W, E, I, It(R), SA 1, 2, R, PI(R), A, 2007 I2, SA, [Pt, R, It, Arg], 2008 F, W, I, E, It, Arg 1, 2, NZ, SA, C, 2009 W, F, It, I, E, Fj(R), 2010 W(R), It(R), I(R), Arg 1(R), 2(R), NZ, Sm(R), 2011 F(R), W(R), I1, E(R), It1(R), 2, [R, Arg(R), E], 2012 E(R), W(R), F, I, It, A, Fj, Sm(R), NZ, SA

Blair, P C B (Cambridge U) 1912 SA, 1913 F, W, I, E

Blake, H P (Glasgow Warriors) 2015 I 2

Bolton, W H (W of Scotland) 1876 E

Borthwick, J B (Stewart's Coll FP) 1938 W, I

Bos, F H ten (Oxford U, London Scottish) 1959 E, 1960 F, W, SA, 1961 F, SA, W, I, E, 1962 F, W, I, E, 1963 F, W, I, E

Boswell, J D (W of Scotland) 1889 W, I, 1890 W, I, E, 1891 W, I, E, 1892 W, I, E, 1893 I, E, 1894 I, E

Bowie, T C (Watsonians) 1913 I, E, 1914 I, E

Boyd, G M (Glasgow HSFP) 1926 E

Boyd, J L (United Services) 1912 E, SA

Boyle, A C W (London Scottish) 1963 F, W, I

Boyle, A H W (St Thomas's Hospital, London Scottish) 1966 A, 1967 F, NZ, 1968 F, W, I

Brash, J C (Cambridge U) 1961 E

Breakey, R W (Gosforth) 1978 E

Brewis, N T (Edinburgh Inst FP) 1876 E, 1878 E, 1879 I, E, 1880 I, E

Brewster, A K (Stewart's-Melville FP) 1977 E, 1980 I, F, 1986 E, I, R

Brotherstone, S J (Melrose, Brive, Newcastle) 1999 I (R), 2000 F, W, E, US, A, Sm, 2002 C (R)

Brown, A H (Heriot's FP) 1928 E, 1929 F, W

Brown, A R (Gala) 1971 E (2[1C]), 1972 F, W, E

Brown, C H C (Dunfermline) 1929 E

Brown, D I (Cambridge U) 1933 W, E, I

Brown, F J M (Glasgow Warriors) 2013 It2(R), 2014 NZ(R), Tg(R), 2015 F 1(R), W(R), It 1(R), E(R), I 1(R), 2, F 2(R), [J(R), US(R), SA, Sm(R), A(R)]

Brown, G L (W of Scotland) 1969 SA, 1970 F, W (R), I, E, A, 1971 F, W, I, E (2[1C]), 1972 F, W, E, NZ, 1973 E (R), P, 1974 W, E, I, F, 1975 I, F, W, E, A, 1976 F, W, E, I

Brown, J A (Glasgow Acads) 1908 W, I

Brown, J B (Glasgow Acads) 1879 I, E, 1880 I, E, 1881 I, E, 1882 I, E, 1883 W, I, E, 1884 W, I, E, 1885 I 1, 2, 1886 W, I, E

Brown, K D R (Borders, Glasgow Warriors, Saracens) 2005 R, Sm(R), R(R), 2006 SA 1(R), 2(R), R, PI, A, 2007 E, W, It, I1, 2(R), SA, [Pt(R), R(R), NZ, It(R), Arg(R)], 2008 F(R), W, I, E(R), It(R), Arg 1(R), 2(R), 2009 W(R), F(R), It(R), E(R), 2010 F, W, It, E, I, Arg 1, 2, NZ, SA, Sm, 2011 F, W, I1, E, It1, 2, [R, Gg, Arg], 2012 NZ, SA, Tg, 2013 It1, I, W, F, Sm, J, A, 2014 I, F, W, C

Brown, P C (W of Scotland, Gala) 1964 F, NZ, W, I, E, 1965 I, E, SA, 1966 A, 1969 I, E, 1970 W, E, 1971 F, W, I, E (2[1C]), 1972 F, W, E, NZ, 1973 F, W, I, E, P

Brown, T G (Heriot's FP) 1929 W

Brown, T G (Edinburgh) 2012 A(R)

Brown, W D (Glasgow Acads) 1871 F, 1872 E, 1873 E, 1874 E, 1875 E

Brown, W S (Edinburgh Inst FP) 1880 I, E, 1882 I, E, 1883 W, E

Browning, A (Glasgow HSFP) 1920 I, 1922 F, W, I, 1923 W, I, E

Bruce, C R (Glasgow Acads) 1947 F, W, I, E, 1949 F, W, I, E

Bruce, N S (Blackheath, Army and London Scottish) 1958 F, A, I, E, 1959 F, W, I, E, 1960 F, W, I, E, SA, 1961 F, SA, W, I, E, 1962 F, W, I, E, 1963 F, W, I, E, 1964 F, NZ, W, I, E

Bruce, R M (Gordonians) 1947 A, 1948 F, W, I

Bruce-Lockhart, J H (London Scottish) 1913 W, 1920 E

Bruce-Lockhart, L (London Scottish) 1948 E, 1950 F, W, 1953 I, E

Bruce-Lockhart, R B (Cambridge U and London Scottish) 1937 I, 1939 I, E

Bryce, C C (Glasgow Acads) 1873 E, 1874 E

Bryce, K (Glasgow Warriors) 2014 C(R), SA(R), 2015 [US(R)]

Bryce, R D H (W of Scotland) 1973 I (R)

Bryce, W E (Selkirk) 1922 W, I, E, 1923 F, W, I, E, 1924 F, W, I, E

Brydon, W R C (Heriot's FP) 1939 W

Buchanan, A (Royal HSFP) 1871 E

Buchanan, F G (Kelvinside Acads and Oxford U) 1910 F, 1911 F, W

Buchanan, J C R (Stewart's Coll FP) 1921 W, I, E, 1922 W, I, E, 1923 F, W, I, E, 1924 W, I, E, 1925 F, I

Buchanan-Smith, G A E (London Scottish, Heriot's FP) 1989 Fj (R), 1990 Arg

Bucher, A M (Edinburgh Acads) 1897 E

Budge, G M (Edinburgh Wands) 1950 F, W, I, E

Bullmore, H H (Edinburgh U) 1902 I

Bulloch, A J (Glasgow) 2000 US, A, Sm, 2001 F (t+R), E

Finlay, R (Watsonians) 1948 E

Fisher, A T (Waterloo, Watsonians) 1947 I, E

Fisher, C D (Waterloo) 1975 NZ, A, 1976 W, E, I

Fisher, D (W of Scotland) 1893 I

Fisher, J P (Royal HSFP, London Scottish) 1963 E, 1964 F, NZ, W, I, E, 1965 F, W, I, E, SA, 1966 F, W, I, E, A, 1967 F, W, I, E, NZ, 1968 F, W, I, E

Fleming, C J N (Edinburgh Wands) 1896 I, E, 1897 I

Fleming, G R (Glasgow Acads) 1875 E, 1876 E

Fletcher, H N (Edinburgh U) 1904 E, 1905 W

Flett, A B (Edinburgh U) 1901 W, I, E, 1902 W, I

Forbes, J L (Watsonians) 1905 W, 1906 I, E

Ford, D St C (United Services, RN) 1930 I, E, 1931 E, 1932 W, I

Ford, J R (Gala) 1893 I

Ford, R W (Borders, Glasgow, Edinburgh) 2004 A3(R), 2006 W(R), E(R), PI(R), A(R), 2007 E(R), W(R), It(R), I1(R), F, I2, SA, [Pt(R), R, It, Arg], 2008 F, W, I, E, Arg 1, 2, NZ, SA, C, 2009 W, F, It, I, E, Fj, A, Arg, 2010 F, W, It, E, I, Arg 1, 2, NZ, SA, Sm, 2011 F, W, I1, E, It1, I2, [R, Gg, Arg, E], 2012 E, W, F, I, It, A, Fj, Sm, NZ, SA, 2013 E(R), It1, I, W, F, J, SA2, A, 2014 I, E, F(R), W(R), Arg1, SA, Arg 2, NZ, Tg, 2015 F 1, W, It 1, E, I 1, 2(R), It 2(R), 3, F 2, [J, US, SA(R), Sm, A]

Forrest, J E (Glasgow Acads) 1932 SA, 1935 E, NZ

Forrest, J G S (Cambridge U) 1938 W, I, E

Forrest, W T (Hawick) 1903 W, I, E, 1904 W, I, E, 1905 W, I

Forsayth, H H (Oxford U) 1921 F, W, I, E, 1922 W, I, E

Forsyth, I W (Stewart's Coll FP) 1972 NZ, 1973 F, W, I, E, P

Forsyth, J (Edinburgh U) 1871 E

Foster, R A (Hawick) 1930 W, 1932 SA, I, E

Fox, J (Gala) 1952 F, W, I, E

Frame, J N M (Edinburgh U, Gala) 1967 NZ, 1968 F, W, I, E, 1969 W, I, E, SA, 1970 F, W, I, E, A, 1971 F, W, I, E (2[1C]), 1972 F, W, E, 1973 P (R)

France, C (Kelvinside Acads) 1903 I

Fraser, C F P (Glasgow U) 1888 W, 1889 W

Fraser, J W (Edinburgh Inst FP) 1881 E

Fraser, R (Cambridge U) 1911 F, W, I, E

French, J (Glasgow Acads) 1886 W, 1887 I, W, E

Frew, A (Edinburgh U) 1901 W, I, E

Frew, G M (Glasgow HSFP) 1906 SA, 1907 W, I, E, 1908 W, I, E, 1909 W, I, E, 1910 F, W, I, 1911 I, E

Friebe, J P (Glasgow HSFP) 1952 E

Fullarton, I A (Edinburgh) 2000 NZ 1(R), 2, 2001 NZ (R), 2003 It 2(R), I 2(t), 2004 Sm(R), A1(R), 2

Fulton, A K (Edinburgh U, Dollar Acads) 1952 F, 1954 F

Fusaro, C C (Glasgow Warriors) 2014 E, It, Arg1(R), SA

Fyfe, K C (Cambridge U, Sale, London Scottish) 1933 W, E, 1934 E, 1935 W, I, E, NZ, 1936 W, E, 1939 I

Gallie, G H (Edinburgh Acads) 1939 W

Gallie, R A (Glasgow Acads) 1920 F, W, I, E, 1921 F, W, I, E

Gammell, W B B (Edinburgh Wands) 1977 I, F, W, 1978 W, E

Geddes, I C (London Scottish) 1906 SA, 1907 W, I, E, 1908 W, E

Geddes, K I (London Scottish) 1947 F, W, I, E

Gedge, H T S (Oxford U, London Scottish, Edinburgh Wands) 1894 W, I, E, 1896 E, 1899 W, E

Gedge, P M S (Edinburgh Wands) 1933 I

Gemmill, R (Glasgow HSFP) 1950 F, W, I, E, 1951 F, W, I

Gibson, W R (Royal HSFP) 1891 I, E, 1892 W, I, E, 1893 W, I, E, 1894 W, I, E, 1895 W, I, E

Gilbert-Smith, D S (London Scottish) 1952 E

Gilchrist, G S (Edinburgh) 2013 F, Sm, It2(R), A, 2014 US(R), C, Arg1, SA, 2015 I 2, It 3, [J, US]

Gilchrist, J (Glasgow Acads) 1925 F

Gill, A D (Gala) 1973 P, 1974 W, E, I, F

Gillespie, J I (Edinburgh Acads) 1899 E, 1900 W, E, 1901 W, I, E, 1902 W, I, 1904 I, E

Gillies, A C (Watsonians) 1924 W, I, E, 1925 F, W, E, 1926 F, W, 1927 F, W, I, E

Gilmour, H R (Watsonians) 1998 Fj

Gilray, C M (Oxford U, London Scottish) 1908 E, 1909 W, E, 1912 I

Glasgow, I C (Heriot's FP) 1997 F (R)

Glasgow, R J C (Dunfermline) 1962 F, W, I, E, 1963 I, E, 1964 I, E, 1965 W, I

Glen, W S (Edinburgh Wands) 1955 W

Gloag, L G (Cambridge U) 1949 F, W, I, E

Godman, P J (Edinburgh) 2005 R(R), Sm(R), NZ(R), 2006 R, PI(R), A(t&R), 2007 W, It, 2008 Arg 2, NZ, SA, C, 2009 W, F, It, I, E, Fj, A, Arg, 2010 F, W(R), E(R)

Goodfellow, J (Langholm) 1928 W, I, E

Goodhue, F W J (London Scottish) 1890 W, I, E, 1891 W, I, E, 1892 W, I, E

Gordon, R (Edinburgh Wands) 1951 W, 1952 F, W, I, E, 1953 W

Gordon, R E (Royal Artillery) 1913 F, W, I

Gordon, R J (London Scottish) 1982 A 1, 2

Gore, A C (London Scottish) 1882 I

Gossman, B M (W of Scotland) 1980 W, 1983 E, F, W

Gossman, J S (W of Scotland) 1980 E (R)

Gowans, J J (Cambridge U, London Scottish) 1893 W, 1894 W, E, 1895 W, I, E, 1896 I, E

Gowland, G C (London Scottish) 1908 W, 1909 W, E, 1910 F, W, I, E

Gracie, A L (Harlequins) 1921 F, W, I, E, 1922 F, W, I, E, 1923 F, W, I, E, 1924 F

Graham, G (Newcastle) 1997 A (R), SA (R), 1998 I, F (R), W (R), 1999 F (R), Arg (R), R, [SA, U, Sm, NZ (R)], 2000 I (R), US, A, Sm, 2001 I (R), Tg (R), Arg (R), NZ (R), 2002 E (R), It (R), I (R), F (R), W (R)

Graham, I N (Edinburgh Acads) 1939 I, E

Graham, J (Kelso) 1926 I, E, 1927 F, W, I, E, A, 1928 F, W, I, E, 1930 I, E, 1932 SA, W

Graham, J H S (Edinburgh Acads) 1876 E, 1877 I, E, 1878 E, 1879 I, E, 1880 I, E, 1881 I, E

Grant, D (Hawick) 1965 F, E, SA, 1966 F, W, I, E, A, 1967 F, W, I, E, NZ, 1968 F

Grant, D M (East Midlands) 1911 W, I

Grant, M L (Harlequins) 1955 F, 1956 F, W, 1957 F

Grant, R (Glasgow Warriors) 2012 A, Fj, Sm, NZ, SA, 2013 E, It1, I, W, F, J, SA2(R), A, 2014 I, E, It, F, W, Tg(R), 2015 It 1(R), E(R), I 1, 2, [J(R), US]

Grant, T O (Hawick) 1960 I, E, SA, 1964 F, NZ, W

Grant, W St C (Craigmount) 1873 E, 1874 E

Gray, C A (Nottingham) 1989 W, E, I, F, Fj, R, 1990 I, F, W, E, NZ 1, 2, Arg, 1991 F, W, E, I, [J, I, WS, E, NZ]

Gray, D (W of Scotland) 1978 E, 1979 I, F, NZ, 1980 I, F, W, E, 1981 F

Gray, G L (Gala) 1935 NZ, 1937 W, I, E

Gray, J D (Glasgow Warriors) 2013 SA2(R), A(R), 2014 E(R), Arg1, SA(R)), Arg 2, NZ, Tg, 2015 F 1, W, It 1, E, I 1, It 3, F 2, [J, SA, Sm, A]

Gray, R J (Glasgow Warriors, Sale, Castres) 2010 F(R), W(R), I(R), NZ, SA, Sm, 2011 F, I1, E, It1, I2, It2(R), [R, Gg(R), Arg, E], 2012 E, W, F, I, It, A, Fj, Sm, NZ, Sa, 2013 E, It1, I, W, J(R), SA2, 2014 I(R), It, F, W, US, C, Arg 2, NZ, Tg, 2015 F 1, W, It 2, F 2, [J(R), US, SA, Sm, A]

Gray, S D (Borders, Northampton) 2004 A3, 2008 NZ(R), SA(R), C(R), 2009 W(R), It(R), I(R), E

Gray, T (Northampton, Heriot's FP) 1950 E, 1951 F, E

Greenlees, H D (Leicester) 1927 A, 1928 F, W, 1929 I, E, 1930 E

Greenlees, J R C (Cambridge U, Kelvinside Acads) 1900 I, 1902 W, I, E, 1903 W, I, E

Greenwood, J T (Dunfermline and Perthshire Acads) 1952 F, 1955 F, W, I, E, 1956 F, W, I, E, 1957 F, W, E, 1958 F, W, A, I, E, 1959 F, W, I

Greig, A (Glasgow HSFP) 1911 I

Greig, L L (Glasgow Acads, United Services) 1905 NZ, 1906 SA, 1907 W, 1908 W, I

Greig, R C (Glasgow Acads) 1893 W, 1897 I

Grieve, C F (Oxford U) 1935 W, 1936 E

Grieve, R M (Kelso) 1935 W, I, E, NZ, 1936 W, I, E

Grimes, S B (Watsonians, Newcastle) 1997 A (t+R), 1998 I (R), F (R), W (R), E(R, Fj, A 1, 2, 1999 W (R), E, It, I, F, Arg, R, [SA, U, Sm (R), NZ (R)], 2000 It, I, F (R), W, US, A, Sm (R), 2001 F (R), W (R), E (R), It, I (R), Tg, Arg, NZ, 2002 E, It, I, F (R), W (R), C, US, R, SA, Fj, 2003 I 1, F, W 1, E(R), It 1(R), W 2, I 2, It 2(R), F (R, F, A], 2004 W, E, It, F, I, Sm, A1, J, A4, SA, 2005 F, I, It, W, E(R)

Grove, A (Worcester) 2009 Fj, A, Arg

Gunn, A W (Royal HSFP) 1912 F, W, I, SA, 1913 F

Hall, A J A (Glasgow) 2002 US (R)

Hall, D W H (Edinburgh, Glasgow Warriors) 2003 W 2(R), 2005

R(R), Arg, Sm(R), NZ(R), 2006 F, E, I, It(R), SA 1(R), 2, R, PI, A, 2007 E, W, It, I1, F(R), 2008 Arg 2(R), NZ(R), SA(R), C(R), 2009 W(R), F(R), It(R), I(R), E(R), Fj(R), A(R), Arg(R), 2010 SA(R), Sm(R), 2011 F(R), I2(R), It2(R), [Arg(R)], 2012 SA(R), Tg(R), 2013 E, I(R), F(R)

Hamilton, A S (Headingley) 1914 W, 1920 F

Hamilton, C P (Newcastle) 2004 A2(R), 2005 R, Arg, Sm, NZ

Hamilton, H M (W of Scotland) 1874 E, 1875 E

Hamilton, J L (Leicester, Edinburgh, Gloucester, Saracens) 2006 R(R), A(R), 2007 E, W, It(R), I1(R), F(R), I2, SA, [R, NZ(R)], It, Arg], 2008 F, W, I(R), NZ, SA, C, 2009 W, F, I, E, 2010 W, It, E, I, Arg 1, 2, NZ, Sm(R), 2011 I2, [Gg, Arg], 2012 E, W, F, I, It, NZ, SA, 2013 E, It1, I, W, F, Sm(R), SA1, 2, A, 2014 I, E, It, F, W, US, Arg 2(R), 2015 F 1(R), W(R), E, I 1, 2, It 2

Hannah, R S M (W of Scotland) 1971 I

Hardie, J I (Unattached) 2015 It 2, F 2, [J, Sm, A]

Harley, R J (Glasgow Warriors) 2012 Sm(R), 2013 It1, I, W, It2(R), 2014 Arg1, SA, Arg 2, NZ, Tg, 2015 F 1, W, It 1, E, I 1(R), 2(R), It 3(R)

Harrower, P R (London Scottish) 1885 W

Hart, G J (Edinburgh) 2014 C(R), Arg1, SA(R)

Hart, J G M (London Scottish) 1951 SA

Hart, T M (Glasgow U) 1930 W, I

Hart, W (Melrose) 1960 SA

Harvey, L (Greenock Wands) 1899 I

Hastie, J I (Melrose) 1961 W, I, E, 1964 I, E, 1965 E, SA, 1966 F, W, I, E, A, 1967 F, W, I, NZ, 1968 F, W

Hastie, I R (Kelso) 1955 F, 1958 F, E, 1959 F, W, I

Hastie, J D H (Melrose) 1938 W, I, E

Hastings, A G (Cambridge U, Watsonians, London Scottish) 1986 F, W, E, I, R, 1987 I, F, W, E, [F, Z, R, NZ], 1988 I, F, W, E, A, 1989 Fj, R, 1990 I, F, W, E, NZ 1, 2, Arg, 1991 F, W, E, I, [J, I, WS, E, NZ], 1992 E, I, F, W, A 1, 1993 I, F, W, E, NZ, 1994 W, E, I, F, SA, 1995 C, I, F, W, E, R, [Iv, Tg, F, NZ]

Hastings, S (Watsonians) 1986 F, W, E, I, R, 1987 I, F, W, [R], 1988 I, F, W, A, 1989 W, E, I, F, Fj, R, 1990 I, F, W, E, NZ 1, 2, Arg, 1991 F, W, E, I, [J, Z, I, WS, E, NZ], 1992 E, I, F, W, A 1, 2, 1993 I, F, W, E, NZ, 1994 E, I, F, SA, 1995 W, E, R (R), [Tg, F, NZ], 1996 I, F, W, E, NZ 2, It, 1997 W, E (R)

Hay, B H (Boroughmuir) 1975 NZ, A, 1976 F, 1978 I, F, W, E, NZ, 1979 W, E, I, F, NZ, 1980 I, F, W, E, 1981 W, E, I, NZ 1, 2

Hay, J A (Hawick) 1995 WS

Hay-Gordon, J R (Edinburgh Acads) 1875 E, 1877 I, E

Heathcote, T A (Bath) 2012 Tg(R), 2013 Sm, It2

Hegarty, C B (Hawick) 1978 I, F, W, E

Hegarty, J J (Hawick) 1951 F, 1953 F, W, I, E, 1955 F

Henderson, A R (Glasgow Warriors) 2001 I (R), Tg (R), NZ (R), 2002 It, I, US (R), 2003 SA 1, 2, It 2, I 2, [US, F, Fj, A], 2004 W, E(t&R), It(R), F, I, Sm, A1, 2, 3, J, A4, SA, 2005 W(R), R, Arg, Sm, NZ, 2006 F, W, E, I, It, SA 1, 2, PI, A, 2007 E, It(R), I1(R), F, I2, SA, [NZ, It(R), Arg(R)], 2008 F, W, I, It(R)

Henderson, B C (Edinburgh Wands) 1963 E, 1964 F, I, E, 1965 F, W, I, E, 1966 F, W, I, E

Henderson, F W (London Scottish) 1900 W, I

Henderson, I C (Edinburgh Acads) 1939 I, E, 1947 F, W, E, A, 1948 I, E

Henderson, J H (Oxford U, Richmond) 1953 F, W, I, E, 1954 F, NZ, I, E, W

Henderson, J M (Edinburgh Acads) 1933 W, E, I

Henderson, J Y M (Watsonians) 1911 E

Henderson, M M (Dunfermline) 1937 W, I, E

Henderson, N F (London Scottish) 1892 I

Henderson, R G (Newcastle Northern) 1924 I, E

Hendrie, K G P (Heriot's FP) 1924 F, W, E

Hendry, T L (Clydesdale) 1893 W, I, E, 1895 I

Henriksen, E H (Royal HSFP) 1953 I

Hepburn, D P (Woodford) 1947 A, 1948 F, W, I, E, 1949 F, W, I, E

Heron, G (Glasgow Acads) 1874 E, 1875 E

Hidalgo-Clyne, S P (Edinburgh) 2015 F 1(R), W(R), It 1(R), E(R), I 1(R), 2(R), It 2, [SA(R)]

Hill, C C P (St Andrew's U) 1912 F, I

Hilton, D I W (Bath, Glasgow) 1995 C, I, F, W, E, R, [Tg, F, NZ], WS, 1996 I, F, W, E, NZ 1, 2, A, It, 1997 W, A, SA, 1998 It, I (R), F, W, E, A 1, 2, SA (R), 1999 W (R), E (R), It (R), I (R), F, R (R), [SA (R), U (R), Sp], 2000 It (R), F (R), W (R), 2002 SA(R)

Hines, N J (Edinburgh, Glasgow, Perpignan, Leinster, Clermont-Auvergne) 2000 NZ 2(R), 2002 C, US, R(R), SA(R), Fj(R), 2003

W 1(R), E, It 1, SA 1, 2, It 2, W 2(R), I 2, [US, F(R), Fj, A], 2004 E(R), It(R), F(R), I(R), A3, J, A4, SA, 2005 F(R), I(R), It(R), W(R), E, 2006 E(R), F, I, It, SA 1, 2, R, 2007 W(R), It, I, F, I2, SA, [Pt, R, It, Arg], 2008 F, W, I, E, It, NZ, SA, C, 2009 I(R), E(R), Fj, A, Arg, 2010 F, It(R), E(R), NZ(R), SA, Sm, 2011 F, W, I1(R), E, It1, 2, [R(R), Gg, Arg(R), E(R)]

Hinshelwood, A J W (London Scottish) 1966 F, W, I, E, A, 1967 F, W, I, E, NZ, 1968 F, W, I, E, A, 1969 F, W, I, SA, 1970 F, W

Hinshelwood, B G (Worcester) 2002 C (R), R(R), SA(R), Fj, 2003 It 2, [J, US(R), Fj(R), A(R)], 2004 W, E, It, Sm, A1, 2, J, A4, SA, 2005 It(R)

Hodge D W (Watsonians, Edinburgh) 1997 F (R), A, SA (t+R), 1998 A 2(R), SA, 1999 W, Arg, R, [Sp, Sm (R)], 2000 F (R), W, E, I 1, 2, US (R), Sm (R), 2001 F (R), W, E, It, I (R), 2002 E, W (R), C, US

Hodgson, C G (London Scottish) 1968 I, E

Hogg, A (Edinburgh) 2004 W, E(R), It, F(R), I, Sm, A1, 2, 3, J, A4, SA, 2005 F, I, It, W, E, R, Arg, Sm, NZ, 2006 F, W, E, I, It, SA 1, 2, 2007 E(R), W(R), It(R), I1(R), F, I2, SA(t&R), [Pt, R, It, Arg], 2008 W(R), I, E, It, Arg 1, 2, NZ, SA, 2009 W

Hogg, C D (Melrose) 1992 A 1, 2, 1993 NZ, W, 1994 Arg 1, 2

Hogg, C G (Boroughmuir) 1978 F (R), W (R)

Hogg, S W (Glasgow Warriors) 2012 W(R), F, I, It, A, Fj, Sm, NZ, SA, Tg, 2013 E, It1, I, W, F, 2014 I, E, It, F, W, US, C, Arg1, SA, Arg 2, NZ, Tg, 2015 F 1, W,It 1, E, I 1, It 3, [J, US, SA, Sm, A]

Holmes, S D (London Scottish) 1998 It, I, F

Holmes, T T (Glasgow Warriors) 2014 SA(R)

Holms, W F (RIE Coll) 1886 W, E, 1887 I, E, 1889 W, I

Horne, P (Glasgow Warriors) 2013 Sm(R), SA1(R), 2014 C, Arg1, SA, 2015 F 1(R), It 1, I 2, It 2(R), 3, [J(R), US, SA(R), Sm(R), A]

Horsburgh, G B (London Scottish) 1937 W, I, E, 1938 W, I, E, 1939 W, I, E

Howie, D D (Kirkcaldy) 1912 F, W, I, E, SA, 1913 F, W

Howie, R A (Kirkcaldy) 1924 F, W, I, E, 1925 W, I, E

Hoyer-Millar, G C (Oxford U) 1953 I

Hoyland, D N (Edinburgh) 2015 It 2(R)

Huggan, J L (London Scottish) 1914 E

Hughes, R C (Glasgow Warriors) 2015 It 2

Hume, J (Royal HSFP) 1912 F, 1920 F, 1921 F, W, I, E, 1922 F

Hume, J W G (Oxford U, Edinburgh Wands) 1928 I, 1930 F

Hunter, F (Edinburgh U) 1882 I

Hunter, I G (Selkirk) 1984 I (R), 1985 F (R), W, E

Hunter, J M (Cambridge U) 1947 F

Hunter, M D (Glasgow High) 1974 F

Hunter, W J (Hawick) 1964 F, NZ, W, 1967 F, W, I, E

Hutchison, W R (Glasgow HSFP) 1911 E

Hutton, A H M (Dunfermline) 1932 I

Hutton, J E (Harlequins) 1930 E, 1931 F

Inglis, H M (Edinburgh Acads) 1951 F, W, I, E, SA, 1952 W, I

Inglis, J M (Selkirk) 1952 E

Inglis, W M (Cambridge U, Royal Engineers) 1937 W, I, E, 1938 W, I, E

Innes, J R S (Aberdeen GSFP) 1939 W, I, E, 1947 A, 1948 F, W, I, E

Ireland, J C H (Glasgow HSFP) 1925 W, I, E, 1926 F, W, I, E, 1927 F, W, I, E

Irvine, A R (Heriot's FP) 1972 NZ, 1973 F, W, I, E, P, 1974 W, E, I, F, 1975 I, F, W, E, NZ, A, 1976 F, W, E, I, 1977 E, I, F, W, 1978 I, F, E, NZ, 1979 W, E, I, F, NZ, 1980 I, F, W, E, 1981 F, W, E, I, NZ 1, 2, A, 1982 E, I, F, W, A 1, 2

Irvine, D R (Edinburgh Acads) 1878 E, 1879 I, E

Irvine, R W (Edinburgh Acads) 1871 E, 1872 E, 1873 E, 1874 E, 1875 E, 1876 E, 1877 I, E, 1878 E, 1879 I, E, 1880 I, E

Irvine, T W (Edinburgh Acads) 1885 I 1, 2, 1886 W, I, E, 1887 I, W, E, 1888 W, I, E, 1889 I

Jackson, R J H (Glasgow Warriors, Wasps) 2010 NZ(R), Sm(R), 2011 F(R), I1, E, It1, I2, It2(R), [R, Arg, E], 2012 I(R), It(R), NZ(R), SA(R), 2013 E, It1, I, W(R), F(R), SA1, J, SA2, 2014 US(R), C(R), 2015 I 2, It 3(R)

Jackson, K L T (Oxford U) 1933 W, E, I, 1934 W

Jackson, T G H (Army) 1947 F, W, E, A, 1948 F, W, I, E, 1949 F, W, I, E

Jackson, W D (Hawick) 1964 I, 1965 E, SA, 1968 A, 1969 F, W, I, E

Jacobsen, A F (Edinburgh) 2002 C (R), US, 2003 I 2, 2004 It, F, I, A3, J, A4, SA, 2005 R, Arg(R), Sm, 2006 R(R), PI(R), A(R), 2007 E(R), W(R), It(t&R), I1(R), F(R), I2, SA(R), [Pt], 2008 F, W, I, E, It, Arg 1, 2, NZ, SA, C, 2009 W, F, It, Fj, A, Arg, 2010 F(R), W(R), It, E, I, Arg 1, 2, NZ, SA, Sm, 2011 F, W, I1, E, It1, I2, [R, Gg, Arg, E], 2012 E, W, F, I, NZ(R)

Jamieson, J (W of Scotland) 1883 W, I, E, 1884 W, I, E, 1885 W, I 1, 2

Jardine, I C (Stirling County) 1993 NZ, 1994 W, E (R), Arg 1, 2, 1995 C, I, F, [Tg, F (t & R), NZ (R)], 1996 I, F, W, E, NZ 1, 2, 1998 Fj

Jeffrey, J (Kelso) 1984 A, 1985 I, E, 1986 F, W, E, I, R, 1987 I, F, W, E, [F, Z, R], 1988 I, W, A, 1989 W, E, I, F, Fj, R, 1990 I, F, W, E, NZ 1, 2, Arg, 1991 F, W, E, I, [J, I, WS, E, NZ]

Johnston, D I (Watsonians) 1979 NZ, 1980 I, F, W, E, 1981 R, A, 1982 E, I, F, W, A 1, 2, 1983 I, F, W, NZ, 1984 W, E, I, F, R, 1986 F, W, E, I, R

Johnston, H H (Edinburgh Collegian FP) 1877 I, E

Johnston, J (Melrose) 1951 SA, 1952 F, W, I, E

Johnston, W C (Glasgow HSFP) 1922 F

Johnston, W G S (Cambridge U) 1935 W, I, 1937 W, I, E

Joiner, C A (Melrose, Leicester) 1994 Arg 1, 2, 1995 C, I, F, W, E, R, [Iv, Tg, F, NZ], 1996 I, F, W, E, NZ 1, 1997 SA, 1998 It, I, A 2(R), 2000 NZ 1(R), 2, US (R)

Jones, L (Edinburgh) 2012 E, W, F, I

Jones, P M (Gloucester) 1992 W (R)

Junor, J E (Glasgow Acads) 1876 E, 1877 I, E, 1878 E, 1879 E, 1881 I

Kalman, E D (Glasgow Warriors) 2012 W(R), F(R)

Keddie, R R (Watsonians) 1967 NZ

Keith, G J (Wasps) 1968 F, W

Keller, D H (London Scottish) 1949 F, W, I, E, 1950 F, W, I

Kellock, A D (Edinburgh, Glasgow Warriors) 2004 A3(t&R), 2005 R(R), Arg(R), Sm(R), NZ(R), 2006 F, W, E, It(R), SA 1(R), 2, PI(R), A, 2007 E, 2008 Arg 1(t&R), 2(R), 2009 It, Fj, A, Arg(R), 2010 F, W, It, E, I, Arg 1, 2, 2011 F, W, I1, E, It1, I2(R), It2, [R, E], 2012 E(R), W(R), F(R), I(R), It(R), A, Fj, Sm, NZ(R), SA(R), Tg, 2013 E(R), It1(R), I(R), W(R), F(R), Sm, SA1(R), It2, J

Kelly, R F (Watsonians) 1927 A, 1928 F, W, E

Kemp, J W Y (Glasgow HSFP) 1954 W, 1955 F, W, I, E, 1956 F, W, I, E, 1957 F, W, I, E, 1958 F, W, I, E, 1959 F, W, I, E, 1960 F, W, I, E, SA

Kennedy, A E (Watsonians) 1983 NZ, 1984 W, E, A

Kennedy, F (Stewart's Coll FP) 1920 F, W, I, E, 1921 E

Kennedy, N (W of Scotland) 1903 W, I, E

Ker, A B M (Kelso) 1988 W, E

Ker, H T (Glasgow Acads) 1887 I, W, E, 1888 I, 1889 W, 1890 I, E

Kerr, D S (Heriot's FP) 1923 F, W, 1924 F, 1926 I, E, 1927 W, I, E, 1928 I, E

Kerr, G (Leeds, Borders, Glasgow, Edinburgh) 2003 I 1(R), F(R), W 1(R), E(R), SA 1, 2, W 2, [J(R), US, F], 2004 W(R), E(R), It(R), F(R), I(R), J, A4, SA, 2005 F, I, It, W, E, Arg, Sm(R), NZ, 2006 F, W, E, I, It, SA 1, 2, PI, A, 2007 E, W, It, F, SA, [Pt(R), R, NZ(R), It, Arg], 2008 F(R), W(R), I(R)

Kerr, G C (Old Dunelmians, Edinburgh Wands) 1898 I, E, 1899 I, W, E, 1900 W, I, E

Kerr, J M (Heriot's FP) 1935 NZ, 1936 I, E, 1937 W, I

Kerr, R C (Glasgow) 2002 C, US, 2003 W 2

Kerr, W (London Scottish) 1953 E

Kidston, D W (Glasgow Acads) 1883 W, E

Kidston, W H (W of Scotland) 1874 E

Kilgour, I J (RMC Sandhurst) 1921 F

King, J H F (Selkirk) 1953 F, W, E, 1954 E

Kininmonth, P W (Oxford U, Richmond) 1949 F, W, I, E, 1950 F, W, I, E, 1951 F, W, I, E, SA, 1952 F, W, I, 1954 F, NZ, I, E, W

Kinnear, R M (Heriot's FP) 1926 F, W, I

Knox, J (Kelvinside Acads) 1903 W, I, E

Kyle, W E (Hawick) 1902 W, I, E, 1903 W, I, E, 1904 W, I, E, 1905 W, I, E, NZ, 1906 W, I, E, 1908 E, 1909 W, I, E, 1910 W

Laidlaw, A S (Hawick) 1897 I

Laidlaw, F A L (Melrose) 1965 F, W, I, E, SA, 1966 F, W, I, E, A,

1967 F, W, I, E, NZ, 1968 F, W, I, A, 1969 F, W, I, E, SA, 1970 F, W, I, E, A, 1971 F, W, I

Laidlaw, G D (Edinburgh, Gloucester) 2010 NZ(R), 2011 I2(R), 2012 E(R), W, F, I, It, A, Fj, Sm, NZ, SA, Tg, 2013 E, It1, I, W, F, Sm, SA1, It2, J, SA2, A, 2014 I, E, It, F, W, US, C , Arg 2, NZ, Tg, 2015 F 1, W, It 1, E, I 1, It 3, F 2, [J, US(R), SA, Sm, A]

Laidlaw, R J (Jedforest) 1980 I, F, W, E, 1981 F, W, E, I, NZ 1, 2, R, A, 1982 E, I, F, W, A 1, 2, 1983 I, F, W, NZ, 1984 W, E, I, F, R, A, 1985 I, F, 1986 F, W, E, I, R, 1987 I, F, W, E, [F, R, NZ], 1988 I, F, W, E

Laing, A D (Royal HSFP) 1914 W, I, E, 1920 F, W, I, 1921 F

Lambie, I K (Watsonians) 1978 NZ (R), 1979 W, E, NZ

Lambie, L B (Glasgow HSFP) 1934 W, I, E, 1935 W, I, E, NZ

Lamond, G A W (Kelvinside Acads) 1899 W, E, 1905 E

Lamont, R P (Glasgow, Sale, Toulon, Glasgow Warriors) 2005 W, E, R, Arg, Sm, 2007 E(R), I1(R), F(R), I2, SA, [Pt, R, It, Arg], 2008 F, I, E, SA, C, 2009 Fj, A, Arg, 2010 W, NZ, 2011 It2, [Gg], 2012 E, W, F

Lamont, S F (Glasgow, Northampton, Llanelli Scarlets, Glasgow Warriors) 2004 Sm, A1, 2, 3, J, A4, SA, 2005 F, I, It, W, E, R, Arg, Sm, NZ, 2006 F, W, E, I, It, SA1, R, PI, A, 2007 E, W, It, I1, F, I2, [Pt, R, It, Arg], 2008 NZ, 2009 W, Fj, A, Arg, 2010 F, W, It, E, I, Arg1, 2, NZ, SA, Sm, 2011 F(R), W(R), I1, E, It1, I2, [R, Gg, Arg, E], 2012 E, W, F, I, It, A, Fj(R), Sm, NZ, SA, Tg, 2013 E, It1, I, W, F, Sm, SA1, It2, J, SA2, A, 2014 I, E, It, F, US, C, Arg 2(R), NZ(R), Tg, 2015 W, It 1, I 2, It 2, 3, F 2(R), [J, SA(R), Sm(R), A(R)]

Laney, B J (Edinburgh) 2001 NZ, 2002 E, It, I, F, W, C, US, R, SA, Fj, 2003 I 1, F, SA 2(R), It 2(R), W 2, 2004 W, E, It, I(R)

Lang, D (Paisley) 1876 E, 1877 I

Langrish, R W (London Scottish) 1930 F, 1931 F, W, I

Lauder, W (Neath) 1969 I, E, SA, 1970 F, W, I, A, 1973 F, 1974 W, E, I, F, 1975 I, F, NZ, A, 1976 F, 1977 E

Laughland, I H P (London Scottish) 1959 F, 1960 F, W, I, E, 1961 SA, W, I, E, 1962 F, W, I, E, 1963 F, W, I, 1964 F, NZ, W, I, E, 1965 F, W, I, E, SA, 1966 F, W, I, E, 1967 E

Lawrie, J R (Melrose) 1922 F, W, I, E, 1923 F, W, I, E, 1924 W, I, E

Lawrie, K G (Gala) 1980 F (R), W, E

Lawrie, S (Edinburgh) 2013 Sm(R)

Lawson, A J M (Edinburgh Wands, London Scottish) 1972 F (R), E, 1973 F, 1974 W, E, 1976 E, I, 1977 E, 1978 NZ, 1979 W, E, I, F, NZ, 1980 W (R)

Lawson, R G M (Gloucester, Newcastle) 2006 A(R), 2007 E(R), W(R), It(R), I1(R), F, SA(R), [Pt(R), NZ(R)], 2008 E(R), Arg1(R), 2(R), NZ(R), SA(R), C(R), 2009 A(R), Arg(R), 2010 E(R), Arg 1, 2, SA, Sm, 2011 F, W, I1(R), E, It1, I2, [Gg, Arg], 2012 Tg(R)

Lawson, S (Glasgow, Sale, Gloucester, London Irish, Newcastle) 2005 R, Arg(R), Sm, NZ, 2006 F(R), W, I(R), It, SA 1, 2(R), R(R), 2007 [Pt, R(R), NZ, Arg(R)], 2008 It(R), 2010 F(R), W(R), E(R), I(R), Arg1(R), 2(R), NZ2(R), 2011 W (R), I1(R), E(R), It1(R), 2, [R(R)], 2012 E(R), W(R), F(R), Fj(R), Sm(R), NZ(R), Tg, 2013 SA1, It2, SA2(R), 2014 E(R), It, F, W, US, C, Arg 2(R)

Lawther, T H B (Old Millhillians) 1932 SA, W , Arg 2(R)

Ledingham, G A (Aberdeen GSFP) 1913 F

Lee, D J (London Scottish, Edinburgh) 1998 I (R), F, W, E, Fj, A 1, 2, SA, 2001 Arg, 2004 It(R), F, I(R)

Lees, J B (Gala) 1947 I, A, 1948 F, W, E

Leggatt, H T O (Watsonians) 1891 W, I, E, 1892 W, I, 1893 W, E, 1894 I, E

Lely, W G (Cambridge U, London Scottish) 1909 I

Leslie, D G (Dundee HSFP, W of Scotland, Gala) 1975 I, F, W, E, NZ, A, 1976 F, W, E, I, 1978 NZ, 1980 E, 1981 W, E, I, NZ 1, 2, R, A, 1982 E, 1983 I, F, W, E, 1984 W, E, I, F, R, 1985 F, W, E

Leslie, J A (Glasgow, Northampton) 1998 SA, 1999 W, E, It, I, F, [SA], 2000 It, F, W, US, A, Sm, 2001 F, W, E, It, I, Tg, Arg, NZ, 2002 F, W

Leslie, M D (Glasgow, Edinburgh) 1998 SA (R), 1999 W, E, It, I, F, R, [SA, U, Sm, NZ], 2000 It, I, F, W, E, NZ 1, 2, 2001 F, W, E, It, 2002 It (R), I (R), F, W, E, SA, Fj(R), 2003 I 1, F, SA 1(R), 2 (R), It 2(R), W 2, [J(R), US(R)]

Liddell, E H (Edinburgh U) 1922 F, W, I, 1923 F, W, I, E

Lind, H (Dunfermline) 1928 I, 1931 F, W, I, E, 1932 SA, W, E, 1933 W, E, I, 1934 W, I, E, 1935 I, 1936 E

Lindsay, A B (London Hospital) 1910 I, 1911 I

Lindsay, G C (London Scottish) 1884 W, 1885 I 1, 1887 W, E

Lindsay-Watson, R H (Hawick) 1909 I

Lineen, S R P (Boroughmuir) 1989 W, E, I, F, Fj, R, 1990 I, F, W, E, NZ 1, 2, Arg, 1991 F, W, E, I, R, [J, Z, I, E, NZ], 1992 E, I, F, W, A 1, 2

Little, A W (Hawick) 1905 W

Logan, K M (Stirling County, Wasps) 1992 A 2, 1993 E (R), NZ (t), 1994 W, E, I, F, Arg 1, 2, SA, 1995 C, I, F, W, E, R, [Iv, Tg, F, NZ], WS, 1996 W (R), NZ 1, 2, A, It, 1997 W, E, I, F, A, 1998 I, F, SA (R), 1999 W, E, It, I, F, Arg, R, [SA, U, Sm, NZ], 2000 It, I, F, Sm, 2001 F, W, E, It, 2002 I (R), F (R), W, 2003 I 1, F, W 1, E, It 1, SA 1, 2, It 2, I 2, [J, US(R), F, Fj, A]

Logan, W R (Edinburgh U, Edinburgh Wands) 1931 E, 1932 SA, W, I, 1933 W, E, I, 1934 W, I, E, 1935 W, I, E, NZ, 1936 W, I, E, 1937 W, I, E

Longstaff, S L (Dundee HSFP, Glasgow) 1998 F (R), W, E, Fj, A 1, 2 1999 It (R), I (R), Arg (R), R, [U (R), Sp], 2000 It, I, NZ 1

Lorraine, H D B (Oxford U) 1933 W, E, I

Loudoun-Shand, E G (Oxford U) 1913 E

Low, K (London Irish) 2013 A(R), 2014 US(R), C(R), Arg1, Tg(R)

Low, M J (Glasgow Warriors, Exeter) 2009 F(R), E(R), Fj, A, Arg, 2010 F, Arg 1, 2, SA(R), Sm(R), 2011 F(R), W(R), I1, E, It2, 2013 It1(R), I(t&R), F(R), Sm(R), SA1(R), It2(R), SA2, A, 2014 I, E, It, US(R), C, SA(R)

Lowe, J D (Heriot's FP) 1934 W

Lumsden, I J M (Bath, Watsonians) 1947 F, W, A, 1949 F, W, I, E

Lyall, G G (Gala) 1947 F, 1948 F, W, I, E

Lyall, W J C (Edinburgh Acads) 1871 E

Mabon, J T (Jedforest) 1898 I, E, 1899 I, 1900 I

Macarthur, J P (Waterloo) 1932 E

MacArthur, P C (Glasgow Warriors) 2013 Sm, J(R), A(R), 2014 I(R), US(R), Arg1(R)

MacCallum, J C (Watsonians) 1905 E, NZ, 1906 W, I, E, SA, 1907 W, I, E, 1908 W, I, E, 1909 W, I, E, 1910 F, W, I, E, 1911 F, I, E, 1912 F, W, I, E

McClung, T (Edinburgh Acads) 1956 I, E, 1957 W, I, E, 1959 F, W, I, 1960 W

McClure, G B (W of Scotland) 1873 E

McClure, J H (W of Scotland) 1872 E

McCowan, D (W of Scotland) 1880 I, E, 1881 I, E, 1882 I, E, 1883 I, E, 1884 I, E

McCowat, R H (Glasgow Acads) 1905 I

McCrae, I G (Gordonians) 1967 E, 1968 I, 1969 F (R), W, 1972 F, NZ

McCrow, J W S (Edinburgh Acads) 1921 I

Macdonald, A E D (Heriot's FP) 1993 NZ

MacDonald, A R (Edinburgh) 2009 Arg, 2010 W(t&R), E(R), I(t)

McDonald, C (Jedforest) 1947 A

Macdonald, D (Edinburgh U) 1953 F, W, 1958 I, E

Macdonald, D S M (Oxford U, London Scottish, W of Scotland) 1977 E, I, F, W, 1978 I, W, E

Macdonald, J D (London Scottish, Army) 1966 F, W, I, E, 1967 F, W, I, E

Macdonald, J M (Edinburgh Wands) 1911 W

Macdonald, J S (Edinburgh U) 1903 E, 1904 W, I, E, 1905 W

Macdonald, K R (Stewart's Coll FP) 1956 F, W, I, 1957 W, I, E

Macdonald, R (Edinburgh U) 1950 F, W, I, E

McDonald, W A (Glasgow U) 1889 W, 1892 I, E

Macdonald, W G (London Scottish) 1969 I (R)

MacDougall, B (Borders) 2006 W, SA2(R)

Macdougall, J B (Greenock Wands, Wakefield) 1913 F, 1914 I, 1921 F, I, E

McEwan, M C (Edinburgh Acads) 1886 E, 1887 I, W, E, 1888 W, I, 1889 W, I, 1890 W, I, E, 1891 W, I, E, 1892 E

MacEwan, N A (Gala, Highland) 1971 F, W, I, E (2[1C]), 1972 F, W, E, NZ, 1973 F, W, I, E, P, 1974 W, E, I, F, 1975 W, E

McEwan, W M C (Edinburgh Acads) 1894 W, E, 1895 W, E, 1896 W, I, E, 1897 I, E, 1898 I, E, 1899 I, W, E, 1900 W, E

MacEwen, R K G (Cambridge U, London Scottish) 1954 F, NZ, I, W, 1956 F, W, I, E, 1957 F, W, I, E, 1958 W

Macfadyen, D J H (Glasgow) 2002 C (R), US, 2004 Sm, A1, 2, 3, J, A4, SA, 2006 SA 1, 2(R)

Macfarlan, D J (London Scottish) 1883 W, 1884 W, I, E, 1886 W, I, 1887 I, 1888 I

McFarlane, J L H (Edinburgh U) 1871 E, 1872 E, 1873 E

McGaughey, S K (Hawick) 1984 R

McGeechan, I R (Headingley) 1972 NZ, 1973 F, W, I, E, P, 1974 W, E, I, F, 1975 I, F, W, E, NZ, A, 1976 F, W, E, I, 1977 E, I, F, W, 1978 I, F, W, NZ, 1979 W, E, I, F

McGlashan, T P L (Royal HSFP) 1947 F, I, E, 1954 F, NZ, I, E, W

MacGregor, D G (Watsonians, Pontypridd) 1907 W, I, E

MacGregor, G (Cambridge U) 1890 W, I, E, 1891 W, I, E, 1893 W, I, E, 1894 W, I, E, 1896 E

MacGregor, I A A (Hillhead HSFP, Llanelli) 1955 I, 1956 F, W, I, E, 1957 F, W, I

MacGregor, J R (Edinburgh U) 1909 I

McGuinness, G M (W of Scotland) 1982 A 1, 2, 1983 I, 1985 I, F, W, E

McHarg, A F (W of Scotland, London Scottish) 1968 I, E, A, 1969 F, W, I, E, 1971 F, W, I, E (2[1C]), 1972 F, E, NZ, 1973 F, W, I, E, P, 1974 W, E, I, F, 1975 I, F, W, E, NZ, A, 1976 F, W, E, I, 1977 E, I, F, 1978 I, F, W, NZ, 1979 W, E

McIlwham, G R (Glasgow Hawks, Glasgow, Bordeaux-Bègles) 1998 Fj, A 2(R), 2000 E (R), NZ 2(R), US (R), A (R), Sm (R), 2001 F (R), W (R), E (R), It (R), 2003 SA 2(R), It 2(R), W 2(R), I 2, [A(R)]

McInally, S (Edinburgh) 2015 It 2, 3(R)

McIndoe, F J (Glasgow Acads) 1886 W, I

MacIntyre, I (Edinburgh Wands) 1890 W, I, E, 1891 W, I, E

McIvor, D J (Edinburgh Acads) 1992 E, I, F, W, 1993 NZ, 1994 SA

Mackay, E B (Glasgow Acads) 1920 W, 1922 E

McKeating, E (Heriot's FP) 1957 F, W, 1961 SA, W, I, E

McKelvey, G (Watsonians) 1997 A

McKendrick, J G (W of Scotland) 1889 I

Mackenzie, A D G (Selkirk) 1984 A

Mackenzie, C J G (United Services) 1921 E

Mackenzie, D D (Edinburgh U) 1947 W, I, E, 1948 F, W, I

Mackenzie, D K A (Edinburgh Wands) 1939 I, E

Mackenzie, J M (Edinburgh U) 1905 NZ, 1909 W, I, E, 1910 W, I, E, 1911 W, I

McKenzie, K D (Stirling County) 1994 Arg 1, 2, 1995 R, [Iv], 1996 I, F, W, E, NZ 1, 2, A, It, 1998 A 1(R), 2

Mackenzie, R C (Glasgow Acads) 1877 I, E, 1881 I, E

Mackie, G Y (Highland) 1975 A, 1976 F, W, 1978 F

MacKinnon, A (London Scottish) 1898 I, E, 1899 I, W, E, 1900 E

Mackintosh, C E W C (London Scottish) 1924 F

Mackintosh, H S (Glasgow U, W of Scotland) 1929 F, W, I, E, 1930 F, W, I, E, 1931 F, W, I, E, 1932 SA, W, I, E

MacLachlan, L P (Oxford U, London Scottish) 1954 NZ, I, E, W

Maclagan, W E (Edinburgh Acads) 1878 E, 1879 I, E, 1880 I, E, 1881 I, E, 1882 I, E, 1883 W, I, E, 1884 W, I, E, 1885 W, I 1, 2, 1887 I, W, E, 1888 W, I, 1890 W, I, E

McLaren, A (Durham County) 1931 F

McLaren, E (London Scottish, Royal HSFP) 1923 F, W, I, E, 1924 F

McLaren, J G (Bourgoin, Glasgow, Bordeaux-Bègles, Castres) 1999 R, [Sp, Sm], 2000 It (R), F, E, NZ 1, 2001 F, W, E (R), I, Tg, Arg, NZ, 2002 E, It, I, F, W, 2003 W 1, E, It 1, SA 1(R), It 2, I 2(R), [J, F(R), Fj(t&R), A(R)]

McLauchlan, J (Jordanhill) 1969 E, SA, 1970 F, W, 1971 F, W, I, E (2[1C]), 1972 F, W, E, NZ, 1973 F, W, I, E, P, 1974 W, E, I, F, 1975 I, F, W, E, NZ, A, 1976 F, W, E, I, 1977 W, 1978 I, F, W, E, NZ, 1979 W, E, I, F, NZ

McLean, D I (Royal HSFP) 1947 I, E

Maclennan, W D (Watsonians) 1947 F, I

MacLeod, D A (Glasgow U) 1886 I, E

MacLeod, G (Edinburgh Acads) 1878 E, 1882 I

McLeod, H F (Hawick) 1954 F, NZ, I, E, W, 1955 F, W, I, E, 1956 F, W, I, E, 1957 F, W, I, E, 1958 F, W, A, I, E, 1959 F, W, I, E, 1960 F, W, I, E, SA, 1961 F, SA, W, I, E, 1962 F, W, I, E

MacLeod, K G (Cambridge U) 1905 NZ, 1906 W, I, E, SA, 1907 W, I, E, 1908 I, E

MacLeod, L M (Cambridge U) 1904 W, I, E, 1905 W, I, NZ

MacLeod, S J (Borders, Llanelli Scarlets, Edinburgh) 2004 A3, J(t&R), A4(R), SA(R), 2006 F(R), W(R), E, SA2(R), 2007 I2(R), [Pt(R), R(R), NZ, It(R), Arg(R)], 2008 F(R), W(R), I, E, It, Arg 1, 2, 2010 Arg 2(t&R), SA, 2011 W(R)

Macleod, W M (Fettesian-Lorettonians, Edinburgh Wands) 1886 W, I

McMillan, K H D (Sale) 1953 F, W, I, E

MacMillan, R G (London Scottish) 1887 W, I, E, 1890 W, I, E,

1891 W, E, 1892 W, I, E, 1893 W, E, 1894 W, I, E, 1895 W, I, E, 1897 I, E

MacMyn, D J (Cambridge U, London Scottish) 1925 F, W, I, E, 1926 F, W, I, E, 1927 E, A, 1928 F

McNeil, A S B (Watsonians) 1935 I

McPartlin, J J (Harlequins, Oxford U) 1960 F, W, 1962 F, W, I, E

Macphail, J A R (Edinburgh Acads) 1949 E, 1951 SA

Macpherson, D G (London Hospital) 1910 I, E

Macpherson, G P S (Oxford U, Edinburgh Acads) 1922 F, W, I, E, 1924 W, E, 1925 F, W, E, 1927 F, W, I, E, 1928 F, W, E, 1929 I, E, 1930 F, W, I, E, 1931 W, E, 1932 SA, E

Macpherson, N C (Newport) 1920 W, I, E, 1921 F, E, 1923 I, E

McQueen, S B (Waterloo) 1923 F, W, I, E

Macrae, D J (St Andrew's U) 1937 W, I, E, 1938 W, I, E, 1939 W, I, E

Madsen, D F (Gosforth) 1974 W, E, I, F, 1975 I, F, W, E, 1976 F, 1977 E, I, F, W, 1978 I

Mair, N G R (Edinburgh U) 1951 F, W, I, E

Maitland, G (Edinburgh Inst FP) 1885 W, I 2

Maitland, R (Edinburgh Inst FP) 1881 E, 1882 I, E, 1884 W, 1885 W

Maitland, R P (Royal Artillery) 1872 E

Maitland, S D (Glasgow Warriors) 2013 E, It1, I, W, F, J, SA2, A, 2014 I, US, C, Arg1, SA, Arg 2, NZ, 2015 F 2, [J(R), US, Sm, A]

Malcolm, A G (Glasgow U) 1888 I

Manson, J J (Dundee HSFP) 1995 E (R)

Marsh, J (Edinburgh Inst FP) 1889 W, I

Marshall, A (Edinburgh Acads) 1875 E

Marshall, G R (Selkirk) 1988 A (R), 1989 Fj, 1990 Arg, 1991 [Z]

Marshall, J C (London Scottish) 1954 F, NZ, I, E, W

Marshall, K W (Edinburgh Acads) 1934 W, I, E, 1935 W, I, E, 1936 W, 1937 E

Marshall, T R (Edinburgh Acads) 1871 E, 1872 E, 1873 E, 1874 E

Marshall, W (Edinburgh Acads) 1872 E

Martin, H (Edinburgh Acads, Oxford U) 1908 W, I, E, 1909 W, E

Masters, W H (Edinburgh Inst FP) 1879 I, 1880 I, E

Mather, C G (Edinburgh, Glasgow) 1999 R (R), [Sp, Sm (R)], 2000 F (t), 2003 [F, Fj, A], 2004 W, E, F

Maxwell, F T (Royal Engineers) 1872 E

Maxwell, G H H P (Edinburgh Acads, RAF, London Scottish) 1913 I, E, 1914 W, I, E, 1920 W, E, 1921 F, W, I, E, 1922 F, E

Maxwell, J M (Langholm) 1957 I

Mayer, M J M (Watsonians, Edinburgh) 1998 SA, 1999 [SA (R), U, Sp, Sm, NZ], 2000 It, I

Mein, J (Edinburgh Acads) 1871 E, 1872 E, 1873 E, 1874 E, 1875 E

Melville, C L (Army) 1937 W, I, E

Menzies, H F (W of Scotland) 1893 W, I, 1894 W, E

Metcalfe, G H (Glasgow Hawks, Glasgow) 1998 A 1, 2, 1999 W, E, It, I, F, Arg, R, [SA, U, Sm, NZ], 2000 It, I, F, W, E, 2001 I, Tg, 2002 E, It, I, F, W (R), C, US, 2003 I 1, F, W 1, E, It 1, SA 1, 2, W 2, I 2, [US, F, Fj, A]

Metcalfe, R (Northampton, Edinburgh) 2000 E, NZ 1, 2, US (R), A (R), Sm, 2001 F, W, E

Methuen, A (London Scottish) 1889 W, I

Michie, E J S (Aberdeen U, Aberdeen GSFP) 1954 F, NZ, I, E, 1955 W, I, E, 1956 F, W, I, E, 1957 F, W, I, E

Millar, J N (W of Scotland) 1892 W, I, E, 1893 W, 1895 I, E

Millar, R K (London Scottish) 1924 I

Millican, J G (Edinburgh U) 1973 W, I, E

Milne, C J B (Fettesian-Lorettonians, W of Scotland) 1886 W, I, E

Milne, D F (Heriot's FP) 1991 [J(R)]

Milne, I G (Heriot's FP, Harlequins) 1979 I, F, NZ, 1980 I, F, 1981 NZ 1, 2, R, A, 1982 E, I, F, W, A 1, 2, 1983 I, F, W, E, NZ, 1984 W, E, I, F, A, 1985 F, W, E, 1986 F, W, E, I, R, 1987 I, F, W, E, [F, Z, NZ], 1988 A, 1989 W, 1990 NZ 1, 2

Milne, K S (Heriot's FP) 1989 W, E, I, F, Fj, R, 1990 I, F, W, E, NZ 2, Arg, 1991 F, W (R), E, [Z], 1992 E, I, F, W, A 1, 1993 I, F, W, E, NZ, 1994 W, E, I, F, SA, 1995 C, I, F, W, E, [Tg, F, NZ]

Milne, W M (Glasgow Acads) 1904 I, E, 1905 W, I

Milroy, E (Watsonians) 1910 W, 1911 E, 1912 W, I, E, SA, 1913 F, I, E, 1914 I, E

Mitchell, G W E (Edinburgh Wands) 1967 NZ, 1968 F, W

Mitchell, J G (W of Scotland) 1885 W, I 1, 2

Moffat, J S D (Edinburgh, Borders) 2002 R, SA, Fj(R), 2004 A3

Moir, C C (Northampton) 2000 W, E, NZ 1

Moncreiff, F J (Edinburgh Acads) 1871 E, 1872 E, 1873 E

Monteith, H G (Cambridge U, London Scottish) 1905 E, 1906 W, I, E, SA, 1907 W, I, 1908 E

Monypenny, D B (London Scottish) 1899 I, W, E

Moodie, A R (St Andrew's U) 1909 E, 1910 F, 1911 F

Moore, A (Edinburgh Acads) 1990 NZ 2, Arg, 1991 F, W, E

Morgan, D W (Stewart's-Melville FP) 1973 W, I, E, P, 1974 I, F, 1975 I, F, W, E, NZ, A, 1976 F, W, 1977 I, F, W, 1978 I, F, W, E

Morrison, G A (Glasgow Warriors) 2004 A1(R), 2(R), 3, J(R), A4(R), SA(R), 2008 W(R), E, It, Arg 1, 2, 2009 W, F, It, I, E, Fj, A, 2010 F, W, It, E, I, Arg 1, 2, NZ, SA, Sm, 2011 I2, It2, [Gg, Arg], 2012 F, I, It

Morrison, I R (London Scottish) 1993 I, F, W, E, 1994 W, SA, 1995 C, I, F, W, E, R, [Tg, F, NZ]

Morrison, M C (Royal HSFP) 1896 W, I, E, 1897 I, E, 1898 I, E, 1899 I, W, E, 1900 W, E, 1901 W, I, E, 1902 W, I, E, 1903 W, I, 1904 W, I, E

Morrison, R H (Edinburgh U) 1886 W, I, E

Morrison, W H (Edinburgh Acads) 1900 W

Morton, D S (W of Scotland) 1887 I, W, E, 1888 W, I, 1889 W, I, 1890 I, E

Mowat, J G (Glasgow Acads) 1883 W, E

Mower, A L (Newcastle) 2001 Tg, Arg, NZ, 2002 It, 2003 I 1, F, W 1, E, It 1, SA 1, 2, W 2, I 2

Muir, D E (Heriot's FP) 1950 F, W, I, E, 1952 W, I, E

Munnoch, N M (Watsonians) 1952 F, W, I

Munro, D S (Glasgow High Kelvinside) 1994 W, E, I, F, Arg 1, 2, 1997 W (R)

Munro, P (Oxford U, London Scottish) 1905 W, I, E, NZ, 1906 W, I, E, SA, 1907 I, E, 1911 F, W, I

Munro, R (St Andrew's U) 1871 E

Munro, S (Ayr, W of Scotland) 1980 I, F, 1981 F, W, E, I, NZ 1, 2, R, 1984 W

Munro, W H (Glasgow HSFP) 1947 I, E

Murchie, P E (Glasgow Warriors) 2013 SA1, It2, 2014 SA(R)

Murdoch, W C W (Hillhead HSFP) 1935 E, NZ, 1936 W, I, 1939 E, 1948 F, W, I, E

Murray, C A (Hawick, Edinburgh) 1998 E (R), Fj, A 1, 2, SA, 1999 W, E, It, I, F, Arg, [SA, U, Sp, Sm, NZ], 2000 NZ 2, US, A, Sm, 2001 F, W, E, It (R), Tg, Arg

Murray, E A (Northampton, Newcastle, Worcester. Glasgow Warriors) 2005 R(R), 2006 R, PI, A, 2007 E, W, It, I1, F, I2, SA, [Pt, R, It, Arg], 2008 F, W, I, E, It, Arg 1, 2, NZ, SA, C, 2009 It, I, E, 2010 W, It, E, I, NZ, SA, Sm, 2011 F, W, It1(R), 2(R), [Gg, E], 2012 E, I(R), It(R), A, Fj, Sm, SA, Tg, 2013 E, It1, W, F, Sm, SA1, It2, J, A(R), 2014 W(R), SA(R), Arg 2, NZ, 2015 F 1, It 1, E, I 1

Murray, G M (Glasgow Acads) 1921 I, 1926 W

Murray, H M (Glasgow U) 1936 W, I

Murray, K T (Hawick) 1985 I, F, W

Murray, R O (Cambridge U) 1935 W, E

Murray, S (Bedford, Saracens, Edinburgh) 1997 A, SA, 1998 It, Fj, A 1, 2, SA, 1999 W, E, It, I, F, Arg, R, [SA, U, Sm, NZ], 2000 It, I, F, W, NZ 1, 2, US, A, Sm, 2001 F, W, E, It, I, Tg, Arg, NZ, 2002 E, It, I, F, W, R, SA, 2003 I 1, F, W 1, E, It 1, SA 1, 2, It 2, W 2, [J, F, A(R)], 2004 W, E, It, F, I, Sm, A1, 2, 2005 F, I, It, W, E, R, Arg, Sm, NZ, 2006 F, W, I, It, SA1, R, PI, A, 2007 Et&R), W, It, I1, F, SA(R), [Pt, NZ]

Murray, W A K (London Scottish) 1920 F, I, 1921 F

Mustchin, M L (Edinburgh) 2008 Arg 1, 2, NZ(R), SA(R), C(R)

Napier, H M (W of Scotland) 1877 I, E, 1878 E, 1879 I, E

Neill, J B (Edinburgh Acads) 1963 E, 1964 F, NZ, W, I, E, 1965 F

Neill, R M (Edinburgh Acads) 1901 E, 1902 I

Neilson, G T (W of Scotland) 1891 W, I, 1892 W, E, 1893 W, 1894 W, I, 1895 W, I, E, 1896 W, I, E

Neilson, J A (Glasgow Acads) 1878 E, 1879 E

Neilson, R T (W of Scotland) 1898 I, E, 1899 I, W, 1900 I, E

Neilson, T (W of Scotland) 1874 E

Neilson, W (Merchiston Castle School, Cambridge U, London Scottish) 1891 W, E, 1892 W, I, E, 1893 I, E, 1894 E, 1895 W, I, E, 1896 I, 1897 I, E

Neilson, W G (Merchistonians) 1894 E
Nel, W P (Edinburgh) 2015 It 2(R), 3, F 2, [J, US(R), SA, Sm, A]
Nelson, J B (Glasgow Acads) 1925 F, W, I, E, 1926 F, W, I, E, 1927 F, W, I, E, 1928 I, E, 1929 F, W, I, E, 1930 F, W, I, E, 1931 F, W, I
Nelson, T A (Oxford U) 1898 E
Nichol, J A (Royal HSFP) 1955 W, I, E
Nichol, S A (Selkirk) 1994 Arg 2(R)
Nicol, A D (Dundee HSFP, Bath, Glasgow) 1992 E, I, F, W, A 1, 2, 1993 NZ, 1994 W, 1997 A, SA, 2000 I (R), F, W, E, NZ 1, 2, 2001 F, W, E, I (R), Tg, Arg, NZ
Nimmo, C S (Watsonians) 1920 E

Ogilvy, C (Hawick) 1911 I, E, 1912 I
Oliver, G H (Hawick) 1987 [Z], 1990 NZ 2(R), 1991 [Z]
Oliver, G K (Gala) 1970 A
Orr, C E (W of Scotland) 1887 I, E, W, 1888 W, I, 1889 W, I, 1890 W, I, E, 1891 W, I, E, 1892 W, I, E
Orr, H J (London Scottish) 1903 W, I, 1904 W, I
Orr, J E (W of Scotland) 1889 I, 1890 W, I, E, 1891 W, I, E, 1892 W, I, E, 1893 I, E
Orr, J H (Edinburgh City Police) 1947 F, W
Osler, F L (Edinburgh U) 1911 F, W

Park, J (Royal HSFP) 1934 W
Parks, D A (Glasgow Warriors, Cardiff Blues) 2004 W(R), E(R), F(R), I, Sm(t&R), A1, 2, 3, J, A4, SA, 2005 F, I, It, W, R, Arg, Sm, NZ, 2006 F, W, E, I, It(R), SA1, PI, A, 2007 E, I1, F, I2(R), SA(R), [Pt, R, NZ(R), It, Arg], 2008 F, W, I(R), E(R), It, Arg 1, 2(R), NZ(R), SA(t), C(R), 2010 W, It, E, I, Arg 1, 2, NZ, SA, Sm, 2011 F, W, I1(R), E(R), It1(R), 2, [R(R), Gg, Arg(R), E(R)], 2012 E
Paterson, C D (Edinburgh, Gloucester) 1999 [Sp], 2000 F, W, E, NZ 1, 2, US, A, Sm, 2001 F, W, E, It, I, NZ, 2002 E, It, I, F, W, C, US, R, SA, Fj, 2003 I 1, F, W 1, E, It 1, SA 1, 2, It 2(R), W 2(R), I 2, [J, US, F, Fj, A], 2004 W, E, It, F, I, Sm, A3, J, A4, SA, 2005 F, I, It, W, E, R, Arg, Sm, NZ, 2006 F, W, E, I, NZ, It, Arg], 2008 F(R), W, I, E, It, Arg 1, 2, NZ, SA, 2009 W(R), F(R), It(t&R), I, E, Fj(R), A(R), Arg(R), 2010 F, W, SA(R), 2011 I1, E, It1, I2, [R, Gg(R), Arg, E]
Paterson, D S (Gala) 1969 SA, 1970 I, A, 1971 F, W, I, E (2[1C]), 1972 W
Paterson, G Q (Edinburgh Acads) 1876 E
Paterson, J R (Birkenhead Park) 1925 F, W, I, E, 1926 F, W, I, E, 1927 F, W, I, E, A, 1928 F, W, I, E, 1929 F, W, I, E
Patterson, D (Hawick) 1896 W
Patterson, D W (West Hartlepool) 1994 SA, 1995 [Tg]
Pattullo, G L (Panmure) 1920 F, W, I, E
Paxton, I A M (Selkirk) 1981 NZ 1, 2, R, A, 1982 E, I, F, W, A 1, 2, 1983 I, E, NZ, 1984 W, E, I, F, 1985 I (R), F, W, E, 1986 W, E, I, R, 1987 I, F, W, E, [F, Z, R, NZ], 1988 I, E, A
Paxton, R E (Kelso) 1982 I, A 2(R)
Pearson, J (Watsonians) 1909 I, E, 1910 F, W, I, E, 1911 F, 1912 F, W, SA, 1913 I, E
Pender, I M (London Scottish) 1914 E
Pender, N E K (Hawick) 1977 I, 1978 F, W, E
Penman, W M (RAF) 1939 I
Peterkin, W A (Edinburgh U) 1881 E, 1883 I, 1884 W, I, E, 1885 W, I 1, 2
Peters, E W (Bath) 1995 C, I, F, W, E, R, [Tg, F, NZ], 1996 I, F, W, E, NZ 1, 2, A, It, 1997 A, SA, 1998 W, E, Fj, A 1, 2, SA, 1999 W, E, It, I
Petrie, A G (Royal HSFP) 1873 E, 1874 E, 1875 E, 1876 E, 1877 I, E, 1878 E, 1879 I, E, 1880 I, E
Petrie, J M (Glasgow) 2000 NZ 2, US, A, Sm, 2001 F, W, It (R), I (R), Tg, Arg, 2002 F (t), W (R), C, R(R), Fj, 2003 F(t+R), 1(R), SA 1(R), 2 (R), It 2, W 2, I 2(R), [J, US, F(t&R), A(R)], 2004 It(R), I(R), Sm(R), A1(R), 2(t&R), 3(R), J, A4, SA(R), 2005 F, I, It, W, E(R), R, 2006 F(R), W(R), I(R), SA 2
Philip, T K (Edinburgh) 2004 W, E, It, F, I
Philp, A (Edinburgh Inst FP) 1882 E
Pinder, S J (Glasgow) 2006 SA 1(R), 2(R)
Pocock, E I (Edinburgh Wands) 1877 I, E
Pollock, J A (Gosforth) 1982 W, 1983 F, NZ, 1984 E (R), I, F, R, 1985 F

Polson, A H (Gala) 1930 E
Pountney, A C (Northampton) 1998 SA, 1999 W (t+R), E (R), It (t+R), I (R), F, Arg, [SA, U, Sm, NZ], 2000 It, I, F, W, E, US, A, Sm, 2001 F, W, E, It, I, 2002 E, I, F, W, R, SA, Fj
Proudfoot, M C (Melrose, Glasgow) 1998 Fj, A 1, 2, 2003 I 2(R)
Purdie, W (Jedforest) 1939 W, I, E
Purves, A B H L (London Scottish) 1906 W, I, E, SA, 1907 W, I, E, 1908 W, I, E
Purves, W D C L (London Scottish) 1912 F, W, I, SA, 1913 I, E
Pyrgos, H B (Glasgow Warriors) 2012 NZ(R), SA(R), Tg, 2013 E(R), It1(R), F(R), Sm(R), SA1(R), It2(R), J(R), 2014 Arg1(R), SA, Arg 2(R), 2015 I 2, It 2(R), 3(R), [US]

Rea, C W W (W of Scotland, Headingley) 1968 A, 1969 F, W, I, SA, 1970 F, W, I, A, 1971 F, W, E (2[1C])
Redpath, B W (Melrose, Narbonne, Sale) 1993 NZ (t), 1994 E (t), F, Arg 1, 2, 1995 C, I, F, W, E, R, [Iv, F, NZ], WS, 1996 I, F, W, E, A (R), It, 1997 E, I, F, 1998 Fj, A 1, 2, SA, 1999 R (R), [U (R), Sp], 2000 It, I, US, A, Sm, 2001 F (R), E (R), It, I, 2002 E, It, I, F, W, R, SA, Fj, 2003 I 1, F, W 1, E, It 1, SA 1, 2, [J, US(R), F, Fj, A]
Reed, A I (Bath, Wasps) 1993 I, F, W, E, 1994 E, I, F, Arg 1, 2, SA, 1996 It, 1997 W, E, I, F, 1999 It (R), F (R), [Sp]
Reid, C (Edinburgh Acads) 1881 I, E, 1882 I, E, 1883 W, I, E, 1884 W, I, E, 1885 W, I 1, 2, 1886 W, I, E, 1887 I, W, E, 1888 W, I
Reid, G J (Glasgow Warriors) 2014 US,C,Arg1(R), 2(R), NZ(R), Tg(R), 2015 F 1(R), W(R), I 2(R), It 2, 3(R), F 2(R), [SA, Sm(t), A(R)]
Reid, J (Edinburgh Wands) 1874 E, 1875 E, 1876 E, 1877 I, E
Reid, J M (Edinburgh Acads) 1898 I, E, 1899 I
Reid, M F (Loretto) 1883 I, E
Reid, R E (Glasgow) 2001 Tg (R), Arg
Reid, S J (Boroughmuir, Leeds, Narbonne) 1995 WS, 1999 F, Arg, [Sp], 2000 It (t), F, W, E (t)
Reid-Kerr, J (Greenock Wand) 1909 E
Relph, W K L (Stewart's Coll FP) 1955 F, W, I, E
Rennie, R M (Edinburgh) 2008 I(R), 2010 NZ(R), SA(R), Sm(R), 2011 F(R), W(R), I2, It2(R), [R(R), Gg, E(R)], 2012 E, W, F, I, It, A, Fj, Sm, NZ
Renny-Tailyour, H W (Royal Engineers) 1872 E
Renwick, J M (Hawick) 1972 F, W, E, NZ, 1973 F, 1974 W, E, I, F, 1975 I, F, W, E, NZ, A, 1976 F, W, E (R), 1977 I, F, W, 1978 I, F, W, E, NZ, 1979 W, E, I, F, NZ, 1980 I, F, W, E, 1981 F, W, E, I, NZ 1, 2, R, A, 1982 E, I, F, W, 1983 I, F, W, E, 1984 R
Renwick, W L (London Scottish) 1989 R
Renwick, W N (London Scottish, Edinburgh Wands) 1938 E, 1939 W
Richardson, J F (Edinburgh Acads) 1994 SA
Ritchie, G (Merchistonians) 1871 E
Ritchie, G F (Dundee HSFP) 1932 E
Ritchie, J M (Watsonians) 1933 W, E, I, 1934 W, I, E
Ritchie, W T (Cambridge U) 1905 I, E
Robb, G H (Glasgow U) 1881 I, 1885 W
Roberts, G (Watsonians) 1938 W, I, E, 1939 W, E
Robertson, A H (W of Scotland) 1871 E
Robertson, A W (Edinburgh Acads) 1897 E
Robertson, D (Edinburgh Acads) 1875 E
Robertson, D D (Cambridge U) 1893 W
Robertson, I (London Scottish, Watsonians) 1968 E, 1969 E, SA, 1970 F, W, I, E, A
Robertson, I P M (Watsonians) 1910 F
Robertson, J (Clydesdale) 1908 E
Robertson, K W (Melrose) 1978 NZ, 1979 W, E, I, F, NZ, 1980 W, E, 1981 F, W, I, R, A, 1982 E, I, F, A 1, 2, 1983 I, F, W, E, 1984 R, I, F, R, A, 1985 I, F, W, E, 1986 I, 1987 F (R), W, E, [F, Z, NZ], 1988 E, A, 1989 E, I, F
Robertson, L (London Scottish United Services) 1908 E, 1911 W, 1912 W, I, E, SA, 1913 W, I, E
Robertson, M A (Gala) 1958 F
Robertson, R D (London Scottish) 1912 F
Robson, A (Hawick) 1954 F, 1955 F, W, I, E, 1956 F, W, I, E, 1957 F, W, I, E, 1958 W, A, I, E, 1959 F, W, I, E, 1960 F
Rodd, J A T (United Services, RN, London Scottish) 1958 F, W, A, I, E, 1960 F, W, 1962 F, 1964 F, NZ, W, 1965 F, W, I
Rogerson, J (Kelvinside Acads) 1894 W
Roland, E T (Edinburgh Acads) 1884 I, E

Rollo, D M D (Howe of Fife) 1959 E, 1960 F, W, I, E, SA, 1961 F, SA, W, I, E, 1962 F, W, E, 1963 F, W, I, E, 1964 F, NZ, W, I, E, 1965 F, W, I, E, SA, 1966 F, W, I, E, A, 1967 F, W, E, NZ, 1968 F, W, I

Rose, D M (Jedforest) 1951 F, W, I, E, SA, 1953 F, W

Ross, A (Kilmarnock) 1924 F, W

Ross, A (Royal HSFP) 1905 W, I, E, 1909 W, I

Ross, A R (Edinburgh U) 1911 W, 1914 W, I, E

Ross, E J (London Scottish) 1904 W

Ross, G (Edinburgh, Leeds) 2001 Tg, 2002 R, SA, Fj(R), 2003 I 1, W 1(R), SA 2(R), It 2, I 2, [J], 2004 Sm, A1(R), 2(R), J(R), SA(R), 2005 It(R), W(R), E, 2006 F(R), W(R), E(R), I(R), It, SA 1(R), 2

Ross, G T (Watsonians) 1954 NZ, I, E, W

Ross, I A (Hillhead HSFP) 1951 F, W, I, E

Ross, J (London Scottish) 1901 W, I, E, 1902 W, 1903 E

Ross, K I (Boroughmuir FP) 1961 SA, W, I, E, 1962 F, W, I, E, 1963 F, W, E

Ross, W A (Hillhead HSFP) 1937 W, E

Rottenburg, H (Cambridge U, London Scottish) 1899 W, E, 1900 W, I, E

Roughead, W N (Edinburgh Acads, London Scottish) 1927 A, 1928 F, W, I, E, 1930 I, E, 1931 F, W, I, E, 1932 W

Rowan, N A (Boroughmuir) 1980 W, E, 1981 F, W, E, I, 1984 R, 1985 I, 1987 [R], 1988 I, F, W, E

Rowand, R (Glasgow HSFP) 1930 F, W, 1932 E, 1933 W, E, I, 1934 W

Roxburgh, A J (Kelso) 1997 A, 1998 It, F (R), W, E, Fj, A 1(R), 2(R)

Roy, A (Waterloo) 1938 W, I, E, 1939 W, I, E

Russell, F A (Glasgow Warriors) 2014 US, C, Arg 2, NZ, Tg, 2015 F 1, W, E, I 1, It 3, F 2, [J, US, Sm, A]

Russell, R R (Saracens, London Irish) 1999 R, [U (R), Sp, Sm (R), NZ (R)], 2000 I (R), 2001 F (R), 2002 F (R), W (R), 2003 W 1(R), It 1(R), SA 1 (R), 2 (R), It 2 I 2(R), [J, F(R), Fj(t), A(R)] , 2004 W(R), E(R), F(R), I(R), J(R), A4(R), SA(R), 2005 It(R)

Russell, W L (Glasgow Acads) 1905 NZ, 1906 W, I, E

Rutherford, J Y (Selkirk) 1979 W, E, I, F, NZ, 1980 I, F, E, 1981 F, W, E, I, NZ 1, 2, A, 1982 E, I, F, W, A 1, 2, 1983 E, NZ, 1984 W, E, I, F, R, 1985 I, F, W, E, 1986 F, W, E, I, R, 1987 I, F, W, E, [F]

Ryder, T P (Glasgow Warriors) 2012 Fj(R), Sm(R)

Sampson, R W F (London Scottish) 1939 W, 1947 W

Sanderson, G A (Royal HSFP) 1907 W, I, E, 1908 I

Sanderson, J L P (Edinburgh Acads) 1873 E

Schulze, D G (London Scottish) 1905 E, 1907 I, E, 1908 W, I, E, 1909 W, I, E, 1910 W, I, E, 1911 W

Scobie, R M (Royal Military Coll) 1914 W, I, E

Scotland, K J F (Heriot's FP, Cambridge U, Leicester) 1957 F, W, I, E, 1958 E, 1959 F, W, I, E, 1960 F, W, I, E, 1961 F, SA, W, I, E, 1962 F, W, I, E, 1963 F, W, I, E, 1965 F

Scott, D M (Langholm, Watsonians) 1950 I, E, 1951 W, I, E, SA, 1952 F, W, I, 1953 F

Scott, J M B (Edinburgh Acads) 1907 E, 1908 W, I, E, 1909 W, I, E, 1910 F, W, I, E, 1911 F, W, I, 1912 W, I, E, SA, 1913 W, I, E

Scott, J S (St Andrew's U) 1950 E

Scott, J W (Stewart's Coll FP) 1925 F, W, I, E, 1926 F, W, I, E, 1927 F, W, I, E, A, 1928 F, W, E, 1929 E, 1930 F

Scott, M (Dunfermline) 1992 A 2

Scott, M C M (Edinburgh) 2012 I(R), A, Fj, Sm, NZ, SA, Tg, 2013 E, It1, I, W, F, Sm, SA1, Tg, J, 2014 I(R), E, It, F, W, 2015 W(R), It 1(R), E, I 1, 2(R), It 2, 3(R), F 2, [J, US(R), SA, Sm]

Scott, R (Hawick) 1898 I, 1900 I, E

Scott, S (Edinburgh, Borders) 2000 NZ 2 (R), US (t+R), 2001 It (R), I (R), Tg (R), NZ (R), 2002 US (R), R(R), Fj(R), 2004 Sm(R), A1(R)

Scott, T (Langholm, Hawick) 1896 W, 1897 I, E, 1898 I, E, 1899 I, W, E, 1900 I, W, E

Scott, T M (Hawick) 1893 E, 1895 W, I, E, 1896 W, E, 1897 I, E, 1898 I, E, 1900 W, I

Scott, W P (W of Scotland) 1900 I, E, 1902 I, E, 1903 W, I, E, 1904 W, I, E, 1905 W, I, E, NZ, 1906 W, I, E, SA, 1907 W, I, E

Scoular, J G (Cambridge U) 1905 NZ, 1906 W, I, E, SA

Selby, J A R (Watsonians) 1920 W, I

Seymour, T S F (Glasgow Warriors) 2013 SA1, It2, J, SA2, A, 2014 E, It, F, Arg1, SA, Arg 2, NZ, Tg, 2015 F 1, It 1, E, I 1, F 2, [J, SA, Sm, A]

Shackleton, J A P (London Scottish) 1959 E, 1963 F, W, 1964 NZ, W, 1965 I, SA

Sharp, A V (Bristol) 1994 E, I, F, Arg 1, 2 SA

Sharp, G (Stewart's FP, Army) 1960 F, 1964 F, NZ, W

Shaw, G D (Sale) 1935 NZ, 1936 W, 1937 W, I, E, 1939 I

Shaw, I (Glasgow HSFP) 1937 I

Shaw, J N (Edinburgh Acads) 1921 W, I

Shaw, R W (Glasgow HSFP) 1934 W, I, E, 1935 W, I, E, NZ, 1936 W, I, E, 1937 W, I, E, 1938 W, I, E, 1939 W, I, E

Shedden, D (W of Scotland) 1972 NZ, 1973 F, W, I, E, P, 1976 W, E, I, 1977 I, F, W, 1978 I, F, W

Shepherd, R J S (Melrose) 1995 WS, 1996 I, F, W, E, NZ 1, 2, A, It, 1997 W, E, I, F, SA, 1998 It, I, W (R), Fj (t), A 1, 2

Shiel, A G (Melrose, Edinburgh) 1991 [I (R), WS], 1993 I, F, W, E, NZ, 1994 Arg 1, 2, SA, 1995 R, [Iv, F, NZ], WS, 2000 I, NZ 1(R), 2

Shillinglaw, R B (Gala, Army) 1960 I, E, SA, 1961 F, SA

Simmers, B M (Glasgow Acads) 1965 F, W, 1966 A, 1967 F, W, I, 1971 F (R)

Simmers, W M (Glasgow Acads) 1926 W, I, E, 1927 F, W, I, E, A, 1928 F, W, I, E, 1929 F, W, I, E, 1930 F, W, I, E, 1931 F, W, I, E, 1932 SA, W, I, E

Simpson, G L (Kirkcaldy, Glasgow) 1998 A 1, 2, 1999 Arg (R), R, [SA, U, Sm, NZ], 2000 It, I, NZ 1(R), 2001 I, Tg (R), Arg (R), NZ

Simpson, J W (Royal HSFP) 1893 I, E, 1894 W, I, E, 1895 W, I, E, 1896 W, I, 1897 E, 1899 W, E

Simpson, R S (Glasgow Acads) 1923 I

Simson, E D (Edinburgh U, London Scottish) 1902 E, 1903 W, I, E, 1904 W, I, E, 1905 W, I, E, NZ, 1906 W, I, E, 1907 W, I, E

Simson, J T (Watsonians) 1905 NZ, 1909 W, I, E, 1910 F, W, 1911 I

Simson, R F (London Scottish) 1911 E

Sloan, A T (Edinburgh Acads) 1914 W, 1920 F, W, I, E, 1921 F, W, I, E

Sloan, D A (Edinburgh Acads, London Scottish) 1950 F, W, E, 1951 W, I, E, 1953 F

Sloan, T (Glasgow Acads, Oxford U) 1905 NZ, 1906 W, SA, 1907 W, E, 1908 W, 1909 I

Smeaton, P W (Edinburgh Acads) 1881 I, 1883 I, E

Smith, A R (Oxford U) 1895 W, I, E, 1896 W, I, 1897 I, E, 1898 I, E, 1900 I, E

Smith, A R (Cambridge U, Gosforth, Ebbw Vale, Edinburgh Wands) 1955 W, I, E, 1956 F, W, I, E, 1957 F, W, I, E, 1958 F, W, A, I, 1959 F, W, I, E, 1960 F, W, I, E, SA, 1961 F, SA, W, I, E, 1962 F, W, I, E

Smith, C J (Edinburgh) 2002 C, US (R), 2004 Sm(t&R), A1(R), 2(R), 3(R), J(R), 2005 Arg(R), Sm, NZ(R), 2006 F(R), W(R), E(R), I(R), It(R), SA 1(R), 2, R(R), 2007 I2(R), [R(R), NZ, It(R), Arg(R)], 2008 E(R), It(R)

Smith, D W C (London Scottish) 1949 F, W, I, E, 1950 F, W, I, 1953 I

Smith, E R (Edinburgh Acads) 1879 I

Smith, G K (Kelso) 1957 I, E, 1958 F, W, A, 1959 F, W, I, E, 1960 F, W, I, E, 1961 F, SA, W, I, E

Smith, H O (Watsonians) 1895 W, 1896 W, I, E, 1898 I, E, 1899 W, 1900 E, 1902 E

Smith, I R (Gloucester, Moseley) 1992 E, I, W, A 1, 2, 1994 E (R), I, F, Arg 1, 2, 1995 [Iv], WS, 1996 I, F, W, E, NZ 1, 2, A, It, 1997 E, I, F, A, SA

Smith, I S (Oxford U, Edinburgh U) 1924 W, I, E, 1925 F, W, I, E, 1926 F, W, I, E, 1927 F, I, E, 1929 F, W, I, E, 1930 F, W, I, 1931 F, W, I, E, 1932 SA, W, I, E, 1933 W, E, I

Smith, I S G (London Scottish) 1969 SA, 1970 F, W, I, E, 1971 F, W, I

Smith, M A (London Scottish) 1970 W, I, E, A

Smith, R T (Kelso) 1929 F, W, I, E, 1930 F, W, I

Smith, S H (Glasgow Acads) 1877 I, 1878 E

Smith, T J (Gala) 1983 E, NZ, 1985 I, F

Smith T J (Watsonians, Dundee HSFP, Glasgow, Brive, Northampton) 1997 E, I, F, 1998 SA, 1999 W, E, It, I, Arg, R, [SA, U, Sm, NZ], 2000 It, I, F, W, E, NZ 1, 2, US, A, Sm, 2001 F, W, E, It, I, Tg, Arg, NZ, 2002 E, It, I, F, W, R, SA, Fj,

2003 I 1, F, W 1, E, It 1, 2, [J, US, F, Fj, A], 2004 W, E, Sm, A1, 2, 2005 F, I, It, W, E

Sole, D M B (Bath, Edinburgh Acads) 1986 F, W, 1987 I, F, W, E, [F, Z, R, NZ], 1988 I, F, W, E, A, 1989 W, E, I, F, Fj, R, 1990 I, F, W, E, NZ 1, 2, Arg, 1991 F, W, E, I, R, [J, I, WS, E, NZ], 1992 E, I, F, W, A 1, 2

Somerville, D (Edinburgh Inst FP) 1879 I, 1882 I, 1883 W, I, E, 1884 W

Southwell, H F G (Edinburgh, Stade Français) 2004 Sm(t&R), A1, 2, 3(R), J, A4, SA, 2005 F, I, It, W, E, R(R), Arg(R), Sm(R), NZ, 2006 F, W, E, I, It, SA 1, 2, 2006 R, PI(t&R), A(R), 2007 E, W, It, 11, SA(R), [Pt(R), R(R), NZ, It(R), Arg(R)], 2008 F(R), W, I, E, It, Arg 2, NZ(R), SA(R), 2009 W, F, It, E(R), 2010 F(R), It, E, I, Arg 1, 2, NZ, SA, Sm, 2011 F, W

Speirs, L M (Watsonians) 1906 SA, 1907 W, I, E, 1908 W, I, E, 1910 F, W, E

Spence, K M (Oxford U) 1953 I

Spencer, E (Clydesdale) 1898 I

Stagg, P K (Sale) 1965 F, W, E, SA, 1966 F, W, I, E, A, 1967 F, W, I, E, NZ, 1968 F, W, I, E, A, 1969 F, W, I (R), SA, 1970 F, W, I, E, A

Stanger, A G (Hawick) 1989 Fj, R, 1990 I, F, W, E, NZ 1, 2, Arg, 1991 F, W, E, I, R, [J, Z, I, WS, E, NZ], 1992 E, I, F, W, A 1, 2, 1993 I, F, W, E, NZ, 1994 W, E, I, F, SA, 1995 R, [Iv], 1996 NZ 2, A, It, 1997 W, E, I, F, A, SA, 1998 It, I (R), F, W, E

Stark, D A (Boroughmuir, Melrose, Glasgow Hawks) 1993 I, F, W, E, 1996 NZ 2(R), It (R), 1997 W (R), E, SA

Steel, J F (Glasgow) 2000 US, A, 2001 I, Tg, NZ

Steele, W C C (Langholm, Bedford, RAF, London Scottish) 1969 E, 1971 F, W, I, E (2[1C]), 1972 F, W, E, NZ, 1973 F, W, I, E, 1975 I, F, W, E, NZ (R), 1976 W, E, I, 1977 E

Stephen, A E (W of Scotland) 1885 W, 1886 I

Steven, P D (Heriot's FP) 1984 A, 1985 F, W, E

Steven, R (Edinburgh Wands) 1962 I

Stevenson, A K (Glasgow Acads) 1922 F, 1923 F, W, E

Stevenson, A M (Glasgow U) 1911 F

Stevenson, G D (Hawick) 1956 E, 1957 F, 1958 F, W, A, I, E, 1959 W, I, E, 1960 W, I, E, SA, 1961 F, SA, W, I, E, 1963 F, W, I, 1964 E, 1965 F

Stevenson, H J (Edinburgh Acads) 1888 W, I, 1889 W, I, 1890 W, I, E, 1891 W, I, E, 1892 W, I, E, 1893 I, E

Stevenson, L E (Edinburgh U) 1888 W

Stevenson, R C (London Scottish) 1897 I, E, 1898 E, 1899 I, W, E

Stevenson, R C (St Andrew's U) 1910 F, I, E, 1911 F, W, I

Stevenson, W H (Glasgow Acads) 1925 F

Stewart, A K (Edinburgh U) 1874 E, 1876 E

Stewart, A M (Edinburgh Acads) 1914 W

Stewart, B D (Edinburgh Acads, Edinburgh) 1996 NZ 2, A, 2000 NZ 1, 2

Stewart, C A R (W of Scotland) 1880 I, E

Stewart, C E B (Kelso) 1960 W, 1961 F

Stewart, J (Glasgow HSFP) 1930 F

Stewart, J L (Edinburgh Acads) 1921 I

Stewart M J (Northampton) 1996 It, 1997 W, E, I, F, A, SA, 1998 It, I, F, W, Fj (R), 2000 It, I, F, W, E, NZ 1(R), 2001 F, W, E, It, I, Tg, Arg, NZ, 2002 E, It, I, F, W, C, US, R(R)

Stewart, M S (Stewart's Coll FP) 1932 SA, W, I, 1933 W, E, I, 1934 W, I, E

Stewart, W A (London Hospital) 1913 F, W, I, 1914 W

Steyn, S S L (Oxford U) 1911 E, 1912 I

Strachan, G M (Jordanhill) 1971 E (C) (R), 1973 W, I, E, P

Strauss, J Z (Glasgow Warriors) 2015 [J(R)], US, SA, Sm(R), A(R)]

Strokosch, A K (Edinburgh, Gloucester, Perpignan) 2006 A(R), 2008 I, E, It, Arg 1, 2, C, 2009 F, It, I, E, Fj, A, Arg, 2010 It(R), Arg 1(R), 2(R), 2011 E(R), It1(R), I2, [Gg, Arg, E], 2012 E, W, A, Fj, Sm, NZ, Tg, 2013 E, F, Sm, SA1, It2, J, SA, 2014 W(R), US, C, Arg 2(R), Tg(R), 2015 F 1(R), W(R), It 2, F 2(R), [US]

Stronach, R S (Glasgow Acads) 1901 W, E, 1905 W, I, E

Stuart, C D (W of Scotland) 1909 I, 1910 F, W, I, E, 1911 I, E

Stuart, L M (Glasgow HSFP) 1923 F, W, I, E, 1924 F, 1928 E, 1930 I, E

Suddon, N (Hawick) 1965 W, I, E, SA, 1966 A, 1968 E, A, 1969 F, W, I, 1970 I, E, A

Sutherland, W R (Hawick) 1910 W, E, 1911 F, E, 1912 F, W, E, SA, 1913 F, W, I, E, 1914 W

Swan, J S (Army, London Scottish, Leicester) 1953 E, 1954 F, NZ, I, E, W, 1955 F, W, I, E, 1956 F, W, I, E, 1957 F, W, 1958 F

Swan, M W (Oxford U, London Scottish) 1958 F, W, A, I, E, 1959 F, W, I

Sweet, J B (Glasgow HSFP) 1913 E, 1914 I

Swinson, T J M (Glasgow Warriors) 2013 SA1, It2, J, 2014 I, E, F(R), W(R), Arg1(R), SA, 2015 It 1, E(t&R), I1(R), F 2(R), [US(R), SA(R), Sm(R), A(R)]

Symington, A W (Cambridge U) 1914 W, E

Tait, A V (Kelso, Newcastle, Edinburgh) 1987 [F(R), Z, R, NZ], 1988 I, F, W, E, 1997 I, F, A, 1998 It, I, F, W, E, SA, 1999 W (R), E, It, I, F, Arg, R, [A, U, NZ]

Tait, J G (Edinburgh Acads) 1880 I, 1885 I 2

Tait, P W (Royal HSFP) 1935 E

Taylor, D M (Saracens) 2013 Sm(R), SA1(R), It2(R), J(R), SA2, A, 2014 I, E(R), It(R), W(R), US, Tg(R)

Taylor, E G (Oxford U) 1927 W, A

Taylor, R C (Kelvinside-West) 1951 W, I, E, SA

Taylor, S M (Edinburgh, Stade Français) 2000 US, A, 2001 E, It, I, NZ (R), 2002 E, It, I, F, W, C, US, R, SA, Fj, 2003 I 1, F, W 1, E, It 1, SA 1, 2, It 2, I 2, [J, US, F, Fj, A], 2004 W, E, It, F, I, 2005 It, W, E, Arg, Sm, NZ, 2006 F, W, E, I, It, PI, A, 2007 E, W, It, I1, F, I2, [Pt, R, It, Arg], 2008 F(R), W, It, I, E

Telfer, C M (Hawick) 1968 A, 1969 F, W, I, E, 1972 F, W, E, 1973 W, I, E, P, 1974 W, E, I, 1975 A, 1976 F

Telfer, J W (Melrose) 1964 F, NZ, W, I, E, 1965 F, W, I, 1966 F, W, I, E, 1967 W, I, E, 1968 E, A, 1969 F, W, I, E, SA, 1970 F, W, I

Tennent, J M (W of Scotland) 1909 W, I, E, 1910 F, W, E

Thom, D A (London Scottish) 1934 W, 1935 W, I, E, NZ

Thom, G (Kirkcaldy) 1920 F, W, I, E

Thom, J R (Watsonians) 1933 W, E, I

Thomson, A E (United Services) 1921 F, W, E

Thomson, A M (St Andrew's U) 1949 I

Thomson, B E (Oxford U) 1953 F, W, I

Thomson, F M A (Glasgow Warriors) 2007 I2(t&R), SA(R), [NZ(R)], 2008 F(R), W(R), I(R), E(R), It

Thomson, I H M (Heriot's FP, Army) 1951 W, I, 1952 F, W, I, 1953 I, E

Thomson, J S (Glasgow Acads) 1871 E

Thomson, R H (London Scottish, PUC) 1960 I, E, SA, 1961 F, SA, W, I, E, 1963 F, W, I, E, 1964 F, NZ, W

Thomson, W H (W of Scotland) 1906 SA

Thomson, W J (W of Scotland) 1899 W, E, 1900 W

Timms, A B (Edinburgh U, Edinburgh Wands) 1896 W, 1900 W, I, 1901 W, I, E, 1902 W, E, 1903 W, I, E, 1904 I, E, 1905 I, E

Tod, H B (Gala) 1911 F

Tod, J (Watsonians) 1884 W, I, E, 1885 W, I 1, 2, 1886 W, I, E

Todd, J K (Glasgow Acads) 1874 E, 1875 E

Tolmie, J M (Glasgow HSFP) 1922 E

Tomes, A J (Hawick) 1976 E, I, 1977 E, 1978 I, F, W, E, NZ, 1979 W, E, I, F, NZ, 1980 F, W, E, 1981 F, W, E, I, NZ 1, 2, R, A, 1982 E, I, F, W, A 1, 2, 1983 I, F, W, 1984 W, E, I, F, R, A, 1985 W, E, 1987 I, F, E (R), [F, Z, R, NZ]

Tonks, G A (Edinburgh) 2013 Sm, 2015 It 1(R), E(R), I 1(R), 2, It 2

Toolis, B (Edinburgh) 2015 It 1(R)

Torrie, T J (Edinburgh Acads) 1877 E

Townsend, G P J (Gala, Northampton, Brive, Castres, Borders) 1993 E (R), 1994 W, E, I, F, Arg 1, 2, 1995 C, I, F, W, E, WS, 1996 I, F, W, E, NZ 1, 2, A, It, 1997 W, E, I, F, A, SA, 1998 It, I, F, W, E, Fj, A 1, 2, SA (R), 1999 W, E, It, I, F, [SA, U, Sp (R), Sm, NZ], 2000 It, I, F, W, E, NZ 1, 2, US, A, Sm, 2001 F, It, I, Arg, NZ, 2002 E, It, I, F, W, R(R), SA(R), Fj, 2003 I 1(R), F, W 1, E, It 1, SA 1, 2, W 2, [J(R), US, F, Fj, A]

Traynor, K (Edinburgh, Bristol) 2009 Fj(R), A(R), Arg(R), 2012 Tg

Tukalo, I (Selkirk) 1985 I, 1987 I, F, W, E, [F, Z, R, NZ], 1988 F, W, E, A, 1989 W, E, I, F, Fj, 1990 I, F, W, E, NZ 1, 1991 I, R, [J, Z, I, WS, E, NZ], 1992 E, I, F, W, A 1, 2

Turk, A S (Langholm) 1971 E (R)

Turnbull, D J (Hawick) 1987 [NZ], 1988 F, E, 1990 E (R), 1991 F, W, E, I, R, [Z], 1993 I, F, W, E, 1994 W

Turnbull, F O (Kelso) 1951 F, SA

Turnbull, G O (W of Scotland) 1896 I, E, 1897 I, E, 1904 W

Turnbull, P (Edinburgh Acads) 1901 W, I, E, 1902 W, I, E

Turner, F H (Oxford U, Liverpool) 1911 F, W, I, E, 1912 F, W, I, E, SA, 1913 F, W, I, E, 1914 I, E

Turner, J W C (Gala) 1966 W, A, 1967 F, W, I, E, NZ, 1968 F, W, I, E, A, 1969 F, 1970 E, A, 1971 F, W, I, E (2[1C])

Usher, C M (United Services, Edinburgh Wands) 1912 E, 1913 F, W, I, E, 1914 E, 1920 F, W, I, E, 1921 W, E, 1922 F, W, I, E

Utterson, K N (Borders) 2003 F, W 1, E(R)

Valentine, A R (RNAS, Anthorn) 1953 F, W, I

Valentine, D D (Hawick) 1947 I, E

Veitch, J P (Royal HSFP) 1882 E, 1883 I, 1884 W, I, E, 1885 I 1, 2, 1886 E

Vernon, R J (Glasgow Warriors, Sale) 2009 Fj(R), A(R), Arg(R), 2010 NZ, SA(R), Sm, 2011 F(R), W, I1(R), E(R), It1(R), 2, [R, Arg(R), E], 2012 F(R), I(R), It(R), Fj(R), Sm, 2015 I 2,It 2, [SA, A(R)]

Villar, C (Edinburgh Wands) 1876 E, 1877 I, E

Visser, T J W (Edinburgh, Harlequins) 2012 Fj, Sm, NZ, SA, Tg, 2013 E, It1, I, W, F, Sm, It2(R), 2014 US, C, Tg, 2015 F 1, W, I 1(t&R), 2, It 3, F 2, [US,SA]

Waddell, G H (London Scottish, Cambridge U) 1957 E, 1958 F, W, A, I, E, 1959 F, W, I, E, 1960 I, E, SA, 1961 F, 1962 F, W, I, E

Waddell, H (Glasgow Acads) 1924 F, W, I, E, 1925 I, E, 1926 F, W, I, E, 1927 F, W, I, E, 1930 W

Wade, A L (London Scottish) 1908 E

Wainwright, R I (Edinburgh Acads, West Hartlepool, Watsonians, Army, Dundee HSFP) 1992 I (R), F, A 1, 2, 1993 NZ, 1994 W, E, 1995 C, I, F, W, E, R, [Iv, Tg, F, NZ], WS, 1996 I, F, W, E, NZ 1, 2, 1997 W, E, I, F, SA, 1998 It, I, F, W, E, Fj, A 1, 2

Walker, A (W of Scotland) 1881 I, 1882 E, 1883 W, I, E

Walker, A W (Cambridge U, Birkenhead Park) 1931 F, W, I, E, 1932 I

Walker, J G (W of Scotland) 1882 E, 1883 W

Walker, M (Oxford U) 1952 F

Walker, N (Borders, Ospreys) 2002 R, SA, Fj, 2007 W(R), It(R), F, I2(R), SA, [R(R), NZ], 2008 F, W, I, E, C, 2010 NZ(R), SA, Sm, 2011 F, W, I1, It1, I2, It2(R)

Wallace, A C (Oxford U) 1923 F, 1924 F, W, E, 1925 F, W, I, E, 1926 F

Wallace, W M (Cambridge U) 1913 E, 1914 W, I, E

Wallace, M I (Glasgow High Kelvinside) 1996 A, It, 1997 W

Walls, W A (Glasgow Acads) 1882 E, 1883 W, I, E, 1884 W, I, E, 1886 W, I, E

Walter, M W (London Scottish) 1906 I, E, SA, 1907 W, I, 1908 W, I, 1910 I

Walton, P (Northampton, Newcastle) 1994 E, I, F, Arg 1, 2, 1995 [Iv], 1997 W, E, I, F, SA (R), 1998 I, F, SA, 1999 W, E, It, I, F (R), Arg, R, [SA (R), U (R), Sp]

Warren, J R (Glasgow Acads) 1914 I

Warren, R C (Glasgow Acads) 1922 W, I, 1930 W, I, E

Waters, F H (Cambridge U, London Scottish) 1930 F, W, I, E, 1932 SA, W, I

Waters, J A (Selkirk) 1933 W, E, I, 1934 W, I, E, 1935 W, I, E, NZ, 1936 W, I, E, 1937 W, I, E

Waters, J B (Cambridge U) 1904 I, E

Watherston, J G (Edinburgh Wands) 1934 I, E

Watherston, W R A (London Scottish) 1963 F, W, I

Watson, D H (Glasgow Acads) 1876 I, E, 1877 I, E

Watson, H F W (Edinburgh) 2015 It 1(R), 2(R)

Watson, W S (Boroughmuir) 1974 W, E, I, F, 1975 NZ, 1977 I, F, W, 1979 I, F

Watt, A G J (Glasgow High Kelvinside) 1991 [Z], 1993 I, NZ, 1994 Arg 2(t & R)

Watt, A G M (Edinburgh Acads) 1947 F, W, I, A, 1948 F, W

Weatherstone, T G (Stewart's Coll FP) 1952 E, 1953 I, E, 1954 F, NZ, I, E, W, 1955 F 1958 W A, I, E, 1959 W I, E

Webster, S L (Edinburgh) 2003 I, 2(R), 2004 W(R), E, It, F, I, Sm, A1, 2, 2005 It, NZ(R), 2006 F(R), W(R), E(R), I(R), It(R), SA 1(R), 2, R, PI, A, 2007 W(R), I2, SA, [Pt, R, NZ, It, Arg], 2008 F, I, E, It, Arg 1(R), 2, C, 2009 W

Weir, D (Glasgow Warriors) 2012 F(R), Fj(R), 2013 I(R), W, F, J(R), SA2(R), A, 2014 I, E, It, F, W, Arg1, SA , Arg 2(R), NZ(t&R), Tg(R), 2015 It 2, [US(R), SA]

Weir, G W (Melrose, Newcastle) 1990 Arg, 1991 R, [J, Z, I, WS, E, NZ] 1992 E, I, F, W, A 1, 2, 1993 I, F, W, E, NZ, 1994 W (R), E, I, F, SA, 1995 F (R), W, E, R, [Iv, Tg, F, NZ], WS, 1996 I, F, W, E, NZ 1, 2, A, It (R), 1997 W, E, I, F, 1998 It, I, F, W, E, SA, 1999 W, Arg (R), R, R (R), [SA (R), Sp, Sm, NZ], 2000 It (R), I (R), F

Welsh, J S (Glasgow Warriors, Newcastle) 2012 It, 2013 It2(R), 2014 Arg1(R), 2015 W(R), I 2, It 3(R), F 2(R), [J(R), US, SA(R), A(R)]

Welsh, R (Watsonians) 1895 W, I, E, 1896 W

Welsh, R B (Hawick) 1967 I, E

Welsh, W B (Hawick) 1927 A, 1928 F, W, I, 1929 I, E, 1930 F, W, I, E, 1931 F, W, I, E, 1932 SA, W, I, E, 1933 W, E, I

Welsh, W H (Edinburgh U) 1900 I, E, 1901 W, I, E, 1902 W, I, E

Wemyss, A (Gala, Edinburgh Wands) 1914 W, I, 1920 F, E, 1922 F, W, I

West, L (Edinburgh U, West Hartlepool) 1903 W, I, E, 1905 I, E, NZ, 1906 W, I, E

Weston, V G (Kelvinside Acads) 1936 I, E

White, D B (Gala, London Scottish) 1982 F, W, A 1, 2, 1987 W, E, [F, R, NZ], 1988 I, F, W, E, A, 1989 W, E, I, F, Fj, R, 1990 I, F, W, E, NZ 1, 2, 1991 F, W, E, I, R, [J, Z, I, WS, E, NZ], 1992 E, I, F, W

White, D M (Kelvinside Acads) 1963 F, W, I, E

White, J P R (Glasgow, Sale, Clermont-Auvergne) 2000 E, NZ 1, 2, US (R), A (R), Sm, 2001 F (R), I, Tg, Arg, NZ, 2002 E, It, I, F, W, C, US, SA(R), Fj, 2003 F(R), W 1, E, It 1, SA 1, 2, It 2, [J, US(R), F, Fj(R), A], 2004 W(R), E, It, F, I, Sm, A 1, 2, A(R), A4(R), SA, 2005 F, I, E, Arg, Sm, NZ, 2006 F, W, E, I, It, SA 1, 2, R, 2007 I2, SA, [Pt, R, It, Arg], 2008 F, W, E(R), It(R), NZ, SA, 2009 W, F, It, I, E, Fj(R), A(R), Arg(R)

White, T B (Edinburgh Acads) 1888 W, I, 1889 W

Whittington, T P (Merchistonians) 1873 E

Whitworth, R J E (London Scottish) 1936 I

Whyte, D J (Edinburgh Wands) 1965 W, I, E, SA, 1966 F, W, I, E, A, 1967 F, W, I, E

Will, J G (Cambridge U) 1912 F, W, I, E, 1914 W, I, E

Wilson, A W (Dunfermline) 1931 F, I, E

Wilson, A W (Glasgow) 2005 R(R)

Wilson, G A (Oxford U) 1949 F, W, E

Wilson, G R (Royal HSFP) 1886 E, 1890 W, I, E, 1891 I

Wilson, J H (Watsonians) 1953 I

Wilson, J S (St Andrew's U) 1931 F, W, I, E, 1932 E

Wilson, J S (United Services, London Scottish) 1908 I, 1909 W

Wilson, R (London Scottish) 1976 E, I, 1977 E, I, F, 1978 I, F, 1981 R, 1983 I

Wilson, R (Glasgow Warriors) 2013 W(R), F(R), Sm(R), SA1, 2014 I, E, It, F(R), W, 2015 It 3, F 2, [J, US, SA(t&R), Sm]

Wilson, R L (Gala) 1951 F, W, I, E, SA, 1953 F, W, E

Wilson, R W (W of Scotland) 1873 E, 1874 E

Wilson, S (Oxford U, London Scottish) 1964 F, NZ, W, I, E, 1965 W, I, E, SA, 1966 F, W, I, A, 1967 F, W, I, E, NZ, 1968 F, W, I, E

Wood, A (Royal HSFP) 1873 E, 1874 E, 1875 E

Wood, G (Gala) 1931 W, I, 1932 W, I, E

Woodburn, J C (Kelvinside Acads) 1892 I

Woodrow, A N (Glasgow Acads) 1887 I, W, E

Wotherspoon, W (W of Scotland) 1891 I, 1892 I, 1893 W, E, 1894 W, I, E

Wright, F A (Edinburgh Acads) 1932 E

Wright, H B (Watsonians) 1894 W

Wright, K M (London Scottish) 1929 F, W, I, E

Wright, P H (Boroughmuir) 1992 A 1, 2, 1993 F, W, E, 1994 W, 1995 C, I, F, W, E, R, [Iv, Tg, F, NZ], 1996 W, E, NZ 1

Wright, R W J (Edinburgh Wands) 1973 F

Wright, S T H (Stewart's Coll FP) 1949 E

Wright, T (Hawick) 1947 A

Wyllie, D S (Stewart's-Melville FP) 1984 A, 1985 W (R), E, 1987 I, F, [F, Z, R, NZ], 1989 F, R, 1991 R, [J (R), Z], 1993 NZ (R), 1994 W (R), E, I, F

Young, A H (Edinburgh Acads) 1874 E

Young, E T (Glasgow Acads) 1914 E

Young, R G (Watsonians) 1970 W

Young, T E B (Durham) 1911 F

Young, W B (Cambridge U, London Scottish) 1937 W, I, E, 1938 W, I, E, 1939 W, I, E, 1948 E

Scotland centre Mark Bennett celebrates after scoring the try that edged his side ahead late in their quarter-final with Australia.

Getty Images

SOUTH AFRICA

SOUTH AFRICA'S 2014–15 TEST RECORD

OPPONENTS	DATE	VENUE	RESULT
Ireland	8 Nov	A	Lost 29–15
England	15 Nov	A	Won 31–28
Italy	22 Nov	A	Won 22–6
Wales	29 Nov	A	Lost 12–6
Australia	18 Jul	A	Lost 24–20
New Zealand	25 Jul	H	Lost 20–27
Argentina	8 Aug	H	Lost 25–37
Argentina	15 Aug	A	Won 26–12
Japan	19 Sep	N	Lost 34–32
Samoa	26 Sep	N	Won 46–6
Scotland	3 Oct	N	Won 34–16
USA	7 Oct	N	Won 64–0
Wales	17 Oct	N	Won 23–19
New Zealand	24 Oct	N	Lost 20–18
Argentina	30 Oct	N	Won 24–13

BOKS MUST SHOW MORE AMBITION

By Joel Stransky

Bryan Habana scores his third against the USA to equal Jonah Lomu's record of 15 Rugby World Cup tries.

I think to describe South Africa's experience at Rugby World Cup 2015 as mixed would qualify as a significant understatement. The utter shock of the Boks losing their Pool B opener against Japan in Brighton was one many supporters will probably never forget but you have to give the players an enormous amount of credit for the way they regrouped, fought their way through to the semi-finals and pushed the All Blacks close on the scoreboard at Twickenham.

The team needed huge heart to turn things around after the Japan game and the courage on display was admirable. It wasn't always pretty as the Boks muscled their way out of the pool and then past Wales in the quarter-final but they got the job done and there was no disgrace in losing to New Zealand in the last four after what the Kiwis had showed they were capable of over the course of the tournament.

These were the positives for South Africa but you would have to be short-sighted not to acknowledge that the side looked bereft of creativity

for long periods of the World Cup and in my opinion Heyneke Meyer
has to take responsibility for the side's tactical naivety. I felt 18 months
ago that the Boks were really getting to grips with an expansive, creative
brand of rugby where they were looking to score tries but it seemed as
soon as his team got to the World Cup they went into their shells and
simply reverted to trying to batter the opposition into submission. Coaches
cannot always be held responsible for the form of their players but they
are responsible for setting the game plan. We just were not smart enough
with the ball and although there was no shortage of heart and soul, the
performances were crying out for someone to bring the brains.

The optimists may point to the narrow margin of defeat to the All
Blacks but while a 20–18 loss might look respectable, the wet conditions
at Twickenham were a real leveller and although it sounds close, I always
felt New Zealand had another gear in reserve had they needed it.

The Kiwis, and to a lesser extent the Wallabies, proved at the World
Cup that if you aspire to be a really top side in test rugby today that
you have to be willing to repeatedly put width on the ball and you have
to be able to convert the chances you create. The Boks got away with
a comparatively limited game plan against the lesser sides but against
the bigger fish I just didn't feel they were capable of creating enough
chances. And for me that is the biggest frustration. I have no doubt at
all we have the players but it was the game plan, the way we set out
to unlock teams, that was lacking in England.

I think the Boks' problems were mirrored by the individual displays
of Willie le Roux at full-back. When Le Roux first came into the test
side in the summer of 2013 after a barrage of calls for his selection he
brought a new dimension to the team, he was a breath of fresh air, but
he had a disappointing World Cup and looked like a shadow of the
player he was two years ago. I was surprised he made the team for the
semi-final against the All Blacks and the more conservative South Africa
became, the more Le Roux struggled to make any impact.

That all said, should the South African Rugby Union decide to extend
Meyer's contract, which runs out at the end of 2015, he has proved in
the past that he can send out teams with ambition and attacking intent.
It didn't happen at the World Cup because I believe his conservative
tendencies on the big occasion ultimately got the better of him.

The World Cup was the test swansong of Jean de Villiers, and with
more than a century of caps for South Africa it was a sad way for him
to go, forced to announce his immediate retirement after breaking his
jaw in the pool game against Samoa. I'm not convinced he ever really
fully recovered from the horrendous knee injury he suffered against
Wales in Cardiff at the end of 2014 and he never looked to have

completely regained his confidence. He was an incredible servant to South African rugby but I don't think the side was weakened at the World Cup by his absence because Jesse Kriel and Damian de Allende had already proved themselves a solid midfield partnership before the start of the tournament. De Villiers returned to camp as soon as he'd had surgery on his jaw so the Boks weren't deprived of his experience or leadership qualities for long.

It was also a third and final World Cup for Bryan Habana and with five tries he drew level with Jonah Lomu as the tournament's joint-record finisher with 15 tries. Ironically it wasn't a tournament in which he saw much of the ball because of the Boks' limited game plan but yet again he was the consummate professional, chasing every kick like a champion and putting in a lot of unglamorous work for the team. To be honest, I was glad he didn't eclipse Lomu's record because the Kiwi is such an icon of the game and for me it felt more apt for them to share the record.

There was, of course, a lot of rugby played before the World Cup and the Boks were very inconsistent both on the end-of-season European tour and in The Rugby Championship. They weren't helped by injuries, particularly to De Villiers and Duane Vermeulen, but in my opinion there's a rich crop of talented young players in South African rugby at the moment and it was frustrating to see them not brought through.

The headline result was the Boks' 37–25 defeat against Argentina in Durban in August, the country's first ever loss to the Pumas. I thought Argentina were superb at the World Cup and there's no doubt the Championship has accelerated their development but I did not see that result coming at all. There's no way the Pumas should be beating the Boks in South Africa, but they picked a team that played without fear, perhaps the Boks underestimated them at the start and once they got their noses in front, we were always chasing the game.

In terms of individual performances over the year and during the World Cup I thought Lood de Jager in the second row was outstanding when he was given a chance and although he missed an important tackle on Kaino in the semi-final he and Eben Etzebeth look set to be an important pairing in the Boks' pack for years to come. Francois Louw was really good at times on the flank, Vermeulen was impressive once he recovered from his neck injury, Handré Pollard showed some good signs while Fourie du Preez made a massive difference to the side once he came back into contention.

Off the pitch, politics reared its ugly head once again with a renewed debate in South Africa about quotas in rugby. At one stage one of the political parties tried to petition the courts to stop the Boks playing at the World Cup because the squad did not properly represent the country and while in my opinion that was more about political posturing than a realistic attempt to prevent the team going to England, it was sad to see the row erupt again. It's a sensitive subject but I do feel that it all overshadows the fact we have so many exciting young players of all races coming up through the ranks in South Africa.

The next generation of Boks were in the news in January when SARU announced it was designating the under-20 side as the official South Africa second string, meaning that once a player had been selected for the under-20s they would not be eligible to switch allegiance to another country in the future. It was a decision designed to keep the best young players at home but I think rich clubs offering young Boks lucrative deals abroad rather than other countries actively trying to poach players is the bigger threat to South African rugby going forward. I wouldn't begrudge any player heading to Europe if Toulon can afford to pay them more than the Sharks. Players are entitled to take the best offer on the table and individuals have to accept that might hurt their chances of selection for the test team.

I also strongly believe that rather than worrying about which young South African players they might be able to sign, teams in France in particular and to a lesser extent England, should be focused on developing homegrown talent. There was a lot of debate about the failings of the northern hemisphere sides at the World Cup and it is certainly no coincidence that the French have struggled in recent years as the Top 14 competition has become more and more bloated with foreign imports.

Eben Etzebeth, who scored a try in the bronze final victory, formed a formidable second-row partnership with Lood de Jager.

SOUTH AFRICA

SOUTH AFRICA INTERNATIONAL STATISTICS

MATCH RECORDS UP TO 1 NOVEMBER, 2015

MOST CONSECUTIVE TEST WINS

17 1997 A2, It, F 1, 2, E, S, 1998 I 1, 2, W 1, E 1, A 1, NZ 1,2, A 2, W 2, S, I 3
15 1994 Arg 1,2, S, W 1995 WS, A, R, C, WS, F, NZ, W, It, E, 1996 Fj

MOST CONSECUTIVE TESTS WITHOUT DEFEAT

Matches	Wins	Draws	Period
17	17	0	1997 to 1998
16	15	1	1994 to 1996
15	12	3	1960 to 1963

MOST POINTS IN A MATCH
BY THE TEAM

Pts	Opponents	Venue	Year
134	Uruguay	E London	2005
105	Namibia	Cape Town	2007
101	Italy	Durban	1999
96	Wales	Pretoria	1998
87	Namibia	Albany	2011
74	Tonga	Cape Town	1997
74	Italy	Port Elizabeth	1999
73	Argentina	Soweto	2013
72	Uruguay	Perth	2003
68	Scotland	Murrayfield	1997
64	USA	Montpellier	2007
64	USA	London	2015
63	Argentina	Johannesburg	2008
62	Italy	Bologna	1997
61	Australia	Pretoria	1997

BY A PLAYER

Pts	Player	Opponents	Venue	Year
35	PC Montgomery	Namibia	Cape Town	2007
34	JH de Beer	England	Paris	1999
31	PC Montgomery	Wales	Pretoria	1998
31	M Steyn	N Zealand	Durban	2009
30	T Chavhanga	Uruguay	E London	2005
29	GS du Toit	Italy	Port Elizabeth	1999
29	PC Montgomery	Samoa	Paris	2007
28	GK Johnson	W Samoa	Johannesburg	1995
28	M Steyn	Argentina	Soweto	2013
26	JH de Beer	Australia	Pretoria	1997
26	PC Montgomery	Scotland	Murrayfield	1997
26	M Steyn	Italy	East London	2010
25	J T Stransky	Australia	Bloemfontein	1996
25	C S Terblanche	Italy	Durban	1999

MOST TRIES IN A MATCH
BY THE TEAM

Tries	Opponents	Venue	Year
21	Uruguay	E London	2005
15	Wales	Pretoria	1998
15	Italy	Durban	1999
15	Namibia	Cape Town	2007
12	Tonga	Cape Town	1997
12	Uruguay	Perth	2003
12	Namibia	Albany	2011
11	Italy	Port Elizabeth	1999
10	Ireland	Dublin	1912
10	Scotland	Murrayfield	1997
10	USA	London	2015

BY A PLAYER

Tries	Player	Opponents	Venue	Year
6	T Chavhanga	Uruguay	E London	2005
5	CS Terblanche	Italy	Durban	1999
4	CM Williams	W Samoa	Johannesburg	1995
4	PWG Rossouw	France	Parc des Princes	1997
4	CS Terblanche	Ireland	Bloemfontein	1998
4	BG Habana	Samoa	Paris	2007
4	JL Nokwe	Australia	Johannesburg	2008

MOST CONVERSIONS IN A MATCH
BY THE TEAM

Cons	Opponents	Venue	Year
13	Italy	Durban	1999
13	Uruguay	E London	2005
12	Namibia	Cape Town	2007
12	Namibia	Albany	2011
9	Scotland	Murrayfield	1997
9	Wales	Pretoria	1998
9	Argentina	Johannesburg	2008
8	Italy	Port Elizabeth	1999
8	USA	Montpellier	2007
8	Argentina	Soweto	2013
7	Scotland	Murrayfield	1951
7	Tonga	Cape Town	1997
7	Italy	Bologna	1997
7	France	Parc des Princes	1997
7	Italy	Genoa	2001
7	Samoa	Pretoria	2002
7	Samoa	Brisbane	2003
7	England	Bloemfontein	2007
7	Italy	East London	2010
7	USA	London	2015

BY A PLAYER

Cons	Player	Opponents	Venue	Year
12	PC Montgomery	Namibia	Cape Town	2007
9	PC Montgomery	Wales	Pretoria	1998
9	AD James	Argentina	Johannesburg	2008
8	PC Montgomery	Scotland	Murrayfield	1997
8	GS du Toit	Italy	Port Elizabeth	1999
8	GS du Toit	Italy	Durban	1999
8	M Steyn	Argentina	Soweto	2013
7	AO Geffin	Scotland	Murrayfield	1951
7	JMF Lubbe	Tonga	Cape Town	1997
7	HW Honiball	Italy	Bologna	1997
7	HW Honiball	France	Parc des Princes	1997
7	AS Pretorius	Samoa	Pretoria	2002
7	JNB van der Westhuyzen	Uruguay	E London	2005
7	PC Montgomery	England	Bloemfontein	2007

MOST PENALTIES IN A MATCH
BY THE TEAM

Penalties	Opponents	Venue	Year
8	Scotland	Port Elizabeth	2006
8	N Zealand	Durban	2009
7	France	Pretoria	1975
7	France	Cape Town	2006
7	Australia	Cape Town	2009
6	Australia	Bloemfontein	1996
6	Australia	Twickenham	1999
6	England	Pretoria	2000
6	Australia	Durban	2000
6	France	Johannesburg	2001
6	Scotland	Johannesburg	2003
6	N Zealand	Bloemfontein	2009
6	Australia	Bloemfontein	2010
6	Australia	Perth	2014
6	N Zealand	Twickenham	2015

MOST PENALTIES IN A MATCH
BY A PLAYER

Pens	Player	Opponents	Venue	Year
8	M Steyn	N Zealand	Durban	2009
7	PC Montgomery	Scotland	Port Elizabeth	2006
7	PC Montgomery	France	Cape Town	2006
7	M Steyn	Australia	Cape Town	2009
6	GR Bosch	France	Pretoria	1975
6	JT Stransky	Australia	Bloemfontein	1996
6	JH de Beer	Australia	Twickenham	1999
6	AJJ van Straaten	England	Pretoria	2000
6	AJJ van Straaten	Australia	Durban	2000
6	PC Montgomery	France	Johannesburg	2001
6	LJ Koen	Scotland	Johannesburg	2003
6	M Steyn	Australia	Bloemfontein	2010
6	M Steyn	Australia	Perth	2014

MOST DROP GOALS IN A MATCH
BY THE TEAM

Drops	Opponents	Venue	Year
5	England	Paris	1999
4	England	Twickenham	2006
3	S America	Durban	1980
3	Ireland	Durban	1981
3	Scotland	Murrayfield	2004

BY A PLAYER

Drops	Player	Opponents	Venue	Year
5	JH de Beer	England	Paris	1999
4	AS Pretorius	England	Twickenham	2006
3	HE Botha	S America	Durban	1980
3	HE Botha	Ireland	Durban	1981
3	JNB van der Westhuyzen	Scotland	Murrayfield	2004
2	BL Osler	N Zealand	Durban	1928
2	HE Botha	NZ Cavaliers	Cape Town	1986
2	JT Stransky	N Zealand	Johannesburg	1995
2	JH de Beer	N Zealand	Johannesburg	1997
2	PC Montgomery	N Zealand	Cardiff	1999
2	FPL Steyn	Australia	Cape Town	2007

CAREER RECORDS

MOST CAPPED PLAYERS

Caps	Player	Career Span
127	V Matfield	2001 to 2015
117	BG Habana	2004 to 2015
111	JW Smit	2000 to 2011
109	J de Villiers	2002 to 2015
102	PC Montgomery	1997 to 2008
89	JH van der Westhuizen	1993 to 2003
88	R Pienaar	2006 to 2015
86	SWP Burger	2003 to 2015
85	JP Botha	2002 to 2014
80	JP du Randt	1994 to 2007
79	BW du Plessis	2007 to 2015
77	MG Andrews	1994 to 2001
76	PF du Preez	2004 to 2015
75	CJ van der Linde	2002 to 2012
75	T Mtawarira	2008 to 2015
72	J Fourie	2003 to 2013
70	JH Smith	2003 to 2014
70	JN du Plessis	2007 to 2015

MOST CONSECUTIVE TESTS

Tests	Player	Span
46	JW Smit	2003 to 2007
39	GH Teichmann	1996 to 1999
28	V Matfield	2008 to 2010
26	AH Snyman	1996 to 1998
26	AN Vos	1999 to 2001
25	SH Nomis	1967 to 1972
25	AG Venter	1997 to 1999
25	A-H le Roux	1998 to 1999

MOST TESTS AS CAPTAIN

Tests	Captain	Span
83	JW Smit	2003 to 2011
37	J de Villiers	2012 to 2015
36	GH Teichmann	1996 to 1999
29	JF Pienaar	1993 to 1996
23	V Matfield	2007 to 2015
22	DJ de Villiers	1965 to 1970
18	CPJ Krigé	1999 to 2003
16	A N Vos	1999 to 2001
15	M du Plessis	1975 to 1980
12	RB Skinstad	2001 to 2007
11	JFK Marais	1971 to 1974

MOST POINTS IN TESTS

Points	Player	Tests	Career
893	PC Montgomery	102	1997 to 2008
694	M Steyn	60	2009 to 2015
320	BG Habana	117	2004 to 2015
312	HE Botha	28	1980 to 1992
240	JT Stransky	22	1993 to 1996
221	AJJ van Straaten	21	1999 to 2001
190	JH van der Westhuizen	89	1993 to 2003
188	H Pollard	20	2014 to 2015
181	JH de Beer	13	1997 to 1999
171	AS Pretorius	31	2002 to 2007
160	J Fourie	72	2003 to 2013
156	HW Honiball	35	1993 to 1999
154	AD James	42	2001 to 2011

MOST TRIES IN TESTS

Tries	Player	Tests	Career
64	BG Habana	117	2004 to 2015
38	JH van der Westhuizen	89	1993 to 2003
32	J Fourie	72	2003 to 2013
27*	BJ Paulse	64	1999 to 2007
27	J de Villiers	109	2002 to 2015
25	PC Montgomery	102	1997 to 2008
23	J-PR Pietersen	66	2006 to 2015
21	PWG Rossouw	43	1997 to 2003
20	JT Small	47	1992 to 1997
19	DM Gerber	24	1980 to 1992
19	CS Terblanche	37	1998 to 2003
16	PF du Preez	76	2004 to 2015
16	SWP Burger	86	2003 to 2015

* includes a penalty try

MOST CONVERSIONS IN TESTS

Cons	Player	Tests	Career
153	PC Montgomery	102	1997 to 2008
102	M Steyn	60	2009 to 2015
50	HE Botha	28	1980 to 1992
38	HW Honiball	35	1993 to 1999
33	JH de Beer	13	1997 to 1999
31	AS Pretorius	31	2002 to 2007
30	JT Stransky	22	1993 to 1996
29	H Pollard	20	2014 to 2015
26	AD James	42	2001 to 2011
25	GS du Toit	14	1998 to 2006
23	AJJ van Straaten	21	1999 to 2001
23	LJ Koen	15	2000 to 2003
23	PJ Lambie	50	2010 to 2015
22	R Pienaar	88	2006 to 2015
20	PJ Visagie	25	1967 to 1971

MOST PENALTY GOALS IN TESTS

Penalties	Player	Tests	Career
148	PC Montgomery	102	1997 to 2008
142	M Steyn	60	2009 to 2015
55	AJJ van Straaten	21	1999 to 2001
50	HE Botha	28	1980 to 1992
47	JT Stransky	22	1993 to 1996
37	H Pollard	20	2014 to 2015
31	LJ Koen	15	2000 to 2003
28	AD James	42	2001 to 2011
27	JH de Beer	13	1997 to 1999
25	HW Honiball	35	1993 to 1999
25	AS Pretorius	31	2002 to 2007
23	GR Bosch	9	1974 to 1976
23	PJ Lambie	50	2010 to 2015
21	FPL Steyn	53	2006 to 2012
19	PJ Visagie	25	1967 to 1971

MOST DROP GOALS IN TESTS

Drops	Player	Tests	Career
18	HE Botha	28	1980 to 1992
8	JH de Beer	13	1997 to 1999
8	AS Pretorius	31	2002 to 2007
8	M Steyn	60	2009 to 2015
6	PC Montgomery	102	1997 to 2008
5	JD Brewis	10	1949 to 1953
5	PJ Visagie	25	1967 to 1971
4	BL Osler	17	1924 to 1933

RUGBY CHAMPIONSHIP (FORMERLY TRI NATIONS) RECORDS

RECORD	DETAIL	HOLDER	SET
Most points in season	203	in six matches	2013
Most tries in season	23	in six matches	2013
Highest score	73	73–13 v Argentina (h)	2013
Biggest win	60	73–13 v Argentina (h)	2013
Highest score conceded	55	35–55 v N Zealand (a)	1997
Biggest defeat	49	0–49 v Australia (a)	2006
Most appearances	51	J de Villiers	2004 to 2015
Most points in matches	348	M Steyn	2009 to 2014
Most points in season	95	M Steyn	2009
Most points in match	31	M Steyn	v N Zealand (h) 2009
Most tries in matches	19	BG Habana	2005 to 2015
Most tries in season	7	BG Habana	2012
Most tries in match	4	JL Nokwe	v Australia (h) 2008
Most cons in matches	41	M Steyn	2009 to 2014
Most cons in season	17	M Steyn	2013
Most cons in match	8	M Steyn	v Argentina (h) 2013
Most pens in matches	83	M Steyn	2009 to 2014
Most pens in season	23	M Steyn	2009
Most pens in match	8	M Steyn	v N Zealand (h) 2009

SOUTH AFRICA

MISCELLANEOUS RECORDS

RECORD	HOLDER	DETAIL
Longest Test Career	V Matfield	2001–2015
Youngest Test Cap	AJ Hartley	18 yrs 18 days in 1891
Oldest Test Cap	V Matfield	38 yrs 172 days in 2015

CAREER RECORDS OF SOUTH AFRICA INTERNATIONAL PLAYERS

UP TO 1 NOVEMBER, 2015

PLAYER BACKS:	DEBUT	CAPS	T	C	P	D	PTS
D de Allende	2014 v Arg	13	1	0	0	0	5
J de Villiers	2002 v F	109	27	0	0	0	135
PF du Preez	2004 v I	76	16	0	0	0	80
JL Goosen	2012 v A	6	0	1	2	0	8
BG Habana	2004 v E	117	64	0	0	0	320
C Hendricks	2014 v W	12	6*	0	0	0	30
F Hougaard	2009 v It	35	5	0	0	0	25
Z Kirchner	2009 v BI	31	5	0	0	0	25
JA Kriel	2015 v A	11	3	0	0	0	15
PJ Lambie	2010 v I	50	2	23	23	3	134
WJ Le Roux	2013 v It	34	9	0	0	0	45
LG Mapoe	2015 v NZ	1	0	0	0	0	0
LN Mvovo	2010 v S	15	5	0	0	0	25
R Paige	2015 v US	2	0	0	0	0	0
R Pienaar	2006 v NZ	88	8	22	17	0	135
J-PR Pietersen	2006 v A	66	23	0	0	0	115
H Pollard	2014 v S	20	2	29	37	3	188
JM Reinach	2014 v A	10	2	0	0	0	10
JL Serfontein	2013 v It	26	2	0	0	0	10
FPL Steyn	2006 v I	53	10	5	21	3	132
M Steyn	2009 v BI	60	8	102	142	8	694

THE COUNTRIES

FORWARDS :

WS Alberts	2010 v W	38	7	0	0	0	35
JP Botha	2002 v F	85	7	0	0	0	35
SB Brits	2008 v It	10	1	0	0	0	5
HW Brüssow	2008 v E	23	1	0	0	0	5
SWP Burger	2003 v Gg	86	16	0	0	0	80
N Carr	2014 v It	2	0	0	0	0	0
MC Coetzee	2012 v E	28	6	0	0	0	30
L de Jager	2014 v W	19	4	0	0	0	20
BW du Plessis	2007 v A	79	11	0	0	0	55
JN du Plessis	2007 v A	70	1	0	0	0	5
P-S du Toit	2013 v W	8	0	0	0	0	0
E Etzebeth	2012 v E	44	2	0	0	0	10
VP Koch	2015 v NZ	2	0	0	0	0	0
S Kolisi	2013 v S	13	0	0	0	0	0
L-FP Louw	2010 v W	43	8	0	0	0	40
JF Malherbe	2013 v W	12	0	0	0	0	0
V Matfield	2001 v It	127	7	0	0	0	35
TS Mohoje	2014 v S	8	0	0	0	0	0
T Mtawarira	2008 v W	75	2	0	0	0	10
TN Nyakane	2013 v It	23	1	0	0	0	5
CV Oosthuizen	2012 v E	23	3	0	0	0	15
J Redelinghuys	2014 v It	2	0	0	0	0	0
GG Steenkamp	2004 v S	53	6	0	0	0	30
JA Strauss	2008 v A	54	6	0	0	0	30
HS van der Merwe	2007 v W	5	0	0	0	0	0
M van der Merwe	2014 v S	7	0	0	0	0	0
PR van der Merwe	2010 v F	37	1	0	0	0	5
DJ Vermeulen	2012 v A	35	2	0	0	0	10
WR Whiteley	2014 v A	3	0	0	0	0	0

* Cornal Hendricks's figures include a penalty try awarded against Wales at Nelspruit in 2014

SOUTH AFRICA

SOUTH AFRICAN INTERNATIONAL PLAYERS
UP TO 1 NOVEMBER, 2015

Entries in square brackets denote matches played in RWC Finals.

Ackermann, D S P (WP) 1955 BI 2, 3, 4, 1956 A 1, 2, NZ 1, 3, 1958 F 2
Ackermann, J N (NT, BB, N) 1996 Fj, A 1, NZ 1, A 2, 2001 F 2(R), It 1, NZ 1(R), A 1, 2006 I, E1, 2, 2007 Sm, A2
Adriaanse, L C (Griquas) 2013 F(R)
Aitken, A D (WP) 1997 F 2(R), E, 1998 I 2(R), W 1(R), NZ 1, 2(R), A 2(R)
Alberts, W S (NS) 2010 W2(R), S(t&R), E(R), 2011 NZ2, [W(R), Fj(R), Nm, Sm(t&R), A(t&R)], 2012 E1, 2, Arg1, 2, A1, NZ1,
A2, NZ2, I, S, E4, 2013 Sm, Arg1, 2, A1, NZ1, A2, NZ2, W, S2, F, 2014 W1, 2, 2015 Arg 2, [S(R), US(R), W(R)), NZ(t&R), Arg(R)]
Albertyn, P K (SWD) 1924 BI 1, 2, 3, 4
Alexander, F A (GW) 1891 BI 1, 2
Allan, J (N) 1993 A 1(R), Arg 1, 2(R), 1994 E 1, 2, NZ 1, 2, 3, 1996 Fj, A 1, NZ 1, A 2, NZ 2
Allen, P B (EP) 1960 S
Allport, P H (WP) 1910 BI 2, 3

Anderson, J W (WP) 1903 BI 3
Anderson, J H (WP) 1896 BI 1, 3, 4
Andrew, J B (Tvl) 1896 BI 2
Andrews, E P (WP) 2004 I1, 2, W1(t&R), PI, NZ1, A1, NZ2, A2, W2, I3, E, 2005 F1, A2, NZ2(t), Arg(R), F3(R), 2006 S1, 2, F, A1(R), NZ1(t), 2007 A2(R), NZ2(R)
Andrews, K S (WP) 1992 E, 1993 F 1, 2, A 1(R), 2, 3, Arg 1(R), 2, 1994 NZ 3
Andrews, M G (N) 1994 E 2, NZ 1, 2, 3, Arg 1, 2, S, W, 1995 WS, [A, WS, F, NZ], W, It, E, 1996 Fj, A 1, NZ 1, A 2, NZ 2, 3, 4, 5, Arg 1, 2, F 1, 2, W, 1997 Tg (R), BI 1, 2, NZ 1, A 1, NZ 2, A 2, It, F 1, 2, E, S, 1998 I 1, 2, W 1, E 1, A 1, NZ 1, 2, A 2, W 2, S, I 3, E 2, 1999 NZ 1, 2(R), A 2(R), [S, U, E, A 3, NZ 3], 2000 A 2, NZ 2, A 3, Arg, I, W, E 3, 2001 F 1, 2, It 1, NZ 1, A 1, 2, NZ 2, F 3, E
Antelme, J G M (Tvl) 1960 NZ 1, 2, 3, 4, 1961 F
Apsey, J T (WP) 1933 A 4, 5, 1938 BI 2
Aplon, G G (WP) 2010 W1, F, It 1, 2, NZ1(R), 2(R), A1, NZ3, A3(R), I, W2, S, E, 2011 A1, 2(R), [Nm], 2012 E3
Ashley, S (WP) 1903 BI 2
Aston, F T D (Tvl) 1896 BI 1, 2, 3, 4
Atherton, S (N) 1993 Arg 1, 2, 1994 E 1, 2, NZ 1, 2, 3, 1996 NZ 2
Aucamp, J (WT) 1924 BI 1, 2

Baard, A P (WP) 1960 I
Babrow, L (WP) 1937 A 1, 2, NZ 1, 2, 3
Badenhorst, C (OFS) 1994 Arg 2, 1995 WS (R)
Bands, R E (BB) 2003 S 1, 2, Arg (R), A 1, NZ 1, A 2, NZ 2, [U, E, Sm(R), NZ(R)]
Barnard, A S (EP) 1984 S Am 1, 2, 1986 Cv 1, 2
Barnard, J H (Tvl) 1965 S, A 1, 2, NZ 3, 4
Barnard, R W (Tvl) 1970 NZ 2(R)
Barnard, W H M (NT) 1949 NZ 4, 1951 W
Barry, D W (WP) 2000 C, E 1, 2, A 1, W(R) NZ 1, A 2, 2001 F 1, 2, US (R), 2002 W 2, Arg, Sm, NZ 1, A 1, NZ 2, A 2, 2003 A 1, NZ 1, A 2, [U, E, Sm, NZ], 2004 PI, NZ1, A1, NZ2, A2, W2, I3, E, Arg(t), 2005 F1, 2, A1, NZ2, W(R), F3(R), 2006 F
Barry, J (WP) 1903 BI 1, 2, 3
Bartmann, W J (Tvl, N) 1986 Cv 1, 2, 3, 4, 1992 NZ, A, F, 1, 2
Basson, B A (GW, BB) 2010 W1(R), It 1(R), I, W2, 2011 A1, NZ1, 2013 It, S1, Sm, Arg1, 2
Bastard, W E (N) 1937 A 1, NZ 1, 2, 3, 1938 BI 1, 3
Bates, A J (WT) 1969 E, 1970 NZ 1, 2, 1972 E
Bayvel, P C R (Tvl) 1974 BI 2, 4, F 1, 2, 1975 F 1, 2, 1976 NZ 1, 2, 3, 4
Beck, J J (WP) 1981 NZ 2(R), 3(R), US
Bedford, T P (N) 1963 A 1, 2, 3, 4, 1964 W, F, 1965 I, A 1, 2, 1968 BI 1, 2, 3, 4, F 1, 2, 1969 A 1, 2, 3, 4, S, E, 1970 I, W, 1971 F 1, 2
Bekker, A (WP) 2008 W1, 2(R), It(R), NZ1(R), 2(t&R), A1(t&R), Arg(R), NZ3, A2, W3(R), S(R), E(R), 2009 BI 1(R), 2(R), NZ2(R), A1(R), 2(R), F(t&R), It 1, 2010 It2, NZ1(R), 2(R), 2012 Arg1, 2, NZ1(t&R), A2, NZ2
Bekker, H J (WP) 1981 NZ 1, 3
Bekker, H P J (NT) 1952 E, F, 1953 A 1, 2, 3, 4, 1955 BI 2, 3, 4, 1956 A 1, 2, NZ 1, 2, 3, 4
Bekker, M J (NT) 1960 S
Bekker, R P (NT) 1953 A 3, 4
Bekker, S (NT) 1997 A 2(t)
Bennett, R G (Border) 1997 Tg (R), BI 1(R), 3, NZ 1, A 1, NZ 2
Bergh, W F (SWD) 1931 W, I, 1932 E, S, 1933 A 1, 2, 3, 4, 5, 1937 A 1, 2, NZ 1, 2, 3, 1938 BI 1, 2, 3
Bestbier, A (OFS) 1974 F 2(R)
Bester, J J N (WP) 1924 BI 2, 4
Bester, J L A (WP) 1938 BI 2, 3
Beswick, A M (Bor) 1896 BI 2, 3, 4
Bezuidenhout, C E (NT) 1962 BI 2, 3, 4
Bezuidenhout, C J (MP) 2003 NZ 2(R), [E, Sm, NZ]
Bezuidenhout, N S E (NT) 1972 E, 1974 BI 2, 3, 4, F 1, 2, 1975 F 1, 2, 1977 Wld
Bierman, J N (Tvl) 1931 I
Bisset, W M (WP) 1891 BI 1, 3
Blair, R (WP) 1977 Wld
Bobo, G (GL, WP) 2003 S 2(R), Arg, A 1(R), NZ 2, 2004 S(R), 2008 It
Boome, C S (WP) 1999 It 1, 2, W, NZ 1(R), A 1, NZ 2, A 2,

2000 C, E 1, 2, 2003 S 1(R), 2(R), Arg (R), A 1(R), NZ 1(R), A 2, NZ 2(R), [U(R), Gg, NZ(R)]
Bosch, G R (Tvl) 1974 BI 2, F 1, 2, 1975 F 1, 2, 1976 NZ 1, 2, 3, 4
Boshoff, M L (GL) 2014 S(R)
Bosman, H M (FS) 2005 W, F3, 2006 A1(R)
Bosman, N J S (Tvl) 1924 BI 2, 3, 4
Botha, A F (BB) 2013 It, S1
Botha, B J (N, Ulster) 2006 NZ2(R), 3, A3, I(R), E1, 2, 2007 E1, Sm, A1, NZ1, Nm(R), S(t&R), [Sm(R), E1, Tg(R), US], 2008 W2, 2009 It(R), I, 2010 W1, F, It 2(R), NZ1(R), 2(R), A1
Botha, D S (NT) 1981 NZ 1
Botha, G van G (BB) 2005 A3(R), F3(R), 2007 E1(R), 2(R), Sm(R), A1(R), NZ1, A2, NZ2(R), Nm, S, [Tg]
Botha, H E (NT) 1980 S Am 1, 2, BI 1, 2, 3, 4, S Am 3, 4, F, 1981 I 1, 2, NZ 1, 2, 3, US, 1982 S Am 1, 2, 1986 Cv 1, 2, 3, 4, 1989 Wld 1, 2, 1992 NZ, A, F 1, 2, E
Botha, J A (Tvl) 1903 BI 3
Botha, J P (BB, Toulon) 2002 F, 2003 S 1, 2, A 1, NZ 1, A 2(R), [U, E, Gg, Sm, NZ], 2004 I1, PI, NZ1, A1, NZ2, A2, W2, I3, E, S, Arg, 2005 A1, 2, 3, NZ1, A4, NZ2, Arg, W, F3, 2007 E1, 2, A1, NZ1, Nm, S, [Sm, E1, Tg, US(R)], Fj, Arg, E2], W, 2008 W1, 2, It, NZ1, 2, A1, Arg, W3, S, E, 2009 BI 1, 2, NZ1, 2, A1, 2, 3, NZ3, F, It, 2010 It1, 2, NZ1, I, W2, S, E, 2011 A2, NZ2, [Fj, Nm], 2013 S2, F(R), 2014 W1, Arg1, 2(R), A2(R), NZ2(R), I(R), E(R)
Botha, J P F (NT) 1962 BI 2, 3, 4
Botha, P H (Tvl) 1965 A 1, 2
Boyes, H C (GW) 1891 BI 1, 2
Brand, G H (WP) 1928 NZ 2, 3, 1931 W, I, 1932 E, S, 1933 A 1, 2, 3, 4, 5, 1937 A 1, 2, NZ 1, 2, 3, 1938 BI 1
Bredenkamp, M J (GW) 1896 BI 1, 3
Breedt, J C (Tvl) 1986 Cv 1, 2, 3, 4, 1989 Wld 1, 2, 1992 NZ, A
Brewis, J D (NT) 1949 NZ 1, 2, 3, 4, 1951 S, I, W, 1952 E, F, 1953 A 1
Briers, T P D (WP) 1955 BI 1, 2, 3, 4, 1956 NZ 2, 3, 4
Brink D J (WP) 1906 S, W, E
Brink, R (WP) 1995 [R, C]
Brits, S B (WP, Saracens) 2008 It(R), NZ2(R), A1, 2012 S(R), E4(R), 2014 W1(R), 2(R), 2015 Arg 2(R), [Sm(R), US(R)]
Britz, G J J (FS, WP) 2004 I1(R), 2(R), W1(R), PI, A1, NZ2, A2(R), I3(t), S(t&R), Arg(R), 2005 U, 2006 E2(R), NZ2(R)
Britz, W K (N) 2002 W 1
Brooks, D (Bor) 1906 S
Brosnihan, W (GL, N) 1997 A 2, 2000 NZ 1(t+R), A 2(t+R), NZ 2(R), A 3(R), E 3(R)
Brown, C B (WP) 1903 BI 1, 2, 3
Brüssow, H W (FS, Red Hurricanes) 2008 E(R), 2009 BI 1, 2(R), 3, NZ 1, 2, A 2, NZ 3, F, It, I, 2011 A 2, NZ 2, [W, Fj, Nm(R), Sm, A], 2015 NZ, Arg 1, 2
Brynard, G S (WP) 1965 A 1, NZ 1, 2, 3, 4, 1968 BI 3, 4
Buchler, J U (Tvl) 1951 S, I, W, 1952 E, F, 1953 A 1, 2, 3, 4, 1956 A 2
Burdett, A F (WP) 1906 S, I
Burger, J M (WP) 1989 Wld 1, 2
Burger, M P (NT) 1980 BI 2(R), S Am 3, 1981 US (R)
Burger, S W P (WP) 1984 E 1, 2, 1986 Cv 1, 2, 3, 4
Burger, S W P (WP, Sungoliaths) 2003 [Gg(R), Sm(R), NZ(R)], 2004 I1, 2, W1, PI, NZ1, A1, NZ2, A2, W2, I3, E, 2005 F1, 2, A1, 2(R), 3(R), NZ1, A4, NZ2, Arg(R), W, F3, 2006 S1, 2, 2007 E1, 2, A1, NZ1, Nm, S, [Sm, US, Fj, Arg, E2], W, 2008 It(R), NZ1, 2, A1, NZ3, A2, 3, W3, S, E, 2009 BI 2, A2(R), 3(R), NZ3, F, I, 2010 F, It2, NZ1, 2, A1, NZ3, A2, 3, 2011 [W, Fj, Nm, Sm, A], 2014 W1(R), 2(R), S, A2(R), NZ22(R), I(R), E, 2015 A, NZ, Arg 1, 2, [J, Sm, S, US, W, NZ, Arg]
Burger, W A G (Bor) 1906 S, I, W, 1910 BI 2

Carelse, G (EP) 1964 W, F, 1965 I, S, 1967 F 1, 2, 3, 1968 F 1, 2, 1969 A 1, 2, 3, 4, S
Carlson, R A (WP) 1972 E
Carolin, H W (WP) 1903 BI 3, 1906 S, I
Carr, N (WP) 2014 It(R), W 3(R)
Carstens, P D (NS) 2002 S, E, 2006 E1(t&R), 2(R), 2007 E1, 2(t&R), Sm(R), 2009 BI 1(R), 3(t)
Castens, H H (WP) 1891 BI 1

Chavhanga, T (WP) 2005 U, 2007 NZ2(R), 2008 W1, 2
Chignell, T W (WP) 1891 BI 3
Cilliers, G D (OFS) 1963 A 1, 3, 4
Cilliers, N V (WP) 1996 NZ 3(t)
Cilliers, P M (GL) 2012 Arg1(t&R), 2(R), A1(t&R), 2(R), I(R), E4(R)
Claassen, J T (WT) 1955 BI 1, 2, 3, 4, 1956 A 1, 2, NZ 1, 2, 3, 4, 1958 F 1, 2, 1960 S, NZ 1, 2, 3, W, I, 1961 E, S, F, I, A 1, 2, 1962 BI 1, 2, 3, 4
Claassen, W (N) 1981 I 1, 2, NZ 2, 3, US, 1982 S Am 1, 2
Claassens, M (FS) 2004 W2(R), S(R), Arg(R), 2005 Arg(R), W, F3, 2007 A2(R), NZ2(R)
Clark, W H G (Tvl) 1933 A 3
Clarkson, W A (N) 1921 NZ 1, 2, 1924 BI 1
Cloete, H A (WP) 1896 BI 4
Cockrell, C H (WP) 1969 S, 1970 I, W
Cockrell, R J (WP) 1974 F 1, 2, 1975 F 1, 2, 1976 NZ 1, 2, 1977 Wld, 1981 NZ 1, 2(R), 3, US
Coetzee, D (BB) 2002 Sm, 2003 S 1, 2, Arg, A 1, NZ 1, A 2, NZ 2, [U, E, Sm(R), NZ(R)], 2004 S(R), Arg(R), 2006 A1(R)
Coetzee, J H H (WP) 1974 BI 1, 1975 F 2(R), 1976 NZ 1, 2, 3, 4
Coetzee, M C (NS) 2012 E1, 2, 3, Arg1, 2, A1, NZ1(R), A2(R), NZ2(t&R), I(R), S(R), E4(R), 2013 It(t&R), S1, 2(R), 2014 S, Arg1, 2(R), A1, NZ1, A2, NZ2, I, E, It, W 3, 2015 A, Arg 1
Conradie, J H (WP) 2002 W 1, 2, Arg (R), Sm, NZ 1, A 1, NZ 2(R), A 2(R), S, E, 2004 W1(R), PI, NZ2, A2, 2005 Arg, 2008 W1, 2(R), NZ1(R)
Cope, D K (Tvl) 1896 BI 2
Cotty, W (GW) 1896 BI 3
Crampton, G (GW) 1903 BI 2
Craven, D H (WP) 1931 W, I, 1932 S, 1933 A 1, 2, 3, 4, 5, 1937 A 1, 2, NZ 1, 2, 3, 1938 BI 1, 2, 3,
Cronjé, G (BB) 2003 NZ 2, 2004 I2(R), W1(R)
Cronjé, J (BB, GL) 2004 I1, 2, W1, PI, NZ1, A1, NZ2(R), A2(t&R), S(t&R), Arg, 2005 U, F1, 2, A1, 3, NZ1(R), 2(t), Arg, W, F3, 2006 S2(R), F(R), A1(t&R), NZ1, A2, NZ2, A3(R), I(R), E1, 2007 A2(R), NZ2, Nm
Cronje, P A (Tvl) 1971 F 1, 2, A 1, 2, 3, 1974 BI 3, 4
Crosby, J H (Tvl) 1896 BI 2
Crosby, N J (Tvl) 1910 BI 1, 3
Currie, C (GW) 1903 BI 2

D'Alton, G (WP) 1933 A 1
Dalton, J (Tvl, GL, Falcons) 1994 Arg 1(R), 1995 [A, C], W, It, E, 1996 NZ 4(R), 5, Arg 1, 2, F 1, 2, W, 1997 Tg (R), BI 3, NZ 2, A 2, It, F 1, 2, E, S, 1998 I 1, 2, W 1, E 1, A 1, NZ 1, 2, A 2, W 2, S, I 3, E 2, 2002 W 1, 2, Arg, NZ 1, A 1, NZ 2, A 2, F, E
Daneel, M (WP) 1928 NZ 1, 2, 3, 4, 1931 W, I, 1932 E, S
Daneel, H J (WP) 1906 S, I, W, E
Daniel, K R (NS) 2010 I(R), 2012 E1(R), 2(R), Arg1, 2(R)
Davidson, C D (N) 2002 W 2(R), Arg, 2003 Arg, NZ 1(R), A 2
Davids, Q (WP) 2002 W 2, Arg (R), Sm (R), 2003 Arg, 2004 I1(R), 2, W1, PI(t&R), NZ1(R)
Davison, P M (EP) 1910 BI 1
De Allende, D (WP) 2014 Arg1, 2, W 3(R), 2015 A, NZ, Arg 1, 2, [Sm, S, US, W, NZ, Arg]
De Beer, J H (OFS) 1997 BI 3, NZ 1, A 1, NZ 2, A 2, F 2(R), S, 1999 A 2, [S, Sp, U, E, A 3]
De Bruyn, J (OFS) 1974 BI 3
De Jager, L (FSC) 2014 W1(R), 2(t), S, Arg1, 2, A1(R), NZ1(R), It(R), W 3(R), 2015 A(R), NZ, Arg 1, [J, Sm(R), S, US, W, NZ, Arg(R)]
De Jongh, H P K (WP) 1928 NZ 3
De Jongh, J L (WP) 2010 W1, F(R), It 1(R), 2, A1(R), NZ3, 2011 A1, NZ1, [Fj(R), Nm(R)], 2012 A2(R), NZ2(R), S, E4
De Klerk, I J (Tvl) 1969 E, 1970 I, W
De Klerk, K B H (Tvl) 1974 BI 1, 2, 3(R), 1975 F 1, 2, 1976 NZ 2(R), 3, 4, 1980 S Am 1, 2, BI 2, 1981 I 1, 2
De Kock, A N (GW) 1891 BI 2
De Kock, D (Falcons) 2001 It 2(R), US
De Kock, J S (WP) 1921 NZ 3, 1924 BI 3
De Kock, N A (WP) 2001 It 1, 2002 Sm (R), NZ 1(R), 2, A 2, F, 2003 [U(R), Gg, Sm(R), NZ(R)]
Delport, G M (GL, Worcester) 2000 C (R), E 1(t+R), A 1, NZ 1, A 2, NZ 2, A 3, Arg, I, W, 2001 F 2, It 1, 2003 A 1, NZ 2, [U, E, Sm, NZ]
Delport, W H (EP) 1951 S, I, W, 1952 E, F, 1953 A 1, 2, 3, 4

De Melker, S C (GW) 1903 BI 2, 1906 E
Devenish, C E (GW) 1896 BI 2
Devenish, G St L (Tvl) 1896 BI 2
Devenish, G E (Tvl) 1891 BI 1
De Villiers, D I (Tvl) 1910 BI 1, 2, 3
De Villiers, D J (WP, Bol) 1962 BI 2, 3, 1965 I, NZ 1, 3, 4, 1967 F 1, 2, 3, 4, 1968 BI 1, 2, 3, 4, F 1, 2, 1969 A 1, 4, E, 1970 I, W, NZ 1, 2, 3, 4
De Villiers, H A (WP) 1906 S, W, E
De Villiers, H O (WP) 1967 F 1, 2, 3, 4, 1968 F 1, 2, 1969 A 1, 2, 3, 4, S, E, 1970 I, W
De Villiers, J (WP, Munster) 2002 F, 2004 PI, NZ1, A1, NZ2, A2, W2(R), E, 2005 U, F1, 2, A1, 2, 3, NZ1, A4, NZ2, Arg, W, F3, 2006 S1, NZ2, 3, A3, I, E1, 2, 2007 E1, 2, A1, NZ1, Nm, [Sm], 2008 W1, 2, It, NZ1, 2, A1, Arg, NZ3, A2, 3, W3, S, E, 2009 BI 1, 2, NZ1, 2, A1, 2, 3, NZ3, I(R), 2010 F(t&R), It1, 2, NZ1, 2, 3, A2, 3, I, W2, S, E, 2011 A2, NZ2, [W, Sm(R), A], 2012 E1, 2, 3, Arg1, 2, A1, NZ1, A2, NZ2, I, S, E4, 2013 It, S1, Sm, Arg1, 2, A1, NZ1, A2, NZ2, W, S2, F, 2014 Arg1, 2, A1, NZ1, A2, NZ2, I, E, It, W 3, 2015 Arg 1, [J, Sm]
De Villiers, P du P (WP) 1928 NZ 1, 3, 4, 1932 E, 1933 A 4, 1937 A 1, 2, NZ 1
Devine, D (Tvl) 1924 BI 3, 1928 NZ 2
De Vos, D J J (WP) 1965 S, 1969 A 3, S
De Waal, A N (WP) 1967 F 1, 2, 3, 4
De Waal, P J (WP) 1896 BI 4
De Wet, A E (WP) 1969 A 3, 4, E
De Wet, P J (WP) 1938 BI 1, 2, 3
Deysel, J R (NS) 2009 It(R), 2011 A1(R), NZ1, A2(R)
Dinkelmann, E E (NT) 1951 S, I, 1952 E, F, 1953 A 1, 2
Dirksen, C W (NT) 1963 A 4, 1964 W, 1965 I, S, 1967 F 1, 2, 3, 4, 1968 BI 1, 2
Dlulane, V T (MP) 2004 W2(R)
Dobbin, F J (GW) 1903 BI 1, 2, 1906 S, W, E, 1910 BI 1, 1912 S, I, W
Dobie, J A R (Tvl) 1928 NZ 2
Dormehl, P J (WP) 1896 BI 3, 4
Douglass, F W (EP) 1896 BI 1
Drotské, A E (OFS) 1993 Arg 2, 1995 [WS (R)], 1996 A 1(R), 1997 Tg, BI 1, 2, 3(R), NZ 1, A 1, NZ 2(R), 1998 I 2(R), W 1(R), I 3(R), 1999 It 1, 2, W, NZ 1, A 1, NZ 2, A 2, [S, Sp (R), U, E, A 3, NZ 3]
Dryburgh, R G (WP) 1955 BI 2, 3, 4, 1956 A 2, NZ 1, 4, 1960 NZ 1, 2
Duff, B R (WP) 1891 BI 1, 2, 3
Duffy, B A (Bor) 1928 NZ 1
Du Plessis, B W (NS) 2007 A2(t&R), NZ2, Nm(R), S(R), [Sm(R), E1(R), US(R), Arg(R), E2(t)], W(R), 2008 W1(R), 2(R), It, NZ1(R), 2, Arg, NZ3, A2, 3, W3, S, 2009 BI 1, 2, 3(R), NZ1, 2, A1, 2, 3, NZ3, F, I(R), 2010 I, W2, S, E, 2011 A2(R), NZ2, [W(R), Fj(R), Sm, A(R)], 2012 E1, 2, 3, Arg1, 2013 S1(R), Sm(R), Arg1(R), 2(R), A1, NZ1, A2(R), NZ2, W, S2(R), F, 2014 W1, 2, S, Arg1, 2, A1(R), NZ1(R), A2(R), NZ2, I, E(R), It(R), W 3, 2015 A, NZ, Arg 1, [J, S, US, W, NZ, Arg]
Du Plessis, C J (WP) 1982 S Am 1, 2, 1984 E 1, 2, S Am 1, 2, 1986 Cv 1, 2, 3, 4, 1989 Wld 1, 2
Du Plessis, D C (NT) 1977 Wld, 1980 S Am 2
Du Plessis, F (Tvl) 1949 NZ 1, 2, 3
Du Plessis, J N (FS, NS) 2007 A2, NZ2, [Fj, Arg(t&R)], W, 2008 A3(R), E, 2009 NZ1(t), 2(R), A1(R), 2(R), NZ3(R), 2010 W1(R), F(R), It 1, 2, NZ1, 3, A2, 3, I, W2, S, E, 2011 A2, NZ2, [W, Fj, Sm, A], 2012 E1, 2, 3, Arg1, 2, A1, NZ1, A2, NZ2, I, S, E4, 2013 It, S1, Sm, Arg1, 2, A1, NZ1, A2, NZ2, 2014 W1, 2, S, Arg1, 2, A1, NZ1, A2, NZ2, Arg], I, E, 2015 A, NZ, [J, Sm, S, W(R), NZ(R), Arg(R)]
Du Plessis, M (WP) 1971 A 1, 2, 3, 1974 BI 1, 2, F 1, 2, 1975 F 1, 2, 1976 NZ 1, 2, 3, 4, 1977 Wld, 1980 S Am 1, 2, BI 1, 2, 3, 4, S Am 4, F
Du Plessis, M J (WP) 1984 S Am 1, 2, 1986 Cv 1, 2, 3, 4, 1989 Wld 1, 2
Du Plessis, N J (WT) 1921 NZ 2, 3, 1924 BI 1, 2, 3
Du Plessis, P G (NT) 1972 E
Du Plessis, T D (NT) 1980 S Am 1, 2
Du Plessis, W (WP) 1980 S Am 1, 2, BI 1, 2, 3, 4, S Am 3, 4, F, 1981 NZ 1, 2, 3, 1982 S Am 1, 2

502

Du Plooy, A J J (EP) 1955 BI 1

Du Preez, F C H (NT) 1961 E, S, A 1, 2, 1962 BI 1, 2, 3, 4, 1963 A 1, 1964 W, F, 1965 A 1, 2, NZ 1, 2, 3, 4, 1967 F 4, 1968 BI 1, 2, 3, 4, F 1, 2, 1969 A 1, 2, S, 1970 I, W, NZ 1, 2, 3, 4, 1971 F 1, 2, A 1, 2, 3

Du Preez, G J D (GL) 2002 Sm (R), A 1(R)

Du Preez, J G H (WP) 1956 NZ 1

Du Preez, P F (BB, Suntory Sungoliaths) 2004 I1, 2, W1, PI(R), NZ1, A1, NZ2(R), A2(R), W2, I3, E, S, Arg, 2005 U(R), F1, 2(R), A1(R), 2(R), 3, NZ1(R), A4(R), 2006 S1, 2, F, A1(R), NZ1, A2, NZ2, 3, A3, 2007 Nm, S, [Sm, E1, US, Fj, Arg, E2], 2008 Arg(R), NZ3, A2, 3, W3, 2009 BI 1, 2, 3, NZ1, 2, A1, 2, 3, NZ3, F, It, I, 2011 A2, NZ2, [W, Fj, Nm(R), Sm, A], 2013 Arg1(R), A2, NZ2, W, S2, 2014 W1, 2, S, 2015 [J(R), Sm, S, US, W, NZ]

Du Preez, R J (N) 1992 NZ, A, 1993 F 1, 2, A 1, 2, 3

Du Preez, W H (FS) 2009 It

Du Rand, J A (R, NT) 1949 NZ 2, 3, 1951 S, I, W, 1952 E, F, 1953 A 1, 2, 3, 4, 1955 BI 1, 2, 3, 4, 1956 A 1, 2, NZ 1, 2, 3, 4

Du Randt, J P (OFS, FS) 1994 Arg 1, 2, S, W, 1995 WS, [A, WS, F, NZ], 1996 Fj, A 1, NZ 1, A 2, NZ 2, 3, 4, 1997 Tg, BI 1, 2, 3, NZ 1, A 1, NZ 2, A 2, It, F 1, 2, E, S, 1999 NZ 1, A 1, NZ 2, A 2, [S, Sp (R), U, E, A 3, NZ 3], 2004 I1, 2, W1, PI, NZ1, A1, NZ2, A2, W2, I3, E, S(R), Arg(R), 2005 U(R), F1, A1, NZ1, A4, NZ2, Arg, W(R), F3, 2006 S1, 2, F, A1, NZ1, A2, NZ2, 3, A3, 2007 Sm, NZ1, Nm, S, [Sm, E1, US, Fj, Arg, E2]

Du Toit, A F (WP) 1928 NZ 3, 4

Du Toit, B A (Tvl) 1938 BI 1, 2, 3

Du Toit, G S (GW, WP) 1998 I 1, 1999 It 1, 2, W (R), NZ 1, 2, 2004 I1, W1(R), A1(R), S(R), Arg, 2006 S1(R), 2(R), F(R)

Du Toit, P A (NT) 1949 NZ 2, 3, 4, 1951 S, I, W, 1952 E, F

Du Toit, P G (WP) 1981 NZ 1, 1982 S Am 1, 2, 1984 E 1, 2

Du Toit, P-S (NS) 2013 W(R), F(R), 2015 Arg 1(R), 2(R), [J, S(R), US(R), W(R)]

Du Toit, P S (WP) 1958 F 1, 2, 1960 NZ 1, 2, 3, 4, W, I, 1961 E, S, F, I, A 1, 2

Duvenhage, F P (GW) 1949 NZ 1, 3

Edwards, P (NT) 1980 S Am 1, 2

Ellis, J H (SWA) 1965 NZ 1, 2, 3, 4, 1967 F 1, 2, 3, 4, 1968 BI 1, 2, 3, 4, F 1, 2, 1969 A 1, 2, 3, 4, S, 1970 I, W, NZ 1, 2, 3, 4, 1971 F 1, 2, A 1, 2, 3, 1972 E, 1974 BI 1, 2, 3, 4, F 1, 2, 1976 NZ 1

Ellis, M C (Tvl) 1921 NZ 2, 3, 1924 BI 1, 2, 3, 4

Els, W W (OFS) 1997 A 2(R)

Engelbrecht, J J (BB) 2012 Arg1(R), 2013 It, S1, Sm, Arg1, 2, A1, NZ1, A2, NZ2, W(R), S2(R)

Engelbrecht, J P (WP) 1960 S, W, I, 1961 E, S, F, A 1, 2, 1962 BI 2, 3, 4, 1963 A 2, 3, 1964 W, F, 1965 I, S, A 1, 2, NZ 1, 2, 3, 4, 1967 F 1, 2, 3, 4, 1968 BI 1, 2, F 1, 2, 1969 A 1, 2

Erasmus, F S (NT, EP) 1986 Cv 3, 4, 1989 Wld 2

Erasmus, J C (OFS, GL) 1997 BI 3, A 2, It, F 1, 2, S, 1998 I 1, 2, W 1, E 1, A 1, NZ 2, A 2, S, W 2, I 3, E 2, 1999 It 1, 2, W, A 1, NZ 2, A 2, [S, U, E, A 3, NZ 3], 2000 C, E 1, A 1, NZ 1, 2, A 3, 2001 F 1, 2

Esterhuizen, G (GL) 2000 NZ 1(R), 2, A 3, Arg, I, W (R), E 3(t)

Etlinger, T E (WP) 1896 BI 4

Etzebeth, E (WP) 2012 E1, 2, 3, Arg1, 2, A1, 2, NZ2, I, S, E4, 2013 It, S1, Sm, Arg1, 2, A1, NZ1, A2, NZ2, W, S2(R), F, 2014 Arg1(R), 2, A1, NZ1, A2, NZ2, I, E, It, W 3, 2015 A, NZ, Arg1, 2, [J(R), Sm, S, US, W, NZ, Arg]

Ferreira, C (OFS) 1986 Cv 1, 2

Ferreira, P S (WP) 1984 S Am 1, 2

Ferris, H H (Tvl) 1903 BI 3

Fleck R F (WP) 1999 It 1, 2, NZ 1(R), A 1, NZ 2(R), A 2, [S, U, E, A 3, NZ 3], 2000 C, E 1, 2, A 1, NZ 1, A 2, NZ 2, A 3, Arg, I, W, E 3, 2001 F 1(R), 2, It 1, NZ 1, A 1, 2, 2002 S, E

Floors, L (FS) 2006 E2

Forbes, H H (Tvl) 1896 BI 2

Fortuin, B A (FS) 2006 I, 2007 A2

Fourie, C (EP) 1974 F 1, 2, 1975 F 1, 2

Fourie, J (GL, WP, Kobe Steel) 2003 [U, Gg, Sm(R), NZ(R)], 2004 I2, E(R), S, Arg, 2005 U(R), F2(R), A1(R), 2, 3, NZ1, A4, NZ2, Arg, W, F3, 2006 S1, A1, NZ1, A2, NZ2, 3, A3, 2007 Sm(R), A1, NZ1, Nm, S, [Sm, E1, US, Fj, Arg, E2],

W, 2008 Arg(R), W3(R), S(R), E(R), 2009 BI 1(R), 2(R), 3, NZ1, 2, A1, 2, 3, NZ3, F, It, I, 2010 W1, F, It2, NZ1, 2, A1, 2, 3, 2011A2, NZ2, [W, Fj, Nm, Sm, A], 2013 W, S2, F

Fourie, T T (SET) 1974 BI 3

Fourie, W L (SWA) 1958 F 1, 2

Francis, J A J (Tvl) 1912 S, I, W, 1913 E, F

Frederickson, C A (Tvl) 1974 BI 2, 1980 S Am 1, 2

Frew, A (Tvl) 1903 BI 1

Froneman, D C (OFS) 1977 Wld

Froneman, I L (Bor) 1933 A 1

Fuls, H T (Tvl, EP) 1992 NZ (R), 1993 F 1, 2, A 1, 2, 3, Arg 1, 2

Fry, S P (WP) 1951 S, I, W, 1952 E, F, 1953 A 1, 2, 3, 4, 1955 BI 1, 2, 3, 4

Fynn, E E (N) 2001 F 1, It 1(R)

Fyvie, W (N) 1996 NZ 4(t & R), 5(R), Arg 2(R)

Gage, J H (OFS) 1933 A 1

Gainsford, J L (WP) 1960 S, NZ 1, 2, 3, 4, W, I, 1961 E, S, F, A 1, 2, 1962 BI 1, 2, 3, 4, 1963 A 1, 2, 3, 4, 1964 W, F, 1965 I, S, A 1, 2, NZ 1, 2, 3, 4, 1967 F 1, 2, 3

Garvey, A C (N) 1996 Arg 1, 2, F 1, 2, W, 1997 Tg, BI 1, 2, 3(R), A 1(t), It, F 1, 2, E, S, 1998 I 1, 2, W 1, E1, A 1, NZ 1, 2 A 2, W 2, S, I 3, E 2, 1999 [Sp]

Geel, P J (OFS) 1949 NZ 3

Geere, V (Tvl) 1933 A 1, 2, 3, 4, 5

Geffin, A O (Tvl) 1949 NZ 1, 2, 3, 4, 1951 S, I, W

Geldenhuys, A (EP) 1992 NZ, A, F 1, 2

Geldenhuys, S B (NT) 1981 NZ 3, US, 1982 S Am 1, 2, 1989 Wld 1, 2

Gentles, T A (WP) 1955 BI 1, 2, 4, 1956 NZ 2, 3, 1958 F 2

Geraghty, E M (Bor) 1949 NZ 4

Gerber, D M (EP, WP) 1980 S Am 3, 4, F, 1981 I 1, 2, NZ 1, 2, 3, US, 1982 S Am 1, 2, 1984 E 1, 2, S Am 1, 2, 1986 Cv 1, 2, 3, 4, 1992 NZ, A, F 1, 2, E

Gerber, H J (WP) 2003 S 1, 2

Gerber, M C (EP) 1958 F 1, 2, 1960 S

Gericke, F W (Tvl) 1960 S

Germishuys, J S (OFS, Tvl) 1974 BI 2, 1976 NZ 1, 2, 3, 4, 1977 Wld, 1980 S Am 1, 2, BI 1, 2, 3, 4, S Am 3, 4, F, 1981 I 1, 2, NZ 2, 3, US

Gibbs, B (GW) 1903 BI 2

Goosen, C P (OFS) 1965 NZ 2

Goosen, J L (FS, Racing 92) 2012 A1(R), NZ1(R), A2, NZ2, 2014 W1(R), It

Gorton, H C (Tvl) 1896 BI 1

Gould, R L (N) 1968 BI 1, 2, 3, 4

Grant, P J (WP) 2007 A2(R), NZ2(R), 2008 W1(t&R), It(R), A1(R)

Gray, B G (WP) 1931 W, 1932 E, S, 1933 A 5

Greeff, W W (WP) 2002 Arg (R), Sm, NZ 1, A 1, NZ 2, A 2, F, S, E, 2003 [U, Gg]

Greenwood, C M (WP) 1961 I

Greyling, M D (BB) 2011 A1, NZ1, 2012 NZ1(R)

Greyling, P J F (OFS) 1967 F 1, 2, 3, 4, 1968 BI 1, F 1, 2, 1969 A 1, 2, 3, 4, S, E, 1970 I, W, NZ 1, 2, 3, 4, 1971 F 1, 2, A 1, 2, 3, 1972 E

Grobler, C J (OFS) 1974 BI 4, 1975 F 1, 2

Guthrie, F H (WP) 1891 BI 1, 3, 1896 BI 1

Habana, B G (GL, BB, WP, Toulon) 2004 E(R), S, Arg, 2005 U, F1, 2, A1, 2, 3, NZ1, A4, NZ2, Arg, W, F3, 2006 S2, F, A1, NZ1, A2, NZ2, 3, I, E1, 2, 2007 E1, 2, S, [Sm, E1, Tg(R), US, Fj, Arg, E2], W, 2008 W1, 2, It, NZ1, 2, A1, NZ3, W3, S, E, 2009 BI 1, 2, NZ1, 2, A1, 2, 3, NZ3, F, It, I, 2010 F, It 1, 2, NZ1, A1, NZ3, A2, 3, I, W2, 2011 A2, NZ2, [W, Nm, Sm, A], 2012 E1, 2, 3, Arg1, 2, A1, NZ1, A2, NZ2, 2013 It, S1, Sm, Arg1, 2, A1, NZ1, A2, NZ2, W, S2, F, 2014 W1, 2, Arg1, 2, A1, NZ1, A2, NZ2, I, E, It, 2015 A, NZ, Arg 1, 2, [J, Sm, S, US, W, NZ, Arg]

Hahn, C H L (Tvl) 1910 BI 1, 2, 3

Hall, D B (GL) 2001 F 1, 2, NZ 1, A 1, 2, NZ 2, It 2, E, US, 2002 Sm, NZ 1, 2, A 2

Halstead, T M (N) 2001 F 3, It 2, E, US (R), 2003 S 1, 2

Hamilton, F (EP) 1891 BI 1

Hargreaves, A J (NS) 2010 W1(R), It 1(R), 2011 A1, NZ1

Harris, T A (Tvl) 1937 NZ 2, 3, 1938 BI 1, 2, 3

Hartley, A J (WP) 1891 BI 3

Hattingh, H (NT) 1992 A (R), F 2(R), E, 1994 Arg 1, 2

Hattingh, L B (OFS) 1933 A 2

Heatlie, B H (WP) 1891 BI 2, 3, 1896 BI 1, 4, 1903 BI 1, 3

Hendricks, C (FSC) 2014 W1, 2, S, Arg1, 2, A1, NZ1, A2, NZ2, I, W 3, 2015 NZ

Hendricks, M (Bol) 1998 I 2(R), W 1(R)

Hendriks, P (Tvl) 1992 NZ, A, 1994 S, W, 1995 [A, R, C], 1996 A 1, NZ 1, A 2, NZ 2, 3, 4, 5

Hepburn, T B (WP) 1896 BI 4

Heunis, J W (NT) 1981 NZ 3(R), US, 1982 S Am 1, 2, 1984 E 1, 2, S Am 1, 2, 1986 Cv 1, 2, 3, 4, 1989 Wld 1, 2

Hill, R A (R) 1960 W, I, 1961 I, A 1, 2, 1962 BI 4, 1963 A 3

Hills, W G (NT) 1992 F 1, 2, E, 1993 F 1, 2, A 1

Hirsch, J G (EP) 1906 I, 1910 BI 1

Hobson, T E C (WP) 1903 BI 3

Hoffman, R S (Bol) 1953 A 3

Holton, D N (EP) 1960 S

Honiball, H W (N) 1993 A 3(R), Arg 2, 1995 WS (R), 1996 Fj, A 1, NZ 5, Arg 1, 2, F 1, 2, W, 1997 Tg, BI 1, 2, 3(R), NZ 1(R), A 1(R), NZ 2, A 2, It, F 1, 2, E, 1998 W 1(R), E 1, A 1, NZ 1, 2, A 2, W 2, S, I 3, E 2, 1999 [A 3(R), NZ 3]

Hopwood, D J (WP) 1960 S, NZ 3, 4, W, 1961 E, S, F, I, A 1, 2, 1962 BI 1, 2, 3, 4, 1963 A 1, 2, 4, 1964 W, F, 1965 S, NZ 3, 4

Hougaard, D J (BB) 2003 [U(R), E(R), Gg, Sm, NZ], 2007 Sm, A2, NZ2

Hougaard, F (BB) 2009 It(R), 2010 A1(R), NZ3, A2, 3, W2(R), S, E(t&R), 2011 A2(t), NZ2(R), [W(R), Fj(R), Nm, Sm(R), A(R)], 2012 E1, 2, 3, Arg1, 2, A1, NZ1, A2, NZ2, I, S, E4, 2014 S(R), Arg2(R), NZ1(R), A2, NZ2, I, It(R), W 3(R)

Howe, B F (Bor) 1956 NZ 1, 4

Howe-Browne, N R F G (WP) 1910 BI 1, 2, 3

Hugo, D P (WP) 1989 Wld 1, 2

Human, D C F (WP) 2002 W 1, 2, Arg (R), Sm (R)

Hurter, M H (NT) 1995 [R, C], W, 1996 Fj, A 1, NZ 1, 2, 3, 4, 5, 1997 NZ 1, 2, A 2

Immelman, J H (WP) 1913 F

Jackson, D C (WP) 1906 I, W, E

Jackson, J S (WP) 1903 BI 2

Jacobs, A A (Falcons, NS) 2001 It 2(R), US, 2002 W 1(R), Arg, Sm (R), NZ 1(t+R), A 1(R), F, S, E (R), 2008 W1, 2, NZ1, 2, Arg, NZ3, A2, 3, W3, S, E, 2009 BI 1, 2, NZ2(R), A1(R), 2(R), 3(R), NZ3(R), F, It, 2010 I(R), E(R), 2011 A1(R), NZ1

James, A D (N, Bath, GL) 2001 F 1, 2, NZ 1, A 1, 2, NZ 2, 2002 F (R), S, E, 2006 NZ1, A2, NZ2, 3(R), E1, 2007 E1, 2, A1, NZ1, Nm, S, [Sm, E1, US, Fj, Arg, E2], 2008 W1, 2, NZ1, 2, A1, Arg, NZ3, A2, 3, 2010 It1, 2(R), NZ1(R), A1(R), 2(R), 2011 A2, [W(R)]

Jansen, E (OFS) 1981 NZ 1

Jansen, J S (OFS) 1970 NZ 1, 2, 3, 4, 1971 F 1, 2, A 1, 2, 3, 1972 E

Jantjes, C A (GL, WP) 2001 It 1, A 1, 2, NZ 2, F 3, It 2, E, US, 2005 Arg, W, 2007 W(R), 2008 W1, 2, It, NZ1, 2(R), A1, Arg, NZ3(R), A2, 3, W3, S, E

Jantjies, E T (GL) 2012 A2(R), NZ2(R)

Januarie, E R (GL, WP) 2005 U, F2, A1, 2, 3(R), NZ1, A4, NZ2, 2006 S1(R), 2(R), F(R), A1, I, E1, 2, 2007 E1, 2, Sm, Nm(R), [Sm(R), Tg], W, 2008 W2, It, NZ1, 2, Arg, NZ3(R), A2(R), 3(R), W3(R), S, E, 2009 BI 1(R), NZ1(R), 2(R), A1(R), 2(R), NZ3(R), 2010 W1, F, It 1, 2, NZ1, 2, 3(R)

Jennings, C B (Bor) 1937 NZ 1

Johnson, A F (FS) 2011 A1, NZ1(t&R), 2(t&R)

Johnson, G K (Tvl) 1993 Arg 2, 1994 NZ 3, Arg 1, 1995 WS, [R, C, WS]

Johnstone, P G A (WP) 1951 S, I, W, 1952 E, F, 1956 A 1, NZ 1, 2, 4

Jones, C H (Tvl) 1903 BI 1, 2

Jones, P S T (WP) 1896 BI 1, 3, 4

Jordaan, N (BB) 2002 E (R)

Jordaan, R P (NT) 1949 NZ 1, 2, 3, 4

Joubert, A J (OFS, N) 1989 Wld 1(R), 1993 A 3, Arg 1, 1994 E 1, 2, NZ 1, 2(R), 3, Arg 2, S, W, 1995 [A, C, WS, F, NZ], W, It, E, 1996 Fj, A 1, NZ 1, 3, 4, 5, Arg 1, 2, F 1, 2, W, 1997 Tg, BI 1, 2, A 2

Joubert, M C (Bol, WP) 2001 NZ 1, 2002 W 1, 2, Arg (R), Sm, NZ 1, A1, NZ 2, A 2, F (R), 2003 S 2, Arg, A 1, 2004 I1,

2, W1, PI, NZ1, A1, NZ2, A2, W2, I3, E, S, Arg, 2005 U, F1, 2, A1

Joubert, S J (WP) 1906 I, W, E

Julies, W (Bol, SWD, GL) 1999 [Sp], 2004 I1, 2, W1, S, Arg, 2005 A2(r), 3(t), 2006 F(R), 2007 Sm, [Tg]

Kahts, W J H (NT) 1980 BI 1, 2, 3, S Am 3, 4, F, 1981 I 1, 2, NZ 2, 1982 S Am 1, 2

Kaminer, J (Tvl) 1958 F 2

Kankowski, R (NS) 2007 W, 2008 W2(R), It, A1(R), W3(R), S(R), E(R), 2009 BI3, NZ3(R), F, It, 2010 W1(R), It 1(R), NZ2(R), A1, 3(R), S, 2011 A1(R), NZ1(R), 2012 E3(R)

Kayser, D J (EP, N) 1999 It 2(R), A 1(R), NZ 2, A 2, [S, Sp (R), U, E, A 3], 2001 It 1(R), NZ 1(R), A 2(R), NZ 2(R)

Kebble, G R (N) 1993 Arg 1, 2, 1994 NZ 1(R), 2

Kelly, E W (GW) 1896 BI 3

Kempson, R B (N, WP, Ulster) 1998 I 2(R), W 1, E 1, A 1, NZ 1, 2 A 2, W 2, S, I 3, E 2, 1999 It 1, 2, W, 2000 C, E 1, 2, A 1, NZ 1, A 2, 3, Arg, I, W, E 3, 2001 F 1, 2(R), NZ 1, A 1, 2, 2003 S 1(R), 2(R), Arg, A 1(R), NZ 1(R), A 2

Kenyon, B J (Bor) 1949 NZ 4

Kipling, H G (GW) 1931 W, I, 1932 E, S, 1933 A 1, 2, 3, 4, 5

Kirchner, Z (BB, Leinster) 2009 BI 3, F, It, I, 2010 W1(R), F, It1, NZ1, 2, A1, I, W2(R), S, E, 2012 E1, Arg1, 2, A1, NZ1, A2, NZ2, I, S, E4, 2013 A1, NZ1, A2, NZ2, 2014 S(t&R), 2015 Arg 2, [J]

Kirkpatrick, A I (GW) 1953 A 2, 1956 NZ 2, 1958 F 1, 1960 S, NZ 1, 2, 3, 4, W, I, 1961 E, S, F

Knight, A S (Tvl) 1912 S, I, W, 1913 E, F

Knoetze, F (WP) 1989 Wld 1, 2

Koch, A C (Bol) 1949 NZ 2, 3, 4, 1951 S, I, W, 1952 E, F, 1953 A 1, 2, 4, 1955 BI 1, 2, 3, 4, 1956 A 1, NZ 2, 3, 1958 F 1, 2, 1960 NZ 1, 2

Koch, H V (WP) 1949 NZ 1, 2, 3, 4

Koch, V P (Steval Pumas) 2015 NZ(R), Arg 1

Koen, L J (GL, BB) 2000 A 1, 2001 It 2, E, US, 2003 S 1, 2, Arg, A 1, NZ 1, A 2, NZ 2, [U, E, Sm(R), NZ(R)]

Kolisi, S (WP) 2013 S1(R), Sm(R), Arg1(R), 2(R), A1(R), NZ1(R), A2(R), NZ2(R), W(R), F(R), 2015 Arg 1(R), [J(R), Sm(R)]

Kotze, G J M (WP) 1967 F 1, 2, 3, 4

Krantz, E F W (OFS) 1976 NZ 1, 1981 I 1,

Kriel, J A (BB) 2015 A, NZ, Arg 1, 2, [J, Sm(R), S, US, W, NZ, Arg]

Krige, C P J (WP) 1999 It 2, W, NZ 1, 2000 C (R), E 1(R), 2, A 1(R), NZ 1, A 2, NZ 2, A 3, Arg, I, W, E 3, 2001 F 1, 2, It 1(R), A 1(t+R), It 2(R), E (R), 2002 W 2, Arg, Sm, NZ 1, A 1, NZ 2, A 2, F, S, E, 2003 Arg, A 1, NZ 1, A 2, NZ 2, [E, Sm, NZ]

Krige, J D (WP) 1903 BI 1, 3, 1906 S, I, W

Kritzinger, J L (Tvl) 1974 BI 3, 4, F 1, 2, 1975 F 1, 2, 1976 NZ 4

Kroon, C M (EP) 1955 BI 1

Kruger, P E (Tvl) 1986 Cv 3, 4

Kruger, P J J (BB, Racing Metro) 2012 E1, 2, 3, A1, NZ1, I, S, E4, 2013 S1, Sm(t&R),
Arg1, 2, A1(R), NZ1(R), A2(R), NZ2

Kruger, R J (NT, BB) 1993 Arg 1, 2, 1994 S, W, 1995 WS, [A, R, WS, F, NZ], W, It, E, 1996 Fj, A 1, NZ 1, A 2, NZ 2, 3, 4, 5, Arg 1, 2, F 1, 2, W, 1997 Tg, BI 1, 2, NZ 1, A 1, NZ 2, 1999 NZ 2, A 2(R), [Sp, NZ 3(R)]

Kruger, T L (Tvl) 1921 NZ 1, 2, 1924 BI 1, 2, 3, 4, 1928 NZ 1, 2

Kruger, W (BB) 2011 A1, NZ1, 2012 E2(R), 3(R)

Kuhn, S P (Tvl) 1960 NZ 3, 4, W, I, 1961 E, S, F, I, A 1, 2, 1962 BI 1, 2, 3, 4, 1963 A 1, 2, 3, 1965 I, S

Labuschagne, J J (GL) 2000 NZ 1(R), 2002 W 1, 2, Arg, NZ 1, A 1, NZ 2, A2, F, S, E

La Grange, J B (WP) 1924 BI 3, 4

Lambie, P J (NS) 2010 I(R), W2(R), S(R), E(R), 2011 A1(R), NZ1, 2, [Fj, Nm, Sm, A], 2012 E1(R), 2, A1(R), NZ1(R), A2(R), NZ2(R), I, S, E4, 2013 It(R), S1(R), Sm(R), Arg1(R), 2(R), A1(R), NZ1(R), A2(R), NZ2(R), W, S2, F(t&R), 2014 A1(R), NZ1(R), A2(R), NZ2(R), I(R), E, It, W 3, 2015 A(R), NZ(t&R), Arg 1(R), 2, [J, Sm(R), S(R), W(R), NZ(R), Arg(R)]

Larard, A (Tvl) 1896 BI 2, 4

Lategan, M T (WP) 1949 NZ 1, 2, 3, 4, 1951 S, I, W, 1952 E, F, 1953 A 1, 2

Laubscher, T G (WP) 1994 Arg 1, 2, S, W, 1995 It, E

Lawless, M J (WP) 1964 F, 1969 E (R), 1970 I, W
Ledger, S H (GW) 1912 S, I, 1913 E, F
Leonard, A (WP, SWD) 1999 A 1, [Sp]
Le Roux, A H (OFS, N) 1994 E 1, 1998 I 1, 2, W 1(R), E 1(R), A 1(R), NZ 1(R), 2(R), A 2(R), W 2(R), S (R), I 3(R), E 2(t+R), 1999 It 1(R), 2(R), W (R), NZ 1(R), A 1(R), NZ 2(R), A 2(R), [S(R), Sp, U (R), E (R), A 3(R), NZ 3(R)], 2000 E 1(t+R), 2(R), A 1(R), 2(R), NZ 2, A 3(R), Arg (R), I (t), W (R), E 3(R), 2001 F 1(R), 2, It 1, NZ 1(R), A 1(R), 2(R), NZ 2(R), F 3, It 2, E, US (R), 2002 W 1(R), 2(R), Arg, NZ 1(R), A 1(R), NZ 2(R), A 2(R)
Le Roux, H P (Tvl) 1993 F 1, 2, 1994 E 1, 2, NZ 1, 2, 3, Arg 2, S, W, 1995 WS [A, R, C (R), WS, F, NZ], W, It, E, 1996 Fj, NZ 2, Arg 1, 2, F 1, 2, W
Le Roux, J H S (Tvl) 1994 E 2, NZ 1, 2
Le Roux, M (OFS) 1980 Bl 1, 2, 3, 4, S Am 3, 4, F, 1981 I 1
Le Roux, P A (WP) 1906 I, W, E
Le Roux, W J (Griquas, FSC) 2013 It, S1, Sm, Arg1, 2, A1, NZ1, A2, NZ2, W(R), S2, F, 2014 W1, 2, S, Arg1, 2, A1, NZ1, A2, NZ2, I, E, It(R), W 3, 2015 A, NZ, Arg 1, [Sm, S, US, W, NZ, Arg]
Lewies, J S T (NS) 2014 S(R)
Liebenberg, C R (WP) 2012 Arg2(R), A1(R), NZ1(R), A2(R), NZ2(R)
Little, E M (GW) 1891 Bl 1, 3
Lobberts, H (BB) 2006 E1(R), 2007 NZ2(R)
Lochner, G P (WP) 1955 Bl 3, 1956 A 1, 2, NZ 1, 2, 3, 4, 1958 F 1, 2
Lochner, G P (EP) 1937 NZ 3, 1938 Bl 1, 2
Lockyear, R J (GW) 1960 NZ 1, 2, 3, 4, 1960 I, 1961 F
Lombard, A C (EP) 1910 Bl 2
Lombard, F (FS) 2002 S, E
Lötter, D (Tvl) 1993 F 2, A 1, 2
Lotz, J W (Tvl) 1937 A 1, 2, NZ 1, 2, 3, 1938 Bl 1, 2, 3
Loubscher, R I P (EP, N) 2002 W 1, 2003 S 1, [U(R), Gg]
Loubser, J A (WP) 1903 Bl 3, 1906 S, I, W, E, 1910 Bl 1, 3
Lourens, M J (NT) 1968 Bl 2, 3, 4
Louw, F H (WP) 2002 W 2(R), Arg, Sm
Louw, J S (Tvl) 1891 Bl 1, 2, 3
Louw, L-F P (WP, Bath) 2010 W1, F, It 1, 2, NZ1, 2, 3(R), 2011 [Fj(t), Nm(t&R), A(R)], 2012 A1(R), NZ1, A2, NZ2, I, S, E4, 2013 It, Sm, Arg1, 2, A1, NZ1, A2, NZ2, W, S2, F, 2014 W1, 2, Arg1, 2, A1, NZ1, 2015 A, NZ, [J, Sm, US, W, NZ, Arg]
Louw, M J (Tvl) 1971 A 2, 3
Louw, M M (WP) 1928 NZ 3, 4, 1931 W, I, 1932 E, S, 1933 A 1, 2, 3, 4, 5, 1937 A 1, 2, NZ 2, 3, 1938 Bl 1, 2, 3
Louw, R J (WP) 1980 S Am 1, 2, Bl 1, 2, 3, 4 S Am 3, 4, F, 1981 I 1, 2, NZ 1, 3, 1982 S Am 1, 2, 1984 E 1, 2, S Am 1, 2
Louw, S C (WP) 1933 A 1, 2, 3, 4, 5, 1937 A 1, NZ 1, 2, 3, 1938 Bl 1, 2, 3
Lubbe, E (GW) 1997 Tg, Bl 1
Luyt, F P (WP) 1910 Bl 1, 2, 3, 1912 S, I, W, 1913 E
Luyt, J D (EP) 1912 S, W, 1913 E, F
Luyt, R R (W P) 1910 Bl 2, 3, 1912 S, I, W, 1913 E, F
Lyons, D J (EP) 1896 Bl 1
Lyster, P J (N) 1933 A 2, 5, 1937 NZ 1

McCallum, I D (WP) 1970 NZ 1, 2, 3, 4, 1971 F 1, 2, A 1, 2, 3, 1974 Bl 1, 2
McCallum, R J (WP) 1974 Bl 1
McCulloch, J D (GW) 1913 E, F
MacDonald, A W (R) 1965 A 1, NZ 1, 2, 3, 4
Macdonald, D A (WP) 1974 Bl 2
Macdonald, I (Tvl) 1992 NZ, A, 1993 F 1, A 3, 1994 E 2, 1995 WS (R)
McDonald, J A J (WP) 1931 W, I, 1932 E, S
McEwan, W M C (Tvl) 1903 Bl 1, 3
McHardy, E E (OFS) 1912 S, I, W, 1913 E, F
McKendrick, J A (WP) 1891 Bl 3
McLeod, C (NS) 2011 NZ1(R)
Maku, B G (BB) 2010 It1(R)
Malan, A S (Tvl) 1960 NZ 1, 2, 3, 4, W, I, 1961 E, S, F, 1962 Bl 1, 1963 A 1, 2, 3, 1964 W, 1965 I, S
Malan, A W (NT) 1989 Wld 1, 2, 1992 NZ, A, F 1, 2, E
Malan, E (NT) 1980 Bl 3(R), 4
Malan, G F (WP) 1958 F 2, 1960 NZ 1, 3, 4, 1961 E, S, F, 1962 Bl 1, 2, 3, 1963 A 1, 2, 4, 1964 W, 1965 A 1, 2, NZ 1, 2

Malan, P (Tvl) 1949 NZ 4
Malherbe, J F (WP) 2013 W, S2, 2014 Arg1(R), 2(R), 2015 A(t&R), Arg 2(R), [Sm(R), S(R), US, W, NZ, Arg]
Mallett, N V H (WP) 1984 S Am 1, 2
Malotana, K (Bor) 1999 [Sp]
Mans, W J (WP) 1965 I, S
Mapoe, L G (GL) 2015 NZ(R)
Marais, C F (WP) 1999 It 1(R), 2(R), 2000 C, E 1, 2, A 1, NZ 1, A 2, NZ 2, A 3, Arg (R), W (R)
Marais, F P (Bol) 1949 NZ 1, 2, 1951 S, 1953 A 1, 2
Marais, J F K (WP) 1963 A 3, 1964 W, F, 1965 I, S, A 2, 1968 Bl, 1, 2, 3, 4, F 1, 2, 1969 A 1, 2, 3, 4, S, E, 1970 I, W, NZ 1, 2, 3, 4, 1971 F 1, 2, A 1, 2, 3, 1974 Bl 1, 2, 3, 4, F 1, 2
Maré, D S (Tvl) 1906 S
Marsberg, A F W (GW) 1906 S, W, E
Marsberg, P A (GW) 1910 Bl 1
Martheze, W C (GW) 1903 Bl 2, 1906 I, W
Martin, H J (Tvl) 1937 A 2
Matfield, V (BB) 2001 It 1(R), NZ 1, A 2, NZ 2, F 3, It 2, E, US, 2002 W 1, Sm, NZ 1, A 1, NZ 2(R), 2003 S 1, 2, Arg, A 1, NZ 1, A 2, NZ 2, [U, E, Sm, NZ], 2004 I1, 2, W1, NZ2, A2, W2, I3, E, S, Arg, 2005 F1, 2, A1, 2, 3, NZ1, A4, NZ2, Arg, W, F3, 2006 S1, 2, F, A1, NZ1, A2, NZ2, 3, A3, 2007 E1, 2, A1, NZ1, Nm, S, [Sm, E1, Tg(R), US, Fj, Arg, E2], 2008 W1(R), 2, It, NZ1, 2, A1, Arg, NZ3, A2, 3, W3, S, E, 2009 Bl 1, 2, 3, NZ1, 2, A1, 2, 3, NZ3, F, It(R), I, 2010 W1, F, It 1, NZ1, 2, A1, NZ3, A2, 3, I, W2, S, E, 2011 A2, NZ2, [W, Sm, A], 2014 W1, 2, S, A1, NZ1, A2, NZ2, I, E, It, W 3, 2015 A, Arg 2, [J, Sm, NZ(R), Arg]
Mellet, T B (GW) 1896 Bl 2
Mellish, F W (WP) 1921 NZ 1, 3, 1924 Bl 1, 2, 3, 4
Mentz, H (N) 2004 I1, W1(R)
Merry, J (EP) 1891 Bl 1
Metcalf, H D (Bor) 1903 Bl 2
Meyer, C du P (WP) 1921 NZ 1, 2, 3
Meyer, P J (GW) 1896 Bl 1
Meyer, W (OFS, GL) 1997 S (R), 1999 It 2, NZ 1(R), A 1(R), 2000 C (R), E 1, NZ 1(R), 2(R), Arg, I, W, E 3, 2001 F 1(R), 2, It 1, F 3(R), It 2, E, US (t+R), 2002 W 1, 2, Arg, NZ 1, 2, A 2, F
Michau, J M (Tvl) 1921 NZ 1
Michau, J P (WP) 1921 NZ 1, 2, 3
Millar, W A (WP) 1906 E, 1910 Bl 2, 3, 1912 I, W, 1913 F
Mills, W J (WP) 1910 Bl 2
Mohoje, T S (FSC) 2014 S(R), A2, NZ2, I, E(R), It, W 3, 2015 A(t&R)
Moll, T (Tvl) 1910 Bl 2
Montini, P E (WP) 1956 A 1, 2
Montgomery, P C (WP, Newport, N, Perpignan) 1997 Bl 2, 3, NZ 1, A 1, NZ 2, A 2, F 1, 2, E, S, 1998 I 1, 2, W 1, E 1, A 1, NZ 1, 2, A 2, W 2, S, I 3, E 2, 1999 It 1, 2, W, NZ 1, A 1, NZ 2, A 2, [S, U, E, A 3, NZ 3], 2000 C, E 1, 2, A 1, NZ 1, A 2(R), Arg, I, W, E 3, 2001 F 1, 2(t), It 1, NZ 1, F 3(R), It 2(R), 2004 I2, W1, PI, NZ1, A1, NZ2, A2, W2, I3, E, S, 2005 U, F1, 2, A1, 2, 3, NZ1, A4, NZ2, Arg, W, F3, 2006 S1, 2, F, A1, NZ1, A2, NZ2, 2007 E1, 2, Sm(R), A1, NZ1, Nm, S, [Sm, E1, Tg(R), US, Fj, Arg, E2], 2008 W1(R), 2(R), NZ1(R), 2, Arg(R), NZ3, A2(R), 3(R)
Moolman, L C (NT) 1977 Wld, 1980 S Am 1, 2, Bl 1, 2, 3, 4, S Am 3, 4, F, 1981 I 1, 2, NZ 1, 2, 3, US, 1982 S Am 1, 2, 1984 S Am 1, 2, 1986 Cv 1, 2, 3, 4
Mordt, R H (Z-R, NT) 1980 S Am 1, 2, Bl 1, 2, 3, 4, S Am 3, 4, F, 1981 I 2, NZ 1, 2, 3, US, 1982 S Am 1, 2, 1984 S Am 1, 2
Morkel, D A (Tvl) 1903 Bl 1
Morkel, D F T (Tvl) 1906 I, E, 1910 Bl 1, 3, 1912 S, I, W, 1913 E, F
Morkel, H J (WP) 1921 NZ 1
Morkel, H W (WP) 1921 NZ 1, 2
Morkel, J A (WP) 1921 NZ 2, 3
Morkel, J W H (WP) 1912 S, I, W, 1913 E, F
Morkel, P G (WP) 1912 S, I, W, 1913 E, F, 1921 NZ 1, 2, 3
Morkel, P K (WP) 1928 NZ 4
Morkel, W H (WP) 1910 Bl 3, 1912 S, I, W, 1913 E, F, 1921 NZ 1, 2, 3
Morkel, W S (Tvl) 1906 S, I, W, E
Moss, C (N) 1949 NZ 1, 2, 3, 4

Mostert, G (Stade Français) 2011 NZ1, A2(R)

Mostert, P J (WP) 1921 NZ 1, 2, 3, 1924 BI 1, 2, 4, 1928 NZ 1, 2, 3, 4, 1931 W, I, 1932 E, S

Mtawarira, T (NS) 2008 W2, It, A1(R), Arg, NZ3, A2, 3, W3, S, E, 2009 BI 1, 2, 3, NZ1, 2, A1, 2, 3, NZ3, F, It(R), I, 2010 I, W2, S, E, 2011 A2, NZ2(R), [W, F](R), Nm(R), Sm], 2012 E1, 2, 3, Arg1, 2, A1, NZ1, A2, NZ2, 2013 It, S1, Sm, Arg1, 2, A1, NZ1, A2, NZ2, W, S2(R), F, 2014 W1(R), 2, Arg1, 2(R), A1, NZ1, A2, NZ2, I, E, W 3, 2015 A, NZ, Arg 1, 2(R), [J, Sm, S, US, W, NZ, Arg]

Muir, D J (WP) 1997 It, F 1, 2, E, S

Mujati, B V (WP) 2008 W1, It(R), NZ1(R), 2(t), A1(R), Arg(R), NZ3(R), A2(R), 3, W3(t), S(R), E(R)

Mulder, J C (Tvl, GL) 1994 NZ 2, 3, S, W, 1995 WS, [A, WS, F, NZ], W, It, E, 1996 Fj, A 1, NZ 1, A 2, NZ 2, 5, Arg 1, 2, F 1, 2, W, 1997 Tg, BI 1, 1999 It 1(R), 2, W, NZ 1, 2000 C(R), A 1, E 3, 2001 F 1, It 1

Muller, G H (WP) 1969 A 3, 4, S, 1970 W, NZ 1, 2, 3, 4, 1971 F 1, 2, 1972 E, 1974 BI 1, 3, 4

Muller, G J (NS, Ulster) 2006 S1(R), NZ1(R), A2, NZ2, 3, A3, I(R), E1, 2, 2007 E1(R), 2(R), Sm(R), A1(R), NZ1(R), A2, NZ2, Nm(R), [Sm(R), E1(R), Fj(t&R), Arg(t&R)], W, 2009 BI 3, 2011 [W(R)]

Muller, G P (GL) 2003 A 2, NZ 2, [E, Gg(R), Sm, NZ]

Muller, H L (OFS) 1986 Cv 4(R), 1989 Wld 1(R)

Muller, H S V (Tvl) 1949 NZ 1, 2, 3, 4, 1951 S, I, W, 1952 E, F, 1953 A 1, 2, 3, 4

Muller, L J J (N) 1992 NZ, A

Muller, P G (N) 1992 NZ, A, F 1, 2, E, 1993 F 1, 2, A 1, 2, 3, Arg 1, 2, 1994 E 1, 2, NZ 1, S, W, 1998 I 1, 2, W 1, E 1, A 1, NZ 1, 2, A 2, 1999 It 1, W, NZ 1, A 1, [Sp, E, A 3, NZ 3]

Murray, W M (N) 2007 Sm, A2, NZ2

Mvovo, L N (NS) 2010 S, E, 2011 A1, NZ1, 2012 Arg1, 2, A1(R), 2014 W1(R), S, W 3, 2015 A(R), Arg 1(R), 2, [J, US]

Myburgh, F R (EP) 1896 BI 1

Myburgh, J L (NT) 1962 BI 1, 1963 A 4, 1964 W, F, 1968 BI 1, 2, 3, F 1, 2, 1969 A 1, 2, 3, 4, E, 1970 I, W, NZ 3, 4

Myburgh, W H (WT) 1924 BI 1

Naude, J P (WP) 1963 A 4, 1965 A 1, 2, NZ 1, 3, 4, 1967 F 1, 2, 3, 4, 1968 BI 1, 2, 3, 4

Ndungane, A Z (BB) 2006 A1, 2, NZ2, 3, A3, E1, 2, 2007 E2, Nm(R), [US], W(R)

Ndungane, O M (NS) 2008 It, NZ1, A3, 2009 BI 3, A3, NZ3, 2010 W1, 2011 NZ1(R), [Fj]

Neethling, J B (WP) 1967 F 1, 2, 3, 4, 1968 BI 4, 1969 S, 1970 NZ 1, 2

Nel, J A (Tvl) 1960 NZ 1, 2, 1963 A 1, 2, 1965 A 2, NZ 1, 2, 3, 4, 1970 NZ 3, 4

Nel, J J (WP) 1956 A 1, 2, NZ 1, 2, 3, 4, 1958 F 1, 2

Nel, P A R 0 (Tvl) 1903 BI 1, 2, 3

Nel, P J (N) 1928 NZ 1, 2, 3, 4, 1931 W, I, 1932 E, S, 1933 A 1, 3, 4, 5, 1937 A 1, 2, NZ 2, 3

Nimb, C F (WP) 1961 I

Nokwe, J L (FS) 2008 Arg, A2, 3, 2009 BI 3

Nomis, S H (Tvl) 1967 F 4, 1968 BI 1, 2, 3, 4, F 1, 2, 1969 A 1, 2, 3, 4, S, E, 1970 I, W, NZ 1, 2, 3, 4, 1971 F 1, 2, A 1, 2, 3, 1972 E

Nyakane, T N (FSC, BB) 2013 It(R), S1(R), Sm(R), 2014 S(R), Arg1(R), A1(R), NZ1(R), A2(R), NZ2(R), I(R), E(R), It, W 3(R), 2015 NZ(R), Arg 1(R), 2, [J(R), Sm(R), S(R), US(R), W(R), NZ(R), Arg(R)]

Nykamp, J L (Tvl) 1933 A 2

Ochse, J K (WP) 1951 I, W, 1952 E, F, 1953 A 1, 2, 4

Oelofse, J S A (Tvl) 1953 A 1, 2, 3, 4

Oliver, J F (Tvl) 1928 NZ 3, 4

Olivier, E (WP) 1967 F 1, 2, 3, 4, 1968 BI 1, 2, 3, 4, F 1, 2, 1969 A 1, 2, 3, 4, S, E

Olivier, J (NT) 1992 F 1, 2, E, 1993 F 1, 2 A 1, 2, 3, Arg 1, 1995 W, It (R), E, 1996 Arg 1, 2, F 1, 2, W

Olivier, W (BB, Montpellier) 2006 S1(R), 2, F, A1, NZ1, A2, NZ2(R), 3, A3, I(R), E1, 2, 2007 E1, 2, NZ1(R), A2, NZ2, [E1(R), Tg, Arg(R)], W(R), 2009 BI3, NZ1(R), 2(R), F(R), It(R), I, 2010 F, It2(R), NZ1, 2, A1, 2011 A1, NZ1(R), 2012 E1(t), 2(R), 3, 2014 W2(R)

Olver, E (EP) 1896 BI 1

Oosthuizen, C V (FSC) 2012 E1(t&R), NZ2(R), 2013 It(R), S1(R), Sm(R), Arg1(R), 2(R), A1(t&R), NZ1(R), A2(R), NZ2(R), W(R), S2(R), F, 2014 W1(R), 2(R), S, I(R), E(R), It, W 3, 2015 [J(R), US(R)]

Oosthuizen, J J (WP) 1974 BI 1, F 1, 2, 1975 F 1, 2, 1976 NZ 1, 2, 3, 4

Oosthuizen, O W (NT, Tvl) 1981 I 1(R), 2, NZ 2, 3, US, 1982 S Am 1, 2, 1984 E 1, 2

Osler, B L (WP) 1924 BI 1, 2, 3, 4, 1928 NZ 1, 2, 3, 4, 1931 W, I, 1932 E, S, 1933 A 1, 2, 3, 4, 5

Osler, S G (WP) 1928 NZ 1

Otto, K (NT, BB) 1995 [R, C (R), WS (R)], 1997 BI 3, NZ 1, A 1, NZ 2, It, F 1, 2, E, S, 1998 I 1, 2, W 1, E 1, A 1, NZ 1, 2, A 2, W 2, S, I 3, E 2, 1999 It 1, W, NZ 1, A 1, [S (R), Sp, U, E, A 3, NZ 3], 2000 C, E 1, 2, A 1

Oxlee, K (N) 1960 NZ 1, 2, 3, 4, W, I, 1961 S, A 1, 2, 1962 BI 1, 2, 3, 4, 1963 A 1, 2, 4, 1964 W, 1965 NZ 1, 2

Pagel, G L (WP) 1995 [A (R), R, C, NZ (R)], 1996 NZ 5(R)

Paige, R (BB) 2015 [US(R), Arg(R)]

Parker, W H (EP) 1965 A 1, 2

Partridge, J E C (Tvl) 1903 BI 1

Paulse, B J (WP) 1999 It 1, 2, NZ 1, A 1, 2(R), [S (R), Sp, NZ 3], 2000 C, E 1, 2, A 1, NZ 1, A 2, NZ 2, A 3, Arg, W, E 3, 2001 F 1, 2, It 1, NZ 1, A 1, 2, NZ 2, F 3, It 2, E, 2002 W 1, 2, Arg, Sm (R), A 1, NZ 2, A 2, F, S, E, 2003 [Gg], 2004 I1, 2, W1, PI, NZ1, A1, NZ2, A2, W2, I3, E, 2005 A2, 3, NZ1, A4, F3, 2006 S1, 2, A1(R), NZ1, 3(R), A3(R), 2007 A2, NZ2

Payn, C (N) 1924 BI 1, 2

Pelser, H J M (Tvl) 1958 F 1, 1960 NZ 1, 2, 3, 4, W, I, 1961 F, I, A 1, 2

Pfaff, B D (WP) 1956 A 1

Pickard, J A J (WP) 1953 A 3, 4, 1956 NZ 2, 1958 F 2

Pienaar, J F (Tvl) 1993 F 1, 2, A 1, 2, 3, Arg 1, 2, 1994 E 1, 2, NZ 2, 3, Arg 1, 2, S, W, 1995 WS, [A, C, WS, F, NZ], W, It, E, 1996 Fj, A 1, NZ 1, A 2, NZ 2

Pienaar, R (NS, Ulster) 2006 NZ2(R), 3(R), A3(R), I(t), E1(R), 2007 E1(R), 2(R), Sm(R), A1, NZ1, A2, NZ2, Nm(R), S(R), [E1(t&R), Tg, US(R), Arg(R)], W, 2008 W1(R), It(R), NZ2(R), A1(R), 3(R), W3, S, E, 2009 BI 1, 2, 3(R), NZ1, A1(R), 2, 3, It(R), I(R), 2010 W1, F(R), It 1(R), 2(R), NZ1(R), 2(R), A1, I, W2, S(R), E, 2011 W1, NZ1, [F](R), Nm(R)], 2012 E1(R), 2(R), 3(R), Arg1(R), 2(R), A1, NZ1, A2, NZ2, I, S, E4, 2013 It(R), S1, Sm, Arg1, 2, A1, NZ1, 2(R), W(R), S2(R), F, 2014 W1(R), 2(t), Arg1, 2, A1, NZ1, 2015 A, NZ, Arg 1, 2, [J, Sm(R), S(R), Arg]

Pienaar, Z M J (OFS) 1980 S Am 2(R), BI 1, 2, 3, 4, S Am 3, 4, F, 1981 I 1, 2, NZ 1, 2, 3

Pietersen, J-P R (NS, Wild Knights) 2006 A3, 2007 Sm, A1, NZ1, A2, NZ2, Nm, S, [Sm, E1, Tg, US(R), Fj, Arg, E2], W, 2008 NZ2, A1, Arg, NZ3, A2, W3, S, E, 2009 BI 1, 2, NZ1, 2, A1, 2, F, It, I, 2010 NZ3, A2, 3, 2011 A2, NZ2, [W, Fj, Sm, A], 2012 E1, 2, 3, I, S, E4, 2013 W, S2, F, 2014 W1, 2, S, A2(t&R), NZ2(R), I(R), E, It, 2015 A, [J(R), Sm, S, W, NZ, Arg]

Pitzer, G (NT) 1967 F 1, 2, 3, 4, 1968 BI 1, 2, 3, 4, F 1, 2, 1969 A 3, 4

Pollard, H (BB) 2014 S, Arg1, 2, NZ1, A2, NZ2, I, It(R), W 3(R), 2015 A, NZ, Arg 1, 2, [J(R), Sm, S, US, W, NZ, Arg]

Pope, C F (WP) 1974 BI 1, 2, 3, 4, 1975 F 1, 2, 1976 NZ 2, 3, 4

Potgieter, D J (BB) 2009 I(t), 2010 W1, F(t&R), It 1, 2(R), A1(R)

Potgieter, H J (OFS) 1928 NZ 1, 2

Potgieter, H L (OFS) 1977 Wld

Potgieter, U J (BB) 2012 E3, Arg1(R), 2

Powell, A W (GW) 1896 BI 3

Powell, J M (GW) 1891 BI 2, 1896 BI 3, 1903 BI 1, 2

Prentis, R B (Tvl) 1980 S Am 1, 2, BI 1, 2, 3, 4, S Am 3, 4, F, 1981 I 1, 2

Pretorius, A S (GL) 2002 W 1, 2, Arg, Sm, NZ 1, A 1, NZ 2, F, S (R), E, 2003 NZ 1(R), A 1, 2005 A2, 3, NZ1, A4, NZ2, Arg, 2006 NZ2(R), 3, A3, I, E1(t&R), 2, 2007 S(R), [Sm(R), E1(R), Tg, US(R), Arg(R)], W

Pretorius, J C (GL) 2006 I, 2007 NZ2

Pretorius, N F (Tvl) 1928 NZ 1, 2, 3, 4

Prinsloo, J (Tvl) 1958 F 1, 2
Prinsloo, J (NT) 1963 A 3
Prinsloo, J P (Tvl) 1928 NZ 1
Putter, D J (WT) 1963 A 1, 2, 4

Raaff, J W E (GW) 1903 BI 1, 2, 1906 S, W, E, 1910 BI 1
Ralepelle, M C (BB) 2006 NZ2(R), E2(R), 2008 E(t&R), 2009 BI 3, NZ1(R), 2(R), A2(R), NZ3(R), 2010 W1(R), F(R), It 1, 2(R), NZ1(R), 2(R), A1(R), 2(R), 3(R), W2(R), 2011 A1(R), NZ1(R), [Nm(R)], 2013 It(R)
Ras, W J de Wet (OFS) 1976 NZ 1(R), 1980 S Am 2(R)
Rautenbach, S J (WP) 2002 W 1(R), 2(t+R), Arg (R), Sm, NZ 1(R), A 1, NZ 2(R), A 2(R), 2003 [U(R), Gg, Sm, NZ], 2004 W1, NZ1(R)
Redelinghuys, J (GL) 2014 It(R), W 3(R)
Reece-Edwards, H (N) 1992 F 1, 2, 1993 A 2
Reid, A (WP) 1903 BI 3
Reid, B C (Bor) 1933 A 4
Reinach, J (OFS) 1986 Cv 1, 2, 3, 4
Reinach, J M (NS) 2014 A2(R), NZ2(R), I(R), E, It, W 3, 2015 A(R), NZ(R), Arg 1(R), 2(R)
Rens, I J (Tvl) 1953 A 3, 4
Retief, D F (NT) 1955 BI 1, 2, 4, 1956 A 1, 2, NZ 1, 2, 3, 4
Reyneke, H J (WP) 1910 BI 3
Richards, A R (WP) 1891 BI 1, 2, 3
Richter, A (NT) 1992 F 1, 2, E, 1994 E 2, NZ 1, 2, 3, 1995 [R, C, WS (R)]
Riley, N M (ET) 1963 A 3
Riordan, C A (Tvl) 1910 BI 1, 2
Robertson, I W (R) 1974 F 1, 2, 1976 NZ 1, 2, 4
Rodgers, P H (NT, Tvl) 1989 Wld 1, 2, 1992 NZ, F 1, 2
Rogers, C D (Tvl) 1984 E 1, 2, S Am 1, 2
Roos, G D (WP) 1910 BI 2, 3
Roos, P J (WP) 1903 BI 3, 1906 I, W, E
Rosenberg, W (Tvl) 1955 BI 2, 3, 4, 1956 NZ 3, 1958 F 1
Rossouw, C L C (Tvl, N) 1995 WS, [R, WS, F, NZ], 1999 NZ 2(R), A 2(t), [Sp, NZ 3(R)]
Rossouw, D H (WP) 1953 A 3, 4
Rossouw, D J (BB) 2003 [U, Gg, Sm(R), NZ], 2004 E(R), S, Arg, 2005 U, F1, 2, A1, W(R), F3(R), 2006 S1, 2, F, A1, I, E1, 2, 2007 E1, Sm, A1(R), NZ1, S, [Sm, E1, Tg, Fj, Arg, E2], 2008 W1(t&R), NZ3(R), A3(R), S(R), E, 2009 BI 1(R), 2(R), NZ1(R), 2(R), A1(R), 3(R), W2(R), F(R), It, I, 2010 W1, F, NZ1(R), 2, A1, NZ3(t&R), A2(R), 3, 2011 A1, NZ1, A2, NZ2(t&R), [W, Fj, Nm, Sm, A]
Rossouw, P W G (WP) 1997 BI 2, 3, NZ 1, A 1, NZ 2(R), A 2(R), It, F 1, 2, E, S, 1998 I 1, 2, W 1, E 1, A 1, NZ 1, 2, A 2, W 2, S, I 3, E 2, 1999 It 1, W, NZ 1, A 1(R), NZ 2, A 2, [S, U, E, A 3], 2000 C, E 1, 2, A 2, Arg (R), I, W, 2001 F 3, US, 2003 Arg
Rousseau, W P (WP) 1928 NZ 3, 4
Roux, F du T (WP) 1960 W, 1961 A 1, 2, 1962 BI 1, 2, 3, 4, 1963 A 2, 1965 A 1, 2, NZ 1, 2, 3, 4, 1968 BI 3, 4, F 1, 2 1969 A 1, 2, 3, 4, 1970 I, NZ 1, 2, 3, 4
Roux, J P (Tvl) 1994 E 2, NZ 1, 2, 3, Arg 1, 1995 [R, C, F (R)], 1996 A 1, NZ 1, A 2, NZ 3
Roux, O A (NT) 1969 S, E, 1970 I, W, 1972 E, 1974 BI 3, 4
Roux, W G (BB) 2002 F (R), S, E
Russell, R B (MP, N) 2002 W 1(R), 2, Arg, A 1(R), NZ 2(R), A 2, F, E (R), 2003 Arg (R), A1(R), NZ 1, A 2(R), 2004 I2(t&R), W1, NZ1(R), W2(R), Arg(R), 2005 U(R), F2(R), A1(t), Arg(R), W(R), 2006 F

Samuels, T A (GW) 1896 BI 2, 3, 4
Santon, D (Bol) 2003 A 1(R), NZ 1(R), A 2(t), [Gg(R)]
Sauermann, J T (Tvl) 1971 F 1, 2, A 1, 1972 E, 1974 BI 1
Schlebusch, J J J (OFS) 1974 BI 3, 4, 1975 F 2
Schmidt, L U (NT) 1958 F 2, 1962 BI 2
Schmidt, U L (NT, Tvl) 1986 Cv 1, 2, 3, 4, 1989 Wld 1, 2, 1992 NZ, A, 1993 F 1, 2, A 1, 2, 3, 1994 Arg 1, 2, S, W
Schoeman, J (WP) 1963 A 3, 4, 1965 I, S, A 1, NZ 1, 2
Scholtz, C P (WP, Tvl) 1994 Arg 1, 1995 [R, C, WS]
Scholtz, H (FS) 2002 A 1(R), NZ 2(R), A(R), 2003 [U(R), Gg]
Scholtz, H H (WP) 1921 NZ 1, 2
Schutte, P J W (Tvl) 1994 S, W
Scott, P A (Tvl) 1896 BI 1, 2, 3, 4
Sendin, W D (GW) 1921 NZ 2

Sephaka, L D (GL) 2001 US, 2002 Sm, NZ 1, A 1, NZ 2, A 2, F, 2003 S 1, 2, A 1, NZ 1, A 2(t+R), NZ 2, [U, E(t&R), Gg], 2005 F2, A1, 2(R), W, 2006 S1(R), NZ3(t&R), A3(R), I
Serfontein, D J (WP) 1980 BI 1, 2, 3, 4, S Am 3, 4, F, 1981 I 1, 2, NZ 1, 2, 3, US, 1982 S Am 1, 2, 1984 E 1, 2, S Am 1, 2
Serfontein, J L (BB) 2013 It(R), S1(R), Sm(R), Arg1(R), 2(R), A1(R), NZ1(t&R), A2(R), NZ2(R), 2014 W1, 2, S, A1, NZ1, A2, NZ2, I, E, It, W 3, 2015 Arg 2(R), [S(R), US(t&R), W(R), NZ(R), Arg(R)]
Shand, R (GW) 1891 BI 2, 3
Sheriff, A R (Tvl) 1938 BI 1, 2, 3
Shimange, M H (FS, WP) 2004 W1(R), NZ2(R), A2(R), W2(R), 2005 U(R), A1(R), 2(R), Arg(R), 2006 S1(R)
Shum, E H (Tvl) 1913 E
Sinclair, D J (Tvl) 1955 BI 1, 2, 3, 4
Sinclair, J H (Tvl) 1903 BI 1
Skene, A L (WP) 1958 F 2
Skinstad, R B (WP, GL, N) 1997 E (t), 1998 W 1(R), E 1(t), NZ 1(R), 2(R), A 2(R), W 2(R), S, I 3, E 2, 1999 [S, Sp (R), U, E, A 3], 2001 F 1(R), 2(R), It 1, NZ 1, A 1, 2, NZ 2, F 3, It 2, E, 2002 W 1, 2, Arg, Sm, NZ 1, A 1, NZ 2, A 2, 2003 Arg (R), 2007 E2(t&R), Sm, NZ1, A2, [E1(R), Tg, US(R), Arg(R)]
Slater, J T (EP) 1924 BI 3, 4, 1928 NZ 1
Smal, G P (WP) 1986 Cv 1, 2, 3, 4, 1989 Wld 1, 2
Small, J T (Tvl, N, WP) 1992 NZ, A, F 1, 2, E, 1993 F 1, 2, A 1, 2, 3, Arg 1, 2, 1994 E 1, 2, NZ 1, 2, 3(t), Arg 1, 1995 WS, [A, R, F, NZ], W, It, E (R), 1996 Fj, A 1, NZ 1, A 2, NZ 2, Arg 1, 2, F (R), W, 1997 Tg, BI 1, NZ 1(R), A 1(R), NZ 2, A 2, It, F 1, 2, E, S
Smit, F C (WP) 1992 E
Smit, J W (NS, Clermont-Auvergne) 2000 C (t), A 1(R), NZ 1(t+R), A 2(R), NZ 2(R), A 3(R), Arg, I, W, E 3, 2001 F 1, 2, It 1, NZ 1(R), A 1(R), 2(R), NZ 2(R), F 3(R), E 2, US (R), 2003 [U(R), E(t&R), Gg, Sm, NZ], 2004 I1, 2, W1, PI, NZ1, A1, NZ2, A2, W2, I3, E, S, Arg, 2005 U, F1, 2, A1, 2, 3, NZ1, A4, NZ2, Arg, W, F3, 2006 S1, 2, F, A1, NZ1, A2, NZ2, 3, A3, I, E1, 2, 2007 E1, 2, Sm, A1, [Sm, E1, Tg(R), US, Fj, Arg, E2], W, 2008 W1, 2, NZ1, W3, S, E, 2009 BI 1, 2, 3, NZ1, 2, A1, 2, 3, NZ3, F, It, I, 2010 W1, F, It 2, NZ1, 2, A1, NZ3, A2, 3, 2011 A1, NZ1, A2, NZ2(R), [W, Fj, Nm, Sm(R), A]
Smith, C M (OFS) 1963 A 3, 4, 1964 W, F, 1965 A 1, 2, NZ 2
Smith, C W (GW) 1891 BI 2, 1896 BI 2, 3
Smith, D (GW) 1891 BI 2
Smith, D J (Z-R) 1980 BI 1, 2, 3, 4
Smith, G A C (EP) 1938 BI 3
Smith, J H (FS, Toulon) 2003 S 1(R), 2(R), A 1, NZ 1, A 2, NZ 2, [U, E, Sm, NZ], 2004 W2, 2005 U(R), F2(R), A2, 3, NZ1, A4, NZ2, Arg, W, F3, 2006 S1, 2, F, A1, NZ1, A1, I, E2, 2007 E1, 2, A1, Nm, S, [Sm, E1, Tg(t&R), US, Fj, Arg, E2], W, 2008 W1, 2, It, NZ1, 2, A1, Arg, NZ3, A2, 3, W3, S, 2009 BI 1, 2, 3, NZ1, 2, A1, 2, 2010 NZ3, A2, 3, I, W2, S, E, 2014 Arg2
Smith, P F (GW) 1997 S (R), 1998 I 1(t), 2, W 1, NZ 1(R), 2(R), A 2(R), W 2, 1999 NZ 2
Smollan, F C (Tvl) 1933 A 3, 4, 5
Snedden, R C D (GW) 1891 BI 2
Snyman, A H (NT, BB, N) 1996 NZ 3, 4, Arg 2(R), W (R), 1997 Tg, BI 1, 2, 3, NZ 1, A 1, NZ 2, A 2, It, F 1, 2, E, S, 1998 I 1, 2, W 1, E 1, A 1, NZ 1, 2, A 2, W 2, S, I 3, E 2, 1999 NZ 2, 2001 NZ 2, F 3, US, 2002 W 1, 2003 S 1, NZ 1, 2006 S1, 2
Snyman, D S L (WP) 1972 E, 1974 BI 1, 2(R), F 1, 2, 1975 F 1, 2, 1976 NZ 2, 3, 1977 Wld
Snyman, J C P (OFS) 1974 BI 2, 3, 4
Sonnekus, G H H (OFS) 1974 BI 3, 1984 E 1, 2
Sowerby, R S (N) 2002 Sm (R)
Spies, J J (NT) 1970 NZ 1, 2, 3, 4
Spies, P J (BB) 2006 A1, NZ2, 3, A3, I, E1, 2007 E1(R), 2, 2008 W1, 2, A1, Arg, NZ3, A2, 3, W3, S, E, 2009 BI 1, 2, 3(R), NZ1, 2, A1, 2, 3, NZ3, 2010 F, It 1, 2, NZ1, 2, A1, NZ3, A2, 3, I, W2, E, 2012 E1, 2, 3, 2013 It, S1, Sm
Stander, J C J (OFS) 1974 BI 4(R), 1976 NZ 1, 2, 3, 4
Stapelberg, W P (NT) 1974 F 1, 2

Starke, J J (WP) 1956 NZ 4
Starke, K T (WP) 1924 BI 1, 2, 3, 4
Steenekamp, J G A (Tvl) 1958 F 1
Steenkamp, G G (FS, BB, Toulouse) 2004 S, Arg, 2005 U, F2(R), A2, 3, NZ1(R), A4(R), 2007 E1(R), 2, A1, [Tg, Fj(R)], 2008 W1, 2(R), NZ1, 2, A1, W3(R), S(R), 2009 BI 1(R), 3(R), 2010 F, It 1, 2, NZ1, 2, A1, NZ3, A2, 3, 2011 A2(R), NZ2, [W(R), Fj, Nm, Sm(R), A], 2012 S, E4, 2013 Arg1(R), 2(R), A1(R), NZ1(R), A2(R), NZ2(R), W(R), S2, F(R), 2014 W1, 2(R), Arg2, It(R)
Stegmann, A C (WP) 1906 S, I
Stegmann, G J (BB) 2010 I, W2, S, E, 2011 A1, NZ1
Stegmann, J A (Tvl) 1912 S, I, W, 1913 E, F
Stewart, C (WP) 1998 S, I 3, E 2
Stewart, D A (WP) 1960 S, 1961 E, S, F, I, 1963 A 1, 3, 4, 1964 W, F, 1965 I
Steyn, F P L (NS, Racing Metro) 2006 I, E1, 2, 2007 E1(R), 2(R), Sm, A1(R), NZ1(R), S, [Sm(R), E1, Tg(R), US, Fj, Arg, E2], W, 2008 W2(R), It, NZ1(R), 2(R), A1, NZ3(R), A2(R), W3(R), S(R), E(R), 2009 BI 1, 2, 3(t&R), NZ1, 2, A1, 2(R), 3(R), NZ3, 2010 W1, A2, 3, W2, S, E, 2011 A2, [W, Fj, Nm, Sm], 2012 E1, 2, Arg1, 2, A1, NZ1
Steyn, M (BB, SF) 2009 BI 1(t&R), 2(R), 3, NZ1(R), 2, A1, 2, 3, NZ3, F, It, 1, 2010 F, It 1, 2, NZ1, 2, A1, NZ3, A2, 3, I, W2, S, E, 2011 A1, NZ1, A2(R), NZ2, [W, Fj, Nm, Sm, A], 2012 E1, 2, 3, Arg1, 2, A1, NZ1, S(R), 2013 It, S1, Sm, Arg1, 2, A1, NZ1, A2, NZ2, W, S2(R), F, 2014 W1, 2, Arg1(R), 2(R), A1, 2015 [US(R)]
Stofberg, M T S (OFS, NT, WP) 1976 NZ 2, 3, 1977 Wld, 1980 S Am 1, 2, BI 1, 2, 3, 4, S Am 3, 4, F, 1981 I 1, 2, NZ 1, 2, US, 1982 S Am 1, 2, 1984 E 1, 2
Strachan, L C (Tvl) 1932 E, S, 1937 A 1, 2, NZ 1, 2, 3, 1938 BI 1, 2, 3
Stransky, J T (N, WP) 1993 A 1, 2, 3, Arg 1, 1994 Arg 1, 2, 1995 WS, [A, R (t), C, F, NZ], W, It, E, 1996 Fj (R), NZ 1, A 2, NZ 2, 3, 4, 5(R)
Straeuli, R A W (Tvl) 1994 NZ 1, Arg 1, 2, S, W, 1995 WS, [A, WS, NZ(R)], E (R)
Strauss, C P (WP) 1992 F 1, 2, E, 1993 F 1, 2, A 1, 2, 3, Arg 1, 2, 1994 E 1, NZ 1, 2, Arg 1, 2
Strauss, J A (WP) 1984 S Am 1, 2
Strauss, J A (FSC, BB) 2008 A1(R), Arg(R), NZ3(R), A2(R), 3(R), 2009 F(R), It, 2010 S(R), E(R), 2012 E1(R), 2(R), 3(R), Arg1(R), 2, A1, NZ1, A2, NZ2, I, S, E4, 2013 It, S1, Sm, Arg1, 2, A1(R), NZ1(t&R), A2(R), NZ2(R), W(R), S2, F(R), 2014 S(R), Arg1(R), 2(R), A1, NZ1, A2, NZ2(R), I(R), E, It, W 3(R), 2015 A(R), NZ(R), Arg 1(R), 2, [J(R), Sm, S(R), W(t&R), NZ(R), Arg(R)]
Strauss, J H P (Tvl) 1976 NZ 3, 4, 1980 S Am 1
Strauss, S S F (GW) 1921 NZ 3
Strydom, C F (OFS) 1955 BI 3, 1956 A 1, 2, NZ 1, 4, 1958 F 1,
Strydom, J J (Tvl, GL) 1993 F 2, A 1, 2, 3, Arg 1, 2, 1994 E 1, 1995 [A, C, F, NZ], 1996 A 2(R), NZ 2(R), 3, 4, W (R), 1997 Tg, BI 1, 2, 3, A 2
Strydom, L J (NT) 1994 NZ 1, 2
Styger, J J (OFS) 1992 NZ (R), A, F 1, 2, E, 1993 F 2(R), A 3(R)
Suter, M R (N) 1965 I, S
Swanepoel, W (OFS, GL) 1997 BI 3(R), A 2(R), F 1(R), 2, E, S, 1998 I 2(R), W 1(R), E 2(R), 1999 It 1, 2(R), W, A 1, [Sp, NZ 3(t)], 2000 A 1, NZ 1, A 2, NZ 2, A 3
Swart, J (WP) 1996 Fj, NZ 1(R), A 2, NZ 2, 3, 4, 5, 1997 BI 3(R), It, S (R)
Swart, J J N (SWA) 1955 BI 1
Swart, I S (Tvl) 1993 A 1, 2, 3, Arg 1, 1994 E 1, 2, NZ 1, 3, Arg 2(R), 1995 WS, [A, WS, F, NZ], W, 1996 A 2

Taberer, W S (GW) 1896 BI 2
Taute, J J (GL) 2012 A2, NZ2, I
Taylor, O B (N) 1962 BI 1
Terblanche, C S (Bol, N) 1998 I 1, 2, W 1, E 1, A 1, NZ 1, 2, A 2, W 2, S, I 3, E 2, 1999 It 1(R), 2, W, A 1, NZ 2(R), [Sp, E (R), A 3(R), NZ 3], 2000 E 3, 2002 W 1, 2, Arg, Sm, NZ 1, A 1, 2(R), 2003 S 1 1, 2, Arg, A 1, NZ 2, [Gg]
Teichmann, G H (N) 1995 W, 1996 Fj, A 1, NZ 1, A 2, NZ 2, 3, 4, 5, Arg 1, 2, F 1, 2, W, 1997 Tg, BI 1, 2, 3, NZ 1, A 1,

NZ 2, A 2, It, F 1, 2 E, S, 1998 I 1, 2, W 1, E 1, A 1, NZ 1, 2, A 2, W 2, S, I 3, E 2, 1999 It 1, W, NZ 1
Theron, D F (GW) 1996 A 2(R), NZ 2(R), 5, Arg 1, 2, F 1, 2, W, 1997 BI 2(R), 3, NZ 1(R), A 1, NZ 2(R)
Theunissen, D J (GW) 1896 BI 3
Thompson, G (GW) 1912 S, I, W
Tindall, J C (WP) 1924 BI 1, 1928 NZ 1, 2, 3, 4
Tobias, E G (SARF, Bol) 1981 I 1, 2, 1984 E 1, 2, S Am 1, 2
Tod, N S (N) 1928 NZ 2
Townsend, W H (N) 1921 NZ 1
Trenery, W E (GW) 1891 BI 2
Tromp, H (NT) 1996 NZ3, 4, Arg 2(R), F 1(R)
Truter, D R (WP) 1924 BI 2, 4
Truter, J T (N) 1963 A 1, 1964 F, 1965 A 2
Turner, F G (EP) 1933 A 1, 2, 3, 1937 A 1, 2, NZ 1, 2, 3, 1938 BI 1, 2, 3
Twigge, R J (NT) 1960 S
Tyibilika, S (N) 2004 S, Arg, 2005 U, A2, Arg, 2006 NZ1, A2, NZ2

Ulyate, C A (Tvl) 1955 BI 1, 2, 3, 4, 1956 NZ 1, 2, 3
Uys, P de W (NT) 1960 W, 1961 E, S, I, A 1, 2, 1962 BI 1, 4, 1963 A 1, 2, 1969 A 1(R), 2
Uys, P J (Pumas) 2002 S

Van Aswegen, H J (WP) 1981 NZ 1, 1982 S Am 2(R)
Van Biljon, L (N) 2001 It 1(R), NZ 1, A 1, 2, NZ 2 F 3, It 2(R), E (R), US, 2002 F (R), S, E (R), 2003 NZ 2(R)
Van Broekhuizen, H D (WP) 1896 BI 4
Van Buuren, M C (Tvl) 1891 BI 1
Van de Vyver, D F (WP) 1937 A 2
Van den Berg, D S (N) 1975 F 1, 2, 1976 NZ 1, 2
Van den Berg, M A (WP) 1937 A 1, NZ 1, 2, 3
Van den Berg, P A (WP, GW, N) 1999 It 1(R), 2, NZ 2, A 2, [S, U (t+R), E (R), A 3(R), NZ 2], 2000 E 1(R), A 1, NZ 1, A 2, NZ 2(R), A 3(t+R), Arg, I, W, E 3, 2001 F 1(R), 2, A 2(R), NZ 2(R), US, 2004 NZ1, 2005 U, F1, 2, A1(R), 2(R), 3(R), 4(R), Arg(R), F3(R), 2006 S2(R), A1(R), NZ1, A2(R), NZ2(R), A3(R), I, E1(R), 2(R), 2007 Sm, A2(R), NZ2, Nm(t&R), S(R), [Tg, US(R)]
Van den Bergh, E (EP) 1994 Arg 2(t & R)
Van der Linde, A (WP) 1995 It, E, 1996 Arg 1(R), 2(R), F 1(R), W (R), 2001 F 3(R)
Van der Linde, C J (FS, Leinster, WP, GL) 2002 S (R), E(R), 2004 I1(R), 2(R), PI(R), A1(R), NZ2(t&R), A2(R), W2(R), I3(R), E(t&R), S, Arg, 2005 U, F1(R), 2, A1(R), 3, NZ1, A4, NZ2, Arg, W, F3, 2006 S2(R), F(R), A1, NZ1, A2, NZ2, I, E1, 2, 2007 E1(R), 2, A1(R), NZ1(R), A2, NZ2, Nm, S, [Sm, E1(R), Tg, US(R), Arg, E2], W, 2008 W1(t&R), It, NZ1, 2, A1, Arg, NZ3, A2, 2009 F(R), I(t), 2010 W1, It1(R) , NZ2, A1(t&R), NZ3(R), A2(R), 3(R), I(R), W2(R), S(R), E(R), 2011 A1(t&R), NZ1(R), 2(R), [Nm], 2012 I, S(R)
Van der Merwe, A J (Bol) 1955 BI 2, 3, 4, 1956 A 1, 2, NZ 1, 2, 3, 4, 1958 F 1, 1960 S, NZ 2
Van der Merwe, A V (WP) 1931 W
Van der Merwe, B S (NT) 1949 NZ 1
Van der Merwe, F (GL) 2013 NZ 2(R)
Van der Merwe, H S (N) 1960 NZ 4, 1963 A 2, 3, 4, 1964 F
Van der Merwe, H S (GL, Leinster, SF) 2007 W(t+R), 2012 I(R), S(R), E4(R), 2015 A(R)
Van der Merwe, J P (WP) 1970 W
Van der Merwe, M (BB) 2014 S(R), A1(R), NZ1(R), A2(R), NZ2(R), 2015 Arg 1(R), 2
Van der Merwe, P R (SWD, WT, GW) 1981 NZ 2, 3, US, 1986 Cv 1, 2, 1989 Wld 1
Van der Merwe, P R (BB) 2010 F(R), It 2(R), A1(R), NZ3, A2, 3(R), I(R), W2(R), S(R), E(R), 2011 A1, 2012 E1(R), 2(R), 3(R), Arg1(R), 2(R), A1(R), NZ1, A2(R), NZ2(R), I(R), S(R), E4(R), 2013 It(R), S1(R), Sm, Arg1(R), 2(R), A1, NZ1, A2, W, S2, F, 2014 W2, 2015 NZ(R), Arg 2(R)
Vanderplank, B E (N) 1924 BI 3, 4
Van der Schyff, J H (GW) 1949 NZ 1, 2, 3, 4, 1955 BI 1
Van der Watt, A E (WP) 1969 S (R), E, 1970 I
Van der Westhuizen, J C (WP) 1928 NZ 2, 3, 4, 1931 I
Van der Westhuizen, J H (WP) 1931 I, 1932 E, S
Van der Westhuizen, J H (NT, BB) 1993 Arg 1, 2, 1994 E 1, 2(R), Arg 2, S, W, 1995 WS, [A, C (R), WS, F, NZ], W, It, E, 1996

507

SOUTH AFRICA

Fj, A 1, 2(R), NZ 2, 3(R), 4, 5, Arg 1, 2, F 1, 2, W, 1997 Tg, BI 1, 2, 3, NZ 1, A 1, NZ 2, A 2, It, F 1, 1998 I 1, 2, W 1, E 1, A 1, NZ 1, 2, A 2, W 2, S, I 3, E 2, 1999 NZ 2, A 2, [S, Sp (R), U, E, A 3, NZ 3], 2000 C, E 1, 2, A 1(R), NZ 1(R), A 2(R), Arg, I, W, E 3, 2001 F 1, 2, It 1(R), NZ 1, A 1, 2, NZ 2, F 3, It 2, E, US (R), 2003 S 1, 2, A 1, NZ 1, A 2(R), NZ 2, [U, E, Sm, NZ]

Van der Westhuyzen, J N B (MP, BB) 2000 NZ 2(R), 2001 It 1(R), 2003 S 1(R), 2, Arg, A 1, 2003 [E, Sm, NZ], 2004 I1, 2, W1, PI, NZ1, A1, NZ2, A2, W2, I3, E, S, Arg, 2005 U, F1, 2, A1, 4(R), NZ2(R), 2006 S1, 2, F, A1

Van Druten, N J V (Tvl) 1924 BI 1, 2, 3, 4, 1928 NZ 1, 2, 3, 4

Van Heerden, A J (Tvl) 1921 NZ 1, 3

Van Heerden, F J (WP) 1994 E 1, 2(R), NZ 3, 1995 It, E, 1996 NZ 5(R), Arg 1(R), 2(R), 1997 Tg, BI 2(t+R), 3(R), NZ 1(R), 2(R), 1999 [Sp]

Van Heerden, J L (NT, Tvl) 1974 BI 3, 4, F 1, 2, 1975 F 1, 2, 1976 NZ 1, 2, 3, 4, 1977 Wld, 1980 BI 1, 3, 4, S Am 3, 4, F

Van Heerden, J L (BB) 2003 S 1, 2, A 1, NZ 1, A 2(t), 2007 A2, NZ2, S(R), [Sm(R), E1, Tg, US, Fj(R), E2(R)]

Van Jaarsveld, C J (Tvl) 1949 NZ 1

Van Jaarsveldt, D C (R) 1960 S

Van Niekerk, J A (WP) 1928 NZ 4

Van Niekerk, J C (GL, WP, Toulon) 2001 NZ 1(R), A 1(R), NZ 2(t+R), F 3(R), It2, US, 2002 W 1(R), 2(R), Arg (R), Sm, NZ 1, A 1, NZ 2, A 2, F, S, E, 2003 A 2, NZ 2, [U, E, Gg, Sm], 2004 NZ1(R), A1(t), NZ2, A2, W2, I3, E, S, Arg(R), 2005 U(R), F2(R), A1(R), 2, 3, NZ1, A4, NZ2, 2006 S1, 2, F, A1, NZ1(R), A2(R), 2008 It(R), NZ1, 2, Arg(R), A2(R), 2010 W1

Van Reenen, G L (WP) 1937 A 2, NZ 1

Van Renen, C G (WP) 1891 BI 3, 1896 BI 1, 4

Van Renen, W (WP) 1903 BI 1, 3

Van Rensburg, J T J (Tvl) 1992 NZ, A, E, 1993 F 1, 2, A 1, 1994 NZ 2

Van Rooyen, G W (Tvl) 1921 NZ 2, 3

Van Ryneveld, R C B (WP) 1910 BI 2, 3

Van Schalkwyk, D (NT) 1996 Fj (R), NZ 3, 4, 5, 1997 BI 2, 3, NZ 1, A 1

Van Schoor, R A M (R) 1949 NZ 2, 3, 4, 1951 S, I, W, 1952 E, F, 1953 A 1, 2, 3, 4

Van Straaten, A J J (WP) 1999 It 2(R), W, NZ 1(R), A 1, 2000 C, E 1, 2, NZ 1, A 2, NZ 2, A 3, Arg (R), I (R), W, E 3, 2001 A 1, 2, NZ 2, F 3, It 2, E

Van Vollenhoven, K T (NT) 1955 BI 1, 2, 3, 4, 1956 A 1, 2, NZ 3

Van Vuuren, T F (EP) 1912 S, I, W, 1913 E, F

Van Wyk, C J (Tvl) 1951 S, I, W, 1952 E, F, 1953 A 1, 2, 3, 4, 1955 BI 1

Van Wyk, J F B (NT) 1970 NZ 1, 2, 3, 4, 1971 F 1, 2, A 1, 2, 3, 1972 E, 1974 BI 1, 3, 4, 1976 NZ 3, 4

Van Wyk, S P (WP) 1928 NZ 1, 2

Van Zyl, B P (WP) 1961 I

Van Zyl, C G P (OFS) 1965 NZ 1, 2, 3, 4

Van Zyl, D J (WP) 2000 E 3(R)

Van Zyl, G H (WP) 1958 F 1, 1960 S, NZ 1, 2, 3, 4, W, I, 1961 E, S, F, I, A 1, 2, 1962 BI 1, 3, 4

Van Zyl, H J (Tvl) 1960 NZ 1, 2, 3, 4, I, 1961 E, S, I, A 1, 2

Van Zyl, P J (Bol) 1961 I

Van Zyl, P E (FSC) 2013 S1(R), Sm(R)

Veldsman, P E (WP) 1977 Wld

Venter, A G (OFS) 1996 NZ 3, 4, 5, Arg 1, 2, F 1, 2, W, 1997 Tg, BI 1, 2, 3, NZ 1, A 1, NZ 2, It, F 1, 2, E, S, 1998 I 1, 2, W 1, E 1, A 1, NZ 1, 2, A 2, W 2, S (R), I 3(R), E 2(R), 1999 It 1, 2(R), W (R), NZ 1, A 1, NZ 2, A 2, [S, U, E, A 3, NZ 3], 2000 C, E 1, 2, A 1, NZ 1, A 2, NZ 2, F 3(R), It 2(R), E (t+R), US (R)

Venter, A J (N) 2000 W (R), E 3(R), 2001 F 3, It 2, E, US, 2002 W 1, 2, Arg, NZ 1(R), 2, A 2, F, S (R), E, 2003 Arg, 2004 PI, NZ1, A1, NZ2(R), A2, I3, E, 2006 NZ3, A3

Venter, B (OFS) 1994 E 1, 2, NZ 1, 2, 3, Arg 1, 2, 1995 [R, C, WS (R), NZ (R)], 1996 A 1, NZ 1, A 2, 1999 A 2, [S, U]

Venter, F D (Tvl) 1931 W, 1932 S, 1933 A 3

Vermaak, J (BB) 2013 It, A1(R), NZ1(R)

Vermeulen, D J (WP) 2012 A1, NZ1, A2, NZ2, I, S, E4, 2013 Arg1, 2, A1, NZ1, A2, NZ2, W, S2, F, 2014 W1, 2, S, Arg1, 2, A1, NZ1, A2, NZ2, I, E, It, W 3, 2015 [Sm, S, US, W, NZ, Arg]

Versfeld, C (WP) 1891 BI 3

Versfeld, M (WP) 1891 BI 1, 2, 3

Vigne, J T (Tvl) 1891 BI 1, 2, 3

Viljoen, J F (GW) 1971 F 1, 2, A 1, 2, 3, 1972 E

Viljoen, J T (N) 1971 A 1, 2, 3

Villet, J V (WP) 1984 E 1, 2

Visagie, I J (WP) 1999 It 1, W, NZ 1, A 1, NZ 2, A 2, [S, U, E, A 3, NZ 3], 2000 C, E 2, A 1, NZ 1, A 2, NZ 2, A 3, 2001 NZ 1, A 1, 2, NZ 2, F 3, It 2(R), E (t+R), US, 2003 S 1(R), 2(R), Arg

Visagie, P J (GW) 1967 F 1, 2, 3, 4, 1968 BI 1, 2, 3, 4, F 1, 2, 1969 A 1, 2, 3, 4, S, E, 1970 NZ 1, 2, 3, 4, 1971 F 1, 2, A 1, 2, 3

Visagie, R G (OFS, N) 1984 E 1, 2, S Am 1, 2, 1993 F 1

Visser, J de V (WP) 1981 NZ 2, US

Visser, M (WP) 1995 WS (R)

Visser, P J (Tvl) 1933 A 2

Viviers, S S (OFS) 1956 A 1, 2, NZ 2, 3, 4

Vogel, M L (OFS) 1974 BI 2(R)

Von Hoesslin, D J B (GW) 1999 It 1(R), 2, W (R), NZ 1, A 1(R)

Vos, A N (GL) 1999 It 1(t+R), 2, NZ 1(R), 2(R), A 2, [S (R), Sp, E (R), A 3(R), NZ 3], 2000 C, E 1, 2, A 1, NZ 1, A 2, NZ 2, A 3, Arg, I, W, E 3, 2001 F 1, 2, It 1, NZ 1, A 1, 2, NZ 2, F 3, It 2, E, US

Wagenaar, C (NT) 1977 Wld

Wahl, J J (WP) 1949 NZ 1

Walker, A P (N) 1921 NZ 1, 3, 1924 BI 1, 2, 3, 4

Walker, H N (OFS) 1953 A 3, 1956 A 2, NZ 1, 4

Walker, H W (Tvl) 1910 BI 1, 2, 3

Walton, D C (N) 1964 F, 1965 I, S, NZ 3, 4, 1969 A 1, 2, E

Wannenburg, P J (BB) 2002 F (R), E, 2003 S 1, 2, Arg, A 1(t+R), NZ 1(R), 2004 I1, 2, W1, PI(R), 2006 S1(R), F, NZ2(R), 3, A3, 2007 Sm(R), NZ1(R), A2, NZ2

Waring, F W (WP) 1931 I, 1932 E, 1933 A 1, 2, 3, 4, 5

Watson, L A (WP) 2007 Sm, 2008 W1, 2, It, NZ1(R), 2(R), Arg, NZ3(R), A2(R), 3(t&R)

Wegner, N (WP) 1993 F 2, A 1, 2, 3

Wentzel, M van Z (Pumas) 2002 F (R), S

Wessels, J J (WP) 1896 BI 1, 2, 3

Whipp, P J M (WP) 1974 BI 1, 2, 1975 F 1, 1976 NZ 1, 3, 4, 1980 S Am 1, 2

White, J (Bor) 1931 W, 1933 A 1, 2, 3, 4, 5, 1937 A 1, 2, NZ 1, 2

Whiteley, W R (GL) 2014 A1(R), NZ1(R), 2015 NZ(R)

Wiese, J J (Tvl) 1993 F 1, 1995 WS, [R, C, WS, F, NZ], W, It, E, 1996 NZ 3(R), 4(R), 5, Arg 1, 2, F 1, 2, W

Willemse, A K (GL) 2003 S 1, 2, NZ 1, A 2, NZ 2, [U, E, Sm, NZ], 2004 W2, I3, 2007 E1, 2(R), Sm, A1, NZ1, Nm, S(R), [Tg]

Williams, A E (GW) 1910 BI 1

Williams, A P (WP) 1984 E 1, 2

Williams, C M (WP, GL) 1993 Arg 2, 1994 E 1, 2, NZ 1, 2, 3, Arg 1, 2, S, W, 1995 WS, [WS, F, NZ], It, E, 1998 A 1(t), NZ 1(t), 2000 C (R), E 1(t), 2(R), A 1(R), NZ 2, A 3, Arg, I, W (R)

Williams, D O (WP) 1937 A 1, 2, NZ 1, 2, 3, 1938 BI 1, 2, 3

Williams, J G (NT) 1971 F 1, 2, A 1, 2, 3, 1972 E, 1974 BI 1, 2, 4, F 1, 2, 1976 NZ 1, 2

Wilson, L G (WP) 1960 NZ 3, 4, W, I, 1961 E, F, I, A 1, 2, 1962 BI 1, 3, 4, 1963 A 1, 2, 3, 4, 1964 W, F, 1965 I, S, A 1, 2, NZ 1, 2, 3, 4

Wolmarans, B J (OFS) 1977 Wld

Wright, G D (EP, Tvl) 1986 Cv 3, 4, 1989 Wld 1, 2, 1992 F 1, 2, E

Wyness, M R K (WP) 1962 BI 1, 2, 3, 4, 1963 A 2

Zeller, W C (N) 1921 NZ 2, 3

Zimerman, M (WP) 1931 W, I, 1932 E, S

TONGA

TONGA'S 2014–15 TEST RECORD

OPPONENT	DATE	VENUE	RESULT
Georgia	8 Nov	A	Won 23–9
USA	15 Nov	N	Won 40–12
Scotland	22 Nov	A	Lost 37–12
Fiji	18 Jul	A	Lost 30–22
Canada	24 Jul	A	Won 28–18
USA	29 Jul	N	Won 33–19
Japan	3 Aug	N	Won 31–20
Romania	5 Sep	A	Won 21–16
Georgia	19 Sep	N	Lost 17–10
Namibia	29 Sep	N	Won 35–21
Argentina	4 Oct	N	Lost 45–16
New Zealand	9 Oct	N	Lost 47–9

KEY MOMENTS SLIP AWAY FROM TONGA

By Alex Broun

The Tongan team perform the Sipi Tau before their RWC 2015 match against Namibia at Sandy Park, Exeter.

Looking at the bare statistics, 2015 was a good year for Tongan rugby. Since November 2014 they played 12 tests, winning seven and losing five. They also scored 280 points, including 30 tries, while conceding 291.

But despite a winning percentage of 58.33 per cent for the 12-month period, and victories over Georgia, USA (twice), Canada, Japan, Romania and Namibia, they lost two crucial matches that saw disappointing end results for Tonga at both of their major tournaments for the year.

The first loss, a 30–22 reverse to Fiji in Suva, meant that they could only finish third in the World Rugby Pacific Nations Cup despite winning their remaining three matches and a shock 17–10 loss to Georgia in Gloucester on the opening weekend of Rugby World Cup 2015 saw them eventually finish fourth in Pool C, a disappointing result considering the stunning performance of RWC 2011 and their hopes going into the global showpiece.

The fourth-place finish meant they were deprived an automatic place at RWC 2019 in Japan, which went to Georgia, and will now have to come through some tough Rugby World Cup qualifiers with their fellow Pacific nations Samoa and Fiji to qualify automatically for Japan 2019.

The 'Ikale Tahi's build-up to RWC 2015 started impressively on their end of year tour in 2014 with solid wins over Georgia in Tbilisi 23–9 (a score that made the RWC 2015 result even more surprising) and a comfortable 40–12 victory over the USA in Gloucester. They were far from disgraced in their final tour match, a 37–12 loss to Scotland in Kilmarnock.

Their next match came in the first round of the Pacific Nations Cup, a tricky assignment against Fiji in Suva. Tonga have never won the Pacific Nations Cup and hopes were high for their first title in 2015.

But despite three tries apiece, Tonga's scored by wingers Fetu'u Vainikolo and Telusa Veainu and scrum-half Sonatane Takulua, the difference in the 30–22 loss was the accurate boot of Fiji fly-half Ben Volavola.

However Tonga fought back superbly from this setback to defeat their hosts Canada 28–18 in Burnaby in their next PNC match with Takulua crossing for a double. Their form continued in their next match, a 33–19 victory over the USA in Toronto with Vainikolo scoring twice this time.

Vainikolo's first try in the fifth minute was a spectacular effort, beginning in Tonga's 22 with fly-half Kurt Morath kicking across field for the pacey winger, who then beat four tacklers on his way to the line. Not surprisingly the try was later nominated for the IRPA Try of the Year Award.

But the earlier loss to Fiji meant Tonga missed out on the final, instead taking part in the third place play-off against Japan in Burnaby, with Vainikolo and Takulua again among the try scorers as the 'Ikale Tahi emerged 31–20 victors.

Despite finishing third Mana 'Otai's team had shown impressive passages of play and after a final warm-up win, 21–16 over Romania in Bucharest with Takulua again crossing for a try, they came into RWC 2015 with hopes high.

This made the loss to Georgia even more disappointing. Tonga knew the ground well, after defeating the USA there in 2014; they also had local knowledge with winger David Halaifonua, back-row Sione Kalamafoni, hooker Aleki Lutui and prop Sila Puafisi all playing for Gloucester. They also had form on Georgia, having defeated them comfortably in Tbilisi in late 2014.

But all this meant nothing as Tonga just could not get into the match, smothered by some desperate Georgian defence inspired by their talismanic leader, try scorer and man of the match, Mamuka Gorgodze.

It could have been different if a superbly worked lineout move on the stroke of half-time, which saw back rower Viliami Ma'afu touchdown, was allowed to stand. But it was struck off for a forward pass.

The only bright spot for Tonga in the 17–10 loss was a late try for

Vainikolo which saw him bring his tally to 15 tries, becoming Tonga's highest ever test try scorer.

"Credit to Georgia," reflected Kalamafoni after the match. "They had the better of the lineout and scrum and deserved the win. Our ball handling was poor, we were missing opportunities due to dropping the ball, so we need to go back and fix that."

Tonga did bounce back in their next match, a solid 35–21 win over Namibia in Exeter, with man of the match, back-row Jack Ram and Veainu both crossing for doubles and fly-half Latiume Fosita also dotting down.

The win meant Tonga still had an outside chance of reaching the quarter-finals but to do that they would have to upset either Argentina or New Zealand in their final Pool C matches.

"After Georgia, we kept saying the dream is still alive," said a brave 'Otai after the win. "Gaining five points is another step towards that. We'll celebrate the victory tonight, have a few words and share some beverages and be back on the horse tomorrow. We played one final today and we'll play another on Sunday."

That match was against Los Pumas and after tries for Morath and prop Soane Tonga'uiha the upset looked on as Tonga trailed just 20–16 early in the second half. But in perfect conditions in Leicester, Argentina pulled away with a trio of long-range tries.

This left just one final match against the All Blacks in Newcastle where more than 50,000 crammed into St James' Park to see if Tonga could follow in Japan's footsteps and defeat one of world rugby's superpowers.

The 'Ikale Tahi started well with their scrum holding and even shading the famed All Blacks' pack. The match was extremely tight in the first 50 minutes with a second Morath penalty bringing Tonga back to 14–6. Was RWC 2015 about to see another earth-shattering shock?

But New Zealand, as only they can, shifted up the gears and scored five second-half tries to ease home 47–9. Just as disappointing as the result was the fact that despite dominating both possession and territory Tonga could not get across the line.

'Otai however remained upbeat. "We always look at a silver lining behind every dark cloud," the coach insisted. "I thought there has been a huge improvement from the way we played against Georgia to the way we played against the tier one nations.

"I thought we had shifted the way we played and performed beyond our wildest imagination. We showed glimpses of how good we can be. There are just a few little bits in the middle and fitness is an issue. I don't think we have gone downhill."

The challenge now for Tonga is to re-group and look forward to perhaps their first PNC crown in 2016.

TONGA INTERNATIONAL STATISTICS

MATCH RECORDS UP TO 1 NOVEMBER, 2015

WINNING MARGIN

Date	Opponent	Result	Winning Margin
21/03/2003	Korea	119–0	119
08/07/2006	Cook Islands	90–0	90
01/01/1979	Solomon Islands	92–3	89
10/02/2007	Korea	83–3	80
15/03/2003	Korea	75–0	75

MOST POINTS IN A MATCH
BY THE TEAM

Date	Opponent	Result	Points
21/03/2003	Korea	119–0	119
01/01/1979	Solomon Islands	92–3	92
08/07/2006	Cook Islands	90–0	90
06/12/2002	Papua New Guinea	84–12	84
10/02/2007	Korea	83–3	83

BY A PLAYER

Date	Player	Opponent	Points
21/03/2003	Pierre Hola	Korea	39
10/02/2007	Fangatapu Apikotoa	Korea	28
04/05/1999	Sateki Tuipulotu	Korea	27
21/03/2003	Benhur Kivalu	Korea	25
06/12/2002	Pierre Hola	Papua New Guinea	24

MOST TRIES IN A MATCH
BY THE TEAM

Date	Opponent	Result	Tries
21/03/2003	Korea	119–0	17
08/07/2006	Cook Islands	90–0	14
10/02/2007	Korea	83–3	13
24/06/2006	Cook Islands	77–10	13
	12 on 2 occasions		

BY A PLAYER

Date	Player	Opponent	Tries
21/03/2003	Benhur Kivalu	Korea	5
08/06/2011	Viliame Iongi	USA	4
	3 on 5 occasions		

MOST CONVERSIONS IN A MATCH
BY THE TEAM

Date	Opponent	Result	Cons
21/03/2003	Korea	119–0	17
08/07/2006	Cook Islands	90–0	10
	9 on 3 occasions		

BY A PLAYER

Date	Player	Opponent	Cons
21/03/2003	Pierre Hola	Korea	17
05/07/1997	Kusitafu Tonga	Cook Islands	9
06/12/2002	Pierre Hola	Papua New Guinea	9
08/07/2006	Fangatapu Apikotoa	Cook Islands	9
10/02/2007	Fangatapu Apikotoa	Korea	9

MOST PENALTIES IN A MATCH
BY THE TEAM

Date	Opponent	Result	Pens
05/06/2012	Samoa	18–20	6
	5 on 4 occasions		

BY A PLAYER

Date	Player	Opponent	Pens
05/06/2012	Kurt Morath	Samoa	6
13/07/2011	Kurt Morath	Samoa	5
19/08/2011	Kurt Morath	Fiji	5

MOST DROP GOALS IN A MATCH
BY THE TEAM

1 on 8 occasions

BY A PLAYER

1 on 8 occasions

MOST CAPPED PLAYERS

Name	Caps
Nili Latu	43
'Elisi Vunipola	42
Vungakoto Lilo	42
Benhur Kivalu	39
Pierre Hola	39

LEADING TRY SCORERS

Name	Tries
Fetu'u Vainikolo	15
Siua Taumalolo	13
Vungakoto Lilo	12
Fepikou Tatafu	11

LEADING CONVERSIONS SCORERS

Name	Cons
Pierre Hola	68
Kurt Morath	47
Fangatapu Apikotoa	39
Sateki Tuipulotu	33
Kusitafu Tonga	26

LEADING PENALTY SCORERS

Name	Pens
Kurt Morath	78
Pierre Hola	38
Sateki Tuipulotu	32
Fangatapu Apikotoa	22

LEADING DROP GOAL SCORERS

Name	DGs
Pierre Hola	3

LEADING POINTS SCORERS

Name	Points
Kurt Morath	338
Pierre Hola	309
Sateki Tuipulotu	190
Fangatapu Apikotoa	159
Siua Taumalolo	113

TONGA INTERNATIONAL PLAYERS
UP TO 1 NOVEMBER, 2015

I Afeaki 1995 *F, , S, Iv*, 1997 *Fj*, 2001 *S, W*, 2002 *J, Fj, Sa, Fj*, 2003 *Kor, Kor, M, I, Fj, Fj, It, C*, 2004 *Sa, Fj*, 2005 *It*, 2007 *Sa, SA, E*

P Afeaki 1983 *Fj, Sa*

S Afeaki 2002 *Fj, Sa, Fj, PNG, PNG*, 2003 *Kor, Kor, M, I, Fj, It, W, NZ*

V Afeaki 1997 *Sa*, 2002 *Sa, Fj*

JL Afu 2008 *J, Sa, Fj*, 2009 *Fj, Sa, J*, 2011 *US*, 2012 *Sa, J, Fj, US*, 2013 *J, C, US, Fj*, 2014 *Sa, Fj*

T Afu Fifita 1924 *Fj, Fj, Fj*

S 'Aho 1974 *S, W*

T Ahoafi 2007 *AuA, Sa*

P Ahofono 1990 *Sa*

E Aholelei 2013 *J, C, R, W*, 2014 *Sa, Fj*

K Ahota'e'iloa 1999 *Sa, F, Fj*, 2000 *C, Fj, J*

M Ahota'e'iloa 2010 *Sa, Fj, J*

S Aisake 1934 *Fj*

M Akau'ola 1934 *Fj*

P 'Ake 1926 *Fj, Fj, Fj*

M Alatini 1969 *M*, 1972 *Fj, Fj*, 1973 *M, A, A, Fj*, 1974 *S, W, C*, 1975 *M*, 1977 *Fj*

PF Alatini 1995 *Sa*

S Alatini 1994 *Sa, Fj*, 1998 *Sa, Fj*, 2000 *NZ, US*

S Alatini 1977 *Fj*, 1979 *NC, M, E*

T Alatini 1932 *Fj*

A Alatini 2001 *S*, 2002 *J, Sa, Fj*, 2003 *M, I, Fj*

V 'Alipate 1967 *Fj*, 1968 *Fj, Fj, Fj*, 1969 *M*

A Amone 1987 *W, I, Sa, Fj*

A Amore 1988 *Fj*

F Anderson 2013 *US, Fj*, 2014 *Sa, Fj*

T Anitoni 1995 *J, Sa, Fj*, 1996 *Sa, Fj*

VN Anitoni 1990 *Sa*

F Apikotoa 2004 *Sa, Fj*, 2005 *Fj, Sa, Fj, Sa, It, F*, 2006 *Coo, Coo*, 2007 *Kor, AuA, J, JAB*, 2008 *J, Sa, Fj*, 2009 *Fj, J*, 2010 *Fj, ChI*, 2012 *It, US, S*, 2013 *J, R, F, W*, 2014 *Sa, Fj*

T Apitani 1947 *Fj, Fj*

S Asi 1987 *C*

T Asi 1996 *Sa*

H 'Asi 2000 *C*

S Ata 1928 *Fj*

S Atiola 1987 *Sa, Fj*, 1988 *Fj, Fj*, 1989 *Fj, Fj*, 1990 *Fj, J*

H 'Aulika 2011 *Fj, Fj, C, J, F*, 2012 *It, US, S*, 2015 *Fj, C, US, J, R, Geo, Nm, Ar, NZ*

K Bakewa 2002 *PNG, PNG*, 2003 *Fj*

O Beba 1932 *Fj, Fj, Fj*

O Blake 1983 *M, M*, 1987 *Sa, Fj*, 1988 *Sa, Fj, Fj*

T Bloomfield 1973 *M, A, A, Fj*, 1986 *W*

D Briggs 1997 *W*

J Buloka 1932 *Fj, Fj*

D Edwards 1998 *A*, 1999 *Geo, Geo, Kor, US, Sa, F, Fj, C, NZ, It, E*

T Ete'aki 1984 *Fj*, 1986 *W, Fj, Fj*, 1987 *C, W, I*, 1990 *Fj, J, Sa, Kor, Sa*, 1991 *Sa*

TONGA

U Fa'a 1994 *Sa, W*, 1995 *J*, 1998 *Sa, A, Fj*
PO Faanunu 2014 *Geo, US, S*
L Fa'aoso 2004 *Sa, Fj*, 2005 *Fj, Sa, Fj, Sa*, 2007 *US, E*, 2009 *Pt*, 2011 *Fj, J, Fj*, 2014 *Sa, Geo, US, S*
P Fa'apoi 1963 *Fj*
V Fa'aumu 1986 *Fj, Fj*
SSA Fahiua 2013 *US, Fj*
V Faingaa 2012 *Sa, Fj*
OHL Faingaanuku 2011 *US*, 2012 *Fj*, 2014 *Fj*
T Fainga'anuku 1999 *NZ, It, E*, 2000 *C, Fj, J, NZ*, 2001 *Fj, Sa, Fj, Sa*
S Faka 'osi'folau 1996 *M*, 1997 *Z, Nm, SA, Fj, Sa, Coo, W*, 1998 *A, Fj*, 1999 *Geo, Kor, Fj*, 2001 *Sa*
DAT Fakafanua 2010 *Chl*, 2012 *Sa*
P Fakalelu 2005 *It*, 2006 *Coo, Coo*, 2009 *Sa, J*, 2013 *US, Fj*
J Fakalolo 1926 *Fj, Fj, Fj*
P Fakana 1963 *Fj, Fj*
F Fakaongo 1993 *S, Fj*, 1995 *Iv, Sa, Fj*, 2000 *Fj, J, NZ, Sa*, 2001 *S, W*, 2002 *J, Fj, Sa*
HV Fakatou 1998 *Sa, A, Fj*, 1999 *Kor, NZ*
V Fakatulolo 1975 *M*
S Fakaua 2005 *Sa*
P Faka'ua 1967 *Fj, Fj*, 1968 *Fj, Fj, Fj*, 1969 *M, M*, 1972 *Fj*
N Fakauho 1977 *Fj, Fj*
P Fakava 1988 *Sa, Fj*
DT Faleafa 2013 *US, Fj*, 2014 *Sa, Fj*
K Faletau 1988 *Sa, Fj*, 1989 *Fj, Fj*, 1990 *Sa*, 1991 *Fj*, 1992 *Fj*, 1997 *Nm, SA, Fj, Sa, Coo, W*, 1999 *Sa, F, Fj, C*
FP Faletau 1999 *Geo, Kor, Kor, J, US, Sa, F, Fj, C*
M Fanga'uta 1982 *Fj*
K Fangupo 2009 *Pt*
MU Fangupo 2009 *Sa, J*, 2010 *J, Chl*
F Faotusa 1990 *Sa*
LAHN Fatafehi 2009 *Fj, Sa, Pt*, 2010 *Sa, Fj, J*, 2011 *Fj, NZ, C, J, F*, 2012 *Sa, J, Fj, It, US, S*, 2015 *Fj, US*
IT Fatani 1992 *Fj*, 1993 *Sa, S, Fj, A, Fj*, 1997 *Fj, Coo*, 1999 *Geo, Kor, Kor, J, US, Sa, F, Fj, C, NZ, It, E*, 2000 *C, Fj, J, NZ, Sa, US*
O Faupula 1924 *Fj, Fj, Fj*
SLJ Faupula 2010 *Chl*
AOM Feao 2010 *Sa, Fj*
S Fe'ao 1995 *F, S*
SL Fekau 1983 *M, M*
K Feke 1988 *Fj, Fj*, 1989 *Fj*, 1990 *Fj, Sa*
SH Fekitoa 2010 *Sa, J*
T Feleola 1934 *Fj*
I Fenukitau 1993 *Sa, S, Fj, A, Fj*, 1994 *Sa, Fj*, 1995 *J, J, F, S*, 2002 *J, Fj, Sa*, 2003 *It, W, NZ, C*
Fetu'ulele 1967 *Fj*
KV Fielea 1987 *C, W, I, Sa, Fj*, 1990 *J, Sa, Kor, Sa*, 1991 *Sa*
L Fifita 1934 *Fj*
P Fifita 1983 *Fj*
S Fifita 1974 *S, W, C*, 1975 *M*
T Fifita 1984 *Fj, Fj*, 1986 *W, Fj, Fj*, 1987 *C, W, I*, 1991 *Sa, Fj, Fj*
T Fifita 2001 *Fj, Fj*, 2003 *Fj*, 2006 *J*, 2008 *J*
V Fifita 1982 *Fj*
V Fifita 2005 *F*
V Fihaki 2013 *J, C, Fj*, 2014 *Sa, Fj*, 2015 *Fj, C, US*
F Filikitonga 1990 *Fj, Sa*
L Fililava 1960 *M*
M Filimoehala 1968 *Fj*, 1974 *W, C*, 1975 *M, M*
OAML Filipine 2000 *C*, 2006 *J, Fj, Coo, Sa*, 2007 *US, SA*, 2008 *J*
M Filise 1986 *Fj, Fj*, 1987 *W, I*
T Filise 2001 *Fj, Fj, S, W*, 2002 *Sa, Fj*, 2004 *Sa, Fj*, 2005 *Fj, Sa, Fj, Sa*, 2007 *Fj, Sa, E*, 2011 *NZ, J*
S Filo 2004 *Sa, Fj*
I Finau 1987 *Sa, Fj*, 1990 *Fj, J, Sa*
M Finau 2007 *AuA*, 2008 *J*, 2009 *Fj, J*, 2010 *J, Chl*
M Finau 1979 *NC, M, E, Sa*, 1980 *Sa*, 1984 *Fj*
S Finau 1998 *Sa*, 1999 *Geo, Sa, F, Fj, C, E*, 2001 *Fj, Fj, S*, 2005 *It, F*
S Finau 1924 *Fj, Fj, Fj*, 1926 *Fj, Fj, Fj*
S Finau 1989 *Fj, Fj*, 1990 *Fj, J, Sa, Kor, Sa*
T Finau 1967 *Fj*

T Finau 1924 *Fj, Fj, Fj*
V Finau 1987 *Sa, Fj*
I Fine 2007 *Kor, AuA, JAB, Sa*
K Fine 1987 *C, W, I*, 1988 *Fj*
L Fineanganofo 1924 *Fj, Fj, Fj*
J Finisi 1932 *Fj, Fj, Fj*
S Finisi 1928 *Fj*
P Fisi'iahi 1992 *Sa*
K Fisilau 1999 *J, US*, 2000 *C*, 2005 *Fj, Sa, It*
S Fisilau 2010 *Sa, Fj, J*, 2011 *Fj, J, Sa, Fj, NZ, J*, 2012 *It*, 2013 *R, F, W*, 2014 *Sa, Fj*, 2015 *Nm, Ar, NZ*
K Fokofuka 1995 *Sa*
K Folea 1991 *Fj*
S Foliaki 1973 *A, A*, 1977 *Fj*
Fololisi 1991 *Fj*
U Fono 2005 *Sa, Fj, It, F*
H Fonua 1973 *M, A, A, Fj*, 1974 *S, W, C*
O Fonua 2009 *Fj, Sa, Pt*, 2013 *R, F, W*, 2015 *Nm, Ar*
S Fonua 1928 *Fj, Fj, Fj*
SO Fonua 2002 *Sa, Sa*, 2003 *It, W, NZ, C*, 2007 *Kor, AuA, J, JAB, Fj, Sa*
T Fonua 2007 *Kor*
LJ Fosita 2013 *F, W*, 2014 *Sa, Fj, Geo, US, S*, 2015 *Fj, C, US, R, Nm, Ar, NZ*
TK Fotu 1987 *C*, 1988 *Sa, Fj*, 1989 *Fj*, 1990 *Fj, J, Sa, Kor, Sa*
L Fotu 1991 *Sa*, 1992 *Fj*, 1993 *S, Fj*
R Fotu 1979 *M*, 1983 *Fj, Sa*
S Fotu 1947 *Fj*
S Fotu 1968 *Fj, Fj, Fj*, 1969 *M, M*
P Fua'ava 1985 *Fj*
T Fuataimi 1928 *Fj*, 1932 *Fj, Fj, Fj*
F Fukofuka 1926 *Fj, Fj, Fj*, 1928 *Fj*
SM Maama 2010 *Sa, Fj*
T Fukofuka 1993 *Fj*, 1995 *J, J, F, S, Iv, Fj*
A Fungavaka 1982 *Sa, Fj*, 1984 *Fj, Fj*, 1985 *Fj*, 1986 *W, Fj, Fj*, 1987 *C, W, I, Sa, Fj*
L Fusimalohi 1987 *Fj*, 1988 *Fj*, 1990 *J, Sa*

W Gibbons 2002 *PNG*, 2003 *M, Fj*

F Hafoka 1932 *Fj, Fj, Fj*
I Hafoka 1928 *Fj, Fj*, 1932 *Fj, Fj, Fj*, 1934 *Fj*
K Hafoka 1967 *Fj, Fj*, 1968 *Fj, Fj, Fj*
M Hafoka 1977 *Fj, Fj*, 1979 *M*, 1980 *Sa*
S Hafoka 1997 *W*
T Hafoka 1987 *Fj*
VA Hakalo 2006 *J, Coo, Sa*, 2010 *Chl*, 2013 *C, US*
S Hala 1999 *Geo, Geo, Kor*, 2002 *J, Fj, Sa, Sa, Fj*, 2003 *Kor, Kor*
H Halaeua 2010 *Fj, J*
M Halafatu 1989 *Fj*
KM Halafihi 2010 *Sa, J*
T Halafihi 1982 *Sa, Fj*, 1983 *Sa*, 1985 *Fj*
S Halahingano 1924 *Fj, Fj, Fj*
T Halaifonua 2009 *Fj, J*, 2013 *J, C, R, F, W*, 2014 *Sa, Fj, Geo, US, S*, 2015 *R, Nm, Ar*
A Halangahu 2007 *Kor*, 2011 *US*
C Halangi 2002 *Fj*
S Halanukonuka 2014 *Geo*
T Halasika 1988 *Fj, Fj*
C Hala'ufia 2000 *C*, 2001 *Fj, Sa, Fj, Sa, W*, 2002 *Sa*, 2004 *Sa, Fj*, 2005 *Fj, Sa, It, F*, 2006 *J, Fj, Coo, Sa, Coo*, 2007 *JAB, Fj*, 2009 *J*
S Hala'ufia 1977 *Fj*, 1979 *NC, M, E, Sa*, 1981 *Fj*
L Halavatau 1982 *Sa, Fj*
N Hau 2002 *Sa*
T Haumono 1924 *Fj, Fj, Fj*, 1926 *Fj, Fj, Fj*, 1928 *Fj*, 1932 *Fj, Fj, Fj*
T Havea 1924 *Fj, Fj, Fj*
SPPB Havea 2000 *NZ, US*, 2004 *Sa, Fj*, 2005 *Fj, Sa, Fj, Sa, It, F*, 2006 *J, Fj, Coo, Sa*, 2007 *Kor, JAB, Fj, Sa, US, SA, E*, 2008 *J, Sa, Fj*, 2010 *Chl*, 2011 *US, J, Sa*
M Havili 1987 *Sa*, 1988 *Fj*
P Havili 1981 *Fj, Fj, Fj*
R Havili 2013 *Fj*
AP Havili 2000 *C, Fj, J, Sa, US*, 2001 *Fj, Sa, Fj*, 2007 *AuA, J, JAB, US, SA, E*

THE COUNTRIES

TONGA

S **Tavo** 1959 *Fj*, 1960 *M*, 1963 *Fj*, *Fj*, 1967 *Fj*, *Fj*, *Fj*, 1968 *Fj*, *Fj*, *Fj*, 1969 *M*, *M*
M **Te Pou** 1998 *A*, *Fj*, 1999 *Geo*, *Geo*, *Kor*, *Kor*, *J*, *US*, *F*, *NZ*, *It*, 2001 *S*, *W*
Telanisi 1967 *Fj*
SF **Telefoni** 2008 *J*, *Sa*, *Fj*, 2009 *Pt*, 2011 *Fj*
Teri 1991 *Fj*
Teutau 1991 *Fj*
UV **Moa** 2011 *Fj*, *Fj*, *NZ*, *C*, *J*, *F*, 2012 *Sa*, *J*, *Fj*, *It*, *US*, *S*, 2013 *J*, *C*, *US*, *Fj*, *F*, *W*, 2014 *Geo*, *US*, 2015 *Fj*
SLN **Timani** 2008 *J*, 2009 *Fj*, 2011 *US*, *Fj*, *Fj*, *NZ*, *C*, 2012 *S*
D **Tiueti** 1997 *Fj*, *Sa*, *W*, 1999 *Geo*, *Geo*, *Kor*, *Sa*, *F*, *Fj*, *C*, *NZ*, *It*, *E*, 2000 *C*, *Fj*, *J*, *NZ*, *Sa*, *US*, 2001 *S*, *W*
T **Tofua** 1924 *Fj*, *Fj*, *Fj*, 1926 *Fj*, *Fj*, *Fj*
T **Toga** 1968 *Fj*
T **Tohi** 1997 *Nm*, *SA*
T **Toke** 2007 *Kor*, *J*, *JAB*, *Fj*, *Sa*, *US*, *Sa*, 2009 *Fj*, 2010 *Sa*, *Fj*, *J*
M **Toloke** 2010 *Chl*
V **Toloke** 1995 *J*, *Sa*, *Fj*, 1996 *Sa*, *Fj*, *M*, 1999 *Geo*, *Geo*, *Kor*, *Kor*, *US*, *NZ*, *C*, 2000 *NZ*, *US*, 2002 *J*, *Sa*, *Sa*
M **Toma** 1988 *Sa*, *Fj*, *Fj*, 1991 *Sa*, *Fj*, *Fj*
T **Tonga** 1990 *Sa*
G **Tonga** 1997 *Z*, *W*
K **Tonga** 2003 *Fj*, *C*, 2004 *Sa*, *Fj*, 2005 *Fj*, *Fj*
K **Tonga** 1947 *Fj*, *Fj*
K **Tonga** 1996 *Fj*, *M*, 1997 *Nm*, *SA*, *Fj*, *Sa*, *Coo*, 1999 *Geo*, *Geo*, *Kor*, 2001 *Fj*, *Sa*
M **Tonga** 1947 *Fj*
M **Tonga** 2001 *Fj*, *Sa*, *Fj*, *Sa*, 2003 *Kor*, *Kor*
P **Tonga** 1973 *A*
S **Tonga** 2005 *Sa*, *Fj*, *Sa*
S **Tonga Simiki** 1924 *Fj*, 1926 *Fj*, *Fj*, *Fj*
H **Tonga'uiha** 2005 *Fj*, *Sa*, *Sa*, 2006 *J*, *Fj*, *JAB*, *Coo*, *Sa*, *Coo*, 2007 *Kor*, *AuA*, *J*, *JAB*, *Fj*, *Sa*, *E*, 2008 *J*, *Sa*, *Fj*, 2009 *Fj*, *Sa*, *J*, 2011 *J*, *Sa*
SL **Tonga'uiha** 2005 *It*, *F*, 2007 *JAB*, *US*, *Sa*, *SA*, *E*, 2011 *Fj*, *NZ*, *C*, *J*, *F*, 2012 *It*, 2015 *US*, *R*, *Nm*, *Ar*, *NZ*
O **Topeni** 2000 *J*
S **Tuamoheloa** 2003 *Fj*, *Fj*, *C*, 2005 *Fj*
T **Tuavao** 1986 *Fj*
N **Tufui** 1990 *Fj*, *J*, *Sa*, *Sa*, 1992 *Fj*, 1994 *Fj*, 1995 *S*, *Iv*
S **Tufui** 1926 *Fj*, *Fj*, *Fj*, 1928 *Fj*, *Fj*, *Fj*, 1932 *Fj*, *Fj*, *Fj*, 1934 *Fj*
TH **Tu'ifua** 2003 *M*, *Fj*, *It*, *W*, *NZ*, 2006 *J*, *Fj*, *JAB*, *Coo*, *Sa*, 2007 *Fj*, *Sa*, *US*, *Sa*, *SA*, *E*
P **Tuihalamaka** 1972 *Fj*, 1973 *M*, *A*, *A*, *Fj*, 1974 *S*, *C*, 1975 *M*, *M*, 1977 *Fj*, *Fj*, 1979 *NC*, 1981 *Fj*, *Fj*, 1987 *C*
S **Tu'ihalamaka** 1999 *Kor*, *Kor*, *J*, *US*, 2001 *Sa*, *Fj*
Tu'ikolovatu 1983 *Fj*
JML **Tuineau** 2011 *Fj*, *J*, *Sa*, *Fj*, *NZ*, *J*, *F*, 2012 *Sa*, *J*, *Fj*, *It*, *US*, *S*, 2013 *F*, *W*, 2014 *Geo*, *US*, *S*, 2015 *Fj*, *C*, *US*, *R*, *Nm*, *Ar*, *NZ*
T **Tu'ineua** 1992 *Fj*, 1993 *Sa*, *S*, *Fj*, *A*, *Fj*
E **Tu'ipolotu** 1926 *Fj*, *Fj*, *Fj*, 1928 *Fj*, *Fj*
S **Tu'ipolotu** 1981 *Fj*
S **Tu'ipolotu** 1947 *Fj*, *Fj*
K **Tuipulotu** 1994 *Fj*, 1997 *Fj*, *Sa*, *Coo*
S **Tuipulotu** 1993 *Fj*, 1994 *Sa*, *W*, *Fj*, 1995 *J*, *J*, *F*, *S*, *Iv*, 1999 *Kor*, *F*, *Fj*, *C*, *It*, *E*, 2001 *S*, 2003 *Fj*, *Fj*, *It*, *NZ*
SM **Tuipulotu** 1997 *W*, 1998 *Sa*, *A*, 1999 *Sa*, *F*, *NZ*, *E*, 2000 *C*, *NZ*, *Sa*, *US*, 2001 *Fj*, *Fj*, *Sa*, 2005 *Fj*, *Sa*, *It*, *F*, 2006 *J*, *Fj*, *JAB*, *Coo*, *Sa*, 2007 *US*, *Sa*, *SA*, *E*, 2008 *J*, *Sa*
K **Tu'ipulotu** 1994 *W*, 1997 *Sa*, *Fj*, *Coo*, *W*, 1999 *Kor*, *Kor*, *J*, *US*, *Fj*, *It*, *E*, 2000 *Fj*, *J*, 2001 *Fj*
M **Tu'ipulotu** 1977 *Fj*, *Fj*, *Fj*
P **Tu'ipulotu** 1979 *Sa*, 1980 *Sa*
V **Tu'ipulotu** 1977 *Fj*, *Fj*, *Fj*, 1979 *M*, *E*, *Fj*
J **Tu'itavake** 1932 *Fj*
L **Tu'itavake** 1959 *Fj*, 1960 *M*, 1963 *Fj*, *Fj*
P **Tu'itavake** 1995 *Fj*
I **Tuivai** 1993 *Sa*
K **Tuivailala** 1987 *Sa*, 1988 *Sa*, *Fj*, *Fj*, 1989 *Fj*, *Fj*, 1990 *Fj*, *J*, *Sa*, *Kor*, 1991 *Fj*
K **Tuivailala** 1988 *Fj*
M **Tuku'aho** 1979 *NC*, *Sa*, 1980 *Sa*, 1982 *Sa*
M **Tuku'aho** 1979 *Fj*

T **Tulia** 2002 *PNG*, 2003 *Kor*, *Kor*, *M*, *I*, *Fj*, 2004 *Sa*, *Fj*, 2005 *Fj*, *Sa*
A **Tulikaki** 1993 *S*
S **Tulikifanga** 1997 *SA*, *Fj*, *Sa*, *Coo*
S **Tunufa'i** 1934 *Fj*
F **Tupi** 1973 *A*, *Fj*, 1974 *S*, *W*, 1975 *M*, *M*
H **Tupou** 1982 *Sa*, *Fj*, 1983 *M*, *M*, 1984 *Fj*, *Fj*, 1987 *C*, *W*, *I*
J **Tupou** 1994 *Fj*
IM **Tupou** 2006 *Coo*, *Coo*, 2007 *Kor*, *AuA*, *J*, *JAB*, *US*, *Sa*, *SA*, 2008 *J*, 2009 *Fj*, *Sa*
M **Tupou** 2005 *Fj*, *Fj*, *Sa*, 2010 *Chl*
P **Tupou** 1984 *Fj*, 1986 *W*, 1988 *Fj*
S **Tupou** 1975 *M*
THN **Pole** 2007 *Kor*, *AuA*, *J*, *JAB*, *Fj*, *Sa*, *US*, *Sa*, *E*, 2008 *Sa*, *Fj*, 2009 *Fj*, *Sa*, *J*, 2012 *It*, *US*, *S*, 2013 *J*, *C*, *US*, *Fj*, *F*, *W*, 2014 *Geo*, *US*, *S*, 2015 *Fj*, *C*, *US*, *J*, *R*, *Geo*, *Nm*
M **Tu'ungafasi** 1986 *W*, *Fj*, 1987 *W*, *I*
L **Tu'uta** 1928 *Fj*, *Fj*
T **Tu'utu Kakato** 1987 *C*, *W*, *I*, 1990 *Sa*, *Kor*, 1991 *Sa*, *Fj*, 1992 *Fj*

A **Uasi** 1993 *S*, 1994 *Sa*, *Fj*
L **Uhatafe** 1987 *Sa*, *Fj*
V **Uhi** 1996 *M*, 1997 *Z*, *Nm*, *SA*, *Fj*, *Sa*, *Coo*
S **Ula** 1959 *Fj*, 1960 *M*, 1963 *Fj*, *Fj*
T **Ula** 2011 *Fj*
L **Ulufonua** 2002 *PNG*, 2003 *Kor*, *Kor*, *Fj*
T **Unga** 1934 *Fj*

S **Vaea** 1928 *Fj*, *Fj*, *Fj*
S **Vaea** 1974 *S*, *W*, *C*, 1975 *M*, 1977 *Fj*, *Fj*
S **Vaeno** 1991 *Sa*
L **Vaeno** 1986 *Fj*
L **Va'eono** 1987 *W*
S **Va'enuku** 2003 *Fj*, *It*, *W*, *NZ*, 2004 *Sa*, *Fj*, 2005 *Sa*, *Fj*, *Sa*, *It*, 2007 *AuA*, *Sa*
T **Va'enuku** 1991 *Sa*, *Fj*, 1992 *Sa*, *Fj*, 1993 *S*, *Fj*, *A*, *Fj*, 1994 *Sa*, *W*, *Fj*, 1995 *F*, *S*, *Iv*
U **Va'enuku** 1995 *F*, *S*, *Iv*
L **Vaeuo** 1985 *Fj*
S **Vaha'akolo** 1990 *J*, *Kor*
SK **Vahafolau** 2007 *J*, *Fj*, *Sa*, 2008 *Sa*, *Fj*, 2009 *Pt*, 2011 *Fj*, *Sa*, *Fj*, *NZ*, *C*, *J*, *F*
N **Vahe** 1977 *Fj*, *Fj*
S **Vai** 1981 *Fj*, *Fj*, 1988 *Sa*, *Fj*
A **Vaihu** 1975 *M*
T **Vaikona** 2006 *J*, *Fj*, *JAB*, *Coo*
H **Vaingalo** 1988 *Fj*
F **Vainikolo** 2011 *Fj*, *Fj*, *C*, *J*, 2012 *It*, *US*, *S*, 2013 *J*, *C*, *R*, *F*, *W*, 2014 *Sa*, *Fj*, *Geo*, *US*, *S*, 2015 *Fj*, *C*, *US*, *J*, *R*, *Geo*, *Ar*, *NZ*
SAF **Vaioleti** 2010 *Chl*
T **Vaioleti** 2005 *F*, 2010 *Chl*
SFKHF **Vaiomounga** 2009 *Pt*, 2010 *Sa*, *Fj*, 2011 *Fj*, *Sa*, *Fj*, *C*, *J*, 2012 *Sa*, *J*, *Fj*, *It*
L **Vaipulu** 1987 *C*
JW **Vaka** 2004 *Sa*, *Fj*, 2005 *Sa*, 2007 *US*, *Sa*, *SA*, *E*, 2009 *Fj*, *Sa*, *J*, 2012 *Sa*, *J*, *Fj*
PM **Vakaloa** 2009 *Pt*
P **Vakamalolo** 1993 *Sa*
S **Vaka'uta** 1924 *Fj*, *Fj*, *Fj*
I **Vaka'uta** 1959 *Fj*, 1963 *Fj*, *Fj*
V **Vaka'uta** 1959 *Fj*, 1960 *M*
V **Vake** 1932 *Fj*
VL **Vaki** 2001 *Fj*, *Sa*, *Fj*, *Sa*, *S*, *W*, 2002 *J*, *Fj*, *Sa*, *Fj*, *PNG*, 2003 *M*, *I*, *Fj*, *It*, *W*, *NZ*, *C*, 2005 *Fj*, *Sa*, *It*, *F*, 2006 *JAB*, *Coo*, *Sa*, *Coo*, 2007 *US*, *Sa*, *SA*, *E*, 2008 *Fj*
Valeli 1947 *Fj*
F **Valu** 1973 *M*, *A*, *A*, *Fj*, 1974 *S*, *W*, *C*, 1975 *M*, *M*, 1977 *Fj*, *Fj*, *Fj*, 1979 *NC*, *M*, *E*, *Sa*, *Fj*, 1980 *Sa*, 1981 *Fj*, 1983 *Sa*, *M*, *M*, 1987 *C*, *W*, *I*
V **Vanisi** 1969 *M*, *M*
L **Vano** 1986 *Fj*
A **Vasi** 1993 *Fj*
I **Vave** 1973 *A*, *A*, *Fj*, 1974 *S*, *C*
T **Vave** 1993 *A*
M **Vea** 1992 *Fj*

T Vea 2013 *J, C, US, Fj, F, W*
KTP Veainu 2015 *Fj, C, US, R, Geo, Nm, Ar, NZ*
S Veehala 1987 *Sa, Fj*, 1988 *Fj, Fj*, 1989 *Fj*, 1990 *J, Kor*, 1991 *Sa, Fj, Fj*
J Vikilani 1932 *Fj, Fj*
T Vikilani 1992 *Fj*, 1994 *Sa, W*
T Viliame 1979 *M*
O Vitelefi 1986 *W*
F Vuna 1977 *Fj, Fj*, 1979 *NC, M, Sa*, 1981 *Fj*
V Vuni 1932 *Fj, Fj, Fj*, 1934 *Fj*
A Vunipola 1982 *Fj*
E Vunipola 1990 *Fj, Kor*, 1993 *Sa, S, Fj, A, Fj*, 1994 *Sa, W*, 1995 *J, J, F, S, Iv*, 1996 *Sa, Fj, M*, 1997 *Z*, 1999 *Geo, Geo, Kor, Kor, J, F, Fj, NZ, It, E*, 2000 *C, Fj, J, NZ, Sa, US*, 2001 *Fj, Sa, Fj, Sa, S*, 2004 *Sa, Fj*, 2005 *F*

F Vunipola 1988 *Fj*, 1991 *Sa, Fj, Fj*, 1994 *Sa, W, Fj*, 1995 *J, J, F, S, Iv, Sa, Fj*, 1996 *Sa, Fj, M*, 1997 *SA, Fj, Coo*, 1998 *Sa, Fj*, 1999 *Geo, Kor, Kor, Fj, C, NZ, E*, 2000 *NZ, Sa, US*, 2001 *Sa*
K Vunipola 1982 *Sa, Fj*, 1983 *Fj, Sa, M, M*
M Vunipola 1987 *W, Sa*, 1988 *Sa, Fj, Fj, Fj*, 1989 *Fj, Fj*, 1990 *Kor*, 1991 *Fj, Fj*, 1992 *Sa*, 1993 *Sa, S, Fj, A, Fj*, 1994 *Sa, W*, 1995 *J, J, F, S, Sa, Fj*, 1996 *Sa, Fj, M*, 1997 *Nm, SA, Coo*, 1999 *Geo, Kor, Kor, US, Fj*
S Vunipola 1977 *Fj*, 1981 *Fj*, 1982 *Sa*
V Vunipola 1982 *Fj*
VS Vunipola 2004 *Sa, Fj*, 2005 *It*
S Vunipoli 1960 *M*, 1963 *Fj*

B Woolley 1998 *Sa, Fj*, 1999 *Geo, Geo, Kor, J, US, Sa, C, It*

Tonga flanker Jack Ram dives over to score one of his two tries in the 35–21 defeat of Namibia in Exeter.

URUGUAY

URUGUAY'S 2014–15 TEST RECORD

OPPONENTS	DATE	VENUE	RESULT
Paraguay	11 Apr	H	Won 77–3
Brazil	18 Apr	H	Won 48–9
Chile	9 May	A	Lost 30–15
Argentina	16 May	H	Lost 14–36
Georgia	13 Jun	A	Lost 19–10
Japan	22 Aug	A	Lost 30–8
Japan	29 Aug	A	Lost 40–0
Wales	20 Sep	A	Lost 54–9
Australia	27 Sep	N	Lost 65–3
Fiji	6 Oct	N	Lost 47–15
England	10 Oct	N	Lost 60–3

URUGUAY RETURN HOME AS HEROES

By Frankie Deges

THE COUNTRIES

Uruguay hooker Carlos Arboleya scores Los Teros' first Rugby World Cup try in 12 years against Fiji at Stadium MK.

Pablo Lemoine was not given the keys to the City of Montevideo on his arrival back from Rugby World Cup 2015, but he and his team did return to a heroes' welcome in the Uruguayan capital. Rugby in Uruguay gained a profile it did not have before the tournament and Lemoine, the burly former prop and now leader of the Uruguayan rugby renaissance, has been instrumental in achieving this.

Of course, Uruguay did not win a match at Rugby World Cup 2015, and they only scored two tries in four heavy losses against Wales (54–9), Australia (65–3), Fiji (47–15) and England (60–3). But the manner in which they performed – in a tough Pool A from which hosts England failed to escape – was commendable.

They came to England wide-eyed and ready to enjoy the experience – a first for every one of the players and management team except the three coaches – and returned home street-wise, better players and hungry for more rugby at the highest level. One of the many achievements of what was an incredible festival of rugby over 40-plus days was the performances of the tier two nations, and Uruguay earned every one of the accolades that came their way. World Rugby deserves a big round of applause for all their efforts in making Rugby World Cup 2015 the most competitive tournament to date.

It wasn't a successful World Cup in terms of the win-loss ratio for Uruguay, but it was positive if you analyse the difference in how the public perceived the team before 18 September and where they placed them at the end of the tournament. From expected defeats in three, maybe four games, and the possibility of record losing margins, the amateurs from Uruguay finished on decent scores and fought well above their weight.

"When you play against physical monsters as we did, there is nothing you can do or there is no way you can produce players that big," says Lemoine as he plots the road to Japan 2019. For example, at 1.87m and 100kg captain Santiago Vilaseca had to out-jump the likes of Wallaby Will Skelton (2.03m and 140kg) in the lineout. In fact, only 10 of the original Welsh squad were shorter than Vilaseca – and not by much.

The intensive preparation would not make them giants overnight, but did provide them with physical and technical weapons to take with them to England and Cardiff. "We tirelessly worked on ensuring each and every one of our squad was as fit as he had ever been and technically ready for the challenge," said Lemoine. The players trained at the Estadio Charrúa, where Uruguayan rugby continues to enlarge its high performance centre, both in size and its ability to include more players of different ages, and they worked with professional levels of commitment.

After qualifying by beating Russia in the final repechage match in Montevideo in October 2014, an enlarged squad had a week off and immediately started what was the most important year in Uruguayan rugby history. As relentless as the preparations were, however, it was the busiest playing calendar Los Teros had ever faced and included 11 tests and a handful of other internationals, a two-month tour and RWC 2015.

"Maybe that we were not in 2007 and 2011 was good for us because it forced us to work very hard on who we are and what we want to be," said Lemoine, the former captain who retired in 2010.

Lemoine's 49th and last test was in Bucharest when Los Teros failed to secure a ticket to New Zealand 2011 and he vowed, there and then, to take his team back to a Rugby World Cup. He moved back to Uruguay after 12 years of professional rugby in Europe, and worked hard in setting up a high-performance mentality while facilities were being upgraded. The whole of Uruguayan rugby bought into the idea and the project has proved to be successful.

It wasn't easy as only four members of the squad held professional contracts at the start of the tournament. The rest were amateurs who prepared as professionals, putting on hold a number of personal and work-related projects.

"It was hard to combine life as a doctor and father of one, with a wife that is also a doctor, with my rugby commitments," explained hooker Nicolás Klappenbach. "I was helped by family, friends, workmates, bosses, club mates . . . everybody. And if you ask each and every one of the players they will talk about similar commitment and assistance to help us get to where we were."

When you look at personal sacrifices made – leaving jobs, taking unpaid holiday, postponing career opportunities, even delaying a wedding – it is clear that this team would not go down without a fight.

The year began with the traditional South American Championship and after easily dispatching Paraguay and Brazil, Los Teros went down 30–15 to Chile, a disastrous result in any other season. But the coaching trio of Lemoine, Juan Carlos Bado and Emiliano Caffera were after other things – the goal was clear and the calendar set for 20 September in Cardiff.

Travelling to Georgia for the World Rugby Tbilisi Cup in June also saw them lose their three games, but progress was evident, and more so in the first game against Georgia. As each piece of the jigsaw began to fit into place, Los Teros overcame an Argentina XV in Montevideo in August – a huge achievement, not only in the manner in which they played but because it was the first time a senior team had beaten their neighbour.

The trip to England took a long detour via Japan, where the two tests were lost by large margins. "It involved a lot of travelling, playing in extreme heat and Japan were fizzing as they showed in their opening game against South Africa," explained retiring prop Alejo Corral, one of six who made a test bow against England in Manchester.

"The World Cup was incredible – all I dreamt of and better," said fly-half Felipe Berchesi, who before the tournament was worried about how to stop himself taking selfies with all of his better-known opponents during games! "We played to our strengths and as hard as it was, we managed to keep our composure."

The opening game against Wales in the Millennium Stadium did not see Los Teros subdued. They were well beaten but they didn't revert to negative rugby. They tried to play their burgeoning brand of rugby with the ball, and without it they were committed in the tackle. Two tries in the final nine minutes denied them the possibility of a fairer result and they would also have to wait longer for their first try of RWC 2015. Following the match, however, the Welsh squad invited the Uruguayans to their dressing room to share a few beers and watch neighbours Argentina take on New Zealand.

Villa Park saw them tackle, and tackle, and tackle a strong Wallabies side and had it not been for their notable defence, one of the best attacking teams in the tournament would have run in more than the 11 tries they finished with.

A long break helped recharge the batteries before playing Fiji in Milton Keynes, where Los Teros scored two well-deserved tries. Hooker Carlos Arboleya was at the end of a furious attack close to the Fijian line and went over to score Uruguay's first try since Lemoine's five-pointer against England 12 years ago. Again, Fiji were stronger physically but a second try came courtesy of Agustín Ormaechea, whose father Diego had scored against Spain in RWC 1999, though the scrum-half was later sent-off for a second yellow card.

With England already eliminated from Rugby World Cup 2015, it was only pride that was at stake for both teams in their final Pool A encounter in Manchester. The difference in strength was apparent as England scored nine unanswered tries, the ninth a penalty try in the last second of the game to even further stretch their lead.

"We are not used to playing at that level, at that intensity but we are happy in the team with our performance," Ormaechea said afterwards. "Our aim was also to grow rugby in Uruguay and we have achieved that."

Pride and growth: two very important things to came out of this Rugby World Cup experience for Uruguayan rugby. "Back home interest levels rose and we are expecting more players to join the game," said Lemoine. "Our objective was always to leave a good impression of our rugby, more than winning, and we sought to do the best we could. I think we have had a very good participation, doing good things and we need to maintain that level."

A mixture of good management, a solid coaching staff, a high-performance training centre, players that have sampled rugby at the highest level and a renewed fixture list will allow Uruguay to look positively towards the future.

URUGUAY INTERNATIONAL STATISTICS

MATCH RECORDS UP TO 1 NOVEMBER, 2015

WINNING MARGINS

Date	Opponent	Result	Winning Margin
14/05/2011	Paraguay	102–6	96
10/10/1998	Paraguay	93–3	90
25/04/2004	Venezuela	92–8	84
25/04/2009	Paraguay	85–7	78
21/05/1981	Brazil	77–0	77

MOST POINTS IN A MATCH
BY THE TEAM

Date	Opponent	Result	Points
14/05/2011	Paraguay	102–6	102
10/10/1998	Paraguay	93–3	93
25/04/2004	Venezuela	92–8	92
25/04/2009	Paraguay	85–7	85
03/05/2002	Paraguay	81–6	81

BY A PLAYER

Date	Player	Opponent	Points
11/04/2015	Jeronimo Etcheverry	Paraguay	32
02/05/2009	Matias Arocena	Chile	31
07/09/2002	Juan Menchaca	Chile	29
02/10/1993	Marcelo Nicola Horta	Paraguay	28
09/10/1971	Oscar Bacot	Paraguay	27

MOST TRIES IN A MATCH
BY THE TEAM

Date	Opponent	Result	Tries
14/05/2011	Paraguay	102–6	16
10/10/1998	Paraguay	93–3	15
25/04/2004	Venezuela	92–8	14
21/05/1981	Brazil	77–0	13

BY A PLAYER

Date	Player	Opponent	Tries
21/05/1981	Carlos Bonaso	Brazil	4
28/09/1991	Diego Ormaechea	Brazil	4
03/05/2002	Benjamin Bono	Paraguay	4
14/05/2011	Pablo Bueno	Paraguay	4

MOST CONVERSIONS IN A MATCH
BY THE TEAM

Date	Opponent	Result	Cons
25/04/2004	Venezuela	92–8	11
14/05/2011	Paraguay	102–6	11
11/04/2015	Paraguay	77–3	11
9 on 3 occasions			

BY A PLAYER

Date	Player	Opponent	Cons
11/04/2015	Jeronimo Etcheverry	Paraguay	11
21/05/1981	Jose Peirano	Brazil	8
29/04/2009	Matias Arocena	Brazil	8
06/10/2001	Juan Menchacha	Paraguay	7

MOST PENALTIES IN A MATCH
BY THE TEAM

Date	Opponent	Result	Pens
27/10/1977	Chile	21–18	7
27/09/2014	Russia	21–22	7
6 on 10 occasions			

BY A PLAYER

Date	Player	Opponent	Pens
27/09/2014	Felipe Berchesi	Russia	7
6 on 8 occasions			

MOST DROP GOALS IN A MATCH
BY THE TEAM

Date	Opponent	Result	DGs
07/09/2002	Chile	34–23	4
08/09/1991	Chile	34–18	3
18/08/1964	Chile	15–8	2
12/10/1979	Chile	9–9	2

BY A PLAYER

Date	Player	Opponent	DGs
07/09/2002	Juan Menchaca	Chile	4
12/10/1979	Rafael Ubilla	Chile	2
08/09/1991	Cesar Cat	Chile	2

MOST CAPPED PLAYERS	
Name	Caps
Rodrigo Sanchez	67
Diego Aguirre	59
Diego Ormaechea	54
Carlos Arboleya	54
Nicolas Grille	53

LEADING TRY SCORERS	
Name	Tries
Diego Ormaechea	30
Alfonso Cardoso	13
Federico Sciarra	13
Leandro Leivas	13

LEADING CONVERSIONS SCORERS	
Name	Conversions
Marcelo Nicola Horta	35
Matias Arocena	35
Federico Sciarra	33
Juan Menchaca	28
Agustin Ormaechea	16

LEADING PENALTY SCORERS	
Name	Penalties
Juan Menchaca	50
Matias Arocena	48
Federico Sciarra	44
Felipe Berchesi	33

LEADING DROP GOAL SCORERS	
Name	DGs
Juan Menchaca	5
Rafael Ubilla	4

LEADING POINTS SCORERS	
Name	Points
Federico Sciarra	261
Juan Menchaca	256
Matias Arocena	255
Jeronimo Etcheverry	187
Marcelo Nicola Horta	156

URUGUAY INTERNATIONAL PLAYERS
UP TO 1 NOVEMBER, 2015

URUGUAY

P Abatte 1987 *Sp*
P Acerenza 1981 *Par, Bra, Chl,* 1983 *Par, Chl, Ar,* 1985 *F,* 1987 *Ar, Sp, Ar, Chl, Par,* 1988 *Bel,* 1990 *Chl, Chl,* 1991 *Par, Chl, Ar, Bra,* 1992 *Chl, Chl,* 1993 *Bra, Par, Chl, Ar,* 1995 *Ar, C, Ar, Sp, Chl, Par, Ar,* 1996 *Ar, C, Ar, US,* 1997 *Chl, Par, Ar,* 1998 *Par, Chl*
B Acle 2001 *Ar*
D Aguirre 1992 *Chl,* 1995 *Ar, C, Ar, Sp, Chl, Par, Ar,* 1996 *Ar, C, Ar, US,* 1997 *Ar,* 1998 *Par, Chl, Ar, C, Ar, US, Chl, Par, Ar,* 1999 *Pt, Pt, Mor, Mor, It, Fj, Sp, Sp, S, SA,* 2001 *It, Sp,* 2002 *Ar, Chl, Par, Chl, C, US, C, US, Chl,* 2003 *Fj, C, Ar, US, SA, Sa, Geo, E,* 2005 *J,* 2006 *Ar, Chl, Pt, US, US,* 2007 *Pt, Pt*
M Aguirre 2002 *Ar, Chl, Par*
S Aguirre 1997 *Chl,* 1998 *Ar, Ar, Par, Ar,* 1999 *Pt, Pt, Mor, SA,* 2001 *It, Sp,* 2002 *Ar, Chl, Par, Chl, C, US, C, US, Chl,* 2003 *Chl, Par, Ar, Fj, C, Ar, SA, Geo, E,* 2006 *Ar, Chl, Pt, US, US,* 2007 *Pt, Pt*
G Albanell 2013 *SAP, Geo, Elr*
G Alonso 1987 *Sp,* 1989 *Par, Ar, US,* 1990 *Chl, Chl,* 1991 *Par, Chl, Ar, Bra*
A Alonso 2014 *Par, R, Elr,* 2015 *Par, Bra, USE, Chl, Ar, FIJ, FIJ, Elr, ARG, W, E*
R Álvarez 2004 *Ar, Chl, Pt,* 2005 *J, Chl, Ar, SA, Pt,* 2006 *Ar, Chl, Pt, US, US,* 2007 *Pt, Pt,* 2009 *Ar, R, S, Rus*
JM Alvarez 2001 *Par, Chl, Chl,* 2002 *Ar, Chl, Par, C, US,* 2003 *C, Ar, Sa, E,* 2006 *Ar, Chl, Pt, US, US,* 2007 *Pt, Pt, Sp,* 2008 *US,* 2009 *R, S, Rus*
J Alzueta 1999 *Pt, It, Fj, Sp, SA,* 2001 *Ar, Ar, C, US, It, Sp, Chl, Chl,* 2002 *Ar, Chl, Par, Chl, C, US, C, Chl,* 2003 *Chl,*

Ar, C, Ar, US, SA, Sa, Geo, E, 2004 *Geo, Pt,* 2005 *J, Chl, Ar, SA,* 2006 *Ar, Chl, Pt, US, US,* 2007 *It,* 2008 *Ar,* 2009 *US*
B Amarillo 1998 *Par, Ar, C, Ar, US,* 1999 *Fj, Sp,* 2000 *Nm, Chl, Ar,* 2001 *Ar, Ar, C, US,* 2003 *Chl, Ar, Fj, C, Ar, US, SA, Sa, Geo*
J Ameglio 2011 *Par, Chl*
I Amorin 1975 *Ar, Bra, Chl, Par,* 1976 *Ar*
A Aquistapache 2007 *Chl*
L Ara 2004 *Ven, Ar, Chl, Geo, Pt,* 2005 *J, Chl, Ar*
P Aramendia 1958 *Ar, Chl, Per,* 1960 *F*
CM Arboleya 2004 *Geo,* 2007 *Pt, It, Chl,* 2008 *Ar, R, Geo, Rus, US, Chl,* 2009 *Par, Bra, Chl, Ar, R, S, Rus, US, US,* 2010 *Bra, Par, Chl, Ar, C, Rus, Kaz, R, R,* 2011 *Par, Bra, Chl, Ar,* 2014 *Par, Bra, R, Elr, Rus, HK, Rus, Rus,* 2015 *Par, Bra, USE, Chl, FIJ, Geo, Elr, Elt, J, J, W, A, Fj, E*
E Arechavaleta 1976 *Ar,* 1979 *Ar, Ar, Par, Chl,* 1981 *Par, Chl,* 1985 *F, Par*
S Ariano 2007 *It*
F Armas 1951 *Chl, Bra*
M Arocena 2005 *Chl, Pt,* 2006 *Ar, Chl, Pt, US, US,* 2007 *Pt, It, Sp, Chl,* 2008 *Ar, R, Geo, Rus, US, Chl,* 2009 *Par, Bra, Chl, Ar,* 2010 *R, R,* 2011 *Par, Bra, Chl, Ar, Pt, Sp,* 2012 *Ar, Chl, Bra,* 2013 *Bra,* 2014 *Par, Bra, Chl*
S Arocena 2010 *Bra, Par, Chl, Ar,* 2011 *Par, Bra, Chl,* 2012 *Ar, Bra, Rus*
JP Artagaveytia 1961 *Ar,* 1963 *Bra*
G Artola 1993 *Bra*
F Auesperg 2001 *Ar, C,* 2002 *Par,* 2003 *Par*
A Avalo 2011 *Par, Bra, Ar, Sp,* 2012 *Ar, Bra, R, Rus, Pt, Pt,*

2013 Ar, Bra, Chl, SAP, Geo, Elr, Sp, 2014 US, US, Chl, Ar, HK, Rus, Rus, 2015 Par, Chl, Ar, ARG
J Ayling 1958 Ar, Chl, Per

J Bachini 2004 Ven
O Bacot 1967 Chl, 1969 Ar, Chl, 1971 Par, Chl, Ar
N Badano 2010 Bra, Par, Chl, Ar, C, Rus, R
JC Bado 1992 Chl, Chl, 1993 Par, Chl, 1995 Ar, C, Ar, Chl, Par, Ar, 1996 Ar, C, Ar, US, 1997 Chl, Par, Ar, 1998 Par, Chl, C, US, Chl, Ar, 1999 Pt, Pt, Mor, Mor, Sp, S, SA, 2001 Ar, C, US, It, Ar, 2002 Chl, US, Chl, 2003 Fj, C, Ar, US, SA, Sa, Geo, E, 2007 Pt, 2008 Chl, 2009 Bra, 2010 Kaz
C Baldasarri 2003 Ar, US, Sa, Geo, 2004 Ven, Ar, Chl, 2005 J, Chl, Ar, SA
A Baldomir 1983 Chl
M Balinas 1976 NZ, 1979 Ar, Ar, Par, Chl
C Baraibar 1961 Bra
J Barbe 1979 Ar, Bra, Par, 1981 Par, Bra
I Barcos 2009 Par, Bra, Chl, Ar, R, Rus, 2011 Par, Bra, Chl
DD Bascou 2011 Par, Chl, Ar, 2012 Ar, Bra, R, Rus, Pt
FD Bascou 2011 Pt, Sp, 2012 Ar, Chl, Bra, R, Rus, Pt, 2013 SAP, Geo, Elr, Sp, 2014 R, Elr, Rus, 2015 Par, Bra, USE, Chl, Ar, FIJ, Geo, Elr, Elt, ARG, A
M Beer 2014 Par, Bra, Chl, Elr, 2015 Ar, FIJ, FIJ, Geo, Elt, J, J, W, A, Fj, E
A Behrens 1951 Ar
P Behrens 1973 Chl, Ar, Bra, Par, 1977 Par, Chl, Bra
M Belluscio 1985 Ar, Par, Chl, 1987 Sp, Ar, Chl, Par, 1989 Par, Chl, Ar, US, 1990 Chl, Chl, 1991 Par, Chl, Ar, Bra, 1992 Chl, Chl, 1993 Ar, 1995 Ar, C
E Benitez 2010 Bra, Par, Chl, Ar, C, Kaz
A Benquet 1963 Ar, 1964 Ar, Chl, Bra, 1967 Chl, Ar, 1971 Chl
J Benquet 1971 Bra, Ar
F Berchesi 2011 Pt, Sp
F Berchesi 2011 Pt, 2012 Ar, Bra, R, Rus, Pt, 2013 Sp, 2014 US, US, HK, Rus, Rus, 2015 ARG, J, J, W, A, E
H Bergman 1958 Ar, Chl, Per, 1960 F
E Berruti 1989 Par, Chl, Ar, US, 1990 Chl, Chl, 1995 Ar, C, Ar, Par, Ar, 1999 Pt, Pt, Mor, Mor, It, Sp, S, SA, 2000 Nm, Chl, Ar, 2001 Ar, Ar, C, US, Sp, Par, 2002 Chl, Par, Chl, C, US, C, US, Chl, 2003 Chl, Ar, US, SA, Geo, E, 2004 Ven, Ar, Chl
D Bertacchi 2005 Chl, Ar
A Bertolotti 2000 Nm, Chl, Ar, 2001 Ar, Par, 2002 Ar, Chl, Par, C
D Bessio 2000 Nm, Ar, 2001 Ar, It
A Beyhaut 1973 Ar
J Beyhaut 2001 Ar, 2002 Chl, Par
J Bird 1976 Ar, NZ, 1977 Par, Chl, Ar, Bra, 1979 Ar, Ar, Bra, Chl, 1981 Par, Bra, Chl, 1983 Par, Chl, Ar, 1985 F, 1987 Ar, 1988 Bel
P Blanco 1958 Ar, Chl, Per
JP Blengio 1990 Chl
M Blengio 2015 Par, Bra, USE, Chl, Ar, FIJ, FIJ, Geo, Elr, Elt, E
M Bocking 1985 Chl
R Bocking 2015 Bra
C Bomio 1983 Par, Ar, 1985 F, 1987 Sp, Ar, Chl, Par, 1988 Bel
C Bonaso 1981 Bra
R Bonner 1967 Chl, 1969 Ar, Chl, 1971 Par, Bra, Ar, 1975 Ar, Chl, 1979 Bra
B Bono 2001 Sp, Par, Chl, Chl, 2002 Ar, Par
R Booth 1951 Ar, Chl, Bra
J Bordaberry 1976 NZ
SJ Bordaberry 1981 Par, Chl, 1985 F, 1991 Ar, Bra
L Borges 1969 Ar
H Borrat 1977 Chl, Bra
HS Bowles 1958 Ar, Chl
J Brancato 1983 Par, 1987 Sp, Ar, Chl, Par
M Braun 2010 Bra, Par, Chl, Ar, C, Rus, Kaz, R, R, 2011 Par, Bra, Chl, Ar, 2012 Ar, Chl, Bra, 2014 Par, Chl, Ar, R, Elr, Rus, 2015 Par, Bra, USE, Chl, Ar, FIJ, Geo, Elr
N Brignoni 1998 Ar, Ar, Chl, Par, Ar, 1999 Mor, Mor, It, Fj, Sp, Sp, S, SA, 2000 Nm, Chl, Ar, 2001 Ar, Ar, C, US, It, 2002

Ar, Chl, Chl, C, US, C, US, Chl, 2003 C, Ar, US, SA, Sa, Geo, E, 2004 Geo, Pt, 2007 Pt, Pt, 2008 Chl, 2009 US, US, 2010 Kaz, R
P Bueno 2007 Sp, 2008 Geo, Rus, 2011 Par, Bra, Ar, 2012 R, Rus, 2013 SAP, Elr
FJ Bulanti 2004 Ven, Ar, 2006 Ar, 2007 Pt, It, Sp, Chl, 2008 US, 2011 Pt, 2012 R, Pt, Pt, 2013 Ar, Bra, 2014 US, US, 2015 Par, Ar, FIJ, FIJ, ARG, W, Fj

F Cadenas 2005 Pt
E Caffera 2000 Nm, Chl, Ar, 2001 Ar, Ar, US, It, Sp, Chl, Chl, 2002 Ar, Par, C, US, C, US, Chl, 2003 Fj, Ar, SA, E, 2004 Geo, Pt, 2005 SA, 2007 Chl, 2008 Ar, R, Rus, 2010 Bra, Par, Chl, C, Rus, Kaz, R
M Calandra 1987 Ar, Chl, 1988 Bel, 1989 Bra, Par, Chl, Ar, US, 1991 Par, Chl, Ar, 1992 Chl, Chl, 1993 Par, Chl, Ar, 1995 Chl, Ar, 1996 C, US, 1997 Chl
C Calvo 1979 Ar
G Campomar 2009 Ar, S, Rus
J Campomar 2003 Ar, C, US, Sa, Geo, E, 2004 Ar, Chl, Geo, Pt, 2005 J, SA, 2006 Ar, Chl, Pt, US, US, 2007 Pt, Pt, Chl, 2008 Ar, R, Geo, Rus, US, Chl, 2009 Par, Bra, Chl, Ar, R, S, Rus, US, US
A Canessa 1960 F
A Canessa 1960 F
H Canessa 2000 Nm, Ar, 2001 Ar, C, It, 2002 Ar, Par, 2003 Par, Ar, Ar, US, 2004 Geo, Pt, 2005 J, Chl, Ar, SA
R Canessa 1971 Bra, Ar, 1976 NZ, 1977 Par, Ar, Bra, 1979 Ar
D Cano 2005 Pt, 2008 Ar
J Capezzuto 1976 Ar, NZ, 1977 Ar, Bra
F Capó 2004 Ven, Ar, Geo, Pt, 2005 J, 2006 Ar, Pt, 2007 Pt, Pt, Sp, Chl, 2008 Ar, R, Geo, 2009 Par, Bra, Chl, R, Rus
R Capo Ortega 2000 Chl, Ar, 2001 Ar, Ar, US, Sp, Par, Chl, Chl, 2002 Chl, C, US, C, US, Chl, 2003 Fj, C, Ar, US, SA, Sa, Geo, E, 2006 Ar, Chl, US, US, 2007 Pt, Pt, 2009 Bra, Chl, Ar, S, Rus, US, US, 2014 Rus, Rus
A Cardoso 1995 Sp, Chl, Par, Ar, 1996 Ar, Ar, 1997 Chl, Ar, 1998 Chl, Ar, C, US, Chl, Ar, 1999 Pt, Pt, Mor, Mor, It, Sp, Sp, S, SA, 2002 Ar, Chl, C, US, C, US, Chl, 2003 Chl, Par, Ar, Fj, C, SA, Geo
J Cardoso 1956 Chl
S Carracedo 2005 Pt, 2007 Sp, Chl, 2008 Ar, R, Geo, Rus
G Carrere 1973 Ar, 1976 Ar
G Cassarino 1971 Par, Chl, Ar, 1973 Chl, Bra, Par
J Cassarino 1967 Chl, Ar, 1971 Par, Chl, Bra, Ar
R Cassarino 1963 Bra, 1964 Ar, Chl, Bra
J Castilla 1971 Par, Bra
FL Castilla 1963 Bra
D Castro 2001 Par, Chl
A Cat 1951 Ar, Chl, 1953 Bra, 1958 Ar, Chl
CA Cat 1951 Ar, Chl, Bra, 1953 Bra, 1961 Bra, Chl, Ar
C Cat 1989 Bra, 1991 Par, Chl, 1992 Chl
J Cat 1987 Sp, 1991 Ar, Bra, 1995 Ar
S Cat 1995 Ar, C, Sp, Chl, Par, Ar, 1996 Ar, 1998 Ar, Ar
C Cattivelli 2004 Chl
O Caviglia 2001 Par, Chl, 2004 Ven, Ar, Chl
E Cerutti 1979 Ar, Ar, Bra, 1981 Par, Bra, Chl, 1983 Par, Chl, Ar, 1985 F, Ar, Par, Chl, 1987 Ar, Sp, Ar, Chl, Par, 1988 Bel, 1989 Bra, Par, Chl, Ar, US
M Cervino 1999 Pt, It, Fj, 2001 Chl
E Cevallos 2001 Ar
P Chapt 1953 Bra
G Chiarino 1969 Ar
JA Chiarino 1969 Ar, Chl, 1971 Par, Chl, Ar, 1975 Ar, Bra, Chl, Par
A Chouldjian 1998 Ar, Ar, Chl
A Cibils 1976 NZ, 1977 Ar
D Cibils 1987 Ar, Chl, Par
JI Conti 2000 Nm, 2001 Ar, 2002 Par, C, US, 2003 Par, Ar, Sa, 2004 Ven, Ar, Geo, Pt, 2005 J, Chl, Ar, SA, 2006 Ar, Chl, Pt, US, US, 2007 It, Sp, Chl, 2008 Ar, R, Geo, Rus, US, Chl, 2009 Bra, Chl, R, S
S Core 2013 SAP
F Corletto 1998 Ar, Ar
J Coronel 2013 SAP, Elr
A Corral 2009 US, US, 2010 Bra, Par, Chl, Ar, C, Rus, Kaz,

R, R, 2011 Par, Bra, Chl, Pt, Sp, 2012 Chl, R, Rus, Pt, Pt, 2013 Ar, Bra, Chl, SAP, Geo, Elr, Sp, 2014 US, US, Chl, R, Rus, HK, Rus, Rus, 2015 Bra, USE, Chl, FIJ, FIJ, Geo, Elr, Elt, ARG, J, J, W, Fj, E

P Costábile 1989 Bra, US, 1990 Chl, Chl, 1995 C, 1996 C, US, 1997 Chl, 1998 Par, Chl, C, US, Chl, Par, Ar, 1999 Pt, Pt, Mor, Mor, It, Sp, Sp, S, SA, 2000 Nm, Chl, 2001 Ar, It, Sp, Par, Chl, Chl, 2002 C, US, Chl, 2003 Chl, Par, Ar

G Costemalle 1967 Chl, Ar, 1969 Ar

M Crosa 2007 Pt, It, 2009 US, 2010 Par, Chl, Ar, Kaz, R, R

I Crosa Gaminara 2004 Ven, Ar, Chl, Geo, 2005 Pt

P Crosta 2011 Par, Bra, Ar

P Crosta 1977 Par, Ar

A Dabo 1989 Bra, Ar, US, 1990 Chl, Chl, 1991 Par, Chl, Ar, Bra, 1992 Chl, Chl, 1993 Par, Ar, 1995 Sp, Ar, 1996 Ar, C, 1998 US, 1999 Pt, It

N Datindrade 2011 Ar

AM Davies 1963 Bra

N Davies 1951 Chl, Bra, 1953 Bra

R Davies 1961 Chl, 1963 Bra

W Davies 1963 Bra

RW Day 1951 Ar, Bra

J de Freitas 2000 Nm, Ar, 2001 Ar, US, Par, Chl, Ar, 2002 Chl, Par, C, US, C, 2003 Chl, Sa, E, 2006 Pt

JA De Freitas 2009 US, 2010 Bra, Chl, Ar, C, Rus, Kaz, R, R, 2011 Bra, Chl, Ar, Pt, 2012 Chl, Pt, 2013 Ar, Bra, Chl, SAP, Geo, Elr, Sp, 2014 US, US, Par, Bra, Chl, Ar, R, Elr, Rus, HK, Rus, Rus, 2015 ARG, J, J, W, A, Fj

F de los Santos 1990 Chl, Chl, 1991 Par, Chl, Bra, 1993 Chl, 1995 Ar, Ar, Sp, Chl, Par, Ar, 1996 Ar, 1998 Ar, C, Ar, Chl, Ar, 1999 Mor, It, Fj, Sp, Sp, S, 2000 Chl, Ar, 2001 Ar, Ar, C, US, It, Sp, 2002 Ar, Chl

M de los Santos 1995 C

R De Mula 2011 Par, Bra, Chl, Ar, 2012 Ar, Bra, R, Rus, Pt, 2013 Ar, Bra, Chl, SAP, Geo, Elr, Sp, 2014 US, US, Par, Bra, Chl, Ar, HK, 2015 Par, Ar

L de Olivera 1998 Ar, Ar, Par, 1999 Pt, Pt, Mor, 2000 Chl, Ar, 2001 Par, Chl, 2002 Ar, Chl, 2008 Chl, 2009 Bra, Chl

F de Posadas 2006 Chl, US, US, 2008 Ar, US, Chl, 2009 Par, Bra, Chl

P Deal 2014 Bra, Elr, 2015 ARG

J Decia 1988 Bel

S Deicas 2010 Bra, Par, Chl, Ar, C, Rus

A del Castillo 2013 SAP, Geo

AP del Castillo 2004 Ven, Ar, Chl, Geo, Pt, 2005 J, SA, 2008 Ar, R, Geo, Rus

A Delgado 2001 Ar, Par, 2004 Ven, Ar, Chl, Geo, Pt, 2005 Chl, Ar

JP Deus 1963 Bra

P Devita 1953 Bra

M Diab 1973 Chl, Bra, Par

P Diana 1989 Bra, Chl, 1990 Chl, Chl, 1991 Par

J Diaz 2001 Ar

C Dodero 1971 Par, Chl, Bra

I Dotti 2015 Par, Bra, ARG

C Drever 1958 Chl, Per

I Dugonjic 2004 Geo, Pt, 2005 J, Chl, Ar, SA, Pt, 2007 It, 2008 R, 2010 Bra, Par, Chl, Ar, C, Rus, Kaz, R, R

G Dupont 1960 F, 1961 Bra, Chl

OA Duran 2001 Ar, 2004 Ven, Ar, Chl, 2006 Pt, US, US, 2011 Pt, Sp, 2012 Chl, Pt, 2013 Ar, Bra, Chl, 2014 US, US, Chl, Ar, Elr, Rus, HK, Rus, Rus, 2015 Par, Bra, USE, Chl, FIJ, ARG, J, J, W, A, Fj, E

A Duran 2012 R, Rus, Pt, Pt, 2013 Ar, Bra, Chl, SAP, Geo, Elr, 2014 US, Par, Bra, Chl, R, Elr, Rus, HK, Rus, 2015 Par, Bra, USE, Chl, Ar, FIJ, FIJ, Geo, Elr, Elt, J, J, W, A, Fj, E

J Echevarria 1975 Ar, Chl, 1976 Ar, NZ

JA Echeverria 2014 Par, Bra, Ar, R, Elr, Rus, 2015 Bra, USE, Ar, ARG

A Eirea 1985 F, 1987 Sp, Ar, Chl, Par, 1988 Bel, 1989 Bra, Par, Chl, Ar, US, 1991 Par, 1993 Bra, Par, Chl, Ar, 1995 C

M Espiga 2005 Pt, 2007 It, Sp, Chl, 2008 Ar, R, Geo, Rus,

US, Chl, 2009 Par, Bra, Chl, R, S, Rus, US, US, 2010 Bra, Par, Chl, Ar, C, Kaz, R, 2011 Par, Bra, Chl

R Espiga 2011 Pt, Sp, 2013 SAP, Geo, Elr

G Estape 1964 Ar, Chl, Bra

J Etcheverry 2008 US, 2009 Par, Bra, Chl, Ar, R, S, Rus, US, US, 2010 R, 2011 Sp, 2012 Ar, Chl, Bra, R, Pt, Pt, 2013 Ar, SAP, Geo, Elr, Sp, 2014 US, R, Elr, Rus, HK, Rus, Rus, 2015 Par, Bra, USE, Chl, Ar, FIJ, Geo, Elr, ARG, J, Fj

R Fajardo 1975 Ar, Chl, 1977 Par, Chl, Ar, Bra, 1979 Ar, Ar, Bra, Par, Chl, 1981 Par, Chl

A Farraco 1967 Ar

E Favaro 1983 Chl, Ar

F Favaro 2013 Bra, 2014 Par, Chl, R, Elr, Rus, 2015 Par, Bra, Chl

M Ferres 1993 Bra, Par, Chl, Ar, 1995 Ar, Sp, Chl, Ar, 1996 Ar, C, Ar, US, 1997 Chl, Par, Ar, 1998 Par, Chl, C, Ar, US, Chl, Par, 1999 Mor, Mor, Sp

M Fonseca 2008 US, Chl, 2009 Par, Bra, Chl, Ar, R, S, Rus, US, US, 2010 Rus, Kaz, R, R

B Fontana 1960 F

C Fosatti 1967 Chl, Ar

E Francisco Rocco 1951 Ar, Chl, Bra

D Frederick 1985 F, Ar, Par, Chl, 1987 Sp, 1988 Bel

SN Freitas 2014 Par, Bra

G Furest 1951 Chl, 1953 Bra, 1956 Chl, 1958 Ar, Chl, Per, 1961 Chl

E Fynn 1958 Per

G Gallo 2005 Pt

JM Gaminara 2010 R, R, 2011 Bra, Chl, Ar, 2013 Ar, Bra, Chl, SAP, Geo, Elr, Sp, 2014 US, US, Chl, Ar, HK, Rus, Rus, 2015 Geo, Elt, J, J, W, A, Fj, E

A Garcia Aust 1976 Ar

L Garcia Mansilla 1961 Bra, Chl, Ar

JJ Gari 1975 Ar, Bra, Chl, Par, 1977 Chl

J Gatti 1977 Par, Chl, Bra, 1979 Ar

A Gianoli 1976 Ar, NZ, 1977 Chl, Ar

C Giavi 1964 Ar, Chl, Bra

G Gibernau 2013 Geo, Elr, 2014 Par, Bra, R, Elr

S Gibernau 2009 Par, Bra, Chl, Ar, R, US, 2011 Sp, 2012 R, Rus, Pt, Pt, 2013 Ar, Chl, Sp, 2014 Bra, Ar, R, Rus, HK, Rus, Rus, 2015 Par, Bra, USE, Chl, FIJ, FIJ, Geo, Elr, Elt, J, J, W, Fj, E

A Giuria 2004 Ven, Ar, Chl, Geo, Pt, 2005 J, SA, 2006 Ar, Pt, 2007 Pt, Pt, It, 2008 R, Chl, 2009 Par, Bra, Chl, US, US, 2010 Kaz

CA Gomez 1961 Bra, Chl, Ar, 1963 Bra, 1964 Ar, Chl, Bra

JM Gomez 1969 Ar, Chl

M Gonzalez 2013 Geo, Elr

S Gortari 2010 Bra, Kaz

I Grignola 2010 Bra, Par, Chl, Ar, C, Rus

M Grille 2001 Ar

N Grillé 1996 Ar, US, 1998 Ar, C, Ar, US, Chl, 1999 Pt, Pt, Mor, Mor, Sp, S, SA, 2000 Chl, Ar, 2001 Ar, Ar, C, US, It, Par, Chl, Chl, 2002 Ar, Chl, Chl, C, US, 2003 Chl, Par, Ar, Fj, C, Ar, US, SA, Sa, Geo, E, 2004 Ven, Ar, Chl, 2005 J, Chl, 2006 Ar, Chl, Pt, US, US, 2007 Pt, Sp

M Guelfi 1969 Chl

C Guillemette 1953 Bra

E Guillemette 1956 Chl

M Gurmendez 1956 Chl

CA Gutierrez 1961 Chl, Ar

M Gutierrez 2000 Nm, Ar, 2001 It, Sp, 2002 Chl, C, US, C, US, Chl, 2003 Chl, Par, Ar, Fj, C, Ar, US, SA, Sa, Geo, E, 2005 J, 2006 Pt

M Henderson 1951 Ar, Chl, Bra, 1953 Bra, 1956 Chl

G Hernandez 1967 Chl, Ar, 1969 Ar, Chl

M Hernandez 1998 Ar

R Hernandez 1967 Ar

J Horta 2001 Sp

JP Horta 2008 Ar, R, Geo, Rus, 2009 Par, Ar, R, Rus, US, 2010 Par, Chl, C, Rus, Kaz

R Hubber 1960 F

R Hudson 1975 Ar, Bra, Par

JL Nicola 1979 *Bra, Par, Chl*, 1981 *Par, Bra, Chl*, 1993 *Ar*
M Nicola Horta 1989 *Bra, Par, Chl, Ar, US*, 1990 *Chl, Chl*, 1991 *Par, Chl, Ar, Bra*, 1993 *Bra, Par, Chl*, 1995 *Ar, C, Ar, Sp, Chl, Par, Ar*
A Nicolich 1977 *Par, Ar, Bra*, 1979 *Ar, Bra, Chl*, 1981 *Bra*
A Nieto 2012 *Ar, Chl, Bra, R, Rus, Pt, Pt*, 2013 *Ar, Bra, Chl, Sp*, 2014 *US, US, Bra, Chl, Ar, R, Elr, Rus, HK, Rus, Rus*, 2015 *Elr, Elt, ARG, J, J, W, A, Fj, E*
J Novoa 2011 *Ar*

F Obes 1975 *Ar, Chl*, 1976 *Ar, NZ*, 1979 *Ar, Par, Chl*
J Obes 1975 *Ar*, 1979 *Ar*
H Octetich 1973 *Ar, Par*
A Ormaechea 2011 *Pt, Sp*, 2012 *Ar, Chl, R, Rus, Pt*, 2013 *Ar, Bra, Chl, Sp*, 2014 *US, US, HK, Rus, Rus*, 2015 *FIJ, Geo, Elr, Elt, ARG, J, J, W, A, Fj, E*
D Ormaechea 1979 *Ar*, 1981 *Bra*, 1983 *Par, Chl, Ar*, 1985 *F, Ar, Chl*, 1987 *Ar, Sp, Ar, Chl, Par*, 1989 *Par, Chl, Ar, US*, 1990 *Chl, Chl*, 1991 *Chl, Ar, Bra*, 1992 *Chl, Chl, Ar, Bra*, 1993 *Par, Chl, Ar*, 1995 *Ar, C, Ar, Sp, Par, Ar*, 1996 *Ar, C, Ar, US*, 1997 *Chl, Par, Ar*, 1998 *Par, Chl, C, US*, 1999 *Pt, Pt, Mor, Mor, It, Sp, Sp, S, SA*
JD Ormaechea 2011 *Pt, Sp*, 2012 *Ar, Chl, Bra, R, Rus, Pt, Pt*, 2013 *Ar, Bra, Chl*
Z Orr 1969 *Ar, Chl*
Ostazo 1985 *F*

P Pagani 2000 *Nm*, 2001 *Ar, US, Sp, Par, Chl, Ar*, 2002 *Par*
J Paladino 1983 *Par, Chl*
G Palmer 1951 *Ar, Chl, Bra*
M Palomeque 2011 *Bra, Ar*, 2012 *Pt*, 2013 *Ar, Chl, Sp*, 2014 *US, US, Bra, Chl, Ar, HK, Rus, Rus*, 2015 *Par, Bra, USE, Chl, FIJ, FIJ, Geo, Elr, ARG, J, Fj, E*
M Panizza 1990 *Chl, Chl*, 1991 *Par, Chl, Ar, Bra*, 1992 *Chl, Chl*, 1993 *Bra, Par, Chl, Ar*, 1995 *Ar, C, Ar, Sp, Chl, Par, Ar*, 1996 *C, Ar*, 1997 *Chl, Par, Ar*, 1998 *Par, Chl, Ar, C, Ar, US, Chl, Ar*, 1999 *Pt, Pt, Mor, Mor, Fj, Sp, Sp, S, SA*
N Pardo de Iriondo 1964 *Ar, Chl, Bra*, 1967 *Chl, Ar*
A Passadore 1981 *Par, Chl*, 1983 *Par, Ar*, 1985 *F, Ar, Chl*, 1987 *Ar, Sp*, 1988 *Bel*, 1989 *Par, Chl, Ar, US*, 1993 *Bra, Par, Ar*, 1995 *Ar, C*
J Pastore 2003 *Chl, Par, Ar, C, Ar, US, SA, Sa, Geo, E*, 2004 *Ven, Ar, Chl, Geo, Pt*, 2005 *J, Chl, Ar, SA*, 2006 *Chl, Pt, US, US*, 2007 *Pt, Pt, It, Sp, Chl*, 2008 *Ar, R, Geo, Rus, US, US*, 2009 *Bra, Chl, Ar, R, S, Rus, US, US*
M Patino 1979 *Ar, Ar, Bra, Par, Chl*, 1981 *Par, Chl, Ar*, 1983 *Par, Chl, Ar*, 1985 *F, Ar, Par, Chl*, 1987 *Ar*, 1988 *Bel*, 1990 *Chl, Chl*
F Paullier 1989 *Bra, Par, Chl, Ar, US*, 1991 *Ar*, 1992 *Chl, Chl*, 1993 *Bra, Par, Chl, Ar*, 1995 *Sp*, 1996 *Ar, C, Ar*, 1997 *Chl*, 1999 *Pt, Fj, SA*
M Paullier 1987 *Ar, Sp, Ar, Chl, Par*, 1988 *Bel*, 1989 *Bra, Chl, Ar, US*, 1991 *Ar*
M Paullier 1979 *Bra, Par*, 1981 *Bra, Chl*, 1983 *Chl*
JC Paysse 1961 *Bra, Chl, Ar*, 1964 *Ar, Chl, Bra*
J Peirano 1979 *Bra, Par*, 1981 *Bra, Chl*, 1983 *Par*
G Pena 1985 *F, Par*
HC Pepe 1961 *Ar*
H Pepe 1964 *Ar, Chl, Bra*, 1967 *Chl, Ar*
A Pereira 2004 *Ven, Ar, Chl, Geo*, 2005 *Chl, Ar*
M Pereyra 1977 *Par, Ar*
J Pérez 2004 *Ven*
JA Pérez 2001 *Sp, Par, Chl, Chl*, 2002 *C, C, US, Chl*, 2003 *Chl, Par, Ar, C, Ar, SA, Sa, Geo, E*, 2004 *Geo, Pt*, 2005 *J, Chl, Ar, SA*, 2006 *Ar, Chl, Pt, US, US*, 2007 *Pt, Pt*
G Peyrou 2005 *Chl, Ar, SA, Pt*, 2007 *Chl*, 2008 *Ar, R, US*
J Peyrou 1975 *Ar, Chl*
P Pick 1958 *Ar, Chl, Per*
A Pieroni 1985 *Par*, 1988 *Bel*, 1989 *US*
R Pieroni 1987 *Ar*
R Pigurina 1985 *Ar, Par, Chl*, 1987 *Ar, Chl*
P Pineyrua 1979 *Ar*
T Pineyrúa 2004 *Ven*
J Pol 1967 *Chl*
A Pollak 1963 *Bra*, 1964 *Ar, Chl, Bra*, 1967 *Chl, Ar*, 1969 *Ar, Chl*, 1971 *Par, Chl, Bra, Ar*, 1973 *Chl, Bra, Par*
AR Pollak 1967 *Chl, Ar*, 1969 *Ar, Chl*

C Pombo 2014 *US*
A Ponce de Leon 1993 *Bra*, 1995 *Ar, Chl*, 1996 *C, Ar, US*, 1997 *Chl*, 1998 *Ar, C, Ar*, 1999 *Pt, It, Fj, Sp, Sp, S*, 2000 *Nm*, 2001 *Ar, C, US, Sp, Chl*
F Ponte 2000 *Nm*
H Ponte 2002 *Ar, Chl, Chl, C, US, C, Chl*, 2003 *Chl, Par, Ar, Fj, C, Ar, US, SA, Geo*, 2006 *Chl, US, US*, 2007 *Pt*
R Pose 2004 *Geo*, 2005 *Pt*, 2007 *It*
J Prada 2013 *SAP, Geo, Elr, Sp*, 2014 *US, US, Par, Bra, Chl, Ar, R, Elr, Rus, HK, Rus, Rus*, 2015 *Bra, USE, Chl, Ar, FIJ, FIJ, Geo, Elr, Elt, ARG, J, J, W, A, Fj, E*
F Praderi 1973 *Par*, 1976 *NZ*
C Protasi 2005 *Ar, SA, Pt*, 2006 *Pt, US*, 2007 *Pt, It, Sp, Chl*, 2009 *Par, Ar, S, US, US*
H Pugh 1953 *Bra*, 1956 *Chl*, 1960 *F*
A Puig 1951 *Chl, Bra*
G Puig 1981 *Par*, 1983 *Par, Chl, Ar*, 1985 *F*, 1987 *Ar, Sp*, 1989 *Bra, Chl, Ar*, 1991 *Chl, Ar*
G Puig 2014 *Par, Bra, Chl, Ar*, 2015 *Chl, Ar, ARG*

B Ramazzi 1951 *Ar*
S Ramos 2004 *Pt*, 2005 *Chl, Ar, SA*
B Rathbone 1951 *Ar, Chl, Bra*, 1953 *Bra*
C Regules 1958 *Per*
C Reyes 1953 *Bra*, 1961 *Bra*
D Reyes 2002 *C*, 2003 *Par, Ar, Fj, C, E*, 2004 *Ven*
J Reyes 1975 *Bra, Par*
M Reyes 1996 *US*, 1997 *Par, Ar*, 1998 *Par*
A Rial 1951 *Chl, Bra*, 1953 *Bra*
A Rienzi 1973 *Ar, Bra*
JP Rignon 1976 *Ar, NZ*
H Rivera 2007 *Sp*
S Rodino 2008 *Geo, Rus*
C Rodriguez 1997 *Par*, 1998 *Par, Ar, C, Ar, Par*, 1999 *Pt, Fj, Sp*, 2000 *Nm*
O Rodriguez 1958 *Chl*
A Roman 2011 *Par, Bra, Chl, Ar, Pt, Sp*, 2012 *Ar, Bra, R, Rus, Pt, Pt*, 2013 *Ar, Bra, Chl, SAP, Geo, Elr, Sp*, 2014 *Ar, R, Elr, Rus, HK, Rus, Rus*, 2015 *Par, USE, Chl, Ar, FIJ, FIJ, Geo, Elr, Elt, J, A*
N Romay 1981 *Par*, 1983 *Chl, Ar*, 1985 *F, Ar, Par, Chl*, 1988 *Bel*
J Rombys 2008 *Ar, R, Geo, Rus, US*, 2009 *Par, Bra, Chl, R, S, US*, 2010 *Bra, Par, Chl, Ar, C, Rus, Kaz, R, R*, 2011 *Sp*, 2012 *Pt*
JP Ruffalini 2010 *Bra, Par, Chl, Ar, Rus*
H Ruggeroni 1958 *Ar, Per*

M Saavedra 1964 *Ar, Chl, Bra*
G Sabasti 1960 *F*, 1961 *Bra, Ar*
F Sader 1995 *Chl*
B Saenz 1987 *Ar*, 1988 *Bel*, 1991 *Par, Chl*, 2001 *C, US, Chl, Ar*
S Sagario 2013 *Geo*
M Sagario 2006 *Chl*, 2007 *It, Sp, Chl*, 2008 *Ar, R, Geo, Rus, US, Chl*, 2009 *Par, Bra, Chl, Ar, R, S, Rus, US, US*, 2010 *R, R*, 2011 *Sp*, 2012 *Ar, Chl, Bra, R, Rus, Pt, Pt*, 2013 *Ar, Bra, Chl, SAP, Geo, Elr, Sp*, 2014 *US, US*, 2015 *Ar, FIJ, FIJ, Geo, Elr, Elt, ARG, J, J, W, A, Fj, E*
J Sagarra 1956 *Chl*, 1958 *Ar, Chl*
Salustio 1985 *F*
A Sanabria 1998 *Ar, Ar*, 2001 *Ar*
R Sanchez 2000 *Nm*
R Sanchez 1996 *Ar*, 1997 *Par, Ar*, 1998 *Par, Chl, C, US, Chl, Par, Ar*, 1999 *Pt, Pt, Mor, Mor, It, Sp, Sp, S, SA*, 2000 *Nm, Chl, Ar*, 2001 *Ar, Ar, C, US, It, Sp, Chl, Chl*, 2002 *Ar, Chl, Chl, C, US, C, US, Chl*, 2003 *Fj, C, SA, Sa, Geo, E*, 2005 *J*, 2006 *Ar, Chl, Pt, US, US*, 2007 *Pt, Pt, It, Sp, Chl*, 2008 *R, Geo, Rus, US, Chl*, 2009 *Chl, Ar, R, S, Rus, US, US*
M Sanguinetti 2014 *Par, Bra, R, Elr*, 2015 *Par, Bra, USE, Chl, Ar, FIJ, Geo, Elr, Elt, J, W, A, Fj, E*
JC Sartori 1969 *Ar, Chl*
R Sayagues 1971 *Par*
JC Scasso 1971 *Chl, Bra, Ar*, 1973 *Chl, Ar, Bra*
JC Scasso 1969 *Ar, Chl*
F Sciarra 1990 *Chl, Chl*, 1991 *Par, Chl, Ar, Bra*, 1992 *Chl*, 1993 *Bra, Par, Chl, Ar*, 1995 *C, Ar, Sp, Chl, Par, Ar*, 1996

Ar, C, Ar, US, 1997 Chl, Par, Ar, 1998 Par, Chl, Ar, C, US, Chl, Par, Ar, 1999 Pt, Pt, Mor, Mor, It, Sp, Sp, S
M Sciarra 2010 Ar
G Sebasti 1961 Chl
D Segdeefield 1964 Ar, Chl, Bra
JL Shaw 1960 F, 1963 Bra
M Shaw 1990 Chl, Chl
R Sierra 2001 Par, Chl, Chl, 2002 Chl, Par
CA Sierra 1951 Ar, Chl, Bra
F Silva 1985 Ar, Par, Chl, 1987 Ar, Chl, Par
G Silva 2000 Ar
R Silva 1987 Ar
S Silva 1992 Chl, 1993 Bra, 1995 Par, 1996 C, Ar
R Silva 2012 Pt, 2014 Par, Bra, Chl, Ar, Elr, Rus, 2015 Bra, USE, Chl, Ar, FIJ, FIJ, ARG, W, A, Fj, E
A Silveira 2009 Par, Bra, Chl, Ar, R, S, Rus, US, US
D Silveira 2004 Ar, Geo, Pt, 2005 J, Chl, Ar, SA
A Silveyra 1987 Ar, 1989 Par, Chl, 1990 Chl, 1991 Par, Chl, Ar, Bra, 1992 Chl
R Skerl 1956 Chl
M Smith 1971 Par, Chl, Bra, Ar, 1973 Chl, Ar, Bra, 1975 Bra, Chl, Par, 1976 Ar, NZ, 1977 Chl, Ar, Bra, 1979 Ar, Ar, Bra, Chl, 1981 Par, Bra, Chl
C Soares De Lima 2011 Par, Bra, Chl, Ar, 2012 Chl, Bra, R, Pt, Pt, 2013 Ar, Bra, Chl, 2014 US, US, Par, Bra, Ar, R, Elr, Rus, HK
U Sokolovich 2001 Ar
A Sommer 1985 F, Ar, Par, Chl, 1987 Ar, Sp, Ar, Chl, Par, 1988 Bel, 1989 Par, Chl, Ar
F Sosa Diaz 1993 Chl, 1997 Chl, Ar, 1999 Fj, SA, 2001 Sp
A Soto 1963 Bra, 1964 Ar, Chl, Bra
PP Stanhan 1956 Chl, 1961 Bra, Chl, Ar
H Stein 1967 Chl, Ar, 1975 Ar
JE Stein 1969 Chl, 1973 Ar, Par
JE Stein 1953 Bra, 1956 Chl
A Stewart 1961 Chl
G Storace 1996 Ar, 1997 Chl, 1998 Par, C, Ar, Chl, Par, Ar, 1999 Pt, Pt, Mor, Mor, Fj, Sp, Sp, S, SA, 2001 Ar, C, US, Sp, Par, Chl, Chl, 2002 C, US, Chl, 2003 Chl, Par, Ar, Ar, SA, Geo, E, 2004 Ar, Chl, Geo, Pt, 2005 SA, 2006 Ar, Chl, Pt, US, US, 2007 Pt
A Suarez 1993 Bra, 1996 Ar, C, Ar, US, 1997 Chl, Par, Ar, 1998 Par, Chl, Ar, Chl, Par, Ar
A Suarez 2003 Par
D Suarez 1993 Chl, 1997 Par, Ar, 1998 Par, Chl
E Suarez 1971 Chl, Ar
A Summers 1967 Chl, Ar
Szabo 2007 It

JI Tabarez 2010 R, 2011 Pt
J Tassistro 2013 SAP, Geo, Elr
A Tato 1969 Ar, Chl, 1973 Ar
A Terra 1987 Ar, 1992 Chl, Chl, 1993 Bra, Ar, 1995 Ar, Ar, Par
S Terra 1985 F, Ar, Par, Chl, 1987 Chl, Par
J Trigo 1958 Per
D Turcatti 1969 Chl

JM Ubilla 1976 Ar, NZ, 1977 Ar
RE Ubilla 1979 Ar, Bra, Par, Chl, 1981 Par, Chl, 1983 Par, Chl, Ar, 1985 F, 1987 Ar, 1988 Bel, 1989 Bra, Par, Chl, Ar, US, 1991 Par, Chl, Ar

M Uria 1976 Ar
M Uriarte 1983 Ar, 1985 F, Ar, Par, Chl
C Uriate 1983 Par
A Urrestara 2001 C, It

C Vaccaro 1979 Ar, Bra, Par, Chl
D van Rompaey 1976 Ar
J Varela 1976 NZ
A Vazquez 2001 Ar
A Vázquez 2007 Chl
L Vazquez 1960 F
P Vecino 1990 Chl, Chl, 1991 Bra, 1992 Chl, Chl, 1993 Bra, Par, Chl, Ar, 1995 Ar, C, Ar, Sp, Chl, Par, Ar, 1996 Ar, Ar, US, 1997 Chl, Par, Ar, 1998 Par, Chl, C, US, Chl, Par, Ar, 1999 Pt, Pt, Mor, Mor, It, Sp, Sp, S, SA, 2000 Chl, Ar, 2001 Ar, Ar, C, US, It, Sp, Chl, Chl, 2002 Chl, 2003 Chl, Ar
T Vecino 2001 Par, Chl
F Vecino 2011 Pt, Sp, 2012 Chl, Pt, 2014 Par, Chl, Ar
H Vega 1958 Ar, Per
F Vejo 1969 Chl
JM Viacava 1990 Chl, Chl, 1991 Ar, 1992 Chl, Chl, 1993 Bra, Par
D Viana 1977 Par, Chl, Bra
J Viana 1997 Chl, Par, 1998 Ar, 1999 Fj, Sp, S, SA, 2000 Chl, 2002 Chl, US, 2003 Ar, US, Sa, E
E Viera 1975 Ar, Bra, Chl, Par, 1977 Par, Chl, Ar, Bra, 1979 Ar, Ar, Par, Chl
P Viglietti 1989 Par, US, 1990 Chl, Chl, 1992 Chl, 1993 Par, Chl, Ar
F Vilaboa 2002 Ar, Par
A Vilaseca 2013 Ar, Bra, Chl, Sp, 2014 US, US, 2015 FIJ, Elr, Elt, ARG, J, J, W, A, Fj, E
S Vilaseca 2008 Ar, US, 2010 R, R, 2011 Pt, Sp, 2012 Ar, Chl, Bra, Pt, 2013 Ar, Bra, Chl, Sp, 2014 US, US, Chl, Ar, HK, Rus, Rus, 2015 Par, Bra, USE, Chl, Ar, FIJ, FIJ, Geo, Elt, Elt, J, J, W, A, Fj, E
P Villa 1987 Par
F Villaboa 2005 Pt
A Villamil 1977 Ar
A Vivo 1973 Chl, Ar, Bra, Par, 1976 Ar, 1977 Par, Bra
R Vivo 1958 Ar, Chl, Per, 1960 F
A Vizintin 1975 Ar, Bra, Chl, Par, 1977 Par, Chl, Ar, Bra, 1981 Par, Bra, Chl
G Voituret 2006 Ar, Chl

R Wenzel 1973 Chl, Bra, Par
C Widemann 1976 NZ

J Yorston 1964 Ar, Chl, Bra

G Zamandrea 2001 Ar
G Zerbino 1973 Chl, Ar, Par, 1977 Par, Bra
J Zerbino 1973 Chl, Bra, Par, 1975 Ar, Bra, Chl, Par, 1976 NZ, 1977 Par, Chl, Ar, Bra, 1979 Ar, Ar, Bra, Par, Chl, 1981 Par, Bra, Chl, 1983 Par, Chl, Ar, 1985 Ar, Par, Chl
J Zerbino 2015 Par, Bra, USE, Chl, Ar, FIJ, FIJ, Geo, Elt, J, J, W, Fj, E
R Zerbino 1975 Bra, Chl, Par, 1976 Ar, NZ, 1977 Chl, Ar, Bra, 1979 Ar, Bra, Chl, 1985 Par
S Zumaran 1992 Chl

USA

USA'S 2014–15 TEST RECORD

OPPONENT	DATE	VENUE	RESULT
New Zealand	1 Nov	H	Lost 6–74
Romania	8 Nov	A	Won 27–17
Tonga	15 Nov	N	Lost 40–12
Fiji	21 Nov	N	Lost 20–14
Samoa	18 Jul	H	Lost 16–21
Japan	24 Jul	H	Won 23–18
Tonga	29 Jul	N	Lost 33–19
Canada	3 Aug	A	Won 15–13
Canada	22 Aug	A	Won 41–23
Australia	5 Sep	H	Lost 10–47
Samoa	20 Sep	N	Lost 25–16
Scotland	27 Sep	N	Lost 39–16
South Africa	7 Oct	N	Lost 64–0
Japan	11 Oct	N	Lost 28–18

EAGLES PAY THE PRICE FOR LAPSES IN DISCIPLINE

By Ian Gilbert

USA's captain Chris Wyles leads by example, scoring a well-worked try against Samoa at the Brighton Community Stadium.

When the draw was made for Rugby World Cup 2015, the USA found themselves grouped with Japan, a side that, like the Eagles, had struggled to make consistent progress.

This was to prove the year one of them finally realised their potential with results that would send shockwaves through the sport but, unfortunately for the USA, it wasn't them.

Before the tournament, the Eagles would have fancied their chances of accounting for the Brave Blossoms, who had previously won only a single World Cup match, particularly after beating Japan in the World Rugby Pacific Nations Cup in July.

But the final game of the pool stages typified how the countries' fortunes contrasted as Japan ran out 28–18 winners.

This meant the USA closed their RWC 2015 account with a fourth defeat in an admittedly tough Pool B that also featured South Africa, Scotland and Samoa.

Given that Japan's advance has coincided with the continued strength of the lucrative Top League, it adds support to the belief that the way forward for the Americans is a professional league and in November it was revealed that a six-team PRO Rugby competition would begin in April 2016.

The Eagles' form was reasonably solid prior to the tournament, with a won four, lost five record since defeat by the All Blacks in November 2014. One of those reverses was against Australia and two others were by less than a score.

The USA faced Samoa first up and although they showed they could match higher-ranked sides for physicality, discipline was another matter as they went down 25–16 at the Brighton Community Stadium on 20 September.

The penalty count against the Eagles reached 11 – five in the first 20 minutes – to Samoa's four, a tally that handed them 15 points from kicks.

USA second-row Greg Peterson was painfully aware of where the match was won and lost. "Samoa kept moving us back into our 22," he said. "We need to control our penalty count and control our discipline, and then we'll do much better."

In their next match, a 39–16 defeat by Scotland in Leeds, the USA inadvertently did their opponents a favour, giving them a tough hit-out ahead of matches against South Africa and Samoa.

The Eagles took the game to the higher-ranked Scots, going into the break 13–6 ahead, but the eventual quarter-finalists ran in five tries for a bonus-point victory.

"Japan were physical as well but these guys were bigger, very hard-hitting and came off the line with speed," Scotland coach Vern Cotter admitted afterwards. "It took time to adapt to them. South Africa are physical, probably even more so, Samoa the same, and we knew this was going to be the kind of rugby we would face in this pool."

Peterson acknowledged the Eagles wanted to impose their physicality. "We came out wanting to bash Scotland as much as we could," he said. "We knew they had a short turnaround between matches so we were looking to come out of the blocks quickly and I thought we did that well. We just couldn't manage to keep it up in the second half."

Captain Chris Wyles was phlegmatic about the result. "In the second half they [Scotland] took hold and won it very comfortably so I don't think it was harsh. Our discipline let us down and we simply were not good enough in the second half."

The Eagles had 10 days to prepare for their third match, against South Africa at The Stadium, Queen Elizabeth Olympic Park. Coach

USA

Mike Tolkin elected to rest several players in anticipation of the Japan encounter and the Springboks, with Bryan Habana to the fore, capitalised ruthlessly with a 64–0 victory.

Eagles scrum-half Niku Kruger could have been forgiven for feeling divided loyalties in his first test start, having been born and raised in South Africa, but afterwards he explained how coach Tolkin had fired up the side to face the Springboks.

"He just spoke about what we have done," he said. "In the last year we have played the All Blacks, we have played Australia, we led at half-time against Scotland."

Habana's hat-trick against the Eagles brought him level with All Black wing Jonah Lomu's record of 15 Rugby World Cup tries in what was the most one-sided victory at the tournament.

And so to Japan, a side the USA had beaten on home soil in the World Rugby Pacific Nations Cup in July and who, pre-tournament, sat only two places higher in the rankings at 13.

But after their exploits against South Africa and Samoa, the Japanese were clear favourites and so it proved, consigning USA to a winless tournament as they became the first to win three matches but fail to make the quarter-finals. The Eagles scored tries through Takudzwa Ngwenya and Wyles but it was not enough to finish on a winning note.

Rugby World Cup disappointment aside, the season was a special one for the Eagles as it began with the historic visit of world champions New Zealand to Chicago's Soldier Field in November.

While the Eagles were convincingly beaten 74–6, it was a success in so far as it drew a crowd of 61,500 and provided the high-quality opposition the USA must face to prosper.

Tolkin alluded to as much after the Scotland match, when his mix of professional and amateur players were eclipsed by the full-timers of the Scotland team. The coach lamented the gulf between his side and those comprising entirely professional players.

"A lot of these guys don't play the grind of a professional season with a hard game week in, week out, so for some of our guys it's a real challenge and it's something that we have got to overcome," he said.

On the domestic front, New York Athletic Club won the Division 1 title, coming from behind to beat Austin Blacks 44–39 in the final couple of minutes in Glendale, Colorado. In the women's competition, Seattle Saracens beat Beantown Rugby 31–24 in a game of great attacking rugby.

USA INTERNATIONAL STATISTICS

MATCH RECORDS UP TO 1 NOVEMBER, 2015

WINNING MARGIN

Date	Opponent	Result	Winning Margin
01/07/2006	Barbados	91–0	91
06/07/1996	Japan	74–5	69
07/11/1989	Uruguay	60–3	57
12/03/1994	Bermuda	60–3	57
08/04/1998	Portugal	61–5	56

MOST POINTS IN A MATCH
BY THE TEAM

Date	Opponent	Result	Points
01/07/2006	Barbados	91–0	91
06/07/1996	Japan	74–5	74
17/05/2003	Japan	69–27	69
12/04/2003	Spain	62–13	62
08/04/1998	Portugal	61–5	61

BY A PLAYER

Date	Player	Opponent	Points
07/11/1989	Chris O'Brien	Uruguay	26
31/05/2004	Mike Hercus	Russia	26
01/07/2006	Mike Hercus	Barbados	26
12/03/1994	Chris O'Brien	Bermuda	25
06/07/1996	Matt Alexander	Japan	24

MOST TRIES IN A MATCH
BY THE TEAM

Date	Opponent	Result	Tries
01/07/2006	Barbados	91–0	13
07/11/1989	Uruguay	60–3	11
06/07/1996	Japan	74–5	11
17/05/2003	Japan	69–27	11
9 on 5 occasions			

BY A PLAYER

Date	Player	Opponent	Tries
11/05/1924	Dick Hyland	Romania	5
11/05/1924	John Patrick	Romania	4
06/07/1996	Vaea Anitoni	Japan	4
07/06/1997	Brian Hightower	Japan	4
08/04/1998	Vaea Anitoni	Portugal	4

MOST CONVERSIONS IN A MATCH
BY THE TEAM

Date	Opponent	Result	Cons
01/07/2006	Barbados	91–0	13
07/11/1989	Uruguay	60–3	8
06/07/1996	Japan	74–5	8
17/05/2003	Japan	69–27	7
6 on 2 occasions			

BY A PLAYER

Date	Player	Opponent	Cons
01/07/2006	Mike Hercus	Barbados	13
06/07/1996	Matt Alexander	Japan	8
07/11/1989	Chris O'Brien	Uruguay	7
17/05/2003	Mike Hercus	Japan	7

MOST PENALTIES IN A MATCH
BY THE TEAM

Date	Opponent	Result	Pens
18/09/1996	Canada	18–23	6
24/07/2015	Japan	23–18	6
5 on 5 occasions			

BY A PLAYER

Date	Player	Opponent	Pens
18/09/1996	Matt Alexander	Canada	6
24/07/2015	AJ MacGinty	Japan	6
5 on 5 occasions			

MOST DROP GOALS IN A MATCH
BY THE TEAM

Date	Opponent	Result	DGs
27/11/2010	Georgia	17–19	2

BY A PLAYER

1 on 20 Occasions

USA

MOST CAPPED PLAYERS

Name	Caps
Mike MacDonald	67
Todd Clever	63
Luke Gross	62
Alec Parker	57
Mike Petri	57

LEADING PENALTY SCORERS

Name	Pens
Mike Hercus	76
Matt Alexander	55
Mark Williams	35
Chris Wyles	31
AJ MacGinty	23

LEADING TRY SCORERS

Name	Tries
Vaea Anitoni	26
Paul Emerick	17
Chris Wyles	16
Takudzwa Ngwenya	13
Todd Clever	11

LEADING DROP GOAL SCORERS

Name	DGs
Mike Hercus	4

LEADING POINTS SCORERS

Name	Points
Mike Hercus	465
Matt Alexander	286
Chris Wyles	222
Chris O'Brien	144
Mark Williams	143

LEADING CONVERSIONS SCORERS

Name	Cons
Mike Hercus	90
Matt Alexander	45
Chris O'Brien	24
Chris Wyles	23
Nese Malifa	17

USA INTERNATIONAL PLAYERS
UP TO 1 NOVEMBER, 2015

M Alexander 1995 *C*, 1996 *I, C, HK, J, HK, J, Ar, C, Ur*, 1997 *W, C, HK, J, J, HK, C, W, W*, 1998 *Pt, Sp, J, HK, C*

AE Allen 1912 *A*

S Allen 1996 *J*, 1997 *HK, J, J, C, W, W*

T Altemeier 1978 *C*

D Anderson 2002 *S*

B Andrews 1978 *C*, 1979 *C*

VN Anitoni 1992 *C*, 1994 *C, Ar, Ar, I*, 1995 *C*, 1996 *I, C, C, HK, J, HK, J, Ar, C, Ur*, 1997 *W, C, J, HK, C, W, W*, 1998 *Pt, Sp, J, HK, C, C, J, HK, Fj, Ar, C, Ur*, 1999 *Tg, Fj, J, C, Sa, E, I, R, A*, 2000 *Fj, Sa*

J Arrell 1912 *A*

D Asbun 2012 *Geo, It, Tg, R*, 2013 *C, Geo, Rus*

S Auerbach 1976 *A*

CA Austin 1912 *A*, 1913 *NZ*

M Aylor 2006 *IrA, M, C, Bar, Ur, Ur*, 2007 *S, C, Sa, SA*, 2008 *IrA*

A Bachelet 1993 *C, A*, 1994 *Ber, C, Ar, Ar, I*, 1995 *C*, 1996 *I, C, C, HK, J, HK, J, Ar, C*, 1997 *W, C, HK, J, J, HK, C, W, W*, 1998 *Pt, Sp, J, HK, C, C, J*

R Bailey 1979 *C*, 1980 *NZ*, 1981 *C, SA*, 1982 *C*, 1983 *C, A*, 1987 *Tun, C, J, E*

B Barnard 2006 *IrA, M, Bar, C*

D Barrett 2014 *S, J, C, NZ*, 2015 *Sa, J, C, C, A, Sa, S, SA, J*

JI Basauri Flores 2007 *S, E, Tg*, 2008 *Ur, J, J*, 2010 *Pt, Geo*, 2011 *Tg, Rus, C, A*, 2012 *Rus, Tg, R*

D Bateman 1982 *C, E*, 1983 *A*, 1985 *J, C*

C Baumann 2015 *Tg, C, C, A, Sa, S, SA*

P Bell 2006 *IrA, M, C, Bar, C, Ur, Ur*

W Bernhard 1987 *Tun*

CM Biller 2009 *I, W, Geo, C, C*, 2010 *Rus, Pt, Geo*, 2011 *Tg,* *Rus, C, C, J, I, Rus, It*, 2012 *C, Geo, It, Rus, Tg, R*, 2013 *I, Tg, Fj, J, C, C*

TW Billups 1993 *C, A*, 1994 *Ber, C, Ar, Ar, I*, 1995 *C*, 1996 *I, C, C, HK, HK, J, Ar, C, Ur*, 1997 *W, C, HK, HK, W, W*, 1998 *Pt, Sp, J, HK, Fj, Ar, C, Ur*, 1999 *Tg, Fj, J, C, Sa, E, I, R, A*

RR Blasé 1913 *NZ*

A Blom 1998 *Sp, J, HK, C, C, HK, Fj, Ar, Ur*, 1999 *Sa*, 2000 *J, C, I*

H Bloomfield 2007 *E, Tg, SA*, 2008 *E, C*

R Bordley 1976 *A, F*, 1977 *C, E*, 1978 *C*

J Boyd 2008 *IrA*, 2009 *I*

S Bracken 1994 *Ar*, 1995 *C*

G Brackett 1976 *A, F*, 1977 *E*

N Brendel 1983 *A*, 1984 *C*, 1985 *J, C*, 1987 *Tun, E*

D Briley 1979 *C*, 1980 *W, C, NZ*

J Buchholz 2001 *C*, 2002 *S*, 2003 *Sp, EngA, Ar, Fj, J, F*, 2004 *C*

B Burdette 2006 *Ur, Ur*, 2007 *E, S, C, E, Tg, Sa, SA*

JR Burke 1990 *C, J*, 1991 *J, J, S, C, F, NZ*, 1992 *C*

J Burke 2000 *C, I*

J Burkhardt 1983 *C*, 1985 *C*

E Burlingham 1980 *NZ*, 1981 *C, SA*, 1982 *C, E*, 1983 *C, A*, 1984 *C*, 1985 *C*, 1986 *J*, 1987 *Tun, C, J, E*

C Campbell 1993 *C, A*, 1994 *Ber, C, Ar*

D Care 1998 *Pt, J, C*

M Carlson 1987 *W, C*

DB Carroll 1913 *NZ*, 1920 *F, F*

L Cass 1913 *NZ*

M Caulder 1984 *C*, 1985 *C*, 1989 *C*

R Causey 1977 *C*, 1981 *C, SA*, 1982 *C, E*, 1984 *C*, 1986 *J*, 1987 *E*

WALES

WALES' 2014–15 TEST RECORD

OPPONENTS	DATE	VENUE	RESULT
Australia	8 Nov	H	Lost 28–33
Fiji	15 Nov	H	Won 17–13
New Zealand	22 Nov	H	Lost 16–34
South Africa	29 Nov	H	Won 12–6
England	6 Feb	H	Lost 16–21
Scotland	15 Feb	A	Won 26–23
France	28 Feb	A	Won 20–13
Ireland	14 Mar	H	Won 23–16
Italy	21 Mar	A	Won 61–20
Ireland	8 Aug	H	Lost 21–35
Ireland	29 Aug	A	Won 16–10
Italy	5 Sep	H	Won 23–19
Uruguay	20 Sep	H	Won 54–9
England	26 Sep	N	Won 28–25
Fiji	1 Oct	H	Won 23–13
Australia	10 Oct	N	Lost 15–6
South Africa	17 Oct	N	Lost 24–15

GATLAND THE MAN TO TAKE WALES FORWARD

By Martyn Williams

Wales completed a famous 28–25 victory over rivals England, with Gareth Davies scoring the decisive try at Twickenham.

It was a marathon rather than a sprint for Wales with 17 test matches in 12 physically demanding months, and although there was no RBS 6 Nations trophy for Warren Gatland's side and no second successive appearance in a Rugby World Cup semi-final at the end of it all, I would still have to say on balance it was a successful year.

A poor second half against England in Cardiff ultimately cost Wales the chance of a Grand Slam in the Six Nations while an appalling catalogue of injuries meant the quarter-final against the Springboks at the World Cup was a game too far, but for me those disappointments don't overshadow the tangible steps forward the team did make.

It wasn't a year which justified wild celebrations at the end of it but 11 victories in those 17 tests, including the scalps of South Africa, England and Ireland, was a significant improvement on what had gone before in the previous 12 months and with a young squad and a new political landscape in Welsh rugby, I'm optimistic about the future.

The long build-up to the World Cup began with the autumn internationals and Wales' narrow 33–28 defeat to Australia in the opening fixture had a depressing sense of déjà vu about it. The team's inability to get over the line against southern hemisphere opposition is well documented and a 10th loss on the bounce to the Wallabies did nothing to dispel their reputation for repeatedly coming up short.

You could sense Gatland's sheer frustration a fortnight later after the team were beaten 34–16 by the All Blacks and he took exception to questions put to him by the BBC about a 22nd straight loss to a SANZAR side. Gatland is usually a measured kind of guy and his tetchiness was symptomatic of his impatience to get the monkey off Wales' back.

A week later his side did just that with a bruising 12–6 win over South Africa in the Millennium Stadium. It wasn't pretty, it wasn't a full-strength Springbok side because the game fell outside the window, and there were no tries, but Gatland didn't care. He'd finally got his southern hemisphere scalp and although it was Leigh Halfpenny who kicked the crucial points, the win owed much to an awesome display from Dan Biggar at 10.

A Six Nations immediately before the World Cup is a strange animal but had it not been for a below-par performance after half-time against England, Wales could have claimed a Grand Slam. Hindsight is obviously a wonderful thing but after going down 21–16 to the English, the way Wales regrouped to string together four consecutive victories was impressive.

A lot of people would pick out the win over the champions Ireland in Cardiff as a highlight but for me it was the second half against Italy in Rome on the final weekend that stood out. To score seven tries after the break en route to a 61–20 victory was the best attacking display I've seen from a Wales side in 10 years and was an incredible way to finish the Championship.

I really thought they'd done enough to claim the title with that result but they were ultimately leapfrogged by Ireland and England in the table on points difference. It's been clear for the last couple of years that there's precious little to separate Wales, Ireland and England and the fact there was a spread of only 10 points between them in 2015 only underlines the parity. It's all about tiny margins and had Wales not fallen off the pace in the second half against England, Ireland made a slow start in Cardiff or the English an equally sluggish start in Dublin, any one of the three could have very conceivably completed a clean sweep.

The headline news for Wales in the build-up to Rugby World Cup 2015 was the injuries to Jonathan Davies and then Leigh Halfpenny and Rhys Webb, and with England and Australia lying in wait in Pool A it's fair to say the Principality looked ahead to the tournament with a mixture of anxiety and anticipation. The injuries kept coming as the competition unfolded and with the boys having to step up and play England, Fiji, Australia and South Africa in the space of three weeks, I think it was a pretty heroic effort to get as far as they did.

Wales were hanging on by a thread against the English at Twickenham but a brilliant display of kicking from Biggar with seven penalties from seven attempts and a moment of magic from Lloyd Williams to set up the try for Gareth Davies were enough to secure a famous 28–25 win which ultimately sent Wales through to the quarters and condemned England to an early exit.

Five days later the team faced the Fijians at the Millennium Stadium and thankfully there was no repeat of the shock defeat they suffered at Rugby World Cup 2007 as they wrapped up a 23–13 win. Speaking to the Wales boys after the tournament, they were adamant the Fiji game was the most physically intense and draining they experienced in the whole tournament.

The last game in the pool was the 15–6 loss to the Wallabies and while some were disappointed because Australia were down to 13 men at one stage, I was actually relieved because I feared the England and Fiji games and the ridiculous injury list had already taken their toll – I was worried Wales would get a thumping.

I think those factors finally did catch up with the team in the last eight against South Africa. It was another hugely committed display full of heart and passion but the physical power and aggression of the Springboks was too much for Gatland's team and they just didn't have enough gas left in the tank when it mattered.

I'd argue Wales' performances at the World Cup summed up the state of northern hemisphere rugby. The fact no European team made the semi-finals was pretty sobering and although Wales and Scotland went close, the World Cup for me highlighted the gap between the north and south.

The All Blacks and the Wallabies proved you've got to score tries in the modern game to be successful. At the highest level you can no longer hope to get by simply scratching out results with penalties and the odd try here or there and it will be interesting to see how all the European sides react. There's nothing between north and south physically or in terms of commitment but if we are being honest, you'd have to say our players lack the 'X factor' the stars of the southern hemisphere bring to test rugby.

After Wales were knocked out of the World Cup, there was speculation about the future of Warren Gatland and there were even whispers about England trying to poach him, but I don't think Wales fans need worry. His contract runs until the end of Rugby World Cup 2019 and

I suspect he still has a sense of unfinished business with Wales. The bulk of his leading players have at least four more years in the legs and I'd be surprised if he didn't stick around.

The other big factor likely to persuade Gatland to stay is the signing of the Rugby Services Agreement between the WRU and the four regions in late 2014. I wrote last year that I feared all the political disputes in Wales were having a negative impact on the national side, so like everyone else I was relieved when peace officially broke out in August.

It's not a perfect solution to all the problems it seeks to address, though. The regions will obviously welcome the extra cash from the WRU which was part of the deal, and having only six non-qualified players in each squad will give Gatland a greater pool of players to choose from. I also like the concept of players on dual contracts with the WRU and their region and I think you only need to look at how successfully Sam Warburton's workload was managed by Wales and the Blues in 2015 to see the benefits of that particular set-up.

The agreement however makes it harder for the regions to compete in Europe now they are only allowed six imports. The likes of Toulon and Toulouse strengthen every year with world-class recruits and without that kind of freedom, the regions will not be able to keep pace. There is also an argument that attracting big names to Wales will accelerate the development of young Welsh players, which in turn strengthens the national team.

The other interesting element of the Rugby Services Agreement was the formalisation of 'Gatland's Law', the rule designed to stem the flow of talent to France and England which states players have to be plying their trade in Wales to be picked for the national side. Gatland has two 'wild cards' – two exceptions to the rule – but I think the WRU should probably have given him more flexibility and the scope to exempt more players. Australia drastically changed their selection criteria to ensure they could put the likes of Matt Giteau and Drew Mitchell into their World Cup squad and I don't think Wales have the resources to potentially rule anyone out of contention.

There's also part of me that's uneasy about the possibility of making a player choose between representing Wales and the chance to experience rugby in a different country. I accept the WRU needs to encourage as many of our top players to stay in Wales but the chance to be part of a different rugby culture doesn't come around every day and, after all, Cardiff really isn't that far away from London or Paris these days.

That said, the Rugby Services Agreement was absolutely a step in the right direction and like many others, I look forward to a prolonged period when everyone in Wales is only talking about the rugby rather than politics and finances.

WALES

WALES INTERNATIONAL STATISTICS

MATCH RECORDS UP TO 1 NOVEMBER, 2015

MOST CONSECUTIVE TESTS WITHOUT DEFEAT

Matches	Wins	Draws	Period
11	11	0	1907 to 1910
10	10	0	1999 to 1999
8	8	0	1970 to 1972
8	8	0	2004 to 2005

MOST CONSECUTIVE TEST WINS

11	1907 I, 1908 E, S, F, I, A, 1909 E, S, F, I, 1910 F
10	1999 F1, It, E, Arg 1, 2, SA, C, F2, Arg 3, J
8	1970 F, 1971 E, S, I, F, 1972 E, S, F
8	2004 J, 2005 E, It, F, S, I, US, C

MOST POINTS IN A MATCH

BY THE TEAM

Pts	Opponents	Venue	Year
102	Portugal	Lisbon	1994
98	Japan	Cardiff	2004
81	Romania	Cardiff	2001
81	Namibia	New Plymouth	2011
77	USA	Hartford	2005
72	Japan	Cardiff	2007
70	Romania	Wrexham	1997
66	Romania	Cardiff	2004
66	Fiji	Hamilton	2011
64	Japan	Cardiff	1999
64	Japan	Osaka	2001

BY A PLAYER

Pts	Player	Opponents	Venue	Year
30	NR Jenkins	Italy	Treviso	1999
29	NR Jenkins	France	Cardiff	1999
28	NR Jenkins	Canada	Cardiff	1999
28	NR Jenkins	France	Paris	2001
28	GL Henson	Japan	Cardiff	2004
27	NR Jenkins	Italy	Cardiff	2000
27	C Sweeney	USA	Hartford	2005
26	SM Jones	Romania	Cardiff	2001
24	NR Jenkins	Canada	Cardiff	1993
24	NR Jenkins	Italy	Cardiff	1994
24	GL Henson	Romania	Wrexham	2003

MOST TRIES IN A MATCH

BY THE TEAM

Tries	Opponents	Venue	Year
16	Portugal	Lisbon	1994
14	Japan	Cardiff	2004
12	Namibia	New Plymouth	2011
11	France	Paris	1909
11	Romania	Wrexham	1997
11	Romania	Cardiff	2001
11	USA	Hartford	2005
11	Japan	Cardiff	2007
10	France	Swansea	1910
10	Japan	Osaka	2001
10	Romania	Cardiff	2004

BY A PLAYER

Tries	Player	Opponents	Venue	Year
4	W Llewellyn	England	Swansea	1899
4	RA Gibbs	France	Cardiff	1908
4	MCR Richards	England	Cardiff	1969
4	IC Evans	Canada	Invercargill	1987
4	N Walker	Portugal	Lisbon	1994
4	G Thomas	Italy	Treviso	1999
4	SM Williams	Japan	Osaka	2001
4	TGL Shanklin	Romania	Cardiff	2004
4	CL Charvis	Japan	Cardiff	2004

MOST CONVERSIONS IN A MATCH
BY THE TEAM

Cons	Opponents	Venue	Year
14	Japan	Cardiff	2004
11	Portugal	Lisbon	1994
11	U S A	Hartford	2005
10	Romania	Cardiff	2001
9	Namibia	New Plymouth	2011
9	Fiji	Hamilton	2011
8	France	Swansea	1910
8	Japan	Cardiff	1999
8	Romania	Cardiff	2004
8	Canada	Cardiff	2006

BY A PLAYER

Cons	Player	Opponents	Venue	Year
14	GL Henson	Japan	Cardiff	2004
11	NR Jenkins	Portugal	Lisbon	1994
11	C Sweeney	USA	Hartford	2005
10	SM Jones	Romania	Cardiff	2001
8	J Bancroft	France	Swansea	1910
8	NR Jenkins	Japan	Cardiff	1999
8	J Hook	Canada	Cardiff	2006
7	SM Jones	Japan	Osaka	2001
7	SM Jones	Romania	Cardiff	2004
7	R Priestland	Uruguay	Cardiff	2015

MOST DROP GOALS IN A MATCH
BY THE TEAM

Drops	Opponents	Venue	Year
3	Scotland	Murrayfield	2001
2	Scotland	Swansea	1912
2	Scotland	Cardiff	1914
2	England	Swansea	1920
2	Scotland	Swansea	1921
2	France	Paris	1930
2	England	Cardiff	1971
2	France	Cardiff	1978
2	England	Twickenham	1984
2	Ireland	Wellington	1987
2	Scotland	Cardiff	1988
2	France	Paris	2001
2	South Africa	Durban	2014

BY A PLAYER

Drops	Player	Opponents	Venue	Year
3	NR Jenkins	Scotland	Murrayfield	2001
2	J Shea	England	Swansea	1920
2	A Jenkins	Scotland	Swansea	1921
2	B John	England	Cardiff	1971
2	M Dacey	England	Twickenham	1984
2	J Davies	Ireland	Wellington	1987
2	J Davies	Scotland	Cardiff	1988
2	NR Jenkins	France	Paris	2001

MOST PENALTIES IN A MATCH
BY THE TEAM

Penalties	Opponents	Venue	Year
9	France	Cardiff	1999
8	Canada	Cardiff	1993
7	Italy	Cardiff	1994
7	Canada	Cardiff	1999
7	Italy	Cardiff	2000
7	Scotland	Murrayfield	2013
7	England	Twickenham	2015
6	France	Cardiff	1982
6	Tonga	Nuku'alofa	1994
6	England	Wembley	1999
6	Canada	Cardiff	2002
6	England	Cardiff	2009
6	Canada	Toronto	2009
6	New Zealand	Cardiff	2010
6	England	Twickenham	2014
6	Italy	Cardiff	2015

BY A PLAYER

Pens	Player	Opponents	Venue	Year
9	NR Jenkins	France	Cardiff	1999
8	NR Jenkins	Canada	Cardiff	1993
7	NR Jenkins	Italy	Cardiff	1994
7	NR Jenkins	Canada	Cardiff	1999
7	NR Jenkins	Italy	Cardiff	2000
7	SL Halfpenny	Scotland	Murrayfield	2013
7	DR Biggar	England	Twickenham	2015
6	G Evans	France	Cardiff	1982
6	NR Jenkins	Tonga	Nuku'alofa	1994
6	NR Jenkins	England	Wembley	1999
6	SM Jones	Canada	Cardiff	2002
6	DR Biggar	Canada	Toronto	2009
6	SM Jones	New Zealand	Cardiff	2010
6	SL Halfpenny	England	Twickenham	2014

WALES

MOST CAPPED PLAYERS

Caps	Player	Career Span
119	GD Jenkins	2002 to 2015
104	SM Jones	1998 to 2011
100	Gareth Thomas	1995 to 2007
100	ME Williams	1996 to 2012
95	AR Jones	2003 to 2014
94	CL Charvis	1996 to 2007
94	WM Phillips	2003 to 2015
94	A-W Jones	2006 to 2015
92	GO Llewellyn	1989 to 2004
87	NR Jenkins	1991 to 2002
87	SM Williams	2000 to 2011
81	JW Hook	2006 to 2015
76	DJ Peel	2001 to 2011
75	RP Jones	2004 to 2013

MOST CONSECUTIVE TESTS

Tests	Player	Span
53	GO Edwards	1967 to 1978
43	KJ Jones	1947 to 1956
39	G Price	1975 to 1983
38	TM Davies	1969 to 1976
33	WJ Bancroft	1890 to 1901

MOST TESTS AS CAPTAIN

Tests	Captain	Span
41	SK Warburton	2011 to 2015
33	RP Jones	2008 to 2013
28	IC Evans	1991 to 1995
22	R Howley	1998 to 1999
22	CL Charvis	2002 to 2004
21	Gareth Thomas	2003 to 2007
19	JM Humphreys	1995 to 2003
18	AJ Gould	1889 to 1897
14	DCT Rowlands	1963 to 1965
14	WJ Trew	1907 to 1913

MOST POINTS IN TESTS

Points	Player	Tests	Career
1049	NR Jenkins	87	1991 to 2002
917	SM Jones	104	1998 to 2011
508	SL Halfpenny	62	2008 to 2015
352	JW Hook	81	2006 to 2015
304	PH Thorburn	37	1985 to 1991
290	SM Williams	87	2000 to 2011
211	AC Thomas	23	1996 to 2000
209	DR Biggar	39	2008 to 2015
200	Gareth Thomas	100	1995 to 2007
166	P Bennett	29	1969 to 1978
157	IC Evans	72	1987 to 1998

MOST TRIES IN TESTS

Tries	Player	Tests	Career
58	SM Williams	87	2000 to 2011
40	Gareth Thomas	100	1995 to 2007
33	IC Evans	72	1987 to 1998
23	GP North	55	2010 to 2015
22	CL Charvis	94	1996 to 2007
20	GO Edwards	53	1967 to 1978
20	TGR Davies	46	1966 to 1978
20	TGL Shanklin	70	2001 to 2010
18	GR Williams	44	2000 to 2005
17	RA Gibbs	16	1906 to 1911
17	JL Williams	17	1906 to 1911
17	KJ Jones	44	1947 to 1957

MOST CONVERSIONS IN TESTS

Cons	Player	Tests	Career
153	SM Jones	104	1998 to 2011
130	NR Jenkins	87	1991 to 2002
46	JW Hook	81	2006 to 2015
43	PH Thorburn	37	1985 to 1991
38	J Bancroft	18	1909 to 1914
35	SL Halfpenny	62	2008 to 2015
30	AC Thomas	23	1996 to 2000
30	DR Biggar	39	2008 to 2015
29	GL Henson	33	2001 to 2011
25	C Sweeney	35	2003 to 2007
21	R Priestland	40	2011 to 2015
20	WJ Bancroft	33	1890 to 1901
20	IR Harris	25	2001 to 2004

MOST PENALTY GOALS IN TESTS

Penalties	Player	Tests	Career
235	NR Jenkins	87	1991 to 2002
186	SM Jones	104	1998 to 2011
126	SL Halfpenny	62	2008 to 2015
70	PH Thorburn	37	1985 to 1991
61	JW Hook	81	2006 to 2015
42	DR Biggar	39	2008 to 2015
36	P Bennett	29	1969 to 1978
35	SP Fenwick	30	1975 to 1981
32	AC Thomas	23	1996 to 2000
22	G Evans	10	1981 to 1983

MOST DROP GOALS IN TESTS

Drops	Player	Tests	Career
13	J Davies	32	1985 to 1997
10	NR Jenkins	87	1991 to 2002
8	B John	25	1966 to 1972
7	WG Davies	21	1978 to 1985
6	SM Jones	104	1998 to 2011
6	DR Biggar	39	2008 to 2015
4	JW Hook	81	2006 to 2015

THE COUNTRIES

RECORD	DETAIL	HOLDER	SET
Most points in season	151	in five matches	2005
Most tries in season	21	in four matches	1910
Highest score	61	61-20 v Italy	2015
Biggest win	48	51–3 v Scotland	2014
Highest score conceded	60	26–60 v England	1998
Biggest defeat	51	0–51 v France	1998
Most appearances	52	GD Jenkins	2003–2015
Most points in matches	467	SM Jones	2000–2011
Most points in season	74	NR Jenkins	2001
	74	SL Halfpenny	2013
Most points in match	28	NR Jenkins	v France, 2001
Most tries in matches	22	SM Williams	2000–2011
Most tries in season	6	MCR Richards	1969
	6	SM Williams	2008
Most tries in match	4	W Llewellyn	v England, 1899
	4	MCR Richards	v England, 1969
Most cons in matches	69	SM Jones	2000–2011
Most cons in season	12	SM Jones	2005
Most cons in match	8	J Bancroft	v France, 1910
Most pens in matches	100	SM Jones	2000–2011
Most pens in season	19	SL Halfpenny	2013
Most pens in match	7	NR Jenkins	v Italy, 2000
	7	SL Halfpenny	v Scotland, 2013
Most drops in matches	8	J Davies	1985–1997
Most drops in season	5	NR Jenkins	2001
Most drops in match	3	NR Jenkins	v Scotland, 2001

WALES

MISCELLANEOUS RECORDS

RECORD	HOLDER	DETAIL
Longest Test Career	ME Williams	1996 to 2012
Youngest Test Cap	TWJ Prydie	18 yrs 25 days in 2010
Oldest Test Cap	TH Vile	38 yrs 152 days in 1921

CAREER RECORDS OF WALES INTERNATIONAL PLAYERS

UP TO 1 NOVEMBER, 2015

PLAYER BACKS :	DEBUT	CAPS	T	C	P	D	PTS
CL Allen	2013 v Arg	4	3	0	0	0	15
HB Amos	2013 v Tg	5	1	0	0	0	5
GW Anscombe	2015 v I	3	0	2	0	0	4
MA Beck	2012 v A	7	2	0	0	0	10
DR Biggar	2008 v C	39	1	30	42	6	209
ACG Cuthbert	2011 v A	40	15	0	0	0	75
DG Davies	2014 v SA	9	5	0	0	0	25
JJV Davies	2009 v C	48	10	0	0	0	50
SL Halfpenny	2008 v SA	62	12	35	126	0	508
JW Hook	2006 v Arg	81	13	46	61	4	352
MJ Morgan	2014 v SA	5	0	0	0	0	0
T Morgan	2015 v I	3	0	0	0	0	0
GP North	2010 v SA	55	23	0	0	0	115
WM Phillips	2003 v R	94	9	0	0	0	45
R Priestland	2011 v S	40	1	21	9	0	74
JH Roberts	2008 v S	74	9	0	0	0	45
EJ Walker	2015 v I	1	0	0	0	0	0
R Webb	2012 v It	16	5	0	0	0	25
LB Williams	2012 v Bb	26	2	0	0	0	10
LD Williams	2011 v Arg	24	2	0	0	0	10
MS Williams	2011 v Bb	34	9	0	0	0	45
R Williams	2013 v Tg	3	1	0	0	0	5
FORWARDS :							
SA Andrews	2011 v Bb	12	0	0	0	0	0
DT Baker	2013 v J	3	0	0	0	0	0
SJ Baldwin	2013 v J	15	1	0	0	0	5
JD Ball	2014 v I	15	0	0	0	0	0
LC Charteris	2004 v SA	62	0	0	0	0	0
KDV Dacey	2015 v I	2	0	0	0	0	0
BS Davies	2009 v S	49	0	0	0	0	0
DW Day	2015 v I	3	0	0	0	0	0
MR Evans	2015 v I	3	0	0	0	0	0
TT Faletau	2011 v Bb	52	4	0	0	0	20
TW Francis	2015 v I	7	0	0	0	0	0
IAR Gill	2010 v I	6	0	0	0	0	0
RM Hibbard	2006 v Arg	38	2	0	0	0	10

P James	2003 v R	65	0	0	0	0	0
AR Jarvis	2012 v Arg	16	0	0	0	0	0
GD Jenkins	2002 v R	119	4	0	0	0	20
A-W Jones	2006 v Arg	94	8	0	0	0	40
Rhodri P Jones	2012 v Bb	13	0	0	0	0	0
JD King	2013 v J	7	0	0	0	0	0
S Lee	2013 v Arg	17	1	0	0	0	5
DJ Lydiate	2009 v Arg	51	0	0	0	0	0
CR Moriarty	2015 v I	4	0	0	0	0	0
KJ Owens	2011 v Nm	34	2	0	0	0	10
DE Phillips	2013 v J	3	0	0	0	0	0
AC Shingler	2012 v S	8	0	0	0	0	0
NP Smith	2014 v Fj	3	0	0	0	0	0
JC Tipuric	2011 v Arg	38	3	0	0	0	15
SK Warburton	2009 v US	60	4	0	0	0	20

WALES INTERNATIONAL PLAYERS
UP TO 1 NOVEMBER, 2015

Note: Years given for International Championship matches are for second half of season; eg 1972 means season 1971–72. Years for all other matches refer to the actual year of the match. Entries in square brackets denote matches played in RWC Finals.

Ackerman, R A (Newport, London Welsh) 1980 NZ, 1981 E, S, A, 1982 I, F, E, S, 1983 S, I, F, R, 1984 S, I, F, E, A, 1985 S, I, F, E, Fj

Alexander, E P (Llandovery Coll, Cambridge U) 1885 S, 1886 E, S, 1887 E, I

Alexander, W H (Llwynypia) 1898 I, E, 1899 E, S, I, 1901 S, I

Allen, A G (Newbridge) 1990 F, E, I

Allen, C L (Cardiff Blues) 2013 Arg, 2014 A(R), 2015 It 2, [U]

Allen, C P (Oxford U, Beaumaris) 1884 E, S

Amos, H B (Newport Gwent Dragons) 2013 Tg, 2015 I 2, 3(R), [U, E]

Andrews, F (Pontypool) 1912 SA, 1913 E, S, I

Andrews, F G (Swansea) 1884 E, S

Andrews, G E (Newport) 1926 E, S, 1927 E, F, I

Andrews, S A (Cardiff Blues) 2011 Bb(R), J1, 2, Sm(R), NZ(R), A4, 2013 E(R), J1, 2, SA(R), 2015 S(R), It 1(R), I 2(R)

Anscombe, G W (Cardiff Blues) 2015 I 2(R), [A, SA]

Anthony, C T (Swansea, Newport, Gwent Dragons) 1997 US 1(R), 2(R), C (R), Tg (R), 1998 SA 2, Arg, 1999 S, I (R), 2001 J 1, 2, I (R), 2002 I, F, It, E, S, 2003 R (R)

Anthony, L (Neath) 1948 E, S, F

Appleyard, R C (Swansea) 1997 C, R, Tg, NZ, 1998 It, E (R), S, I, F

Arnold, P (Swansea) 1990 Nm 1, 2, Bb, 1991 E, S, I, F, A, [Arg, A], 1993 F (R), Z 2, 1994 Sp, Fj, 1995 SA, 1996 Bb (R)

Arnold, W R (Swansea) 1903 S

Arthur, C S (Cardiff) 1888 I, M, 1891 E

Arthur, T (Neath) 1927 S, F, I, 1929 E, S, F, I, 1930 E, S, I, F, 1931 E, S, F, I, SA, 1933 E, S

Ashton, C (Aberavon) 1959 E, S, I, 1960 E, S, I, 1962 I

Attewell, S L (Newport) 1921 E, S, F

Back, M J (Bridgend) 1995 F (R), E (R), S, I

Badger, O (Llanelli) 1895 E, S, I, 1896 E

Baker, A (Neath) 1921 I, 1923 E, S, F, I

Baker, A M (Newport) 1909 S, F, 1910 S

Baker, D T (Ospreys) 2013 J1(R), 2(R), 2015 I 2

Baldwin, S J (Ospreys) 2013 J2(R), 2014 A(R), Fj, NZ(R), SA 3, 2015 S(R), F, I 1, It 1, I 3(R), [U, E, Fj, A, SA]

Ball, J D (Scarlets) 2014 I(R), F, E, S(R), SA2(R), A, NZ, SA 3, 2015 E, S, I 1(R), It 1(R), I 2, It 2, [U]

Bancroft, J (Swansea) 1909 E, S, F, I, 1910 F, E, S, I, 1911 E, F, I, 1912 E, S, I, 1913 I, 1914 E, S, F

Bancroft, W J (Swansea) 1890 S, E, I, 1891 E, S, I, 1892 E, S, I, 1893 E, S, I, 1894 E, S, I, 1895 E, S, I, 1896 E, S, I, 1897 E, 1898 I, E, 1899 E, S, I, 1900 E, S, I, 1901 E, S, I

Barrell, R J (Cardiff) 1929 S, F, I, 1933 I

Bartlett, J D (Llanelli) 1927 S, 1928 E, S

Bassett, A (Cardiff) 1934 I, 1935 E, S, I, 1938 E, S

Bassett, J A (Penarth) 1929 E, S, F, I, 1930 E, S, I, 1931 E, S, F, I, SA, 1932 E, S, I

Bateman, A G (Neath, Richmond, Northampton) 1990 S, I, Nm 1, 2, 1996 SA, 1997 US, S, F, E, R, NZ, 1998 It, E, S, I, 1999 S, Arg 1, 2, SA, C, [J, A (R)], 2000 It, E, S, I, Sm, US, SA, 2001 E (R), It (R), R, I, Art (R), Tg

Bater, J (Ospreys) 2003 R (R)

Bayliss, G (Pontypool) 1933 S

Bebb, D I E (Carmarthen TC, Swansea) 1959 E, S, I, F, 1960 E, S, I, SA, 1961 E, S, I, F, 1962 E, S, F, I, 1963 E, F, NZ, 1964 E, S, F, SA, 1965 E, S, I, F, 1966 F, A, 1967 S, I, F, E

Beck, M A (Ospreys) 2012 A 1(R), 2, 3, Sm, 2013 SA(R), Arg(R), Tg

Beckingham, G (Cardiff) 1953 E, S, 1958 F

Bennett, A M (Cardiff) 1995 [NZ] SA, Fj

Bennett, H (Ospreys) 2003 I 2(R), S 2(R), [C(R), Tg(R)], 2004 S(R), F(R), Arg 1(R), 2, SA1(R), 2006 Arg 2, PI(R), 2007 E2, [J(R)], SA, 2008 E, S, It(R), F, 2009 S(R), E(R), F(R), It, I(R), NZ(R), Sm, Arg(R), A(R), 2010 E(R), S(R), F, I(R), It(R), NZ1(R), 2(R), A(R), SA2(R), Fj, NZ3(R), 2011 Bb, E2, 3(R), Arg(R) , [SA, Sm, Fj, I, F, A], A, 2012 I, S

Bennett, I (Aberavon) 1937 I

Bennett, P (Cardiff Harlequins) 1891 E, S, 1892 S, I

Bennett, P (Llanelli) 1969 F (R), 1970 SA, S, F, 1972 S (R), NZ, 1973 E, S, I, F, A, 1974 S, I, F, E, 1975 S (R), I, 1976 E, S, I, F, 1977 I, F, E, S, 1978 E, S, I, F

Bergiers, R T E (Cardiff Coll of Ed, Llanelli) 1972 E, S, F, NZ, 1973 E, S, I, F, A, 1974 E, 1975 I

Bevan, G W (Llanelli) 1947 E

Bevan, J A (Cambridge U) 1881 E

Bevan, J C (Cardiff, Cardiff Coll of Ed) 1971 E, S, I, F, 1972 E, S, F, NZ, 1973 E, S

Bevan, J D (Aberavon) 1975 F, E, S, A

Bevan, S (Swansea) 1904 I

Bevington, R J (Ospreys) 2011 Bb, E2(R), 3(R), Arg(R), [Nm(R), A(R)], A(R), 2012 Arg(R), 2013 S(R), J1, Tg(R), A(R), 2014 It(R)

Beynon, B (Swansea) 1920 E, S

Beynon, G E (Swansea) 1925 F, I

Bidgood, R A (Newport) 1992 S, 1993 Z 1, 2, Nm, J (R)

Biggar, D R (Ospreys) 2008 C(R), 2009 C, US(R), Sm, 2010 NZ1(R), 2, A(R), Fj, 2011 A(R), 2012 Bb, Sm, 2013 I, F, It, S, E, J1, 2, Arg, A, 2014 F(R), E(R), S, SA1, 2, A, NZ,SA 3, 2015 E, S, F, I 1, It 1, I 3, It 2, [E, Fj, A, SA]

Biggs, N W (Cardiff) 1888 M, 1889 I, 1892 I, 1893 E, S, I, 1894 E, I

Biggs, S H (Cardiff) 1895 E, S, 1896 S, 1897 E, 1898 I, E, 1899 S, I, 1900 I

Birch, J (Neath) 1911 S, F

Birt, F W (Newport) 1911 E, S, 1912 E, S, I, SA, 1913 E

Bishop, A M (Ospreys) 2008 SA2(R), C, A(R), 2009 S(R), C, US, Arg(R), A(R), 2010 I(R), It(R), NZ1, A, SA2(t), Fj, NZ3(R), 2012 Bb

Bishop, D J (Pontypool) 1984 A

Bishop, E H (Swansea) 1889 S

Blackmore, J H (Abertillery) 1909 E

Blackmore, S W (Cardiff) 1987 I, [Tg (R), C, A]

Blake, J (Cardiff) 1899 E, S, I, 1900 E, S, I, 1901 E, S, I

Blakemore, R E (Newport) 1947 E

Bland, A F (Cardiff) 1887 E, S, I, 1888 S, I, M, 1890 S, E, I

Blyth, L (Swansea) 1951 SA, 1952 E, S

Blyth, W R (Swansea) 1974 E, 1975 S (R), 1980 F, E, S, I

Boobyer, N (Llanelli) 1993 Z 1(R), 2, Nm, 1994 Fj, Tg, 1998 F, 1999 It (R)

Boon, R W (Cardiff) 1930 S, F, 1931 E, S, F, I, SA, 1932 E, S, I, 1933 E, I

Booth, J (Pontymister) 1898 I

Boots, J G (Newport) 1898 I, E, 1899 I, 1900 E, S, I, 1901 E, S, I, 1902 E, S, I, 1903 E, S, I, 1904 E

Boucher, A W (Newport) 1892 E, S, I, 1893 E, S, I, 1894 E, 1895 E, S, I, 1896 E, I, 1897 E

Bowcott, H M (Cardiff, Cambridge U) 1929 S, F, I, 1930 E, 1931 E, S, 1933 E, I

Bowdler, F A (Cross Keys) 1927 A, 1928 E, S, I, F, 1929 E, S, F, I, 1930 E, 1931 SA, 1932 E, S, I, 1933 I

Bowen, B (S Wales Police, Swansea) 1983 R, 1984 S, I, F, E, 1985 Fj, 1986 E, S, I, F, Fj, Tg, WS, 1987 [C, E, NZ], US, 1988 E, S, I, F, WS, 1989 S, I

Bowen, C A (Llanelli) 1896 E, S, I, 1897 E

Bowen, D H (Llanelli) 1883 E, 1886 E, S, 1887 E

Bowen, G E (Swansea) 1887 S, I, 1888 S, I

Bowen, W (Swansea) 1921 S, F, 1922 E, S, I, F

Bowen, Wm A (Swansea) 1886 E, S, 1887 E, S, I, 1888 M, 1889 S, I, 1890 S, I, 1891 E, S

Brace, D O (Llanelli, Oxford U) 1956 E, S, I, F, 1957 E, 1960 S, I, F, 1961 I

Braddock, K J (Newbridge) 1966 A, 1967 S, I

Bradshaw, K (Bridgend) 1964 E, S, I, F, SA, 1966 E, S, I, F

Brew, A G (Newport Gwent Dragons, Ospreys) 2007 I(R), A2, E2, 2010 Fj, 2011 Bb, E3(R), Arg(R), [Nm], 2012 Bb

Brew, N R (Gwent Dragons) 2003 R

Brewer, T J (Newport) 1950 E, 1955 E, S

Brice, A B (Aberavon) 1899 E, S, I, 1900 E, S, I, 1901 E, S, I, 1902 E, S, I, 1903 E, S, I, 1904 E, S, I

Bridges, C J (Neath) 1990 Nm 1, 2, Bb, 1991 E (R), I, F 1, A

Bridie, R H (Newport) 1882 I

Britton, G R (Newport) 1961 S

Broster, B G J (Saracens) 2005 US(R), C

Broughton, A S (Treorchy) 1927 A, 1929 S

Brown, A (Newport) 1921 I

Brown, J (Cardiff) 1925 I

Brown, J A (Cardiff) 1907 E, S, I, 1908 E, S, F, 1909 E

Brown, J (Cardiff) 1925 I

Brown, M (Pontypool) 1983 R, 1986 E, S, Fj (R), Tg, WS

Bryant, D J (Bridgend) 1988 NZ 1, 2, WS, R, 1989 S, I, F, E

Bryant, J (Celtic Warriors) 2003 R (R)

Buchanan, D A (Llanelli) 1987 [Tg, E, NZ, A], 1988 I

Buckett, I M (Swansea) 1994 Tg, 1997 US 2, C

Budgett, N J (Ebbw Vale, Bridgend) 2000 S, I, Sm (R), US, SA, 2001 J 1(R), 2, 2002 I, F, It, E, S

Burcher, D H (Newport) 1977 I, F, E, S

Burgess, R C (Ebbw Vale) 1977 I, F, E, S, 1981 I, F, 1982 F, E, S

Burnett, R (Newport) 1953 E

Burns, J (Cardiff) 1927 F, I

Burns, L B (Newport Gwent Dragons) 2011 Bb(R), E2(R), 3, [Sm(R), Nm, Fj(R), A(R)]

Bush, P F (Cardiff) 1905 NZ, 1906 E, SA, 1907 I, 1908 E, S, 1910 S, I

Butler, E T (Pontypool) 1980 F, E, S, I, NZ (R), 1982 S, 1983 E, S, I, F, R, 1984 S, I, F, E, A

Byrne, L M (Llanelli Scarlets, Ospreys, Clermont-Auvergne) 2005 NZ(R), Fj, SA, 2006 E(t&R), S(t&R), I, It, F, Arg 1, 2, PI, 2007 F1, A1, E2, 2008 E, S, It, I, F, SA3, NZ, A, 2009 S, E, F, It, I, 2010 E, S, F, I, It, SA1, NZ1, 2, SA2, F, NZ3, 2011 E1(R), S, It, I, F, Arg, [Nm, Fj]

Cale, W R (Newbridge, Pontypool) 1949 E, S, I, 1950 E, S, I, F

Cardey, M D (Llanelli) 2000 S

Carter, A J (Newport) 1991 E, S

Cattell, A (Llanelli) 1883 E, S

Challinor, C (Neath) 1939 E

Charteris, L C (Newport Gwent Dragons, Perpignan, Racing Métro) 2004 SA2(R), R, 2005 US, C, NZ(R), Fj, 2007 SA(R), 2008 C, NZ(R), 2009 S(R), F(R), It, I(R), US(R), NZ, Sm, Arg, A, 2010 E, F(R), I, It, 2011 Bb, E2(R), 3, [SA, Sm, Nm(R), Fj, I, F, A], 2012 It(R), F(R), A 1, 2(R), 3(t&R), Sm(R), NZ, A4, 2013 SA(R), Arg(R), Tg, 2014 It, F, S, SA1, 2, Fj, NZ(R), 2015 E(R), S(R), F, I 1, It 1, I 3(R), It 2(R), [U, E(R), Fj(t&R), A, SA]

Charvis, C L (Swansea, Tarbes, Newcastle, Newport Gwent Dragons) 1996 A 3(R), SA, 1997 US, S, I, F, 1998 It (R), E, S, I, F, Z (R), SA 1, 2, Arg, 1999 S, I F 1, It, E, Arg 1, SA, F 2, [Arg 3, A], 2000 F It (R), E, S, I, Sm, US, SA, 2001 E, S, F, It, R, I, Arg, A, 2002 E (R), S, SA 1, 2, R, Fj, C, NZ, 2003 It, E 1(R), S 1(R), I 1, F, A, NZ, E 2, S 2, [C, Tg, It, NZ, E], 2004 S, F, E, It, Arg 1, 2, SA1, 2, R, NZ, J, 2005 US, C, NZ, SA, A, 2006 E, S, I, It, 2007 A1, 2, E2, Arg(R), F2(R), [C(t&R), A, J, Fj], SA

Clapp, T J S (Newport) 1882 I, 1883 E, S, 1884 E, S, I, 1885 E, S, 1886 E, 1887 E, S, I, 1888 S, I

Clare, J (Cardiff) 1883 E

Clark, S S (Neath) 1882 I, 1887 I

Cleaver, W B (Cardiff) 1947 E, S, F, I, A, 1948 E, S, F, I, 1949 I, 1950 E, S, I, F

Clegg, B G (Swansea) 1979 F

Clement, A (Swansea) 1987 US (R), 1988 E, NZ 1, WS (R), R, 1989 NZ, 1990 S (R), I (R), Nm 1, 2, 1991 S (R), A (R), F 2, [WS, A], 1992 I, F, E, S, 1993 I (R), F, J, C, 1994 S, I, F, Sp, C (R), Tg, WS, It, 1995 F, E, [J, NZ, I]

Clement, W H (Llanelli) 1937 E, S, I, 1938 E, S, I

Cobner, T J (Pontypool) 1974 S, I, F, E, 1975 F, E, S, I, A, 1976 E, S, 1977 F, E, S, 1978 E, S, I, F, A 1

Cockbain, B J (Celtic Warriors, Ospreys) 2003 R, [C, It, NZ, E], 2004 S, I, F, E, Arg 1, 2, SA2, NZ, 2005 E, It, F, S, I, US, C(R), NZ, Fj, 2007 F1(t&R), A1

Coldrick, A P (Newport) 1911 E, S, I, 1912 E, S, F

Coleman, E O (Newport) 1949 E, S, I

Coles, F C (Pontypool) 1960 S, I, F

Collins, J E (Aberavon) 1958 A, E, S, F, 1959 E, S, I, F, 1960 E, 1961 F

Collins, R G (S Wales Police, Cardiff, Pontypridd) 1987 E (R), I, [I, E, NZ], US, 1988 E, S, I, F, R, 1990 E, S, I, 1991 A, F 2, [WS], 1994 C, Fj, Tg, WS, R, It, SA, 1995 F, E, S, I
Collins, T J (Mountain Ash) 1923 I
Conway-Rees, J (Llanelli) 1892 S, 1893 E, 1894 E
Cook, T (Cardiff) 1949 S, I
Coombs, A J (Newport Gwent Dragons) 2013 I, F, It, E(R), J1, 2(R), 2014 It(R), I, F(R), E(R)
Cooper, G J (Bath, Celtic Warriors, Newport Gwent Dragons, Gloucester, Cardiff Blues) 2001 It, J 1, 2, 2003 E 1, S 1, I 1, F(R), A, NZ, E 2, [C, Tg, It(t&R)], 2004 S, I, F, E, It, R(R), NZ(R), J, 2005 E(R), It(R), F(R), NZ(R), Fj, SA, A, 2006 E(R), PI(R), 2007 A1(R), E2, [J(R)], 2008 SA1, 2, 3, NZ, A, 2009 C, US(R), NZ, Arg, 2010 E, S
Cooper, V L (Llanelli) 2002 C, 2003 I 2(R), S 2
Cope, W (Cardiff, Blackheath) 1896 S
Copsey, A H (Llanelli) 1992 I, F, E, S, A, 1993 E, S, I, J, C, 1994 E (R), Pt, Sp (R), Fj, Tg, WS (R)
Cornish, F H (Cardiff) 1897 E, 1898 I, E, 1899 I
Cornish, R A (Cardiff) 1923 E, S, 1924 E, 1925 E, S, F, 1926 E, S, I, F
Coslett, T K (Aberavon) 1962 E, S, F
Cowey, B T V (Welch Regt, Newport) 1934 E, S, I, 1935 E
Cresswell, B R (Newport) 1960 E, S, I, F
Cummins, W (Treorchy) 1922 E, S, I, F
Cunningham, L J (Aberavon) 1960 E, S, I, F, 1962 E, S, F, I, 1963 NZ, 1964 E, S, I, F, SA
Cuthbert, A C G (Cardiff Blues) 2011 A(R), 2012 I, S, E, It, F, A 1, 2, 3, Arg, Sm, NZ, A4, 2013 I, F, It, S, E, A, 2014 It, I, F, E, S, SA1, 2, A, Fj, NZ, SA 3, 2015 E, I 2, 3, It 2, [U, E(R), Fj, A, SA]
Czekaj, C D (Cardiff Blues) 2005 C, 2006 Arg 1(R), 2007 I, S, A1, 2, 2009 C, 2010 A(R), SA2(R)

Dacey, K D V (Cardiff Blues) 2015 I 2(R), It 2(R)
Dacey, M (Swansea) 1983 E, S, I, F, R, 1984 S, I, F, E, A, 1986 Fj, Tg, WS, 1987 F (R), [Tg]
Daniel, D J (Llanelli) 1891 S, 1894 E, S, I, 1898 I, E, 1899 E, I
Daniel, L T D (Newport) 1970 S
Daniels, P C T (Cardiff) 1981 A, 1982 I
Darbishire, G (Bangor) 1881 E
Dauncey, F H (Newport) 1896 E, S, I
Davey, C (Swansea) 1930 F, 1931 E, S, F, I, SA, 1932 E, S, I, 1933 E, S, 1934 E, S, I, 1935 E, S, I, NZ, 1936 S, 1937 E, I, 1938 E, I
David, R J (Cardiff) 1907 I
David, T P (Llanelli, Pontypridd) 1973 F, A, 1976 I, F
Davidge, G D (Newport) 1959 F, 1960 S, I, F, SA, 1961 E, S, I, 1962 F
Davies, A (Cambridge U, Neath, Cardiff) 1990 Bb (R), 1991 A, 1993 Z 1, 2, J, C, 1994 Fj, 1995 [J, I]
Davies, A C (London Welsh) 1889 I
Davies, A E (Llanelli) 1984 A
Davies, B (Llanelli) 1895 E, 1896 E
Davies, B (Llanelli Scarlets) 2006 I(R)
Davies, B S (Cardiff Blues, Wasps) 2009 S(R), It(R), C, NZ(R), Sm(R), 2010 E(t&R), S(R), F, I, It, SA1, NZ1, 2, A, SA2, Fj(R), NZ3, 2011 E1, S, It, I, F, E2, Arg, [SA(R), Sm(R), Nm, Fj, I(R), F(R), A], 2012 I, A 1, 2, 3, Sm, NZ, 2013 J1, 2, SA, Arg, 2014 A(R), Fj, 2015 F(R), I 3, [E, Fj, SA(R)]
Davies, C (Cardiff) 1947 S, F, I, A, 1948 E, S, F, I, 1949 F, 1950 E, S, I, F, 1951 E, S, I
Davies, C (Llanelli) 1988 WS, 1989 S, I (R), F
Davies, C A H (Llanelli, Cardiff) 1957 I, 1958 A, E, S, I, 1960 SA, 1961 E
Davies, C H (Swansea, Llanelli) 1939 S, I, 1947 E, S, F, I
Davies, C L (Cardiff) 1956 E, S, I
Davies, C R (Bedford, RAF) 1934 E
Davies, D B (Llanelli) 1907 E
Davies, D B (Llanelli) 1962 I, 1963 E, S
Davies, D E G (Cardiff) 1912 E, F
Davies, D G (Cardiff) 1923 E, S
Davies, D G (Scarlets) 2014 SA1(R), 2015 It 1(R), I 3(R), It 2(R), [U, E, Fj, A, SA]
Davies, D H (Neath) 1904 S
Davies, D H (Bridgend) 1921 I, 1925 I
Davies, D H (Aberavon) 1924 E

Davies, D I (Swansea) 1939 E
Davies, D J (Neath) 1962 I
Davies, D M (Somerset Police) 1950 E, S, I, F, 1951 E, S, I, F, SA, 1952 E, S, I, F, 1953 I, F, NZ, 1954 E
Davies, E (Maesteg) 1919 NZA
Davies, E G (Cardiff) 1928 F, 1929 E, 1930 S
Davies, E P (Aberavon) 1947 A, 1948 I
Davies, G (Swansea) 1900 E, S, I, 1901 E, S, I, 1905 E, S, I
Davies, G (Cambridge U, Pontypridd) 1947 S, A, 1948 E, S, F, I, 1949 E, S, F, 1951 E, S
Davies, H (Swansea) 1898 I, E, 1901 S, I
Davies, H (Bridgend) 1984 S, I, F, E
Davies, H G (Llanelli) 1921 F, I, 1925 F
Davies, H (Neath) 1912 E, S
Davies, H J (Newport) 1924 S
Davies, H J (Cambridge U, Aberavon) 1959 E, S
Davies, H S (Treherbert) 1923 I
Davies, I T (Llanelli) 1914 S, F, I
Davies, J (Neath, Llanelli, Cardiff) 1985 E, Fj, 1986 E, S, I, F, Fj, Tg, WS, 1987 F, E, S, I, [I, Tg (R), C, E, NZ, A], 1988 E, S, I, F, NZ 1, 2, WS, R, 1996 A 3, 1997 US (t), S (R), F (R), E
Davies, Rev J A (Swansea) 1913 S, F, I, 1914 E, S, F, I
Davies, J D (Neath, Richmond) 1991 I, F 1, 1993 F (R), Z 2, J, C, 1994 S, I, F, E, Pt, Sp, C, WS, R, It, SA, 1995 F, E, [J, NZ, I] SA, 1996 It, E, S, I, F 1, A 1, Bb, F 2, It, 1998 Z, SA 1
Davies, J H (Aberavon) 1923 I
Davies, J J V (Scarlets , Clermont-Auvergne) 2009 C, US, Sm(R), Arg, A, 2010 NZ1(R), 2, 2011 E1, S, I, F, Bb, E2, Arg, [SA, Sm, Nm, Fj(R), I, F, A], 2012 I, S, E, It, F, A 1, 2, 3, NZ, A4, 2013 I, F, It, S, E, SA, 2014 E, S, SA1, 2, NZ, SA 3, 2015 E, S, F, I 1, It 1
Davies, L (Swansea) 1939 S, I
Davies, L (Bridgend) 1966 E, S, I
Davies, L B (Neath, Cardiff, Llanelli) 1996 It, E, S, I, F 1, A 1, Bb, F 2, It (R), 1997 US 1, 2, C, R, Tg, NZ (R), 1998 E (R), I, F, 1999 C, 2001 I, 2003 It
Davies, L M (Llanelli) 1954 F, S, 1955 I
Davies, M (Swansea) 1981 A, 1982 I, 1985 Fj
Davies, Mefin (Pontypridd, Celtic Warriors, Gloucester) 2002 SA 2(R), R, Fj, 2003 It, S 1(R), I 1(R), F, A(R), NZ(R), I 2, R, [Tg, NZ(R), E(R)], 2004 S, F, It(R), Arg 1, 2(R), SA1, 2(R), R, NZ, J, 2005 E, I, F, S, I, C(R), NZ, SA(R), A(t), 2006 S(R), I(R), It(R), F(R), 2007 A2
Davies, M J (Blackheath) 1939 S, I
Davies, N G (London Welsh) 1955 E
Davies, N G (Llanelli) 1988 NZ 2, WS, 1989 S, I, 1993 F, 1994 S, I, E, Pt, Sp, C, Fj, Tg (R), WS, R, It, 1995 E, S, I, Fj, 1996 E, S, I, F 1, A 1, 2, Bb, F 2, 1997 E
Davies, P T (Llanelli) 1985 E, Fj, 1986 E, S, I, F, Fj, Tg, WS, 1987 F, E, I, [Tg, C, NZ], 1988 WS, R, 1989 S, I, F, E, NZ, 1990 F, E, S, 1991 I, F 1, A, F 2, [WS, Arg, A], 1993 F, Z 1, Nm, 1994 S, I, F, E, C, Fj (R), WS, R, It, 1995 F, I
Davies, R H (Oxford U, London Welsh) 1957 S, I, F, 1958 A, 1962 E, S
Davies, S (Swansea) 1992 I, F, E, S, A, 1993 E, S, I, Z 1(R), 2, Nm, J, 1995 F, [J, I], 1998 I (R), F
Davies, T G R (Cardiff, London Welsh) 1966 A, 1967 S, I, F, E, 1968 E, S, 1969 S, I, F, NZ 1, 2, A, 1971 E, S, I, F, 1972 E, S, F, NZ, 1973 E, S, I, F, A, 1974 S, F, E, 1975 F, E, S, I, 1976 E, S, I, F, 1977 I, F, E, S, 1978 E, S, I, A 1, 2
Davies, T J (Devonport Services, Swansea, Llanelli) 1953 E, S, I, F, 1957 E, S, I, F, 1958 A, E, S, F, 1959 E, S, I, F, 1960 E, SA, 1961 E, S, F
Davies, T M (London Welsh, Swansea) 1969 S, I, F, E, NZ 1, 2, A, 1970 SA, S, E, I, F, 1971 E, S, I, F, 1972 E, S, F, NZ, 1973 E, S, I, F, A, 1974 S, I, F, E, 1975 F, E, S, I, A, 1976 E, S, I, F
Davies, W (Cardiff) 1896 S
Davies, W (Swansea) 1931 SA, 1932 E, S, I
Davies, W A (Aberavon) 1912 S, I
Davies, W G (Cardiff) 1978 A 1, 2, NZ, 1979 S, I, F, E, 1980 F, E, S, NZ, 1981 E, S, A, 1982 I, F, E, S, 1985 S, I, F
Davies, W T H (Swansea) 1936 I, 1937 E, I, 1939 E, S, I
Davis, C E (Newbridge) 1978 A 2, 1981 E, S
Davis, M (Newport) 1991 A
Davis, W E N (Cardiff) 1939 E, S, I

Dawes, S J (London Welsh) 1964 I, F, SA, 1965 E, S, I, F, 1966 A, 1968 I, F, 1969 E, NZ 2, A, 1970 SA, S, E, I, F, 1971 E, S, I, F

Day, D W (Bath) 2015 I 2, It 2, [U(R)]

Day, H C (Newport) 1930 S, I, F, 1931 E, S

Day, H T (Newport) 1892 I, 1893 E, S, 1894 S, I

Day, T B (Swansea) 1931 E, S, F, I, SA, 1932 E, S, I, 1934 S, I, 1935 E, S, I

Deacon, J T (Swansea) 1891 I, 1892 E, S, I

Delahay, W J (Bridgend) 1922 E, S, I, F, 1923 E, S, F, I, 1924 NZ, 1925 E, S, F, I, 1926 E, S, I, F, 1927 S

Delaney, L (Llanelli) 1989 I, F, E, 1990 E, 1991 F 2, [WS, Arg, A], 1992 I, F, E

Delve, G L (Bath, Gloucester) 2006 S(R), I(R), Arg 1(R), 2(R), 2008 S(R), It(R), I(R), SA1(R), 2, 2010 I, It(R)

Devereux, D B (Neath) 1958 A, E, S

Devereux, J A (S Glamorgan Inst, Bridgend) 1986 E, S, I, F, Fj, Tg, WS, 1987 F, E, S, I, [I, C, E, NZ, A], 1988 NZ 1, 2, R, 1989 S, I

Diplock, R S (Bridgend) 1988 R

Dobson, G A (Cardiff) 1900 S

Dobson, T (Cardiff) 1898 I, E, 1899 E, S

Donovan, A J (Swansea) 1978 A 2, 1981 I (R), A, 1982 E, S

Donovan, R E (S Wales Police) 1983 F (R)

Douglas, M H J (Llanelli) 1984 S, I, F

Douglas, W M (Cardiff) 1886 E, S, 1887 E, S

Dowell, W H (Newport) 1907 E, S, I, 1908 E, S, F, I

Durston, A P R (Bridgend) 2001 J 1, 2

Dyke, J C M (Penarth) 1906 SA

Dyke, L M (Penarth, Cardiff) 1910 I, 1911 S, F, I

Edmunds, D A (Neath) 1990 I (R), Bb

Edwards, A B (London Welsh, Army) 1955 E, S

Edwards, B O (Newport) 1951 I

Edwards, D (Glynneath) 1921 E

Edwards, G O (Cardiff, Cardiff Coll of Ed) 1967 F, E, NZ, 1968 E, S, I, F, 1969 S, I, F, E, NZ 1, 2, A, 1970 SA, S, E, I, F, 1971 E, S, I, F, 1972 E, S, F, NZ, 1973 E, S, I, F, A, 1974 S, I, F, E, 1975 F, E, S, I, A, 1976 E, S, I, F, 1977 I, F, E, S, 1978 E, S, I, F

Eidman, I H (Cardiff) 1983 S, R, 1984 I, F, E, A, 1985 S, I, Fj, 1986 E, S, I, F

Elliott, J (Cardiff) 1894 I, 1898 I, E

Elsey, W J (Cardiff) 1895 E

Emyr, Arthur (Swansea) 1989 E, NZ, 1990 F, E, S, I, Nm 1, 2, 1991 F 1, 2, [WS, Arg, A]

Evans, A (Pontypool) 1924 E, I, F

Evans, B (Llanelli) 1933 E, S, 1936 E, S, I, 1937 E

Evans, B R (Swansea, Cardiff Blues) 1998 SA 2(R), 1999 F 1, It, E, Arg 1, 2, C, [J (R), Sm (R), A (R)], 2000 Sm, US, 2001 J 1(R), 2002 SA 1, 2, R(R), Fj, C, NZ, 2003 It, E 1, S 1, I 2, R, 2004 F(R), E(t), It(R)

Evans, B S (Llanelli) 1920 E, 1922 E, S, I, F

Evans, C (Pontypool) 1960 E

Evans, D (Penygraig) 1896 S, I, 1897 E, 1898 E

Evans, D B (Swansea) 1926 E

Evans, D B (Swansea) 1933 S

Evans, D D (Cheshire, Cardiff U) 1934 E

Evans, D J (Scarlets) 2009 C, US

Evans, D P (Llanelli) 1960 SA

Evans, D W (Cardiff) 1889 S, I, 1890 E, I, 1891 E

Evans, D W (Oxford U, Cardiff, Treorchy) 1989 F, E, NZ, 1990 F, E, S, I, Bb, 1991 A (R), F 2(R), [A (R)], 1995 [J (R)]

Evans, E (Llanelli) 1937 E, 1939 S, I

Evans, F (Llanelli) 1921 S

Evans, G (Cardiff) 1947 E, S, F, I, A, 1948 E, S, F, I, 1949 E, S, I

Evans, G (Maesteg) 1981 S (R), I, F, A, 1982 I, F, E, S, 1983 F, R

Evans, G D (Llanelli Scarlets) 2006 PI(R)

Evans, G L (Newport) 1977 F (R), 1978 F, A 2(R)

Evans, G R (Cardiff) 1889 S

Evans, G R (Llanelli) 1998 SA 1, 2003 I 2, S 2, [NZ]

Evans, H I (Swansea) 1922 E, S, I, F

Evans, I (London Welsh) 1934 S, I

Evans, I C (Llanelli, Bath) 1987 F, E, S, I, [I, C, E, NZ, A], 1988 E, S, I, F, NZ 1, 2, 1989 I, F, E, 1991 E, S, I, F 1, A, F 2, [WS,

Arg, A], 1992 I, F, E, S, A, 1993 E, S, I, F, J, C, 1994 S, I, E, Pt, Sp, C, Fj, Tg, WS, R, 1995 E, S, I, [J, NZ, I], SA, Fj, 1996 It, E, S, I, F 1, A 1, 2, Bb, F 2, A 3, SA, 1997 US, S, I, F, 1998 It

Evans, I L (Llanelli) 1991 F 2(R)

Evans, I R (Ospreys) 2006 Arg 1, 2, A, C, NZ, 2007 [J(R), Fj], SA, 2008 E(R), S, It, F(R), SA1(R), 2(R), 3, NZ, 2011 A, 2012 I, S, E, It, F, Bb, Arg, Sm, 2013 I, F, It, S, E, Tg, A, 2014 SA1(R)

Evans, J (Llanelli) 1896 S, I, 1897 E

Evans, J D (Cardiff) 1958 I, F

Evans, J E (Llanelli) 1924 S

Evans, J H (Pontypool) 1907 E, S, I

Evans, J R (Newport) 1934 E

Evans, J W (Blaina) 1904 E

Evans, M R (Scarlets) 2015 I1(R), It 1, I 2(R)

Evans, O J (Cardiff) 1887 E, S, 1888 S, I

Evans, P D (Llanelli) 1951 E, F

Evans, R (Bridgend) 1963 S, I, F

Evans, R L (Llanelli) 1993 E, S, I, F, E, 1994 S, I, F, E, Pt, Sp, C, Fj, WS, R, It, SA, 1995 F, [NZ, I (R)]

Evans, R T (Newport) 1947 F, I, 1950 E, S, I, F, 1951 E, S, I, F

Evans, S (Swansea, Neath) 1985 F, E, 1986 Fj, Tg, WS, 1987 F, E, [I, Tg]

Evans, T D (Swansea) 1924 I

Evans, T G (London Welsh) 1970 SA, S, E, I, 1972 E, S, F

Evans, T H (Llanelli) 1906 I, 1907 E, S, I, 1908 I, A, 1909 E, S, F, I, 1910 F, E, S, I, 1911 E, S, F, I

Evans, T P (Swansea) 1975 F, E, S, I, A, 1976 E, S, I, F, 1977 I

Evans, T W (Llanelli) 1958 A

Evans, V (Neath) 1954 I, F, S

Evans, W F (Rhymney) 1882 I, 1883 S

Evans, W G (Brynmawr) 1911 I

Evans, W H (Llwynypia) 1914 E, S, F, I

Evans, W J (Pontypool) 1947 S

Evans, W R (Bridgend) 1958 A, E, S, I, F, 1960 SA, 1961 E, S, I, F, 1962 E, S, I

Everson, W A (Newport) 1926 S

Faletau, T T (Newport Gwent Dragons) 2011 Bb, E2, 3, [SA, Sm, Nm, Fj, I, F, A], A, 2012 I, S, E, It, F, Arg, Sm, NZ, A4, 2013 I, F, It, S, E, SA, Arg, A, 2014 It, I, F, E, S, SA1, 2, A, Fj, NZ, SA 3, 2015 E, S, F, I 1, It 1, I 2(R), 3, It 2, [E, Fj, A, SA]

Faulkner, A G (Pontypool) 1975 F, E, S, I, A, 1976 E, S, I, F, 1978 E, S, I, F, A 1, 2, NZ, 1979 S, I, F

Faull, J (Swansea) 1957 I, F, 1958 A, E, S, I, F, 1959 E, S, I, 1960 E, F

Fauvel, T J (Aberavon) 1988 NZ 1(R)

Fear, A G (Newport) 1934 S, I, 1935 S, I

Fender, N H (Cardiff) 1930 I, F, 1931 E, S, F, I

Fenwick, S P (Bridgend) 1975 F, E, S, A, 1976 E, S, I, F, 1977 I, F, E, S, 1978 E, S, I, F, A 1, 2, NZ, 1979 S, I, F, E, 1980 F, E, S, I, NZ, 1981 E, S

Finch, E (Llanelli) 1924 F, NZ, 1925 F, I, 1926 F, 1927 A, 1928 I, F

Finlayson, A A J (Cardiff) 1974 I, F, E

Fitzgerald, D (Cardiff) 1894 S, I

Ford, F J V (Welch Regt, Newport) 1939 E

Ford, I R (Newport) 1959 E, S

Ford, S P (Cardiff) 1990 I, Nm 1, 2, Bb, 1991 E, S, I, A

Forster, J A (Newport Gwent Dragons) 2004 Arg 1

Forward, A (Pontypool, Mon Police) 1951 S, SA, 1952 E, S, I, F

Fowler, I J (Llanelli) 1919 NZA

Francis, D G (Llanelli) 1919 NZA, 1924 S

Francis, P W (Maesteg) 1987 S

Francis, T W (Exeter) 2015 I 3, It 2, [U(R), E, Fj, A(R), SA(R)]

Funnell, J S (Ebbw Vale) 1998 Z (R), SA 1

Fury, W L (London Irish) 2008 SA1(R), 2(R)

Gabe, R T (Cardiff, Llanelli) 1901 I, 1902 E, S, I, 1903 E, S, I, 1904 E, S, I, 1905 E, S, I, NZ, 1906 E, I, SA, 1907 E, S, I, 1908 E, S, F, I

Gale, N R (Swansea, Llanelli) 1960 I, 1963 E, S, I, NZ, 1964 E, S, I, F, SA, 1965 E, S, I, F, 1966 E, S, I, F, A, 1967 E, NZ, 1968 E, 1969 NZ 1(R), 2, A

Gallacher, I S (Llanelli) 1970 F

Garrett, R M (Penarth) 1888 M, 1889 S, 1890 S, E, I, 1891 S, I, 1892 E

Geen, W P (Oxford U, Newport) 1912 SA, 1913 E, I

George, E E (Pontypridd, Cardiff) 1895 S, I, 1896 E

George, G M (Newport) 1991 E, S

Gething, G I (Neath) 1913 F

Gibbs, A (Newbridge) 1995 I, SA, 1996 A 2, 1997 US 1, 2, C

Gibbs, I S (Neath, Swansea) 1991 E, S, I, F 1, A, F 2, [WS, Arg, A], 1992 I, F, E, S, A, 1993 E, S, I, F, J, C, 1996 It, A 3, SA, 1997 US, S, I, F, Tg, NZ, 1998 It, E, S, A 2, Arg, 1999 S, I, F 1, It, E, C, F 2, [Arg 3, J, Sm, A], 2000 I, Sm, US, SA, 2001 E, S, F, It

Gibbs, R A (Cardiff) 1906 S, I, 1907 E, S, 1908 E, S, F, I, 1910 F, E, S, I, 1911 E, S, F, I

Giles, R (Aberavon) 1983 R, 1985 Fj (R), 1987 [C]

Gill, I A R (Saracens) 2010 I(R), 2012 I, Bb, 2013 J1(R), 2, 2015 It 1(R)

Girling, B E (Cardiff) 1881 E

Goldsworthy, S J (Swansea) 1884 I, 1885 E, S

Gore, J H (Blaina) 1924 I, F, NZ, 1925 E

Gore, W (Newbridge) 1947 S, F, I

Gough, I M (Newport, Pontypridd, Newport Gwent Dragons, Ospreys) 1998 SA 1, 1999 S, 2000 F, It (R), E (R), S, I, Sm, US, SA, 2001 E, S, F, It, Tg, A, 2002 I (R), F (R), It, S, 2003 R, 2005 It(R), US(R), SA, A, 2006 E, S, I, It, F, Arg 1, 2, A, C, NZ, 2007 I, S(R), F1, It, E1, Arg, F2, [C, A, Fj(R)], 2008 E, S, It, I, F, SA1, 2, 3(R), C, A, 2009 S, E, F, I, C(R), US, 2010 I(R), It(R), Fj

Gould, A J (Newport) 1885 E, S, 1886 E, S, 1887 E, S, I, 1888 I, 1889 I, 1890 S, E, I, 1892 E, S, I, 1893 E, S, I, 1894 E, S, 1895 E, S, I, 1896 E, S, I, 1897 E

Gould, G H (Newport) 1892 I, 1893 S, I

Gould, R (Newport) 1882 I, 1883 E, S, 1884 E, S, I, 1885 E, S, 1886 E, 1887 E, S

Graham, T C (Newport) 1890 I, 1891 S, I, 1892 E, S, 1893 E, S, I, 1894 E, S, 1895 E, S

Gravell, R W R (Llanelli) 1975 F, E, S, I, A, 1976 E, S, I, F, 1978 E, S, I, F, A 1, 2, NZ, 1979 S, I, 1981 I, F, 1982 F, E, S

Gray, A J (London Welsh) 1968 E, S

Greenslade, D (Newport) 1962 S

Greville, H G (Llanelli) 1947 A

Griffin, Dr J (Edinburgh U) 1883 S

Griffiths, C R (Llanelli) 1979 E (R)

Griffiths, D (Llanelli) 1888 M, 1889 I

Griffiths, G (Llanelli) 1889 I

Griffiths, G M (Cardiff) 1953 E, S, I, F, NZ, 1954 I, F, S, 1955 I, F, 1957 E, S

Griffiths, J (Swansea) 2000 Sm (R)

Griffiths, J L (Llanelli) 1988 NZ 2, 1989 S

Griffiths, M (Bridgend, Cardiff, Pontypridd) 1988 WS, R, 1989 S, I, F, E, NZ, 1990 F, E, Nm 1, 2, Bb, 1991 I, F 1, 2, [WS, Arg, A], 1992 I, F, E, S, A, 1993 Z 1, 2, Nm, J, C, 1995 F (R), E, S, I, [J, I], 1998 SA 1

Griffiths, V M (Newport) 1924 S, I, F

Gronow, B (Bridgend) 1910 F, E, S, I

Gwilliam, J A (Cambridge U, Newport) 1947 A, 1948 I, 1949 E, S, I, F, 1950 E, S, I, F, 1951 E, S, I, SA, 1952 E, S, I, F, 1953 E, I, F, NZ, 1954 E

Gwynn, D (Swansea) 1883 E, 1887 S, 1890 E, I, 1891 E, S

Gwynn, W H (Swansea) 1884 E, S, I, 1885 E, S

Hadley, A M (Cardiff) 1983 R, 1984 S, I, F, E, 1985 F, E, Fj, 1986 E, S, I, F, Fj, Tg, 1987 S (R), I, [I, Tg, C, E, NZ, A], US, 1988 E, S, I, F

Halfpenny, S L (Cardiff Blues, Toulon) 2008 SA3, C, NZ, 2009 S, E, F, NZ, Sm, Arg, A, 2010 E(R), S, F, I, SA1, NZ1, 2, 2011 I, F, Arg, [Sm(R), Nm, Fj, I, F, A] , A, 2012 I, S, E, It, F, A 1, 2, 3, Arg, Sm, NZ, A4, 2013 I, F, It, S, E, SA, Arg, Tg, A, 2014 It, I, F, E, A, NZ, SA 3, 2015 E, S, F, I 1, It 1, I 3, It 2

Hall, I (Aberavon) 1967 NZ, 1970 SA, S, E, 1971 S, 1974 S, I, F

Hall, M R (Cambridge U, Bridgend, Cardiff) 1988 NZ 1(R), 2, WS, R, 1989 S, I, F, E, NZ, 1990 F, E, S, 1991 A, F 2, [WS, Arg, A], 1992 I, F, E, S, A, 1993 E, S, I, 1994 S, I, F, E, Pt, Sp, C, Tg, R, It, SA, 1995 F, S, I, [J, NZ, I]

Hall, W H (Bridgend) 1988 WS

Hancock, F E (Cardiff) 1884 I, 1885 E, S, 1886 S

Hannan, J (Newport) 1888 M, 1889 S, I, 1890 S, E, I, 1891 E, 1892 E, S, I, 1893 E, S, I, 1894 E, S, I, 1895 E, S, I

Harding, A F (London Welsh) 1902 E, S, I, 1903 E, S, I, 1904 E, S, I, 1905 E, S, I, NZ, 1906 E, S, I, SA, 1907 I, 1908 E, S

Harding, C T (Newport) 1888 M, 1889 S, I

Harding, G F (Newport) 1881 E, 1882 I, 1883 E, S

Harding, R (Swansea, Cambridge U) 1923 E, S, F, I, 1924 I, F, NZ, 1925 F, I, 1926 E, I, F, 1927 E, S, F, I, 1928 E

Harries, W T M (Newport Gwent Dragons) 2010 NZ2(R), A, 2012 Bb(R)

Harris, C A (Aberavon) 1927 A

Harris, D J E (Pontypridd, Cardiff) 1959 I, F, 1960 S, I, F, SA, 1961 E, S

Harris, I R (Cardiff) 2001 Arg, Tg, A, 2002 I, It (R), E, S (R), Fj(R), C(R), NZ(R), 2003 It, E 1(R), S 1(R), I 1(R), F, I 2, S 2, [C, Tg, It, E], 2004 S, I, F, It

Hathway, G F (Newport) 1924 I, F

Havard, Rev W T (Llanelli) 1919 NZA

Hawkins, F J (Pontypridd) 1912 I, F

Hayward, B I (Ebbw Vale) 1998 Z (R), SA 1

Hayward, D J (Newbridge) 1949 E, F, 1950 E, S, I, F, 1951 E, S, I, F, SA, 1952 E, S, I, F

Hayward, D J (Cardiff) 1963 E, NZ, 1964 S, I, F, SA

Hayward, G (Swansea) 1908 S, F, I, A, 1909 E

Hellings, D (Llwynypia) 1897 E, 1898 I, E, 1899 S, I, 1900 E, I, 1901 E, S

Henson, G L (Swansea, Ospreys, Toulon) 2001 J 1(R), R, 2003 NZ(R), R, 2004 Arg 1, 2, SA1, 2, R, NZ, J, 2005 E, It, F, S, I, 2006 I(R), F(R), A, NZ(R), 2007 A1(t&R), 2(R), SA, 2008 E, S, It, I, F, 2009 F(R), It, I, 2011 Bb, E3

Herrerá, R C (Cross Keys) 1925 S, F, I, 1926 E, S, I, F, 1927 E

Hiams, H (Swansea) 1912 I, F

Hibbard, R M (Ospreys, Gloucester) 2006 Arg 1(R), 2(R), 2007 A1(R), 2(R), 2008 SA1(R), 2, C, 2009 C, US(R), 2011 E1(R) S(R), It(R), I(R), F(R), Arg, 2012 Bb(R), A2(R), Arg(R), Sm, 2013 F, It, S, E, SA, Arg, A, 2014 It, I, F, E, S(R), A, NZ, 2015 E, S, F(R), I 1(R), 2

Hickman, A (Neath) 1930 E, 1933 S

Hiddlestone, D D (Neath) 1922 E, S, I, F, 1924 NZ

Hill, A F (Cardiff) 1885 S, 1886 E, S, 1888 S, I, M, 1889 S, 1890 S, I, 1893 E, S, I, 1894 E, S, I

Hill, S D (Cardiff) 1993 Z 1, 2, Nm, 1994 I (R), F, SA, 1995 F, SA, 1996 A 2, F 2(R), It, 1997 E

Hinam, S (Cardiff) 1925 I, 1926 E, S, I, F

Hinton, J T (Cardiff) 1884 I

Hirst, G L (Newport) 1912 S, 1913 S, 1914 E, S, F, I

Hodder, W (Pontypool) 1921 E, S, F

Hodges, J J (Newport) 1899 E, S, I, 1900 E, S, I, 1901 E, S, 1902 E, S, I, 1903 E, S, I, 1904 E, S, 1905 E, S, I, NZ, 1906 E, S, I

Hodgson, G T R (Neath) 1962 I, 1963 E, S, I, F, NZ, 1964 E, S, I, F, SA, 1966 S, I, F, 1967 I

Hollingdale, B G (Swansea) 1912 SA, 1913 E

Hollingdale, T H (Neath) 1927 A, 1928 E, S, I, F, 1930 E

Holmes, T D (Cardiff) 1978 A 2, NZ, 1979 S, I, F, E, 1980 F, E, S, I, NZ, 1981 A, 1982 I, F, E, 1983 E, S, I, F, 1984 E, 1985 S, I, F, E, Fj

Hook, J W (Ospreys, Perpignan, Gloucester) 2006 Arg 1(R), 2, A(R), PI, C, NZ(R), 2007 I, S, F1, It, E1, A1, 2, Arg, F2, [C, A(R), J, Fj], SA, 2008 E, S, It(R), I(R), F, SA1(R), 2, 3(R), C, NZ(R) , 2009 S(R), F(R), It, NZ, Sm, Arg, A, 2010 E, S, F, I, It, SA1, A, SA2, Fj, NZ3, 2011 E1, S, It, I, F, E3, Arg, [SA, Sm, I(R), F, A], 2012 I(R), S(R), It(R), Bb, A 1(R), 3(R), Arg(R), NZ(R), 2013 I(R), It(R), E(R), SA(R), Arg(R), Tg, 2014 F(R), S(R), SA1(R), NZ(R), 2015 I 2, [Fj(R), A(R), SA(R)]

Hopkin, W H (Newport) 1937 S

Hopkins, K (Cardiff, Swansea) 1985 E, 1987 F, E, S, [Tg, C (R)], US

Hopkins, P L (Swansea) 1908 A, 1909 E, I, 1910 E

Hopkins, R (Maesteg) 1970 E (R)

Hopkins, T (Swansea) 1926 E, S, I, F

Hopkins, W J (Aberavon) 1925 E, S

Horsman, C L (Worcester) 2005 NZ(R), Fj, SA, A, 2006 PI, 2007 I, F1, It, E1, A2(R), E2, F2, [J, Fj]

Howarth, S P (Sale, Newport) 1998 SA 2, Arg, 1999 S, I, F 1, It, E, Arg 1, 2, SA, C, F 2, [Arg 3, J, Sm, A], 2000 F, It, E

Howells, B (Llanelli) 1934 E

Howells, D W (Ospreys) 2013 J1, 2(R)

Howells, W G (Llanelli) 1957 E, S, I, F

Howells, W H (Swansea) 1888 S, I
Howley, R (Bridgend, Cardiff) 1996 E, S, I, F 1, A 1, 2, Bb, F 2, It, A 3, SA, 1997 US, S, I, F, E, Tg (R), NZ, 1998 It, E, S, I, F, Z, SA 2, Arg, 1999 S, I, F 1, It, E, Arg 1, 2, SA, C, F 2, [Arg 3, J, Sm, A], 2000 F, It, E, Sm, US, SA, 2001 E, S, F, R, I, Arg, Tg, A, 2002 I, F, It, E, S
Hughes, D (Newbridge) 1967 NZ, 1969 NZ 2, 1970 SA, S, E, I
Hughes, G (Penarth) 1934 E, S, I
Hughes, H (Cardiff) 1887 S, 1889 S
Hughes, K (Cambridge U, London Welsh) 1970 I, 1973 A, 1974 S
Hullin, W G (Cardiff) 1967 S
Humphreys, J M (Cardiff, Bath) 1995 [NZ, I], SA, Fj, 1996 It, E, S, I, F 1, A 1, 2, Bb, It, A 3, SA, 1997 S, I, F, E, Tg (R), NZ (R), 1998 It (R), E (R), S (R), I (R), F (R), SA 2, Arg, 1999 S, Arg 2(R), SA (R), C, [J (R)], 2003 E 1, I 1
Hurrell, R J (Newport) 1959 F
Hutchinson, F O (Neath) 1894 I, 1896 S, I
Huxtable, R (Swansea) 1920 F, I
Huzzey, H V P (Cardiff) 1898 I, E, 1899 E, S, I
Hybart, A J (Cardiff) 1887 E

Ingledew, H M (Cardiff) 1890 I, 1891 E, S
Isaacs, I (Cardiff) 1933 E, S

Jackson, T H (Swansea) 1895 E
James, C R (Llanelli) 1958 A, F
James, D (Swansea) 1891 I, 1892 S, I, 1899 E
James, D (Cardiff) 1947 A, 1948 E, S, F, I
James, D R (Treorchy) 1931 F, I
James, D R (Bridgend, Pontypridd, Llanelli Scarlets) 1996 A 2(R), It, A 3, SA, 1997 S, I, F 1, Tg (R), 1998 F (R), Z, SA 1, 2, Arg, 1999 S, I, F, It, E, Arg 1, 2, SA, F 2, [Arg 3, Sm, A], 2000 F, It (R), I (R), Sm (R), US, SA, 2001 E, S, F, It, R, I, 2002 I, F, It, E, S (R), NZ(R), 2005 SA, A, 2006 I, F, 2007 E2, Arg, [J]
James, T E (Cardiff Blues, Wasps) 2007 E2(R), SA(R), 2008 SA2(R), 2009 C, US, Sm, Arg(R), A(R), 2010 E, NZ3
James, T O (Aberavon) 1935 I, 1937 S
James, W (Gloucester) 2007 E2, Arg(R), F2(R), [J]
James, W J (Aberavon) 1983 E, S, I, F, R, 1984 S, 1985 S, I, F, E, Fj, 1986 E, S, I, F, Fj, Tg, WS, 1987 E, S, I
James, W P (Aberavon) 1925 E, S
Jarman, H (Newport) 1910 E, S, I, 1911 E
Jarrett, K S (Newport) 1967 E, 1968 E, S, 1969 S, I, F, E, NZ 1, 2, A
Jarvis, A R (Ospreys) 2012 Arg, Sm, NZ, 2014 SA2(R), 3(R), 2015 E(R), S, F(R), I I(R), It 1, I 2, 3(R), It 2(R), [U(R), Fj(R), A(R)]
Jarvis, L (Cardiff) 1997 R (R)
Jeffery, J J (Cardiff Coll of Ed, Newport) 1967 NZ
Jenkin, A M (Swansea) 1895 I, 1896 E
Jenkins, A E (Llanelli) 1920 E, S, F, I, 1921 S, F, 1922 F, 1923 E, S, F, I, 1924 NZ, 1928 S, I
Jenkins, D M (Treorchy) 1926 E, S, I, F
Jenkins, D R (Swansea) 1927 A, 1929 E
Jenkins, E (Newport) 1910 S, I
Jenkins, E M (Aberavon) 1927 S, F, I, A, 1928 E, S, I, F, 1929 F, 1930 E, S, I, F, 1931 E, S, F, I, SA, 1932 E, S, I
Jenkins, G D (Pontypridd, Celtic Warriors, Cardiff Blues, Toulon) 2002 R, NZ(R), 2003 E 1(R), S 1(R), I 1, F, NZ, I 2(R), E 2, [C, Tg, It(R), NZ(R), E(R)], 2004 S(R), I(R), F, E, It, Arg 1(R), 2(R), SA1, 2(R), R, NZ, J, 2005 E, It, F, S, I, 2006 E(R), I(R), It(R), F(R), A, C, NZ(R), 2007 I, S(R), F1, It, E1, 2(R), Arg(R), F2(R), [C, A, J(R), Fj], 2008 E(R), It, I, F, SA1, 2, 3, NZ, A, 2009 S, E, F, It(R), I, NZ, Sm, Arg, A, 2010 S(R), It, A, NZ3, 2011 [Sm(R), Nm, Fj, I, F, A], 2012 S, E, It, F, A 1, 2, 3, Arg, Sm(R)(R), NZ(R), A4, 2013 I, F, It, E, SA, Arg, A, 2014 I, F, E, S, SA1, 2, A(R), It, SA 3, 2015 S, E, F, I I, 3, It 2, [E, Fj, SA]

Jenkins, G R (Pontypool, Swansea) 1991 F 2, [WS (R), Arg, A], 1992 I, F, E, S, A, 1993 C, 1994 S, I, F, E, Pt, Sp, C, Tg, WS, R, It, SA, 1995 F, E, S, I, [J], SA (R), Fj (t), 1996 E (R), 1997 US, US 1, C, 1998 S, I, F, Z, SA 1(R), 1999 I (R), F 1, It, E, Arg 1, 2, SA, F 2, [Arg 3, J, Sm, A], 2000 F, It, E, S, I, Sm, US, SA, A(R), Fj, SA 3, 2015 E, S, F, I 1, 3, It 2, [E ,Fj, SA]
Jenkins, J C (London Welsh) 1906 SA
Jenkins, J L (Aberavon) 1923 S, F
Jenkins, L H (Mon TC, Newport) 1954 I, 1956 E, S, I, F
Jenkins, N R (Pontypridd, Cardiff) 1991 E, S, I, F 1, 1992 I, F, E, S, 1993 E, S, I, F, Z 1, 2, Nm, J, C, 1994 S, I, F, E, Pt, Sp, C, Tg, WS, R, It, SA, 1995 F, E, S, I, [J, NZ, I], SA, Fj, 1996 F 1, A 1, 2, Bb, F 2, It, A 3(R), SA, 1997 S, I, F, E, Tg, NZ, 1998 It, E, S, I, F, SA 2, Arg 1, 2, SA, C, F 2, [Arg 3, J, Sm, A], 2000 F, It, E, I (R), Sm (R), US (R), SA, 2001 E, S, F, It, 2002 SA 1(R), 2(R), R
Jenkins, V G J (Oxford U, Bridgend, London Welsh) 1933 E, I, 1934 S, I, 1935 E, S, NZ, 1936 E, S, I, 1937 E, 1938 E, S, 1939 E
Jenkins, W J (Cardiff) 1912 I, F, 1913 S, I
John, B (Llanelli, Cardiff) 1966 A, 1967 S, 1968 E, S, I, F, 1969 S, I, F, E, NZ 1, 2, A, 1970 SA, S, E, I, 1971 E, S, I, F, 1972 E, S, F
John, D A (Llanelli) 1925 I, 1928 E, S, I
John, D E (Llanelli) 1923 F, I, 1928 E, S, I
John, E R (Neath) 1950 E, S, I, F, 1951 E, S, I, F, SA, 1952 E, S, I, F, 1953 E, S, I, F, NZ, 1954 E
John G (St Luke's Coll, Exeter) 1954 E, F
John, J H (Swansea) 1926 E, S, I, F, 1927 E, S, F, I
John, P (Pontypridd) 1994 Tg, 1996 Bb (t), 1997 US (R), US 1, 2, C, R, Tg, 1998 Z (R), SA 1
John, S C (Llanelli, Cardiff) 1995 S, I, 1997 E (R), Tg, NZ (R), 2000 F, It (R), E (R), Sm (R), SA (R), 2001 E (R), S (R), Tg (R), A, 2002 I, F, It (R), S (R)
Johnson, T A W (Cardiff) 1921 E, F, I, 1923 E, S, F, 1924 E, S, NZ, 1925 E, S, F
Johnson, W D (Swansea) 1953 E
Jones, A E (SEE Emyr)
Jones, A H (Cardiff) 1933 E, S
Jones, A M (Llanelli Scarlets) 2006 E(t&R), S(R)
Jones, A R (Ospreys) 2003 E 2(R), S 2, [C(R), Tg(R), It, NZ, E], 2004 S, I, Arg 1, 2, SA1, 2, R, NZ, J(t&R), 2005 E, It, F, S, I, US, NZ, Fj(R), SA(t&R), A(R), 2006 E, S, I, It, F, Arg 1, 2, A, PI(R), C, NZ, 2007 S, It(R), E1(R), A1, Arg, [C, A], 2008 E, S, I, F, SA1, 3, NZ, A, 2009 S, E, F, I, 2010 E, S, F, I, SA, SA1, NZ1, 2, A, SA2, Fj, NZ3, 2011 F, Arg, [SA, Sm, Fj, I, F], 2012 I, S, E, It, F, A 1, 2, 3, 2013 I, F, It, S, E, SA, 2014 It, I, F, E, S(R), SA1
Jones, A W (Mountain Ash) 1905 I
Jones, A-W (Ospreys) 2006 Arg 1, 2, PI, C(R), NZ(R), 2007 I, S, F1, It, E1, 2, Arg, F2, [C, A, J, Fj], SA, 2008 E, I, F, SA1, 2, 3, NZ, A, 2009 S, E, F, It, I, NZ, Sm, Arg, A, 2010 E, S, SA1(R), NZ1, 2, A, SA2, NZ3, 2011 E1, S, It, I, F, Bb(R), 2, 3, Arg, [SA, Sm, Nm, Fj(R), I, F, A(R)], 2012 E, It, F, Bb, A1(R), 2, 3, Arg, 2013 It(R), S, E, SA, Arg, Tg(R), A, 2014 It, I, E, S, SA1, 2, A, Fj(R), NZ, SA 3, 2015 E, S, F, I 1, I 3, [E, Fj, A, SA]
Jones, B J (Newport) 1960 I, F
Jones, B L (Devonport Services, Llanelli) 1950 E, S, I, F, 1951 E, S, SA, 1952 E, I, F
Jones, C (Harlequins) 2007 A1(R), 2
Jones, C W (Cambridge U, Cardiff) 1934 E, S, I, 1935 E, S, I, NZ, 1936 E, S, I, 1938 E, S, I
Jones, C W (Bridgend) 1920 E, S, F
Jones, D (Aberavon) 1897 E
Jones, D (Treherbert) 1902 E, S, I, 1903 E, S, I, 1905 E, S, I, NZ, 1906 E, S, SA
Jones, D (Neath) 1927 A
Jones, D (Cardiff) 1994 SA, 1995 F, E, S, [J, NZ, I], SA, Fj, 1996 It, E, S, I, F 1, A 1, 2, Bb, It, A 3
Jones, D A R (Llanelli Scarlets) 2002 Fj, C, NZ, 2003 It(R), E 1, S 1, I 1, F, NZ, E 2, [C, Tg, It, NZ(R), E], 2004 S, I, F, E, It, Arg 2, SA1, 2, R, NZ, J, 2005 E, Fj, 2006 F(R), 2008 SA1, 2(R), C, NZ(R), A(R), 2009 S, E(R), F(R), It, I, C, US, NZ(R)
Jones, D C J (Swansea) 1947 E, F, I, 1949 E, S, I, F
Jones, D J (Neath, Ospreys) 2001 A (R), 2002 I (R), F (R), 2003 I 2, S 2, [C, It], 2004 S, E, It, Arg1, 2, SA1(R), 2, R(R), NZ(t&R), J, 2005 US, C, NZ, SA, A, 2006 E, S, I, It, F, Arg 1, 2, A(R),

Lewis, W H (London Welsh, Cambridge U) 1926 I, 1927 E, F, I, A, 1928 F

Lewis-Roberts, E T (Sale) 2008 C(R)

Llewellyn, D S (Ebbw Vale, Newport) 1998 SA 1(R), 1999 F 1(R), It (R), [J (R)]

Llewellyn, G D (Neath) 1990 Nm 1, 2, Bb, 1991 E, S, I, F 1, A, F 2

Llewellyn, G O (Neath, Harlequins, Ospreys, Narbonne) 1989 NZ, 1990 E, S, I, 1991 E, S, A (R), 1992 I, F, E, S, A, 1993 E, S, I, F, Z 1, 2, Nm, J, C, 1994 S, I, F, E, Pt, Sp, C, Tg, WS, R, It, SA, 1995 F, E, S, I, [J, NZ, I], 1996 It, E, S, I, F 1, A 1, 2, Bb, F 2, It, A 3, SA, 1997 US, S, I, F, E, US 1, 2, NZ, 1998 It, E, 1999 C (R), [Sm], 2002 E (R), SA 1, 2, R(R), Fj, C, NZ, 2003 E 1(R), S 1(R), I 1, F, A, NZ, I 2, S 2(R), [C, Tg, It, E(R)], 2004 S, F(R), E(R), It, Arg 1, 2, SA1, R, NZ

Llewellyn, P D (Swansea) 1973 I, F, A, 1974 S, E

Llewellyn, W (Llwynypia) 1899 E, S, I, 1900 E, S, I, 1901 E, S, I, 1902 E, S, I, 1903 I, 1904 E, S, I, 1905 E, S, I, NZ

Llewelyn, D B (Newport, Llanelli) 1970 SA, S, E, I, F, 1971 E, S, I, F, 1972 E, S, F, NZ

Lloyd, A (Bath) 2001 J 1

Lloyd, D J (Bridgend) 1966 E, S, I, F, A, 1967 S, I, F, E, 1968 S, I, F, 1969 S, I, F, E, NZ 1, A, 1970 F, 1972 E, S, F, 1973 E, S

Lloyd, D P M (Llanelli) 1890 S, E, 1891 E, I

Lloyd, E (Llanelli) 1895 S

Lloyd, G L (Newport) 1896 I, 1899 S, I, 1900 E, S, 1901 E, S, 1902 S, I, 1903 E, S, I

Lloyd, R (Pontypool) 1913 S, F, I, 1914 E, S, F, I

Lloyd, T (Maesteg) 1953 I, F

Lloyd, T J (Neath) 1909 F, 1913 F, I, 1914 E, S, F, I

Loader, C D (Swansea) 1995 SA, Fj, 1996 F 1, A 1, 2, Bb, F 2, It, A 3, SA, 1997 US, S, I, F, E, US 1, R, Tg, NZ

Lockwood, T W (Newport) 1887 E, S, I

Long, E C (Swansea) 1936 E, S, I, 1937 E, S, 1939 S, I

Luscombe, H N (Newport Gwent Dragons, Harlequins) 2003 S 2(R), 2004 Arg 1, 2, SA1, 2, R, J, 2005 E, It, S(t&R), 2006 E, S, I, It, F, 2007 I

Lydiate, D J (Newport Gwent Dragons, Racing Métro, Ospreys) 2009 Arg(R), A, 2010 A, Fj, NZ3, 2011 E1, S, It, I, F, Bb, E2, 3, Arg, [SA, Sm, I, F, A], A, 2012 S, E, It, F, A 1, 2, 3, 2013 SA, Tg, A, 2014 It, I, F, E, S, SA1, 2, A, Fj, NZ, SA 3, 2015 E, S, F, I 1, It 1, I 3, [U(R), E, Fj, SA]

Lyne, H S (Newport) 1883 S, 1884 E, S, I, 1885 E

McBryde, R C (Swansea, Llanelli, Neath, Llanelli Scarlets) 1994 Fj, SA (t), 1997 US 2, 2000 I (R), 2001 E, S, F, It, R, I, Arg, Tg, A, 2002 I, F, It, E, S (R), SA 1, 2, C, NZ, 2003 A, NZ, E 2, S 2, [C, It, NZ, E], 2004 I, E, It, 2005 It(R), F(R), S(R), I(R)

McCall, B E W (Welch Regt, Newport) 1936 E, S, I

McCarley, A (Neath) 1938 E, S, I

McCusker, R J (Scarlets) 2010 SA1(R), NZ1(R), 2(R), 2011 F(R), 2012 Arg(R), 2013 J1

McCutcheon, W M (Swansea) 1891 S, 1892 E, S, 1893 E, S, I, 1894 E

McIntosh, D L M (Pontypridd) 1996 SA, 1997 E (R)

Madden, M (Llanelli) 2002 SA 1(R), R, Fj(R), 2003 I 1(R), F(R)

Maddock, H T (London Welsh) 1906 E, S, I, 1907 E, S, 1910 F

Maddocks, K (Neath) 1957 E

Main, D R (London Welsh) 1959 E, S, I, F

Mainwaring, H J (Swansea) 1961 F

Mainwaring, W T (Aberavon) 1967 S, I, F, E, NZ, 1968 E

Major, W C (Maesteg) 1949 F, 1950 S

Male, B O (Cardiff) 1921 F, 1923 S, 1924 S, I, 1927 E, S, F, I, 1928 S, I, F

Manfield, L (Mountain Ash, Cardiff) 1939 S, I, 1947 A, 1948 E, S, F, I

Mann, B B (Cardiff) 1881 E

Mantle, J T (Loughborough Colls, Newport) 1964 E, SA

Margrave, F L (Llanelli) 1884 E, S

Marinos, A W N (Newport, Gwent Dragons)) 2002 I (R), F, It, E, S, SA 1, 2, 2003 R

Marsden-Jones, D (Cardiff) 1921 E, 1924 NZ

Martin, A J (Aberavon) 1973 A, 1974 S, I, 1975 F, E, S, I, A, 1976 E, S, I, F, 1977 I, F, E, S, 1978 E, S, I, F, A 1, 2, NZ, 1979 S, I, F, E, 1980 F, E, S, I, NZ, 1981 I, F

Martin, W J (Newport) 1912 I, F, 1919 NZA

Mason, J E (Pontypridd) 1988 NZ 2(R)

Mathews, Rev A A (Lampeter) 1886 S

Mathias, R (Llanelli) 1970 F

Matthews, C M (Bridgend) 1939 I

Matthews, J (Cardiff), 1947 E, A, 1948 E, S, F, 1949 E, S, I, F, 1950 S, I, F, 1951 E, S, I, F

May, P S (Llanelli) 1988 E, S, I, F, NZ 1, 2, 1991 [WS]

Meek, N N (Pontypool) 1993 E, S, I

Meredith, A (Devonport Services) 1949 E, S, I

Meredith, B V (St Luke's Coll, London Welsh, Newport) 1954 I, F, S, 1955 E, S, I, F, 1956 E, S, I, F, 1957 E, S, I, F, 1958 A, E, S, I, 1959 E, S, I, F, 1960 E, S, F, SA, 1961 E, S, I, 1962 E, S, F, I

Meredith, C C (Neath) 1953 S, NZ, 1954 E, I, F, S, 1955 E, S, I, F, 1956 E, I, 1957 E, S

Meredith, J (Swansea) 1888 S, I, 1890 S, E

Merry, J A (Pill Harriers) 1912 I, F

Michael, G M (Swansea) 1923 E, S, F

Michaelson, R C B (Aberavon, Cambridge U) 1963 E

Millar, W H (Mountain Ash) 1896 I, 1900 E, S, I, 1901 E, S, I

Mills, F M (Swansea, Cardiff) 1892 E, S, I, 1893 E, S, I, 1894 E, S, I, 1895 E, S, I, 1896 E

Mitchell, C (Ospreys, Exeter) 2009 C(R), US(R), Sm(R), 2010 NZ2(R), 2011 E1, S, It, I, E2, 3, [Nm], 2013 I(R), F(R), It(R), J2(R)

Moon, R H St J B (Llanelli) 1993 F, Z 1, 2, Nm, J, C, 1994 S, I, F, E, Sp, C, Fj, WS, R, It, SA, 1995 E (R), 2000 S, I, Sm (R), US (R), 2001 E (R), S (R)

Moore, A P (Cardiff) 1995 [J], SA, Fj, 1996 It

Moore, A P (Swansea) 1995 SA (R), Fj, 1998 S, I, F, Z, SA 1, 1999 C, 2000 S, I, US (R), 2001 E (R), S, F, It, J 1, 2, R, I, Arg, Tg, A, 2002 F, It, E, S

Moore, S J (Swansea, Moseley) 1997 C, R, Tg

Moore, W J (Bridgend) 1933 I

Morgan, C H (Llanelli) 1957 I, F

Morgan, C I (Cardiff) 1951 I, F, SA, 1952 E, S, I, 1953 S, I, F, NZ, 1954 E, I, S, 1955 E, S, I, F, 1956 E, S, I, F, 1957 E, S, I, F, 1958 E, S, I, F

Morgan, C S (Cardiff Blues) 2002 I, F, It, E, S, SA 1, 2, R(R), 2003 F, 2005 US

Morgan, D (Swansea) 1885 S, 1886 E, S, 1887 E, S, I, 1889 I

Morgan, D (Llanelli) 1895 I, 1896 E

Morgan, D E (Llanelli) 1920 I, 1921 E, S, F

Morgan, D R R (Llanelli) 1962 E, S, F, I, 1963 E, S, I, F, NZ

Morgan, E (Swansea) 1914 E, S, F, I

Morgan, E (London Welsh) 1902 E, S, I, 1903 I, 1904 E, S, I, 1905 E, S, I, NZ, 1906 E, S, I, SA, 1908 F

Morgan, F L (Llanelli) 1938 E, S, I, 1939 E

Morgan, G R (Newport) 1984 S

Morgan, H J (Abertillery) 1958 E, S, I, F, 1959 I, F, 1960 E, 1961 E, S, I, F, 1962 E, S, F, I, 1963 S, I, F, 1965 E, S, I, F, 1966 E, S, I, F, A

Morgan, H P (Newport) 1956 E, S, I, F

Morgan, J L (Llanelli) 1912 SA, 1913 E

Morgan, K A (Pontypridd, Swansea, Newport Gwent Dragons) 1997 US 1, 2, C, R, NZ, 1998 S, I, F, 2001 J 1, 2, R, I, Arg, Tg, A, 2002 I, F, It, E, S, SA 1, 2, 2003 E 1, S 1, [C, It], 2004 J(R), 2005 E(R), It(R), F, S, I, US, C, NZ, Fj, 2006 A, PI, NZ, 2007 I, S, It, E1, Arg, F2, [C, A(R), J]

Morgan, M E (Swansea) 1938 E, S, I, 1939 E

Morgan, M J (Ospreys, Bristol) 2014 SA1(R), 2015 I 2(R), It 2(t&R), [U(R), Fj]

Morgan, N H (Newport) 1960 S, I, F

Morgan, P E J (Aberavon) 1961 E, S, F

Morgan, P J (Llanelli) 1980 S (R), I, NZ (R), 1981 I

Morgan, S (Cardiff Blues) 2007 A2(R)

Morgan, T (Llanelli) 1889 I

Morgan, T (Newport Gwent Dragons) 2015 I 2, [Fj, SA]

Morgan, W G (Cambridge U) 1927 F, I, 1929 E, S, F, I, 1930 I, F

Morgan, W I (Swansea) 1908 A, 1909 E, S, F, I, 1910 F, E, S, I, 1911 E, I, F, 1912 S

Morgan, W L (Cardiff) 1910 S

Moriarty, C R (Gloucester) 2015 I 2, It 2(R), [U(R), A(R)]

Moriarty, R D (Swansea) 1981 A, 1982 I, F, E, S, 1983 E, 1984 S, I, F, E, 1985 S, I, F, 1986 Fj, Tg, WS, 1987 [I, Tg, C (R), E, NZ, A]

Moriarty, W P (Swansea) 1986 I, F, Fj, Tg, WS, 1987 F, E, S, I, [I, Tg, C, E, NZ, A], 1988 E, S, I, F, NZ 1

Morley, J C (Newport) 1929 E, S, F, I, 1930 E, I, 1931 E, S, F, I, SA, 1932 E, S, I

Morris, D R (Neath, Swansea, Leicester) 1998 Z, SA 1(R), 2(R), 1999 S, I, It (R), 2000 US, SA, 2001 E, S, F, It, Arg, Tg, A, 2004 Arg 1(R), 2(R), SA1(R)

Morris, G L (Swansea) 1882 I, 1883 E, S, 1884 E, S

Morris, H T (Cardiff) 1951 F, 1955 I, F

Morris, J I T (Swansea) 1924 E, S

Morris, M S (S Wales Police, Neath) 1985 S, I, F, 1990 I, Nm 1, 2, Bb, 1991 I, F 1, [WS (R)], 1992 E

Morris, R R (Swansea, Bristol) 1933 S, 1937 S

Morris, S (Cross Keys) 1920 E, S, F, I, 1922 E, S, I, F, 1923 E, S, F, I, 1924 E, S, F, NZ, 1925 E, S, F

Morris, W (Llanelli) 1896 S, I, 1897 E

Morris, W D (Neath) 1967 F, E, 1968 E, S, I, F, 1969 S, I, F, E, NZ 1, 2, A, 1970 SA, S, E, I, F, 1971 E, S, I, F, 1972 E, S, F, NZ, 1973 E, S, I, A, 1974 S, I, F, E

Morris, W G H (Abertillery) 1919 NZA, 1920 F, 1921 I

Morris, W J (Newport) 1965 S, 1966 F

Morris, W J B (Pontypool) 1963 S, I

Moseley, K (Pontypool, Newport) 1988 NZ 2, R, 1989 S, I, 1990 F, 1991 F 2, [WS, Arg, A]

Murphy, C D (Cross Keys) 1935 E, S, I

Mustoe, L (Cardiff) 1995 Fj, 1996 A 1(R), 2, 1997 US 1, 2, C, R (R), 1998 E (R), I (R), F (R)

Nash, D (Ebbw Vale) 1960 SA, 1961 E, S, I, F, 1962 F

Navidi, J R (Cardiff Blues) 2013 J2

Newman, C H (Newport) 1881 E, 1882 I, 1883 E, S, 1884 E, S, 1885 E, S, 1886 E, 1887 E

Nicholas, D L (Llanelli) 1981 E, S, I, F

Nicholas, T J (Cardiff) 1919 NZA

Nicholl, C B (Cambridge U, Llanelli) 1891 I, 1892 E, S, I, 1893 E, S, I, 1894 E, S, 1895 E, S, I, 1896 E, S, I

Nicholl, D W (Llanelli) 1894 I

Nicholls, E G (Cardiff) 1896 S, I, 1897 E, 1898 I, E, 1899 E, S, I, 1900 S, I, 1901 E, S, I, 1902 E, S, I, 1903 I, 1904 E, 1905 I, NZ, 1906 E, S, I, SA

Nicholls, F E (Cardiff Harlequins) 1892 I

Nicholls, H C W (Cardiff) 1958 I

Nicholls, S H (Cardiff) 1888 M, 1889 S, I, 1891 S

Norris, C H (Cardiff) 1963 F, 1966 F

Norster, R L (Cardiff) 1982 S, 1983 E, S, I, F, 1984 S, I, F, E, A, 1985 S, I, F, E, Fj, 1986 Fj, Tg, WS, 1987 F, E, S, I, [I, C, E], US, 1988 E, S, I, F, NZ 1, WS, 1989 F, E

North, G P (Scarlets, Northampton) 2010 SA2, Fj, NZ3, 2011 F, Bb, E2, 3, Arg, [SA, Sm, Nm(R), Fj, I, F, A], A, 2012 I, S, E, It, F, A 1, 2, 3, Arg, Sm, 2013 I, F, It, S, E, SA, Arg, Tg, A, 2014 It, I, F, E, S, SA1, 2, A, Fj, NZ, 2015 E, F, I 1, It 1, I 3, It 2, [E, Fj, A, SA]

Norton, W B (Cardiff) 1882 I, 1883 E, S, 1884 E, S, I

Oakley, R L (Gwent Dragons) 2003 I 2, S 2(R)

O'Connor, A (Aberavon) 1960 SA, 1961 E, S, 1962 F, I

O'Connor, R (Aberavon) 1957 E

O'Neil, W (Cardiff) 1904 S, I, 1905 E, S, I, 1907 E, I, 1908 E, S, F, I

O'Shea, J P (Cardiff) 1967 S, I, 1968 S, I, F

Oliver, G (Pontypool) 1920 E, S, F, I

Osborne, W T (Mountain Ash) 1902 E, S, I, 1903 E, S, I

Ould, W J (Cardiff) 1924 E, S

Owen, A D (Swansea) 1924 E

Owen, G D (Newport) 1955 I, F, 1956 E, S, I, F

Owen, M J (Pontypridd, Newport Gwent Dragons) 2002 SA 1, 2, R, C(R), NZ(R), 2003 It, I 2, S 2, 2004 S(R), I(R), F, E, It, Arg 1, 2, SA2, R, NZ, J, 2005 E, It, F, S, I, NZ, Fj, SA, A, 2006 E, S, I, It, F, PI, 2007 A1(R), 2, E2, [C(R), A(R), J(R), Fj(R)]

Owen, R M (Swansea) 1901 I, 1902 E, S, I, 1903 E, S, I, 1904 E, S, I, 1905 E, S, I, NZ, 1906 E, S, I, SA, 1907 E, S, 1908 F, I, A, 1909 E, S, F, I, 1910 F, E, 1911 E, S, F, I, 1912 E, S

Owens, K J (Scarlets) 2011 [Nm(R)], 2012 S(t&R), E, It(R), F(R), A1, 3(R), Sm(R), NZ(R), A4(R), 2013 It(t&R), F(R), It(R), S(R), E(R), SA(R), Arg(R), Tg, A(R), 2014 It(R), I(R), F(R), E(R), S, SA1, 2, 2015 It 1(R), I 3, It 2, [U(R), E(R), Fj(R), A(R), SA(R)]

Packer, H (Newport) 1891 E, 1895 S, I, 1896 E, S, I, 1897 E

Palmer, F C (Swansea) 1922 E, S, I

Parfitt, F C (Newport) 1893 E, S, I, 1894 E, S, I, 1895 S, 1896 S, I

Parfitt, S A (Swansea) 1990 Nm 1(R), Bb

Parker, D S (Swansea) 1924 I, F, NZ, 1925 E, S, F, I, 1929 F, I, 1930 E

Parker, E T (Swansea) 1919 NZA, 1920 E, S, I, 1921 E, S, F, I, 1922 E, S, I, F, 1923 E, S, F

Parker, S T (Pontypridd, Celtic Warriors, Newport Gwent Dragons, Ospreys) 2002 R, Fj, C, NZ, 2003 E 2, [C, It, NZ], 2004 S, I, Arg 1, 2, SA1, 2, NZ, 2005 Fj, SA, A, 2006 PI, C, NZ, 2007 A1, 2, F2(t&R), [C, A], SA, 2008 E, S(R), It(R), SA1

Parker, W J (Swansea) 1899 E, S

Parks, R D (Pontypridd, Celtic Warriors) 2002 SA 1(R), Fj(R), 2003 I 2, S 2

Parsons, G (Newport) 1947 E

Pascoe, D (Bridgend) 1923 F, I

Pask, A E I (Abertillery) 1961 F, 1962 E, S, F, I, 1963 E, S, I, F, NZ, 1964 E, S, I, F, SA, 1965 E, S, I, F, 1966 E, S, I, F, A, 1967 S, I

Patchell, M R (Cardiff Blues) 2013 J1(R), 2(R)

Payne, G W (Army, Pontypridd) 1960 E, S, I

Payne, H (Swansea) 1935 NZ

Peacock, H (Newport) 1929 S, F, I, 1930 S, I, F

Peake, E (Chepstow) 1881 E

Pearce, P G (Bridgend) 1981 I, F, 1982 I (R)

Pearson, T W (Cardiff, Newport) 1891 E, I, 1892 E, S, 1894 S, I, 1895 E, S, I, 1897 E, 1898 I, E, 1903 E

Peel, D J (Llanelli Scarlets, Sale) 2001 J 2(R), R (R), Tg (R), 2002 I (R), It (R), E (R), S (R), SA 1, 2, R, Fj, C, NZ, 2003 It, S 1(R), I 1(R), F, NZ(R), I 2, S 2, [C(R), Tg(R), It, NZ(R), E(R)], 2004 S(R), I(R), F(R), E(R), It(R), Arg 1, 2, SA1, 2, R, NZ, 2005 E, It, F, S, I, 2006 E, S, I, It, A, C, NZ, 2007 I, F, S, F1, It, E1, Arg, F2, [C, A, Fj], SA, 2008 S(R), It, SA3(R), C(R), NZ(R), 2009 S(R), F(R), C(R), US, Sm, Arg(R), A, 2010 I(R), It(R), 2011 E1(R), F(R)

Pegge, E V (Neath) 1891 E

Perego, M A (Llanelli) 1990 S, 1993 F, Z 1, Nm (R), 1994 S, I, F, E, Sp

Perkins, S J (Pontypool) 1983 S, I, F, R, 1984 S, I, F, E, A, 1985 S, I, F, E, Fj, 1986 E, S, I, F

Perrett, F L (Neath) 1912 SA, 1913 E, S, F, I

Perrins, V C (Newport) 1970 SA, S

Perry, W J (Neath) 1911 E

Phillips, A J (Cardiff) 1979 E, 1980 F, E, S, I, NZ, 1981 E, S, I, F, A, 1982 I, F, E, S, 1987 [C, E, A]

Phillips, B (Aberavon) 1925 E, S, F, I, 1926 E

Phillips, D E (Scarlets) 2013 J1, 2, Tg(R)

Phillips, D H (Swansea) 1952 F

Phillips, H P (Newport) 1892 E, 1893 E, S, I, 1894 E, S

Phillips, H T (Newport) 1927 E, S, F, I, A, 1928 E, S, I, F

Phillips, K H (Neath) 1987 F, [I, Tg, NZ], US, 1988 E, NZ 1, 1989 NZ, 1990 F, E, S, I, Nm 1, 2, Bb, 1991 E, S, I, F 1, A

Phillips, L A (Newport) 1900 S, I, 1901 S

Phillips, R D (Neath) 1987 US, 1988 E, S, I, F, NZ 1, 2, WS, 1989 S, I

Phillips, W D (Cardiff) 1881 E, 1882 I, 1884 E, S, I

Phillips, W M (Llanelli Scarlets, Cardiff Blues, Ospreys, Bayonne, Racing Métro) 2003 R, 2004 Arg 1(R), 2(R), J(R), 2005 US, C, NZ, Fj(R), SA(R), 2006 S(R), It(R), F, Arg 1, 2, PI, C(R), NZ(R), 2007 I(R), F1(R), E1(R), A1, 2, F2(R), [C(R), A(R), J, Fj(R)], SA(R), 2008 E, S, It(R), I, F, 2009 S, E, F, It, I, 2010 It, SA1, NZ1, 2, A, SA2, Fj(R), NZ3, 2011 E1, S, It, I, F, Bb, E2, 3, [SA, Sm, Fj, I, F, A], 2012 I, S, E, It, F, A 1, 2, 3, Arg(R), Sm, NZ, A4, 2013 I, F, It, S, E, SA, Arg, A, 2014 It, I, F(R), E(R), S, SA1, 2, A(R), Fj, NZ(R), 2015 E(R), S(R), I 1(R), 2

Pickering, D F (Llanelli) 1983 E, S, I, F, R, 1984 S, I, F, E, A, 1985 S, I, F, E, Fj, 1986 E, S, I, F, Fj, 1987 F, E, S

Plummer, R C S (Newport) 1912 S, I, F, SA, 1913 E

Pook, T R (Newport) 1895 S

Popham, A J (Leeds, Llanelli Scarlets) 2003 A (R), I 2, R, S 2, [Tg, NZ], 2004 I(R), It(R), SA1, J(R), 2005 C, Fj(R), 2006 E(R), It(R), F, Arg 1, 2, PI, NZ(R), 2007 I, S, F1, It, E1, 2(R), Arg, F2, [C, A(t), J, Fj], SA(R), 2008 E(R)

Powell, A T (Cardiff Blues, Wasps, Sale) 2008 SA3, C(R), NZ, A, 2009 S, F, E, It, NZ, Sm, Arg, A, 2010 E, S, SA2, NZ3(R), 2011 E1, Arg, [Sm(R), Nm(R), Fj(R), A(R)], 2012 S(R)

Powell, G (Ebbw Vale) 1957 I, F

Powell, J (Cardiff) 1923 I

Powell, J A (Cardiff) 1906 I

Powell, R D (Cardiff) 2002 SA 1(R), 2(R), C(R)

Powell, R W (Newport) 1888 S, I

Powell, W C (London Welsh) 1926 S, I, F, 1927 E, F, I, 1928 S, I, F, 1929 E, S, F, I, 1930 S, I, F, 1931 E, S, F, I, SA, 1932 E, S, I, 1935 E, S, I

Powell, W J (Cardiff) 1920 E, S, F, I

Pretorius, W A (Cardiff Blues) 2013 J1(R), 2

Price, B (Newport) 1961 I, F, 1962 E, S, 1963 E, S, F, NZ, 1964 E, S, I, F, SA, 1965 E, S, I, F, 1966 E, S, I, F, A, 1967 S, I, F, E, 1969 S, I, F, NZ 1, 2, A

Price, G (Pontypool) 1975 F, E, S, I, A, 1976 E, S, I, F, 1977 I, F, E, S, 1978 E, S, I, F, A 1, 2, NZ, 1979 S, I, F, E, 1980 F, E, S, I, NZ, 1981 E, S, I, F, A, 1982 I, F, E, S, 1983 E, I, F

Price, M J (Pontypool, RAF) 1959 E, S, I, F, 1960 E, S, I, F, 1962 E

Price, R E (Weston-s-Mare) 1939 S, I

Price, T G (Llanelli) 1965 E, S, I, F, 1966 E, A, 1967 S, F

Priday, A J (Cardiff) 1958 I, 1961 I

Priestland, R (Scarlets, Bath) 2011 S(R), Bb(R), E2, 3, [SA, Sm, Nm(R), Fj, I], A, 2012 I, S, E, It, F, A 1, 2, 3, Arg, Sm(R), NZ, A4, 2013 SA, Tg(R), A(R), 2014 It, I, F, E, S(R), A(R), Fj, 2015 F(R), It 1(R), I 3(R), [U, E(R), Fj(R), A(R), SA(R)]

Pritchard, C C (Newport, Pontypool) 1904 S, I, 1905 NZ, 1906 E, S

Pritchard, C C (Pontypool) 1928 E, S, I, F, 1929 E, S, F, I

Pritchard, C M (Newport) 1904 I, 1905 E, S, NZ, 1906 E, S, I, SA, 1907 E, S, I, 1908 E, 1910 F, E

Proctor, W T (Llanelli) 1992 A, 1993 E, S, Z 1, 2, Nm, C, 1994 I, C, Fj, WS, R, It, SA, 1995 S, I, [NZ], Fj, 1996 It, E, S, I, A 1, 2, Bb, F 2, It, A 3, 1997 E(R), US 1, 2, C, R, 1998 E (R), S, I, F, Z, 2001 A

Prosser, D R (Neath) 1934 S, I

Prosser, F J (Cardiff) 1921 I

Prosser, G (Pontypridd) 1995 [NZ]

Prosser, I G (Neath) 1934 E, S, I, 1935 NZ

Prosser, T R (Pontypool) 1956 S, F, 1957 E, S, I, F, 1958 A, E, S, I, F, 1959 E, S, I, F, 1960 E, S, I, F, SA, 1961 I, F

Prothero, G J (Bridgend) 1964 S, I, F, 1965 E, S, I, F, 1966 E, S, I, F

Pryce-Jenkins, T J (London Welsh) 1888 S, I

Prydie, T W J (Ospreys, Newport Gwent Dragons) 2010 It, SA1, NZ1, 2, 2013 J2

Pugh, C H (Maesteg) 1924 E, S, I, F, NZ, 1925 E, S

Pugh, J D (Neath) 1987 US, 1988 S (R), 1990 S

Pugh, P (Neath) 1989 NZ

Pugh, R (Ospreys) 2005 US(R)

Pugsley, J (Cardiff) 1910 E, S, I, 1911 E, S, F, I

Pullman, J J (Neath) 1910 F

Purdon, F T (Newport) 1881 I, 1882 I, 1883 E, S

Quinnell, D L (Llanelli) 1972 F (R), NZ, 1973 E, S, A, 1974 S, F, 1975 E (R), 1977 I (R), F, E, S, 1978 E, S, I, F, A 1, NZ, 1979 S, I, F, E, 1980 NZ

Quinnell, J C (Llanelli, Richmond, Cardiff) 1995 Fj, 1996 A 3(R), 1997 US (R), S (R), I (R), E (R), 1998 SA 2, Arg, 1999 I, F 1, It, E, Arg 1, 2, SA, C, F 2, [Arg 3, J, A], 2000 It, E, 2001 S (R), F (R), It (R), J 1, 2, R (R), I (R), Arg, 2002 I, F

Quinnell, L S (Llanelli, Richmond) 1993 C, 1994 S, I, F, E, Pt, Sp, C, WS, 1997 US, S, I, F, E, 1998 It, E, S (R), Z, SA 2, Arg, 1999 S, I, F 1, It, E, Arg 1, 2, SA, C, F 2, [Arg 3, Sm, A], 2000 F, It, E, Sm, US, SA, 2001 E, S, F, It, Arg, Tg, A, 2002 I, F, It, E, R, C(R)

Radford, W J (Newport) 1923 I

Ralph, A R (Newport) 1931 F, I, SA, 1932 E, S, I

Ramsay, S (Treorchy) 1896 E, 1904 E

Randall, R J (Aberavon) 1924 I, F

Raybould, W H (London Welsh, Cambridge U, Newport) 1967 S, I, F, E, NZ, 1968 I, F, 1970 SA, E, I, F (R)

Rayer, M A (Cardiff) 1991 [WS (R), Arg, A (R)], 1992 E (R), A, 1993 E, S, I, Z 1, Nm, J (R), 1994 S (R), I (R), F, E, Pt, C, Fj, WS, R, It

Reed, L (Scarlets, Cardiff Blues) 2012 S(R), A4, 2013 F(R), J1, 2

Rees, A (Maesteg) 1919 NZA

Rees, A (Maesteg) 1962 E, S, F

Rees, A M (London Welsh) 1934 E, 1935 E, S, I, NZ, 1936 E, S, I, 1937 E, S, I, 1938 E, S

Rees, B I (London Welsh) 1967 S, I, F

Rees, C F W (London Welsh) 1974 I, 1975 A, 1978 NZ, 1981 F, A, 1982 I, F, E, S, 1983 E, S, I, F

Rees, D (Swansea) 1900 E, S, 1905 E, S

Rees, D (Swansea) 1968 S, I, F

Rees, E B (Swansea) 1919 NZA

Rees, H E (Neath) 1979 S, I, F, E, 1980 F, E, S, I, NZ, 1983 E, S, I, F

Rees, H T (Cardiff) 1937 S, I, 1938 E, S, I

Rees, J (Swansea) 1920 E, S, F, I, 1921 E, S, I, 1922 E, 1923 E, F, I, 1924 E

Rees, J I (Swansea) 1934 E, S, I, 1935 S, NZ, 1936 E, S, I, 1937 E, S, I, 1938 E, S, I

Rees, L M (Cardiff) 1933 I

Rees, M (Scarlets, Cardiff Blues) 2005 US, 2006 Arg 1, A, C, NZ(R), 2007 I(R), S(t&R), F1, It, E1, A1, Arg, F2, [C, A, Fj], 2008 E(R), S(R), It, I, F(R), SA1, 3, NZ, A, 2009 S, E, F, It(R), I, NZ, Sm(R), Arg, A, 2010 I, It, SA1, NZ1, 2, A, SA2, NZ3, 2011 E1, S, It, I, F, A(R), 2012 It, F, Bb, A 1(R), 2, 3, Arg, NZ, A4, 2013 I, 2014 SA1(R), 2(R)

Rees, P (Llanelli) 1947 F, I

Rees, P M (Newport) 1961 E, S, I, 1964 I

Rees, R (Swansea) 1998 Z

Rees, R S (Cardiff Blues) 2010 E(R), S(R), F, I, NZ2(R), A(R), SA2(R), Fj, NZ3(R)

Rees, T A (Llandovery) 1881 E

Rees, T E (London Welsh) 1926 I, F, 1927 A, 1928 E

Rees, T J (Newport) 1935 S, I, NZ, 1936 E, S, I, 1937 E, S

Rees-Jones, G R (Oxford U, London Welsh) 1934 E, S, 1935 I, NZ, 1936 E

Reeves, F C (Cross Keys) 1920 F, I, 1921 E

Reynolds, A D (Swansea) 1990 Nm 1, 2(R), 1992 A (R)

Rhapps, J (Penygraig) 1897 E

Rice-Evans, W (Swansea) 1890 S, 1891 E, S

Richards, D S (Swansea) 1979 F, E, 1980 F, E, S, I, NZ, 1981 E, S, I, F, 1982 I, F, 1983 E, S, I, R (R)

Richards, E G (Cardiff) 1927 S

Richards, E I (Cardiff) 1925 E, S, F

Richards, E S (Swansea) 1885 E, 1887 S

Richards, H D (Neath) 1986 Tg (R), 1987 [Tg, E (R), NZ]

Richards, K H L (Bridgend) 1960 SA, 1961 E, S, I, F

Richards, M C R (Cardiff) 1968 I, F, 1969 S, I, F, E, NZ 1, 2, A

Richards, R (Aberavon) 1913 S, F, I

Richards, R C (Cross Keys) 1956 F

Richards, T B (Swansea) 1960 F

Richards, T L (Maesteg) 1923 I

Richards, W C (Pontypool) 1922 E, S, I, F, 1924 I

Richardson, S J (Aberavon) 1978 A 2(R), 1979 E

Rickards, A R (Cardiff) 1924 F

Ring, J (Aberavon) 1921 E

Ring, M G (Cardiff, Pontypool) 1983 E, 1984 A, 1985 S, I, F, 1987 I, [I, Tg, A], US, 1988 E, S, I, F, NZ 1, 2, 1989 NZ, 1990 F, E, S, I, Nm 1, 2, Bb, 1991 E, S, I, F 1, 2, [WS, Arg, A]

Ringer, J (Bridgend) 2001 J 1(R), 2(R)

Ringer, P (Ebbw Vale, Llanelli) 1978 NZ, 1979 S, I, F, E, 1980 F, E, NZ

Roberts, C R (Neath) 1958 I, F

Roberts, D E A (London Welsh) 1930 E

Roberts, E (Llanelli) 1886 E, 1887 I

Roberts, E J (Llanelli) 1888 S, I, 1889 I

Roberts, G J (Cardiff) 1985 F (R), E, 1987 [I, Tg, C, E, A]

Roberts, H M (Cardiff) 1960 SA, 1961 E, S, I, F, 1962 S, F, 1963 I

Roberts, J (Cardiff) 1927 E, S, F, I, A, 1928 E, S, I, F, 1929 E, S, F, I

Roberts, J H (Cardiff Blues Racing Métro, Harlequins) 2008 S, SA1, 2, 3, C(R), NZ, A, 2009 S, E, F, It, I(R), NZ, Sm, Arg, A, 2010 E, S, F, I, It, SA1, NZ1, 2, 2011 E1, S, It, I, F, E2, 3, Arg, [SA, Sm, Fj, I, F, A], A, 2012 I, S, E, It, F, Arg, Sm, NZ, A4, 2013 I, F, It, S, E, 2014 It, I, F, E, S, SA1, 2, A, Fj, NZ, SA 3, 2015 E, S, F, I 1, It 1, I 3, [E, Fj, A, SA]

Roberts, M (Scarlets) 2008 C, 2009 NZ(R), A(t&R)

Roberts, M G (London Welsh) 1971 E, S, I, F, 1973 I, F, 1975 S, 1979 E

Roberts, T (Newport, Risca) 1921 S, F, I, 1922 E, S, I, F, 1923 E, S
Roberts, W (Cardiff) 1929 E
Robins, J D (Birkenhead Park) 1950 E, S, I, F, 1951 E, S, I, F, 1953 E, I, F
Robins, R J (Pontypridd) 1953 S, 1954 F, S, 1955 E, S, I, F, 1956 E, F, 1957 E, S, I, F
Robinson, H R (Cardiff Blues) 2012 Bb, 2013 J1, 2
Robinson, I R (Cardiff) 1974 F, E
Robinson, J P (Cardiff Blues) 2001 J 1(R), 2(R), Arg (R), Tg (R), A, 2002 I, Fj(R), C, NZ, 2003 A, NZ, I 2, S 2, 2006 Arg 1, 2, 2007 I, S, F1(R), A1, 2, Arg(t&R), F2, [J]
Robinson, M F D (Swansea) 1999 S, I, F 1, Arg 1
Robinson, N J (Cardiff Blues) 2003 I 2, R, 2004 Arg 1(R), 2, SA1, 2005 US, C, NZ(R), Fj, 2006 S(R), Arg 1, 2, 2009 US
Rocyn-Jones, D N (Cambridge U) 1925 I
Roderick, W B (Llanelli) 1884 I
Rogers, P J D (London Irish, Newport, Cardiff) 1999 F 1, It, E, Arg 1, 2, SA, C, F 2, [Arg 3, J, Sm, A], 2000 F, It, E, S, I, SA
Rosser, M A (Penarth) 1924 S, F
Rowland, E M (Lampeter) 1885 E
Rowlands, C F (Aberavon) 1926 I
Rowlands, D C T (Pontypool) 1963 E, S, I, F, NZ, 1964 E, S, I, F, SA, 1965 E, S, I, F
Rowlands, G (RAF, Cardiff) 1953 NZ, 1954 E, F, 1956 F
Rowlands, K A (Cardiff) 1962 F, I, 1963 I, 1965 I, F
Rowles, G A (Penarth) 1892 E
Rowley, M (Pontypridd) 1996 SA, 1997 US, S, I, F, R
Roy, W S (Cardiff) 1995 [J (R)]
Russell, S (London Welsh) 1987 US

Samuel, D (Swansea) 1891 I, 1893 I
Samuel, J (Swansea) 1891 I
Samuel, T F (Mountain Ash) 1922 S, I, F
Scourfield, T B (Torquay Athletic) 1930 F
Scrine, F G (Swansea) 1899 E, S, 1901 I
Selley, T J (Llanelli Scarlets) 2005 US(R)
Shanklin, J L (London Welsh) 1970 F, 1972 NZ, 1973 I, F
Shanklin, T G L (Saracens, Cardiff Blues) 2001 J 2, 2002 F, It, SA 1(R), 2(R), R, Fj, 2003 It, E 1, S 1, I 1, F(t+R), A, NZ, S 2, [Tg, NZ], 2004 I(R), F(R), E, It(R), Arg 1(R), 2, SA1, 2(R), R, NZ, J, 2005 E, It, F, S, I, 2006 A, C, NZ, 2007 S(R), F1, It, E1, 2, Arg, [C, A, J(R), Fj], 2008 E(R), S, It, I, F, SA1, 2, 3, C, NZ, A, 2009 S, E, F, It(R), I, NZ, Sm, 2010 It(R), A, SA2, Fj(R), NZ3
Shaw, G (Neath) 1972 NZ, 1973 E, S, I, F, A, 1974 S, I, F, E, 1977 I, F
Shaw, T W (Newbridge) 1983 R
Shea, J (Newport) 1919 NZA, 1920 E, S, 1921 E
Shell, R C (Aberavon) 1973 A (R)
Shingler, A C (Scarlets) 2012 SA, Bb(R), NZ(R), A4, 2013 I, F(R), E(R), 2014 SA1
Sidoli, R A (Pontypridd, Celtic Warriors, Cardiff Blues) 2002 SA 1(R), 2(R), R, Fj, NZ, 2003 It, E 1, S 1, I 1, F, A, NZ, E 2, [C(R), Tg, It(R), NZ, E], 2004 I, It(R), 2005 E, It, F, S, I, C, NZ, Fj(R), SA, A, 2006 E, S, I, It, F, PI, C(R), 2007 I(t&R), S, A1, 2, E2
Simpson, H J (Cardiff) 1884 E, S, I
Sinkinson, B D (Neath) 1999 F 1, It, E, Arg 1, 2, SA, F 2, [Arg 3, J, Sm, A], 2000 F, It, E, 2001 R (R), I, Arg (R), Tg, A, 2002 It (R)
Skrimshire, R T (Newport) 1899 E, S, I
Skym, A (Llanelli) 1928 E, S, I, F, 1930 E, S, I, F, 1931 E, S, F, I, SA, 1932 E, S, I, 1933 E, S, I, 1935 E
Smith, J S (Cardiff) 1884 E, I, 1885 E
Smith, N P (Ospreys) 2014 Fj(R), NZ(R), 2015 I 2
Smith, R (Ebbw Vale) 2000 F (R)
Sowden-Taylor, R (Cardiff Blues) 2005 It(R), C(R), NZ(R), 2007 A2(R), SA, 2008 C, 2009 C, US
Sparks, B A (Neath) 1954 I, 1955 E, F, 1956 E, S, I, 1957 S
Spiller, W (Cardiff) 1910 S, I, 1911 E, S, F, I, 1912 E, F, SA, 1913 E
Spratt, J P (Ospreys) 2009 C(R), US(R), 2013 J1, 2
Squire, J (Newport, Pontypool) 1977 I, F, 1978 E, S, I, F, A 1, NZ, 1979 S, I, F, E, 1980 F, E, S, I, NZ, 1981 E, S, I, F, A, 1982 I, F, E, 1983 E, S, I, F
Stadden, W J (Cardiff) 1884 I, 1886 E, S, 1887 I, 1888 S, M, 1890 S, E

Stephens, C (Bridgend) 1998 E (R), 2001 J 2(R)
Stephens, C J (Llanelli) 1992 I, F, E, A
Stephens, G (Neath) 1912 E, S, I, F, SA, 1913 E, S, F, I, 1919 NZA
Stephens, I (Bridgend) 1981 E, S, I, F, A, 1982 I, F, E, S, 1984 I, F, E, A
Stephens, Rev J G (Llanelli) 1922 E, S, I, F
Stephens, J R G (Neath) 1947 E, S, F, I, 1948 I, 1949 S, I, F, 1951 F, SA, 1952 E, S, I, F, 1953 E, S, I, F, NZ, 1954 E, I, 1955 E, S, I, F, 1956 S, I, F, 1957 E, S, I, F
Stock, A (Newport) 1924 F, NZ, 1926 E, S
Stoddart, M L (Llanelli Scarlets) 2007 SA, 2008 SA1(R), C, 2011 E1, S, It, Bb, E2
Stone, P (Llanelli) 1949 F
Strand-Jones, J (Llanelli) 1902 E, S, I, 1903 E, S
Sullivan, A C (Cardiff) 2001 Arg, Tg
Summers, R H B (Haverfordwest) 1881 E
Sutton, S (Pontypool, S Wales Police) 1982 F, E, 1987 F, E, S, I, [C, NZ (R), A]
Sweeney, C (Pontypridd, Celtic Warriors, Newport Gwent Dragons) 2003 It(R), E 1, NZ(R), I 2, S 2, [C, It, NZ(t&R), E(t)], 2004 I(R), F(R), E(R), It(R), Arg 1, SA1(R), 2(R), R(R), J, 2005 It(R), F(t), S(R), US, C, NZ, Fj(R), SA(t&R), A(R), 2006 PI, C(R), 2007 S(t), A2(R), E2, F2(R), [J(R)], SA(R)
Sweet-Escott, R B (Cardiff) 1891 S, 1894 I, 1895 I

Tamplin, W E (Cardiff) 1947 S, F, I, A, 1948 E, S, F
Tanner, H (Swansea, Cardiff) 1935 NZ, 1936 E, S, I, 1937 E, S, I, 1938 E, S, I, 1939 E, S, I, 1947 E, S, F, I, 1948 E, S, F, I, 1949 E, S, I, F
Tarr, D J (Swansea, Royal Navy) 1935 NZ
Taylor, A R (Cross Keys) 1937 I, 1938 I, 1939 E
Taylor, C G (Ruabon) 1884 E, S, I, 1885 E, S, 1886 E, S, 1887 E, I
Taylor, H T (Cardiff) 1994 Pt, C, Fj, Tg, WS (R), R, It, SA, 1995 E, S, [J, NZ, I], SA, Fj, 1996 It, E, S, I, F, A 1, 2, It, A 3
Taylor, J (London Welsh) 1967 S, I, F, E, NZ, 1968 I, F, 1969 S, I, F, E, NZ 1, A, 1970 F, 1971 E, S, I, F, 1972 E, S, F, NZ, 1973 E, S, I, F
Taylor, M (Pontypool, Swansea, Llanelli Scarlets, Sale) 1994 SA, 1995 F, E, SA, 1998 Z, SA 1, 2, Arg, 1999 I, F 1, It, E, Arg 1, 2, SA, F 2, [Arg 3, J, Sm, A], 2000 F, It, E, S, Sm, US, 2001 E, S, F, It, 2002 S, SA 1, 2, 2003 E 1, S 1, I 1, F, A, NZ, E 2, [C(R), Tg, NZ, E], 2004 F, It, R(R), 2005 I, US, C, NZ

Thomas, A C (Bristol, Swansea) 1996 It, E, S, I, F 2(R), SA, 1997 US, S, I, F, US 1, 2, C, R, NZ (t), 1998 It, E, S (R), SA 1, 2000 Sm, US, SA (R)
Thomas, A R F (Newport) 1963 NZ, 1964 E
Thomas, A G (Swansea, Cardiff) 1952 E, S, I, F, 1953 S, I, F, 1954 E, I, F, 1955 S, I, F
Thomas, B (Neath, Cambridge U) 1963 E, S, I, F, NZ, 1964 E, S, I, F, SA, 1965 E, 1966 E, S, I, 1967 NZ, 1969 S, I, F, E, NZ 1, 2
Thomas, B M G (St Bart's Hospital) 1919 NZA, 1921 S, F, I, 1923 F, 1924 E
Thomas, C (Newport) 1888 I, M, 1889 S, I, 1890 S, E, I, 1891 E, I
Thomas, C R (Bridgend) 1925 E, S
Thomas, D J (Swansea) 1904 E, 1908 A, 1910 E, S, I, 1911 E, S, F, I, 1912 E
Thomas, D J (Swansea) 1930 S, I, F, 1932 E, S, I, 1933 E, S, 1934 E, 1935 E, S, I
Thomas, D L (Newport) 1937 E
Thomas, D L (Aberavon) 1961 I
Thomas, E (Newport) 1904 S, I, 1909 S, F, I, 1910 F
Thomas, E J R (Mountain Ash) 1906 SA, 1908 F, I, 1909 S
Thomas, G (Newport) 1888 M, 1890 I, 1891 S
Thomas, G (Bridgend, Cardiff, Celtic Warriors, Toulouse, Cardiff Blues) 1995 [J, NZ, I], SA, Fj, 1996 F 1, A 1, 2, Bb, F 2, It, A 3, 1997 US, S, I, F, E, US 1, 2, C, R, Tg, NZ, 1998 It, E, S, I, F, SA 2, Arg, 1999 F 1(R), It, E, Arg, SA, F 2, [Arg 3, J (R), Sm, A], 2000 F, It, E, S, I, US (R), SA, 2001 E, F, It, J 1, 2, R, Arg, Tg, A, 2002 E, R, Fj, C, 2003 It, E 1, S 1, I 1, F, I 2, E 2, [C, It, NZ(R), E], 2004 S, I, F, E, It, SA2, R, NZ, 2005 E, It, F, NZ, SA, A, 2006 E, S, A, C, 2007 It(t&R), E1, A1, 2, E2, Arg, F2, [C(R), A, Fj]]

Thomas, G M (Bath, Ospreys, Llanelli Scarlets, Newport Gwent Dragons) 2001 J 1, 2, R, I (R), Arg, Tg (R), A (R), 2002 S (R), SA 2(R), R(R), 2003 It(R), E 1, S 1, F, E 2(R), R, 2006 Arg 1, 2, PI, 2007 I(t&R), A1, 2, 2010 NZ1, 2

Thomas, H H M (Llanelli) 1912 F

Thomas, H W (Swansea) 1912 SA, 1913 E

Thomas, H W (Neath) 1936 E, S, I, 1937 E, S, I

Thomas, I (Bryncethin) 1924 E

Thomas, I D (Ebbw Vale, Llanelli Scarlets) 2000 Sm, US (R), SA (R), 2001 J 1, 2, R, I, Arg (R), Tg, 2002 It, E, S, SA 1, 2, Fj, C, NZ, 2003 It, E 1, S 1, I 1, F, A, NZ, E 2, [Tg, NZ, E], 2004 I, F, 2007 A1, 2, E2

Thomas, J D (Llanelli) 1954 I

Thomas, J J (Swansea, Ospreys) 2003 A, NZ(R), E 2(R), R, [It(R), NZ, E], 2004 S(t&R), I, F, E, Arg 2(R), SA1(R), R(t&R), J, 2005 E(R), It, F(R), S(R), US, C, NZ, 2006 It(R), F(R), A, PI(R), C, NZ, 2007 S(R), F1(R), It(R), E1(R), A1, 2, Arg, F2, [C, A], SA, 2008 E, S, It, I, F, SA1, 2, 2009 It, Sm(R), Arg(R), A(R), 2010 E(R), S, F, I, It, SA1, NZ1, 2, A, SA2, Fj, NZ3(R), 2011 E1(R), S(R), I(R), F(R), Arg(R)

Thomas, L C (Cardiff) 1885 E, S

Thomas, M C (Newport, Devonport Services) 1949 F, 1950 E, S, I, F, 1951 E, S, I, F, SA, 1952 E, S, I, F, 1953 E, 1956 E, S, I, F, 1957 E, S, 1958 E, S, I, F, 1959 I, F

Thomas, N (Bath) 1996 SA (R), 1997 US 1(R), 2, C (R), R, Tg, NZ, 1998 Z, SA 1

Thomas, R (Swansea) 1900 E, S, I, 1901 E

Thomas, R (Pontypool) 1909 F, I, 1911 S, F, 1912 E, S, SA, 1913 E

Thomas, R C C (Swansea) 1949 F, 1952 I, F, 1953 S, I, F, NZ, 1954 E, I, F, S, 1955 S, I, 1956 E, S, I, 1957 E, 1958 A, E, S, I, F, 1959 E, S, I, F

Thomas, R L (London Welsh) 1889 S, I, 1890 I, 1891 E, S, I, 1892 E

Thomas, R M (Newport Gwent Dragons) 2006 Arg 2(R), 2007 E2(R), SA, 2008 It, SA2, C, 2009 It

Thomas, S (Llanelli) 1890 S, E, 1891 I

Thomas, S G (Llanelli) 1923 E, S, F, I

Thomas, T R (Cardiff Blues) 2005 US(R), C, NZ(R), Fj, SA, A, 2006E, S, I, It, F, PI, C(R), NZ, 2007 I, S, F1(R), It(R), E1(R), 2(R), F2(R), [C(R), A(R), J, Fj(R)], SA(R), 2008 SA2(R)

Thomas, W D (Llanelli) 1966 A, 1968 S, I, F, 1969 E, NZ 2, A, 1970 SA, S, E, I, F, 1971 E, S, I, F, 1972 E, S, F, NZ, 1973 E, S, I, F, 1974 E

Thomas, W G (Llanelli, Waterloo, Swansea) 1927 E, S, F, I, 1929 E, 1931 E, S, SA, 1932 E, S, I, 1933 E, S, I

Thomas, W H (Llandovery Coll, Cambridge U) 1885 S, 1886 E, S, 1887 E, S, 1888 S, I, 1890 E, I, 1891 S, I

Thomas, W J (Cardiff) 1961 F, 1963 F

Thomas, W J L (Llanelli, Cardiff) 1995 SA, Fj, 1996 It, E, S, I, F 1, 1996 Bb (R), 1997 US

Thomas, W L (Newport) 1894 S, 1895 E, I

Thompson, J F (Cross Keys) 1923 E

Thorburn, P H (Neath) 1985 F, E, Fj, 1986 E, S, I, F, 1987 F, [I, Tg, C, E, NZ, A], US, 1988 S, I, F, WS, R (R), 1989 S, I, F, E, NZ, 1990 F, E, S, I, Nm 1, 2, Bb, 1991 E, S, I, F 1, A

Tipuric, J C (Ospreys) 2011 Arg(R), A(R), 2012 I(R), It, Bb, A 3(R), Arg(R), Sm, NZ(R), A4(R), 2013 I(R), F, It, S(R), E, SA(R), Arg, Tg, A(R), 2014 It, I(R), F(R), E(R), S(R), A(R), Fj, NZ(R), 2015 S(R), F(R), I 1(R), It 1(R), I 2, 3, [U, E(R), Fj(R), A, SA(R)]

Titley, M H (Bridgend, Swansea) 1983 R, 1984 S, I, F, E, A, 1985 S, I, Fj, 1986 F, Fj, Tg, WS, 1990 F, E

Towers, W H (Swansea) 1887 I, 1888 M

Travers, G (Pill Harriers, Newport) 1903 E, S, I, 1905 E, S, I, NZ, 1906 E, S, I, SA, 1907 E, S, I, 1908 E, S, F, I, A, 1909 E, S, 1911 S, F, I

Travers, W H (Newport) 1937 S, I, 1938 E, S, I, 1939 E, S, I, 1949 E, S, I, F

Treharne, E (Pontypridd) 1881 E, 1883 E

Trew, W J (Swansea) 1900 E, S, I, 1901 E, S, 1903 S, 1905 S, 1906 S, 1907 E, S, 1908 E, S, F, I, A, 1909 E, S, F, I, 1910 F, E, S, 1911 E, S, F, I, 1912 S, 1913 S, F

Trott, R F (Cardiff) 1948 E, S, F, I, 1949 E, S, I, F

Truman, W H (Llanelli) 1934 E, 1935 E

Trump, L C (Newport) 1912 E, S, I, F

Turnbull, B R (Cardiff) 1925 I, 1927 E, S, 1928 E, F, 1930 S

Turnbull, J (Scarlets) 2011 S(R), Bb(R), E3(R), 2012 Bb, Arg, 2014 SA1(R), 2

Turnbull, M J L (Cardiff) 1933 E, I

Turner, P (Newbridge) 1989 I (R), F, E

Uzzell, H (Newport) 1912 E, S, I, F, 1913 S, F, I, 1914 E, S, F, I, 1920 E, S, F, I

Uzzell, J R (Newport) 1963 NZ, 1965 E, S, I, F

Vickery, W E (Aberavon) 1938 E, S, I, 1939 E

Vile, T H (Newport) 1908 E, S, 1910 I, 1912 I, F, SA, 1913 E, 1921 S

Vincent, H C (Bangor) 1882 I

Voyle, M J (Newport, Llanelli, Cardiff) 1996 A 1(t), F 2, 1997 E, US 1, 2, C, Tg, NZ, 1998 It, E, S, I, F, Arg (R), 1999 S (R), I (t), It (R), SA (R), F 2(R), [J, A (R)], 2000 F (R)

Wakeford, J D M (S Wales Police) 1988 WS, R

Waldron, R G (Neath) 1965 E, S, I, F

Walker, E J (Ospreys) 2015 I 2

Walker, N (Cardiff) 1993 I, F, J, 1994 S, F, E, Pt, Sp, 1995 F, E, 1997 US 1, 2, C, R (R), Tg, NZ, 1998 E

Waller, P D (Newport) 1908 A, 1909 E, S, F, I, 1910 F

Walne, N J (Richmond, Cardiff) 1999 It (R), E (R), C

Walters, N (Llanelli) 1902 E

Wanbon, R (Aberavon) 1968 E

Warburton, S K (Cardiff Blues) 2009 US(R), Sm, A(R), 2010 S(R), I(R), It, SA1, A, NZ3, 2011 E1, S, It, I, F, Bb, E2, 3, [SA, Sm, Nm, I, F], A, 2012 I, E, F, A1, 2, 3, Arg, Sm(R), NZ, A4, 2013 I, It(R), S, E, SA, Arg, A, 2014 It(R), I, F, E, S, A, NZ, SA 3, 2015 E, S, F, I 1, It 1, 2, [U, E, Fj, A, SA]

Ward, W S (Cross Keys) 1934 S, I

Warlow, D J (Llanelli) 1962 I

Warren, A R (Scarlets) 2012 Bb(R)

Waters, D R (Newport) 1986 E, S, I, F

Waters, K (Newbridge) 1991 [WS]

Watkins, D (Newport) 1963 E, S, I, F, NZ, 1964 E, S, I, F, SA, 1965 E, S, I, F, 1966 E, S, I, F, 1967 I, F, E

Watkins, E (Neath) 1924 E, S, I, F

Watkins, E (Blaina) 1926 S, I, F

Watkins, E V (Cardiff) 1935 NZ, 1937 S, I, 1938 E, S, I, 1939 E, S

Watkins, H V (Llanelli) 1904 S, I, 1905 E, S, I, 1906 E

Watkins, I J (Ebbw Vale) 1988 E (R), S, I, F, NZ 2, R, 1989 S, I, F, E

Watkins, L (Oxford U, Llandaff) 1881 E

Watkins, M J (Newport) 1984 I, F, E, A

Watkins, M J (Llanelli Scarlets) 2003 It(R), E 1(R), S 1(R), I 1(R), R, S 2, 2005 US(R), C(R), Fj, SA(R), A, 2006 E, S, I, It, F, Arg 1, 2(R)

Watkins, S J (Newport, Cardiff) 1964 S, I, F, 1965 E, S, I, F, 1966 E, S, I, F, A, 1967 S, I, F, E, NZ, 1968 E, S, 1969 S, I, F, E, NZ 1, 1970 E, I

Watkins, W R (Newport) 1959 F

Watts, D (Maesteg) 1914 E, S, F, I

Watts, J (Llanelli) 1907 E, S, I, 1908 E, S, F, I, A, 1909 S, F, I

Watts, W H (Newport) 1892 E, S, I, 1893 E, S, I, 1894 E, S, I, 1895 E, I, 1896 E

Watts, W J (Llanelli) 1914 E

Weatherley, D J (Swansea) 1998 Z

Weaver, D S (Swansea) 1964 E

Webb, A (Jim) (Abertillery) 1907 S, 1908 E, S, F, I, A, 1909 E, S, F, I, 1910 F, E, S, I, 1911 E, S, F, I, 1912 E, S

Webb, J (Newport) 1888 M, 1889 S

Webb, R (Ospreys) 2012 It(R), Bb(R), A2(R) , 2014 It(R), F, E, A, NZ, SA 3, 2015 E, S, F, I 1, It 1, I 3, It 2

Webbe, G M C (Bridgend) 1986 Tg (R), WS, 1987 F, E, S, [Tg], US, 1988 F (R), NZ 1, R

Webster, R E (Swansea) 1987 [A], 1990 Bb, 1991 [Arg, A], 1992 I, F, E, S, A, 1993 E, S, I, F

Wells, G T (Cardiff) 1955 E, S, 1957 I, F, 1958 A, E, S

Westacott, D (Cardiff) 1906 I

Wetter, J J (Newport) 1914 S, F, I, 1920 E, S, F, I, 1921 E, 1924 I, NZ

Wetter, W H (Newport) 1912 SA, 1913 E

Wheel, G A D (Swansea) 1974 I, E (R), 1975 F, E, I, A, 1976 E, S, I, F, 1977 I, E, S, 1978 E, S, I, F, A 1, 2, NZ, 1979 S, I, 1980 F, E, S, I, 1981 E, S, I, F, A, 1982 I

Wheeler, **P J** (Aberavon) 1967 NZ, 1968 E

Whitefoot, **J** (Cardiff) 1984 A (R), 1985 S, I, F, E, Fj, 1986 E, S, I, F, Fj, Tg, WS, 1987 F, E, S, I, [I, C]

Whitfield, **J J** (Newport) 1919 NZA, 1920 E, S, F, I, 1921 E, 1922 E, S, I, F, 1924 S, I

Whitson, **G K** (Newport) 1956 F, 1960 S, I

Wilkins, **G** (Bridgend) 1994 Tg

Williams, **A** (Ospreys, Bath) 2003 R (R), 2005 v US(R), C(R), 2006 Arg 2(R), 2007 A2(R)

Williams, **B** (Llanelli) 1920 S, F, I

Williams, **B H** (Neath, Richmond, Bristol) 1996 F 2, 1997 R, Tg, NZ, 1998 It, E, Z (R), SA 1, Arg (R), 1999 S (R), I, It (R), 2000 F (R), It (R), E (t+R), 2001 R (R), I (R), Tg (R), A (R), 2002 I (R), F (R), It (R), E (R), S

Williams, **B L** (Cardiff) 1947 E, S, F, I, A, 1948 E, S, F, I, 1949 E, S, I, 1951 I, SA, 1952 S, 1953 E, S, I, F, NZ, 1954 S, 1955 E

Williams, **B R** (Neath) 1990 S, I, Bb, 1991 E, S

Williams, **C** (Llanelli) 1924 NZ, 1925 E

Williams, **C** (Aberavon, Swansea) 1977 E, S, 1980 F, E, S, I, NZ, 1983 E

Williams, **C D** (Cardiff, Neath) 1955 F, 1956 F

Williams, **D** (Ebbw Vale) 1963 E, S, I, F, 1964 E, S, I, F, SA, 1965 E, S, I, F, 1966 E, S, I, A, 1967 F, E, NZ, 1968 E, 1969 S, I, F, E, NZ 1, 2, A, 1970 SA, S, E, I, 1971 E, S, I, F

Williams, **D** (Llanelli) 1998 SA 1(R)

Williams, **D A** (Bridgend, Swansea) 1990 Nm 2(R), 1995 Fj (R)

Williams, **D B** (Newport, Swansea) 1978 A 1, 1981 E, S

Williams, **E** (Neath) 1924 NZ, 1925 F

Williams, **E** (Aberavon) 1925 E, S

Williams, **F L** (Cardiff) 1929 S, F, I, 1930 E, S, I, F, 1931 F, I, SA, 1932 E, S, I, 1933 I

Williams, **G** (London Welsh) 1950 I, F, 1951 E, S, I, F, SA, 1952 E, S, I, F, 1953 NZ, 1954 E

Williams, **G** (Bridgend) 1981 I, F, 1982 E (R), S

Williams, **G J** (Bridgend, Cardiff Blues) 2003 It(R), E 1(R), S 1, F(R), E 2(R), 2009 C(R), US, 2010 E, S

Williams, **G M** (Aberavon) 1936 E, S, I

Williams, **G P** (Bridgend) 1980 NZ, 1981 E, S, A, 1982 I

Williams, **G R** (Cardiff Blues) 2000 I, Sm, US, SA, 2001 S, F, It, R (R), I (R), Arg, Tg (R), A (R), 2002 F (R), It (R), E (R), S, SA 1, 2, R, Fj, C, NZ, 2003 It, E 1, S 1, I 1, F, A, NZ, E 2, [Tg, It(R)], 2004 S, I, F, E, It, Arg1, R, J, 2005 F(R), S, US, C

Williams, **H R** (Llanelli) 1954 S, 1957 F, 1958 A

Williams, **J F** (London Welsh) 1905 I, NZ, 1906 S, SA

Williams, **J J** (Llanelli) 1973 F (R), A, 1974 S, I, F, E, 1975 F, E, S, I, A, 1976 E, S, I, F, 1977 I, F, E, S, 1978 E, S, I, F, A 1, 2, NZ, 1979 S, I, F, E

Williams, **J L** (Cardiff) 1906 SA, 1907 E, S, I, 1908 E, S, I, A, 1909 E, S, F, I, 1910 I, 1911 E, S, F, I

Williams, **J L** (Blaina) 1920 E, S, F, I, 1921 S, F, I

Williams, **J P R** (London Welsh, Bridgend) 1969 S, I, F, E, NZ 1, 2, A, 1970 SA, S, E, I, F, 1971 E, S, I, F, 1972 E, S, F, NZ, 1973 E, S, I, F, A, 1974 S, I, F, 1975 F, E, S, I, A, 1976 E, S, I, F, 1977 I, F, E, S, 1978 E, S, I, F, A 1, 2, NZ, 1979 S, I, F, E, 1980 NZ, 1981 E, S

Williams, **L B** (Scarlets) 2012 Bb, NZ, A4, 2013 J1, 2, SA, Arg, A(R), 2014 I(R), F, E(R), S, SA1, 2, A, Fj, NZ(R), SA 3, 2015 E(t), S, F, I 1, It 1, [U, E, A]

Williams, **L D** (Cardiff Blues) 2011 Arg(R), [Nm(R), Fj(R), A(R)], A, 2012 S(R), F(R), Bb, 2013 I(R), F(R), It(R), S(R), E(R), J1, 2, SA(R), Arg(R), Tg, 2015 I 2(R), [U(R), E(R), Fj(t), A(R), SA(R)]

Williams, **L H** (Cardiff) 1957 S, I, F, 1958 E, S, I, F, 1959 E, S, I, 1961 F, 1962 E, S

Williams, **M E** (Pontypridd, Cardiff Blues) 1996 Bb, F 2, It (t), 1998 It, E, Z, SA 2, Arg, 1999 S, I, C, J, [Sm], 2000 F (R), 2001 E, S, F, It, 2002 I, F, It, E, S, SA 1, 2, Fj, C, NZ, 2003 It, E 1, S 1, I 1, F, A, NZ, E 2, [C, Tg(R), It, E(R)], 2004 S, I, F(t&R), E(R), It, SA2(t&R), R(R), NZ(R), J(R), 2005 E, It, F, S, I, Fj, SA, A, 2006 E, S, I, It, F, A, C, NZ, 2007 I, S, F1, It, E1, Arg, F2, [C, A, J, Fj], 2008 E, S, It, I, F, SA3, NZ, A, 2009 S, E, F, I, NZ, Arg, A, 2010 E, S, F, I, A(R), SA2, NZ3 (R), 2011 Arg, 2012 Bb(R)

Williams, **M S** (Scarlets) 2011 Bb(R), E2(R), 3(R), Arg(R) , [Nm, Fj, A(R)], A, 2012 S(R), E(R), It(R), F(t), A 1, 3(R), Arg, NZ(R), 2013 F(R), It(R), S(R), E(R), SA, Arg, A, 2014 It, I, Fj, SA 3(R), 2015 I 1(R), It 1(R), I 2, 3, It 2, [U, E]

Williams, **M T** (Newport) 1923 F

Williams, **O** (Llanelli) 1947 E, S, A, 1948 E, S, F, I

Williams, **O L** (Bridgend) 1990 Nm 2

Williams, **O R** (Cardiff Blues) 2013 J1, 2, Tg, A

Williams, **R** (Scarlets) 2013 Tg(R), A(R), 2014 S(R)

Williams, **R D G** (Newport) 1881 E

Williams, **R F** (Cardiff) 1912 SA, 1913 E, S, 1914 I

Williams, **R H** (Llanelli) 1954 I, F, S, 1955 S, I, F, 1956 E, S, I, 1957 E, S, I, F, 1958 A, E, S, I, F, 1959 E, S, I, F, 1960 E

Williams, **S** (Llanelli) 1947 E, S, F, I, 1948 S, F

Williams, **S A** (Aberavon) 1939 E, S, I

Williams, **S M** (Neath, Cardiff, Northampton) 1994 Tg, 1996 E (t), A 1, 2, Bb, F 2, It, A 3, SA, 1997 US, S, I, F, E, US 1, 2(R), C, R (R), Tg (R), NZ (t+R), 2002 SA 1, 2, R, Fj(R), 2003 It, E 1, S 1, F(R)

Williams, **S M** (Neath, Ospreys) 2000 F (R), It, E, S, I, Sm, SA (R), 2001 J 1, 2, I, 2003 R, [NZ, E], 2004 S, I, F, E, It, Arg 1, 2, SA1, 2, NZ, J, 2005 E, It, F, S, I, NZ, Fj, SA, A, 2006 E, S, It, F, Arg 1, 2, A, PI(R), C, NZ, 2007 F1, It, E1, F2, [C, A, J, Fj], 2008 E, S, It, I, F, SA1, 2, 3, NZ, A, 2009 S, F, It, I, NZ, Arg, A, 2010 E, S, F, I, It, A, SA2, 2011 E1, S, It, I, E2, 3, [SA, Sm, I, F, A], A

Williams, **T** (Pontypridd) 1882 I

Williams, **T** (Swansea) 1888 S, I

Williams, **T** (Swansea) 1912 I, 1913 F, 1914 E, S, F, I

Williams, **T** (Swansea) 1921 F

Williams, **T G** (Cross Keys) 1935 S, I, NZ, 1936 E, S, I, 1937 S, I

Williams, **W A** (Crumlin) 1927 E, S, F, I

Williams, **W A** (Newport) 1952 I, F, 1953 E

Williams, **W E O** (Cardiff) 1887 S, I, 1889 S, 1890 S, E

Williams, **W H** (Pontymister) 1900 E, S, I, 1901 E

Williams, **W L T** (Llanelli, Cardiff) 1947 E, S, F, I, A, 1948 I, 1949 E

Williams, **W O G** (Swansea, Devonport Services) 1951 F, SA, 1952 E, S, I, F, 1953 E, S, I, F, NZ, 1954 E, I, F, S, 1955 E, S, I, F, 1956 E, S, I

Williams, **W P J** (Neath) 1974 I, F

Williams-Jones, **H** (S Wales Police, Llanelli) 1989 S (R), 1990 F (R), I, 1991 A, 1992 S, A, 1993 E, S, I, F, Z 1, Nm, 1994 Fj, Tg, WS (R), It (t), 1995 E (R)

Willis, **W R** (Cardiff) 1950 E, S, I, F, 1951 E, S, I, F, SA, 1952 E, S, 1953 S, NZ, 1954 E, I, F, S, 1955 E, S, I, F

Wiltshire, **M L** (Aberavon) 1967 NZ, 1968 E, S, F

Windsor, **R W** (Pontypool) 1973 A, 1974 S, I, F, E, 1975 F, E, S, I, A, 1976 E, S, I, F, 1977 I, F, E, S, 1978 E, S, I, F, A 1, 2, NZ, 1979 S, I, F

Winfield, **H B** (Cardiff) 1903 I, 1904 E, S, I, 1905 NZ, 1906 E, S, I, 1907 S, I, 1908 E, S, F, I, A

Winmill, **S** (Cross Keys) 1921 E, S, F, I

Wintle, **M E** (Llanelli) 1996 It

Wintle, **R V** (London Welsh) 1988 WS (R)

Wooller, **W** (Sale, Cambridge U, Cardiff) 1933 E, S, I, 1935 E, S, I, NZ, 1936 E, S, I, 1937 E, S, I, 1938 S, I, 1939 E, S, I

Wyatt, **C P** (Llanelli) 1998 Z (R), SA 1(R), 2, Arg, 1999 S, I, F 1, It, E, Arg 1, 2, SA, C (R), F 2, [Arg 3, J (R), Sm, A], 2000 F, It, E, US, SA, 2001 E, F, I, Arg (R), Tg (R), A (R), 2002 I, It (R), E, S (R), 2003 A(R), NZ(t+R), E 2, [Tg(R), NZ(R)]

Wyatt, **G** (Pontypridd, Celtic Warriors) 1997 Tg, 2003 R (R)

Wyatt, **M A** (Swansea) 1983 E, S, I, F, 1984 A, 1985 S, I, 1987 E, S, I

Yapp, **J V** (Cardiff Blues) 2005 E(R), It(R), F(R), S(R), I(R), C(R), Fj, 2006 Arg 1(R), 2008 C, NZ(R), 2009 S(R), It, C, US, 2010 SA1(R), NZ1(R), SA2(R), 2011 E1(t&R), S(R), I(R), F(R)

Young, **D** (Swansea, Cardiff) 1987 [E, NZ], US, 1988 E, S, I, F, NZ 1, 2, WS, R, 1989 S, NZ, 1990 F 1996 A 3, SA, 1997 US, S, I, F, E, R, NZ, 1998 It, E, S, I, F, 1999 I, E (R), Arg 1(R), 2(R), SA, C (R), F 2, [Arg 3, J, Sm, A], 2000 F, It, E, S, I, 2001 E, S, F, It, R, I, Arg

Young, **G A** (Cardiff) 1886 E, S

Young, **J** (Harrogate, RAF, London Welsh) 1968 S, I, F, 1969 S, I, F, E, NZ 1, 1970 E, I, F, 1971 E, S, I, F, 1972 E, S, F, NZ, 1973 E, S, I, F

Young, **P** (Gwent Dragons) 2003 R (R)

MAJOR TOURS

By Chris Rhys

BLEDISLOE CUP

18 October, Suncorp Stadium, Brisbane, Australia 28 (2G 1T 3PG) New Zealand 29 (3G 1T 1PG)

AUSTRALIA: I Folau (NSW Waratahs); AP Ashley-Cooper (NSW Waratahs), RTRN Kuridrani (Brumbies), CP Leali'ifano (Brumbies), JM Tomane (Brumbies); BT Foley (NSW Waratahs), NJ Phipps (NSW Waratahs); JA Slipper (Queensland Reds), SM Fainga'a (Queensland Reds), SM Kepu (NSW Waratahs), STG Carter (Brumbies), RA Simmons (Queensland Reds), SM Fardy (Brumbies), MK Hooper (NSW Waratahs, captain), S Higginbotham (Melbourne Rebels)

SUBSTITUTIONS: NW White (Brumbies) for Phipps (53 mins); MJ Hodgson (Western Force) for Higginbotham (59 mins); BE Alexander (Brumbies) and JE Horwill (Queensland Reds) for Kepu and Carter (63 mins); BA Robinson (NSW Waratahs) for Slipper (66 mins); JW Mann-Rea (Brumbies) for Fainga'a (71 mins)

SCORERS: *Tries:* Phipps, Foley, Ashley-Cooper *Conversions:* Foley (2), *Penalty Goals:* Foley (2), White

NEW ZEALAND: IJA Dagg (Hawke's Bay); CS Jane (Wellington), CG Smith (Wellington), MF Fekitoa (Auckland), SJ Savea (Wellington); BJ Barrett (Taranaki), AL Smith (Manawatu); WWV Crockett (Canterbury), DS Coles (Wellington), OT Franks (Canterbury), BA Retallick (Bay of Plenty), SL Whitelock (Canterbury), LJ Messam (Waikato), RH McCaw (Canterbury, captain), KJ Read (Canterbury)

SUBSTITUTIONS: ST Piutau (Auckland) for Jane (40 mins); KF Mealamu (Auckland) and CC Faumuina (Auckland) for Coles and O Franks (47 mins); BJ Franks (Hawke's Bay) for Crockett (52 mins); PT Tuipulotu (Auckland) for Whitelock (56 mins); SJ Cane (Bay of Plenty) for Messam (61 mins); TTR Perenara (Wellington) and CR Slade (Canterbury) for AL Smith and Barrett (71 mins)

SCORERS: *Tries:* Jane, Coles, AL Smith, Fekitoa *Conversions:* Barrett (2), Slade *Penalty Goal:* Barrett

REFEREE: CP Joubert (South Africa)

AUSTRALIA TO EUROPE 2014

TOUR PARTY

FULL-BACK: I Folau (NSW Waratahs)

THREEQUARTERS: AP Ashley-Cooper (NSW Waratahs), JM Tomane (Brumbies), RTRN Kuridrani (Brumbies), MP Toomua (Brumbies), CP Leali'ifano (Brumbies), RG Horne (NSW Waratahs), T English (Melbourne Rebels), HV Speight (Brumbies)

HALF-BACKS: QS Cooper (Queensland Reds), BT Foley (NSW Waratahs), K Godwin (Western Force), SW Genia (Queensland Reds), NW White (Brumbies), NC Phipps (Melbourne Rebels)

FORWARDS: SM Fainga'a (Queensland Reds), JE Hanson (Queensland Reds), JW Mann-Rea (Brumbies), JA Slipper (Queensland Reds), BE Alexander (Brumbies), SM Kepu (NSW Waratahs), BA Robinson (NSW Waratahs), TJ Faulkner (Western Force), JE Horwill (Queensland Reds), RA Simmons (Queensland Reds), STG Carter (Brumbies), LM Jones (Melbourne Rebels), WRJ Skelton (NSW Waratahs), MJ Hodgson (Western Force), MK Hooper (NSW Waratahs), BJ McCalman (Western Force), S Higginbotham (Melbourne Rebels), SP McMahon (Melbourne Rebels), JW Schatz (Queensland Reds)

HEAD COACH: M Cheika

8 November, Millennium Stadium, Cardiff, Wales 28 (4G), Australia 33 (3G 3PG 1DG)

WALES: SL Halfpenny (RC Toulon); ACG Cuthbert (Cardiff Blues), GP North (Northampton Saints), JH Roberts (Racing Métro), LB Williams (Scarlets); DR Biggar (Ospreys), R Webb (Ospreys); P James (Bath Rugby), RM Hibbard (Gloucester Rugby), S Lee (Scarlets), JD Ball (Scarlets), AW Jones (Ospreys), DJ Lydiate (Racing Métro), S Warburton (Cardiff Blues, captain), TT Faletau (Newport Gwent Dragons)

SUBSTITUTIONS: CL Allen (Cardiff Blues) for Halfpenny (29 mins); R Priestland (Scarlets) for Biggar (47 mins); WM Phillips (Racing Métro) for Webb (53 mins); SJ Baldwin (Ospreys) and GD Jenkins (Cardiff Blues) for Hibbard and James (57 mins); BS Davies (Wasps) and RP Jones (Scarlets) for Ball and Lee (68 mins); JC Tipuric (Ospreys) for Lydiate (75 mins)

SCORERS: *Tries:* Webb, Cuthbert, AW Jones, Penalty Try *Conversions:* Halfpenny (2), Biggar, Priestland

AUSTRALIA: Folau; Ashley-Cooper, Kuridrani, Leali'ifano, Tomane; Foley, Phipps; Slipper, Fainga'a, Kepu, Carter, Simmons, McMahon, Hooper (captain), McCalman
SUBSTITUTIONS: Skelton for Carter (30 mins); Hanson for Fainga'a (59 mins); Alexander for Kepu (65 mins); Horwill for Simmons (67 mins); Genia for Phipps (68 mins); Hodgson for McMahon (70 mins); Faulkner for Slipper (73 mins); Horne for Leali'ifano (75 mins)
SCORERS: *Tries*: Folau (2), Kuridrani *Conversions*: Foley (3) *Penalty Goals*: Foley (3) *Drop Goals*: Foley
REFEREE: CP Joubert (South Africa)

15 November, Stade de France, Paris, France 29 (2G 5PG) Australia 26 (2G 4PG)

FRANCE: SL Spedding (Aviron Bayonnais); Y Huget (Stade Toulousain), A Dumoulin (Racing Métro), W Fofana (ASM Clermont Auvergne), T Thomas (Racing Métro); C Lopez (ASM Clermont Auvergne), S Tillous-Borde (RC Toulon); A Menini (RC Toulon), G Guirado (RC Toulon), N Mas (Montpellier HRC), P Papé (Stade Français), Y Maestri (Stade Toulousain), T Dusautoir (Stade Toulousain, captain), B le Roux (Racing Métro), D Chouly (ASM Clermont Auvergne)
SUBSTITUTIONS: U Atonio (Stade Rochelais) and M Bastareaud (RC Toulon) for Mas and Dumoulin (40 mins); B Kayser (ASM Clermont Auvergne) for Guirado (49 mins); RM Kockott (Castres Olympique) for Tillous-Borde (53 mins); X Chiocci (RC Toulon) and S Vahaamahina (ASM Clermont Auvergne) for Menini and Papé (56 mins); R Talès (Castres Olympique) for Lopez (69 mins); Y Nyanga (Stade Toulousain) for Le Roux (74 mins)
SCORERS: *Tries*: Tillous-Borde, Thomas *Conversions*: Lopez (2) *Penalty Goals*: Lopez (4), Kockott
AUSTRALIA: Folau; Ashley-Cooper, Kuridrani, Leali'ifano, Tomane; Foley, Phipps; Slipper, Fainga'a, Kepu, Horwill, Simmons, McMahon, Hooper (captain), McCalman
SUBSTITUTIONS: Horne for Leali'ifano (44 mins); Skelton for Horwill (49 mins); Cooper for Tomane (60 mins); Robinson for Slipper (61 mins); Alexander for Kepu (65 mins); Hanson, Hodgson and Genia for Fainga'a, McMahon and Phipps (69 mins)
SCORERS: *Tries*: Ashley-Cooper, Simmons *Conversions*: Foley (2) *Penalty Goals*: Foley (4)
REFEREE: N Owens (Wales)

22 November, Aviva Stadium, Dublin, Ireland 26 (2G 4PG) Australia 23 (1G 2T 2PG)

IRELAND: RDJ Kearney (Leinster); TJ Bowe (Ulster), R Henshaw (Connacht), GWD D'Arcy (Leinster), SR Zebo (Munster); JJ Sexton (Racing Métro), GC Murray (Munster); JC McGrath (Leinster), RD Best (Ulster), MA Ross (Leinster), D Toner (Leinster), PJ O'Connell (Munster, captain), P O'Mahony (Munster), RJ Ruddock (Leinster), JPR Heaslip (Leinster)
SUBSTITUTIONS: I Madigan (Leinster) for D'Arcy (58 mins); SM Cronin (Leinster) and D Foley (Munster) for Best and Toner (67 mins); EGE Reddan (Leinster) for Murray (temp 71–75 and 77 mins); FA Jones (Munster) for Sexton (77 mins)
SCORERS: *Tries*: Zebo, Bowe *Conversions*: Sexton (2) *Penalty Goals*: Sexton (4)
AUSTRALIA: Folau; Ashley-Cooper, Kuridrani, Toomua, Speight; Foley, Phipps; Slipper, Fainga'a, Kepu, Carter, Simmons, Jones, Hooper (captain), McCalman
SUBSTITUTIONS: Beale for Kuridrani (45 mins); Schatz for Jones (53 mins); Cooper for Foley (64 mins); Genia for Phipps (68 mins); Hanson and Faulkner for Fainga'a and Kepu (70 mins); Skelton for Carter (71 mins); Robinson for Slipper (75 mins)
SCORERS: *Tries*: Phipps (2), Foley *Conversion*: Foley *Penalty Goals*: Foley (2)
REFEREE: GW Jackson (New Zealand)

29 November, Twickenham, England 26 (2G 4PG) Australia 17 (2G 1PG)

ENGLAND: MN Brown (Harlequins); AKC Watson (Bath Rugby), BM Barritt (Saracens), WWF Twelvetrees (Gloucester Rugby), JJ May (Gloucester Rugby); GT Ford (Bath Rugby), BR Youngs (Leicester Tigers); JWG Marler (Harlequins), DM Hartley (Northampton Saints), DG Wilson (Bath Rugby), DMJ Attwood (Bath Rugby), CL Lawes (Northampton Saints), TA Wood (Northampton Saints), CDC Robshaw (Harlequins, captain), BJ Morgan (Gloucester Rugby)
SUBSTITUTIONS: MJ Mullan (Wasps) and GEJ Kruis (Saracens) for Marler and Lawes (53 mins); K Brookes (Newcastle Falcons) for Wilson (60 mins); OA Farrell (Saracens) for Barritt (temp 61–67 mins) and Twelvetrees (67 mins); REP Wigglesworth (Saracens) for Youngs (69 mins); RW Webber (Bath Rugby) for Hartley (71 mins); JAW Haskell (Wasps) for Wood (77 mins); MXG Yarde (Harlequins) for Barritt (78 mins); Wood for Kruis (temp 78–80 mins)
SCORERS: *Tries*: Morgan (2) *Conversions*: Ford (2) *Penalty Goals*: Ford (4)
AUSTRALIA: Folau; Speight, Ashley-Cooper, Toomua, Horne; Foley, Phipps; Slipper, Fainga'a, Kepu, Carter, Simmons, Jones, Hooper (captain), McCalman
SUBSTITUTIONS: Jones for Simmons (40 mins); Cooper for Foley (45 mins); White for Phipps (49 mins);

Alexander for Kepu (51 mins); Skelton for McMahon (57 mins); Beale for Speight (63 mins); Robinson for Slipper (67 mins); Hanson for Fainga'a (72 mins)

SCORERS: *Tries:* Foley, Skelton *Conversions:* Foley, Cooper *Penalty Goal:* Foley

REFEREE: J Garcès (France)

NEW ZEALAND TO USA AND EUROPE 2014

Tour Party

FULL-BACKS: IJA Dagg (Hawke's Bay)

THREEQUARTERS: SJ Savea (Wellington), CS Jane (Wellington), BR Smith (Otago), ST Puitau (Auckland), RS Crotty (Canterbury), MF Fekitoa (Auckland), CG Smith (Wellington), SB Williams (Counties Manukau)

HALF-BACKS: AL Smith (Manawatu), AW Pulu (Counties Manukau), TTR Perenara (Wellington), AW Cruden (Manawatu), DW Carter (Canterbury), BJ Barrett (Taranaki)

FORWARDS: DS Coles (Wellington), KF Mealamu (Auckland), N Harris (Bay of Plenty), *JW Parsons (North Harbour), WWV Crockett (Canterbury), CC Faumuina (Auckland), BJ Franks (Hawke's Bay), OJ Franks (Canterbury), J Moody (Canterbury), BA Retallick (Bay of Plenty), L Romano (Canterbury), JI Thrush (Wellington), PT Tuipulotu (Auckland), SL Whitelock (Canterbury), *DJ Bird (Canterbury), SJ Cane (Bay of Plenty), J Kaino (Wellington), RH McCaw (Canterbury, captain), LJ Messam (Waikato), KJ Read (Canterbury), VVJ Vito (Wellington)

*Replacements on tour

HEAD COACH: SW Hansen

1 November, Soldier Field, Chicago, USA 6 (2PG) New Zealand 74 (7G 5T)

USA: CT Wyles (Saracens); BH Scully (Leicester Tigers), S Kelly (unattached), A Suniula (Old Blue), B Thompson (Edinburgh Rugby); A Siddall (Old Blue), MZ Petri (New York AC); EC Fry (Newcastle Falcons), P Thiel (Life University), O Kilifi (Seattle Saracens), SV Manoa (Northampton Saints), HW Smith (Saracens), T Clever (NTT Shining Arcs, captain), SC LaValla (Stade Français), D Barrett (USA Sevens)

SUBSTITUTIONS: T Tuisamoa (London Scottish) for Barrett (4 mins); F Niua (USA Sevens) for Thompson (30 mins); N Wallace (Glendale Raptors), T Coolican (Sydney Stars) and T Moeakiola (RC Castenet) for Fry, Thiel and Kilifi (for Petri (59 mins); S Suniula (Seattle Saracens) for Petri (59 mins); LE Stanfill (Seattle Saracens) for Tuisamioa (66 mins); Kilifi for Moeakiola (72 mins); T Hall (New York AC) for Niua (76 mins)

SCORER: *Penalty Goals:* Siddall (2)

NEW ZEALAND: Dagg; Jane, Crotty, Williams, Piutau; Cruden, Perenara; Moody, Harris, Faumuina, Thrush, Tuipulotu, Vito, Cane, Read

SUBSTITUTIONS: Mealamu for Harris (10 mins); Savea for Jane (30 mins); Carter for Cruden (49 mins); B Franks for Moody (51 mins); Messam for Read (54 mins); Pulu for Perenara (60 mins); O Franks and Retallick for Faumuina and Tuipulotu (72 mins)

SCORERS: *Tries:* Williams (2), Savea (2), Harris, Jane, Tuipulotu, Piutau, Moody, Cruden, Dagg, Cane *Conversions:* Cruden (4), Carter (3)

REFEREE: CP Joubert (South Africa)

8 November, Twickenham, England 21 (1G 1T 3PG) New Zealand 24 (3T 3PG)

ENGLAND: MN Brown (Harlequins); S Rokoduguni (Bath Rugby), BM Barritt (Saracens), KO Eastmond (Bath Rugby), JJ May (Gloucester Rugby); OA Farrell (Saracens), DS Care (Harlequins); JWG Marler (Harlequins), DM Hartley (Northampton Saints), DG Wilson (Bath Rugby), DMJ Attwood (Bath Rugby), CL Lawes (Northampton Saints), TA Wood (Northampton Saints), CDC Robshaw (Harlequins, captain), VML Vunipola (Saracens)

SUBSTITUTIONS: GEJ Kruis (Saracens) for Lawes (22 mins); BJ Morgan (Gloucester Rugby) for Vunipola (52 mins); MJ Mullan (Wasps) for Marler (54 mins); BR Youngs (Leicester Tigers) and AKC Watson (Bath Rugby) for Care and Rokoduguni (61 mins); GT Ford (Bath Rugby) for Eastmond (64 mins); RW Webber (Bath Rugby) and K Brookes (Newcastle Falcons) for Hartley and Wilson (73 mins)

SCORERS: *Tries:* May, Penalty Try *Conversion:* Ford *Penalty Goals:* Farrell (3)

NEW ZEALAND: Dagg; B Smith, C Smith, Williams, Savea; Cruden, A Smith; Crockett, Coles, O Franks, Retallick, Whitelock, Kaino, McCaw (captain), Read

SUBSTITUTIONS: Tuipulotu for Retallick (40 mins); Crotty and Faumuina for C Smith and O Franks (46 mins); B Franks and Barrett for Crockett and Cruden (59 mins); Mealamu for Kaino (temp 60–66 mins) and Coles (66 mins); Messam and Perenara for Kaino and A Smith (66 mins)

SCORERS: *Tries:* Cruden, McCaw, Faumuina *Penalty Goals:* Cruden (2), Barrett

REFEREE: N Owens (Wales)

15 November, Murrayfield, Scotland 16 (1G 3PG) New Zealand 24 (1G 1T 4PG)

SCOTLAND: SW Hogg (Glasgow Warriors); SD Maitland (Glasgow Warriors), MS Bennett (Glasgow Warriors), AJ Dunbar (Glasgow Warriors), TSF Seymour (Glasgow Warriors); FA Russell (Glasgow Warriors), GD Laidlaw (Gloucester Rugby, captain); AG Dickinson (Edinburgh Rugby), RW Ford (Edinburgh Rugby), EA Murray (Glasgow Warriors), RJ Gray (Castres Olympique), JD Gray (Glasgow Warriors), RJ Harley (Glasgow Warriors), BA Cowan (London Irish), A Ashe (Glasgow Warriors)
SUBSTITUTIONS: SF Lamont (Glasgow Warriors) for Bennett (12 mins); D Weir (Glasgow Warriors) for Russell (temp 25–31 mins and 60 mins); GDS Cross (London Irish) for Murray (30 mins); JW Beattie (Castres Olympique) for Ashe (57 mins); DK Denton (Edinburgh Rugby) for Cowan (72 mins); FJM Brown (Glasgow Warriors) and CP Cusiter (Sale Sharks) for Ford and Laidlaw; GJ Reid (Glasgow Warriors) for Dickinson (76 mins)
SCORERS: *Try*: Seymour *Conversion*: Laidlaw *Penalty Goals*: Laidlaw (3)
NEW ZEALAND: B Smith; Slade, Fekitoa, Crotty, Piutau; Carter, Perenara; Moody, Parsons, Faumuina, Thrush, Bird, McCaw (captain), Cane, Vito
SUBSTITUTIONS: Messam for Vito (37 mins); Coles for Parsons (46 mins); Romano and Crockett for Bird and Moody (51 mins); Williams, Savea and B Franks for Fekitoa, Carter and Faumuina (55 mins); Pulu for Perenara (78 mins)
SCORERS: *Tries*: Vito, Thrush *Conversion*: Slade *Penalty Goals*: Carter (3), Slade
REFEREE: R Poite (France)

22 November, Millennium Stadium, Cardiff, Wales 16 (1G 3PG) New Zealand 34 (3G 2T 1PG)

WALES: SL Halfpenny (RC Toulon); ACG Cuthbert (Cardiff Blues), JJV Davies (ASM Clermont Auvergne), JH Roberts (Racing Métro), GP North (Northampton Saints); DR Biggar (Ospreys), R Webb (Ospreys); P James (Bath Rugby), RM Hibbard (Gloucester Rugby), S Lee (Scarlets), JD Ball (Scarlets), AW Jones (Ospreys), DJ Lydiate (Racing Métro), S Warburton (Cardiff Blues, captain), TT Faletau (Newport Gwent Dragons)
SUBSTITUTIONS: WM Phillips (Racing Métro) for Webb (56 mins); JC Tipuric (Ospreys), LC Charteris (Racing Métro) and SJ Baldwin (Ospreys) for Lydiate, Ball and Hibbard (61 mins); LB Williams (Scarlets) for North (65 mins); JW Hook (Gloucester Rugby), NP Smith (Ospreys) and RP Jones (Scarlets) for Biggar, James and Lee (73 mins)
SCORERS: *Try*: Webb *Conversion*: Halfpenny *Penalty Goals*: Halfpenny (3)
NEW ZEALAND: B Smith; Piutau, C Smith, Williams, Savea; Barrett, A Smith; Crockett, Coles, O Franks, Retallick, Whitelock, Kaino, McCaw (captain), Read
SUBSTITUTIONS: Moody for Crockett (40 mins); Faumuina for O Franks (46 mins); Slade for Piutau (55 mins); Mealamu, Tuipulotu and Messam for Coles, Whitelock and Kaino (65 mins); Crotty for Williams (70 mins); Perenara for A Smith (72 mins)
SCORERS: *Tries*: Barrett (2), Savea, Kaino, Read *Conversions*: Slade (2), Barrett *Penalty Goal*: Barrett
REFEREE: W Barnes (England)

SOUTH AFRICA TO EUROPE 2014

Tour Party

FULL-BACKS: WJ le Roux (FS Cheetahs) JL Goosen (Racing Métro)
THREEQUARTERS: BG Habana (RC Toulon), JPR Pietersen (Panasonic Wild Knights), C Hendricks (FS Cheetahs), L Mvovo (Sharks), S Senatla (SA Sevens), D de Allende (Western Province), J de Villiers (Western Province, captain), JL Serfontein (Blue Bulls)
HALF-BACKS: R Pienaar (Ulster), F Hougaard (Blue Bulls), JM Reinach (Sharks), PJ Lambie (Sharks), M Steyn (Stade Français), H Pollard (Blue Bulls)
FORWARDS: BW du Plessis (Sharks), JA Strauss (FS Cheetahs), R Coetzee (Golden Lions), JN du Plessis (Sharks), T Mtawarira (Sharks), CV Oosthuizen (FS Cheetahs), GG Steenkamp (Stade Toulousain), TN Nyakane (FS Cheetahs), J Redelinghuys (Golden Lions), E Etzebeth (Western Province), JP Botha (RC Toulon), V Matfield (Blue Bulls), L de Jager (FS Cheetahs), MC Coetzee (Sharks), SWP Burger (Suntory Sungoliath), N Carr (Western Province), J Kriel (Golden Lions), TS Mohoje (FS Cheetahs), W Whiteley (Golden Lions), DJ Vermeulen (Western Province)
HEAD COACH: H Meyer

8 November, Aviva Stadium, Dublin, Ireland 29 (2G 5PG) South Africa 15 (1G 1T 1PG)

IRELAND: RDJ Kearney (Leinster); TJ Bowe (Ulster), JB Payne (Ulster), R Henshaw (Connacht), SR Zebo (Munster); JJ Sexton (Racing Métro), GC Murray (Munster); JC McGrath (Leinster), SM Cronin (Leinster),

MA Ross (Leinster), D Toner (Leinster), PJ O'Connell (Munster, captain), P O'Mahony (Munster), RJ Ruddock (Leinster), JPR Heaslip (Leinster)
SUBSTITUTIONS: CR Strauss (Leinster) for Cronin (58 mins); T O'Donnell (Munster) for O'Mahony 70 mins); I Madigan (Leinster), R Ah You (Connacht), D Kilcoyne (Munster), MP McCarthy (Leinster) and FA Jones (Munster) for Sexton, Ross, McGrath, Toner and Kearney (73 mins); EG Reddan (Leinster) for Payne (78 mins)
SCORERS: *Tries*: Ruddock, Bowe *Conversions*: Sexton (2) *Penalty Goals*: Sexton (4), Madigan
SOUTH AFRICA: Le Roux; Hendricks, Serfontein, De Villiers (captain), Habana; Pollard, Hougaard; Mtawarira, B du Plessis, J du Plessis, Etzebeth, Matfield, M Coetzee, Mohoje, Vermeulen
SUBSTITUTIONS: Burger for Mohoje (46 mins); Pietersen for Hendricks (49 mins); J Strauss for B du Plessis (50 mins); Reinach for Hougaard (56 mins); Botha for Etzebeth (64 mins); Nyakane and Lambie for Mtawarira and Pollard (66 mins); Oosthuizen for J du Plessis (70 mins)
SCORERS: *Tries*: M Coetzee, Pietersen *Conversion*: Pollard *Penalty Goal*: Pollard
REFEREE: R Poite (France)

15 November, Twickenham, England 28 (2G 1T 3PG) South Africa 31 (2G 1T 3PG 1DG)

ENGLAND: MN Brown (Harlequins); AKC Watson (Bath Rugby), BM Barritt (Saracens), KO Eastmond (Bath Rugby), JJ May (Gloucester Rugby); OA Farrell (Saracens), DS Care (Harlequins); JWG Marler (Harlequins), DM Hartley (Northampton Saints), DG Wilson (Bath Rugby), DMJ Attwood (Bath Rugby), CL Lawes (Northampton Saints), TA Wood (Northampton Saints), CDC Robshaw (Harlequins, captain), VML Vunipola (Saracens)
SUBSTITUTIONS: BJ Morgan (Gloucester Rugby) for V Vunipola (43 mins); BR Youngs (Leicester Tigers) and GT Ford (Bath Rugby) for Care and Farrell (64 mins); RW Webber (Bath Rugby) for Wood (temp 60–70 mins) and Hartley (70 mins); GEJ Kruis (Saracens) and MJ Mullan (Wasps) for Attwood and Marler (66 mins); K Brookes (Newcastle Falcons) for Wilson (72 mins)
SCORERS: *Tries*: Wilson, Morgan, Barritt *Conversions*: Farrell (2) *Penalty Goals*: Farrell (2), Ford
SOUTH AFRICA: Le Roux; Pietersen, Serfontein, De Villiers (captain), Habana; Lambie, Reinach; Mtawarira, Strauss, J du Plessis, Etzebeth, Matfield, Burger, M Coetzee, Vermeulen
SUBSTITUTIONS: B du Plessis for Strauss (60 mins); Oosthuizen and Botha for J du Plessis and Etzebeth (64 mins); Nyakane for Mtawarira (74 mins); Mohoje for Burger (77 mins)
SCORERS: *Tries*: Serfontein, Reinach, Burger *Conversions*: Lambie (2) *Penalty Goals*: Lambie (3) *Drop Goal*: Lambie
REFEREE: SR Walsh (Australia)

22 November, Stadio Euganeo, Padua, Italy 6 (2PG) South Africa 22 (2G 1T 1PG)

ITALY: A Masi (Wasps); L Sarto (Zebre), M Campagnaro (Treviso), L Morisi (Treviso), LJ McLean (Sale Sharks); KJ Haimona (Zebre), E Gori (Treviso); M Aguero (Zebre), L Ghiraldini (Leicester Tigers), ML Castrogiovanni (RC Toulon), Q Geldhenhuys (Zebre), J Furno (Newcastle Falcons), S Vunisa (Zebre), A Zanni (Treviso), S Parisse (Stade Français, captain)
SUBSTITUTIONS: A de Marchi (Sale Sharks) for Aguero (34 mins); F Minto (Treviso) for Zanni (40 mins); A Manici (Zebre) and D Chistolini (Zebre) for Ghirlaldini and Castrogiovanni (63 mins); G Palazzani (Zebre) for Gori (64 mins); M Bortolami (Zebre) for Furno (70 mins); L Orquera (Zebre) and G Toniolatti (Zebre) for Haimona and Sarto (75 mins)
SCORERS: *Penalty Goals*: Haimona (2)
SOUTH AFRICA: Goosen; Pietersen, Serfontein, De Villiers (captain), Habana; Lambie, Reinach; Nyakane, Strauss, Oosthuizen, Etzebeth, Matfield, Mohoje, M Coetzee, Vermeulen
SUBSTITUTIONS: B du Plessis for Strauss (50 mins); Steenkamp and Carr for Nyakane and Mohoje (56 mins); Pollard and Le Roux for Lambie and Goosen (57 mins); Redelinghuys and Hougaard for Oosthuizen and Reinach (70 mins); De Jager for Etzebeth (70 mins)
SCORERS: *Tries*: Oosthuizen, Reinach, Habana *Conversions*: Pollard (2) *Penalty Goal*: Lambie
REFEREE: J Garcès (France)

29 November, Millennium Stadium, Cardiff, Wales 12 (4PG) South Africa 6 (2PG)

WALES: SL Halfpenny (RC Toulon); ACG Cuthbert (Cardiff Blues), JJV Davies (ASM Clermont Auvergne), JH Roberts (Racing Métro), LB Williams (Scarlets); DR Biggar (Ospreys), R Webb (Ospreys); GD Jenkins (Cardiff Blues), SJ Baldwin (Ospreys), S Lee (Scarlets), JD Ball (Scarlets), AW Jones (Ospreys), DJ Lydiate (Racing Métro), S Warburton (Cardiff Blues, captain), TT Faletau (Newport Gwent Dragons)
SUBSTITUTIONS: MS Williams (Scarlets) for Halfpenny (66 mins); AR Jarvis (Ospreys) for Jenkins (74 mins)
SCORER: *Penalty Goals*: Halfpenny (4)

SOUTH AFRICA: Le Roux; Hendricks, Serfontein, De Villiers (captain), Mvovo; Lambie, Reinach; Mtawarira, B du Plessis, Oosthuizen, Etzebeth, Matfield, M Coetzee, Mohoje, Vermeulen
SUBSTITUTIONS: Nyakane and Carr for Mtawarira and Mohoje (53 mins); Pollard and Strauss for Lambie and B du Plessis (56 mins); De Allende for De Villiers (57 mins); Hougaard for Reinach (61 mins); De Jager for Etzebeth (68 mins); Redelinghuys for Oosthuizen (69 mins)
SCORER: *Penalty Goals*: Lambie (2)
REFEREE: J Lacey (Ireland)

ARGENTINA TO EUROPE 2014

Tour Party

FULL-BACKS: S Cordero (Regatas de Bella Vista), LP González Amorosino (Cardiff Blues), J Tuculet (Bordeaux-Bègles)
THREEQUARTERS: JJ Imhoff (Racing Métro), H Agulla (Bath Rugby), M Montero (Pucara), JM Hernández (unattached), J de la Fuente (RC Elves)
HALF-BACKS: TM Cubelli (Belgrano Athletic), MT Bosch (Saracens), FN Sánchez (RC Toulon), M Landajo (CA San Isidro), S González Iglesias (AA Alumni), M Moroni (CUBA)
FORWARDS: A Creevy (Worcester Warriors), M Cortese (RC Liceo), S Iglesias Valdez (Universitario Tucumán), MI Ayerza (Leicester Tigers), R Herrera (Castres Olympique), FN Tetaz Chaparro (Lyon OU), L Noguera (RC Lynx), TE Lavanini (Racing Métro), J Cruz Guillemain (Stade Français), L Ponce (CUBA), M Alemanno (La Tablada), G Petti (San Isidro Club), JM Leguizamón (Lyon OU), R Baez (RC Liceo), J Ortega Desio (unattached), F Isa (unattached), B Macome (Aviron Bayonnais), LV Senatore (Worcester Warriors), T Lezana (Santiago LTC)
HEAD COACH: D Hourcade

8 November, Murrayfield, Scotland 41 (5G 2PG) Argentina 31 (4G 1PG)

SCOTLAND: SW Hogg (Glasgow Warriors); SD Maitland (Glasgow Warriors), MS Bennett (Glasgow Warriors), AJ Dunbar (Glasgow Warriors), TSF Seymour (Glasgow Warriors); FA Russell (Glasgow Warriors), GD Laidlaw (Gloucester Rugby, captain); AG Dickinson (Edinburgh Rugby), RW Ford (Edinburgh Rugby), EA Murray (Glasgow Warriors), RJ Gray (Castres Olympique), JD Gray (Glasgow Warriors), RJ Harley (Glasgow Warriors), BA Cowan (London Irish), A Ashe (Glasgow Warriors)
SUBSTITUTIONS: AK Strokosch (USA Perpignan) for Cowan (59 mins); S Lawson (Newcastle Falcons) and HB Pyrgos (Glasgow Warriors) for Ford and Laidlaw (63 mins); D Weir (Glasgow Warriors) for Russell (64 mins); JL Hamilton (Saracens) and GJ Reid (Glasgow Warriors) for RJ Gray and Dickinson (68 mins); GDS Cross (London Irish) for Murray (70 mins); SF Lamont (Glasgow Warriors) for Dunbar (75 mins)
SCORERS: *Tries*: RJ Gray, JD Gray, Maitland, Hogg, Seymour *Conversions*: Laidlaw (4), Weir *Penalty Goals*: Laidlaw (2)
ARGENTINA: Tuculet; Imhoff, Bosch, Hernández, Montero; Sánchez, Landajo; Ayerza, Creevy (captain), Herrera, Lavanini, Cruz Guillemain, Baez, Ortega Desio, Senatore
SUBSTITUTIONS: Isa for Baez (16 mins); Cortese for Creevy (19 mins); Tetaz Chaparro for Herrera (45 mins); González Iglesias for Sánchez (52 mins); Cubelli for Landajo (57 mins); Noguera and Agulla for Ayerza and Bosch (61 mins); Ponce for Cruz Guillemain (68 mins)
SCORERS: *Tries*: Cubelli (2), Ortega Desio, Penalty Try *Conversions*: Hernández (3), Sánchez *Penalty Goal*: Sánchez
REFEREE: W Barnes (England)

14 November, Stadio Marassi, Genoa, Italy 18 (6PG) Argentina 20 (2G 2PG)

ITALY: A Masi (Wasps); L Sarto (Zebre), M Campagnaro (Treviso), L Morisi (Treviso), LJ McLean (Sale Sharks); KJ Haimona (Zebre), E Gori (Treviso); M Aguero (Zebre), L Ghiraldini (Leicester Tigers), ML Castrogiovanni (RC Toulon), Q Geldhenhuys (Zebre), J Furno (Newcastle Falcons), A Zanni (Treviso), S Favero (Treviso), S Parisse (Stade Français, captain)
SUBSTITUTIONS: D Chistolini (Zebre) and F Minto (Treviso) for Castrogiovanni and Favaro (56 mins); A de Marchi (Sale Sharks) for Aguero (61 mins); M Bortolami (Zebre), G Palazzani (Zebre) and L Orquera (Zebre) for Furno, Gori and Haimona (70 mins); G Toniolatti (Zebre) and A Manici (Zebre) for McLean and Ghiraldini (73 mins)
SCORERS: *Penalty Goals*: Haimona (5), Orquera
ARGENTINA: Tuculet; González Amorosino, Agulla, De la Fuente, Montero; Hernández, Cubelli (captain); Ayerza, Cortese, Tetaz Chaparro, Petti, Lavanini, Isa, Ortega Desio, Senatore

SUBSTITUTIONS: Moroni for Tuculet (40 mins); Sánchez for Moroni (temp 44–50 mins) and Hernández (61 mins); Herrera for Tetaz Chaparro (52 mins); Iglesias Valdez for Cortese (56 mins); Landajo for Cubelli (61 mins); Noguera for Ayerza (67 mins); Ponce for Petti (68 mins)
SCORERS: *Tries:* González Amorosino, De la Fuente *Conversions:* Hernández (2) *Penalty Goals:* Hernández, Sánchez
REFEREE: CP Joubert (South Africa)

22 November, Stade de France, Paris, France 13 (1G 2PG) Argentina 18 (2PG 4DG)

FRANCE: SL Spedding (Aviron Bayonnais); Y Huget (Stade Toulousain), M Mermoz (RC Toulon), W Fofana (ASM Clermont Auvergne), M Médard (Stade Toulousain); C Lopez (ASM Clermont Auvergne), S Tillous-Borde (RC Toulon); X Chiocci (RC Toulon), B Kayser (ASM Clermont Auvergne), N Mas (Montpellier HRC), P Papé (Stade Français), S Vahaamahina (ASM Clermont Auvergne), T Dusautoir (Stade Toulousain, captain), B le Roux (Racing Métro), D Chouly (ASM Clermont Auvergne)
SUBSTITUTIONS: A Menini (RC Toulon) for Chiocci (37 mins); U Atonio (Stade Rochelais) for Mas (40 mins); M Bastareaud (RC Toulon) for Mermoz (temp 42–57 mins) and Médard (57 mins); RM Kockott (Castres Olympique) and G Guirado (RC Toulon) for Tillous-Borde and Kayser (46 mins); Y Maestri (Stade Toulousain) for Vahaamahina (49 mins); R Talès (Castres Olympique) for Lopez (69 mins); C Ollivon (Aviron Bayonnais) for Chouly (74 mins)
SCORERS: *Try:* Fofana *Conversion:* Lopez *Penalty Goals:* Lopez, Kockott
ARGENTINA: Tuculet; Imhoff, Bosch, Hernández, Montero; Sánchez, Cubelli; Ayerza, Creevy (captain), Tetaz Chaparro, Petti, Lavanini, Isa, Ortega Desio, Senatore
SUBSTITUTIONS: González Iglesias for Bosch (16 mins); Lezana for Senatore (19 mins); Herrera for Tetaz Chaparro (57 mins); Landajo and González Amorosino for Cubelli and Tuculet (61 mins); Noguera for Ayerza (63 mins); Ponce for Petti (74 mins)
SCORERS: *Penalty Goals:* Sánchez (2) *Drop Goals:* Sánchez (3), Hernández
REFEREE: GJ Clancy (Ireland)

SAMOA TO EUROPE 2014

Tour Party

FULL-BACKS: KS Pisi (Northampton Saints), A Tuala (Counties Manukau), F Autagavaia (RC Nevers)
THREEQUARTERS: A Leiua (Wasps), D Lemi (Bristol Rugby, captain), A Alofa (Stade Rochelais), R Lee-Lo (Counties Manukau), JW Leota (Sale Sharks), WTN Stanley (Auckland)
HALF-BACKS: K Fotuali'i (Northampton Saints), J Taulapapa (Wellington), P Crowley (Auckland), T Pisi (Suntory Sungoliath), MJ Stanley (Counties Manukau)
FORWARDS: TT Paulo (ASM Clermont Auvergne), WO Avei (Bordeaux-Bègles), M Leiataua, (RC Aurillac) V Afatia (SU Agen), S Taulafo (Stade Français), L Mulipola (Leicester Tigers), CAI Johnston (Stade Toulousain), J Johnston (Saracens), AI Perenise (Bristol Rugby), A Anae (Treviso), AP Toetu (Bordeaux-Bègles), TAM Paulo (Cardiff Blues), KG Thompson (Newcastle Falcons), DA Leo (London Irish), F Lemalu (Sanix Blues), M Fa'asavalu (Oyonnax), P Fa'asalele (Castres Olympique), JT Lam (Bristol Rugby), TJ Ioane (Otago), O Treviranus (London Irish), T Tuifua (Bordeaux-Bègles)
HEAD COACH: S Betham

8 November, Stadio del Duca, Ascoli Piceno, Italy 24 (1G 1T 4PG) Samoa 13 (1G 2PG)

ITALY: A Masi (Wasps); L Sarto (Zebre), M Campagnaro (Treviso), L Morisi (Treviso), LJ McLean (Sale Sharks); KJ Haimona (Zebre), E Gori (Treviso); M Aguero (Zebre), L Ghiraldini (Leicester Tigers), D Chistolini (Zebre), Q Geldenhuys (Zebre), J Furno (Newcastle Falcons), A Zanni (Treviso), S Favaro (Treviso), S Parisse (Stade Français, captain)
SUBSTITUTIONS: G Toniolatti (Zebre) for Sarto (temp 19–24 mins); A Manici (Zebre) and M Bortolami (Zebre) for Ghiraldini and Furno (64 mins); RJ Barbieri (Leicester Tigers) for Favaro (68 mins); A de Marchi (Sale Sharks) and L Cittadini (Wasps) for Aguero and Chistolini (69 mins)
SCORERS: *Tries:* Favaro, Parisse *Conversion:* Haimona *Penalty Goals:* Haimona (4)
SAMOA: Autagavaia; K Pisi; Leiua, Leota, Lemi (captain); T Pisi, Fotuali'i; Taulafo, TT Paulo, Perenise, Lemalu, Thompson, Fa'asalele, Lam, Tu'ifua
SUBSTITUTIONS: TAM Paulo for Thompson (40 mins); Afatia and Avei for Taulafo and TT Paulo (52 mins); Fa'asavalu for Tu'ifua (67 mins); MJ Stanley and WTN Stanley for T Pisi and Leota (73 mins); Toetu for Perenise (74 mins); Crowley for Autagavaia (80 mins)
SCORERS: *Try:* Lam *Conversion:* T Pisi *Penalty Goals:* T Pisi (2)
REFEREE: SR Walsh (Australia)

CANADA: J Pritchard (Bedford Blues); J Hassler (Ospreys), C Trainor (BC Bears), C Hearn (Atlantic Rock), DTH van der Merwe (Glasgow Warriors); C Braid (Glasgow Warriors), G McRorie (Prairie Wolf Pack); H Buydens (Manawatu, captain), A Carpenter (Cornish Pirates), J Marshall (Hawke's Bay), J Cudmore (ASM Clermont Auvergne), B Beukeboom (Plymouth Albion), K Gilmour (Prairie Wolf Pack), N Dala (Prairie Wolf Pack), J Sinclair (London Irish)

SUBSTITUTIONS: J Ilnicki (NSW Country) for Marshall (temp 5–10 mins) and Buydens (71 mins); J Phelan (Doncaster Knights) for Beukeboom (31 mins); RJ Thorpe (London Welsh) for Gilmour (55 mins); S White (BC Bears) for McRorie (63 mins); P Parfrey (Atlantic Rock) for Braid (64 mins); R Barkwill (Ontario Blues) for Carpenter (69 mins); A Tiedemann (Plymouth Albion) for Marshall (71 mins); J Wilson-Ross (Ontario Blues) for Hearn (74 mins)

SCORERS: *Try:* Trainor *Conversion:* Pritchard *Penalty Goals:* McRorie (2)

SAMOA: Tuala; Alofa, Leiua, Lee-Lo, Lemi (captain); MJ Stanley, Fotuali'i; Taulafo, Avei, C Johnston, TAM Paulo, Leo, Fa'asavalu, Ioane, Treviranus

SUBSTITUTIONS: Perenise, Thompson and WTN Stanley for C Johnston, Leo and Alofa (55 mins), Lam for Ioane (65 mins); Leiataua for Avei (69 mins); Autagavaia for Tuala (73 mins); Afatia and Crowley for Taulafo and Fotuali'i (76 mins)

SCORERS: *Tries:* Perenise, WTN Stanley *Conversions:* MJ Stanley (2) *Penalty Goals* MJ Stanley (3)

REFEREE GJ Clancy (Ireland)

ENGLAND MN Brown (Harlequins); AKC Watson (Bath Rugby), BM Barritt (Saracens), OA Farrell (Saracens), JJ May (Gloucester Rugby); GT Ford (Bath Rugby), BR Youngs (Leicester Tigers); JWG Marler (Harlequins), RW Webber (Bath Rugby), DG Wilson (Bath Rugby), DMJ Attwood (Bath Rugby), CL Lawes (Northampton Saints), JAW Haskell (Wasps), CDC Robshaw (Harlequins, captain), BJ Morgan (Gloucester Rugby)

SUBSTITUTIONS: MXJ Yarde (Harlequins) for May (temp 8–17 mins and 60 mins); GEJ Kruis (Saracens) for Lawes (53 mins); MJ Mullan (Wasps) and K Brookes (Newcastle Falcons) for Marler and Wilson (58 mins); REP Wigglesworth (Saracens) for Youngs (61 mins); WWF Twelvetrees (Gloucester Rugby) for Farrell (64 mins); TA Wood (Northampton Saints) for Haskell (67 mins); DM Hartley (Northampton Saints) for Webber (69 mins)

SCORERS *Tries:* May (2), Brown *Conversions:* Ford (2) *Penalty Goals:* Ford (3)

SAMOA: K Pisi; Leiua, Lee-Lo, Leota, Lemi (captain); T Pisi, Fotuali'i; Taulafo, TT Paulo, C Johnston, TAM Paulo, Thompson, Fa'asavalu, Lam, Treviranus

SUBSTITUTIONS: Leo for TAM Paulo (51 mins); Perenise and Ioane for C Johnston and Lam (55 mins); Leiataua for TT Paulo (60 mins); Lemalu for Thompson (61 mins); MJ Stanley for T Pisi (67 mins); Afatia for Taulafo (77 mins)

SCORER: *Penalty Goals:* T Pisi (3)

REFEREE: J Peyper (South Africa)

JAPAN TO EUROPE 2014

FULL-BACKS: A Goromaru (Yamaha Jubilo)

THREEQUARTERS: KL Hesketh (Munakata Sanix Blues), A Yamada (Panasonic Wild Knights), T Hirose (Toshiba Brave Lupus), K Matsushima (Suntory Sungoliath), M Sau (Yamaha Jubilo), Y Tamura (NEC Green Rockets)

HALF-BACKS: K Ono (Suntory Sungoliath), H Tatekawa (Kubota Spears), M Mikami (Suntory Sungoliath), Y Yatomi (Yamaha Jubilo)

FORWARDS: T Kizu (Kobe Steel), H Yuhara (Toshiba Brave Lupus), M Mikami (Toshiba Brave Lupus), K Inagaki (Panasonic Wild Knights), K Hatakeyama (Suntory Sungoliath), S Kakinaga (Suntory Sungoliath), H Yamashita (Kobe Steel), M Ito (Kobe Steel), S Makabe (Suntory Sungoliath), L Thompson (Kintetsu Liners), H Ono (Toshiba Brave Lupus), H Tui (Suntory Sungoliath), M Leitch (Toshiba Brave Lupus), HK Hopgood (Kamaishi Seawaves), AL Mafi (NTT Shining Arcs)

HEAD COACH: E Jones

ROMANIA: C Fercu (Saracens); D Manole (RC Orthez), C Gal (Baia Mare), CR Dascalu (Steaua Bucharest), I Botezatu (Baia Mare); F Vlaicu (Farul Constanta), V Calefeteanu (RCM Timisoara Saracens); A Ursache

(RC Carcassonne), A Radoi (Ealing Trailfinders), P Ion (USA Perpignan), M Sirbe (Blagnac), V Poparlan (RCM Timisoara Saracens), O Tonita (Pays d'Aix en Provence), M Macovei (RC Massy, captain), D Carpo (RCM Timisoara Saracens)

SUBSTITUTIONS: S Burcea (RCM Timisoara Saracens) for Carpo (38 mins); O Turashvili (Farul Constanta) for Radoi (54 min); A Coste (RC Carcassonne) for Tonita (58 mins); H Pungea (Lyon OU) for Ion (63 mins); M Lazar (Castres Olympique) for Ursache (67 mins); F Ionita (Steaua Bucharest) for Botezatu (71 mins)

SCORERS: *Try*: Penalty Try *Conversion*: Vlaicu *Penalty Goals*: Vlaicu (2)

JAPAN: Goromaru; Hesketh, Matsushima, M Sau, Yamada; K Ono, Hiwasa; M Mikami, Kizu, Hatakeyama, Ito, Makabe, Tui, Leitch (captain), Mafi

SUBSTITUTIONS: Tatekawa for Yamada (38 mins); H Ono for Makabe (49 mins); Hopgood for Leitch (50 mins); Inagaki for Mikami (60 mins); Hirose for Hesketh (70 mins); Yuhara for Kizu (77 mins); Yamashita for Hatakeyama (77 mins)

SCORER: *Penalty Goals*: Goromaru (6)

REFEREE: S Berry (South Africa)

---

23 November, Meskhi Stadium, Tbilisi, Georgia 35 (2G 3T 2PG) Japan 24 (3G 1PG)

GEORGIA: M Kvirikashvili (RC Montlucon); T Mchedlidze (SU Agen), D Kacharava (STM Enisey, captain), M Sharikadze (RC Aurillac), A Todua (Lelo Saracens); L Khmaladze (Lelo Saracens), V Khutsishvili (Kharebi); M Natriashvili (Montpellier HRC), S Mamukashvili (Sale Sharks), D Kubriashvili (Stade Francais), G Nemsadze (RC Tarbes), L Datunashvili (RC Aurillac), G Tkhilaishvili (Batumi), V Kolelishvili (ASM Clermont Auvergne), L Lomidze (Beziers HRC)

SUBSTITUTIONS: G Aptsiauri (Aia Kutaisi) for Kacharava (3 mins); L Chilachava (RC Toulon) for Kubriashvili (56 mins); K Mikautadze (RC Toulon) for Nemsadze (56 mins); B Tsiklauri (Lokomotiv Tibilisi) for Aptsiauri (59 mins); S Maisuradze (Valence) for Mamukashvili (65 mins); Z Zhvania (Stade Francais) for Nariashvili (66 mins); G Chkhaidze (RC Lille) for Tkhilaishvili (69 mins); G Begadze (Kochebi) for Sharikadze (80 mins)

SCORERS: *Tries*: Mamukashvili, Penalty Try, Khmaladze, Kvirikashvili, Tsiklauri *Conversions*: Kvirikashvili (2) *Penalty Goals*: Kvirikashvili (2)

JAPAN: Goromaru; Matsushima, Sau, Tatekawa, Hesketh; Tamura, Hiwasa; Mikami, Kizu, Hatakeyama (captain), Thompson, Ito, Tui, Hopgood, Mafi

SUBSTITUTIONS: Makabe for Ito (51 mins); K Ono for Tamura (54 mins); Inagaki for Mikami (63 mins); Kakinaga for Hatakeyama (63 mins); H Ono for Hopgood (65 mins); Yuhara for Kizu (72 mins); Yatomi for Hiwasa (75 mins); Hirose for Hesketh (75 mins)

SCORERS: *Tries*: Tatekawa, Hesketh (2) *Conversions*: Goromaru (3) *Penalty Goal*: Goromaru

REFEREE: R Poite (France)

FIJI TO EUROPE 2014

Tour Party

FULL-BACKS: T Nagusa (Montpellier HRC), M Talebula (Bordeaux-Bègles)

THREEQUARTERS: WN Nayacalevu (Stade Français), AT Tikoirotuma (London Irish), W Votu (Section Pau), A Ratini (FC Grenoble), L Botia (Stade Rochelais), N Nadolo (Crusaders), V Goneva (Leicester Tigers)

HALF-BACKS: J Ralulu (Farul Constanta), JL Matavesi (Ospreys), N Kenatale (Steaua Bucharest), NL Matawalu (Bath Rugby), HW Seniloli (Treviso)

FORWARDS: V Veikoso (Doncaster Knights), T Talemaitoga (Pays d'Aix en Provence), SK Koto (RC Narbonne), JNBN Yanuyanutawa (Glasgow Warriors), GDC Ma'afu (Pays d'Aix en Provence), M Saulo (Timisoara Saracens), T Koroi (Wellington), I Colati (RC Nevers), P Ravai (Fiji Warriors), DM Waqaniburotu (CA Brive), A Ratuniyarawa (SU Agen), L Nakawara (Glasgow Warriors), T Cavubati (Ospreys), NR Soqeta (Biarritz Olympique), A Qera (Montpellier HRC), RMM Ravulo (Farul Constanta), MS Matadigo (Lyon OU), N Nagusa (Nadroga)

HEAD COACH: J McKee

---

8 November, Stade de Velodrome, Marseille, France 40 (3G 2T 3PG) Fiji 15 (1G 1T 1PG)

FRANCE: SL Spedding (Aviron Bayonnais); Y Huget (Stade Toulousain), A Dumoulin (Racing Métro), W Fofana (ASM Clermont Auvergne), T Thomas (Racing Métro); C Lopez (ASM Clermont Auvergne), S Tillous-Borde (RC Toulon); A Menini (RC Toulon), G Guirado (RC Toulon), N Mas (Montpellier HRC), P Papé (Stade Français), Y Maestri (Stade Toulousain), T Dusautoir (Stade Toulousain, captain), B le Roux (Racing Métro), D Chouly (ASM Clermont Auvergne)

SUBSTITUTIONS: U Atonio (Stade Rochelais) for Mas (47 mins); B Kayser (ASM Clermont Auvergne) for

Guirado (50 mins); X Chiocci (RC Toulon) for Menini (57 mins); RM Kockott (Castres Olympique) and R Talès (Castres Olympique) for Tillous-Borde and Lopez (67 mins); C Ollivon (Aviron Bayonnais) for Chouly (68 mins); A Flanquart (Stade Français) and M Bastareaud (RC Toulon) for Maestri and Dumoulin (72 mins)
SCORERS: *Tries*: Thomas (3), Papé, Fofana *Conversions*: Lopez (2), Kockott *Penalty Goals*: Lopez (3)
FIJI: Talebula; Votu, Tikoroituma, Botia, Ratini; Ralulu, Matawalu; Ma'afu, Koto, Saulo, Nakarawa, Ratuniyarawa, Waqaniburotu, Qera (captain), Matadigo
SUBSTITUTIONS: Nadolo for Botia (40 mins); Nagusa for Votu (58 mins); Yanyanutawa for Ma'afu (64 mins); Soqeta for Ratuniyarawa (68 mins), Colati and Ravulo for Saulo and Matadigo (75 mins); Seniloli for Matawalu (76 mins)
SCORERS: *Tries*: Votu, Nagusa *Conversion*: Nadolo *Penalty Goal*: Nadolo
REFEREE: GW Jackson (New Zealand)

15 November, Millennium Stadium, Cardiff, Wales 17 (1G 2T) Fiji 13 (1G 2PG)

WALES: LB Williams (Scarlets); ACG Cuthbert (Cardiff Blues), MS Williams (Scarlets), JH Roberts (Racing Métro), GP North (Northampton Saints); R Priestland (Scarlets), WM Phillips (Racing Métro); GD Jenkins (Cardiff Blues, captain), SJ Baldwin (Ospreys), S Lee (Scarlets), BS Davies (Wasps), LC Charteris (Racing Métro), DJ Lydiate (Racing Métro), JC Tipuric (Ospreys), TT Faletau (Newport Gwent Dragons)
SUBSTITUTIONS: RP Jones (Scarlets) and JD King (Ospreys) for Lee and Lydiate (60 mins); NP Smith (Ospreys) and AW Jones (Ospreys) for Jenkins and Charteris (65 mins)
SCORERS: *Tries*: North, Cuthbert, Penalty Try *Conversion*: Priestland
FIJI: Talebula; Nayacalevu, Goneva, Nadolo, Tikoroituma: Matavesi, Matawalu; Ma'afu, Koto, Saulo, Cavubati, Nakarawa, Waqaniburotu, Qera (captain), Matadigo
SUBSTITUTIONS: Yanuyanutawa for Matadigo (temp 43–46 mins and 60 mins); Soqeta for Cavubati (65 mins); Colati, Ravulo, Seniloli and Nagusa for Saulo, Waqaniburotu, Matawalu and Goneva (71 mins)
SCORERS: *Try*: Nadolo *Conversion*: Nadolo *Penalty Goals*: Nadolo (2)
RED CARD: Ma'afu (52 mins)
REFEREE: P Gaüzère (France)

21 November, Stade de la Rabine, Vannes, France, Fiji 20 (1G 2T 1PG) USA 14 (2G)

FIJI: Nagusa; Votu, Goneva, Nadolo, Tikoroituma; Matavesi, Seniloli; Ravai, Tuapati, Saulo, Cavubati, Nakarawa, Qera (captain), Ravulo, Matadigo
SUBSTITUTIONS: Ralulu for Nagusa (temp 31–40 mins); Waqaniburotu for Matadigo (temp 39–48 mins and 57 mins); Koto and Koroi for Tuapati and Saulo (64 mins); Soqeta for Cavubati (71 mins); Nayacalevu for Nadolo (73 mins); Kenatale and Colati for Seniloli and Ravai (78 mins)
SCORERS: *Tries*: Nagusa, Votu (2) *Conversion*: Nadolo *Penalty Goal*: Nadolo
USA: R McLean (Ealing Trailfinders); T Ngwenya, (Biarritz Olympique), S Kelly (unattached), T Palamo (Seattle Saracens), T Stanfill (Seattle Saracens); S Suniula (Seattle Saracens), M Petri (New York AC); O Kilifi (Seattle Saracens), P Thiel (Life University), M Moeakiola (RC Castenet), J Cullen (Seattle Saracens), G Petersen (North Harbour Rays), S LaValla (Stade Français), J Quill (Dolphin), T Clever (NTT Shining Arcs, captain)
SUBSTITUTIONS: K Sumsion (Brigham Young University) for Quill (temp 39–41 mins); M Trouville (Seattle Saracens) for Clever (48 mins); N Wallace (Glendale Raptors) for Kilifi (59 mins); Sumsion and LE Stanfill (Seattle Saracens) for Peterson and Cullen (78 mins)
SCORERS: *Tries*: Kelly, Ngwenya *Conversions*: McLean (2)
REFEREE: J Lacey (Ireland)

USA TO EUROPE 2014

8 November, Stadionul National Arcul de Triumf, Bucharest, Romania 17 (2G 1PG) USA 27 (3G 1PG 1DG)

ROMANIA: C Fercu (Saracens); A Apostol (Farul Constanta), C Gal (Baia Mare), F Vlaicu (Farul Constanta), R Neagu (Farul Constanta); D Manole (RC Orthez), V Calefeteanu (RCM Timisoara Saracens); M Lazar (Castres Olympique,), O Turashvili (Farul Constanta), P Ion (USA Perpignan), M Sirbe (Blagnac), A Coste (RC Carcassonne), M Macovei (RC Massy, captain), O Tonita (Pays d'Aix en Provence), D Carpo (RCM Timisoara Saracens)
SUBSTITUTIONS: A Radoi (Ealing Trailfinders) for Turashvili (temp 12–24 and 63 mins); V Nistor (Castres Olympique) for Tonita (48 mins); A Ursache (RC Carcassonne) for Lazar (53 mins); V Poparlan (RCM Timisoara Saracens) for Coste (55 mins)
SCORERS: *Tries*: Penalty Try, Radoi *Conversions*: Vlaicu (2) *Penalty Goal*: Vlaicu

MAJOR TOURS

USA: F Niua (USA Sevens); T Ngwenya (Biarritz Olympique), S Kelly (unattached), A Suniula (Old Blue), T Stanfill (Seattle Saracens); A Siddall (Old Blue), M Petri (New York AC); N Wallace (Glendale Raptors), P Thiel (Life University), O Kilifi (Seattle Saracens), T Tuisamoa (London Scottish), L Stanfill (Seattle Saracens), T Clever (NTT Shining Arcs, captain), J Quill (Dolphin), M Trouville (Seattle Saracens)
SUBSTITUTIONS: B Tarr (Souths Rugby) for Kilifi (39 mis); T Coolican (Sydney Saracens) for Thiel (52 mins); J Cullen (Seattle Saracens) for Tuisamoa (52 mins); G Peterson (NSW Waratahs) for Stanfill (62 mins); S Suniula (RC Chalon) for Siddall (68 mins)
SCORERS: *Tries*: Ngwenya, Stanfill, Niua *Conversions*: Siddall (3) *Penalty Goal*: Siddall *Drop Goal*: Siddall
REFEREE: L Hodges (Wales)

15 November, Kingsholm, Gloucester Tonga 40 (3G 2T 3PG) USA 12 (1G 1T)

Details in Tonga tour record

21 November, Stade de la Rabine, Vannes, France, Fiji 20 (1G 2T 1PG) USA 14 (2G)

Details in Fiji tour record

GEORGIA NOVEMBER 2014 INTERNATIONALS

8 November, Meskhi Stadium, Tbilisi, Georgia 9 (3PG) Tonga 23 (1G 2T 2PG)

Details in Tonga tour record

16 November, Aviva Stadium, Dublin, Ireland 49 (5G 1T 3PG) Georgia 7 (1G)

IRELAND: FA Jones (Munster); CJH Gilroy (Ulster), DM Cave (Ulster), GWD D'Arcy (Leinster), SR Zebo (Munster); I Madigan (Leinster), EG Reddan (Leinster, captain); D Kilcoyne (Munster), CR Strauss (Leinster), MA Ross (Leinster), D Foley (Munster), MP McCarthy (Leinster), D Ryan (Leinster), T O'Donnell (Munster), RJE Diack (Ulster)
SUBSTITUTIONS: R Ah You (Connacht) for Ross (46 mins); S Olding (Ulster), R Copeland (Munster), SM Cronin (Leinster), D Toner (Leinster), IJ Keatley (Munster) and KD Marmion (Connacht) for Zebo, McCarthy, Strauss, Foley, D'Arcy and Reddan (61 mins)
SCORERS: *Tries*: Jones (2), Kilcoyne, Strauss, Zebo, Olding *Conversions*: Madigan (5) *Penalty Goals*: Madigan (3)
GEORGIA: M Kvirikashvili (RC Montlucon); T Mchedlidze (SU Agen), D Kacharava (Yenisey Krasnoyarsk, captain), M Sharikadze (RC Aurillac), S Todua (Lelo Saracens); L Khmaladze (Lelo Saracens), G Begadze (Qochebi Bolnisi); M Nariashvili (Montpellier HRC), S Mamukashvili (Sale Sharks), D Kubriashvili (Stade Français), K Mikautadze (RC Toulon), G Nemsadze (RC Tarbes), G Tkhilaishvili (Batumi), V Kolelishvili (ASM Clermont Auvergne), D Basilaia (USA Perpignan)
SUBSTITUTIONS: L Datunashvili (RC Aurillac) for Mikautadze (49 mins); Z Zhvania (Stade Français), L Chilachava (RC Toulon) and S Maisuradze (RC Valence) for Nariashvili, Kubriashvili and Mamukashvili (51 mins); L Malaguradze (RC Bagneres) and M Giorgadze (Armazi) for Khmaladze and Mchedlidze (54 mins); V Khutsishvili (Kharebi Rustavi) and G Chkhaidze (RC Lille) for Begadze and Kolelishvili (57 mins)
SCORERS: *Try*: Nemsadze *Conversion*: Kvirikashvili
REFEREE: JP Doyle (England)

23 November, Meskhi Stadium, Tbilisi, Georgia 35 (2G 3T 2PG) Japan 24 (3G 1PG)

Details in Japan tour record

TONGA TO EUROPE 2014

Tour Party

FULL-BACKS: VF Lilo (RC Tarbes), DT Halaifonua (RC Bergerac),
THREEQUARTERS: O Katoa (Southland), FM Vainikolo (Exeter Chiefs), SV Piutau (Yamaha Jubilo), S Piukala (USA Perpignan), H Paea (Oyonnax), D Kilioni (FC Grenoble)
HALF-BACKS: KS Morath (Biarritz Olympique), L Fosita (Northland), TUV Moa (Section Pau), S Takulua (Northland), L Simote (Toloa Old Boys), TT Palu (Doncaster Knights)
FORWARDS: AA Lutui (Gloucester Rugby), EVT Taione (Exeter Chiefs), P Ngauamo (Oyonnax), T Vea (London Welsh), S Taumalolo (Racing Métro), H 'Aulika (London Irish), TS Mailau (RC Mont de Marsan),

S Halanukonuka (Tasman), P Fa'anunu (Castres Olympique), S Lea (Taranaki), SKV Puafisi (Gloucester Rugby), TA Lokotui (Beziers HRC), JML Tuineau (Lyon OU), L Fa'aoso (Aviron Bayonnais), SM Kalamafoni (Gloucester Rugby), C Hala'ufia (London Welsh), HTNT Pole (Southland), NO Latu (NEC Rockets), VS Ma'afu (Oyonnax), M Vaipulu (Counties Manukau), V Fihaki (Sale Sharks)

HEAD COACH: M 'Otai

---

8 November, Meskhi Stadium, Tbilisi, Georgia 9 (3PG) Tonga 23 (1G 2T 2PG)

GEORGIA: M Kvirikashvili (RC Montlucon); I Machkhaneli (RC Armasy Tbilisi, captain), D Kacharava (STM Enisey), M Sharikadze (RC Aurillac), T Mchedlidze (SU Agen); L Khmaladze (Lelo Saracens), G Begadze (Kochebi); M Nariashvili (Montpellier HRC), S Mamukashvili (Sale Sharks), D Kubriashvili (Stade Francais), K Mikautadze (RC Toulon), L Datunashvili (RC Aurillac), G Tkhilaishvili (Batumi), V Kolelishvili (ASM Clermont Auvergne), G Chkhaidze (RC Lille)

SUBSTITUTIONS: Z Zhvania (Stade Français) for Nariashvili (67 mins); L Chilachava (RC Toulon) for Kubriashvili (67 mins); L Lomidze (Beziers HRC) for Chkhaidze (67 mins); S Maisuradze (Valence) for Mamukashvili (70 mins); G Nemsadze (RC Tarbes) for Mikautadze (70 mins); A Todua (Lelo Saracens) for Machkhaneli (72 mins); L Malaguradze (Beziers HRC) for Khmaladze (74 mins); V Khutsishvili (Kharebi) for Begadze (75 mins)

SCORER: *Penalty Goals:* Kvirikashvili (3)

TONGA: Lilo; Halaifonua, Piutau, Paea, Vainikolo; Morath, Takulua; Mailau, Lutui, Puafisi, Lokotui, Tuineau, Kalamafoni, Latu (captain), Ma'afu

SUBSTITUTIONS: Halanukonuka for Mailau (54 mins); Faanunu for Puafisi (54 mins); Moa for Takulua (61 mins); Fosita for Morath (62 mins); Katoa for Paea (62 mins); Taione for Lutui (70 mins); Fa'aoso for Tuineau (77 mins); T Pole for Latu (77 mins)

SCORERS: *Tries:* Moa (2), Lilo *Conversion:* Fosita *Penalty Goals:* Morath (2)

REFEREE: P Gaüzère (France)

---

15 November, Kingsholm, Gloucester, Tonga 40 (3G 2T 3PG) USA 12 (1G 1T)

TONGA: Lilo; Halaifonua, Piutau, Paea, Vainikolo; Morath, Takulua; Mailau, Lutui, Faanunu, Lokotui, Tuineau, Kalamafoni, Latu (captain), Ma'afu

SUBSTITUTIONS: Fosita for Morath (55 mins); Taione for Lutui (58 mins); Lea for Mailau (58 mins); Puafisi for Faanunu (58 mins); Katoa for Halaifonua (65 mins); Fa'aoso for Tuineau (70 mins); T Pole for Kalamafoni (70 mins); Moa for Takulua (70 mins)

SCORERS: *Tries:* Vainikolo, Ma'afu, Lilo (2), Latu *Conversions:* Morath (2), Fosita *Penalty Goals:* Morath (2)

USA: F Niua (USA Sevens); T Maupin (Trinity College), S Kelly (unattached), A Suniula (Old Blue), T Stanfill (Seattle Saracens); S Suniula (Seattle Saracens), M Petri (New York AC); N Wallace (Glendale Raptors), P Thiel (Life University), M Moeakiola (RC Castenet), J Cullen (Seattle Saracens), G Peterson (North Harbour), S LaValla (Stade Français, captain), J Quill (Dolphin), M Trouville (Seattle Saracens)

SUBSTITUTIONS: T Tuisamoa (London Scottish) for Peterson (58 mins); T Palamo (Saracens) for A Suniula (58 mins); T Coolican (Sydney Stars) for Thiel (63 mins); T Clever (NTT Shining Arcs) for Trouville (63 mins); K Sumsion (Brigham Young University) for Quill (65 mins); B Tarr (Glendale Raptors) for Moeakiola (70 mins)

SCORERS: *Tries:* T Stanfill, Quill *Conversion:* Niua

REFEREE: MI Fraser (New Zealand)

---

22 November, Rugby Park, Kilmarnock, Scotland 37 (3G 2T 2PG), Tonga 12 (4PG)

SCOTLAND: SW Hogg (Glasgow Warriors); TSF Seymour (Glasgow Warriors), SF Lamont (Glasgow Warriors), AJ Dunbar (Glasgow Warriors), TJW Visser (Edinburgh Rugby); FA Russell (Glasgow Warriors), GD Laidlaw (Gloucester Rugby, captain); AG Dickinson (Edinburgh Rugby), RW Ford (Edinburgh Rugby), GDS Cross (London Irish), RJ Gray (Castres Olympique), JD Gray (Glasgow Warriors), RJ Harley (Glasgow Warriors), BA Cowan (London Irish), JW Beattie (Castres Olympique)

SUBSTITUTIONS: GJ Reid (Glasgow Warriors) and AK Strokosch (USA Perpignan) for Dickinson and Beattie (64 mins); FJM Brown (Glasgow Warriors) for Ford (70 mins); CP Cusiter (Sale Sharks), DM Taylor (Saracens) and K Low (London Irish) for Laidlaw, Lamont and RJ Gray (73 mins); D Weir (Glasgow Warriors) and R Grant (Glasgow Warriors) for Russell and Cros (77 mins)

SCORERS: *Tries:* Cowan, Hogg, Dunbar, Cross, Seymour *Conversions:* Laidlaw (3) *Penalty Goals:* Laidlaw (2)

TONGA: Lilo; Halaifonua, Piutau, Paea, F Vainikolo; Fosita, Takulua; Mailau, Lutui, Faanunu, Lokotui, Tuineau, Kalamafoni, Latu (captain), Ma'afu

SUBSTITUTIONS: Lea and Puafisi for Mailau and Fa'anunu (51 mins); Taione for Lutui (54 mins); Fa'aoso and T Pole for Tuineau and Ma'afu (64 mins); Mailau and Piukala for Lea and Halaifonua (68 mins); Palu and Morath for Takulua and Fosita (69 mins)
SCORER: *Penalty Goals:* Fosita (4)
REFEREE: JP Doyle (England)

CANADA TO EUROPE 2014

2 November, Sixways, Worcester, RFU Championship XV 28 (4G), Canada XV 23 (1G 2T 2PG)

CHAMPIONSHIP XV SCORERS: *Tries:* M Bright, J Tovey, M Mama, J Phillips *Conversions:* L Rayner (3), K Hallett
CANADA XV SCORERS: *Tries:* Gilmour, McRorie (2) *Conversion:* Pritchard *Penalty Goals:* Pritchard (2)
REFEREE: M Carley (England)

7 November, Colwyn Bay, Canada 17 (1T 4PG) Namibia 13 (1G 2PG)

CANADA: DTH van der Merwe (Glasgow Warriors); J Wilson-Ross (Ontario Blues), C Trainor (BC Bears), C Hearn (Atlantic Rock), S Duke (BC Bears); C Braid (Glasgow Warriors), G McRorie (Prairie Wolf Pack); H Buydens (Manawatu, captain), R Barkwill (Ontario Blues), J Marshall (Hawke's Bay), T Hotson (Doncaster Knights), J Sinclair (London Irish), K Gilmour (Prairie Wolf Pack), N Dala (Prairie Wolf Pack), J Moonlight (Canada Sevens)
SUBSTITUTIONS: B Beukeboom (Plymouth Albion) for Hotson (62 mins); S White (BC Bears) for McRorie (63 mins); A Carpenter (Cornish Pirates) for Barkwill (66 mins)
SCORERS: *Try:* Dala *Penalty Goals:* McRorie (4)
NAMIBIA: C Botha (Exeter Chiefs); D Dames, D de la Harpe (Western Suburbs), J Deysel (Leopards), D Philander (Spotswood United); T Kotze (Bourg-en-Bresse), E Buitendag (Wanderers); J Redelinghuys (Wanderers), T van Jaarsveld (Cheetahs), A Schlechter, M Blom, T Uanivi (unattached), R Kitshoff (Durbanville-Belleville), J Burger (Saracens), PJ van Lill (Bayonne)
SUBSTITUTIONS: R de la Harpe (40 mins); J Tromp (Wanderers) for Botha (48 mins); F Bertholini (Windhoek United) for Schlechter (75 mins); C Vivier (Trustco United) for Redelinghuys (75 mins); S Neustadt (Trustco United) for Uanivi (79 mins)
SCORERS: *Try:* Burger *Conversions:* Kotze *Penalty Goals:* Kotze (2)
REFEREE: S Berry (South Africa)

14 November, Stade de la Rabine, Vannes, France, Canada 13 (1G 2PG) Samoa 23 (2G 3PG)

Details in Samoa tour record

22 November, Stadionul National Arcul de Triumf, Bucharest, Romania 18 (6PG) Canada 9 (3PG)

ROMANIA: C Fercu (Saracens); D Manole (RC Orthez), C Gal (Baia Mare), CR Dascalu (Steaua Bucharest), I Botezatu (Baia Mare); F Vlaicu (Farul Constanta), V Calefeteanu (RCM Timisoara Saracens); M Lazar (Castres Olympique), O Turashvili (Farul Constanta), H Pungea (Lyon OU), A Coste (RC Carcassonne), V Poparlan (RCM Timisoara Saracens), M Macovei (RC Massy, captain), V Ursache (Oyonnax), S Burcea (RCM Timisoara Saracens)
SUBSTITUTIONS: F Ionita (Steaua Bucharest) for Gal (12 mins); V Nistor (Castres Olympique) for Macovei (temp 52–60 mins); P Ion (USA Perpignan) for Pungea (60 mins); A Radoi (Ealing Trailfinders) for Turashvili (62 mins); A Ursache (RC Carcassonne) for Lazar (69 mins); M Atonescu (RC Tarbes) for Coste (69 mins); F Surugiu (Bucharest Wolves) for Calefeteanu (77 mins)
SCORERS: *Penalty Goals:* Vlaicu (6)
CANADA: Pritchard; Hassler, Trainor, Hearn, Van der Merwe; Parfrey, McRorie; Buydens, Carpenter, Marshall, Cudmore, Phelan, Sinclair, Dala, Ardron (captain)
SUBSTITUTIONS: Tiedemann for Marshall (40 mins); Thorpe for Ardron (40 mins); Barkwill for Carpenter (46 mins); Gilmour for Dala (62 mins); White for Parfrey (66 mins); Wooldridge for Thorpe (72 mins); Wilson-Ross for Pritchard (75 mins); Blevins for Hassler (77 mins)
SCORERS: *Penalty Goals:* Pritchard (2), McRorie
REFEREE: NP Briant (New Zealand)

8 August, Millennium Stadium, Cardiff, Wales 21 (3G) Ireland 35 (2G 3T 2PG)

WALES: HB Amos (Newport Gwent Dragons); ACG Cuthbert (Cardiff Blues), T Morgan (Newport Gwent Dragons), MS Williams (Scarlets, captain), E Walker (Ospreys); JW Hook (Gloucester Rugby), WM Phillips (Racing Métro); NP Smith (Ospreys), RM Hibbard (Gloucester Rugby), AR Jarvis (Ospreys), JD Ball (Scarlets), D Day (Bath Rugby), CR Moriarty (Gloucester Rugby), JC Tipuric (Ospreys), D Baker (Ospreys)

SUBSTITUTIONS: TT Faletau (Newport Gwent Dragons) for Baker (40 mins); G Anscombe (Cardiff Blues) and LD Williams (Cardiff Blues) for Hook and Phillips (49 mins); MR Evans (Scarlets) and KDV Dacey (Cardiff Blues) for Smith and Hibbard (50 mins); MJ Morgan (Bristol Rugby) for MS Williams (56 mins); J King (Ospreys) and SA Andrews (Cardiff Blues) for Ball and Jarvis (57 mins)

SCORERS: *Tries*: Hibbard, Tipuric, Cuthbert *Conversions*: Hook, Anscombe (2)

IRELAND: FA Jones (Munster); AD Trimble (Ulster), KG Earls (Munster), DM Cave (Ulster), FL McFadden (Leinster); DPL Jackson (Ulster), EG Reddan (Leinster); JC McGrath (Leinster), CR Strauss (Leinster), MA Ross (Leinster), D Ryan (Ulster), WI Henderson (Munster), J Murphy (Leinster), T O'Donnell (Munster), JPR Heaslip (Leinster, captain)

SUBSTITUTIONS: RD Best (Ulster) for Strauss (temp 19–25 mins and 61 mins); SR Zebo (Munster) for Trimble (34 mins); DM Tuohy (Ulster) for Henderson (49 mins); D Kilcoyne (Munster) for McGrath (51 mins); CG Henry (Ulster) for Heaslip (54 mins); MR Bent (Leinster) for Ross (57 mins); KD Marmion (Connacht) and I Madigan (Leinster) for Reddan and Earls (67 mins)

SCORERS: *Tries*: Heaslip, Cave, Earls, Zebo, Jones *Conversions*: Jackson (2) *Penalty Goals*: Jackson (2)

REFEREE: GW Jackson (New Zealand)

15 August, Twickenham, England 19 (2G 1T) France 14 (1T 3PG)

ENGLAND: AD Goode (Saracens); AKC Watson (Bath Rugby), HJH Slade (Exeter Chiefs), S Burgess (Bath Rugby), JJ May (Gloucester Rugby); OA Farrell (Saracens), REP Wigglesworth (Saracens); MWIW Vunipola (Saracens), RW Webber (Bath Rugby), K Brookes (Northampton Saints), GEJ Kruis (Saracens), GMW Parling (Exeter Chiefs), TA Wood (Northampton Saints, captain), CT Clark (Northampton Saints), BJ Morgan (Gloucester Rugby)

SUBSTITUTIONS: JAW Haskell (Wasps) for Morgan (40 mins); DS Care (Harlequins) and DJ Cipriani (Sale Sharks) for Wigglesworth and Goode (49 mins); LA Cowan-Dickie (Exeter Chiefs), DG Wilson (Bath Rugby) and DMJ Attwood (Bath Rugby) for Webber, Brookes and Parling (55 mins); AR Corbisiero (Northampton Saints) for Vunipola (62 mins); WWF Twelvetrees (Gloucester Rugby) for Slade (65 mins)

SCORERS: *Tries*: Watson (2), May *Conversions*: Farrell (2)

FRANCE: SL Spedding (ASM Clermont Auvergne); S Guitoune (Bordeaux-Bègles), R Lamerat (Castres Olympique), A Dumoulin (Racing Métro), B Dulin (Racing Métro); F Trinh-Duc (Montpellier HRC), M Parra (ASM Clermont Auvergne); V Debaty (ASM Clermont Avergne), D Szarzewksi (Racing Métro), N Mas (Montpellier HRC), Y Maestri (Stade Toulousain), A Flanquart (Stade Français), F Ouedraogo (Montpellier HRC), Y Nyanga (Stade Toulousain), L Picamoles (Stade Toulousain)

SUBSTITUTIONS: G Fickou (Stade Toulousain) for Dulin (temp 16–25 mins); U Atonio (Stade Rochelais) for Mas (50 mins); X Chiocci (RC Toulon) and G Guirado (RC Toulon) for Debaty and Szarzewski (52 mins); L Goujon (Bordeaux-Bègles) for Nyanga (55 mins); RM Kockott (Castres Olympique) and R Talès (Racing Métro) for Parra and Trinh-Duc (60 mins); S Vahaamahina (ASM Clermont Auvergne) and Fickou for Maestri and Dumoulin (65 mins)

SCORERS: *Try*: Ouedraogo *Penalty Goals*: Parra (3)

REFEREE: J Lacey (Ireland)

15 August, Aviva Stadium, Dublin, Ireland 28 (4G) Scotland 22 (2G 1T 1PG)

IRELAND: SR Zebo (Munster); TJ Bowe (Ulster), JB Payne (Ulster), GW D'Arcy (Leinster), LM Fitzgerald (Leinster); I Madigan (Leinster), IJ Boss (Leinster); D Kilcoyne (Munster), SM Cronin (Leinster), MA Ross (Leinster), D Toner (Leinster), DM Tuohy (Ulster), JE Conan (Leinster), CG Henry (Ulster), SK O'Brien (Leinster, captain)

SUBSTITUTIONS: NJ White (Connacht) for Ross (51 mins); PJ O'Connell (Munster) for Tuohy (55 mins); D Kearney (Leinster), CR Strauss (Leinster) and MR Bent (Leinster) for Bowe, Cronin and Kilcoyne (59 mins); J Murphy (Leinster) and EG Reddan (Leinster) for Conan and Boss (65 mins); DPL Jackson (Ulster) for Zebo (77 mins)

SCORERS: *Tries*: Henry, Cronin, Zebo, Fitzgerald *Conversions*: Madigan (4)

SCOTLAND: RJH Jackson (Wasps); SF Lamont (Glasgow Warriors), RJ Vernon (Glasgow Warriors), P Horne (Glasgow Warriors), TJW Visser (Harlequins); GA Tonks (Edinburgh Rugby), HB Pyrgos (Glasgow Warriors, captain); R Grant (Glasgow Warriors), FJM Brown (Glasgow Warriors), J Welsh (Newcastle Falcons), JL Hamilton (Saracens), GS Gilchrist (Edinburgh Rugby), BA Cowan (London Irish), H Blake (Glasgow Warriors), DK Denton (Edinburgh Rugby)

SUBSTITUTIONS: GJ Reid (Glasgow Warriors) for Grant (44 mins); MPT Cusack (Glasgow Warriors) for Welsh (46 mins); RW Ford (Edinburgh Rugby) for Brown (51 mins); RJ Harley (Glasgow Warriors) for Hamilton (55 mins); JA Barclay (Scarlets) for Cowan (57 mins); MCM Scott (Edinburgh Rugby) for Vernon (59 mins); SP Hidalgo-Clyne (Edinburgh Rugby) for Pyrgos (65 mins)

SCORERS: *Tries:* Cowan, Pyrgos, Horne *Conversions:* Horne, Jackson *Penalty Goal:* Horne

REFEREE: P Gaüzère (France)

BLEDISLOE CUP

15 August, Eden Park, Auckland, New Zealand 41 (5G 2PG) Australia 13 (1G 2PG)

NEW ZEALAND: BR Smith (Otago); N Milner-Skudder (Manawatu), CG Smith (Wellington), MA Nonu (Wellington), SJ Savea (Wellington); DJ Carter (Canterbury), AL Smith (Manawatu); TD Woodcock (North Harbour), DS Coles (Wellington), OT Franks (Canterbury), BA Retallick (Bay of Plenty), SL Whitelock (Canterbury), VVJ Vito (Wellington), RH McCaw (Canterbury, captain), KJ Read (Canterbury)

SUBSTITUTIONS: WWV Crockett (Canterbury) and CR Slade (Canterbury) for Woodcock and Milner-Skudder (51 mins); NE Laulala (Canterbury) for O Franks (62 mins); SJ Cane (Bay of Plenty) for Vito (63 mins); KF Mealamu (Auckland) and TTR Perenara (Wellington) for Coles and AL Smith (65 mins); MF Fekitoa (Auckland) and J Kaino (Auckland) for CG Smith and McCaw (67 mins)

SCORERS: *Tries:* Coles, Penalty Try, Nonu (2), CG Smith *Conversions:* Carter (5) *Penalty Goals:* Carter (2)

AUSTRALIA: I Folau (NSW Waratahs); AP Ashley-Cooper (NSW Waratahs), RT Kuridrani (Brumbies), MP Toomua (Brumbies), HV Speight (Brumbies); QS Cooper (Queensland Reds), NW White (Brumbies); ST Sio (Brumbies), ST Moore (Brumbies, captain), SM Kepu (NSW Waratahs), WRJ Skelton (NSW Waratahs), JE Horwill (Queensland Reds), SM Fardy (Brumbies), MK Hooper (NSW Waratahs), WL Palu (NSW Waratahs)

SUBSTITUTIONS: DW Pocock (Brumbies) for Hooper (temp 27–31 mins); KJ Beale (NSW Waratahs) for Speight (temp 37–40 mins); DW Mumm (NSW Waratahs) and Pocock for Skelton and Palu (40 mins); MJ Giteau (RC Toulon) for Speight (48 mins); GS Holmes (Queensland Reds) and JA Slipper (Queensland Reds) for Kepu and Sio (54 mins); KJ Beale for Cooper (57 mins); KP Douglas (Queensland Reds) for Horwill (62 mins); ST Polota-Nau (NSW Waratahs) for Moore (66 mins)

SCORERS: *Try:* Folau *Conversion:* White *Penalty Goals:* Cooper (2)

REFEREE: N Owens (Wales)

15 August, Estadio Velez Sarsfield, Buenos Aires, Argentina 12 (4PG) South Africa 26 (2G 3PG 1DG)

ARGENTINA: J Tuculet (unattached); S Cordero (Regatas de Bella Vista), M Moroni (CUBA), JP Socino (Newcastle Falcons), J Imhoff (Racing Métro); N Sánchez (unattached), M Landajo (CA San Isidro); L Noguera (Lince RC), A Creevy (unattached, captain), FN Tetaz Chaparro (unattached), B Macome (Aviron Bayonnais), T Lavanini (unattached), T Lezana (Santiago LTC), JM Fernández Lobbe (RC Toulon), JM Leguizamón (unattached)

SUBSITUTIONS: J Montoya (Club Newman) for Creevy (40 mins); M Alemanno (La Tablada) and P Matera (unattached) for Macome and Leguizamón (51 mins); JP Orlandi (unattached) for Tetaz Chaparro (52 mins); L González Amorosino (unattached) and T Cubelli (Belgrano Athletic) for Tuculet and Landajo (58 mins); S Garcia Botta (Belgrano Athletic) for Noguera (73 mins); S González Iglesias (AA Alumni) for Moroni (74 mins)

SCORER: *Penalty Goals:* Sánchez (4)

SOUTH AFRICA: Z Kirchner (Leinster); LN Mvovo (Sharks), JA Kriel (Blue Bulls), D de Allende (Stormers), BG Habana (RC Toulon); PJ Lambie (Sharks), R Pienaar (Ulster); TN Nyakane (Blue Bulls), JA Strauss (Blue Bulls), M van der Merwe (Blue Bulls), V Matfield (Blue Bulls, captain), E Etzebeth (Stormers), HW Brussow (FS Cheetahs), WS Alberts (Sharks), SWP Burger (Stormers)

SUBSTITUTIONS: SB Brits (Saracens) for Strauss (40 mins); T Mtawarira (Sharks) for Nyakane (47 mins); JF Malherbe (Stormers) for M van der Merwe (48 mins); PR van der Merwe (Blue Bulls) for Matfield (55 mins); P-S du Toit (Sharks) and JL Serfontein (Blue Bulls) for Alberts and De Allende (63 mins); H Pollard (Blue Bulls) for Kirchner (74 mins); JM Reinach (Sharks) for Lambie (75 mins)

SCORERS: *Tries:* Habana, Mvovo *Conversions:* Lambie (2) *Penalty Goals:* Lambie (3) *Drop Goal:* Lambie

REFEREE: GW Jackson (New Zealand)

22 August, Stadio Olympico, Turin, Italy 12 (4PG) Scotland 16 (1G 3PG)

ITALY: A Masi (Wasps); L Sarto (Zebre), T Benvenuti (Bristol Rugby), G Garcia (Zebre), G Venditti (Newcastle

Falcons); T Allan (USA Perpignan), G Palazzani (Zebre); M Aguero (unattached), D Giazzon (Treviso), L Cittadini (Wasps), Q Geldenhuys (Zebre, captain), V Bernabò (Zebre), F Minto (Treviso), A Zanni (Treviso), S Vunisa (Saracens)

SUBSTITUTIONS: L Ghiraldini (Leicester Tigers), ML Castrogiovanni (Racing Métro) and M Rizzo (Leicester Tigers) for Giazzon, Cittadini and Aguero (49 mins); M Bortolami (Zebre) for Bernabò (51 mins); M Bergamasco (unattched) for Zanni (60 mins); LJ McLean (Treviso) for Benvenuti (66 mins); M Violi (Zebre) and C Canna (Zebre) for Palazzani and Garcia (75 mins)

SCORERS: *Penalty Goals:* Garcia, Allan (3)

SCOTLAND: GA Tonks (Edinburgh Rugby); SF Lamont (Glasgow Warriors), RJ Vernon (Glasgow Warriors), MCM Scott (Edinburgh Rugby), R Hughes (Glasgow Warriors); D Weir (Glasgow Warriors), SP Hidalgo-Clyne (Edinburgh Rugby); G Reid (Glasgow Warriors), S McInally (Edinburgh Rugby), MPT Cusack (Glasgow Warriors), RJ Gray (Castres Olympique), JL Hamilton (Saracens), AK Strokosch (USA Perpignan, captain), JI Hardie (unattached), A Ashe (Glasgow Warriors)

SUBSTITUTIONS: AG Dickinson (Edinburgh Rugby) for Reid (43 mins); WP Nel (Edinburgh Rugby) for Cusack (46 mins); RW Ford (Edinburgh Rugby) for McInally (51 mins); HFW Watson (Edinburgh Rugby) for Hardie (55 mins); HB Pyrgos (Glasgow Warriors) for Hidalgo-Clyne (61 mins); D Hoyland (Edinburgh Rugby) for Hughes (62 mins); P Horne (Glasgow Warriors) for Vernon (68 mins)

SCORERS: *Try:* Pyrgos *Conversion:* Weir *Penalty Goals:* Weir (3)

REFEREE: JP Doyle (England)

---

22 August, Stade de France, Paris, France 25 (1G 6PG) England 20 (2G 2PG)

FRANCE: SL Spedding (ASM Clermont Auvergne); Y Huget (Stade Toulousain), M Bastareaud (RC Toulon), W Fofana (ASM Clermont Auvergne), SN Nakaitaci (ASM Clermont Auvergne); F Michalak (RC Toulon), S Tillous-Borde (RC Toulon); E Ben Arous (Racing Métro), G Guirado (RC Toulon), R Slimani (Stade Français), P Papé (Stade Français), Y Maestri (Stade Toulousain), D Chouly (ASM Clermont Auvegne), B le Roux (Racing Métro), L Picamoles (Stade Toulousain)

SUBSTITUTIONS: B Kayser (ASM Clermont Auvergne), V Debaty (ASM Clermont Auvergne) and Y Nyanga (Stade Toulousain) for Guirado, Ben Arous and Picamoles (56 mins); U Atonio (Stade Rochelais) for Slimani (63 mins); A Flanquart (Stade Français) and G Fickou (Stade Toulousain) for Papé and Bastareaud (67 mins); R Talès (Racing Métro) for Michalak (68 mins); RM Kockott (Castres Olympique) for Tillous-Borde (70 mins)

SCORERS: *Try:* Huget *Conversion:* Michalak *Penalty Goals:* Spedding, Michalak (5)

ENGLAND: MN Brown (Harlequins); JT Nowell (Exeter Chiefs), JBA Joseph (Bath Rugby), LD Burrell (Leicester Tigers), JJ May (Gloucester Rugby); GT Ford (Bath Rugby), BR Youngs (Leicester Tigers); JWG Marler (Harlequins), TN Youngs (Leicester Tigers), DR Cole (Leicester Tigers), JO Launchbury (Wasps), CL Lawes (Northampton Saints), JAW Haskell (Wasps), CDC Robshaw (Harlequins, captain), VML Vunipola (Saracens)

SUBSTITUTIONS: JE George (Saracens) and DS Care (Harlequins) for T Youngs and B Youngs (48 mins); DMJ Attwood (Bath Rugby) and NJ Easter (Harlequins) for Launchbury and Haskell (53 mins); DJ Cipriani (Sale Sharks) and WWF Twelvetrees (Gloucester Rugby) for May and Burrell (63 mins); MWIW Vunipola (Saracens) and DG Wilson (Bath Rugby) for Marler and Cole (65 mins)

SCORERS: *Tries:* Cipriani, Joseph *Conversions:* Ford (2) *Penalty Goals:* Ford (2)

REFEREE: J Peyper (South Africa)

---

22 August, Twin Elms Park, Nepean, Canada 23 (1G 2T 1PG 1DG) USA 41 (5G 2PG)

CANADA: H Jones (Canada Sevens); P Mackenzie (Sale Sharks), C Trainor (BC Bears), N Blevins (Prairie Wolf Pack), T Paris (SU Agen); N Hirayama (Canada Sevens), G McRorie (Prairie Wolf Pack); H Buydens (Manawatu), R Barkwill (Ontario Blues), D Wooldridge (Ontario Blues), T Hotson (Doncaster Knights), J Phelan (Doncaster Knights), N Dala (Prairie Wolf Pack), J Moonlight (Canada Sevens), A Carpenter (Cornish Pirates, captain)

SUBSTITUTIONS: B Piffero (Castanet) for Barkwill (temp 15–24 and 71 mins); E Olmstead (Greater Sydney Rams) for Phelan (53 mins); P Mack (Canada Sevens) for McRorie (53 mins); D Sears-Duru (Leicester Tigers) for Wooldridge (57 mins); A Tiedemann (Prairie Wolf Pack) for Buydens (57 mins); C Hearn (Atlantic Rock) for Trainor (67 mins); M Evans (Cornish Pirates) for Mackenzie (67 mins); K Gilmour (Prairie Wolf Pack) for Dala (72 mins)

SCORERS: *Tries:* Blevins, Carpenter, Paris *Conversion:* Hirayama *Penalty Goals:* McRorie *Drop Goal:* Hirayama

USA: C Wyles (Saracens); B Scully (Leicester Tigers), S Kelly (unattached), T Palamo, B Thompson (Edinburgh Rugby); AJ MacGinty (Connacht), M Petri (New York AC); E Fry (Newcastle Falcons), Z Fenoglio (Glendale Raptors), T Lamositele (Saracens), C Dolan (Cardiff Blues), G Peterson (NSW Waratahs), AI McFarland (New York AC), A Durutalo (USA Sevens), D Barrett (USA Sevens)

SUBSTITUTIONS: J Quill (Dolphin) for Barrett (57 mins); A Suniula (Old Blue) for Palamo (57 mins); P Thiel (Life University) for Fenoglio (59 mins); C Baumann (Santa Monica) for Lamositele (59 mins); L Stanfill (Seattle Saracens) for Peterson (61 mins); O Kilifi (Seattle Saracens) for Fry (71 mins); N Kruger (Glendale Raptors) for Petri (75 mins); M Trouville (Seattle Saracens) for Durutalo (78 mins)

SCORERS: *Tries*: Dolan, Durutalo, Peterson, Petri, Suniula *Conversions*: MacGinty (5) *Penalty Goals*: A MacGinty (2)

REFEREE: S Berry (South Africa)

---

22 August, Level-5 Stadium, Fukuoka, Japan 30 (3G 3PG) Uruguay 8 (1T 1PG)

JAPAN: A Goromaru (Yamaha Jubilo); K Hesketh (Munakata Sanix Blues), M Sau (Yamaha Jubilo), Y Tamura (NEC Green Rockets), K Uchida (Panasonic Wild Knights); H Tatekawa (Kubota Spears), A Hiwasa (Suntory Sungoliath); M Mikami (Suntory Sungoliath), S Horie (Panasonic Wild Knights), H Yamashita (Kobe Steel), H Ono (Toshiba Brave Lupus), S Ito (Kobe Steel), M Leitch (Toshiba Brave Lupus, captain), H Hopgood (Kamaishi Seawaves), H Tui (Suntory Sungoliath)

SUBSTITUTIONS: Y Fujita (Waseda University) for Uchida (50 mins); F Tanaka (Panasonic Wild Knights) for Hiwasa (52 mins); S Kakinaga (Suntory Sungoliath) for Yamashita (54 mins); T Murata (Yamaha Jubilo) for Hopgood (54 mins); L Thompson (Kintetsu Liners) for Ono (57 mins); H Yuhara (Toshiba Brave Lupus) for Horie (62 mins); T Hirose (Toshiba Brave Lupus) for Tamura (62 mins); T Watanabe (Toshiba Brave Lupus) for Mikami (68 mins);

SCORERS: *Tries* Tui (2), Horie *Conversions*: Goromaru (3) *Penalty Goals*: Goromaru (3)

URUGUAY: G Mieres (Valpolicella); S Gibernau (Carrasco Polo), J Prada (Los Cuervos), A Vilaseca (Old Boys), J Etcheverry (Carrasco Polo); F Berchesi (Carcassonne), A Ormaechea (Stade Montois); A Corral (San Isidro), N Klappenbach (Champagnat), M Sagario (Munster), S Vilaseca (Old Boys, captain), J Zerbino (Old Christians), JM Gaminara (Old Boys), D Magno (Montevideo)

SUBSTITUTIONS: J de Freitas (Champagnat) for Nieto (temp 6–8 mins and 57 mins); C Arboleya (Trébol de Paysandú) for Klappenbach (18 mins); F Lamanna (Carrasco Polo) for Zerbino (52 mins); G Kessler (Los Cuervos) for Sagario (62 mins); M Beer (Old Christians) for Magno (64 mins); L Leivas (Old Christians) for Etcheverry (64 mins); O Duran (Carrasco Polo) for Corral (68 mins); A Duran (Trébol de Paysandú) for Ormaechea (70 mins)

SCORERS: *Try*: Etcheverry *Penalty Goal*: Berchesi

REFEREE: J Garcès (France)

---

20 August, Prince Chichibu Memorial Stadium, Tokyo, Japan 40 (5G 1T) Uruguay 0

JAPAN: A Goromaru (Yamaha Jubilo); K Matsushima (Suntory Sungoliath), M Sau (Yamaha Jubilo), C Wing (Kobelco Steelers), K Fukuoka (Tsukuba University); K Ono (Suntory Sungoliath), F Tanaka (Panasonic Wild Knights); M Mikami (Suntory Sungoliath), S Horie (Panasonic Wild Knights), K Hatakeyama (Suntory Sungoliath), L Thompson (Kintetsu Liners), H Ono (Toshiba Brave Lupus), M Leitch (Toshiba Brave Lupus, captain), M Broadhurst (Ricoh Black Rams), H Tui (Suntory Sungoliath)

SUBSTITUTIONS: H Tatekawa (Kubota Spears) for Wing (40 mins); S Makabe (Suntory Sungoliath) for Ono (47 mins); T Watanabe (Toshiba Brave Lupus) for Mikami (51 mins); A Hiwasa (Suntory Sungoliath) for Tanaka (54 mins); H Yamashita (Kobe Steel) for Hatakeyama (57 mins); T Kizu (Kobe Steel) for Horie (60 mins); K Hesketh (Munakata Sanix Blues) for Sau (60 mins); H Hopgood (Kamaishi Seawaves) for Makabe (67 mins)

SCORERS: *Tries*: Broadhurst, Fukuoka, Goromaru, Matsushima, Ono, Tui *Conversions*: Goromaru (5)

URUGUAY: G Mieres (Valpolicella); L Leivas (Old Christians), J Prada (Los Cuervos), A Vilaseca (Old Boys), S Gibernau (Carrasco Polo); F Berchesi (Carcassonne), A Ormaechea (Stade Montois); A Corral (San Isidro), C Arboleya (Trébol de Paysandú), M Sagario (Munster), S Vilaseca (Old Boys, captain), J Zerbino (Old Christians), (Old Boys), D Magno (Montevideo)

SUBSTITUTIONS: M Beer (Old Christians) for Nieto (temp 22–26 mins) and Magno (40 mins); G Kessler (Los Cuervos) for Arboleya (45 mins); A Roman (Pucaru Stade Gaulois) for Mieres (45 mins); M Palomeque (Trébol de Paysandú) for S Vilaseca (48 mins); M Sanguinetti (Los Cuervos) for Corral (51 mins); J de Freitas (Champagnat) for Zerbino (54 mins); O Duran (Carrasco Polo) for Sagario (70 mins); A Duran (Trébol de Paysandú) for Prada (70 mins)

REFEREE: GJ Clancy (Ireland)

---

29 August, Aviva Stadium, Dublin, Ireland 10 (1G 1PG) Wales 16 (1G 3PG)

IRELAND: RDJ Kearney (Leinster); D Kearney (Leinster), LM Fitzgerald (Leinster), R Henshaw (Connacht), KG Earls (Munster); JJ Sexton (Leinster), GC Murray (Munster); JC McGrath (Leinster), CR Strauss (Leinster), NJ White (Connacht), WI Henderson (Ulster), PJ O'Connell (Munster, captain), P O'Mahony (Munster), J Murphy (Leinster), JPR Heaslip (Leinster)

SUBSTITUTIONS: SK O'Brien (Leinster) and SM Cronin (Leinster) for O'Mahony and Strauss (50 mins); T Furlong (Leinster) for White (56 mins); D Kilcoyne (Munster) for McGrath (60 mins); EG Reddan (Leinster), DPL Jackson (Ulster) and FA Jones (Munster) for Murray, Sexton and Earls (63 mins); D Ryan (Munster) for Fitzgerald (67 mins)

SCORERS: *Try:* Henderson *Conversion:* Sexton *Penalty Goal:* Sexton

WALES: SL Halfpenny (RC Toulon); ACG Cuthbert (Cardiff Blues), MS Williams (Scarlets), JH Roberts (Harlequins), GP North (Northampton Saints); DR Biggar (Ospreys), R Webb (Ospreys); GD Jenkins (Cardiff Blues), KJ Owens (Scarlets), TW Francis (Exeter Chiefs), BS Davies (Wasps), AW Jones (Ospreys, captain), DJ Lydiate (Ospreys), JC Tipuric (Ospreys), TT Faletau (Newport Gwent Dragons)

SUBSTITUTIONS: P James (Bath Rugby) for Jenkins (46 mins); J King (Ospreys) for Lydiate (temp 50–60 mins); LC Charteris (Racing Métro), SJ Baldwin (Ospreys) and AR Jarvis (Ospreys) for BS Davies, Owens and Francis (53 mins); HB Amos (Newport Gwent Dragons) for Roberts (61 mins); G Davies (Scarlets) and R Priestland (Scarlets) for Webb and Biggar (63 mins); King for Jones (72 mins)

SCORERS: *Try:* Tipuric *Conversion:* Halfpenny *Penalty Goals:* Halfpenny (3)

REFEREE: CP Joubert (South Africa)

---

29 August, Murrayfield, Scotland 48 (3G 3T 4PG) Italy 7 (1G)

SCOTLAND: SW Hogg (Glasgow Warriors); SF Lamont (Glasgow Warriors), MS Bennett (Glasgow Warriors), P Horne (Glasgow Warriors), TJW Visser (Harlequins); FA Russell (Glasgow Warriors), GD Laidlaw (Gloucester Rugby, captain); AG Dickinson (Edinburgh Rugby), RW Ford (Edinburgh Rugby), WP Nel (Edinburgh Rugby), GS Gilchrist (Edinburgh Rugby), JD Gray (Glasgow Warriors), R Wilson (Glasgow Warriors), JA Barclay (Scarlets), DK Denton (Edinburgh Rugby)

SUBSTITUTIONS: MCM Scott (Edinburgh Rugby) for Horne (51 mins); S McInally (Edinburgh Rugby) for Ford (57 mins); BA Cowan (London Irish) and RJ Harley (Glasgow Warriors) for Barclay and Gilchrist (60 mins); GJ Reid (Glasgow Warriors) and J Welsh (Glasgow Warriors) for Dickinson and Nel (62 mins); HB Pyrgos (Glasgow Warriors) for Laidlaw (65 mins); RJH Jackson (Wasps) for Hogg (68 mins)

SCORERS: *Tries:* S Lamont (2), Visser (2), Barclay, Bennett *Conversions:* Laidlaw (2) Russell *Penalty Goals:* Laidlaw (4)

ITALY: LJ McLean (Treviso); A Esposito (Treviso), M Campagnaro (Exeter Chiefs), L Morisi (Treviso), L Sarto (Zebre); T Allan (USA Perpignan), G Palazzani (Zebre); M Aguero (unattached), L Ghiraldini (Leicester Tigers, captain); ML Catrogiovanni (Racing Métro), M Fuser (Treviso), J Furno (Newcastle Falcons), A Zanni (Treviso), F Minto (Treviso), S Vunisa (Saracens)

SUBSTITUTIONS: M Rizzo (Leicester Tigers) for Aguero (33 mins); A Masi (Wasps) for Esposito (51 mins); D Chistolini (Zebre) and Q Geldenhuys (Zebre) for Castrogiovanni and Fuser (55 mins); A Manici (Zebre) and M Bergamasco (unattached) for Ghiraldini and Minto (64 mins); M Violi (Zebre) and C Canna (Zebre) for Palazzani and Allan (73 mins); Castrogiovanni for Vunisa (74–78 mins)

SCORERS: *Try:* Campagnaro *Conversion:* Allan

REFEREE: R Poite (France)

---

2 September, Molesey Road, Esher, Canada 16 (1G 3PG) Georgia 15 (1G 1T 1PG)

CANADA: M Evans (Cornish Pirates); J Hassler (Ospreys), C Hearn (Atlantic Rock), N Blevins (Prairie Wolf Pack), P Mackenzie (Sale Sharks); N Hirayama (Canada Sevens), J Mackenzie (Ontario Blues); D Sears-Duru (Leicester Tigers), R Barkwill (Ontario Blues), A Tiedemann (Plymouth Albion), B Beukeboom (Plymouth Albion), J Cudmore (ASM Clermont Auvergne), J Sinclair (London Irish), J Moonlight (Canada Sevens), A Carpenter (Cornish Pirates)

SUBSTITUTIONS: B Piffero (Castenet) for Barkwill; H Buydens (Manawatu) for Sears-Duru; E Olmstead (Greater Sydney Rams) for Cudmore; K Gilmour (Prairie Wolf Pack) for Sinclair; G McRorie (Prairie Wolf Pack) for Mackenzie; C Trainor (BC Bears) for Hassler; H Jones (Canada Sevens) for Evans

CANADA SCORERS: *Try:* Tiedemann *Conversion:* Hirayama *Penalty Goals:* Hirayama (3)

YELLOW CARD: N Blevins

GEORGIA: B Tsiklauri (Locomotive Tbilisi); G Pruidze (Kutaisi), M Sharikadze (RC Aurillac), T Mchedlidze (SU Agen), G Aptsiauri (Aia Kutaisi); L Malaguradze (RC Bagneres), G Begadze (Kochebi); K Asieshvili (CA Brive), S Mamukashvili (Sale Sharks), L Chilachava (RC Toulon), G Nemsadze (RC Tarbes), L Datunashvili (RC Aurillac), G Tkhilaishvili (Batumi), M Gorgodze (RC Toulon, captain), L Lomidze (Beziers HRC)

SUBSTITUTIONS: J Bregvadze (Stade Toulousain) for Mamukashvili; M Nariashvili (Montpellier HRC) for Asieshvili; D Zirakashvili (ASM Clermont Auvergne) for Chilachava; K Mikautadze (RC Toulon) for Nemsadze; G Chkhaidze (RC Lille) for Lomidze; V Khutsishvili (Kharebi) for Begadze; L Khmaladze (Lelo Saracens) for Malaguradze; D Kacharava (STM Enisey) for Mchedlidze

GEORGIA SCORERS: *Tries:* Tkhilaishvili, Tsiklauri *Conversion:* Malaguradze *Penalty Goal:* Malaguradze

REFEREE: JP Doyle (England)

5 September, Soldier Field, Chicago, USA 10 (1G 1T) Australia 47 (6G 1T)

USA: BH Scully (Cardiff Blues); T Ngwenya (Biarritz Olympique), S Kelly (SF Golden Gate), T Palamo (London Welsh), CT Wyles (Saracens, captain); AJ MacGinty (Life University), MZ Petri (New York AC); EC Fry (Newcastle Falcons), Z Fenoglio (Glendale Raptors), T Lamositele (Saracens), CA Dolan (Cardiff Blues), G Peterson (Glasgow Warriors), A McFarland (New York AC), AMV Durutalo (USA Sevens), SV Manoa (RC Toulon)
SUBSTITUTIONS: P Thiel (Life University) for Fenoglio (temp 4–10 mins and 56 mins); F Niua (USA Sevens) for Scully (temp 15–21 mins); D Barrett (USA Sevens) for McFarland (38 mins); JF Quill (New York AC) for Manoa (40 mins); O Kilifi (Seattle Saracens) for Fry (56 mins); C Baumann (Santa Monica) and LE Stanfill (Seattle Saracens) for Lamositele and Dolan (58 mins); S Suniula (Seattle Saracens) for MacGinty (71 mins), Niua fior Palamo (75 mins)
SCORERS: *Try*: Petri *Conversion*: MacGinty *Penalty Goal*: MacGinty
AUSTRALIA: KJ Beale (NSW Waratahs); J Tomane (Brumbies), HV Speight (Brumbies), MJ Giteau (RC Toulon), RG Horne (NSW Waratahs); BT Foley (NSW Waratahs), NJ Phipps (NSW Waratahs); JA Slipper (Queensland Reds, captain), ST Polota-Nau (NSW Waratahs), GS Holmes (Queensland Reds), KP Douglas (Queensland Reds), RA Simmons (Queensland Reds), BJ McCalman (Western Force), SP McMahon (Melbourne Rebels), WL Palu (NSW Waratahs)
SUBSTITUTIONS: SW Genia (Queensland Reds) and DW Mumm (NSW Waratahs) for Phipps and Simmons (46 mins); STG Carter (Brumbies) for Palu (50 mins); TJ Smith (Melbourne Rebels) and QS Cooper (Queensland Reds) for Holmes and Giteau (56 mins); JE Hanson (Queensland Reds) for Polota-Nau (58 mins); ST Sio (Brumbies) for Slipper (64 mins); TT Naiyaravoro (NSW Waratahs) for Horne (70 mins)
SCORERS: *Tries*: Foley, Phipps, McMahon, Foley, Beale, Cooper, Naiyaravoro *Conversions*: Foley (6)
REFEREE: J Peyper (South Africa)

5 September, Twickenham, England 21 (1G 1T 3PG) Ireland 13 (1G 2PG)

ENGLAND: MN Brown (Harlequins); AKC Watson (Bath Rugby), JBA Joseph (Bath Rugby), BM Barritt (Saracens), JJ May (Gloucester Rugby); GT Ford (Bath Rugby), BR Youngs (Leicester Tigers); JWG Marler (Harlequins), TN Youngs (Leicester Tigers), DR Cole (Leicester Tigers), GMW Parling (Exeter Chiefs), CL Lawes (Northampton Saints), TA Wood (Northampton Saints), CDC Robshaw (Harlequins, captain), BJ Morgan (Gloucester Rugby)
SUBSTITUTIONS: JO Launchbury (Wasps) for Parling (temp 12–19 mins and 44 mins); MWIW Vunipola (Saracens) and VML Vunipola (Saracens) for Marler and Morgan (55 mins); REP Wigglesworth (Saracens), OA Farrell (Saracens), JE George (Saracens) and S Burgess (Bath Rugby) for D Youngs, Ford, T Youngs and Barritt (59 mins); K Brookes (Northampton Saints) for Cole (61 mins)
SCORERS: *Tries*: May, Watson *Conversion*: Ford *Penalty Goals*: Ford, Farrell (2)
IRELAND: SR Zebo (Munster); TJ Bowe (Ulster), JB Payne (Ulster), R Henshaw (Connacht), D Kearney (Leinster); JJ Sexton (Leinster), GC Murray (Munster); JC McGrath (Leinster), RD Best (Ulster), MA Ross (Leinster), D Toner (Leinster), PJ O'Connell (Munster, captain), P O'Mahony (Munster), SK O'Brien (Leinster), JPR Heaslip (Leinster)
SUBSTITUTIONS: EG Reddan (Leinster) for Murray (16 mins); NJ White (Connacht), I Madigan (Leinster) and DM Cave (Ulster) for Ross, Henshaw and D Kearney (59 mins); CR Strauss (Leinster) and CG Henry (Ulster) for Best and O'Brien (60 mins); D Kearney and D Ryan (Munster) for Sexton and O'Connell (65 mins); T Furlong (Leinster) for Zebo (69 mins)
SCORERS: *Try*: O'Connell *Conversion*: Sexton *Penalty Goals*: Sexton (2)
REFEREE: N Owens (Wales)

5 September, Millennium Stadium, Cardiff, Wales 23 (1T 6PG) Italy 19 (2T 2PG 1DG)

WALES: SL Halfpenny (RC Toulon); ACG Cuthbert (Cardiff Blues), CL Allen (Cardiff Blues), MS Williams (Cardiff Blues), GP North (Northampton Saints); DR Biggar (Ospreys), R Webb (Ospreys); GD Jenkins (Cardiff Blues), KJ Owens (Scarlets), TW Francis (Exeter Chiefs), JD Ball (Scarlets), D Day (Bath Rugby), J King (Ospreys), S Warburton (Cardiff Blues, captain), TT Faletau (Newport Gwent Dragons)
SUBSTITUTIONS: MJ Morgan (Bristol Rugby) for Cuthbert (temp 20–26 mins), G Davies (Cardiff Blues) for Webb (26 mins); LC Charteris (Racing Métro) and P James (Bath Rugby) for Ball and Jenkins (53 mins); CR Moriarty (Gloucester Rugby) and AR Jarvis (Ospreys) for Faletau and Francis (63 mins); KDV Dacey (Cardiff Blues) for Owens (68 mins); Morgan for Halfpenny (69 mins)
SCORERS: *Try*: North *Penalty Goals*: Halfpenny (5), Biggar
ITALY: A Masi (Wasps); L Sarto (Zebre), L Morisi (Treviso), G Garcia (Zebre), G Venditti (Newcastle Falcons); T Allan (USA Perpignan), E Gori (Treviso); M Rizzo (Leicester Tigers), L Ghiraldini (Leicester Tigers), ML Castrogiovanni (Racing Métro), Q Geldenhuys (Zebre), J Furno (Newcastle Falcons), A Zanni (Treviso), F Minto (Treviso), S Parisse (Stade Français, captain)

SUBSTITUTIONS: LJ McLean (Treviso) for Morisi (4 mins); L Cittadini (Wasps) for Castrogiovanni (40 mins); M Aguero (unattached) for Rizzo (52 mins); C Canna (Zebre) for Allan (58 mins); V Bernabò (Zebre), S Vunisa (Saracens) and G Palazzani (Zebre) for Furno, Parisse and Garcia (64 mins); A Manici (Zebre) for Ghiraldini (75 mins)
SCORERS: *Tries:* Sarto, Palazzani *Penalty Goals:* Allan (2) *Drop Goal:* Canna
REFEREE: J Garcès (France)

MAJOR TOURS

5 September, Stade de France, Paris, France 19 (1G 4PG) Scotland 16 (1G 3PG)

FRANCE: SL Spedding (ASM Clermont Auvergne); Y Huget (Stade Toulousain), M Bastareaud (RC Toulon), W Fofana (ASM Clermont Auvergne), N Nakaitici (ASM Clermont Auvergne); F Michalak (RC Toulon), S Tillous-Borde (RC Toulon); E Ben Arous (Racing Métro), G Guirado (RC Toulon), R Slimani (Stade Français), P Papé (Stade Français), A Flanquart (Stade Français); T Dusautoir (Stade Toulousain, captain), D Chouly (ASM Clermont Auvergne), L Picamoles (Stade Toulousain)
SUBSTITUTIONS: N Mas (Montpellier HRC) for Slimani (temp 3–8 mins and 56 mins), A Doumoulin (Racing Métro) for Fofana (34 mins), B le Roux (Racing Métro) for Papé (52 mins), V Debaty (ASM Clermont Auvergne) and D Szarzewski (Racing Métro) for Ben Arous and Guirado (56 mins), M Parra (ASM Clermont Auvergne) for Tillous-Borde (59 mins), Y Nyanga (Stade Toulousain) for Picamoles (65 mins), R Talès (Racing Métro) for Michalak (72 mins)
SCORERS: *Try:* Nakaitaci *Conversion:* Parra *Penalty Goals:* Michalak (3), Spedding
SCOTLAND: SD Maitland (London Irish); TSF Seymour (Glasgow Warriors), MS Bennett (Glasgow Warriors), MCM Scott (Edinburgh Rugby), TJW Visser (Harlequins); FA Russell (Glasgow Warriors), GD Laidlaw (Gloucester Rugby, captain); AG Dickinson (Edinburgh Rugby), RW Ford (Edinburgh Rugby), WP Nel (Edinburgh Rugby), RJ Gray (Castres Olympique), JD Gray (Glasgow Warriors), R Wilson (Glasgow Warriors), JI Hardie (unattached), DK Denton (Edinburgh Rugby)
SUBSTITUTIONS: GJ Reid (Edinburgh Rugby) for Dickinson (6 mins); AK Strokosch (USA Perpignan) for (53 mins); J Welsh (Newcastle Falcons) for Nel (59 mins); TJM Swinson (Edinburgh Rugby) for JD Gray (62 mins); FJM Brown (Glasgow Warriors) for Ford (64 mins); SF Lamont (Glasgow Warriors) for Seymour (67 mins)
SCORERS: *Try:* Seymour *Conversion:* Laidlaw *Penalty Goals:* Laidlaw (3)
REFEREE: W Barnes (England)

5 September, Kingsholm, Gloucester, Japan 13 (1G 2PG) Georgia 10 (1G 1PG)

JAPAN: A Goromaru (Yamaha Jubilo); Y Fujita (Waseda University), M Sau (Yamaha Jubilo), C Wing (Kobelco Steelers), H Tui (Suntory Sungoliath); H Tatekawa (Kubota Spears), F Tanaka (Panasonic Wild Knights); M Mikami (Toshiba Brave Lupus), S Horie (Panasonic Wild Knights), H Yamashita (Kobe Steel), L Thompson (Kintetsu Liners), H Ono (Toshiba Brave Lupus), M Leitch (Toshiba Brave Lupus, captain), M Broadhurst (Ricoh Black Rams), RK Holani (Panasonic Wild Knights)
SUBSTITUTIONS: K Hatakeyama (Suntory Sungoliath) for Yamashita (34 mins); A Mafi (NTT Shining Arcs) for Holani (46 mins); K Matsushima (Suntory Sungoliath) for Fujita (46 mins); K Ono (Suntory Sungoliath) for Tatekawa (49 mins); S Makabe (Suntory Sungoliath) for H Ono (54 mins); A Hiwasa (Suntory Sungoliath) for Tanaka (62 mins); T Kizu (Kobe Steel) for Horie (74 mins)
SCORERS: *Try:* Mafi *Conversion:* Goromaru *Penalty Goals:* Goromaru (2)
GEORGIA: M Kvirikashvili (RC Montlucon); M Giorgadze (Armazi), D Kacharava (STM Enisey), M Sharikadze (RC Aurillac), G Aptsiauri (Aia Kutaisi); L Malaguradze (RC Bagneres), V Lobzhanidze (Armazi); M Nariashvili (Montpellier HRC), J Bregvadze (Stade Toulousain), D Zirakashvili (ASM Clermont Auvergne), G Nemsadze (RC Tarbes), K Mikautadze (RC Toulon), S Sutiashvili (RC Massy), V Kolelishvili (ASM Clermont Auvergne), M Gorgodze (RC Toulon, captain)
SUBSTITUTIONS: S Mamukashvili (Sale Sharks) for Bregvadze (49 mins); G Begadze (Kochebi) for Lobzhanidze (55 mins); T Mchedlidze (SU Agen) for Kvirikashvili (58 mins); K Asieshvili (CA Brive) for Nariashvili (60 mins); D Kubriashvili (Stade Francais) for Zirakashvili (60 mins); L Datunashvili (RC Aurillac) for Nemsadze (60 mins); G Chkhaidze (RC Lille) for Gorgodze (67 mins)
SCORERS: *Try:* Giorgadze *Conversions:* Kvirikashvili *Penalty Goal:* Malaguradze
REFEREE: J Lacey (Ireland)

5 September, Stadionul National Arcul de Triumf, Bucharest, Romania 16 (1G 3PG) Tonga 21 (1G 1T 3PG)

ROMANIA: C Fercu (Saracens); M Lemnaru (Bucharest Wolves), P Kinikinilau (Bucharest Wolves), F Vlaicu (Farul Constanta), A Apostol (Farul Constanta); D Dumbrava (Steaua Bucharest), F Surugiu (Bucharest Wolves); A Ursache (RC Carcassonne), O Turashvili (Farul Constanta), P Ion (USA Perpignan), V Poparlan (RCM Timisoara Saracens), J van Heerden (Bucharest Wolves), V Ursache (Oyonnax), V Lucaci (Bucharest Wolves), M Macovei (RC Massy, captain)

SUBSTITUTIONS: A Radoi (Ealing Trailfinders) for Turashvili (temp 29–40 and 67 mins); D Carpo (RCM Timisoara Saracens) for Lucaci (45 mins); M Lazar (Castres Olympique) for A Ursache (49 mins); C Gal (Baia Mare) for Dumbrava (62 mins); H Pungea (Lyon OU) for Ion (67 mins); M Antonescu (RC Tarbes) for Poparlan (75 mins)

SCORERS: *Try:* Radoi *Conversions:* Vlaicu *Penalty Goals:* Vlaicu (3)

TONGA: T Veainu (Rebels); D Halaifonua (RC Bergerac), W Helu (Wasps), S Piutau (Yamaha Jubilo), F Vainikolo (Exeter Chiefs); K Morath (Biarritz Olympique), S Takulua (Northland); S Tonga'uiha (Oyonnax), E Taione (Exeter Chiefs), H 'Aulika (London Irish), T Lokotui (Beziers HRC), J Tuineau (Lyon OU), S Mafi (Leicester Tigers), N Latu (NEC Rockets, captain), S Kalamafoni (Gloucester Rugby)

SUBSTITUTIONS: S Taumalolo (Racing Métro) for Tonga'uiha (45 mins); S Puafisi (Gloucester Rugby) for 'Aulika (55 mins); H T Pole (Southland) for Tuineau (58 mins); P Ngauamo (Oyonnax) for Taione (62 mins); V Lilo (RC Tarbes) for Halaifonua (62 mins); V Ma'afu (Oyonnax) for Mafi (70 mins); L Fosita (Northland) for Helu (70 mins)

SCORERS: *Tries:* Penalty Try, Takulua *Conversion:* Morath *Penalty Goals:* Morath (3)

REFEREE: P Gaüzère (France)

---

6 September, The Twickenham Stoop, Canada 18 (3T 1PG) Fiji 47 (5G 4PG)

CANADA: H Jones (Greater Sydney Rams); DTH van der Merwe (Glasgow Warriors), C Trainor (BC Bears), C Braid (Glasgow Warriors), P Mackenzie (Sale Sharks); L Underwood (Ontario Blues), G McRorie (Prairie Wolf Pack); H Buydens (Manawatu), B Piffero (Atlantic Rock), J Marshall (Hawke's Bay), E Olmstead (Greater Sydney Rams), J Cudmore (ASM Clermont Auvergne, captain), K Gilmour (Prairie Wolf Pack), N Dala (Prairie Wolf Pack), R Thorpe (London Welsh)

SUBSTITUTIONS: J Ilnicki (NSW Country) for Marshall (16 mins); C Hearn (Atlantic Rock) for Jones (46 mins); A Carpenter (Cornish Pirates) for Piffero (53 mins); D Sears-Duru (Ontario Blues) for Buydens (53 mins); J Sinclair (London Irish) for Cudmore (53 mins); P Mack (BC Bears) for McRorie (56 mins); N Blevins (Prairie Wolf Pack) for Mackenzie (73 mins)

SCORERS: *Tries:* Van der Merwe (2), Trainor *Conversions: Penalty Goal:* McRorie

FIJI: M Talebula (Bordeaux-Bègles); W Nayacalevu (Stade Français), V Goneva (Leicester Tigers), G Lovobalavu (unattached), N Nadolo (Crusaders); J Matavesi (Ospreys), N Matawalu (Bath Rugby); C Ma'afu (Pays d'Aix en Provence), S Koto (RC Narbonne), M Saulo (Timisoara Saracens), L Nakarawa (Glasgow Warriors), A Ratuniyarawa (SU Agen), D Waqaniburotu (CA Brive), A Qera (Montpellier HRC, captain), S Matadigo (Lyon OU)

SUBSTITUTIONS: N Kenatale (Steaua Bucharest) for Matawalu (40 mins); N Talei (Harlequins) for Matadigo (44 mins); P Ravai (Fiji Warriors) for Ma'afu (53 mins); T Cavubati (Ospreys) for Nakarawa (58 mins); V Veikoso (Doncaster Knights) for Koto (61 mins); A Tikoirotuma (London Irish) for Matavesi (64 mins); Koto (RC Narbonne) for Qera (temp 64–68 mins); L Atalifo (unattached) for Saulo (71 mins); K Murimurivalu (La Rochelle) for Goneva (78 mins)

SCORERS: *Tries:* Matawalu (2), Nayacalevu (2), Talebula *Conversions:* Nadolo (5) *Penalty Goals:* Nadolo (4)

REFEREE: M Raynal (France)

A YEAR TO CELEBRATE

By Iain Spragg

Australian Ben Tapuai finishes off a stunning Barbarians move for the match-winning try against Samoa in London.

The Barbarians commemorated their 125th anniversary in 2015 in style by claiming the scalp of Samoa in an historic fixture at The Stadium, Queen Elizabeth Olympic Park as rugby broke new ground. They also overcame an Ireland XV and faced an Australia XV and England XV at Twickenham.

It was a frenetic but prestigious season for the team a century and a quarter after their inaugural fixture against Hartlepool Rovers in 1890 and evidence the Barbarian ethos was very much alive and kicking.

The season, if not the anniversary year, kicked off with a pulsating encounter against an Australia XV in November which produced five tries apiece as the Australians clinched an entertaining 40–36 victory.

Later in the month the Baa-Baas beat Leicester Tigers (59–26) at Welford Road and the Combined Services (31–15) in Bath before turning their attention to the first fixture of 2015 against Heriot's at Goldenacre in April, a match to mark the 125th anniversary of both clubs and which finished 97–31 to the visitors.

A month later the team, coached by Robbie Deans, faced an Ireland XV at Thomond Park and the Barbarians secured a 22–21 victory, their fifth win in six meetings with the men in green, thanks to a brace of tries from Wales wing Alex Cuthbert.

"We worked hard," Cuthbert said after the win at the home of Munster. "Everyone knows what the Baa-Baas are like and this week we gelled really well."

The side went into their next match, against an England XV at Twickenham in June, looking for a second successive triumph over the Red Rose following a 39–29 victory 12 months earlier, but there was to be no repeat performance as the hosts cut loose to post a comprehensive 73–12 win.

The next assignment took the Baa-Baas into uncharted territory with a first ever meeting with Samoa at an iconic setting, The Stadium, Queen Elizabeth Olympic Park, which was staging a rugby match for the very first time ahead of its duties as a Rugby World Cup 2015 venue.

"It is a significant honour for the Barbarians to take part in the first rugby match at the Olympic Stadium," said club president Micky Steele-Bodger. "The match should be a great spectacle for supporters and we hope to light up the stadium with the Barbarians brand of rugby in our first meeting with Samoa."

The action in London did not disappoint as eight tries were scored. Five went to the Baa-Baas – two apiece from Kiwi flanker Adam Thomson and Australian centre Ben Tapuai – and it was 27–24 to the side in the famous black and white at full-time.

A week later the Barbarians gave a typically flamboyant display in an 11-try thriller against Worcester Warriors at Sixways with Melbourne Rebels winger Dom Shipperley scoring a hat-trick in the 43–35 win.

The famous invitational side will face Gloucester Rugby at Kingsholm and Argentina at Twickenham in November hoping to bring down the curtain on a successful 125th year in style.

BARBARIANS 2014–15 RESULTS

01/11/2014	Barbarians	36–40	Australia XV
04/11/2014	Barbarians	59–26	Leicester Tigers
11/11/2014	Barbarians	31–15	Combined Services
21/04/2015	Barbarians	97–31	Heriot's
28/05/2015	Barbarians	22–21	Ireland XV
01/06/2015	Barbarians	12–73	England XV
29/08/2015	Barbarians	27–24	Samoa
05/09/2015	Barbarians	43–35	Worcester Warriors

THE COMBINED TEAMS

Elite Competitions

Argentina fly-half Nicolás Sánchez was Rugby World Cup 2015's top point scorer with 97.

FARRELL STEERS SARRIES TO GLORY

By Iain Spragg

Saracens captain Alistair Hargreaves and Brad Barritt lift the Aviva Premiership trophy after victory over Bath at Twickenham.

Saracens defied pre-match predictions of a Bath victory at Twickenham to emerge victorious in the Premiership final, a second title triumph in four years for the capital club which also saw Mark McCall's side join the coterie of multiple English champions.

Since the inauguration of league rugby in 1987 only Leicester, Bath and Wasps had lifted the trophy more than once. Wasps had become the newest member of the exclusive club 12 years earlier when they won their second league title but the trio finally became a quartet in May as Saracens overpowered their West Country rivals to replicate their 2011 triumph.

Their convincing 28–16 victory was built on the platform of 18 points from man of the match Owen Farrell and in the process McCall's team exorcised the ghosts of 2014 and the heartache of losing two major finals.

Those bitter disappointments came in the space of seven agonising days as they were defeated in the last minute of extra-time in the Premiership final by Northampton and then dismantled by Toulon in the climax of the Heineken Cup. Twelve months later, however, and Saracens were finally able to celebrate.

"Last year was painful and there was a lot of hurt afterwards," admitted McCall, the Saracens director of rugby. "It's always in the back of your mind and people deal with it in different ways but we were very clear that we were owed nothing because of the way it ended [in the Premiership] last year. We had to deserve it and earn it.

"To perform the way we did in the first half was exceptional and Bath were always going to come back in the second half and they showed what they were capable of. We knew we had a big chance today and knew we had to contain Bath's outstanding attack but we hung in there and are absolutely thrilled to win."

For Bath, defeat was equally as painful as 2014 had been for their opponents. The West Country heavyweights were looking to end an 18-year wait to add to their collection of seven league titles, as well as expunge memories of losses in the finals of 2001 and 2004, but they were unable to reproduce the vibrant attacking form which had swept Mike Ford's side towards Twickenham.

"It's hugely disappointing but we need to make sure that we realise that it was not a wasted year," said captain Stuart Hooper. "We worked hard and got to this point but we didn't really do ourselves justice today. I guess one of the reasons we play sport is that if you win you get your moment and credit to Saracens, they will be on the podium today with the trophy."

The 22-game battle for an all-important top-four finish and a coveted place in the play-offs began in early September and as the season unfolded a two-tier contest emerged as defending champions Northampton and Bath set the pace at the top while Leicester, Exeter, Saracens and Wasps arm wrestled for third and fourth.

It was the Saints, beaten just five times, who ultimately clinched top spot by a single point ahead of Bath, but the tussle below them went down to the wire and the semi-final line-up was only decided in a dramatic, final day denouement.

A solitary point separated the Tigers, the Chiefs and Sarries ahead of their last fixtures and Leicester sealed their place in the top four with a 22–14 victory against old rivals Northampton at Welford Road. Exeter beat Sale 44–16 but Saracens also triumphed, the Londoners' crushing 68–17 win away to relegated London Welsh enough to leapfrog the Chiefs into fourth on points difference in the final reckoning.

The first of the semi-finals saw Saracens head north to face Northampton at Franklin's Gardens in a repeat of the 2014 final and the rematch provided an equally tumultuous contest as the one which had been played out at Twickenham.

A second-minute, opportunistic try from winger David Strettle gave the visitors an early advantage but the Saints were back on terms 10 minutes later when Mako Vunipola was yellow carded for collapsing a maul and referee Greg Garner awarded the home side a penalty try.

The opposing fly-halves, Farrell and Stephen Myler, traded a series of penalties to keep the scoreboard ticking over but the pivotal moment came seven minutes into the second half when hooker Jamie George rumbled over to give Saracens a 20–16 lead.

It was an advantage McCall's side refused to surrender. The Saints responded with a Tom Wood score but Farrell replied with his fourth and fifth penalties of the match to keep his side in front, and at full-time it was 29–24 to Saracens and Northampton's reign as champions was over.

"I think we knew Saracens' plan and they did what we expected but they did it very well and it was very disappointing," said Jim Mallinder, the Saints director of rugby. "It's all about small margins and we just didn't get enough of those right and in the first half we attacked too much from deep. We needed to stick the ball back to them and make them turn but at the breakdown they were physical."

The second semi-final saw Bath entertain Leicester at The Rec and in stark contrast to the preceding last four clash, the result was never in doubt from the moment winger Matt Banahan galloped over for the opening try for the home side with just 90 seconds on the clock.

The hallmark of Bath's 2014–15 campaign had been their ambitious, entertaining brand of rugby and it was very much in evidence in the semi-final as they put the Tigers to the sword with six more tries, including a hat-trick for Banahan, to register a crushing 47–10 victory over the 10-time champions.

"I think that was the best team performance I've presided over considering the occasion, against a team who've been there and done it," said head coach Ford. "My job with this young side is to keep them pressure-free, make them have fun and enjoy it and go out and do what they do.

"We were so clinical in the first half – the attack was outstanding. I thought Leicester played better than the scoreboard suggested. We would

AVIVA PREMIERSHIP

be stupid to change [our style in the final] unless it is absolutely a monsoon next Saturday."

The final seven days later was billed as a beauty and the beast encounter, Saracens' muscle and ferocious defence pitted against a Bath side with an entertaining appetite for putting width on the ball, but predicting finals is a fickle business and after 80 minutes at Twickenham McCall's side had outscored their opponents three tries to one en route to securing the silverware.

The match was only five minutes old when Saracens scored their first. A wayward kick from fly-half George Ford gave away possession and Sarries counter-attacked, Farrell delivering the *coup de grâce* with a dummy to touch down. The fly-half converted and Saracens were on their way.

Their second try came eight minutes later when George intercepted a pass from his opposite number Ross Batty and raced over from 30 metres, and although Ford knocked over a penalty to open Bath's account there was more misery for his father's charges before half-time.

What proved to be the killer blow came on the half hour. Another Bath pass was intercepted by Duncan Taylor and his offload to Strettle saw the winger hauled down just short of the line. Saracens recycled possession and created a huge overlap, winger Chris Wyles with the simple task of finishing off the move. Farrell made no mistake with the conversion and also added a 37th-minute penalty, and as the two sides headed to the dressing room Saracens had built an imposing 25-3 lead.

Bath had the proverbial mountain to climb but gave themselves fleeting hope of what would have been a famous fight-back when Ford landed a 44th-minute penalty followed, nine minutes later, by a converted try from Jonathan Joseph, the England centre slicing through the midfield before a trademark sidestep took him over. Ford was on target with the conversion and then added his third penalty and Bath had reduced the deficit to only nine points.

With the score at 25-16 and 22 minutes to play, another Bath score would have rung the alarm bells resoundingly in the opposition camp, but the Saracens pack sensed the danger and won a crucial penalty in front of the posts after Bath were caught offside at a ruck. Farrell duly bisected the uprights to make it 28-16 and as the clock wound down, McCall's team were able to keep Bath at arm's length to seal a cathartic victory at Twickenham.

"It's been a good season for us," Farrell said. "We've had to work hard to get where we are today and that has pulled us together as a group. It's made us work hard and we've drawn on a couple of experiences we've had before and thankfully we've come good on the day.

"We built a good lead and we had to stay on it in the second half. **595** We knew they were going to come after us and throw everything at us from the start of the second half, but thankfully we held on in there and got the win."

AVIVA PREMIERSHIP 2014–15 RESULTS

5 September, 2014: **Northampton** 53 **Gloucester** 6. 6 September: **Sale** 20 **Bath** 29, **Saracens** 34 **Wasps** 28, **Leicester** 36 **Newcastle** 17, **London Irish** 15 **Harlequins** 20. 7 September: **London Welsh** 0 **Exeter** 52. 12 September: **Harlequins** 0 **Saracens** 39. 13 September: **Bath** 53 **London Welsh** 26, **Gloucester** 34 **Sale** 27, **Exeter** 20 **Leicester** 24. 14 September: **Wasps** 20 **Northampton** 16, **Newcastle** 18 **London Irish** 20. 19 September: **Gloucester** 22 **Exeter** 25. 20 September: **Sale** 46 **London Welsh** 8, **Harlequins** 26 **Wasps** 23, **London Irish** 32 **Saracens** 36, **Bath** 45 **Leicester** 0. 21 September: **Newcastle** 10 **Northampton** 35. 26 September: **London Welsh** 10 **Gloucester** 46. 27 September: **Leicester** 19 **London Irish** 22, **Saracens** 40 **Sale** 19, **Northampton** 31 **Bath** 24. 28 September: **Exeter** 36 **Harlequins** 13, **Wasps** 35 **Newcastle** 18. 3 October: **Bath** 21 **Saracens** 11. 4 October: **Harlequins** 52 **London Welsh** 0, **London Irish** 12 **Northampton** 19, **Gloucester** 33 **Leicester** 16. 5 October: **Sale** 25 **Wasps** 14, **Newcastle** 29 **Exeter** 24. 10 October: **Leicester** 22 **Harlequins** 16. 11 October: **London Welsh** 3 **Newcastle** 23, **Exeter** 44 **London Irish** 24, **Saracens** 28 **Gloucester** 21, **Northampton** 43 **Sale** 10. 12 October: **Wasps** 29 **Bath** 22. 14 November: **Gloucester** 15 **Harlequins** 22, **Northampton** 18 **Exeter** 24. 15 November: **Sale** 36 **London Irish** 8, **Bath** 23 **Newcastle** 14. 16 November: **Leicester** 21 **Saracens** 21, **Wasps** 71 **London Welsh** 7. 21 November: **Harlequins** 12 **Sale** 16, **Newcastle** 20 **Gloucester** 10. 22 November: **Exeter** 31 **Wasps** 15, **London Irish** 23 **Bath** 33. 23 November: **Saracens** 24 **Northampton** 31, **London Welsh** 5 **Leicester** 26. 28 November: **Bath** 25 **Harlequins** 6. 29 November: **Leicester** 18 **Wasps** 16, **Exeter** 27 **Saracens** 19. 30 November: **London Irish** 9 **Gloucester** 21, **London Welsh** 14 **Northampton** 43, **Newcastle** 13 **Sale** 18. 19 December: **Sale** 18 **Exeter** 11. 20 December: **Harlequins** 15 **Newcastle** 7, **Saracens** 78 **London Welsh** 7, **Northampton** 23 **Leicester** 19, **Gloucester** 16 **Bath** 39. 21 December: **Wasps** 48 **London Irish** 16. 26 December: **London Irish** 24 **London Welsh** 9. 27 December: **Bath** 31 **Exeter** 14, **Sale** 30 **Leicester** 32, **Newcastle** 23 **Saracens** 25, **Harlequins** 25 **Northampton** 30. 28 December: **Gloucester** 23 **Wasps** 30. 2 January, 2015: **Northampton** 39 **Newcastle** 31. 3 January: **Saracens** 22 **London Irish** 6, **Exeter** 25 **Gloucester** 26. 4 January: **Leicester** 17 **Bath** 8, **Wasps** 41 **Sale** 16, **London Welsh** 13 **Harlequins** 24. 9 January: **Gloucester** 24 **Saracens** 23. 10 January: **Sale** 20 **Northampton** 7, **Bath** 39 **Wasps** 26, **Harlequins** 32 **Leicester** 12. 11 January: **Newcastle** 38 **London Welsh** 7, **London Irish** 28 **Exeter** 26. 13 February: **Leicester** 18 **Gloucester** 15, **Northampton** 15 **London Irish** 9. 14 February: **Exeter** 46 **Newcastle** 17. 15 February: **London Welsh** 12 **Sale** 52, **Saracens** 34 **Bath** 24, **Wasps** 37 **Harlequins** 6. 20 February: **Newcastle** 23 **Wasps** 23. 21 February: **Sale** 14 **Saracens** 10, **Gloucester** 48 **London Welsh** 10, **Harlequins** 21 **Exeter** 32, **Bath** 13 **Northampton** 21. 22 February: **London Irish** 6 **Leicester** 12. 27 February: **Northampton** 17 **Harlequins** 13. 28 February: **London Welsh** 12 **London Irish** 50, **Leicester** 28 **Sale** 8, **Saracens** 22 **Newcastle** 17, **Exeter** 16 **Bath** 6. 1 March: **Wasps** 32 **Gloucester** 21. 6 March: **Bath** 12 **Sale** 3. 7 March: **Exeter** 74 **London Welsh** 19, **Harlequins** 26 **London Irish** 20, **Gloucester** 33 **Northampton** 33. 8 March: **Wasps** 17 **Saracens** 26, **Newcastle** 12 **Leicester** 16. 27 March: **Northampton** 52 **Wasps** 30. 28 March: **Leicester** 25 **Exeter** 18, **London Irish** 22 **Newcastle** 21, **Saracens** 42 **Harlequins** 14. 29 March: **Sale** 23 **Gloucester** 6, **London Welsh** 14 **Bath** 29. 10 April: **Newcastle** 19 **Bath** 29. 11 April: **Harlequins** 29 **Gloucester** 26, **Saracens** 22 **Leicester** 6. 12 April: **Exeter** 21 **Northampton** 10, **London Welsh** 13 **Wasps** 40, **London Irish** 25 **Sale**

23. 24 April: **Bath** 43 **London Irish** 18. 25 April: **Sale** 23 **Harlequins** 25, **Gloucester** 42 **Newcastle** 40, **Leicester** 38 **London Welsh** 17, **Northampton** 25 **Saracens** 20. 26 April: **Wasps** 36 **Exeter** 29. 8 May: **Harlequins** 26 **Bath** 27. 9 May: **Sale** 34 **Newcastle** 28, **Gloucester** 35 **London Irish** 13, **Northampton** 46 **London Welsh** 0, **Wasps** 21 **Leicester** 26. 10 May: **Saracens** 20 **Exeter** 24. 16 May: **Bath** 50 **Gloucester** 30, **Exeter** 44 **Sale** 16, **Leicester** 22 **Northampton** 14, **London Irish** 40 **Wasps** 40, **London Welsh** 17 **Saracens** 68, **Newcastle** 37 **Harlequins** 21.

FINAL TABLE

	P	W	D	L	F	A	BP	PTS
Northampton	22	16	1	5	621	400	10	76
Bath	22	16	0	6	625	414	11	75
Leicester	22	15	1	6	453	421	6	68
Saracens	22	14	1	7	664	418	10	68
Exeter	22	14	0	8	663	437	12	68
Wasps	22	11	2	9	672	527	13	61
Sale	22	11	0	11	497	482	10	54
Harlequins	22	10	0	12	444	514	9	49
Gloucester	22	9	1	12	553	575	10	48
London Irish	22	7	1	14	442	578	10	40
Newcastle	22	5	1	16	475	545	12	34
London Welsh	22	0	0	22	223	1021	1	1

23 May, Franklin's Gardens, Northampton

NORTHAMPTON 24 (1G 1T 4PG) SARACENS 29 (2G 5PG)

NORTHAMPTON: A Tuala; K Pisi, G Pisi, L Burrell, J Elliott; S Myler, L Dickson; A Corbisiero, D Hartley (captain), S Ma'afu, C Lawes, C Day, T Wood, C Clark, S Manoa

SUBSTITUTIONS: J Wilson for Tuala (4 mins); A Waller for Corbisiero (32 mins); T Stephenson for Wilson (40 mins); K Fotuali'i for Dickson (51 mins); G Denman for Ma'afu (54 mins); M Haywood for Hartley (68 mins); J Fisher for Day (69 mins); S Dickinson for Clark (74 mins)

SCORERS: *Tries*: Penalty Try, Wood *Conversion*: Myler *Penalty Goals*: Myler (4)

SARACENS: A Goode; C Wyles, D Taylor, B Barritt, D Strettle; O Farrell, R Wigglesworth; M Vunipola, J George, P du Plessis, G Kruis, A Hargreaves (captain), M Itoje, J Burger, B Vunipola

SUBSTITUTIONS: R Barrington for Itoje (temp 17–24 mins); J Figallo for Du Plessis (59 mins); C Ashton for Strettle (59 mins); J Hamilton for Hargreaves (62 mins); J Wray for Itoje (65 mins)

SCORERS: *Tries*: Strettle, George *Conversions*: Farrell (2) *Penalty Goals*: Farrell (5)

YELLOW CARD: M Vunipola (12 mins)

REFEREE: G Garner (England)

23 May, Recreation Ground, Bath

BATH 47 (6G 1T) LEICESTER 10 (1G 1PG)

BATH: A Watson; S Rokoduguni, J Joseph, K Eastmond, M Banahan; G Ford, P Stringer; P James, R Batty, D Wilson, S Hooper (captain), D Attwood, S Burgess, F Louw, L Houston

SUBSTITUTIONS: N Auterac for James (45 mins); H Thomas for Wilson (48 mins); D Day for Hooper (52 mins); R Webber for Batty (53 mins); M Garvey for Burgess (54 mins); C Fearns for Houston (57 mins); O Devoto for Eastmond (67 mins); C Cook for Stringer (71 mins)

SCORERS: *Tries*: Banahan (3), Eastmond, Stringer, Ford, Watson *Conversions*: Ford (6)

YELLOW CARDS: Watson (32 mins), Houston (33 mins)

LEICESTER: N Morris; A Thompstone, M Tait, C Loamanu, V Goneva; F Burns, B Youngs (captain); M Ayerza, T Youngs, D Cole, B Thorn, G Kitchener, E Slater, J Salvi, J Crane

SUBSTITUTIONS: T Bell for Morris (44 mins); J Gibson for Crane (54 mins); S Harrison for B Youngs (61 mins); G Catchpole for Tait (67 mins); N Briggs for T Youngs (69 mins); F Balman for Cole (70 mins); M Rizzo for Ayerza (70 mins); S de Chaves for Kitchener (70 mins)

SCORERS: *Try*: T Youngs *Conversion*: Burns *Penalty Goal*: Burns

REFEREE: JP Doyle (England)

FINAL

30 May, Twickenham, London

BATH 16 (1G 3PG) SARACENS 28 (2G 1T 3PG)

BATH: A Watson; S Rokoduguni, J Joseph, K Eastmond, M Banahan; G Ford, P Stringer; P James, R Batty, D Wilson, S Hooper (captain), D Attwood, S Burgess, F Louw, L Houston

SUBSTITUTIONS: O Devoto for Watson (9 mins); N Auterac for James (47 mins); R Webber for Batty (47 mins); H Thomas for Wilson (53 mins); D Day for Hooper (58 mins); M Garvey for Attwood (58 mins); C Fearns for Houston (60 mins); C Cook for Stringer (67 mins)

SCORERS: *Try*: Joseph *Conversion*: Ford *Penalty Goals*: Ford (3)

SARACENS: A Goode; C Wyles, D Taylor, B Barritt, D Strettle; O Farrell, R Wigglesworth; M Vunipola, J George, P du Plessis, G Kruis, A Hargreaves (captain), M Itoje, J Burger, B Vunipola

SUBSTITUTIONS: J Wray for Hargreaves (33 mins); J Figallo for Du Plessis (50 mins); S Brits for George (53 mins); N de Kock for Wigglesworth (55 mins); C Ashton for Strettle (64 mins); J Hamilton for Itoje (67 mins); C Hodgson for Barritt (69 mins); R Barrington for M Vunipola (76 mins)

SCORERS: *Tries*: Farrell, George, Wyle *Conversions*: Farrell (2) *Penalty Goals*: Farrell (3)

REFEREE: W Barnes (England)

Bath's Matt Banahan scores the second try of his remarkable hat-trick against Leicester in the Aviva Premiership semi-final.

STADE COMPOUND CLERMONT MISERY

By Iain Spragg

Stade Français edged Clermont Auvergne in a close encounter to lift the Top 14 title at the Stade de France.

Stade Français lifted Le Bouclier de Brennus for a 14th time in the club's history after carving out a 12–6 victory over Clermont Auvergne in the Top 14 final, a tense triumph in the Stade de France which elicited unbridled celebrations from the Parisian contingent in the crowd but left despondent supporters of Les Jaunards with a depressing sense of déjà vu.

In what proved an attritional rather than free-flowing final, four penalties from Springbok fly-half Morné Steyn coupled with Clermont's profligacy from the tee saw Stade claim the trophy for the first time since 2007 as Gonzalo Quesada's side ensured their opponent's horrendous record in the competition continued.

Victory for the Parisians in their home city was only the second time in eight years in which the team finishing fourth in the table became champions and according to Stade number eight and captain Sergio Parisse, a survivor from the club's last Top 14 win, the result represented a renaissance for one of the traditional powerhouses of French club rugby.

"This shield will be the beginning of a new era for the club," he said. "I'm finding it tough to talk, it's just incredible. It wasn't a great final to watch but we don't care because we dealt with it and we let nothing go. It is a mixture of everything, joy, pride and also relief. It's huge. This is what we have dreamed of for quite some time."

In contrast defeat for Clermont, their 11th failure in 12 appearances in the showpiece game of the French domestic season, only cemented their unwanted reputation as the competition's perennial bridesmaids. It was their fourth loss in the final in nine years and to add considerable insult to injury came just six weeks after they were beaten by Toulon in the climax of the European Rugby Champions Cup campaign.

"I felt like we let them off the hook too easily," said full-back Nick Abendanon, the recently-crowned European Player of the Year. "We had them pinned down a couple of times but gave away easy penalties. We seem to say that too many times this season – it should have been us in the Champions Cup, it should have been us today.

"We got ourselves into a position to go and win this game but once again we were not clinical enough. There is only one team we can blame and that is ourselves. It is a matter of learning, but we just have not learned. I hear the words next season too often – everyone keeps on saying next season but when you make two finals you have got to convert at least one of them."

The long and arduous 26-game battle to secure a top six finish and place in the play-offs began in August and as ever in the fiercely competitive Top 14, defeats for the leading title contenders were almost as frequent as victories. Defending champions Toulon were beaten twice in their opening five fixtures, Toulouse had lost five in a row by the end of September and only once throughout the course of the campaign were Stade able to register three consecutive wins.

By May however the setbacks and shocks were forgotten as Toulon topped the table for the second successive season, Clermont came second, Toulouse third and Stade fourth. Racing Métro also made the play-offs in fifth while the surprise package of the campaign were Oyonnax, playing only their second season of Top 14 rugby, narrowly edged out Bordeaux-Bègles by a single point in the final reckoning.

The Oyonnax dream of reaching the last four for the first time was extinguished by Toulouse's narrow 20–19 victory in the play–offs while Stade despatched Racing more convincingly with a 38–15 win and the stage was set for the last four encounters.

The first semi-final saw Toulon tackle Stade. Le Rouge et Noir were targeting a fourth successive appearance in the final while the Parisians were featuring in the knockout stages for the first time since 2009 but pre-match predictions of victory for the champions proved erroneous as Quesada's team clinically dethroned the champions.

An early converted Drew Mitchell try was as good as it got for Toulon as Stade came roaring back into the contest, 18 points from the boot of Steyn and scores from openside Raphaël Lakafia, blindside Antoine Burban in the first half and a third from wing Julien Arias in the second sealing an impressive 33–16 triumph.

Stade were through to the final while Le Rouge et Noir's reign as champions was over, an inauspicious end to the club careers of three of the game's most iconic and decorated players, the retiring Bakkies Botha, Ali Williams and captain Carl Hayman.

"Above all it's the end of an era," said head coach Bernard Laporte. "It was a very difficult day. We lost to a good team, that's sport, but I'll remember everything that these players did at Toulon. It's been a pleasure to know them, to coach them, to train them, because they are great guys. They arrived at the club at the same time as me. We had just finished ninth, we were fighting relegation more than playing for titles. Now we've won three European titles and one French title."

The second semi paired Clermont and Toulouse, the most successful side in Top 14 history, and it was a far tighter clash between the teams which had finished second and third respectively as they vied for the right to play in Paris the following week.

The only try of the match belonged to Toulouse when full-back Maxime Médard went over five minutes after half-time and when Luke McAlister knocked over a third penalty in the 63rd minute, Guy Novès' side had established a slender 14–12 advantage. Les Jaunards were reeling but just moments after McAlister's kick they sent on fly-half Brock James to replace Camille Lopez and the Australian's introduction proved decisive as he landed a 70th-minute penalty and a 74th-minute drop goal to wrap up an 18–14 win.

Defeat brought a disappointing end to Novès' long association with Toulouse as the head coach said goodbye after 22 years with the club, his next assignment to replace Philippe Saint-André as France coach after

TOP 14

Rugby World Cup 2015, while victory for Clermont saw them through to the final for the first time since they won their solitary title in 2010.

"They missed eight points with the boot, we hit everything," said captain Damien Chouly. "If they had been successful with all we would have lost tonight, we realise that. What was good today was the team spirit because there was a lot of waste, we know that, but there was always someone to make up for the blow. It was the solidarity that saw us through."

The build-up to the Stade de France showdown, a repeat of the final in 2007 in which Stade beat Clermont 23–18, brought contrasting fortunes for the two sides. The Parisians were able to name the same starting XV which had overcome Toulon while Franck Azéma's Jaunards lost wing Noa Nakaitaci to a knee injury sustained in the victory over Toulouse and centre Wesley Fofana to a hamstring strain in midweek training.

Clermont's lamentable record in both domestic and European finals however dominated discussion before kick-off. "The Champions Cup final is not forgotten, it's in the back of our minds, but we have to now look ahead," insisted scrum-half Morgan Parra. "We often lose in the final but I'd prefer to go to 15 finals and think that I might win one than not be there at all. The more times you get there, the more chance you have of winning one. We know that sport at the highest level is cruel."

A total of 126 points were scored in the two meetings between the sides in the regular season but the final yielded just 18 as nerves and ill-discipline held sway in Paris.

Stade drew first blood when Clermont flanker Julien Bardy was shown a yellow card in the 13th minute for a reckless shoulder charge, Steyn landing the resulting penalty, while two further three-pointers from the South African playmaker before the break against one successful kick from three from Parra saw the Parisians 9–3 ahead as they retreated to the dressing room.

Clermont's inability to accumulate points from the tee clearly concerned Azéma, who replaced Lopez with James at half-time and charged him with the kicking duties and the Australian responded with a 61st-minute penalty to cut his side's arrears to just three points.

The result hung in the balance but the pivotal moment came 10 minutes from the final whistle when James was off target with another penalty attempt which would have levelled the scores. It was to be Clermont's final chance of redemption and when Steyn bisected the uprights with his fourth successful kick of the night in the closing seconds, there was no time for the restart.

Both sets of players inside the Stade de France fell to their knees, the Stade side in joyous relief after ending the club's eight-year wait for the title, the Clermont team in despair after allowing yet another trophy to **603** slip through their fingers.

"We knew that our strength would be our bond as a group and not necessarily the individuals," said Stade centre Jonathan Danty. "What really has made us into a group was all the work that we did in pre-season. We laughed a lot, spent a lot of time together. All this created the soul of the group, it has welded us."

TOP 14 2014–15 RESULTS

15 August, 2014: **Bayonne** 15 **Toulon** 29. 16 August: **Clermont** 30 **Grenoble** 26, **Bordeaux** 18 **Lyon** 9, **Brive** 37 **La Rochelle** 15, **Castres** 22 **Stade Français** 25, **Toulouse** 20 **Oyonnax** 19, **Montpellier** 16 **Racing Métro** 19. 22 August: **Toulouse** 35 **Castres** 6. 23 August: **Brive** 6 **Clermont** 21, **Bayonne** 38 **Oyonnax** 12, **Bordeaux** 30 **Racing Métro** 21, **Montpellier** 20 **Grenoble** 17, **Toulon** 60 **La Rochelle** 19, **Stade Français** 23 **Lyon** 20. 29 August: **Clermont** 20 **Montpellier** 21. 30 August: **La Rochelle** 37 **Toulouse** 25, **Castres** 30 **Bayonne** 6, **Grenoble** 37 **Bordeaux** 23, **Lyon** 24 **Brive** 6, **Oyonnax** 33 **Stade Français** 6, **Racing Métro** 17 **Toulon** 10. 5 September: **Montpellier** 43 **Castres** 10. 6 September: **Brive** 26 **Toulouse** 19, **Clermont** 32 **Racing Métro** 6, **Grenoble** 30 **La Rochelle** 12, **Lyon** 26 **Oyonnax** 23, **Stade Français** 34 **Bayonne** 29, **Toulon** 18 **Bordeaux** 13. 12 September: **La Rochelle** 41 **Castres** 16. 13 September: **Toulouse** 9 **Clermont** 13, **Bayonne** 23 **Brive** 6, **Oyonnax** 40 **Grenoble** 27, **Racing Métro** 28 **Lyon** 11, **Toulon** 24 **Stade Français** 28. 14 September: **Bordeaux** 27 **Montpellier** 21. 19 September: **Brive** 13 **Toulon** 53. 20 September: **Racing Métro** 27 **Toulouse** 16, **Castres** 27 **Oyonnax** 18, **Clermont** 43 **Lyon** 12, **Grenoble** 24 **Bayonne** 15, **La Rochelle** 26 **Bordeaux** 29, **Montpellier** 23 **Stade Français** 3. 26 September: **Bayonne** 35 **Toulouse** 19. 27 September: **Toulon** 40 **Montpellier** 17, **Brive** 34 **Bordeaux** 24, **Grenoble** 27 **Racing Métro** 25, **Lyon** 28 **Castres** 18, **Stade Français** 43 **La Rochelle** 10, **Oyonnax** 8 **Clermont** 19. 3 October: **Oyonnax** 18 **Toulon** 21. 4 October: **Bordeaux** 51 **Clermont** 21, **Bayonne** 10 **Montpellier** 15, **Castres** 51 **Grenoble** 10, **La Rochelle** 29 **Lyon** 10, **Racing Métro** 46 **Brive** 32, **Toulouse** 22 **Stade Français** 10. 10 October: **Grenoble** 26 **Brive** 25. 11 October: **Bordeaux** 59 **Castres** 7, **Clermont** 30 **La Rochelle** 10, **Lyon** 24 **Bayonne** 19, **Montpellier** 25 **Oyonnax** 9, **Stade Français** 23 **Racing Métro** 19. 12 October: **Toulouse** 21 **Toulon** 10. 1 November: **Lyon** 17 **Toulouse** 41, **Brive** 21 **Castres** 15, **La Rochelle** 21 **Montpellier** 15, **Racing Métro** 17 **Oyonnax** 21, **Stade Français** 39 **Bordeaux** 22, **Bayonne** 24 **Clermont** 13. 2 November: **Toulon** 61 **Grenoble** 28. 7 November: **Montpellier** 10 **Brive** 25. 8 November: **Castres** 22 **Toulon** 14, **Clermont** 51 **Stade Français** 9, **Grenoble** 34 **Lyon** 30, **Oyonnax** 37 **La Rochelle** 9, **Racing Métro** 27 **Bayonne** 10, **Bordeaux** 20 **Toulouse** 21. 29 November: **Toulon** 27 **Clermont** 19, **Castres** 9 **Racing Métro** 14, **La Rochelle** 19 **Bayonne** 19, **Lyon** 23 **Montpellier** 20, **Oyonnax** 28 **Bordeaux** 23, **Toulouse** 22 **Grenoble** 25. 30 November: **Stade Français** 20 **Brive** 17. 19 December: **Grenoble** 30 **Stade Français** 43. 20 December: **Montpellier** 23 **Toulouse** 20, **Bayonne** 15 **Bordeaux** 12, **Brive** 19 **Oyonnax** 6, **Racing Métro** 27 **La Rochelle** 8, **Toulon** 30 **Lyon** 6, **Clermont** 19 **Castres** 10. 28 December: **Toulouse** 15 **Racing Métro** 9, **Bordeaux** 46 **Brive** 10, **Castres** 27 **Montpellier** 9, **La Rochelle** 19 **Grenoble** 15, **Oyonnax** 12 **Bayonne** 9, **Lyon** 16 **Clermont** 13, **Stade Français** 30 **Toulon** 6. 2 January, 2015: **Lyon** 12 **Stade Français** 9. 3 January: **Racing Métro** 12 **Bordeaux** 9, **Brive** 25 **Bayonne** 9, **Castres** 30 **La Rochelle** 15, **Grenoble** 33 **Oyonnax** 19,**Montpellier** 16 **Toulon** 12. 4 January: **Clermont** 24 **Toulouse** 6. 9 January: **Stade Français** 49 **Castres** 13. 10 January: **Toulon** 32 **Racing Métro** 23, **Bayonne** 23 **Lyon** 22, **Bordeaux** 34 **Grenoble** 16, **Oyonnax** 20 **Montpellier** 13, **Toulouse** 29 **La Rochelle** 26, **Clermont** 44 **Brive** 20. 30 January: **Toulon** 24 **Bayonne** 17. 31 January: **Montpellier** 34 **Bordeaux** 24, **Brive** 23 **Grenoble** 0, **La Rochelle** 16 **Clermont** 12, **Lyon** 11 **Racing Métro** 13, **Stade Français** 13 **Oyonnax** 15, **Castres**

9 **Toulouse** 13. 19 February: **La Rochelle** 19 **Brive** 12. 21 February: **Bordeaux** 28 **Toulon** 23, **Bayonne** 23 **Stade Français** 6, **Toulouse** 23 **Lyon** 20, **Grenoble** 20 **Montpellier** 18, **Oyonnax** 23 **Castres** 13 , **Racing Métro** 13 **Clermont** 13. 6 March: **Oyonnax** 9 **Toulouse** 3. 7 March: **Bordeaux** 22 **Stade Français** 23, **Castres** 23 **Lyon** 20, **Clermont** 28 **Bayonne** 16, **Montpellier** 15 **La Rochelle** 15, **Racing Métro** 34 **Grenoble** 29, **Toulon** 34 **Brive** 11. 13 March: **Clermont** 31 **Bordeaux** 23. 14 March: **Toulouse** 18 **Montpellier** 13, **Bayonne** 21 **Castres** 19, **Brive** 36 **Racing Métro** 12, **La Rochelle** 35 **Oyonnax** 20, **Stade Français** 21 **Grenoble** 30, **Lyon** 14 **Toulon** 22. 27 March: **Bayonne** 6 **Racing Métro** 12. 28 March: **Stade Français** 40 **Clermont** 26, **Bordeaux** 21 **La Rochelle** 22, **Montpellier** 45 **Lyon** 17, **Oyonnax** 24 **Brive** 3, **Toulon** 24 **Toulouse** 34, **Grenoble** 12 **Castres** 16. 10 April: **La Rochelle** 19 **Stade Français** 19. 11 April: **Racing Métro** 24 **Montpellier** 24, **Brive** 22 **Lyon** 20, **Clermont** 10 **Oyonnax** 11, **Toulouse** 20 **Bayonne** 17, **Grenoble** 24 **Toulon** 35, **Castres** 22 **Bordeaux** 20. 24 April: **Stade Français** 12 **Toulouse** 21. 25 April: **La Rochelle** 32 **Toulon** 29, **Bayonne** 42 **Grenoble** 33, **Brive** 15 **Montpellier** 10, **Lyon** 22 **Bordeaux** 37, **Oyonnax** 21 **Racing Métro** 16, **Castres** 31 **Clermont** 10. 9 May: **Toulon** 37 **Castres** 21, **Bordeaux** 26 **Oyonnax** 23, **Lyon** 16 **La Rochelle** 16, **Montpellier** 33 **Bayonne** 16, **Toulouse** 67 **Brive** 19, **Grenoble** 17 **Clermont** 37. 10 May: **Racing Métro** 19 **Stade Français** 28. 15 May: **Oyonnax** 28 **Lyon** 10. 16 May: **Grenoble** 32 **Toulouse** 11, **Bordeaux** 38 **Bayonne** 20, **Castres** 32 **Brive** 12, **La Rochelle** 18 **Racing Métro** 18, **Stade Français** 35 **Montpellier** 21. 17 May: **Clermont** 22 **Toulon** 19. 23 May: **Bayonne** 45 **La Rochelle** 12, **Brive** 27 **Stade Français** 0, **Lyon** 29 **Grenoble** 24, **Montpellier** 17 **Clermont** 29, **Racing Métro** 53 **Castres** 10, **Toulon** 46 **Oyonnax** 17, **Toulouse** 23 **Bordeaux** 22.

FINAL TABLE

	P	W	D	L	F	A	BP	PTS
Toulon	26	16	0	10	740	525	12	76
Clermont	26	16	1	9	630	464	9	75
Toulouse	26	16	0	10	573	504	6	70
Stade Français	26	15	1	10	591	576	8	70
Racing Métro	26	13	3	10	551	497	7	65
Oyonnax	26	14	0	12	514	507	6	62
Bordeaux	26	12	0	14	701	578	13	61
Montpellier	26	11	2	13	537	516	7	55
La Rochelle	26	10	5	11	520	659	4	54
Brive	26	12	0	14	502	619	5	53
Grenoble	26	11	0	15	626	735	9	53
Castres	26	11	0	15	509	627	8	52
Bayonne	26	10	1	15	522	548	10	52
Lyon	26	8	1	17	469	630	7	41

29 May, 2015
Stade Français 38 **Racing Métro** 15
30 May, 2015
Toulouse 20 **Oyonnax** 19

SEMI-FINALS

5 June, Nouveau Stade de Bordeaux, Bordeaux

TOULON 16 (1G 3PG) STADE FRANÇAIS 33 (3G 4PG)

TOULON: L Halfpenny; D Mitchell, M Bastareaud, JM Hernández, B Habana; M Giteau, S Tillous-Borde; X Chocci, G Guirado, C Hayman (captain), B Botha, A Williams, J Smith, S Armitage, C Masoe

SUBSTITUTIONS: M Mermoz for Hernandez (40 mins); A Menini for Chiocci (52 mins); J Suta for Botha (58 mins); J-C Orioli for Guirado (60 mins); JM Fernández Lobbe for Smith (66 mins); M Claassens for Tillous-Borde (71 mins)

SCORERS: *Try*: Mitchell *Conversion*: Halfpenny *Penalty Goals*: Halfpenny (3)

STADE FRANÇAIS: D Camara; J Arias, W Nayacalevu, J Danty, J Sinzelle; M Steyn, J Dupuy; H van der Merwe, R Bonfils, R Slimani, H Pyle, A Flanquart, A Burban, R Lakafia, S Parisse (captain)

SUBSTITUTIONS: J Ross for Lakafia (49 mins); L Sempéré for Bonfils (60 mins); P Papé for Pyle (63 mins); J Fillol for Dupuy (65 mins); S Taulafo for Van der Merwe (69 mins); D Kubriashvili for Slimani (71 mins); S LaValla for Burban (76 mins); M Bosman for Nayacalevu (79 mins)

SCORERS: *Tries*: Lakafia, Burban, Arias *Conversions*: Steyn (3) *Penalty Goals*: Steyn (4)

REFEREE: M Raynal (France)

TOP 14

6 June, Nouveau Stade de Bordeaux, Bordeaux

CLERMONT AUVERGNE 18 (5PG 1DG) TOULOUSE 14 (3PG 1T)

CLERMONT AUVERGNE: N Abendanon; A Rougerie, B Stanley, W Fofana, N Nakaitaci; C Lopez, M Parra; T Domingo, J Ulugia, D Zirakashvili, P Jedrasiak, S Vahaamahina, D Chouly (captain), J Bardy, F Lee

SUBSTITUTIONS: J Pierre for Jedrasiak (51 mins); R Chaume for Domingo (51 mins); B Kayser for Ulugia (51 mins); A Lapandry for Bardy (64 mins); B James for Lopez (64 mins); C Ric for Zirakashvili (66 mins); L Radosavljevic for Parra (70 mins); J-M Buttin for Stanley (76 mins)

SCORERS: *Penalty Goals:* Parra (4), James *Drop Goal:* James

TOULOUSE: M Médard; V Clerc, Y David, L McAlister, Y Huget; J-M Doussain, S Bézy; G Steenkamp, C Flynn, C Johnston, J Tekori, P Albacete, T Dusautoir (captain), Y Nyanga, G Galan

SUBSTITUTIONS: F Fritz for David (47 mins); L Picamoles for Galan (47 mins); Y Maestri for Tekori (47 mins); D Aldegheri for Johnston (51 mins); C Baille for Steenkamp (51 mins); J Marchand for Flynn (66 mins); Y Camara for Nyanga (71 mins); T Matanavou (76 mins)

SCORERS: *Try:* Médard *Penalty Goals:* McAlister (3)

REFEREE: A Ruiz (France)

FINAL

13 June, Stade de France, Paris

CLERMONT AUVERGNE 6 (2PG) STADE FRANÇAIS 12 (4PG)

CLERMONT AUVERGNE: N Abendanon; J-M Buttin, A Rougerie, B Stanley, N Nalaga; C Lopez, M Parra; T Domingo, J Ulugia, D Zirakashvili, P Jedrasiak, S Vahaamahina, D Chouly (captain), J Bardy, F Lee

SUBSTITUTIONS: B Kayser for Ulugia (20 mins); J Pierre for Jedrasiak (51 mins); B James for Lopez (51 mins); A Lapandry for Bardy (69 mins); M Delany for Stanley (69 mins); L Radosavljevic for Parra (69 mins); R Chaume for Domingo (73 mins); C Ric for Zirakashvili (73 mins)

SCORERS: *Penalty Goals:* Lopez, James

YELLOW CARD: J Bardy (13 mins)

STADE FRANÇAIS: D Camara; J Arias, W Nayacalevu, J Danty, J Sinzelle; M Steyn, J Dupuy; H van der Merwe, R Bonfils, R Slimani, H Pyle, A Flanquart, A Burban, R Lakafia, S Parisse (captain)

SUBSTITUTIONS: P Papé for Pyle (26 mins); L Sempéré for Bonfils (56 mins); S Taulafo for Van der Merwe (63 mins); J Ross for Burban (65 mins); G Doumayrou for Camara (67 mins); J Fillol for Dupuy (69 mins); M Bosman for Nayacalevu (79 mins)

SCORERS: *Penalty Goals:* Steyn (4)

REFEREE: P Gaüzère (France)

WARRIORS END SCOTTISH TROPHY DROUGHT

By Iain Spragg

Glasgow Warriors swept aside Munster 31–13 in Belfast to lift the PRO12 trophy for the first time.

Glasgow defied both the might of three-time champions Munster and the weight of history to claim a maiden Guinness PRO12 title, becoming the first side from Scotland in the professional era to lift major silverware and in the process end the Irish and Welsh stranglehold on the competition.

All 13 previous editions of the competition had seen either an Irish province or Welsh region crowned champions, but 2015 was the year the Warriors finally gatecrashed the party to restore beleaguered Scottish pride, outscoring Munster four tries to one in Belfast to record a stunning and unashamedly cathartic 31–13 victory.

The triumph came exactly a year after Glasgow's loss in the final to Leinster. In the aftermath of defeat, Warriors head coach Gregor Townsend had insisted "that anything less than a trophy would be deemed a failure" in the following campaign and, after finishing top of the PRO12 table at the end of the regular season before emphatically outplaying Munster in the final, his side did not disappoint.

Victory at the Kingspan Stadium also ensured an emotional but euphoric farewell for club captain Alastair Kellock, who came off the bench in the 65th minute of the final to make his 174th and last PRO12 appearance before heading into retirement after a decade of unstinting service for the Warriors.

"There'll be plenty of time for individual reflection but we're just collectively enjoying something incredibly special," said the veteran second-row. "That was our best performance in knockout rugby. It was top class, not only the way we played but the way we stopped a top-quality Munster team.

"To get as close as we did last year meant we were that bit more desperate and we talked all year about learning the lessons from the last final and it's so pleasing to see us do it. We have great people here and the advantage of playing rugby in a small country is that we can share it. If there is one thing that this trophy needs to do, it is to push the game further."

Glasgow's long march to glory began in early September in dramatic style with a repeat of the 2014 final as they entertained Leinster at Scotstoun, with Townsend's side emerging 22–20 winners against the reigning champions courtesy of a nerveless injury-time penalty from substitute Stuart Hogg.

Four successive victories followed to underline the Warriors' title credentials and send the side top, but a 29–9 loss to Ulster at the Kingspan Stadium in October was an abrupt reality check. And with Munster, Ospreys and Ulster all jockeying for position, it was evident that Glasgow could ill afford to become complacent despite their strong start.

The balance of power ebbed and flowed throughout the campaign and when Munster beat Glasgow 22–10 in late February at Musgrave Park, it was a result that propelled Anthony Foley's team above the Scots into pole position in the table.

The battle for the order of the top four places was only resolved on the final weekend of the regular season as Munster beat the Dragons 50–27 and the Ospreys won 24–20 in Connacht. The pivotal result, however, was the Warriors' 32–10 home victory over Ulster, which ensured Townsend's side ended the season on top despite finishing level on points with Munster, their elevated status coming courtesy of 16 wins to 15 for the Irish province.

Just six days later Glasgow and Ulster renewed acquaintances in the first of the semi-finals. The margin of victory in their previous encounter had been a comfortable 22 points in favour of the Warriors, but the rematch at Scotstoun was an altogether more tense affair which was only settled in the dying minutes.

First blood went to the visitors when scrum-half Ruan Pienaar knocked over a penalty after only 30 seconds of play, and Ulster also scored the first try of the match when quick hands from full-back Louis Ludik sent Chris Henry over in the corner after 19 minutes. Worse followed for the home side when captain Kellock was forced off with a head injury and at half-time the Warriors trailed Neil Doak's side 8–6.

Two more Pienaar penalties and a second from Finn Russell for the home side left the score 14–9 in Ulster's favour, and it was not until the 75th minute that Glasgow were able to deliver what proved to be a stunning *coup de grâce*.

A series of drives from the pack inside the 22 laid the platform before Russell's exquisite 30-yard pass off his left hand found DTH van der Merwe out wide and the wing was able to burst through Craig Gilroy's despairing tackle for the equalising score in the corner. There was palpable tension as Russell lined up the touchline conversion, but the Scotland fly-half's superb kick sailed over and the Warriors were 16–14 winners.

"It was a tough game and I'm glad the boys stuck in there," said Scarlets-bound van der Merwe, who like Kellock was making his final appearance for Glasgow at Scotstoun. "Every opportunity when I got the ball in my hands, I just try to do as much as I can. That try was a team try, I was just lucky to be on the end of it. I'm going to really miss this place, but there are still great things to come from this club."

The second semi-final between Munster and Ospreys was equally dramatic as two sides with seven titles between them crossed swords at Thomond Park.

The opening 39 minutes in Limerick were deceptively sedate as two penalties from Munster fly-half Ian Keatley to one from his opposite number Dan Biggar gave the home side a slender 6–3 advantage, but it was merely the calm before the storm and in the 13 minutes that followed either side of half-time five tries were scored.

Munster scored the first of the remarkable salvo when Simon Zebo went over seconds before the break, and the Irish side extended their lead just two minutes after the restart when Denis Hurley muscled his way through Eli Walker's attempted tackle. The Ospreys responded quickly with a try from Rhys Webb after the scrum-half had intercepted from CJ Stander, only for Munster to storm back with a score from flanker Paddy Butler. The scoring spree was completed when Ospreys winger Jeff Hassler collected Zebo's attempted grubber kick in the 52nd minute.

The crowd finally had time to catch its breath with the home side 21–15 in front, but the alarm bells rang loudly again when Biggar landed a 66th minute penalty to reduce the Ospreys' arrears and put the result firmly in the balance.

Munster held firm until added time but then had to endure an agonising TMO referral after Josh Matavesi appeared to have scored the winning try for the Ospreys. However, the verdict was a knock-on by Webb in the build-up, the try was chalked off and the home side had clung on for a 21–18 triumph.

"You had two very good sides out there playing a good brand of rugby and for it to go to the wire like that sums up how tight a competition it was," said Foley after the nerve-shredding climax to the match. "It was a good spectacle. We'll go at it hard with Glasgow on Saturday. I'll guarantee you one thing, the team who wins it this year will have earned it. It's going to be a tough, physical contest."

If the two semis were titanic tussles, the final was in truth a one-sided affair as Glasgow blew away Munster in Belfast with an irresistible blend of intensity and precision, scoring three first-half tries to effectively end the Irish challenge.

The first came on eight minutes when the magnificent Leone Nakarawa burst through the cover to feed Rob Harley, while the second on 25 minutes went to van der Merwe after another decisive offload from Nakarawa. The third to scrum-half Henry Pyrgos after an incisive break from Stuart Hogg, and although Munster scored themselves before the break through centre Andrew Smith, it was 21–10 to the Warriors at half-time.

Any hopes of a Munster fightback were extinguished midway through the second period when Russell ghosted through the defence for a fourth Glasgow try, and the remainder of the match was something of a procession as the Scottish side closed out their historic 31–13 victory.

Defeat was a particularly bitter pill to swallow for Paul O'Connell, playing his final game for Munster after 14 years, but the veteran Ireland and Lions second-row conceded the province had not done enough to lift the trophy for a fourth time.

"It's very disappointing," he said. "We didn't play well at all. We didn't show up in the first half and nothing seemed to work for us. That's just the way it goes, it's a shame to perform like that in a final but that's life. We missed some tackles, we did some simple things poorly and that's what costs you in these big games."

The contrast in emotion in the Warriors camp could not have been starker after the side had finally secured Scottish rugby's first major club trophy and expunged memories of their loss to Leinster 12 months earlier. Victory also represented a personal triumph for Townsend three years after he was appointed head coach at Scotstoun and charged with reviving Glasgow's fortunes.

"We will be a much better team having won this match," the former Scotland fly-half said after the final. "There's a lot more to come from this group of players and they have now had the experience of winning something, which is fantastic."

GUINNESS PRO12 2014–15 RESULTS

5 September, 2014: **Munster** 13 **Edinburgh** 14, **Ospreys** 44 **Treviso** 13. 6 September: **Scarlets** 32 **Ulster** 32, **Connacht** 16 **Dragons** 11, **Glasgow** 22 **Leinster** 20. 7 September: **Zebre** 26 **Blues** 41. 12 September: **Treviso** 10 **Munster** 21, **Dragons** 15 **Ospreys** 17, **Edinburgh** 13 **Connacht** 14, **Ulster** 33 **Zebre** 13. 13 September: **Leinster** 42 **Scarlets** 12. 14 September: **Blues** 12 **Glasgow** 33. 19 September: **Munster** 31 **Zebre** 5, **Blues** 9 **Ulster** 26, **Connacht** 10 **Leinster** 9. 20 September: **Dragons** 13 **Glasgow** 33. **Scarlets** 43 **Treviso** 0. 21 September: **Ospreys** 62 **Edinburgh** 13. 26 September: **Edinburgh** 20 **Scarlets** 20, **Glasgow** 39 **Connacht** 21, **Leinster** 37 **Blues** 23. 27 September: **Zebre** 13 **Ulster** 6, **Munster** 14 **Ospreys** 19. September: **Dragons** 33 **Treviso** 15. 3 October: **Connacht** 24 **Blues** 24, **Ulster** 30 **Edinburgh** 0, **Zebre** 14 **Ospreys** 15. 4 October: **Leinster** 23 **Munster** 34. 5 October: **Treviso** 23 **Glasgow** 40, **Scarlets** 26 **Dragons** 13. 10 October: **Treviso** 6 **Connacht** 9, **Munster** 17 **Scarlets** 6. 11 October: **Edinburgh** 24 **Dragons** 10, **Zebre** 3 **Leinster** 20, **Ulster** 29 **Glasgow** 9. 12 October: **Ospreys** 26 **Blues** 15. 31 October: **Glasgow** 17 **Treviso** 9, **Leinster** 33 **Edinburgh** 8, **Ospreys** 26 **Connacht** 11. 1 November: **Blues** 24 **Munster** 28, **Scarlets** 28 **Zebre** 13, **Ulster** 23 **Dragons** 6. 21 November: **Dragons** 12 **Munster** 38, **Connacht** 43 **Zebre** 3, **Scarlets** 19 **Glasgow** 9, **Ulster** 25 **Ospreys** 16. 23 November: **Treviso** 24 **Leinster** 24, **Edinburgh** 28 **Blues** 13. 28 November: **Blues** 36 **Treviso** 25, **Munster** 21 **Ulster** 20. 29 November: **Zebre** 18 **Edinburgh** 10, **Leinster** 18 **Ospreys** 12, **Connacht** 14 **Scarlets** 8. 30 November: **Glasgow** 19 **Dragons** 15. 19 December: **Blues** 21 **Scarlets** 9, **Edinburgh** 48 **Treviso** 0, **Leinster** 21 **Connacht** 11. 20 December: **Glasgow** 21 **Munster** 18, **Ospreys** 31 **Ulster** 20. 21 December: **Dragons** 25 **Zebre** 11. 26 December: **Blues** 17 **Dragons** 23, **Munster** 28 **Leinster** 13, **Ulster** 13 **Connacht** 10. 27 December: **Glasgow** 16 **Edinburgh** 6, **Ospreys** 17 **Scarlets** 15. 28 December: **Zebre** 16 **Treviso** 26. 1 January, 2015: **Dragons** 9 **Blues** 11, **Connacht** 24 **Munster** 16. 2 January: **Edinburgh** 20 **Glasgow** 8.

3 January: **Treviso** 17 **Zebre** 15, **Leinster** 24 **Ulster** 11, **Scarlets** 22 **Ospreys** 10. 9 January: **Connacht** 13 **Edinburgh** 16, **Glasgow** 22 **Scarlets** 7. 10 January: **Blues** 13 **Leinster** 22, **Zebre** 7 **Munster** 31. 11 January: **Treviso** 20 **Ulster** 24, **Ospreys** 22 **Dragons** 11. 13 February: **Ulster** 43 **Treviso** 3, **Edinburgh** 24 **Ospreys** 16. 14 February: **Munster** 33 **Blues** 16. 15 February: **Scarlets** 32 **Connacht** 14, **Zebre** 10 **Glasgow** 54, **Leinster** 14 **Dragons** 16. 20 February: **Treviso** 40 **Blues** 24, **Edinburgh** 17 **Ulster** 20, **Leinster** 29 **Zebre** 8. 21 February: **Scarlets** 25 **Munster** 25, **Glasgow** 19 **Ospreys** 16. 22 February: **Dragons** 25 **Connacht** 30. 27 February: **Ospreys** 9 **Leinster** 9, **Ulster** 25 **Scarlets** 20. 28 February: **Munster** 22 **Glasgow** 10. 1 March: **Blues** 21 **Edinburgh** 15, **Zebre** 23 **Dragons** 17, **Connacht** 53 **Treviso** 5. 6 March: **Blues** 18 **Connacht** 17, **Glasgow** 26 **Zebre** 5. 7 March: **Ospreys** 26 **Munster** 12, **Scarlets** 23 **Leinster** 13, **Treviso** 8 **Edinburgh** 29. 8 March: **Dragons** 26 **Ulster** 22. 27 March: **Leinster** 34 **Glasgow** 34, **Ulster** 36 **Blues** 17. 28 March: **Scarlets** 15 **Edinburgh** 26, **Munster** 42 **Connacht** 20, **Ospreys** 53 **Zebre** 22, **Treviso** 17 **Dragons** 32. 10 April: **Treviso** 13 **Ospreys** 33, **Glasgow** 36 **Blues** 17. 11 April: **Connacht** 20 **Ulster** 27, **Zebre** 26 **Scarlets** 28, **Edinburgh** 3 **Munster** 34. 12 April: **Dragons** 25 **Leinster** 22. 24 April: **Edinburgh** 37 **Zebre** 0, **Ulster** 26 **Leinster** 10. 25 April: **Connacht** 13 **Glasgow** 31, **Blues** 23 **Ospreys** 31, **Munster** 30 **Treviso** 19, **Dragons** 10 **Scarlets** 29. 8 May: **Dragons** 19 **Edinburgh** 5, **Leinster** 10 **Treviso** 0, **Ospreys** 21 **Glasgow** 10. 9 May: **Ulster** 23 **Munster** 23, **Zebre** 10 **Connacht** 40. 10 May: **Scarlets** 16 **Blues** 6. 16 May: **Treviso** 13 **Scarlets** 17, **Blues** 29 **Zebre** 5, **Connacht** 20 **Ospreys** 24, **Edinburgh** 23 **Leinster** 36, **Glasgow** 32 **Ulster** 10, **Munster** 50 **Dragons** 27.

FINAL TABLE

	P	W	D	L	F	A	BP	PTS
Glasgow	22	16	1	5	540	360	9	75
Munster	22	15	2	5	581	367	11	75
Ospreys	22	16	1	5	546	358	8	74
Ulster	22	14	2	6	524	372	9	69
Leinster	22	11	3	8	483	375	12	62
Scarlets	22	11	3	8	452	388	7	57
Connacht	22	10	1	11	447	419	8	50
Edinburgh	22	10	1	11	399	419	6	48
Dragons	22	8	0	14	393	484	10	42
Blues	22	7	1	14	430	545	5	35
Treviso	22	3	1	18	306	641	5	19
Zebre	22	3	0	19	266	639	3	15

GLASGOW 16 (1G 3PG) ULSTER 14 (1T 3PG)

GLASGOW: S Hogg; T Seymour, R Vernon, P Horne, N Matawalu; F Russell, H Pyrgos; R Grant, F Brown, R de Klerk, J Gray, A Kellock (captain), J Strauss, C Fusaro, A Ashe

SUBSTITUTIONS: L Nakarawa for Kellock (21 mins); P McArthur for Brown (21 mins); R Wilson for Fusaro (41 mins); G Reid for Grant (47 mins); M Cusack for de Klerk (54 mins); DTH van der Merwe for Seymour (68 mins); S Lamont for Horne (71 mins); D Weir for Matawalu (79 mins)

SCORERS: *Try:* Van der Merwe *Conversion:* Russell *Penalty Goals:* Russell (2), Hogg

ULSTER: L Ludik; T Bowe, J Payne, D Cave, C Gilroy; P Jackson, R Pienaar; C Black, R Best (captain), R Lutton, L Stevenson, D Tuohy, I Henderson, C Henry, R Wilson

SUBSTITUTIONS: A Warwick for Black (73 mins); R Diack for Stevenson (78 mins); S McCloskey for Cave (78 mins); S Reidy for Henry (78 mins)

SCORERS: *Try:* Henry *Penalty Goals:* Pienaar (3)

REFEREE: G Clancy (Ireland)

MUNSTER 21 (3T 2PG) OSPREYS 18 (1G 1T 2PG)

MUNSTER: F Jones; K Earls, A Smith, D Hurley, S Zebo, I Keatley, C Murray; D Kilcoyne, E Guinazu, S Archer, D Ryan, P O'Connell, P O'Mahony (captain), P Butler, CJ Stander

SUBSTITUTIONS: D Williams for Murray (16 mins); B Holland for P O'Mahony (44 mins); BJ Botha for Archer (52 mins); R O'Mahony for Zebo (67 mins); J Ryan for Kilcoyne (72 mins); D Casey for Guinazu (72 mins); JJ Hanrahan for Keatley (74 mins)

SCORERS: *Tries:* Zebo, Hurley, Butler *Penalty Goals:* Keatley (2)

OSPREYS: D Evans; J Hassler, B John, J Matavesi, E Walker; D Biggar, R Webb; N Smith, S Baldwin, D Arhip, T Ardron, AW Jones (captain), D Lydiate, J Tipuric, D Baker

SUBSTITUTIONS: J King for Lydiate (42 mins); M Thomas for Baldwin (55 mins); A Jarvis for Arhip (57 mins); R Thornton for Ardron (66 mins); S Davies for Evans (67 mins); M Thomas for Smith (73 mins); J Spratt for Biggar (76 mins)

SCORERS: *Tries:* Webb, Hassler *Conversion:* Biggar *Penalty Goals:* Biggar (2)

REFEREE: N Owens (Wales)

FINAL

MUNSTER 13 (1G 2PG) GLASGOW 31 (4G 1PG)

MUNSTER: F Jones; K Earles, A Smith, D Hurley (captain), S Zebo; I Keatley, D Williams; D Kilcoyne, E Guinazu, BJ Botha, B Holland, P O'Connell, D Ryan, P Butler, CJ Stander

SUBSTITUTIONS: R O'Mahony for Zebo (56 mins); JJ Hanrahan for Keatley (56 mins); J Cronin for Kilcoyne (62 mins); D Casey for Guinazu (62 mins); C Sheridan for Williams (72 mins); S Dougall for Butler (72 mins)

SCORERS: *Try:* Smith *Conversion:* Keatley *Penalty Goals:* Keatley (2)

GLASGOW: S Hogg; DTH van der Merwe, R Vernon, P Horne, T Seymour; F Russell, H Pyrgos; G Reid, D Hall, R De Klerk, J Gray, L Nakarawa, R Harley, R Wilson, J Strauss (captain)

SUBSTITUTIONS: J Welsh for De Klerk (52 mins); C Fusaro for Harley (60 mins); S Lamont for Hogg (62 mins); D Weir for Russell (67 mins); A Kellock for Nakarawa (67 mins); N Matawalu for Van der Merwe (70 mins); J Yanuyanutawa for Reid (77 mins).

SCORERS: *Tries:* Harley, Van der Merwe, Pyrgos, Russell *Conversions:* Russell (4) *Penalty Goal:* Weir

REFEREE: N Owens (Wales)

Glasgow Warriors players join their jubilant fans to celebrate victory over Munster at the Kingspan Stadium.

TOULON SECURE HISTORIC HAT-TRICK

By Iain Spragg

Jubilation for the Toulon players after a closely contested 24–18 victory over Clermont Auvergne at Twickenham.

European rugby marked its 20th season of cross-border club competition in 2014–15 and two decades after Toulouse had become the inaugural winners of the Heineken Cup, Toulon registered a new continental milestone as they became the first club to claim three successive crowns.

It was also the season in which the Heineken Cup made way for the new European Rugby Champions Cup, but the star-studded Le Rouge et Noir found the remodelled tournament as much to their liking as they had its predecessor, beating Clermont Auvergne 24–18 in the final at Twickenham to underline their status as the undisputed number one side in the northern hemisphere. Their unprecedented hat-trick of triumphs also saw Bernard Laporte's side join Leinster as three-time European winners, leaving them just one adrift of Toulouse's record of four final successes.

This final was a repeat of the clash between Toulon and Clermont at the same stage two years earlier which had finished 16–15 in the former's favour. The rematch was equally absorbing but with just a single point separating the two protagonists 10 minutes from time, it was dramatically settled by a sensational solo score by Drew Mitchell for Le Rouge et Noir.

"We've been questioned a lot lately as a squad, where we've been, how we've come together and what we've played for," Mitchell said after the final whistle. "But we know internally that we're a pretty driven side out there. We were certainly pushed by Clermont there, they're a fantastic side, right to the end again, the same as a couple of years ago. They could have snatched it at the end there. It's good for us to know that we've got that belief and that respect and that trust in one another."

Defeat for Clermont condemned Les Jaunards to their second disappointment in the space of three years and in the process they reluctantly joined fellow French sides Biarritz and Stade Français as two-time losing finalists.

"It's hard to watch a team celebrate something that we desperately wanted to win but that is finals rugby," said Clermont full-back and try scorer Nick Abendanon. "It is on a knife-edge and mistakes can hurt you – that is what happened today. This is my first season here but I feel that this team will be lifting trophies.

"We have a great group of individuals in the squad. We came here with the mental belief that we could beat Toulon today. There are no words but there are a lot of tears in the changing room. This means so much to this group of players who have been at this club for a lot longer than I have and played in more semi-finals and finals than I have so it's hard to put that sort of emotion into words."

Toulon began the defence of their title in Pool Three of the Champions Cup, drawn alongside former champions Leicester and Ulster, and Scarlets. Aside from a 25–21 reverse to the Tigers at Welford Road in December, the champions were untroubled as they progressed to the knockout stages with five wins from their six outings.

Four English Premiership teams, two from the Top 14 and Leinster, the sole representatives from the PRO12, joined Toulon in the quarter-finals and after the make-or-break fixtures were staged in early April,

Laporte's side, Clermont, Leinster and Saracens were the four sides still standing.

The first semi-final saw Les Jaunards host Saracens at the Stade Geoffroy-Guichard. The English club were aiming to repeat their comprehensive 46–6 demolition of Clermont at Twickenham at the same stage 12 months earlier and reach a second successive final, but Mark McCall's team were on French soil this time and found Les Jaunards a far sterner proposition in Saint-Étienne.

Saracens edged the first half 6–3 courtesy of a drop goal and penalty from fly-half Charlie Hodgson but his opposite number Brock James was in the ascendency after the break, setting up Wesley Fofana for the only try of the match and kicking eight points to exact Clermont's revenge and seal a 13–9 triumph for the home side.

"I thought the effort and many, many aspects of the performance were phenomenal," said McCall after the game. "We made Clermont play a game that they didn't really want to play. The game was on a knife-edge all the way through. We made maybe a few too many errors at crucial times, but in terms of the big things that we judge ourselves on, we were magnificent."

The second semi-final took Leinster to Marseille to tackle Toulon with the Irish side looking to reach the final for the first since 2012 when they beat provincial rivals Ulster, but they were denied after an epic encounter in the Stade Vélodrome which was only settled by an interception try deep into extra-time.

The first 80 minutes of hostilities in the south of France was a showdown between the two respective kickers as Leigh Halfpenny and Ian Madigan both landed four penalties apiece for their sides to make it 12–12 and send the match into an additional 20 minutes. Another three points from each continued the duel but Toulon then found themselves on the back foot when former All Black second-row Ali Williams was yellow carded in the 85th minute.

Leinster, however, failed to exploit their numerical superiority and it was Le Rouge et Noir who pounced with a sixth Halfpenny penalty followed by Bryan Habana's decisive intercept on halfway from Madigan's pass. Toulon had suddenly surged into a 10-point lead and although Sean O'Brien powered over for a Leinster try six minutes from time, it was too little too late and the French side were 25–20 winners and en route to the final once again.

"It was a pretty impressive performance from my guys," said Leinster head coach Matt O'Connor. "They gave every bit of effort they had and we led for large parts of the game. They are gutted in the dressing room. The conditions made it difficult to play out there and the defences dominated. It was hard to put passes together and get the ball to the edges.

"We dug in for large parts of the game, but the interception try changed the game. We wanted to drive at them, make their forwards work really hard and break them down in the last 15 minutes. Unfortunately we weren't good enough to do that but the effort that those 23 players put in shows how much it means to them to play for Leinster. We may have lost, but this performance has shown we can compete against the best club side ever put together."

The final was staged at Twickenham a fortnight later and when Laporte and his opposite number Franck Azéma revealed their respective starting XVs, there was a grand total of 1,193 test caps in the ranks of the two teams.

It was Clermont who made the early running in London with two penalties from fly-half Camille Lopez, drafted into the side at the eleventh hour after Les Jaunards had lost James with a thigh injury in the warm-up, and although Halfpenny replied for the champions, Azéma's side surged further ahead with the opening try from Fofana after a Morgan Parra charge down. A typically muscular charge from Mathieu Bastareaud and the boot of Halfpenny redressed the balance and at the break Toulon had established a 16–11 lead.

The second half was to produce two stunning individual scores and the first was conjured up by Abendanon for Clermont in the 62nd minute when the full-back collected possession and dissected the entire Toulon defence with a sublime chip and gather to race over for a converted try.

As a result there was just two points separating the sides when Mitchell took a flat pass from Sébastien Tillous-Borde on the Clermont 10-metre line. The Wallaby wing appeared well marshalled by the defence but he burst through the initial tackle on the gain-line and accelerated, leaving five further tacklers in his slipstream as he powered over the line for one of the greatest scores ever witnessed in a final.

The conversion went wide but Mitchell's try had already done the damage. Toulon were able to keep Clermont at arm's length for the remaining 10 minutes and when the final whistle sounded, they had secured a 24–18 victory and an unprecedented third consecutive European trophy.

"Right to the end it was anyone's game, that's finals rugby," said Toulon captain Carl Hayman. "From our behalf, it's good that we've been in that position a lot in the last three or four years. The guys know what's needed and we were able to hang in there.

"I think being the third one, it's even greater. It's such a difficult competition, especially now with the pools being reduced, it's a lot harder. Teams now have bigger budgets, teams are getting more competitive and more balanced throughout the competition. To win three Champions Cups in a row, it's pretty special."

The final was Hayman's final European appearance for Toulon. He was joined in retirement at the end of the season by former Springbok lock Bakkies Botha and Williams but despite the departure of the vastly experienced forwards, Hayman was confident Le Rouge et Noir could challenge for even more European honours. "There's three or four older fellas moving on, but they are being replaced and it will be up to the guys who are staying to move things forward."

EUROPEAN RUGBY CHAMPIONS CUP 2014–15 RESULTS

ROUND ONE

17 October, 2014
Harlequins 25 Castres 9

18 October, 2014
Sale 26 Munster 27 | Racing Métro 20 Northampton 11
Glasgow 37 Bath 10 | Leicester 25 Ulster 18
Saracens 30 Clermont Auvergne 23

19 October, 2014
Ospreys 42 Treviso 7 | Toulon 28 Scarlets 18
Toulouse 30 Montpellier 23 | Leinster 25 Wasps 20

ROUND TWO

24 October, 2014
Munster 14 Saracens 3

25 October, 2014
Ulster 13 Toulon 23 | Northampton 34 Ospreys 6
Bath 19 Toulouse 21 | Scarlets 15 Leicester 3
Montpellier 13 Glasgow 15

26 October, 2014
Castres 16 Leinster 21 | Treviso 10 Racing Métro 26
Clermont Auvergne 35 Sale 3 | Wasps 16 Harlequins 23

ROUND THREE

5 December, 2014	
Montpellier 5 **Bath** 30	

6 December, 2014	
Treviso 15 **Northampton** 38	Munster 9 **Clermont Auvergne** 16
Sale 15 **Saracens** 19	**Ulster** 24 Scarlets 9
Ospreys 19 Racing Métro 19	

7 December, 2014	
Castres 17 **Wasps** 32	**Toulouse** 19 Glasgow 11
Harlequins 24 Leinster 18	**Leicester** 25 Toulon 21

ROUND FOUR

12 December, 2014	
Bath 32 Montpellier 12	

13 December, 2014	
Glasgow 9 **Toulouse** 12	**Racing Métro** 18 Ospreys 14
Northampton 67 Treviso 0	**Saracens** 28 Sale 15
Toulon 23 Leicester 8	**Leinster** 14 Harlequins 13

14 December, 2014	
Wasps 44 Castres 17	**Scarlets** 22 Ulster 13
Clermont Auvergne 26 Munster 19	

ROUND FIVE

16 January, 2015	
Leicester 40 Scarlets 23	

17 January, 2015	
Saracens 33 Munster 10	Sale 13 **Clermont Auvergne** 22
Toulon 60 Ulster 22	Harlequins 3 **Wasps** 23
Leinster 50 Castres 8	

18 January, 2015	
Glasgow 21 Montpellier 10	Ospreys 9 **Northampton** 20
Toulouse 18 **Bath** 35	**Racing Métro** 53 Treviso 7

ROUND SIX

24 January, 2015	
Castres 19 **Harlequins** 47	**Northampton** 8 **Racing Métro** 32
Wasps 20 **Leinster** 20	**Scarlets** 3 **Toulon** 26
Treviso 23 **Ospreys** 20	**Ulster** 26 **Leicester** 7
25 January, 2015	
Bath 20 **Glasgow** 15	**Clermont Auvergne** 18 **Saracens** 6
Montpellier 27 **Toulouse** 26	**Munster** 65 **Sale** 10

POOL TABLES

POOL ONE

	P	W	D	L	F	A	BP	PTS
Clermont	6	5	0	1	140	80	2	22
Saracens	6	4	0	2	119	95	1	17
Munster	6	3	0	3	144	114	3	15
Sale	6	0	0	6	82	196	2	2

POOL TWO

	P	W	D	L	F	A	BP	PTS
Leinster	6	4	1	1	148	101	2	20
Wasps	6	3	1	2	155	105	4	18
Harlequins	6	4	0	2	135	99	2	18
Castres	6	0	0	6	86	219	1	1

POOL THREE

	P	W	D	L	F	A	BP	PTS
Toulon	6	5	0	1	181	89	2	22
Leicester	6	3	0	3	108	126	1	13
Ulster	6	2	0	4	116	146	4	12
Scarlets	6	2	0	4	90	134	0	8

POOL FOUR

	P	W	D	L	F	A	BP	PTS
Bath	6	4	0	2	146	108	3	19
Toulouse	6	4	0	2	126	124	1	17
Glasgow	6	3	0	3	108	84	3	15
Montpellier	6	1	0	5	90	154	2	6

POOL FIVE

	P	W	D	L	F	A	BP	PTS
Racing Métro	6	5	1	0	168	69	2	24
Northampton	6	4	0	2	178	82	3	19
Ospreys	6	1	1	4	110	121	3	9
Treviso	6	1	0	5	62	246	0	4

QUARTER-FINALS

4 April, 2015	
Leinster 18 **Bath** 15	**Clermont Auvergne** 37 **Northampton** 5
5 April, 2015	
Racing Métro 11 **Saracens** 12	**Toulon** 32 **Wasps** 18

18 April, Stade Geoffroy-Guichard, Saint-Étienne

CLERMONT AUVERGNE 13 (1G 2PG) SARACENS 9 (2PG 1DG)

CLERMONT AUVERGNE: N Abendanon; N Niakaitaci, J Davies, W Fofana, N Nalaga; B James, L Radoslavjevic; V Debaty, B Kayser, D Zirakashvili, J Cudmore, S Vahaamahina, J Bonnaire, J Bardy, D Chouly (captain)

SUBSTITUTIONS: J Pierre for Cudmore (temp 22–32 mins); M Parra for Radoslavjevic (54 mins); A Lapandry for Bardy (55 mins); J Ulugia for Kayser (66 mins); A Rougerie for Nalaga (74 mins)

SCORERS: *Try*: Fofana *Conversion*: James *Penalty Goals*: James (2)

SARACENS: A Goode; C Ashton, M Bosch, B Barritt (captain), C Wyles; C Hodgson, R Wigglesworth; M Vunipola, J George, P du Plessis, G Kruis, J Hamilton, M Itoje, J Burger, B Vunipola

SUBSTITUTIONS: S Brits for George (50 mins); J Johnston for du Plessis (50 mins); J Wray for Hamilton (55 mins); O Farrell for Hodgson (57 mins); N de Kock for Wigglesworth (68 mins); D Strettle for Wyles (72 mins); R Gill for M Vunipola (72 mins); K Brown for Burger (74 mins)

SCORERS: *Penalty Goals*: Hodgson, Farrell *Drop Goal*: Farrell

REFEREE: G Clancy (Ireland)

19 April, Stade Vélodrome, Marseille

TOULON 25 (1G 6PG) LEINSTER 20 (1T 5PG) AET

Toulon: L Halfpenny; D Armitage, M Bastareaud, M Giteau, B Habana; F Michalak, S Tillous-Borde; X Chiocci, G Guirado, C Hayman (captain), B Botha, A Williams, J Smith, JM Fernández Lobbe, C Masoe

SUBSTITUTIONS: S Armitage for Smith (35 mins); R Wulf for Michalak (48 mins); A Menini for Chiocci (51 mins); J Suta for Botha (61 mins); J-C Orioli for Guirado (68 mins); L Chilachava for Hayman (75 mins); D Mitchell for Habana (91 mins)

SCORERS: *Try*: Habana *Conversion*: Halfpenny *Penalty Goals*: Halfpenny (6)

YELLOW CARD: A Williams (85 mins)

LEINSTER: R Kearney; F McFadden, B Te'o, I Madigan, L Fitzgerald; J Gopperth, I Boss; C Healy, S Cronin, M Ross, D Toner, M McCarthy, J Murphy, S O'Brien, J Heaslip (captain)

SUBSTITUTIONS: M Moore for Ross (57 mins); Z Kirchner for McFadden (61 mins); E Reddan for Boss (66 mins); J McGrath for Healy (66 mins); R Strauss for Cronin (66 mins); G D'Arcy for Gopperth (90 mins); B Marshall for M McCarthy (91 mins)

SCORERS: *Try*: O'Brien *Penalty Goals*: Madigan (5)

REFEREE: W Barnes (England)

CLERMONT AUVERGNE 18 (1G 1T 2PG) TOULON 24 (1G 1T 4PG)

CLERMONT AUVERGNE: N Abendanon; N Nakaitaci, J Davies, W Fofana, N Nalaga; C Lopez, M Parra; V Debaty, B Kayser, D Zirakashvili, J Cudmore, S Vahaamahina, J Bonnaire, D Chouly (captain), F Lee

SUBSTITUTIONS: J Pierre for Cudmore (temp 10–16 & 57–65 mins); T Domingo for Debaty (47 mins); A Rougerie for Nalaga (54 mins); J Bardy for Lee (54 mins); L Radoslavejevic for Parra (56 mins); J Ulugia for Kayser (63 mins); C Ric for Zirakashvili (66 mins); M Delany for Nakaitaci (67 mins)

SCORERS: *Tries*: Fofana, Abendanon *Conversion*: Lopez *Penalty Goals*: Lopez (2)

TOULON: L Halfpenny; D Mitchell, M Bastareaud, JM Hernández, B Habana; M Giteau, S Tillous-Borde; X Chiocci, G Guirado, C Hayman (captain), B Botha, A Williams, J Smith, S Armitage, C Masoe

SUBSTITUTIONS: R Taofifenua for Botha (47 mins); A Menini for Chiocci (48 mins); JM Fernández Lobbe for Smith (58 mins); J-C Orioli for Guirado (63 mins); L Chilachava for Hayman (temp 63–76 mins); R Wulf for Hernandez (66 mins)

SCORERS: Tries: Bastareaud, Mitchell *Conversion*: Halfpenny *Penalty Goals*: Halfpenny (4)

REFEREE: N Owens (Wales)

EUROPEAN CHAMPIONS CUP

CONCUSSION
RECOGNISE
+ REMOVE

#RECOGNISEANDREMOVE

DOWNLOAD THE OFFICIAL WORLD RUGBY
CONCUSSION MANAGEMENT APP
GO TO
PLAYERWELFARE.WORLDRUGBY.ORG

WORLD
RUGBY™

GLOUCESTER SURVIVE EDINBURGH FIGHT-BACK

By Iain Spragg

Captain Billy Twelvetrees leads Gloucester's celebrations after their Challenge Cup victory over Edinburgh.

The new-look European Rugby Challenge Cup saw Gloucester overcome Edinburgh and their own indiscipline to be crowned champions as the Cherry and Whites emerged 19–13 winners at the Twickenham Stoop in a nerve-wracking conclusion to the second tier tournament.

Victory presented the English club with its first silverware since they had triumphed in the old Challenge Cup nine years earlier, but Gloucester almost contrived to snatch defeat from the jaws of victory in the final, finishing the contest with 14 men after having been briefly reduced to 13 players during the second half.

626

The first Scottish side to reach a European final, Edinburgh pressed home their numerical advantage to move to within a converted try of glory, but Gloucester were able to hold on to become the fourth Premiership team to record multiple Challenge Cup successes.

Gloucester reached the knockout stages with six wins from six in Pool Five and although Edinburgh did suffer one defeat in Pool Four en route to the quarter-final, they both qualified for the last eight in convincing style.

The Cherry and Whites subsequently dispatched Connacht (14–7) and Exeter Chiefs (30–19) to maintain their charge, while Edinburgh overcame a stubborn London Irish side 23–18 before scoring five tries in a 45–16 demolition of the Dragons in the last four.

Two weeks later the two sides convened at The Stoop for the final and although the match yielded a modest two tries, there was no shortage of drama as Gloucester ultimately clung on for victory.

An early penalty from scrum-half Sam Hidalgo-Clyne for Alan Solomons' PRO12 side was cancelled out by his opposite number and former Edinburgh player Greig Laidlaw six minutes later, before a break from wing Jonny May allowed captain Billy Twelvetrees to take a scoring pass on the Edinburgh 22 and outpace the cover. Laidlaw converted and Gloucester had established a seven-point advantage.

A 25th minute yellow card for second-row Anton Bresler did not help the Edinburgh cause but they held out during his 10-minute absence and, after Hidalgo-Clyne and Laidlaw had exchanged penalties once again, Gloucester went in 13–6 in front at half-time.

Two further three-pointers from Laidlaw after the break put the English side in the driving seat at 19–6, but an eight-minute spell of Gloucester indiscipline threatened to undo all their good work.

First flanker Ross Moriarty saw yellow for foul play and then centre Bill Meakes was sent off for a high tackle. To rub salt into the wound, Edinburgh scored a try through Scotland hooker Ross Ford while Gloucester were reduced to 13 men, and after Hidalgo-Clyne's conversion sailed over the deficit was only six points.

Moriaty's return to the fray did little to quell Edinburgh's increasing momentum, but the Cherry and Whites' defence stood firm until referee Jérôme Garcès blew for full-time.

"This is a huge achievement because it is not something we talked about doing at the start of the season when we had 25 new players and a completely new coaching team," said Gloucester director of rugby David Humphreys. "At that stage all we talked about was improving week in, week out, so that by the end of the season we were a better side. It has been a bit of a rollercoaster this season."

EUROPEAN RUGBY CHALLENGE CUP
2014–15 RESULTS

ROUND ONE

16 October, 2014	
Gloucester 55 Brive 0	
17 October, 2014	
Bordeaux 13 Edinburgh 15	Newcastle 43 Bucharest 19
18 October, 2014	
Lyon 28 London Welsh 18	Connacht 48 La Rochelle 12
Cardiff 37 Grenoble 14	Bayonne 30 Exeter 24
Zebre 24 Oyonnax 33	Stade Français 22 Dragons 38
19 October, 2014	
London Irish 70 Rovigo 14	

ROUND TWO

23 October, 2014	
London Welsh 20 Bordeaux 52	
24 October, 2014	
Brive 21 Zebre 26	Dragons 26 Newcastle 30
Grenoble 15 London Irish 25	Edinburgh 25 Lyon 17
La Rochelle 25 Bayonne 13	
25 October, 2014	
Bucharest 9 Stade Français 13	Exeter 33 Connacht 13
Rovigo 18 Cardiff 33	Oyonnax 15 Gloucester 25

ROUND THREE

4 December, 2014	
La Rochelle 10 Exeter 36	
5 December, 2014	
Brive 22 Oyonnax 30	Newcastle 30 Stade Français 23
Grenoble 68 Rovigo 10	
6 December, 2014	
Bucharest 10 Dragons 37	Connacht 42 Bayonne 19
Cardiff 24 London Irish 14	Bordeaux 37 Lyon 29
7 December, 2014	
Edinburgh 25 London Welsh 13	Gloucester 35 Zebre 10

EUROPEAN CHALLENGE CUP

ROUND FOUR

11 December, 2014

Stade Français 31 **Newcastle** 24

12 December, 2014

Lyon 37 **Bordeaux** 28   **Dragons** 69 **Bucharest** 17

13 December, 2014

Rovigo 17 **Grenoble** 20   **Zebre** 16 **Gloucester** 32

Exeter 41 **La Rochelle** 17   **Oyonnax** 22 **Brive** 17

London Irish 34 **Cardiff** 23   **Bayonne** 27 **Connacht** 29

14 December, 2014

London Welsh 6 **Edinburgh** 24

ROUND FIVE

16 January, 2015

Cardiff 104 **Rovigo** 12   **Bordeaux** 26 **London Welsh** 3

17 January, 2015

Stade Français 47 **Bucharest** 12   **Newcastle** 29 **Dragons** 40

Gloucester 33 **Oyonnax** 3   **Bayonne** 14 **La Rochelle** 0

London Irish 43 **Grenoble** 41   **Lyon** 21 **Edinburgh** 19

Zebre 23 **Brive** 13

18 January, 2015

Connacht 24 **Exeter** 33

ROUND SIX

22 January, 2015

Brive 20 **Gloucester** 31   **Oyonnax** 20 **Zebre** 3

23 January, 2015

Edinburgh 38 **Bordeaux** 20

24 January, 2015

Grenoble 3 **Cardiff** 28   **Dragons** 30 **Stade Français** 19

Rovigo 6 **London Irish** 34   **Exeter** 45 **Bayonne** 3

Bucharest 10 **Newcastle** 52   **La Rochelle** 20 **Connacht** 30

25 January, 2015

London Welsh 12 **Lyon** 17

FINAL TABLES

ELITE COMPETITIONS

POOL ONE

	P	W	D	L	F	A	BP	PTS
London Irish	6	5	0	1	220	123	4	24
Cardiff Blues	6	5	0	1	249	95	4	24
Grenoble	6	2	0	4	161	160	4	12
Rovigo	6	0	0	6	77	329	1	1

POOL TWO

	P	W	D	L	F	A	BP	PTS
Exeter Chiefs	6	5	0	1	212	97	5	25
Connacht	6	4	0	2	186	144	4	20
Bayonne	6	2	0	4	106	165	1	9
La Rochelle	6	1	0	5	84	182	0	4

POOL THREE

	P	W	D	L	F	A	BP	PTS
Dragons	6	5	0	1	240	127	5	25
Newcastle	6	4	0	2	208	149	5	21
Stade Français	6	3	0	3	155	143	3	15
Bucharest	6	0	0	6	77	261	1	1

POOL FOUR

	P	W	D	L	F	A	BP	PTS
Edinburgh	6	5	0	1	146	90	2	22
Lyon	6	4	0	2	149	139	2	18
Bordeaux	6	3	0	3	176	142	4	16
London Welsh	6	0	0	6	72	172	1	1

POOL FIVE

	P	W	D	L	F	A	BP	PTS
Gloucester	6	6	0	0	211	64	5	29
Oyonnax	6	4	0	2	123	124	0	16
Zebre	6	2	0	4	102	154	0	8
Brive	6	0	0	6	93	187	2	2

QUARTER-FINALS

3 April, 2015

Gloucester 14 **Connacht** 7

4 April, 2015

Dragons 25 **Cardiff Blues** 21   **Exeter Chiefs** 48 **Newcastle Falcons** 13

5 April, 2015

London Irish 18 **Edinburgh** 23

SEMI-FINALS

17 April, Murrayfield, Edinburgh

EDINBURGH 45 (4G 1T 4PG) DRAGONS 16 (1G 3PG)

EDINBURGH: J Cuthbert; D Fife, S Beard, A Strauss, T Visser; P Burleigh, S Hidalgo-Clyne; A Dickinson, R Ford, WP Nel, A Bresler, B Toolis, S McInally, R Grant, M Coman (captain)

SUBSTITUTIONS: T Brown for Cuthbert (50 mins); F McKenzie for Bresler (69 mins); C du Preez for McInally (69 mins); N Fowles for Hidalgo-Clyne (72 mins); R Sutherland for Dickinson (73 mins); T Heathcote for Beard (75 mins); J Andress for Nel (75 mins)

SCORERS: *Tries:* McInally, Visser, Toolis, Hidalgo-Clyne, Fife *Conversions:* Hidalgo-Clyne (4) *Penalty Goals:* Hidalgo-Clyne (4)

DRAGONS: J Tovey; T Prydie, T Morgan, J Dixon, H Amos; D Jones, J Evans; B Harris, T Rhys Thomas (captain), D Way, J Thomas, C Hill, N Crosswell, J Benjamin, T Faletau

SUBSTITUTIONS: P Price for Way (47 mins); M Screech for Hill (62 mins); GR Jones for Tovey (62 mins); I Gough for Cresswell (66 mins); A Hewitt for Prydie (72 mins); L Jones for Evans (72 mins); L Fairbrother for Harris (74 mins); R Buckle for Benjamin (75 mins)

SCORERS: *Try:* Harris *Conversion:* D Jones *Penalty Goals:* D Jones (3)

YELLOW CARDS: T Faletau (9 mins), Evans (51 mins), Rhys Thomas (72 mins)

REFEREE: JP Doyle (England)

18 April, Kingsholm, Gloucester

GLOUCESTER 30 (3G 3PG) EXETER 19 (1G 4PG)

GLOUCESTER: C Sharples; J May, B Meakes, B Twelvetrees (captain), H Purdy; J Hook, G Laidlaw; N Wood, R Hibbard, J Afoa, T Savage, M Galarza, S Kalamafoni, M Kvesic, G Evans

SUBSTITUTIONS: R Moriarty for Evans (10 mins); D Murphy for Wood (61 mins); D Dawidiuk for Hibbard (77 mins)

SCORERS: *Tries:* Meakes, Savage, May *Conversions:* Laidlaw (3) *Penalty Goals:* Laidlaw (2), Hook

EXETER CHIEFS: P Dollman; I Whitten, J Nowell, S Hill, M Jess; H Slade, W Chudley; B Moon, J Yeandle, T Francis, D Mumm (captain), M Lees, D Ewers, K Horstmann, T Waldrom

SUBSTITUTIONS: T James for Nowell (temp 36–39 mins); James for Dollman (40 mins); A Brown for Francis (60 mins); C Rimmer for Moon (66 mins); T Johnson for Horstmann (71 mins); G Steenson for Slade (72 mins); E Taione for Yeandle (72 mins)

SCORERS: *Try:* Taione *Conversion:* Steenson *Penalty Goals:* Slade (4)

REFEREE: J Lacey (Ireland)

FINAL

1 May, Twickenham Stoop, London

EDINBURGH 13 (1G 2PG) GLOUCESTER 19 (1G 4PG)

EDINBURGH: G Tonks; D Fife, S Beard, A Strauss, T Visser; P Burleigh, S Hidalgo-Clyne; A Dickinson, R Ford, W P Nel, A Bresler, B Toolis, M Coman (captain), R Grant, C du Preez

SUBSTITUTIONS: T Brown for Tonks (40 mins); F McKenzie for Bresler (49 mins); S McInally for Coman (58 mins); H Watson for Grant (58 mins); T Heathcote for Beard (temp 63–67 mins)

SCORERS: *Try:* Ford *Conversion:* Hidalgo-Clyne *Penalty Goals:* Hidalgo-Clyne (2)

YELLOW CARD: A Bresler (25 mins)

GLOUCESTER: C Sharples; J May, B Meakes, B Twelvetrees (captain), H Purdy; J Hook, G Laidlaw; N Wood, R Hibbard, J Afoa, T Savage, T Palmer, R Moriarty, M Kvesic, G Evans

SUBSTITUTIONS: M Galarza for Palmer (40 mins); Y Thomas for Wood (47 mins); J Rowan for Evans (temp 69–73 mins); D Dawidiuk for Hibbard (71 mins)

SCORERS: *Try:* Twelvetrees *Conversion:* Laidlaw *Penalty Goals:* Laidlaw (4)

YELLOW CARD: R Moriarty (56 mins)

RED CARD: B Meakes (63 mins)

REFEREE: J Garcès (France)

SUPERUGBY

MAIDEN TITLE A SURREAL EXPERIENCE

By Highlanders co-captain Nasi Manu

Getty Images

Highlanders co-captains Nasi Manu and Ben Smith lift the Super Rugby trophy after victory over the Hurricanes in Wellington.

It **would be** fair to say the Highlanders began the Super Rugby season as underdogs. We had no shortage of self-belief within the squad and the hunger to do well but we knew we weren't a team of superstars and that other sides had a better recent track record than us in the competition.

It didn't worry us. We had a common goal, a desire to improve together and we initially approached the season on a week-by-week, match-by-match basis. We definitely were not there to make up the numbers but could I say, hand on heart, we had set our sights on the title at the start of the year? Maybe not.

This made our victory in the final against the Hurricanes in Wellington a surreal experience. I can remember hearing the final whistle and feeling in a state of shock, not really being able to take in what had happened and what we had just achieved. It was only a couple of days later with the trophy on the victory parade through Dunedin, in front of thousands of our fans, that it all began to properly sink in. We had exceeded a lot of people's expectations and for the first time the Highlanders were champions.

There was no big secret to our success. We've always been an honest, hard-working team full of good players who apply themselves and I think that's what got us over the line in the end. The way we grew together as the season went on was important and we peaked at the right time, going into the knockout stages with confidence and a collective determination.

There were obviously setbacks along the way and we started the year with a 26–20 loss to the Crusaders in Dunedin. We had seven new players in the squad that day and it was maybe inevitable it would take time for the new boys to settle in – but we didn't panic. We had three wins on the bounce after that and the belief grew as we got stronger and stronger.

There wasn't a single, magic moment when I thought 'we're going to be champions', but I remember beating the Cheetahs and the Force on the road in May and then getting a 36–9 win against the Chiefs in Invercargill and thinking we were in really good shape. Like I said before, I felt we peaked at just the right time and I started to get the sense something special could be right around the corner.

We played the Chiefs again in the quarter-finals to set up a semi-final against the champions, the Waratahs, and everyone outside the camp had pretty low expectations of us coming through the game over in Australia, even though we had beaten them earlier in the year.

The build-up to the match was superb. I could sense a real hunger in the squad, the atmosphere among the boys was spot on and before the game Jamie Joseph gave the most memorable speech I've ever heard from a coach. We had a team meeting and he asked how many of us had received messages and texts from family and friends telling us how proud they were of us no matter what happened on Saturday. We all nodded, and Jamie laughed and said, "They're already happy but they don't believe you can win." We then all laughed because we knew exactly what he was getting at, that even our families were writing us off. He didn't need to say anything else.

We won the match 35–17 in Sydney because we got our game management just right. Our line speed was superb, we ran their big forwards around the park and we turned them with our kicking. We outscored the champions five tries to one, which shows we took our chances, and we could now start to think about the final.

There were two big talking points in the build-up to the game against the Canes. The first was the fact that the two teams in the final were the only New Zealand sides to have never won the Super Rugby title. The press boys were pretty keen to ask us about that, whether it put extra pressure on us, but I have to admit we just played dumb and said we hadn't given it any thought. It wasn't keeping me awake at night but of course I knew victory would give one of us a first ever title.

There was also a lot made of our two losses to the Canes in the regular season, particularly our 56–20 hammering in Napier the month before. It was weird because we never mentioned those games inside the squad and I think if we had gone over the details of what had gone wrong, it could have given us an inferiority complex. As it was, every individual player was in their own world, focusing on the job they had to do, and we didn't dwell on it. It might sound hard to believe but the losses really weren't a factor.

You can dissect the final in minute detail if you like, looking at all the statistics and the rest of it, but for me the deciding factor was that we handled the pressure better. I'm not saying the Canes choked but I felt the two teams were evenly matched in most areas and what got us over the line was the way we dealt with the crunch moments. Maybe that calmness came from being the underdogs but whatever it was, I felt we were in control.

Lifting the trophy was the climax of four years of hard work from Jamie Joseph and the rest of the coaching staff. Jamie can be a very intimidating figure but he always had a clear vision of where he wanted to take the Highlanders and from the moment in 2013 when he decided to change the culture of the squad, forget about signing star players and get back to basics, we were on an incredible journey.

Jamie has always known what he wants and in his case it is always more and then more from his players. I always enjoyed a good relationship with him but if you don't give everything he wants in terms of preparation and commitment, he leaves you in no doubt that he's not happy. As a player, you can never short-change him. He's been mentioned as a possible head coach of the All Blacks in the future and while it's not for me to get involved in all the politics, Jamie definitely has the ability to work at that level in the game.

I was asked many times during the season about the co-captaincy set-up at the Highlanders and how the relationship with Ben Smith worked, but it was a lot less complicated than I think some people imagined. It's not a new innovation – the Chiefs had two captains in 2013 when they became champions – and obviously it worked well for us as well.

It was a simple arrangement really. One week would be 'my week' in which I'd deal with the media and any other off-pitch stuff and captain the side at the weekend, and the following week it would be Ben's turn. Every week started with a management meeting with the coaching staff, Ben and I and some other senior players, and then whoever was captain for the week would just get on with it.

What I think really worked well is that alternating the captaincy duties allowed both of us to stay fresher as individual players. It was not a case of being silent in the dressing room when it wasn't 'my week' but a few days without leadership responsibilities, taking a step back from it all, does help to recharge the batteries.

After six seasons of Super Rugby with the club, the final was my last game for the Highlanders before heading to the northern hemisphere to play for Edinburgh. I'd signed my deal with Edinburgh earlier in the year, so I knew it was my last season, and there was a mix of emotions after the game when the reality of heading off to Europe hit.

Of course it was great to say goodbye on such a high but it was also tough to leave after what we had achieved. To be honest, I was a bit scared about leaving New Zealand even before the season had started but I also wanted to experience something different and the decision was made. Some people suggested I was mad to leave when I had the chance to defend the title with the team but plenty of great players never lift the trophy once, so I'm happy with what I achieved.

Super Rugby will have a new look in 2016 with the addition of a team from Argentina and one from Japan, making it 18 sides in the tournament in total. I support the expansion because no competition can afford to stand still but I hope the organisers get things right in terms of the fixture list. Not all 18 teams will play each other and it's important everybody's travel commitments and quality of opposition are comparable. The new format might take a couple of years to settle down but I'm looking forward to seeing what happens.

SUPER RUGBY 2015 RESULTS

13 February: **Lions** 8 **Hurricanes** 22, **Brumbies** 47 **Reds** 3, **Crusaders** 10 **Rebels** 20. 14 February: **Bulls** 17 **Stormers** 29, **Sharks** 29 **Cheetahs** 35, **Blues** 18 **Chiefs** 23. 15 February: **Waratahs** 13 **Force** 25. 20 February: **Chiefs** 19 **Brumbies** 17, **Rebels** 28 **Waratahs** 38, **Bulls** 13 **Hurricanes** 17. 21 February: **Highlanders** 20 **Crusaders** 26, **Reds** 18 **Force** 6, **Stormers** 27 **Blues** 16, **Sharks** 29 **Lions** 12. 27 February: **Highlanders** 20 **Reds** 13, **Force** 13 **Hurricanes** 42, **Cheetahs** 25 **Blues** 24. 28 February: **Chiefs** 40 **Crusaders** 16, **Rebels** 15 **Brumbies** 20, **Bulls** 43 **Sharks** 35, **Lions** 19 **Stormers** 22. 6 March: **Chiefs** 17 **Highlanders** 20, **Brumbies** 27 **Force** 15. 7 March: **Blues** 10 **Lions** 13, **Reds** 5 **Waratahs** 23, **Cheetahs** 20 **Bulls** 39, **Stormers** 29 **Sharks** 13. 13 March: 13 March: **Hurricanes** 30 **Blues** 23, **Force** 17 **Rebels** 21. 14 March: **Crusaders** 34 **Lions** 6, **Highlanders** 26 **Waratahs** 19, **Reds** 0 **Brumbies** 29, **Stormers** 19 **Chiefs** 28, **Cheetahs** 10 **Sharks** 27. 20 March: **Highlanders** 13 **Hurricanes** 20, **Rebels** 16 **Lions** 20. 21 March: **Crusaders** 57 **Cheetahs** 14, **Bulls** 25 **Force** 24, **Sharks** 12 **Chiefs** 11. 22 March: **Waratahs** 28 **Brumbies** 13. 27 March: **Hurricanes** 36 **Rebels** 12, **Reds** 17 **Lions** 18. 28 March: **Chiefs** 37 **Cheetahs** 27, **Highlanders** 39 **Stormers** 21, **Waratahs** 23 **Blues** 11, **Sharks** 15 **Force** 9, **Bulls** 31 **Crusaders** 19. 3 April: **Hurricanes** 25 **Stormers** 20, **Rebels** 23 **Reds** 15. 4 April: **Chiefs** 23 **Blues** 16, **Brumbies** 20 **Cheetahs** 3, **Sharks** 10 **Crusaders** 52, **Lions** 22 **Bulls** 18. 10 April: **Blues** 16 **Brumbies** 14. 11 April: **Crusaders** 20 **Highlanders** 25, **Waratahs** 18 **Stormers** 32, **Force** 15 **Cheetahs** 24, **Lions** 23 **Sharks** 21, **Bulls** 43 **Reds** 22. 17 April: **Crusaders** 9 **Chiefs** 26. 18 April: **Hurricanes** 24 **Waratahs** 29, **Highlanders** 30 **Blues** 24, **Brumbies** 8 **Rebels** 13, **Force** 6 **Stormers** 13, **Sharks** 10 **Bulls** 17, **Cheetahs** 17 **Reds** 18. 24 April: **Chiefs** 35 **Force** 27, **Brumbies** 31 **Highlanders** 18. 25 April: **Crusaders** 29 **Blues** 15, **Waratahs** 18 **Rebels** 16, **Lions** 34 **Cheetahs** 29, **Stormers** 15 **Bulls** 13. 26 April: **Reds** 19 **Hurricanes** 35. 1 May: **Highlanders** 48 **Sharks** 15, **Brumbies** 10 **Waratahs** 13. 2 May: **Blues** 41 **Force** 24, **Hurricanes** 29 **Crusaders** 23, **Rebels** 16 **Chiefs** 15, **Cheetahs** 25 **Stormers** 17, **Bulls** 35 **Lions** 33. 8 May: **Crusaders** 58 **Reds** 17, **Rebels** 42 **Blues** 22. 9 May: **Hurricanes** 32 **Sharks** 24, **Force** 18 **Waratahs** 11, **Lions** 28 **Highlanders** 23, **Stormers** 25 **Brumbies** 24. 15 May: **Blues** 23 **Bulls** 18, **Reds** 46 **Rebels** 29. 16 May: **Hurricanes** 22 **Chiefs** 18, **Waratahs** 33 **Sharks** 18, **Lions** 20 **Brumbies** 30, **Cheetahs** 24 **Highlanders** 45. 22 May: **Chiefs** 34 **Bulls** 20, **Reds** 14 **Sharks** 21. 23 May: **Blues** 5 **Hurricanes** 29, **Waratahs** 32 **Crusaders** 22, **Force** 3 **Highlanders** 23, **Cheetahs** 17 **Lions** 40, **Stormers** 31 **Rebels** 15. 29 May: **Crusaders** 35 **Hurricanes** 18, **Brumbies** 22 **Bulls** 16, **Sharks** 25 **Rebels** 21. 30 May: **Highlanders** 36 **Chiefs** 9, **Force** 10 **Reds** 32, **Stormers** 42 **Cheetahs** 12, **Lions** 27 **Waratahs** 22. 5 June: **Hurricanes** 56 **Highlanders** 20, **Force** 20 **Brumbies** 33. 6 June: **Rebels** 21 **Bulls** 20, **Blues** 11 **Crusaders** 34, **Reds** 3 **Chiefs** 24, **Cheetahs** 33 **Waratahs** 58, **Stormers** 19 **Lions** 19. 12 June: **Blues** 7 **Highlanders** 44, **Rebels** 11 **Force** 13. 13 June: **Brumbies** 24 **Crusaders** 37, **Chiefs** 13 **Hurricanes** 21, **Waratahs** 31 **Reds** 5, **Bulls** 29 **Cheetahs** 42, **Sharks** 34 **Stormers** 12.

FINAL TABLE

	P	W	D	L	F	A	BP	PTS
Hurricanes	16	14	0	2	458	288	10	66
Waratahs	16	11	0	5	409	313	8	52
Stormers	16	10	1	5	373	323	3	45
Highlanders	16	11	0	5	450	333	9	53
Chiefs	16	10	0	6	372	299	8	48
Brumbies	16	9	0	7	369	261	11	47
Crusaders	16	9	0	7	481	338	10	46
Lions	16	9	1	6	342	364	4	42
Bulls	16	7	0	9	397	388	10	38
Rebels	16	7	0	9	319	354	8	36
Sharks	16	7	0	9	338	401	6	34
Cheetahs	16	5	0	11	357	531	6	26
Reds	16	4	0	12	247	434	6	22
Blues	16	3	0	13	282	428	8	20
Force	16	3	0	13	245	384	7	19

PLAY-OFFS

20 June, 2015	
Highlanders 24 **Chiefs** 14	**Stormers** 19 **Brumbies** 39

27 June, Westpac Stadium, Wellington

HURRICANES 29 (3G 1T 1PG) BRUMBIES 9 (3PG)

HURRICANES: J Marshall; N Milner-Skudder, C Smith (capt), M Nonu, J Savea; B Barrett, TJ Perenara; R Goodes, D Coles, B Franks, J Thrush, J Broadhurst, B Shields, A Savea, V Vito

SUBSTITUTIONS: M Proctor for Milner-Skudder (40 mins); B Thomson for A Savea (49 mins); C Eves for Goodes (49 mins); J Toomaga-Allen for Franks (65 mins); R Lee-Lo for Nonu (75 mins); B Mitchell for Coles (75 mins); C Smylie for Perenara (75 mins); M Abbott for Broadhurst

SCORERS: *Tries*: J Savea, Perenara, A Savea, Proctor *Conversions*: Barrett, Proctor (2) *Penalty Goal*: Marshall

BRUMBIES: J Mogg; L Taliauli, T Kuridrani, M Toomua, J Tomane; C Leali'ifano, N White; S Sio, S Moore (capt), B Alexander, R Arnold, B Enever, S Fardy, D Pocock, I Vaea

SUBSTITUTIONS: R Coleman for Leali'ifano (temp 36–40 mins); J Smiler for Arnold (44 mins); N Ah Wong for Taliauli (56 mins); J Butler for Vaea (65 mins); R Smith for Alexander (65 mins); A Alaalatoa for Sio (65 mins); J Mann-Rea for Moore (71 mins); R Coleman for Mogg (75 mins); M Dowsett for White (75 mins)

SCORERS: *Penalty Goals*: Mogg, Leali'ifano (2)

REFEREE: G Jackson (New Zealand)

27 June, Allianz Stadium, Sydney

WARATAHS 17 (1T 4PG) HIGHLANDERS 35 (2G 3T 1PG 1DG)

WARATAHS: I Folau; T Naiyaravoro, A Ashley-Cooper, M Carraro, R Horne; B Foley, N Phipps; B Robinson, T Polota-Nau, S Kepu, W Skelton, D Dennis (capt), J Potgieter, M Hooper, W Palu

SUBSTITUTIONS: P Betham for Carraro (55 mins); S Hoiles for Palu (61 mins); T Latu for Polota-Nau (62 mins); P Ryan for Kepu (67 mins); B McKibbin for Phipps (71 mins); M Chapman for Dennis (71 mins); J Lance for Horne (76 mins)

SCORERS: *Try*: Horne *Penalty Goals*: Foley (4)

YELLOW CARD: J Potgieter (57 mins)

HIGHLANDERS: B Smith (capt); W Naholo, M Fekitoa, R Buckman, P Osborne; L Sopoaga, A Smith; B Edmonds, L Coltman, J Hohneck, A Ainley, M Reddish, E Dixon, J Lentjes, N Manu

SUBSTITUTIONS: T Renata for Sopoaga (temp 12–21 mins); A Dixon for Coltman (50 mins); S Christie for Lentjes (50 mins); D Leinert-Brown for Edmonds (61 mins); G Evans for Manu (69 mins); J Wheeler for Ainley (71 mins); R Geldenhuys for Hohneck (71 mins); F Tanaka for A Smith (80 mins); Renata for Sopoaga (80 mins)

SCORERS: *Tries*: A Smith, Buckman, Naholo, Penalty Try, Osborne *Conversions*: Sopoaga (2) *Penalty Goals*: Sopoaga *Drop Goal*: Sopoaga

REFEREE: C Joubert (South Africa)

SUPER RUGBY

FINAL

HURRICANES 14 (1T 3PG) HIGHLANDERS 21 (1G 1T 2PG 1DG)

HURRICANES: J Marshall; N Milner-Skudder, C Smith (capt), M Nonu, J Savea; B Barrett, TJ Perenara; R Goodes, D Coles, B Franks, J Thrush, J Broadhurst, B Shields, C Gibbins, V Vito

SUBSTITUTIONS: C Eves for Goodes (40 mins); J Toomaga-Allen for Franks (51 mins); B Thomson for Gibbins (51 mins); M Proctor for Milner-Skudder (70 mins); Franks for Eves (72 mins)

SCORERS: *Try*: Nonu *Penalty Goals*: Barrett (3)

HIGHLANDERS: B Smith (capt); W Naholo, M Fekitoa, R Buckman, P Osborne; L Sopoaga, A Smith; B Edmonds, L Coltman, J Hohneck, A Ainley, M Reddish, E Dixon, J Lentjes, N Manu

SUBSTITUTIONS: S Christie for Lentjes (40 mins); J Wheeler for Reddish (51 mins); A Dixon for Coltman (57 mins); R Geldenhuys for Hohneck (61 mins); D Lienert-Brown for Edmonds (64 mins); M Banks for Sopoaga (70 mins); G Evans for E Dixon (71 mins)

SCORERS: *Tries*: E Dixon, Naholo *Conversion*: Sopoaga *Penalty Goals*: Sopoaga (2) *Drop Goal*: Banks

REFEREE: J Peyper (South Africa)

Referees

THE MAN IN THE MIDDLE

By Nigel Owens

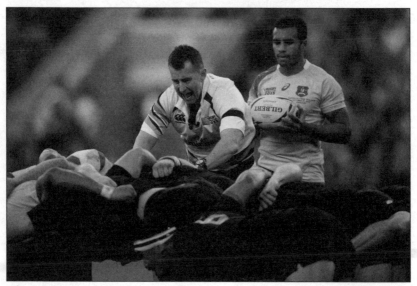

Nigel Owens became the second Welshman to referee a Rugby World Cup final after taking charge in 2015.

REFEREES

It was a privilege and an honour to be given the opportunity to take charge of the final of Rugby World Cup 2015 and after what was a brilliant tournament, I think it got the final it richly deserved. Like the majority of people, I thought the best team won and even the most passionate fans of the Wallabies I have spoken to since the match have had no complaints about the result.

I was only partially aware out on the pitch quite how good the final was as it unfolded. The level of concentration you need to referee a test match means you have a different perspective from the spectators in the stadium or the fans watching at home but I do remember thinking when Australia scored their second try in the second half, cutting the All Blacks' lead to four points, that something special was happening. The noise at Twickenham was incredible but it was only afterwards, watching the final played back, that I really understood what a great contest it had been.

To be honest, it was a pretty easy game from my perspective. There were no controversial moments to deal with, both teams came out to play and I was just delighted that nobody was talking about me at the end of the match. That is exactly as it should be. It's fantastic when you get retrospective praise for making the correct call on difficult decisions but it's even better if people forget you were even on the pitch at all. Players make great games, not the referee.

I'm often asked which laws of the game I would modify or change but I think the final summed up my views. If rugby can be played like that then in my opinion there's not much wrong with the laws as they stand.

I would be lying if I said I'd always dreamed of refereeing a World Cup final. I started refereeing when I was 16-years-old in 1987, the same year as the inaugural World Cup, but my first, burning ambition was to take charge of a big Welsh derby. I remember going to see Llanelli play Neath at Stradey Park back in the late 1980s and hearing 10,000 odd fans booing the referee because he penalised the Scarlets for something or other. I told my family and friends they'd be booing me one day.

I suppose the dream of getting the World Cup final began after the tournament in France in 2007. I nearly missed out on selection as one of the 12 referees that year because my form with the whistle was not very good in 2004 and 2005 as I was dealing with being who I really was, but once I accepted who I was and came out my form improved dramatically and I had a very decent year in 2006 and I managed to be selected as the 11th/12th pick for the tournament.

I got three pool stage games in 2007 – Australia against Fiji in Montpellier, Scotland and Romania at Murrayfield and the Argentina and Georgia game in Lyon – and I felt I performed well. Some people told me I was unlucky not to get one of the quarter-finals and after taking charge of the All Blacks against the Pumas in the last eight in 2011, I obviously knew I had at least a chance of landing the big one. I wanted to emulate Derek Bevan, who refereed the 1991 final between England and Australia at Twickenham, and it is a huge honour to have now followed in my countryman's footsteps.

I think what swung things in my favour in large part was luck. Specifically I was fortunate to have refereed some big test matches between 2011 and 2015 which developed into classics and in which I put in decent performances. I'm talking about tests like the Springboks against the All Blacks at Ellis Park in 2013, Ireland v New Zealand in November 2013 and the high scoring England against France game at Twickenham in the Six Nations in 2015. To be involved in matches like that doesn't do your reputation any harm.

So a lot of people thought I was the favourite to get the final in 2015 and although I never, ever thought it was guaranteed, it was heavy burden carrying the tag of frontrunner around for four years. There was an enormous sense of relief when I learned I had been selected to referee the final because whatever anyone else says, you are still at the mercy of your own form and your own country not progressing to the final. The pressure is off now and I can enjoy the rest of my career.

The preparation for the final was the same as any test match. I suppose there was extra pressure but I've done 68 tests now and you learn to deal with the nerves. I sat in the officials changing room at Twickenham with my two assistants, Wayne Barnes and Jérôme Garcès, and Shaun Veldsman, the television match official, and as always I put on my iPod. I put together a playlist to listen to before every game and although I always have the same song, the Welsh hymn *How Great Thou Art*, I ask whoever I'm working with for a song they'd like. For the final, Wayne went for *Wake Me Up* by the DJ Avici, Jérôme chose a song by a French pop star whose name now escapes me and Shaun asked for *Shilo* by Neil Diamond. There was plenty of contrast, put it that way.

After the game it was a shower and change, a quick beer in the changing room and then back to the hotel. There's dinner or a black tie reception after a Six Nations game but they don't do that in the southern hemisphere for the most part and after the final it was an unglamorous but enjoyable return to the hotel for me for a few beers with all the other referees and family.

The following evening it was the World Rugby Awards in London and I was humbled to receive the Referee Award. I'd received an email earlier in the week telling me I'd been nominated and asking whether I was going to attend, but I was stunned when my name was read out. People started shouting and I got a standing ovation when I went up to collect the award and to be honest it still hasn't really sunk in yet. It was a very special moment in my life.

I'd like to accept the award on behalf of all the referees in the game. There are so many more deserving me and I'm particularly thinking of those who give up their time for free to take charge of an under-10s game on a freezing Sunday morning. Without those people, the kids wouldn't get a game and rugby wouldn't survive. It's those people who deserve the recognition.

The weekend after the final I was refereeing Gowerton against Crymych in the Welsh National League Division One West. I'd been talking to my referees' manager Nigel Whitehouse and I knew there wasn't a local PRO12 game scheduled. We agreed it probably wasn't the best idea for me to be jumping on a plane to do another game so soon after the World Cup and he gave me the choice of the weekend off or doing the Gowerton game. I enjoy refereeing at any level, so it was any easy choice.

Hopefully it was a good day for the club and my family and friends really enjoyed themselves. We also took the opportunity to promote some of the courses on offer to young referees in Wales. There's still pressure on me though because that game was as important to the Gowerton and Crymych players as a test match is to internationals and you've got to give both the same respect as a referee.

I've decided to continue refereeing for another four years. At 44, I was the oldest referee at the World Cup but I enjoy the job as much as ever and I feel my fitness is still good. I would never carry on for the sake of it, or if I felt my level of performance was suffering, but right now the body and mind are willing. A lot can change in four years but I'd love to be involved in Rugby World Cup 2019 in Japan and I will do all I can to keep on top of my game and get there.

REFEREE FOCUS

Getty Images

Nigel Owens receives the World Rugby Referee Award from John Jeffrey at the World Rugby Awards 2015 in London.

I'M OVER-THE-MOON EXCITED BY THE OLYMPIC DREAM

By Leah Berard

Martin Seras Lima

Referee Leah Berard looks on as Canada attack at the World Rugby Women's Sevens Series round in London.

With the Summer Olympics being on the not-too-distant horizon (although there are still quite a few sunrises and sunsets between now and then), the 2015–16 HSBC World Rugby Women's Sevens Series will surely be the most exciting to date. The 2016 Olympics not only marks the first time sevens will be showcased, but it also marks the first time women's rugby will be included.

I personally am over-the-moon excited and fortunate to have been involved in the lead up to this realisation. Players talk about it being their dream to be chosen to represent their sport and country, and I assure you it's no different for the referees. We work toward the same goal and achievement as the players. We are athletes and students of the game just the same as they are. We hold the same passion toward the game as they do.

My passion for rugby started when I was 19 years old at the University of Wisconsin-La Crosse. I had a couple of friends who went to a practice and came back boasting about how different and fun this sport of rugby was. Coming from a country where rugby isn't big, as well as a state that some years has more months with snow on the ground than none, I had never heard of this sport.

I was intrigued, though, by what they were telling me about it. Being a multi-sport athlete my entire childhood, and being one of the most aggressive and intense players in every one of them (yes, even in figure skating!), this 'new' sport seemed like a good fit. Actually, it was the perfect fit as I had one practice and I was hooked! I remember feeling, 'where has this sport been my whole life?' It was an instant connection. I went to one practice, and started on the wing two days later in my first game.

A season-ending injury to the inside-centre during that match opened up the opportunity for me to make the move. Wearing the No.12 jersey would be something I did for every game, except one, for the next four years. Then came that day that most athletes do not enjoy, when I had to make the decision between continuing to play with recurring injuries or to give up playing the sport I loved.

I made the right decision, and a new door opened for me. I eventually got recruited from the sidelines to give this refereeing thing a 'try'. I never imagined picking up the whistle would lead me to where it has nine years later.

I am one of the lucky ones, as my good Spanish friend and colleague, Alhambra Nievas, would say. I get to travel the world, meeting new, amazing people everywhere I go, doing what I love. Rugby means family anywhere you go, and it's the same in the referee micro-community.

What's great about rugby sevens is you are not alone. You get to meet up with some of your best, life-long friends at every tournament. You go through the ups and downs together. You learn together. You get stronger together as a team. The referees also work with the teams on the Women's Sevens Series to become better as one.

Our overarching goal is to make our sport better so the world can witness how exciting and unique our great sport is. We are all looking forward to showing the world a new Olympic sport, a sport that many people may have never seen before.

Sevens truly is a perfect fit and addition to the Olympics. It's a sport that any country can compete in, and we see some of the most athletic and humbled athletes competing. The pace, the scoring, the intensity, the strength, the speed . . . how absolutely enthralling! I get chills just thinking about it.

There is still time and work to do before we are ready to take to the

REFEREE FOCUS

Olympic stage. There is a whole Women's Sevens Series, and there are challenges confronting us, to which we continue to find solutions.

One of the greatest challenges referees face is training separately in our respective countries and only coming together for tournaments. Players have the opportunity to bond and grow together on an everyday basis as a single unit following the same system.

As referees, we must find a way to do this in the limited time we have together. We have our team bonding activities and team value sessions in the days leading up to a tournament. We stay connected when we're back home as well. We support each other in whatever we have going on in our lives, both on and off the pitch.

Trust and faith in each other and our management team is critical. It's not difficult, though, in the open, supportive environment we've worked hard to create since the inception of the World Rugby Women's Sevens Series. We know the best – and only – way to realise and achieve our collective dream is by doing it together . . . 12 on-field match officials strong.

At the moment, there really are no words to describe the feeling we will have when we make it to the summit of our fantastic voyage – Rio 2016, the 31st Summer Olympic Games and first in South America.

It still doesn't seem real, and as I said previously, we still have a whole season in front of us to keep us grounded and focused. We will remain training and performing in the moment. We will continue to enjoy the time we have doing what we love, doing it together, and learning from each other throughout this fortunate journey we're all navigating and embracing together. We have the winning combination of youth, experience, personality and philosophy to make for a cohesive and successful team when Rio rolls around.

Our 'Road to Rio' is the same path as the players take, even if the detours we face and take look a little differently than theirs. We will achieve our dream and celebrate it as one big, happy rugby family. As the African proverb goes, "If you want to go quickly, go alone. If you want to go far, go together."

DISMISSALS IN MAJOR INTERNATIONAL MATCHES

Up to 1 November, 2015 in major international matches. These cover all matches for which the eight senior members of the International Board have awarded caps, and also all matches played in Rugby World Cup final stages.

AE Freethy	sent off	CJ Brownlie (NZ)	E v NZ	1925
KD Kelleher	sent off	CE Meads (NZ)	S v NZ	1967
RT Burnett	sent off	MA Burton (E)	A v E	1975
WM Cooney	sent off	J Sovau (Fj)	A v Fj	1976
NR Sanson	sent off	GAD Wheel (W)	W v I	1977
NR Sanson	sent off	WP Duggan (I)	W v I	1977
DIH Burnett	sent off	P Ringer (W)	E v W	1980
C Norling	sent off	J-P Garuet (F)	F v I	1984
KVJ Fitzgerald	sent off	HD Richards (W)	NZ v W	*1987
FA Howard	sent off	D Codey (A)	A v W	*1987
KVJ Fitzgerald	sent off	M Taga (Fj)	Fj v E	1988
OE Doyle	sent off	A Lorieux (F)	Arg v F	1988
BW Stirling	sent off	T Vonolagi (Fj)	E v Fj	1989
BW Stirling	sent off	N Nadruku (Fj)	E v Fj	1989
FA Howard	sent off	K Moseley (W)	W v F	1990
FA Howard	sent off	A Carminati (F)	S v F	1990
FA Howard	sent off	A Stoop (Nm)	Nm v W	1990
AJ Spreadbury	sent off	A Benazzi (F)	A v F	1990
C Norling	sent off	P Gallart (F)	A v F	1990
CJ Hawke	sent off	FE Mendez (Arg)	E v Arg	1990
EF Morrison	sent off	C Cojocariu (R)	R v F	1991
JM Fleming	sent off	PL Sporleder (Arg)	WS v Arg	*1991
JM Fleming	sent off	MG Keenan (WS)	WS v Arg	*1991
SR Hilditch	sent off	G Lascubé (F)	F v E	1992
SR Hilditch	sent off	V Moscato (F)	F v E	1992
DJ Bishop	sent off	O Roumat (Wld)	NZ v Wld	1992
EF Morrison	sent off	JT Small (SA)	A v SA	1993
I Rogers	sent off	ME Cardinal (C)	C v F	1994
I Rogers	sent off	P Sella (F)	C v F	1994
D Mené	sent off	JD Davies (W)	W v E	1995
S Lander	sent off	F Mahoni (Tg)	F v Tg	*1995
DTM McHugh	sent off	J Dalton (SA)	SA v C	*1995
DTM McHugh	sent off	RGA Snow (C)	SA v C	*1995
DTM McHugh	sent off	GL Rees (C)	SA v C	*1995
J Dumé	sent off	GR Jenkins (W)	SA v W	1995
WJ Erickson	sent off	VB Cavubati (Fj)	NZ v Fj	1997
WD Bevan	sent off	AG Venter (SA)	NZ v SA	1997
C Giacomel	sent off	R Travaglini (Arg)	F v Arg	1997

WJ Erickson	sent off	DJ Grewcock (E)	NZ v E	1998
S Walsh	sent off	J Sitoa (Tg)	A v Tg	1998
RG Davies	sent off	M Giovanelli (It)	S v It	1999
C Thomas	sent off	T Leota (Sm)	Sm v F	1999
C Thomas	sent off	G Leaupepe (Sm)	Sm v F	1999
S Dickinson	sent off	J-J Crenca (F)	NZ v F	1999
EF Morrison	sent off	M Vunibaka (Fj)	Fj v C	*1999
A Cole	sent off	DR Baugh (C)	C v Nm	*1999
WJ Erickson	sent off	N Ta'ufo'ou (Tg)	E v Tg	*1999
P Marshall	sent off	BD Venter (SA)	SA v U	*1999
PC Deluca	sent off	W Cristofoletto (It)	F v It	2000
JI Kaplan	sent off	A Troncon (It)	It v I	2001
R Dickson	sent off	G Leger (Tg)	W v Tg	2001
PC Deluca	sent off	NJ Hines (S)	US v S	2002
PD O'Brien	sent off	MC Joubert (SA)	SA v A	2002
PD O'Brien	sent off	JJ Labuschagne (SA)	E v SA	2002
SR Walsh	sent off	V Ma'asi (Tg)	Tg v I	2003
N Williams	sent off	SD Shaw (E)	NZ v E	2004
SJ Dickinson	sent off	PC Montgomery (SA)	W v SA	2005
SM Lawrence	sent off	LW Moody (E)	E v Sm	2005
SM Lawrence	sent off	A Tuilagi (Sm)	E v Sm	2005
SR Walsh	sent off	S Murray (S)	W v S	2006
JI Kaplan	sent off	H T Pole (Tg)	Sm v Tg	*2007
AC Rolland	sent off	J Nieuwenhuis (Nm)	F v Nm	*2007
N Owens	sent off	N Nalaga (PI)	F v PI	2008
W Barnes	sent off	JPR Heaslip (I)	NZ v I	2010
C Joubert	sent off	DA Mitchell (A)	A v NZ	2010
N Owens	sent off	PB Williams (Sm)	SA v Sm	*2011
AC Rolland	sent off	S Warburton (W)	W v F	*2011
P Gaüzère	sent off	AT Tuilagi (Sm)	SA v Sm	2013
R Poite	sent off	BW du Plessis (SA)	NZ v SA	2013
GW Jackson	sent off	Y Maestri (F)	F v Tg	2013
GW Jackson	sent off	FKA Taumalolo (Tg)	F v Tg	2013
CJ Pollock	sent off	RTRN Kuridrani (A)	I v A	2013
J Peyper	sent off	R Slimani (F)	F v It	2014
J Peyper	sent off	M Rizzo (It)	F v It	2014
J Garcès	sent off	SW Hogg (S)	W v S	2014
MI Fraser	sent off	JL Sinclair (C)	C v S	2014
P Gaüzère	sent off	GDC Ma'afu (Fj)	W v Fj	2014
JP Doyle	sent off	A Ormaechea (U)	Fj v U	*2015

* Matches in a Rugby World Cup

The Back Row

OBITUARIES

By Adam Hathaway

CLIVE ASHBY, who died on 21 May, 2015 aged 78, was an England scrum-half who won three caps between 1966 and 1967 and scored his only test try in his final appearance, against Australia. Born in Mozambique to South African parents, Ashby moved to England in 1951 and attended RGS High Wycombe – the same school where future England scrum-halves Matt Dawson and Nick Duncombe were educated. He did National Service in the Royal Navy, and when selected for England for his second cap in France he had to be smuggled back from the match through passport control as he did not have any English documentation. Ashby had studied agriculture at Harper Adams Agricultural College in Newport, Shropshire, before joining the family business. He was an honorary life president of High Wycombe RUFC and a director of A&P Tools and Products Ltd in Chertsey before his death.

NORM BERRYMAN, who died of a heart attack in Perth, Australia, aged 42, played one test for New Zealand in a 24–23 defeat to South Africa in Durban in 1998. 'Stormin' Norm played Super Rugby for a decade, winning three titles with the Crusaders from 1998–2000, and also represented the Chiefs and the Blues before finishing his professional career with a stint in France with Castres and Bourgoin. The midfielder also played for the Maori All Blacks and had a spell with the Kalamunda Bulls in Western Australia, where he was working as a forklift driver when he died. Berryman's last game of rugby had come as part of a NZ Invitational XV, which was played in Milan to commemorate fellow All Black Jerry Collins. He is survived by six children.

JERRY COLLINS, who died in a car crash on 5 June, 2015 in Béziers, France, aged 34, won 48 caps for New Zealand as a powerful and tough-tackling loose forward, and played in Rugby World Cup 2003 and 2007. The Samoan-born Collins started his career with the Norths club in Wellington before graduating to the provincial side and making his Super Rugby debut with the Hurricanes in 2001. Collins, who captained New Zealand against Argentina in 2006, played for the Ospreys in Wales, French giants Toulon, and also had a stint in Japan. He had signed for Narbonne as medical cover for Rocky Elsom before his death. In 2007, Collins famously played for Barnstaple 2nd XV when he was taking a break in Devon, took a coaching clinic and wore the club's socks when he played for the Barbarians a few weeks later. The flanker had worked on the dustcarts in Wellington, New Zealand, and would play rugby anywhere, anytime which sometimes brought him into conflict with his employers. In 2008 he played a rugby league match, under an assumed name, for North City Vikings in the Wellington competition, but was found out and his club were fined. Collins' partner Alana was also killed in the car crash. In their memory several French-based All Blacks, including Ali Williams and Carl Hayman, performed a haka at the scene shortly after his death.

BRIAN COX, who died on 13 June, 2015 aged 86, was an Australian scrum-half who played nine tests for the Wallabies from 1952–57, scoring one try. He also represented New South Wales on 14 occasions and turned out for Manly 142 times. A quantity surveyor by profession, Cox worked at Manly in various administrative roles after his career ended and was eventually made a life member. He also worked as the voluntary timekeeper for Manly's club matches, NSW Waratahs home matches and Sydney-based test matches from 1989–2006. His son Phillip, also a scrum-half, won 16 caps for Australia between 1979 and 1984, and another son Mitchell played twice on the wing for the Wallabies in 1981.

JIMMY DOCHERTY, who died on 18 October, 2014 aged 83, was a Scottish centre who won eight caps between 1955 and 1958 and scored a drop goal in his country's 14–8 win over Wales in his first year of international rugby. An elusive runner, Docherty played for Glasgow High School FP, for Glasgow against Australia in 1957 and also represented the Barbarians, although persistent knee injuries curtailed his playing days. He later coached at Glasgow High School FP and was the club's president in 1980–81. Docherty ran the family tailoring manufacturing business until his retirement.

ARTHUR DORWARD, who died on 4 August, 2015 aged 90, was a 15-times capped Scotland scrum-half whose international career spanned from 1950–57 and also included the captaincy on three occasions. Dorward, who won Barbarians and South of Scotland honours too, succeeded his older brother Tom in the Scotland scrum-half jersey, with Tom having won five caps between 1938 and 1939 before he was killed during World War II. His finest Scotland performance – in a poor era for the side – came in the 1957 meeting with Wales at Murrayfield when his drop goal earned a 9–6 win.

OBITUARIES

In the days of amateurism, Dorward was a stand-out character and often led the singing in the bar after games. He was a good all-round sportsman who also represented Galashiels at cricket, tennis, squash, golf and hockey, but his rugby playing days ended when he injured his pelvis in a road accident. A director in the family textile and clothing business, Dorward was schooled at St Mary's Prep School in Melrose and Sedbergh School in Cumbria, a famous rugby nursery.

JOHN ELDERS, who died on 3 May, 2015 aged 84, was a former Leicester centre who coached England to historic away wins over South Africa in 1972 and New Zealand in 1973. Elders joined Leicester from Loughborough Colleges in 1953 and played 144 times for the Tigers, scoring 38 tries and captaining the side from 1955–57. He worked as a teacher at South Wigston and Alderman Newton's schools before leaving the Midlands in 1958 to teach at Newcastle's Royal Grammar School and play for Northern. Elders had an England trial in 1956 and, although he did not win a cap, he made his mark on the international stage when, along with captain John Pullin, he led England to an 18–9 victory over the Springboks at Ellis Park and a 16–10 win over the All Blacks at Eden Park. England would not win in New Zealand again until 2003. In 1981, Elders moved to Australia before returning to England in 1990.

STAN HODGSON MBE, who died on 25 March, 2015 aged 86, was a Durham City and England hooker who played 11 times for his country between 1960 and 1964, winning his last cap against Wales at Twickenham at the age of 35. Hodgson, who reportedly took 10 blows to the head in the first half of the match against Ireland in 1962, toured South Africa with the Lions that summer but broke his leg during the first game, a match against Rhodesia in Bulawayo. Despite the tour-ending injury, he was kept on for the remainder of the trip because of his positive influence on the squad. Renowned for his fitness – he didn't drink, smoke and walked or ran everywhere – in those amateur days he worked as a maintenance fitter at a carpet factory in Durham. Hodgson played rugby in the lower levels for Durham City into his 60s.

PHIL JUDD, who died on 14 June, 2015 aged 81, was a Coventry prop who played 22 times for England between 1962 and 1967 and a then-record 442 times for his club before he retired in 1968 immediately after Warwickshire's win over Middlesex in the County Championship final. Judd, who had 10 England trials before making his test debut, started his rugby life at Broadstreet RFC prior to moving to the powerful

Coventry set-up. An engineer by profession, Judd captained Coventry for five seasons, from 1957–60 and 1966–68, played 77 times for Warwickshire and captained England in his last five tests. The 'Judd Project', which he was involved in setting up, is a scheme to develop rugby in the Midlands.

MARK KEYWORTH, who died on 24 November, 2014 aged 66, was the second man capped for England while playing for Swansea when he played four tests as a flanker in 1976. Keyworth had formed an all-international back row at the Welsh club, alongside Mervyn Davies and Trefor Evans, whom he had joined from Aberystwyth RFC. Keyworth played for the North Midlands before making his international debut in the 23–6 win over Australia, then playing three Five Nations games. He lost his place to Peter Dixon after the 13–12 defeat to Ireland. In all, Keyworth, who farmed in Cardiganshire, played 259 times for Swansea between 1972 and 1981, scoring 37 tries, and was a regular at All Whites Former Players' Association events until his death.

JACK KYLE OBE, who died on 27 November, 2014 aged 88, was a genius of a fly-half who won 46 caps for Ireland between 1947 and 1958. He was the pivotal player in his country's Grand Slam of 1948, toured with the Lions in 1950 and spent 30 years working as a doctor in Zambia. Kyle, voted Ireland's greatest ever player in 2002, also helped his country to the Triple Crown in 1949 and the Championship in 1951. The Belfast-born Kyle studied medicine at Queen's University in his home city, and on retiring from rugby in the early 1960s moved to Indonesia as a medical missionary before heading to Chigola, Zambia, in the Copper Belt close to the Congolese border, where he often worked

Inpho Photography

Jack Kyle was voted Ireland's greatest ever player in 2002.

as the only surgeon in a 500-bed hospital. Kyle was one of the most famous men in Ireland when he left, but said: "In Ireland I was Jack Kyle the rugby player. In Africa I was more than that."

Kyle returned to Northern Ireland in 2000 and lived in Bryansford in County Down. He was made an OBE in 1959, awarded an honorary doctorate from Queen's University, membership of the World Rugby Hall of Fame and a lifetime achievement award from the Royal Academy of Medicine in Ireland. In 2010 Kyle attended the Rugby Union Writers' Club 50th anniversary lunch in London and stole the show with his anecdotes about the 1950 Lions tour when interviewed on stage.

EDUARDO LABORDE, who died on 4 February, 2015 aged 47, played three games for Argentina at Rugby World Cup 1991 as a goal-kicking centre in defeats to Australia, Wales and Western Samoa, and played club rugby for Pucara in his home country. He continued to play with the Pumas' veterans team after retiring from the top flight, but was tragically killed when his bicycle was hit by another vehicle at the holiday resort of Pinamar, Argentina. He is survived by two children.

TREVOR LLOYD, who died on 6 October, 2015 aged 91, was the oldest living Lion at the time of his passing, having toured South Africa with the pioneering team of 1955. On that trip Lloyd, a scrum-half, played six matches and, at the age of 30, was the oldest player in the squad. Lloyd won two caps for Wales in 1953 – against Scotland and France – but had to play second fiddle to England's Dickie Jeeps on that great Lions adventure. A former schoolmate of the actor Richard Burton, Lloyd played for Aberavon, Maesteg and Bristol and captained Wales in the 75 anniversary match against the Lions in 1955. He worked as a blast furnaceman and served in the Royal Navy in World War II.

JONAH LOMU ONZM, who died on 18 November, 2015 aged 40, was a winger who played 63 tests for New Zealand, scoring 37 international tries, but those figures do not do justice to the impact the All Black had on world rugby. Lomu was the sport's first global superstar, whose fame reached beyond rugby, and his displays at Rugby World Cup 1995 produced an audience from all over the planet and helped hurry the game into professionalism.

A champion athlete at Wesley College, Lomu played for New Zealand under-17s but he announced his arrival at the top level at the Hong Kong Sevens in 1994, when as an 18-year-old he decimated all-comers.

In those days backs were not supposed to be built like second-rows with the speed of a sprinter, but Lomu broke the mould.

Lomu nearly did not make Rugby World Cup 1995 in South Africa at all. He was due to play in a sevens tournament but when Eric Rush pulled a hamstring Lomu was called in by the All Blacks and he caused mayhem, scoring seven tries in all, including four against England in the 45–29 semi-final win in Cape Town which led English captain Will Carling to describe him as 'a freak'. South Africa snuffed out the threat of Lomu in the final but he continued to destroy defences and scored another eight tries in Rugby World Cup 1999 – to give him 15 in all, a total recently equalled by Bryan Habana.

Lomu had long been suffering with nephrotic syndrome, a kidney disorder which meant, as he said, he played most of his career with the handbrake on. His last test match came in 2002 and in 2004 he had a kidney transplant before joining Cardiff a year later. He made just 10 appearances for the Blues before breaking his ankle and having further spells with North Harbour and Vitrolles in France, though he didn't reach the heights he had a decade before.

Lomu continued to struggle with his health and during the recent Rugby World Cup in England was on dialysis but kept up a hectic schedule of personal appearances. Those who did not know him were surprised that he was not the rampaging ogre of his playing days but a modest and quiet man whose priority was looking after his family. He died shortly after returning to New Zealand after a trip to Dubai following Rugby World Cup 2015, and is survived by his third wife, Nadene, and their two sons.

OBITUARIES

Getty Images

Gentle giant Jonah Lomu changed the game of rugby forever.

THOMPSON 'SANDI' MAGXALA, who died on 13 June, 2015 aged 73, was a legend of black rugby in South Africa, playing 32 tests – six of those against then-IRB nations – for the African Springboks, later known as the Leopards. He started his career as a lock and ended it as a hooker. After starting his rugby career in 1962 with the Flying Eagles RFC, he captained both Western Province and the Leopards, for whom he played against the 1974 Lions. On retiring from rugby in 1979, Magxala became president of the Flying Eagles, and later Lagunya RFC president, and was elected president of the Western Province Rugby Association in 1987. Following South African rugby unity in 1992, he was appointed as a senior selector of the Western Province Rugby Union.

NORMAN MAIR, who died on 7 December, 2014 aged 86, was a Scottish hooker who won four caps in 1951 before embarking on a highly successful career in journalism. Mair, who studied law at Edinburgh University, played in the 19–0 win over Wales, then-Grand Slam champions, at Murrayfield, and also played cricket for Scotland before turning to teaching at Moray House in Edinburgh. He switched to journalism with STV and *The Sunday Telegraph* before becoming *The Scotsman's* rugby correspondent until 1982. Mair later worked for the *Sunday Standard* and *The Observer*, covering golf as well as rugby, and later renewed his association with *The Scotsman*. He had the ear of the great and good in Scottish rugby, with Jim Telfer once saying: "If I wanted advice I would turn to him because I knew it would not go any further."

ABIE MALAN, who died on 23 October, 2014 aged 78, was a hooker, captain and selector for the Springboks and won 18 test caps, between 1958 and 1965, as well as playing 26 other matches for South Africa. Malan captained the Boks four times in 1963, including the shared series against Australia, and in a test against Wales. A product of Stellenbosch University, Malan first played for Western Province in 1955 before making his international debut against the touring French team in 1958, finishing his career on the poor tour of Australia and New Zealand, by which time he was playing for Transvaal. He worked as grape farmer on the family estate in Upington in South Africa's Northern Cape.

PIET MALAN, who died on 5 July, 2015 aged 96, was the oldest living Springbok until his death and won his only cap as a flanker against New Zealand in Port Elizabeth as part of the brilliant 1949 South African team. The 11–8 win gave the Boks a famous 4–0 series, but Malan perhaps made a bigger contribution to the game when he came up with the idea of starting an inter-provincial schools tournament, which was taken up by Danie Craven and continues to this day as the 'Craven Week'. Malan was educated at Potchefstroom Gymnasium and Potchefstroom University, and played for Western Transvaal at the age of 20 before moving to Transvaal to take up his first teaching appointment.

He played for Diggers and Transvaal in the period following World War II, but the conflict had robbed him of best playing years. He retired from rugby in 1951 to become the first director of sport at Potchefstroom University.

JIM MCCARTHY, who died on 20 April, 2015 aged 90, was a member of the Irish side that won the Grand Slam in 1948 and played 28 times in the back row for his country from 1948–55. McCarthy, who played at Dolphin RFC in Cork, was the first man from Munster to captain Ireland. He also led the side four times in his final year in international rugby, and toured New Zealand and Australia with the Lions in 1950, playing 13 times without appearing in a test match. Before the match against Wales in 1948, which secured Ireland's first Grand Slam, McCarthy had ordered six eggs to be eaten raw beforehand. When he got his expenses claim back from the IRFU he was paid the money for his train fare from Cork, but the union refused to pay for his pre-match snack.

DOUGLAS MUIR, who died on 6 September, 2014 aged 89, was a seven-time capped lock for Scotland between 1950 and 1952. Muir had served as a captain with the Gurkhas in World War II before joining the Edinburgh packaging company William Thyne & Co. at the end of hostilities. Muir won his debut match against France in 1950, but only tasted international victory once more, against England the same year. Muir rose to become managing director of Thyne & Co. before it was taken over, and he then moved to Bristol as a divisional chairman of the new group overseeing companies in Scotland, France and Germany. He served as a Scottish selector and helped players such as Ken Scotland and Eddie McKeating gain employment in his company. On retirement he moved to Guernsey.

HOWARD NORRIS, who died on 30 January, 2015 aged 80, was a prop who played twice for Wales, against France in 1963 and again in 1966. He also played three tests for the Lions in 1966, all against New Zealand, and made 17 appearances on the tour in all. He had turned

32 on the tour, but lied to the selectors about his age as they said they would not pick anyone over 30. Norris was injured for the final test but at the end of the tour was invited to play for the New Zealand Barbarians. However, his hopes were dashed when the Lions told him his contract had finished at the last minute of the final test and he was not insured against injury. Between 1958 and 6 November, 1971, when he played his last game for Cardiff, against Oxford University, he played a club record 413 games and captained the side in the 1967-68 and 1968–69 seasons. Norris, who had graduated from St Luke's College, Exeter, taught at Fitzalan High School in Cardiff.

MARTIN REGAN, who died on 29 October, 2014 aged 85, was an England fly-half who won 12 caps between 1953 and 1956 before moving to rugby league with Warrington. Regan started playing rugby at his local club, West Park, before moving to Liverpool, from where he played all his tests ahead of switching codes. He played 64 times for Warrington between 1956 and 1961 before his retirement. Regan worked as a gym master at St Edward's College, Liverpool before becoming a rep for a food company, but returned to teaching at St John's School, Warrington from 1956–69. He then spent 22 years at St Anselm's College, Birkenhead before his retirement in 1991. At St Anselm's he was on the staff with the former England wing, Ted Rudd.

NOEL TURLEY, who died on 12 May, 2015 aged 80, won one cap as a flanker for Ireland, his only appearance coming in the 16–0 defeat to England at Twickenham in a match dominated by the home fly-half, Richard Sharp. Turley was one of nine Irish debutants that day – Willie-John McBride and Ray McLoughlin were among the others – but the huge defeat by those days' standards was his sole taste of test rugby. A schoolteacher at St Michaels' College and Blackrock College, Dublin, Turley also worked as an Irish Schools' and Leinster Schools' coach and selector and served as Blackrock president.

ROSS TURNBULL, who died on 7 March, 2015 aged 74, played once for Australia, as a prop against Ireland in 1968, before becoming a powerful contributor in rugby's move to professionalism. In 1975, aged 34, Turnbull was one of the youngest Wallaby managers ever when he led the team, captained by John Hipwell, to the British Isles. He was also appointed treasurer of the NSW Rugby Union in 1976, and in 1984 joined the ARU Executive Committee. That same year he became one of Australia's two delegates to the International Rugby Board, a position he held until 1989, chaired the IRB's Amateurism Committee from 1987–88 and was deputy chairman of the ARU from 1984–89. In 1995, and with the game on the brink of turning professional, Turnbull was part of the World Rugby Corporation (WRC), bankrolled by Kerry Packer, that claimed to have signed up 500 players to an unofficial rugby tournament. However, the scheme was scuppered when the world champion Springbok team elected to stay with the official schedule backed by Rupert Murdoch's News Corporation. Nevertheless, WRC had helped force the game into a new era.

GORDON STONE, who died on 7 February, 2015 aged 100, was the oldest surviving Wallaby at the time of his death, having won one cap against the All Blacks in 1938. Stone, a scrum-half for Randwick in Sydney and the NSW Waratahs, served in World War II with the 119th Australian General Hospital Unit in New Guinea, New Britain and Darwin, where he was stationed during the bombings of February 1942. Stone, who won three Premierships with Randwick, started his working life as a medical technologist at the Prince Henry Hospital in Sydney and continued as a haematologist in the area until retiring in 1979.

DEREK 'CD' WILLIAMS, who died on 19 September, 2014 aged 89, won two caps on the flank for Wales and was part of the Cardiff team that beat the All Blacks in 1953 and Australia in 1957. He also scored the try against France that clinched the 1957 Five Nations for his country. An Oxford Blue in 1945, Williams also won a half-Blue for boxing and played cricket for the university, and carried the Olympic Torch towards Wembley Stadium ahead of the 1948 Games. Williams played 248 times for Cardiff and joined its rugby committee in 1974–75, becoming chairman and later president of the club.

RAY WILLIAMS OBE, who died on 3 December, 2014 aged 87, was the world's first full-time professional rugby union coach after a playing career with London Welsh, Northampton and Moseley. A trained PE teacher, Williams coached the West Midlands before being appointed as the Welsh Rugby Union Coaching Organiser in 1967, where he introduced a more scientific approach to the game which heralded a period of unprecedented success for a national side containing the likes of Gareth Edwards, Barry John and JPR Williams. Williams was secretary of the WRU from 1980–88 before becoming a national representative on the General Committee of the WRU. He was also the WRU's representative on the IRB Council from 1993–97 and the tournament director of Rugby World Cup 1991.

OBITUARIES

THE DIRECTORY

WORLD RUGBY MEMBER UNIONS

AMERICAN SAMOA American Samoa Rugby
Football Union
www.amerika-samoa-rugby-union.com

ANDORRA Federació Andorrana de Rugby

ARGENTINA Unión Argentina de Rugby
www.uar.com.ar

AUSTRALIA Australian Rugby Union
www.rugby.com.au

AUSTRIA Osterreichischer Rugby Verband
www.rugby-austria.at

BAHAMAS Bahamas Rugby Football Union
www.rugbybahamas.com

BARBADOS Barbados Rugby Football Union
www.rugbybarbados.com

BELGIUM Fédération Belge de Rugby
www.fbrb.be

BERMUDA Bermuda Rugby Union
www.bermudarfu.com

BOSNIA & HERZEGOVINA Ragbi Savez
Republike Bosne i Hercegovine
www.zeragbi.blogspot.com

BOTSWANA Botswana Rugby Union

BRAZIL Confederação Brasileira de Rugby
www.brasilrugby.com.br

BULGARIA Bulgarian Rugby Federation

CAMEROON Fédération Camerounaise de
Rugby

CANADA Rugby Canada
www.rugbycanada.ca

CAYMAN Cayman Rugby Union
www.caymanrugby.com

CHILE Federación de Rugby de Chile
www.feruchi.cl

CHINA Chinese Rugby Football Association
http://rugby.sport.org.cn

CHINESE TAIPEI Chinese Taipei Rugby
Football Union
www.rocrugby.org.tw

COLOMBIA Federación Colombiana de
Rugby
www.fecorugby.co

COOK ISLANDS Cook Islands Rugby Union
www.rugby.co.ck

CROATIA Hrvatski Ragbijaski Savez
www.rugby.hr

CZECH REPUBLIC C̆eská Rugbyová Unie
www.rugbyunion.cz

DENMARK Dansk Rugby Union
www.rugby.dk

ENGLAND Rugby Football Union
www.englandrugby.com

FIJI Fiji Rugby Union
www.fijirugby.com

FINLAND Suomen Rugbyliitto
www.rugby.fi

FRANCE Fédération Française de Rugby
www.ffr.fr

GEORGIA Georgian Rugby Union
www.rugby.ge

GERMANY Deutscher Rugby Verband
www.rugby.de

GREECE Hellenic Federation of Rugby

GUAM Guam Rugby Football Union

GUYANA Guyana Rugby Football Union

HONG KONG Hong Kong Rugby Union
www.hkrugby.com

HUNGARY Magyar Rögbi Szövetség
www.mrgsz.hu

INDIA Indian Rugby Football Union
www.rugbyindia.in

INDONESIA Persatuan Rugby Union
Indonesia
rugbyindonesia.or.id

IRELAND Irish Rugby Football Union
www.irishrugby.ie

ISRAEL Israel Rugby Union
www.rugby.org.il

ITALY Federazione Italiana Rugby
www.federugby.it

IVORY COAST Fédération Ivoirienne de
Rugby

JAMAICA Jamaica Rugby Football Union
www.jamaicarugby.weebly.com

JAPAN Japan Rugby Football Union
www.jrfu.org

KAZAKHSTAN Kazakhstan Rugby Federation
www.kaz-rugby.kz

KENYA Kenya Rugby Football Union
www.kru.co.ke

KOREA Korea Rugby Union
www.rugby.or.kr

LATVIA Latvijas Regbija Federäcija
www.rugby.lv

LITHUANIA Lietuvos Regbio Federacija

LUXEMBOURG Fédération Luxembourgeoise
de Rugby
www.rugby.lu

MADAGASCAR Fédération Malagasy de Rugby
www.fmrugby.mg

MALAYSIA Malaysia Rugby Union

MALTA Malta Rugby Football Union
www.maltarugby.com

MAURITIUS Rugby Union Mauritius
www.rugbymauritius.com

MEXICO Federación Mexicana de Rugby
www.mexrugby.com

MOLDOVA Federatia de Rugby din Moldovei
www.rugby.md

MONACO Fédération Monégasque de Rugby
www.monaco-rugby.com

MOROCCO Fédération Royale Marocaine de
Rugby

NAMIBIA Namibia Rugby Union
www.namibianrugby.com

NETHERLANDS Nederlands Rugby Bond
www.rugby.nl

NEW ZEALAND New Zealand Rugby Union
www.nzru.co.nz

NIGERIA Nigeria Rugby Football Federation

NIUE ISLANDS Niue Rugby Football Union

NORWAY Norges Rugby Forbund
www.rugby.no

PAKISTAN Pakistan Rugby Union
www.pakistanrugby.com

PAPUA NEW GUINEA Papua New Guinea
Rugby Football Union
www.rugbypng.com.pg

THE DIRECTORY

PARAGUAY Union de Rugby del Paraguay
www.urp.org.py

PERU Federación Peruana de Rugby
www.rugbyperu.org

PHILIPPINES Philippine Rugby Football Union
www.prfu.com

POLAND Polski Zwia̱zek Rugby
www.pzrugby.pl

PORTUGAL Federação Portuguesa de Rugby
www.fpr.pt

ROMANIA Federatia Romana de Rugbi
www.frr.ro

RUSSIA Rugby Union of Russia
www.rugby.ru

RWANDA Fédération Rwandaise de Rugby
www.rwandarugby.org

SAMOA Samoa Rugby Union
www.manusamoa.com

SCOTLAND Scottish Rugby Union
www.scottishrugby.org

SENEGAL Fédération Sénégalaise de Rugby
www.senegal-rugby.com

SERBIA Rugby Union of Serbia
www.rugbyserbia.com

SINGAPORE Singapore Rugby Union
www.singaporerugby.com

SLOVENIA Rugby Zveza Slovenije
www.rugby.si

SOLOMON ISLANDS Solomon Islands Rugby Union Federation
solomonislandsrugby.com

SOUTH AFRICA South African Rugby Union
www.sarugby.co.za

SPAIN Federación Española de Rugby
www.ferugby.es

SRI LANKA Sri Lanka Rugby Football Union
www.rugby.lk

ST. VINCENT & THE GRENADINES St. Vincent & The Grenadines Rugby Union Football
http://svgnationalrugbyunion.weebly.com/

SWAZILAND Swaziland Rugby Union
www.swazilandrugby.com

SWEDEN Svenska Rugby Forbundet
www.rugby.se

SWITZERLAND Fédération Suisse de Rugby
www.suisserugby.com

TAHITI Fédération Tahitienne de Rugby de Polynésie Française

THAILAND Thai Rugby Union
www.thairugbyunion.com

TONGA Tonga Rugby Union
www.tongarugbyunion.net

TRINIDAD & TOBAGO Trinidad and Tobago Rugby Football Union
www.ttrfu.com

TUNISIA Fédération Tunisienne de Rugby

UGANDA Uganda Rugby Football Union
www.ugandarugby.com

UKRAINE National Rugby Federation of Ukraine
www.rugby.org.ua

UNITED ARAB EMIRATES United Arab Emirates Rugby Federation
www.uaerugby.ae

URUGUAY Union de Rugby del Uruguay
www.uru.org.uy

USA USA Rugby
www.usarugby.org

UZBEKISTAN Uzbekistan Rugby Union

VANUATU Vanuatu Rugby Football Union

VENEZUELA Federación Venezolana de Rugby
www.feverugby.com

WALES Welsh Rugby Union
www.wru.co.uk

ZAMBIA Zambia Rugby Football Union

ZIMBABWE Zimbabwe Rugby Union
www.zimbabwerugby.com

REGIONAL ASSOCIATIONS

ASIA RUGBY
www.asiarugby.com

RUGBY AFRICA
www.rugbyafrique.com

SUDAMÉRICA RUGBY
www.sudamericarugby.org

RUGBY EUROPE
www.rugbyeurope.eu

OCEANIA RUGBY
www.oceaniarugby.com

RUGBY AMERICAS NORTH
www.nacrugby.com

ASSOCIATE MEMBERS

AZERBAIJAN Azerbaijan Rugby Union
www.rugby.az

BRITISH VIRGIN ISLANDS British Virgin Islands Rugby Union
www.bvirugby.com

BRUNEI Brunei Rugby Football Union
bruneirugby.wordpress.com

BURUNDI Fédération Burundaise de Rugby

CAMBODIA Cambodia Federation of Rugby
www.cambodiafederationrugby.com

COSTA RICA Federación de Rugby de Costa Rica
www.federacionrugbycr.com

CYPRUS Cyprus Rugby Federation
www.cyprus-rugby.org

GHANA Ghana Rugby Union
www.ghanarugby.org

IRAN Iran Rugby Federation
www.rugbyiran.ir

KYRGYZSTAN Kyrgyzstan Rugby Union

LAO Lao Rugby Federation
www.laorugby.com

MALI Fédération Malienne de Rugby

MAURITANIA Fédération Mauritanienne de Rugby (Suspended October 2013)
www.mauritanie-rugby.org

MONGOLIA Mongolia Rugby Union
www.mrfu.mn

ST. LUCIA St. Lucia Rugby Football Union
www.stluciarugby.moonfruit.com

TANZANIA Tanzania Rugby Union

TOGO Fédération Togolaise de Rugby
www.fetogrugby.com

ACKNOWLEDGEMENTS

A book of this magnitude, which covers every facet of the rugby world in 2014–15 and is put together at breakneck speed during the greatest Rugby World Cup in history, would not have been possible without the dedication and energy of a long list of contributors.

First and foremost, Karen Bond at World Rugby is the driving force behind the book – arranging interviews, editing and writing articles, checking statistics and records – and her extraordinary knowledge of the game is invaluable; ask Karen a question about any tournament, team, player or try in world rugby and you'll receive an instant answer. And for Karen to combine work on a 672-page *World Rugby Yearbook* in conjunction with all-consuming RWC 2015 commitments is certainly a feat to behold.

My thanks go to the army of writers and contributors that cover every tournament from the HSBC Sevens World Series to the Aviva Premiership, and every nation from Argentina to Wales, and who submit quality writing on time and to the exact word count. These include Stephen Jones, Jon Newcombe, Seb Lauzier, Melodie Robinson, Ali Donnelly, Frankie Deges, Ian Gilbert, Lúcás Ó'Ceallacháin, Ruaidhri O'Connor, Rich Freeman, Chris Thau, Chris Rhys and Adam Hathaway – it's a pleasure to work with you all.

The writers above are ably led by Iain Spragg, whose expertise, calmness, excellent rugby connections and ability to conduct interviews and pen first-class articles to tight deadlines makes my job infinitely easier. I wouldn't want anyone else on the front line with me.

A number of other contributors give the *World Rugby Yearbook* its star quality, with players, coaches and legends from the rugby family giving their honest thoughts and inside knowledge. These include RWC winners Joel Stransky and George Gregan as well as Ben Ryan, Martyn Williams, Mauro Bergamasco and Ian Jones.

A huge thanks go to Janice Dyer at Palimpsest Book Production Limited and Neal Cobourne for the high-quality typesetting job. Readers will never know the sheer amount of concentration and time taken to design and lay out a book of this size and complexity, but with Janice and Neal at the helm not a word or image is out of place.

Special thanks go to the stats men, co-editor John Griffiths and Tom Coggle at Sportradar, who provide in-depth records and statistics for everything in the rugby world. Their dedication to detail and accuracy provides readers of the yearbook with a wealth of information about rugby past and present.

Thank you to David Moor for providing the kit graphics for each national team – attention to detail is again a continuing theme in this publication.

Here at the coalface in the Vision Sports Publishing office I'm brilliantly supported by Jim, Toby and Ulrika, whose publishing expertise and general camaraderie help immeasurably as the spectre of myriad deadlines loom.

Finally, a big thank you to Dominic Rumbles, Head of Communications at World Rugby, for his continuing belief in the project.

I hope you enjoy this *World Rugby Yearbook* as much as we have enjoyed putting it together, and here's to many more years of this weighty tome landing on my desk.

Paul Baillie-Lane